WORLD HISTORY
People & Nations

WORLD HISTORY
People & Nations

HOLT, RINEHART AND WINSTON
Harcourt Brace & Company
Austin • New York • Orlando • Atlanta • San Francisco • Boston • Dallas • Toronto • London

Staff Credits

Editorial
Sue Miller, *Executive Editor*
Jim Eckel, *Managing Editor*
Rhonda Haynes, *Senior Editor*
Christopher J. Parker, *Associate Editor*

Editorial Permissions
Janet Harrington

Art, Design, and Photo
Book and Media Design
Joe Melomo, *Art Director*

Cover Design
Joe Melomo, *Art Director*

Photo Research
Peggy Cooper, *Photo Research Manager*
Tim Taylor, *Senior Photo Researcher*
Kristin Hay, *Assistant Photo Researcher*
Stephanie Friedman, *Assistant Photo Researcher*

Image Services
Elaine Tate, *Art Buyer Supervisor*
CoCo Weir, *Art Buyer*

New Media Design
Susan Michael, *Art Director*

Design and Page Production
The Quarasan Group, Inc.

New Media
Kate Bennett, *Associate Director*
Armin Gutzmer, *Manager Training and Technical Support*
Cathy Kuhles, *Technical Assistant*
Nina Degollado, *Intern*

Production
Gene Rumann, *Production Manager*
Leanna Ford, *Production Assistant*

Media Production
Kim Anderson-Scott, *Media Production Manager*
Nancy Hargis, *Production Supervisor*
Adriana Bardin, *Production Coordinator*

Manufacturing
Shirley Cantrell, *Manufacturing Coordinator*

Front Cover: K. Scholz/H. Armstrong Roberts; Background: Michael Holford
Spine: K. Scholz/H. Armstrong Roberts
Back Cover Background: Michael Holford
Half Title: K. Scholz/H. Armstrong Roberts; Background: Michael Holford
Title: Bibliotheque Nationale, Paris, France/The Bridgeman Art Library, New York

ISBN 0-03-053359-7

13 14 15 16 17 048 09 08 07 06

Content Reviewers

Dr. Pierre Cagniart
Southwest Texas State University
Ancient history

Dr. Laurel Carrington
St. Olaf College
Medieval, early modern Europe, intellectual

Dr. Robert Divine
University of Texas
American diplomatic

Dr. Roberta Ann Dunbar
University of North Carolina
at Chapel Hill
African, Afro-American studies

Dr. Michael Hall
University of Texas
Colonial America

Professor Robin Higham, Emeritus
Kansas State University
Military, aviation, technology

Dr. Julian Martin
University of Alberta
Science and medicine, early modern Britain

Dr. Alida Metcalf
Trinity University
Latin America, Brazil

Dr. Gail Minault
University of Texas
India

Dr. Mark Parillo
Kansas State University
United States military,
diplomatic, Japan

Dr. E. Bruce Reynolds
San Jose State University
Japan, China, Southeast Asia

Dr. Richard Saller
University of Chicago
Ancient, early Roman Empire

Dr. Robert Mark Spaulding
University of North Carolina
at Wilmington
Modern German, modern Europe

Dr. Peter Stearns
Carnegie Mellon University
Comparative social, aging, emotions

Dr. Lynn Struve
Indiana University
Premodern China, Chinese
political and intellectual history

Educational Reviewers

James Alloco
Dumont High School
Dumont, New Jersey

Linda Crockford
St. Brendan High School
Miami, Florida

Mary H. Naylor
Deep Creek High School
Chesapeake, Virginia

David Olson
Angola High School
Angola, Indiana

Elizabeth Silva
Dartmouth High School
Dartmouth, Massachusetts

Laura Watkins
Acton Boxborough Regional High School
Acton, Massachusetts

Scott Whitlow
Round Rock High School
Round Rock, Texas

Contents

UNIT 1 The Beginnings of Civilization   xxx

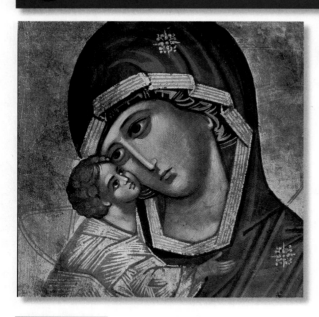

UNIT ❸

Reference Section

Features

Maps

Geography and World History: An Introduction

World History: People and Nations tells the story of the world's people from the very earliest times to the present. History describes the events that make up this story, while geography describes the places in which the events take place. History, then, represents the unfolding drama of people and events through the ages. Geography describes the stage on which this drama is played out. History and geography are so intertwined that to separate them would leave the story only partially told.

Time and Space
Even though history and geography are closely related, they are still two distinct subjects. The basic difference between them may be stated quite simply. As you study history, you acquire an orientation to time; as you study geography, you acquire an orientation to space. Geographers organize their thoughts with respect to spatial arrangements and distributions over Earth's surface. Historians, on the other hand, organize their ideas with respect to time.

Although history is mostly concerned with time, and geography mostly with space, each subject employs aspects of the other as analytical tools. Historians know full well that events occur in places as well as in time. Events, like people, are widely distributed across Earth. In other words, events have a spatial, or geographic, dimension. And geographers, in examining distributions and arrangements throughout the world today, find that they often must look back to a period in time in order to explain these current patterns.

World History: People and Nations tells the story of the world's history. Geography helps to bring this story into focus. Therefore, understanding the special themes and tools of geography will be of great value to you as you read and think about the great personalities and events of the past.

The Five Basic Themes in Geography
Modern geography focuses on five basic themes, or topics: location, place, human-environment interaction, movement, and regions. Each of these five basic themes helps to clarify the relationship between the world's physical landscape and its human occupants. These relationships, of course, have a time span as well as a spatial context.

Location. The first theme, location, has two aspects. Absolute location deals with the exact, or precise, spot on Earth that a place occupies. Relative location, on the other hand, describes the position of a particular place in relation to other places.

The latitude and longitude of a place best describes its absolute location. To calculate latitude and longitude, geographers use a grid formed by a series of imaginary lines drawn around Earth. (See globe on this page.) The equator, an imaginary line that circles Earth halfway between the North and South Poles, divides Earth into two halves, or hemispheres. Geographers call these hemispheres the Northern Hemisphere and the Southern Hemisphere. Several shorter imaginary lines called parallels, or lines of latitude, circle Earth, parallel to the equator.

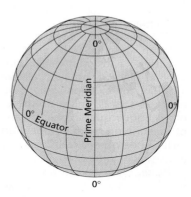

Geographers identify the parallels through a special numbering system based on degrees. In the Northern Hemisphere, the parallels number from zero degrees (0°) at the equator to ninety degrees north (90°N) at the North Pole. Similarly, in the Southern Hemisphere, they run from 0° at the equator to 90° S at the South Pole.

Another set of imaginary lines—called meridians, or lines of longitude—is used to measure Earth east and west. The prime meridian—which runs from pole to pole through the Royal Observatory in Greenwich, England—serves as 0° longitude. The meridian directly opposite the prime meridian, on the other side of the globe, is the 180° meridian. The prime meridian and the 180° meridian together divide Earth into the Eastern and Western Hemispheres. The Eastern Hemisphere is the half of Earth that extends east of the prime meridian to the 180° meridian. The Western Hemisphere is the half of Earth west of the prime meridian to the 180° meridian.

Together, parallels and meridians form an imaginary grid over Earth. Since each degree of latitude and longitude can be broken into 60' (60 minutes), and each minute can be broken into 60" (60 seconds), the grid fixes the precise location of any place on Earth's surface. For example, the absolute location of Santa Fe, New Mexico, is 35°41' north and 105°57' west. No other place on Earth is located at exactly this same place.

The relative location of a place is often described in terms of direction and distance from another place. Santa Fe's relative location, for example, might be expressed as 58 miles northeast of Albuquerque. Other ways of describing relative location include nearness to resources and accessibility to trade routes.

Place. Place has to do with a location's physical and human characteristics. Every location on Earth has its own unique, or distinctive, physical and human characteristics. Physical characteristics include the shape of the land, climate, soils, vegetation, and animal life. Land use, street layout, architecture, and population distribution are a location's human characteristics. Physically, Santa Fe is in the foothills of the southern Rocky Mountains. Its human characteristics include its traditional Pueblo and Spanish architecture. Together, the physical and human characteristics make up a location's place identity. This identity changes through time and is therefore very important to an understanding of history.

Human-Environment Interaction. Throughout time, people have adapted their way of life to accommodate their environment. For example, people who live in hot, dry climates such as in Sante Fe and other parts of the American Southwest have built houses of adobe, or sun-dried clay bricks. Even in extreme heat, the adobe helps to keep the house cool.

People also have made changes to their physical environment. For instance, they have cleared forests, dug irrigation ditches, and built huge cities. Geographers consider all the ways in which people interact with their natural environment.

The theme of human-environment interaction is of great importance to historians, for it concerns not only the ways in which people interact with their physical surroundings but also the consequences of such interactions. For example, the decision to mine and use fossil fuels to produce energy had the negative consequence of polluting the environment. This consequence, in turn, gave rise to people acting together to protect their environment. Such actions are of great interest to historians.

Tea fields in Sri Lanka

Movement. The fourth theme of modern geography, movement, concerns the interactions of people with one another as they travel, communicate, and exchange goods and services on a worldwide basis. Through much of its history, for example, Santa Fe has been a trading center for ranchers, farmers, and American Indians. Movement also includes an examination of the spread of ideas and the great human migrations that have occurred through the centuries—two vital issues in the study of history.

Regions. In order to better study and understand Earth, geographers think of it in units called regions. A region is an area having a specific characteristic or characteristics. The characterisics used to define a region may be physical features such as climate, vegetation, and landforms, or they may be cultural features such as a dominant religion or language. The particular features that characterize a region set it apart from other regions. Since there are different kinds of regions, any given area might be part of several regions. For example, Sante Fe is the state capital of New Mexico (a political region), at the foot of the Sangre de Cristo Range of the Rocky Mountains (a climate region), and it has a large Spanish-American population (a cultural region).

The Tools of Geography
To develop these five basic themes, geographers use a wide

Skyline of Houston, Texas

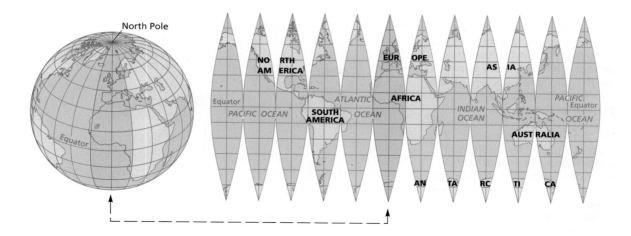

variety of tools. These tools include such modern and sophisticated items as aerial photographs, satellite images, and extremely intricate computer programs. However, a geographer's most basic and essential tools—globes and maps—have been used for centuries. Globes and maps, of course, are very familiar objects. You have seen them in your classroom or in the school library, and perhaps also in your home. Globes and maps are essential to the study of geography because they provide fairly accurate representations of Earth. However, globes and maps are not perfect models of Earth, and, therefore, each has advantages and disadvantages as a geographical tool.

The most important advantage of a globe is its shape. It is the only model of Earth that is spherical. Because a globe's shape follows the shape of Earth, the landmasses and bodies of water shown on it are correct in terms of shape and relative area. A globe also accurately shows distance and direction from one place to another.

In spite of its accuracy, the globe has some limitations. To begin with, a globe is bulky and awkward to carry. In addition, a globe does not allow you to see the entire Earth at once. For example, if you look at South America, Australia is hidden from your view. When you turn the globe to find Australia, South America is not visible. A globe's greatest problem, however, is that it lacks detail. Even the largest globes could not show the detailed features of the ancient Nile Valley. There would be no way to indicate the location of each of the 35 major pyramids that stand near the Nile River, the huge stone figure of the Sphinx, or the numerous irrigation channels and reservoirs used by the farmers of the region.

In contrast, the intricate details shown on maps make them useful to geographers. Through the use of symbols and colors, a huge range of information can be shown clearly on a map. By comparing maps, geographers can see movement, the effects of human-environment interaction, and the locations of various physical and cultural regions. In addition, maps are far more manageable than globes. They can be rolled or folded, and therefore they are easy to carry.

Still, maps do have one serious drawback: they are never totally accurate. Regardless of the skill of the cartographer, or mapmaker, no map can accurately show the qualities of shape, area, distance, and direction at the same time because mapmaking involves recording on a flat surface what is curved on Earth's surface. (See map on this page.)

To appreciate the problems faced by cartographers, place a piece of paper directly over one of the Great Lakes of North America on a globe. Now trace the outline of the lake onto your paper. You should be able to trace its outline accurately without once bending or twisting your paper. Next, try tracing the outline of the entire North American continent. You can see immediately that some cutting or folding of the paper is required. Otherwise, you will drastically distort the outline of the continent. On the other hand, in cutting or folding the map, you create other distortions.

Distortion, then, is a major problem for cartographers when depicting large areas of Earth's curved surface on a flat map. Since maps cannot accurately show all four kinds of map information—shape, area, distance, and direction—at the same time, cartographers must decide which information they want their maps to distort least. Cartographers use a variety of projections—methods by which Earth's surface is recorded, or projected, onto paper to create flat maps.

Map Projections

Literally thousands of map projections exist. Each one distorts one or more of the four major map attributes. The projection that a cartographer chooses depends on the size and location of the area to be projected and on the purpose of the map.

Cartographers often choose the Robinson projection. (See map at right.) This projection is unique because it is a compromise projection. It maintains no single property but minimizes overall distortion.

If true shape is the most important objective of the cartographer, he or she will select a conformal projection, such as the Mercator projection. (See map below.) On a map that uses such a projection, land masses are shown in their true shapes. Size relationships, however, are distorted. If the purpose of the map is to show

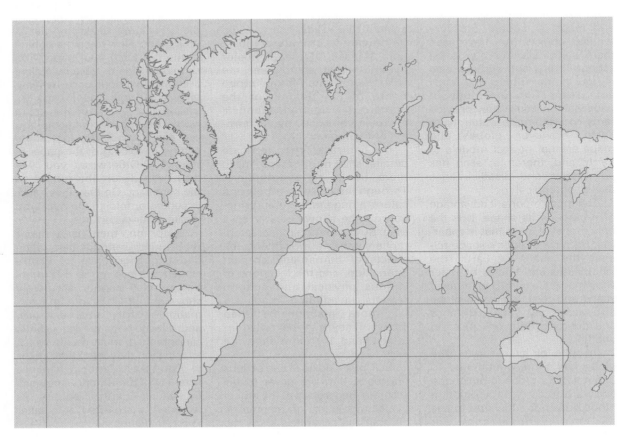

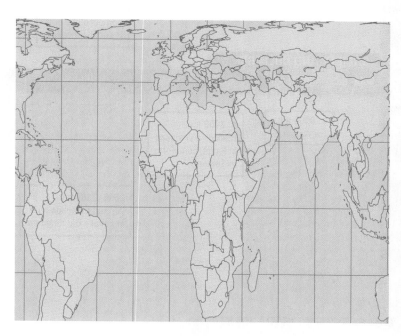

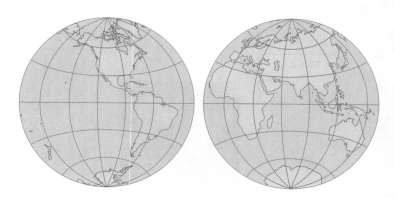

correct relative size, an equal-area projection, such as the Molleweide projection or the Peters projection, will be used. (See maps on this page.) Maps whose projections show correct distances between places are called equidistant maps. Equidistant maps work well for projecting areas of limited size, such as a city or a state. A map of the entire world could never be equidistant, however, because it is impossible to show the lengths of lines of latitude and longitude on a flat map as accurately as they appear on a globe. Finally, maps that show true distances and direction measurements from a central point on the map are called azimuthal maps. (See map at the bottom of this page.) These maps are often used to show the polar regions.

Each kind of projection has its strengths and weaknesses. On a conformal map, for example, angles and directions are correct, but size relationships are quite distorted. Compare, for example, the relative sizes of Africa and Greenland on the Mercator projection with their relative size on the Molleweide or Peters projection or on a globe.

Equal-area maps, on the other hand, are especially useful for comparing factors that may be affected by an area's size, such as temperature patterns, population size, or mineral production. The greatest drawback of equal-area maps is that they distort the shapes of the areas shown.

Equidistant projections are used for road maps because they allow the driver to get a clear and accurate picture of the distances to be traveled. Certain types of azimuthal maps, in contrast, are especially useful to pilots because they show the shortest distance between two places on Earth as a straight line.

In spite of their drawbacks, then, there is indeed a map projection to meet every need. In studying maps, however, always remember to note the type of projection that was used so that you will be aware of how it is different from a globe, the one precise model of Earth. To aid you in this task, each of the maps in this book identifies the map projection used.

UNIT

1

The Beginnings of Civilization

Chapter 1

c.* 3,700,000 B.C.–1200 B.C.

The Emergence of Civilization

Chapter 2

c. 6000 B.C.–587 B.C.

The First Civilizations

Chapter 3

c. 2500 B.C.–A.D. 550

Ancient Indian Civilization

Chapter 4

c. 1500 B.C.–A.D. 589

Ancient Chinese Civilization

*c. stands for *circa* and means "about."

POLITICS AND GOVERNMENT

9000 B.C. | 8000 B.C. | 3000 B.C. | 2500 B.C.

c. 3000 B.C. Sumerian civilization begins in Mesopotamia

2650 B.C. Beginning of Old Kingdom in Egypt

c. 2500 B.C. Harappan civilization develops in Indus River valley

SOCIETY AND CULTURE

9000 B.C. | 8000 B.C. | 3000 B.C. | 2500 B.C.

c. 8000 B.C. Ice Age ends

c. 3000 B.C. Hieroglyphics used in Egypt, cuneiform in Sumer

2650–2180 B.C. Largest pyramids built in Egypt's Old Kingdom

SCIENCE AND TECHNOLOGY

9000 B.C. | 8000 B.C. | 3000 B.C. | 2500 B.C.

c. 8000 B.C. New Stone Age begins

c. 3000 B.C. Beginning of Bronze Age in Nile and Tigris-Euphrates River valleys

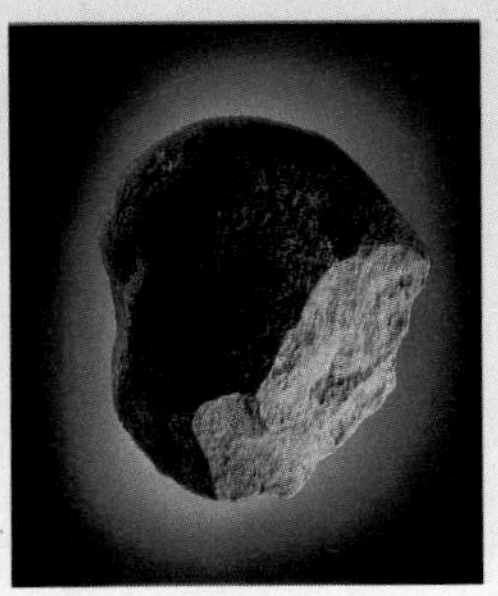

Stone tool

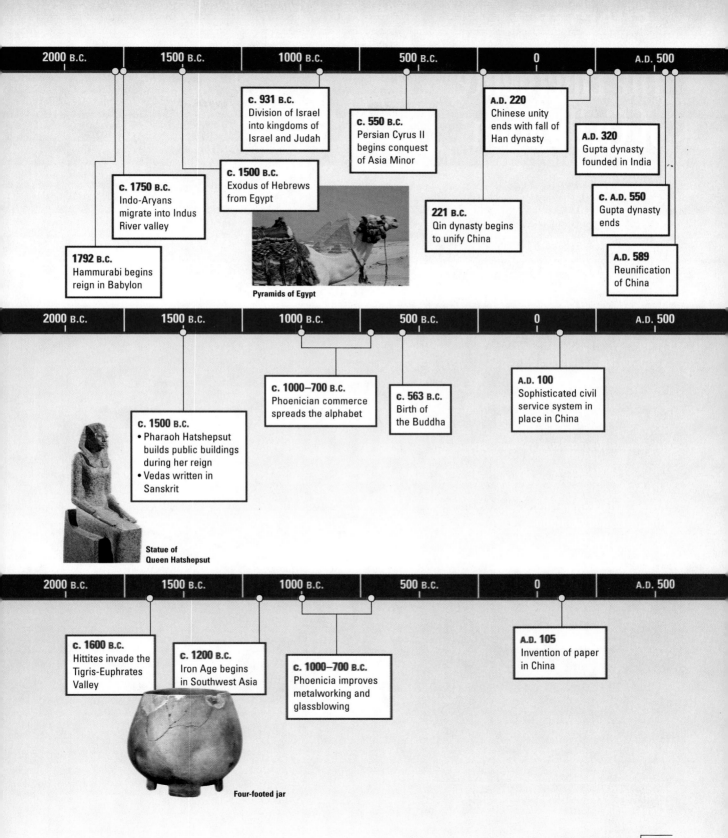

Timeline 1 (Top)

2000 B.C. — 1500 B.C. — 1000 B.C. — 500 B.C. — 0 — A.D. 500

c. 931 B.C.
Division of Israel into kingdoms of Israel and Judah

c. 550 B.C.
Persian Cyrus II begins conquest of Asia Minor

A.D. 220
Chinese unity ends with fall of Han dynasty

A.D. 320
Gupta dynasty founded in India

c. 1750 B.C.
Indo-Aryans migrate into Indus River valley

c. 1500 B.C.
Exodus of Hebrews from Egypt

221 B.C.
Qin dynasty begins to unify China

C. A.D. 550
Gupta dynasty ends

1792 B.C.
Hammurabi begins reign in Babylon

A.D. 589
Reunification of China

Pyramids of Egypt

Timeline 2 (Middle)

2000 B.C. — 1500 B.C. — 1000 B.C. — 500 B.C. — 0 — A.D. 500

c. 1500 B.C.
• Pharaoh Hatshepsut builds public buildings during her reign
• Vedas written in Sanskrit

c. 1000–700 B.C.
Phoenician commerce spreads the alphabet

c. 563 B.C.
Birth of the Buddha

A.D. 100
Sophisticated civil service system in place in China

Statue of Queen Hatshepsut

Timeline 3 (Bottom)

2000 B.C. — 1500 B.C. — 1000 B.C. — 500 B.C. — 0 — A.D. 500

c. 1600 B.C.
Hittites invade the Tigris-Euphrates Valley

c. 1200 B.C.
Iron Age begins in Southwest Asia

c. 1000–700 B.C.
Phoenicia improves metalworking and glassblowing

A.D. 105
Invention of paper in China

Four-footed jar

The Emergence of Civilization

TIME

c.* 3,700,000 B.C.–1200 B.C.

3,700,000 B.C.–1200 B.C.

| 3.7 million B.C. | 4000 B.C. | A.D. 2100 |

*c. stands for *circa* and means "about."

PLACE

Africa, Asia, Europe, the
Americas, and Australia

Prehistoric cave drawings from Altamirea
Caves, Spain

Significance

This book deals primarily with **history**—the record of events since people first developed writing, about 5,000 years ago. However, evidence indicates that people lived on Earth long before the development of writing. We call the period before writing **prehistory**.

Because we have no written records of prehistoric times, many of the events of that remote past remain cloaked in mystery. Nevertheless, we know that prehistoric people invented tools, produced beautiful art, built cities, and developed governments. They gradually created what we call **civilizations**—highly organized societies with complex institutions and attitudes that link a large number of people together.

As civilizations developed, the first forms of writing also developed, thus ending prehistory. What we call history, our main story, began.

Terms to Define

history	Ice Age
prehistory	agriculture
civilizations	nomads
anthropologists	domestication
hominids	Neolithic Revolution
archaeologists	division of labor
artifacts	irrigation
culture	artisans
radiocarbon dating	cultural diffusion
glaciers	

People to Identify

Mary Leakey
Donald Johanson

Places to Locate

Jarmo	Euphrates River
Çatalhüyük	Indus River
Nile River	Huang He
Tigris River	

Chapter Theme Questions

- **Geography** What natural feature might have encouraged the settling of early humans?
- **Technology** How might technology impact the development of early civilizations?
- **Science** How does science affect the study of past cultures?

In 1979 in a remote, almost inaccessible region of northern Tanzania, the scientist Mary Leakey made a remarkable discovery. As she stared down into the rugged terrain, she was amazed to see that a simple series of footprints lay imbedded in the volcanic rock. What fascinated her was that these footprints had not been left earlier that day or even earlier that week. Instead, she found that they were millions of years old. Made in the soft ash of a volcanic eruption, the prints had been preserved as the ash had hardened.

Although we will never know exactly who made these prints, Leakey believes that they belonged to a hominid, one of the humanlike creatures who, scientists theorize, preceded us on Earth.

"Following the path produces, at least for me, a kind of poignant time wrench. At one point, and you need not be an expert tracker to discern this, the traveler stops, pauses, turns to the left to glance at some possible threat or irregularity, then continues to the north. This motion, so intensely human, transcends time. Three million seven hundred thousand years ago, a remote ancestor—just as you or I—experienced a moment of doubt."

Leakey is only one of many dedicated scholars who have tried to piece together the distant past.

Section 1

Prehistoric Peoples

Focus Questions

- **How do anthropologists and archaeologists study prehistoric peoples?**
- **What were the achievements of the Neanderthal and Cro-Magnon peoples?**
- **What important developments occurred in the Middle and New Stone Ages?**

How can we learn anything about what happened on Earth before people learned to keep written records? Surprisingly, we can find out a great deal.

Examining Prehistory

Scientists have discovered many things about prehistory, often by using scientific methods. Most recently, advances in genetic research have allowed biologists to cast new light on the origins and development of early humans. **Anthropologists** study the skeletal remains of **hominids**—human beings and earlier human-like creatures—to determine how long they lived, how they looked, and what their other physical characteristics were. **Archaeologists** excavate ancient settlements and study **artifacts**—material objects shaped by human beings or the hominids who preceded them. Examples of artifacts include furniture, clothing, tools, weapons, works of art, and toys. By studying these objects, archaeologists can piece together information on the cultures of earlier people. **Culture** is the beliefs, knowledge, and patterns of living that people develop through living together. It includes language, skills, art, literature, law, and ways of life.

Archaeologists study past cultures by analyzing human remains and artifacts.

To assign a date to prehistoric remains, scientists use a variety of scientific techniques, including **radiocarbon dating**. Each living thing contains radiocarbon atoms that begin to decay when the organism dies. Radiocarbon dating measures the rate of this decay for organic matter up to about 50,000 years old. For remains older than that, scientists use other methods that record the rate of decay of certain key elements and compounds. For example, the potassium-argon dating method can be used to date some of the oldest objects on Earth.

Despite these sophisticated methods, scientists still must rely on educated guesses. However, scientists often are quite confident about the conclusions they reach. They can tell us when important changes took place many thousands of years ago and describe some of the ways the first human beings lived.

Early Humanlike Creatures

Anthropologists have found evidence that humanlike creatures appeared on Earth millions of years ago. In 1974 in Ethiopia, anthropologist Donald Johanson discovered female skeletal remains that may be 3 million years old. Johanson classified his find as Australopithecus (aw·stray·loh·PI·thuh·kuhs). The skeleton became known as Lucy, after the Beatles' song "Lucy in the Sky with Diamonds." Johanson heard the song shortly after making the discovery.

After examining Lucy's bones, particularly fragments of her leg and foot, Johanson concluded that she walked upright, like modern humans. In 1975 at Laetoli in Tanzania, Mary Leakey found other Australopithecine skeletal fragments dating back 3.7 million years. These creatures also walked upright.

Other hominids similar to the Australopithecines lived in eastern Africa 2 million years ago. In 1986, for example, Donald Johanson discovered the skeleton of a hominid who probably lived about 1.8 to 2 million years ago in Olduvai (OHL·duh·way) Gorge in Tanzania. Scientists also uncovered tools made of chipped stone in the gorge.

Scientists are still not certain whether modern humans are related to Australopithecines. However, many scientists believe that upright posture and the ability to make tools occurred millions of years ago, very early in human development.

The Old Stone Age

The period of prehistory that begins with the development of stone tools about 2.5 million years ago is called the Stone Age. Almost all the artifacts that have survived from this time were made of stone. The Stone Age is divided into three parts. The oldest part is called the Old Stone Age, or Paleolithic (pay·lee·uh·LI·thik) Age. It lasted for more than 2 million years—until about 12,000 years ago. The word *paleolithic* comes from the Greek words *palaios*, meaning "ancient," and *lithos*, meaning "stone."

The Middle Stone Age, or Mesolithic Age (from the Greek *mesos*, meaning "middle") and the New Stone Age, or Neolithic Age (from the Greek *neos*, meaning "new") followed the Old Stone Age. The dates for each age vary in different regions of the world, but the Middle Stone Age lasted from about 12,000 to about 10,000 years ago. The New Stone Age lasted from about 10,000 years ago to about 5,000 years ago. Each succeeding age is distinguished partly by a new level of sophistication in tools and other artifacts.

The First People

Because early human and other hominid remains are fragmentary, scientists often disagree about what conclusions can be drawn from them and other materials found. Future excavations may lead to theories different from those commonly held today.

Anthropologists have used excavated bones to learn about the first humans. These individuals had powerful jaws, sharply receding chins, low foreheads, and heavy eyebrow ridges.

Scientists believe these early people sometimes used caves as shelters and probably ate seeds, fruits, nuts, and other edible plants. Eventually, they hunted first small and then large animals. To hunt successfully, people had to make tools, work together, and communicate. Inquiring minds—and hands freed by an upright posture—helped make these developments possible.

As humans became successful hunters, they moved, or migrated, over great distances over generations in search of food. Their populations expanded from Africa to Asia. Paleolithic people may have lived in Asia as early as 2 million years ago. Scientists discovered the remains of prehistoric people on the Indonesian island of Java in 1891 and near Beijing (BAY·JING), China, in 1927. Scientists named these people Java man and Peking man. (*Peking* was an earlier spelling of *Beijing*.) At some point, probably between 300,000 and 200,000 years ago, the species known as *Homo sapiens* appeared in Africa. Neanderthal and Cro-Magnon people, as well as all people living today, belong to this species. *Homo sapiens* spread, over thousands of years, to Europe and Asia.

The Ice Age

Extremes of climate have greatly influenced human history and the history of Earth itself. Four times within the last 1.7 million years, Earth has had periods of extremely cold weather. During each extremely cold period the northern polar icecap moved south and joined **glaciers**—large, slowly moving masses of snow and ice—that formed in the mountain ranges. The icecap and glaciers gradually melted between glacial advances. Each of these four cold-weather periods lasted from 50,000 to 110,000 years. Together these periods are known as the **Ice Age**. Scientists believe that we now live in a warm era that began after the fourth period of the Ice Age, which ended about 10,000 years ago.

Today glacier ice covers a little more than one-tenth of Earth's land surface. During the fourth and longest period of the Ice Age, ice covered nearly one third of Earth's surface. In some places the ice was nearly two miles thick. Large areas of northern North America, Europe, and Asia were engulfed in ice.

The Ice Age affected Earth in various ways. Some humans and animals migrated to warmer, ice-free areas. Many kinds of animals and plants disappeared completely. The grinding, chiseling effect of the moving ice changed the surface of Earth greatly. While ice covered much of the northern half of the planet, the rest of the planet received unusually large amounts of rainfall. Rivers and lakes rose, and large inland bodies of water formed. Former desert regions began to produce vegetation and support animal life.

During these periods of extremely cold weather, the sea level dropped because so much water was frozen in the icecaps. As the sea level fell, ridges that had been under water were uncovered and formed "land bridges." These bridges linked some continents and islands that are today separated by water. People and animals migrated over some of these land bridges. However, only when prehistoric people learned to use fire and make warm clothing could they successfully settle in the colder regions.

What If?

The Ice Age
If there had been no Ice Age, how might prehistory have been different?

Neanderthal People

In caves located in many parts of Europe, Southwest Asia, and North Africa, anthropologists have found the remains of the Neanderthal (nee·AN·duhr·tawl) people—early humans who lived some 35,000 to 130,000 years ago, during the Old Stone Age. These people were named after the Neander Valley in Germany, where their remains were first found in 1856. Neanderthal remains reveal that these people had powerful builds, heavy jaws, thick eyebrow ridges, and large noses.

Neanderthal people made more efficient tools than did the hominids who preceded them. They lived in caves, wore clothing made of animal skins, and used fire.

Neanderthals also cooked food. Some anthropologists believe that Neanderthals placed frozen meat on hot coals to thaw and that when they discovered the cooked meat tasted better than raw meat, they adopted cooking.

Neanderthal people differed from earlier hominids in a very significant way—Neanderthals buried their dead. What is more, they buried meat and tools with the dead. Many scientists believe this practice shows that the Neanderthals expected the food to be eaten and for the tools to be used by the dead person after his or her death. If the theories of these scientists are correct, this practice shows a belief in some form of life after death—a belief basic to many of the world's religions.

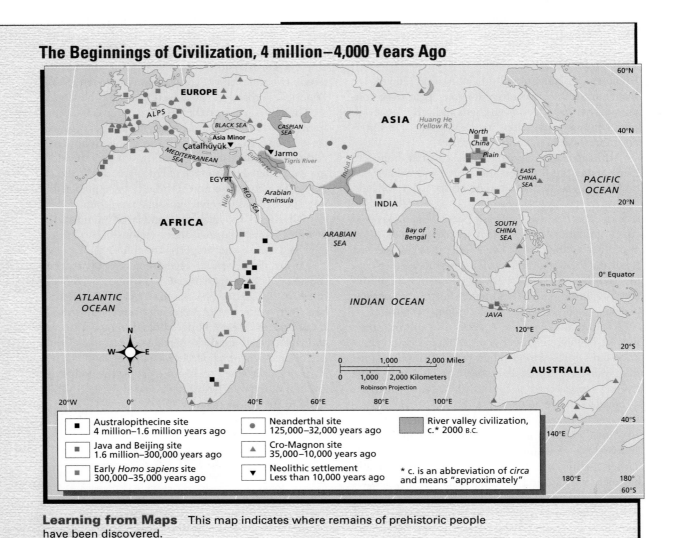

The Beginnings of Civilization, 4 million–4,000 Years Ago

Legend:

- ■ Australopithecine site
  4 million–1.6 million years ago
- ■ Java and Beijing site
  1.6 million–300,000 years ago
- ■ Early *Homo sapiens* site
  300,000–35,000 years ago
- ● Neanderthal site
  125,000–32,000 years ago
- ▲ Cro-Magnon site
  35,000–10,000 years ago
- ▼ Neolithic settlement
  Less than 10,000 years ago
- ▨ River valley civilization,
  c.* 2000 B.C.

* c. is an abbreviation of *circa* and means "approximately"

Learning from Maps This map indicates where remains of prehistoric people have been discovered.

? Region On which continent were most of the Neanderthal sites located?

Prehistoric Ivory Head

A Cro-Magnon artist carved this ivory head of a woman about 24,000 years ago, during the Old Stone Age. Found in France, it is small enough to hold in the palm of your hand. From artifacts such as this, we learn that some prehistoric peoples had an appreciation of beauty similar to our own. Such artifacts also tell us that some prehistoric groups had time for activities other than looking for food and making tools. This carving is one of the earliest known attempts to create a portrait. It may have been an object of worship that the owner could easily carry from place to place as he or she searched for food.

Perhaps the Neanderthals were the first people to believe in a god or gods.

Like earlier hominids, Neanderthal people disappeared. We do not know why. Massive glaciers had again advanced southward and covered much of Europe and North America. The cold, hostile environment may have had an effect. Or perhaps physically stronger or more mentally alert people overwhelmed and destroyed the Neanderthals.

Cro-Magnon People

About 35,000 years ago, a new kind of people—the Cro-Magnons—appeared in Europe. These new people made better tools and weapons and thus were better equipped to survive. The invention of spear-throwers, for example, made Cro-Magnons more effective hunters than Neanderthal people were. This new group of humans is named for a cave in southern France where their remains were first found in 1868. (See map on page 6.)

By about 20,000 years ago, humans had migrated to northeastern Europe, northern Asia, North America, and Australia. This movement of people into new areas highlights humans' ability to live and succeed in many different environments.

We know something about Cro-Magnon people through their drawings and paintings. In Spain and southern France, where many Cro-Magnon sites have been found, paintings of the animals they hunted cover the walls of limestone caves. In these paintings we can see bulls tossing their heads, wounded bison charging a hunter, and herds of fleeing reindeer. Paintings of red and black horses up to 18 feet long leap majestically. Faint drawings of human hands appear and disappear, depending on the angle of light.

Scientists and scholars are uncertain about why the Cro-Magnons created these artworks. The art may have been a chronicle of the hunt. The art might also have represented a means not only of teaching hunting techniques to young people but also of passing on tales about how the world began and how people and animals were created.

With high foreheads, well-defined chins, and small brow ridges, Cro-Magnon people looked almost the same as men and women living today. The Cro-Magnons lived on Earth for many thousands of years. By the end of the Old Stone Age, however, the Cro-Magnon as a distinct type of people no longer existed. In appearance, people looked basically like they do today.

The Middle Stone Age

The period lasting from the end of the Old Stone Age until the development of **agriculture**, the raising of crops for food, is called the Middle Stone Age, or Mesolithic Age. Because people in different parts of the world developed agriculture at different times, the dates of the Middle Stone Age vary according to region. In most of northern Europe, however, the era lasted until about 5,000 years ago.

People made much progress during the Middle Stone Age. They tamed the dog, which proved valuable in hunting smaller animals. They invented the bow and arrow, fishhooks, fish spears, and harpoons made from bones and antlers. By hollowing out logs, they made dugout canoes so that they could fish in deep water and cross rivers.

The New Stone Age

During the New Stone Age, or Neolithic Age, basic changes occurred in the way people lived. In the Old Stone Age and Middle Stone Age, people chipped stone to produce an edge or a point. In the New Stone Age, people discovered better ways to make tools and weapons from many kinds of stone and from wood. What distinguished the Neolithic Age from earlier ones is people's ability to shape stone tools by polishing or grinding. With new methods and materials, people made more specialized tools.

Other, even more important changes also occurred during the New Stone Age. Earlier people had been **nomads**, or wanderers who travel from place to place in search of food. Some Neolithic people, however, began settling in permanent villages. Two important developments are associated with this period: (1) agriculture and (2) the **domestication**, or taming, of cattle, goats, sheep, and pigs.

The development of agriculture changed the basic way people lived. Exactly how people learned that seeds could be planted and made to grow year after year, however, remains a mystery. In prehistoric times men went out in search of animals, while women remained near the campsite to care for the children. Women and children gathered plants and fruit for food. Perhaps a woman first noticed that seeds could be planted and grown. In any case, people somehow learned to plant wheat, barley, rice, and millet, grasses cultivated for grain. They also learned to use fertilizer and invented the plow.

Different plant species were domesticated in different parts of the world, and their use gradually spread to other areas. Wheat and barley originated in Southwest Asia, rice developed in South Asia, and corn was first cultivated in the Americas. Other domesticated plants included bananas in Southeast Asia and potatoes in South America.

The important shift from food gathering to food producing has often been called the **Neolithic Revolution**. (Although the word *revolution* is often used to mean the overthrow of a government, it also means a very important change in people's lives.)

In the period between 9000 B.C. and 5000 B.C., many of the old hunting-and-gathering settlements turned to farming and grew larger and more complex. In fact, many Neolithic villages had developed into small cities. For example, on the site of the biblical town of Jericho, scientists have found evidence of a town that may date from around 9000 B.C., making it one of the earliest continuous settlements. In Iraq, archaeologists unearthed remains of a town called Jarmo that had around 150 inhabitants in about 7000 B.C. In Turkey, scientists excavated Çatalhüyük (chah·TUHL·hoo·YOOHK), a town that flourished from about 6700 B.C. to 5600 B.C. with nearly 3,000 residents. Evidence shows that the people of Çatalhüyük built shrines to many gods and probably offered food and other forms of wealth to win the gods' favor or to express thanks.

Archaeologists have discovered the remains of mud-brick houses and shrines at Çatalhüyük.

1. **Define** history, prehistory, civilizations, anthropologists, hominids, archaeologists, artifacts, culture, radiocarbon dating, glaciers, Ice Age, agriculture, nomads, domestication, Neolithic Revolution
2. **Identify** Mary Leakey, Donald Johanson
3. **Locate and Explain the Significance** Jarmo, Çatalhüyük
4. **Understanding Ideas** Through what methods and using what types of evidence left by prehistoric people do anthropologists and archaeologists conduct their research?
5. **Summarizing Ideas** Compare the Neanderthal and Cro-Magnon peoples by describing the achievements of both groups.
6. **Identifying Ideas** Describe the advances made in the Mesolithic and Neolithic periods as related to the way people lived.

Section 2

The Foundations of Civilization

Focus Questions

- **Where did the first civilizations develop?**
- **What were the characteristics of the first civilizations?**
- **What were the great achievements of the first civilizations?**

By the end of the Stone Age, people had learned to make tools and weapons, use fire, create works of art, tame animals, grow their own food, and establish permanent settlements. Not all people lived in such settlements in the Neolithic Age, however. Some areas of the world lacked a soil and a climate suitable for farming. In some regions with grassy pasturelands, people maintained a herding culture, moving their flocks from one place to another to graze. They continued to live as nomads.

The River Valley Civilizations

Although Neolithic people lived in many areas, the settlements in four specific regions had particular importance for later human development. These four regions were (1) the Nile River valley in Africa, (2) the valley of the Tigris and Euphrates (yoo·FRAYT·eez) Rivers in southwestern Asia, (3) the Indus River valley in southern Asia, and (4) the Huang He, or Yellow River, valley in eastern Asia. (See map on p. 10–11.)

In these four river valleys, people first developed civilizations. Although all people have some sort of culture, when a culture becomes highly complex, we call it a civilization.

Most civilizations have at least three characteristics: (1) People have been able to produce surplus food. (2) People have created large towns or cities with some form of government. (3) A **division of labor** exists, in which different people perform different jobs, instead of each person doing all kinds of work. Some historians also consider the development of a calendar or the development of some form of writing to be characteristic of civilization.

Learning to Use Metals

People probably discovered metals by accident. It may have happened when someone built a fire over an area that contained the metal copper. Later the fire builder might have noticed lumps of this metal in the ashes. People may have learned how to shape the heated metal.

More than 6,000 years ago, people in both the Nile and Tigris-Euphrates River valleys knew how to make copper weapons, tools, utensils, and jewelry. Copper tools and weapons proved unsatisfactory, however, mainly because copper is a soft metal and cannot keep a sharp edge in heavy work. In time people learned to make a better metal—bronze. An alloy, or mixture, of copper and tin, bronze is harder than copper. People in the Nile and Tigris-Euphrates River valleys knew how to make bronze jewelry and weapons as early as 5,000 years ago. People in India and China also used bronze at an early date. The invention of bronze tools marked the end of the Stone Age and the beginning of the Bronze Age.

Iron, a stronger metal than either copper or bronze, is found in the earth mixed with other minerals. This mixture, iron ore, exists in more places and in larger amounts than either copper or tin. Separating the iron from the ore, however, required an extremely long and difficult process. The invention of the forge, a kind of furnace in which forcing air through fire produces great heat, helped make the use of iron possible. After the extreme heat of the forge had softened the ore, the iron could be separated from it. The iron then had to be hammered to eliminate impurities that would weaken the metal and render it useless.

We do not know when people discovered the process of making iron or who invented it. It may have originated separately in several different areas. We do know, however, that about 3,200 years ago people in southwestern Asia learned to make iron and craft it into tools and weapons stronger and more durable than those made of copper or bronze. The Iron Age had begun.

The Family in Early Civilizations

Women managed the family, cared for the children, and made items necessary for survival. They prepared food, made clothing, and probably invented pottery and weaving. As agriculture developed, men hunted less. Women did much of the farming, both planting and harvesting crops. As women became responsible for much of the food supply for the community, their authority and independence seems to have increased. The evidence for women's improved status is the rise of female goddesses, which corresponds with the early development of agriculture. When the plow was invented and animals were harnessed to pull it, men again became the primary food providers and assumed their former dominance in the family.

Religion played an important part in the lives of families in early civilizations. Early people believed in many gods and goddesses and in unseen forces of nature. They believed that gods and goddesses and these forces controlled all aspects of their lives. People worried that the rains would not come and that their crops would not grow. Because crop failure would mean starvation, they begged their gods and goddesses to provide water and to make seeds grow. Often these people offered sacrifices to their gods and goddesses to ensure good harvests, and they offered thanks when they believed their prayers had been answered.

People in early civilizations lived in large family groups. In addition to mothers, fathers, and children, families included grandparents, aunts, uncles, and cousins. However, because people had limited medical knowledge, many children died as infants. People of all ages depended on their relatives for help in everyday affairs.

Irrigation, Government, and Cities

The valleys of the Nile, Tigris and Euphrates, Indus, and Huang He have a common feature that greatly influenced their early development. Once a year the

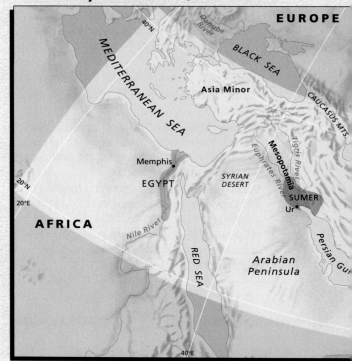

River Valley Civilizations, c. 2500 B.C.

Learning from Maps The earliest civilizations arose in similar latitudes and along rivers that nourished agriculture.

rivers rise and flood the valleys. Except for this rainy period, however, little if any rain falls. Hot, dry conditions prevail the rest of the year.

This climate challenged the farmers of these valleys. Somehow they had to get water to their crops during the dry season. At some point in the distant past, the farmers in these valleys learned to dig ditches and canals to transport needed water from the rivers to their fields. Thus they developed the first systems of **irrigation**. In the Tigris and Euphrates River valley and along the Indus River and the Huang He, farmers also built dikes to keep the rivers within their banks during the rainy season.

Farming in these river valleys, then, depended both on irrigation and the ability to control floods. Building large irrigation and flood-control projects required a high level of cooperation.

Governments may have developed gradually as a result of such cooperation. To work together effectively, people made rules to govern their behavior and to plan, direct, and regulate their work.

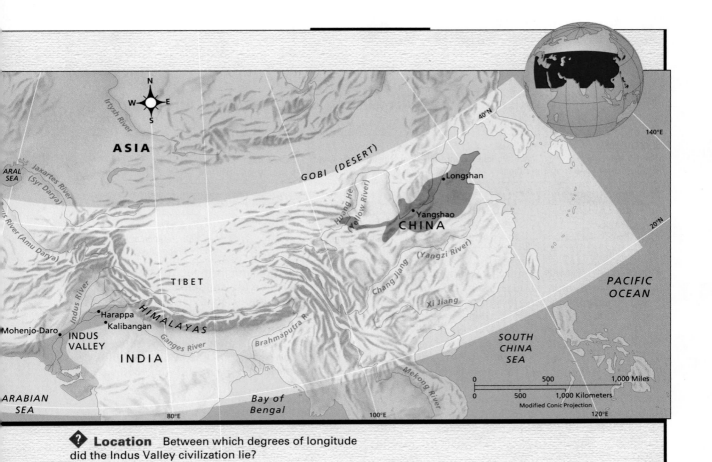

Location Between which degrees of longitude did the Indus Valley civilization lie?

The development of cities along the river valleys may have followed this course. The first dwellers probably moved into the valleys in tribes. Over time tribes established villages along the river. People lived in the villages and together worked the surrounding land and worked on group projects. Improved farming, made possible by techniques such as irrigation and better tools, meant more and better food and therefore a healthier and more comfortable life for each person.

More and better food also led to an increase in population, and some of the village communities grew to become cities. The large number of people living in cities provided the labor to create great palaces, temples, and other public buildings.

Origins of War

Not all people settled into agricultural communities and cities. Some groups of people were herders who used the territory outside agricultural communities for pastureland for their domesticated animals. Herders were hardy people, perhaps because they had to know how to protect their animals from predators. They no doubt attached some importance to the skills and practices of warfare because the takeover of someone else's herd or pastureland was an easy and quick way to gain wealth. In all likelihood, conflicts also arose between herders and farmers when herders let their animals graze on the farmers' carefully cultivated land.

As agricultural cities grew, settlers moved outward in all directions. More land was needed to feed the growing populations of cities. As the fields of one community came to encroach on the fields of another community, conflicts arose. Communities also frequently went to war over water rights.

Division of Labor

As methods of farming improved, fewer people had to work in the fields in order to produce enough food for all. Some people could specialize in other kinds of work besides farming. For example, people skilled in making tools and weapons could devote all their time to such work. They would then trade their products

Interpreting Visuals: Using a Time Line to Understand B.C. and A.D.

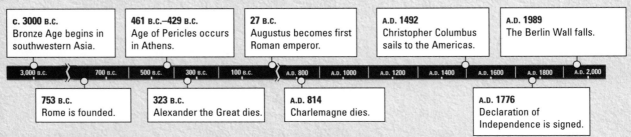

c. 3000 B.C.
Bronze Age begins in southwestern Asia.

461 B.C.–429 B.C.
Age of Pericles occurs in Athens.

27 B.C.
Augustus becomes first Roman emperor.

A.D. 1492
Christopher Columbus sails to the Americas.

A.D. 1989
The Berlin Wall falls.

3,000 B.C. — 700 B.C. — 500 B.C. — 300 B.C. — 100 B.C. — A.D. 800 — A.D. 1000 — A.D. 1200 — A.D. 1400 — A.D. 1600 — A.D. 1800 — A.D. 2,000

753 B.C.
Rome is founded.

323 B.C.
Alexander the Great dies.

A.D. 814
Charlemagne dies.

A.D. 1776
Declaration of Independence is signed.

To understand history, you need to know when events happened. In this book, we will be using a system of dating years from the traditional birth date of Christ. Years following Christ's birth are identified in numerical order and start with the letters A.D. The letters A.D. stand for the Latin phrase ***A**nno **D**omini,* which means "in the year of the Lord," or "since the birth of Christ." The year A.D. 1900 thus means the year 1,900 years after Christ's birth. Years before Christ's birth are identified in reverse numerical order and are followed by the letters B.C., which stand for "**B**efore the birth of **C**hrist." Thus the date 2000 B.C. means 2,000 years before Christ's birth.

To calculate how many years separate events in modern times from events in ancient history requires adding the B.C. date to the A.D. date. For example, 5000 B.C. was 6,990 years before A.D. 1990 (5,000 + 1,990 = 6,990), whereas 1000 B.C. was 2,500 years before A.D. 1500 (1,000 + 1,500 = 2,500).

The method of dating events from the birth of Christ is only one of several ways of calculating time. The Muslim, Chinese, Jewish, and Hindu calendars count the years in different ways. For example, the Christian year A.D. 1900 corresponds with the Muslim year 1318, the Hebrew year 5660, and the Chinese year 4597. Some scholars designate years with the abbreviation B.P., meaning "before the present."

How to Use a Time Line to Understand B.C. and A.D.

To help you understand when events occurred, each Chapter Review in this book includes a time line that shows the order, or sequence, of important events discussed in the chapter. A time line can also help you see relationships between certain events. In order to use a time line to understand B.C. and A.D., follow these steps.

1. Read the time line from left to right so that you can determine the sequence of events.
2. Identify the important events that the time line shows. Which events occurred in B.C.? Which events occurred in A.D.?
3. Identify relationships in time between the events on the time line. For example, how many years before A.D. 158 was 1350 B.C.?

Developing the Skill

The time line at the top of this page documents events that occurred between 3000 B.C. and A.D. 2000, a period of 5,000 years (3,000 + 2,000 = 5,000).

As you read the time line from left to right, notice that 1000 B.C. is earlier in time than 100 B.C. and that 500 B.C. is later in time than 800 B.C. This is true because the years before the birth of Christ are numbered in reverse numerical order. Also note that A.D. 1900 is later in time than A.D. 100 because the years after the birth of Christ (A.D.) are numbered in numerical order.

The time line helps you understand the order in which events occurred. For example, the Bronze Age began in southwestern Asia in about 3000 B.C.—2,247 years before the legendary founding of Rome (753 B.C.). Also note that the Bronze Age began about 4,776 years before the signing of the Declaration of Independence. You know that this is true because from 3000 B.C. to the end of the B.C. period was 3,000 years, and from the beginning of A.D. to A.D. 1776 was 1,776 years (3,000 + 1,776 = 4,776).

Practicing the Skill

How many years after the beginning of the Bronze Age in southwestern Asia was the fall of the Berlin Wall?

To apply this skill, see Applying History Study Skills on page 15.

for food. Thus a class of skilled craft workers called **artisans** appeared.

Other people became merchants and traders. They made their living by buying goods from farmers or artisans and then selling the goods for a profit to people who needed them. Traders not only transported goods to be sold but also passed along ideas. We call the spread of aspects of culture from one area of the world to another **cultural diffusion**.

Developing a Calendar

Early in their history, the people in the great river valleys developed calendars. Because these people farmed, they had to observe carefully the changes of the seasons. They needed to know, for example, when the yearly floods would start and stop. One way was to regard the time from flood to flood as a year and to divide the year according to the phases of the moon. The moon's phases are caused by its movements around Earth. The changes in the moon's appearance were the most regular repetitions that early people could easily see in the sky.

The time from one full moon to the next full moon would be a month—the time it takes the moon to revolve once completely around Earth. Twelve of these lunar months would roughly equal a year.

This system presented a major problem, however. A month based on the movement of the moon lasts only about 29 1/2 days. Twelve "moon" months thus equal 354 days. Yet by measuring the time it takes Earth to revolve once completely around the Sun, we know a year actually has approximately 365 1/4 days. The moon-based calendar of the river valley civilizations therefore fell about 11 days short. As a result, the months came earlier each year, and 12 months did not fill the time until the next flood. As you read more about river valley civilizations, you will see how early people coped with this problem.

People also needed to devise a way to date years. In this book, we will be using a system of dating years with the letters B.C. and A.D. (See Building History Study Skills on page 12.)

Inventing Writing

Life had become increasingly complex. For centuries human memory and verbal instructions had served society well. People in settled communities were now developing rules and agreements for living together and for protecting property. Trade also developed between various communities, and with the expansion of trade came a need for a method of keeping records.

As a result, speech was no longer sufficient as the only means of communication. People needed a written language to preserve and pass on ideas and information. By developing this written language, these early river valley civilizations created a record of their culture and society.

The development of writing was a long and complex process. The following story of the development of the letter *T* is imaginary and simplified, but it illustrates how alphabets might have been invented.

Pictures represent things. A picture of a tree can stand for the word *tree*. Picture signs of this sort are called pictographs, or pictograms. Pictographs, however, have disadvantages. It is easy to show a tree or a person, but how would you represent an idea, such as truth, honesty, liberty, or life after death?

Pictures symbolize ideas. People did learn to use pictures to stand for ideas. Suppose a successful farmer kept orchards. The farmer might use a drawing of a tree to represent the idea of wealth. We call signs of this sort ideographs, or ideograms.

Pictures stand for sounds. A great many signs are needed to express thoughts using pictographs and ideographs. Fewer signs are required if one sign can represent a sound, not just one meaning. Thus the tree sign could stand not only for *tree* but also for the syllable *trea* in the word *treason*. Signs of this sort are called phonograms.

Signs represent consonants or vowels. Signs that represent consonants or vowels are called letters and form an alphabet. Imagine what might have happened over many years to the tree symbol, for example. The picture came to stand for more than one idea; it came to stand for the syllable *trea*. Finally, a simplified version of the picture—the letter *T*—came to represent just the first sound of *tree*.

Section 2 Review

1. **Define** division of labor, irrigation, artisans, cultural diffusion
2. **Locate and Explain the Significance** Nile River, Tigris River, Euphrates River, Indus River, Huang He
3. **Understanding Ideas** In which four geographical regions did the first civilizations develop?
4. **Seeing Relationships** How did the need for irrigation and flood control lead to the development of governments?
5. **Summarizing Ideas** Briefly describe how calendars and writing developed.

Chapter 1 Review

c. 1,600,000 B.C.
Java man and
Peking man emerge.

| 4,000,000 B.C. | 3,000,000 B.C. | 2,000,000 B.C. | 130,000 B.C. |

c. 3,700,000 B.C.
Australopithecus skeletal remains from this date are found by archaeologists.

c. 2,500,000 B.C.
First stone tools appear.

c. 128,000 B.C.
Neanderthal people appear.

Chapter Summary

The following list contains the key concepts you have learned about the cultures and civilizations that began during prehistoric times.

1. The first humans left behind bones, artifacts, and pictures. From these, anthropologists have been able to determine something about what the first human beings looked like, what they ate, where they lived, and what some of their customs were.
2. Many scientists believe that during prehistoric times people gradually developed greater skills, such as producing more effective tools, learning to hunt more efficiently, and creating the earliest works of art.
3. Eventually, people learned to domesticate animals and to farm. As a result, they began settling in villages and gave up their nomadic lifestyles.
4. Changes during Neolithic times brought about one of the most important turning points in human history—the development of agriculture.
5. People developed the first civilizations in four great river valleys in Africa and Asia. There people learned how to use metals, build cities, promote economic activity, and establish governments.
6. One of the most significant developments was writing. The ability to keep written records gave civilizations continuity. It also allows us, for the first time, to find out what early people thought about their own times. With the development of writing, prehistory ended and history began.

Reviewing Important Terms

On a separate sheet of paper, match each of the following terms with the correct definition in column two.

a. prehistory
b. civilization
c. artifact
d. history
e. division of labor
f. anthropologist
g. radiocarbon dating
h. glaciers
i. agriculture
j. Neolithic Revolution

_____1. Record of what has taken place in the world since the invention of writing
_____2. Highly organized society with complex institutions and attitudes that link a large number of people together
_____3. Period before the invention of writing
_____4. Technique that measures the rate of decay of certain atoms present in organic matter
_____5. Large, slowly moving masses of snow and ice
_____6. Shift from food gathering to food producing
_____7. Material object shaped by human being or earlier hominid
_____8. System in which different people perform different jobs, instead of each person having to do all kinds of work
_____9. Scientist who studies the skeletal remains of early humans to determine how they looked, how tall they were, how long they lived, and other physical characteristics
_____10. Raising of crops for food

Developing Critical Thinking Skills

1. **Understanding Ideas (a)** Why do the events of prehistory remain cloaked in mystery? **(b)** What methods do archaeologists and anthropologists use to unlock these mysteries?
2. **Seeing Relationships** How did the lives of early people change after they learned to domesticate animals and raise food crops?
3. **Contrasting Ideas** How did the people of the Neolithic Age differ from those of the Paleolithic Age in these categories: **(a)** method of obtaining food; **(b)** tools?
4. **Understanding Chronology** Place the items in each of the following three lists in chronological order from most ancient to most recent: **(a)** plow, upright posture, meat eaters, use of fire; **(b)** Peking man, Australopithecus, Neanderthal people, Cro-Magnon people; **(c)** farming, hunting, cooking of food, gathering of fruits and seeds.
5. **Synthesizing Ideas (a)** What are the three major characteristics of civilizations? **(b)** How does life in the United States today meet each of these characteristics of civilizations?

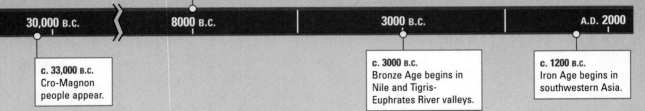

c. 8000 B.C.
Last Ice Age ends.
New Stone Age begins.

30,000 B.C.   8000 B.C.   3000 B.C.   A.D. 2000

c. 33,000 B.C.
Cro-Magnon
people appear.

c. 3000 B.C.
Bronze Age begins in
Nile and Tigris-
Euphrates River valleys.

c. 1200 B.C.
Iron Age begins in
southwestern Asia.

Relating Geography to History

Study the map of the four river valley civilizations on pages 10–11. **(a)** List the large bodies of water that are closest to the four major river valley civilizations. **(b)** Which two of these civilizations seem most likely, based on their location, to have had some trading contact with each other? **(c)** Which civilization seems the most isolated from the others?

Relating Past to Present

1. **(a)** What was the role of women in Neolithic society? **(b)** How have the roles of women in the United States changed in the past 30 years? **(c)** What new inventions, developments, and attitudes have helped bring about these changes?
2. What do you think a civilization from outer space would learn of the culture of the United States today from investigating the contents of our garbage dumps, cemeteries, and junkyards?
3. Over thousands of years, prehistoric people discovered new skills and inventions that greatly changed their lives. Among these were methods of agriculture, the use of metals, and the calendar. **(a)** Choose a modern skill or invention and explain how it has changed our lives today. **(b)** Why do you think it took prehistoric people thousands of years to make a few important discoveries?

Applying History Study Skills

Before completing this activity, review Building History Study Skills on page 12.

Look at the events shown on the time line on these Chapter Review pages (pages 14 and 15). Remember that B.C. years are numbered in reverse numerical order before the birth of Christ and that A.D. (Anno Domini) years are numbered in numerical order after the birth of Christ. Then calculate how many years separate the two events in each of the following.

(a) Neanderthal <u>and</u> Cro-Magnon people appear.
(b) Iron Age begins in southwestern Asia <u>and</u> first stone tools appear.
(c) Bronze Age begins in Nile and Tigris-Euphrates River valleys <u>and</u> first stone tools appear.
(d) Last Ice Age ends <u>and</u> archaeologists find remains of Australopithecus skeleton from this date.

(e) New Stone Age begins <u>and</u> Java man and Peking man emerge.

Building Your Portfolio

1. **Writing a Report** In your school or local library, locate information about hunting and gathering societies in the world today. For example, you might read Clive Cowley's *Fabled Tribe: A Voyage to Discover the River Bushmen of the Okavango Swamps* (Atheneum, 1968), which is about the San people of southern Africa. Or you might choose to read about the Pygmies of Central Africa, who are described in Colin M. Turnbull's *The Forest People* (Peter Smith, 1988). Other groups that you might read about are New Guinea tribes, Amazon tribes, or Philippine tribes. Periodicals such as *National Geographic* would be good sources for your research. Then write a report describing: **(a)** how the group is organized and governed; **(b)** the roles of men and women; **(c)** how food is obtained and distributed within the group; **(d)** the group's religious practices; **(e)** the physical environment and how it affects the way the people live; **(f)** the types of tools made and used. Place the report in your portfolio.
2. **Making Charts** Reread the information on inventing writing on page 13. Then use resources in your school or public library to find more information on the systems of writing that early people developed. Use the information you find to help you construct a chart illustrating the major steps in the development of writing. Place the chart in your portfolio.

The First Civilizations

TIME

c. 6000 B.C.–587 B.C.

c. 6000 B.C.–587 B.C.

3.7 million B.C. | 4000 B.C. | A.D. 2100

PLACE

Africa and
Southwest Asia

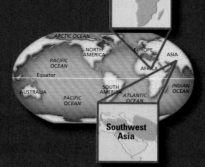

Figures of Ramses II in front of main temple,
at Abu Simbel, Egypt

Significance

Civilization first appeared in two great river valleys of Africa and the Middle East. In both of these river valleys—the Nile and the Tigris-Euphrates—people gradually developed different complex societies with strong governments.

Terms to Define

oasis	caravans
silt	scribes
hieroglyphics	mummification
papyrus	city-state
kingdom	cuneiform
monarchy	arch
pharaoh	ziggurats
dynasty	cavalry
empire	barter
polytheism	money economy
monotheism	ethical monotheism

People to Identify

Menes	Cyrus the Great
Hyksos	Darius I
Hatshepsut	Xerxes I
Amenhotep IV	Zoroaster
Tutankhamen	Abraham
Ramses II	Moses
Sargon	Saul
Hammurabi	David
Nebuchadnezzar	Solomon

Places to Locate

Egypt	Mesopotamia
Nile River	Babylonia
Upper Egypt	Sumer
Lower Egypt	Israel
Giza	Samaria
Fertile Crescent	Judah
Persian Gulf	Jerusalem

Chapter Theme Questions

- **Cross-Cultural Interaction** What might contribute to the development of culture in an area of frequent migration?
- **Politics and Law** What makes law an important part of civilization?
- **Religion** What characteristics might major religions have in common?

Almost 4,000 years ago in the town of Sumer in the fertile valley of the Tigris and Euphrates Rivers, a worried father turned to his son and gave the advice that would be repeated by generations of fathers down through the centuries of history.

❝The father begins by asking his son: 'Where did you go?' 'I did not go anywhere.' 'If you did not go anywhere, why do you idle about? Go to school, stand before your "school-father," recite your assignment, open your schoolbag, write your tablet, let your "big brother" write your new tablet for you. After you have finished your assignment and reported to your monitor, come to me, and do not wander about in the street. . . . Don't stand about in the public square, or wander about the boulevard.'❞

The story of the Sumerians, as well as of the other great civilizations of Africa and southwestern Asia, shows how early people developed cultures and passed them on to future generations.

Section 1

Ancient Kingdoms of the Nile

Focus Questions

- **What geographical factors influenced Egyptian civilization?**
- **What were the great achievements of the early Egyptians?**
- **What were the main periods in the early history of Egyptian civilization?**

Of all the ancient river valley civilizations, the Nile Valley civilization in Africa is probably the best known because most people have seen pictures of its ancient landmarks, such as the pyramids and the

Ancient Egypt, c. 3000 B.C.

Nile floodplain

0   150   300 Miles
0   150   300 Kilometers
Lambert Conformal Conic Projection

Learning from Maps The Nile River is the longest river in the world.

? Movement The Nile River flows in a northward direction on which continent? Into which body of water does the Nile River enter?

Great Sphinx. For many, these huge constructions symbolize both the ancient culture that produced them and the modern nation of Egypt, although the two societies are quite different.

The Origins of Civilization in the Nile Valley

The Nile Valley civilization did not develop in a vacuum. Like other civilizations, it was the result of the coming together of ideas and influences from other parts of the world. Archaeological finds have suggested that a number of ancient cultures influenced the development of Nile Valley civilization. Early hunter-gatherers appear to have moved into the

Nile Valley in groups by at least 12,000 B.C. Over time, these groups formed settlements and turned to farming. Furthermore, studies of ancient seeds have shown that plants cultivated in the Nile Valley, such as cotton, were grown earlier elsewhere in Africa.

Civilizations to the north of Egypt may also have influenced its development. Archaeological finds in ancient Palestine suggest that an older culture there contributed to Nile Valley civilization. Most scholars believe, however, that it was mainly the Nile Valley people themselves who created and developed their magnificent culture.

The Physical Setting

The boundaries of modern Egypt are quite different from those of ancient Egypt. (See map on this page.) Today desert predominates in the region, with only an occasional green **oasis**, a place where there is water, breaking the barren landscape. Some 12,000 years ago, however, much of the area was covered by swampland that probably teemed with the animals we associate with central Africa—the hippopotamus and the crocodile, for example. Even so, for the last 5,000 years one physical feature has dominated the area: the Nile River.

The main sources of this river, the longest in the world, are the White Nile, which begins near Lake Victoria in eastern Africa, and the Blue Nile, the source of which is Lake Tana in the Ethiopian highlands. From the source of the White Nile to where the river enters the Mediterranean Sea through the Nile Delta is about 4,160 miles. Along its length lie six great cataracts (rapids), where the river is forced into narrow channels cut through rock. The Nile Valley people built their civilization in the 750 mile stretch between the sea and the first cataract.

"The gift of the Nile." Many centuries after the early period of Nile Valley history, an ancient Greek historian named Herodotus (hee·RAHD·uh·tuhs) wrote of his travels in northeastern Africa. He said that all Egypt was "the gift of the Nile." His writings accurately described a remarkable feature of Nile Valley geography—the annual flood.

Until the construction of the Aswan High Dam in the 1960s, each year from June to October, rain falling on the Ethiopian plateau near the source of the Nile caused the river to flood the flatland of the Nile Valley. As the waters receded, they left behind a layer of **silt**, or fertile soil, carried as sediment in the river's waters.

From earliest times, Egyptian farmers planned their work around the flood. They knew when it would come every year. They harvested their crops (such as wheat and barley) before the flood began; then they waited for the water to soak the hard, dry earth before draining off and leaving its new, fertile soil.

Little or no rain falls in Egypt directly, and the moisture produced by the flood was sufficient for only one planting. Early in their history, however, the Egyptians learned to use water from the Nile for irrigation. Farmers dug networks of short canals to carry water to their fields. The water from the canals helped farmers grow two or even three crops a year, thus making it possible to feed a large population.

Other natural advantages. Even in ancient times the Nile Valley had other natural resources besides its fertile soil. Its sunny, frost-free climate, for example, nurtured many kinds of crops.

An interesting and important feature of the climate was, and still is, the prevailing wind that blows from the Mediterranean Sea upstream into the Nile Valley. A boat on the Nile can either go upstream with the wind by using a sail or be rowed with oars downstream against the wind, aided by the river current. This fact allowed the ancient Egyptians to make the Nile River as far as the first cataract a pathway of travel and trade that linked all parts of the valley. It also helped the ancient Egyptians unite the region.

The Nile Valley also contains deposits of granite, sandstone, and limestone. The Egyptians used these minerals for building. They had no lumber because there were few forests in the region. Finally, the ancient Egyptians enjoyed one other natural advantage—the valley's location. The deserts and seas that surrounded the Nile Valley provided a natural protection against invaders. Only the Isthmus of Suez broke the natural barriers. (See map on opposite page.) The isthmus forms a land bridge between Asia and Africa and thus provided a route for trade, for the exchange of ideas, and even for invading armies.

Early Steps Toward Civilization

People have lived in the valley of the Nile River since earliest times. A Neolithic culture probably developed in the valley about 6000 B.C.

By about 3800 B.C. the people of the Nile Valley had begun to take important steps along the road to civilization. They mined copper, perhaps to make tools and jewelry. They discovered how to make bronze, the strong alloy of copper and tin. Evidence indicates that they also learned how to glaze pottery.

Nile Valley writing. By about 3000 B.C. Nile Valley people were using a form of writing referred to as **hieroglyphics** (hy·ruh·GLI·fiks). The word comes

The ancient Egyptians used many symbols to reflect their beliefs, such as the ankh above, which represents life.

from two Greek words: *hieros,* meaning "sacred," and *gluphein,* meaning "to carve." Hieroglyphic writing used more than 600 hieroglyphic signs, pictures, or symbols to indicate words or sounds. The Egyptians used 24 signs that each stood for only one sound—all consonants. Other signs represented two consonants. They had no signs for vowels.

At first Egyptians carved hieroglyphics in stone and other hard materials, but this was a long and difficult process. Searching for a better material on which to write, they discovered how to make use of the papyrus plant that grew in the marshes near the Nile. They first cut the stem of the plant into long, thin slices. Then they moistened the strips, arranged them in layers on top of each other, and pressed them together to form a mat with a smooth surface. The Egyptians called this product **papyrus** (plural *papyri*), from which we derive our word *paper.*

Egyptians wrote on papyrus with ink made from soot, water, and vegetable gum—a sticky juice from certain trees and plants. The Egyptians diluted the gum with water before mixing it with soot. They used a sharpened reed as a pen.

Solving the hieroglyphic puzzle. Modern scholars learned to read the language of the ancient Egyptians through a clever bit of detective work. In A.D. 1798 a French army, commanded by Napoleon Bonaparte, invaded Egypt. The next year a French officer discovered a stone that had inscriptions written in Greek,

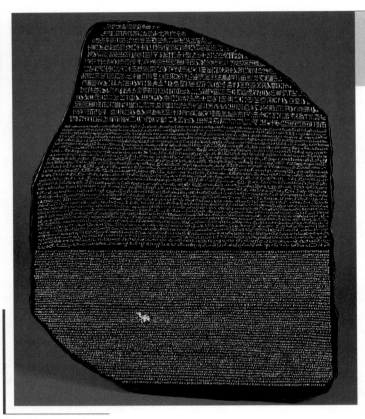

hieroglyphics, and a later Egyptian writing called *demotic*. The Rosetta Stone, named for the Rosetta branch of the Nile Delta (where the officer stumbled upon the stone), provided the means to understanding the language of the ancient Egyptians.

Almost 23 years after the discovery of the Rosetta Stone, a French language expert, Jean François Champollion (sham·pawl·YAWN), solved the mystery. The Greek text, which scholars could read, stated that all three inscriptions said the same thing and also described honors granted by the priesthood to the ruler Ptolemy (TAL·uh·mee) V in 196 B.C. Champollion was able to decipher the hieroglyphic symbols in the inscription and went on to establish the principles by which all other hieroglyphics could be read. Because scholars could now understand hieroglyphics, they could read eyewitness accounts of Egypt's history.

The Egyptian Kingdom

Over the centuries strong leaders united early Egyptian settlements to form two kingdoms—Upper Egypt and Lower Egypt. (A king or queen heads a **kingdom**, one of the earliest forms of government. Another word for kingdom is **monarchy**.) Upper Egypt lay farther south from the Mediterranean Sea, along the upper Nile River. Lower Egypt lay to the north, in the delta of the Nile River. (See map on page 18.)

Then, sometime after 3200 B.C., a ruler known as Menes (MEE·neez), a king of Upper Egypt, united all Egypt into one kingdom. Menes and his successors crushed rebellions, gained new territory, regulated irrigation, and encouraged trade, bringing increased prosperity.

Much of the power of these rulers came from their roles as religious as well as political leaders. The people regarded them as gods. In later years Egyptian rulers took the title **pharaoh**, which means "great house," after the place where they lived. The pharaohs led the government and served as judges, high priests, and generals of the armies. Although the pharaohs had absolute, or unlimited, power, their duties included protecting and caring for their people.

Menes founded a **dynasty**, or family of rulers in which the right to rule passes on within the family, usually from father to son or daughter. This hereditary rule ends only when the family is driven from power or when there is no family member left to become ruler. In more than 2,500 years, beginning with the time of Menes and continuing to almost 300 B.C., about 30 Egyptian dynasties rose and fell. Historians divide this span of time into three kingdoms: the Old Kingdom, the Middle Kingdom, and the New Kingdom. The periods between the kingdoms are referred to as the intermediate periods.

The Old Kingdom

The Old Kingdom existed from about 2650 to 2180 B.C. Many important developments in science and the arts took place during this time. For example, Egyptians of the Old Kingdom built the largest pyramids, which still stand as symbols of the glory of Egyptian civilization.

During this time, the upper class in Egyptian society consisted of the pharaoh, the royal family, and the priests and officials who helped govern the country. The lower class was most of the population—mainly peasants, or farmers. They owed the pharaoh certain services, such as duty in the army or work on the irrigation system or on the pyramids and public buildings.

As time passed, officials in the upper class gradually became a hereditary group of nobles. Toward the end of the Old Kingdom, the pharaohs grew weaker and the nobles grew stronger. For well over 100 years after the end of this period, civil wars divided the country as rivals claimed the throne.

The Middle Kingdom

In about 2040 B.C. a new line of pharaohs reunited Egypt for a while, beginning a period known as the Middle Kingdom. Once again, however, the rise of a hereditary class of nobles and priests weakened the power of the pharaoh. Rivalries, conflicts, and the division of power caused the Middle Kingdom to fall into disorder around 1780 B.C. Then, about 1650 B.C., much of Egypt fell under the rule of an Asiatic people—the Hyksos (HIK·sohs)—whose horse-drawn chariots overwhelmed the Egyptians.

The Hyksos. The story of the Hyksos' rule in Egypt provides an excellent example of differing interpretations of history. Historians investigate past events and interpret these events according to the evidence they find. Often, different historians disagree as to exactly what happened.

According to Egyptian records written hundreds of years later, the brutal and warlike Hyksos savagely invaded Lower Egypt. In about the 200s B.C. an Egyptian priest, Manetho, wrote that Egypt had been invaded by people from the east. Manetho described how these people had used force to conquer the rulers of Egypt and destroy cities and temples. He wrote that they treated the natives of Egypt cruelly, slaughtering some and enslaving women and children. Based on this and other ancient Egyptian sources, some scholars believe that the Hyksos invaded and conquered Egypt.

Other scholars, however, point out that little evidence confirms the destruction of Egyptian temples during this period. They discount Egyptian stories of the Hyksos' brutality as excuses for why the Hyksos were able to conquer Egypt. After all, how could a land ruled by a god fall under foreign rule unless those foreigners had mighty armies?

These scholars believe that nomadic Hyksos migrated into the Nile Delta around 1800 B.C. In the confusion following the collapse of the Middle Kingdom, the Hyksos emerged as the most powerful people in the region and ruled most of Lower Egypt for more than 100 years.

The New Kingdom

Although historians disagree about how the Hyksos came to rule Egypt, most agree that they remained outsiders in Egypt. Eventually leaders in Upper Egypt forged an army, rebelled against the Hyksos, and drove them from the country. A line of strong pharaohs who lived in the city of Thebes far up the Nile ruled a reunited Egypt. The period in which they ruled—from about 1570 B.C. to about 1100 B.C.—is called the New Kingdom.

For a time, the pharaohs once more had absolute power. They kept strict control over the government, and adopting the horse-drawn chariots of the Hyksos, they created a strong army. With the aid of this army, the pharaohs extended their territory to include land along the eastern end of the Mediterranean Sea and south into Nubia. (See map on page 22.) In doing so, they created an **empire**, a form of government in which an individual or a single people rules over many other peoples and their territories.

Like many other peoples, however, the Egyptians found it easier to conquer territory than to rule and keep it. Usually they allowed the local prince of a conquered region to act as governor. To be sure of his loyalty and obedience, they took his sons and brothers back to Egypt as hostages to be trained at the palace of Thebes.

Only the strongest pharaohs, however, could hold the empire together. Whenever the government of Egypt showed signs of weakness, some part of the empire would revolt and try to break away.

Egypt: The New Kingdom, c. 1450 B.C.

Learning from Maps The New Kingdom extended Egypt's borders.

? Location Approximately how many miles is it from the northernmost point to the southernmost point of the New Kingdom?

Hatshepsut rules Egypt. One of the first woman rulers about whom we have written records, Hatshepsut (hat·SHEP·soot), reigned as pharaoh from c. 1503 B.C. to 1482 B.C. Although Egyptian queens often gained fame as the wives of kings, few ever became pharaohs. Hatshepsut proved to be an able ruler. In addition to maintaining the security of Egypt, she had temples to the gods constructed, as well as other public buildings.

Hatshepsut first ruled with her husband, Thutmose (thoot·MOH·suh) II, who was also her half brother. This marriage illustrates a unique custom of Egyptian rulers. As a god, the pharaoh could not marry an ordinary human being. Instead, the pharaoh usually married a sister or brother, or half sister or half brother. After

Thutmose II died, his son, Thutmose III, wanted to become ruler, but Hatshepsut continued to rule alone. Angry at Hatshepsut for refusing to allow him power, Thutmose III tried to have her name removed from all public monuments after she died.

Amenhotep and religious innovation. The pharaoh Amenhotep (ahm·uhn·HOH·tep) IV ruled from about 1380 B.C. to 1362 B.C. Neither a great conqueror nor a good ruler, Amenhotep is nevertheless important because he attempted to bring about a social and religious revolution.

Before Amenhotep became pharaoh, Egyptians believed in the existence of many gods. We call such a belief **polytheism,** from the Greek words *polys,* meaning "many," and *theos,* meaning "god." The greatest of the Egyptian gods was Amon-Re.

Amenhotep tried to change Egyptian religion. He believed in only one god—the sun, symbolized by a sun disk called the Aton—and he believed that the pharaoh was that god's earthly son. We call this belief in only one god **monotheism,** from the Greek *monos,* meaning "one," plus *theos.* To honor Aton, Amenhotep changed his own name to Akhenaton (ahk·NAHT·uhn), which means "he who is pleasing to Aton."

The priests of Amon-Re had become so powerful that they constantly interfered in public affairs. To break up their power, Akhenaton moved his capital from Thebes, the site of the great temple of Amon-Re, to a new city, Akhetaton, a site known today as Tell el-'Amarna. At Akhetaton, Akhenaton devoted his time to religion and neglected the ruling of the empire.

Akhenaton's actions infuriated the priests of Amon-Re. The wealth that formerly had come to them at their great temple of Thebes now went to the temple of the new god in the new capital. Their easy way of life suddenly ended. Appointments to high positions, which formerly had been theirs, now went to followers of Aton.

Akhenaton soon learned that he could not change all of his people's religious beliefs by command. A bitter struggle between pharaoh and priests disrupted Egypt during the later years of his reign. During the reign of a successor of Akhenaton—the boy king Tutankhamen (too·tang·KAHM·uhn)—the priests of Amon-Re regained their power. The capital was moved to Memphis, and the old polytheistic religion was reestablished. The religious and cultural upheaval begun by Akhenaton was now ended.

After the death of Akhenaton, few strong pharaohs ruled Egypt. Ramses II, however, was a powerful leader

Funeral Mask of a Pharaoh

One of the most beautiful treasures in the world is this life-size funeral mask of the pharaoh Tutankhamen. The discovery of his tomb in 1922 captured the imagination of people around the world. What was extraordinary about the find was that although the tomb had been robbed in ancient times, the inner chambers remained untouched. The tomb contained works of art that revealed many aspects of Egyptian life.

The mask is made of beaten gold, inlaid with beads and blue glass. It shows Tutankhamen as the handsome youth he was when he died in his late teens, more than 3,000 years ago. The decorative beard on the mask is a symbol of the great god Osiris, who judged the dead. On the headdress are depicted a vulture and a cobra, symbols of sovereignty over Upper and Lower Egypt.

who ruled from about 1279 to 1213 B.C. He waged war for years against the Hittites, who were invading the Egyptian territory of Syria. Ramses managed to hold Egypt and the empire intact and ordered the construction of many temples and monuments. He is sometimes called Ramses the Great.

Egypt's Decline

Most of Ramses II's successors could not maintain the empire or prevent corruption in the government. Slowly Egypt slipped into decline. Egyptian records from this period suggest there was widespread upheaval in the Eastern Mediterranean. A series of invasions weakened Egypt, and finally foreign empires, including the Nubians, the Assyrians, and the Persians, ravaged Egypt. Egypt was no longer a major imperial power. Even during these times, however, dynasties of Egyptian pharaohs continued to reign. It was not until the 300s B.C. that rule in Egypt by Egyptians finally came to an end.

Section 1 Review

1. **Define** oasis, silt, hieroglyphics, papyrus, kingdom, monarchy, pharaoh, dynasty, empire, polytheism, monotheism

2. **Identify** Menes, Hyksos, Hatshepsut, Amenhotep IV, Tutankhamen, Ramses II

3. **Locate and Explain the Significance** Egypt, Nile River, Upper Egypt, Lower Egypt

4. **Interpreting Ideas** Is Herodotus's statement that Egypt is the gift of the Nile an accurate description? Use information from the chapter to support your answer.

5. **Understanding Ideas** Explain the significance of one of the achievements of the early Egyptians.

6. **Summarizing Ideas** Briefly characterize each of the three kingdoms of Egypt: the Old Kingdom, the Middle Kingdom, and the New Kingdom.

Egyptian Life and Culture

Focus Questions

- **How were farming and trade carried on in Egypt?**
- **What were the great Egyptian cultural and scientific achievements?**
- **How did the Egyptians express their religious beliefs?**

Although dynasties rose and fell, the remarkably stable Nile Valley culture extended over many centuries. This stability resulted in part from favorable conditions, particularly the regular Nile floods and the region's protected geographic location.

Farming and Trade

Farmland in Egypt was divided into large estates. Peasants did most of the farming, using crude hoes or wooden plows. The peasants, however, could keep only part of the crop. The rest went to the pharaoh as rents and taxes.

Wheat and barley were the chief grain crops. Flax was grown and then spun and woven into linen. Farmers also raised cotton, important to Egypt in ancient times just as it is today, for weaving into cloth.

Ancient Egypt usually produced more food than its people required. The Egyptians traded the surplus with other peoples for products that Egypt needed. Trade was carried on by land and sea. Egyptians were among the first people to build seagoing ships. Their ships sailed the Mediterranean, Aegean, and Red Seas. On land, merchants riding donkeys and camels joined **caravans**—groups of people traveling together for safety over long distances—into western Asia and deep into Africa. (See map on page 22.)

Social Classes

For the most part, rigid divisions separated Egyptian social classes. Although people in the lower class sometimes could improve their status, they almost never entered the ranks of the upper class.

Women, however, enjoyed many legal rights and ranked as the equals of their husbands in social and business affairs. An Egyptian woman could own property in her own right and could leave it to her daughter. In many ways, Egyptian women at that

The upper class, or nobles, in ancient Egypt followed many rituals. This scene depicts a wife anointing her husband.

Connections: Then and Now

Cotton

The painted figures on ancient Egyptian temple walls (shown in this feature) and mummy cases appear to be wearing cotton clothing. Egypt has long been a major source of cotton, one of the world's most important agricultural products. Egypt's warm climate and the water of the Nile River create an excellent environment for the cultivation of cotton. Egypt's cotton is of very high quality and is in great demand worldwide.

Cotton probably first grew wild in East Africa. Nearly 5,000 years ago the people of the Indus Valley cultivated cotton. Ancient peoples used cotton to make clothing and sandal bindings. Types of cotton are often named after the places from which they come, such as American upland, Egyptian, and Asiatic.

The fabric woven from the fluffy fiber of the cotton plant absorbs moisture and remains cool even in hot weather. It is so comfortable that manufacturers today use it in clothing of all kinds. Cotton is used in many other products as well, including bandages, towels, and even explosives. Cotton's popularity spans thousands of years, and the demand for it still continues.

---

time had more freedom and more power than women in other cultures in the region.

Architecture and the Arts

When most people think of Egypt, they often first call to mind the huge stone figure of the Sphinx and the majestic pyramids, which still stand after nearly 5,000 years. The huge limestone beast crouching in the sand near the present-day city of Giza is called the Great Sphinx. The statue has the 240-foot body of a lion, stands 66 feet tall, and has a human face measuring almost 14 feet across. Scholars believe that the Great Sphinx is about 4,500 years old, and think that it may represent the ancient Egyptian sun god.

The Egyptians built the pyramids as tombs for the pharaohs. Most of the 80 or so pyramids that still stand are clustered in groups along the west bank of the Nile. The best-known ones tower above the sands at Giza. Among them is the Great Pyramid, built about 2600 B.C. This gigantic structure covers about 13 acres at its base and is almost 460 feet high. It consists of over 2 million blocks of stone, each of which weighs 500 pounds.

The building of such gigantic structures obviously required great skill. Egyptian architects and engineers ranked among the best in the ancient world. Scholars believe they built ramps, or sloping walkways, along which thousands of slaves pushed or pulled enormous stones into place. They also used levers to move heavy objects.

The Egyptians perfected other art forms as well. In addition to large-scale works, sculptors made small, lifelike statues of rulers and animals.

Egyptians decorated many of their buildings with paintings showing scenes of everyday life—artisans at work, farmers harvesting grain, and people enjoying banquets. Egyptians developed a distinctive way of drawing the human figure. They showed the head and feet in profile and the shoulders facing forward. Despite this angular, somewhat stiff interpretation, surviving paintings provide us with colorful examples of the Egyptian way of life.

Science, Mathematics, and Medicine

Early in their history, the Egyptians invented a lunar calendar—that is, one based on the moon's movements. As discussed in Chapter 1, such a calendar caused difficulties because it did not fill the entire year. Some time later, however, an observant Egyptian noticed that a very bright star began to appear above the horizon just before the floods came. The time between one rising of this star (which we now call Sirius, the Dog Star) and the next is 365 days, almost exactly a full year. The ancient Egyptians then based their year on this cycle, dividing it into 12 months of 30 days each. This system left them with five extra days, which they used for holidays and feasting.

To keep track of the years, Egyptians adopted the practice of counting the years of the pharaohs' reigns. For example, they might refer to the first, second, or twentieth year of the reign of a certain pharaoh.

The Egyptians developed a number system based on 10, similar to the decimal system we use today, and they used fractions as well as whole numbers. They also used geometry to calculate how to restore the boundaries of fields after floods, and also to build the pyramids.

The Egyptians also made important discoveries in medicine. They knew a great deal about the human body and used this knowledge to treat illnesses and in preserving bodies. Several Egyptian papyri that have survived classify diseases according to symptoms and recommend treatments. Although the treatments include some "magic spells," many specify the use of herbs and medicine.

Education and Religion

The Egyptians could not have gathered and passed on their knowledge without a system of education. Religious instruction formed an important part of Egyptian education, and schools were usually in or attached to temples. Most education, however, focused on training an elite group of people to read and write so that they could work for the government. These people were **scribes**, or clerks.

Religion was an extremely important part of Egyptian life. Egyptians believed in many gods. In early days each village and district had its own local god or gods. In time, people throughout the country accepted and worshiped some of these gods. The most important god was Amon, or Amon-Re, the creator, sky, and sun. Another very important god was Osiris. He was the god of the Nile River, who periodically died and was resurrected, very much the way the river regularly flooded and receded. Osiris also judged people after death. Osiris's wife and sister, Isis, was the moon goddess, the Great Mother, and a symbol of fertility. As you have read, the priests of Amon-Re fought Akhenaton's attempt to replace Amon-Re and the other gods with the worship of a sole sun god, Aton.

Each god was associated with animal symbols that people considered sacred. Sacred animals included the cat, the bull, the crocodile, and the scarab (beetle).

These pillars stand in the Great Hall of Pillars at the Temple of Amon-Re in Luxor.

The afterlife. At first, Egyptians believed that only the pharaohs had an afterlife, or life after death. Later, Egyptians believed that everyone, including animals, went on living after death. They believed that the human body had to be preserved to make existence after death possible. To do this, they developed a process called **mummification**, which involved removing the organs and treating the body with chemicals so that it would remain preserved for centuries.

Workers placed the mummy in a tomb stocked with clothing, food, jewelry, tools, weapons, and even servants in the form of sculptured or painted figures. The number and richness of the articles in the tomb depended on the importance of the dead person. The Egyptians considered these articles necessary for the person's existence after death. In later periods, they also placed in the tomb papyrus scrolls known as the *Book of the Dead*—a collection of hymns, prayers, and spells that formed a kind of guide to the afterlife.

In the afterlife, it was thought, a person's soul was judged on the basis of the kind of life the person had lived. The soul testified as to whether the person had lied, murdered, or been excessively proud. After the soul had testified, the god Osiris weighed its statement on a great scale against a sacred feather, the symbol of truth. If the scales balanced, the soul had spoken the truth. It could then enter into a place of eternal happiness. But if the scale did not balance, the soul was thrown to a horrible monster called the Eater of the Dead. Thus the Egyptians' religion emphasized the importance of having a good character and living a morally pure life, qualities that led to rewards in the afterlife.

Egyptian tombs. Because of the precious articles buried inside Egyptian graves, robbers frequently plundered them. Looters opened the pyramids built during the Old Kingdom and stole their contents. During the New Kingdom, the Egyptians cut elaborate secret tombs into cliff walls in the Valley of the Kings, but thieves robbed most of these tombs also. In A.D. 1922, however, archaeologists discovered the previously unopened burial chamber of the pharaoh Tutankhamen. This tomb, cut into rock, dated from around 1300 B.C. and contained gold, objects decorated with jewels, furniture, and household items. Although Tutankhamen had a short and relatively unimportant reign, the objects in his tomb have taught us much about life in ancient Egypt.

Section 2 Review

1. **Define** caravans, scribes, mummification
2. **Locate and Explain the Significance** Giza
3. **Understanding Ideas** Describe the methods used by Egyptians to trade their surplus crops.
4. **Summarizing Ideas** Describe the Great Pyramid and the process used by Egyptian architects and engineers to construct pyramids.
5. **Interpreting Ideas** Describe the role of gods, including Amon-Re and Osiris, in Egyptian life.

Section 3

Sumerian Civilization

Focus Questions

- **What was significant about the environment in which Sumerian civilization developed?**
- **What were the achievements of Sumerian civilization?**

The story of ancient Egypt describes one people living in one place—the Nile Valley—for many centuries. A very different story developed in the area of western Asia called the Fertile Crescent. Here, wave upon wave of invaders crisscrossed the land.

The Physical Setting

Look at the map on page 28. Note the strip of land that begins at the Isthmus of Suez and arcs through Southwest Asia before dipping to the Persian Gulf. Because much fertile land lies within this crescent-shaped area, it is known as the Fertile Crescent.

Arid land, as in Egypt, and also mountains surrounded the Fertile Crescent. One great difference in geography, however, made the history of the two areas quite dissimilar. The dry lands and hills around the Fertile Crescent were not as barren as those in and around Egypt. The grasses and other plant life there sustained tribes of wandering herders who were tough and hardy and had developed skill in warfare.

Perhaps the herders envied the richer, easier life of the people who lived in the Tigris-Euphrates Valley within the Fertile Crescent. The people of the river valley could not always defend themselves against the herders, who came into the region, conquered it, and established empires. Over time, these invaders also grew weak, and new waves of invaders conquered them. Thus the history of the Fertile Crescent is a story of repeated migration and conquest.

The Tigris and Euphrates Rivers both begin in the hills of modern Turkey. The Tigris flows about 1,180 miles to the Persian Gulf. The Euphrates, to the west of the Tigris, flows about 1,740 miles before reaching the Persian Gulf. At one point the two rivers come within 20 miles of each other and then spread apart until the valley between them—the Tigris-Euphrates Valley—widens to about 250 miles. (See map on this page.)

Of the two rivers, the Tigris has the greater amount of water. It cuts a deep path into the earth, lowering the water level below that of the land and making irrigation difficult. The Euphrates, too, creates problems for those who live along its banks. It carries a great deal of silt—twice as much as the Nile does. Because this silt builds up along the bottom of the river, the Euphrates often overflows and sends floodwaters swirling across the surrounding land. Valley dwellers must dig canals and dikes to bring water to the fields and also to carry excess water back to the river after floods.

The flooding of the Tigris and the Euphrates, unlike that of the Nile, cannot be easily predicted. It may come anytime between the beginning of April and the early part of June. Not only is the exact time of year unpredictable, but the extent of the flood cannot be estimated. Not surprisingly, the people of the valley viewed nature and the gods as angry and unreasonable.

Various names have been given to the Tigris-Euphrates Valley. Sometimes it is called Mesopotamia, from a Greek word meaning "between rivers." The southeastern part of the valley has usually been known as Babylonia. Today, almost the entire valley is within the nation of Iraq.

Sumer and Its People

The lowest part of the Tigris-Euphrates Valley benefits from the rich soil the rivers carry as they flow into the Persian Gulf. In ancient times, especially fertile soil covered this area, called Sumer (SOO·muhr). Here Neolithic people settled, grew crops, and over time created what we call Sumerian culture. We do not know much about the origins of the Sumerians except that a group of nomadic people probably migrated to Sumer and mingled with the original inhabitants. By 3000 B.C. these people knew how to use metal and had developed a kind of writing.

City-States

Early in their history the Sumerians developed a form of community called the **city-state**, which included a town or city and the surrounding land the city controlled. The major Sumerian city-states, including Ur, Erech, and Kish, had thousands of residents.

The people believed that much of the land in each of these early city-states belonged to a god or to several gods. Priests managed the gods' land, interpreted the gods' will to the people, and directed worship. The many Sumerian city-states seldom united under a single government. Evidence indicates that, originally, priests ruled these city-states. As the city-states competed for water and land, war leaders became more important and eventually came to rule as kings.

The Fertile Crescent, c. 2900 B.C.

Learning from Maps The Fertile Crescent arcs from the Isthmus of Suez through Mesopotamia to the Persian Gulf.

🔍 **Location** Near what Sumerian city do the Tigris and Euphrates Rivers come within 20 miles of each other?

Technology of the First Civilizations

Stone arches, cement, highways, aqueducts, the waterwheel, the sailing ship, the compass—each of these technological innovations was made by people in the ancient world.

The oldest technology of which evidence survives—dating back to the Paleolithic and Mesolithic periods of the Stone Age—is that of making stone tools. Early toolmakers chipped pieces or flakes of rock, often flint, into specific shapes, depending upon the purpose of the tool. The Paleolithic hunters and herders made spears, daggers, hand axes, cutting tools, and scrapers for cleaning animal hides. The later Neolithic farmers, who inhabited an area from Egypt to Mesopotamia, refined the technology of toolmaking by sharpening and polishing their stone tools on rocks.

The invention of the wheel forever revolutionized the technology of transportation. It is not known where or when the wheel was

first invented, but there is evidence of its use in many areas by around 3000 B.C. The earliest known drawing of a wheel dates from about 3500 B.C. in Mesopotamia, and wheeled vehicles were in use there and in India and China at that time. Egyptians used the wheel for transportation 1,000 years later. The great civilizations of Mesopotamia, India, China, and Egypt used first four-wheeled and then two-wheeled chariots in battle. Chariots became more maneuverable with the introduction of light, spoked wheels in Egypt in about 2000 B.C.

In Egypt also, building technology soared to new heights with the construction of the pyramids. The first Egyptian pyramid was begun around 2500 B.C. or 2600 B.C. The huge limestone blocks of the pyramids were quarried by hand with wooden, stone, and copper tools.

Social Classes

Like many other societies, the Sumerians had a range of social classes. At the top were high priests, kings, and nobles. Sumer had a middle class of lower priests, merchants, and scholars. Below them were the peasant farmers, and at the bottom of society were slaves, people who were kidnapped from other regions or captured in war.

Sumerian Writing

Sumerian writing was quite different from Egyptian writing. Egyptian hieroglyphics consisted of symbols carved on stone or written on papyrus. But the papyrus reed, which the Egyptians used to make their equivalent of paper, did not grow in Sumer.

Instead, throughout their history the Sumerians wrote primarily by pressing marks into clay tablets. Because the writers used a wedge-shaped tool called a

stylus, most of the signs were combinations of wedge shapes. Today we call Sumerian writing **cuneiform** (kyooh·NEE·uh·fawrm) from the Latin word for wedge, *cuneus*. The Sumerians had about 600 cuneiform signs.

They rolled out a lump of soft clay, made their wedge-shaped marks on it, and then allowed the clay tablet to dry until hard. Hardened clay would last for many years. It might shatter, but the pieces could usually be fitted together.

Farming and Trade

Most Sumerians farmed, growing grains, vegetables, and dates. Their domestic animals included cows, sheep, and goats, as well as oxen and donkeys to pull plows, carts, and chariots. The Sumerians raised flax for linen and wove fine woolen goods. Sumer produced enough food to allow many people to work as traders and artisans. Before 3000 B.C., Sumerians had

begun trading with other peoples of Southwest Asia. Some merchants had agents in faraway places, while others traveled from city to city by land and boat to sell Sumerian products.

Architecture, Engineering, and Science

The Sumerians used sun-dried clay bricks to build houses. Their brick structures did not last as long as the stone buildings of the Egyptians, but they were nonetheless well planned and well built.

The Sumerians may have invented several important architectural designs, including one of the strongest forms in building—the **arch**, a curved structure over an opening. By combining several arches, the Sumerians built rounded roofs in the shape of domes or vaults.

The most striking Sumerian buildings were the temples, known as **ziggurats**. Builders erected a ziggurat in layers, each one smaller than the one below, so that it looked something like a wedding cake. They sometimes painted the bricks in different colors. A ziggurat could be up to 150 feet high. The top served as a shrine to one of their gods.

Sumerian engineers and scientists made many important discoveries. Some scholars think that Sumerians were the first people to develop and use the wheel. In mathematics they used a system of numbers based on 60. Large numbers were thought of as

multiples of 60—for example, 120 was expressed as two 60s and 180 as three 60s. Sumerians divided a circle into 360 degrees (six 60s), each degree into 60 minutes, and each minute into 60 seconds. Today, when you look at a compass or a watch, you are seeing a principle that the Sumerians developed thousands of years ago. The Sumerians also created a lunar calendar. To keep it accurate, every few years they added a month.

Education and Religion

The Sumerians considered education very important, although apparently only upper-class boys—and no girls—attended school. Students learned to write and spell by copying religious books and songs. They also studied drawing and arithmetic.

Like the Egyptians, the Sumerians practiced polytheism. The Sumerians associated their gods with the forces of nature and with heavenly bodies, such as the sun and moon. Anu, lord of heaven; Enlil, god of air and storms; and Enki, god of the water and of wisdom, ranked as the most important Sumerian gods.

The Sumerians buried food and tools with their dead. Unlike the Egyptians, however, they did not imagine an afterlife in detail. The Sumerians believed in a kind of shadowy lower world. They did not believe in rewards and punishments after death.

Reading About History: Evaluating Sources of Evidence

Evaluating sources of evidence about historical events helps us interpret those events. Sources of evidence fall into two basic categories. Primary sources include items such as artifacts, official documents, letters, diaries, and eyewitness accounts of an event or a period of history. Secondary sources are accounts written after the events by people who played no part in them.

How to Evaluate Sources of Evidence

To evaluate sources of evidence, follow these steps:

1. Identify the source. For example, is it a diary, a government record, a biography, or a work of art?
2. Review the definitions of primary and secondary sources to determine what kind of evidence you have identified.
3. Consider the usefulness of the evidence. What question(s) will it help you answer? Is a primary source always more reliable as evidence than a secondary source? Why or why not?

Developing the Skill

The Standard of Ur was found in a Sumerian royal cemetery. It dates from about 2500 B.C. It is a mosaic of shell, lapis lazuli, and colored stone. The panel is double-sided, with scenes of peace on one side (shown above) and war on the other. From the various images shown on the mosaic—such as domestic animals, chariots advancing into battle, and prisoners of war being taken into captivity—historians can learn much about Sumerian society.

The *Standard of Ur* is a primary source. Sometimes, however, a piece of evidence can be classified as both a primary source and a

secondary source, depending on the purpose it is used for and the question that scholars wish to answer. For example, Howard Carter's description of the opening of Egyptian pharaoh Tutankhamen's tomb is classified as a primary source when the question concerns the discovery of the tomb. But this same description is considered a secondary source when it is used to answer questions about Egyptian life during ancient times. Can you see these two classifications of sources of evidence in the excerpt below?

"With suppressed excitement I carefully cut the cord, removed that precious seal, drew back the bolts, and opened the doors, when a fourth shrine was revealed. . . . There, filling the entire area within stood an immense yellow quartzite sarcophagus [stone coffin]. . . Amid intense silence the huge slab . . . rose from its bed. The lid being suspended in mid-air, we rolled back those covering shrouds, one by one . . . so gorgeous was the sight that met our eyes: a golden effigy of the young boy king."

The hands, crossed over the breast, held the royal emblems—the Crook and the Flail. Upon the forehead of this recumbent figure. . . were two emblems delicately worked in brilliant inlay—the Cobra and the Vulture—symbols of Upper and Lower Egypt."

Practicing the Skill

Describe how an account of the 1988 discovery of a Spanish galleon that sank off the coast of Florida in 1568 might be considered both a primary and a secondary source.

To apply this skill, see Applying History Study Skills on page 47.

1. **Define** city-state, cuneiform, arch, ziggurats
2. **Locate and Explain the Significance** Fertile Crescent, Persian Gulf, Mesopotamia, Babylonia, Sumer
3. **Understanding Ideas** Why did the inhabitants of the Tigris-Euphrates Valley regard nature as a hostile force?
4. **Summarizing Ideas** Describe the Sumerians' contributions to architecture and mathematics.
5. **Synthesizing Ideas (a)** How did the religious beliefs of the Sumerians resemble those of the Egyptians? **(b)** How were they different?

Section 4

Empires of the Fertile Crescent

Focus Questions

- Which were the most powerful empires in the Fertile Crescent?
- What were the cultural achievements of the empires of the Fertile Crescent?

The lack of unity among Sumerian city-states made them vulnerable to attack by hardy nomadic peoples who were attracted to the advantages of civilization. These nomadic peoples expanded their territories and built empires.

The Akkadians

Some time around 2330 B.C. the Akkadians, a people who also lived in Mesopotamia, conquered the Sumerians. Unlike the Sumerians, the Akkadians spoke a Semitic language closely related to modern Hebrew and Arabic. The most powerful of the Akkadian kings was Sargon, who ruled from about 2350 B.C. to 2300 B.C. Sargon established a great empire that extended as far west as the Mediterranean Sea. (See map on this page.)

The Akkadian Empire lasted about 100 years. When this empire ended, Sumerian city-states once again became prosperous, but new waves of invaders soon swept through the eastern Fertile Crescent. Another

powerful state of Semitic-speaking people arose, this time centered at the large new city of Babylon.

The Babylonians

Around 1792 B.C. a strong ruler named Hammurabi (ham·uh·RAHB·ee) came to power in Babylon and conquered most of the upper Tigris-Euphrates Valley. (See map on opposite page.) More than just a great military leader, Hammurabi was an outstanding political leader as well. He is best known for the Code of Hammurabi, a collection of laws compiled under his direction.

The Code of Hammurabi consisted of nearly 282 laws that concerned all aspects of life in Babylon. Some laws dealt with commerce and industry and included provisions regarding wages, hours, and working conditions. The fee that a surgeon might charge a patient was

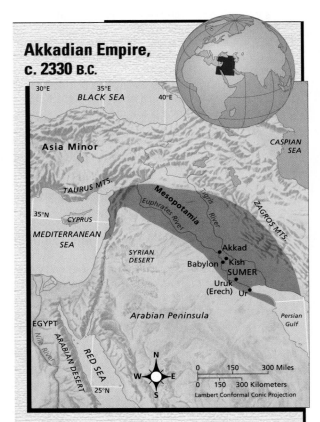

Akkadian Empire, c. 2330 B.C.

Learning from Maps Although the Akkadian king Sargon first settled near the city of Kish, he later established his capital at Akkad.

? Location What was the southernmost city in the Akkadian Empire?

spelled out. Other laws covered property rights and inheritance. Still others dealt with marriage and divorce. Judges enforced the laws under the supervision of the king's advisers and officials.

The Code of Hammurabi provided for harsh punishments. For example:

"[1] If a man bring an accusation against a man, and charge him with a [capital] crime, but cannot prove it, he, the accuser, shall be put to death. [22–23] If a man practice brigandage and be captured, that man shall be put to death. If the brigand be not captured, the man who has been robbed, shall, in the presence of god, make an itemized statement of his loss, and the city and the governor, in whose province and jurisdiction the robbery was committed, shall compensate him for whatever was lost. [229–230] If a builder build a house for a man and do not make its construction firm, and the house which he has built collapse and cause the death of the owner of the house, that builder shall be put to death. If it cause the death of a son of the owner of the house, they shall put to death a son of that builder."

As this quotation illustrates, the concept sometimes referred to as "an eye for an eye" provided the basis of punishment. If a man caused another to lose an eye, then his own eye was put out. Punishment often varied according to wealth, however. If a wealthy man destroyed the eye of a poor man, the wealthy man did not lose his eye but merely paid a fine. A thief who could not repay what was stolen was put to death. If the thief had the means to repay, however, he was required to repay more than was stolen.

Babylonian culture. Babylonian culture resembled that of the Sumerians in some respects. Most Babylonians farmed. They kept domestic animals, grew a wide variety of food crops, and wove cotton and wool textiles. The Babylonians were very active traders. Their merchants exchanged goods with distant parts of the Fertile Crescent as well as trading with Egypt and even India.

The social order of the Babylonians was also like that of the Sumerians. The upper class consisted of priests, nobles, high government officials, and also rich traders. Next came a middle class of merchants, artisans, clerks, and farmers who owned their own land. Below them were tenant farmers, and at the bottom were slaves.

Women in Babylon. Babylonian women probably were less privileged than Egyptian women, but they enjoyed a higher position in society than most women in ancient civilizations. Babylonian women had legal and economic rights, and laws protected their property.

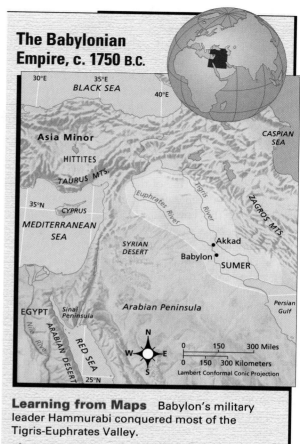

The Babylonian Empire, c. 1750 B.C.

Learning from Maps Babylon's military leader Hammurabi conquered most of the Tigris-Euphrates Valley.

Linking Geography and History Which geographical features bordered the Babylonian Empire?

Women could be traders and merchants and could work at other jobs. They could also become scribes.

Marriages, however, were arranged by parents. The father of the bride was expected to provide a large dowry, which the bride brought with her into the marriage. Husbands could divorce their wives, but wives could not divorce their husbands. A woman could, however, leave her husband if he was cruel, and she could take her property with her.

Babylonian religion. The Babylonians adopted many Sumerian religious beliefs. The chief god was Marduk, god of the city of Babylon, but there were many others, as every locality had its own gods. The Babylonians made many sacrifices to their gods for such favors as a good harvest or success in business. They were also extremely superstitious and believed in spells and charms for all kinds of situations. Like the Sumerians, the Babylonians believed in a shadowy life after death. Their religious practices were directed toward leading a successful life on Earth.

Babylonians believed that their priests could foretell the future. Perhaps for this reason, Babylonian priests wielded enormous power, in some ways even more than the monarch. They controlled enormous wealth in land, precious metals and jewelry, and slaves.

The Hittites

Many times throughout history, conquerors adopted parts of the culture of the people they conquered. This was certainly true of the Babylonians after they conquered the Sumerians. However, it was definitely not true of the Hittites, a warlike Indo-European-speaking people who invaded the Tigris-Euphrates Valley from Asia Minor sometime in the 1600s B.C.

The Hittites were among the first people to make extensive use of iron weapons. Their most important achievement, however, may have been their laws, which were less brutal than the Code of Hammurabi. Only major crimes, such as offenses against the gods and the practice of witchcraft, warranted execution. Hittite law called for a person to pay a fine—rather than experience retaliation—for causing damage or injury. For example, if one man injured another, and the injured man became ill, the guilty party had to work in the injured man's house until he became well. Then the guilty man had to pay six shekels of silver as well as any doctor's fees.

When the Hittites invaded the Tigris-Euphrates Valley, they conquered and looted the city of Babylon. The Hittites were too far from their home-land to control Babylonia permanently, however, and they soon withdrew to the western part of the Fertile Crescent. They remained a powerful force in the west until about 1200 B.C.

The Assyrians

After the Hittites, Babylon suffered further invasions by migratory peoples. Then, around 900 B.C., a Semitic-speaking people who were great conquerors—the Assyrians—overwhelmed Mesopotamia.

The Assyrians first settled along the Tigris River, northwest of Babylon. There they built the city-state of Assur, named for their chief god. (Both the region, Assyria, and the people took their name from Assur.) The Assyrians spread throughout the region until they controlled Syria, Babylonia, and even Egypt. (See map on this page.)

The Assyrians excelled in warfare. In addition to using chariots in battle, as had other peoples, they were

Assyrian Empire, c. 650 B.C.

Learning from Maps The skilled Assyrian army acquired new lands for their empire and put their captives to work on various construction projects.

❓ Human-Environment Interaction What major cities did the Assyrians settle along the Tigris River?

the first to make major use of **cavalry**—units of soldiers on horses. They also used many iron weapons and began the use of heavy battering rams to break through the defenses and walls of their opponents.

The Assyrians frequently killed the enemies they captured in battle and sometimes even massacred the inhabitants of the places they conquered. Whole conquered populations were enslaved and deported to other areas. By these methods, the Assyrians added new lands to their empire and gained many slaves, whom they put to work on vast construction projects, such as changing the courses of rivers. In about 700 B.C. the Assyrians captured Babylon, looted it, and finally destroyed it completely. Such acts of destruction earned the Assyrians the hatred and fear of people throughout the ancient world.

Assyrian government. The Assyrians were the first people to develop an effective method for governing a large empire. The Assyrian king had absolute, or total, power. Priests and government officials took orders from him and answered to him. The monarch was responsible only to the god Ashur, whose representative on Earth he claimed to be.

The Assyrians created an extremely efficient government to administer their vast empire. Governors ruled conquered lands and made regular and frequent reports to the king. To ensure loyalty, the king had inspectors secretly check on the governors' activities. The army was the most important part of the government. Soldiers were rewarded with wealth from the places they conquered.

Assyrian greatness and decline. After the Assyrians became powerful, they made the city of Nineveh their capital. Attempting to fortify the city as strongly as possible, the Assyrians constructed a huge double wall around it. The wall was more than 70 feet high and 7.5 miles long, and in places it was as much as 148 feet wide. It had 15 decorated gates.

To assure a supply of water for Nineveh, the Assyrians diverted the flow of a river, built canals, and constructed a 30-mile long aqueduct. In the city the Assyrians built a large library, in which scholars kept writings on clay tablets collected from all over the empire. This library helped to preserve texts for future generations. Among them was the great *Epic of Gilgamesh*, the story of a Sumerian king and one of the oldest works of literature known. Scholars have drawn conclusions about Sumerian beliefs—about life and death and other matters—from reading *Epic of Gilgamesh*.

Powerful Assyria and its great capital, Nineveh, eventually fell. Around 650 B.C., civil war broke out, weakening Assyria so that it could not resist outside enemies. Finally, in 612 B.C., a group of enemies led by the Chaldeans and the Medes captured and totally destroyed Nineveh.

The Chaldeans

The Chaldeans took control of much of the territory that the Assyrians had ruled. Under the leadership of the wise ruler Nebuchadnezzar (neb·uh·kuhd·NEZ·uhr), the Chaldeans conquered most of the Fertile Crescent. (See map on this page.) Nebuchadnezzar governed from the rebuilt city of Babylon from 605 B.C. to 562 B.C.

Under Nebuchadnezzar, Babylon once again became a large and rich city. Trade flourished, and within the city were impressive canals and magnificent buildings.

The king's palace included beautiful terrace gardens, known as the Hanging Gardens. According to legend, Amytis, one of Nebuchadnezzar's wives, had lived in the mountains. Now living on the drier plains of Babylonia, she yearned for the greenery of her homeland. To please her, the king planted thousands of brightly colored tropical trees and flowers on the palace grounds. The Greeks and other peoples of the ancient world regarded the Hanging Gardens of Babylon as one of the Seven Wonders of the World.

The Chaldeans were skilled astronomers. They kept careful records of the apparent movement of the stars and planets and could predict solar and lunar eclipses. They also calculated the length of a year with a very high degree of accuracy.

All the strength of the Chaldeans, however, seemed to lie in the leadership ability of Nebuchadnezzar. After he died, the Chaldeans had difficulties. When one of

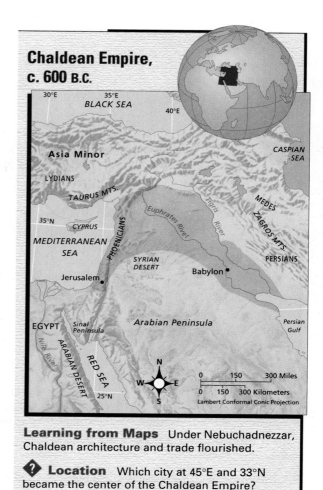

Chaldean Empire, c. 600 B.C.

BLACK SEA

Asia Minor

LYDIANS

TAURUS MTS.

CYPRUS

MEDITERRANEAN SEA

PHOENICIANS

Jerusalem

SYRIAN DESERT

Euphrates River

Tigris River

Babylon

CASPIAN SEA

MEDES

ZAGROS MTS.

PERSIANS

EGYPT

Sinai Peninsula

Nile River

ARABIAN DESERT

RED SEA

Arabian Peninsula

Persian Gulf

0   150   300 Miles
0   150   300 Kilometers
Lambert Conformal Conic Projection

Learning from Maps Under Nebuchadnezzar, Chaldean architecture and trade flourished.

? Location Which city at 45°E and 33°N became the center of the Chaldean Empire?

his successors quarreled with the Chaldean priests, the priests betrayed the city of Babylon to the enemy Persians. Within 30 years of Nebuchadnezzar's death in 562 B.C., the Chaldean Empire fell.

The Persians

The Persians who conquered Babylon in 539 B.C. spoke an Indo-European language and, like the Medes, had migrated into what is now Iran sometime before 1500 B.C.* The region became known as Persia and Media, after these two tribes. (In the A.D. 1900s, the country of Persia changed its name to Iran.) At first the Medes ruled over the Persians.

---

*The Indo-Europeans originally lived in the steppe lands north of the Black Sea. The Indo-European peoples included the Medes and the Persians, whom you will read about in this chapter, and the ancestors of the ancient Greeks and Romans.

Cyrus, Darius, and Xerxes. In about 550 B.C., however, the great Persian ruler Cyrus the Great rebelled against the Medes. Cyrus then began a series of conquests, capturing Babylon and taking over the rest of the Fertile Crescent and Asia Minor.

Cyrus and the later rulers Darius I and Xerxes I (ZUHRK·seez) expanded Persian rule as far as the Indus River in India and parts of southeastern Europe. (See map on this page.) Both Darius and his son Xerxes invaded Greece in the 400s B.C. but failed to conquer it. Nevertheless, the Persians ruled the mightiest empire in history up to that time.

Persian government. The early Persian kings distinguished themselves not only as great generals but also as effective rulers. Although all-powerful in government, they showed great concern for justice. They collected taxes and administered the law fairly.

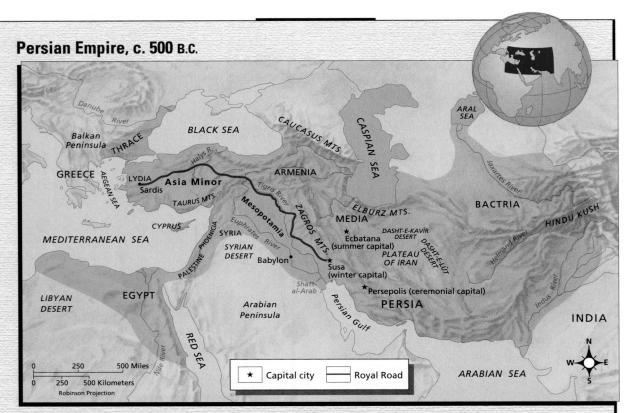

Persian Empire, c. 500 B.C.

Learning from Maps The Persian rulers expanded their empire from southeastern Europe to the Indus River in India.

? Movement To aid travel within their great realm, the Persian rulers built the Royal Road. Which cities did this road link?

Darius I is shown here in a stone carving receiving homage in his palace at Persepolis.

The Persians treated the peoples they ruled better than earlier empires had done. They paid close attention to local customs and allowed the conquered peoples to keep their own religions and laws. One practice they took over from the Assyrians was the use of secret agents of the king, known as the King's Eyes and Ears, to keep the ruler informed.

The Persians built roads to connect the widely separated cities of the immense realm. The great Royal Road, for example, extended more than 1,250 miles, all the way from Sardis in western Asia Minor to Susa, one of the capitals of the empire. The Persians built these roads mainly for the army and postal riders, but merchants also used them. The roads aided the process of cultural diffusion in the empire by promoting the exchange of customs and ideas as well as goods.

Persian religion. Perhaps the greatest cultural contribution of the Persians concerned religion. At first, like other early peoples, the Persians worshiped many gods. Then, around 600 B.C., a great prophet and religious reformer named Zoroaster (ZOHR·uh·was·tuhr) completely changed the religious outlook and consequently the lives of the Persian people. The teachings of Zoroaster are called Zoroastrianism.

Zoroaster taught that on Earth, people receive training for a future life. He said that in the world the forces of good and evil struggle savagely, and people must choose between them. Zoroastrianism also included the idea of a final judgment, a reward or punishment that depended on human choice. Those who chose good (symbolized by light) would be rewarded with a life of eternal blessings. Those who chose evil would face punishment. Once a person had chosen, the decision could not be reversed. In the distant future, the forces of good would triumph. Then Earth would disappear.

Zoroaster felt that nothing was more shameful than lying. The Persians taught their children that they must always tell the truth. They also considered getting into debt disgraceful and a form of lying.

Zoroaster's vision of a struggle between good and evil has been highly significant in history. It probably influenced other major religions, including Judaism and, later, Christianity.

The decline of the Persians. The Persian kings who followed Darius and Xerxes lacked their abilities. Consequently, the empire began to lose its strength. In 331 B.C., more than 200 years after Cyrus led the revolt against the Medes, Alexander the Great led his army out of Greece and conquered the Persian Empire.

Section 4 Review

1. **Define** cavalry
2. **Identify** Sargon, Hammurabi, Nebuchadnezzar, Cyrus the Great, Darius I, Xerxes I, Zoroaster
3. **Understanding Ideas (a)** List several provisions of the Code of Hammurabi. **(b)** How did the Hittite laws differ from the Code of Hammurabi?
4. **Summarizing Ideas** Describe the status of women in Babylonian society.
5. **Evaluating Ideas (a)** List briefly the accomplishments of the Babylonians, the Hittites, the Assyrians, the Chaldeans, and the Persians. **(b)** Which accomplishment do you believe was the most important? Why?

The Phoenicians, Lydians, and Hebrews

Focus Questions

- **What were the contributions of the Phoenicians and Lydians to language and economics?**
- **How did the Hebrews make a lasting difference in the history of religion?**

The peoples who lived in the western end of the Fertile Crescent and in western Asia Minor did not create large empires, but they had a great influence on the modern world. Today this region along and near the Mediterranean Sea forms the nations of Israel, Jordan, Lebanon, Syria, and portions of Egypt and Turkey. In ancient times, however, people called the northern portions Phoenicia (fi·NI·shuh) and Lydia (LI·dee·uh). The southern sections had different names during the course of history, including Canaan, Israel, and Palestine.

The Phoenicians

Phoenicia consisted of a loose union of city-states, each governed by a different king. Phoenicia had hills and mountains but lacked much fertile land. Perhaps because of the barrier posed by the high ridges of the Lebanon Mountains, the Phoenicians did not migrate eastward. Instead, they turned to the sea and to commerce for their living. On the map on this page, notice the cities of Tyre and Sidon (SYD·uhn). Both of these seaports became world famous.

The Phoenicians sailed in ships that today would seem small and frail, but their sailors were highly skilled. Propelled by sails and oars, Phoenician ships plied the Mediterranean Sea. Some historians believe that the Phoenicians sailed as far as Britain in search of tin. They may also have sailed around the western coast of Africa. In time the Phoenicians became the greatest traders in the ancient world.

Articles of trade. Phoenicia had one major natural resource—lumber that came from the beautiful cedar forests and other trees of the Lebanon Mountains. Many ancient peoples used this lumber for building.

However, Phoenicia developed several other valuable exports. Using methods that were learned from the Egyptians, with materials that were probably imported, the Phoenicians became skilled workers in

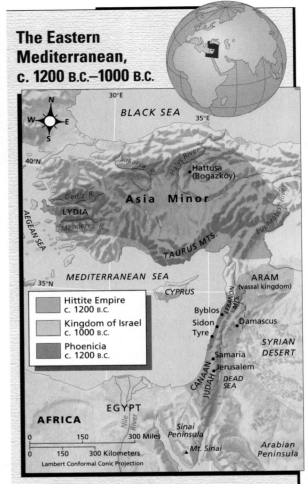

The Eastern Mediterranean, c. 1200 B.C.–1000 B.C.

Learning from Maps Because of their location along the Mediterranean, many of the region's peoples turned to the sea for commercial activity.

? Region Which mountain range created a natural boundary between Phoenicia and the Kingdom of Israel?

What If?

The Phoenician Alphabet
Phoenician trade helped spread the use of the alphabet throughout the Mediterranean region. How might the history of writing have been different if the Phoenicians had not been traders?

metal. They created beautiful objects of gold and silver. They also invented the art of glassblowing and learned how to make exquisite glass objects. Sidon became the home of a well-known glass industry.

On their coast the Phoenicians found a shellfish called murex from which they made a purple dye. Sidon and Tyre became the centers of the dyeing trade. People throughout the ancient world prized cloth dyed with this purple. A favorite of the wealthy and royalty, the color became known as the royal purple. The Phoenicians also exported wine, linen, olive oil, and dried fish.

Phoenician colonies. Phoenicia reached its peak as a great sea trading power in the three centuries after 1000 B.C. Tyre was the leading Phoenician city-state. The Phoenicians established colonies throughout the Mediterranean region—at Carthage in North Africa and on the islands of Sicily, Sardinia, and Malta. Farther west, the Phoenicians also established a colony at the site of the modern city of Cádiz, Spain. These colonies themselves served as centers for trade.

Phoenician culture. Perhaps reflecting their role as intermediaries and traders, the Phoenicians imitated the cultures of other peoples. They patterned their government and most of their customs after those of the Egyptians and the Babylonians. Through trading, the Phoenicians indirectly spread Egyptian and Babylonian culture throughout the Mediterranean area.

Phoenician religion offered the people few comforts. Phoenicians did not believe in an afterlife, and they sometimes sacrificed their own children to win favor from the many gods they worshiped.

The Phoenicians never established a major empire. Their cities were eventually conquered by the Assyrians. However, the Phoenicians made one very important contribution to world civilization: the alphabet. Earlier writing systems had been developed in Mesopotamia and Egypt, but the Phoenicians developed the alphabet that became the model for later Western alphabets.

The spread of the alphabet provides a good example of how commerce can speed the process of cultural diffusion. The practical Phoenicians used writing in their businesses to record contracts and draw up bills. We can imagine that their trading partners saw the advantages of written records. Phoenician commerce made it possible for the knowledge of alphabetical writing to spread throughout the Mediterranean world.

The Greeks adopted the Phoenician alphabet and improved it by adding signs for vowel sounds. Later, the Romans copied this alphabet from the Greeks and developed the Roman alphabet we use now.

The Lydians

The Lydians of Asia Minor are remembered as the first people in history to use coined money. Before this invention in about 600 B.C., traders had to rely on **barter**, or the exchange of one commodity or service for another. Barter, however, limited trade because two people could strike a bargain only if each could offer goods or services that the other wanted. The use of money allowed traders to set prices for goods and services and to develop a **money economy**, an economic system based on the use of money as a measure of value and a unit of account.

Like the Phoenicians, the Lydians did not rule an empire. Through trade, however, they passed on the concept of a money economy to the Greeks and the Persians, who in turn helped spread this concept to other parts of the world.

The Physical Setting

To the south of Phoenicia lay a small strip of land, known as Canaan, that had no forests and few minerals or other natural resources. As you can see on the map on page 38, Canaan consisted of two regions. The Jordan River watered the northern valley. There the fertile soil helped farmers grow grains, olives, figs, and grapes. Desert covered most of the southern region, around and south of the Dead Sea. This arid plateau had poor and rocky soil.

Canaan lay along the great land bridge between Asia and Africa. In one way this location gave the people an advantage because the merchants who carried goods and ideas between Egypt and the Fertile Crescent traveled this route.

In another way, however, Canaan's location was a disadvantage, because armies also passed along the route. The people of Canaan lacked powerful armies, and at one time or another, groups including the Egyptians, Syrians, Assyrians, Persians, and Babylonians all conquered Canaan.

The Hebrews

Just as in the eastern part of the Fertile Crescent, a series of peoples inhabited Canaan. The Hebrews, the ancestors of modern Jews, had a great influence on the region and on history. The Hebrews did not always live in Canaan. Abraham, the leader of the Hebrew people according to the Bible, once lived in Sumer. After leaving there, he led his nomadic people through the desert to the borders of northern Canaan. The descendants of Abraham traveled farther west, across the Isthmus of Suez and into Egypt.

Money

What is money? Quite simply, it is any object that people are willing to accept as payment for goods or services.

Throughout history, money has taken many different forms. Today money of some kind is accepted as payment by virtually all people. In the past, however, this was not always the case.

Early societies—in which people hunted, fished, and farmed for their own needs—used a barter system. A fisherman might trade a basket of fish for a farmer's extra vegetables. This system did not always work very well, however. What if the farmer did not want fish that day? The fisherman would have to look around for someone else who did.

To make trade easier, people began to look for objects with a common value that could be traded. To work well, the object had to be useful to everyone, rare enough to be valuable, and small and light enough to be carried. Salt was one of the first kinds of this "commodity money," as it has been called, that people used. Early Roman leaders paid their soldiers in salt. In fact, our word *salary* comes ultimately from the Latin word for salt, *sal*. Salt money, however, was useful only in areas where salt was hard to find. Other kinds of commodity money were also used. Some ancient peoples used cattle as money. In fact, our word *pecuniary*, which means "measured in money," comes from the Latin word for cattle, *pecus*.

A very unusual form of money was employed on the island of Yap in the South Pacific. People there used wheel-shaped boulders as money until the early years of the twentieth century. The wheels were from 1 to 12 feet in diameter and had a hole in the center. The larger the stone, the greater its value. Difficult to move, they usually remained in one place although different people might own them over time.

Shells were another widely accepted form of money. In India, people used colorful cowrie shells. The shell money with which Americans are most familiar is wampum, carefully cut and highly polished colored shells. For hundreds of years, American Indians in the region that is today the northeastern United States used these beautiful and rare tiny objects, strung together on their belts and jewelry, as money.

Swiss bank worker

Counting and bagging pennies

Wheel-shaped boulders used as money on the island of Yap

images of gods and goddesses, pictures of sacred objects, or portraits of rulers.

In the early days of the American colonies and even of the United States, official money was often very hard to find. The inventive population came up with a variety of answers to this problem. Some people accepted rice or tobacco. Others used beaver skins or the Indians' wampum.

Over time, many governments throughout the world began issuing notes or IOUs for their coins.

Early United States paper money

Unlike earlier forms of money, the notes had no value in themselves. On a note the government might declare that it would pay the owner of the note its stated value in gold or silver. Paper money was in use all over the world by the 1700s. But the value of paper money depended on the confidence people had in the government that issued it. During difficult periods in the American Revolution, for example, paper money issued by the new United States government had very little value, and people did not want to use it. The same was true of Confederate "scrip" issued by the South during the Civil War. After the South lost the war, of course, Confederate paper money became totally worthless.

Easy to carry, durable, and scarce, shells made excellent money. But in other parts of the world, another material—metal—met these requirements. Metal rings were used as money as early as 2500 B.C. in Egypt. Gold or silver bars were also used for exchange. After some time, merchants began stamping these bars with their personal imprints, and this stamp also stated the bar's weight.

As the countries around the Mediterranean Sea began to trade with one another, they needed to find a kind of money that was mutually accepted and that could be readily carried in ships. In the 600s B.C., the government of the kingdom of Lydia in what is now western Turkey began issuing small kidney-bean-shaped pieces of money made of electrum, a mixture of gold and silver. This form of money is usually considered to be the first coinage. Within about 100 years, Greek city-states began minting coins that were known as staters. These coins were made of electrum, gold, or silver. In about 150 B.C., Rome issued the silver denarius. It eventually became one of the most widely accepted coins in the world. These ancient coins often were stamped with

Coins today are little more than symbols themselves. The value stamped on the coin's face is far more than the coin's metal is worth. Since 1965, dimes and quarters minted by the United States government have contained no silver at all.

Today, credit cards and ATMs (automatic teller machines) are used worldwide. The money of one country can be electronically converted into another's almost instantaneously. We rarely think about the problems of storing, using, and transporting money. Less than 300 years ago, however, a sack of rice might have brought more for you than a government-issued bill!

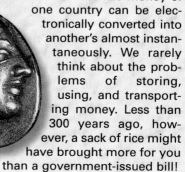

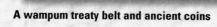

A wampum treaty belt and ancient coins

According to the Bible, in their siege of the city of Jericho, the Hebrews blew trumpets as they marched around the walls of the city.

They settled in the "Land of Goshen," east of the Nile Delta, where the Nile flows into the Mediterranean Sea.

These Hebrews lived peacefully in Egypt for some time, but eventually they fell from favor. Some scholars believe that one group of Hebrews entered Egypt along with the Hyksos in the 1700s B.C. When the Egyptians finally expelled the Hyksos in the 1500s B.C., the pharaohs enslaved the Hebrews.

Establishing a homeland. A great leader, Moses, later arose among the Hebrews and led his people out of slavery and into the deserts of the Sinai Peninsula.

The books of Exodus, Numbers, and Deuteronomy in the Bible tell the story of Moses, the escape from Egypt, and the wandering in the wilderness.

According to the Bible, Moses climbed to the top of Mount Sinai and returned to the Hebrews bearing the Ten Commandments—the moral laws that the Hebrew god, referred to by biblical scholars as Yahweh (yah·way), had revealed to him. As the Bible records,

❝God spoke, and these were his words:
I am the Lord your God who brought you out of Egypt, out of the land of slavery.
[1] You shall have no other god to set against me.

[2] You shall not make a carved image for yourself nor the likeness of anything in the heavens above, or on the earth below, or in the waters under the earth.

[3] You shall not make wrong use of the name of the Lord your God; the Lord will not leave unpunished the man who misuses his name.

[4] Remember to keep the sabbath day holy. You have six days to labour and do all your work. But the seventh day is a sabbath of the Lord your God; that day you shall not do any work.

[5] Honour your father and your mother.

[6] You shall not commit murder.

[7] You shall not commit adultery.

[8] You shall not steal.

[9] You shall not give false evidence against your neighbour.

[10] You shall not covet your neighbour's house; you shall not covet your neighbor's wife, . . . or anything that belongs to him. **"**

These commandments begin by establishing for the Hebrews an exclusive relationship to God and go on to emphasize principles of self-restraint and the importance of the family, human life, and formal worship. When the Hebrews agreed to follow these commandments, they entered into a covenant, or solemn agreement, with Yahweh. Moses announced that Canaan was a promised land—promised to his forefathers—and that Yahweh had commissioned him to found a holy nation. Inspired by his words, the Hebrews set out for Canaan. According to the Bible, Moses and his followers wandered in the desert for many years until finally entering Canaan.

The Hebrews who had come from Egypt joined those who had lived for so long on the borders of northern Canaan. By this time the harsh wilderness life had hardened the Hebrews into tough desert tribes. But establishing a homeland in Canaan proved difficult. People known as Canaanites held the northern Jordan Valley, while the Philistines lived along the southern coast. Both groups vigorously defended their land in a struggle that lasted more than 200 years. The Hebrews first conquered the Canaanites, making it possible for some of the Hebrews to settle in the Jordan Valley. However, the Philistines proved to be fiercer opponents. The Hebrews drove them closer to the seacoast but never conquered them completely.

A new government and new customs. As nomads, the Hebrews had been divided into 12 tribes. During the long years of fighting, the tribes united under the rule of one king. The first king of this united kingdom called Israel was Saul.

David, who formed a new dynasty, succeeded Saul. David occupied the city of Jerusalem and made it a capital and a religious center. His son, Solomon, built palaces there and also built a great temple for Yahweh.

After the end of Solomon's reign in the middle of the 900s B.C., the 10 northern tribes revolted, and the kingdom split in two. The northern part became the kingdom of Israel, with its capital located at Samaria. The southern part, situated around the Dead Sea, became the kingdom of Judah, with Jerusalem as its capital. (See map on page 38.)

These two Hebrew kingdoms lacked the strength to withstand invasions from the east. Around 722 B.C. the Assyrians ravaged Samaria and conquered Israel, capturing many Hebrews and deporting them as slaves. Later, in 587 B.C., the Chaldeans under Nebuchadnezzar conquered Judah and destroyed its capital, Jerusalem. They destroyed Solomon's temple and took the southern Hebrews into captivity. Cyrus, the Persian king, conquered the Chaldeans and allowed the Hebrews to return to their homeland in 538 B.C. to rebuild the temple in Jerusalem.

The Old Testament and Jewish Law

The Hebrew scriptures (also known as the Old Testament of the Christian Bible) tell the story of the creation of the world, the special mission of Hebrews, their escape from slavery in Egypt, and the progress of their culture and beliefs over 1,000 years. About one third of these scriptures is devoted to Hebrew history. The remainder includes poetry, prophecy, and religious instruction and laws.

The Hebrews did not think of prophets as people who predicted the future, though some prophets claimed that they could. Rather, they viewed the prophets as messengers sent to reveal God's will. Their messages, especially those of the prophets who wrote before the exile to Babylon, often warned the Hebrews about the consequences of their behavior. Many messages of the prophets—messages such as "There is no peace unto the wicked," as well as other principles expressed in the books of instruction and law—have remained the foundation for Jewish moral and ethical behavior. Prophets who wrote during the exile spoke also of hope for the future.

The first five books of the Old Testament, known as the Torah, list the Hebrew code of laws. This code of laws, named for Moses, is called Mosaic law and includes the Ten Commandments and laws developed during later periods. Mosaic law, like the Code of Hammurabi, demanded "an eye for an eye," but it set a much higher value on human life. Although Mosaic law accepted slavery as the custom

The Amazing Variety of Earth's Surface

Plains, plateaus, hills, mountains, canyons, and valleys are but a few of our planet's amazing variety of landforms, the shapes Earth's surface takes. As you read about these landforms, think about the ones you see in the area where you live.

Types of Landforms

Geographers recognize many different types of landforms, including plains, plateaus, hills, and mountains. They categorize these landforms in terms of such characteristics as slope and local relief. Slope is the slant of the land. Relief means the difference between the highest and lowest points of a landform.

Plains. Geographers classify a landform that is level or gently rolling as plains. This type of landform has little slope. Most plains occur at low elevations—less than 1,000 feet above sea level. The Gulf Coastal Plain of the United States, for example, stretches from the Gulf of Mexico to southern Illinois, but no part of it is higher than 656 feet above sea level. A few plains, such as the western Great Plains of the United States, however, have higher elevations.

Plateaus. A plateau is a generally flat landform that rises far above the surrounding land on at least one side. The term tableland—another name for a plateau—provides a helpful image of the characteristics of this landform. Like a table, a plateau has a flat surface high off the ground.

A feature characteristic of plateaus is their high elevation. The Colorado Plateau of the western United States, for example, ranges from 2,000 feet to more than 12,000 feet above sea level. The Plateau of Tibet in China rises to more than 15,000 feet above sea level. Some plateaus, however, occur at lower elevations.

Some plateaus are broken up by deep canyons. These canyons have high slope and high relief. For example, the Grand Canyon, which the Colorado River carved into the Colorado Plateau, has a local relief of from 5,000 feet to 9,000 feet.

Mountains and hills. Geographers classify as a mountain an elevated mass of land that projects above its surroundings. A hill is usually lower than

The Austrian Alps

a mountain and has a more rounded top. The slope of a hill can vary from very gentle to very steep.

Mountains rise dramatically from the surrounding land to an elevation thousands of feet above sea level. Mountains have steep slope. The summit is the highest point of a mountain. The highest mountain in the world is Mount Everest, in the Himalayas in Asia. Its summit is 29,028 feet above sea level.

Landforms and History

Throughout history, landforms have had an important impact on human activity. For example, the fertile plains areas of North Africa and Southwest Asia nurtured the growth of the early civilizations you have read about in this chapter. High mountains have formed barriers that isolated some civilizations from outside influences for thousands of years. One of the most important themes of history is the way in which people have adapted to the demands of their physical environment. Another important theme, however, has been people's efforts to modify their environment for better living.

This Rabbi reads from the Talmud about the teachings of Judaism.

viewed Yahweh not only as their protector and provider but also as a god to fear.

This understanding of Yahweh slowly changed, partly because of the Hebrews' many sufferings and partly because of the teachings and writings of their prophets. The prophets insisted that Yahweh was more concerned with a person's moral behavior than with religious rituals. The Hebrews believed that people had a choice between good and evil, and that Yahweh held them responsible for their choices.

The Hebrews came to think of Yahweh as a loving parent—a god who lived in the hearts of his worshipers and the god of all peoples. This was very different from the religious concepts of Mesopotamia and Egypt during this period. Other ancient peoples thought of their gods as having human qualities, but as being more powerful than humans. The Hebrews viewed Yahweh as a spiritual force rather than as a glorified human being. The fact that no carved images were made of Yahweh was a clear contrast to other religions. The kings of other ancient peoples were sometimes viewed as gods or as the representatives of gods. Hebrew kings were not gods. Only Yahweh was divine. Yet the Hebrews also believed that Yahweh had made humans in his own image. Humans were not intended to be Yahweh's slaves, but to serve him out of love.

Because of its emphasis on ethics, or proper conduct, the Hebrew form of monotheism is often called **ethical monotheism**. It ranks as the most important contribution of the ancient Hebrews to Western civilization.

of the ancient world, the law demanded kindness toward slaves. Mosaic law also preached kindness toward the poor and hospitality toward strangers, as did other ancient codes of law. Mosaic law reserved severe punishments for witchcraft, sacrifices to idols, adultery, kidnapping, and treason—crimes punishable by death. This system of law reflected the belief that all people, regardless of their status, deserved kindness and respect.

The Development of Judaism

The early Hebrews worshiped Yahweh as the one god to whom they belonged and with whom they had a special relationship of trust. They believed that Yahweh protected them from their enemies, took their side in battle, and provided them with food and water. According to the Ten Commandments, Yahweh was a jealous god—a word that can also be translated from the original text as "impassioned." If people sinned against Yahweh, not only would they suffer the consequences, but so would their children and succeeding generations. The Hebrews therefore

---

Section 5 Review

1. **Define** barter, money economy, ethical monotheism
2. **Identify** Abraham, Moses, Saul, David, Solomon
3. **Locate and Explain the Significance** Israel, Samaria, Judah, Jerusalem
4. **Evaluating Ideas (a)** How did Phoenician sea trade benefit the peoples of the Mediterranean? **(b)** How did the invention of coined money make trade easier?
5. **Analyzing Ideas (a)** Why did the Hebrews leave Egypt? **(b)** What difficulties did the Hebrews experience when they reached Canaan?
6. **Summarizing Ideas** Briefly describe the three basic elements of early Jewish religion.

Chapter 2 Review

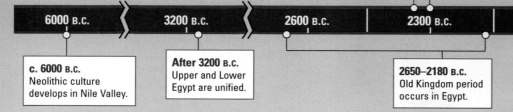

2350–2300 B.C.
Sargon rules Akkadian Empire.

6000 B.C.   **3200 B.C.**   **2600 B.C.**   **2300 B.C.**   **2000 B.C.**

c. 6000 B.C.
Neolithic culture develops in Nile Valley.

After 3200 B.C.
Upper and Lower Egypt are unified.

2650–2180 B.C.
Old Kingdom period occurs in Egypt.

Chapter Summary

The following list contains the key concepts you have learned about the great civilizations that developed in Southwest Asia and the Nile Valley.

1. The geography and climate of the Nile Valley area greatly contributed to the development of a long-lasting and distinctive civilization.
2. Sometime after 3200 B.C. the Nile Valley region was united into one kingdom ruled by pharaohs. Successive dynasties of pharaohs made this kingdom a considerable power for almost 2,000 years.
3. The Egyptian people developed a remarkable culture. Their arts, literature, science, and religion became sophisticated, and a complex and effective agricultural system evolved. At the same time, strict divisions were maintained between social classes.
4. In the Fertile Crescent a succession of conquests and empires led to a variety of societies and cultures.
5. The Sumerians organized city-states, invented a new form of writing, and made many advances in architecture and engineering.
6. The Babylonians were famous for their system of laws, the Code of Hammurabi.
7. The Assyrians were fierce warriors and conquered lands throughout Syria, Babylonia, and even Egypt.
8. The Persians developed a complex and effective government for their empire. They also embraced an influential new religion called Zoroastrianism.
9. The Phoenicians were the world's first great sea traders. They organized a loose union of cities and colonies around the Mediterranean that were linked by the sea. Their trade spread new ideas. The alphabet that the Phoenicians developed became the model for later Western alphabets.
10. The Lydians of Asia Minor were the first to use coined money, making trade easier.
11. The Hebrews developed Judaism—a system of laws and a religious faith that has been a major influence in Western civilization. The Hebrew scriptures introduced the concept of ethical monotheism, which has helped to shape Western history.

Reviewing Important Terms

On a separate sheet of paper, match each of the following terms with the correct definition below.

a. pharaoh
b. hieroglyphics
c. dynasty
d. monotheism
e. caravan
f. mummification
g. barter
h. ziggurat
i. arch
j. cavalry

_____1. family of rulers
_____2. exchange of goods or services for other goods or services
_____3. Sumerian temple
_____4. units of soldiers on horses
_____5. ruler of Nile Valley kingdom
_____6. belief in one god
_____7. writing that uses pictures or symbols to indicate words or sounds
_____8. treating a dead body chemically to preserve it
_____9. curved structure over an opening
_____10. group of people traveling together for safety over long distances

Developing Critical Thinking Skills

1. **Contrasting Ideas** How did the civilization that arose along the banks of the Nile River differ from the civilizations of the Fertile Crescent?
2. **Understanding Ideas** List the peoples of the Fertile Crescent and each group's most important achievements.
3. **Analyzing Maps (a)** Using the maps in Chapter 2, name the geographic barriers between the ancient civilizations of Africa and those of Southwest Asia. **(b)** How do you think the people of these early civilizations overcame these barriers?
4. **Comparing Ideas (a)** Compare the legal systems of the Babylonians, the Hittites, and the Hebrews. **(b)** Under which system would you have preferred to live? Why?

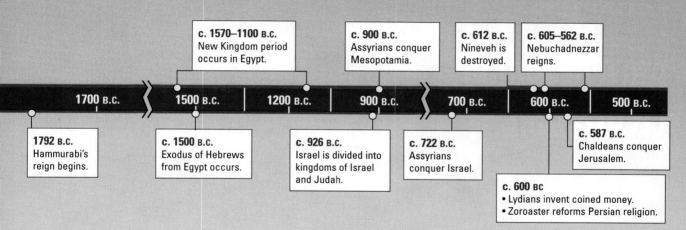

c. 1570–1100 B.C.
New Kingdom period occurs in Egypt.

c. 900 B.C.
Assyrians conquer Mesopotamia.

c. 612 B.C.
Nineveh is destroyed.

c. 605–562 B.C.
Nebuchadnezzar reigns.

1700 B.C.   1500 B.C.   1200 B.C.   900 B.C.   700 B.C.   600 B.C.   500 B.C.

1792 B.C.
Hammurabi's reign begins.

c. 1500 B.C.
Exodus of Hebrews from Egypt occurs.

c. 926 B.C.
Israel is divided into kingdoms of Israel and Judah.

c. 722 B.C.
Assyrians conquer Israel.

c. 587 B.C.
Chaldeans conquer Jerusalem.

c. 600 BC
• Lydians invent coined money.
• Zoroaster reforms Persian religion.

5. **Evaluating Ideas** Choose two groups of people in this chapter and explain how the environment affected their ways of making a living. Which group had the most success with making a living? Why?

Relating Past to Present

1. **(a)** Look up the word *justice* in a dictionary. How would you define it? **(b)** How does the concept of justice in the United States today compare with the concept of justice shown in Hammurabi's code? **(c)** Which concept of justice do you think would be more effective in combating crime?

2. **(a)** How does trade in the world today help the spread of ideas from one culture to another? **(b)** What effects do you think films and music from the United States might have on other cultures? **(c)** Can you give other examples of cultural diffusion?

3. In this chapter you read about the pharaoh Akhenaton's conflict with the priests of the god Amon-Re. This was an early example in history of a conflict between governmental authority and religion. Review and explain how the First Amendment to the United States Constitution deals with the relationship between church and state in the United States.

4. Economic power is necessary for the survival of an empire. **(a)** Explain the basis of the economic power of ancient Egypt. **(b)** What was the basis of the economic power of the Fertile Crescent? **(c)** Explain the economic power of oil-producing countries today.

5. **(a)** Cotton continues to be an important crop in Egypt and in many other parts of the world, including the United States. Using encyclopedias and statistical abstracts, find out about the size and nature of the cotton industry in the United States. **(b)** What are some items produced from the cotton grown in the United States?

Applying History Study Skills

Before completing this activity, review Building History Study Skills on page 31.

Look again at the definitions of a primary source and a secondary source. Then review the guidelines for identifying sources of evidence.

Select a historical event that occurred in the last 100 years. For example, you may be interested in a particular aspect of the Great Depression, World War II, or the Vietnam War. If possible, interview a person who experienced that event. You may wish to prepare a list of questions ahead of time.

After you have discussed the historical event with an eyewitness, locate a secondary source, such as a book or magazine article, on the same topic. Then compare the two types of information. Did both sources present a similar point of view? What advantages or disadvantages can you identify in the use of primary sources and secondary sources? Which type of evidence do you think is more useful?

---

internetconnect

Search the Internet through the HRW Web site for pictures of modern Egyptian cities that also show ancient Egyptian structures. If possible, print out some of these pictures. Write a paragraph contrasting the modern structures with the ancient structures.

GO TO: go.hrw.com
KEYWORD: SC0 Egypt

Building Your Portfolio

1. **Making Comparisons** Use encyclopedias in your school or public library to write a report comparing Judaism, Christianity, Zoroastrianism, and the religion of ancient Egypt. Focus on the beliefs in each religion about the struggle between good and evil. Discuss why the conflict between good and evil is a theme in most religions. Place the report in your portfolio.

2. **Reporting on Technology** The pyramids are among the most impressive structures left by any civilization. Research and write a report on techniques of ancient Egyptian building. You might use the following books as sources: William Fix's *Pyramid Odyssey* (Mercury Media, 1984) and Zaui A. Hawass's *The Pyramids of Ancient Egypt* (Carnegie Museum of Natural History, 1990). Place the report in your portfolio.

CHAPTER 3

Ancient Indian Civilization

TIME

c. 2500 B.C.–A.D. **550**

c. 2500 B.C.–A.D. 550

3.7 million B.C.   4000 B.C.   A.D. 2100

PLACE

India

India

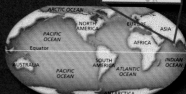

ARCTIC OCEAN

NORTH AMERICA

EUROPE

ASIA

PACIFIC OCEAN

AFRICA

Equator

SOUTH AMERICA

ATLANTIC OCEAN

INDIAN OCEAN

AUSTRALIA

PACIFIC OCEAN

ANTARCTICA

Statue of the Buddha

Significance

In some ways the Indus River valley civilization that developed in India resembled the early civilizations of the Nile and Tigris-Euphrates Valleys. Important differences, however, existed between Eastern, or Asian, civilizations and the Western civilizations you have read about so far.

Terms to Define

monsoons	caste system
citadel	monism
Vedas	maya
Sanskrit	reincarnation
Brahmins	dharma
raja	karma
Upanishads	yoga
epics	nirvana
Mahabharata	polygyny
Ramayana	suttee
Bhagavad Gita	stupa

People to Identify

Indo-Aryans	Shiva
Varuna	Enlightened One
Indra	Chandragupta Maurya
Krishna	Asoka
Rama	Guptas
Sita	Aryabhata
Brahma	Susruta
Vishnu	

Places to Locate

Himalayas	Black Sea
Indo-Gangetic Plain	Caspian Sea
Indus River	Vindhya Range
Deccan	China
Western and Eastern	Korea
Ghats	Japan
Mohenjo-Daro	Ganges River
Harappa	Hindu Kush
Khyber Pass	Ajanta

Chapter Theme Questions

- **Geography** How might weather influence the way a geographic region develops?
- **Religion** How might religious beliefs shape a society?
- **Science and the Arts** What kinds of advances in science and the arts might prove important to early civilizations?

The Hindu religion of India includes many unique practices and rituals. One of these is yoga, a set of physical and mental activities by which an individual, the yogi, attempts to become one with the divine spirit by ignoring everything that goes on around him or her. The following is an excerpt from the famous Hindu sacred text, the *Bhagavad Gita*, "Song of the Lord." Here the Lord Krishna, a Hindu god, discusses the practice and meaning of yoga:

❝The yogi should always practice concentration of mind alone in a quiet spot, restraining body and mind without desire and without possessions. One who wants to practice meditation should place his seat firmly on a clean spot, neither too high nor too low, and cover it with tender grass, deer skin and cloth. . . . Taking his seat there and making the mind one-pointed by restraining its activities and those of the senses, he should practice yoga for self-purification. Holding the spine, the neck and the head steadily in a line and gazing at the tip of the nose without looking in any direction and without movement, the yogi of peaceful mind, fearless . . . should sit absorbed in me by controlling his mind.❞

The religions of India—Hinduism and Buddhism—have been very significant in history. They fascinate people who study them, and they have attracted the attention of many westerners in our own time.

Section 1

Indus Valley Civilization

Focus Questions

- **What are the most important features of India's geography and climate?**
- **What were the characteristics of the first Indus Valley civilization?**

The first Indian civilization developed in the Indus Valley of northern India about 4,500 years ago. In time people settled throughout the subcontinent* of India, a region that includes the modern countries of India, Pakistan, Bangladesh, Nepal, Bhutan, and Sri Lanka.

The Physical Setting

The northern border of the Indian subcontinent nestles in the Himalayas, the tallest mountains on Earth. (These mountains are sometimes called the Himalaya.) Half as large as the United States, the Indian subcontinent has a wide diversity of both terrain and climate. Dense rain forests, great fertile plains, high plateaus, dry deserts, narrow coastal plains, and vast rivers sprawl across this region of timeless beauty in southern Asia.

Physical regions. Geographically, the subcontinent of India can be divided into three main regions. Each of these main regions has its own features, climate, and natural resources.

The northern mountains. Three mountain ranges, the Himalayas, the Karakoram (kah·ruh·KOHR·ahm), and the Hindu Kush, loom in the north. The Himalayas were named for a word meaning "place of the snow" in Sanskrit, an ancient Indian language. They consist of a series of parallel mountain ranges that stretch east and southeast for more than 1,500 miles. There are massive glaciers that rest in the valleys. Avalanches careen down the rugged mountainsides, and high winds lash the towering peaks of these mountain ranges. Few usable mountain passes penetrate the formidable mountain walls.

The majestic Karakoram meet the Himalayas in the east and the Hindu Kush in the west. Forbidding peaks, the highest of which is more than 28,000 feet high, jut boldly to the sky. The Karakoram compose part of the mountain chain that forms a wall between the Indian subcontinent and the rest of Asia.

Not quite as rugged as the other mountain ranges of northern India, the Hindu Kush lie to the northwest of the Karakoram. Several usable passes, including the famous Khyber Pass, once provided migrating and invading tribes access to India.

The Indo-Gangetic Plain. Two great rivers lie south of the three mountain ranges. The Ganges (GAN·jeez) River flows to the southeast through an immensely fertile valley, while the Indus River flows southwest through drier lands. Only a low divide, or ridge, separates the northern ends of the two river valleys. After immigrants and invaders traveled through the narrow mountain passes, they spread out along this broad plain and came into contact with the earlier settlers in this area.

The Deccan. The interior region of the vast Indian subcontinent lies south of the Indo-Gangetic Plain. This high plateau is called the Deccan, from the Sanskrit word meaning "south." A range of hills—the Vindhya Range—separates the Deccan from the Indo-Gangetic Plain. Historically this mountain range has formed a cultural barrier between northern and southern India.

At the western edge of the Deccan lie the Western Ghats, a low mountain range that slopes gradually eastward to the inland plateau but rises abruptly from a narrow coastal plain along the Arabian Sea. An even lower mountain range called the Eastern Ghats marks the eastern edge of the Deccan. On the eastern coast of India, another and broader coastal plain faces the Bay of Bengal. The inhabitants of the coastal plains became sea traders very early in their history.

The climate. Two features dominate India's climate: monsoons and high temperatures. **Monsoons** are seasonal winds named for the direction in which they blow or the season in which they occur. From November until the end of the following February or March, the monsoon blows from the north and northeast. Any moisture it carries falls onto the northern slopes of the Himalayas before reaching the rest of India.

The wet season, called the southwest monsoon, occurs from mid-June through October. In April the monsoon begins to swing around and blow from the southwest. The southwesterly winds carry warm, moist air from the Indian Ocean. Water vapor in the air condenses to form clouds and rain. Heavy rains fall along the coastal plains, while sparse rainfall is typical of the land behind the Western Ghats. Northeastern India—the lower Ganges Valley and the eastern Himalayas—receives the heaviest rainfall because the region lies directly in the path of these winds.

In most of India, about three quarters of the entire year's rainfall comes between mid-June and early October, when the monsoon comes out of the southwest. The timing of the monsoon is critical. If the monsoon arrives late, or if little rain falls, crops wither. If the monsoon brings too much rain, destructive floods rage across the countryside.

The other important feature of India's climate is its high range of temperatures. Although temperatures seldom soar on the Coastal Plain or on the Deccan, scorching heat plagues the Indo-Gangetic Plain.

---

*A subcontinent is a large landmass that is smaller than a continent.

Mount Everest, which lies on the border between Tibet and Nepal, is the highest mountain in the world, reaching an elevation of 29,028 feet.

Temperatures there remain cool in the winter months of December, January, and February, but during the rest of the year they become stifling. From March until June, temperatures may rise to 120°F.

Early Civilization in the Indus Valley

An impressive civilization appeared in the Indus River valley around 2500 B.C., several hundred years after Egypt and Sumer developed civilizations. Although our knowledge of this early civilization is incomplete, scholars now believe that this civilization flourished until about 1500 B.C.

The twin cities. The ruins of two cities, Mohenjo-Daro and Harappa, provide us with the best evidence we have of this early Indus Valley civilization. Scholars often call it the Harappan civilization because they first discovered some of its artifacts in the town of Harappa. (See map on page 54.)

Harappa and Mohenjo-Daro showed evidence of impressive city planning and design. Wide streets, laid out in a regular pattern, intersected at right angles. Each city had a water system, complete with public baths, and a covered brick sewer system for private homes. The brick homes of the wealthy appear to have been two stories tall with bathrooms and garbage chutes. Many buildings were built of bricks baked in kilns, or ovens, which made them stronger than sun-dried bricks. Some of the baked bricks have remained intact over the centuries.

Each city had a strong central fortress, or **citadel**, built on a brick platform. At Harappa—a city of about 35,000 people—farmers kept enough grain in storehouses to feed the entire population.

Indus Valley culture. Farmlands surrounded Harappa and Mohenjo-Daro. The people raised cattle, sheep, pigs, and goats, and cultivated crops including cotton, wheat and rice. Scientists have found evidence of flood control and irrigation projects. City dwellers worked primarily in industry or trade. As early as 2300 B.C. they traded with people of the Tigris-Euphrates Valley. Indus Valley artisans produced fine articles, including cotton cloth, pottery, bronze items, and gold and silver jewelry.

The early Indus Valley people also developed a written language. Pictographs dating from about 2300 B.C. have been found, but scholars have not yet

Economics

Industry and Trade in the Indus Valley

The rich soil of the Indus Valley made productive agriculture possible. Farmers cultivated a variety of crops including wheat, rice, and barley; they also raised chickens, cattle, and buffalo. To irrigate their fields, the farmers created a series of canals and ditches.

Trade was also an essential element of life in the Indus Valley. Using transportation that most likely included carts, boats, and pack animals, the people of the region traded goods with both neighboring and distant communities. These goods included grain, cotton, and farm animals.

Indus Valley artisans created many fine articles, some for ornamental use and others for practical purposes. Decorative articles included ceramic beads, ornaments, and gold and silver jewelry, while useful articles included bronze and copper tools, pots, and pans as well as stone utensils.

Among the most interesting types of Harappan art objects, however, are seals like the ones shown here. These seals are the only known examples of the picture writing of the Harappans. Although scholars have been unable to decipher this writing, many believe that the Harappans used the seals to stamp property or to identify its owners. Because Harappan seals have been found in the Tigris-Euphrates region near the sites of Sumerian civilization, scholars think that the people of the Indus Valley traded with people of Southwest Asia.

deciphered them, partly because most are personal seals and are thought to be signatures. Additional writing has been found on clay pots and fragments, but scholars have been unable to connect this writing to any other language.

Little is known about religion of this period in the Indus Valley. What may have been sacred trees, along with horned deities, are depicted on many seals or tablets. Because archaeologists have found no temples, shrines, or religious writings, scholars believe that the people of the Indus Valley worshiped a great god and performed rituals at home or possibly in temporary public locations, such as at the foot of a sacred tree. In religious ceremonies they probably used images of animals associated with physical power, such as bulls, buffaloes, and tigers. Other evidence indicates that a mother goddess symbolized fertility.

Scholars do not know why the Indus Valley civilization declined. Some have speculated that tribes from outside lands conquered the valley, but this theory is no longer widely accepted. Recent studies have shown that the Indus and other rivers changed course dramatically. Floods caused by these shifts buried many settlements in silt and likely had a devastating effect on agriculture.

Other evidence suggests that major earthquakes struck the region around 1700 B.C. The discovery of several unburied skeletons, together with homes and personal belongings hastily abandoned, seems to indicate that some disastrous event occurred at Mohenjo-Daro. The evidence that would be needed to verify this theory, however, is lacking.

Section 1 Review

1. **Define** monsoons, citadel
2. **Locate and Explain the Significance** Himalayas, Indo-Gangetic Plain, Indus River, Deccan, Western and Eastern Ghats, Mohenjo-Daro, Harappa
3. **Summarizing Ideas (a)** Name and briefly describe the main geographical regions of India. **(b)** Why are monsoons so important to India?
4. **Interpreting Ideas** What do archaeological findings in the Indus Valley suggest about the political, economic, and social aspects of city life in the early Indus Valley civilization?

Building History Study Skills

READ
WRITE
INTERPRET
CONNECT
THINK

Reading About History: Classifying Information

Classifying information involves grouping information about ideas, objects, or people in categories according to the characteristics they have in common. Grouping ideas or events within a category enables you to organize and understand large amounts of information and find added meaning in isolated bits of information. When data are organized in this way, conclusions can be drawn, and comparisons can be made.

How to Classify Information

To classify information, follow these steps.
1. Read the information.
2. Sort the information into groups of related data.
3. Assign a category name to each group.
4. Place the groups within broader categories if possible.
5. Formulate a statement relating the categories to each other to clarify the meaning of the information.

Developing the Skill

Read the following description of Mohenjo-Daro to determine the characteristics of Harappan civilization.

"At Harappa and Mohenjo-daro . . . the basic form of the ideal Indus city was achieved . . . on the west a citadel mound built on a high podium of mud brick . . . and to the east, dominated by the citadel, a lower city. . . . The architects of the citadel platform were . . . troubled by the prospects of flooding and to counter this danger they protected the citadel by a mud-brick embankment. . . . [The Great Bath] occupied a central area in the citadel. Its principal element comprised a . . . sunken pool. . . . Near the southwest corner of the pool an outlet led to a high-arched drain which took excess waters down the western side of the citadel mound. A range of small rooms stood to the east of the pool, and in one of these was a large double-lined well which no doubt was the source of water for the pool. To the north, across a lane, was a building block which contained eight small bathrooms. . . . The Great Bath may have been part of a religious and ceremonial centre, offering ritual immersion and perhaps the services of resident priesthood. . . . To the north and east of the Great Bath were other large and prestigious buildings, which may have been the offices or quarters of administrators. . . . Divided into rectangular blocks by the street pattern, the individual buildings of the lower city differed considerably in size and function. . . . Nearly all the larger houses were equipped with wells, indoor bathing platforms and seated latrines connected to sewers underneath the streets. . . . In addition to residential areas, there were many shops and workshops, producing wares for local consumption and for export: for example, potteries, dyers' vats and metalworkers', shell-ornament makers' and beadmakers' shops. . . . Wheat and barley were two staple crops. . . . The agricultural surplus made it possible to support a number of crafts and specialists. . . . Buildings which may have been temples and stone sculptures, probably cult icons, have been located. . . . One of the most characteristic depictions of an Indus god is to be found on a series of seals."

Study the chart below to see how this information about Harappan civilization can be grouped into four major categories.

By studying the chart, you can draw conclusions about Harappan civilization. The people of this civilization were concerned with cleanliness. This concern is evident in the elaborate technology devoted to cleanliness—bathrooms, sewers, the drainage system, and the ritual bathing pool. In addition, we know that the government was concerned with the people's welfare because it built extensive public facilities. We also know that religion played a role in Harappan life, as shown by the icons and seals depicting Indus gods. This was a highly developed urban civilization, as evidenced by the technology, the city services, and the layout of the city.

Practicing the Skill

Use the categories in the chart to sort the major characteristics of society in your home town or city.

To apply this skill, see Applying History Study Skills on page 67.

Government	Religion	Technology	Economy
government buildings	seals	drainage systems	grain production
city planning	ritual bathing pool	bathrooms	craftsmen
public works	icons	sewer systems	trade

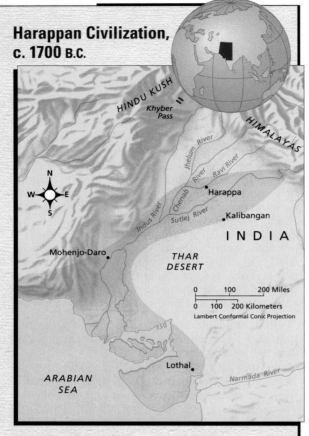

Harappan Civilization, c. 1700 B.C.

HINDU KUSH

Khyber Pass

HIMALAYAS

Jhelum River

Chenab River

Ravi River

Sutlej River

Indus River

Harappa

Kalibangan

INDIA

Mohenjo-Daro

THAR DESERT

N W E S

0   100   200 Miles
0   100   200 Kilometers
Lambert Conformal Conic Projection

Lothal

ARABIAN SEA

Narmada River

Learning from Maps Rivers formed natural highways that encouraged exchange as well as unity in the Harappan civilization.

❓ **Location** Which two Harappan cities are connected by rivers?

Indo-Aryan Migrants

Focus Questions

- Who were the Indo-Aryans, and what impact did they have on Indian civilization?
- What was the importance of the Vedas?
- What were the characteristics of early Indo-Aryan society?

About 1750 B.C., new groups of people came through mountain passes, such as the Khyber Pass, into India. They came from the region north of the Black and Caspian Seas and spoke an Indo-European language.

The Nomadic Indo-Aryans

We call the many Indo-European tribes that migrated one after another to northwestern India, Aryans, or Indo-Aryans. Although these people called themselves "Aryans," scholars sometimes refer to them as "Indo-Aryans" to distinguish them from those Aryans who remained in what is now Iran. One historian observed:

"There is no ancient record of that first successful trip to India. We do not know how difficult the journey was when the Aryan invaders first led their people down . . . beyond the snowline to the hot, rock-strewn [narrow passages] and out onto the broad grasslands which they had come seeking. We have no way of knowing how the animals felt, and whether or not their owners knew that horses would die unless their noses bled at the top of the Pass, to relieve the pressure of the height. We know only that enough people and animals survived that rugged experience to change the course of Indian history."

The nomadic Indo-Aryans herded sheep and cows. In fact, their word for *war* meant "a desire for more cows." Many Indo-Aryan archers followed horse-drawn chariots into battle. Skillful fighters, the Indo-Aryans conquered the Indus Valley and then gradually moved eastward along the Ganges until, after several centuries, they controlled the entire northern plain.

Indo-Aryan Civilization During the Vedic Age

Most of what we know of the Indo-Aryans comes from the **Vedas,** the great literature of the Indo-Aryan religion. For centuries the people memorized the Vedas and handed them down by word of mouth. Later, with the development of writing, Indo-Aryan scholars wrote them in the Indo-Aryan language, **Sanskrit**. So important are the Vedas to Indian history that we call the period from 1500 B.C. to 1000 B.C. the Vedic Age.

Indo-Aryan religion. The earliest gods mentioned in the Vedas include elements of nature, such as the sky, sun, earth, light, fire, wind, storms, water, and rain. The Vedas personified these natural materials and forces—that is, they regarded or represented them as people. Thus the sky became a father, Earth a mother. Although the Vedas mention gods and goddesses, a very important hymn celebrating the creation of the universe suggests a concept of a supreme god, called "That One," who created universal order out of the original chaos.

As the Vedic religion changed and developed, gods were seen as having particular attributes. Varuna was the guardian of cosmic order and the personification of the heavens or sky, where he lived in a great palace. Varuna also came to be seen as the divine judge who punished sin. Indra was the god of storm and war.

Ritual sacrifices were important observances, made in the hope of obtaining such favors as good fortune, health, and long life. Apparently no temples or images characterized the early Vedic religion. The ceremonies were performed in an open space that was newly consecrated on each important occasion. Fires were lit on newly constructed altars, and the juice of the soma plant—thought of as the drink of immortality—was poured into the sacred fire. Foods such as meat, butter, milk, and barley cakes were also offered as sacrifices.

It was important to perform ceremonies properly. As time passed, the rituals of sacrifice became more complicated. **Brahmins**, the priests who knew the proper forms and rules, became more important in Indo-Aryan society. Changes in the Sanskrit language brought by the Indo-Aryan invaders reflected these developments. Originally a spoken tongue used in everyday life, over time Sanskrit became a highly complex and stylized language that was used by the priests in sacred observances.

Early Indo-Aryan society. At first the Indo-Aryans kept the habits and customs of nomadic wanderers. Eventually, however, most of them settled in village communities, where they practiced agriculture as well as herding animals.

In time, Indo-Aryan settlements joined to form small city-states. A **raja**, a prince or king, ruled each city-state. He acted as military leader, lawmaker, and judge. A royal council of his friends and relatives assisted the raja. Although the city-states warred with each other, for hundreds of years they enjoyed internal stability and independence.

Physical and social differences existed between the Indo-Aryan migrants and the earlier inhabitants of the Indo-Gangetic Plain. These differences were the source of the complex system of social orders that later became so important in Indian society. (See Section 3.) The Indo-Aryans were light-skinned, whereas the earlier settlers were dark-skinned. The Indo-Aryans had been a nomadic people, while Indus Valley peoples lived in settled communities. Warriors, and later priests, were at the top of the Indo-Aryan social structure, with merchants, traders, farmers, and servants below them.

In addition to providing information about Indo-Aryan religion, the Vedas tell us a great deal about family life in the Vedic Age. Marriage was a very important institution. Elaborate rules governed marriages among the different orders of society and the marriage ceremonies themselves. Marriages arranged by parents were favored. However, a number of different types of marriages were recognized, including marriage by purchase, marriage by capture, and marriage by mutual consent of the couple.

The Indo-Aryan economy. When the Indo-Aryans began farming the Indo-Gangetic Plain, they raised wheat and barley as their principal crops. Rice was grown in some areas with the help of irrigation. Other crops were sugar cane, leafy vegetables, gourds, peas, beans, and lentils.

In this relief from Gandhara, two young Brahmins raise their right hands to perform the *abhaya mudra*, a gesture of benediction.

Clues to the Past Through Archaeology

Centuries in the future, when archaeologists excavate the buried ruins of a 20-story office building from our civilization, they will undoubtedly discover the remains of countless computer terminals. What might such an archaeological excavation reveal about us and the civilization in which we lived? What tools will the archaeologists use to study the artifacts of our time?

Today archaeologists and their assistants, using modest shovels, trowels, and brushes, dig carefully and work slowly to uncover a structure from the past and preserve its artifacts. In addition to their traditional implements, modern-day archaeologists' toolboxes contain a few sophisticated pieces of technological equipment, such as a mass spectrometer, a sonar scanner, or a particle accelerator. The powerful tools provided by technology help archaeologists gather information, evaluate and classify artifacts and fossils, and determine the age of their finds.

The tools with which archaeologists search for clues to the past have evolved as technology has developed. The first task an archaeologist faces is to locate the site. By means of aerial photographs, magnetometers, and sonar scanners, archaeologists search for sites underground, above ground, and under water.

After a site has been excavated, an archaeologist needs to catalog, classify, and date the uncovered objects. Computers accelerate the otherwise time-consuming process of cataloging and classifying finds. Since the development in 1947 of the carbon-14 dating technique, archaeologists and other scientists are able to date the remains of living beings—human, animal, or plant—up to about 50,000 years old. After a plant or animal dies, its radiocarbon atoms begin to decay. A sophisticated tool called the mass spectrometer measures the amount of radiocarbon still present in the life form. From the measurement of an ancient animal's or plant's radiocarbon content, scientists determine its age. Another tool, the particle accelerator, accurately measures the smallest artifacts up to 60,000 years old. More recently, the potassium-argon dating technique has been used to date rock formations up to millions of years old in which artifacts and fossils are found.

Although poor transportation and trading methods sometimes limited trade, various types of goods gradually appeared in the villages. Early traders bartered, since coins were not widely used until about 500 B.C.

The Indo-Aryan migrants had a significant impact on the civilization of the northern part of the Indian subcontinent. These contributions included a new social order, a new language, and a new religious interpretation of how the world works. Archaeological evidence shows that, over time, the contributions of these Indo-Aryan migrants blended into the previous civilization of the Indus Valley people. Religious values changed, and social classes became more rigid and closely identified with ritual purity.

Southern India. Southern India developed somewhat differently. Separated from the Indo-Gangetic Plain in the north by the forest-covered mountains of the Vindhya Range, the people of the south were able to resist conquest by the Indo-Aryans for centuries. They remained linguistically, ethnically, and culturally distinct from the population of the north. Similarly, the southern part of India is quite hilly, and this worked against political or cultural unification there. As a result, southern India's people remained fragmented into many diverse groups. To some extent, these distinctions still exist today.

Some southern Indians lived as farmers, others as hunter-gatherers. Some southern Indians, however, particularly those living along the coast, turned to trade and commerce. Some traders eventually became wealthy by trading valuable goods such as cotton, spices, and ivory. Through coastal ports, southern Indians eventually made contact with other civilizations in Southeast Asia.

Section 2 Review

1. **Define** Vedas, Sanskrit, Brahmins, raja
2. **Identify** Indo-Aryans, Varuna, Indra
3. **Locate and Explain the Significance** Khyber Pass, Black Sea, Caspian Sea, Vindhya Range
4. **Interpreting Ideas (a)** Who were the Indo-Aryans? **(b)** Describe the contributions of the Indo-Aryans to Indian civilization.
5. **Understanding Ideas (a)** What were the Vedas? **(b)** What do the Vedas tell us about the Indo-Aryans?
6. **Summarizing Ideas** How was Indo-Aryan society structured?

Hinduism and Buddhism

Focus Questions
- **What were the great works of philosophy and literature of India after the Vedic Age?**
- **What social structure emerged in India?**
- **What are the teachings of Hinduism and Buddhism?**

During the Vedic Age, the Indo-Aryans had introduced a new social structure in India. In time this structure evolved into the caste system, part of the foundation of Indian society. In the centuries after the Vedic Age, two of the world's great religions—Hinduism and Buddhism—developed in India.

The *Upanishads* and the Epics

The Vedic Age is named after the Vedas, collections of religious prayers and hymns to the gods. By the end of that period, the basic social structure of India had taken shape. During the next thousand years, until about A.D. 500, great works of religious literature, based on earlier stories, were compiled.

Sometime after 700 B.C., several thinkers began to question the authority of the Brahmins. These thinkers became wanderers who taught their message in the forests of the Ganges Plain. This school of thought was known as the Vedanta, or "end of the Vedas." It was expressed in written form in the *Upanishads* (oo·PAH·ni·shahdz). These were complex philosophical explanations of the Vedic religion.

Ordinary people, however, did not understand the *Upanishads* any more than they could the Vedas. But they could understand simple stories that made these ideas about Vedic religion clearer. These stories, retold from generation to generation, were eventually combined into two **epics**, or long poems describing heroes and great events. These epic poems, based on historical and religious themes, are the *Mahabharata* (muh·HAH·BAHR·uh·tuh) and the *Ramayana*.

The *Mahabharata* tells the story of a great civil war in a kingdom near what is today the city of Delhi, in what is now northern India. The last 18 chapters of this epic, known as the *Bhagavad Gita*, or "Song of the Lord," stress the idea that conducting oneself properly according to one's status in life marks the highest fulfillment in life. In the *Bhagavad Gita*, Krishna, a human incarnation of the god Vishnu, also explains that love and devotion to Vishnu can lead to salvation in the afterlife.

The *Ramayana* tells the story of two royal heroic figures—Rama (another human incarnation of the god Vishnu) and his devoted wife, Sita. Rama, a prince, was exiled, and Sita was kidnapped by a demon. Rama defeated the demon and became king. Their faithfulness to duty and their devotion to each other and the people of their kingdom make Rama and Sita ideals of Indian manhood and womanhood.

From the *Mahabharata* and the *Ramayana,* and from the *Upanishads* and the Vedas themselves, scholars have pieced together the origins of the two most important influences in Indian history—the caste system and Hinduism.

A Changing Social Structure

A complex form of social organization began to take shape after the Indo-Aryan migration to northern India. Four distinct varnas, or social classes, emerged in Indian society. At the top of the social scale stood the rulers and warriors called Kshatriyas (KSHA·tree·uhz). Next came the priests, scholars, and wise men called Brahmins. During the next several centuries, the Brahmins and the Kshatriyas changed positions within society, the Brahmins becoming most important because of their influential role in society. The varna of Vaisyas (VYSH·yuhz), which included merchants, traders, and owners of small farms, came third. The Sudras—peasants bound to work the fields of large landowners and do other kinds of menial labor—stood at the bottom of the social ladder.

A fifth group of people called Pariahs stood apart from and lower than the rest of Indian society. They may initially have been slaves captured in battle by Indo-Aryan warriors, or other circumstances may have forced them to do society's most unpleasant tasks, such as skinning animals or working with human corpses. These people were called "untouchables" because the other people in Indian society thought that merely by touching those who did impure work, they themselves would become impure.

As time passed, the original four varnas divided into smaller groups called *jati,* meaning "subgroups." Eventually some 3,000 hereditary *jati* developed. Each had its own fixed social position and rules about eating, marriage, labor, and worship. For example, people could not eat or drink with someone of another *jati,* nor could they marry outside their *jati.* They could perform services for other people that were consistent with the duties of their *jati,* and they could work only at those occupations recognized as fitting for members of their *jati.* This system later became known to westerners as the **caste system**.

Hinduism

Hinduism, India's major religion, developed through Brahmin priests' interpretations of the Vedas. According to the *Upanishads,* a basic divine essence known as Brahma fills everything in the world. Atman, or Self, refers to the essence of an individual person. When Hindus say that Brahma and Atman are one and indivisible, they mean that God and human beings are one. Another way of expressing this idea is to say that mind and matter are ultimately the same. This belief is called **monism**.

According to Hinduism, the world known to our senses is merely an illusion called **maya**, which—because it is an illusion—betrays people, giving them sorrow and pain. People can be delivered from their suffering if they learn to identify maya, or those things that are illusory. Because this learning takes lifetimes of experience, **reincarnation**—the transmigration or rebirth of the soul—occurs to make it possible. According to Hinduism, the soul does not die with the body but enters the body of another being, either human or animal, and thus lives again and again.

Two major elements in the theory of reincarnation are known as dharma and karma. **Dharma** is fulfillment of one's moral duty in this life so that the soul can make progress toward deliverance from punishment in the next life. **Karma** is the positive or negative force generated by a person's actions, which will determine their status in the next life.

According to Hinduism, people who fulfill their dharma are rewarded with good karma and are reborn into a higher social group. People who do not live moral lives are reborn into a lower social group or even into the bodies of animals or insects.

Hindus hope, by fulfilling their dharma, ultimately to end the repeated transmigrations. In this way they will attain salvation and enable their souls to reunite with the universal spirit, Brahma.

Brahma has a number of representations, most notably Brahma the Creator, Vishnu the Preserver, and Siva the Destroyer. Below these come many other gods, represented in the spirits of trees, animals, and people. Since Hindus believe that all souls make up part of the Universal Soul, or Brahma, Hindus respect the sacredness of life in all forms.

To westerners, this religion of many gods with different names sounds polytheistic. However, Hindus

SCULPTURE

The God Siva

Along with Brahma and Vishnu, Siva is one of the three great gods of Hinduism. Siva has many roles but is best known as both the destroyer and restorer of life. Siva is also the lord of the dance and is often shown dancing, as in this bronze statue.

The circle of flames surrounding Siva represents the continuous creation and destruction of the universe. In one of the god's hands are the flames of destruction; in another, he holds an hourglass-shaped drum that beats the creative heartbeat of the cosmos. Other hands perform movements of benediction and reassurance. With his right foot, Siva is crushing a dwarf that represents the illusionary world of maya.

The sculpture is both a work of art and a way to remind Hindus of the complex, sometimes contradictory nature of the Hindu religion and of life itself.

insist that it is monistic—that all the gods are merely different representations of the oneness of the universe.

Hindu religious practices. Hindus commonly practice **yoga**, a physical and mental discipline designed to harmonize body with soul. In one form of yoga a person might, for example, sit for many hours in a certain position in order to free the mind of bodily concerns.

Hindu festivals combine religious ceremonies, rituals, music, dancing, eating, and drinking. The festivals represent the cyclical course of nature; originally, they were intended to ensure that those cycles would continue. Many ancient festivals, some lasting for days, continue to be celebrated throughout India.

Some Hindus pay special reverence to certain animals. For example, they consider cows especially sacred because cows provide power for the plow and the cart and produce food (milk and butter) and fuel (dung). For these reasons many Hindus will not eat beef.

Establishment of the caste system and Hinduism were the most important developments in early Indian history. The caste system and Hinduism became deeply interwoven in the fabric of Indian society.

The Early Life of The Buddha

Another of the world's great religions, Buddhism, also arose in India. Buddhism's founder, Siddhartha Gautama, who became known as the Buddha, or "the Enlightened One," was born about 563 B.C. in northern India and died about 483 B.C. The son of an Indian prince, he lived in luxury, apart from ordinary people. At the age of 29, he left his palace and was shocked by what he found: an old, decrepit man, a very sick man covered with boils, and a corpse about to be cremated. Profoundly disturbed, he wondered about the great problems of life. "Why does suffering exist?" he asked. "What is the value of life and death?"

Gautama decided to spend the rest of his life seeking answers to these questions. In what is now called the Great Renunciation, he put aside all his possessions, left his wife and infant son, and set out to search for the truth.

Gautama followed all the recommended practices to attain wisdom. He lived as a hermit and a scholar and practiced the mental and physical discipline of yoga. He tried fasting—not eating for a specified amount of time—so strictly that he nearly died. But none of these practices gave him the answers he longed for so much.

One day, after six years of searching, as Gautama meditated under a fig tree, he felt that he understood the truth that forms the basis of life. In that moment, according to his followers, he became the Buddha, "the Enlightened One." He spent the remainder of his life teaching the Enlightenment, the Way of Life.

The Buddha's Teachings

The Buddha accepted the Hindu belief that the progress of the soul depends on the life a person leads, and that good is rewarded and evil punished. He taught that salvation comes from knowing the Four Noble Truths and following the Eightfold Path.

The Four Noble Truths. The Four Noble Truths are (1) that all human life involves suffering and sorrow; (2) that the desire for a life of pleasure and material gain causes suffering and sorrow; (3) that renouncing desire frees people from suffering and helps their souls attain **nirvana**, the perfect peace, which releases the soul from the endless cycle of reincarnation; and (4) that the Eightfold Path leads to renunciation, or denial of desire and attainment of nirvana.

The Eightfold Path. The Eightfold Path consists of eight guides to thought and conduct. They are (1) right views, or seeing life as it really is, with all its imperfections; (2) right intentions; (3) right speech, or avoiding lies and gossip; (4) right action, or avoiding any unlawful acts and, instead, seeking to be honest; (5) right living, which means working at a job that does not harm others; (6) right effort, or working to prevent evil; (7) right mindfulness, or constant awareness of one's self; and (8) right concentration to direct the mind in meditation.

The Buddha's teachings stressed ethics, a code of morals and conduct, rather than ceremonies. He believed that desire caused suffering, and consequently he stressed the denial of self. The Buddha did not accept the Hindu gods, and he taught that priests should live peaceful and highly moral lives of poverty. Although he did not attack the Hindu caste system openly, he did not accept it. According to the teachings of Buddhism, any person, regardless of caste, could reach nirvana if he or she was good. These teachings, however, were opposed by powerful Brahmins.

The Spread of Buddhism

The Buddha gained some followers in his lifetime—but not many. Over several centuries, however, his teachings won wide acceptance in Asia.

Sometime between 200 B.C. and A.D. 200, Buddhism split into two branches: Theraveda and Mahayana. Theraveda followed the traditional beliefs of Buddhism and regarded the Buddha simply as an outstanding spiritual teacher. Theraveda Buddhism was widely accepted in Burma (now Myanmar), Siam (now Thailand), Ceylon (now Sri Lanka), and other countries. Believers in the Mahayana form of Buddhism regarded the Buddha as a god and savior. They developed Buddhism into a religion with priests, temples, creeds, and rituals. Mahayana Buddhism was taken up in China, Korea, and Japan.

As cultural interactions grew between India and Central Asia, particularly under the Kushan Empire, Mahayana Buddhism developed and spread. Mahayana Buddhism was able to incorporate elements of other religions by arguing that their gods were *Bodhisattvas*—those who had attained enlightenment like the Buddha, but had turned back from nirvana in order to help the rest of humanity achieve salvation.

Although the Brahmins strongly opposed it, over several centuries Buddhism gained many followers in India. Eventually, however, it slowly declined there. Buddhism achieved greater acceptance in other areas of Asia. (See map on page 61.)

What If?

Siddhartha Gautama
What if Siddhartha Gautama had not left his luxurious palace as a young man, witnessed scenes of human misery, and thought deeply about the problems of life? What might have changed about his own life, and how might the Buddhist religion have been affected?

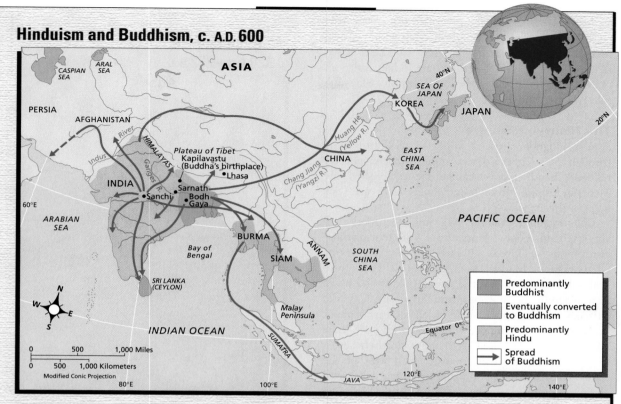

Hinduism and Buddhism, c. A.D. 600

Learning from Maps Buddhism spread throughout Asia along major trade routes.

❓ **Place** How far east had Buddhism spread by A.D. 600?

Section 3 Review

1. **Define** *Upanishads,* epics, *Mahabharata, Ramayana, Bhagavad Gita,* caste system, monism, maya, reincarnation, dharma, karma, yoga, nirvana

2. **Identify** Krishna, Rama, Sita, Brahma, Vishnu, Siva, Enlightened One

3. **Locate and Explain the Significance** China, Korea, Japan

4. **Understanding Ideas** Briefly describe three great works of Indian literature after the Vedic Age.

5. **Identifying Ideas** What five social groups emerged in Indian society after the Indo-Aryan invasions?

6. **Summarizing Ideas (a)** What Hindu belief did the Buddha accept? **(b)** Explain the Four Noble Truths and the principles of the Eightfold Path.

Section 4

Ancient Indian Dynasties and Empires

Focus Questions

- What great empires existed in India from the 320s B.C. to about A.D. 550?
- Who were the great rulers of each empire, and what were their accomplishments?

Neither the Persians nor the Greeks (whom you will read about in Chapter 5) conquered the Indian subcontinent, although both did for a time control lands as far as the Indus River. The Persian ruler Darius the Great sent an army to invade the Indus

Valley in the 510s B.C. and organized the area as part of the Persian Empire. But Indian kingdoms slowly reduced Persian control in India as the Persian Empire declined. The northeastern Indian kingdom of Magadha finally absorbed this region. Magadha rule ended in the 320s B.C.

The Mauryan Empire

A new kingdom arose in India at about this time through the conquests of a powerful young adventurer named Chandragupta Maurya. He established the Mauryan Empire, which lasted almost 150 years. (See map on this page.)

Chandragupta Maurya. We know a good deal about Chandragupta Maurya from a fascinating diary written by a Greek ambassador to his court. Chandragupta Maurya took control of Pataliputra (pah·tah·li·POO·trah) on the Ganges River and made it a magnificent and beautiful city with a grand palace. Chandragupta Maurya raised an army of about 700,000 soldiers, equipped with thousands of chariots and elephants. He used it to unite northern India from the Ganges River to the region west of the Indus. Eventually, Chandragupta Maurya conquered all of northwestern India up to the Hindu Kush. He was an able administrator, and his empire controlled and operated mines and centers for spinning and weaving. A uniform system of weights and measures was used throughout the empire.

A clever but harsh ruler, Chandragupta Maurya made many enemies. The Greek ambassador reported that Chandragupta slept in a different room each night because he feared assassination. Among the guards who protected him were armed women. In 301 B.C. Chandragupta Maurya abdicated the throne in favor of his son.

Asoka. One of India's greatest rulers was Asoka, Chandragupta Maurya's grandson, who came to the throne about 270 B.C. By means of terribly bloody wars, in which many thousands were killed and even more captured or deported, Asoka enlarged the Mauryan Empire until it included all of India except the southern tip of the subcontinent.

However, Asoka was eventually so sickened by the slaughter of battle that he renounced war and became a devout Buddhist. Many other Indian people also became Buddhists around this time. Asoka sent his brother as a missionary to Ceylon and also sent missionaries to other countries.

As a Buddhist, Asoka thought constantly of piety and duty. He urged religious toleration and relaxed

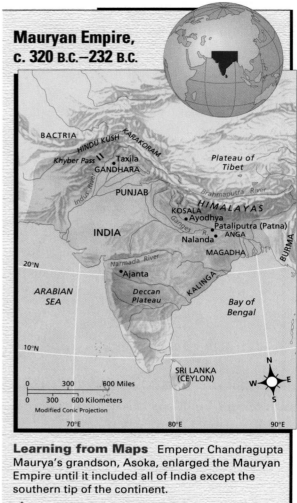

Learning from Maps Emperor Chandragupta Maurya's grandson, Asoka, enlarged the Mauryan Empire until it included all of India except the southern tip of the continent.

? Location Which mountain ranges form the northern boundary of the Mauryan Empire?

the harsh laws that had supported the unlimited power of his father and grandfather. To gain wide publicity, Asoka set up stone pillars inscribed with his laws in public places. He pardoned prisoners and forbade animal sacrifices.

After Asoka died in 232 B.C., the Mauryan Empire began to crumble. Following the assassination of the last Mauryan ruler in 184 B.C., a series of foreign rulers took control of northern India.

The Gupta Rulers

The next great rulers of India were the Guptas, who came to power in A.D. 320. The Guptas first governed

Gupta Empire, c. A.D. 400

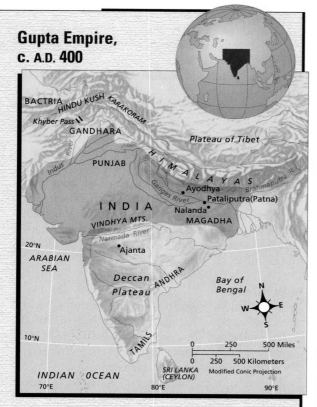

Learning from Maps The Gupta rulers made Pataliputra (now Patna) capital of their empire.

? Region Which mountains created natural boundaries for the Gupta Empire?

in the Ganges Valley, but through intermarriage and conquest they extended their power greatly. (See map on this page.) By A.D. 400 the Gupta empire reached from the Bay of Bengal to the Arabian Sea. Eventually it included all of the northern part of India.

Particularly under the early Gupta rulers, including Chandra Gupta I (no relation to the earlier Chandragupta of the Mauryan dynasty) and Chandra Gupta II, Indian civilization flourished. The Guptas favored Hinduism, although they continued to support Buddhism. Hinduism became the dominant religion of India and remains so today.

This period has been called a golden age because of the brilliant civilization that flourished under the reign of the Guptas. Both society and the arts prospered during Chandra Gupta II's reign (A.D. 374–415).

Under later rulers, however, this great empire became weakened.

Gupta rule ended by A.D. 550, after the death of Skanda Gupta. Waves of invaders from Central Asia had begun to enter northern India in the late A.D. 400s and eventually gained control of the area.

Section 4 Review

1. **Identify** Chandragupta Maurya, Asoka, Guptas
2. **Locate and Explain the Significance** Ganges River, Hindu Kush
3. **Analyzing Ideas (a)** What great empires existed in India from the 320s B.C. to about A.D. 550? **(a)** Give a physical description of these empires using the maps in the section.
4. **Summarizing Ideas** What did Chandragupta Maurya, Asoka, and Chandra Gupta I and Chandra Gupta II accomplish as rulers?

Section 5

Ancient Indian Life and Culture

Focus Questions

- **What position did women occupy in early Indian society?**
- **What was education like in ancient India?**
- **What contributions did early Indian society make to the arts, mathematics, and science?**

Indian civilization reached great heights from the Vedic Age through the Gupta Empire period. During that time the cultural traditions of India were established, and the ancient Indian societies left the world a rich legacy in art, literature, mathematics, and science. The impact of these contributions has endured.

Economy and Women's Position in Society

From ancient times onward, the land provided a living for nearly all the people of northern India. A limited few at the top of the caste system enjoyed great luxury. Most of the population, however, eked out a meager existence. During the Indo-Aryan period the rajas controlled the land and took what they wanted from the farmers. By the time of the Guptas, the rulers claimed one-fourth of each harvest in taxes.

In southern India many people made their living through trade with foreign nations. Foreign trade also flourished in northern India under the Guptas. In the ancient world, Indian goods such as silks, cottons, cashmere, ivory, spices, and precious gems could be found in the Far East, Southwest Asia, Africa, and Europe.

Generally, women in ancient Indian society were subordinate to men. Although Hindu customs provided women with some protection, the laws made it clear that their status was inferior to men. For example, the Hindu Laws of Manu, compiled between 200 B.C. and A.D. 200, stated: "In childhood a female must be subject to her father, in youth to her husband, when her lord is dead, to her sons; a woman must never be independent." **Polygyny**, the marriage of a man to more than one woman, was accepted in Indo-Aryan society and became more widespread during the Gupta period. Another practice that was common under Gupta rule, especially among the upper castes, was **suttee**. This custom required a widow to commit suicide by throwing herself on top of her husband's flaming funeral pyre.

Literature

In addition to the *Mahabharata* and *Ramayana*, people enjoyed the stories of the *Panchatantra*, "Five Books," a series of fables from the Gupta period. These stories contained underlying morals and emphasized desirable traits such as adaptability, shrewdness, and determination. They greatly influenced stories that were popular in many other parts of the world, including the tale "Sinbad the Sailor" from *The Thousand and One Nights*. The *Panchatantra* has been translated into more languages than any other book except the Bible.

Indian drama developed greatly in the Gupta period. The plays might contain tragic scenes, but by custom they always ended happily. Plays were often performed in the open air and made use of little scenery, since there were no regular theaters.

Art and Architecture

Mural paintings in caves tell us something about the artistic style of early Indian painters. Today people continue to visit the caves at Ajanta in central India to admire the mural paintings there. These paintings, from the Gupta period, depict the Buddha and his followers and are a valuable source of information about the daily life of the Indian people at that time. We know little about other kinds of Indian painting before about A.D. 1000, however, because artists used materials such as wood and cloth that have not survived.

Early images of the Buddha show the influence of the art of Greece and Rome. During the reign of the Guptas, however, Indian sculptors developed their own more rigid and formal style, which still characterizes Indian art today. As Hinduism increased in importance, Indians also created a distinctive style of Hindu temple—a square building with heavy walls enclosing the statue of a god.

The great Mauryan ruler Asoka had stone pillars erected throughout his empire with his laws carved on them, and he may have built as many as 84,000 stupas. A **stupa** was a hemispherical, or dome-shaped, shrine that held artifacts and objects associated with the Buddha.

Education

In ancient India, children of the higher castes received formal education in many subjects. They studied the Vedas and other literature including the great epics, astronomy, mathematics, warfare, and government. Poorer children learned only crafts or trades.

By the time of the Guptas, Nalanda, a famous Buddhist monastic university, had become the chief center of Indian higher education. Located in the eastern Ganges Valley near what is today the state of Bihar, it offered free education to as many as 10,000 students in a large complex of buildings. The curriculum included the Vedas, Hindu philosophy, logic, grammar, and medicine.

Mathematics and Astronomy

Indian mathematicians and scientists were highly skilled. The mathematicians understood abstract numbers and negative numbers—without which algebra could not exist—as well as the concepts of zero and infinity. The mathematician Aryabhata, who was born in the late A.D. 400s, is one of the first people known to have used algebra and to have solved quadratic equations. Indians used and probably invented the numbers we call "Arabic": the digits 1 through 9.

Indian astronomers identified the seven planets that can be seen without the aid of a telescope. They understood the daily rotation of Earth on its axis and accurately predicted eclipses of the Sun and moon.

Medicine

Indian physicians understood the importance of the spinal cord, and their surgical procedures included

Connections: Then and Now

Fairy Tales

"Once upon a time . . ." is a phrase that we all probably recognize from the fairy tales that we heard as children. The stories that we call fairy tales occur in many cultures around the world, and often the same basic tale can be found in several cultures.

The Jataka Tales, which were popular Indian stories taken from Buddhist writings, teach lessons about kindness using animals as characters. Their theme is good versus evil. The same theme underlies the story of Cinderella. Her fairy godmother represents good, and the wicked stepmother and stepsisters represent evil.

In a Chinese version of this tale, a talking golden fish and (after the fish is killed) its bones play the fairy godmother's role. However, the lost slipper (golden in the Chinese version), the prince, and the wedding are all in the story. In a Scottish version, the young girl is helped by her dead mother, who appears first as a red calf. More than 500 versions of the Cinderella story have been found in Europe alone.

Another worldwide theme of tales is that of the sleeper and the awakening. In some stories a wicked witch or fairy puts a curse or spell on someone, who sleeps until awakened by a person of good will. We find this theme in the story of Sleeping Beauty. In other stories, a person sleeps for many years and awakes to find the world has greatly changed. A version of this theme occurs in the American story of Rip van Winkle, which was written by Washington Irving.

Cinderella and her fairy godmother

A third universal theme is that of magical transformation. Often this is brought about by love, as Sleeping Beauty also illustrates. The story of Beauty and the Beast tells of a kind but ugly beast who is transformed into a handsome youth by the love of a young woman. In a Kaffir story from southern Africa, the beast is a crocodile.

Scholars see fairy tales as a way in which societies instruct and remind children of wise codes of conduct. In so doing, the tales provide vivid examples of different kinds of human character. At the same time they communicate eternal human concerns, dreams, and experiences—the triumph of good, the power of nature, and the chance of success for even the most unlikely people.

---

bone setting and plastic surgery. They developed the technique of inoculation—infecting a person with a mild form of a disease so that he or she will not fall ill with the more serious form. For example, early Indian physicians successfully inoculated people against the deadly smallpox. Smallpox vaccines were unknown in the Western world until the end of the 1700s.

Indian rulers built free hospitals in the early A.D. 400s. Susruta, a great Indian doctor, practiced strict cleanliness before an operation and also disinfected wounds, another procedure unknown in the West until modern times.

Section 5 Review

1. **Define** polygyny, suttee, stupa
2. **Identify** Aryabhata, Susruta
3. **Locate and Explain the Significance** Ajanta
4. **Summarizing Ideas** What was the status of women in early Indian society?
5. **Understanding Ideas** How did the education of Indian children vary among different castes?
6. **Classifying Ideas** What did the early Indians achieve in the fields of literature, mathematics, astronomy, and medicine?

Chapter 3 Review

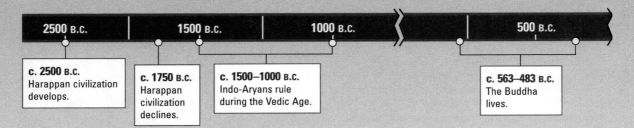

| 2500 B.C. | 1500 B.C. | 1000 B.C. | 500 B.C. |

c. 2500 B.C.
Harappan civilization develops.

c. 1750 B.C.
Harappan civilization declines.

c. 1500–1000 B.C.
Indo-Aryans rule during the Vedic Age.

c. 563–483 B.C.
The Buddha lives.

Chapter Summary

The following list contains the key concepts you have learned about the ancient civilizations of India.

1. The Indian subcontinent is divided into three geographical regions—the northern mountains, the Indo-Gangetic Plain, and the Deccan—plus coastal plains along the west and east coasts.
2. Monsoons and high temperatures dominate India's climate.
3. In about 2500 B.C. the Harappan civilization appeared in the Indus Valley. Industry and trade were centered in such cities as Harappa and Mohenjo-Daro. The Harappans developed a written language and a religion that involved the images of powerful animals, horned deities, and what may have been sacred trees.
4. Around 1750 B.C. the Indo-Aryans began to enter the Indus Valley. Knowledge of the early history of the Indo-Aryans comes mainly from the Vedas, their sacred books, which describe their religious beliefs. Originally herders and nomads, the Indo-Aryans became farmers and founded small tribal states. In their religion, the Indo-Aryans personified natural forces and practiced ritual sacrifices, directed by priests called Brahmins. Important social divisions began to form during the Vedic Age.
5. The Indo-Aryan social divisions developed into the Indian caste system. Each subgroup, or *jati,* had its own fixed position in society and its own rules about eating, marriage, labor, and worship. Caste remains an important part of social organization in India today.
6. Religious thinkers composed the *Upanishads* to explain the Vedic religion. From the *Upanishads* and Brahmin priests' explanations of the Vedas

grew a complex set of ideas known as Hinduism, which remains the major Indian religion.

7. Hinduism teaches that the world of our senses is an illusion. Only through reincarnation can a person gain the experience needed to escape suffering and be reunited with Brahma. Two important elements of reincarnation are karma and dharma, which determine whether a person will achieve salvation.
8. Siddhartha Gautama, an Indian prince who became known as the Buddha, taught that people could attain salvation by accepting the Four Noble Truths and following the Eightfold Path. These teachings, which became known as Buddhism, exerted an even more powerful influence on the rest of Asia than on India itself.
9. From c. 320 B.C. to 184 B.C., the Mauryan Empire ruled India. Asoka, a Mauryan emperor, was one of India's greatest rulers. After expanding his empire through bloody wars, he embraced Buddhism, relaxed the harsh laws, and urged religious toleration.
10. The Gupta dynasty lasted from A.D. 320 to c. 550. Under the Guptas, Indian culture flourished, and this period is known as the golden age in India. It was during this period that Hinduism again became the major religion of India.
11. Indian culture achieved great works in ancient times. Great epics, such as the *Mahabharata* and the *Ramayana,* and the famous fables of the *Panchatantra* were written. Drama, painting, and other arts flourished. Great advances were made in mathematics, astronomy, and medicine. Indians had a great university, understood abstract mathematical concepts, and practiced surgery and inoculation.

Reviewing Important Terms

On a separate sheet of paper, supply the term that correctly completes each statement.

1. A(n) _____ is a seasonal wind named for the direction in which it blows.
2. A(n) _____ is a strong central fortress.
3. The _____ _____ in Indian history lasted from 1500 B.C. to 1000 B.C. and takes its name from religious literature.
4. Indian priests were called _____.
5. In Indo-Aryan times princes, or _____, ruled each city-state.
6. The _____ _____ is the complex form of social organization that developed in India after the Indo-Aryan invasions.

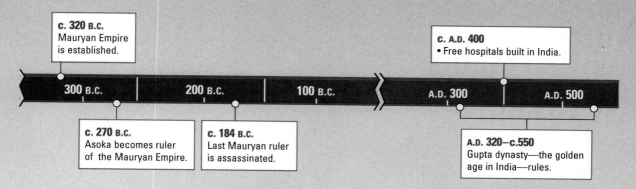

c. 320 B.C.
Mauryan Empire is established.

c. A.D. 400
• Free hospitals built in India.

300 B.C.   200 B.C.   100 B.C.   A.D. 300   A.D. 500

c. 270 B.C.
Asoka becomes ruler of the Mauryan Empire.

c. 184 B.C.
Last Mauryan ruler is assassinated.

A.D. 320–c.550
Gupta dynasty—the golden age in India—rules.

7. The Hindu belief that God and human beings are one and indivisible is called _____.
8. Marriage to more than one wife is called _____.
9. In Hindu belief, the transmigration or rebirth of the soul is called _____.
10. Hindus believe in _____, which is the positive or negative force generated by a person's actions.
11. Hindus commonly practice _____, a physical and mental discipline designed to harmonize the body with the soul.
12. In Hinduism, the world known to our senses is an illusion called _____.
13. _____ was a custom in which a widow would commit suicide by throwing herself on top of her husband's flaming funeral pyre.

Developing Critical Thinking Skills

1. **Describing Ideas** Describe the geographical features of India that were barriers to the spread of Indian culture.
2. **Determining Cause and Effect** How does climate influence agricultural production in the various geographical regions of India?
3. **Summarizing Ideas** What changes did the Indo-Aryans bring to Indus Valley civilization?
4. **Making Charts** Make a chart showing the major accomplishments of the Indus Valley civilization and the Indo-Aryans.
5. **Analyzing Information** (a) What differences and similarities can you find between the civilizations of the Indus Valley and the civilizations that you read about in Chapter 2? (b) How would you account for these differences?

Relating Geography to History

(a) Trace a map of India. (b) Indicate the areas that have heavy rainfall. (c) Indicate the areas that need irrigation in order to grow crops. (d) Show the areas that might be used for grazing. (e) Indicate the wind direction for summer and winter monsoons.

Relating Past to Present

1. The Mauryan ruler Chandragupta Maurya worried about being assassinated. (a) What did he do to guard against assassination? (b) What measures do national leaders today take to avoid assassination? Have any been assassinated?

2. (a) What city planning problems did the people of Harappa and Mohenjo Daro solve? (b) What are some modern city planning problems that were unknown to the people of these ancient civilizations? (c) How are these problems being solved?

Applying History Study Skills

Before completing this activity, review Building History Study Skills on page 53.

The *Rig-Veda,* the oldest Indo-Aryan collection of hymns, consists of stanzas of praise to the Indo-Aryan gods. This literature helps us to understand the religious beliefs and the culture of the early Indian people. Locate a modern translation of the *Rig-Veda* or a book about Indian religion. Study the names and functions of the gods mentioned. Then construct a chart in which you classify the gods according to the characteristics they share.

internetconnect

Search the Internet through the HRW Web site to find out more about Chandragupta Maurya and Asoka. Prepare a written report on the life and accomplishments of one of these Indian rulers.

GO TO: go.hrw.com
KEYWORD: SCØ Mauryan Empire

Building Your Portfolio

1. **Presenting an Oral Report** Present an oral report on the achievements, mysterious beginnings, and sudden end of the Harappan civilization. Good sources for your report are "Mohenjo-Daro," in *The Atlas of Past Worlds* by John Manley (Cassell Publishers), and "The First Indian Cities: Mohenjo-Daro and Harappa," in *World Civilizations, Volume I* by F. Roy Willis (D.C. Heath and Company). Place a record of your report (such as your notes or a video) in your portfolio.
2. **Constructing a Model** Use resources in your school or public library to find out more information on the architecture of Mohenjo-Daro or Harappa. Then construct a model showing what the city may have looked like. Place your notes or model plans in your portfolio.

Ancient Chinese Civilization

TIME

c. 1500 B.C.–A.D. 589

c. 1500 B.C.–A.D. 589

3.7 million B.C.	4000 B.C.	A.D. 2100

PLACE

China

China

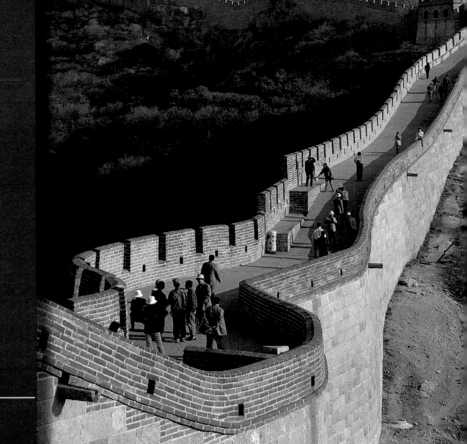

ARCTIC OCEAN

NORTH AMERICA · EUROPE · ASIA

PACIFIC OCEAN · AFRICA

Equator

INDIAN OCEAN

AUSTRALIA · PACIFIC OCEAN · SOUTH AMERICA · ATLANTIC OCEAN

ANTARCTICA

The Great Wall of China

Significance

Beginning in some of the world's most fertile river valleys, many great civilizations struggled in the first stages of development. Not all of these civilizations survived, but they developed ideas and traditions that most nations of the world share today.

Chinese civilization began in the vastness of the North China Plain, to the northeast of the rugged, snowcapped peaks of the Himalayas. As in India, many of the customs and traditions developed in ancient China remain a part of Chinese life today. One reason for this continuity was the influence on Chinese life of two great leaders, Siddhartha Gautama (called the Buddha) and Confucius. In one of the great coincidences of history, both leaders lived at about the same time, in the 500s B.C.

Terms to Define

loess	autocracy
silt	civil service
calligraphy	*The Analects*
oracle bones	the Five Classics
Mandate of Heaven	acupuncture

People to Identify

Xia dynasty	Liu Bang
Shang dynasty	Wu Di
Zhou dynasty	Confucius
Shi Huangdi	Laozi

Places to Locate

Qinling Shandi	Gobi Desert
China Proper	Chang-an
Korea	
Huang He	
Chang Jiang	
Xi Jiang	

Chapter Theme Questions

- **Politics and Law** What political patterns might be distinguished over a period of time within a civilization?
- **Technology** What factors might promote the development of technology?
- **Philosophy** How might philosophy influence social relationships and government?

Not long ago, in 1974, some Chinese farmers near the ancient city of Chang-an (modern-day Xi'an) made a momentous discovery. As the farmers were digging new wells to bring badly needed water to their village, they uncovered the sculpted head of a man. Archaeologists later uncovered a life-sized terra-cotta clay figure of an ancient Chinese knight. Soon the archaeologists began to uncover other life-sized figures.

News of this discovery spread quickly, and a large-scale excavation was launched. Archaeologists found row after row of terra-cotta knights, horses, and servants, along with real chariots and weapons. But who had created these sculptures—thousands in all—and why were there so many? Scholars believe that an early Chinese emperor, Shi Huangdi, had them made in the hope of re-creating his earthly palace in the afterlife. These sculptures provide just one example of the magnificent accomplishments of the ancient Chinese civilization.

Geographic and Cultural Influences

Focus Questions

- **What important geographic features shaped China's history?**
- **How did China's isolation influence Chinese people's attitudes toward their own and other cultures?**
- **What basic patterns have historians identified in Chinese history?**

Paleolithic people lived near what is today the city of Beijing, as well as other parts of China. During the Neolithic period, people settled along the Yellow River, or Huang He.* The people domesticated animals, improved their tools, developed agriculture, and eventually settled in permanent communities.

Before continuing the story of China, however, it is important to take a look at the geography of China.

---

*The words *he* and *jiang* are Chinese for "river." Throughout this book we will be using the Pinyin system of spelling Chinese names.

It will also be helpful to learn about the basic patterns of Chinese history.

The Physical Setting

Intersecting mountain ranges crisscross China. (See map on this page.) The great mountain ranges of the west, northwest, and southwest slope down to high desert or semidesert plateaus. In the south the plateaus give way to a region of many low hills and valleys. In the north the plateaus slope gradually down to the North China Plain, a coastal plain along the Yellow Sea (Huang Hai), which became the center of early Chinese civilization.

Look again at the map on this page. Notice the range of mountains that cuts from west to east across the center of China. This range separates the valleys of the two greatest rivers of China—the Huang He and

the Chang Jiang, or Yangzi (Yangtze) River. Known as the Qinling (CHIN·LING) Shandi, it marks the boundary between northern and southern China. The range also marks the boundary between the two major agricultural areas of China. In the north, where the growing season is shorter and relatively little rain falls, wheat is the principal crop. In the center and south, where rainfall is more plentiful, rice is the leading farm product.

Throughout its history China has also been divided politically into two main sections. The smaller and historically more significant section stretches from the seacoast inland, up the valleys of the Huang He, Chang Jiang, and Xi Jiang. We call this region China Proper—the heart of China.

The second political section surrounds China Proper with a great semicircle of regions, including Tibet, Xinjiang (SHIN·JYAHNG), Mongolia, Manchuria,

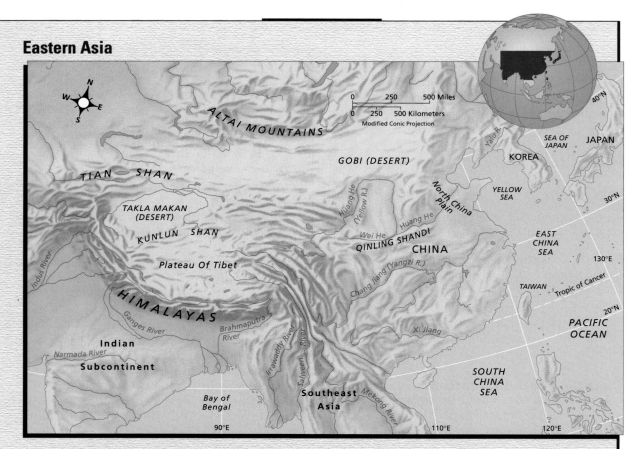

Eastern Asia

Learning from Maps Because China developed in relative isolation from civilizations of India and the West, the country formed and retained its own distinctive culture.

? Place Which natural boundaries helped China remain isolated from outside influences?

The Huang He in northeastern China has shifted course many times through the centuries, affecting millions of acres of rich farmland.

and Korea. At various times throughout their history, the Chinese conquered and ruled these regions, usually to protect themselves from attack or to secure important trade routes. On a few occasions, nomads from one or another of these outlying regions conquered and ruled China's heartland.

The rivers of China. China has many rivers, but the three principal rivers—the Huang He, the Chang Jiang, and the Xi (SHEE) Jiang—have played particularly important roles in China's history. The Huang He meanders for more than 2,900 miles across China before emptying into an arm of the Yellow Sea. The climate in the Huang He Valley includes long, cold winters and short, hot summers. Dust storms sweep across the valley in the spring. However, enough rain falls to nourish most crops. More important, the region has extraordinarily fertile yellow soil called **loess** (LES).

So much of this yellow soil washes into the Huang He that it is known as the world's muddiest river. A cubic foot of water contains two pounds of **silt**, soil carried as sediment in a river's water. The yellow silt also gives the river a yellowish tint, which is why the Chinese named it the Huang He, meaning "Yellow River."

Early Chinese farmers in the Huang He Valley built earthen dikes to protect their crops from periodic floods. These dikes, however, caused the Huang He to deposit silt on the river bottom. Over the years, so much silt accumulated that the river level reached

the tops of the dikes. Even moderate rains brought the Huang He to flood stage, sending torrents of water raging over the dikes and into the fields. Successive generations of Chinese farmers responded to the threat of floods by building higher dikes. As a result, today the Huang He flows up to 33 feet above the land outside the dikes.

The higher dikes did not end the flooding, however. Every few years the Huang He still broke through the dikes, and the rampaging floodwater destroyed everything in its path. The floodwater remained on the land until it evaporated because it could not drain back into the higher riverbed. Such devastating floods led the ancient Chinese to nickname the river "China's Sorrow."

The Chang Jiang, in central China, flows for 3,434 miles and cuts a deep channel. In modern times, large oceangoing ships have been able to navigate nearly 700 miles upstream to the great city of Wuhan. Smaller ships can travel as far as Chongqing (CHOOHNG·CHING), about 1,700 miles from the sea.

The Xi Jiang, in southern China, is about 1,200 miles long. Like the Chang Jiang, it forms an important commercial waterway. Large ships can navigate about one third of its length.

China's isolation. Civilization in China developed in relative isolation from the civilizations of India and the West. Great distances, the towering mountains of Central Asia, and formidable deserts such as the

Gobi made China almost inaccessible. As a result, China developed and retained its own distinctive culture. Although the Chinese did adopt some of the ideas and skills of other peoples, they probably owed less to outside influence than any other people in ancient times.

Along their northern and northwestern borders, the Chinese did have constant contact with nomadic and semi-nomadic peoples. These peoples spoke their own languages and had their own tribal cultures. Usually they traded peacefully with the Chinese, exchanging livestock for grain and other agricultural products. Sometimes, however, they organized bands of mounted warriors and attacked Chinese settlements. The Chinese called these nomadic peoples barbarians and considered them culturally inferior.

Their lack of contact with foreigners helped give the Chinese a strong sense of identity and superiority. They regarded their land as the only civilized land and called it *Zhongguo,* the "Middle Kingdom." To the Chinese it represented the center of the world. In their eyes, other people could become civilized only by learning the Chinese language and adopting Chinese customs. Even when outsiders overran China, as sometimes happened, the Chinese believed that the strangers would in time lose their identity and be absorbed into China's vast population.

Patterns of Chinese History

From very early times, the Chinese developed their own historical traditions. Given the central importance of imperial rule, it is little wonder that Chinese scholars saw a cyclical pattern in their history. This pattern was the rise and fall of ruling dynasties. At the same time, like all great civilizations, China was also subject to patterns of cultural evolution.

The dynastic cycle. From the beginning of its recorded history until the early A.D. 1900s, a succession of dynasties ruled China. The first dynasty, the Shang, came to power sometime between about 1750 B.C. and 1500 B.C. The last dynasty, the Qing (CHING), ruled China from A.D. 1644 to 1912. Some of these dynasties lasted only a few years; others held power for centuries. Most dynasties, however, went through a cycle that consisted of several stages.

The first stage was the founding of the dynasty. By defeating military rivals in war, an individual leader gained control of China. The right to rule the country then became hereditary within the leader's family, and a new dynasty emerged. Next came a period of internal peace, expansion, and great power. The new dynasty collected taxes and labor services from the people. The dynasty used its wealth to improve roads and irrigation systems, to support education and the arts, and to build splendid palaces to enhance its prestige.

A period of regression marked by decline followed the period of great power. During this stage, the rulers thought less of the people and more about a life of luxury for themselves. The government raised taxes whenever it could, creating hardship among the people. It stopped maintaining dikes and irrigation systems, increasing the risk of floods. The ruling dynasty gradually became unable to defend the frontiers of China, and nomadic invasions increased. When its decline reached the point at which chaos and rebellion took over many parts of the land, the ruling dynasty collapsed. At that point, a new leader emerged, and another dynastic cycle then began.

Cultural evolution. More recent historians, on the other hand, tend to view Chinese history from the perspective of cultural evolution. The dynastic cycle may describe the political history of China, but it does not explain many other aspects of China's history. Beneath the recurring pattern of events in politics was a continuous evolution, or development, of culture over the centuries. For example, structures such as the family, the farm, and the village developed their own patterns of change. During some stages of the dynastic cycle, the pace of cultural evolution quickened; during others, it slowed. Over the centuries, however, civilization in China has maintained a level of continuity unmatched in many other parts of the world.

Section 1 Review

1. **Define** loess, silt
2. **Locate and Explain the Significance** Qinling Shandi, China Proper, Korea, Huang He, Chang Jiang, Xi Jiang, Gobi Desert
3. **Understanding Ideas** Explain why the Huang He has been called "China's Sorrow."
4. **Summarizing Ideas** What factors led to China's relative isolation from the civilizations of the West?
5. **Interpreting Ideas** How did early Chinese historians explain developments in Chinese history?

The Shang Dynasty

Focus Questions

- **What do Chinese legends say about ancient China?**
- **How did the Shang rulers gain and keep power?**
- **What were some of the major cultural achievements that occurred under the Shang rulers?**

The Chinese placed great importance on explanations of the distant past and on China's role in history. They passed on many legends about the beginnings of the world and about ancient China and its people.

Legends of Ancient China

The legends of ancient China tell of Pangu, the first man, who worked for 18,000 years to create the universe. They also describe the labor of Yu, a figure like the biblical Noah, who drained away the floodwaters so that people could live in China and established a line of kings called the Xia (SHAH). They ruled over a late Neolithic people, who inhabited the Huang He region for several hundred years, starting in about 2000 B.C.

Although these legends contain few proven facts, scholars do not doubt that the Xia people of the Huang He Valley existed and that they made great advances over time. They improved methods of agriculture, and some evidence indicates that they began to use written symbols. With the development of writing, the history of China became easier to verify.

China's first historic dynasty, the Shang, began along the Huang He sometime between 1750 and 1500 B.C. The Shang were not natives but invaders, who swept into the Huang He Valley in war chariots. In very early times, without a government to regulate irrigation, drainage, or flood control, the people lived well in good years but starved when droughts or floods struck. Many scholars believe that the Shang introduced simple irrigation and flood control systems to their people. Control of these systems meant control of the region.

Government During the Shang Dynasty

At its height, the Shang empire stretched over 40,000 square miles, an area about the size of Kentucky. Apparently the Shang moved their capital many times, either because it was difficult to defend or

because of floods. During the last centuries of Shang rule, the capital was situated near what is today the city of Anyang. (See map on this page.)

Shang rulers created a complex bureaucracy, in which a hereditary king owned the land in the empire. The Shang used war chariots and bronze weapons to maintain their power over the peoples who lived on the borders of the kingdom. Their military force enabled them to gain territory and to spread the knowledge of their civilization. At one point they ruled most of eastern central China. (See map on this page.)

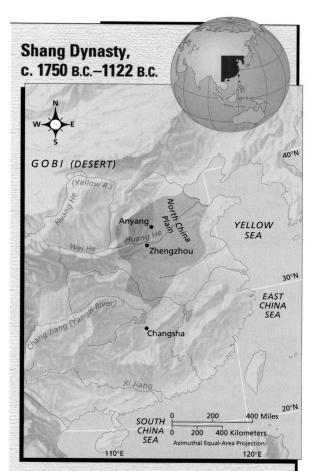

Shang Dynasty, c. 1750 B.C.–1122 B.C.

Learning from Maps The Shang invaded the Huang He Valley and established their dynasty in the region.

Location Which city located north of the Huang He River and between the 30°N and 40°N lines of latitude in the Shang dynasty became the capital during the last centuries of the Shang rule?

Ancient Bronze Vessel

This small vessel—just over a foot long—is an example of the highly developed bronze sculpture of the late Shang dynasty. Shang artists produced sculpture of unparalleled quality.

This vessel shows animal motifs common in the bronzes of the Shang dynasty. The tiger at the right becomes an owl in the middle and yet another bird at the left. The surface of the vessel is covered with a pattern of squared-off spirals.

These vessels, found in tombs, probably contained offerings made to ancestral spirits. This vessel was most likely used for mixing and pouring wine. The neck of the bird at the left provides a handle for pouring out the liquid when the cover—the head of the tiger—is removed.

This ceremonial vessel is from the Anyang period. Anyang is a town in eastern central China where many bronze vessels were found.

Culture During the Shang Dynasty

Shang rulers held power until 1122 B.C. During this time the Chinese people made new discoveries and developed new skills while refining the discoveries and skills of earlier periods.

Economy and handicrafts. The Shang economy was based mainly on agriculture. The chief crops included millet, barley, and rice. Domestic animals included pigs and chickens for meat and horses for labor. Sometime during the Shang dynasty, the Chinese learned to raise silkworms, spin thread from their cocoons, and weave silk cloth from the thread.

Not all the Chinese farmed, however. Many merchants and artisans lived in the capital and in the towns of the Shang realm. Artisans crafted jewelry from jade, ivory, and bone. Shang artisans also established the foundation for later Chinese ceramic art, including the development of forms and shapes used in Chinese ceremonial vases. Shang potters learned to use kaolin, a fine white clay. They glazed some of their pottery to give it a shiny, durable finish.

Today, people throughout the world regard the bronze castings of Shang artisans as outstanding works of art. The Chinese may have developed their technique of casting independently, or they may have learned the technique from peoples as far away as Sumer. However, the forms of the vessels and their decorative designs were uniquely Chinese. Chinese workers mined copper and tin ores that artisans used to mix for making the bronze. Artisans cast small figures as well as large ceremonial vessels whose surfaces featured complex raised patterns.

Astronomy and the calendar. The Chinese used two calendars, one based on the Sun and one based on the movement of the moon. The lunar, or moon-based, calendar was used to record private and public events, such as the birth of a child or the death of a ruler. The shortest period in this calendar was 10 days long. Three such periods, sometimes shortened by a day, made a month. A year consisted of 12 months. To include enough days for a full 365-day year, skilled priest-astronomers employed by the government were responsible for adding days as needed. Since the king's popularity depended on the success of the harvest, which in part depended on the time of planting as determined by the calendar, the priest-astronomers played a very important role.

Language and writing. The Chinese are recognized as one of the few early peoples known to have developed an original written language. To understand the ancient Chinese writing system, one must first understand some characteristics of spoken Chinese.

First, many Chinese words consist of one syllable. Second, the Chinese language does not include as many variations or uses of the same word as some other languages. For example, the same noun could be either singular or plural.

Because many dialects of spoken Chinese existed, a written language needed to be created that would be common to all spoken dialects. The Chinese assigned a special symbol, or character, to every word in their language. At first these characters were pictographs, or drawings of objects. Later, as their culture and therefore their language became more complex, the Chinese developed ideographs. Many written characters then consisted of two parts. One was a signifier, or idea sign. It showed the meaning of the character. The other was a phonetic sign, or sound sign. It told how to pronounce the character.

The Chinese developed their system of writing in an effective way that allowed them to combine signs to invent new characters. However, because each character had to be memorized, it took years of painstaking study to learn to read and write. Thus, for many centuries, reading and writing was the work of a relatively small number of specialists in the service of the ruling classes.

The early Chinese used writing to compose and preserve literary works. They used a brush to write characters in lines that ran from the top to the bottom of a page, beginning on the right side. Eventually, writing itself became an art, called **calligraphy**, and artists used the same kind of brush for calligraphy as was used for painting.

Religion in the Shang period. The religion that developed during the Shang dynasty combined animism—the belief that spirits inhabit everything—with ancestor worship. People believed in an all-powerful and kindly dragon that lived in the seas and rivers and could rise into the clouds. They believed that dragons fighting in the heavens caused the summer thunderstorms that brought rain. In time, this good dragon became the symbol of Chinese rulers.

The Chinese also worshipped gods of the wind, Sun, clouds, and moon, and some of these gods were honored by festivals. The people held a great religious festival in spring, the planting season, to ensure good crops. In an autumn religious festival, the people thanked the gods for the harvest.

In addition to animism, the Shang believed that the principal god, Shang Ti, was responsible for their destiny and controlled the forces of nature. Rulers tried to appeal to the god through the intercession of their ancestors. Because this made them dependent on the good will of those ancestors, rulers regularly offered sacrifices to please the ancestors, who they hoped would in turn try to please the god. Shang Ti's control over destiny gave the rulers divine justification.

Priests played an important role in Chinese religion. Some worked as priest-astronomers. Others foretold the future in order to learn the wishes of the spirits, especially the spirits of ancestors. The priests wrote questions on **oracle bones**, the shoulder bones of cattle or the bottoms of tortoise shells, which were then heated. They used the pattern of cracks that appeared to interpret the answers, which the priests then inscribed on the bone or shell. The inscriptions often included the name of the ruler who had asked the questions. These recorded questions and answers have helped scholars solve many historical and cultural mysteries of the Shang dynasty.

Fall of the Shang Dynasty

The Shang kingdom collapsed in 1122 B.C., apparently because the last king had exhausted his kingdom in wars

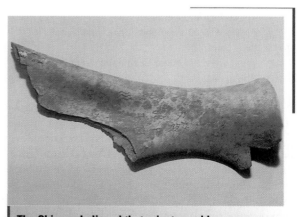

The Chinese believed that priests could answer questions based on the pattern of cracks that appeared when oracle bones were heated.

against the nomads to the north and east. He failed to guard the northwest frontier, where a powerful tribe of people called the Zhou (JOH) led a rebellion. The Zhou ultimately conquered the Shang, claiming that the last Shang king had lost the right to rule because he was a monster of corruption, wickedness, and cruelty. Yet another dynastic cycle had begun.

Section 2 Review

1. **Define** calligraphy, oracle bones
2. **Identify** Xia dynasty, Shang dynasty, Zhou dynasty
3. **Understanding Ideas** How do ancient Chinese legends help us understand the Chinese people who lived prior to the development of written language?
4. **Analyzing Ideas** How did Chinese religious beliefs help Shang rulers maintain power?
5. **Evaluating Ideas** What major cultural achievements occurred under the Shang dynasty?

The Zhou, Qin, and Han Dynasties

Focus Questions

- **In what ways did Chinese civilization advance under the Zhou dynasty?**
- **How did the Qin expand and maintain order in their empire?**
- **What were the major accomplishments of the Han dynasty?**

The Zhou conquest of China in 1122 B.C. marked the beginning of a dynamic era in Chinese history. Under the rule of three successive dynasties—the Zhou, the Qin (CHIN), and the Han—China gradually became a large and powerful state. Tremendous philosophical activity took place as the Chinese formulated ideas and theories that would be of lasting importance to their civilization. According to tradition, the Qin were the first to unify China under imperial rule. Under the Qin and their successors, the Han dynasty, China experienced great technological

and economic growth. Eventually, however, internal weaknesses and foreign invasions brought this first imperial age to an end.

The Zhou Dynasty

The most enduring Chinese dynasty—the Zhou—lasted about 900 years, from about the 1100s B.C. to the 200s B.C. (See map on this page.) The Zhou continued many aspects of Shang culture.

Zhou rulers called themselves the Sons of Heaven. They believed that the gods determined who should rule China, a right known as the **Mandate of Heaven**. This mandate, or command, obligated them

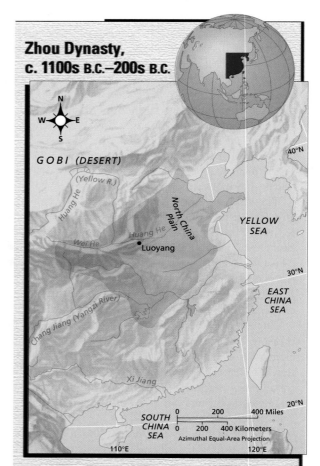

Zhou Dynasty, c. 1100s B.C.–200s B.C.

GOBI (DESERT)

(Yellow R.)

Huang He

Wei He

Huang He

North China Plain

• Luoyang

Chang Jiang (Yangzi River)

Xi Jiang

YELLOW SEA

EAST CHINA SEA

SOUTH CHINA SEA

40°N

30°N

20°N

110°E

120°E

0   200   400 Miles
0   200   400 Kilometers
Azimuthal Equal-Area Projection

Learning from Maps The introduction of iron during the Zhou dynasty was an important development in agriculture and in construction.

? Region What physical feature may have limited the northern expansion of the Zhou empire?

to keep the gods contented, perform rites to ensure the fertility of the soil, and control the rivers. Throughout Chinese history, when usurpers or rebels overthrew a dynasty, they justified their actions by saying that the old dynasty had lost the Mandate of Heaven.

During the many years of Zhou rule, internal trade expanded, and copper coins came into use as money. The introduction of iron, which helped transform Chinese agriculture, probably ranks as the most important development. Using iron tools and iron plows pulled by oxen, Chinese peasants cultivated new lands and produced more grain than ever before. They built canals, dikes, and reservoirs for irrigation. As a result, China's population grew steadily.

After conquering the Shang state, the Zhou rulers did not impose a centralized form of government. Instead, they granted territories to members of the royal family and to their allies. These subordinates ruled their territories as they liked, but they were obliged to give military service and tribute to the Zhou kings. Their positions were hereditary, but each generation had to renew its pledge of loyalty to the monarch.

By the 800s B.C., Zhou kings were losing control over their territories. Local rulers began to fight among themselves, and the state suffered periodic raids by non-Chinese peoples. In addition, Chinese traditions relate a decline in the quality of leadership of the Zhou kings. According to legend, for example, the wicked King Yu had set aside his wife and given his affections to another woman. Yu entertained his new favorite, Pao-Ssu, by lighting warning fires and beating a large drum, signaling the nobles that nomadic raiders were attacking. Yu and Pao-Ssu laughed as the powerful nobles galloped into town to protect the capital. Angered by such treatment, the nobles ignored the warning fires when a real army attacked the capital.

Whether the legend is true or not, in 771 B.C. an invading force did ransack the Zhou capital. The dynasty survived only by fleeing eastward, establishing a new capital farther down the Huang He. This Eastern Zhou dynasty, as it is called, lasted for another 500 years, but without its former strength. As the Zhou declined in power, new states emerged, competing for control of China. Eventually, these powers—known as the Warring States—began to fight among themselves to expand their territories. By the 400s B.C., the Zhou had no real power outside their own city-state. Instead, local rulers wielded great power. One of the Warring States, the Qin, emerged victorious.

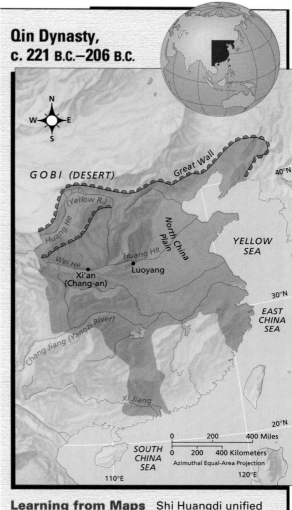

Qin Dynasty, c. 221 B.C.–206 B.C.

Learning from Maps Shi Huangdi unified China under a strong central government with uniform systems of writing and tax collection.

? Location Between which lines of latitude did most of the Qin empire fall?

The Qin Dynasty

The Qin dynasty came to power in 221 B.C. through their military might. Shi Huangdi, whose name means "first emperor," founded this new dynasty.

From its capital at Xi'an (Chang-an), the Qin dynasty ruled a larger area than either of the preceding dynasties and controlled it more firmly. Although the Qin dynasty lasted only a short time, until 206 B.C., it unified China under a strong central government for the first time in history. This dynasty created the first Chinese empire; standardized weights, measures,

The imperial tomb of Shi Huangdi contained more than 6,000 life-sized terra-cotta figures of soldiers and horses.

and coinage; and established a uniform system of writing.

Not satisfied with ruling northern China and parts of the Chang Jiang Valley, Shi Huangdi sent his armies far to the south. In a brilliant military campaign, he soon conquered the central part of southern China as far as the delta of the Xi Jiang. (See map on page 77.) The emperor divided China into military districts, ruled by governors who used stern military and civilian authority. The Code of Qin replaced conflicting local laws with a uniform system of laws. Shi Huangdi also implemented a single system of taxation throughout the country.

The Qin as builders. Like earlier rulers, the Qin attempted to guard against invasion by building a wall on their northern and northwestern frontiers. Later dynasties would add to these structures. Eventually, the connected walls became known as the Great Wall of China. This massive structure, much of which still stands today, was about 1,500 miles long.

Harshness of the Qin. The Qin maintained order in their empire because they established an **autocracy**, in which the emperor held total power. Like autocrats ever since, Shi Huangdi saw the danger of allowing scholars to investigate and discuss problems freely. Consequently, he suppressed scholars who criticized the regime; he even had some of them executed. He also banned or burned many books that the new regime deemed unacceptable or considered a threat to their rule.

Discontent spread quickly under the rule of the Qin dynasty. A great gap existed between the ruler, supported by his warriors, and the mass of people. The Qin also employed forced labor for many public works, a policy resented by the people. At last, in 206 B.C., a revolt erupted against the Qin. In 202 B.C. Liu Bang, a commoner who had risen to become a great general, overthrew the empire and founded the Han dynasty.

The Han Dynasty

The new dynasty took its name from the title that had been taken by Liu Bang—King of Han. Like the Qin, the Han dynasty ruled a centralized and expanding empire. Unlike the Qin, however, it was less oppressive and succeeded in maintaining its power for about four centuries. Han rulers so influenced China that even today, many Chinese refer to themselves as Sons of Han.

The longest-ruling Han emperor was Wu Di, who ruled from 140 B.C. to 87 B.C. He established his capital at Chang-an, now called Xi'an, and extended Chinese territory north into what has become present-day Manchuria and Korea, south into Southeast Asia, and west into Central Asia. (See map on page 79.)

The civil service system. Building on a foundation laid by the Qin, the Han dynasty built up a centralized civil service system to govern China. A **civil service** system administers the day-to-day business of government. Candidates for civil service under the Han dynasty

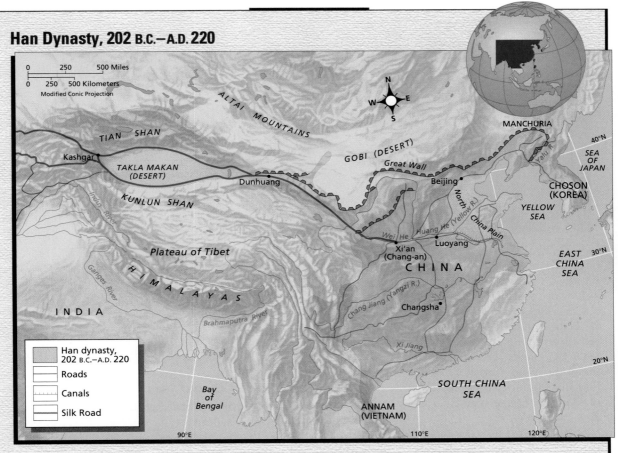

Han Dynasty, 202 B.C.–A.D. 220

0   250   500 Miles

0   250   500 Kilometers
Modified Conic Projection

ALTAI MOUNTAINS

TIAN SHAN

Kashgar

TAKLA MAKAN
(DESERT)

KUNLUN SHAN

Dunhuang

GOBI (DESERT)

Great Wall

MANCHURIA

40°N

SEA
OF
JAPAN

Beijing

Plateau of Tibet

HIMALAYAS

Ganges River

INDIA

Brahmaputra River

Wei He   Huang He (Yellow R.)

Xi'an
(Chang-an)

North R.

Luoyang

CHINA

Chang Jiang (Yangzi R.)

Changsha

Xi Jiang

CHOSON
(KOREA)

YELLOW
SEA

EAST
CHINA
SEA

30°N

20°N

Han dynasty,
202 B.C.–A.D. 220

Roads

Canals

Silk Road

Bay
of
Bengal

90°E

ANNAM
(VIETNAM)

SOUTH CHINA
SEA

110°E

120°E

Learning from Maps   During the Han dynasty, trade prospered throughout Central Asia to the Mediterranean region.

? **Movement**   Name two cities through which a merchant would have to pass while traveling along the Silk Road.

were usually recommended by central or local government officials on the basis of family connections. In addition, however, the Han eventually instituted an examination system for recommended candidates. The emperor Wu established an imperial university to train men for government service. Theoretically, the civil service was open to anyone. In practice, however, only those with the right family connections and those who could afford the necessary schooling and books were able to gain entry to the government bureaucracy. The civil service was improved over the centuries, under many dynasties, and remained important to Chinese government until the early A.D. 1900s.

Other accomplishments. Wu Di began an economic policy that was known as **leveling** because the rise and fall of prices of farm products had caused endless hardships for peasants. Under this policy, government agents were able to level—even out—the effects of years of surplus and years of shortages.

Wu Di fought vigorous battles with the nomadic Xiongnu (shee·UNG·noo) of Central and eastern Asia who threatened the frontiers of his empire. Through military conquest and the establishment of military colonies, Wu Di established what historians would later call the *Pax Sinica*, or "Chinese Peace," throughout much of Asia.

During this period of peace, trade prospered along the famous Silk Road from China across Central Asia to the Mediterranean region. (See map on this page.) Long camel caravans carried silk, jade, and other

This bronze horse from a Han tomb was discovered in 1969. The flying horse appears to rest one of his hooves on a swallow with its wings outstretched.

valuable Chinese goods to be sold ultimately to wealthy Greeks and Romans. The caravans returned with wools, gold, and silver.

China's population grew to almost 60 million during the Han dynasty. The imperial capital at Chang-an became an imposing city, where one could find luxury goods from lands across Europe and Asia, including one of the greatest of all Chinese inventions, paper. This invention spread from China to the Western world in later centuries and had a profound impact on Western cultures.

None of Wu Di's successors in the Han dynasty matched his leadership abilities. Still, with the exception of one brief interruption, the Han dynasty ruled China until A.D. 220, when the last Han emperor was deposed.

For hundreds of years, countless nomadic tribes swept across northern China, ravaging the countryside and terrorizing the people. Not until A.D. 589 did a Chinese general unify China once again.

Section 3 Review

1. **Define** Mandate of Heaven, autocracy, civil service
2. **Identify** Shi Huangdi, Liu Bang, Wu Di
3. **Locate and Explain the Significance** Chang-an
4. **Evaluating Ideas** Why was the introduction of iron under the Zhou an important development?
5. **Summarizing Ideas** Describe the government under the Qin dynasty.
6. **Interpreting Ideas** What accomplishments of the Han dynasty were later dynasties able to use to build upon?

Section 4

Philosophies of Ancient China

Focus Questions

- **What distinct philosophies emerged in ancient China?**
- **Why did the Chinese people find Buddhism appealing?**

Although political disunity and almost constant warfare marked the last years of the Zhou dynasty, this period remains as one of the most creative in the history of Chinese philosophy. As in other ancient civilizations of the same period, new political, economic, and social problems prompted many new ideas and theories. Scholars classify these theories into several main groups.

Ancient Chinese Beliefs

At a time when the political life of China was in turmoil, philosophers were looking for ways to restore harmony. At the root of many of these harmonizing philosophies was an ancient Chinese belief concerning the dualism, or two-sidedness, of nature. This idea says essentially that everything in the world results from a balancing of complementary forces, called yin and yang. Yin is female, dark, and passive. Yang is male, bright, and active.

Yin and yang do not conflict with each other, however, as do the concepts of good and evil in Western thought. Rather, they depend on one another, and under the best of conditions, they maintain a balance. Day, which is yang, gives way to night, which is yin. Summer gives way to winter.

These beliefs led to the conviction that balance in human affairs was the normal condition. For example, extremes such as a harsh government, anarchy (no government), or overindulgence during times of prosperity could not last for long.

Confucianism

Westerners know Kong Fuzi as Confucius. Left in poverty at the age of three when his father died, Confucius, who lived from about 551 B.C. to 479 B.C., still managed to obtain a good education. He began teaching as a young man and soon gained many followers. In time, his ideas and teachings, as written by his followers in a collection of writings called *The Analects,* became known as Confucianism. The philosophy of Confucianism exerted a more powerful influence on later Chinese beliefs and lifestyles than did any other philosophy.

Confucius was not a religious prophet and had little to say about gods, the meaning of death, or the idea of life after death. Instead, he taught about the importance of the family, respect for one's elders, and reverence for the past and for one's ancestors. These three concepts formed the basis of Confucian philosophy.

Confucius had a primary interest in politics and wanted to end the political disorder of his time. He believed that this could be accomplished in two ways. First, every person should accept an appropriate role in society and perform the duties of that role. Second, government should be virtuous. Instead of relying on military power, rulers should be honest and show concern for others. Only well-educated and morally excellent officials should be appointed to run the government.

Confucius taught that government should set a good example, for he believed that the people would willingly obey a ruler who lived and governed virtuously. Virtue, in Confucian teaching, consists of correct behavior toward others. This basic principle resembles the Christian Golden Rule, although stated negatively: "What you do not wish for yourself, do not do to others."

Confucius hoped to put his ideas into practice by becoming an adviser to a local ruler, but he never achieved his goal. He spent most of his life teaching, and eventually his teachings took on almost religious significance. By the time of the emperor Wu Di,

offerings were being made to Confucius in the Grand Academy and other schools.

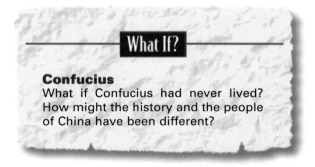

What If?

Confucius
What if Confucius had never lived? How might the history and the people of China have been different?

Daoism

Laozi (LOWD·ZOO), thought to have lived in the 500s B.C., founded a philosophy called Daoism (DOW·ih·zuhm). Daoism got its name from its central idea, the Dao, which can be defined as the "Way of Nature." Laozi saw the Dao as an indescribable force that governed the universe and all of nature. Only by withdrawing from the world and contemplating nature could people understand the Dao and live in harmony with it.

According to Laozi, people should not strive for riches or power. Rather, they should try to bring

Confucius remains China's most famous teacher, philosopher, and political theorist.

themselves into harmony with the Dao by being quiet, thoughtful, and humble. Unlike Confucius, Laozi shunned politics. He advised people not to seek after power or material wealth.

Daoism became second only to Confucianism in its importance to the Chinese. Daoism appealed to the masses of peasants because of its concern with nature and natural forces. It also appealed to many artists and poets because it encouraged artistic expression as a means of understanding the Dao. Daoism appealed to many Confucianists as well because it added balance to their lives. Some Confucianists believed that concerning oneself only with politics, education, and social problems was too restrictive and frustrating. Even officials and the emperor needed a temporary escape from governing the country. They found the escape they desired within the Daoist contemplation of nature.

Laozi, the founder of Chinese Daoism, lived during the 500s B.C.

Like yin and yang, Daoism and Confucianism came to be complementary parts of Chinese culture. Each supplied what the other lacked.

Legalism

Like Confucianism, the school of philosophy known as Legalism concerned itself with politics. Its teachings, however, differed greatly from the teachings of Confucianism. The Legalists believed in power—not virtue—and in harsh laws. In their view, people were by nature selfish and untrustworthy. Peace and prosperity could be achieved only by threatening severe punishment if people did not obey the laws.

The first Qin emperor, Shi Huangdi, followed the ideas of Legalism. He succeeded in creating a powerful empire, but his dynasty ruled for a very short period. Later Chinese philosophers believed that the Qin dynasty failed because of its extremely cruel methods.

The government of the Han dynasty took over the Legalist principles of the Qin dynasty, but tempered the application of those principles with Confucian values. The Han dynasty probably lasted as long as it did because it achieved a balance between the Legalist and Confucian approaches to government.

Buddhism in China

Another great influence on Chinese thought and religious belief came not from China but from India—from the teachings of the Buddha. Missionaries from India first brought Buddhism to China during the Han dynasty.

When the Han dynasty collapsed and nomads from the north raided China, Buddhism found many converts, especially among the peasants. People looking for consolation in this time of crisis found it in Mahayana Buddhism, a branch of Buddhism that became dominant in China, Japan, and Korea. Mahayana Buddhism emphasized worship of the Buddha as a savior who was committed to helping all human beings escape from the miseries of the world by achieving nirvana. Buddhist temples and ceremonies offered a sense of comfort and tranquillity in turbulent times. Buddhism also emphasized universal charity and compassion, which Chinese culture had previously lacked.

The teachings of the Legalists, Confucius, Laozi, and the Buddha had a lasting effect on Chinese attitudes. The centralizing political ideas of the Legalists provided a strong foundation on which Chinese society rested. Confucianism, with its

Building History Study Skills

READ
WRITE
INTERPRET
CONNECT
THINK

Reading About History: Analyzing a Statement

To analyze a statement, you must take it apart in order to find its meaning, identify the main idea, see relationships, or determine the importance of the information. Analysis has a specific goal. For example, you might analyze a statement so that you could understand the author's thoughts and relate them to a movement, idea, or situation. You might tie together the various parts of a theory by analyzing the statements.

How to Analyze a Statement
To analyze a statement, follow these steps.
1. Determine the goal or purpose of the analysis.
2. Read the statement carefully.
3. Identify the key words in the statement.
4. Explain what the statement means.
5. Determine how the statement might be related to other ideas.

Developing the Skill
Read the following statements. The first is attributed to Laozi and the second to Zhuang Zi, who lived about 200 years after Laozi. Laozi founded Daoism, and Zhuang Zi was an influential Daoist thinker. By analyzing both statements, you will be able to understand the meaning of Daoism and its impact on Chinese thought and institutions.

Knowing Oneself
"He who knows others is learned;
He who knows himself is wise.
He who conquers others has power of muscles;
He who conquers himself is strong.
He who is contented is rich.
He who is determined has strength of will.
He who does not lose his center endures.
He who dies yet (his power) remains has long life."

"Once a sea bird alighted in the suburbs of the Lu capital. The marquis of Lu escorted it to the ancestral temple, where he entertained it, performing . . . music for it to listen to and presenting it with [a] sacrifice to feast on. But the bird only looked dazed and forlorn, refusing to eat a single slice of meat or drink a cup of wine, and in three days it was dead. This is to

Miniature house from Han dynasty tomb

try to nourish a bird with what would nourish you instead of what would nourish a bird. If you want to nourish a bird with what nourishes a bird, then you should let it roost in the deep forest, play among the banks and islands, float on the rivers and lakes, eat mudfish and minnows, follow the rest of the flock in flight and rest, and live any way it chooses."

The key words in Laozi's statement are *learned, wise, strong, strength of will, endures,* and *long life*. These are desired virtues or states of being that Laozi believed people would acquire when they had learned self-mastery. One develops this self-mastery through knowledge and determination.

The key words in Zhuang Zi's statement are *dazed, nourish, roost, play, float,* and *eat*. These words refer to being natural and finding happiness through discovering one's own nature. Zhuang Zi was pointing out that every person must realize his or her own human nature in order to be healthy, creative, and happy.

Both statements illustrate one of the key beliefs of Daoism—the importance of internal harmony or peace, which can be reached through self-realization, or knowledge of oneself.

Practicing the Skill
Using the steps for analyzing a statement, find and analyze a statement or quote made by a famous person in the 1900s.

To apply this skill, see Applying History Study Skills on page 89.

Mahayana Buddhism emphasized the celestial qualities of Buddha. These Buddhas are found in the Jade Buddha Temple in Shanghai.

reverence for the past and emphasis on the family, won the most followers. The Chinese had always revered their ancestors and worshipped the emperor as almost a divine being, and these practices continued. Other ideas contained in Daoism and Buddhism—humility, contentment, loyalty, justice, wisdom, and obedience—were also absorbed into Chinese culture.

Section 4 Review

1. **Define** *The Analects*
2. **Identify** Confucius, Laozi
3. **Comparing Ideas** Explain the concept of yin and yang.
4. **Analyzing Ideas (a)** What are the basic teachings of Confucianism? **(b)** How did the ideas of Daoism complement the ideas of Confucianism? **(c)** What were the main beliefs of Legalism?
5. **Evaluating Ideas** What made Buddhism so appealing to the Chinese people?

Chinese Life and Culture

Focus Questions

- How were families organized in ancient China?
- What was the primary economic activity in ancient China?
- What did the ancient Chinese achieve in literature, science, and technology?

Chinese society in ancient times rested upon the idea that the family was of key importance to the welfare of the state. The values that governed family life—reverence for one's family, respect for age, and acceptance of the decisions made by one's superiors—governed national life as well as Chinese social and cultural life, including economics, education, literature, and science.

Harvest Festivals

When Americans sit down to Thanksgiving dinner each year, they are participating in a kind of celebration found in almost every society in the world. All peoples find a way to give thanks when they have finished gathering the harvest. The growing season is over, and there is a sense of gratitude that the earth has once again provided grains, vegetables, and fruits. Festivals devoted to particular crops, such as the Irish strawberry festival shown at right, are an example of festivals of harvest.

Long ago, the ancient Hebrews celebrated a fall thanksgiving, a holiday called Shavuoth that Jews today still celebrate. As early as the Shang dynasty, harvest gods were worshipped in China (right). An important part of harvest festivities in many Buddhist countries is a sacred performance relating an episode in the life of the Buddha. Other Buddhist countries celebrate harvest festivals as part of a New Year's celebration.

Among the early American Indians, there were many rituals of planting and harvest (right). A mythological figure called the Corn Mother was believed by some tribes of North America to have brought maize to the earth.

Although the forms of festivals differ from place to place, the importance of the land is the same for people all over the world.

Family and Social Life

The family, not the individual, constituted the most important unit in Chinese society. Generally, a man rose or fell in the social system not because of wealth or personal accomplishments but because of his family's position. Each upper-class family usually consisted of the father, his wife, the sons with their wives and children, and the unmarried daughters. Often all members of a family lived in the same house and shared day-to-day tasks.

The Chinese father ruled the family. The older he was, the more authority he had, for the Chinese respected age as a source of wisdom. Respect for one's aged parents, and especially for one's father, was an important virtue. Each upper-class family kept a careful genealogy, or record of its family tree, even including third cousins. When family members died, they became honored ancestors. Most families constructed altars where they made offerings of food to their ancestors, expressing reverence for them as links between the family's past, present, and future.

The Chinese father arranged his children's and his grandchildren's marriages, decided how much education his sons would receive, and even chose his sons' careers. Women were subordinate to men and usually had no property rights of their own. On the other hand, Chinese society also taught great respect for mothers and mothers-in-law. Within the household, these women held much power. After she married, a young woman sometimes became almost a servant in the household of her husband's family. Before her wedding she often cried, not because she did not yet know her husband, but because she did not know how her new family would treat her. However, when she became a mother, especially of a son, and later when she became a mother-in-law, she became an important figure in the family.

The Economy

Despite the growth of cities and towns, the vast majority of Chinese people continued as small village farmers. On one hand, they had to contend with nature. If too much or too little rain fell, their crops might be ruined, so that they would starve. On the other hand, they had to contend with government. In addition to paying taxes, peasants had to perform labor. For part of each year, they left their farms and worked on roads, canals, or other local construction projects.

Just as during the Shang dynasty, farmers grew millet and wheat in the north and rice in the south. In both northern and southern China, a group of families might work fields in common. They used ox-drawn plows and complex systems of irrigation and flood control.

Although trade had never been very important to the Chinese economy, it improved when the Qin dynasty standardized the currency system and the system of weights and measures. Trade increased further when the Silk Road linked China with the Mediterranean region during the Han dynasty.

Literature

The Five Classics became the most important works of Chinese literature and the basis on which all Chinese scholars were educated. We do not know who wrote these works or when they were written, but we do know that they were already important by the time of the Zhou dynasty. Officials later used the Five Classics in civil service examinations.

The Five Classics. The *Book of Poetry* contains more than 300 songs about love, joy, politics, and domestic life. The *Book of History* contains semihistorical speeches and documents about government. The *Book of Divination* is about the art of foretelling the future. The *Spring and Autumn Annals* is a record of events in the important city-state of Lu from 722 B.C. to 481 B.C. The *Book of Rites* is about etiquette and ceremonies. Study of the Five Classics became essential for every well-brought-up young man of China. The Chinese also expected such young men to know *The Analects* of Confucius.

The use of these texts tended to produce scholars and civil servants who were dedicated and reliable. Most of all, this system of education emphasized respect for tradition. At the same time, the use of these texts in all parts of China helped maintain a common culture across the country.

Science and Technology

Early Chinese astronomers had computed the year at $365\frac{1}{4}$ days. Later, during the Han dynasty, scientists refined these calculations even further. In 28 B.C., astronomers in China first observed sunspots, which Europeans did not discover until the A.D. 1600s.

Sometime before A.D. 100, Chinese astronomers built special instruments to observe the movement of planets. Another scientific invention was the primitive seismograph that registered earthquakes so faint that royal officials did not even notice them.

The Chinese also invented paper. First produced in A.D. 105 from hemp, old rags, fishing nets, and the bark of mulberry trees, the earliest paper was a bright yellow. By the mid-700s A.D. the use of paper had

The ancient Chinese used sailboats called junks to trade throughout East Asia. This ancient type of Chinese sailboat can carry up to five sails at one time, each of which may be spread open or closed. These vessels continue to sail along China's rivers today.

spread throughout Asia and also to Europe, where it replaced papyrus as the main writing material. The Chinese also invented the sundial, the water clock, and the process of printing.

Chinese scholars, particularly the Daoists, were very interested in chemistry. They discovered substances for dyeing cloth and glazing pottery, as well as developing medicines based on herbs and minerals.

Perhaps the most widely known Chinese contribution to medicine is the therapy known as **acupuncture**. Its development stemmed from the Daoist belief that good health depends on the movement of a life-force energy through the body and that illness or pain results when something interferes with that movement.

In acupuncture, the doctor inserts needles into certain points of the body to enable the life-force energy to move properly. Some modern researchers believe that these needle insertion points may have less electrical resistance than other parts of the body and thus may affect the nervous system. Today, the Chinese use acupuncture as an anesthetic in many types of surgery. Many Americans use it to relieve the pain of arthritis and cancer.

Section 5 Review

1. **Define** the Five Classics, acupuncture
2. **Summarizing Ideas** Describe family structure in ancient China.
3. **Analyzing Ideas** How did the ancient Chinese maintain their economy?
4. **Classifying Ideas** What were some of the major Chinese contributions to science and technology?

Chapter 4 Review

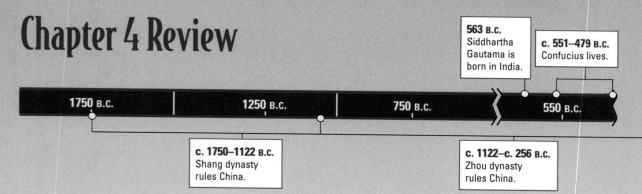

563 B.C.
Siddhartha Gautama is born in India.

c. 551–479 B.C.
Confucius lives.

1750 B.C.   1250 B.C.   750 B.C.   550 B.C.

c. 1750–1122 B.C.
Shang dynasty rules China.

c. 1122–c. 256 B.C.
Zhou dynasty rules China.

Chapter Summary

The following list contains the key concepts you have learned about the great civilization of ancient China.

1. China is divided into two main sections—China Proper and the vast semicircle of regions that surround it. These regions include present-day Tibet, Xinjiang, Mongolia, Manchuria, and Korea.
2. The major rivers of China include the Chang Jiang, the Huang He, and the Xi Jiang. Because of devastating floods, the Huang He is often referred to as "China's Sorrow."
3. China's political history involves a succession of ruling dynasties that rose and fell in a recognizable pattern or cycle. China's cultural history concerns the gradual evolution of civilization over the centuries.
4. The Shang was the first historically verifiable Chinese dynasty. Under Shang rule, simple irrigation and flood control systems, a calendar, and an original written language were developed.
5. The Zhou, Qin, and Han dynasties were important and enduring influences in the development of both Chinese government and thought.
6. China's most influential philosopher was Confucius, who taught that emphasis on family

and the choice of virtuous rulers led to a healthy society. Confucianism became the most important philosophy in China. It later developed religious and spiritual aspects.
7. Laozi, the founder of Daoism, taught that people should withdraw from the world and try to achieve harmony with nature. In time, Daoism became the second most important philosophy in China.
8. Other significant belief systems in China included ancient beliefs about harmony and balance as well as Legalism and Buddhism. Legalism stressed political power, governmental administration, and harsh laws. Mahayana Buddhism emphasized charity and compassion.
9. The most important unit in Chinese society was the family. Age was highly respected, and fathers had great authority.
10. Many cultural and technological advances occurred during the Zhou, Qin, and Han dynasties. The Five Classics became the most important works studied by Chinese scholars. Technological advances included the invention of paper, scientific instruments, and the medical technique of acupuncture.

Reviewing Important Terms

On a separate sheet of paper, supply the term that correctly completes each statement.

1. In a(n) _____ the ruler wields unlimited power.
2. _____ is artistic handwriting.
3. A(n)_____ _____ administers the government on a day-to-day basis, and its members in later dynasties were appointed according to the results of competitive examinations.
4. The fertile yellowish soil found in the Huang He Valley is called _____.
5. The gods were believed to give the Chinese monarch the right to rule, a right known as the _____ _____ _____.
6. During the Shang dynasty, priests wrote questions on _____ _____, made from the shoulder bones of cattle or the bottoms of tortoise shells.
7. _____ is a Chinese therapy in which doctors insert needles into certain points of the body to enable life-force energy to move properly.

Developing Critical Thinking Skills

1. **Seeing Relationships** Describe the geographical barriers of China that limited the spread of Chinese culture.
2. **Synthesizing Ideas (a)** Why did the Chinese call their country the Middle Kingdom? **(b)** How do you think the attitude the Chinese held toward foreigners might have affected ancient Chinese history? **(c)** How might it affect China today?
3. **Making Charts** Make a chart listing the accomplishments of the Shang dynasty.
4. **Evaluating Ideas** Which dynasty—the Zhou, the Qin, or the Han—did the most to advance Chinese culture? Give evidence to support your answer.
5. **Analyzing Ideas (a)** Compare the ideas of Confucianism and Legalism regarding ways in which society should be changed. **(b)** Are any of these ideas or values present in our society today? Give examples from newspapers to support your opinion.

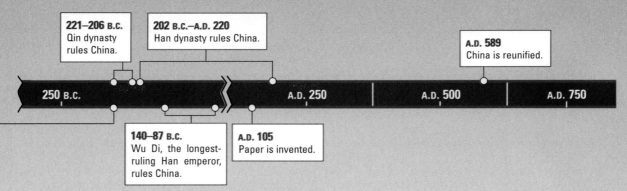

221–206 B.C.
Qin dynasty rules China.

202 B.C.–A.D. 220
Han dynasty rules China.

A.D. 589
China is reunified.

250 B.C.　　　**A.D. 250**　　　**A.D. 500**　　　**A.D. 750**

140–87 B.C.
Wu Di, the longest-ruling Han emperor, rules China.

A.D. 105
Paper is invented.

6. **Classifying Ideas** Put each of the following names or ideas into one of these four categories: literature, technology, philosophy, government.
   (a) leveling
   (b) *Pax Sinica*
   (c) civil service
   (d) yin and yang
   (e) wall building
   (f) uniform law code
   (g) teachings of Confucius
   (h) large-scale irrigation and flood control
   (i) *Book of Poetry* and *Book of History*
   (j) acupuncture
   (k) Legalism

Relating Geography to History
(a) Trace the map of eastern Asia on page 70. Then use atlases to complete the following activities. (b) Indicate the areas that have heavy rainfall. (c) Indicate the areas that need irrigation in order to grow crops. (d) Show the desert area (the Gobi Desert) that might be used for grazing.

Relating Past to Present
1. Animism is the belief that spirits inhabit everything—rocks, plants, animals, and people. Scholars believe that the people who lived in China during the Shang dynasty were animists. (a) List some of these animistic beliefs and compare them with myths that people still believe. (b) What are some of the symbols considered lucky and unlucky today?
2. It is sometimes said that a culture can be judged by the people to whom the greatest honor is paid. (a) Which people were most honored in ancient China? (b) Whom do you think people in the United States today respect or honor most? (c) What qualities make people in the United States regard these people so highly? (d) Compare these qualities to the qualities that were respected in leaders of ancient China.

Applying History Study Skills
Before completing this activity, review Building History Study Skills on page 83.
Read the following statement from the Confucian book *The Great Learning*. Then analyze the statement by answering the questions below it.

"The ancients who wished to manifest their clear character to the world would first bring order to their states. Those who wished to bring order to their states would first regulate their families. Those who wished to regulate their families would first cultivate their personal lives. Those who wished to cultivate their personal lives would first rectify their minds. Those who wished to rectify their minds would first make their wills sincere. Those who wished to make their wills sincere would first extend their knowledge."

1. What is the purpose of the statement?
2. One of the key words in the statement is *cultivate*. (a) What does the word mean? (b) What are the other key words in the statement?
3. (a) According to Confucius, how is harmony in a society achieved? (b) Do you agree? Why or why not?

 internet connect

Search the Internet through the HRW Web site for information about Chinese calligraphy. Learn how to read 10 characters of the Chinese language. Display the characters you have learned, and participate in a class discussion about the skills you learned during your research.

HRW **GO TO:** go.hrw.com
KEYWORD: SCØ Chinese Calligraphy

Building Your Portfolio
1. **Writing a Report** Find pictures of bronze items from the Shang dynasty in reference books in your school or public library. Study the pictures to determine the religious functions and the aesthetic value of the bronzes. Write a report describing your findings. Place the report in your portfolio.
2. **Interviewing** Visit a Chinese restaurant in your community and interview a native Chinese employee to find out what types of food are typically Chinese. How do these foods differ from American food? How are they prepared differently from American foods? Place a tape recording or your notes of the interview in your portfolio.

Unit Summary

The following list contains the key concepts you have learned about ancient civilizations.

1. Using skeletal remains and artifacts, anthropologists study early human behavior, customs, and patterns of living.
2. People in four great river valleys developed the first civilizations.
3. Protected by geographic barriers, the Nile Valley people developed a remarkable culture that made advances in literature, science, art, agricultural practices, and religious thought.
4. In the Fertile Crescent, a succession of leaders formed empires and cultures. Major developments included cuneiform (Sumerians), codification of law (Babylonians), the alphabet (Phoenicians), use of coined money (Lydians), and ethical monotheism (Hebrews).
5. Around 2500 B.C., people in the Indus Valley cities of Harappa and Mohenjo-Daro developed a complex civilization. In about 1750 B.C., nomadic Indo-Aryans swept through the Khyber Pass and settled in India.

By 1000 B.C. they had developed a caste system that regulated everyday contacts among more than 3,000 hereditary classes.

6. The religious books of Hinduism, the *Upanishads,* contain many stories. The stories were eventually combined into two great epics, the *Mahabharata* and the *Ramayana.*
7. Siddhartha Gautama, who became known as the Buddha, founded Buddhism. According to this religion, people can reach salvation through knowledge of the Four Noble Truths and by following the Eightfold Path.
8. Geographical barriers isolated China from India and the West. The Chinese built irrigation ditches and dikes in an attempt to control flooding of the Huang He and developed a lunar calendar and written language.
9. During the Zhou, Qin, and Han dynasties, philosophy flourished. Ancient Chinese beliefs about harmony, Confucianism, Daoism, and Legalism coexisted as systems of thought.

Reviewing Concepts

On a separate sheet of paper, complete the following exercises.

1. Supply the term that correctly completes each statement.
   (a) Belief in many gods is called _____.
   (b) A seasonal wind is called a(n) _____.
   (c) Skilled craft workers are called _____.
   (d) A(n) _____ was a town or city and the surrounding land it controlled.
   (e) _____ was the Sumerian form of writing.
2. Identify the specific society or culture with which each of the following ideas or developments is associated.
   (a) Constructed pyramids as royal tombs
   (b) Had a collection of laws known as the Code of Hammurabi
   (c) Worshiped in layered temples called ziggurats
   (d) Established the caste system
   (e) Lacked direct contact with other great civilizations and believed that peoples of other cultures were barbarians
   (f) Had a religion that placed great emphasis on the earthly struggle between good and evil
   (g) Developed the alphabet that became the model for later Western alphabets
   (h) Believed that Canaan was their promised land
3. Explain the beliefs about God (or gods) and an afterlife in three of the following cultures or civilizations:
   (a) Egyptian; (b) Sumerian; (c) Hebrew; (d) Indo-Aryan;
   (e) Shang; (f) Persian.

Applying Critical Thinking Skills

1. **Understanding Ideas** Discuss how cultural diffusion took place in the Fertile Crescent.
2. **Analyzing Ideas** (a) Describe some of the laws included in the Code of Hammurabi and in Mosaic law. (b) Explain why such codes of law became important as people began living together in groups.
3. **Evaluating Ideas** Choose two of the following religious or political leaders: Akhenaton, Hammurabi, Moses, Darius, Buddha, Asoka, Shi Huangdi, Wu Di, Confucius. (a) Describe each person's accomplishments. (b) Do you think that these leaders achieved their goals? Why or why not?
4. **Synthesizing Ideas** Using examples from the civilizations described in Unit 1, discuss the idea that cultures frequently adopt ideas and customs from other cultures rather than create ideas and methods unique to themselves.

Relating Geography to History

The earliest civilizations developed in four great river valleys—the Huang He, the Nile, the Indus, and the Tigris-Euphrates. Almost all other civilizations also originally developed in river valleys. (a) Why do you think this was so? (b) What advantages did rivers provide to the people of early civilizations?

Writing About History

1. Write a dialogue to take place between or among the people described below:

   (a) Akhenaton of Egypt and a priest of Amon-Re, discussing monotheism versus polytheism;

   (b) a Hebrew prophet, a follower of Zoroastrianism, a Buddhist priest, and a Brahman, discussing the role of religion in shaping the values of their particular societies.

2. Write a newspaper story dated A.D. 550, summarizing the great accomplishments of the Gupta rulers.

Further Readings

Casson, Lionel. *Daily Life in Ancient Egypt.* Paperbook Press, Inc., 1994. Describes daily life during the New Kingdom.

Gore, Rick. "The Dawn of Humans: The First Steps." *National Geographic,* February 1997: 72–99. Gives an overview of archaeological findings about early hominids.

Mazzatenta, O. Louis. "China's Warriors Rise from the Earth." *National Geographic,* October 1996: 68–85. Describes the unearthing of the tomb of Shi Huangdi.

Olivelle, Patrick, (trans.). *Pancatantra: The Book of India's Folk Wisdom (World's Classics).* Oxford University Press, 1997. Includes readable translations of tales from the Pancatantra *(Panchatantra).*

The World's Last Mysteries. Reader's Digest Association, 1978. Analyzes mythical ancient kingdoms and peoples that vanished mysteriously.

UNIT 1 CHRONOLOGY

Date	Politics	Science and Technology	Society and Culture
6000–3000 B.C.		Neolithic developments 1*	Prehistoric times 1 Cave paintings 1 River valley civilizations 1
3000–1000 B.C.	Sumerian civilization 2 Egyptian Old Kingdom 2 Egyptian Middle Kingdom 2 Code of Hammurabi 2 Indo-Aryan migrations 3 Shang dynasty 4	Sumerian ziggurats 2 Sumerian arch 2 Cuneiform 2 Egyptian irrigation 2 Egyptian pyramids 2 Egyptian calendar 2 Hieroglyphics 2 Hittites use iron weapons 2 Chinese bronze casting 4 Chinese calendar 4 Chinese astronomy 4	The Book of the Dead 2 Mohenjo-Daro 3 Polytheism in Egypt 2 Animism in India and China 3, 4 Chinese ancestor worship 4 Amenhotep; Israelites develop monotheism 2 Indian Vedic religion 3
1000–500 B.C.	Solomon in Israel 2 Chinese Zhou dynasty 4 Persian Empire 2	Assyrians use cavalry 2 Iron in China 4 Chaldean math and astronomy 2	Phoenicians and trade 2 Phoenician alphabet 2 Nineveh library 2 *Upanishads* 3 Hinduism 3 Zoroaster in Persia 2
500–1 B.C.	Qin dynasty 4 Han dynasty 4 *Pax Sinica* 4 Mauryan Empire and Asoka 3	Great Wall begun 4	Stupas constructed 3 Confucius 4 Laozi 4 Buddhism in India 3 Chinese civil service 4
A.D. 1–500	Gupta rulers 3	Chinese paper 4 Indian numeral system 3	Ajanta cave painting 3 Indian *Panchatantra* 3

*Indicates chapter in which development is discussed

The Beginnings of Civilization

CHAPTER 1

The Emergence of Civilization

Scholars believe that people lived on Earth long before the development of writing, during the period known as prehistory. Although unable to write, prehistoric people made significant discoveries and advances.

Prehistoric Peoples

From scientific studies, researchers have concluded that humanlike creatures appeared on the earth millions of years ago during a period of prehistory called the Old Stone Age, or the Paleolithic (pay·lee·uh·li·thik) Age. Then, between 200,000 and 300,000 years ago, *Homo sapiens* appeared. This species included the Neanderthal and Cro-Magnon peoples, as well as all humans living today. Over many thousands of years, the first prehistoric people migrated to many parts of the world. During long periods of extremely cold weather, known as the Ice Age, the Neanderthals, and later the Cro-Magnons, learned to use fire and make warm clothing and so could successfully settle in the colder regions of the world.

Early humans had been nomads who traveled from place to place in search of food. About 10,000 years ago, however, in the period called the New Stone Age, or Neolithic Age, people began to settle in villages. Two important developments—the domestication, or taming, of a number of different animals and the development of agriculture—helped to make permanent settlements possible.

The Foundations of Civilization

Although Neolithic people settled in many regions, the settlements in the Nile River valley in Africa, the valley of the Tigris and Euphrates (yoo·frayt·eez) Rivers in southwestern Asia, the Indus River valley in southern Asia, and the Huang He (or Yellow River) Valley in eastern Asia had particular significance. In these four river valleys, people first developed civilizations.

The people of these early civilizations developed advanced technical skills, such as the ability to use metals. In addition, improved farming methods led to an increase in population, which in turn encouraged the growth of cities. Eventually, the people of these communities developed calendars to predict when crops should be planted and harvested.

With the many changes of late Neolithic times, life became increasingly complex. People in settled communities developed rules for living together and for protecting property. They also developed governments and traded with other communities. Disputes over land and water rights sometimes caused conflicts and even war. To keep government records and to better communicate with one another, the people of these civilizations developed writing. The development of writing marked the end of prehistory and the beginning of history.

CHAPTER 2

The First Civilizations

Civilizations first appeared along the Nile River and along the Tigris and Euphrates Rivers.

Ancient Kingdoms of the Nile

Along the narrow strip of fertile land that straddles the Nile River in northeastern Africa, people created a thriving civilization. Each year the river swept over its banks and deposited a layer of fertile silt in the valley. This fertile silt made it possible for the early inhabitants of the valley to establish agriculture.

The people of the Nile Valley mined copper and learned to make bronze, the strong alloy of copper and tin. Around 3000 B.C., they also developed a system of writing known as hieroglyphics and later learned to make papyrus, a smooth-surfaced writing material made from a reed plant.

Over the centuries, early Egyptian settlements were united to form the two kingdoms of Upper Egypt and Lower Egypt. Then, around 3200 B.C., a ruler known as Menes (mee·neez) united all Egypt into one kingdom.

In more than 2,500 years, beginning with the time of Menes and continuing to about 300 B.C., there were about 30 Egyptian dynasties ruled by pharaohs. This span of time is divided into three kingdoms: the Old Kingdom, the Middle Kingdom, and the New

Figures of Ramses II in front of main temple, Abu Simbel

The Sumerians used sun-dried clay bricks to build houses and may have invented several important architectural designs, including the arch. The most striking Sumerian buildings were the temples known as ziggurats. A ziggurat was constructed in layers, each one smaller than the one below. The top layer served as a shrine to a god. Sumerians used a system of mathematics based on 60 and divided a circle into 360 degrees, each degree into 60 minutes, and each minute into 60 seconds (as we do today).

The Sumerians developed a form of writing known as cuneiform and considered education very important, although only upper-class boys were educated. Students learned to write and spell by copying religious books and songs. They also studied arithmetic.

Empires of the Fertile Crescent

The disunity of the Sumerian city-states allowed a series of invaders to conquer the region.

The Akkadians. Around 2330 B.C., the Akkadians conquered the Sumerians and established a great empire that lasted about 100 years. When it ended, new waves of invaders swept through the region.

The Babylonians. Around 1792 B.C., a strong ruler named Hammurabi (ham·uh·rahb·ee) came to power in Babylon and conquered the upper Tigris-Euphrates Valley. Hammurabi's greatest accomplishment was the Code of Hammurabi, a collection of laws concerned with all aspects of life in Babylon.

The Hittites. In the 1600s B.C., the Hittites from Asia Minor invaded the Tigris-Euphrates Valley. The Hittites were the first people to make extensive use of iron for weapons. Like the Babylonians, the Hittites had a code of laws. Their laws, however, were less severe than those in the Code of Hammurabi. The Hittites were too far from their homeland to control Babylonia permanently, however, and they soon withdrew to the western part of the Fertile Crescent.

The Assyrians. Following the decline of the Hittites, Babylon suffered further invasions. Then, around 900 B.C., a Semitic-speaking people who were great conquerors—the Assyrians—overwhelmed Mesopotamia. They spread throughout the region until they controlled Syria, Babylonia, and even Egypt.

The Assyrians excelled in warfare. They were the first to make major use of cavalry—units of soldiers on horses—and began the use of heavy battering rams to break through defenses of their enemies.

Kingdom. The periods between kingdoms are known as intermediate periods.

Egyptian Life and Culture

The Nile Valley people built great monuments to their gods and rulers. These monuments included the Great Sphinx near Giza and the pyramids, which were designed as tombs for the pharaohs. In addition to large-scale works, sculptors also made small, lifelike statues of kings and sacred animals from copper, bronze, stone, or wood.

The Nile Valley people developed a calendar with 12 months of 30 days each. They also developed a number system based on 10, used geometry, and made significant advances in science and medicine.

Sumerian Civilization

To the east of the Nile Valley, the fertile valley of the Tigris and Euphrates nurtured equally advanced civilizations. There, in a region called the Fertile Crescent that stretches from the Mediterranean Sea to the Persian Gulf, many civilizations rose and fell. The earliest was that of Sumer.

Early in their history the Sumerians developed a social system called the city-state, which included a town or city and the surrounding land it controlled. Unlike Egypt, the many Sumerian city-states were seldom united.

The Assyrians were the first people to develop an effective method of governing an empire. The army was the most important part of the government. Soldiers were rewarded with the wealth of the places they conquered. In their capital of Nineveh, the Assyrians built a large library, in which writings on clay tablets collected from all over the empire were stored. In 612 B.C., a group of opponents captured and destroyed Nineveh.

The Chaldeans. A people known as the Chaldeans took control of much of the territory that the Assyrians had ruled. Under the leadership of a wise ruler, Nebuchadnezzar (neb·uh·kuhd·nez·uhr), who ruled from the rebuilt city of Babylon from 605 B.C. to 562 B.C., the Chaldeans conquered most of the Fertile Crescent.

All of the strength of the Chaldeans seemed to lie in the ability of Nebuchadnezzar. Within 30 years of Nebuchadnezzar's death, the empire fell.

The Persians. In about 550 B.C., Cyrus the Great, a Persian, began a series of conquests, capturing Babylon and conquering the rest of the Fertile Crescent and Asia Minor. Later Persian rulers, Darius I and Xerxes I, expanded Persian rule as far as the Indus River in India, as well as into parts of southeastern Europe. The Persians ruled the mightiest empire known up to that time.

Although all-powerful in government, Persian rulers showed great concern for justice. They collected taxes and administered their laws fairly. Persian rulers paid close attention to local customs and allowed conquered peoples to keep their own religions and laws.

The Phoenicians, Lydians, and Hebrews

The peoples who lived in the western end of the Fertile Crescent and in western Asia Minor did not create large empires, but they had great influence on the modern world.

The Phoenicians turned to the sea and to commerce for their living and became the greatest traders in the ancient world. Most important, the Phoenicians developed the alphabet upon which our alphabet is patterned.

The Lydians of Asia Minor are remembered as the first people in history to use coined money, in about 600 B.C. Through trade they passed on the concept of a money economy to the Greeks and the Persians.

As in the eastern part of the Fertile Crescent, a series of peoples inhabited Canaan, which lay south of Phoenicia along the land bridge between Asia and Africa. The Hebrews, the ancestors of modern Jews, had a great influence on the region and on all of history.

The Hebrews worshiped one god, Yahweh. The Hebrews thought of Yahweh not as a glorified human being but as the one god. The Torah, part of the Hebrew scriptures, outlines the Hebrew code of law. This code set a higher value on human life than did earlier law codes. Because of its emphasis on ethics, or proper conduct, the Hebrew form of monotheism is often called ethical monotheism and is often considered the Hebrews' most important contribution to Western civilization.

CHAPTER 3

Ancient Indian Civilization

In ancient India, people learned how to farm, developed a written language and calendars, and created a complex civilization.

Indus Valley Civilization

An impressive civilization appeared in the Indus Valley around 2500 B.C., several hundred years after Egypt and Sumer developed civilizations. This early civilization is best known from the ruins of two cities, Mohenjo-Daro and Harappa. Scholars often call it the Harappan civilization because they first discovered some of its artifacts in the town of Harappa.

Harappa and Mohenjo-Daro showed evidence of city planning and design, including a water system and a covered brick sewer system for private homes. City dwellers worked primarily in industry or trade. These early Indus Valley people also developed a written language before the civilization's collapse about 1700 B.C.

Indo-Aryan Migrants

Around 1750 B.C. new groups of people, the Indo-Aryans, who spoke an Indo-European language, came into India. Most of what we know of the Indo-Aryans comes from the Vedas, the great literature of the Indo-Aryan religion. Eventually, Indo-Aryan settlements joined to form small city-states, each ruled by a raja—a prince or king. Differences existed between the Indo-Aryans and the early inhabitants of the area. Over time, a complex system of social orders evolved, with warriors and priests at the top of the order and merchants, traders, farmers, and peasants below them. Southern India developed somewhat differently from the area to the north. Trade and commerce were important in southern India.

Hinduism and Buddhism

Two of the world's great religions—Hinduism and Buddhism—developed in ancient India.

Hinduism. According to Hinduism, the world known to our senses is an illusion called maya, which betrays people, giving them sorrow and pain. People can be delivered from their suffering if they learn to identify maya. Because this learning takes lifetimes of experience, reincarnation—the rebirth of the soul—occurs to make it possible. According to Hinduism, the soul does not die with the body but is reborn in the body of another being, either human or animal, and thus lives again and again. Ultimately, Hindus hope to end the repeated reincarnations and enable their souls to reunite with the universal spirit, Brahma.

Buddhism. The other great religion of India, Buddhism, was founded by Siddhartha Gautama, who became known as the Buddha, or "the Enlightened One." The Buddha accepted the Hindu belief that the progress of the soul depends on the life a person leads and that good is rewarded and evil punished. He taught that salvation comes from knowing the Four Noble Truths and following the Eightfold Path.

Ancient Indian Dynasties and Empires

The subcontinent of India was never conquered by the Persians or Greeks, although both conquered land as far as the Indus River.

The Mauryan Empire. A kingdom arose in India in the 320s B.C. as a result of the conquests of a young adventurer named Chandragupta. He established the Mauryan Empire. Chandragupta's grandson, Asoka, who came to the throne in about 270 B.C., enlarged the empire until it included nearly all of India.

The Gupta rulers. The next great rulers of India were the Guptas, who came to power in A.D. 320. The time during which the Guptas ruled has been called a golden age because of the brilliant civilization that flourished during the period. Gupta rule ended in about A.D. 550. Invaders had begun to enter India in the late A.D. 400s and gained control of the area after the death of Skanda Gupta.

Ancient Indian Life and Culture

India has left the world a rich legacy in art, literature, mathematics, and science.

Economy and social life. From ancient times, the land had provided a living for nearly all of the people of India. Foreign trade flourished in northern India during the time of the Guptas. Generally, women in ancient India were subordinate to men.

Literature. In addition to the two great epics, the *Mahabharata* and the *Ramayana*, people enjoyed the stories of the *Panchatantra*, a series of fables from the Gupta period that has been translated into more languages than any other book except the Bible.

Art and architecture. Much Indian art and architecture reflects religious influences. For example, stupas—hemispherical, or dome-shaped, shrines—held artifacts and objects associated with Buddha. Indians also created a distinctive style of Hindu temple, a square building with heavy walls enclosing the statue of a god.

Mathematics and astronomy. Indians used and probably invented the numbers we call "Arabic," the digits 1 through 9. They understood the concepts of zero and infinity. Indians also understood abstract numbers and negative numbers, without which algebra could not exist. The Indian mathematician Aryabhata is one of the first people known to have used algebra.

Indian astronomers identified the seven planets that can be seen without the aid of a telescope. They

Statue of the Buddha

understood the daily rotation of the earth on its axis and accurately predicted eclipses of the sun and moon.

Medicine. Indian physicians understood the importance of the spinal cord, and their surgical procedures included bone setting and plastic surgery. They developed the technique of inoculation—infecting a person with a mild form of a disease so that he or she will not fall ill with the more serious form.

CHAPTER 4

Ancient Chinese Civilization

Great distances, the towering mountains of Central Asia, and such formidable deserts as the Gobi made China almost inaccessible. As a result, China developed and retained its own distinctive culture in relative isolation.

Geographic and Cultural Influences

From the beginning of its recorded history until the early 1900s, a succession of dynasties ruled China. Most dynasties went through a cycle that consisted of several stages. The first stage was the founding of the dynasty. Next came a period of internal peace, expansion, and great power. A period of regression marked by decline followed the period of great power. When its decline reached the low point at which chaos and rebellion took over many parts of the land, the dynasty collapsed. A new leader emerged, and another dynastic cycle then began.

Beneath the recurring pattern of the dynastic cycle lay a continuous evolution, or development, of culture over the centuries. For example, structures such as the family, the farm, and the village developed their own patterns of change. During some stages of the dynastic cycle, the pace of cultural evolution quickened; during others it slowed.

The Shang Dynasty

China's first historic dynasty, the Shang, began along the Huang He sometime between 1750 B.C. and 1500 B.C. Although the Shang economy was based mainly on agriculture, Shang artisans established the foundation for later Chinese ceramic art, including the development of forms and shapes used in Chinese ceremonial vases. The bronze castings made by Shang artisans are regarded as outstanding works of art throughout the world.

The Zhou, Qin, and Han Dynasties

The Zhou conquest of China in 1122 B.C. marked the beginning of a dynamic era in Chinese history. The Zhou dynasty was the most enduring Chinese dynasty, lasting about 900 years. During the many years of Zhou rule, internal trade expanded, and copper coins came into use as money. The most important development was probably the introduction of iron, which helped transform Chinese agriculture. Using iron tools and iron plows pulled by oxen, Chinese peasants cultivated new lands and produced more grain than ever before.

The Qin dynasty. The Qin (chin) dynasty came to power in 221 B.C. through military might. The dynasty's founder was Shi Huangdi, which means "first emperor." Although the Qin dynasty lasted only a short time, until 206 B.C., it succeeded in unifying China under a strong central government. The Qin dynasty was also noted for standardizing weights, measures, and coinage, and for establishing a uniform system of writing. Like earlier rulers, the Qin attempted to guard against invasion by building a wall on their northern and northwestern frontiers. Later dynasties added to these structures, which were eventually connected and became known as the Great Wall of China, much of which still stands today.

The Great Wall of China

The Han dynasty. In 202 B.C. a general of peasant background, Liu Bang, founded the Han dynasty. Like the Qin, the Han dynasty ruled a centralized and expanding empire. Unlike the Qin, however, it succeeded in maintaining its power for almost 400 years. Han influence was so great that even today many Chinese refer to themselves as Sons of Han.

Building on a foundation laid by the Qin, the Han dynasty built up a centralized civil service system to govern China. The Han eventually instituted an examination system for recommended candidates for civil service positions. Theoretically, the civil service was open to anyone, but in practice, only those with family connections and those who could afford the necessary schooling were able to gain entry.

Philosophies of Ancient China

Although political disunity and almost constant warfare marked the last years of the Zhou dynasty, this period remains one of the most creative in the history of Chinese philosophy.

Ancient Chinese beliefs. At a time when the political life of China was in turmoil, philosophers were looking for ways to restore harmony. One of their basic ideas concerned the dualism, or two-sidedness, of nature. This idea holds that everything in the world results from a balancing of complementary forces, called yin and yang. Yin and yang do not conflict with each other, as do the concepts of good and evil in Western thought, but balance and depend on one another.

Confucianism. Westerners know Kong Fuzi as Confucius. Confucius was not a religious prophet and had little to say about gods, the meaning of death, or the idea of life after death. Instead he taught about the importance of the family, respect for one's elders, and reverence for the past. These three concepts formed the basis of Confucian philosophy, which exerted a more powerful influence on later Chinese beliefs and lifestyles than did any other philosophy.

Daoism. Daoism (DOW·ih·zuhm) got its name from its central idea, the Dao, which can be defined as the "Way of Nature." Laozi, the founder of Daoism, believed that only by withdrawing from the world and contemplating nature could people understand the Dao and live in harmony with it. Like yin and yang, Daoism and Confucianism came to be complementary parts of Chinese culture. Each supplied what the other lacked.

Legalism. Like Confucianism, the school of philosophy known as Legalism was concerned with politics. Its teachings, however, differed greatly from the teachings of Confucianism. The Legalists believed in power—not virtue—and in harsh laws. In their view, people were by nature selfish and untrustworthy. Peace and prosperity could be achieved only by threatening severe punishment in case people failed to do what the laws expected of them.

Chinese Life and Culture

The family, not the individual, constituted the most important unit in Chinese society. The Chinese father ruled the family. He arranged his children's and his grandchildren's marriages, decided how much education his sons would receive, and even chose his sons' careers. Women were subordinate to men, although Chinese society also taught great respect for mothers and mothers-in-law.

The Five Classics—the *Book of Poetry,* the *Book of History,* the *Book of Divination,* the *Spring and Autumn Annals,* and the *Book of Rites*—became the most important works of Chinese literature and the basis on which all Chinese scholars were educated. The study of The Analects of Confucius was also important.

Early Chinese astronomers had computed the year at 365 1/4 days. During the Han dynasty, these calculations were refined even further. Sometime before A.D. 100, Chinese astronomers built special instruments to observe the movement of planets. Other achievements included the invention of a primitive seismograph that registered earthquakes so faint that they were unnoticed by the royal officials, and the earliest production of paper, in A.D. 105.

> ### Synthesis Review
>
> 1. **Understanding Ideas** What advances were made by the people of the earliest civilizations?
> 2. **Contrasting Ideas** How was the Nile Valley civilization different from those of the Fertile Crescent?
> 3. **Summarizing Ideas** What were the major beliefs of Hinduism and Buddhism?
> 4. **Analyzing Ideas** Why did Chinese civilization develop in relative isolation?
> 5. **Synthesizing Ideas** What characteristics of Egyptian, Indian, and Chinese cultures identify them as advanced civilizations?

UNIT

2

Civilizations of the Mediterranean World

Chapter 5

c. 2000 B.C.–404 B.C.

The Greek City-States

Chapter 6

478 B.C.–146 B.C.

Greece's Golden and Hellenistic Ages

Chapter 7

1000 B.C.–A.D. 476

The Roman World

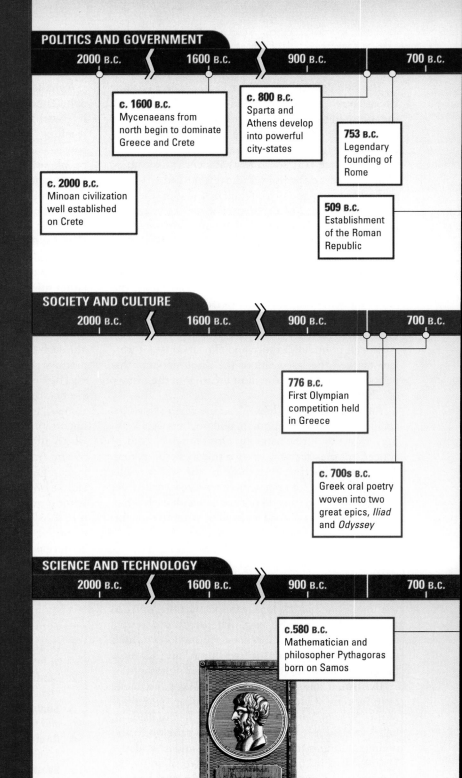

POLITICS AND GOVERNMENT

2000 B.C.	1600 B.C.	900 B.C.	700 B.C.

c. 1600 B.C.
Mycenaeans from north begin to dominate Greece and Crete

c. 800 B.C.
Sparta and Athens develop into powerful city-states

753 B.C.
Legendary founding of Rome

c. 2000 B.C.
Minoan civilization well established on Crete

509 B.C.
Establishment of the Roman Republic

SOCIETY AND CULTURE

2000 B.C.	1600 B.C.	900 B.C.	700 B.C.

776 B.C.
First Olympian competition held in Greece

c. 700s B.C.
Greek oral poetry woven into two great epics, *Iliad* and *Odyssey*

SCIENCE AND TECHNOLOGY

2000 B.C.	1600 B.C.	900 B.C.	700 B.C.

c.580 B.C.
Mathematician and philosopher Pythagoras born on Samos

Pythagoras

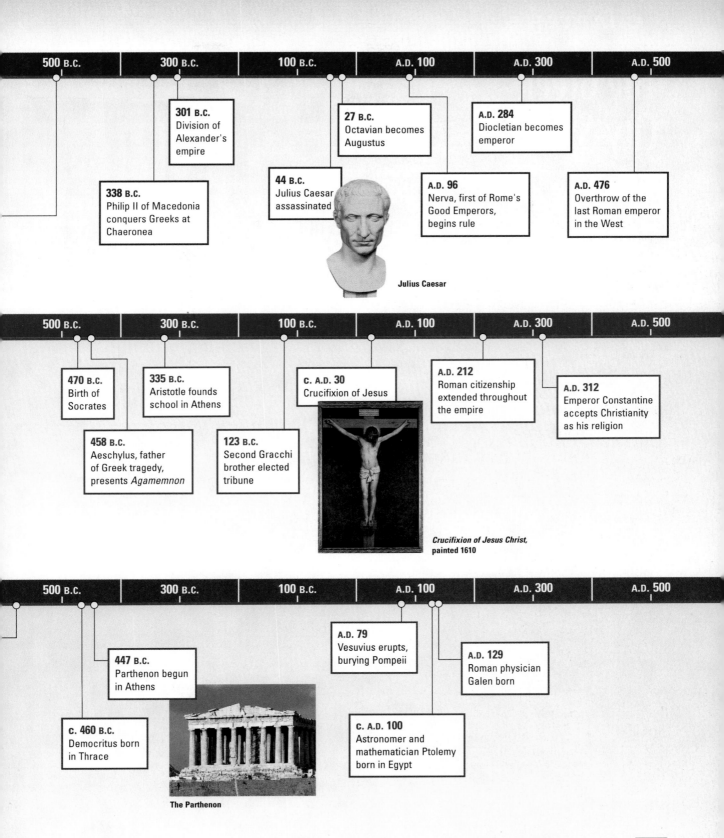

500 B.C.   **300** B.C.   **100** B.C.   A.D. **100**   A.D. **300**   A.D. **500**

301 B.C.
Division of
Alexander's
empire

338 B.C.
Philip II of Macedonia
conquers Greeks at
Chaeronea

27 B.C.
Octavian becomes
Augustus

44 B.C.
Julius Caesar
assassinated

A.D. 284
Diocletian becomes
emperor

A.D. 96
Nerva, first of Rome's
Good Emperors,
begins rule

A.D. 476
Overthrow of the
last Roman emperor
in the West

Julius Caesar

---

500 B.C.   **300** B.C.   **100** B.C.   A.D. **100**   A.D. **300**   A.D. **500**

470 B.C.
Birth of
Socrates

335 B.C.
Aristotle founds
school in Athens

C. A.D. 30
Crucifixion of Jesus

A.D. 212
Roman citizenship
extended throughout
the empire

A.D. 312
Emperor Constantine
accepts Christianity
as his religion

458 B.C.
Aeschylus, father
of Greek tragedy,
presents *Agamemnon*

123 B.C.
Second Gracchi
brother elected
tribune

Crucifixion of Jesus Christ,
painted 1610

---

500 B.C.   **300** B.C.   **100** B.C.   A.D. **100**   A.D. **300**   A.D. **500**

A.D. 79
Vesuvius erupts,
burying Pompeii

447 B.C.
Parthenon begun
in Athens

A.D. 129
Roman physician
Galen born

c. 460 B.C.
Democritus born
in Thrace

C. A.D. 100
Astronomer and
mathematician Ptolemy
born in Egypt

The Parthenon

The Greek City-States

TIME

c. 2000 B.C.–404 B.C.

c. 2000 B.C.–404 B.C.

| 3.7 million B.C. | 4000 B.C. | A.D. 2100 |

PLACE

Greece and
Asia Minor

Greece

ARCTIC OCEAN

NORTH
AMERICA

EUROPE

ASIA

PACIFIC
OCEAN

AFRICA

Equator

AUSTRALIA

PACIFIC
OCEAN

SOUTH
AMERICA

ATLANTIC
OCEAN

INDIAN
OCEAN

ANTARCTICA

Asia Minor

Ruins of the Parthenon,
Acropolis, Athens

CHAPTER FOCUS

Significance

We take a special interest in the Greeks because much of **Western civilization**—the civilization that in later centuries evolved in Europe and spread to the Americas—had its foundations in early Greece. For example, the Greeks were the first people to experiment successfully with the idea that citizens could govern themselves, an idea that the United States and many other countries have since adopted and refined.

Terms to Define

Western civilization	popular government
frescoes	democracy
polis	helots
acropolis	ephors
agora	metics
epics	archons
myths	direct democracy
oracles	representative
import	democracy
export	terracing
aristocracies	pedagogue
hoplite	rhetoric
tyrants	

People to Identify

Minoans	Solon
Mycenaeans	Peisistratus
Dorians	Cleisthenes
Homer	Darius
Zeus	Xerxes
Athena	Themistocles
Draco	Pericles

Places to Locate

Aegean Sea	Mount Olympus
Balkan Peninsula	Piraeus
Crete	Marathon
Mycenae	Thermopylae
Athens	Salamis
Sparta	Delos

Chapter Theme Questions

- **Geography** How might geographic factors influence the growth of civilizations?
- **Social Relations** What are some of the different ways that communities might organize their societies?
- **War and Diplomacy** What might cause communities to go to war?

When the world's best athletes test their skills at the Olympic Games every four years, they repeat a tradition that began thousands of years ago in Greece. As historian Lionel Casson said in these excerpts from a Smithsonian article:

❝ One midsummer day in the year we calculate to have been 776 B.C., a 200-meter dash was run in a rural backwater in southwestern Greece, and a young local named Coroebus won it. It was an obscure event in an obscure spot but it earned him immortality: he is the first Olympic victor on record. ❞

❝ Winners formed a procession and marched to the Temple of Zeus [the chief Greek god]. . . . At the temple, each was handed what ancient athletes considered the most precious object in the world, the victor's olive wreath. . . .

Winning was everything; there were no seconds or thirds, no Greek equivalents of silver or bronze medals. . . . Losers were jeered and, hiding their heads in shame, slunk away. Even their mothers treated them with scorn. 'The wreath or death' was the motto. ❞

The Olympic Games are only one of the many traditions we owe to the people of ancient Greece.

Early Greeks and the Rise of City-States

Focus Questions

- How did geography influence Greek history?
- Who were the Minoans, Mycenaeans, and Dorians?
- What was the polis?

Geography influences history. This is certainly true of the history of Greece and its city-states, where the

The Mediterranean Region

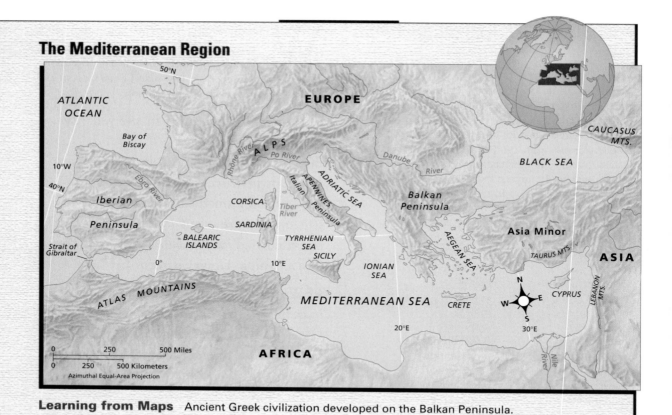

Learning from Maps   Ancient Greek civilization developed on the Balkan Peninsula.

? Region   What two other peninsulas extend southward into the Mediterranean Sea?

location and the surroundings of each city influenced its growth, development, and ultimate fate.

The Physical Setting

At the extreme northeastern end of the Mediterranean, the Aegean Sea separates the Balkan Peninsula from Asia Minor. The southern tip of the Balkan Peninsula consists of many small peninsulas that form the mainland of Greece. In addition, many small islands dot the Aegean Sea and are considered part of Greece.

In many ways, nature did not smile kindly on the Greeks. Look at the map of the Mediterranean region on this page. Notice that short mountain ranges cut up the Greek mainland. These mountains separated communities and prevented them from developing a sense of unity. Also notice that although Greece has many small rivers, it has no great river systems such as those around which the ancient civilizations of Egypt and Mesopotamia developed.

However, Greece had a mild climate and enough good soil and sufficient rainfall for farmers to grow grain, grapes, and olives in the small valleys and in the foothills of the mountains. The foothills also provided pasture for sheep and goats. Still Greece could not produce the amount or the variety of food that its increasing population needed.

Greece's geography encouraged the development of trade. The long, irregular coastline allowed every part of the mainland to be close to the sea, and both the mainland and the islands had many good harbors. With the sea so much a part of their lives, the Greeks became fishers, sailors, traders, and eventually colonizers of new lands.

These early sailors and traders traveled throughout the eastern Mediterranean. From Egypt and the Fertile Crescent, people brought knowledge and ideas to the Aegean Islands, to the mainland of Greece, and to the Aegean shores of Asia Minor.

Minoan Civilization

Look again at the map on this page, and locate the long, narrow island of Crete in the eastern Mediterranean

Sea. Ancient Greek myths told of a great and powerful civilization that had existed there in the distant past. Around A.D. 1900 a series of archaeological discoveries began to provide a factual basis for the ancient stories. British archaeologist Arthur Evans discovered the ruins of a great palace with hundreds of rooms. Evans believed that he had unearthed Knossos (NAHS·uhs)—the palace of Minos, legendary king of Crete. Scholars named this civilization Minoan in honor of its king, Minos, who allegedly kept imprisoned a giant creature—half human and half bull—called the Minotaur.

Since Evans's discovery, other archaeologists have unearthed artifacts and ruins of buildings showing that a great civilization did indeed flourish on the island. The early Minoans developed writing in a script known today as linear A, which has not yet been deciphered. Later, after the Minoans came into contact with Indo-European-speaking groups, a new form of writing called linear B came into use. This new writing, an early form of Greek, recorded details of Minoan civilization.

Evidence indicates that Minoan civilization was well established by about 2000 B.C. Although the great civilizations of the nearby Nile Valley and Fertile Crescent influenced Minoan civilization, this civilization developed many unique features. Excavations in Knossos show that the royal palace and the homes of the nobles had running water and walls decorated with colorful **frescoes**—paintings made on wet plaster walls. Minoan artisans made beautiful, delicately carved figures from ivory, stone, gold, silver, and bronze. These artifacts show the Minoans as a cheerful people who enjoyed festivals and worshipped the bull and an earth goddess. They also show that women played an important role in Minoan society. The natural world was especially important in Minoan society and art.

Because the soil of Crete was unsuitable for growing many kinds of crops, the Minoans turned to the sea for their livelihood. They may have dominated the Aegean Islands and probably founded colonies both there and in Asia Minor. Excellent sailors, the Minoans also traded widely. The kings of Crete had so much confidence in the strength of their navy that they did not bother to fortify their cities.

Sometime around 1500 B.C., however, a volcanic eruption on a nearby island sent giant tidal waves crashing across Crete, causing great destruction and loss of life. Though the Minoans rebuilt after this disaster, their civilization was weakened. Knossos, the

The Toreador Fresco, c. 1500 B.C., remains the largest and most dynamic Minoan mural still in existence. It shows three athletes (the two women are differentiated by lighter skin tones) vaulting over a bull, a popular activity in Minoan religion.

last palace, was destroyed in about 1400 B.C., possibly by Indo-Europeans who had migrated to Greece and established their own civilization.

Early Migrations into Greece

Around the same time that the Minoan civilization developed, important changes took place on the Greek mainland. Beginning around 2000 B.C., new people entered Greece from the north. They spoke an Indo-European language.

The invaders were organized into clans and tribes. Several related families formed a clan headed by a warrior. A number of clans made up a tribe, which had its own chief. These wandering people learned how to grow grain, grapes, and olives. They also learned how to sail.

Known as Mycenaeans (my·suh·NEE·uhnz), they dominated the Greek mainland from about 1600 B.C. to 1200 B.C. They built fortified cities in the Peloponnesus (pel·uh·puh·NEE·suhs), the southern part of Greece. These cities included Mycenae, Tiryns, and Pylos. (See map on page 105.) A warlike people who carried out raids by sea throughout the eastern Mediterranean area, the Mycenaeans conquered Crete

and in turn adopted many elements of Minoan civilization. The Mycenaeans kept records in linear B, the written language of the later Minoan civilization.

Mycenaean civilization, like that of the Minoans, suffered the effects of earthquakes. The civilization was also weakened by continual warfare. By 1200 B.C. most of the major Mycenaean cities, including Mycenae, had been destroyed. Perhaps these cities perished in the general upheaval caused by the arrival of other migrating tribes.

After the collapse of Mycenaean society around 1100 B.C., more primitive Greeks—the Dorians—moved into the fertile areas of the Peloponnesus, Crete, and southwestern Asia Minor. The newcomers were illiterate, and knowledge of writing disappeared when the Mycenaean cities fell. A dark age descended on Greece until Phoenician traders introduced an alphabet around 750 B.C.

The City-States of Greece

Influenced by the geography of Greece and their own tribal organization, the early Greeks established city-states, such as Athens and Sparta, in the 800s and 700s B.C. (See map on page 110.) The Greek word for

The Mycenaeans buried their dead in conical stone chambers. Artifacts with ornate decoration such as silver and gold masks, drinking vessels, jewelry, and weapons were found in these tombs.

Aegean Civilization, c. 1450 B.C.

BLACK SEA

Bosporus

THRACE

SEA OF MARMARA

MACEDONIA

Mt. Olympus 40°N

Dardanelles (Hellespont) Troy

THESSALY

Asia Minor

GREECE

AEGEAN SEA

IONIA

MYCENAEANS

ATTICA

Mycenae
Tiryns Athens

Peloponnesus

Pylos

DELOS

IONIAN SEA

KOS

36°N

THERA

RHODES

N
W E
S

MINOANS

Knossos

CRETE

0   75   150 Miles
0   75   150 Kilometers
Lambert Conformal Conic Projection

MEDITERRANEAN SEA

24°E   28°E

Learning from Maps Because Greece's geography encouraged the development of trade, many cities were established along the coast.

? Place What four Minoan and Mycenaean cities were located near the sea?

city-state is **polis**. The polis typically developed around a fort, a refuge in time of danger. As a village or city grew up around the fort, *polis* came to mean the fort and the city as well as the surrounding land outside the city walls. The concept of *polis* also included the government. Our words *police*, *politics*, and *policy* are related to the word *polis*.

All Greek city-states shared certain features: (1) *Small size*. Typically a city-state occupied from 30 to 500 square miles. The mighty city-state of Athens at its greatest extent was smaller than Rhode Island. Sparta, the largest city-state, was smaller than Connecticut. These two poleis (plural of polis), were exceptionally large compared to the others. (2) *Small population*. Most city-states had a total population—men, women, and children, including slaves and other noncitizens—of fewer than 10,000 people. Only free adult males had all the rights of citizenship; women were considered citizens without political rights. Most

city-states had fewer than 1,000 male citizens. Athens was an unusually populous city-state. At its height it had approximately 40,000 male citizens and a total population of 400,000. (3) *Setting on a hill*. In most city-states the original fort stood on an **acropolis**, a hill or mountain, together with temples and other public buildings. (4) *Public meeting place*. Each city-state had an **agora**, or marketplace. In almost all cases, the agora was also the public meeting place, where citizens could gather to discuss common issues.

The polis was far more than a place where people lived. It served as the focus of Greek identity, and the Greeks believed that citizens owed total loyalty to their polis. Citizens loved their city-state and often were willing to give up their lives for it.

The Greeks also placed great value on the distinctness and political independence of each polis. Although physically similar, the city-states developed different forms of government. Each city-state had its own laws, calendar, money, and system of weights and measures. These differences helped make each city-state unique.

Nevertheless, all ancient Greeks had certain things in common. They all spoke the same language and tended to regard people who did not speak Greek as barbarians. A Greek myth claimed that all Greeks were descended from the same ancestor, Hellen. They also shared many religious ideas and joined in common management of certain temples, such as those of the god Zeus at Olympia and the god Apollo at Delphi. Great festivals such as the Olympic Games brought the Greeks together.

Section 1 Review

1. **Define** Western civilization, frescoes, polis, acropolis, agora
2. **Identify** Minoans, Mycenaeans, Dorians
3. **Locate and Explain the Significance** Aegean Sea, Balkan Peninsula, Crete, Mycenae, Athens, Sparta
4. **Understanding Ideas** How did geography influence the way of life of the early Greeks?
5. **Summarizing Ideas (a)** What were the accomplishments of Minoan civilization? **(b)** Who were the Mycenaeans and the Dorians?
6. **Comparing Ideas (a)** What four things did all Greek city-states have in common? **(b)** How do these characteristics compare to those of modern cities in the United States?

Greek Government and Society

Focus Questions

- Who was Homer, and what were the *Iliad* and the *Odyssey*?
- What were the main characteristics of Greek religion?
- How were the city-states governed, and how did this change over time?

At first, chiefs ruled the tribes that lived in Greece. Later, as the independent Greek city-states emerged, a variety of governments developed.

The Homeric Age

In the period between 1000 B.C. and 700 B.C., the Greek city-states had similar forms of government based on the tribal systems introduced during the early migrations. These tribal systems gradually developed into small kingdoms, or monarchies, that constantly waged war among themselves.

The Greeks of this period did not have a very advanced civilization. Because few people could write, most communication was oral. Poets wandered from village to village, singing or reciting folk songs, ballads, and **epics**—long poems describing heroes and great events.

Sometime during the 700s B.C., much of this oral poetry was gathered together and woven into two great epics—the *Iliad* and the *Odyssey*. While other epic poetry existed, these epics are the two that have endured. According to tradition, the blind poet Homer composed these epics, although scholars stress that we really do not know who their author or authors were. Nevertheless, this period is often called the Homeric Age.

The Trojan War provided the setting for the *Iliad* and the background for the *Odyssey*. Legends told how Paris, a Trojan prince, stole Helen, the beautiful wife of a Greek king. The Greeks then sent a great expedition against Troy. After years of fighting, Troy was defeated by a clever trick. The Greeks built a giant wooden horse outside Troy's walls. Then, after secretly filling the horse with soldiers, the bulk of the Greek forces broke camp and seemingly departed. Thinking the Greeks had given up the fight, the unsuspecting Trojans dragged the horse into the city as a trophy. When night fell, however, the Greeks inside the horse burst out and threw open the city gates. Returning, the rest of the Greek forces poured into Troy and destroyed it.

The *Iliad* relates incidents in the tenth year of the Trojan War. The *Odyssey* depicts the end of the war, including the episode of the Trojan horse, and then chronicles the many adventures of the Greek hero Odysseus on his long journey home from the war. According to legend, several gods, angered by Odysseus's trickery, condemned him to wander for 10 years before he finally arrived home.

The *Iliad* and the *Odyssey* supposedly describe actual events of the distant past. Yet many scholars also value these works as rich sources of information about the life, customs, and ideals of the Greeks between 1000 B.C. and 700 B.C.

Religious and moral beliefs. The religion that developed among the Greeks during the Homeric Age differed greatly from the religions of the Egyptians, Persians, and Hebrews. The Greeks asked three things of their religion: (1) an explanation for such mysteries of the physical world as thunder, lightning, and the change of the seasons; (2) an explanation of the passions that could make people lose the self-control that the Greeks considered so important; and (3) a means for gaining such benefits as long life, good fortune, and abundant harvests.

The Greek religion did not focus on morality. Greeks did not expect their religion to save them from sin, to bring them spiritual blessings, or to ensure a life after death. Greeks of the Homeric Age were not as concerned, for example, as the Egyptians were about what happened to them after death. Often they cremated, or burned, their dead with only a simple ritual. They thought that with few exceptions the spirits of all people went to a gray and gloomy place—the underworld—ruled by the god Hades (HAY·deez). The "house of Hades" was not a place of punishment.

The Greek gods. The Egyptians worshiped the Sun and the moon, attributed both human and animal characteristics to many of their gods, and believed their pharaoh represented these gods. In contrast, the Greeks attributed human qualities and personal characteristics to all their gods and goddesses.

The Greeks thought of gods as having weaknesses and wants much like their own but on a larger scale. Greek gods lived not in some remote heaven but on the top of Mount Olympus, a peak in northern Greece. (See map on page 105.)

The *Odyssey*

Homer's *Odyssey* details the many adventures of Odysseus and his men as they made their way home from the Trojan War. In one adventure, excerpted below, they landed on the island of the Kyklops, who are legendary one-eyed giants known for their cruelty. (These monsters are sometimes called Kyclops or Cyclops.) A Kyklops named Polyphêmos (pah·luh·fee·muhs) captured Odysseus and part of his crew and viciously devoured some of the men. Through a clever trick, however, Odysseus saved the remaining members of his crew.

Mosaic from Homer's *Odyssey*

"Three bowls [of wine] I brought him, and he
poured them down.
I saw the fuddle and flush come over him,
then I sang out in cordial tones:

'Kyklops,

you ask my honorable name? Remember
the gift you promised me, and I shall tell you.
My name is Nohbdy: mother, father, and friends,
everyone calls me Nohbdy,'

And he said:

'Nohbdy's my meat, then, after I eat his friends.
Others come first. There's a noble gift, now.'

Even as he spoke, he reeled and tumbled
backward,
his great head lolling to one side; and sleep
took him like any creature. Drunk, hiccuping,
he dribbled streams of liquor and bits of men.

Now, by the gods, I drove my big hand spike
deep in the embers, charring it again,
and cheered my men along with battle talk
to keep their courage up: no quitting now.
The pike of olive, green though it had been,
reddened and glowed as if about to catch.
I drew it from the coals and my four fellows
gave me a hand, lugging it near the Kyklops
as more than natural force nerved them; straight
forward they sprinted, lifted it, and rammed it deep
in his crater eye, and I leaned on it
turning it as a shipwright turns a drill
in planking, having men below to swing
the two-handled strap that spins it in the groove.
So with our brand we bored that great eye socket
while blood ran out around the red-hot bar.
Eyelid and lash were seared; the pierced ball
hissed broiling, and the roots popped.

In a smithy

one sees a white-hot axehead or an adze
plunged and wrung in a cold tub, screeching steam—
the way they make soft iron hale and hard—:
just so that eyeball hissed around the spike.

The Kyklops bellowed and the rock roared
round him,
and we fell back in fear. Clawing his face
he tugged the bloody spike out of his eye,
threw it away, and his wild hands went groping;
then he set up a howl for Kyklopês
who lived in caves on windy peaks nearby.
Some heard him; and they came by divers ways
to clump around outside and call:

'What ails you,

Polyphêmos? Why do you cry so sore
in the starry night? You will not let us sleep.
Sure no man's driving off your flock? No man
has tricked you, ruined you?'

Out of the cave

the mammoth Polyphêmos roared in answer:

'Nohbdy, Nohbdy's tricked me, Nohbdy's
ruined me!'

To this rough shout they made a sage reply:

'Ah well, if nobody has played you foul
there in your lonely bed, we are no use in pain
given by great Zeus. Let it be your father,
Poseidon Lord, to whom you pray.'

So saying

they trailed away. And I was filled with laughter
to see how like a charm
the name deceived them. . . . "

This frieze from the Altar of Zeus at Pergamum depicts the struggle of Athena and Alcyoneus. The movement of the composition seen in the flowing drapery and twisting figures exemplifies the drama of Hellenistic sculpture.

To explain their world, the Greeks developed **myths**—traditional stories about the deeds and misdeeds of gods, goddesses, and heroes. Zeus, the king of the gods, was the most powerful god and the father of some other gods as well as some humans. Hera, his sister and wife, protected women and marriage. Poseidon (puh·SY·duhn), brother of Zeus, was god of the sea.

Athena, a daughter of Zeus, was the goddess of wisdom, womanly virtue, and technical skill. She was also the special protector of the great city-states, especially Athens, which was named in her honor. Aphrodite (a·fruh·DY·tee), another daughter of Zeus, was the goddess of love and beauty. Her brother Apollo was the god of light, music, and poetry, as well as the symbol of manly beauty. Dionysus (dy·uh·NY·suhs) was the god of fertility and wine.

Religious practices. The Greeks believed that the gods spoke through priests or priestesses at special sanctuaries called **oracles**, usually in answer to questions about the future. The most famous oracle was that of Apollo at Delphi in the rugged mountains north of the Gulf of Corinth.

Because displays of strength and courage pleased the gods, the Greeks held athletic contests in their honor. Most notable were the games at Olympia, held every fourth year in honor of Zeus. Only men could attend and compete in the Olympic Games.

The Olympic Games consisted of footraces, jumping, javelin and discus throwing, boxing, wrestling, and horse and chariot racing. The winners received wreaths of wild olive branches, but when they returned home their fellow citizens showered them with money and valuable gifts. The games became so important that the Greeks used them as one basis for dating events. The first games are thought to have been held in 776 B.C., and the four-year periods between them were called Olympiads.

Stadiums

All over the world, millions of people crowd stadiums each year to watch sporting events. The desire to watch such events—and the need to provide a place where a large number of people can do their watching—is a very old one. The stadium is the best way of meeting that need.

The idea of a big "bowl" with terraced steps on which people can sit goes back more than 2,500 years to the time of the ancient Greeks. When the first Olympic Games were held, the events took place in a magnificent stadium built for the occasion in the city-state of Olympia. In the earliest stadiums, people sat on the ground rather than on stone steps. Many ancient stadiums still stand, such as the one in Tunisia (top).

The Greeks, and later the Romans, erected many of these structures. Plays, performed on a stage at one end, were mounted there as well as sporting events.

Today stadiums continue to have various uses. Yankee Stadium in New York City, for example, is mainly a place to play baseball. Yet it has also held huge crowds attending a concert or hearing the pope during his visit to the United States.

Most ancient stadiums were smaller than modern ones. One exception was the Circus Maximus in Rome, which may have held 250,000 people. However, the Colosseum in Rome could hold only about 50,000. Modern stadiums have room for many more. For example, the soccer stadium in Rio de Janeiro, Brazil, can hold 200,000 people, and one in Prague, Czechoslovakia, has a capacity of 240,000.

In the United States, this stadium in Los Angeles, California (center), was used to hold the large crowds attending the Olympic Games held there in 1984. The Astrodome (bottom), the indoor stadium in Houston, Texas, has the capacity to hold more than 60,000.

Rise of the Nobles

City-states in Greece had begun as small kingdoms. The kings relied on wealthy landowners in battle. By 700 B.C. these landowners, or nobles, had generally overthrown the kings. One reason for the nobles' power was that they supplied cavalry for the military forces. Another reason was economic: although the population steadily increased, the amount of land that could be farmed did not. When the harvest was meager, farmers with small plots of land frequently had to mortgage or sell their land to a noble.

Farmers and laborers who could not support themselves sometimes moved to the cities to find work. There a commercial class of merchants was developing.

Ancient Greece, c. 750 B.C.–450 B.C.

Learning from Maps Greek culture spread throughout the Mediterranean region as city-states were established on islands across the Black, Aegean, and Mediterranean Seas.

? Region What Black Sea colony exported grain, timber, and slaves?

Although the merchants could become wealthy, they always remained beneath the nobles in social position.

The nobles encouraged discontented farmers and laborers to establish colonies outside of Greece. Colonies, set up as city-states such as those in Greece, were established on islands and shorelines throughout the Black, Aegean, and Mediterranean Seas. (See map on this page.) In this manner Greek culture spread throughout the Mediterranean region. The Greeks also gained valuable knowledge through contact with the advanced civilizations to the east and the south, such as Egypt, and carried this knowledge along with their own to less highly developed peoples.

Colonization also promoted trade. The new colonies often imported goods from Greece and exported grain and other products to it. An **import** is a good or service brought from and an **export** is a good or service sold to another country or region.

The many Greek city-states controlled by nobles were called **aristocracies**, which originally meant "rule by the best." (Later the word *aristocracy* came to mean a privileged social class.) Eventually, however, changes took place that weakened the nobles' power. By the 600s B.C., wealthy nonaristocrats could afford some weaponry of their own. A new kind of nonaristocratic soldier emerged, the **hoplite**, or heavy infantryman. Hoplites fought in closely-spaced rows. In this formation, called a phalanx, they could withstand cavalry charges by aristocratic horsemen. As the hoplites' role in the service of the polis increased, these nonaristocrats began to demand more say in government. Meanwhile, even poor citizens, especially farmers, were becoming discontented with the rule of the nobles. Soon many nonaristocratic citizens began to look for leaders who could promise them a better life.

The Age of Tyrants

The leaders who appeared with promises of a better life were called **tyrants**. The ancient Greeks defined a tyrant as someone who seized power in defiance of law but ruled with the people's support. Many of the tyrants governed well for a time. They put an end to the nobles' struggles for political power, encouraged trade, and in general improved life in the city-states.

The rule by tyrants occurred in many of the Greek city-states between 650 B.C. and 500 B.C. In some cases, as has often happened in history, the powerful rulers who began by governing in the people's interest in time became harsh and unjust. Over time the word *tyrant* took on its present meaning—a ruler who exercises absolute power brutally and oppressively.

Popular Government

Many city-states ousted their tyrants. In some the idea of **popular government**—that people could and should rule themselves rather than be ruled by others—began to take root. This led to the form of government called **democracy**, which is defined as a government in which all citizens take part. Full political rights, however, were restricted to a small proportion of the Greek city-state; women, for example, did not have them. Other city-states restored the rule of kings or aristocracies. Even in monarchies and aristocracies, however, a council of citizens now limited the power of the rulers.

Section 2 Review

1. **Define** epics, myths, oracles, import, export, aristocracies, hoplite, tyrants, popular government, democracy
2. **Identify** Homer, Zeus, Athena
3. **Locate and Explain the Significance** Mount Olympus
4. **Understanding Ideas** What are epics? Briefly describe the two great epics of the 700s B.C.
5. **Comparing Ideas** Compare Greek religious beliefs with those of earlier civilizations.
6. **Interpreting Ideas (a)** How did the nobles win power in Greece? **(b)** Why did they lose power? **(c)** What part did tyrants play in the process?

Sparta and Athens

Focus Questions
- **What kind of society emerged in Sparta?**
- **How did democracy develop in Athens?**

Greek city-states had both similarities and differences. The wide range of differences shows clearly in a comparison of the two city-states that became most important, Sparta and Athens.

Sparta: The Military Ideal

The Dorian invaders from the north had overrun most of the Peloponnesus by the end of the 1100s B.C. They conquered the village that became their capital, Sparta, and also the neighboring areas. (See map on page 110.) The invaders forced many of the people they conquered to work for them. They called these people **helots**. Although the Spartans built their city-state in a valley and did not surround it with a wall, Sparta developed into a highly militarized society.

Spartan society. Three social groups emerged in Sparta. The first group, known as the equals, consisted of citizens descended from the Dorian invaders. They controlled the city-state. Land was divided equally among these citizens and their families. With each allotment of land went helots to work it.

The rugged mountains of Greece created a geographical barrier that hindered communication among the city-states, allowing each to develop its own unique way of life.

The second group of people was made up of the half-citizens. Although they were free, paid taxes, and served in the army, they had no political power. The half-citizens both farmed and lived in the towns, where they worked in commerce and industry. Some even became rich.

The third and lowest group consisted of the helots. The helots became slaves of the Spartan city-state, which determined how they should work and live. Because the helots greatly outnumbered the Spartans, the Spartans had to use force to control them and constantly lived in fear of a helot rebellion. This fear was one reason that Spartan society so strongly emphasized militarism. The Spartans systematically terrorized the helots to keep them from rebelling. Not surprisingly, the helots hated the Spartans.

Government in Sparta. Sparta had an assembly consisting of all adult male citizens, a Council of Elders that proposed laws, and two kings. Five **ephors**, or overseers, elected by the assembly for one-year terms, monitored the kings and the citizens. The ephors had unlimited power to act as guardians of the state, and they used that power freely.

The military machine. Sparta regulated the lives of its citizens from birth to death. All the rules had the same basic aim: to make every adult male citizen part of an efficient military machine designed to control the helots and extend Spartan power.

The development of Spartan fighting men, and of women fit to marry them, began at birth, when a group of officials examined newborn babies. Any child who seemed weak, unhealthy, or deformed in any way was abandoned in the countryside to die. At the age of seven, boys went to live in military barracks. Although they learned to read and write, military training formed the basis of their education.

It was a harsh education. To learn endurance, boys were given inadequate clothing. To teach them to feed themselves in wartime, the authorities provided coarse and scanty food, and the boys had to steal food to keep from starving. Anyone caught received a severe punishment, not for stealing but rather for being clumsy enough to get caught.

The male citizen began his military service at the age of 20, and remained available for military service until the age of 60. He could marry at 20 but could neither live at home nor frequent the marketplace until he was 30. The authorities did not allow him to engage in any trade or business because business activities and love of money interfered with military discipline. Even older men were expected to direct most of their attention to the public welfare rather than their private lives.

Spartan girls, as the future mothers of Spartan soldiers, had to be healthy too. They received strict physical training to develop strength and endurance. They also had training in patriotic devotion. Both girls and boys studied music, which would presumably teach them discipline and coordination.

The strict discipline of Sparta did lead to efficient government and an almost unconquerable army. The Spartans paid heavily for this military might, however. First, they sacrificed individual freedom to the state. Second, their society produced nothing in art, literature, philosophy, or science.

Athens: The Birth of Democracy

Athens developed in a way quite different from that of Sparta. To begin with, Athens was bypassed by the Dorian invaders and had no class of conquering invaders who imposed their rule on a conquered people, as had occurred in Sparta.

Athens is located on the Attic peninsula, one of the least fertile areas in Greece. The Athenians turned to the sea, and some became sea traders. The invention of coined money in the 600s B.C. also stimulated trade by making it easier to buy and sell goods. The Athenians built their city inland to protect it against pirates and constructed Piraeus (py·REE·uhs) as its special port. Athens itself was a typical polis built around the rocky, fortified hill of the Acropolis. In time of war, people from the surrounding region took refuge inside the city's strong walls.

Athenian society. In Athens, as elsewhere in Greece, social standing and political power were closely linked. At the top stood the citizens. During Athens' greatest period, all Athenian-born men had full political rights, whether they were wealthy aristocrats or poor commoners. Although women were citizens, they could not vote or hold office and were regarded legally as minors.

People born outside Athens were noncitizens. Called **metics**, they worked as merchants or artisans. Although free, they could not own land or take part in government, even though they paid the same taxes as citizens.

At the bottom stood the slaves, whom the Athenians—like all Greeks—considered a necessity and part of the natural order of things. At the time of Athens' greatest glory, more than half its population consisted of metics and slaves. Slaves were people captured in war. In Athens, as in all Greece, slaves were property, dependent on their master's will. While Athenian masters could force slaves to do brutal work and treat them as they wished, it was not in their best interest to harm their own property. In disputes, courts accepted the word of the master. If the master agreed, the slave might acquire property and even become wealthy, though this was not common. A freed slave became a metic.

Early government in Athens. After its monarchy ended, Athens had an aristocratic government. Only those citizens who had a certain amount of land held office.

All adult male citizens met in an assembly and elected generals whenever necessary, as well as nine **archons**, or rulers, each of whom served a one-year term of office. The archons appointed the other officials and made all the laws. These laws, however, were not written down. The judges, who were always a group of nobles, interpreted the laws and applied them to specific situations.

Political reform. In the late 600s B.C., Athens suffered from economic discontent. Many nonaristocrats began to complain about the arbitrary decisions often made by aristocratic judges. To calm matters, the aristocrats began writing down the laws so that everyone could know what they were. Draco, who served as archon in 621 B.C., is traditionally given credit for Athens' first written law code. Draco's laws were harsh and severe, however, and today we call a harsh law a Draconian law.

Conditions in Athens remained unsatisfactory as nobles and metics became wealthy from trade but small farmers grew poorer. More and more citizens were sold into slavery to pay off their debts. Discontent and anger spread among the poorer population.

In this critical situation, Solon, a respected and trusted leader, became archon about 594 B.C. Solon mediated the dispute between debtors and creditors. He canceled the debts of the poor, outlawed enslavement for debt, and freed those who had been enslaved for nonpayment. Solon divided the Athenian citizenry into four groups based on wealth. While public office was only available to the three wealthiest groups, all could sit in the assembly that elected these officials. This opened the door to the rising nonaristocratic class. To limit the power of the judges, Solon set up a court composed of a large number of citizens to which a citizen could appeal an unfavorable decision.

Solon's reforms did not end the unrest, however. Nobles formed rival political groups and struggled for control of the government. Then around 546 B.C., after

Solon, an Athenian statesman known for his economic and political reforms, was Athens' first poet and was later named one of the Seven Wise Men of Greece.

two earlier attempts, Peisistratus (py·SIS·truht·uhs) seized power as a tyrant. Peisistratus was a wealthy aristocrat and a relative of Solon who had developed a following among the lower classes. He remained in power until 527 B.C. and was followed in power by his sons. Peisistratus improved the economy and exiled nobles who disagreed with him. He may also have distributed some of the nobles' land to poor farmers.

A democratic state. Around 508 B.C. Cleisthenes (KLYS·thuh·neez) overthrew the aristocrats who had replaced Peisistratus's second son. Cleisthenes made sweeping changes that turned Athens into a democracy. He ended the old division of Athenians into four territorial tribes, which was the basis of the aristocracy's power. Instead, he divided the citizens into 10 tribes,

Reading About History: Making Comparisons

Making comparisons helps you understand information and remember ideas and facts because you are able to place them in a historical context. Making comparisons means identifying the similarities and differences between events, ideas, and actions.

How to Make Comparisons

To make comparisons, follow these guidelines.
1. Identify the purpose of the comparison.
2. Select the categories to be compared, such as government, family life, or education.
3. Identify similarities and differences by asking questions about the categories.
4. Draw a conclusion based on the similarities and differences.

Developing the Skill

Read the following excerpts to make a comparison between life in ancient Athens and in Sparta. The first excerpt, about Athens, is from Thucydides' account of a funeral oration given by Pericles. The second excerpt, which describes the Spartan system, is from a biography of the Spartan lawmaker Lycurgus. The biography was written by the ancient writer Plutarch.

"Our constitution does not copy the laws of neighbouring states; we are rather a pattern to others than imitators ourselves. Its administration favours the many instead of the few; this is why it is called a democracy. If we look to the laws, they afford equal justice to all in their private differences; if to social standing, advancement in public life falls to reputation for capacity, class considerations not being allowed to interfere with merit. . . . The freedom which we enjoy in our government extends also to our ordinary life. There, far from exercising a jealous surveillance over each other, we do not feel called upon to be angry with our neighbor for doing what he likes. . . . But all this ease in our private relations does not make us lawless as citizens. Against this fear is our chief safeguard, teaching us to obey the magistrates and the laws. . . .

Further, we provide plenty of means for the mind to refresh itself from business. . . .

. . . We cultivate refinement without extravagance and knowledge without effeminacy. . . ."

"Nor was it lawful, indeed, for the father himself to breed up the children after his own fancy; but as soon as they were seven years old they were to be enrolled in certain companies . . . where they all lived under the same order and discipline. . . . Reading and writing they gave them, just enough to serve their turn; their chief care was to make them good subjects, and to teach them to endure pain and conquer in battle. To this end, as they grew in years, their discipline was proportionately increased. . . .

. . . No one was allowed to live after his own fancy; but the city was a sort of camp, in which every man had his share of . . . business set out, and looked upon himself not so much born to serve his own ends as the interest of his country."

The first step in comparing life in ancient Athens with life in Sparta is to establish categories for analysis. The categories here are the relationship of the citizen to the government and the value system.

You can discover the similarities and differences between Athens and Sparta by asking questions. For example: What was the purpose of government in each city-state? The purposes were similar in that the good of the group and the strength of the state were important to both societies. Both valued obedience to the law and loyalty to the government. The relationship of the citizen to the state, however, was different. Individuals in Athens could pursue their own interests freely as long as they obeyed the law. Sparta allowed no private interest apart from the state. Individuals were trained to think of the city-state above themselves. In addition, the Spartans valued the body over the mind; the strong body better protected the state. The Athenians felt that the mind should be cultivated so that individual initiative could develop.

What conclusion can you draw about Sparta and Athens by comparing the two societies? Sparta denied the individual full development, while the Athenian was encouraged to be creative and to develop the mind.

Practicing the Skill

What other conclusion can you draw about life in Athens and life in Sparta?

To apply this skill, see Applying History Study Skills on page 123.

which in turn were subdivided into more than 100 smaller units widely distributed geographically. The units had self-governing power and chose by lot the members of the Council of Five Hundred—50 from each tribe. Members served for one year and could not serve more than twice. The council proposed laws to the assembly, which met at least 10 times a year and was the source of ultimate authority.

Even the courts of Athens were now democratic. Jurors were chosen by lot, in keeping with the Athenian belief in the equality and fitness of all citizens for government service. Each man could plead his own case, and the jury of citizens voted by secret ballot.

Athenian democracy under Cleisthenes was what is called **direct democracy**. That is, all citizens participated directly in making decisions. In contrast, present-day democratic nations such as the United States are **representative democracies**, in which the citizens elect representatives to run the government for them.

Section 3 Review

1. **Define** helots, ephors, metics, archons, direct democracy, representative democracies
2. **Identify** Draco, Solon, Peisistratus, Cleisthenes
3. **Locate and Explain the Significance** Sparta, Athens, Piraeus
4. **Summarizing Ideas** Describe the government of Sparta, including the focus on militarism.
5. **Analyzing Ideas (a)** Describe the features of the early government of Athens. **(b)** What reforms occurred to transform this government into a democracy?

Section 4

Daily Life in Athens

Focus Questions

- What were the main economic activities in Athens?
- What were the characteristics of family life and education in Athenian society?

As far as we know, the citizens of Athens and most of the other Greek city-states (except Sparta) lived in much the same way. Private life and public life were carefully balanced.

Farming

More than half of all Athenian citizens farmed, despite the poor soil of the area. Many owned the small plots of land that they worked.

Athenian farmlands had to lie unplanted every second year so that the soil could regain fertility. To make matters worse, much of the land was unsuitable for raising grain. Thus farmers concentrated instead on growing olives, grapes, and figs on terraced hillsides. **Terracing** means creating small, flat plots of land by building low walls on the hillsides and filling the space behind them with soil. Athens exported olive oil and wine and imported much of the grain needed to feed its people.

The principal domestic animals were sheep and goats. People used goat's milk for making cheese, and they valued sheep for their wool and meat, although Athenians ate little meat. Fish, cheese, and grain made up much of their diet.

Manufacturing and Trade

Athenian manufacturing took place in small workshops. Many artisans worked in their homes, where family members labored side by side with slaves and free employees. Today the vases and household utensils of ancient Athens are greatly admired for their extraordinary grace and beauty. Yet ordinary workers, not famous artists, made most of these objects.

The Athenian economy depended on trade. The need to maintain and increase a reliable food supply influenced the policies of the Athenian government. This need made foreign trade a necessity and led to the building of the Athenian fleet. Athenian ships went everywhere in the Mediterranean world, from the Black Sea in the east to Spain in the west.

Homes and Streets

Although the Athenians built magnificent temples and other public buildings, they lived in simple homes. Generally, Athenians believed money should be spent on buildings to benefit the whole community, not on private homes. Buildings were crowded on narrow, crooked, dirty streets that lacked sanitation services.

Houses made of sun-dried brick sat close to the street and usually were one story high. The wall facing the street was often plain except for a door leading into an open court. From the court other doors opened into the living room, dining room, bedrooms,

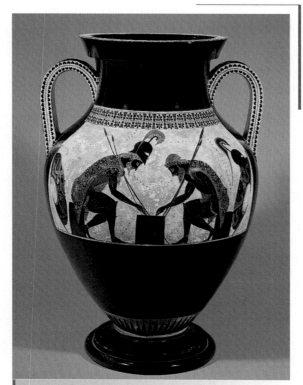

This vase, decorated in black-figured style by Exekias, an Athenian artisan of the mid-500s B.C., was exported to the Etruscan city of Vulci. The scene depicts the Greek heroes Achilles (with the feathered helmet) and Ajax absorbed in a board game.

storerooms, and kitchen. Lamps that burned olive oil furnished dim light. Houses had no plumbing. Although Peisistratus had built an aqueduct that brought water to a fountain near the agora, residents had to collect the water in jars from the fountain or elsewhere from wells or springs.

Family Life

Athenians considered marriage a very important institution. Its main purpose was the bearing and rearing of children. The parents always arranged the marriages. A girl married early, typically at age 13 or 14. The groom might be at least twice her age. As was true elsewhere at the time, many women died in childbirth because of poor medical knowledge. If a family could not afford to raise a baby, they often abandoned it to die, especially if it was a girl.

Legally and socially, Athenian women were considered inferior to men. Although women were citizens, they could not normally own or inherit property. (In Sparta, in contrast, women could inherit land.) A woman could not make a contract or bring a suit in court. In social life, too, Athenians usually expected women to remain in the background. They rarely appeared in public and then only with the permission of their husbands. Even during banquets or entertainment in the home, the wife stayed out of sight. Women's duties included managing the household and the slaves and raising the children.

In many Athenian households, the mother, aided by a female slave, took care of the children of both sexes until they were six. At the age of seven, a boy was placed in the care of a male slave, or **pedagogue**, who taught him manners and went everywhere with him, including to school. Girls stayed at home, where they learned how to run a household but usually received no other schooling. Some daughters of wealthy families, however, were taught to read and write.

Education and Military Service

Most Greeks were poor and hardworking. They labored long hours and had little leisure time. Wealthy men spent their time in the pursuit of intellectual and physical excellence. They engaged in politics, gossip in the marketplace, conversations with friends, and athletic activities.

Literacy and education were highly valued. Many boys therefore attended elementary schools, which charged fees. The cost was low, however, because teachers were not well paid. The schools taught literature—which included reading, writing, grammar, and poetry—music, and gymnastics. Students wrote on wax-covered wooden tablets. Poetry, including Homer's *Iliad* and *Odyssey,* was learned by heart.

The Athenian ideal stressed a sound mind in a healthy body. Grammar and music developed the mind and the emotions. Gymnastics developed the body. In open fields at the edge of the city, boys practiced running, jumping, boxing, and throwing the discus and the javelin.

In the 400s B.C., men who called themselves Sophists, from the Greek word *sophos,* meaning "wise," opened schools for older boys. Here the students studied poetry, government, ethics, mathematics, rhetoric, and other subjects. **Rhetoric** was the study of oratory, or public speaking, and debating. Today the word *rhetoric* means the art of speaking or writing effectively.

At the age of 18, a boy received a year of military training. A young man who could afford to pay for weapons and armor then served as a hoplite in the

Greek artists illustrated scenes from everyday life, such as hunting (top) and baking bread (bottom).

Section 4 Review

1. **Define** terracing, pedagogue, rhetoric
2. **Understanding Ideas** Why was Athens so dependent on trade?
3. **Interpreting Ideas** Describe Greek attitudes toward women in their society, as shown in marriage customs, the rights of citizenship, social life, and education.
4. **Analyzing Ideas** What does Greek education reveal about Greek society?

Section 5

The Expansion of Greece

Focus Questions

- **How did the Persian Wars begin, and what were their results?**
- **What was the Age of Pericles?**
- **What was the Peloponnesian War?**

The Greek city-states and their colonies around the Aegean, Black, and Mediterranean Seas developed for a long time without interference from the empires of Southwest Asia. Then the powerful Persian Empire intervened in Greek affairs, leading to war between the city-states and the Persians. Once they defeated the Persians, however, the Greeks warred among themselves.

The Persian Wars

In 546 B.C. Cyrus of Persia conquered Lydia in Asia Minor, acquiring the Greek city-states on the western coast of the Aegean as well. The Persians did not treat the Greeks cruelly and permitted them to keep their own local governments. When the Persian ruler Darius tightened Persian rule and raised taxes, however, the Greeks rebelled. Around 500 B.C. revolts broke out in several city-states of Asia Minor. These rebellions, which Athens aided, began a series of conflicts that lasted until 479 B.C. Together they are known as the Persian Wars.

Darius easily crushed the revolts. He wanted, however, to punish Athens for its support of the Greek rebels and to control the city-states on the Greek mainland as well as those of Asia Minor. Darius sent a Persian army and a fleet toward Greece in 492 B.C.,

army for a year. The hoplites made up the center of the infantry in battle. Poorer men, who were not as well equipped, served on the army's flanks. Citizens also rowed the warships of the Athenian fleet.

Education played an important role in the spreading of both the Greek language and Greek civilization throughout the Mediterranean world. Traders commonly spoke Greek, which was a second language for educated non-Greeks everywhere. Even today we use many words that are derived from Greek. We can hardly write or talk about government without using such Greek-derived terms as *politics*, *democracy*, and *aristocracy*. Most terms used in medicine also come from the Greek language. For example, the Greek ending *-itis* means "an inflammation" and is part of the words *appendicitis* and *tonsillitis*, among many others.

reestablishing control over Thrace and Macedonia. Much of the fleet was shipwrecked off the Greek coast, however, and the expedition was delayed, but only temporarily. (See map on this page.) In 490 B.C. Darius launched an invasion of Greece itself. The Persians landed on the coast of Attica and set up camp on the plain of Marathon, some 24 miles northeast of Athens. Although the Persians greatly outnumbered the Athenians, the Athenian army defeated the Persians at the Battle of Marathon.

For 10 years an uneasy peace existed. Then in 480 B.C., the dreaded news spread throughout Greece that Darius's son Xerxes was coming with a vast army and fleet gathered from every part of the Persian Empire. An exaggerated report stated that the Persian army was so large that when it stopped to drink water,

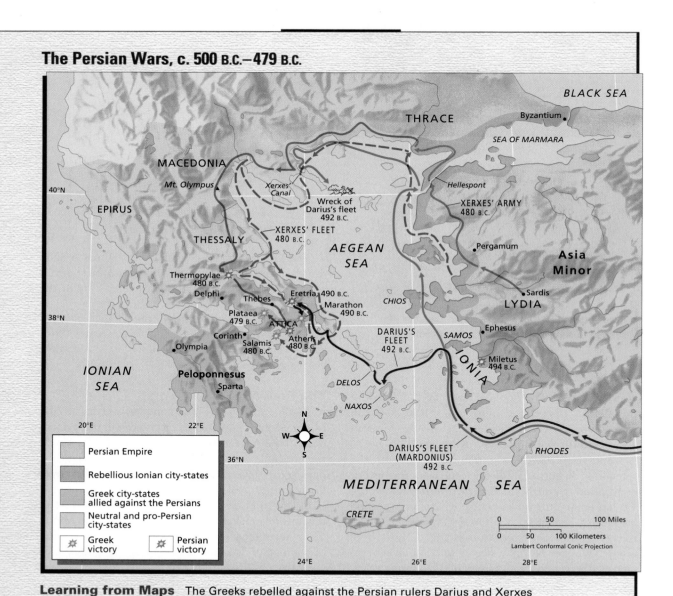

The Persian Wars, c. 500 B.C.–479 B.C.

Learning from Maps The Greeks rebelled against the Persian rulers Darius and Xerxes in a series of conflicts between 500 B.C. and 479 B.C.

? Location Identify the three battles that the Greeks won.

whole rivers ran dry. Modern historians estimate Xerxes' army numbered somewhere around 100,000 troops. This army marched through Thrace and Macedonia toward northern Greece.

Greeks from several city-states united to face the Persians. To advance from northern Greece into central Greece, the Persians had to march through the narrow mountain pass of Thermopylae (thuhr·MAH·puh·lee). There King Leonidas of Sparta, leading a force of 300 Spartans and several hundred other Greeks, met a vastly larger Persian army.

The Greeks valiantly held the narrow pass against the Persians for three days. Finally, a Greek traitor showed the Persians another way through the mountains. Aware that the Greek forces could not possibly turn back the Persians, Leonidas sent many of them home, but the Spartans and some others remained. Surrounded, the Spartans and the other Greeks refused to surrender and fought until every one of them was killed. Although the Persian army could now continue its march into Greece, the Spartans' courage inspired the other city-states to fight on. Even today the Battle of Thermopylae is a symbol of resistance against overwhelming odds.

Now the Persians moved on Athens, which was in turmoil. The Athenian leader Themistocles (thuh·MIS·tuh·kleez) persuaded his people to abandon their city and take refuge elsewhere. With Athens evacuated, Xerxes' army entered the city and destroyed it.

The next crucial battle was fought at sea. Themistocles tricked Xerxes into attacking the Athenian fleet in the Salamis strait. The narrow waters of the strait nullified the numerical advantage of the Persian navy and prevented their ships from maneuvering. From atop a nearby mountain, Xerxes watched in horror as the Athenians took advantage of their position to ram the Persian ships and engage in hand-to-hand combat, defeating and sinking much of the Persian fleet.

After the lost naval battle, Xerxes returned home with part of his army. The next year, 479 B.C., Athenians and Spartans combined to defeat a Persian army at Plataea, northwest of Athens. The survivors of the Persian forces fled in disorder. The Persian Wars were over.

Significance of the Greek Victory

Winning the Persian Wars did not immediately seem like a great victory for Greece. Although the Greek cities of Asia Minor were freed for a time from Persian rule, the Persian Empire remained powerful, and its rulers continued to meddle in Greek affairs. The Persians actively worked to prevent unity in Greece.

From a long-range viewpoint, however, the Battles of Marathon, Salamis, and Plataea are considered decisive. Success against the Persians gave the Greeks confidence. Athens went on to create its own empire in the Aegean Sea area and entered a period of unparalleled cultural achievement.

Athens as Leader

After the destruction caused by the Persian occupation, the Athenians rebuilt their city with magnificent temples and other public buildings. Although the Persians had been defeated, the threat of invasion from the Persian Empire continued. Unity among the Greek city-states seemed necessary for survival.

Sparta wanted Greek unity under its own leadership, but fear of helot revolt kept the Spartans from sending expeditions far from home for very long. Even Sparta's strong army could not extend its power much beyond the Peloponnesus.

Athens was more successful, using diplomacy to form the Delian League, a system of alliances that ultimately included some 140 other city-states. Each city-state contributed either ships or money to the alliance. The league's funds were deposited on the island of Delos (from which the name *Delian* is derived). As the league's leading city-state, Athens had the power to decide how many ships and how much money other city-states would contribute.

When Xerxes died in 465 B.C., the threat of Persian invasion ended. The Delian League, however, continued under Athens' domination. By the 450s B.C., it had become an Athenian empire.

What If?

The Persian Wars
The Greek victory over Persia ensured the survival of Greek civilization. As a result, the Greek ideal of democracy, rather than the Persian concept of rule by an absolute monarch, was passed on to the Western world. How do you think a Persian victory would have affected the establishment of governments in the Western world?

Age of Pericles

During this time, the great general, orator, and statesman Pericles was the leader in Athens. Pericles served as general for many years, and he dominated Athenian public affairs from about 461 B.C. to 429 B.C., even when he was not actually holding office. This was the time of Athens' greatest power and prosperity. So significant was Pericles' leadership that this period of Athenian history is called the Age of Pericles.

Under Pericles, Athenian democracy reached its height. (The chart on this page shows the major steps in the growth of Athenian democracy.) All male citizens could hold public office. Officeholders received salaries. Most offices were in fact chosen by lot, ensuring that no one had an advantage. Athens was probably the most completely democratic government in history. Remember, however, that women rarely participated in public life and many Athenian residents did not hold citizenship. Also, Athens was a society supported by slavery.

The Athenian Empire

Although Athens' own government was democratic, within the Delian League, Athens made the decisions. The Athenian historian Thucydides (thoo·SID·uh·deez) recorded an Athenian advising his colleagues:

> **"Your empire is a tyranny . . . over subjects who do not like it and who are always plotting against you; you will not make them obey you by injuring your own interests . . . ; your leadership depends on superior strength and not on any goodwill of theirs."**

Pericles moved the Delian League's treasury from Delos to Athens and used its money to benefit Athens. He enlarged the league by forcing more city-states to join. Athenian forces crushed revolts by other city-states against its policies. Discontent grew.

Pericles seems to have hoped to unify Greece under Athenian leadership. This hope failed, however. Other city-states increasingly resented Athens' domination. Quarrels with Athens' commercial rival, Corinth, and with Sparta and its allies worsened tensions until a devastating war broke out in 431 B.C. The war is called the Peloponnesian War.

The Peloponnesian War

Athens and Sparta shared responsibility for the Peloponnesian War. There was commercial rivalry among a number of city-states. However, Athens and Sparta were long-standing rivals, opposite of each other in many respects. Athens was broadly democratic, open, and culturally progressive; by comparison, Sparta was a less democratic, more closed, and culturally backward society.

Provoked by the Athenians' flaunting of power, Sparta began the fighting. Neither side tried very hard to avoid war. Thucydides wrote: "The Peloponnesus and Athens were both full of young men whose inexperience made them eager to take up arms."

The Spartans, with the stronger army, invaded Attica, the region surrounding Athens. With their fields and villages destroyed, the Athenians withdrew behind their defensive walls. The Spartans could not starve them out because Athens, with its superior navy, controlled the sea and could therefore bring in food by ship. A terrible plague broke out in 430 B.C. among the Athenians, however. Many people, including Pericles, died of the disease.

The war went on intermittently for a generation, with great loss of life. Even during a period of peace, Athens could not resist the temptation to attack the Greek city of Syracuse, friendly to Sparta, in Sicily. The attack, which occurred between 415 B.C. and 413 B.C., was a total failure, however. At home the Athenian democratic government was discredited,

Democracy in Athens

621 B.C.	Law code attributed to Draco was drawn up.
594 B.C.	Solon abolished enslavement for debt, defined political rights in terms of wealth rather than birth, established court of appeals.
546–527 B.C.	Peisistratus, tyrant who ruled with support of lower classes, may have divided nobles' estates among poor farmers.
508 B.C.	Cleisthenes broke up power of aristocrats and created Council of Five Hundred, chosen from local government units, with wide power.
461–429 B.C.	Pericles opened offices to all male citizens and provided that office holders be paid.

Delos, an island in the Aegean Sea, was once a center of religious, political, and commercial life. Excavations since 1873 have unearthed nine marble lions similar to the one seen here.

and aristocrats seized power in the city. They were soon overthrown, and democracy was restored, but Athens was seriously weakened. Eventually, Sparta, with the help of Persia, managed to block food supplies from reaching Athens. Starving, Athens finally surrendered to Sparta in 404 B.C.

Greek Disunity

After the defeat of Athens, Sparta attempted to dominate Greece. Sparta's harsh rule provoked resistance, however. Thebes defeated Sparta in 371 B.C. and tried to control all of Greece. Theban rule was not successful either, however, and the ruinous wars continued.

Greece was politically unsettled. Desiring unity, some Greeks believed it could come only under a foreign power. Persia was one possibility. The power that did bring unity to Greece, however, was not to appear for more than a generation. In the meantime, as you will read in Chapter 6, the Greek civilization created tremendous achievements.

Section 5 Review

1. **Identify** Darius, Xerxes, Themistocles, Pericles
2. **Locate and Explain the Significance** Marathon, Thermopylae, Salamis, Delos
3. **Understanding Ideas** Why are the Battles of Marathon, Salamis, and Plataea considered decisive in the history of the world?
4. **Interpreting Ideas** Why was the period from 461 B.C. to 429 B.C. called the Age of Pericles?
5. **Analyzing Ideas** How did differences between Athens and Sparta contribute to the Peloponnesian War?

Chapter 5 Review

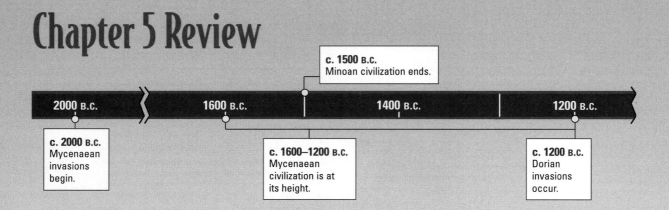

c. 1500 b.c.
Minoan civilization ends.

| 2000 B.C. | 1600 B.C. | 1400 B.C. | 1200 B.C. |

c. 2000 b.c.
Mycenaean invasions begin.

c. 1600–1200 b.c.
Mycenaean civilization is at its height.

c. 1200 b.c.
Dorian invasions occur.

Chapter Summary

The following list contains the key concepts you have learned about ancient Greece.

1. The geography of Greece was not as favorable to settlement as that of the great river valleys in Egypt and Southwest Asia.
2. The Greeks became traders in order to increase their food supply and to improve the quality of their lives.
3. The Minoan culture of Crete was an important early influence on the Greeks.
4. Around 2000 B.C. various invaders entered Greece. The invaders known as Mycenaeans dominated Greece during this period.
5. The polis was considered the basic political unit of ancient Greece.
6. After being ruled by kings, nobles, and tyrants for hundreds of years, some Greek city-states adopted popular governments, or democracies.
7. Sparta was a powerful militaristic city-state in which a select few inhabitants were considered citizens and ran the government.
8. Athens gradually adopted a democratic system of government.
9. The Athenian economy depended on farming, manufacturing, and trade.
10. After the Greeks defeated the Persian invaders, Athens became the leader of the Delian League.
11. Athens enjoyed a prosperous period under the leadership of Pericles. Although many in Athens could not participate in government, those who did participate enjoyed one of the most democratic governments the world has ever seen.
12. Rivalries among the city-states led to the disastrous Peloponnesian War, which lasted from 431 B.C. to 404 B.C.

Reviewing Important Terms

On a separate sheet of paper, supply the term that correctly completes each statement.

1. The civilization that evolved in Europe and spread to the Americas is called _____ _____.
2. City-states governed by nobles were _____.
3. To the ancient Greeks, a(n) _____ was someone who seized power in defiance of law but ruled with the support of the people.
4. The idea that people could and should rule themselves rather than be ruled by others is called _____ _____.
5. A government in which all citizens take part is a(n) _____.
6. A system in which people select representatives to run the government is a(n) _____ _____.
7. Most city-states were originally built on a hill or mountain called a(n) _____.

Developing Critical Thinking Skills

1. **Understanding Chronology** Identify each of the following items and place them in the correct chronological order: (a) Mycenaean civilization; (b) early aristocratic city-states; (c) Minoan civilization; (d) early age of democracy; (e) Age of Tyrants.
2. **Comparing Ideas** (a) Compare the form of government in Sparta with the government in Athens under Pericles. (b) How do you account for the differences?
3. **Interpreting Ideas** Explain how democracy developed in Athens.
4. **Analyzing Primary Sources** Reread the excerpt from Thucydides on page 120. (a) Why do you think the Athenians championed democratic ideals in their city-state but denied them to other members of the Delian League? (b) How might this have contributed to the eventual defeat of Athens?

Relating Geography to History

Study the maps on pages 102, 105, 110, and 118. How did the geography of Greece influence the patterns of

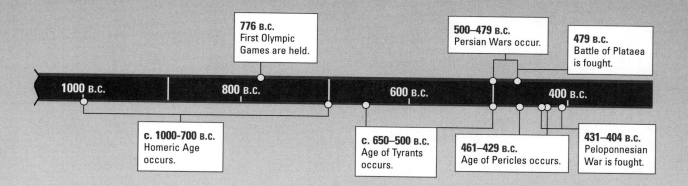

776 B.C.
First Olympic Games are held.

500–479 B.C.
Persian Wars occur.

479 B.C.
Battle of Plataea is fought.

1000 B.C.   800 B.C.   600 B.C.   400 B.C.

c. 1000–700 B.C.
Homeric Age occurs.

c. 650–500 B.C.
Age of Tyrants occurs.

461–429 B.C.
Age of Pericles occurs.

431–404 B.C.
Peloponnesian War is fought.

settlement and the types of government that the ancient Greeks developed?

Relating Past to Present

1. Sports were important in the culture of ancient Greece, where Olympic Games originated. The modern Olympics trace their origins to these ancient Greek games. **(a)** How does the importance of sports and physical fitness in our society compare with that in ancient Greece? **(b)** In what ways do the modern Olympics differ from the ancient Greek Olympics?

2. Compare the ideas and practices of Greek democracy with the democratic ideals of American government in the following areas: **(a)** right of citizenship; **(b)** right to hold public office; **(c)** right to vote; **(d)** passage and review of laws.

Applying History Study Skills

Before completing this activity, review Building History Study Skills on page 114.

Read the following descriptions of the treatment of women in Athens and Sparta. Then answer the questions below to compare the two societies' views of the status and role of women.

Athens

"And since both the indoor and the outdoor tasks demand labour and attention, God from the first adapted the woman's nature, I think, to the indoor and man's to the outdoor tasks and cares.

For he made the man's body and mind more capable of enduring the cold and heat, and journeys and campaigns; . . . To the woman, since he has made her body less capable of such endurance, . . . God has assigned the indoor tasks. And knowing that he had created in the woman and had imposed on her the nourishment of the infants, he meted out to her a larger portion of affection for new-born babes than to the man. . . .Thus, to the woman it is more honourable to stay indoors than to abide in the fields, but to the man it is unseemly rather to stay indoors than to attend to the work outside."

(from Xenophon, *Oeconomicus*)

Sparta

"The truth is, he [Lycurgus] took in their case, also, all the care that was possible; he ordered the maidens to exercise themselves with wrestling, running, throwing the quoit, and casting the dart. . . . Hence it was natural for them to think and speak as Gorgo, for example, the wife of Leonidas, is said to have done, when some foreign lady . . . told her that the women of Lacedaemon [the Spartans' name for their city] were the only women in the world who could rule men; `With good reason,' she said, `for we are the only women who bring forth men.'"

(Plutarch's *Lives*)

1. **(a)** What were the similarities between the role and status of women in Athens and the role and status of women in Sparta? **(b)** What were the differences?

2. Do you think Spartan women were more respected than Athenian women? Why or why not?

3. How does the status of women in Athens and in Sparta compare with that of women in the United States today?

---

internetconnect

Search the Internet through the HRW Web site for information on the Minoan civilization of Crete. Write a short report on the aspect of Minoan civilization that you found most interesting.

 **GO TO:** go.hrw.com
KEYWORD: SCØ Minoan

Building Your Portfolio

1. **Writing a Report** Find books or magazine articles about the excavations at Mycenae. Then write a report on this important archaeological site. Be sure to discuss how archaeologists were involved in these excavations. Place the report in your portfolio.

2. **Constructing a Chart** Construct a chart that compares Greek religion with the religions of the Egyptians, Persians, and Hebrews that you studied in Chapter 2. What are the differences and similarities? Place the chart in your portfolio.

Greece's Golden and Hellenistic Ages

TIME

478 B.C.–146 B.C.

478 B.C.–146 B.C.

3.7 million B.C. | 4000 B.C. | A.D. 2100

PLACE

Greece, Southwest Asia, Egypt, and Persia

Greece

ARCTIC OCEAN
NORTH AMERICA
EUROPE
ASIA
PACIFIC OCEAN
AFRICA
Equator
SOUTH AMERICA
INDIAN OCEAN
AUSTRALIA
PACIFIC OCEAN
ATLANTIC OCEAN
ANTARCTICA

Egypt

Persian Empire

Southwest Asia

Alexander the Great from mosaic at Casa del Fauno in Pompeii

Significance

Greek culture reached new heights during the 400s B.C.—a period so magnificent that it is often called Greece's golden age.

In the 300s B.C., an outside power, Macedonia, conquered the Greek city-states. An extraordinary commander, Alexander the Great, made possible the development of the **Hellenistic culture**—a new culture combining Greek ideas and features from other cultures of the Mediterranean region.

Terms to Define

Hellenistic culture	hubris
philosopher	comedies
philosophy	infantry
dramas	phalanx
tragedies	orators

People to Identify

Myron	Aristophanes
Phidias	Philip II of Macedonia
Praxiteles	Demosthenes
Socrates	Alexander the Great
Plato	Diogenes
Aristotle	Pyrrho
Pythagoras	Zeno
Democritus	Epicurus
Hippocrates	Euclid
Herodotus	Archimedes
Thucydides	Aristarchus
Aeschylus	Hipparchus
Sophocles	Eratosthenes
Euripides	

Places to Locate

Athens	Egypt
Macedonia	Indus River
Syria	Susa

Chapter Theme Questions

- **The Arts** How might the arts reflect a civilization's ideals?
- **Philosophy and Science** How might great intellectual achievements affect life within a culture as well as cultures that follow it?
- **Cross-Cultural Interaction** What kind of interplay might occur between conquering and conquered cultures?

History records the feats of the Macedonian conqueror known as Alexander the Great primarily in terms of military conquest. Those who knew Alexander, however, saw the soul of the man, the emotion inspired by poetry and music, the uncontrollable temper, the grief he bore when his army suffered, and the frenzied excitement of victory.

Much of what is known about Alexander's early life is legend. One famous story is recounted by the Greek historian Plutarch. When Alexander was a young teenager, a fine stallion was presented to his father, Philip II of Macedonia. The horse reared, thrashed its hooves, and shied away from everyone. Watching the stallion, Alexander realized that it was not unmanageable but merely afraid of the movement of its own shadow. "I could manage this horse," Alexander stated, "better than others do." Given the opportunity, he turned the horse to face the sun, causing the horse's shadow to fall out of its sight. Alexander then easily mounted the horse.

Seeing his young son's success, Philip turned proudly to Alexander and said, "O my son, look thee out a kingdom equal to and worthy of thyself, for Macedonia is too little for thee." Philip saw something in the young prince that day that historians can write about but never define—the elements of greatness that shape human history. These qualities in Alexander the Great sparked the spread of Greek culture throughout the Mediterranean world.

Section 1

Greek Art of the Golden Age

Focus Questions

- **What were great works of Greek architecture?**
- **What were the primary characteristics of Greek art?**

After the Persian Wars, the wealth and power of Athens attracted artists and teachers from throughout Greece. As Greece's center of art and culture, Athens inspired many people whose artistic and literary contributions had a tremendous and lasting impact on Western civilization. The peak of cultural activity in Athens occurred during the 400s B.C.

Greek Funeral Stele

In the 400s B.C., the Greeks had somewhat vague ideas about their immortality, assuming some sort of "shadowy" existence after death. Greek funerals did not involve priests, hymns, or prayers. They emphasized the memory of the deceased. The Greeks erected steles (stee·leez), or stone slabs, to commemorate their dead permanently and publicly. Many steles were elaborate, with stylized figures symbolizing how the dead person had lived and worked—for example, as a soldier, a farmer, or a politician. By 400 B.C. simple scenes showing the deceased with their families, in courageous feats, or preparing for death decorated steles.

The *Grave Stele of Hegeso* is from the late 400s B.C. It captures a lovely Athenian woman as she carefully selects a precious jewel from a jewelry box held by her servant. Perhaps Hegeso is planning to wear the jewel on her journey to the next world. The stele is set inside an architectural frame, typical of the classic style. Symmetry and balance, so important in Greek art, are evident in this stele. Hegeso's right hand is located precisely in the center of the relief. In keeping with the Greek idealization of human beings, the unknown sculptor suggests that Hegeso was beautiful in spirit as well as in body.

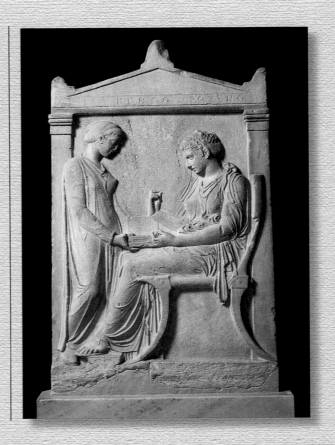

Architecture

The Athenians surrounded themselves with beauty. They showed their love of Athens and their pride in it by erecting impressive temples, gymnasiums, and theaters. They decorated these structures with their finest works of art, especially sculpture.

The Acropolis, the center of the original polis, provided the backdrop for special artistic creations. A magnificent gate graced the entrance to the path up the hill. Nearby towered a bronze statue of the goddess Athena that stood 30 feet high.

At the top of the Acropolis stood the Parthenon, a white marble temple built in honor of Athena. Begun in 447 B.C. and completed about 15 years later, it is considered the finest example of Greek architecture.

This splendid structure measures approximately 230 feet long, 100 feet wide, and 60 feet high. Its exquisite beauty lay not in its great size but in its graceful design and balanced proportions—the relation of length to width, and of length and width to height.

Like most Greek temples, built as shrines rather than meeting places for worshippers, the Parthenon had doors but no windows. A series of columns, or a colonnade, encircled the structure. Sculpted figures painted in a variety of vivid colors adorned the slabs of marble above the columns. Inside the Parthenon stood an even larger statue of Athena. Made of ivory and gold, it stood 38 feet high. Today people consider this type of sculpture and architecture one of the greatest gifts of the Greeks to Western civilization.

Painting

Modern scholars know that painting was an important form of art in ancient Greece. Unfortunately, because almost all of the originals have been lost or severely damaged, our knowledge of Greek painting comes mainly from literary descriptions and from later Roman copies. The best-preserved Greek paintings are found on vases. Greek vase painters illustrated scenes from everyday life as well as mythological events. These artists delighted in showing graceful and natural movements of their subjects. Some vase painters could depict light and shade on the pottery, which was a technique used to show contour and depth.

Sculpture

As with Greek painting, few original works of Greek sculpture still exist. What we know about Greek sculpture has come chiefly from studying the copies made during Roman times.

The Greek sculpture of earlier centuries had been highly structured, with figures in stiff, unnatural poses. By the 400s B.C., Greek sculptors were creating more dynamic, natural figures.

Myron and Phidias (FID·ee·uhs), two of history's greatest sculptors, lived during the golden age. Myron sculpted the famous figure *The Discus Thrower*. Phidias created the two exquisite statues of Athena that were on the Acropolis and in the Parthenon. His greatest work, however, was the statue of Zeus at the Temple of Olympia. Greeks who attended the Olympic Games viewed the statue, which was nearly 40 feet high, with awe. In ancient times, people considered this statue one of the Seven Wonders of the World.

Praxiteles (prak·SIT·uhl·eez), who lived about 100 years after Phidias, created quite a different kind of

This marble statue, *Hermes Carrying the Infant Dionysus,* c. 340 B.C., embodies Praxiteles' admiration for the human body through graceful modeling of forms and delicate surface finish.

sculpture. While Phidias created large, formal, dignified works appropriate for the gods, Praxiteles created more delicate, lifelike, often life-sized figures. Above all, Praxiteles expressed the Greek admiration for the beauty of the human body.

The Nature of Greek Art

Throughout Greek history architecture, painting, and sculpture reflected the Greeks' view of themselves and the world. Four characteristics in particular helped establish the style of this great art. First, Greek art glorified human beings. Much of the painting and sculpture portrayed gods and goddesses, but the Greeks clearly placed great importance on the actions and works of human beings. Greek painters and sculptors idealized their human subjects, omitting any blemishes. The faces and figures of men and women represented the Greek ideal of beauty. The statues also suggested other ideal traits admired by the Greeks—strength, intelligence, pride, grace, and courage.

Second, Greek art symbolized the people's pride in their city-states. At the same time, it honored the gods, thanked them for life and fortune, and tried to win their favor. Thus, in giving Athena a beautiful shrine in the Parthenon, the Athenians showed their love for their city and their hope for its continuing good fortune.

Third, Greek art expressed Greek ideals of harmony, balance, order, and moderation. By moderation, the Greeks meant simplicity and restraint—qualities that they emphasized in their day-to-day lives.

Finally, Greek art expressed the Greek belief in combining beauty and usefulness. In Greek culture the useful, the beautiful, and the good were closely bound together. Most Greek art was functional, with a purpose that was clearly defined.

Section 1 Review

1. **Define** Hellenistic culture
2. **Identify** Myron, Phidias, Praxiteles
3. **Locate and Explain the Significance** Athens
4. **Understanding Ideas** Briefly explain how the following quotation can be applied to Greek architecture: "Nothing in excess, and everything in proportion."
5. **Comparing Ideas** How did the style of Phidias differ from that of Praxiteles?
6. **Analyzing Ideas (a)** List four characteristics of Greek art. **(b)** How did each reflect Greek ideals?

Section 2

Philosophers and Writers of the Golden Age

Focus Questions

- **What basic ideas did Socrates, Plato, and Aristotle express?**
- **What did mathematicians and scientists of the golden age accomplish?**
- **What important literary forms originated or flourished during Greece's golden age?**

The Greeks have been honored through the ages for their artistic and intellectual achievements. Few people before them—and few since—have demonstrated so clearly the capacity of the human hand and mind. One of their greatest achievements was the development of philosophy, an attempt to understand themselves and the world around them.

The Cosmologists

According to tradition, the first Greek **philosopher**—a word meaning "lover of wisdom"—was Thales of Miletus, a city in Ionia on the western coast of present-day Turkey. [From the term philosopher comes our word **philosophy**, or the study of the most fundamental questions of reality and human existence.] Thales and others like him wanted to understand the origins and nature of the cosmos, or universe. Consequently, they are known as cosmologists. Their ideas and questions about the universe stimulated others throughout the Greek world. For example, Pythagoras, a Greek living in one of the colonies in southern Italy, developed a mathematical explanation for the universe. He believed that everything could be explained on the basis of numerical relationships or ratios. This rational approach to the universe in turn inspired Parmenides of Elea to develop formal rules of logic for philosophical arguments. Using both formal logic and mathematics, a Greek philosopher from Thrace, Democritus, later developed atomic theory—the idea that the entire universe is made up of tiny particles of matter, which he called atoms. As Greece entered its golden age, however, the focus of philosophical inquiry began to shift from cosmology and investigations of the physical universe to questions about the nature of human beings themselves and their societies. One of the most important philosophers of this new era was an Athenian, Socrates.

Socrates

Socrates (SAHK·ruh·teez), one of history's greatest thinkers and teachers, lived in Athens from 470 B.C. to 399 B.C. The son of a sculptor and a midwife, Socrates served as an infantry soldier during the Peloponnesian Wars before becoming a teacher.

Socrates criticized Athenian education, especially the teachings of the Sophists. One of his criticisms was that they took money for teaching, something he refused to do. Unlike the Sophists, Socrates did not rely on the teaching method of memorization. He wanted people to think for themselves. Only then could they acquire wisdom, which would lead to "right living." According to Socrates, evil could result only from ignorance. He believed that "the unexamined life is not worth living." Consequently, Socrates taught by engaging his students in logical discussions. He asked questions that required careful thought. As his students provided answers, he would ask further questions. Constantly repeating his motto, "Know thyself," Socrates tried to get people to understand the real meaning for them of love, friendship, duty, patriotism, honor, justice, and other concepts. This way of teaching involving persistent questioning became known as the Socratic method.

Although greatly loved because of his wisdom, honesty, and kindness, Socrates also had enemies. His questions often made public officials look foolish. He also criticized democracy. He believed it unwise for unskilled people to hold positions of power.

Though Socrates honored the gods of Athens, his enemies accused him of denying the existence of many Greek gods. The Athenian leaders brought him to trial on charges of impiety—or not showing proper respect—and for corrupting the minds of Athenian youth.

Socrates did little to defend himself and refused to allow any compromise in his sentencing. Found guilty and condemned to die by drinking a poison made from the hemlock plant, he accepted his fate.

Plato

Although Socrates never recorded his ideas, later generations learned of them from the writings of Plato, a wealthy young aristocrat and the greatest of Socrates' students. After the death of Socrates, Plato traveled throughout the Mediterranean region. He then returned to Athens and founded the Academy, a school devoted to teaching philosophy.

Plato wrote dialogues, or imaginary conversations among several people, covering such topics as government, education, justice, virtue, and religion. In most of the dialogues, Socrates is the primary speaker who asks questions of the others. The dialogues, however, expressed many of Plato's theories as well. Perhaps his most important idea was the "Theory of Forms," that everything physical was merely an imperfect expression of a perfect universal form, or idea.

Plato was also interested in politics. In one of the dialogues, for example, Socrates asks "What is justice?" To answer the question, Plato wrote the *Republic*, a long dialogue describing his concept of the ideal organization of society. People, he said, should do the work for which they are best suited. For example, those noted for their bravery should be in the army. People interested in material goods such as food, clothing, and luxuries should conduct the business and perform the labor. Plato's ideal government was an aristocracy—a government ruled by an upper class. However, it was not an aristocracy of birth or of wealth but one based on intelligence, reasoning, education, and high ideals. Plato's ideal "aristocrats" were philosophers, chosen for their wisdom, ability, and "correct" ideas about justice.

Aristotle

Among Plato's students in the Academy was a young man named Aristotle, who founded his own school at Athens in 335 B.C. Aristotle believed that logic was not separate from but preliminary to the study of every kind of knowledge. He vigorously collected as many facts as possible and then organized them into systems, comparing one fact with another to find out what each meant or showed. Aristotle demonstrated a special skill for defining words and grouping similar or related facts. This process of organization forms an important part of modern scientific thinking.

Aristotle almost accomplished his goal of investigating every known field of knowledge in his time. He collected, described, and classified plants and animals. For his book *Ethics*, Aristotle examined the acts and beliefs of individuals to learn what brought them the greatest happiness. He concluded that the Greek ideal of style in the arts—balance, order, and restraint—also represented the ideal in terms of human behavior. In his work *Poetics*, he examined Greek drama to show the differences between a good play and a bad one. Aristotle studied the political organization of 150 city-states to describe the principles of government, and he recorded his conclusions in a book called *Politics*. He concluded that the best type of government contained a middle class—people neither wealthy nor poor—who played an important role. As he wrote in the following excerpt:

"The middle class is least likely to shrink from rule, or to be overambitious for it; both of which are injuries to the state. . . . But a city ought to be composed, as far as possible, of equals and similars; and these are generally the middle classes. . . .

Thus it is manifest that the best political community is formed by citizens of the middle class, and that those states are likely to be well administered in which the middle class is large, and stronger if possible than both the other classes, or at any rate than either singly; for the addition of the middle class turns the scale, and prevents either of the extremes from being dominant."

Aristotle's political writings, like those of other major philosophers of the golden age, reflected his study of Greek culture and his experiences in public life. Aristotle believed that although pure monarchy, aristocracy, and democracy were equally good forms of government, each could too easily be corrupted. For example, he believed that the power of the people in a democracy could easily lead to a dictatorship of the "mob." Aristotle's perfect government harmonized the best aspects of the three types and was a kind of limited democracy.

This belief contrasted with Plato's belief that one level of government should control a person's life for the benefit of the whole state. According to Plato, people of the lower classes could never rise above their position in society and achieve a good life without the guidance of intellectual leaders who represented a higher level of authority.

Mathematics and Science

For the Greeks, philosophy encompassed all categories of knowledge, including what we know today as mathematics and science. The philosopher Pythagoras, for example, is perhaps best remembered for his development of the Pythagorean theorem, which states that

This mosaic depicts Plato's Academy, founded around 387 B.C. as an institute to instruct students in the systematic pursuit of philosophical knowledge and scientific research.

the square of the hypotenuse of a right triangle is equal to the sum of the squares of the other two sides.

The lack of specialization in philosophical inquiry, however, kept the Greeks from fully developing practical scientific knowledge until much later. Aristotle did little more than lay the foundations for the development of botany, zoology, and anatomy.

The Greeks did make very important advances in medicine. Hippocrates (hip·AHK·ruh·teez), considered the founder of medicine, taught that all disease comes from natural causes, not as punishment from the gods. He believed that rest, fresh air, and a proper diet made the best cures.

Hippocrates had high ideals for physicians. Today medical doctors still take the Hippocratic oath—a pledge to follow the code of medical ethics based on Hippocrates' teachings. Part of this Hippocratic oath follows.

❝I swear by . . . that I will carry out, according to my ability and judgment, this oath and this indenture. . . . I will use treatment to help the sick according to my ability and judgment, but never with a view to injury and wrongdoing. . . . In whatsoever houses I enter, I will enter to help the sick, and I will abstain from all intentional wrongdoing and harm, especially from abusing the bodies of man or woman, bond or free. And whatsoever I shall see or hear in the course of my profession in my intercourse with men, if it be what should not be published abroad, I will never divulge, holding such things to be holy secrets. . . .**❞**

History

The Greeks became the first people to take the writing of history seriously. Herodotus, an enthusiastic traveler and the first historian of the Western world, visited Babylonia, Phoenicia, and Egypt. He included his impressions of these countries and their people in his histories.

A fascinating writer and a wonderful storyteller, Herodotus exaggerated at times but always carefully distinguished between the things he had personally seen or investigated and those he had been told. He often expressed doubt about legends but reported them for whatever they might be worth. Historians still consult his writings for information about the world during his time, and he is often called the Father of History.

Another Greek historian, Thucydides, became famous for his *History of the Peloponnesian War.* Thucydides believed that studying the past yields an understanding of human nature, and he strove to

The theater at Epidaurus, a commercial city on the eastern coast of the Peloponnesus, dates from the mid-300s B.C. Built into the side of a hill, it is one of the best-preserved Greek theaters, with 55 rows of benches seating about 14,000 people.

make his account of history reflect this belief. To aid this understanding, he tried to make his history unbiased and accurate.

Greek Drama

Greeks living in Athens during the golden age wrote a surprising proportion of the world's greatest works of literature. A flood of creative writing occurred during that brief period. Greek literature still endures today because of its simple, graceful, and realistic portrayal of human beings.

The Greeks were the first people to write **dramas**, or plays containing action or dialogue and usually involving conflict and emotion. They excelled in this form of literature and always wrote plays in poetic form. Two or three actors and a chorus—a group of singers who described the scene and commented on the action—spoke or sang the lines for an audience.

The Greeks carved outdoor theaters into hillsides and they built seats for the audience into the slopes of these hillsides. At the bottom of the hill was the *orchestra*, the area where the chorus and the actors performed. Greek theaters did not have raised stages such as the Romans used for plays. Also, unlike the "sets" of many plays today, sets for Greek dramas featured little scenery. Audiences relied on choral descriptions to set the time and place of various scenes.

The male actors, their voices trained to produce variety in tone and pitch, also played women's roles. They wore elaborate padded costumes to make them look larger than life. Actors also used masks to indicate the characters and emotions they portrayed.

Greek actors wore masks, such as this one, as theatrical devices to represent various characters and emotions.

Performed in connection with religious festivals, Greek dramas often focused on a religious theme. Each spring three playwrights were invited to compete at the annual festival held in honor of Dionysus, the god of fertility and wine. Called the Great Dionysia, this became Athens' major dramatic competition. Each playwright produced three tragedies, plus a lighthearted play for comic relief. A panel of judges, made up of ordinary citizens chosen by lottery, awarded prizes, judging each play by the beauty of the language and the wisdom of its ideas.

Tragedies. In Greek **tragedies**, the main character struggled against fate. Usually a combination of outside forces overcame the central character. Tragic heroes often suffered from **hubris** (HYOO·bruhs), or excessive pride in themselves or their accomplishments. Hubris offended the gods and doomed the character to a tragic fate.

Three well-known writers of tragedy lived during the 400s B.C. One writer, Aeschylus (ES·ke·luhs), wrote of old religious beliefs concerning the relationship between gods and people. His three most famous plays centered on the murder of Agamemnon, the king who led the Greeks against Troy, and the revenge that followed.

Another writer of tragedies, Sophocles (SAHF·uh·kleez), defended traditional values. Aristotle called Sophocles' most famous play, *Oedipus Rex*, a perfect example of tragedy.

Euripides (yoo·RIP·uh·deez), the third playwright, was more of a realist than Aeschylus or Sophocles. Like Socrates, he questioned many old beliefs and ideas. Earlier writers often glorified war for its deeds of courage and heroism. In *The Trojan Women*, Euripides showed the reality of war, exposing all its pain and misery.

Comedies. Greek **comedies**, which also originated at the festival honoring Dionysus, mocked ideas and people. The comedies usually introduced both tragic and comic figures. Unlike their counterparts in tragedies, however, the central characters in comedies succeeded in solving their problems.

No person or institution could escape the wit of Aristophanes (ar·uh·STAHF·uh·neez), the finest writer of comedies. In *Clouds* he poked fun at Socrates for his theories about educating the youth of Athens. Aristophanes also disliked war and used comedy to make Athenians think about its causes and consequences. In some of his plays, women controlled the government or persuaded their husbands to make peace during war. This amused the Athenians greatly because of their opinion that women had no interest in and no skill at politics.

Section 2 Review

1. **Define** philosopher, philosophy, dramas, tragedies, hubris, comedies
2. **Identify** Socrates, Plato, Aristotle, Pythagoras, Democritus, Hippocrates, Herodotus, Thucydides, Aeschylus, Sophocles, Euripides, Aristophanes
3. **Understanding Ideas** (a) What teaching method did Socrates use? (b) What was its purpose?
4. **Explaining Ideas** What were the main characteristics of the ideal government described in Plato's *Republic*?
5. **Contrasting Ideas** In what ways did Aristotle's view of the principles of government differ from Plato's view of government?
6. **Evaluating Ideas** What value do the accomplishments of Greek mathematicians and scientists have for us today?
7. **Interpreting Ideas** Choose three aspects of Greek drama and speculate on how they reveal Greek culture.

Alexander the Great

Focus Questions

- **How did Philip II of Macedonia pave the way for a Hellenistic empire?**
- **What were the accomplishments of Alexander the Great?**
- **What factors contributed to the breakup of Alexander's empire?**

Between 404 B.C. and 362 B.C., Sparta and then Thebes attempted to dominate Greece. However, unsuccessful leadership and continuous Persian interference in Greek affairs prevented unity. Wars raged, and although Persia seemed the most logical victor, another foreign power—Macedonia—brought unity to Greece.

Philip II of Macedonia

The power that finally unified Greece came from an unexpected direction. Look at the map on page 134. A mountainous land called Macedonia lies north of Greece. In the 300s B.C., the Macedonians, a hardy, warlike people closely related to the Greeks, inhabited this land. The Macedonians lived in small villages, each ruled by a powerful noble. Macedonia also had a king whose power depended on his own leadership abilities as well as on the help of the nobles.

In 359 B.C. a remarkable young man known as Philip II of Macedonia became king. As a youth, Philip was a hostage to Thebes for three years. During that time, he came to admire both the Greek lifestyle and the organization of the Theban military.

Philip II wanted to be a strong king and to control the unruly Macedonian nobles and people. Instead of depending on the nobles to supply troops for an army, Philip recruited the first regular paid army in Macedonian history.

He drilled his soldiers into one of the strongest armies of the time. One of the elements of Philip's army was the cavalry—fighters mounted on horseback. Another element was the **infantry**—a group of soldiers trained and equipped to fight on foot. Philip organized part of the infantry into phalanxes similar to those used by the armies of the Greek city-states. A **phalanx** (FAY·langks) consisted of rows of soldiers standing shoulder to shoulder and equipped with pikes as long as 21 feet. The tightly spaced soldiers, with pikes held up and forward, were particularly effective against oncoming cavalry. A third element of Philip's army was his archers.

After unifying his own kingdom, Philip II used his army to conquer surrounding peoples. He first gained control of some towns in northern Greece that Athens claimed as colonies. Then he turned south and began unifying the Greek city-states under his rule.

The Greeks had varying opinions of Philip. Some people regarded him as a savior who could bring unity to Greece. Others opposed him as a menace to liberty. Demosthenes (di·MAHS·thuh·neez), one of the finest **orators**, or public speakers, in all Athenian history, led the opposition to Philip in Athens.

Demosthenes tried to make Athenians aware of the danger he believed Philip II of Macedonia posed. He bitterly attacked Philip in a series of speeches to the Assembly and tried to get Athens to lead the Greeks once more in a fight for liberty. Demosthenes did spur the Athenians to action. As so often happened in Greek history, however, the city-states failed to present a unified defense. As Philip and his army relentlessly marched south, traitors betrayed some city-states. This supported Philip's boast that with enough gold he could take any fortress. One by one, other city-states fell to Philip's army. Finally, Philip's army defeated the forces of Thebes and Athens at the Battle of Chaeronea (ker·uh·NEE·uh) in 338 B.C. and Philip II became master of Greece. (See map on page 134.)

The Greeks were at last united, but they had lost their freedom. Although Philip organized the cities into a league to support his plans for an invasion of Persia, he never achieved his goal. At his daughter's wedding in 336 B.C., Philip II was assassinated. The identity of the assassin and the reason behind the assassination are unclear. Philip's 20-year-old son, Alexander, known to history as Alexander the Great, succeeded him.

Alexander the Great

Alexander proved to be even more remarkable than his father. Although very much alike, Alexander and Philip rarely agreed and often quarreled bitterly. Despite their differences, however, Philip did everything to give his son the best training and education possible. Alexander received his military training in the Macedonian army and his formal education from the great Greek philosopher Aristotle. The combination of military skills and cultural education gave Alexander a unique preparation for leadership.

As a military commander, Alexander was even more skilled than his father. His military campaigns are among the most admired in history. He was physically strong and brave to the point of rashness. Alexander's dramatic acts in battle so captured the imagination of his troops that they willingly followed him into unknown lands.

Alexander's conquests. Alexander began his reign by crushing rebellions in Greek city-states and declaring himself master of Greece. He then set out to conquer the world. By 331 B.C. he had defeated the Persian armies and conquered Asia Minor, Syria, Egypt, Mesopotamia, and the rest of Persia.

Although Alexander now ruled a huge territory, he still longed to acquire more. Beyond Persia lay India. For almost four years, he led his troops east, meeting little resistance and going as far as the Indus River. From there it was his intention to march on and gain control of the entire vast plain of northern India. After four years, however, Alexander's long-suffering army had finally had enough fighting. He pleaded with his exhausted soldiers, but they would not follow. Reluctantly, Alexander turned back in 326 B.C.

Alexander led his army to the Indian Ocean, where he divided his troops. Half of them traveled west by sea, explored the shores of the Persian Gulf as far as the mouth of the Euphrates, and sailed inland to meet Alexander at Susa. Alexander led the rest of his army through the desert, where many of his troops, as well as women and children among the camp followers, died from exposure and lack of food and water.

The tattered remnants of his forces finally reached Susa in the spring of 324 B.C. Alexander's fleet had also suffered losses but joined the king at Susa. However, the great army would never be reassembled. Amid growing discontent in his empire, Alexander withdrew to a lonely life dominated by fear for his life.

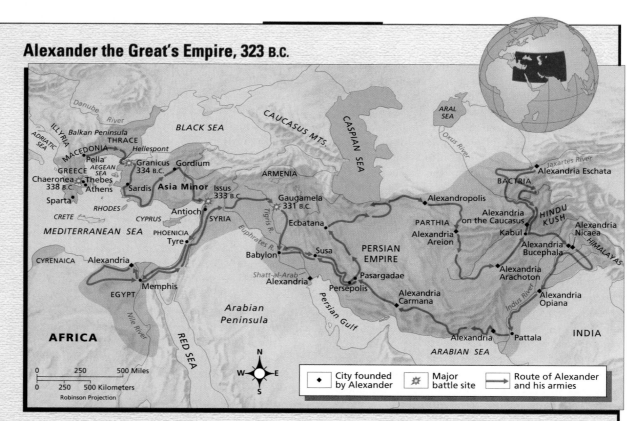

Alexander the Great's Empire, 323 B.C.

Learning from Maps Alexander's military campaigns led him through Asia Minor, Syria, Egypt, the Persian Empire, and India.

? Movement Trace the route of Alexander and his armies from Macedonia to India. In which city did Alexander's last major battle take place?

The gold crown (above) found in the city of Vergina in Macedonia may have belonged to Alexander the Great (whose bust appears left). Alexander had his own coin (lower left) minted because traders in the empire accepted silver as the medium of exchange.

In the spring of 323 B.C. Alexander was in Babylon. He became ill with an infection now thought to be cholera or malaria. After struggling with a raging fever for 10 days, Alexander the Great died in June of 323 B.C. He was not yet 33 years old.

Alexander's empire. In 13 years Alexander had never lost a battle and had conquered much of the world known to him. Alexander's actions as a ruler tell us something. First, he purposely spread Greek culture as he and his army traveled. He established more than 70 cities, many of them named Alexandria in his honor. Groups of Greeks and Macedonians settled in each city.

Second, Alexander encouraged integration of the Macedonians and the Persians into one ruling group to run his empire more efficiently. To set an example, he married the Persian princess Roxana and also required his generals to marry Persian royalty. In a dramatic gesture, Alexander officiated at a mass wedding of 9,000 of his troops with Persian women.

Third, Alexander wanted his subjects to consider him to be a divine monarch, a god-king. Over time he became convinced that his real father was not Philip but the god Zeus. Alexander believed that his subjects should honor him as being part human and part divine. This idea would not have been strange to many of the peoples he encountered. The Egyptians believed in god-kings, and the Greeks thought of some heroes as divine.

Although Alexander's dream of ruling the entire world remained unfulfilled and his empire soon crumbled, his reign spread Hellenistic culture throughout much of the world. So great was the influence of this culture that we refer to the time between Alexander's death and the Roman conquest of Greece in 146 B.C. as the Hellenistic Age. The achievements of this period influenced Western civilization for centuries.

The Breakup of Alexander's Empire

After Alexander's death, his generals murdered his family and divided the "one world" that composed his empire. A fierce power struggle raged until 301 B.C., when the last attempt to hold the empire together under one ambitious general failed. The three surviving generals, honored as god-kings, divided Alexander's empire into three main kingdoms—Macedonia, Egypt

What If?

Alexander's Empire
What if Alexander the Great had not died so young? Would he have continued to expand his empire? Explain your answer.

Building History Study Skills

READ
WRITE
INTERPRET
CONNECT
THINK

Making Connections with History: Identifying Cultural Diffusion

The term *cultural diffusion* refers to the exchange of ideas, values, and products between societies and the changes that result from such cross-cultural contact. Cultural diffusion occurs when one society attempts to spread its own culture, or it results from military ventures, trade, or the migration of people. For example, Greek culture fused with Southwest Asian cultures as a result of Alexander the Great's conquests.

How to Identify Cultural Diffusion
To identify cultural diffusion, follow these steps.
1. Identify the cultures involved and the method of diffusion.
2. Identify the subject.
3. Compare the cultures by stating similarities and differences.
4. Determine what the connection is between the cultures.

Developing the Skill
Study the sculptures in the photographs on this page and note their similarities and differences. The statue in the upper right illustrates classic Greek sculpture. The bronze head in the center reveals the cultural diffusion Alexander the Great initiated through military conquests.

Sculpted by Myron in the 400s B.C., *The Discus Thrower* mixes idealism and realism. The human body is depicted as it appears to the human eye, but the sculpture stresses the Greek ideals of perfection and self-restraint. The athlete is at the moment before he makes his supreme effort. He appears dynamically poised and is in full self-control. Yet he represents the Greek ideal rather than an individual. He symbolizes the balance between the individual and the community so characteristic of the Greeks.

A product of cultural diffusion, the portrait bust shown at the right, sculpted in about 80 B.C., shows much more individuality. It is clear that this

represents a particular person, seemingly one who is worried, anxious, and somewhat sad.

How do statues of the Hellenistic Age show cultural diffusion? First, the statues retain the technical excellence that tends to characterize Greek ideals. However, they also emphasize the individual rather than an abstract perfection.

Practicing the Skill
Locate photographs of sculptures depicting ancient Egyptian culture and ancient Sumerian and Babylonian cultures around 2000 B.C. Explain how the statues of Babylon show the influence of Egyptian and Sumerian cultures.

To apply this skill, see Applying History Study Skills on page 141.

Memorials

What is the name of your school? Many schools, libraries, colleges, and towns are named for famous people. In this way, we remember individuals and honor their contributions long after they have died. In the United States, two of our most famous leaders are honored in the Washington Monument and the Lincoln Memorial in Washington, D.C., as well as in the state and cities called Washington and in the many cities and towns named Lincoln.

Alexander the Great has been memorialized throughout the world both during his life and after his death. As he conquered cities and towns, he gave many of them his name. Beginning in Alexandria, Egypt, his route can be traced eastward by following the towns bearing his name.

Names sometimes change with history. For example, Idlewild Airport in New York was renamed Kennedy Airport in honor of John F. Kennedy.

Notice the names of streets or buildings in your town that have been named to memorialize someone. Perhaps you can think of other people who have been memorialized in this way.

(the lower Nile Valley), and Syria—and several smaller kingdoms. These kingdoms, often at war with one another, used the cities of Greece as pawns in their struggles and wasted much wealth and energy on war. Around 200 B.C. Roman legions invaded Greece and, over time, conquered most of the Hellenistic empire.

Section 3 Review

1. **Define** infantry, phalanx, orators
2. **Identify** Philip II of Macedonia, Demosthenes, Alexander the Great
3. **Locate and Explain the Significance** Macedonia, Syria, Egypt, Indus River, Susa
4. **Understanding Ideas** How did the actions of Philip II of Macedonia prepare for the spread of Hellenistic culture?
5. **Analyzing Ideas** What special qualities made Alexander the Great a remarkable leader, and what did he accomplish?
6. **Interpreting Ideas** Why did Alexander's empire collapse after his death?

Section 4

The Spread of Hellenistic Culture

Focus Questions

- **What changes occurred in society during the Hellenistic Age?**
- **What ideas about ethics did the philosophers of the Hellenistic Age have?**
- **In what ways did Hellenistic scientists add to the existing body of knowledge?**

The conquests of Alexander the Great brought Greek culture to the Nile Valley, Southwest Asia, and the lands that bordered on India. Greek culture continued to influence these areas long after Alexander's death. At the same time, the ideas that Alexander's followers brought from other lands modified Greek culture at home. Although the greatest achievements of Hellenistic culture included new advances in philosophy and science, the works of Greek writers also influenced Western thought for centuries.

The Economy

Throughout the Hellenistic world, rulers or governments owned much of the land. In addition, wealthy aristocrats held land on which slaves or poorly paid free laborers worked. Hellenistic society included a small class of very wealthy people and a large class of miserably poor people. In between was a middle class that thrived because of the many opportunities for acquiring wealth.

Trade, the most profitable activity, originated from the main trading centers in the cities of Alexandria, in Egypt; Rhodes, on the island of Rhodes, off the coast of Asia Minor; and Antioch, in Syria. Trade routes now connected the entire Mediterranean world, reaching as far east as India. Bigger and better ships contributed greatly to this increase in trade.

The cities Alexander had built or rebuilt became the wonders of the Hellenistic world. Carefully planned and laid out, these cities included market squares and large public buildings such as theaters, libraries, and gymnasiums where men exercised and discussed important issues. Alexandria, in Egypt, became the largest city. Its museum and its library, which housed several hundred thousand papyrus rolls, made Alexandria a great center of learning and an important center of commerce.

Changing Attitudes

As the middle class expanded, education became more widespread. Novels appeared. The old and now less respected values of Greece faded. The status of women improved. Hellenistic women appeared more often in public and acquired more rights regarding property.

Another major change centered on a new definition of what it meant to be a Greek. Now a Hellenized Egyptian or Syrian was considered a "Greek." The old Greek bias against "barbarians" had not actually disappeared—it was just that more of the world became "Greek." Nevertheless, tensions still surfaced when Greeks, Hellenized Greeks, and non-Greeks lived side by side.

Hellenistic Religion and Philosophy

The rise of the Hellenistic kingdoms and the decline of the Greek concept of the polis caused many people in the Hellenistic world to feel that they had lost control over their own lives. Many people sought comfort in new religious ideas. Hellenistic kings, for example, encouraged the practice of ruler-worship in an effort to bind their new subjects to them. Perhaps more important were the so-called mystery religions. These were cults that generally promised their worshippers immortality through the practice of secret teachings and rituals. While some thus looked for a new sense of belonging in religion, others turned to philosophy.

Hellenistic philosophers concerned themselves more with ethics than with the basic questions of reality and human existence. Four chief schools of philosophy existed: Cynicism, Skepticism, Stoicism, and Epicureanism.

The Cynics taught that people should live according to nature. They scorned pleasure, wealth, and social position. The best-known Cynic was Diogenes (dy·AHJ·uh·neez). Today the word *cynic* means a sarcastic person who believes that selfish and insincere motives underlie people's actions.

Skeptics believed that no definite knowledge is possible because everything is always changing. Pyrrho (PIR·oh), credited as the founder of Skepticism, taught that people cannot know how things really are. By accepting this fact, they can achieve peace of mind. Today the word *skeptic* refers to someone who doubts generally accepted ideas.

Zeno established the Stoic philosophy in Athens in the late 300s B.C. He and his followers believed that divine reason directs the world. For example, they believed that whatever fate dictates is right. In their opinion, people should not complain but should learn to accept whatever nature might bring. Stoics believed that every person has some "spark" of the divine within. Happiness can be attained only by attempting to discover how one can best fulfill the role given by this spark of the divine.

The Stoics greatly influenced Roman and Christian thinking. Today the word *stoic* means much the same as it did in Hellenistic times—one who remains outwardly unaffected by either pain or pleasure.

Epicurus, founder of Epicurean philosophy, taught that the aim of life focuses on seeking pleasure and avoiding pain. A primary way to achieve this, according to Epicurus, is to limit one's desires, not to try to fulfill all of them. In later centuries, however, this philosophy came to be seen as focused on self-indulgence. Today the word *epicure* means a person who enjoys the pleasures of the senses—particularly someone who enjoys fine food and chooses to postpone worry.

Mathematics and Physics

Greeks of the Hellenistic Age became outstanding scientists and mathematicians. Euclid, a noted Greek mathematician, contributed extremely important work to the field of mathematics. He developed geometry into a system by showing how geometric statements of truth, or theorems, develop logically from one another. Euclid's *Elements*, a textbook that has been used for more than 2,000 years, is the basis for many of today's geometry books.

Archimedes (ahr·kuh·MEED·eez), considered to be the greatest scientist of the Hellenistic period, used geometry to measure spheres, cones, and cylinders. He also calculated the value of pi (π)—the ratio of the circumference of a circle to its diameter—and used mathematics to explain the principle of the lever. Archimedes built many machines that employed the use of levers. His numerous inventions included the compound pulley (or block and tackle) and the Archimedes screw, which is a device still used today for drawing water upward in a continuous flow.

Medicine

Hellenistic scientists greatly enhanced the medical knowledge of the Greeks. Alexandria became the center for the study of medicine and surgery. To learn about human anatomy, physicians dissected and studied the bodies of executed criminals. Studies by Alexandrian physicians revealed information about the human anatomy that advanced the study of medicine, such as that the brain is the center of the nervous system. This and other advances in medicine allowed Hellenistic physicians to perform delicate surgery on patients.

Astronomy and Geography

Hellenistic scientists also added to the knowledge of astronomy and geography. They used mathematics to calculate the daily position of stars and planets. Aristarchus (ar·uh·STAHR·kuhs) of Samos believed that Earth and other planets moved around the Sun; however, he failed to convince other scientists of his day of his theory. Hipparchus (hi·PAHR·kuhs) of Rhodes, who was the first scientist to use trigonometry in a systematic way, calculated the times of eclipses of the Sun and the moon and the length of the year according to both the Sun and the moon.

Hellenistic geographers knew that Earth was round. At Alexandria, Eratosthenes (er·uh·TAHS·thuh·neez) calculated the circumference of Earth with amazing accuracy.

This mosaic shows the death of Archimedes, c. 212 B.C. Archimedes is considered the greatest Greek scientist of the Hellenistic period.

Characteristics of Hellenistic Science

Two features of Hellenistic science remain particularly remarkable. First, scientists learned a great deal about how the world worked using very simple instruments. They had no microscopes, telescopes, compasses, or delicate balances for weighing small quantities. Second, scientists showed little interest at this time in turning any of their practical inventions into labor-saving devices—as happened so often in the centuries to come. For example, an Alexandrian scientist named Hero invented a steam engine, but people regarded it only as an interesting toy. Some scholars believe that since slavery served as the basis for Hellenistic civilization, these labor-saving inventions would have helped the slaves, and the Greeks did not think it necessary or fitting to improve the slaves' situation.

Section 4 Review

1. **Identify** Diogenes, Pyrrho, Zeno, Epicurus, Euclid, Archimedes, Aristarchus, Hipparchus, Eratosthenes
2. **Understanding Ideas** What changes in attitude occurred during the Hellenistic Age?
3. **Classifying Ideas** What were the primary ideas of the four major Hellenistic philosophies?
4. **Summarizing Ideas** In what areas did Hellenistic scientists make advances?

Chapter 6 Review

399 B.C.
Socrates dies.

336–323 B.C.
Alexander the Great rules.

500 B.C.　**450 B.C.**　**400 B.C.**　**350 B.C.**

478 B.C.
Greek city-states form Delian League.

447–432 B.C.
Parthenon is built.

400s B.C.
Golden age of Greece occurs.

338 B.C.
Philip II of Macedonia defeats the Greeks at Chaeronea.

Chapter Summary

The following list contains the key concepts that you have learned about the Greek civilization and the Hellenistic Age.

1. The peak of cultural activity in Athens occurred in the 400s B.C., a period that is known as the golden age.
2. Athenians surrounded themselves with beauty and showed their love for Athens by building temples, gymnasiums, and public theaters adorned with sculpture and other fine works of art.
3. The Parthenon, which is a shrine constructed in honor of the goddess Athena, still stands atop the Acropolis, the hill where the original polis was located.
4. Greek art glorified humans, symbolized the pride of the Greeks, honored the gods, expressed the ideals of balance and order, and combined beauty with usefulness.
5. The works of Greek philosophers and writers, such as Plato and Aristotle, remain among the world's greatest works of literature.
6. Philip II of Macedonia invaded Greece, conquered all the city-states, and united them under his rule.
7. Philip's son, Alexander the Great, went on to conquer the entire Persian Empire and beyond. He died before he could accomplish his goal of a worldwide Hellenistic empire. In time his empire was divided into several kingdoms.
8. As a result of Alexander's conquests, Greek culture, modified by ideas from other lands and known as Hellenistic culture, spread throughout the Mediterranean.
9. Hellenistic philosophers and scientists made significant contributions to our understanding of ethics, mathematics, and science—especially geometry, physics, medicine, and astronomy.

Reviewing Important Terms

On a separate sheet of paper, supply the term that correctly completes each statement.

1. The new culture combining Greek ideas and features from other cultures of the Mediterranean is known as _____ _____.
2. _____ is the inquiry into the most fundamental questions of reality and human existence.
3. A play containing action and dialogue and usually involving conflict and emotion is called a(n) _____.
4. The Greeks called excessive pride _____.
5. A Greek _____ shows the main character struggling against a fate that results in a sad ending.
6. A(n) _____ is a form of Greek drama that mocks ideas and people.
7. _____ is a term for soldiers trained and equipped to fight on foot.

Developing Critical Thinking Skills

1. **Evaluating Ideas** How did architecture and art of the golden age in Athens reflect the values of Greek culture? Include specific examples to support your answer.
2. **Contrasting Ideas** How does Socrates' concept of the ideal form of government, as it was described in Plato's *Republic,* differ from that of modern democratic governments?
3. **Applying Ideas** How is Aristotle's view of good government reflected in the checks and balances in the federal government of the United States?
4. **Interpreting Ideas** How did middle-class expansion change Greek attitudes during the Hellenistic Age?
5. **Comparing Ideas** How did the views of the Greek philosophers of the golden age differ from the views of philosophers of the Hellenistic Age?
6. **Relating Ideas** How might Thucydides' scientific approach to history apply to other contributions of Greek culture?

Relating Geography to History

Compare the map on page 134 with a modern map of the same area. **(a)** What countries now lie in the land that once formed Alexander's empire? **(b)** What geographic barriers prevented Alexander from conquering the Indian subcontinent?

Relating Past to Present

1. The architects of many of the public buildings in our nation's capital, Washington, D.C., were influenced by the architecture of ancient Greece. In your school

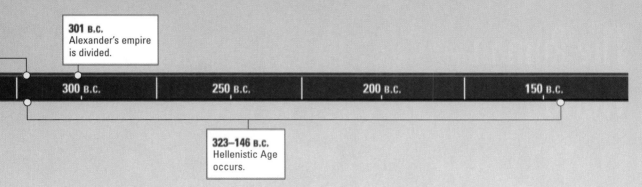

301 B.C.
Alexander's empire
is divided.

300 B.C.   250 B.C.   200 B.C.   150 B.C.

323–146 B.C.
Hellenistic Age
occurs.

or local library, find a book with photographs of buildings located in Washington, D.C. Find another book with photographs of ancient buildings still standing in Greece today. Compare the buildings shown in each book. **(a)** List the ways in which the buildings in the two books are similar and the ways in which they are different. **(b)** What functions did the ancient Greek buildings serve? **(c)** What functions do the buildings in Washington, D.C., serve?

2. Explore the history of your town or city to find streets, parks, or buildings named after people. Which of these people have been memorialized in other parts of the United States?

3. Give examples of how Hellenistic culture influenced the governments and economies of the regions with which it came in contact. What aspects of American culture have spread to other countries today?

Applying History Study Skills

Before completing this activity, review Building History Study Skills on page 136.

Look again at the steps explaining how to identify cultural diffusion. Then read the following selections from Plato's *Republic* and Epicurus's *The Prudent Pursuit of Pleasure,* respectively, to answer the questions below.

"Unless . . . either philosophers become kings in our states or those whom we now call our kings and rulers take to the pursuit of philosophy seriously and adequately, and there is a conjunction of these two things, political power and philosophical intelligence, . . . there can be no cessation of [rest from] troubles . . . for our states, nor, I fancy, for the human race either."

"When we say that pleasure is the goal, we are not talking about . . . continuous drinking and revels . . . but sober reasoning, which examines the motives for every choice and avoidance, and which drives away those opinions resulting in the greatest disturbance to the soul.

The beginning and the greatest good of all these is prudence [self-discipline] .. . . From it derive all the other virtues. Prudence teaches us how impossible it is to live pleasantly without living wisely, virtuously, and justly."

1. **(a)** How are the purposes of Plato and Epicurus similar? **(b)** How do their goals differ?

2. How does Plato's philosophy represent a response to a polis or city-state?

3. How does Epicurus's philosophy represent a response to a society that is multiracial and a center of trade?

4. What evidence of cultural diffusion is present in the quotations by these two philosophers?

Search the Internet through the HRW Web site for information on one of the mathematicians or scientists, such as Hippocrates or Aristarchus, mentioned in this chapter. Learn how the ideas of these ancient scholars were developed and are used today. You may want to direct or supplement your research with an interview with a math or science teacher in your school. Prepare a short report summarizing your findings.

GO TO: go.hrw.com
KEYWORD: SCØ Greek Scientists

Building Your Portfolio

1. **Preparing an Oral Presentation** Read selections from Plato's *Republic.* Then choose one idea from his work on each of the following subjects: **(a)** education; **(b)** the role of women; **(c)** the organization of society; **(d)** the definition of a state. Prepare an oral report on the ways these ideas were reflected in the city-state governments of ancient Greece. Place your research notes in your portfolio.

2. **Writing a Report** Report on the speeches that Demosthenes made in defense of Athens and discuss the arguments that he advanced against Philip II of Macedonia. You can locate the appropriate speeches in books such as Lewis Copeland and Lawrence Lamm's *The World's Great Speeches* (Dover). Place your report in your portfolio.

3. **Studying Literature** During the golden age in Athens, women were subordinate to men in matters of education, legal rights, government participation, and business affairs. Yet during this same period Euripides composed great plays about strong women (for example, *Medea*) and Sophocles wrote *Antigone*. In a short essay answer: What role did these women play in Greek tradition? Place the essay in your portfolio.

CHAPTER 7

The Roman World

TIME

1000 B.C.–A.D. 476

1000 B.C.–A.D. 476

| 3,700,000 B.C. | 4000 B.C. | A.D. 2100 |

PLACE

Italy and the Mediterranean Region

Italy and the Mediterranean Region

The Colosseum, Rome

Significance

The date 146 B.C. is often given as the end of the Hellenistic Age because by that year the Romans had extended their power over a large part of the eastern Mediterranean.

Today we trace the origins of many of our legal and political institutions to those institutions of ancient Rome.

Terms to Define

republic	latifundia
tribunes	equites
consuls	Pax Romana
veto	aqueducts
checks and balances	colonus
praetors	rabbis
censors	martyrs
patricians	patriarchs
plebeians	pope
legion	inflation
paterfamilias	collegia
indemnity	anarchy

People to Identify

Romulus	Marcus Aurelius
Spartacus	Galen
Marius	Ptolemy
Sulla	Constantine
Pompey	Commodus
Cleopatra	Huns
Marc Antony	Alaric
Nero	Attila
Hadrian	Romulus Augustulus

Places to Locate

Tiber River	Nazareth
Rubicon River	Constantinople
Carthage	Rhine River
Actium	Black Sea
Jerusalem	

Chapter Theme Questions

- **Politics and Law** What elements might contribute to the stability and peacefulness of an empire?
- **Religion** How might religions become popular and spread?
- **War and Diplomacy** What factors can lead to the decline of an empire?

No one knows exactly when the city of Rome was founded, but several colorful legends exist. The most famous legend holds that Romulus, the son of a priestess and Mars—the god of war—founded the city. A neighboring king, the legend says, imprisoned or killed Romulus's mother. Romulus and his twin brother, Remus, were set adrift in a basket on the Tiber River. The infants washed ashore and were nursed by a wolf and raised by a shepherd. As adults, the brothers planned to build a city at the spot where they had washed ashore. An omen indicated that Romulus would be the city's king. The brothers soon quarreled, and Remus—to show how little he thought of Romulus's efforts—jumped over the unfinished wall of his city, mocking his brother. Furious, Romulus killed his brother. The city of Rome was named after its founder and first king, Romulus.

Section 1

The Founding of the Roman Republic

Focus Questions

- **What advantages did Italy and Rome have in terms of location?**
- **How did the Romans organize the government of their republic?**
- **What factors allowed Rome's power to expand?**

The geography of Italy and the location of Rome itself had a great deal to do with the rise of Roman power. In time Rome became the heart of a vast empire. Like most empires, it took shape gradually.

The Physical Setting

Italy is the central peninsula of the three great peninsulas in the Mediterranean region. As you can see from the map on page 144, Italy resembles a boot, with its top nestled in the Alps to the north and its toe and heel jutting into the Mediterranean Sea to the south. The toe of Italy rests only about 2 miles from Sicily, which is approximately 90 miles from Africa. Italy lies at the center of the Mediterranean region, slicing the sea nearly in half. Because of its location, Italy is the obvious base from which to control both the eastern and the western halves of the region.

At first glance, the snowcapped Alps separating Italy from the rest of Europe have appeared to offer good protection against invasion. However, for centuries invaders have streamed through several passes that cut across the rugged mountains. Italy's location also makes it vulnerable to sea invasion, for invaders can land anywhere along the peninsula's lengthy seacoast.

Geographical factors made unity possible within Italy, whereas in Greece the geography prevented it. Notice on the map that the Apennines, the mountains that run the full length of the boot, divide the peninsula. Because the Apennines are less rugged than the mountains of Greece, they did not hinder trade and travel. In addition, although Italy has a long coastline, it has fewer good harbors than Greece has. For these reasons, the people living in the peninsula's earliest coastal settlements turned inland for trade and growth rather than toward the sea as the Greeks had done.

Except for the long coastal plain to the west and the great valley of the Po River to the north, mountains dominate the landscape of Italy. Heavy rains easily wash away the sandy soil, and most land can only be used for grazing. Nevertheless, Italy's pleasant climate and plentiful winter rains enable farmers to raise vegetables, olives, grapes, and citrus fruits.

Early Peoples in Italy

People lived in Italy as early as the Paleolithic period, and a Neolithic culture had developed there before 3000 B.C. After 2000 B.C., waves of invaders swept through the mountain passes and overran the peninsula. As in Greece, these invaders came from north of the Black and Caspian Seas.

Sometime around the mid-700s B.C., a group of people called Latins occupied an area in the west-central plains region called Latium (LAY·shee·uhm). Some of the Latin settlers built villages along the Tiber River. In time these villages united to form the city of Rome. (See map on this page.)

In the late 600s B.C., Rome came under the rule of Etruscan kings. These kings controlled the area for about 100 years. The Etruscans were later absorbed into the mixture of peoples who came to be known as Romans. Although the Etruscans eventually disappeared as a distinct people, their culture continued to influence the Latins, who made up the main body of the Romans. The Etruscans had developed a written language using an alphabet based on Greek characters. Although the Etruscan language is unique, later Romans borrowed and adapted the Etruscan alphabet.

The Etruscans also made fine clothing and jewelry and were skilled workers in metal, pottery, and wood. The Etruscans also knew how to pave roads, drain marshes, and construct sewers.

One Etruscan custom later became an important Roman custom as well. A triumph was a splendid parade held for a conquering military leader returning victorious from battle. Preceded by the spoils and prisoners of war, the leader rode in a special chariot at the head of the troops. To keep the leader from being completely carried away by the cheers of the people, a servant rode in the chariot and constantly repeated, "Remember that you are mortal."

Ancient Italy, c. 600 B.C.

Learning from Maps Rome's location on the Italian peninsula, slightly inland on a shallow section of the Tiber River, protected the Romans from sea invasions and encouraged trade in all directions.

Place On what island did the Greeks establish colonies?

Some Greeks also settled in ancient Italy. Greek colonies in Sicily and southern Italy became city-states, as disunited and quarrelsome as those of the homeland. Nonetheless, the Greek culture of these colonies strongly influenced the Romans.

A Strategic Location

Latins, Etruscans, and other peoples living around Rome gradually came to be called Romans. At first Rome was only one of many city-states on the plains of Latium. Rome's location, however, gave it an advantage over other city-states on the Italian peninsula.

Locate Rome on the map on the opposite page. Built on seven hills along the Tiber River, Rome lies about 15 miles inland from the western coast of Italy. This location protected the Romans from sea invasions.

Rome's location gave the city economic advantages as well. The city lay along one of the shallowest parts of the Tiber, near a small island in the river. This location at the easiest river crossing for many miles put the city at the center of land trade routes that spread out in all directions.

Roman Government

In 509 B.C. the Roman aristocracy overthrew the last Etruscan monarch and established a republic. A **republic** is a form of government in which voters elect officials to run the state. In the Roman Republic, only adult male citizens were entitled to vote and participate in government.

Three groups of citizens helped govern Rome: the Senate, various popular assemblies, and the officials themselves, called magistrates.

The Senate. The most important and powerful of the three governing bodies was the 300-member Senate. The Senate controlled public funds, determined foreign policy, and sometimes acted as a court. In times of emergency, the Senate could propose that a citizen be named dictator. A dictator could rule for a maximum of six months and for that time had both military and judicial authority.

Popular assemblies. Several assemblies existed in the republic. Citizens in these assemblies voted on laws and elected officials. Some assemblies voted to make war or peace, and some had a judicial role. Assemblies elected 10 officials called **tribunes.** The 10 tribunes could refuse to approve Senate bills and the actions of public officials if they believed that the acts were contrary to the public interest.

The magistrates. The various types of magistrates were the public officials who governed in the name of Rome. After the monarchy ended in 509 B.C., two **consuls** were elected for one-year terms. They served as the chief executives who ran the government and acted as military commanders. They also appointed dictators. Each consul could **veto**, or refuse to approve, acts of the other. (The Latin word *veto* means "I forbid.") Although powerful, the consuls governed with the advice of the Senate. This division of power was an example of the principle of **checks and balances** that prevented any one part of the government from becoming too powerful. Many nations of the modern world, including the United States, later adopted the principle of checks and balances as well as the veto.

To help the consuls, the Romans elected officials called **praetors** (PREE·tuhrz). In times of war, praetors commanded armies, and in times of peace, they oversaw the legal system. In addition to drawing up lists of potential jurors and judges, the praetors' interpretations of legal questions created much of the civil law of Rome.

Censors were officials elected every 5 years for terms of 18 months. They registered citizens according to their wealth, could appoint candidates to the Senate, and oversaw the moral conduct of all citizens. Censors became very powerful magistrates in the Roman Republic.

The composition of the assemblies and elected officials changed throughout the life of the republic. The changes stemmed from the common people's attempts to win more rights. These struggles became known as the Conflict of the Orders.

The Conflict of the Orders

Roman society was left divided between two social classes after 509 B.C. A powerful aristocratic class organized in clans, the **patricians**, controlled the government. All other citizens were **plebeians**.

Patricians maintained their power over politics—and all other aspects of society—through a patronage system. Patricians provided their client families with financial, social, and legal support in exchange for political backing and loyalty.

Plebeians suffered discrimination for many years. Laws prevented them from holding public office and from joining military service. They could not even know what the laws said because the laws were not written down. In court a judge stated and applied all laws, and only patricians served as judges.

Gradually, the plebeians increased their power by making demands and by leading strikes. They gained

Citizens' Rights in the Roman Republic

Around 500 B.C. the Romans, who valued their freedom above all, established a republic—a government in which voters have a voice in selecting their leaders. However democratic the Roman civic ideal of freedom for all, the rights and privileges of Roman citizens were not equal.

Within this class-based society, power belonged to the patricians—members of privileged families, many of whom belonged to the Senate. Walking along the streets of Rome, the most powerful patricians, the senators and magistrates, were easily recognized by their flowing, purple-hemmed togas. Not surprisingly, Roman law favored the patrician class. Other Roman citizens, known as plebeians, were not at first allowed to hold public office. To protect plebeians from the power of the patricians, the office of tribune was established. Elected by the plebeians, tribunes had the power to veto Roman laws as well as the actions of magistrates.

Elected leaders held great power, but it was not unlimited. For example, in the very first year of the Roman Republic a law was passed that gave citizens the right of appeal (*provocatio*) against a decision of a magistrate. (See silver coin illustrating provocatio court.)

the right to participate in the military and to hold office in the government. In one of their greatest victories, they forced the government to write down the laws. Around 450 B.C. the Romans engraved these laws on tablets known as the Twelve Tables and placed them in the Forum—the chief public square—for all to view.

Over the years, the plebeians won additional rights. Laws banned debt slavery and permitted plebeians to fill public offices, including the office of consul. One of the new laws, however, was a ban on intermarriage between patricians and plebeians—an attempt by the patricians to preserve their special status.

By about 300 B.C., wealthy and powerful plebeians had joined with the patricians to form the Roman nobility. From that time on, the distinction between patricians and plebeians was of little importance, while membership in the nobility was of great importance. Although the common people had the right to elect officials, they did not exert much influence. Only wealthy nobles could hold office because of a class requirement and the lack of salary. The nobles controlled the Senate, and the Senate overshadowed the magistrates. At times ambitious tribunes, hoping for higher office, cooperated with the Senate in using their veto power. Through skillful political maneuvering, the nobles therefore dominated the republic.

Extending the Republic

For more than 200 years after the founding of the republic, the Romans fought many wars against neighboring peoples in Italy. By 265 B.C. the Romans controlled all of Italy south of the Rubicon, a river on the northeast coast. Both military organization and wise policies helped the Romans achieve their victories.

The army. Roman law obligated every adult male citizen who possessed a minimum amount of property to serve in the army. Discipline was strict, and the soldiers themselves enforced it. The most important military unit of the Roman army was the **legion**, consisting of 4,500 to 6,000 men called legionnaires. In addition to legions, which were made up of citizens, the Romans also eventually established the *auxilia*, units made up of noncitizens. Because of excellent organization, training, and high morale, the Roman army eventually defeated even the mighty Macedonian army.

Wise policies. To ensure the loyalty of their subjects, the Romans shared citizenship and political power with the people they conquered. The Romans granted full citizenship to the inhabitants of nearby

Italian cities and partial citizenship to the inhabitants of more distant cities, including the Greek city-states in Italy. Partial citizens could own property and marry under Roman law, but they could not vote. The Romans also made treaties of alliance with more distant cities. The allies remained independent, but they promised to provide military assistance to the Romans and to support Rome's foreign policy whenever their services were needed.

The early Romans did not demand tribute from conquered peoples, but they did expect subject peoples to provide land for Roman farmers' resettlement. This land settlement policy enabled the Romans to maintain military control over their conquests and to spread the Latin language, Roman law, and other aspects of Roman culture throughout Italy.

The Family

As the center of religion, morals, and education, the family was the most important unit in Roman society during the days of the republic. A Roman family included all unmarried children, married sons and their families, all dependent relatives, and the family slaves.

The father, known as the **paterfamilias** (pah·tuhr·fuh·MI·lee·uhs), had absolute authority. He conducted religious ceremonies, made all important decisions, and supervised his sons' education. Roman women enjoyed a higher status than did Greek women. The mother managed the household, did the buying, and helped her husband entertain guests.

Religion

The early Romans believed that spirits inhabited everything. Some spirits were especially connected with the home. These included the *lares*, who were ancestral spirits, and the *penates*, guardians of the storeroom. Family worship focused on Vesta, guardian of fire and the hearth.

After the Romans conquered the Greeks, they eventually identified their gods with those of Olympus. For example, Jupiter, an Indo-European sky god, took on the characteristics of the chief Greek god, Zeus. The

Roman soldiers' helmets were made of either bronze or iron; their body armor was first made of hardened leather and later of overlapping bronze sections sewn together and covering leather or fabric.

Romans also believed they could learn a god's will by observing the internal organs of sacrificed animals or the flight of birds.

The old family religion evolved into a state religion with temples, ceremonies, and processions. The high priest, elected for life by a special assembly, was called the *Pontifex Maximus*. Like the religion of the Greeks, Roman religion was very concerned with the proper performance of rituals.

Section 1 Review

1. **Define** republic, tribunes, consuls, veto, checks and balances, praetors, censors, patricians, plebeians, legion, paterfamilias
2. **Identify** Romulus
3. **Locate and Explain the Significance** Tiber River, Rome, Rubicon River
4. **Understanding Ideas** "In terms of defense, trade, and governing outlying districts, Rome's location was ideal." Do you agree? Why or why not?
5. **Organizing Ideas** What was the structure of the government of the Roman Republic?
6. **Analyzing Ideas** What factors helped Rome expand successfully?

Section 2

Roman Expansion

Focus Questions

- **What were the Punic Wars?**
- **What political, economic, and social changes occurred in the Roman Republic as a result of Roman expansion?**

By the middle 200s B.C., the Roman Republic had extended its power over all the Italian Peninsula south of the Rubicon. However, the burden of defending the republic had also increased.

Rome Versus Carthage

Rome soon came into conflict with Carthage, a large and powerful city on the coast of North Africa. (See map on opposite page.) Originally a Phoenician colony, Carthage became a great commercial power with an empire that spanned the western Mediterranean.

Perhaps war between the rival states was inevitable. Each was aggressive and expansionistic. After the Romans occupied southern Italy, Carthage feared that they would also try to take Sicily, with its Carthaginian colonies and markets. The Romans feared that the Carthaginian navy would dominate the Mediterranean and prevent the expansion of Roman influence overseas. These fears sparked a series of devastating wars between the two cities.

Rome and Carthage fought three wars between 264 B.C. and 146 B.C. In between the wars were peaceful periods that lasted for 23 and 52 years, respectively. We refer to the wars as the Punic Wars because the Latin adjective for *Phoenician* is *punicus*.

The opponents were well matched. Rome had the better army; Carthage had the better navy. Carthage had more wealth, but Roman lands were more compact and more easily defended.

The First Punic War. The First Punic War began in 264 B.C. Initially, Rome had no navy, but it soon built one, using a captured Carthaginian vessel as a model. The Romans used land tactics at sea, equipping their ships with "boarding bridges." The Romans would ram their ship into a Carthaginian ship and then let down the bridge so that heavily armed soldiers could stampede across it and take the enemy. Although these bridges were later abandoned, Rome prevailed, and in 241 B.C. Carthage asked for peace. The Romans made Carthage pay a large **indemnity**—money for the damages it had caused—and forced Carthage to give up control of Sicily. Within a few years, the Romans conquered all of Italy and had major overseas holdings.

The Second Punic War. The Second Punic War began in 218 B.C. In Spain Hannibal, one of the greatest generals of all time, assembled an army including infantry, cavalry, and war elephants. They marched across what is now southern France and crossed the Alps into Italy. The crossing proved to be difficult, and Hannibal's force suffered an enormous loss of life.

Despite Hannibal's difficult journey, the Roman armies were no match for him. Hannibal won several victories, causing the Roman armies to retreat to their fortified cities. Because Hannibal had no siege equipment, he could not attack the cities. Instead, he spent years ravaging the southern Italian countryside. He also tried to win away the Roman Republic's allies. The Roman policy of sharing citizenship and political power proved its value, however, and the majority of the republic's allies remained loyal.

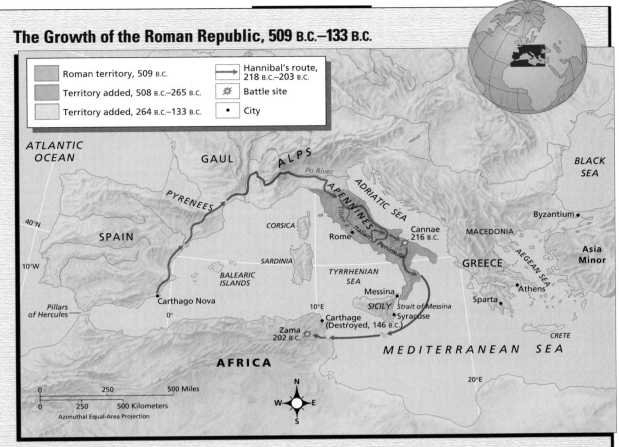

The Growth of the Roman Republic, 509 B.C.–133 B.C.

Legend:
- Roman territory, 509 B.C.
- Territory added, 508 B.C.–265 B.C.
- Territory added, 264 B.C.–133 B.C.
- → Hannibal's route, 218 B.C.–203 B.C.
- ✳ Battle site
- • City

Learning from Maps Rome and Carthage fought three Punic Wars between 264 B.C. and 146 B.C.

❓ **Movement** Trace Hannibal's route from Spain to Carthage. Across which mountain ranges did his army advance during the journey?

Although the situation was desperate, Rome continued to fight. Finally, the Romans turned the tables by invading Africa and threatening Carthage. Hannibal's government ordered him home to defend the city. In Africa he finally met his match—the Roman general Scipio (SIP·ee·oh). In 202 B.C. at the battle of Zama, near Carthage, the brilliant Scipio defeated Hannibal and his army, ensuring the supremacy of Greco-Roman civilization in the Mediterranean. (See map on this page.)

Once more Carthage asked for peace and had to pay a huge indemnity. It also gave up most of its navy and its Spanish colonies. The city of Carthage remained independent, but it had lost all its power. Rome was now the most powerful force in the western area of the Mediterranean.

What If?

Hannibal
Hannibal's army suffered heavy losses as it crossed the Alps. Even so, the Roman legions were no match for the remnants of the Carthaginian forces. How do you think the course of world history would have been different if Hannibal had lost none of his men or war elephants when he crossed the Alps?

The Third Punic War. Although Carthage no longer threatened the power of Rome, some Romans held a lasting hatred for Carthage. Influenced by this hatred, the Senate finally decided to crush Carthage. In 149 B.C. Rome again declared war on Carthage. After a bitter siege, the city fell in 146 B.C. The Romans razed Carthage and enslaved the surviving population. Finally, the Romans sowed the fields around Carthage with salt in a gesture of hatred.

Conquest of the Hellenistic East

During the Second Punic War, Macedonia had been allied with Carthage. To get revenge, Rome started a war against Macedonia and defeated it in 197 B.C. The Greek cities now came under Roman "protection." Over time Rome extended its power over the entire region. By 133 B.C. Rome's supremacy in the Mediterranean was complete.

Problems of Roman Expansion

The Roman state had grown from a loose alliance of Italian cities into a great Mediterranean power. The expansion, however, created many problems for the Roman Republic.

Government. Rome itself retained a republican form of government. However, the operation of the government changed in certain ways to handle the rule of a larger territory. The Senate had almost complete control of the army and foreign policy. The nobles gained even more power.

The Romans governed the recently organized territories, called provinces, loosely. They did not grant the people of the provinces citizenship, nor did they make them allies as they had with the people of conquered Italian cities. Instead, the Romans simply made the people of each province subjects and drew up a set of rules for how that province would be administered and taxed.

Each province was governed by either a proconsul or propraetor appointed by the Senate and backed by a Roman army of occupation. During the time of the republic, these governing officials were not closely monitored by the Senate. Because these officials expected to make a profit from their terms, they often took bribes and neglected the needs of the people.

The proconsuls and propraetors were not the only Romans who became wealthy by stealing from the provinces, however. In Rome the censors contracted with officials called publicans, who agreed to collect taxes according to a province's set of rules. They could then keep whatever they collected in excess of this

fixed sum. Consequently, these tax collectors would attempt to squeeze as much money as they could from the people of the provinces.

Changes in agriculture. Rome's annexation of distant territories lessened the role of the small citizen-farmer in Roman life. Some Romans acquired very large estates called **latifundia**. Only wealthy people could afford these estates and the slaves who did the work on them. As time passed, Rome came to depend on the provinces for grain, Rome's chief food staple.

The Punic Wars also contributed to changes in agriculture. The farmer-soldiers who returned from the Punic Wars were sickened to find their livestock killed, their homes in ruins, olive groves or vineyards uprooted or burned, and the land untended. Because the farmers did not have enough money to bring the war-torn land back into cultivation, they had little choice but to sell it.

Some of the now landless farmers moved to the cities. Not all of them could find jobs there, however, and they depended on the government for food. To make matters worse, the displaced farmers could no longer serve in the army because the republic allowed only landowners to fight. All that some of these landless veterans could do was sell their votes to the highest bidder.

Growth of commerce and social change. After the Punic Wars, trade within Rome's vast empire increased. The business and landowning people of Rome formed a class called **equites** (EK·wuh·teez). They had great wealth and therefore increased political influence. In addition to wealth from imports and exports, they made money from contracts for public works, tax farming, and the loot of war.

The decline of the independent farmers and the growth of jobless masses in the cities weakened the ideals of discipline and devotion to the state. New religions and philosophies from the conquered territories began to influence Roman culture. Other changes had also taken place. As Rome expanded, victorious generals enslaved their enemies. Some of these slaves enjoyed relatively humane treatment. For example, owners often let skilled slaves keep part of what they earned to buy their freedom later, and by Roman law, a freed slave became a citizen.

Other slaves led wretched lives. Some revolted. The most brutal revolt, led by a slave named Spartacus, began in 73 B.C. More than 70,000 slaves took part in this revolt. However, by 71 B.C. the Roman army had crushed the uprising. Spartacus died in battle. Later 6,000 of his followers were crucified. Crucifixion, in which the accused was nailed or tied to a cross and left to die an agonizing death from suffocation, was a common Roman method of executing slaves.

Section 2 Review

1. **Define** indemnity, latifundia, equites
2. **Identify** Spartacus
3. **Locate and Explain the Significance** Carthage, Sicily, Zama
4. **Summarizing Ideas (a)** In what ways were Rome and Carthage in competition with each other? **(b)** What were the final results of the Punic Wars?
5. **Determining Cause and Effect** How did the government and social structure of Rome change as a result of the conquest of new territories?

Section 3

The Roman Empire

Focus Questions

- What political changes occurred during the first century B.C. that led to the end of the republic?
- How did Julius Caesar's reign serve as a transition between the Roman Republic and the Roman Empire?
- What characterized the first two centuries of the Roman Empire?

By 133 B.C. the Roman Republic faced many problems. Although courageous leaders attempted reform, the days of the republic were numbered.

The Gracchi

Two brothers, Tiberius and Gaius Gracchus (GRAK·uhs), were among the first to attempt reforms. Elected tribune in 133 B.C., Tiberius saw that some senators used public land for their own benefit. He therefore limited the amount of public land they could use. He also proposed moving many landless citizens to work the land confiscated from the senators. Although this proposal made him popular with the masses, it angered and frightened many senators. A mob of senators and their sympathizers clubbed Tiberius and as many as several hundred of his followers to death.

His brother Gaius, elected tribune in 123 B.C. and again in 122 B.C., introduced such measures as using public funds to purchase grain to be sold to the poor at low prices. Other measures improved the political status of the equites. Again these policies outraged the senators. Gaius and many of his supporters were later killed in a riot while opposing the cancellation of some of the laws Gaius had passed.

The violent deaths of the Gracchi marked a turning point in Roman history. From this point on, violence became a primary tool of Roman politics and replaced respect for the law.

The Social War

During this period, Rome's relationship with its Italian allies entered a crisis. These allies had been trying to obtain Roman citizenship for decades. Men from the Italian cities had fought in the Roman armies, and now the ruling groups of these cities wanted access to public offices in Rome. The Senate refused, wanting to maintain its hold on power. Finally, in 90 B.C., the Italian allies rebelled against Roman control. The war that followed was called the Social War, from the Latin word for "ally." The rebelling troops were as well trained as the Romans, and the fighting was extremely bloody. The Italian cities were finally beaten, but the Senate also agreed to grant them the benefits of citizenship.

Marius and Sulla

Gaius Marius, a military hero, also attempted reform. Marius was elected to the consulship in 107 B.C. As a military commander, he revolutionized the Roman army. To improve recruitment for the legions, Marius signed up any citizen, regardless of whether he had land or not. The soldiers served not only for pay but also for booty—whatever they could take from the enemy and all the slaves they could bring home. When they were discharged, the soldiers expected their general to reward them with land, probably newly conquered land. In other words, Marius had replaced an army of draftees with a volunteer army. Through his reforms, Marius had provided opportunities for advancement in the army, even for the poorest citizens. As other generals followed these practices, armies became loyal to their leaders instead of to the Roman government.

The consul Lucius Cornelius Sulla showed what an ambitious general could do with his own recruited army. In 88 B.C. Sulla was elected to the consulship. After his term expired, however, his enemies, led by Marius, tried to prevent him from taking a customary military command that would have brought him fame and fortune. In response, Sulla marched his legions on Rome, a violation of the most sacred Roman law. In the civil war that followed, Sulla triumphed. Afterward, he executed hundreds of Roman citizens who had opposed him or whom he regarded as dangers to the state.

From 82 B.C. to 79 B.C., Sulla ruled as dictator. He carried out a reform program aimed at restoring senatorial power. He placed all the powers of government in the hands of the Senate, which he enlarged by 300 members. After carrying out these reforms, Sulla retired voluntarily and eventually died peacefully on his farm. Increasingly, however, army commanders who could count on the loyalty of their troops could force the Senate to do their bidding.

The First Triumvirate

Julius Caesar, a nephew of Marius, gained popularity during this period. An opponent of Sulla's, Caesar felt safest removing himself from Rome in about 81 B.C. After Sulla's death in 78 B.C., Caesar returned to Rome and, by means of spellbinding oratory and much spending of money, built a huge following among the poor citizens of Rome.

Realizing that his popularity with the people had made him many enemies in the Senate, Caesar joined forces with two popular generals, Gaius Pompey (PAHM·pee) and Licinius Crassus, in 60 B.C. The three formed a political alliance that became known as the

Gaius Marius became a successful Roman general. He was elected consul seven times between 107 B.C. and 86 B.C. This coin from 101 B.C. shows an image of Marius in a chariot celebrating his triumph over Cimbri and Teutones.

First Triumvirate. (The word *triumvirate* means "rule of three.") With the support of the other triumvirs, Caesar became consul in 59 B.C.

Caesar in Power

Caesar felt that he could not win power without a loyal army, so he obtained a special command in Gaul, a region in what is today France. (See map on page 149.) During the next 10 years, he brought all Gaul under Roman rule and showed his superb abilities as a military leader and organizer. Caesar also issued written reports about his campaigns and victories. Students of Latin still read these clearly detailed reports known collectively as *Commentaries on the Gallic Wars*.

Crassus died in battle in 53 B.C. Pompey, meanwhile, grew jealous of Caesar's rising fame, and in 52 B.C. he was made sole consul. He then persuaded the Senate to order Caesar to return home without his army. Caesar refused to give up his military command and take second place to Pompey. Instead, he led his army toward Rome in 49 B.C.

When Caesar reached the Rubicon, he ordered his army to march on to Rome, knowing that he would be declared a rebel. Today when people make an irreversible decision, we sometimes say that they have "crossed the Rubicon."

Pompey and his followers fled to Greece, leaving the way open for Caesar to assume power. He first secured his power in Italy and Spain and defeated Pompey in Greece. From there Caesar went to Egypt, which had increasingly come under Roman domination, and put Cleopatra, a daughter of the ruling Ptolemy family, on the throne as a Roman ally.

In 46 B.C. Caesar returned to Rome, where two years later the Senate declared him dictator for life. Caesar kept the republican form of government, but he was king in everything but name.

Caesar proved to be an able politician. He granted citizenship to many people in the provinces and gave land to veterans and grain to the poor. He reduced the Senate to the position of an advisory council and increased its membership to 900 senators. He also ordered the establishment of a calendar of $365\frac{1}{4}$ days, which was used throughout Europe until A.D. 1582.

The conservative families of Rome did not welcome Caesar's new status. Some senators who envied his great power formed a conspiracy against him. Two of these were men Caesar considered friends: Gaius Cassius Longinus and Marcus Brutus. On the Ides of March (March 15), 44 B.C., the conspirators stabbed Caesar to death in the Senate.

The Second Triumvirate

Although Caesar had chosen his 18-year-old grand-nephew, Octavian, as his heir, a scramble for power erupted after Caesar's death. While Octavian was in Greece, Marc Antony, a general and an ally of Caesar's, drove out the conspirators and took control in Rome. Octavian and Marc Antony—along with Lepidus, Caesar's second-in-command—then formed the Second Triumvirate in 43 B.C.

Marc Antony led an army east and reconquered Asia Minor from the armies of Brutus and Cassius. Then, having formed a liaison with Cleopatra, he joined her in Egypt. Meanwhile, Octavian forced Lepidus to retire from political life and built up his own power in Italy.

Octavian: The First Augustus

Antony and Octavian divided the Roman world. Antony took the east and Octavian the west. In time, however, Octavian persuaded the Senate to declare war on Antony and Cleopatra. In 31 B.C., in a naval battle at Actium in Greece, Octavian defeated their fleet. Within a year, Octavian captured Alexandria. Seeing that they could not escape, both Antony and Cleopatra committed suicide. The wars had finally ended but so had the republic.

Determined to avoid his granduncle's fate, Octavian proceeded cautiously. When the Senate appointed him consul, Octavian presented himself not as a king or emperor but as *princeps*, or "first citizen."

The Senate in 27 B.C. gave Octavian the title Augustus, or "the revered one." He has been known ever since as Augustus Caesar, or simply Augustus. Many later Roman rulers used the name Caesar as part of their titles.

Historians generally refer to Augustus as the first Roman emperor, although he did not actually use the title. Beginning with the reign of Augustus, the Roman state became the Roman Empire. He launched a series of new military conquests that expanded the empire's frontiers. Rome's territory stretched from Spain in the west to Syria in the east and from the Rhine and Danube Rivers in the north to Egypt and the Sahara in the south. Augustus had hoped to push the border further into the territory of the German tribes, to the Elbe River, but in A.D. 9 the Roman forces suffered a defeat that ended their expansion into Germany. Three Roman legions were wiped out at the Battle of Teutoburg Forest, and the Romans were forced to accept the boundary of the Rhine.

This sculpture demonstrates the new Roman concept of divine ruler. Augustus's body is idealized and heroic in form.

The Julio-Claudians

Augustus died in A.D. 14. For the next 54 years, relatives of Julius Caesar, called the Julio-Claudians Emperors, ruled the empire. Tiberius, who reigned from A.D. 14 to A.D. 37, was the adopted son of Augustus. Tiberius proved to be an adequate, though disliked, ruler. His brutal and insane successor, Caligula—who according to reports appointed his favorite horse as consul—was murdered in A.D. 41.

Claudius, an intelligent and scholarly man who administered the empire wisely, followed Caligula. During his rule the Roman legions conquered Britain, but even Claudius could not escape the violence that almost always marked imperial succession.* It is believed that his wife, Agrippina, poisoned him, perhaps with tainted mushrooms, in A.D. 54.

---

*The Romans never developed a formal policy of succession. Although many emperors named their successors, the Roman army often refused to accept the new emperors and assassinated them.

Ancient Views of World Geography

People have always been curious about the world, and since the beginning of time, they have tried to describe it. The ancient Greeks were the first to study geography in an organized way. As early as the 500s B.C., the philosopher Anaximander of Miletus wrote a work that contained the first maps and descriptions of both the heavens and Earth. The Greek mathematician Eratosthenes calculated the circumference of Earth in about 200 B.C. with astounding accuracy. Strabo, a Greek scholar who lived about 200 years later, wrote a 17-volume work that described the geography of the world then known to the Greeks and Romans.

In the A.D. 100s, the Egyptian geographer Ptolemy advanced many theories in the eight books of his *Geography*. These theories formed the basis for geographical knowledge for almost a thousand years.

The Greek philosopher Aristotle argued in the 300s B.C. for the spherical shape of Earth. Some of Aristotle's arguments for a round Earth were fanciful, but other arguments were based on observations of phenomena. For example, Aristotle pointed out that when the shadow of Earth crosses the moon during an eclipse, the edge of that shadow is circular. He also recognized that the height of some stars along the horizon increases as one travels north. Aristotle correctly stated that this could only occur if the observer was traveling over the curved surface of a sphere.

Aristotle, and later Ptolemy, divided Earth into climatic zones. These were based on the latitude and the length of the day in various areas. Some areas, early geographers believed, were too hot to be habitable, and others were much too cold. For example, Aristotle believed that humans could not survive in the zone around the equator and within the Arctic Circle.

As time went on, geography came to have very practical applications. Strabo's *Geography*, written in the first century A.D., summarized the world of the time. Strabo was a Greek, but he became a Roman citizen. He felt that a knowledge of geography would help Roman generals and political leaders expand their empire and administer it more effectively.

Strabo drew from and critiqued the writings of earlier geographers and incorporated the reports of travelers. His work is fascinating in that it not only describes such measurements as the shapes of coastlines and distances between cities but also comments on the agricultural and industrial activities of different areas, the types of people who lived there, and the culture they possessed—all aspects of geography as the field is defined today. Like Aristotle and many other early geographers, however, Strabo believed that the equatorial zone was not habitable.

These early geographers would therefore be surprised by the modern world. For instance, Indonesia, one of the most populous nations on Earth, sits on the equator. Alaska and portions of Canada and Finland, located in a zone these geographers thought was too cold for humans, enjoy pleasant, warm summers filled with sunshine.

Early geographers relied on logic as well as observation to develop new theories. However, modern geographers also base their theories on data such as statistics gathered over long periods of time, precise measurements, and satellite photography. They test the accuracy of these theories through experimentation and also through careful observation.

Schematic of Ptolomaic view of the universe

The Height of the Roman Empire, A.D. 117

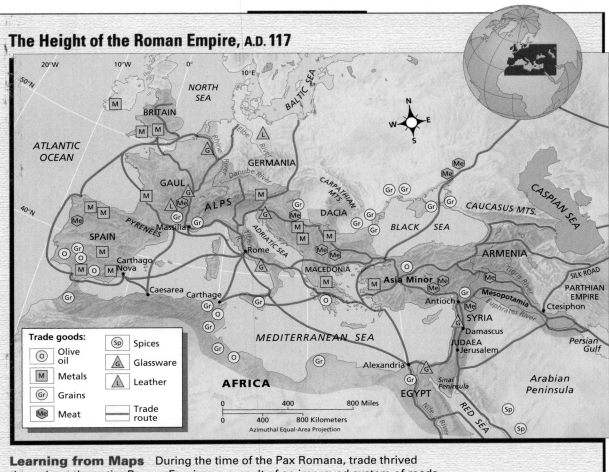

Trade goods:
- O Olive oil
- M Metals
- Gr Grains
- Me Meat
- Sp Spices
- G Glassware
- L Leather
- ▬ Trade route

0 — 400 — 800 Miles
0 — 400 — 800 Kilometers
Azimuthal Equal-Area Projection

Learning from Maps During the time of the Pax Romana, trade thrived throughout the entire Roman Empire as a result of an improved system of roads.

 Region What two areas were large producers of glassware and leather?

A disastrous fire swept Rome during the reign of Nero (A.D. 54–A.D. 68). Many people believed that the emperor started the fire. Whether or not Nero did, the Romans hated him because of his cruel and unpredictable policies. Facing certain assassination, Nero committed suicide in A.D. 68.

The Good Emperors

After Nero's death, a number of emperors supported by the army ruled Rome, including a series of four emperors in A.D. 69. Then in A.D. 96, Emperor Nerva came to power. He was the first of a series of five, known as the Good Emperors, who ruled Rome for almost 100 years. A Spanish general, Trajan, ruled from A.D. 98 to A.D. 117 and added new areas that brought the empire

to its largest size—about the size of the United States today. (See map on this page.)

Hadrian, Trajan's successor, who ruled from A.D. 117 to A.D. 138, supported the arts and proved an able emperor. Born in Spain, he understood the provinces and spent much time organizing and Romanizing them. To help protect the boundaries of the empire, Hadrian built fortifications along the frontiers and encouraged frontier peoples to enter the army. He disapproved of conquering neighboring regions and gave up the areas that Trajan had acquired in Asia.

After the uneventful reign of Antoninus Pius, Marcus Aurelius, the last of the Good Emperors, began his reign in A.D. 161. A well-educated man who

Building History Study Skills

READ
WRITE
INTERPRET
CONNECT
THINK

Writing About History: Formulating a Thesis Statement

The first step in writing an essay is to determine what you wish to describe, explain, or prove. The information or the data you have gathered and your stated purpose help you formulate a thesis statement. A thesis statement expresses the main idea of your essay. It serves the same function as the topic sentence of a paragraph.

A thesis statement follows these criteria:
- It is a generalization.
- It uses significant data in order to express a point of view.
- It measures how the various parts of the data interact with or relate to each other.

How to Formulate a Thesis Statement

To formulate a thesis statement, follow these steps.
1. Choose a topic of interest. Begin to collect facts about the general topic, and be sure to keep detailed notes.
2. Begin to refine the topic. Look for related facts. Make a generalization based on the related facts.
3. Organize the collected facts. Discard those facts that have no bearing on the general statement, or refine the statement even further to include the facts.
4. Write a thesis statement using the characteristics given above. Refine the generalization, turning it into a thesis statement that can be proved and that meets the criteria listed above.

Developing the Skill

Study the data below about significant events during the Roman Republic. As you read the data, think about what thesis statement you can formulate using these events.
- The Senate, the popular assemblies, and the magistrates helped govern Rome.
- Over hundreds of years, the plebeians gained many rights.
- After the Punic Wars, slavery became more widespread, and a new class of urban poor was created.
- The gap between the rich and the poor widened.
- Although the common people of Rome had many rights, it was the nobility that dominated the government.
- Julius Caesar became so powerful that the Senate named him dictator for life.

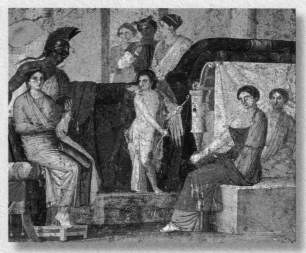

Wall painting from a home in Pompeii

- The attempts by the Gracchi to bring about land and government reform failed because of resistance from wealthy landowners.
- After Marius promised his soldiers plots of land from their conquests, soldiers began to be more loyal to their generals than to Rome.
- Civil war followed Caesar's assassination, and the republic ended with the reign of Octavian.

The facts all relate to conditions during the Roman Republic. The first two statements show that many groups shared in governing Rome and that the republic gave many rights to its citizens. The next seven facts, however, detail events that led to the end of the republic. A generalization relating all these facts might be: The Roman Republic had a democratic government, but various events combined to end the republic. Another way of formulating this generalization, thus turning it into a thesis statement, is this: Although many people were allowed to take part in Roman government, the power of the landowning nobility and the growth of a volunteer army loyal to generals doomed the Roman Republic.

Practicing the Skill

What other thesis statement can you formulate from these facts?

To apply this skill, see *Applying History Study Skills on page 175.*

preferred studying Stoic philosophy to fighting wars, he nevertheless had to defend the empire against invaders from the north and east. These invaders would play a key role in the future of the empire.

Section 3 Review

1. **Identify** Marius, Sulla, Pompey, Cleopatra, Marc Antony, Nero, Hadrian, Marcus Aurelius
2. **Locate and Explain the Significance** Actium
3. **Summarizing Ideas (a)** What was the First Triumvirate? **(b)** Why was it formed?
4. **Understanding Ideas** Describe the significance of the reign of Julius Caesar.
5. **Comparing Ideas** Contrast the rule of the Julio-Claudians with the rule of the Good Emperors.

Section 4

Roman Society and Culture

Focus Questions

- **What aspects of Roman rule helped unify and solidify the empire?**
- **How did citizens of the Roman Empire make a living and entertain themselves?**
- **What role did learning, education, and the arts play in imperial Rome?**

Several essential characteristics helped the Romans build their empire and maintain it in peace. The Romans had a talent for ruling others and maintained their authority through a strong government both at home and abroad. Law, military organization, and widespread trade and transportation held the empire together and brought peace for more than 200 years.

The period from the beginning of Augustus's reign until the death of Marcus Aurelius (27 B.C. to A.D. 180) is known as the **Pax Romana**, or "Roman Peace." The world has rarely witnessed such continuing unity, peace, and stability. During this period the empire's economy prospered, through farming, manufacturing, and trade, and the Roman Army was strong enough to defend the frontier.

Emperors of the Pax Romana 27 B.C.–A.D. 180

27 B.C.–A.D. 14	Augustus
A.D. 14–68	**Julio-Claudian Emperors** Tiberius (14–37)* Caligula (37–41) Claudius (41–54) Nero (54–68)
A.D. 68–69	**Army Emperors** Galba, Otho, Vitellius (Chosen by various legions during a succession crisis)
A.D. 69–96	**Flavian Emperors** Vespasian (69–79) Titus (79–81) Domitian (81–96)
A.D. 96–180	**The Good Emperors** Nerva (96–98) Trajan (98–117) Hadrian (117–138) Antoninus Pius (138–161) Marcus Aurelius (161–180)

*Dates of reign

Government

The Roman government provided the strongest unifying force in the empire. The government maintained order, enforced the laws, and defended the frontiers.

The position of emperor was a demanding one. In the central government and in the provinces, officials drawn from the aristocracy played a role in governing. However, the emperor had to make all policy decisions, appoint the officials who controlled the provinces, and run the entire government. The role entailed too many responsibilities for all but the ablest person. If a weak, incompetent, or selfish emperor reigned, effective government depended on the strength of the other government officials.

The Provinces

The provinces were governed more honorably during the time of the Pax Romana than they had been under the republic partly because the government in Rome kept a closer check on provincial governors. Any citizen in the provinces could appeal a governor's decision directly to the emperor.

The western provinces, especially Gaul and Spain, were influenced greatly because of their closeness to Roman civilization. The Romans constructed many new cities in the western provinces, each a smaller version of imperial Rome, complete with a senate building, theaters, and public baths. Most of the cities had **aqueducts**—bridgelike structures that carried water from the mountains. Most cities also had paved streets and sewer systems. Wealthy citizens of the provinces donated large sums of money to be used for public buildings, streets, schools, and entertainment.

Law

Roman law also unified the empire. The code of the Twelve Tables had been created in the 400s B.C. in a small agricultural society, and these laws had to be changed to address the many needs of a huge empire.

The Romans modified and expanded the Twelve Tables in two ways. First, the government passed new laws as needed. Second, judges interpreted the old laws to fit new circumstances. Both actions ensured that Roman law could adapt to fit the customs of all peoples throughout the provinces.

Roman judges helped develop the belief that certain basic legal principles apply to all humans. This meant that foreigners who came to Rome had the same rights as Roman citizens. This idea was linked to the theoretical notion that law was dictated by nature and therefore common to all people, an idea developed from Greek philosophy.

In later years the Roman system of law became the foundation for the laws of most of the European countries that had been part of the Roman Empire. Roman law also had a strong influence on the laws of the Christian church.

The Army

Augustus had reorganized the Roman army. The Praetorian Guard—first organized by Augustus to guard the praetorium, or headquarters of the commander in chief—was a small, elite force stationed in Rome to protect the emperor. Citizens who served for 20 years made up the legions that were stationed in large fortified camps along the frontiers. People often settled

Over the period between 312 B.C. and 226 A.D., 11 aqueducts were built to carry water to the city of Rome. In addition, Romans built aqueducts throughout their empire in such present-day countries as France, Spain, and Greece.

around these camps, and the settlements eventually grew into towns and cities.

Other forces from the provinces or the border tribes aided the Roman army. These soldiers enlisted for 25 years in return for the promise of Roman citizenship at the end of their enlistment. Thus a population of trained soldiers was established to help guard the frontiers. An estimated 250,000 to 300,000 soldiers guarded the empire at the time of Augustus's death. Although this number increased under later emperors, the total number of Roman soldiers probably never exceeded 500,000.

In some regions the Romans built great lines of fortifications for protection. In Britain, for example, Hadrian's Wall stretched across the entire island in the north. A line of forts ran between the Rhine and Danube Rivers. Between the great camps of the legions lay protective ditches, fortresses, and walls. Many portions of these walls still stand as reminders of Rome's vast presence.

Trade and Transportation

Throughout the time of the Pax Romana, agriculture remained the primary occupation of people in the empire. In Italy itself most farmers worked on large estates devoted to olive and wine production. Small farms were more common in the provinces.

A new type of agricultural worker, a tenant farmer known as a **colonus**, began to replace slaves on the large estates. Each of these farmers rented a small plot of land from the owner. The colonus had to remain on the land for a certain period and had to pay the owner of the land with crops. A colonus worked long, hard hours and had little to show for it.

The vast empire provided great opportunities for commerce, and the exchange of goods was easy. Taxes on trade remained low, and people used Roman currency everywhere. Rome and Alexandria became the empire's greatest commercial centers.

From the provinces, Italy imported grain and raw materials, such as meat, wool, and hides. From Asia came silks, linens, glassware, jewelry, and furniture to satisfy the tastes of the wealthy. India exported many products, including spices, cotton, and other luxury goods that Romans had never known before.

Manufacturing also increased throughout the empire. Italy, Gaul, and Spain made inexpensive pottery and textiles. As in Greece, most work was done by hand in small shops.

Transportation significantly improved during the early period of the empire. An estimated 50,000 miles of paved highways joined military outposts with cities in the interior, and highways linked all provincial cities to Rome—thus the saying "All roads lead to Rome." Bridges spanned rivers, and an imperial post carried correspondence from the emperor and his officials to all parts of the empire. However, even with improved transportation, it took a Roman messenger many weeks to cross the empire, even traveling at top speed and using every known means of transportation.

Living Conditions

The Pax Romana provided prosperity to many people, but citizens did not share equally in this wealth. The rich citizen usually had both a city home and a country home. Each residence included many conveniences, such as running water and baths.

The lives of the wealthy included much time for leisure—rest, exercise, public baths, and banquets. Reclining on couches, many wealthy Romans ate and drank enormous quantities at banquets. These lavish affairs frequently offered exotic foods. For example:

Appetizers

Jellyfish and eggs
Sow's udders stuffed with salted sea urchins
Patina of brains cooked with milk and eggs
Boiled tree fungi with peppered fish-fat sauce
Sea urchins with spices, honey, oil and egg sauce

Main Course

Fallow deer roasted with onion sauce, rue, Jericho dates, raisins, oil and honey
Boiled ostrich with sweet sauce
Turtle dove boiled in its feathers
Roast parrot
Dormice stuffed with pork and pine kernels
Ham boiled with figs and bay leaves, rubbed with honey, baked in pastry crust
Flamingo boiled with dates

Dessert

Fricassee of roses with pastry
Stoned dates stuffed with nuts and pine kernels, fried in honey
Hot African sweet-wine cakes with honey

Most Romans, of course, would never taste these exotic and expensive dishes. The majority of Romans ate three simple meals each day. These meals included foods such as bread, cheese, and fruit. Many ate only cereal and vegetables.

Extreme differences separated the lives of the wealthy from those of the poor. The average Roman had beds, tables, and chairs, which were chiefly camp stools or benches. Many of the 1 million residents of Rome lived in crowded three- or four-story wooden apartment houses, where fire posed a constant threat because of cooking fires and the candles and torches used for light. Most residents of the city of Rome were artisans or farmers. Though the city was large and busy, these people barely eked out a living. Though the government provided free grain to residents of the capital, that alone was not always enough.

Amusements

Romans enjoyed the theater, especially light comedies and satires. Performers such as mimes, jugglers, dancers, acrobats, and clowns became quite popular. Romans also enjoyed savage and brutal sports. Many spectators watched chariot racing in the huge Circus Maximus of Rome, a racetrack that could accommodate 250,000 spectators. Spectacular and often deadly crashes were a frequent part of these races.

Thousands of Romans also enjoyed spectacles in the Colosseum, the great amphitheater in Rome. Wild beasts, made more savage by hunger, fought each other in the arena. Sometimes humans fought against animals. Condemned criminals or slaves were often thrown into the arena to be killed by the beasts.

Combat between gladiators—trained fighters who were usually slaves—drew the largest crowds. The gladiators' fights usually ended in death for one or both men. When a gladiator was wounded, he appealed for mercy to the crowd, who signaled whether he should be killed or spared.

Public entertainment came to be so important to the Romans that the government sponsored free spectacles, in part to distract the people of the lower classes from their miserable living conditions. Juvenal, a Roman satirical poet, once said that only two things interested the Roman masses: "bread and circuses."

Science, Engineering, and Architecture

The Romans were less interested in scientific research to increase knowledge than in collecting and organizing information. Galen, a physician who lived in Rome during the A.D. 100s, wrote several volumes that summarized all the medical knowledge of his day. For centuries people regarded him as the greatest authority on medicine. People also accepted Ptolemy's theories in astronomy. A scientist from Alexandria, Ptolemy believed that Earth lay at the center of the universe. Most people accepted this theory until the A.D. 1500s.

The practical Romans applied the scientific knowledge they gained from the Greeks in planning cities, building water and sewage systems, and improving farming and livestock breeding. Roman engineers surpassed all ancient peoples in their ability to construct roads, bridges, aqueducts, amphitheaters, and public buildings.

The most important contribution of Roman architects was the use of concrete, which made large buildings possible in terms of both cost and engineering. Architects designed great public buildings—law courts, palaces, temples, amphitheaters, and triumphal arches—for the emperor, imperial officials, and the government. The Romans often based their buildings on Greek models. However, unlike the Greeks, the Romans knew how to build the arch and vaulted dome and emphasized size as well as pleasing proportion.

Popular Roman entertainment included games, music, and dance. This mosaic from Pompeii shows musicians playing percussion and wind instruments.

Baths

Ancient peoples were just as fond of taking a plunge into water as we are. The Romans were particularly fond of bathing and built many large public pools and baths. These pools and baths were often filled with water of different temperatures, heated either by natural hot springs or by furnaces. The Roman bather would go from one pool to the other, combining dips with exercises followed by massages with fine oils.

Some Roman bathhouses also contained libraries, sports facilities, and shops. Public baths were social gathering places where people could meet, gossip, and even do business. The largest public bath in Rome is credited as the main

achievement of its builder, the emperor Caracalla, who ruled in the A.D. 200s.

The Romans built baths wherever they settled. One such place in England, which had natural hot springs, became known as the city of Bath (top). People enjoyed its refreshing waters long after the Romans left England.

Today public baths are used as neighborhood gathering places and are extremely popular throughout Japan. There is also a very ornate public bath in Moscow, the capital of Russia, and in Budapest, Hungary (below). In the United States, outdoor and indoor public swimming pools provide the same enjoyment and recreation the ancient Romans knew.

Education

The Romans trained their children to be loyal citizens and to be obedient to their elders and superiors. Early education took place at home. The Roman father taught his sons about the duties of citizenship. The matron of the family taught her daughters to manage a household. Although most Roman women did not receive a formal education, many upper-class women were well educated.

Many towns and cities throughout the Roman Empire had elementary, secondary, and higher level schools. A boy or girl of the free classes entered elementary school at the age of 7 and studied reading, writing, arithmetic, and music. At about age 13, many boys entered a secondary school, where they studied grammar, Greek, literature, composition, and expressive speech. Former Greek slaves often taught the courses.

Literature

Augustus and several of the Good Emperors encouraged the development of art and literature. Although the Greeks strongly influenced Roman artists and writers, a number of Romans produced works of great originality, particularly in the field of literature.

Virgil, who lived during the reign of Augustus, ranked as the greatest Roman poet. He wrote the epic poem the *Aeneid*, which tells the story of Aeneas, a prince of Troy and a legendary ancestor of the Latins. When the Greeks captured Troy, Aeneas fled and, after many adventures, came to Italy. His descendants Romulus and Remus reportedly founded Rome. Another Roman poet, Horace, wrote of human emotions in odes, satires, and epistles (letters). Yet another poet, Ovid, wrote love lyrics and the *Metamorphoses*, a collection of myths written in verse.

The Metamorphoses

Ovid, who lived from 43 B.C. to A.D. 17, was one of the best-known Roman poets. Although he wrote many works, one of his most famous is the *Metamorphoses,* a series of 15 books of mostly Greek and some Roman mythology related in verse. With this work, Ovid produced a masterpiece, or great work, by which he hoped to obtain immortality. Using lively descriptions, he particularly demonstrated the richness of Greek mythology. Generations of poets and painters used his work for inspiration. The excerpt below recounts the story of Daedalus and Icarus, whom the legendary King Minos of Crete held prisoner.

Scene depicting Ovid's *Metamorphoses*

❝Such spectacular flight is what Daedalus, back in Crete, was thinking about. Though the sea surrounded the island, and Minos controlled all shipping, the air was nonetheless open and free. Why not soar up in the sky and fly like a bird to escape this barbarous land? He schemed and planned, made small drawings, and . . . started to build an object of feathers and wax by means of which he might perhaps take wing, leap up in the air, and glide through it to swoop and swim in the sky like a gull. Icarus, his son, watching close by, would play with the feathers, flinging them up into the air to see how they swirled as they fell, or else he would fool with the warm wax that was fun to mold—like clay. . . . At last, with two pairs of wings completed, [Daedalus] told the boy how he had planned their escape and what to do and what to avoid. 'Do not fly too low, where the sea spray can soak your wings and make the feathers soggy and heavy. But don't go too high, where the heat of the Sun's fire can melt the wax. Keep to a middle range if you can, and don't try to show off— it isn't a game but a matter of life and death. Do you understand what I'm trying to tell you?' The young man nods his head and promises he'll be good, will take no foolish chances but do what he's told and follow his father's lead. The parent wants to believe the child, hopes for once to rely on the promise the son has made. His hands nevertheless tremble some as he straps the wings onto his son. He hugs the boy, and his eyes fill with tears as he kisses his cheek and wishes him luck. Daedalus then takes off, ascends into the air, and, like a huge bird that leads his uncertain fledgling, wheels, makes a few turns and maneuvers to show how these feats are managed. The son flaps his wings and rises up to follow his father. Far below, on the ground, a farmer looks up from his plow at these figures high in the sky and supposes gods have come on a visit. Out in the country, a shepherd glances up from his flock, sees these creatures, and wonders if they are about to attack his sheep. Or out at sea beyond the mole of the harbor, a fisherman out in his boat stares up at the flying people but doesn't believe it. . . . The father and son are passing Samos, Delos, Paros, and now Lebinthos, and honey-rich Calymne. . . . But here the youngster's initial fears have mostly been calmed. His confidence now has developed. He wonders what he can do with this splendid toy, what limits there are to his father's invention. He flaps his wings and rises higher—but nothing bad happens. He figures he still has plenty of margin and rises higher still. It's exciting, wonderful fun, as he soars and wheels, but he doesn't notice the wax of his wings is melting and feathers are falling out. And then, it's too late, and he's flapping naked arms, which do nothing to hold him up. He is losing altitude. . . . He is falling. He cries out. His father hears him, and watches in horror the plummeting body splash into the sea that takes its name from its victim. He calls down to his son, 'Icarus! where are you?' but he sees only melted blobs that had been the wings, and the larger blob of the body he grabs and buries then in the tomb on the beach of the small island nearby—that people now call Icaria, in his honor.❞

Tacitus, one of the greatest Roman historians, wrote *Annals*, a history of Rome under the Julio-Claudian Emperors, which expresses his criticism of the government established by Augustus. Tacitus worried about the luxurious living of the wealthy and the lack of public virtue, as well as the decline of Roman political freedom under imperial autocracy. Another of his works, *Germania*, provides the best account of the Germanic tribes along the borders. However, Tacitus may have exaggerated the virtues of the Germanic peoples because he wrote the book to shame the Romans for their low moral standards.

Plutarch, a Greek, wrote *Parallel Lives*, a work that includes a series of biographical sketches. A description of a famous Greek is followed by one of a Roman whose life in some way resembled the Greek's life.

Language

Romans learned the alphabet from the Etruscans (who had adapted the Greeks' alphabet) and later changed some of the letters. Today we use the Roman, or Latin, alphabet of 23 letters, plus *J, U,* and *W,* which the English added after Roman times.

Long after the end of the Roman Empire, the Latin language continued to be used, with some changes, in most of Europe. Nearly all medieval European universities used Latin in their classes, and the Roman Catholic Church conducted services in Latin until the 1960s. Latin is the parent of the modern Romance (from the word *Roman*) languages: Italian, French, Spanish, Portuguese, and Romanian.

Many of the scientific terms we use today have either Latin or Greek origins. Although the language of the early Germanic peoples had a significant effect on the development of the English language, approximately one-half of all English words have Latin origins.

Section 4 Review

1. **Define** Pax Romana, aqueducts, colonus
2. **Identify** Praetorian Guard, Galen, Ptolemy
3. **Understanding Ideas** How did the army contribute to the protection and expansion of the Roman Empire?
4. **Comparing Ideas** How did the life of wealthy Romans compare to that of poor Romans?
5. **Evaluating Ideas** List five Roman contributions to science, engineering, architecture, literature, or language that you think are important.

The Rise of Christianity

Focus Questions

- How did Christianity arise out of the Jewish tradition in Judaea?
- What difficulties and successes did Christians experience while under the influence of the Roman Empire?
- What changes occurred in the church during the late Roman Empire that helped stabilize and solidify the church?

The Romans respected the various religions practiced in the provinces, if only to keep peace. However, as Roman power expanded, the Roman emperor became more widely regarded as a divine monarch. The Romans expected all residents of the empire—with one important exception—to honor the gods of Rome and the "divine spirit" of the emperor.

Jews and the Roman Empire

In Roman times most Jews lived in Judaea, which became a Roman province in A.D. 6. As monotheists, or those believing in a single god, Jews could not honor the Roman gods or the divine spirit of the emperor, and the Romans excused them from doing so.

Many Jews in Judaea hoped they could win their independence and have a king in the tradition of David. They yearned for a king like David—for a Messiah. (Each Jewish king was anointed with oil as part of his coronation. The word *Messiah* means "the Anointed One.")

As the years of Roman rule continued and independence became increasingly unlikely, the Jews began to think of the Messiah as a divinely appointed liberator. Various individuals claiming to be the Messiah appeared from time to time in Judaea, but their claims were false. Occasionally, the Jews would turn to radical measures and revolt against the Romans. After the great revolt of A.D. 66 to A.D. 70, the Romans sacked Jerusalem, slaughtered thousands of Jews, and destroyed the Second Temple. Only the western wall of the temple withstood the onslaught. Today Jews consider this wall, also known as the Wailing Wall, a sacred site of Judaism.

The destruction of the Second Temple marked a major turning point in Jewish history. With the temple gone, priests ceased to be the religious leaders of Judaism. **Rabbis**—scholars learned in the scriptures and in commentaries on religious law—filled their role.

Under the rule of the emperors Trajan and Hadrian, more Jewish revolts erupted in Judaea.* In the last one, led by Simeon Bar Kokhba, the Jews struggled fiercely against Emperor Hadrian. After the Romans brutally suppressed the revolt in A.D. 135, they banned all Jews from Jerusalem. Jewish communities outside Jerusalem, however, carried on the Jewish faith and culture.

Christianity, the religion founded by the Jewish teacher known as Jesus of Nazareth, arose out of this setting. Christianity drew on the expectations for a Messiah in the region during these centuries.

---

*Hadrian changed the name of the region from Judaea to Palestine.

The Life and Teachings of Jesus

Roman histories say very little about Jesus and the early Christians. Our knowledge of Jesus comes mainly from the Gospels of Matthew, Mark, Luke, and John—the first four books of the New Testament of the Christian Bible.

According to the Gospels, Jesus was born in Bethlehem, near Jerusalem, and grew up in the town of Nazareth. He was said to have been a carpenter and a student of the writings of the Jewish prophets. In time he began preaching. As he traveled through the villages of Judaea, he gathered a small group of disciples, or followers. From these he chose 12 to help him preach.

Jesus wandered the countryside with his disciples, depending on the charity of the people for his needs. According to the Gospels, he created great excitement among the people, performing miracles of healing and defending the poor and the oppressed.

This Christian mosaic depicts Jesus on the road to Calvary.

The teachings of Jesus have become one of the greatest influences on the Western world. He accepted the Ten Commandments as guides to right living but gave them further meaning. According to the Gospel of Matthew, Jesus said:

"Don't misunderstand why I have come—it isn't to cancel the laws of Moses and the warnings of the prophets. No, I come to fulfill them, and to make them all come true."

He summarized the Ten Commandments in two great rules: People must love God above all else, and they must love others as they love themselves. His many teachings include the following: (1) God cares more for people than for their laws and rituals. He desires a new relationship between himself and humans based on his promises and his love, to which people respond in faith. (2) Jesus saw himself as coming to establish the "Kingdom of God"—this loving relationship that God desires. The Kingdom of God would be both in this world and in a life beyond it. (3) God is a God of grace—a forgiving God—who wants people to forgive one another in recognition of what God has already done for them.

The Death of Jesus

When Jesus traveled to Jerusalem in about A.D. 30, many Jews there hailed him as the Messiah—the son of God—and as "King of the Jews." Others, especially the conservative priestly class of Jews, denied that he was the Messiah and regarded him as a revolutionary.

The Romans feared that Jesus wanted to lead an uprising, and they considered him an enemy of the state. He was tried before Pontius Pilate, the Roman governor. Pilate acted reluctantly, perhaps because he feared the trial would ignite yet another revolt. Eventually, however, he agreed to Jesus' crucifixion.

The Spread of Christianity

According to the Gospels, Jesus arose from the dead, remained on Earth for 40 more days, and then ascended into heaven. His followers believed that the resurrection and the ascension proved that Jesus was the Messiah, calling him Jesus Christ, after the Greek word for Messiah—*Christos*. The resurrection became the central event of Christianity. Through the death of Jesus Christ, who had died for the sins of the human race, all people could achieve redemption. Believing that the day of God's final judgment was close at hand, the disciples of Jesus set out to spread this message. At first the disciples worked mainly in the Jewish communities of Palestine.

One of the people who did the most to spread Christianity was a Jew named Saul. Born in the town of Tarsus in Asia Minor, Saul converted to Christianity, took the name Paul, and became a Christian missionary. Paul carried on his work not only among Jews but among all peoples. He emphasized that Christianity is not just a sect of Judaism. For about two decades, starting in the mid-40s A.D., he journeyed throughout the eastern Mediterranean region, spreading the teachings of Jesus and founding Christian communities. According to tradition, while visiting Rome, Paul was put to death.

Paul's Epistles, or letters, to Christian congregations in Greece and Asia Minor form an important part of the New Testament. Paul insisted that Jesus was not just the Jewish Messiah but a divine universal savior who would soon return to judge the entire human race. By following the teachings of Jesus, all people could be saved from the consequences of their sins. They could avoid damnation and instead enjoy the bliss of salvation in paradise after death.

Christianity and Its Rivals

Christianity spread slowly, but its appeal increased as life in the Roman Empire became more difficult. Emperor worship and many of the old religions of the empire no longer offered comfort to many people. The Persian cult of Mithras did promise happiness after death, but it excluded women. The cult of Cybele (SI·buh·lee) in Asia Minor and the Egyptian cult of Isis worshiped goddesses, but these cults did not necessarily appeal to everyone.

Christianity, on the other hand, accepted everyone. It welcomed the poor and the rich alike and promised salvation after death. In this world, Christians were expected to be good citizens and to obey the laws. They were encouraged to practice charity and to care for the poor and outcast.

Persecution of the Christians

At first the Roman government viewed Christians as a Jewish sect and thus freed them from the obligation to worship the emperor. However, by the A.D. 100s, it recognized them as different, and Christians had to make a difficult choice.

The early Christians were good citizens. Their religion taught them to respect government. They refused to worship the emperor as a god, however, and they spoke out against the idea of worshiping multiple gods. They also were more likely than the Jews to try to convert others to their point of view.

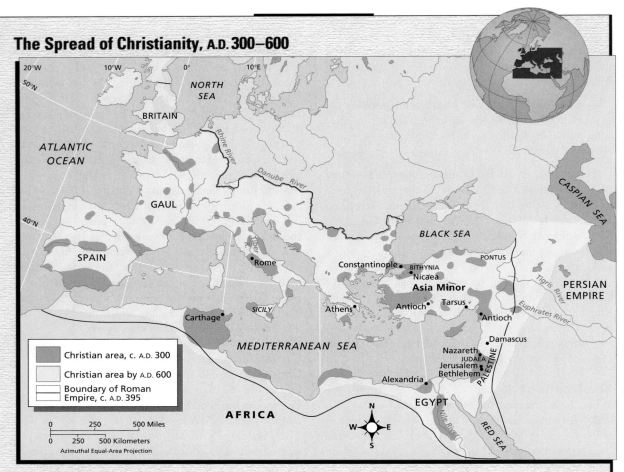

The Spread of Christianity, A.D. 300–600

NORTH SEA

BRITAIN

ATLANTIC OCEAN

20°W 10°W 0° 10°E

50°N

Rhine River

Danube River

GAUL

40°N

SPAIN

Tiber R.

Rome

SICILY

Carthage

MEDITERRANEAN SEA

Constantinople BITHYNIA
Nicaea
Asia Minor
Athens Antioch Tarsus
Antioch

BLACK SEA PONTUS

CASPIAN SEA

Tigris River

PERSIAN EMPIRE

Euphrates River

Damascus

Nazareth
JUDAEA
Jerusalem PALESTINE
Bethlehem

Alexandria

EGYPT

AFRICA

Nile River

RED SEA

N
W E
S

- Christian area, c. A.D. 300
- Christian area by A.D. 600
- Boundary of Roman Empire, c. A.D. 395

0 250 500 Miles
0 250 500 Kilometers
Azimuthal Equal-Area Projection

Learning from Maps Christianity spread throughout the entire Roman Empire.

Human-Environment Interaction Around which physical feature did the Christian church establish the five patriarchal cities of Rome, Constantinople, Alexandria, Antioch, and Jerusalem?

These Christian actions appeared to be an attack against Roman religion and law, and the Romans outlawed Christianity, occasionally seized Christian property, and executed some Christians. Sometimes the Romans used Christians as scapegoats,* blaming them for natural or political disasters. Many Christians became **martyrs**, put to death because they refused to renounce their beliefs. The Roman efforts, however, failed to stop the spread of Christianity.

---

*Many ancient religions sacrificed goats to their god or gods or drove them into the wilderness to obtain forgiveness. The term *scapegoat* came to mean a person or thing bearing blame for the action of others.

In the A.D. 200s, civil wars shook the Roman Empire, and many people turned to Christianity, which gave them hope. By the beginning of the A.D. 300s, the Christian church had become too large for the government to punish all its members, and Roman law accepted Christianity as a religion.

The Success of Christianity

The situation of the Christians vastly improved when Emperor Constantine became a supporter of Christianity. According to Constantine, in A.D. 312 he was leading his army into battle when he saw a blazing cross in the sky. Beneath it were the words *In Hoc Signo Vinces*, Latin words meaning "In this sign, conquer." He placed himself and his army under the protection of the Christian God. After his victory, Constantine declared himself a Christian and supported Christianity throughout the empire. He was baptized on his deathbed in A.D. 337.

In A.D. 391 the emperor Theodosius banned pagan worship. Christian emperors persecuted the pagans and ordered the pagan temples destroyed. Within 400 years, Christianity had spread from its birthplace in Judaea to all parts of the huge empire. (See map on page 166.)

Organization of the Church

In the early years of Christianity, there was little organization among its followers. They did live together in groups, however, often sharing their possessions and holding property in common.

During the latter part of the Roman Empire, a more definitive church organization developed. Priests conducted services and performed baptisms and marriages. Above the priests were the bishops, who headed the church in each city.

Rome, Constantinople, Alexandria, Antioch, and Jerusalem gained special importance as administrative centers for the Christian church. The bishops of these empire cities were called **patriarchs**. Over time the patriarch of Rome assumed the title of **pope** (from a Latin word meaning "father") and claimed supremacy over the other patriarchs. As successors of Peter, whom Jesus had named as his successor on Earth, later bishops of Rome claimed broad powers.

Church councils played a vital role in strengthening the early Christian church. In A.D. 325 the council at Nicaea (ny·SEE·uh) proclaimed the doctrine of the Trinity, the existence of three persons—God the Father, the Son, and the Holy Spirit—in one god, as a main article of faith. Today the concept of the Trinity is a central belief of Christians.

Section 5 Review

1. **Define** rabbi, martyr, patriarch, pope
2. **Identify** disciples, Constantine, Theodosius
3. **Locate and Explain the Significance** Jerusalem, Bethlehem, Nazareth, Tarsus
4. **Comparing Ideas** In what ways was Christianity like Judaism?
5. **Analyzing Ideas** Why were Christians persecuted in the Roman Empire?
6. **Evaluating Ideas** How did church organization strengthen Christianity?

The Fall of the Roman Empire in the West

Focus Questions

- **What problems plagued the empire during the A.D. 200s?**
- **How did the reigns of Diocletian and Constantine serve to slow the decline of the empire?**
- **To what do historians attribute the decline of the Roman Empire?**

The western part of the Roman Empire weakened until it finally collapsed in the A.D. 400s. To understand this long period of decline, we must turn back to the time of the Good Emperors.

When Marcus Aurelius chose his successor in A.D. 180, he knew the man had shortcomings. He appointed his weak, spoiled son, Commodus (KAHM·uh·duhs). The end of the reign of Marcus Aurelius signaled the beginning of the disintegration of the empire. Many different factors, however, contributed to its decline.

Problems of the Empire

Many capable soldier-emperors, including Septimus Severus, Diocletian (dy·uh·KLEE·shuhn), and Constantine, helped slow the decline of the Roman Empire. Even the best emperors, however, had to face population decline, unrest within the empire, and attacks from outside forces.

During most of the A.D. 200s, the empire experienced dreadful confusion and civil war. Between A.D. 235 and 284, for example, 20 emperors reigned. All but one died violently. The legions, moreover, were not always able to defend the borders successfully. Barbarian tribes invaded every frontier of the empire.

The civil wars and barbarian invasions affected many aspects of Roman life. Travel became unsafe, and merchants hesitated to send goods by land or sea. The rural population grew even poorer than before. Population decreased throughout the empire, partly because a great plague spread through the provinces and caused several million deaths.

In A.D. 212 the government granted citizenship to all the free peoples of the empire in order to collect from everyone the inheritance tax that citizens had to pay. While taxes rose, however, money declined in value.

This relief sculpture shows a Roman legionary and an attacking barbarian.

The end of Roman expansion meant no new sources of gold. In addition, gold was being transported out of the empire because the rich continued to buy luxuries from abroad. To maintain the money supply, emperors minted new coins containing copper or lead as well as gold. When people realized that their coins had less gold in them, they refused to accept them at their face value.

To receive the same amount of gold as before, merchants raised their prices. A rise in prices caused by a decrease in the value of the exchange medium is called **inflation**. Inflation became so severe in some parts of the empire that people stopped using money and reverted to bartering.

The wealthy fared better than the poor. As small farmers were forced to sell their land, large estates grew even larger. With the decline in population, there were fewer farmers to feed the remaining population. The emperor refused to permit farmers who inherited their land to leave it.

The people in the cities fared no better. Many artisans tried to leave their jobs in the cities, where food was scarce, to find work in the country. To prevent this, the government made use of the workers' trade associations, called **collegia** (kuh·LEE·jee·uh). A law made workers' membership in the collegia compulsory. The government required members of the collegia to stay at their jobs and to perform certain public services. When some people tried to resign from the collegia, another law made membership not only compulsory but also hereditary.

Diocletian

The Roman Empire would probably have collapsed in the late A.D. 200s except for the efforts of two able emperors, Diocletian and Constantine. Their reforms and reorganizations postponed the collapse for nearly 200 years.

Born to a poor family, Diocletian had risen through the ranks of the army to become a general. The army made him emperor in A.D. 284, and he proved to be an able administrator.

Diocletian reorganized the administration of the empire. Realizing that the empire had grown too large for one person to manage, he appointed a co-emperor. Each co-emperor, known as an augustus, chose an assistant, called a caesar, to help him rule and to become his successor. Diocletian ruled in the east, and Maximian ruled in the west.

Although Diocletian shared his power with others, he held supreme authority. He transformed Roman imperial society into a rigid and bureaucratic order in which almost every aspect of life was controlled by the government. Sons had to follow the trades and social positions of their fathers. Peasants were permanently tied to the land they farmed. Individual freedom became secondary to the defense and security of the empire.

Diocletian ended lawlessness within the empire and drove out the invading barbarian tribes. He also tried to improve commerce and manufacturing and to increase the wealth of the empire through price and wage controls. However, his achievements did not endure. His policies proved impractical and difficult to enforce, and Rome drifted closer to economic ruin.

Constantine

The system of divided rule Diocletian established did not work well after he retired in A.D. 305. The rivalry between co-emperors and their caesars became intense, and civil war racked the empire. Constantine, who came to power as a caesar in A.D. 306, became sole emperor in A.D. 324. His reign is known for two great achievements: his protection of the Christian religion and his creation of a new capital on the site of the former Greek city of Byzantium. Named Constantinople, the new capital was dedicated in A.D. 330. Today it is the Turkish city of Istanbul.

After Constantine's death in A.D. 337, the empire enjoyed some 50 years of stability. However, inefficiency and corruption plagued the government. The Spanish-born emperor Theodosius was the last ruler to control a unified empire. After his death in A.D. 395, his two weak sons shared the throne. By A.D. 400 two empires existed, one in the west and one in the east. The one in the west grew constantly weaker. Power had shifted to the east, the center of wealth. Although the empire in the west collapsed in the A.D. 400s, the empire in the east remained until 1453. (See Chapter 8.)

The Germans

It might seem that the Western Roman Empire would have fallen apart from inner weaknesses alone. However, pressures from the outside also mounted as enemies attacked every frontier of the empire. The most important of these outsiders were the Germans, who lived beyond the Rhine and Danube Rivers. One Germanic tribe, the Ostrogoths, eventually migrated southeast to settle north of the Black Sea. Another tribe, the Visigoths, occupied land north of the Danube River. (See map on page 170.)

Germans in the empire. The northern frontier of the Roman Empire along the Rhine and Danube Rivers had strong fortifications designed to stop the Germans. As early as the reign of Augustus, however, many Germans began crossing the frontier peacefully.

Around A.D. 375 the Huns, an Asiatic tribe, began moving into the region north of the Black Sea. The nomadic Huns lived by raiding and plundering, and their fierceness terrified the people of Europe.

Pressure by the Huns pushed many German tribes into the empire. Roman officials mistreated the new settlers, however, and in A.D. 378 the Visigoths revolted. In a battle at Adrianople, they destroyed a Roman army and killed its leader, the eastern emperor Valens.

An ambitious leader named Alaric now became king of the Visigoths. In A.D. 401 he led the Visigoths west into Italy. (See map on page 170.) Alaric captured Rome in A.D. 410 and savagely sacked the city. A few months later, he died.

Final invasions of the west. The two parts of the empire drifted further apart. The east revived and gained strength, while the west sank into ruin as barbarians poured in everywhere. (See map on page 170.) One tribe of barbarians, the Vandals, so savagely destroyed everything in their path that today we use the word *vandal* to mean one who causes senseless destruction.

In the mid-400s, Attila, a fierce leader of the Huns, led an attack on Gaul. An army of Romans and Visigoths defeated the Huns in a great battle at Châlons-sur-Marne in A.D. 451. Attila himself died two years later. His army quickly broke up, and the Huns no longer threatened the empire. However, it was now too late to save the Western Roman Empire, which was weakened and shattered beyond repair.

A barbarian commander overthrew Romulus Augustulus, the last Roman emperor in the west, in A.D. 476. Because of this event, people sometimes refer to the "fall" of the Roman Empire in A.D. 476.

Invasions into the Roman Empire, A.D. 340–481

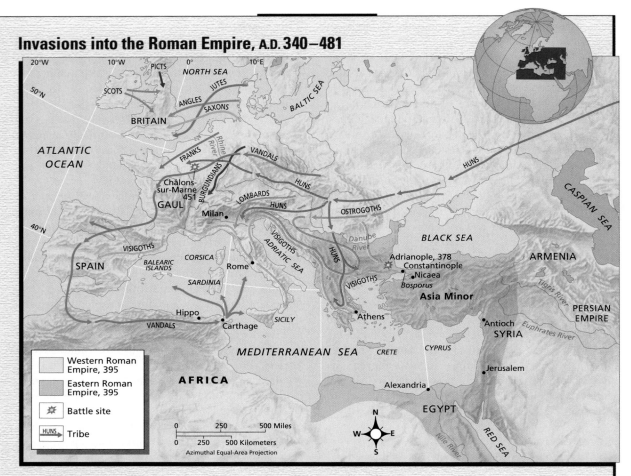

Learning from Maps Although the Roman Empire was affected by civil wars and barbarian invasions during the A.D. 200s, Diocletian and Constantine slowed its decline by means of their able governing.

? Location Locate the place and date of the major battle that took place in the Eastern Roman Empire.

Actually, no such thing as a single fall occurred, but instead the empire had gradually disintegrated.

Results of Rome's Decline

European civilization suffered a grave setback when the Western Roman Empire collapsed. The Germans who invaded the west established tribal kingdoms, but they proved incapable of ruling an empire. The result was **anarchy**—the absence of any government at all.

Most people left the cities in search of both food and greater safety. In the country, however, soldiers often trampled crops during battles, and weeds choked the fields. Learning declined, for no governments existed to set up and maintain schools. Libraries, with their great stores of knowledge, were destroyed. The number of literate and learned people grew smaller and smaller. Knowledge of the world and the past declined and was replaced by ignorance and superstition. Without cities, trade, communication, and literacy of some kind, civilization could not survive.

Why Rome Declined

Why did Rome decline? How did this mighty empire that had accomplished so much disappear? For centuries historians have debated these questions. Some historians blame the army as a weakening factor.

After the time of the Good Emperors, poor leaders and lax discipline plagued the once mighty legions. Military interference in the choice of emperor made the government unstable.

Barbarian invaders also played an important role in the Roman collapse. However, tribes of barbarians lived on the frontiers throughout the time of both the Roman Republic and the Roman Empire. Their numbers were small compared to the millions of people who lived within the empire. Not until the empire had declined did the mass of barbarians choose to break through or become able to break through the frontiers.

The important point to remember is that no one factor caused Rome to decline. Like many other complex movements and events in history, the disintegration of the empire resulted from a combination of different forces. Between A.D. 200 and A.D. 400, almost no aspect of Roman life—political, economic, or social—escaped decay, each one acting upon the others.

Political weakness. Rome tried to control the entire Mediterranean world with a government designed for a small city-state. The miracle is that it worked for 600 years. In an age of slow transportation, the empire grew too fast and became too large for the kind of governmental organization the Romans had set up.

Another political weakness was the lack of civilian control of the military. Many emperors did win the loyalty of the army, but they had to be strong to keep the legions loyal. Ambitious generals often seized control, assassinated the emperor, and assumed the throne. The common soldiers lost a sense of loyalty to Rome and instead served anyone who could pay them more.

Economic decline. The economic decline proved even more devastating than the political decline. Government expenses were heavy. Taxes had to finance the construction of public buildings, the maintenance of the army, and later the cost of two capitals—one in the west and one in the east. Even heavy taxes could not support the government. For centuries the Roman government maintained itself on rich plunder from foreign wars. After Trajan, however, this source of revenue was exhausted.

Decreased revenue for the government resulted in unrepaired roads and bridges and increased banditry. The greater danger in travel led in turn to a decrease in trade. When trade declined, manufacturing suffered, and both virtually disappeared. Agriculture suffered the same fate as trade and commerce. Small farmers—once the strength of the empire—gradually lost their lands to a few very powerful landowners.

The Roman economy did not produce enough wealth to support a great civilization permanently. Wealth was concentrated in too few hands, and poverty steadily increased.

When the barbarians invaded the empire, the Roman armies fought hard, but when they lost, the empire lacked the leadership to recover. Taxes and public service crushed the urban middle class. The corrupt courts did not serve justice. Yet the government seemed to be locked into this system and unable to change it.

Social change. A third force of great importance was social decay. Early Romans may have been rude and uncultured, but they were stern, virtuous, hardworking, and patriotic. They had a strong sense of duty and believed in serving their government. Romans of the later empire lost this patriotism, took little interest in government, and lacked political honesty.

The Roman Heritage and Christianity

In the ruins of the Roman world, two key ideas did survive in the west—the Roman heritage and the presence of Christianity. The barbarians whose kingdoms had once been part of the Roman Empire were influenced by its customs and civilizations. The leaders of the barbarian peoples remembered that unity under an emperor had once existed. Ambitious rulers in later centuries tried to regain this unity.

Christianity became the official religion recognized by the state. Its leaders would play key roles in the post-Roman world. The Christian church became the main preserver of Roman ideas and civilization.

Section 6 Review

1. **Define** inflation, collegia, anarchy
2. **Identify** Commodus, Ostrogoths, Visigoths, Huns, Alaric, Attila, Romulus Augustulus
3. **Locate and Explain the Significance** Constantinople, Rhine River, Danube River, Black Sea, Adrianople, Châlons-sur-Marne
4. **Understanding Ideas** Describe the problems of the Roman Empire in the A.D. 200s.
5. **Interpreting Ideas (a)** What was the system of divided rule? **(b)** What problems were caused by this organization?
6. **Synthesizing Ideas** What were the major reasons for the collapse of the Roman Empire in the west? Give examples to help support your answer.

Rome: An Enduring Legacy

The Roman Empire collapsed more than 1,500 years ago, but in many ways it never died. Instead, it continues to influence people throughout the world even today.

Take language, for example. The Romans based their alphabet on that of the Etruscans—who had borrowed theirs from the Greeks, who had borrowed theirs from the Phoenicians. However, the modern letters you see on this page are a direct gift from the Romans. So are Roman numerals. Even the planets of our solar system show the influence of imperial Rome because they bear the names of Roman gods—Mars, Mercury, and Venus, for example. Our calendar is based on the one developed by Julius Caesar in 46 B.C. July bears the name of Julius Caesar himself, August that of his successor, Augustus Caesar. The last day of the week, Saturday, honors the Roman god Saturn.

Latin, the language of the Romans, developed directly into the Romance languages

Bronze statue of Charlemagne

of Italian, Romanian, French, Spanish, and Portuguese. The common origins of these languages become evident when you examine a few of their words. For example, the Latin word *lux*, meaning "light," is similar to the Italian word *luce*, the Spanish word *luz*, and the French word *lumière*. Although the English language is a mixture of Old Norse, Old German, Latin, and Norman French, about 50 percent of English words have Latin

origins. For example, the word *republic* comes from *res publica*, Latin for "thing belonging to the people." *Senate* comes from the Roman council of elders, the *senatus*.

Rome's legacy remains highly visible throughout the countryside of southern Europe, North Africa, and Southwest Asia. Roman bridges still span French and Spanish rivers, and roads that once connected Rome with its provinces are still in existence today. In each city the Romans conquered, they added their own urban plan—a grid system of roads, temples, a central forum, baths, and theaters. Many cities that flourished under the Romans, such as Alexandria, Antioch, and the rebuilt Carthage, owe their city's layout to the engineers of the Roman period.

The ruins of Roman buildings, themselves largely based on Greek models, have continued to inspire generations of architects. Michelangelo used Roman models to design St. Peter's Basilica in Rome in 1547. Moreover, Thomas Jefferson studied Roman architecture when he built his home, Monticello, in 1770. Roman law also left its imprint on the world. Codified in the second and third centuries, Roman laws were adopted by many countries in Europe and Southwest Asia after the empire fell.

Some of those European nations eventually established colonies in Asia, Africa, and the Americas. They modeled the laws of their

Monticello

St. Peter's Basilica

colonies after the laws of their own countries. In this way, although greatly modified, the Roman influence has been transmitted to the legal system of most of the countries of the world.

In hundreds of ways, Rome speaks to us all. Why? What made Rome so special? For one thing, the Roman Empire was huge. It once included what is today Italy, France, Spain, Portugal, Switzerland, Austria, Greece, Romania, Turkey, Libya, Syria, Morocco, and Tunisia, as well as parts of Great Britain and Germany. Across its far-reaching roads Rome sent not just legions but also commerce and culture.

Rome also lasted a long time. Founded, according to legend, in 753 B.C., it survived for more than 1,200 years, until the last Roman emperor, Romulus Augustulus, was deposed in A.D. 476. When Rome fell, the city of Constantinople laid claim to the entire Roman world. The Eastern Roman, or Byzantine, Empire carried on the heritage and organization of Rome for another 1,000 years, until it fell to the Turks in 1453.

Roman lighthouse in England

The Near East was not the only place to keep the Roman tradition alive. The Germanic rulers who overran the empire saw themselves as successors to the Romans. The Frankish ruler Charlemagne, who spoke fluent Latin, was crowned "Emperor of the Romans" in A.D. 800.

In A.D. 962 Otto the Great founded the Holy Roman Empire, uniting the lands of Germany and Italy in a loose confederation of states. This empire lasted, at least in name, almost 1,000 years, until the reign of Napoleon.

Roman influence lived on not only in politics but also in religion. Christianity, first scorned by Roman authorities, was made an official state religion in the A.D. 300s and took on many Roman features. Church structure and organization were modeled after Roman government. Roman law became the model for canon, or church, law, and the pope became the center of Western Christianity. Christian churches were styled after Roman government centers, or basilicas.

Over the centuries, our Roman heritage has been idealized, romanticized, and often sanitized. While much about Rome was corrupt and unappealing, it was Rome's sense of grandeur, its power, and its organization that made everyone want to be a Roman and that ultimately passed its legacy down to us.

Chapter 7 Review

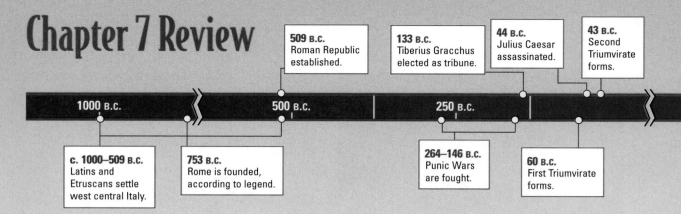

509 B.C.
Roman Republic established.

133 B.C.
Tiberius Gracchus elected as tribune.

44 B.C.
Julius Caesar assassinated.

43 B.C.
Second Triumvirate forms.

1000 B.C.   **500 B.C.**   **250 B.C.**

c. 1000–509 B.C.
Latins and Etruscans settle west central Italy.

753 B.C.
Rome is founded, according to legend.

264–146 B.C.
Punic Wars are fought.

60 B.C.
First Triumvirate forms.

Chapter Summary

The following list contains the key concepts you have learned about Rome.

1. The early inhabitants of Italy included the Latins, the Etruscans, and the Greeks.
2. The Romans dominated the entire Mediterranean region by the mid-200s B.C.
3. Early Rome was a republic. The most important governing bodies were the Senate, the popular assemblies, and the magistrates.
4. After the Conflict of the Orders, the plebeians gained more rights. The nobility, however, continued to control the republic.
5. During the years of the Punic Wars and Rome's expansion, Rome experienced problems in government, changes in agriculture and commerce, and social changes. Many of these changes weakened the empire.
6. Julius Caesar formed the First Triumvirate in 60 B.C. but was assassinated in 44 B.C. Octavian, who succeeded Caesar, became the first emperor, called Augustus Caesar. From the 20s B.C. onward, Rome was an empire, not a republic.
7. The abilities of the emperors varied greatly, but they all maintained internal stability and a continued expansion of Roman territory until the late A.D. 100s.
8. Education and literature flourished, as did engineering and architecture. However, corruption and political disorder gradually increased.
9. One of the world's great religions—Christianity—began in Judaea. It was based on the teachings of Jesus. Despite persecution of its followers, Christianity spread.
10. Around A.D. 300 two reforming emperors, Diocletian and Constantine, helped restore the empire.
11. Political, economic, and social factors all led to the collapse of the Roman Empire in the west.
12. The Christian church helped preserve Roman civilization after the western half of the empire lost its strength and was overrun by invaders in the A.D. 400s. Only in the eastern half did the descendants of the Romans preserve their independence in an empire centered in the city of Constantinople.

Reviewing Important Terms

On a separate sheet of paper, match each of the following terms with the correct definition below.

a. latifundia
b. veto
c. indemnity
d. inflation
e. aqueduct
f. Pax Romana
g. patriarch
h. republic
i. checks and balances

_____1. Rise in prices that a decrease in the value of exchange medium causes
_____2. Roman Peace
_____3. Bishop of one of the five most important early Christian cities
_____4. Form of government in which voters elect officials to run the state
_____5. Refuse to approve
_____6. Money for the damages of war
_____7. Large estate during the later Roman Republic and the Roman Empire
_____8. Bridgelike structure that carried water to the cities from the mountains
_____9. Principle that prevents any one part of the government from becoming too powerful

Developing Critical Thinking Skills

1. **Interpreting Ideas** How did the use of written law help strengthen the Roman government?
2. **Comparing Ideas** Compare the role of citizens in Athenian democracy with that of citizens in the Roman Republic. What are the similarities and differences? (You may want to refer to Chapters 5 and 6 for information on Athenian democracy.)
3. **Contrasting Ideas** How did the government of the Roman Republic differ from the government of the Roman Empire?
4. **Understanding Chronology** Place the three items in each of the following lists in chronological order.

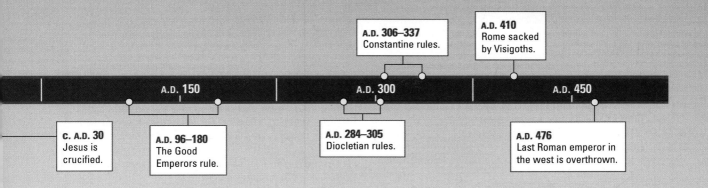

A.D. 306–337
Constantine rules.

A.D. 410
Rome sacked
by Visigoths.

A.D. 150

A.D. 300

A.D. 450

C. A.D. 30
Jesus is
crucified.

A.D. 96–180
The Good
Emperors rule.

A.D. 284–305
Diocletian rules.

A.D. 476
Last Roman emperor in
the west is overthrown.

a. The First Triumvirate, the Third Punic War, the Julio-Claudians
b. The German invasions, the life of Jesus, the reign of Julius Caesar
c. The Hun invasions, the Carthaginian invasions, the Etruscan monarchy
d. The letters of Paul, Virgil's *Aeneid,* the Battle of Adrianople
e. The reforms under the Gracchi, the founding of Constantinople, the division of the empire

5. **Analyzing Ideas** (a) What do you consider to be the most important contribution that the Romans made to civilization today? (b) Support your answer.

Relating Geography to History
Compare the extent of Roman territory shown on the maps on pages 149, 155, and 170. (a) What was the farthest extent of Roman territory to the east? (b) When did these boundaries represent the farthest extent of Roman territory?

Relating Past to Present
1. The Roman Republic had a citizen army rather than a professional army. (a) What kind of army do we have in the United States today? (b) What are the advantages and disadvantages of each type of army?
2. (a) Discuss how the persecution of the Christians in Rome affected the spread of Christianity. (b) Choose a country where religious persecution exists today. What effect does this persecution have on the members of the religious group being persecuted? (c) On the religion worldwide?
3. The Roman historian Tacitus used his treatise *Germania,* which is about the Germanic tribes, to criticize the corruption and immorality of Roman society. Choose a modern book, play, or movie that comments on contemporary events or people and describe the "message" that it puts forward.

Applying History Study Skills
Before completing this activity, review Building History Study Skills on page 156.

Study the following data on the policies and practices of Julius Caesar. Then formulate a thesis statement based on the data.

• Caesar won military distinction in Gaul.
• Caesar employed people on public works.
• Caesar made use of the personal loyalty of his own legions.
• Caesar expanded Roman citizenship to the peoples outside Italy.
• The Senate declared Caesar dictator for life.
• Senators who felt that Julius Caesar was trying to destroy the republic assassinated him on the Ides of March, 44 B.C.

internet**connect**

In A.D. 79 an eruption of Mount Vesuvius destroyed the city of Pompeii in southern Italy. The volcanic ash that buried Pompeii preserved the ruins, and from them we can learn much about daily life during the period. Search the Internet through the HRW Web site for information on the destruction of Pompeii. Write a report on your findings. Include information that clearly indicates that the citizens of Pompeii were caught by surprise when the volcano erupted.

HRW **GO TO:** go.hrw.com
KEYWORD: SCØ Pompeii

Building Your Portfolio
1. **Determining Historical Accuracy** Read Shakespeare's play *Julius Caesar.* (a) How did Shakespeare depict Caesar? (b) How did Shakespeare depict Cassius? (c) Based on what you have read about Caesar in this chapter, is the character in the play historically accurate? (d) Do you feel that Caesar was really trying to become a dictator? (e) According to the play, how did Brutus justify his role in the assassination of Caesar? Place your answers to all of these questions in your portfolio.
2. **Dramatizing History** Use resources in your school or public library to find more information on the plot to assassinate Julius Caesar. Then write a script of a scene in which the conspirators decide when they will kill Caesar. Place the script of the scene that you write in your portfolio.

Unit Summary

The following list contains the key concepts you have learned about the civilizations of the Mediterranean world.

1. The Minoans and the Mycenaeans created the first Greek civilizations.

2. The polis, or city-state, was the basic political unit of ancient Greece. The ancient Greeks were loyal to their own city-states, and they could seldom unite for very long.

3. The two most famous city-states were Sparta and Athens. Sparta was a militaristic state, whereas Athens gradually evolved into a democracy.

4. After stopping two Persian invasions, many of the city-states united under the leadership of Athens. This union was short-lived, however; the city-states were soon caught up in the devastating Peloponnesian War. Only when an outside invader, Philip II of Macedonia, conquered Greece was the region once again united.

5. Against the background of the Peloponnesian War, Athens underwent an unprecedented golden age. Athenian ideals of art, literature, and democracy have been valuable contributions to Western civilization.

6. Alexander the Great created an empire that included Egypt, Asia Minor, and Persia. While this empire lasted, classical Greek culture merged with other cultures of the Mediterranean region to form Hellenistic culture.

7. On the Italian Peninsula, the Latins, Etruscans, and Greeks influenced the culture of Rome. In time, the Romans conquered the entire Mediterranean region and formed a great empire.

8. The Romans made many contributions to Western civilization. Engineers constructed aqueducts; artists, sculptors, and writers created many original works; and architects first used concrete to build public buildings. Roman law formed the basis of our legal code, and from the Latin language emerged our present Romance languages.

9. Christianity developed in Judaea and spread throughout the Roman Empire.

10. Although the Roman Empire in the west collapsed in A.D. 476, the empire in the east preserved the Roman heritage and traditions.

Reviewing Concepts

On a separate sheet of paper, name the individuals who might have made the following statements. Explain why each statement is significant.

1. "King Philip of Macedonia should not be allowed to rule over the Greeks."

2. "If I succeed at Salamis, I will achieve victory over all the Greeks."

3. "All the world should enjoy the benefits of Hellenistic culture under my rule."

4. "We must make Athens a center of culture, beauty, and good government."

5. "You must love God first and then love your neighbor as you love yourself."

6. "I call myself *princeps*, or 'first citizen,' but the Senate has given me a name that means 'the revered one.'"

7. "I will compose poems about the great legends of the ancient Greeks and their conquest of Troy."

8. "I believe that logic is preliminary to the study of every kind of knowledge and that organizing information into systems shows what the individual facts mean."

9. "I will invade Italy from the north and conquer Rome with my infantry, cavalry, and elephants."

10. "I will spread the teachings of Jesus throughout the Mediterranean region, write letters to Christian congregations, and found Christian communities."

Applying Critical Thinking Skills

1. **Comparing Ideas** In what way did the Greek concept of democracy differ from the Roman concept of a republic?

2. **Interpreting Ideas (a)** Trace the development of written law from Draco, through Pericles and the Twelve Tables, to Roman imperial law. Consider the individual rights of citizens, women, and slaves. **(b)** Why was Roman law considered superior to Greek law?

3. **Analyzing Ideas** How did sculpture, architecture, painting, mosaics, drama, and poetry reflect the religions and philosophies of Greece and Rome?

4. **Synthesizing Ideas** Explain what these two periods in history have in common: the rule of Pericles in Athens; the rule of Augustus in Rome.

Relating Geography to History

(a) How was the geography of ancient Greece different from that of ancient Italy? **(b)** How was the geography of these two countries similar? **(c)** How did the geography of each region influence the civilization that developed?

Writing About History

1. Assume that you are either a member of the Greek Council of Five Hundred or a Roman noble during the reign of Augustus. Write a diary describing what you do during a typical week. Describe the major landmarks you pass, the people you meet, and the government activities in which you take part. Include a description of your home, your family, and any family activities in which you participate. Also, describe your job and your friends.

2. Write an essay describing Greek and Roman contributions to the development of government in the United States. Focus especially on the separation of powers, checks and balances, the role of citizens, and the powers of the legislature.

Further Readings

Grant, Michael. *World of Rome.* NAL-Dutton, 1987. A discussion of Rome by a leading classical scholar.

Hamilton, Edith. *Mythology: Timeless Tales of Gods and Heroes.* NAL-Dutton, 1989. Describes various Greek myths, gods, and goddesses.

Martin, Thomas R. *Ancient Greece: From Prehistoric to Hellenistic Times.* Yale University Press, 1996. Describes Greece through Hellenistic times.

Renault, Mary. *The Nature of Alexander.* Pantheon, 1980. Fascinating historical novel about Alexander.

Time-Life, eds. *Pompeii: The Vanished City.* Time-Life, 1992. Illustrated history of Pompeii and its destruction.

UNIT 2 CHRONOLOGY

Date	Politics	Science and Technology	Society and Culture
2000–1400 B.C.	Minoan civilization 5* Mycenaean invasion of Greece 5		Minoan art 5 Minoan bull worship 5
1400–500 B.C.	Latin invasion of Italy 7 Trojan War 5 Etruscans rule Italy 7 Draco's law codes 5	Pythagoras 6	*Iliad* and *Odyssey* 5 Greek polytheism 5
500–250 B.C.	Roman Republic begins 7 Cleisthenes 5 Golden Age of Greece 6 Persian Wars 5 Peloponnesian War 5 Alexander the Great 6	Hippocrates 6	Sophocles 6 Euripides 6 Socrates 6 Parthenon 6 Plato's *Republic* 6 Aristotle's *Politics* 6 Cynicism, Skepticism, Stoicism, Epicureanism 6
250–28 B.C.	Punic Wars 7 Rome invades Greece and Egypt 7	Roman roads 7	Virgil's *Aeneid* 7 Ovid's *Metamorphoses* 7
28 B.C.–A.D. 25	Pax Romana 7 Augustus 7	Galen and medicine 7 Ptolemy 7	Roman emperor worship 7 Tacitus's *Germania* 7 Plutarch's *Parallel Lives* 7 Christianity and Paul's mission 7
A.D. 250–500	Roman civil wars 7 Constantine moves to Byzantium 7 Barbarian invasions 7 Rome falls 7		Christianity official religion of Roman Empire 7

*Indicates chapter in which development is discussed

Civilizations of the Mediterranean World

CHAPTER 5

The Greek City-States

On the southern end of the mountainous Balkan Peninsula, as well as in Asia Minor and on the nearby islands, the Greek civilization—one of the greatest the world has ever known—developed.

Early Greeks and the Rise of City-States

A great civilization, the Minoan civilization, flourished on the island of Crete in the Mediterranean Sea between about 2000 B.C. and 1400 B.C. Although it was influenced by the great civilizations of the nearby Nile Valley and Fertile Crescent, Minoan civilization developed many unique features.

Excavations show that the royal palace and the homes of the nobles had running water and that walls were decorated with colorful frescoes—paintings made on wet plaster walls. Artisans made beautiful, delicately carved figures of ivory, stone, gold, silver, and bronze.

While Minoan civilization was developing, important changes were taking place on the Greek mainland. Beginning around 2000 B.C., a new people known as the Mycenaeans entered Greece from the north. The Mycenaeans built fortified cities in the southern part of Greece. Around 1100 B.C., however, the major Mycenaean cities had been destroyed, and more primitive Greeks—the Dorians—moved into the peninsula.

Influenced by the geography of Greece and by their own tribal organization, the early Greeks established city-states, such as Athens and Sparta, in the 800s and 700s B.C. The Greek word for city-state is polis. The polis typically developed around a fort, a refuge in time of danger. As a village or city grew up around the fort, the word polis came to mean the fort, the city, and its surrounding region.

Greek Government and Society

The early city-states were monarchies that constantly waged war among themselves. According to tradition, at some time during the 700s B.C. the poet Homer gathered and wove oral poetry into two great epics, the Iliad and the Odyssey. This period is often called the Homeric Age. During the Homeric Age, Greeks developed religious beliefs that sought to explain the mysteries of the physical world, the passions that could make people lose self-control, and ways to gain such benefits as long life, good fortune, and abundant harvests. Because the Greeks believed that the gods were pleased by displays of strength and courage, they held athletic contests to honor the gods. Most famous were the games at Olympia, held every fourth year in honor of Zeus.

Over time, the Greeks developed new forms of government. The many city-states governed by nobles—the chief landowners—were called aristocracies. As the Greek people chafed under the rule of the aristocracies, leaders called tyrants who promised them a better life, seized power. Many tyrants were excellent rulers who began by governing in the people's interests, but some over time became harsh and unjust.

Ruins of the Parthenon, Acropolis, Athens

As Greek government changed from monarchy to aristocracy to tyranny, the concept of popular government—the idea that people could and should rule themselves and not be ruled by others—began to take root. When cities ousted their tyrants, some restored the old monarchies and others the aristocracies. Still others developed the form of government called democracy, defined as a government in which all citizens take part.

Sparta and Athens

Similarities and differences existed among Greek city-states. The wide range of differences shows clearly in a comparison of the two city-states that became the most important, Sparta and Athens.

Sparta. The population of Sparta was divided into three groups. The first group, known as the equals, consisted of citizens descended from the Dorian invaders. They controlled the government. The second group of people was made up of the half-citizens. They were free and paid taxes but had no political power. They farmed or lived in the towns, where they worked in commerce and industry. Some even became rich. The third and most numerous group were slaves called helots. Because the Spartans lived in constant fear of a helot revolt, Spartan society strongly emphasized militarism.

Sparta regulated the lives of its citizens from birth to death. All of its rules had the same basic aim: to make every adult male citizen part of an efficient military machine designed to control the helots and extend Spartan power.

Athens. In Athens, as elsewhere in Greece, social standing and political power were closely linked. At the top stood the citizens. During Athens' greatest period, all Athenian-born men had full political rights. Those born outside Athens were noncitizens. Called metics, they worked as merchants or skilled workers. They were free but could not own land or take part in government, even though they paid the same taxes as citizens. At the bottom were the slaves.

After its monarchy ended, Athens had an aristocratic government. Four rulers—Draco, Solon, Pisistratus (py·sis·truht·uhs), and Cleisthenes (klys·thuh·neez)—brought about political reforms. Cleisthenes made sweeping changes that turned Athens into a direct democracy. That is, all citizens participated directly in making decisions.

Daily Life in Athens

The citizens of Athens and of most other Greek city-states lived in much the same way. Private and public life were carefully balanced.

More than half of all citizens were farmers. Manufacturing and foreign trade were also important to the Athenian economy. Athenian ships went everywhere in the Mediterranean world, spreading Greek language and Greek civilization. Traders commonly spoke Greek, which was a second language of educated non-Greeks everywhere.

Although the Athenians built magnificent temples and other public buildings, their private homes remained simple. Athenians believed that money should be spent on buildings that would benefit the whole community, not on private homes.

The Expansion of Greece

In 546 B.C. Cyrus of Persia conquered the Greek city-states on the eastern coast of the Aegean. The Persian emperors Darius and Xerxes sent huge armies to conquer the mainland Greeks. However, in 479 B.C., Athenians and Spartans combined to defeat the Persian army at Plataea.

After these wars, called the Persian Wars, the Greek city-states made attempts to unify. Athens used diplomacy to form the Delian League, an alliance with some 140 city-states. By the 450s B.C., it had become an Athenian empire. During this time, Pericles was the leader of Athens. Under his influence, Athenian democracy reached its height.

Pericles hoped to unify Greece under Athenian leadership. However, other city-states increasingly resented Athens' domination. Tensions rose until the devastating Peloponnesian War broke out in 431 B.C. After almost a generation of warfare, Athens finally surrendered to Sparta in 404 B.C.

CHAPTER 6

Greece's Golden and Hellenistic Ages

Greek culture reached new heights during the 400s B.C.—a period so magnificent that it is often called Greece's golden age.

Greek Art

As a center of art and culture, Athens inspired many people whose contributions had a tremendous and lasting impact on Western civilization.

Architecture. The Athenians surrounded themselves with beauty. They showed their love of Athens, and their pride in it, by erecting many impressive temples, gymnasiums, and theaters. They decorated these structures—such as the magnificent Parthenon that crowned the Acropolis—with their finest works of art, especially sculpture.

Painting. The best-preserved Greek paintings are found on vases. Vase painters illustrated everyday life as well as myths. They delighted in showing figures that moved gracefully and naturally.

Sculpture. Two of history's greatest sculptors lived during the golden age: Myron, who sculpted the famous *Discus Thrower,* and Phidias (FID·ee·uhs), who created the statue of Zeus at the Temple of Olympia. Praxiteles (prak·SIT·uhl·eez), who lived about 100 years after Phidias, crafted delicate, lifelike, and often life-sized figures.

The nature of Greek art. Greek art reflected the way in which Greeks viewed themselves and the world. First, it glorified human beings, omitting any blemishes. Second, it symbolized the pride of the people in their city-states. At the same time, it honored the gods, thanked them for life and fortune, and tried to win their favor. Third, Greek art expressed the Greek ideals of harmony, balance, order, and moderation—the qualities of simplicity and restraint. Finally, the Greeks believed in combining beauty and usefulness. In their view, the useful, the beautiful, and the good were closely bound together. Most Greek art was functional—it had a purpose that was clearly defined.

Philosophers and Writers of the Golden Age

The Greeks have been honored through the ages for their artistic and intellectual achievements. Few people before them—and few since—have shown so clearly the capacity of the human hand and mind.

Socrates, Plato, and Aristotle. One of history's greatest thinkers and teachers was Socrates (SAHK·ruh·teez), who lived in Athens from 470 B.C. to 399 B.C. Socrates wanted people to learn to think for themselves. Only then could they acquire wisdom.

Socrates inspired great love among his followers, but he also made enemies. Although he honored the gods of the city, his enemies accused him of denying the existence of the many Greek gods. He was tried and found guilty of not showing proper respect and of corrupting the minds of Athenian youth, and he was sentenced to death.

After Socrates' death, his student Plato founded the Academy, a school devoted to teaching philosophy. One of Plato's major works is the *Republic,* in which he described his belief that the ideal government would be led by the most intelligent people.

Among Plato's students in the Academy was a young man named Aristotle, who founded his own school at Athens in 335 B.C. In order to describe the principles of government, Aristotle studied the political organization of 150 city-states and recorded his conclusions in a book called *Politics.* He concluded that the best government was one in which the middle class—those people who were neither wealthy nor poor—played an important role.

Mathematics, science, and history. In the 500s B.C., before the golden age, Pythagoras (puh·thag·uh·ruhs), a philosopher and mathematician, wrote that everything could be explained or expressed through numbers. Hippocrates, considered the founder of medicine, taught that disease comes from natural causes, not as punishment from the gods.

The Greeks were the first people to take the writing of history seriously. Herodotus and Thucydides were the first great historians of the Western world.

Greek drama. The Greeks were the first people to write dramas—plays that contained action and dialogue, usually involving conflict and emotion. They excelled in this form of literature. Playwrights wrote both tragedies, in which the major character struggles unsuccessfully against fate, and comedies, in which the central characters succeed in solving their problems.

Alexander the Great

In 359 B.C., Philip II became king of Macedonia (to the north of Greece) and proceeded to conquer the quarrelsome Greek city-states. However, it is Philip's son Alexander who is best known—his military campaigns are among the most admired in history. By 331 B.C., Alexander had conquered Asia Minor, Syria, Egypt, Mesopotamia, and the rest of the Persian

Alexander the Great from mosaic at Casa del Fauno in Pompeii

Empire and was attempting to conquer the plains of northern India. After a long campaign, however, he turned back and started the long journey home. In 323 B.C., Alexander died in Babylon.

The Spread of Hellenistic Culture

Hellenistic society—founded on the ideas of Greek culture with features of other Mediterranean cultures—included a small class of very wealthy people and a large class of miserably poor people. However, the middle class thrived because of the many opportunities for acquiring wealth.

Trade, the most profitable activity, originated from the main trading centers in the cities of Alexandria, in Egypt; Rhodes, on the island of Rhodes off the coast of Asia Minor; and Antioch, in Syria. Trade routes now connected the entire Mediterranean world and reached as far as India.

Hellenistic philosophers were more concerned with ethics than with basic questions of reality and human existence. Four chief schools of philosophy existed: Cynicism, Skepticism, Stoicism, and Epicureanism. The Cynics scorned pleasure, wealth, and social position. Skeptics believed that no definite knowledge is possible because everything is always changing. Stoics believed that divine reason directs the world. Epicureans taught that the aim of life is to seek pleasure and avoid pain.

Greeks of the Hellenistic Age were outstanding scientists and mathematicians. For example, Euclid developed geometry into a system by showing how geometric statements of truth, or theorems, develop logically from one another. Archimedes (ahr·kuh·MEED·eez) used geometry to measure spheres, cones, and cylinders. He also calculated the value of π (pi)—the ratio of the circumference of a circle to its diameter—and used mathematics to explain the principle of the lever.

CHAPTER 7

The Roman World

The date 146 B.C. is often given as the end of the Hellenistic Age because by that year the Romans had extended their power over a large part of the eastern Mediterranean area.

The Founding of the Roman Republic

Many peoples had inhabited Italy since ancient times. Latins, Etruscans, and other peoples living around Rome gradually came to be called Romans. The Romans set up a republic, a form of government in which voters elect their leaders, in 509 B.C. Three groups of citizens helped govern Rome: the Senate, various popular assemblies, and the officials themselves, called magistrates.

For more than 200 years after the founding of the republic, the Romans fought many wars against neighboring peoples in Italy. By 265 B.C., the Romans controlled all of Italy south of the Rubicon, a river on the northeast coast. Both military organization and wise policies helped the Romans achieve their victories.

Roman Expansion

Rome soon came into conflict with Carthage, a large and powerful city on the coast of North Africa. In a series of three wars, called the Punic Wars, the Romans completely destroyed their rival city. At the same time, Rome conquered Macedonia and the entire Mediterranean region.

Rome's annexation of distant territories lessened the role of the small citizen-farmer in Roman life. As land and slaves became more expensive, many citizen-farmers lost their lands and moved to the cities, where they joined the unemployed masses. The ideals of discipline and devotion to the state were weakened.

The Roman Empire

By 133 B.C. the Roman Republic faced many problems. Although leaders attempted reforms, their programs angered many senators, and leaders were overthrown violently. Julius Caesar, who became dictator for life, proved to be an able politician. He granted citizenship to many people in the provinces; he gave land to veterans and grain to the poor. The conservative families of Rome did not welcome Caesar's new status, however, and he was assassinated in 44 B.C.

A scramble for power between Marc Antony and Caesar's chosen heir, Octavian, erupted soon after Caesar's death. However, by 30 B.C., Octavian had defeated Marc Antony, and in 27 B.C. he was given the title of Augustus, or "the revered one." He has been known ever since as Augustus Caesar, or simply Augustus, and he is considered the first Roman emperor.

Roman Society and Culture

The Romans had a talent for ruling others and maintained their authority through a strong government, both at home and abroad. Law, military organization,

The Colosseum, Rome

and widespread trade and transportation held the empire together and brought peace for over 200 years— a period known as the Pax Romana, or Roman Peace.

The vast empire provided great opportunities for commerce, and the exchange of goods was easy. Taxes on trade were low, and people used Roman currency everywhere. Rome and Alexandria in Egypt became the empire's greatest commercial centers.

An estimated 50,000 miles of paved highways joined miliary outposts with cities in the interior, and highways linked all provincial cities to Rome—originating the saying "All roads lead to Rome."

The Pax Romana meant prosperity to many people, but wealth was not evenly distributed. The rich citizen usually had both a city home and a country home. Each residence boasted many conveniences, such as running water and baths. In contrast, the average Roman lived in a poorly constructed apartment building with very little furniture.

The Romans were less interested in scientific research to increase knowledge than in collecting and organizing information. Galen, a physician, wrote several volumes that summarized all of the medical knowledge of his day, and for centuries he was considered the greatest authority on medicine. Ptolemy's theories in astronomy were also widely accepted. A scientist from Alexandria, Ptolemy believed that Earth was the center of the universe. Most people accepted this theory until the A.D. 1500s.

Many towns and cities throughout the Roman Empire had elementary, secondary, and higher-level schools. A boy or girl of the free classes entered elementary school at the age of 7 and studied reading, writing, arithmetic, and music. At about age 13, many boys entered a secondary school, where they studied grammar, Greek, literature, good writing, and expressive speech. Former Greek slaves often taught the courses in these schools.

Although Greek influence was strong, a number of Romans produced literary works of originality. Of particular note are the works of Cicero, Tacitus, Virgil, Ovid, and Plutarch.

Latin is the parent of the modern Romance (from the word *Roman*) languages: Italian, French, Spanish, Portuguese, and Romanian. Although the language of the early Germanic peoples had a significant effect on the development of English, approximately one half of all English words have Latin origins.

Judaism and Christianity

In Roman times most Jews lived in Judaea, which became a Roman province in A.D. 6. Occasionally, the Jews would turn to radical measures and revolt against the Romans. After the great revolt of A.D. 66 to A.D. 70, the Romans sacked Jerusalem, slaughtered thousands of Jews, and destroyed the Second Temple. Only the western wall of the temple withstood the onslaught. Today Jews consider this wall, also known as the Wailing Wall, a sacred site. Under the rule of the emperors Trajan and Hadrian more Jewish revolts erupted in Judaea, now called Palestine.

One of the world's great religions, Christianity, originated during the Roman Empire in the Roman-controlled territory of Judaea. It was founded by a Jewish teacher known as Jesus of Nazareth.

Roman histories say very little about Jesus. Our knowledge of Jesus comes mainly from the Gospels of Matthew, Mark, Luke, and John—the first four books of the New Testament of the Christian Bible.

According to the Gospels, Jesus was born in Bethlehem, grew up in Nazareth, worked for a time as a carpenter, and began preaching as an adult. The teachings of Jesus have become one of the greatest influences on the Western world. He accepted the Hebrew Ten Commandments as guides to right living, but he gave them added meaning. He summarized the Ten Commandments in two great rules: people must love God above all else, and they must love others as they love themselves.

The Romans feared that Jesus wanted to lead an uprising, and they considered him an enemy of the state. Consequently, Jesus was tried before Pontius Pilate, the Roman governor, and crucified.

During the latter years of the Roman Empire, Christianity developed a definitive church organization. Priests conducted services and performed baptisms and marriages. Above the priests were the bishops, who headed the church in each city. Over time, the bishop of Rome assumed the title of pope and claimed supremacy over the church.

The Fall of the Roman Empire in the West

During most of the A.D. 200s, the empire experienced dreadful confusion, civil war, and barbarian invasions. Travel became unsafe, and merchants hesitated to send goods by land or sea. The rural population grew even poorer than before. Population decreased throughout the empire, partly because a great plague spread through the provinces and caused several million deaths.

The Roman Empire would probably have collapsed in the late A.D. 200s except for the efforts of two able emperors, Diocletian and Constantine. Their reforms and reorganizations postponed the collapse for nearly 200 years. However, in A.D. 476, in an event sometimes referred to as the fall of Rome, a barbarian commander overthrew the last Roman emperor in the west. Actually, no single fall occurred, but the empire had gradually disintegrated.

Why did Rome decline? How did this mighty empire that had accomplished so much disappear? For centuries historians have debated these questions. Some cite political weaknesses: the empire was too large to be governed efficiently. Others cite economic decline, including decreased income for the government and the financial burden of maintaining a large army. Still others cite social decay. Romans of the later empire took little interest in government and lacked political honesty. Waves of barbarian invasions were another problem. The important point to remember, however, is that no one factor caused Rome to decline. Like many other complex movements and events in history, it resulted from a combination of political, economic, and social forces.

In the ruins of the Roman world, however, two key ideas did survive in the west: the Roman heritage and the presence of Christianity. The Christian church became the main preserver of Roman ideas and civilization.

Synthesis Review

1. **Summarizing Ideas** Describe the development of democracy in ancient Greece.
2. **Analyzing Ideas** How did Greek art reflect the ideals of Greek society?
3. **Interpreting Ideas** How did foreign conquests weaken the Roman Republic?
4. **Synthesizing Ideas** Why were the Romans able to establish a great empire, whereas the Greeks could never unify their city-states for very long?

UNIT

3

The World in Transition

POLITICS AND GOVERNMENT

A.D. 100 | A.D. 300 | A.D. 500 | A.D. 700

C. A.D. 150
Decline of Kush civilization

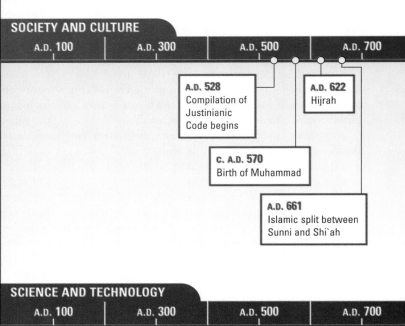

Pyramids at Meroe, the capital of Kush

A.D. 395
Split of the Roman Empire

C. A.D. 450
Angles and Saxons settle in England

A.D. 481
Clovis begins rule of Franks

A.D. 589
China reunited by Sui dynasty

C. A.D. 650
Toltecs move south into Central Mexico

SOCIETY AND CULTURE

A.D. 100 | A.D. 300 | A.D. 500 | A.D. 700

A.D. 528
Compilation of Justinianic Code begins

C. A.D. 570
Birth of Muhammad

A.D. 622
Hijrah

A.D. 661
Islamic split between Sunni and Shi`ah

SCIENCE AND TECHNOLOGY

A.D. 100 | A.D. 300 | A.D. 500 | A.D. 700

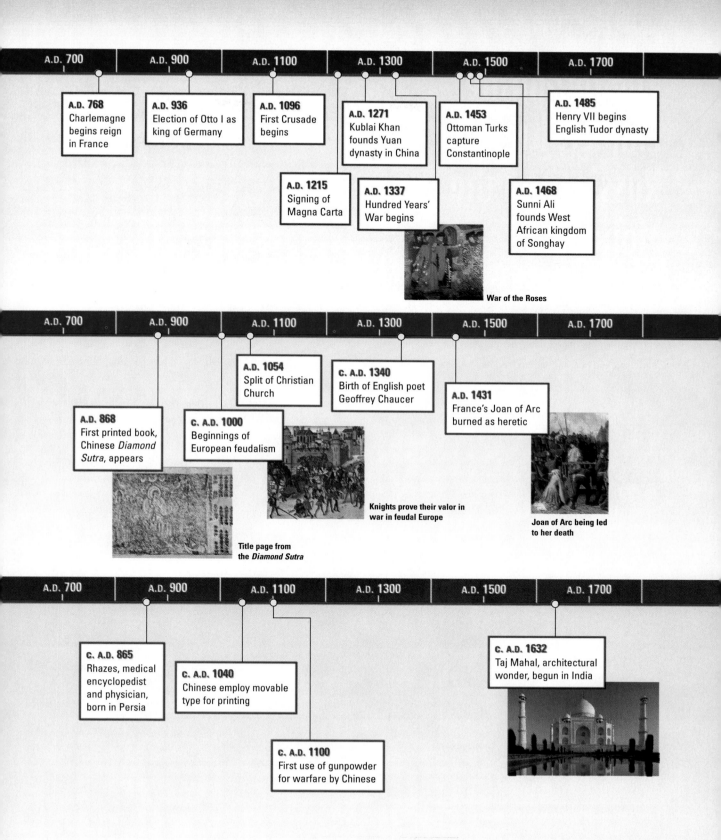

Timeline 1

A.D. 700 | A.D. 900 | A.D. 1100 | A.D. 1300 | A.D. 1500 | A.D. 1700

A.D. 768 Charlemagne begins reign in France

A.D. 936 Election of Otto I as king of Germany

A.D. 1096 First Crusade begins

A.D. 1271 Kublai Khan founds Yuan dynasty in China

A.D. 1453 Ottoman Turks capture Constantinople

A.D. 1485 Henry VII begins English Tudor dynasty

A.D. 1215 Signing of Magna Carta

A.D. 1337 Hundred Years' War begins

A.D. 1468 Sunni Ali founds West African kingdom of Songhay

War of the Roses

Timeline 2

A.D. 700 | A.D. 900 | A.D. 1100 | A.D. 1300 | A.D. 1500 | A.D. 1700

A.D. 1054 Split of Christian Church

C. A.D. 1340 Birth of English poet Geoffrey Chaucer

A.D. 1431 France's Joan of Arc burned as heretic

A.D. 868 First printed book, Chinese *Diamond Sutra*, appears

C. A.D. 1000 Beginnings of European feudalism

Knights prove their valor in war in feudal Europe

Joan of Arc being led to her death

Title page from the *Diamond Sutra*

Timeline 3

A.D. 700 | A.D. 900 | A.D. 1100 | A.D. 1300 | A.D. 1500 | A.D. 1700

C. A.D. 865 Rhazes, medical encyclopedist and physician, born in Persia

C. A.D. 1040 Chinese employ movable type for printing

C. A.D. 1632 Taj Mahal, architectural wonder, begun in India

C. A.D. 1100 First use of gunpowder for warfare by Chinese

The Byzantine Empire, Kievan Russia, and the Mongols

TIME

A.D. 395–1589

| 3.7 million B.C. | 4000 B.C. | A.D. 395–1589 A.D. 2100 |

PLACE

Eastern Europe, Asia Minor, and Russia

Eastern Europe

Russia

Asia Minor

Early Christian/Byzantine wall mosaic

+SANCTVS APOLENAR

Significance

The Byzantine Empire lasted more than 1,000 years. Byzantine culture had great influence upon Kievan (KEE-ef·uhn) Russia, a land that eventually became known as Russia. As the peoples of this region struggled for political identity, they looked to the Byzantine Empire for religious and cultural inspiration. Although the Mongols plundered Kievan Russia in the 1200s, the Mongol influence was more political than cultural. In the 1400s, as Mongol control weakened, a strong Russian state centered in Moscow was established.

Terms to Define

dowry	Hagia Sophia
Greek fire	steppe
patriarchs	boyars
icons	*Pravda Russkaia*
iconoclasts	metropolitan
iconoclastic controversy	taiga
heresy	czar
excommunication	third Rome
mosaics	

People to Identify

Justinian	Yaroslav the Wise
Theodora	Vladimir I
Cyril and Methodius	Polovtsians
Ottoman Turks	Ivan III
Rurik	Ivan IV
Rus	

Places to Locate

Constantinople	Volga River
Bosporus	Caspian Sea
Ural Mountains	Lake Ladoga
Vistula River	Novgorod
Baltic Sea	Kiev
Dnieper River	Lithuania
Don River	Poland
Black Sea	Moscow

Chapter Theme Questions

- **Politics and Government** What might make an empire strong, and what factors might lead to its decline?
- **Cross-Cultural Interaction** What factors, including trade and foreign invasion, might mold a culture?
- **Religion** How might religion affect the government, art, and architecture of a culture?

A mid the ruins of the Roman world, the magnificent city of Constantinople rose to become a great cultural and economic center. One historian noted the city's splendor.

“Around 1000 A.D. Christian Constantinople undoubtedly boasted over 500,000 inhabitants and may well have approximated 1,000,000. It was incomparably the largest city in Christendom, and, since the waning of the splendors of Bagdad, probably surpassed any other in the known world. . . .

Strangers were lost in . . . eloquence when describing the magnificence of New Rome [Constantinople] and the impression which a visit to it produced upon them. Its [residents] took this homage as a matter of course. To them their capital was not only 'The City guarded by God,' it was 'The City'—as if all other communities in the world were merely secondary towns.”

Constantinople, center of the Byzantine Empire, preserved the traditions of the Greco-Roman world for future generations.

Section 1

The Byzantine Empire

Focus Questions

- **What great contributions were made by Justinian?**
- **What were the strengths of the Byzantine Empire?**
- **What factors led to the decline of the Byzantine Empire?**

While barbarians plundered the western part of the Roman Empire in the A.D. 400s and 500s, the Byzantine Empire thrived in the East. Although surrounded by enemies, the Byzantine Empire maintained its independence for more than 1,000 years.

Germanic Kingdoms, A.D. 526

Learning from Maps Germanic tribes established kingdoms across Europe and in northern Africa.

? Region What group controlled most of France?

The Reign of Justinian

In the year A.D. 500, the Eastern Roman Empire included Greece and the northern Balkan Peninsula, Asia Minor, Syria, Palestine, Egypt, and Cyrenaica. Although Germanic tribes had attacked the Eastern Empire even before marching on the Western Empire, the East had withstood the attacks. By the early 500s, the Western Roman Empire had broken down into a group of Germanic tribal kingdoms. (See map on this page.) The Eastern Roman Empire, on the other hand, had defeated the barbarians and was primed for a great political, economic, intellectual, and artistic revival.

Emperor Justinian, who ruled from 527 to 565, led this revival and accomplished so much that the years of his reign marked one of the most splendid periods in Byzantine history. His cultural achievements will be described later in this section. Justinian's instinct for judging the abilities of others allowed him to choose exceptional people to help him rule the empire. Two wise choices were his wife, Theodora, and the commander in chief of his army, Belisarius (bel·uh·SAR·ee·uhs).

Theodora. The Byzantine Empire had several famous empresses, but the most extraordinary was Justinian's wife, Theodora. Theodora spent her early years with the circus, where her father trained bears. Strong and intelligent, she became an actress in her early teens. Justinian first made Theodora his mistress and then married her in 525, even though Byzantine law forbade marriage between high imperial officials and actresses.

With Theodora's encouragement, Justinian changed Byzantine law to improve the status of women. Justinian decreed that a husband could not beat his wife and that a woman could sue for divorce if her husband mistreated her. He changed the rule that prohibited women from owning property. The new law allowed a woman to own property equal to the value of her **dowry,** the money or goods that she brought to her husband when the couple married. Furthermore, Justinian repealed an old law that forced a widow to surrender her children to a male relative. His new law allowed the widow to raise her own children.

Theodora's most dramatic contribution to her husband's success took place in 532. A rebellion, known as the Nika Revolt, threatened to overthrow Justinian. As the leaders of the rebellion prepared to crown a new emperor, the frightened Justinian made plans to flee Constantinople. Theodora, however, urged him to stay and fight. In a fierce battle, Justinian's troops defeated the rebels, killing 30,000 of them. Justinian remained on the throne.

Belisarius. Justinian's appointment of Belisarius as commander in chief of the army was another excellent choice. A member of Justinian's bodyguard, Belisarius had spent time as a commander on the empire's eastern front. Two important factors, however, probably influenced his appointment as commander in chief. Belisarius's wife, Antonina, was a friend of Theodora, and he had made a name for himself by leading the troops that crushed the Nika Revolt.

While the new Germanic kingdoms in the West quarreled among themselves, Justinian's armies, under the capable leadership of Belisarius, regained many former Roman territories in the Mediterranean region. As a result of these victories, the Byzantine Empire reached its greatest territorial extent during Justinian's reign. (See map on page 189.)

Decline after Justinian. After Justinian's death in 565, the empire suffered for decades both from civil wars and from conflicts with other powers. In the east

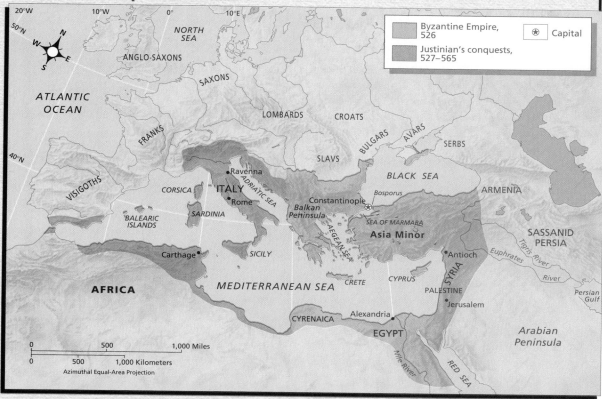

The Byzantine Empire, A.D. 526–565

Legend:
- Byzantine Empire, 526
- Justinian's conquests, 527–565
- ⊛ Capital

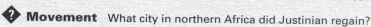

Learning from Maps As a result of Emperor Justinian's victories over Germanic invaders, he recaptured many of the lands around the Mediterranean coast.

 **Movement** What city in northern Africa did Justinian regain?

---

there were wars with the Persians, whom Emperor Heraclius managed to defeat in 627. Elsewhere, however, an Asian group, the Avars, and a European people, the Slavs, invaded the Balkan Peninsula. The Lombards, a Germanic tribe, rampaged through Italy. By the early 600s, the Lombards had settled in much of the territory that Justinian's armies had spent so much time conquering, introducing a new and powerful force into the region.

During the 600s the Byzantine Empire faced a new and highly energetic force—the armies of the Muslim Empire. (See Chapter 9.) The Muslims soon conquered Armenia, Syria, Palestine, and much of North Africa, including Egypt. After 650 the Eastern Empire consisted of little more than Asia Minor, the southern Balkan Peninsula, parts of Italy, and the nearby islands.

Strengths of the Empire

Several factors, however, helped the Byzantine Empire survive for more than 1,000 years. It had political, military, and economic strength, and its people adapted skillfully to change.

Political strength. A highly centralized government, headed by an all-powerful emperor, ruled the Byzantine Empire. Skilled, efficient, well-paid, and usually loyal officials carried out imperial commands and policies. Even under the rule of weak emperors or during times of civil war, these officials made sure that the empire ran smoothly.

The Byzantines practiced especially shrewd diplomacy. To cement alliances, emperors often arranged marriages between Byzantine princesses and foreign princes. Their excellent intelligence service kept the

Byzantine Silk Manufacturing and Trade

Ivory diptych showing the Miracles of Christ, from Rome, c. 450–460

The establishment of a silk industry in the Byzantine Empire began in the A.D. 500s with a few hardy silkworms, which were smuggled from China into Constantinople at the request of the Byzantine emperor Justinian. The silkworm secretes a silk thread, which it uses to make a cocoon for itself. Thousands of years earlier the Chinese had learned how to weave fine cloth from the silk. With its own silkworms, the Byzantine Empire was freed from dependence on China and Persia for its silk. The silk industry became one of several vital Byzantine economic enterprises.

Low internal taxes and a common currency stimulated trade within the empire. Local craftspeople and merchants exchanged their goods, such as high-quality glass and papyrus, at countryside fairs.

Because of its fine harbor and access to the Black and Mediterranean Seas, Constantinople, the capital city of the Byzantine Empire, was a thriving trade center. Traders—en route from India, China, and Persia to Italy and other parts of Europe—carried spices, silks, furs, pearls, precious stones, and timber through the port at Constantinople. Exported from Constantinople were luxury items, such as silk textiles, carved ivory, enamel, glassware, and bronze church doors. Byzantine luxury goods sold especially well in the Italian cities of Amalfi and Venice. As cities grew in western Europe and commercial trade with the region increased, raw materials and agricultural products were exported there from Constantinople.

emperor well informed of important foreign developments. The Byzantines also frequently engaged in intrigues, provoking one neighbor to attack another in order to prevent either one from attacking the empire. Today people use the term *byzantine* to describe tricky or devious policies.

Military strength. Byzantine rulers developed effective frontier forces, infantry, cavalry, and engineering corps to defend the empire. The government rewarded its soldiers with land grants. Starting in 590, military authorities developed instruction manuals to teach officers the latest strategies. They improved the army's weaponry by supplementing the bow and lance with the sword and javelin, and they furnished soldiers with a more effective armor.

During the 500s the Byzantines built an effective navy. Although ships were equipped with battering rams, the navy's strongest feature was a secret weapon—a flammable liquid called "**Greek fire.**" Sprayed over enemy ships or hurled at them in cartridges, it set them ablaze. So carefully did the Byzantines guard their secret that even today no one knows the exact formula of Greek fire. The best guess is that it contained a combination of naphtha, sulfur, and saltpeter (potassium nitrate).

Economic strength. Because of its prosperous agriculture, manufacturing, and trade, the east had always been the richest part of the Roman Empire. At the heart of the empire lay Constantinople, a city of grandeur that was also strategically located. Situated where Asia and Europe meet, the city overlooked the strategic Bosporus, the narrow strait that links the Black Sea with the Sea of Marmara. (See map at right.) This location allowed the Byzantines to control the vital sea trade routes between Europe and Asia.

Merchandise from as far away as Scandinavia, China, and India came into the markets of Constantinople. Throughout the empire, the government regulated trade and manufacturing to produce large tax revenues. The emperor used this income to pay the salaries of his officials and soldiers and to construct magnificent public buildings.

The Christian Church

In the early Christian church, the most important leaders were the **patriarchs** of Rome, Constantinople, Alexandria, Antioch, and Jerusalem. In time, the pope, the patriarch of Rome, gained supreme authority in the West. The Byzantines, however, did not recognize this authority. In the East the patriarch of Constantinople became the most powerful church leader.

The Byzantine faith was a source of both weakness and strength for the Byzantine Empire. Because Christianity formed such a vital part of Byzantine life, the Byzantines often argued intensely about church doctrine and rituals. These questions were as important to Byzantine leaders as matters of imperial policy, such as taxes or defense—or were even more important.

A significant religious debate concerned holy pictures—called **icons,** from *eikon,* the Greek word meaning "portrait"—of Jesus, the Virgin Mary, and the saints. Many Byzantines revered icons, which they kept in their homes and also worshipped in churches. Some Byzantines, however, were **iconoclasts,** people who felt that the presence of icons constituted idol worship and should be suppressed.

The **iconoclastic controversy,** between the defenders and the opponents of icons, rocked the empire for more than a century. In 726 Emperor Leo III, an iconoclast, outlawed the worship of icons. For a time this decree had the effect of weakening the power of both the church and the monasteries, which owned most of the icons. However, many people refused to abandon the worship of icons, and in 843 the Byzantine emperors gave up their efforts to suppress icon worship.

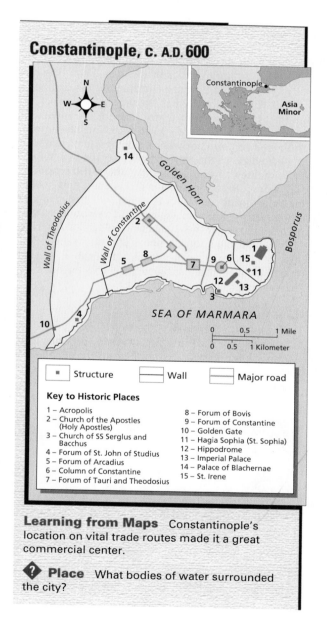

Constantinople, c. A.D. 600

SEA OF MARMARA

| Structure | Wall | Major road |

Key to Historic Places

1 – Acropolis
2 – Church of the Apostles (Holy Apostles)
3 – Church of SS Serglus and Bacchus
4 – Forum of St. John of Studius
5 – Forum of Arcadius
6 – Column of Constantine
7 – Forum of Tauri and Theodosius
8 – Forum of Bovis
9 – Forum of Constantine
10 – Golden Gate
11 – Hagia Sophia (St. Sophia)
12 – Hippodrome
13 – Imperial Palace
14 – Palace of Blachernae
15 – St. Irene

Learning from Maps Constantinople's location on vital trade routes made it a great commercial center.

? Place What bodies of water surrounded the city?

This Byzantine ivory carving depicts Empress Irene, who supported the use of icons during her reign in the last quarter of the A.D. 700s.

Building History Study Skills

READ
WRITE
INTERPRET
CONNECT
THINK

Thinking About History: Identifying Bias

Bias is a word that often has negative connotations. People often equate bias with prejudice, an opinion that is based on ignorance or is without foundation in truth. In its simplest sense, however, bias is nothing more than the outlook that a speaker or writer presents. Thus, identifying bias means determining whether a speaker or writer has a positive or a negative attitude toward the subject being discussed. The following three sentences demonstrate this point:

- The emperor addressed the Senate.
- The brilliant emperor addressed the Senate.
- The foolish emperor addressed the Senate.

The first statement is a simple report of an action. The statement is not biased; it shows neither favor nor disfavor. In the second statement, the word *brilliant* conveys a positive feeling about the emperor. In the third statement, the word *foolish* indicates a negative feeling about the emperor.

Being able to identify bias in writing and speaking is an important skill to have, not only as you study history, but also as you read newspapers and magazines, watch newscasts on television, or simply hear people speak. It helps you decide whether you are reading or hearing a factual, impartial report or one that is biased by the author's or speaker's opinion.

How to Identify Bias

To identify bias, follow these guidelines.

1. Look for clues. Check for words or phrases that convey a positive or negative attitude.
2. Assess the evidence. Decide for yourself whether you agree or disagree with the attitude on the basis of the evidence presented.

Emperor Justinian I (pictured fifth from left) and his entourage

Empress Theodora (pictured third from left) with her attendants

Developing the Skill

Procopius, an official in Constantinople, wrote *The Secret History*, in which he described the rule of Justinian and Theodora. Read the excerpt below in order to identify bias.

"... they were a pair of blood-thirsty demons. ... For they plotted together to find the easiest and swiftest means of destroying all races of men and all their works, assumed human shape, became man-demons, and in this way convulsed the whole world. ... [Justinian] never even gave a hint of anger or irritation to show how he felt towards those who had offended him; but with a friendly expression on his face and without raising an eyebrow, in a gentle voice he would order tens of thousands of quite innocent persons to be put to death, cities to be razed to the ground, and all their possessions to be confiscated for the Treasury. ... His ambition being to force everybody into one form of Christian belief he wantonly destroyed everyone who would not conform, and that while keeping up a pretense of piety. For he did not regard it as murder, so long as those who died did not happen to share his beliefs."

This excerpt includes many words and phrases that condemn Justinian and Theodora. For example, the words *bloodthirsty demons* and *man-demons* display the author's bias that Justinian and Theodora were truly evil people.

Practicing the Skill

Read an article in your local newspaper and determine whether the article shows bias.

To apply this skill, see Applying History Study Skills on page 203.

In the meantime, the iconoclastic controversy had drastically affected the empire's relations with Rome.

Most people in western Europe received no formal education, and they could not read or write. Western clergy, therefore, considered visual images essential to the teaching of Christianity. After Emperor Leo III forbade the use of icons in the Byzantine Empire, the pope in Rome summoned a council of bishops in 787. The council declared opposition to icons a **heresy,** meaning that it was an opinion that conflicted with church doctrine. The council threatened iconoclasts with **excommunication**. Excommunication involves barring a person from being a member of the church and excludes him or her from sacred church ceremonies such as baptism, marriage, and communion.

The declaration of iconoclasm as a heresy led to serious friction between the pope in Rome and the patriarch of Constantinople. Combined with growing cultural and language differences, this friction grew steadily worse over the years, until finally the Christian church split into two churches in 1054. In the West it became known as the Roman Catholic Church, with the pope as its head. In the East it became known as the Eastern Orthodox Church, with the patriarch of Constantinople as its head. The two churches remain separate today.

Byzantine Culture

For more than 1,000 years, while western Europe struggled to develop a new way of life, Constantinople served as the center of a brilliant civilization. The Byzantine Empire performed a great service for succeeding civilizations. Although its scholars produced little work that was original, they preserved and passed on the classical learning of ancient Greece, Rome, and the East for succeeding generations.

Not only did the Byzantines preserve the culture of the Mediterranean world, they also carried this culture beyond the borders of their empire. Cyril (SIR·uhl) and Methodius (muh·THOH·dee·uhs), two brothers who lived in the A.D. 800s, illustrate the role of the Byzantines in this cultural diffusion. As missionaries the brothers worked to convert the Slavs of central and eastern Europe to Christianity. They wanted to teach the Slavs to read the Bible, but the Slavs had no written language. They therefore created an alphabet that eventually evolved into what is now known as the Cyrillic (suh·RIL·ik) alphabet. Today many Slavic peoples of central and eastern Europe, including Russia, still use the Cyrillic alphabet or one derived from it.

Cyril and Methodius converted many Slavs to Christianity. Descendants of these converts still follow the Eastern Orthodox faith.

Art. Byzantine art was devoted to religion. Murals covered the walls and ceilings of churches. Floors, walls, and arches glistened with colored **mosaics—** pictures or designs composed of inlaid pieces of stone, glass, or enamel. Artists used both painting and mosaics to create icons. The location of a particular person's image in the church indicated that person's importance in church doctrine. For example, an image of Jesus always occupied the dome of the church.

Byzantine artists, in depicting their subjects, did not make it their goal to imitate physical reality. Their images sometimes appear stiff or artificial to modern eyes. Their purpose was in some ways similar to that of Buddhist art—to inspire reverence and to emphasize the importance of renouncing the pleasures of this life and preparing for the afterlife.

Architecture. The Byzantines excelled in architecture, especially religious architecture. One of the greatest architectural masterpieces in the world is the church of **Hagia Sophia** (meaning "holy wisdom") in Constantinople.

Justinian ordered the construction of the Hagia Sophia in 532. A huge building in the form of a cross, the church measures 240 feet wide by 270 feet long. The interior originally glittered with breathtaking decorations that reflected the sunlight as it streamed through lofty windows. Murals, mosaics, stone carvings, and metalwork covered every surface. The gold altar was inlaid with precious stones.

A huge dome, some 180 feet high with a diameter of about 108 feet, dominates the structure. Supported by massive columns instead of walls, the dome illustrates the great skill of Byzantine architects, who were the first to solve the difficult problem of placing a round dome over a rectangular building.

What If?

The Byzantine Empire
The Byzantine Empire helped preserve the Greco-Roman heritage of the ancient world. How do you think the course of world history would have changed if the Germanic tribes had toppled the Byzantine Empire at the same time as they plundered the imperial city of Rome?

Although Anthemius of Tralles and Isidorus of Miletus built the Hagia Sophia in the early 500s as a Christian church, it was used after 1453 as an Islamic mosque, and after 1935 as a museum.

The Hagia Sophia was completed in 537. The Byzantine historian Procopius (pruh·KOH·pee·uhs) described his feelings after first entering the church:

"The church . . . is distinguished by indescribable beauty, for it excels both in its size and in the harmony of its proportion. . . . It is singularly full of light and sunshine; you would declare that the place is not lighted by the sun from without, but that the rays are produced within itself, such an abundance of light is poured into this church. . . .

The entire ceiling is covered with pure gold, which adds glory to its beauty, though the rays of light reflected upon the gold from the marble surpass it in beauty. . . . who could tell of the beauty of the columns and marbles with which the church is adorned? one would think that one had come upon a meadow full of flowers in bloom: who would not admire the purple tints of some and the green of others, the glowing red and glittering white? . . . Whoever enters there to worship perceives at once that it is not by any human strength or skill, but by the favour of God that this work has been perfected; his mind rises sublime to commune with God, feeling that He cannot be far off, but must especially love to dwell in the place which He has chosen."

Justinian himself solemnly consecrated the church. As he first entered the Hagia Sophia, he exclaimed: "Solomon, I have outdone thee!" The emperor was referring to King Solomon of Israel, who built the magnificent temple in Jerusalem that is described in the Bible. (See Chapter 2.)

The Preservation of Roman Law

One of the Byzantines' greatest contributions to civilization was the preservation of Roman law. Early in his reign, Justinian ordered his scholars to collect and organize all the laws of the Roman Empire. The collection, begun in A.D. 528, has four parts: the *Code*, the *Digest*, the *Institutes*, and the *Novels*. The entire collection is known as the *Corpus juris civilis*, Latin for "body of civil law."

The *Code*, the first part to be prepared, is a collection of Roman laws that omitted repetitions, inconsistencies, and any statutes that dealt with Roman religion. It includes the original laws compiled by Justinian, often called the Justinianic Code. The *Digest* consists of a summary of the writings of the great Roman legal experts, organized alphabetically by ideas. The *Institutes* is a textbook on the basic principles of Roman law. The *Novels* are collections of the new laws issued by Justinian between 534 and 565, after the *Code* was revised. During the Middle Ages, the Justinianic Code was used as the basis of many European legal systems, and its influence continues today.

Decline of the Empire

During the 1000s, the Saljuq Turks, originally a nomadic people from Central Asia, captured most of Asia Minor. This area was vital to the Byzantine Empire because it was the main source of the empire's food supply and also of its soldiers. When the Turks prepared to attack Constantinople, the Byzantine emperor appealed to the West for help. (See Chapter 11.) Western Europeans responded in 1096 to 1099 with the army of the First Crusade, which recaptured western Asia Minor for the Byzantines. In 1204, however, during the Fourth Crusade, the crusaders turned on the Byzantines and captured Constantinople.

After more than half a century of Western rule, the Byzantines recaptured the city in 1261 and reorganized the empire. Although the Byzantine Empire continued to exist for almost 200 years, it never regained its former strength. In the 1300s a new Asian people, the Ottoman Turks, rose to power in the region. When they captured Constantinople in 1453, the Byzantine Empire finally came to an end.

Spices

Do you realize that when you eat a bowl of chili, your food is seasoned with the same kinds of spices as the Inca in Peru used hundreds of years ago? Whether you eat at home or you eat in a restaurant (top right), at almost every meal you are enjoying the taste of a spice—ginger in ginger ale or gingerbread, oregano in spaghetti sauce, anise in licorice, or mint in peppermints.

Nearly 800 years ago, the Aztec in Mexico ground hot chili peppers and mixed them with other spices to make chili powder. Today hot peppers are used throughout the world. Many people believe that spicy food stimulates the liver and promotes good health.

Black and white pepper can give us almost the same zing as is found in hot chilis. The black peppercorn is the whole berry, which is picked when it begins to turn red and is then set out to dry. White pepper is made from the core of the ripe berry.

Pepper was first grown on the western coast of India and was brought to Europe by traders who often passed through the markets of Constantinople on their journeys. In ancient Greece and Rome, rulers sometimes collected tribute in the form of pepper. Pepper was later used as money, and merchants had to take precautions so that dock workers would not steal it from the ships they were unloading.

In the 1400s, spices from the East were in great demand in Europe. Explorers began to search for new and faster routes to bring pepper and other spices from India to Europe. Columbus had hoped to find such a route to India when he sailed west and eventually reached the Americas.

As trade has become international, so has the taste for dishes and flavors that were once rare and exotic. Today spices are sold all over the world, as in these markets in Southwest Asia (center and bottom right).

The Rise of Russia

Focus Questions

- **How did Kievan Russia develop?**
- **What were the features of Kievan political, economic, and social life?**

During the early period of the Byzantine Empire, the Slavic people who lived to the north of the Black Sea began to trade with Constantinople. Gradually, the Byzantines greatly influenced the political and social lives of these Slavs.

The Physical Setting

A vast plain stretches across eastern Europe and Central Asia. It extends eastward from the Carpathian (kahr·PAY·thee·uhn) Mountains in Europe to Manchuria in eastern Asia. In the south this plain is grassy and largely treeless and is called the **steppe**. Black, fertile soil makes the grassy steppe ideal for farming, especially in the area that is now the Ukraine.

Only the Ural (YOOR·uhl) Mountains, which run north to south and are often considered the boundary between the continents of Europe and Asia, break the plain. The two continents actually form a single huge landmass, sometimes called Eurasia.

A number of large rivers crisscross the plain and provide a network of transportation within the region. The Vistula (VISH·chuh·luh), Neman, and Dvina Rivers flow into the Baltic Sea. The Dniester (NEES·tuhr),

Dnieper (NEE·puhr), and Don Rivers empty into the Black Sea. The Volga and Ural Rivers (not on map) are not as useful for trade as the other rivers because they flow into the landlocked Caspian Sea.

Slavs and Vikings

People have lived in the southern part of eastern Europe since Neolithic times. Armed nomadic horsemen from this region began invading Southwest Asia in 1700 B.C. Beginning in the A.D. 200s, Slavs settled in much of eastern Europe. Other peoples, including the Huns, Avars, and Magyars, often invaded the region and for a time made the Slavs their subjects. Invaders who came across the flat steppe played a key role in the region's subsequent history.

During the A.D. 800s, Vikings from Scandinavia swept into eastern Europe. The Vikings came more as traders than as conquerors, however. Each fall they sailed up the rivers from the Baltic Sea and from Lake Ladoga. (See map on opposite page.) When winter came, they loaded their ships onto large sleds and hauled them across the snow to one of the rivers that flowed into the Black Sea. When the rivers were navigable, probably when the ice melted in the spring, they sailed south to trade in the Black Sea region. After trading their goods, they retraced their route to their Scandinavian homeland.

The Birth of Kievan Russia

Several cities sprang up along the Viking trade routes. Two such cities were Novgorod (Russian for "new fort"), south of Lake Ladoga, and Kiev, on the Dnieper River.

Rurik, who was a military leader of a people called the Rus, took control of Novgorod in 862. Rurik and his successors became the rulers of Novgorod and other principalities, including Kiev. This dynasty, during the 800s, came to rule over the Slavic tribes of the area all along the Dnieper River. Eventually the entire region that was ruled by this dynasty came to be called the Rus. The word *Russia* is probably derived from this name.

Kiev especially prospered because of its strategic location along the rich trade route that extended from the north to Constantinople and the Baltic Sea. (See map on the opposite page.) Kiev grew to be the most important principality in Kievan Russia. The city of Kiev served as the capital of Russia from about 879 to 1169. Although the rulers of other principalities paid tribute to the prince in Kiev in exchange for military protection, the degree of their loyalty varied,

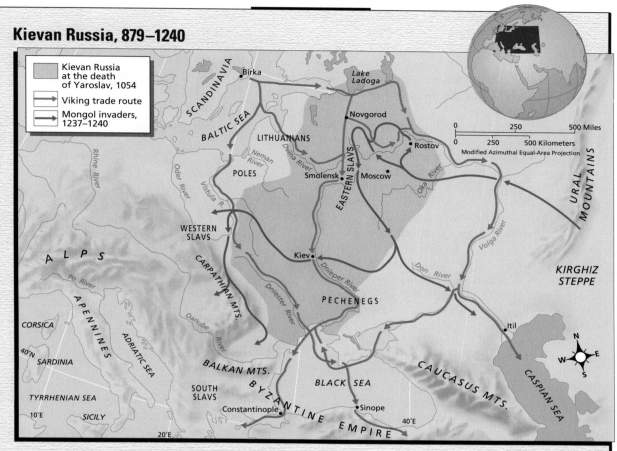

Kievan Russia, 879–1240

Legend:
- Kievan Russia at the death of Yaroslav, 1054
- → Viking trade route
- → Mongol invaders, 1237–1240

Learning from Maps A network of rivers crosses the plain between the Carpathian and Ural Mountains.

? Movement What was the common geographic feature that the Kievan trade routes followed?

---

depending on the Kievan prince's power. Many of the smaller towns remained semi-independent.

Government
The prince of each of the cities of Kievan Russia at times ruled with the advice of a council of **boyars**, or nobles. Another important institution widely used in both Kiev and Novgorod was the *veche*, or town meeting. There, at the request of the prince, the heads of all of the households met in the public marketplace. They considered such matters as calls to war, disputes between princes, and special measures proposed by the prince to deal with emergencies.

A great period in Kievan Russia's history came during the reign of Yaroslav I, called Yaroslav the Wise, who ruled from 1019 to 1054. He issued Russia's first law code, the ***Pravda Russkaia***, which remained in force in parts of the region until 1550. Yaroslav's domain had a population of between 7 and 8 million people.

Religion
Although traders and Greek missionaries had brought the Christian faith to Kievan Russia by the A.D. 800s, little Christian activity took place until the middle of the next century. In the 980s Vladimir I of Kiev invited representatives from several faiths to address his boyar council and offer reasons why his people should convert to their religion.

Vladimir had sent envoys to witness Christian church services in several places. The Roman Catholic services they attended in Germany failed to impress his envoys, but the men who went to Constantinople and attended services in the Hagia Sophia were impressed by the ritual and ideology of Orthodox Christianity.

Influenced by the reports of his envoys and by his desire to marry Anna, the Byzantine emperor's sister, Vladimir converted to Christianity in 988. He may also have been influenced by the Christian church's tolerant attitude toward drinking—alcohol was prohibited by Islam. Vladimir immediately ordered the baptism of Kievans and the destruction of pagan statues.

Although many Kievans continued their ancient practices of worshipping the spirits of their ancestors and gods of nature, the Byzantine church became increasingly important in Kievan Russia as a spiritual force. The patriarch of Constantinople chose the chief bishop, or **metropolitan**, of the Kievan Church. New monasteries in the region soon became centers for social services, education, and artistic expression, and thus further strengthened the church. By the time the Christian church split in 1054, the Kievan church had become associated with Constantinople.

Religious themes dominated Kievan culture in this period. Although authors wrote epic poems and historical chronicles about wars and the personal tragedies associated with war, religious hymns and sermons constituted the bulk of Kievan literature. Icon painting became the most distinctive Kievan art form. Artists also created mosaics and frescoes. They made no attempt to show figures as three-dimensional. The Kievans believed that the second of the Ten Commandments, "You shall not make a carved image for yourself," prohibited any art resembling sculpture, which they identified with pagan worship. They therefore depicted figures in two dimensions in their mosaics, frescoes, and icons.

Economy
Agriculture and trade were the most important economic activities in Kievan society.

Agriculture. Kievan Russia included two major agricultural regions. North of the steppe region lies a zone with great forests known as the **taiga** (TY·guh). Although the taiga receives abundant rainfall, the brutally cold, long winters limit the growing season to about four months of each year. Because of the need to grow and harvest crops in such a short time, everyone in a farm family worked long hours.

This Russian icon shows Christ the Pantocrator, or almighty ruler, with his right hand raised in a gesture of benediction.

In the steppe, less rain falls and less vegetation grows. However the milder climate permits a longer growing season, giving the people more time to sow, cultivate, and harvest their grain crops.

Trade. Kievan Russia traded agricultural goods, wood, iron, salt, and other products with the Byzantine Empire. The most important of these products were fur, wax, honey, animal hides, flax, hemp, burlap, and hops. Kievan Russia also furnished slaves for the Byzantines. In return the traders of Kievan Russia obtained wine, silk, religious art objects, spices, precious stones, steel blades, and horses from the Byzantines. From western Europe they received textiles, glassware, and metals. By the early 1000s, trade had helped make Kievan Russia a strong and wealthy power, and Kiev had become a major city.

Social Classes
In the varied economy of Kievan Russia, several social classes emerged. The highest class was made up of the local princes and their families. Below the princes came the boyars. Next were the artisans and merchants, who lived in the towns and devoted themselves entirely to trade.

The clergy formed another important group in Kievan society. They not only performed religious ceremonies but also ran schools, hospitals, and other charities.

The largest social class, however, consisted of peasants. The peasants lived in small villages and produced the agricultural output of Kievan Russia.

> ### Section 2 Review
>
> 1. **Define** steppe, boyar, *Pravda Russkaia*, metropolitan, taiga
> 2. **Identify** Rurik, Rus, Yaroslav the Wise, Vladimir I
> 3. **Locate and Explain the Significance** Ural Mountains, Vistula River, Baltic Sea, Dnieper River, Don River, Black Sea, Volga River, Caspian Sea, Lake Ladoga, Novgorod, Kiev
> 4. **Analyzing Ideas** How do you think the physical geography of eastern Europe influenced the development of Kievan Russia?
> 5. **Synthesizing Ideas** Describe the political, economic, and social life of Kievan Russia.

Section 3

The Rise of the Mongols

Focus Questions

- **How did the Mongols influence the history of Kievan Russia?**
- **What factors led to the establishment of the Russian state?**

After the rule of Yaroslav the Wise ended in 1054, Kiev declined in power and wealth. The Kievan rulers gave their younger sons outlying towns to rule as independent principalities. These princes and their descendants fought among themselves and with the ruler of Kiev to expand their own territories. Kiev's trade declined because of raids by the Polovtsians, Turkish peoples who controlled the region south of Kiev after 1055. Also, Italian city-states developed new trade routes throughout the Mediterranean region that competed with the Kievan routes.

After groups of princes sacked Kiev in 1169 and again in 1203, the city's prosperity was ruined. As the princes continued to fight among themselves, new invaders took advantage of Kiev's weakness. These invaders, the Mongols, came from the Asian steppe east of the Urals.

The Mongols in Eastern Europe

The Mongols first attacked eastern Europe in force in 1237. Kievan resistance proved too weak to halt the Mongols, and by 1240 they had conquered and burned almost every city in Kievan Russia.

The Mongols pushed on across the Carpathian Mountains into Hungary and across the plains into Poland. After defeating the Hungarian and Polish armies in 1242, however, the Mongol leader Batu called off his attack to return to southern Russia. His decision was a political one, guided by his desire to influence the choice of the next leader of the Mongols. Thus Hungary and Poland, although terribly damaged by war and savage plundering, escaped long-term Mongol rule. The Kievan region, however, remained under Mongol control until the late 1400s.

Kievan Russia Under the Mongols

The Mongols did not try to impose their way of life on the Slavic people they conquered. They wanted only to collect wealth from the region. Taxes were often harsh, but as long as the taxes were paid, the Mongols allowed the people to retain their own government and customs.

In most places, local landlords collected taxes and administered justice. Peasants had two obligations to their landlords: labor at specified times and a payment either in money or in goods. Most peasants in the north, the area between the Volga and Oka Rivers, did not have landlords and paid taxes directly to the government.

Nevertheless, although the Mongols formed only a small ruling class, they did influence the society of the eastern Slavs in several ways. They built important roads and improved methods of taxation and communication. Some of their words filtered into the language that came to be called Russian.

Kievan Russia and Its Neighbors

During the time of Mongol rule, the Slavs of eastern Europe had little contact with central and western Europe. Lithuania and Poland won territory from the northwestern part of Kievan Russia in the late 1300s, forming a kingdom that was hostile to the eastern Slavs. Religious conflicts also existed. The Poles had been converted to western Christianity. The eastern Slavs, however, clung to their Eastern Orthodox faith, which set them apart from both the Poles and the Mongols. The eastern Slavs grew suspicious of western Europeans and their influence. This suspicion became a deep-seated one that has not disappeared to the present day.

The Rise of Moscow

In time Mongol rule grew weaker, and the princes of the region became more independent. During the early 1300s, Moscow, or Muscovy, became the strongest principality, partly because its leader, Prince Ivan I, cooperated with the Mongols. In return for his cooperation, the Mongols awarded Ivan, who ruled Moscow from 1325 to 1341, the title of Grand Prince in 1328. Ivan's power increased further when the chief metropolitan of the Orthodox Church moved to Moscow in about 1328.

By the time of Ivan III of Moscow, also called Ivan the Great, who ruled as Grand Prince from 1462 to 1505, Moscow had become so powerful that it began to assert its independence from the Mongols. In 1480 Ivan III overthrew Mongol rule. He united many of the principalities and emerged as the first ruler of the independent state called Russia. Through military conquest he gained additional territory to the west.

Ivan considered himself "autocrat by the grace of God," and helped establish a pattern of absolute monarchy that would persist in Russia for centuries, long after most of western Europe had begun to move toward some form of representative government.

Ivan the Terrible. In 1533, the three-year-old Ivan IV became ruler of Russia. Because of Ivan's youth, however, it was the boyars who actually wielded power. For several years the young boy stood on the sidelines as the boyars fought among themselves, sometimes torturing and murdering each other.

Finally, after an impressive ceremony in 1547, Ivan began to exercise power himself. He declared that he was the heir of the Roman and Byzantine Empires and took the title of **czar**, the Russian word for caesar. As czar, Ivan IV was an able administrator. He reformed the old laws of Yaroslav, reestablished trade with western Europe, and opened Siberia for Russian settlement.

After a quarrel with boyars whom he suspected of disloyalty, Ivan in 1565 formed a personal army of several thousand men, known as the *oprichniki*. These fearsome men dressed in black and wore an emblem with a broomstick to indicate their intention of sweeping treason from the land.

Ivan used the *oprichniki* to strengthen his control over Russia. They arrested boyars and distributed the boyars' land to Ivan's supporters. In 1570 Ivan led them in an attack on Novgorod, in which the city was destroyed and thousands of its inhabitants executed. For several years some of Ivan's actions were so bizarre

The Cathedral of St. Basil the Blessed in Moscow was built on Red Square between 1554 and 1560 under the reign of Czar Ivan the Terrible.

and cruel that historians have questioned his sanity. In a fit of rage, he even murdered his oldest son in 1581. Such ferocious acts earned him the nickname "Ivan the Terrible."

Ivan IV did, however, establish the foundations of the new Russian state. The state was huge, including old Kievan Russia and Siberia, and extended south to the Caspian Sea. It was also autocratic, with the czar wielding total power.

The Growth of the Church

As with the Roman Catholic Church in western Europe, the Orthodox church in Russia continued to expand its landholdings, primarily through gifts from people who saw these donations as a guarantee of spiritual salvation. By 1500 the church owned a significant portion of all the cultivated land in Russia.

During the Mongol period, the Russian Orthodox Church had become increasingly independent of the patriarch of Constantinople. In 1448 Russian bishops chose the metropolitan of the Orthodox church in Moscow independently of Constantinople. In 1589 Moscow's metropolitan was named patriarch, the

Sacred Icons

When Kievan Russia adopted Christianity in the 900s, the people were baptized and told to destroy their pagan idols. Holy pictures, or icons, were hung in lavish new churches. Gold- or silver-painted backgrounds made the icons easier to see in dimly lighted interiors. Troops marching into battle also carried icons. Despite their flat, two-dimensional style, icons conveyed both individuality and a sense of godliness.

In fact, the unrealistic appearance of icons was intentional, to help convey a message to the viewers. This art was intended to describe religious figures and communicate ideas through simple, familiar images without distractions. In this icon from Kiev, we see Mary and Jesus.

same rank held by the heads of the other Eastern Orthodox churches.

The Russians reinterpreted the history of how their country had been Christianized so as to justify the independence of the Russian Orthodox Church. The Russians now claimed that Andrew, one of the 12 apostles of Jesus, had brought Christianity to Russia directly from Jerusalem. After Constantinople fell to the Turks, they proudly proclaimed Moscow as the **"third Rome."** A Russian churchman wrote that the first Rome had fallen because of heresy and that the second Rome—Constantinople—had fallen to infidels, people who were not Christians. He said that the third Rome—Moscow—was destined to be the final one that would bring spiritual light to the whole world.

This new confidence affected Russian architecture and art. The Cathedral of the Assumption in Moscow exemplifies the artistry and religious fervor of the period. The church was built in the domed-roof style so popular in both Byzantine and Russian cultures.

Every inch of the church's interior walls exhibited some form of artwork. Sparkling chandeliers and candles illuminated every alcove. The face of Jesus adorned the highest central dome. The entire cathedral, full of grandeur and beauty, was designed to produce a strong mystical response from the people.

Section 3 Review

1. **Define** czar, third Rome
2. **Identify** Polovtsians, Ivan III, Ivan IV
3. **Locate and Explain the Significance** Lithuania, Poland, Moscow
4. **Understanding Ideas** How did Mongol rule affect life in eastern Europe? Illustrate your answer with examples from this section.
5. **Contrasting Ideas** Compare and contrast the rule of Ivan the Terrible with that of earlier Russian rulers. How did rulers from Ivan I onward build the power of Russia?

Chapter 8 Review

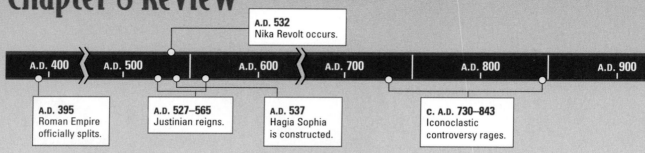

A.D. 532 Nika Revolt occurs.

A.D. 400 — A.D. 500 — A.D. 600 — A.D. 700 — A.D. 800 — A.D. 900

A.D. 395 Roman Empire officially splits.

A.D. 527–565 Justinian reigns.

A.D. 537 Hagia Sophia is constructed.

C. A.D. 730–843 Iconoclastic controversy rages.

Chapter Summary

The following list contains the key concepts you have learned about the Byzantine Empire and its heritage.

1. A brilliant and sophisticated civilization, the Byzantine Empire helped preserve the heritage of Greece and Rome.
2. Justinian, one of the greatest Byzantine emperors, extended the borders of the empire, codified the laws, and ordered the building of the Hagia Sophia.
3. The Byzantine Empire survived for 1,000 years because of its political, military, and economic strengths.
4. The iconoclastic controversy—between supporters and opponents of religious icons—threatened the strength of church and state and affected the empire's relations with Rome.
5. In 1054 the Christian church split into two churches—the Roman Catholic Church and the Eastern Orthodox Church.
6. The main inheritor of Byzantine traditions was Kievan Russia, located on the vast plains of eastern Europe.
7. Kievan Russia became a flourishing society based on agriculture and trade.
8. Although the Mongols conquered Kievan Russia, they had little lasting influence on local institutions and culture in the region around Kiev and Novgorod.
9. As Mongol control weakened, a strong state, centered in Moscow, started to emerge in the 1400s.
10. In the 1500s Ivan IV took the title *czar* and firmly established the large Russian state.

Reviewing Important Terms

On a separate sheet of paper, supply the term that correctly completes each statement.

1. The money or goods that a bride brought to her husband when the couple married was called a _____.
2. Holy pictures of Jesus, the Virgin Mary, and the saints, typically used in devotions, are called _____.
3. _____ felt that the presence of icons constituted idol worship and should be suppressed.
4. The argument between the defenders and the opponents of icons was called the _____.
5. Church leaders label an opinion that conflicts with church doctrine _____.
6. _____ entails barring a person from church membership and excluding the person from taking part in church ceremonies such as baptism, marriage, and communion.
7. _____ are pictures or designs made up of inlaid pieces of stone, glass, or enamel.
8. In Kievan Russia the princes sometimes ruled with the advice of a council of _____, or nobles.
9. Much of southeastern Europe and southern Central Asia consists of a grassy, almost treeless plain called the _____.
10. When the Christian church split in 1054, the Kievan church became a part of the Eastern Orthodox Church, with its chief bishop, the _____, chosen by the patriarch of Constantinople.
11. The forest zone in northern Russia is known as the _____.
12. Ivan IV declared himself the heir of the Roman and Byzantine Empires and took the title _____, the Russian word for caesar.

Developing Critical Thinking Skills

1. **Classifying Ideas** Classify each of the following statements as relating to the Byzantine Empire, Kievan Russia, or the rise of Moscow.
   (a) Justinian established the Justinianic Code.
   (b) Ivan III united territories to form the state of Russia.
   (c) The *veche* settled disputes.
   (d) Yaroslav the Wise issued Russia's first law code.
   (e) Vladimir I accepted Christianity as the official religion for the region.
   (f) Ivan IV became ruler of Russia.
   (g) Rulers gave younger sons outlying towns to rule independently.
   (h) Belisarius was commander in chief of the army.
2. **Summarizing Ideas** (a) Describe Byzantine art, architecture, and law. (b) What features of Byzantine culture did the people who eventually formed Russia adopt?

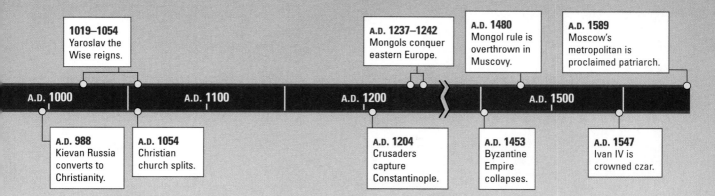

1019–1054
Yaroslav the Wise reigns.

A.D. 1237–1242
Mongols conquer eastern Europe.

A.D. 1480
Mongol rule is overthrown in Muscovy.

A.D. 1589
Moscow's metropolitan is proclaimed patriarch.

A.D. **1000**　　　A.D. **1100**　　　A.D. **1200**　　　A.D. **1500**

A.D. 988
Kievan Russia converts to Christianity.

A.D. 1054
Christian church splits.

A.D. 1204
Crusaders capture Constantinople.

A.D. 1453
Byzantine Empire collapses.

A.D. 1547
Ivan IV is crowned czar.

3. **Relating Cause and Effect** (a) In eastern Europe, how did the Viking trade routes affect the growth of cities such as Kiev? (b) What effects did the Mongol invasion have on Kievan Russia?
4. **Analyzing Ideas** How did Mongol rule and its decline help to strengthen the rule of Moscow?
5. **Understanding Chronology** Indicate whether each of the following events occurred between A.D. 300 and 600, 600 and 900, 900 and 1200, or 1200 and 1500.
   (a) Mongols captured Kiev.
   (b) Justinian ruled the Byzantine Empire.
   (c) Yaroslav I ruled.
   (d) Eastern Church split from the Roman Catholic Church.

Relating Geography to History

(a) On an outline map of present-day eastern Europe and Russia, trace the rivers mentioned in this chapter, and label the body of water into which each river flows.
(b) Using the maps on page 197 and, in Chapter 12, page 284, compare the territories of Kievan Russia (through 1240) with the Mongol Empire in 1294. What part of Kievan Russia was included in the Mongol Empire? What portion of it lay outside the borders of the Mongol Empire in 1294?

Relating Past to Present

1. Use either *The Statesman's Yearbook* or a world almanac from your library to obtain a list of products that Russia and Turkey import and export today. Compare this list with what was traded between the Byzantine Empire and Kievan Russia.
2. Visit a Greek or Russian Orthodox Church and a Roman Catholic Church. Write a report on the types of art, architecture, and decorative pieces you observe. Try to explain any similarities or differences you observe between these modern churches and the description of the ancient churches in this chapter.

Applying History Study Skills

Before completing this activity, review Building History Study Skills on page 192.

Read the following excerpt from *On the Buildings of Justinian* by Procopius. Then identify whether the author was impartial, biased in favor of Justinian, or biased against Justinian when he wrote the piece. Point to evidence, such as words or phrases that convey positive or negative attitudes, that supports your conclusions.

"The Emperor Justinian . . . succeeding to the throne when the state was decayed, added greatly to its extent and glory by driving out from it the barbarians. . . . As for religion, which he found uncertain and torn by various heresies, he destroyed everything which could lead to error, and securely established the true faith upon one solid foundation. Moreover, finding the laws obscure through their unnecessary multitude, and confused by their conflict with one another, he firmly established them by reducing the number of those which were unnecessary, and in the case of those that were contradictory, by confirming the better ones."

internet**connect**

Search the Internet through the HRW Web site for primary sources related to the Byzantine Empire. You may, for example, find contemporary descriptions of the Mongols or the Justinianic Code. Colleges and universities often have Web sites that provide the text of such documents. Print out one or more of these documents, and come to class prepared to discuss them.

HRW　**GO TO:** go.hrw.com
KEYWORD: SCØ Byzantine Empire

Building Your Portfolio

1. **Writing a Report** Use encyclopedias or books about the Byzantine Empire to prepare a written report about the emperor Justinian. Include in your report a description of his life and his accomplishments. Place the completed report in your portfolio.
2. **Drawing a Building Plan** Using pictures in encyclopedias as models, draw a building plan of the church of Hagia Sophia. Place it in your portfolio.
3. **Researching** Research Yaroslav the Wise's law code, the *Pravda Russkaia*. Make special note of its similarities to the Justinianic Code. Be prepared to present an oral report on your findings to the class. Place the completed report in your portfolio.

The Islamic Empire

TIME

A.D. 570–1761

A.D. 570–1761

| 3.7 million B.C. | 4000 B.C. | A.D. 2100 |

PLACE

Arabia, North Africa, Southern Europe, Central Asia, and India

The Alhambra, Granada, Spain

Significance

In the A.D. 600s the prophet Muhammad began preaching the religion of Islam. Through military conquest, the early followers of Islam—known as Muslims—established a vast empire. Muhammad's spiritual teachings, which encouraged people to lead humble, generous, and tolerant lives, proved extremely attractive.

As the new religion spread, an Islamic culture began to flourish. Islamic philosophers, scientists, and artists created works whose influence reached far beyond the Muslim world.

Terms to Define

hijrah	imams
Qur'an	caliphates
jihad	dower
mosques	sultan
caliph	millets
Jabal Tariq	suttee

People to Identify

bedouin	Harsha
Muhammad	Rajputs
Abu Bakr	Timur
Berbers	Urdu
Moors	Babur
Al-Razi	Akbar
Ottomans	Shah Jahan
Janissaries	Nanak

Places to Locate

Arabia	Toledo
Jidda	Seville
Mecca	Delhi
Al-Madīnah	Samarkand
Baghdad	Angora
Cairo	Agra
Córdoba	

Chapter Theme Questions

- **Religion** What factors might contribute to the rapid spread of a religion?
- **The Arts and Science** How might great civilizations advance the arts and sciences?
- **Cross-Cultural Interaction** In what ways could the arrival of Muslims have affected European and Indian history?

A story in Muslim literature tells of a ruler named Shahryar (shahr·i·yahr). Each night he married a new wife, and each morning he ordered her execution because he believed that no wife would remain loyal. To save herself, one wife, Scheherezade (shuh·hehr·uh·zahd), began a story but did not finish it, promising its conclusion the following night. Pleased by the tale and eager for the ending, Shahryar delayed this wife's execution. Night after night she charmed him with stories, each not quite finished. As the story goes, after a thousand and one nights of storytelling, the king was convinced that she would remain faithful and abandoned plans to execute her.

The story of Scheherazade is the tale around which a body of folktales and fairy tales of Arabic, Egyptian, Indian, East Asian, and Persian origin are organized. The first reference to "A Thousand Tales" was made nearly 1,000 years ago about a collection of Persian stories. More tales were added until a "final" Arabic version existed in the 1600s. This collection became what we know today as *The Thousand and One Nights*.

The collection includes the tales about Sinbad the sailor, Aladdin, and Ali Baba and the Forty Thieves. These stories and others from *The Thousand and One Nights* are among the most widely read in history.

Section 1

The Rise and Spread of Islam

Focus Questions

- **What are the central beliefs of Islam?**
- **Why did Islam spread so rapidly?**
- **What ideological differences developed within the Muslim community?**

While the Byzantines ruled Asia Minor and the Balkan region, a new empire—the Muslim, or Arab, Empire—was taking shape to the south and east. Inspired by a new religion, Islam, the Muslim armies rapidly conquered vast territories in southwest Asia and North Africa. The Muslims, like the Byzantines, developed a civilization that for centuries far surpassed that of western Europe. That Muslim civilization began in Arabia.

The Physical Setting

South of the Fertile Crescent lay the great peninsula of Arabia. Most of it consisted of a desert plateau with such sparse vegetation that it could only support herders and their flocks of sheep. These Arabic herders, called bedouins (BE·duh·wuhnz), lived as nomads, moving their flocks from one grazing area to another. They were organized into tribes, each ruled by a sheikh (SHAYK), a man who had the respect of the tribe because of his knowledge, courage, wealth, and family background.

Coastal areas with more temperate climates could support greater numbers of people. Towns grew up in these areas, and the townspeople became traders. Goods from Asia and Africa entered the port of Jidda on the Red Sea and then were transported overland to Mecca, the starting point of a caravan route running north to Syria. Through trade, Arabs in the towns met and were influenced by people from many different cultures.

The Life of Muhammad

Muhammad, the prophet of Islam,* was born in Mecca in about 570. Orphaned at the age of six, he spent the early years of his life in the care of his grandfather and uncle. A member of a respected tribe but a poor family, Muhammad received no formal education. Like many Arabs in Mecca, he made a living as a caravan trader.

As a trader, Muhammad came in contact with followers of monotheistic religions—people, such as Jews and Christians, who worshipped a single god. The teachings of these religions may have intrigued Muhammad. Most Arabs were polytheists, worshipping many gods, but there were some who rejected old gods and worshipped a single deity. These people, called hanifs, were neither Jewish nor Christian. Their practice of solitary meditation increasingly attracted Muhammad.

When he was about 40 years old, Muhammad had a great religious experience. He reported a vision he later identified as the angel Jibreel (Gabriel, in English) ordering him to teach the word of Allah, or the One God, to the Arabs. Muhammad followed this command. Mecca's rulers bitterly opposed Muhammad's preaching. Each year Mecca's merchants profited from the business of Arab pilgrims who came to worship at the sacred Ka'bah (KAH·buh), a stone building filled with the statues of many gods. Muhammad's teaching, the rulers feared, would threaten both the pilgrimage and the merchants' livelihood.

The rulers' opposition soon turned to persecution. Eventually, Muhammad sought a less hostile place. He sent followers to the town of Yathrib (later called Medina, or Al-Madīnah, the "City of the Prophet") and settled there himself at the invitation of the town's leaders. The event became known as the *hijrah* (hi·JY·ruh), meaning "flight" or "migration." In Yathrib many people accepted Muhammad as their spiritual and political leader.

Expanding their influence, Muhammad's followers, later to be called Muslims, began to convert desert tribes. With the help of these tribes, Muhammad's followers raided Meccan caravans. Several years of warfare followed, but Mecca finally submitted to Muslim rule. Muhammad met little resistance when he entered the city in 630. He destroyed the pagan idols in the Ka'bah, which became Islam's holiest shrine and in time the focal point of the Muslim pilgrimage to Mecca.

After the fall of Mecca, many Arabian tribes accepted Islam and the leadership of Muhammad. With a combination of prudent policies, tolerance, and force, he converted many of the bedouin tribes to his new religion. By 632, when Muhammad died, a large part of Arabia had accepted Islam. (See map on page 209.)

The Faith of Islam

The central belief of Islam is that there is only one God: "Say God is One; God the Eternal: He did not beget [have children], and is not begotten, and no one is equal to Him." Like most major religions, Islam has a holy book, definite rules for its believers, and emphasis on certain moral teachings.

The holy book of Islam is the **Qur'an** (kuh·RAN). According to Muslims, the Qur'an presents God's ordinances and teachings as revealed to Muhammad. It includes concepts and teachings also found in the Torah and the Christian Bible. For example, the Qur'an recounts the creation of the world and the teachings of major prophets, including Jesus. Muhammad accepted the Torah and Christian scriptures as part of God's revelations, and he initially taught a special tolerance for Christians and Jews, whom he regarded as "People of the Book." Relations among the religious groups, though, were not always peaceful.

---

*In Arabic the word *Islam* means "submission to [the will of] God."

Building History Study Skills

READ
WRITE
INTERPRET
CONNECT
THINK

Reading About History: Understanding Sequence

A sequence is the order in which things happen in time. Sequencing events, then, is arranging these events in the order in which they occurred. Sequencing helps you to organize information. From the pattern of the data, you can determine how events are related to each other. The relationship among these events can help you identify other important ideas such as cause and effect and historical significance.

How to Sequence Information

To sequence information, follow these steps.
1. Identify what you hope to learn by sequencing the information being studied.
2. Look for calendar references, clue words, and time periods. Calendar references include centuries, years, and dates. Clue words include *first*, *second*, *after*, *before*, *meanwhile*, and *later*.
3. Determine whether there is an implied sequence or a cause-and-effect relationship. For example, could one event have happened without the other taking place?
4. List the events in sequence.
5. Make a statement about the relationship between the items, actions, or events included. What is the significance of the pattern of data?

Developing the Skill

You can better understand the expansion of Islam by organizing significant events sequentially. The following statements about the spread of Islam are not listed in the order that they occurred. As you read the list, try to determine the proper sequence.
1. Muhammad's preaching was opposed, and in 622 he fled to Yathrib (later called Medina or Al-Madīnah).
2. By 632, when Muhammad died, a large part of Arabia had accepted Islam.
3. Muhammad's successors pursued a policy aimed at conquering the territory that belonged to non-Muslims.
4. Muhammad considered himself a prophet and a teacher and believed that there is only one God.
5. Muhammad became the leader of the community in Yathrib (Medina).
6. The Muslims usually allowed conquered peoples to choose either to accept Islam or to pay a tribute.

Persian miniature illustrating "the arrival of the prophet"

7. In 732 the Franks defeated the Moors at the Battle of Tours.
8. Less than a century after the death of Muhammad, his followers had conquered Arabia, Palestine, Syria, Mesopotamia, Persia, part of India, and all of North Africa.

The correct sequence of events would be 4, 1, 5, 2, 3, 8, 6, and 7. The first statement (4) establishes Muhammad as the leader. Muhammad's beliefs are an implied part of the sequence. Muhammad has to be preaching something in order to be expelled from Mecca (1). Muhammad then became the leader of Medina (5). The date 632 completes Muhammad's achievements (2). His successors (3) would have to follow after his death. They conquered neighboring territories and then went to India and North Africa (8). Their conquering policy (6) is then explained as an implied part of the sequence. The defeat at Tours marks the limit of Muslim expansion into other parts of Europe in 732 (7).

Practicing the Skill

Using the guidelines for sequencing information, make a list of important events at your school, and arrange them in sequence. Include events such as special assemblies, school-sponsored club activities, and sports competitions.

To apply this skill, see Applying History Study Skills on page 223.

Muhammad taught that God had revealed the Qur'an as a sacred guide for all humankind. First written in Arabic, the Qur'an was not rapidly translated into other languages because Muslims believed God's revelations might be lost or changed. As a result, Arabic became the common language of Muslims in religion, law, and literature. Muslims memorize and recite the Qur'an in Arabic.

According to the Qur'an, a Muslim must meet five important obligations known as the Five Pillars of Islam: (1) Recite the profession of faith: "I bear witness that there is no deity except Allah [God] and that Muhammad is His Servant and Messenger." (2) Pray five times a day facing Mecca, the holy city of Islam. (3) Give alms—money or food—to the poor. (4) Fast, or go without food and drink, from first light to sunset during the month of Ramadan—the ninth month of the Muslim year. This month is considered sacred because it was the month in which Muhammad had his first vision of the angel Jibreel and received God's revelations, later written in the Qur'an. (5) If possible, make a pilgrimage to Mecca at least once in a lifetime.

Islam requires and emphasizes the virtues of temperance, humility, justice, generosity, tolerance, obedience to law, and courage. Muslims are forbidden to drink alcoholic beverages or to eat pork—for they, like the Jews, believe pigs are unclean.

Polygamy was widespread throughout Arabia, but Islam restricted a Muslim man to four wives, and he had to treat them equally. After marriage, Muslim women gained certain rights with regard to property ownership. Slavery, too, was common in Arabia, but Islam urged freeing slaves as an act of goodness. Those Muslims who chose to keep their slaves were required to treat them humanely.

Muhammad also emphasized the importance of the **jihad** (ji·HAHD), or struggle to defend the faith. Anyone who died in this struggle, Muhammad said, was a martyr who would receive the blessings of God and rewards in heaven.

Muslim **mosques**, or places of worship, have no religious images or statues. Islam discourages representations of human or animal forms. Further, Islam has no elaborate ceremonies or any formal priesthood. At services, religious leaders—men learned in Islamic faith and law—guide the people in worship. On Friday at noon, male Muslims are called to gather for prayer and a sermon. Islam requires that women say the same prayers at home or in a section of the mosque set aside for them.

The Spread of Islam

When Muhammad died in 632, an assembly of Muslims chose Abu Bakr (uh·boo bak·uhr), Muhammad's oldest friend and one of his early converts, as his successor. Abu Bakr used the title **caliph**, meaning "successor to the Prophet." Abu Bakr prevented the young faith from splintering and expanded the influence of Islam northward. His successor as caliph, 'Umar (oo·mahr), continued a policy of conquering neighboring territories of non-Muslims. Within 25 years, the Muslim Empire included Syria, Persia, and much of North Africa. 'Umar's skills allowed for effective government and the distribution of wealth, fueling further expansion.

The Arab policy toward conquered peoples made conquests easier. Fierce and fearless in war, Arabs

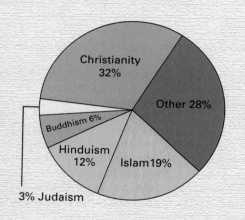

Major Religions of the World

Christianity 32%

Other 28%

Buddhism 6%

Hinduism 12%

Islam 19%

3% Judaism

Religion	Followers
Christianity	1,929,987,000
Islam	1,147,494,000
Hinduism	746,797,000
Buddhism	353,141,000
Judaism	14,890,000
Other	1,653,758,000

Islam grew from a small religion in Arabia to become one of the world's largest religions. This chart shows the approximate number of followers of the world's five largest religions today.

Source: *The World Almanac and Books of Facts,* 1999

What If?

Constantinople

The Muslims attempted to conquer Constantinople in 718, but Byzantine armies successfully defended the city. How do you think the course of history would have been different if the Muslims had toppled the Byzantine Empire?

preferred opponents to yield without battle. They were often more tolerant than other conquerors. Christians, Jews, and some others could choose either to accept Islam or to pay an annual tribute, or tax.

Some who refused to do either were killed, but most either paid or converted to Islam.

Within about 100 years after the death of Muhammad, the Prophet's followers swept through the Arabian Peninsula, Syria, Persia, part of India to the border of China, and all of North Africa, including Egypt. (See map on this page.) They eventually conquered the islands of the Mediterranean Sea, from which they controlled vital trade routes.

An attempt to take Constantinople failed. However, at the western end of the Mediterranean, Muslims successfully entered Europe. A North African people called the Berbers had recently converted to Islam. In 711 a Berber general named Tariq led an expedition against the Visigoths in Spain, past the great rock that guards the strait

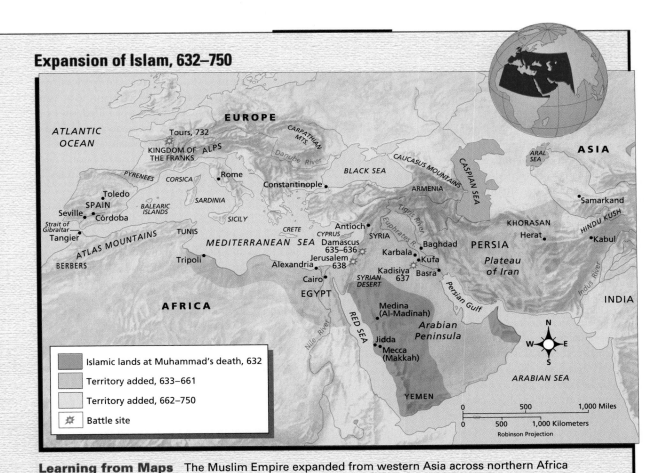

Expansion of Islam, 632–750

Legend:
- Islamic lands at Muhammad's death, 632
- Territory added, 633–661
- Territory added, 662–750
- ☀ Battle site

Learning from Maps The Muslim Empire expanded from western Asia across northern Africa into Spain.

❓ **Region** In what region did the Muslims emerge from a battle without adding any territory?

A *mueddhin*, or crier, calls the hour of daily prayers from this minaret.

between Africa and Europe. The rock became known as **Jabal Tariq**, the "Mountain of Tariq." In Europe the name became Gibraltar.

Spain was an easy conquest, and within seven years the Moors, Muslims of Spain, passed beyond the Pyrenees to raid the plains of what is now central France. In 732 the Franks defeated a raiding party near the town of Tours. (See map on page 209.) European accounts claim a victory that stopped Islam, but skirmishes continued. Tours was in any case the farthest limit of the advance. The Moors eventually withdrew from France and ruled parts of Spain for more than 700 years.

In the 1800s, the American author Washington Irving traveled throughout Spain. After visiting the palace of the Moorish kings in Granada, a province of southern Spain, Irving expressed his feelings in this excerpt from his book *The Alhambra:*

> "Their career of conquest, from the rock of Gibraltar to the cliffs of the Pyrenees, was as rapid and brilliant as the Moslem victories of Syria and Egypt. Nay, had they not been checked on the plains of Tours, all France, all Europe, might have been overrun with the same facility as the empires of the East...
> Where are they? Ask the shores of Barbary and its desert places...They have not even left a distinct name behind them, though for nearly eight centuries they were a distinct people...A few broken monuments are all that remain to bear witness to their power and dominion, as solitary rocks, left far in the interior, bear testimony to the extent of some vast inundation. Such is the

Alhambra...an elegant memento of a brave, intelligent, and graceful people, who conquered, ruled, flourished, and passed away."

Divisions in the Muslim Community

Early in the history of Islam, disputes arose over Muhammad's successors and over interpretation of the Qur'an. Divisions began when rebels killed 'Umar's successor, 'Uthman, for allegedly favoring his own clan. 'Uthman's cousin Mu'awiya (mooh·AH·wee·ya) accused 'Ali, the newly chosen caliph, of protecting the assassins. The rivals went to war. When 'Ali was assassinated in 661, Mu'awiya took power. Most Muslims accepted Mu'awiya's rule and remained "followers of the Sunna" or "way." Sunnis (SOOH·nees) believe that consensus of the Islamic community establishes religious and civil authority.

'Ali's followers believed that only 'Ali's descendants should rule or interpret the Qur'an. This group, the *Shi'at 'Ali,* or "party of Ali," became known as the Shi'ah (SHEE·ah). The Shi'ah looked to 'Ali's successors, called **imams,** (i·MAHMZ) for sole spiritual and secular authority. The sons of Mu'awiya and 'Ali, Yazid and Husayn, also warred. Husayn was killed, and the rift between the two parties, or sects, deepened. Today about 10 percent of the world's Muslims are Shi'ah, and the division between Shi'ah and Sunni concerning secular and spiritual authority continues to separate the two groups.

Later another movement developed among Muslims. Sufis, Muslim mystics, voluntarily adopted an austere lifestyle in which material wealth and grand titles meant nothing. The one reality was God, and personal faith in God was the only mark of a person's worth.

Section 1 Review

1. **Define** *hijrah*, Qur'an, jihad, mosques, caliph, Jabal Tariq, imams
2. **Identify** bedouin, Muhammad, Abu Bakr, Berbers, Moors
3. **Locate and Explain the Significance** Arabia, Jidda, Mecca, Al-Madīnah
4. **Understanding Ideas (a)** Describe the major beliefs of Islam. **(b)** List the five chief obligations or duties of a Muslim.
5. **Interpreting Ideas** What factors allowed Islam to spread widely, from western Asia to Spain?
6. **Comparing Ideas** Explain the differences between Sunni Muslims and Shi'ah Muslims.

Islamic Civilization

Focus Questions

- What contributions did Arab Muslim culture make to the arts and sciences?
- In what ways did the Muslim culture spread to Europe?
- How did the rule of the Turks differ from that of the Arabs?

The system of Islamic government allowed its rulers—the caliphs—to wield great authority. Within the stable society that developed, both economic and cultural activity flourished.

Government and Economy

Arabs ruled the territory of the Muslim Empire, which was organized into provinces. The caliph, the supreme civil, military, and religious leader of this vast empire, headed the government. Although an elected office at first, the position of caliph later became hereditary. However, disagreements over succession developed. In time, disputes led to the breakup of the Muslim Empire into three parts, or **caliphates**, ruled by caliphs in Baghdad, Cairo, and Córdoba.

Trade flourished in the Muslim Empire, which had arisen in the center of a world trade network linking Europe, Asia, and Africa. The Arabs had long been traders, and Muhammad himself had been a trader. India and China sent goods to the ports of Syria and to Cairo and Alexandria in Egypt.

Manufacturing increased because of the demands of trade. The empire produced silk, cotton, and woolen textiles, as well as tapestries and carpets. Luxuries such as jewelry, perfumes, and spices were in great demand. Metal products included objects made of gold, silver, steel, and copper. Steel swords from Damascus in Syria and from Toledo in Spain became world famous. Artisans produced a great variety of pottery and glassware. Other artisans in North Africa and Córdoba, Spain, made fine leather goods.

The Great Mosque of Córdoba took more than 200 years to complete and is considered a masterpiece of Islamic architecture. [Ceiling work (left) and pillars (right) at the Mosque of Córdoba.]

The Arabs also encouraged the development of agriculture. They built irrigation systems in Spain like those they had seen in Persia. They introduced fruits, vegetables, and other products native to one part of the empire to other parts.

Society and Art

In Islamic families, as in many other cultures and religions, the father acted as the head of the household. The family provided both economic security and physical protection to its members. Muslims respected the elderly and showed concern for the needs of all members of the extended family—parents, children, grandparents, aunts, uncles, and cousins.

Women had a clearly defined position in Islamic society. The Qur'an says, "And they [women] have rights similar to those [of men] over them in equity: but men have a degree of advantage above them." A father or husband was responsible for a woman's behavior. Parents usually arranged marriages for their children, though the Qur'an gave women the right to contract their own. The groom gave a marriage gift called a *sadaq* or *mahr*, meaning **dower**, to his bride. Intended as a gesture of love rather than a purchase price, the dower still often served to put a price on a bride.

The Qur'an extended more rights to women than they had received under traditional Arab law. For example, in the event of divorce, women kept the dower and were free to remarry, and they could also inherit and own property. In fact, Muslim women enjoyed freedoms not available to most women of the times, although later they began to be secluded and lost some rights.

The government had educational systems, but the family and the mosque also took responsibility for education in Islamic society. Speaking and writing well were considered the standards for an educated person. Subjects of required study were based on the Qur'an. Other secular studies flourished as well.

Because Islamic law prohibited the use of the human form to depict God, decorative arts and calligraphy assumed a special importance. Islamic art often used complex geometric and floral designs. Pictures of people showed only nonreligious subjects, such as hunting or fighting battles.

Architecture became one of the greatest forms of art in the Islamic world. Mosques, palaces, marketplaces, libraries, and other buildings were designed to emphasize the glory of Islam as well as the power of the ruler who had sponsored the construction.

Advances in Science and Mathematics

Though divided politically, the Muslim world remained united in one great civilization. The Arabs adopted the best ideas, customs, and institutions they found. They combined scientific and philosophical ideas of Greece, Rome, and Asia in their culture.

Muslim scientists wrote books and encyclopedias on many subjects. Their geographers and navigators, known as the finest in the world, perfected the

This Turkish miniature from the 1500s shows a Muslim astronomer at work.

Medicine

Who was the first person in your life to set eyes on you? Most likely it was a doctor. Doctors and medicine have existed since ancient times. Early Egyptian books contain directions for setting fractures, and X-rays of mummies reveal healed bones.

Greeks may have been the first people to record their scientific research so that others could use it. They had medical centers where people went to be cured; they afterward offered sacrifices to the gods in thanks. Diseases gradually began to be seen as natural, not supernatural, phenomena. The Greek physician Galen, who practiced in Rome, conducted studies whose results were used in Europe for the next 1,300 years.

In Southwest Asia, the Arabs developed their own interests in medicine, especially in chemistry. The processes of distillation and sublimation for the purification of substances are Arabic in origin. Ibn-Sina (980–1037) wrote a work called the *Canon of Medicine* that was used in medical schools for centuries. When the Muslims invaded Spain, they brought their scientific knowledge with them. Abu al-Qasim developed and documented surgical techniques in Córdoba, making it the medical equal of Cairo and Baghdad. From Spain, Greek and Middle Eastern medical science spread to other European centers of learning. Monks had preserved the old medical knowledge,

Medieval Arab doctors with patient

Contemporary doctor with child

and now, after combining the old medical knowledge with the new learning, medicine was taught at Italian universities. Farther north, young men began to study at the universities of Paris, Oxford, and Cambridge. These colleges are still well known for medical studies.

astrolabe, a small instrument used to determine latitude by calculating the positions of planets and stars. Muslims learned the art of papermaking from the Chinese.

Muslims added much medical knowledge to that developed by Hippocrates and Galen. At Baghdad in the early 900s, Al-Razi, a physician, wrote about surgery, smallpox, and measles. He compiled a huge

medical encyclopedia that, translated into Latin, was used in Europe for centuries.

Within a century after Al-Razi wrote, Ibn-Sina, an Arab philosopher and physician, used ancient Greek sources to write the *Canon of Medicine*, a medical textbook organized like an encyclopedia. Then in the 1100s, Ibn-Rushd, a Spanish-Arabian physician and philosopher, wrote highly regarded

WEAVING

Carpets of the Muslim World

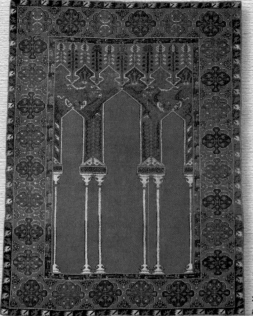

The Metropolitan Museum of Art, Bequest of Joseph V. McMullan, 1973. (1974.149.18). Photograph © 1998 The Metropolitan Museum of Art.

People have been weaving rugs for at least 4,000 years. Although they were used first as protection against cold, carpets soon had other purposes as well. They became symbols of wealth and popular items of trade. In Turkey, Persia, and Central Asia, rug weaving became a great art. Many of these carpets remain unsurpassed for their texture, richness of color, and beauty of design.

Through the centuries, Muslims who could afford them have knelt and prayed on beautiful rugs. During prayer, the rug must be placed on the floor so that the arch in the design points toward Mecca, Muhammad's birthplace. The prayer rug shown here was woven in Turkey during the late 1600s or early 1700s. Typical of many prayer rugs, it has a border of wide and narrow stripes and various geometric and stylized designs. The parts of the carpet have specific meanings. The color red, for example, stands for happiness and wealth. The trees above the arches are probably symbols of the tree of life.

---

commentaries based on Aristotle's works and on Plato's *Republic*. His interpretations of Aristotle influenced later Jewish and Christian writers.

Our word *algebra* comes from the Arabic *al-jabr*, meaning "restoring." Mathematicians of India developed a system of numerals, including zero, which we call Arabic because the Arabs transmitted the system to the West.

Arab scholars were particularly influential in the development of geography as a science. They used the observations of travelers as well as astronomical calculations to improve mapmaking. Arab geographers adopted a Hindu idea that each hemisphere of the world had a center, equally distant from the four cardinal points of north, south, east, and west.

The Spread of Muslim Culture

Europeans encountered Muslim culture in two ways. One was through contact with Spain. The cities of Córdoba and Toledo were famous centers of learning, and prosperous Seville was Spain's capital under

Islam. Christian and Jewish scholars carried Muslim learning from Spain into western Europe. Sicily, too, was a center of Muslim learning—especially astronomy and geography—that influenced European culture. The Crusades—attempts by Europeans to recapture the Holy Land from Muslims—also had an impact on European learning. (See Chapter 11.) Crusaders returning from Palestine and other Muslim regions told of Muslim achievements.

The great era of Arab Muslim culture lasted from about the 700s to the 1100s. Thereafter the Turks became the ruling force in Islam, and invaders entered the Muslim world. However, as Islamic rule changed from Arabic to Turkish, Muslim culture continued to flourish.

The Turks

In the 1000s, the Saljuq Turks of Central Asia migrated to Baghdad and adopted Islam. During the 1000s, they seized Syria, Mesopotamia, and much of Asia Minor. The Saljuq Turks were skillful warriors, and they inflicted a major defeat on the Byzantines at the Battle of Manzikert in 1071. The Saljuqs supported Sunnis and Sufism, but they shifted power away from the caliph. The Turkish **sultan** ruled the empire's secular affairs, claiming to serve the caliph. Islam again displayed its cultural vitality in a flowering of Persian arts and literature. Outside forces ended this era of Turkish expansion. Christians from the West captured cities in the Crusades. Mongols from the East destroyed the city of Baghdad in 1258, killing tens of thousands of people.

During the first half of the 1300s, a group of Turks called Ottomans (after their first ruler, Osman) surged through Asia Minor before invading Europe. The Turks eventually established a capital at Adrianople, northwest of Constantinople, in around 1361. Mehmet II, "the Conqueror," finally took Constantinople in 1453 and made it the capital of the Ottoman Empire. (See Chapter 18.)

The sultans formed a group of slave soldiers called *Janissaries*, who were captives of war or other enslaved Balkan Christians. The Janissaries were carefully instructed in Islamic beliefs and laws and organized as an elite standing army of disciplined, trained infantry. They owed their allegiance exclusively to the sultan, on whom their survival depended. They became influential in government and later gained much power. They eventually became an important faction in the politics of the Ottoman Empire.

Ottoman rulers allowed the religious minorities to practice their religions and to exercise some self-government in groups called **millets**. Each millet, under the general control of the sultan, could establish and administer a civil government with its own courts and collect taxes.

Section 2 Review

1. **Define** caliphates, dower, sultan, millets
2. **Identify** Al-Razi, Ottomans, Janissaries
3. **Locate and Explain the Significance** Baghdad, Cairo, Córdoba, Toledo, Seville
4. **Evaluating Ideas** What do you consider to be the three most important scientific contributions of Islamic culture? Why?
5. **Understanding Ideas** In what two main ways did Europeans encounter Muslim culture?
6. **Analyzing Ideas** Explain how the Ottoman Turks used non-Muslims in the organization of their government.

Islamic and Mughal Rulers in India

Focus Questions

- What effect did Harsha and the Rajputs have on India?
- What were the consequences of Muslim rule in India?
- What were the achievements of the emperors of the Mughal Empire?

Islam also had profound effects far to the east of Arabia. Gupta rule in India ended in the 500s, and a people called the Hunas, or Hua-tun (sometimes called White Huns) repeatedly swept through the mountain passes and into northern India. Disorder ruled the region until a leader named Harsha Vardhana brought stability.

Harsha's Rule

By the early 600s, the Hunas were scattered, and three warring states controlled the Ganges Valley. Sixteen-year-old Harsha Vardhana, or Harsha, became ruler in one of these kingdoms and built an effective army that included cavalry, infantry, and war elephants wearing enormous armor plates.

In six years, Harsha conquered what had been the Gupta Empire. The Deccan, the rugged hill country south of the Narmada River, proved unconquerable, and Harsha never subdued it. A Chinese Buddhist scholar, Hsuan-Tsang, visited India and became a close friend of Harsha. Hsuan-Tsang wrote about Harsha as a model ruler and reported that law-abiding people enjoyed low taxes, a high standard of living, and an excellent educational system. Harsha was a patron of the arts, encouraging writers such as the historian Bana and the poet Mayura. Harsha himself wrote three Sanskrit works. His rule provided relative peace for 41 years.

The Rajputs

After Harsha's death, his empire split into numerous small states that fought for control of northern India. By the early 900s, strong rulers called Rajputs*

Rajput means "son of a king."

(RAHJ·poots) had emerged. Possibly descended from tribes that migrated from Central Asia into northern India during the 400s and 500s, the Rajputs claimed divine origins. They intermarried with Hindus, adopted the religion and caste system, and set up small kingdoms. Although Rajput kingdoms often quarreled with each other, they also staunchly defended their territories against Muslim attacks. Even when defeated in battle or driven from their great forts, they never surrendered.

The Rajputs were a warrior caste organized in clans. They had a fiercely loyal code of conduct, called the *kshatriya-dharma,* or "way of the warrior." The code called for men to protect the weak, show bravery in combat, and respect women. Rajput women had a code of conduct of their own, which included committing ritual suicide, or **suttee**, if their husbands died in battle. The caste system grew in the time of the Rajputs, although not inflexibly so, for marriage or military achievement could lead to advancement. The culture and the caste system remained influential in India for centuries.

Muslim Invasions of India

In the early 700s, Indian pirates from the Indus Valley began attacking Muslim ships in the Arabian Sea. In 711 the Muslims struck back by conquering the Indus Valley. However they ruled the valley so loosely that local government was virtually independent.

For about 300 years, the Muslims made no further conquests in India. Meanwhile, Turkish Muslims had occupied the area now called Afghanistan, northwest of the Indus River. In 997 the Turks began raiding northern India through the northwest mountain passes. Originally attacks for plunder, these raids led to conquest. Over time the small states of the Rajput princes fell to the Turks. The Indians fought fiercely, often outnumbering the Turks, and used their lumbering war elephants. However, the Muslims used cavalry effectively, and their superior mobility and tactics succeeded. In 1193 the Muslims occupied Delhi, and by the early 1200s they controlled most of northern India.

The Delhi sultanate. In 1206 one Muslim leader, a Turkish slave-general, founded the Mamluk dynasty. Because the Mamluk rulers used Delhi as their capital, they are called the Delhi sultanate. Although some sultans were cruel conquerors, they usually allowed Indians to follow their traditional way of life. The Mamluks kept northern India unified for 300 years.

Early in the 1300s, one of the Delhi sultans conquered the Deccan. By 1320 resistance to the Muslims had collapsed throughout most of the Indian subcontinent.

Two notable Delhi sultans represented the extremes of the Delhi sultans' reputations. Muhammad ibn Tughluq ruled from 1325 to 1351. Reputed to have murdered his father to gain rule, his memory survives through grisly tales of his reign. He founded a new capital to strengthen his expansion into the south and ordered the evacuation of Delhi, forcing its inhabitants to march more than 500 miles.

Muhammad ibn Tughluq was succeeded by Firuz Shah Tughluq, a social reformer and cultured man, who reigned from 1351 to 1388. He laid out a network of canals and reservoirs; built hospitals, schools, and mosques; and reversed some of the harsher policies of his predecessor. These reversals also weakened the sultanate, though, and after Firuz's death in 1388, rivalry for succession brought civil war.

Timur. Civil wars and the devastating onslaught of the Turko-Mongol leader Timur (or Timur the Lame)—better known in Europe as Tamerlane—interrupted the rule of the Delhi sultans. Timur was born in Kesh, near Samarkand in what is now Uzbekistan, in 1336. He claimed descent from the great Mongol leader Genghis Khan and was as fierce as his supposed ancestor. Following the pattern of many Asian nomad warriors, Timur created an army and established power in Central Asia, with a capital at Samarkand. In about 1380, he began a career of conquest. North of the Caspian Sea, he defeated the Golden Horde, Mongols who had invaded eastern Europe in the 1200s, and then turned south to India.

Timur's ferocity is almost hard to imagine. Accounts state that before the Battle of Delhi in 1398, he had some 50,000 captives taken en route killed. He destroyed the city and slaughtered most of its people, leaving towers of human heads among the ruins. Taking anything of value, including surviving inhabitants, he left the once-great city in ruins. Afterward, Delhi was, for a long time, a city struggling for survival.

After returning to Samarkand, Timur moved westward. He captured and looted Baghdad and Damascus and massacred their inhabitants. In 1402 his forces defeated the Ottoman Turks and captured the sultan in a great battle at Angora (modern Ankara) in Asia Minor. At the time, the Turks were threatening what was left of the Byzantine Empire.

Timur did not live permanently in any one spot; he moved his army and court from place to place, enduring extreme temperatures of heat and cold.

Profound religious differences separated Muslims and Hindus. The Hindu worship of many gods and of idols offended Muslims. Hindus used music in their religious ceremonies; Muslims did not. Hindus and Muslims had different rules concerning food and drink. For example, Muslims ate beef, which was sacred to Hindus, and Hindus drank fermented beverages, which Muslims rejected. The caste system contradicted Muslim belief in the equality of all people before God, and Hindu fertility goddesses shocked conservative Muslims, who introduced the seclusion of women—called *purdah*—into India. Tensions over these differences sometimes spilled over into violence, and such conflicts remain in India and Pakistan today.

Just as Muslims learned about numerals from Indian mathematicians, the Muslims made their own contributions to Indian life. They introduced a new language, Urdu, the language of present-day Pakistan. Urdu combined Persian and Arabic words and script with a language of the Delhi region. It was used as a means of communication between the authorities and the common people. Muslims brought to India the architectural techniques of the dome and the arch and the Chinese knowledge of gunpowder, paper, and porcelain making.

The Mughal Empire

As the Delhi sultanate grew weaker, Rajput princes again struggled for control of India. These internal conflicts, as in the time of Timur, left India open to Mongol attack. It came under the leadership of the youthful and talented "Babur the Tiger," a descendant of Timur. Babur had fought for years to build an empire in Central Asia, but had been driven out by the Uzbek people. He then decided to focus his ambition on India, and invaded the Delhi sultanate. After a victory at Panipat, Babur occupied Delhi in 1526 and brought the region under his control. He thus founded the Mughal Empire. (See map on page 220.)

Babur died in 1530, and his son Humayun nearly lost the empire. Then a series of energetic and talented rulers saved and expanded it, uniting northern and southern India. Timur had made Indians fear Mongol rulers, but the Mughals encouraged unity, orderly government, and the arts.

Babur's grandson, Akbar, considered the greatest Mughal emperor, took the throne at the age of 13 and reigned from 1556 to 1605. Akbar realized that Indian society was diverse and used various means to win support for his government. He took a Rajput wife and

Their defeat at the hands of Timur's army forestalled the taking of Constantinople for another 50 years.

In his late 60s, Timur planned a campaign against China, wanting to conquer it as Genghis Khan had. However, he died in 1405 before he could accomplish his goal. Timur left India to be ruled by subordinates. After his death, the Delhi sultans regained power and maintained their rule until 1526.

Results of Muslim Rule

Despite the interruption of Timur and his Mongol successors, the first period of Muslim rule in India had important and lasting consequences. Initially, Muslims appeared content to confiscate land and let life go on as it had in the past. Most northern Indians and nearly all southern Indians were Hindus. Few converted to Islam as had happened elsewhere.

The Glory of Islam

Founded in the 600s by the Arabian prophet Muhammad, Islam is today one of the world's largest religions, followed by millions of people throughout the world. Those who adhere to the beliefs of Islam are called Muslims. The largest Muslim communities exist in Southwest Asia, North Africa, Indonesia, the Indian subcontinent, and Central Asia.

Muhammad, who was born in Mecca, Arabia, in about 570, preached that only one God—Allah—exists and that he—Muhammad—was God's messenger. In Arabic the word *Islam,* which means "submission to [the will of] God," illustrates the fundamental tenet of the Islamic religion—that each believer should surrender to the will of God. Islamic scripture, which is written in the Qur'an (the holy book of Islam), teaches God's word as told to Muhammad.

In the early 600s, when Muhammad began preaching in Mecca, most people scorned him and rejected his teachings. However, with his followers from Yathrib (Medina, or Al-Madīnah), Muhammad took over the city of Mecca, destroying idols and turning the shrine at the Ka'bah into a mosque. Since that time, Mecca and Medina have been the sacred cities of Islam, and the Ka'bah its holiest shrine.

After Muhammad died, his successor, Abu Bakr, launched a holy war, or jihad, in an effort to spread Islam and to establish control over Arabian tribes.

Going forth from Mecca and Medina, Muslim armies conquered Syria, Iraq, Egypt, Iran (which was then Persia), Afghanistan, the Indus River Valley, North Africa, and most of Spain. Those conquered were not forced to accept Islam,

Hagia Sophia

but they were obligated to pay a tribute. Gradually, however, the Islamic religion spread to many of those brought under Muslim control. A distinctive Islamic civilization and culture, which was noted for its architecture and art, developed throughout Southwest Asia and North Africa.

During centuries of expansion, consecutive dynasties reigned over the Islamic empire, each headed by a religious and political head called the caliph. Each dynasty and caliph made their mark, large or small, on the empire. The Umayyad dynasty (661–750), for example, successfully conquered parts of North Africa and the Indus River Valley

Calligraphy representing the phrase "Muhammad is the Prophet of God"

region. The Abbasid dynasty (750–1258), however, may be most famous for its fifth caliph, Harun al-Rashid, who ruled the empire during its zenith. A lavish patron of the arts, Harun reigned, for the most part, over a peaceful and prospering empire. The development of various industries, such as textiles, metals, and paper, led to an expansion in trade and an even greater prosperity for the empire under Harun's reign. Stories of the extravagant wealth of Harun and his court are romantically captured in *The Thousand and One Nights.*

The first Islamic mosques, which were modeled after Muhammad's private courtyard at Medina where he worshipped, were simply plots of ground that were marked as sacred. As conquests furthered the spread of Islam, mosques were built in every center taken over by Muslims. In some cases, such as with the Byzantine cathedral Hagia

Sophia at Constantinople, existing sanctuaries were converted to mosques. Mosques are designed to house the thousands of followers who gather and worship, especially for Friday services. The Great Mosque at Samarra, begun in the 800s in central Iraq, was designed so that thousands of troops could worship together. The vast floor plan of one of the largest Islamic mosques, the Great Mosque of Córdoba in Spain, is divided into 19 aisles by 850 marble columns. Considered to be a classic example of early Islamic architecture, the Great Mosque of Córdoba was built in stages, with the first section being built between 785 and 786 and with further additions being made in the 800s and 900s. In 1236 this Córdoba mosque was converted to a Christian cathedral.

In addition to the area for prayer, features of Islamic mosques include a semicircular niche, which points to the direction of Mecca; a pulpit, reserved for the prayer leader; and sometimes a minaret, or tower, attached to the outside of the mosque, from which the call to worship is proclaimed five times each day.

Muslim worshippers

Dome of the Rock in Jerusalem

The Great Mosque at Samarra

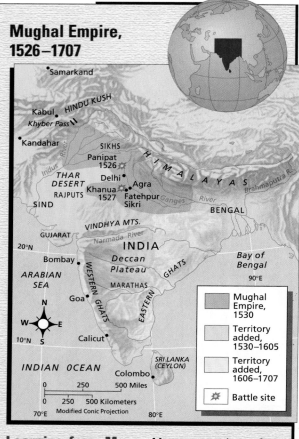

Mughal Empire, 1526–1707

Samarkand

HINDU KUSH
Kabul
Khyber Pass
Kandahar
Indus River
SIKHS
Panipat 1526
THAR DESERT
Delhi
RAJPUTS
Khanua 1527
Agra
Fatehpur Sikri
Ganges River
HIMALAYAS
Brahmaputra R.
SIND
BENGAL
GUJARAT
VINDHYA MTS.
Narmada River
20°N
INDIA
Bombay
Deccan Plateau
WESTERN GHATS
GHATS
EASTERN GHATS
ARABIAN SEA
MARATHAS
Goa
N
W E
10°N S
Calicut
SRI LANKA (CEYLON)
INDIAN OCEAN
Colombo
Bay of Bengal
90°E

0   250   500 Miles
0   250   500 Kilometers
70°E Modified Conic Projection 80°E

Mughal Empire, 1530
Territory added, 1530–1605
Territory added, 1606–1707
✷ Battle site

Learning from Maps Many generations of Mughal emperors supported the arts and united most of India.

? Location What two cities on the west coast of the Indian subcontinent remained independent during Mughal rule?

delicate, colorful miniature paintings based on Persian styles. He fostered literature in the Hindi and Urdu languages and encouraged the translation of popular classics. The architecture of this period shows a blend of Persian, Islamic, and Hindu styles.

More importantly, Akbar fostered tolerance for all religions. He also repealed the special tax that non-Muslims had been forced to pay. Over time, however, he began to think of himself as a divine ruler, and in 1581 he established a creed called the Divine Faith. The motto for the creed was *Allahu Akbar,* meaning either "God is great" or "Akbar is God." The creed blended elements of Islam, Hinduism, Jainism, Christianity, and other religions. It attracted few followers beyond Akbar's court, however, and brought opposition from conservative Muslims.

During the 1600s, Mughal emperors expanded their territory to its greatest extent and concentrated on building lavish monuments. The rule of the emperor Shah Jahan, from 1628 to 1658, is best known for the construction of two famous buildings—the magnificent Taj Mahal at Agra and the Hall of Private Audience in the Red Fort at Delhi. The Taj Mahal, made of marble inlaid with semiprecious gems and built as a tomb for Shah Jahan's beloved wife, Mumtaz Mahal, remains one of the architectural wonders of the world. In the cornices of the Hall of Private Audience are carved these famous lines: "If there be Paradise on Earth, It is Here, It is Here, It is Here!"

These great buildings were enormously expensive both in monetary and in human terms. Their cost, together with military campaigns in the Deccan and against Persia, became a grinding burden on Shah Jahan's subjects, who surrendered half their crops to him. It took 20,000 workers 20 years to finish the Taj Mahal.

Under the Mughals, a synthesis of Hindu and Muslim cultures occurred. In the early 1500s, Nanak, a mystic prophet who was born a Hindu, attempted to bring about a total union of these two faiths. Out of his teachings grew a new religion—the Sikh (SEEK) faith. This faith stressed loving devotion to one god, a lack of representational idols, and a less rigid social system, ideas that conflicted with Hindu beliefs. Nanak became the first guru—leader or teacher—of the Sikh faith. By the late 1600s, the Sikhs had become militant. As their military power developed, they became fierce enemies of the Mughal Empire and the Muslims.

In 1658 Shah Jahan's rule ended. His son Aurangzeb (AWR·uhng·zeb), who had killed his rival

brought Rajputs into his administration. He also used force to maintain power. By 1570 he had suppressed all resistance in the Rajput kingdoms. By the end of his reign in 1605, he controlled all of northern and much of central India.

Akbar introduced a standard tax assessment system on villages, which helped him control his empire. The tax level was based on an average of what a village might produce over 10 years. When the harvest was poor, the tax was waived. In times of good harvest, the villages could keep anything above the designated tax level.

Akbar encouraged Hindu as well as Muslim artists. These artists, supported by the royal household, created

The glorious Taj Mahal stands on a north-south axis and is flanked on either side by symmetric minarets.

older brother, imprisoned his ailing father and declared himself emperor. A devout Sunni Muslim, Aurangzeb persecuted all other faiths in the Mughal Empire. He insisted on strict observance of the holy law of Islam and promoted Islamic scholarship. He restored the hated tax on Hindus and destroyed thousands of Hindu temples. He also oppressed the Shi'ah and Sufi Muslims. When crowds gathered outside the Red Fort to protest these discriminatory policies, Aurangzeb ordered elephants to crush them. Revolts sprang up throughout the empire—by Sikhs and Rajputs in the north and among the peoples of the Deccan in the south. Aurangzeb carried his zealous religious beliefs over into his approach to managing the empire. He dressed simply and with little decoration, setting an example that his courtiers followed. He ended government expenditures on monumental buildings and most celebrations, especially those including wine and music. Although the Mughal Empire reached its greatest territorial extent under Aurangzeb, widespread revolts and

economic problems weakened the empire. Aurangzeb may have come to regret the bloodshed of his reign. When he died in 1707, he wondered whether his actions would please his God.

Section 3 Review

1. **Define** suttee
2. **Identify** Harsha, Rajputs, Timur, Urdu, Babur, Akbar, Shah Jahan, Nanak
3. **Locate and Explain the Significance** Delhi, Samarkand, Angora, Agra
4. **Understanding Ideas** Identify the contributions that Harsha and the Rajputs made to northern India.
5. **Contrasting Ideas** What differences between Muslims and Hindus led to antagonisms?
6. **Summarizing Ideas** List the Mughal emperors discussed in the section and one achievement of each emperor.

Chapter 9 Review

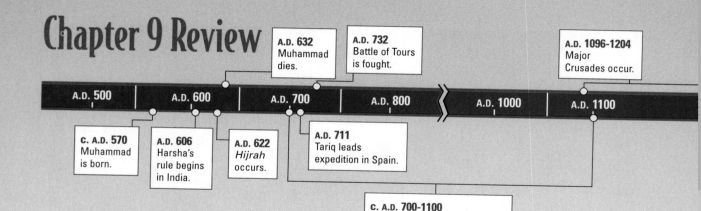

A.D. 632 Muhammad dies.

A.D. 732 Battle of Tours is fought.

A.D. 1096-1204 Major Crusades occur.

A.D. 500 | A.D. 600 | A.D. 700 | A.D. 800 | A.D. 1000 | A.D. 1100

C. A.D. 570 Muhammad is born.

A.D. 606 Harsha's rule begins in India.

A.D. 622 *Hijrah* occurs.

A.D. 711 Tariq leads expedition in Spain.

C. A.D. 700-1100 Arab Muslim culture flourishes.

Chapter Summary

The following list contains the key concepts you have learned about Islam.

1. The rise of Islam transformed much of Asia and parts of Africa and Europe. Early believers spread the Islamic faith aggressively, resulting in the most rapid spread of a new religion the world has ever seen.
2. Although the first wave of Muslim conquests died down in the 700s, the Muslims made further advances in India 400 years later.
3. A new Muslim expansionist force, the Ottoman Turks, rose to prominence in the 1300s and 1400s.
4. The faith of Islam emphasized humility and obedience. The result was the creation of stable societies in much of the Muslim world.
5. The Muslims encouraged economic activity, and they became great traders, linking the East and the West.
6. The stable Islamic societies also promoted notable advances in science, philosophy, and art. The contributions of Muslims to medicine, mathematics, and geography had considerable influence on later scientific work.
7. In India the Muslim presence was first felt in the 700s. This presence came to be of major significance in the 1100s, when the Muslims conquered northern India.
8. Muslim rule brought new ideas and a new language, Urdu, to India. It also brought unrest and upheaval. The ideas of Muslim culture conflicted with those of the Hindus.
9. The Mughal Empire that conquered India in the 1500s was much more stable than earlier rule. The Mughals encouraged tolerance and the arts, notably represented by the building of the Taj Mahal.

Reviewing Important Terms

On a separate sheet of paper, supply the term that correctly completes each statement.

1. Muhammad's migration to Medina is known as the _____ .
2. Muslims believe that the _____ presents God's laws and teachings as revealed to Muhammad.
3. A(n) _____ is a Muslim place of worship.
4. The successor to the Prophet was called a(n) _____.
5. The Shi'ah believed that _____ were intermediaries between God and the people.
6. The Muslim Empire broke up into three parts called _____.

Developing Critical Thinking Skills

1. **Analyzing Ideas** How did trade in the ancient world influence Muhammad's ideas?
2. **Comparing Ideas** In what ways is the Qur'an similar to the Torah and the Christian Bible?
3. **Interpreting Ideas** Why was Muslim Spain important to Europe's cultural development?
4. **Synthesizing Ideas** Although the Muslim world was politically divided, it developed a high level of civilization. Using evidence from the textbook, explain how Muslims made advances in trade, art, mathematics, science, and education.
5. **Classifying Ideas** (a) Discuss the effects of the Muslim conquest on Indian culture. (b) Which effects do you think were positive? (c) Which were negative?
6. **Contrasting Ideas** Compare the treatment of non-Muslims in the Ottoman Empire and the Mughal Empire.
7. **Understanding Chronology** In each of the groups below, place the three events in chronological order.
   (a) Muslim defeat at Tours, *hijrah* of Muhammad, Muslim conquest of Spain
   (b) Taj Mahal built, Delhi sultanate established, Harsha's conquest of Gupta Empire
   (c) Delhi conquered by Timur, Aurangzeb's religious persecutions, Babur establishes Mughal Empire
   (d) Rise of Sufism, Abu Bakr named first caliph, Constantinople captured by Ottoman Turks

Relating Geography to History

Write a general description of the territorial changes that occurred in North Africa, southern and eastern Europe, and western Asia from about 550 to 1450. Use

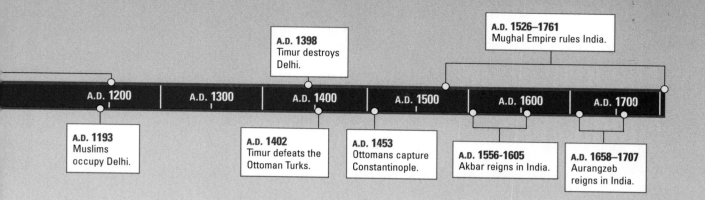

A.D. **1398**
Timur destroys Delhi.

A.D. **1526–1761**
Mughal Empire rules India.

A.D. **1200** A.D. **1300** A.D. **1400** A.D. **1500** A.D. **1600** A.D. **1700**

A.D. **1193**
Muslims occupy Delhi.

A.D. **1402**
Timur defeats the Ottoman Turks.

A.D. **1453**
Ottomans capture Constantinople.

A.D. **1556-1605**
Akbar reigns in India.

A.D. **1658–1707**
Aurangzeb reigns in India.

the maps of the Byzantine Empire on page 189 and the expansion of Islam on page 209 for comparison.

Relating Past to Present

1. In early Islamic society, a set pattern of behavior was established for women. Discuss the role of women today in Muslim countries such as Egypt and Turkey. Compare this role with that of women in countries such as Saudi Arabia and Iran. Use current sources to obtain information.

2. Many English words have been borrowed from other languages. For example, look up the word *coffee* in your dictionary. Where does it come from? Then research the origin of the word *tea* and the use of tea. What can you conclude about the relationship between borrowed words and trade?

Applying History Study Skills

Before completing this activity, review Building History Study Skills on page 207.

All Muslims are expected to make at least one pilgrimage to Mecca during their lifetime. The following selection describes the events that occur during this pilgrimage. Read the selection. Then list the events in sequence.

"Scarcely had the first smile of morning beamed…when we arose, bathed, and proceeded in our pilgrim-garb to the Sanctuary [the Ka'bah]. We entered by the principal…northern door, descended two long flights of steps, traversed the cloister, and stood in the sight of the Bayt Allah [House of God]…We proceeded to the…open pavement…where we performed the usual two-bow prayer in honour of the Mosque. This was followed by a cup of holy water and a present to the…carriers, who for the consideration distributed, in my name, a large earthen vaseful to poor pilgrims.

We then advanced towards the eastern angle of the [Ka'bah], in which is inserted the Black Stone; and, standing about ten yards from it, repeated with upraised hands, 'There is no God but Allah alone, Whose covenant is Truth, and Whose Servant is Victorious'….After which we approached as close as we could to the stone…

Then commenced the ceremony of Tawáf, or circumambulation [a circling on foot], our route being

the…low oval of polished granite immediately surrounding the [Ka'bah]…

At the conclusion of the Tawáf, it was deemed advisable to kiss the stone…

In the evening,…I again…repaired to the [Ka'bah]."

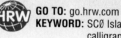

Search the Internet through the HRW Web site to gather information on Islamic calligraphy. Explain the special religious and artistic significance of calligraphy to Islamic culture. Make a chart showing several designs that are important to Islamic culture, and learn what they mean. Share these designs with the class.

HRW **GO TO:** go.hrw.com
KEYWORD: SCØ Islamic calligraphy

Building Your Portfolio

1. **Writing a Report** An important event in a Muslim's life is a pilgrimage to Mecca, the birthplace of Muhammad. Using various reference materials, prepare a report on the holy places in Mecca and the religious ceremonies that take place during the pilgrimage. How do these ceremonies differ from the ceremonies of other religions, such as Christianity, Judaism, and Hinduism? Place your report in your portfolio.

2. **Preparing an Oral Report** Carpets made in Persia (Iran) have long been popular in the United States. Research and report to the class on the history and background of these rugs. Include the following information in your report: **(a)** How were the rugs made? **(b)** What were the importance and symbolic meaning of rugs in the Persian home? **(c)** How did the subject matter and design of the rugs reflect Islamic teaching? Among the books you might use are *Oriental Rugs: Antique and Modern* by Walter Hawley (Dover) and *Oriental Rugs: A Complete Guide* by Charles W. Jacobsen (Tuttle). Place any art and notes from your report in your portfolio.

CHAPTER 10

The Rise of the Middle Ages

TIME
A.D. 432–1328

A.D. 432–1328

| 3.7 million B.C. | 4000 B.C. | A.D. 2100 |

PLACE
Western Europe

Western Europe

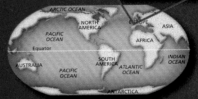

The Bayeux tapestry

Significance

The period in western European history following the collapse of the Roman Empire, from about A.D. 500 to about 1500, is called the **Middle Ages**, or the **medieval** period. (The word *medieval* comes from the Latin words *medium*, meaning "middle," and *aevum*, meaning "age.") The people of the Middle Ages developed new customs and institutions to suit the conditions under which they lived.

Terms to Define

Middle Ages	monasticism
medieval	abbot
feudalism	canon law
vassal	interdict
fief	tithe
primogeniture	simony
manor	Inquisition
serfs	shires
chivalry	Magna Carta
sacraments	common law

People to Identify

Clovis	Alfred the Great
Merovingians	Edward the Confessor
Charles Martel	William the Conqueror
Pepin the Short	Thomas Becket
Charlemagne	Simon de Montfort
Louis the Pious	Otto I
Magyars	Henry III
Vikings	Henry IV
curia	Frederick Barbarossa
cardinals	Pope Innocent III
Saint Benedict	

Places to Locate

Papal States	Île-de-France
Aix-la-Chapelle	Aquitaine
Hastings	Canossa
Canterbury	Worms

Chapter Theme Questions

- **Social Relations** How might a political system affect the social relationships in a culture?
- **Religion** What role might religion play in the political life of a society?
- **War and Diplomacy** How do conflicts establish kingdoms and nations?

In the Middle Ages, most Europeans were peasants who worked in the fields, often toiling from dawn to dusk. As one historian noted:

❝The sun rose early,…but not much earlier than the peasants of the little village of Belcombe…. Within most of these houses men were stirring,…taking a look at the sky before they ate a brief meal…of a lump of bread and a draught of ale. Then they…fetched their scythes and rakes from the sheds, and started off…. On entering the field the peasants broke up in little groups, some going to one and some to another part of the meadow….

In one corner of the field John Wilde and his two sons, Richard and Roger, kept to their task for some time without pause…all three continued until the sun was getting well up in the heavens, when they stopped their work and left the field together with many others. As they passed the church John glanced at the Mass clock on its wall near the door, and saw by the shadow…that they had good time before the service, as it was not yet eight.❞

These hardworking peasants formed the backbone of a society that was attempting to restore order out of the chaos that followed the collapse of the Roman Empire in the west.

Section 1

The Rise of the Franks

Focus Questions

- **How did Frankish rulers gain control of and govern territory in western Europe?**
- **What caused the decline of Charlemagne's great empire?**
- **Why were the Vikings so greatly feared?**

After the Roman Empire collapsed, many Germanic tribes, including Visigoths, Vandals, Burgundians, and

Ostrogoths, plundered Europe, and some established small kingdoms. Most tribes, however, did not create strong governments. Of all the Germanic tribes, the Franks played the greatest role in European history. The Franks first entered the Roman Empire near the mouth of the Rhine River in about 250 B.C. They settled in the area of northern Gaul that corresponds roughly to the present-day nations of Belgium and the Netherlands.

Clovis and the Merovingians
In A.D. 481 an able ruler named Clovis became king of one of the Frankish tribes. He and his successors were called Merovingians because Clovis traced his family back to an ancestor named Merovech. Although brutal, cruel, and apparently without a conscience, Clovis excelled as a military leader. His troops conquered the other Frankish tribes and soon controlled all of northern Gaul.

A few years after Clovis became king, an important event took place, according to legend. Influenced by his Christian wife, he vowed to accept her religion if he won a certain battle. He won the battle, and two years later he kept his vow. He also ordered 3,000 of his warriors to receive baptism. Clovis became a strong supporter of Christianity, and he and the Franks gained the support of the church.

Later, Clovis seized southwestern Gaul from the Visigoths. Even though he ruled most of what is today France (which took its name from the Franks), Clovis failed to pass on to his successors either his strong leadership qualities or his united kingdom. In accordance with Frankish custom, Clovis's sons divided the kingdom among themselves.

The Merovingian kings who followed were weak rulers of the divided kingdom who left the business of governing to palace officials. Eventually, the chief of the royal household, called the mayor of the palace, became the real ruler of each kingdom. Pepin II, the mayor of the palace of one kingdom, ruled from 687 to 714. He and his successors united and ruled the Frankish kingdom, although they did not hold the title of king.

Charles Martel and Pepin the Short
Pepin's able son, Charles Martel (meaning "Charles the Hammer"), succeeded Pepin as the mayor of the palace. In 732 an army of Spanish Moors invaded France. Charles Martel's cavalry defeated the Moors near Tours, in central France, thus halting the Muslim advance in western Europe and removing the immediate danger of invasion, although raids continued to present a constant menace.

What If?

Battle of Tours
The Frankish victory at Tours in 732 halted Muslim expansion in Europe. How do you think modern European culture would be different if the Moors had won the battle?

When Charles Martel died in 741, he left a large and strong kingdom to his sons Pepin and Carloman, who shared power. When Carloman entered a monastery six years later, Pepin III, or Pepin the Short, became the sole ruler. In 751 the pope traveled to France and personally crowned Pepin "king by the grace of God." The coronation established what historians refer to as the Carolingian dynasty. The practice of a king using the blessing of the church to give legitimacy to his rule would eventually become common for monarchs throughout western Europe, and later popes would use it as a basis for their claim to hold authority over kings.

While the pope was in France, he asked Pepin for help against the Lombards, a Germanic tribe that was ravaging central Italy and threatening Rome. Pepin led an army of Franks into Italy and defeated the Lombards. He then took territory around Rome from the Lombard king and gave it to the pope. This gift of land, called the Donation of Pepin, created the Papal States, a region that would be ruled by popes for centuries.

History does not record whether the pope and Pepin made an agreement that Pepin would defend Rome in exchange for his coronation by the pope. Certainly, however, these events began an alliance between the Franks and the pope that greatly strengthened both sides. The way now opened for the greatest of all Frankish kings, Charlemagne.*

Charlemagne's Empire
Pepin's son Charlemagne assumed the Frankish throne in A.D. 768 and ruled until 814. Although he had little formal education, this deeply religious and highly intelligent king became one of history's outstanding rulers.

---

*Charlemagne's Latin name was *Carolus Magnus* (from which comes the name of his dynasty, *Carolingian*). The Germans called him *Karl der Grosse*. Translated into English, all of these names mean "Charles the Great."

Charlemagne, a patron of learning, encouraged the development of art, science, and literature during a period known as the Carolingian Renaissance.

Pope Leo III placed a crown on Charlemagne's head and declared him "Emperor of the Romans." The new title had little to do with the Roman Empire, but it signified that Charlemagne, who had united much of Europe for the first time in 400 years, was regarded as the successor to the emperors of Rome. Charlemagne's coronation by the pope also dramatized the close ties between the Frankish people and the Christian church.

Government. Charlemagne's empire consisted of several hundred regions, each ruled by a representative called a count. Each count raised his own army and administered the laws within his own lands. Charlemagne established a capital at Aix-la-Chapelle (eks·lah·shah·PEL), which today is the city

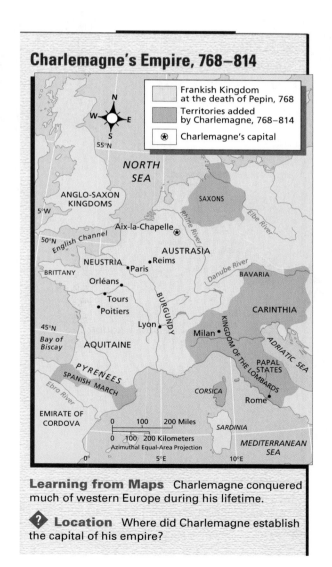

Charlemagne's Empire, 768–814

Frankish Kingdom at the death of Pepin, 768

Territories added by Charlemagne, 768–814

⊛ Charlemagne's capital

Learning from Maps Charlemagne conquered much of western Europe during his lifetime.

? Location Where did Charlemagne establish the capital of his empire?

Like many kings of his day, Charlemagne spent much of his life at war. He defeated the Lombards in Italy, the Saxons in northern Germany, and the Avars in central Europe. Although he failed in his attempt to conquer all of Muslim Spain, he drove the Moors back across the Pyrenees, thus gaining a small strip of Spanish territory. By the end of his reign, Charlemagne controlled much of western Europe. (See map on this page.)

Charlemagne's ambition was to create an empire with the power and glory of the old Roman Empire. His motto was the Latin phrase *Renovatio imperi romani,* "Renewal of the Roman Empire."

On Christmas Day in the year 800, Charlemagne knelt at worship in Saint Peter's Church in Rome.

of Aachen (AH·kuhn), Germany, but he traveled extensively throughout his empire. His government levied no direct taxes on land or people because the emperor's vast estates produced enough revenue to cover most of the government's low expenses. Charlemagne also appointed officials called *missi dominici*, Latin for "the lord's messengers." The *missi dominici* traveled throughout Charlemagne's empire to listen to complaints, review the effectiveness of the laws, and make certain that the counts served the emperor rather than serving themselves.

Education and learning. Greatly interested in education, Charlemagne founded a school at his palace for his own children and for other young nobles. He invited learned scholars, who were almost always monks, from all over western Europe to teach in the school. The emperor also assembled scholars from all parts of Europe to produce a readable and authentic Bible. The Carolingian Bible, as it was called, standardized the Bible for Charlemagne's empire. He ordered bishops to create libraries, by copying ancient Latin manuscripts, and to organize schools for the children of nobles and for intelligent children from the lower classes. Although Charlemagne himself never learned to write, he could read. One of his favorite books, Saint Augustine's *City of God*, urged all Christians to love God, and Charlemagne vigorously encouraged people throughout the empire to convert to Christianity.

The Decline of the Frankish Empire

Charlemagne's energy, ability, and personality unified the empire during his lifetime. However, the empire crumbled during the reign of Charlemagne's only surviving son, Louis the Pious. After Louis died in 840, his three surviving sons, Lothair, Charles the Bald, and Louis the German, agreed to divide the empire into three parts: the eastern kingdom, the middle kingdom, and the western kingdom. (See map on this page.) Their agreement, signed in 843, was called the Treaty of Verdun.

Charlemagne's descendants were poor rulers who fought among themselves instead of uniting against powerful and ambitious local lords. By 870 the middle kingdom had broken up; it was divided between the eastern and western kingdoms. Furthermore, the great lords of these two kingdoms no longer obeyed the Carolingian monarchs. Why should they be governed by a weak central power when they could rule independently and take care of their own local interests?

Charlemagne's empire splintered not only because of internal feuds but also because invaders swarmed into the empire from every direction. In the late 800s, Europe suffered from a new round of invasions. (See map on page 229.)

The Muslims came from North Africa and terrorized the Mediterranean coast, conquering Sicily, Sardinia, and Corsica. From the east came the Slavs, who pressed into central Europe. Also from the east came a new group of nomads, the Magyars. Magyar tactics so resembled those of the earlier Huns that Europeans called them Hungarians. After a century of terrifying raids, the Magyars settled down and established a kingdom in what is now the country of Hungary.

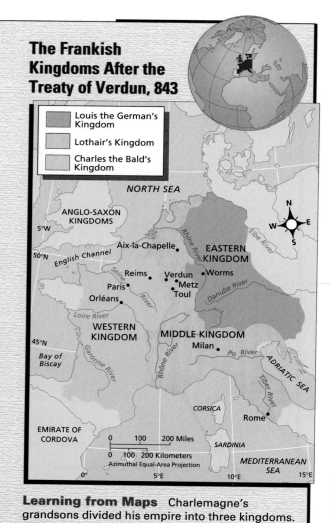

The Frankish Kingdoms After the Treaty of Verdun, 843

- Louis the German's Kingdom
- Lothair's Kingdom
- Charles the Bald's Kingdom

NORTH SEA

ANGLO-SAXON KINGDOMS

5°W

Aix-la-Chapelle

50°N

English Channel

EASTERN KINGDOM

Rhine River

Elbe River

Reims · Verdun · Worms

Seine River · Metz · Toul

Paris ·

Orléans ·

Danube River

Loire River

WESTERN KINGDOM

45°N

MIDDLE KINGDOM

Milan ·

Po River

Bay of Biscay

Garonne River

Rhône River

ADRIATIC SEA

Tiber River

CORSICA

Rome ·

EMIRATE OF CORDOVA

0   100   200 Miles

SARDINIA

0   100   200 Kilometers
Azimuthal Equal-Area Projection

MEDITERRANEAN SEA

0°   5°E   10°E   15°E

Learning from Maps Charlemagne's grandsons divided his empire into three kingdoms.

? Place In which kingdom was Paris located?

Peoples of Europe, 600–1000

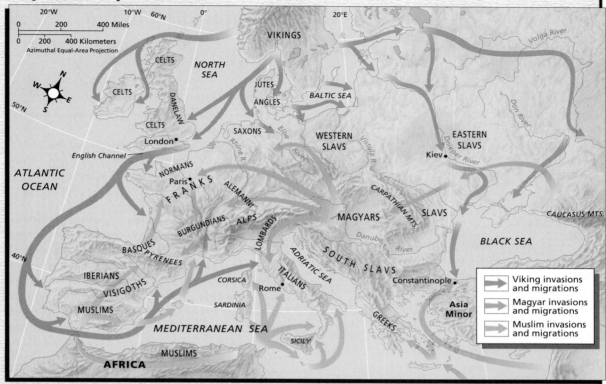

Learning from Maps Muslims, Slavs, Magyars, and Vikings invaded central Europe in the 800s.

? Movement Across which bodies of water did the Vikings travel to settle in England and eastern Europe?

The Vikings

The most fearsome of all invaders, however, came from Scandinavia, in the north. The Germanic peoples of what are now the countries of Norway, Sweden, and Denmark called themselves Vikings. The English called them Danes, while other Europeans called them Northmen, or the Norse.

Although the Vikings were ruled by kings and nobles, their government was surprisingly democratic for its time. The Vikings were primarily farmers, but they also gathered, fished, and hunted. During the spring and summer, when the weather allowed sailing, they went "a-Viking," that is, raiding and pillaging settlements in Europe and the British Isles. During the other months, they worked their farms, using slaves they had captured on their raids. Assemblies of landowners made the laws.

During the 800s a growing population apparently caused a serious food shortage in Scandinavia. Many Vikings sailed from their homeland in search of food and treasure. Sturdy Viking ships, propelled by sails and by oars, skirted the coasts of Europe and plied the rivers of Germany, France, and the eastern Baltic area. They sailed across the Atlantic Ocean to Iceland and then on to Greenland and North America. In time the Vikings settled in England, Ireland, France, and eastern Europe; later, they settled in other parts of Europe. A large settlement of Vikings in northwestern France gave the region its name, Normandy, from the French word *Normans*, meaning "Northmen."

As chaos engulfed medieval Europe, the Vikings continued their conquests, trading with the strong and pillaging the weak. Skilled in siege operations, they sometimes captured strongly fortified towns. Often savage and cruel, the Vikings seem to have enjoyed battle. They used their axes and swords to strike terror into people everywhere.

The Vikings' customs and myths centered on the pagan Norse gods. Archaeologists have excavated Viking burial mounds in Europe that include boats and implements to be used in the afterlife. Sometimes, instead of burial, the Vikings placed the dead person in a boat and burned it. In 922 an Arab, Ibn Fadlan, attended the funeral of a Viking chieftain on the Volga River. A historian wrote the following description about Fadlan's experience:

"A girl slave volunteered to be burned with her master, Ibn Fadlan relates. His ship was hauled onto land and wood placed beneath. A tent was raised on deck and a brocaded mattress set on it. The richly clothed corpse was seated on the mattress…

On the day of the burial,… the slave girl said, 'Lo, I see my lord and master he calls to me. Let me go to him.' Aboard the ship waited the old woman called the Angel of Death, who would kill her. The girl drank from a cup of nabidh and sang a long song. She grew fearful and hesitant. At once the old woman grasped her head and led her into the tent.

Inside the tent the girl died beside her master by stabbing and strangling. Then the ship was fired."

Section 1 Review

1. **Define** Middle Ages, medieval
2. **Identify** Clovis, Merovingians, Charles Martel, Pepin the Short, Charlemagne, Louis the Pious, Magyars, Vikings
3. **Locate and Explain the Significance** Papal States, Aix-la-Chapelle
4. **Summarizing Ideas (a)** What were the accomplishments of Clovis? **(b)** of Charles Martel? **(c)** of Charlemagne?
5. **Evaluating Ideas** Why did Charlemagne's empire disintegrate? What actions might his successors have taken to hold the empire together?
6. **Interpreting Ideas** Why were the Vikings feared more than other invaders?

Feudalism and the Manorial System

Focus Questions

- **How did the feudal system and the manorial system complement each other?**
- **What was life like for the serfs and for the nobility on the manor?**
- **What were the characteristics of the code of chivalry?**

On the continent of Europe, organized government again disappeared within a century after Charlemagne's death in 814. Europe became a continent of small, independent local governments. We call the political structure that evolved in Europe **feudalism.** This was a system in which kings and powerful nobles granted land to other nobles in return for loyalty, military assistance, and other services, and it was firmly established in northern France by the end of the A.D. 900s. By the middle 1000s, feudalism had become the way of life throughout most of western Europe.

Feudalism

The feudal system arose in the absence of a strong central government. Kings held large territories, but they had little power to withstand the invasions of Vikings and other peoples. In return for much-needed military help, weak kings gave grants of land to nobles. The nobles, who often had more land than they needed, then granted part of this land to their own knights—mounted warriors—in return for military service and other forms of support.

The person who granted land was called a lord. The person who received land in return for services was a **vassal.** The grant of land was called a **fief.** This term comes from the Latin word *feudum*, which gave rise to the word *feudal*. The granting and holding of a fief was really a contract between lord and vassal. Because a piece of land could also be further divided—a king's vassal might grant land to knights, for example—a person could be a lord and a vassal at the same time.

In time, the fief became hereditary. Legal ownership passed from the lord to his son, while legal possession and use passed from the vassal to his son. By about 1100, a system called **primogeniture**

This stained-glass window depicts the relationship between a lord and his vassals; land was granted in return for military services and loyalty.

First, it was an honorable relationship between legal equals. Only nobles could be vassals. The greater lords were vassals and tenants of the king. The less powerful lords were vassals and tenants of the greater lords, and so on down.

Second, the same man might be both vassal and lord—vassal to a more powerful lord above him and lord to a less powerful vassal below him.

Third, the relationship was a very personal one. Each man's loyalties and obligations were owed only to the lord immediately above him or to the vassal immediately below him.

Obligations of feudalism. Under a feudal contract, the vassal had more obligations than the lord. The vassal promised to provide the lord with a certain number of fully equipped cavalry riders and infantry soldiers.

The vassal had to make special payments to help cover the lord's extraordinary expenses, such as ransom if the lord became a captive in war. The vassal also had to house and feed the lord and his companions for a certain number of days of each year and serve on the lord's court to administer justice.

Feudal justice. Feudal justice was quite different from Roman justice. Decisions at trials were made in one of three ways: (1) In a trial by battle, the accused and the accuser—or men representing them—fought a duel. The outcome of the duel determined guilt or innocence. (2) In compurgation, or oath taking, the accused and the accuser each gathered a group of people who swore that the man they represented was telling the truth. Compurgators, the oath takers, were similar to the character witnesses who testify in today's trials. (3) In a trial by ordeal, the accused carried a piece of hot iron in his hand, walked through fire, or plunged his arm into a pot of boiling water to pick up a hot stone. If his wounds healed rapidly, he was judged innocent; otherwise, he was guilty.

Warfare. Frequent wars plagued the medieval period. Sometimes two kingdoms fought. At other times, a king tried to subdue a powerful, rebellious vassal. Many wars, however, stemmed from private fights between feudal lords or between lords and vassals.

In the early Middle Ages, a knight wore an iron helmet and a shirt of chain mail—small metal links hooked together to form flexible armor. The knight carried a sword, a large shield, and a lance. Armor became more complicated in later medieval times after gunpowder was introduced, and metal plates replaced chain mail. This armor was so heavy that a knight often had to be hauled onto his horse with a crane.

(pry·moh·JE·nuh·choohr) in which the eldest son always inherited the fief, had become customary. This system kept fiefs from being endlessly subdivided among many sons.

Women had some influence in society and politics, but their legal property rights were limited. A woman could include fiefs in her dowry. However, her husband would take over the dowry, and she controlled it only after he died.

Local lords held many of the same powers that are usually associated with government, and the king became just another feudal lord. In theory every holder of land became a vassal to the king, however, in practice the king really had power only over those who lived on the king's feudal lands.

The church, too, became part of the feudal system. By the 900s the church owned vast amounts of land, some of which it granted as fiefs to nobles in return for military protection.

Feudal relationships. There are three facts to keep in mind to understand the relationship between lord and vassal:

For nobles, wars represented opportunities for glory and wealth, but to the rest of society wars brought suffering and famine. The church tried to limit private wars by issuing several decrees, known together as the Peace of God. These decrees prohibited, under pain of excommunication, acts of violence and private warfare near churches and other holy buildings. They also forbade violence against cattle and agricultural equipment, as well as against certain persons, including clergy, women, merchants, and pilgrims. The church tried to get all lords to accept another decree, the Truce of God, which forbade fighting on certain days, such as weekends and holy days. Gradually other days were added to the Truce of God. Restrictions on fighting, however, could almost

In the medieval illuminated book *Les Très Riches Heures du Duc de Berry*, the Limbourg Brothers depict scenes of people engaged in various activities throughout the seasons. This page, from January, shows the Duke of Berry at a banquet.

never be strictly enforced. Private wars continued until kings became strong enough to stop them.

The Manorial System

While feudalism was essentially a governmental and military system, the manorial system became the economic structure in many parts of Europe. The **manor**, a large estate that included the manor house, pastures, fields, and a village, became the economic unit of the early Middle Ages, just as the fief had become the governmental unit. While a small fief had only one manor, large fiefs had several.

Because no central authority or organized trade existed, each manor tried to be self-sufficient, or able to produce everything it needed. Most manors produced their own food, clothing, and leather goods. Only a few items—such as iron, salt, tar, or wine—were purchased.

The lord and several peasants shared the land of a manor. The lord kept about one third of the manor land, called the domain, for himself. The peasants paid to use the remaining two thirds of the land. They gave the lord a portion of their crops, helped to farm his land, performed other services on the manor, and paid many kinds of taxes.

A typical manor village, usually on a stream that furnished water power for its mill, had houses clustered together for safety a short distance away from the manor house or castle. The land of the manor extended out from the village and included vegetable plots, cultivated fields, pastures, and forests.

The cultivated land of the manor was often divided into three large fields for growing grain. Only two of the three fields were planted each year so that the third field could lie fallow, or unplanted, to regain its fertility. The three large fields in turn were divided into small strips. Peasants had their own strips in each field. If the lord's domain was divided, he too had strips in each field.

Peasant Life

Most of the peasants on a manor were **serfs**, people who were bound to the land. Serfs could not leave the land without the lord's permission. Serfs were not slaves, however, for they could not be sold away from the land. If the land was granted to a new lord, the serfs became the new lord's tenants.

Some free people, too, rented land from the lord. Free people included the skilled workers necessary to the village economy, such as millers, blacksmiths, and carpenters. Most villages also had a priest to provide for the spiritual needs of the villagers.

Long hours spent doing backbreaking work in the fields made daily life on a manor very hard. The laborers' meager diet consisted mainly of coarse black bread, cabbage and a few other vegetables, cheese, and eggs. Beer was plentiful in northern Europe, as was wine in the grape-growing regions of the south. People rarely ate meat because they needed animals to help them work the fields and because they were not allowed to hunt on the lord's land.

The life of ordinary people was brief and narrow in medieval times. Because of disease, starvation, and constant warfare, the average life expectancy was about 30 years. Since people in their forties were regarded as very old, medieval society was a much younger society than ours. Ordinary people rarely escaped the village. They usually died where they had been born.

The Life of the Nobility

When people today think of the Middle Ages, they sometimes picture luxurious castles and knights in burnished armor. However, the nobles did not necessarily lead luxurious or even easy lives.

A castle—the fortified home of a lord—served as a base from which to protect the surrounding countryside and enforce the lord's authority. Most people today picture a castle as a great stone structure. Actually, stone castles were not constructed until late in the Middle Ages. Throughout the early medieval period, castles were relatively simple structures built of earth and wood.

Located on hills or in other places that were easy to defend, castles were built to resist attack, not for pleasant living. If a castle had to be built in flat country, a ditch called a moat, often filled with water, surrounded the outer walls. A drawbridge across the moat enabled people to reach the gate to the courtyard inside the walls. In case of an attack, the drawbridge was raised.

The main part of the castle was the keep—a strong tower that contained storerooms, barracks, and workshops. Sometimes the keep also included the lord's living quarters. In the great hall, the lord received visitors. The thick walls, with their small, usually glassless windows, made the rooms dark, damp, and chilly. The lord spent much of his day looking after his land and dispensing justice to his vassals and serfs.

A man, whether he was a lord or the head of a peasant family, depended a great deal on help from his wife and children. Medieval people viewed marriage as a way to advance one's fortunes, perhaps by acquiring new lands. On the other hand, marriage usually produced children, who had to be cared for. A lord had to provide a dowry for a daughter.

When not fighting, the nobles and vassals amused themselves with mock battles called tournaments. In early medieval times tournaments often led to loss of life, but later they became more like pageants.

Chivalry

By the late 1100s **chivalry**, a code of conduct for knights, had changed feudal society. The word *chivalry* comes from the French word *cheval*, meaning "horse," because knights were mounted soldiers.

In the early days, becoming a knight was quite simple. Any soldier could be knighted by any other knight after proving himself in battle. As time passed, however, chivalry became much more complex.

To become a knight, a boy had to go through two preliminary stages of training, supervised by a knight. First, at the age of seven, a boy became a page, or knight's attendant, learning knightly manners and beginning his training in the use of weapons. Then, in his early teens, the boy became a squire, or knight's assistant. He continued to study both manners and weaponry. He took care of the knight's horses, armor, weapons, and clothing. When he was considered ready, the squire accompanied the knight into battle. After the squire proved himself worthy in battle, an elaborate religious ceremony initiated him into knighthood.

When a knight was in full armor, practically the only way to recognize him was by his coat of arms. A coat of arms might be painted on a shield or an outer coat; it might also be visible on a flag or on the trappings of the knight's horse. Every coat of arms was different and identified the knight. Crests were sometimes worn on the tops of helmets.

Chivalry required a knight to be brave. He had to fight fairly. Tricks and strategy were considered cowardly. A knight had to be loyal to his friends, keep his word, and treat conquered foes gallantly. In addition, he had to be especially courteous to women.

Chivalry greatly improved the rough and crude manners of early feudal lords. Behavior, however, did not become perfect by any modern standards. The knight extended courtesy only to people of his own class. Toward all others his attitude and actions were likely to be coarse and arrogant.

READ
WRITE
INTERPRET
CONNECT
THINK

Thinking About History:
Distinguishing a Fact from a Value Statement

A fact can be verified or proved. A value statement is an opinion that represents a particular point of view. For example, a writer can state that Charlemagne was a successful ruler. That statement is a value statement because it is based upon the writer's definition of success.

Sometimes a fact and a value statement may be included in the same sentence. For example, an author might state that Charlemagne spoke Latin and Greek so eloquently that he could have taught both languages. Charlemagne's mastery of the two languages is a fact that can be verified or disproved. However, the degree of his eloquence in the two languages is a matter of opinion. In your study of history, and later as you assume the responsibilities of citizenship, such as voting, it is important for you to be able to distinguish between facts and value statements.

How to Distinguish a Fact from a Value Statement

To distinguish a fact from a value statement, follow these steps.

1. Review the difference between a fact and a value statement.
2. Identify clue words that suggest values. For example, adjectives such as *great, wonderful,* and *horrible* are words that express feelings. "I" statements such as *I believe* or *In my opinion* indicate a point of view.
3. Ask questions about the sentence. Is it open to more than one interpretation? Does it contain feeling words or "I" statements?

Developing the Skill

The statement below discusses how best to define feudalism. Which sentences contain facts? Which sentences contain value statements?

"The simplest way will be to begin by saying what feudal society was not. Although the obligations arising from blood-relationship played a very active part in it, it did not rely on kinship alone...feudal ties...developed when those of kinship proved inadequate...

European feudalism should therefore be seen as the outcome of the violent dissolution of older societies. It would in fact be unintelli-

Farming on the manor

gible without the great upheaval of the Germanic invasions which, by forcibly uniting two societies originally at very different stages of development, disrupted both of them and brought to the surface a great many...social practices of an extremely primitive character."

In this excerpt, the author emphasizes the social and economic aspects of feudalism. He begins by stating a fact: feudalism did not rely on kinship alone. You know from reading this chapter that this statement is a fact because lord-vassal relations often did not depend on kinship. The value statements are those which include words such as *simplest, unintelligible,* and *primitive.* These statements are open to interpretation and depend on the definitions and data the author provides.

Practicing the Skill

Select a newspaper article about a person or a current event. Then identify the facts and the value statements.

To apply this skill, see Applying History Study Skills on page 249.

Section 2 Review

1. **Define** feudalism, vassal, fief, primogeniture, manor, serfs, chivalry
2. **Classifying Ideas** List three aspects of the feudal system and three aspects of the manorial system. Then show how the two systems worked together.
3. **Comparing Ideas** How did the life of the medieval peasant compare with the life of the medieval lord or lady?
4. **Evaluating Ideas** What impact did the development of the code of chivalry have on everyday life in medieval times? Include all classes of society in your answer.

Section 3

The Church

Focus Questions

- How was the church organized?
- How did the church influence political, economic, and social life in the Middle Ages?
- What major problems faced the church during the Middle Ages?

To people living in the United States today, it may seem strange to learn that the medieval church held a great deal of political power. Central governments in medieval Europe were weak or did not exist at all. Therefore, the church performed many of the functions of modern governments. In one way or another, the church touched the lives of most medieval people.

The Church Hierarchy

Members of the clergy were organized in ranks according to their power and responsibilities. The levels of this hierarchy, starting at the bottom, were as follows.

The parish priest. The parish priest, usually of peasant origin, had little formal education. He served the people in his parish, the smallest division of the church. The poorest clergy member, the priest could hardly be distinguished from the peasants among whom he lived.

Though at the bottom of the hierarchy, the priest was in one sense the church's most important officer, for he administered five of the seven sacraments. The **sacraments** were special ceremonies at which the participants received the direct favor, or grace, of God to help them ward off the consequences of sin. By the 1100s, leaders of the church recognized seven ceremonies as sacraments: baptism (admission to the Christian community), Holy Eucharist (Holy Communion), confirmation (admission to church membership), penance (acts showing repentance for sins), the taking of holy orders (admission to the priesthood), matrimony (marriage), and extreme unction (anointing the sick and dying). These sacraments are still practiced today. The parish priest conducted church services in his parish and administered all of the sacraments except confirmation and holy orders, which were administered by bishops. He supervised the moral and religious instruction of his people and the moral life of the community. Often, however, the beliefs of villagers were as much pagan and superstitious as they were Christian.

The bishop. A number of parishes made up a diocese, which the bishop managed. The cathedral church, or official church of the bishop, was located in the most important city of the diocese. (*Cathedra* is the Latin word for the bishop's throne, or chair.) The king or great nobles usually controlled the selection of the bishop. Bishops, frequently chosen for their family connections and political power, were often feudal lords or vassals who had vassals themselves.

The archbishop. An archbishop managed an archdiocese and had all of the powers of a bishop. In addition, he exercised some authority over the other dioceses and bishops in his province, which consisted of several dioceses.

The pope and his curia. The pope had a group of counselors, called the curia, to advise him. Cardinals, the most important members of the curia, advised the pope on legal and spiritual matters. Beginning in 1059 it was the cardinals who elected each new pope.

Only in the church hierarchy could a commoner move up in the world. It did not happen often, but a man of unusual ability, regardless of birth, might rise to great heights in the church. For example, Pope Callistus I was originally a slave. He was later freed, and in A.D. 217 he was elected pope.

Monasticism

The medieval church was made up of two types of clergy. Priests, bishops, and the pope belonged to what was called the secular clergy (from the Latin word *saeculum*, meaning "the present world"), who lived among ordinary people. They administered the sacraments and preached the gospel. A second group of church people,

Benedictine monks eating a simple meal in the monastery refectory.

Italy. Benedict (known today as Saint Benedict) drew up a set of standards to regulate the lives of his monks. Monasteries throughout Europe adopted this set of standards, called the Benedictine Rule.

According to the Benedictine Rule, a monk could own absolutely nothing. Everything he used or wore belonged to the community of monks. The **abbot**, the elected head of the community, controlled and distributed all property. The monks promised to obey the abbot in all things. Monks spent several hours every day in prayer, but they were also expected to work. The abbot assigned each monk certain tasks in and around the monastery.

Monasteries fulfilled the intellectual needs of medieval society. Monks were often the most learned scholars of the time, and the monastery libraries were the main preservers of the literature of ancient civilizations and the early church. Several monasteries also ran schools.

Over the years monasteries became very rich. As an act of piety, a noble might leave his land to a monastery. Nobles sometimes gave money or land to monasteries to safeguard their own souls or the souls of relatives. Convents also benefited from the gifts of the pious, but there were fewer convents than monasteries, and the convents were not as rich. Monks and nuns often cared for the needy.

Some monks left their monasteries to become missionaries, a practice that existed long before the time of Benedict. Saint Patrick of Ireland and Saint Augustine of England were among those who did important missionary work.

called regular clergy (from the Latin word *regula*, meaning "rule") because they lived according to strict rules, was the monastics—monks and nuns.

Monks and nuns believed that one of the best ways to live a perfect Christian life was to withdraw from the world and its temptations and serve God through prayer, fasting, and self-denial. At first each monk lived alone. During the early centuries of Christianity, some monks and nuns went to extreme lengths to practice their devotion to God. In many cases they inflicted alarming physical suffering on themselves to test their faith and to show that they valued the soul over the body. In time Church authorities decided that people drawn to a life of self-denial would be more productive if they lived together in special religious communities. Monks began to gather in religious communities called monasteries, and nuns lived in convents. The way of life in monasteries and convents is called **monasticism**.

Monasticism lacked organization and direction until the early 500s. Around that time a young Roman noble named Benedict became disgusted with worldly corruption and left Rome to become a hermit. In time his reputation for holiness attracted so many followers that he established a monastery at Monte Cassino in central

Christianity in Ireland and England

Christian missionaries arrived in Ireland in the 400s. Patrick, believed to be the best-known missionary in Ireland, began his work there in 432. Several monastic schools provided the basis of an advanced culture that lasted approximately from 500 to 800. Missionaries and teachers from Irish schools went to all parts of the British Isles. During this time Ireland became the greatest center and preserver of ancient and Christian culture in western Europe.

In 597 Pope Gregory I sent missionaries to England. Led by a monk named Augustine, the missionaries converted many people. Eventually, all of England accepted Christianity. Augustine, who was made the first archbishop of Canterbury, was canonized after his death and became known as Saint Augustine of Canterbury. Canterbury became the center of the Christian church in England.

Print Design: Lindisfarne Gospels

During the early Middle Ages, monks were among the few people in Europe who could read and write. In monastery workshops they copied by hand almost all of the books that date from this period. In this age of great faith, the work that was copied very often was the Bible. The monks were painstakingly careful to create a visually beautiful manuscript, since the Bible was viewed as the word of God, and the book itself was considered sacred. To glorify God, the monks illuminated, or illustrated, the pages with gold leaf and intricate designs.

The Lindisfarne Gospels, among the most beautiful of the early illuminated books, were produced around 700 in the monastery of Lindisfarne, probably for Eadfrion, bishop of Lindisfarne from 698 to 721. Now called Holy Island, Lindisfarne is a peninsula that becomes an island at high tide. One of England's early centers of learning, Lindisfarne lies off the northeastern coast of England.

The beginning of the Gospel According to Saint John, part of the New Testament, shown here, features a decorative border of interlaced ribbons, circles, and other designs. The text begins, "In the beginning was the Word, and the Word was with God..."

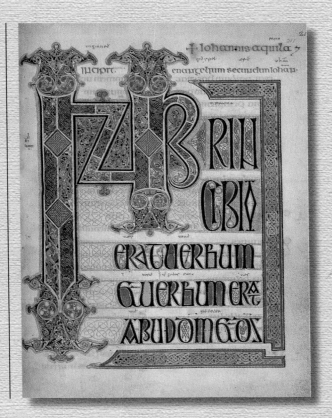

The Church and Medieval Life

Both the secular and the regular clergy played a leading part in medieval institutions and in everyday life. During the early Middle Ages, the clergy were almost the only educated people in Europe. Since printing had not yet been invented in the early Middle Ages, all books had to be copied by hand. Monks did most of this work. To beautify the texts and perhaps as a relief from the tedium of copying, the monks often added small paintings at the beginning of a page or in the margins. The gold leaf and brilliant colors they used brightened the pages so much that such works are called illuminated manuscripts. These manuscripts were some of the finest artistic works produced during the early Middle Ages.

Political role. The church also became a political force during the Middle Ages. In the Papal States, the pope was both the political and the spiritual ruler. Many popes claimed that the church was the supreme political power. They decreed that all monarchs in Europe had to obey the pope. Church leaders also held positions of power as feudal lords and as advisers to kings and nobles. The church preached that people should obey the laws of kings unless these laws conflicted with church laws.

The church had its own code of law, called **canon law**, and its own courts, where members of the clergy were tried for offenses. The church enforced its laws through excommunication and interdict.

Excommunication cut an individual off from the church. He or she could not receive the sacraments or be buried in sacred ground. All Christians had to avoid the excommunicated person.

Reliquary (container in which sacred relics are kept) of St. Faith. This golden image illustrates the devotion Christians had for the relics, or remains, of saints.

The church could also issue an **interdict** against an entire region. All churches of that region were closed. No marriages or burials were performed by the church officials of the region, and everyone who lived there was in danger of eternal damnation. When rulers rebelled against the church, the church used the interdict, hoping that the people of the region would force the ruler to conform.

Like present-day national governments, the medieval church had the power of taxation. Through the parish priest, the church collected the **tithe**, or one tenth of a person's income, from all Christians. In England and Scandinavia the church collected "Peter's Pence," a tax of one penny a year on every household. Also, the church received vast income from church-owned lands. By the early 1200s, when the church reached the peak of its power, it had become enormously wealthy.

Economic and social role. The moral ideas of the church affected all economic life. The church opposed people's gaining wealth by exploiting others. It insisted that labor be in keeping with the dignity of free people. Monks were leaders in agriculture, and they developed techniques for making alcoholic beverages. Some monasteries also carried on widespread trading activities.

The church considered the family a sacred institution. It forbade divorce and took responsibility for widows and orphans. Clergy members also took charge of social work, such as relief for the poor. To help the sick and distressed, the church established hospitals, usually run by special religious orders.

Problems of the Church

At the peak of its power, the church faced several problems. These problems included lay investiture, the worldly lives of the clergy, simony (SY·muh·nee), and heresy.

Lay investiture. The tremendous wealth of the church created a problem, especially after church leaders became feudal lords and vassals. Nobles often rewarded their loyal friends or relatives by appointing them as bishops and abbots, a procedure known as lay investiture. No one questioned a king's or a noble's right to grant a bishop or an abbot a fief and to make him a vassal. The church did object, however, to kings and nobles naming bishops and abbots. Church leaders firmly believed that only a church member could grant spiritual authority to another member of the church. In the case of a bishop, a ring and a crosier, or staff, symbolized this authority. A king or lord who granted a new bishop his fiefs often insisted on giving him his ring and crosier as well.

Worldly lives of the clergy. Some members of the clergy lived in luxury. People criticized them because they seemed more interested in wealth than in holy living.

Simony. In feudal times, people could pay to assume high positions in the church, a practice called **simony**. The purchaser expected to make money through his position, either from church income or by charging high fees for performing religious services.

Heresy. The church did not permit anyone to question the basic principles, or doctrines, that were the foundation of the Christian religion. People who denied the truth of these principles or preached unauthorized doctrines were considered heretics—unbelievers guilty of the unpardonable sin of heresy, which brought eternal damnation. Heresy threatened the church itself, as treason does a modern government.

Attempts at church reform were made by many church leaders and lay rulers, who tried to solve church problems through various measures. Two religious groups, or orders, established in the 1200s dedicated themselves to reform. They were the Franciscans, founded by Saint Francis of Assisi in 1209, and the Dominicans, founded by Saint Dominic in 1216. Members of these religious orders, known as friars, lived and preached among the people instead of secluding themselves in monasteries as members of most other religious orders did.

In the mid-1200s the church ordered the Dominicans to seek out heretics and to eliminate heresy. During this search, known as the **Inquisition**, anyone suspected of heresy could be tried in secret and tortured in order to force a confession. Heretics who confessed that they had done wrong were required to perform penance. The Inquisition condemned heretics who did not confess and turned them over to the civil government to be punished, sometimes by burning at the stake. The church thought that these severe penalties were necessary to prevent the spread of heresy throughout Christendom.

Section 3 Review

1. **Define** sacraments, monasticism, abbot, canon law, interdict, tithe, simony, Inquisition
2. **Identify** curia, cardinals, Saint Benedict, Saint Patrick
3. **Summarizing Ideas** List the positions in the church hierarchy and briefly describe the duties of each position.
4. **Interpreting Ideas** How did the church affect political, economic, and social life in the Middle Ages?
5. **Evaluating Ideas (a)** What four major problems faced the church during the Middle Ages? **(b)** How do you think each problem hurt the power and status of the church?

Section 4

The Struggle for Power in England and France

Focus Questions

- **What contributions did the Anglo-Saxons and the Normans make to England?**
- **How did Parliament and common law develop in England?**
- **How were the Capetian kings able to increase their power?**

In Europe before the A.D. 1000s, kings and lords often struggled for power in a kind of feudal tug of war. Some great lords were as powerful as the kings themselves and served them only when it was convenient. However, a number of kings were able to impose their will on their subjects. From this struggle gradually emerged such kingdoms as England and France, where the king's authority grew stronger than that of the lords.

Anglo-Saxon England

Around A.D. 450, not long after the last Roman legions left Britain, several Germanic tribes invaded the island. Although they first came as raiders, they soon began to settle. Two of these tribes, the Angles and the Saxons, became so powerful that we refer to their descendants as Anglo-Saxons even today. The name *England* means "land of the Angles," and refers to the eastern island of the British Isles, except for Scotland in the north and Wales in the west.

The Anglo-Saxons in Britain formed several small independent kingdoms. Later these kingdoms combined into three important ones: (1) Northumbria, in what is now southern Scotland and northern England; (2) Mercia, in central England; and (3) Wessex, in southern England. In time the Anglo-Saxons divided these kingdoms into governmental districts called **shires**. Officials known as shire-reeves (which became the word *sheriffs*) governed these districts.

Alfred the Great. By the early 800s the Wessex kings controlled practically all of England. However, their rule was soon challenged by the ferocious raiders from the north, the Vikings. At first the Danes—as the Anglo-Saxons called the Vikings—met little resistance, and they quickly conquered much of England. Then, in 871, Alfred the Great came to the throne of Wessex, determined to drive the Danes from English soil. First he persuaded them to leave Wessex by paying them a huge tribute, or sum of money. He spent the next five years reorganizing his army and building a fleet of ships. In 876, when he felt that his forces were strong enough, he attacked the Danes. The war raged for a decade, and in 886 the Danes sued for peace. The peace treaty limited Danish settlement to northeast Mercia and much of Northumbria. In this region, called the Danelaw, the Danes could live under their own laws and govern themselves.

Although best known as a warrior-king, Alfred the Great made many contributions to learning. An educated and scholarly man, he wanted his people to be educated also. To this end he established schools and invited the best scholars from Wales and continental Europe to teach in them. Alfred himself undertook the translation of certain books from Latin to Anglo-Saxon. At his command, too, scholars began a history of England from the earliest times. Work on this history, known as the *Anglo-Saxon Chronicle,* continued for some 250 years after Alfred's death in 899.

Danish rule. During the 900s Alfred's successors won back much of the remaining Danish-held land in England. At the same time, they unified the country, strengthened its government, and spread Christianity throughout the land. However, near the end of the century, England once again came under attack from the Danes. By 1013 they had conquered the whole country.

In 1016, under the rule of King Canute of Denmark, England became part of a large kingdom that included most of Scandinavia. Canute, who

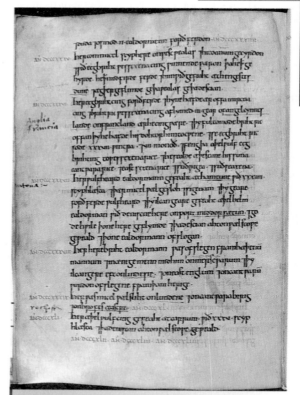

Alfred commissioned the translation of many ecclesiastical and philosophical texts. *The Anglo-Saxon Chronicle,* **begun during Alfred's lifetime, records centuries of English history.**

spent much of his time in England, ruled wisely. Canute's sons, however, had neither his intelligence nor his skill, and they proved to be weak rulers. By 1042 the Danish line had died out, and the Anglo-Saxon nobles had chosen Edward the Confessor as their new king.

The Norman Conquest

Edward the Confessor's background—part Anglo-Saxon and part Norman—created problems upon his death. When he died childless in 1066, Duke William of Normandy, a distant relative, claimed the English throne. The Anglo-Saxon nobles refused to recognize William's claim and selected Edward's brother-in-law, Harold of Wessex, instead. In 1066 William gathered a fleet of ships and an army of nobles and landed near Hastings, on the southeastern coast of England. In the Battle of Hastings, the Norman horsemen defeated the determined Anglo-Saxon defenders. King Harold was shot through the eye with an arrow and died on the battlefield. The victorious William declared himself King William I of England.

It took William, usually called William the Conqueror, several years to overcome Anglo-Saxon resistance entirely. It took many more years for the Norman conquerors to overcome the hatred of the defeated Anglo-Saxons. The Anglo-Saxons did not willingly adopt Norman ideas, customs, or language. Anglo-Saxon, a Germanic language, remained the language of the people. Norman French, a Romance language based on Latin, became the language of the nobles. As time went on, however, the culture of England, including laws and customs, became as much Norman as Anglo-Saxon.

Feudalism in England

William the Conqueror, who ruled from 1066 to 1087, brought feudalism from France to England. However, he carefully altered the system in England so that the king, rather than the nobles, held the authority. To weaken the lords and prevent them from uniting, William gave his followers fiefs scattered widely throughout England.

William the Conqueror laid the foundation for a centralized government by requiring each feudal lord to swear allegiance directly to him. Thus all feudal lords became vassals of the king.

To determine the population and wealth of England, William sent out commissioners to gather information on everyone in the country. This information helped to determine his system of taxation. The survey became known as the Domesday Book (or Doomsday Book).

Reforms Under William's Successors

One of William the Conqueror's sons, Henry I, ruled from 1100 to 1135. He made the central government more efficient by setting up a new department called the exchequer to handle the kingdom's finances. Henry's other important contribution was to the legal system. He wanted to weaken the feudal lords by having cases tried in the king's courts rather than in feudal courts. He sent out traveling judges to hold court sessions throughout the country.

Henry II, who reigned from 1154 to 1189, further increased royal authority. He allowed nobles to pay him a fee instead of doing military service for him; then he used the money to hire mercenaries. In this way he had an army that was loyal to him rather than to the nobles. Henry also reorganized the exchequer so that he could keep careful accounts of the government's financial affairs.

Henry II made great use of the traveling judges. He established definite circuits, or routes, on which the judges were to travel. Thus they became known as circuit judges, and they enforced the king's law throughout England.

In the 1200s the 12-member jury developed in the court system. Juries decided civil cases, such as disputes over land, as well as criminal cases. Trial by jury replaced the old feudal procedures of ordeal and combat to determine guilt or innocence.

In his efforts to increase royal authority, Henry II sought to hold trials of certain members of the clergy in the royal courts after the parties had been judged in the church courts. The archbishop of Canterbury, Thomas Becket, refused to allow a second trial in the royal court. Becket and King Henry, once the best of friends, became bitter enemies. Four of the king's knights, thinking that they were doing the king a great favor, murdered the archbishop in his cathedral.

Henry II denied any part in the assassination of Thomas Becket. Faced with papal excommunication, however, he was forced to abandon further attempts to reduce the power of the church. Thomas Becket became a saint, and his shrine in Canterbury became a very popular destination for pilgrims.

The last years of Henry II's reign were troubled. His sons conspired against him. His marriage to Eleanor of Aquitaine was stormy. Because he had received lands in France as part of Eleanor's dowry, England became further embroiled in wars in France. Nevertheless, Henry II helped consolidate the powers of the crown over the feudal lords. Later kings built upon his governmental and judicial institutions.

King John and Magna Carta

One son of Henry II, King John, is famous for bringing on a revolt among the nobles of the realm. This revolt occurred when King John forced them to pay taxes that they considered unjust. On June 15, 1215, the English nobles forced John to accept a document known as **Magna Carta** (Latin for "great charter"), which protected the liberties of the nobles. Some provisions of Magna Carta, however, dealt with the rights of England's ordinary people. These provisions have come to be considered the most important parts of the document. King John made several promises. He agreed not to collect any new or special tax without the consent of the Great Council, which was a body of important nobles and church leaders who advised the king. He promised not to take property without paying for it, and he agreed not to sell, refuse, or delay justice. The king also promised to grant any accused person a trial by a jury of his peers, or equals. Magna Carta meant that the king was not above the law—the king had to obey the law just as his subjects did, or they would be free to rebel against him.

Although the charter was not considered significant at the time, later political thinkers regarded many of its clauses as important precedents. Today Magna Carta is considered one of the world's great documents, spelling out the basic principles of limited government and the rule of the law.

Parliament and Common Law

In the century that followed the signing of Magna Carta, the two most important developments in English history were the evolution of Parliament and the growth of common law.

Parliament. In the 1260s, nobles revolted against King Henry III. The leader of the nobles, Simon de Montfort, ruled England for several months. He hoped to get greater support for the nobles' cause by broadening representation in the Great Council.

In 1265 de Montfort summoned representatives of the middle class to meet with the higher nobles and clergy in the Great Council. There were four knights

After his brutal murder in 1170, Thomas Becket was made a saint. Many churches, sculptures, and stories were created in his name.

Magna Carta

In June of 1215, King John rode to meet his angry nobles at Runnymede, a wide meadow on the banks of the Thames River. No one present on that day could have guessed that the nobles' demands, written in the form of the document we now call Magna Carta, would later become the cornerstone of constitutional government and representative democracy.

The original purpose of Magna Carta was to limit the powers of the king. Most of its 63 clauses were designed to protect the feudal rights of the nobles; eventually, English legislative and judicial decisions extended these rights. Magna Carta included such concepts as church freedom, trial by jury, and "due process of law"—the orderly, consistent working of law.

Over the centuries, Magna Carta gradually increased in importance as later kings reaffirmed its principles. Eventually it became a symbol of the fight against oppression. Magna Carta forms part of the British Constitution, and the ideas that originated in Magna Carta can be found in the Constitution of the United States.

---

from each shire and two burgesses, or citizens, from each of several towns.

De Montfort was killed in battle and the nobles' revolt was crushed, but the precedent of including knights and burgesses in the Great Council had been set. In time this representative body came to be called Parliament. It was eventually divided into two parts, or houses. The upper house consisted of nobles and clergy and was called the House of Lords. The lower house was made up of knights and burgesses and was called the House of Commons. Within a few years, this was the accepted form of representation, as it is in England today.

The early Parliament did not have the power to pass laws, but it did have the important right of refusing to agree to new and special taxes. As the cost of running the central government increased, new taxes were necessary, and Parliament's approval became vital. Over the years Parliament used this power to its advantage.

Common law. One of England's greatest monarchs was Edward I, who ruled from 1272 to 1307. Edward divided the king's court into three branches. The Court of the Exchequer kept financial accounts and tried tax cases. The Court of Common Pleas tried cases between private citizens. The Court of the King's Bench heard cases that concerned the king or the government.

Each of the three royal courts handed down many verdicts. These decisions became the basis for future decisions made in the king's courts and in the circuit courts. This type of law, based on judges' decisions rather than on a code of statutes like Roman law, is known as **common law**. It was given this name because it was common to all the people of England. Common law forms the basis for the present-day legal systems in the United States and in England.

Rise of the Capetian Kings in France

French kings were also engaged in struggles with their nobles during these centuries. When the last Carolingian king of France died in 987, an assembly of nobles chose Hugh Capet, a French noble, as king. Capet and his descendants, called the Capetians, ruled for more than 300 years.

As king, Hugh Capet ruled only a small region around Paris which was called the Île-de-France (eel·duh·FRAHNS). Île is the French word for "island," and this region was indeed an island of royal authority in the midst of feudal lands. Even in the Île-de-France, the king's vassals resisted his authority. The rest of what is now France was divided into provinces

The Growth of France, 1035–1328

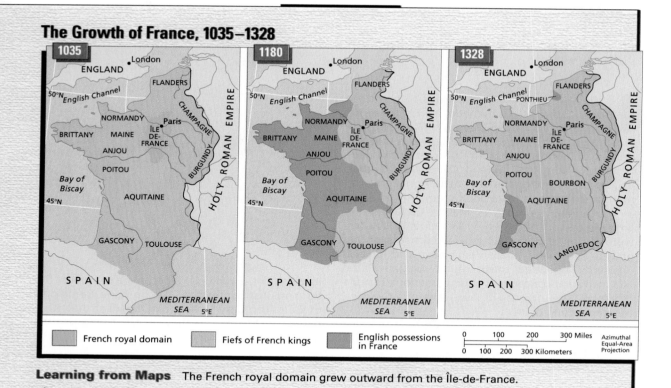

Legend:
- French royal domain
- Fiefs of French kings
- English possessions in France

0 — 100 — 200 — 300 Miles
0 — 100 — 200 — 300 Kilometers
Azimuthal Equal-Area Projection

Learning from Maps The French royal domain grew outward from the Île-de-France.

? Region What lands did the English possess in France in 1328?

ruled by feudal lords. (See map on page 244.) The Capetians set out to unite these provinces and to develop a strong central government.

The history of the Capetian kings demonstrates the feudal struggle for power. Strong kings increased royal lands and authority. Weak kings allowed nobles to regain power. Later Capetian kings added to the royal lands and strengthened the central government.

The growth of royal territory. Kings sometimes married the daughters of great feudal lords to add to the royal lands. In this way, they gained fiefs that were often included in the daughters' dowries. Kings also increased their royal territory by claiming the lands of noble families that died out.

After 1066, when William of Normandy conquered England, the territorial problems of the Capetians became even more complicated. For centuries the English kings had owned vast territories in France. Strong Capetians watched for a chance to regain these lands. The shrewd Philip II, also called Philip Augustus, king of France from 1179 to 1223, seized much English-owned land in France. By 1328, when the last Capetian

king died, the only major English landholdings in France were parts of the provinces of Aquitaine and Gascony. (See map on this page.)

Strengthening the central government. To maintain a strong government, the Capetians sought out loyal, well-trained officials. They could not rely on the nobility. In addition, the Capetians extended the jurisdiction of their courts. The Parlement of Paris became a supreme court, hearing appeals from all parts of the kingdom.

The Capetian Philip the Fair, who ruled from 1285 to 1314, was able to gain control over the clergy, thereby strengthening his own power. Early in his reign Philip imposed a tax on the clergy. When the pope at the time, Boniface VIII, opposed him, Philip had Boniface arrested, and the pope died soon afterward. Philip was able to influence the election of the next pope, Clement V. Philip also convened the Estates General in 1302. The Estates General was a representative body that was drawn from the three major classes of French society of the time: clergy, nobility, and commoners. Convening the Estates

General helped Philip to gain the support of the people in his conflict with the church.

By the early 1300s, the power of the king was greater than that of the nobles in France. However, the three sons of Philip IV died without a male heir, and in 1328 the long line of the Capetians ended.

Section 4 Review

1. **Define** shires, Magna Carta, common law
2. **Identify** Alfred the Great, Edward the Confessor, William the Conqueror, Thomas Becket, Simon de Montfort
3. **Locate and Explain the Significance** Hastings, Canterbury, Île-de-France, Aquitaine
4. **Summarizing Ideas** Summarize the contributions that the Anglo-Saxons and Normans made to England.
5. **Explaining Ideas** Explain how the following developed in England: **(a)** Parliament, **(b)** common law.
6. **Analyzing Ideas** How does the rise of the Capetian kings in France illustrate the feudal struggle for power? How were the Capetians able to add to their power?

Section 5

The Clash over Germany and Italy

Focus Questions

- How did German rulers threaten the power of the medieval popes?
- How did the Concordat of Worms propose to divide power between popes and emperors?
- Why is Pope Innocent III considered one of the church's greatest political leaders?

Although people throughout Europe recognized the spiritual authority of the church, many conflicts arose over the church's temporal authority, or its role in worldly affairs. The greatest threat to the power of the medieval popes came from the German rulers of the revived Holy Roman Empire.

The Holy Roman Empire

Charlemagne's empire had included part of Italy, but after Charlemagne's death in 814, Italy fell into a

Pope John XII crowned Otto emperor 11 days after they signed a treaty regulating the relationship between emperor and pope. This is Emperor Otto's crown.

state of anarchy. Several of Charlemagne's descendants held the title of "Emperor of the Romans" or "Holy Roman Emperor" without really ruling Italy. Later, no one even held the title. The pope ruled the Papal States. The Byzantine Empire held some parts of Italy. Muslims held the island of Sicily and often invaded the Italian mainland.

In Germany the great feudal lords elected Otto I, known as Otto the Great, as their king in 936. A powerful and forceful ruler, Otto might have developed a strong kingdom in Germany like that of the Capetians in France, had he not been more interested in Italy. Otto marched into northern Italy and seized territory in 951. Ten years later, Pope John XII begged Otto's help in his struggle with the Roman nobles. Otto supported the pope, who crowned him Emperor of the Romans in 962.

Although Otto's title was the same one given to Charlemagne 162 years earlier, he ruled a much smaller area—just Germany and northern Italy. This

empire, called the Holy Roman Empire, lasted (in name at least) for centuries. It established a unique relationship between Germany and Italy that continued for more than 800 years.

The power of the Holy Roman Emperors reached a high point under Emperor Henry III, who reigned from 1046 to 1056. Like Charlemagne, Henry regarded the church as a branch of the royal government that should do what the emperor expected. During Henry's reign three different men claimed to be pope. Henry III deposed all three of the these claimants and had a German elected to the papacy. He also chose the next three popes.

Struggle with the Papacy

Henry III's son, Emperor Henry IV, was only six years old when his father died. Powerful nobles in Germany took advantage of Henry's youth and reestablished their feudal powers. At the same time, the church increased its powers. After Henry IV became old enough to rule, Gregory VII, one of the great medieval church leaders, became pope.

A highly devout man, Gregory set out to spiritually reform the church. In the process, he sought to restore the papacy to power. He believed that as God's representative, he had supreme power not only over the church but also over all temporal rulers and their subjects. As pope, Gregory used the terrible punishment of excommunication in his conflicts with emperors, kings, and nobles. Gregory's greatest struggle was with Henry IV.

The struggle between Gregory VII and Henry IV concerned the issue of lay investiture. Henry insisted that he had the right to appoint bishops within the Holy Roman Empire. Gregory disagreed and excommunicated the emperor. He released all of Henry's subjects from their oaths of allegiance and urged them to elect another emperor.

Fearing rebellion, Henry decided to appeal to the pope for mercy. During the bitter winter of 1077, he set off to meet the pope at the castle of Canossa, high in the mountains of northern Italy.

At great risk Henry and his attendants reached the rugged Alpine summit and began the dangerous descent down the jagged, ice-covered peaks. When Henry arrived at the castle at Canossa, he laid his royal regalia down and stood humbly, barefoot and dressed as a pilgrim, waiting for the pope's invitation to enter the castle. For three days Henry suffered the piercing chill of the freezing weather. Finally, he was admitted to the castle. He agreed to several

Although Henry IV (shown submitting to the pope) was forgiven upon repenting to Pope Gregory VII at Canossa, the balance of power between the church and state was tipped in favor of the pope.

conditions of the pope's forgiveness, and Gregory revoked his excommunication.

The struggle over lay investiture, however, continued during the reign of Henry's son. Finally, in 1122 at the German city of Worms, an assembly of church leaders, nobles, and representatives of the Holy Roman Empire reached an agreement known as the Concordat of Worms. The emperor, Henry V, agreed to grant only lands and secular powers to church officials. The church officials would elect bishops and grant them their spiritual powers.

Even though the Concordat of Worms established the popes as spiritual leaders, the bitter struggle between popes and emperors did not end. The emperors still meddled in Italian politics and continued to threaten the popes' rule in the Papal States. The popes therefore opposed all attempts of the Holy Roman Emperors to rule any part of Italy.

Frederick Barbarossa

Frederick I, called Frederick Barbarossa (meaning "Frederick of the Red Beard"), ruled Germany from 1152 to 1190. Like the emperors who preceded him, Frederick was interested in Italy.

The rich city-states of Lombardy in northern Italy—Bologna, Padua, Verona, and Milan—had become increasingly independent trade centers. Each city-state had a wealthy merchant class. Frederick knew that if he could capture these rich city-states, he would be a very wealthy ruler. He sent representatives to take over the governments in the cities. When Milan resisted, Frederick captured the city, destroyed it, and drove out its people.

The other Lombard city-states, aided by the pope, united to form the Lombard League. They raised an army and defeated Frederick in 1176. According to the peace settlement, the cities recognized Frederick as overlord in return for his agreement that they could govern themselves. The success of the Lombard League illustrated the growing political power of cities in medieval Europe.

Innocent III and Papal Power

European rulers met their most formidable opponent in Pope Innocent III, who was pope from 1198 to 1216. Innocent led the papacy to the height of its prestige and power. He was a skillful diplomat and one of the greatest political leaders in all church history.

Innocent III made even more sweeping claims and enforced them more successfully on behalf of papal power than had Gregory VII. Innocent III believed himself supreme over the clergy and temporal rulers. To Innocent, emperors and kings were merely servants of the church, so the pope claimed the right to settle all political and religious problems. No other person or group could do more than advise him.

Innocent intervened in disputes throughout Europe and made free use of his powers of excommunication and interdict. In a quarrel with King John, Innocent placed England under interdict. To have the interdict lifted, John had to become the pope's vassal and pay money every year to Rome. Innocent dominated all of Italy. In Germany he overthrew two kings and put his own chosen rulers on the throne.

Innocent dominated almost all of Europe because of his seemingly superhuman ability and energy. Even so, he was successful partly because conditions in Europe were favorable to his claims and activities. Later popes were less skillful, and circumstances were less favorable. Therefore, they did not attain the power and influence that Innocent had possessed.

Nevertheless, Germany and Italy never united. The Holy Roman Emperor Frederick II attempted to bring the two regions together in the early 1200s. Like earlier emperors, however, Frederick failed.

Not only did the attempts to unite Germany and Italy fail, but both countries remained internally fragmented. Germany remained a jumble of independent cities and feudal states over which the emperor had little authority. Italy was splintered, too, with the Lombard cities in the north, the Papal States in the central region, and the Kingdom of Sicily in the south. Neither Germany nor Italy became a unified nation until the 1800s.

Section 5 Review

1. **Identify** Otto I, Henry III, Henry IV, Frederick Barbarossa, Pope Innocent III

2. **Locate and Explain the Significance** Canossa, Worms

3. **Identifying Ideas** How did conflict develop between Pope Gregory VII and Henry IV? How was it resolved?

4. **Analyzing Ideas** Why did the Concordat of Worms not end the struggle between popes and emperors?

5. **Evaluating Ideas** Explain why the papacy of Innocent III was especially important for Europe.

Chapter 10 Review

A.D. 732
Moors are defeated near Tours.

A.D. 800
Charlemagne is declared Emperor of the Romans.

A.D. 962
Otto I is crowned Emperor of the Romans.

A.D. 400   A.D. 500   A.D. 750   A.D. 850   A.D. 950

A.D. 432
Saint Patrick's missionary work in Ireland begins.

A.D. 481
Clovis becomes king of the Frankish tribes.

A.D. 751
Pepin the Short founds the Carolingian dynasty.

A.D. 768–814
Charlemagne rules.

A.D. 843
The Treaty of Verdun is signed.

A.D. 936
Otto I is elected king of Germany.

Chapter Summary

The following list contains the key concepts you have learned about the rise of the Middle Ages in western Europe.

1. After the Roman Empire declined, Germanic tribes plundered Europe and established a series of short-lived kingdoms.
2. Clovis, king of a Frankish tribe, and the Merovingians who succeeded him, created a large kingdom in France. The greatest Frankish king, Charlemagne, created an empire that included much of western Europe.
3. Two important medieval institutions were feudalism and the manorial system. Feudalism was a political system in which lords granted fiefs to vassals in return for loyalty, military duty, and other services. The manorial system was an economic system based on the self-sufficient manor, worked mainly by serfs (peasants).
4. During the Middle Ages, the church performed many functions, including many of the responsibilities of modern governments.
5. Monasticism attracted many people. Both secular and regular clergy played important roles in education, politics, economics, and the social structure.
6. Problems such as lay investiture, the worldly lives of the clergy, simony, and heresy plagued the medieval church.
7. During the rule of the Anglo-Saxons in England, the people there accepted Christianity, and the Danes (Vikings) invaded England. After the death of Edward the Confessor, the Normans invaded England.
8. Henry I and Henry II increased royal authority. The English ruler himself was made subject to the law when King John was forced to accept Magna Carta. Parliament and common law developed in England during the 1200s.
9. French kings gradually extended their authority. The Capetians—Hugh Capet and his descendants—added territory and developed a strong central government.
10. Holy Roman Emperors controlled much of Germany and Italy and struggled with the papacy for power.

Reviewing Important Terms

On a separate sheet of paper, supply the term that correctly completes each statement.

1. The period in western European history following the collapse of the Roman Empire, from about 500 to about 1500, is called the _____ _____ .
2. _____ was the political system that flourished in much of Europe during the medieval period.
3. The person who held land in return for services was called the _____.
4. A(n) _____ was a grant of land.
5. The custom of allowing only the eldest son to inherit land is called _____.
6. Under the manorial system, the lord kept about one third of the manor land, called the _____.
7. In medieval Europe most peasants who lived on manors were _____, or people who were bound to the land.
8. The code of conduct for knights was known as ____.
9. The elected head of a community of monks was called a(n) _____.
10. Special rites or ceremonies at which participants receive the grace of God to help ward off the consequences of their sins are called _____.
11. A(n) _____ occurred when the church punished an entire region.
12. In feudal times people often paid to be appointed to positions in the church, a practice called _____.

Developing Critical Thinking Skills

1. **Identifying Ideas** Why were the Franks an especially important Germanic tribe in western Europe?
2. **Interpreting Ideas** Why was Charlemagne's title of "Emperor of the Romans" significant?
3. **Evaluating Ideas (a)** How did the church become part of the feudal system in Europe? **(b)** In what ways was the church independent of the feudal system?
4. **Contrasting Ideas** Discuss the conflicts between church and state that arose in the disputes between **(a)** Henry II and Thomas Becket and **(b)** Henry IV and Gregory VII.

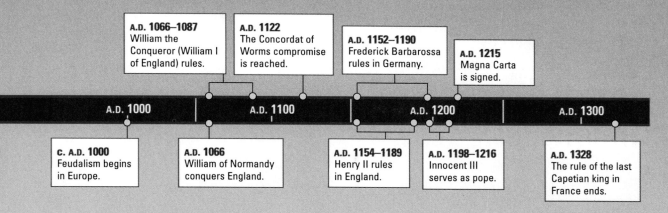

A.D. 1066–1087 William the Conqueror (William I of England) rules.

A.D. 1122 The Concordat of Worms compromise is reached.

A.D. 1152–1190 Frederick Barbarossa rules in Germany.

A.D. 1215 Magna Carta is signed.

A.D. 1000

A.D. 1100

A.D. 1200

A.D. 1300

C. A.D. 1000 Feudalism begins in Europe.

A.D. 1066 William of Normandy conquers England.

A.D. 1154–1189 Henry II rules in England.

A.D. 1198–1216 Innocent III serves as pope.

A.D. 1328 The rule of the last Capetian king in France ends.

5. **Sequencing Information** Give the correct date for each of the following events, and arrange them in chronological order:
   (a) Concordat of Worms signed
   (b) Clovis crowned king of Frankish tribe
   (c) Invasion of England by William the Conqueror
   (d) Battle of Tours
   (e) Charlemagne crowned Emperor of the Romans
   (f) Capetian line of kings founded
   (g) Signing of Magna Carta
6. **Analyzing Ideas** In both England and France, kings increased their own power at the expense of the nobility. (a) List the ways in which William the Conqueror and his successors and the French Capetian kings added to their power and developed central governments. (b) Explain how these measures increased royal authority and decreased the nobles' power.

Relating Geography to History

Compare the map of Charlemagne's empire on page 227 with the map of territorial changes resulting from the Treaty of Verdun on page 228. Then write a paragraph describing how Charlemagne's death affected the boundaries of his empire.

Relating Past to Present

1. Compare life on a medieval manor with life on a modern American farm. In which place would you find greater self-sufficiency? You may refer to books or magazines in your school or public library for information about modern farm life.
2. Use a book on American government to find the following information: (a) What kinds of cases are tried before a modern-day grand jury? (b) Why do some cases use a petit jury while others use only a judge? (c) What is the judge's role? (d) What are the various types of courts in your state? Now compare your findings with the information in this chapter about the early court system in England.

Applying History Study Skills

Before completing this activity, review Building History Study Skills on page 234.

Read the following quotations about women's status during the Middle Ages. Then identify one fact and one value statement in each quotation.

"When it came to making the decision, women entered convents for a variety of reasons, subject to a variety of pressures. Like their male counterparts, the most devout came for spiritual reasons. A few exceptional women challenged their families in pursuing their enthusiasm for the faith. At the beginning of the twelfth century the young Englishwoman, Christina of Markyate, defied her parents, who wished her to marry, …[by] riding off to the protection of her spiritual mentor dressed in men's clothing."

"By the fifteenth century, interiors [of castles] showed care in decoration, and resources were used to make space not only comfortable but pleasurable to look at. Mahaut, the fourteenth-century Countess of Burgundy, had different motifs in the rooms of her castle: roses, shields, and birds decorated the hangings and the furnishings. Women used leather to cover the walls, put colored and brightly striped hangings about the bed, hired workmen to carve wood paneling."

---

internetconnect

Search the Internet through the HRW Web site for information on one of the following subjects: (a) combat and weapons in the Middle Ages, (b) daily life, or (c) the feudal system. Use the information to write an illustrated report.

 GO TO: go.hrw.com
KEYWORD: SCØ Middle Ages

Building Your Portfolio

1. **Studying Literature** Read the medieval play *Everyman*. (a) Describe five of the main characters. (b) What values does the church want people to cherish the most? (c) In the play, what is the importance of good deeds? Place your answers to these questions in your portfolio.
2. **Constructing a Model** Use resources in your school or public library to find more information about medieval manors. Then construct a scale model of a typical manor. Be sure to label all the structures and areas on your model. Place a sketch of the model in your portfolio.

The High Middle Ages

TIME
A.D. **1000–1500**

A.D. **1000–1500**

| 3.7 million B.C. | 4000 B.C. | A.D. 2100 |

PLACE
Western Europe

Western Europe

ARCTIC OCEAN
NORTH AMERICA
PACIFIC OCEAN
EUROPE
ASIA
AFRICA
Equator
AUSTRALIA
SOUTH AMERICA
ATLANTIC OCEAN
PACIFIC OCEAN
INDIAN OCEAN
ANTARCTICA

Crusader siege of Jerusalem

Significance

During the Middle Ages, news traveled by word of mouth, few books existed, and most people could not read.

Great changes occurred during the Middle Ages. Cities became powerful centers of social and political change. Trade revived as people began to look outward, away from Europe.

Christians and Muslims came into conflict in Southwest Asia. Crusader armies fought the Muslims and returned to Europe, little realizing that they had been conquered—by new and remarkable ideas that still influence the world today.

Terms to Define

Crusades	apprentice
barter economy	journeyman
domestic system	vernacular languages
usury	troubadours
capital	scholasticism
market economy	patriotism
merchant guild	Babylonian Captivity
craft guilds	Great Schism

People to Identify

Urban II	Charles VII
Louis VII	Estates General
Conrad III	Ferdinand
Salah al-Din	Isabella
Dante	Habsburgs
Chaucer	Boniface VIII
Abelard	John Wycliffe
Aquinas	Jan Hus
Joan of Arc	

Places to Locate

County of Edessa	English Channel
Principality of Antioch	Flanders
County of Tripoli	Avignon
Kingdom of Jerusalem	Prague

Chapter Theme Questions

- **Cross-Cultural Interaction** How might religious wars bring about an exchange of ideas and goods between peoples?
- **Social Relations** How might the growth of an urban society change how people relate to one another socially and economically?
- **Politics and Law** How might nations begin to form from separate groups of people?

The *Song of Roland* is one of the earliest and best-known epic poems of medieval Europe. Written around 1100, the poem depicts the death of Roland, a courageous and loyal knight in Charlemagne's army. When the army fought the Moors in Spain, Roland was fatally wounded in an ambush of Charlemagne's rear guard. The following verse describes the last act of the dying hero:

> **Roland with pain and anguish winds**
>
> **His Olifant [horn], and blows**
> **with all his might.**
>
> **Blood from his mouth comes spurting**
> **scarlet-bright.**
>
> **He's burst the veins of his**
> **temples outright.**
>
> **From hand and horn the call**
> **goes shrilling high:**
>
> **King Carlon [Charlemagne] hears it**
> **who through the passes rides.**
>
> **Duke Naimon hears, and all the**
> **French beside.**
>
> **Quoth Charles: 'I hear the horn of**
> **Roland cry!**
>
> **He'd never sound it but in the thick**
> **of fight.'**

By the later Middle Ages, knights from all over Europe, like Roland, were answering the call to battle in foreign lands.

Section 1

The Crusades

Focus Questions

- **What were the Crusades, and why did they occur?**
- **What political, social, and economic changes occurred in Europe as a result of the Crusades?**

During the Middle Ages, Christians regarded Palestine, where Jesus had lived and taught, as the Holy

Land. Muslim Arabs conquered Palestine in the 600s. Muslims usually tolerated other religions. If Christians or Jews paid their taxes and observed other regulations, they could live in Palestine and practice their religion openly. For centuries Christian pilgrims visiting Palestine met with little interference from Arab rulers. European traders could generally do business there.

During the 1000s, however, Saljuq Turks, a warlike people from Central Asia who had adopted the Muslim faith, conquered Palestine and attacked Asia Minor, a part of the Byzantine Empire. When the Turks threatened the capital city of Constantinople, the Byzantine emperor appealed to the pope in Rome. Because Christian pilgrims to Palestine came home with reports of persecutions at the hands of the Turks, the Byzantine emperor's appeal for help found a warm reception in Europe.

The Pope's Call for a Crusade

Pope Urban II was eager to regain the Holy Land from the Turks. He called a great meeting of church leaders and nobles at Clermont, France, in 1095. At the meeting he urged the powerful feudal nobles to stop fighting among themselves and to join in one great war to recover the Holy Land for Christians.

Urban's plea fired his listeners with enthusiasm, and they joined in one mighty cry, "God wills it!" From Clermont people traveled throughout France preaching the cause. Those who joined the expeditions sewed a cross of cloth on their garments. They were called crusaders, from the Latin word *cruciata*, meaning "marked with a cross."

People joined the **Crusades**, the expeditions to regain the Holy Land, for many different reasons. Some were inspired by faith. Those who died on a

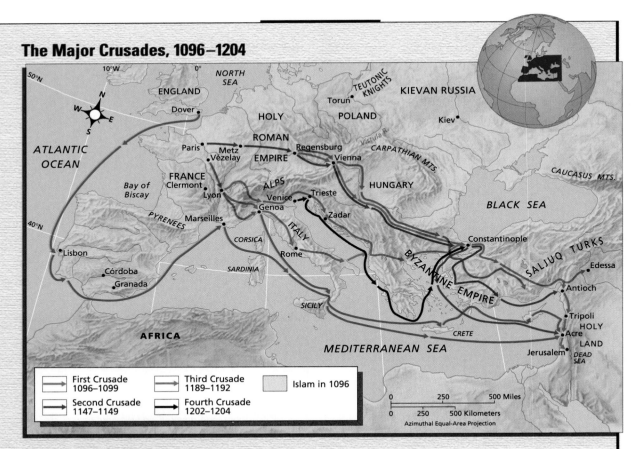

The Major Crusades, 1096–1204

First Crusade 1096–1099
Second Crusade 1147–1149
Third Crusade 1189–1192
Fourth Crusade 1202–1204
Islam in 1096

Learning from Maps Crusaders set out from various cities across Europe to regain the Holy Land from the Turks.

Place Near what city did the paths of the four Crusades cross?

What If?

The Crusades
What if Byzantine Christian forces had gained control of the Holy Land from the Saljuq Turks instead of appealing to Rome for help? The pope would never have called for the First Crusade. Would Europeans have been slower to develop trade and to explore beyond their borders?

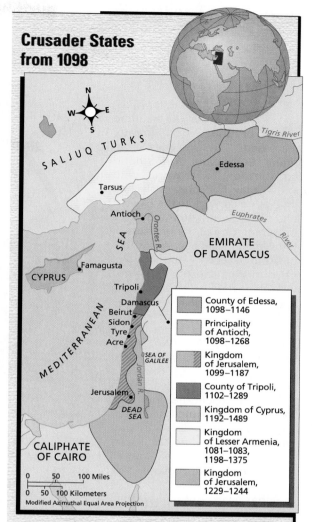

Crusader States from 1098

	County of Edessa, 1098–1146
	Principality of Antioch, 1098–1268
	Kingdom of Jerusalem, 1099–1187
	County of Tripoli, 1102–1289
	Kingdom of Cyprus, 1192–1489
	Kingdom of Lesser Armenia, 1081–1083, 1198–1375
	Kingdom of Jerusalem, 1229–1244

0   50   100 Miles
0   50   100 Kilometers
Modified Azimuthal Equal Area Projection

Learning from Maps Although from a military point of view the Crusades were largely unsuccessful, they did provide a favorable environment for the exchange of ideas and products between Europe and the Middle East.

Location Name three cities along the eastern Mediterranean coast, each in a different state, in which the crusaders settled.

Crusade were said to go straight to heaven. The lure of lands and plunder in Southwest Asia dazzled the knights. Merchants saw a chance to make money. Thus the Crusades appealed to a love of adventure and the promise of rewards, both spiritual and material.

The First Crusade

French and Norman nobles led the First Crusade, which lasted from 1096 to 1099. In several bands, they moved across Europe to Constantinople. (See map on opposite page.)

The crusaders received a hostile reception in Constantinople, however. The Byzantine emperor had asked for some assistance, but now, seeing several armies approaching the city, he feared they might capture and plunder the capital. After much discussion, the Byzantine emperor allowed the crusaders to pass through Constantinople to begin their long, hot march across Asia Minor toward Palestine.

In their wool and leather garments and their heavy armor, the crusaders suffered severely from the heat. A shortage of food and water plagued them because they had few pack animals to carry supplies. Despite these difficulties, however, the crusaders forged on to capture the city of Antioch. They marched toward Jerusalem. If the Turks had not also been quarreling and disunited, the expedition would have failed.

Conditions improved as the crusaders marched down the coast toward Palestine. Fleets of ships from Italy brought reinforcements and supplies. The crusaders captured Jerusalem after a short battle and slaughtered the Muslim and Jewish inhabitants in a terrible massacre. One leader wrote to the pope that his horse's legs had been bloodstained to the knees from riding among the bodies of the dead.

In Southwest Asia, the crusaders set up four small states: the County of Edessa, the Principality of

Antioch, the County of Tripoli, and the Kingdom of Jerusalem. (See map on this page.) They introduced European feudalism and subdivided the land into fiefs, with vassals and lords. For almost a century, the Europeans occupied these lands. Brisk European trade, with goods carried mostly in Italian ships, sprang up. Christians and Muslims lived in close

The World of Arab Geographers

During the Middle Ages, Europeans' knowledge of the world greatly increased. The Crusades gave many Europeans a firsthand introduction to a world with which they had previously had little or no contact. In the East, at this same time, geography was becoming one of the greatest of the Muslim sciences. A number of Arab travelers and geographers distinguished themselves with their detailed observations and mapmaking skills.

Ibn Hawqal, an early Arab traveler, explored some of the most remote parts of Africa and Asia in the mid-900s. On one of his voyages along the east coast of Africa, he reached a point just 20 degrees north of the equator. He noted that thousands of people lived in that latitude. This finding disproved Aristotle's theory that areas near the equator would be totally uninhabitable.

Other Arab geographers also made important discoveries about the climates of the world. In fact, Arabs published the world's first climatic atlas in the 900s. This climatic atlas included observations about temperature patterns from places south of the equator and proved emphatically that Aristotle's uninhabitable zone did not exist. Then in 985 a geographer named al-Muqaddasi drew a map showing 14 world climatic regions in place of the three identified by Aristotle. Al-Muqaddasi included this map in his geographic encyclopedia, which is also distinguished by a broad view of geography. In this work, al-Muqaddasi discusses not only

Al-Idrisi map

land features and climates but also many other aspects of the places covered. For example, he addresses religious and social factors, commerce, agriculture, and even those things he found curious or interesting, such as monuments and local legends. Al-Muqaddasi was also the first geographer to produce maps in natural colors so that people could better understand them.

During the mid-1100s, al-Idrisi, who was a Muslim who lived in Palermo, Sicily, began to compile the huge volume of data accumulated by Arab travelers. The preface to his work states that he spent 15 years compiling it. When al-Idrisi doubted the accuracy or precision of information about the location of a mountain, river, or coastline, he sent out trained geographers to make careful observations. With

this fund of accurate information, al-Idrisi wrote what he called a "new geography." Completed in 1154, it bears the interesting title *Amusement for Him Who Desires to Travel Around the World.*

Al-Idrisi's book corrected a number of mistaken notions. For example, in it he refuted the idea that land completely encircled the Indian Ocean. Al-Idrisi is also credited with creating the world's first globe. Asking for a ball of silver weighing more than 1,000 pounds, he etched on the surface of the ball the continents, land and water features, and major trade routes. Although al-Idrisi's written works have survived, his globe disappeared over the centuries—melted down, no doubt, to enrich a treasury rather than the store of geographical knowledge.

proximity and grew to respect each other. Many Christians adopted Eastern customs and came to prefer Eastern food and clothing.

The Second Crusade

The Second Crusade began in 1147, after the Turks had organized their forces and recaptured the important city of Edessa and threatened the Kingdom of Jerusalem. In this Crusade, King Louis VII of France and the Holy Roman Emperor Conrad III led their armies across Europe to the Holy Land.

The armies of the two monarchs met many misfortunes on the march to the Holy Land. They fought separately and did not join forces until they reached Damascus, which the Turks held. Even then the large combined forces of Louis and Conrad failed to capture the city. After only two years their armies returned to Europe in disgrace.

The Third Crusade

News reached Europe that the Muslim leader Salah al-Din had recaptured Jerusalem in 1187. Europe responded with the Third Crusade, from 1189 to 1192. King Richard the Lion Heart of England, King Philip II of France, and Emperor Frederick Barbarossa of the Holy Roman Empire each started out at the head of a great army to regain the Holy Land.

Once again the Europeans failed. Barbarossa drowned in a river on the way to the Holy Land, and most of his army turned back. Philip and Richard quarreled, and Philip took his army home to seize English lands in France. Richard stayed and continued to fight, but his armies could not recapture Jerusalem. He considered peace proposals from Salah al-Din, including marriage alliances, but these proposals were rejected. Richard settled for a truce that gave the crusaders control of a few coastal towns in Palestine and allowed Christians to enter Jerusalem freely.

Later Crusades

Pope Innocent III persuaded a group of French knights to embark on the Fourth Crusade in 1202. The city-state of Venice provided transportation, at the same time persuading the crusaders to attack Zadar, a Christian city on the Adriatic coast. Zadar was also a commercial rival of Venice. After the crusaders captured Zadar, Pope Innocent excommunicated the entire army for attacking a Christian city.

Next the Venetians and the crusaders planned an attack on Constantinople. The attack was in support of one faction of the Byzantine royal family against another. Although Constantinople was a Christian city, it offered irresistible plunder to the crusaders and commercial advantages to Venice.

In 1204 the crusaders looted Constantinople. Many sacred Christian relics were taken by the looters and sent back to the West. Although the Byzantines regained Constantinople and a part of their lands after 50 years, they never regained their strength. The once-mighty empire finally collapsed when the Turks seized Constantinople in 1453.

A tragic episode in the story of the Crusades occurred in 1212, when a group of young children, believing they could triumph where their elders had failed, undertook their own march to the Holy Land. This Children's Crusade had untrained leaders and no equipment. The pope turned back some of the children. Others reached Marseilles in France, only to be tricked into boarding ships that carried them off to be sold to slave traders.

Despite the failure of the Crusades, the crusading spirit died slowly. Additional Crusades were undertaken after 1204, although historians differ on how many took place. The Crusades continued until 1291, when the Muslims captured the last Christian stronghold, in Acre (AH·kruh). For 200 years, a constant flow of Europeans had streamed into the Holy Land.

Results of the Crusades

From a military standpoint, all the Crusades except the first failed. The Muslims eventually recaptured Jerusalem and the rest of Palestine.

However, Europeans learned about many things of military importance, including the crossbow, a sophisticated bow and arrow held horizontally and fired by pulling a trigger. From the Byzantines as well as the Muslims, Europeans probably learned new siege tactics, such as undermining walls and using catapults to hurl stones. In addition, they may have learned about gunpowder from the Muslims, who probably acquired their knowledge of this explosive from the Chinese.

In Europe the departure of so many nobles and knights for the Crusades did much to strengthen the power of the kings and the middle classes. This hastened the decline of feudalism. Kings imposed new taxes and led armies drawn from their entire countries. Many nobles died fighting. Some had sold or mortgaged their property in order to raise money to go on a Crusade. The success of the First Crusade enhanced papal prestige and allowed the church to assume political power. The later Crusades, however, had somewhat the opposite effect because they failed to secure the Holy Land, and because some popes used the Crusades for their gain.

The Crusades had other important results. Europeans were influenced by the exchange of ideas among the crusaders from different countries and between the crusaders and the other cultures they met.

Commercial changes also occurred. Italian cities benefited from their role in transporting crusading armies. Europeans became increasingly familiar with products from Southwest Asia—rice, sugar, lemons, apricots, and melons, among other things—which stimulated trade in such goods.

Bruges, one of the chief Hanseatic cities, known as the "City of Bridges," became a commercial center in the 1300s. This is a map of Bruges during the 1300s.

Section 1 Review

1. **Define** Crusades
2. **Identify** Urban II, Louis VII, Conrad III, Salah al-Din
3. **Locate and Explain the Significance** County of Edessa, Principality of Antioch, County of Tripoli, Kingdom of Jerusalem
4. **Summarizing Ideas** Describe the Crusades and why they occurred.
5. **Interpreting Ideas** The Crusades are sometimes called "successful failures." **(a)** What does this description mean? **(b)** What political, social, and economic changes occurred in Europe as a result of the Crusades?

Section 2

The Revival of Trade

Focus Questions

- How did a revival of trade come about in Europe?
- Why did fairs arise, and how did they promote the exchange of goods?
- What important developments resulted from the revival of European trade?

Trade nearly died out in western Europe after the A.D. 400s. Manors became increasingly self-sufficient, growing or making nearly everything they used.

Towns and cities, which depended on trade and manufacturing, decreased in both population and size.

Trade Routes

Trade first began to revive in Italy, largely because neither trade nor towns had declined as much there as elsewhere. Moreover, the geographic location of the Italian Peninsula was favorable for trade. Italy lay between northern Europe, where people were becoming interested in goods from Asia, and Southwest Asia, where such goods could be bought. The Italians became the great European distributors, acting as go-betweens for traders from Asia, on the one hand, and traders from central and northern Europe, on the other. By a combination of force and negotiation, the Italian city-states of Venice, Genoa, and Pisa won trading rights in Constantinople, Syria, Palestine, and North Africa.

At the time of the Crusades, ships from Italian city-states carried crusaders to the Holy Land and brought back rich cargoes from the East. From Italian seaports these goods traveled overland into central and northern Europe. This overland trade route led to the growth and increasing wealth of many cities in the region.

Trade also revived in northern Europe. Before the year 1000, Viking traders from Kiev, in what is now Ukraine, traveled regularly to the Black Sea and on to Constantinople to collect goods from the East. They transported these items to the cities of northern Europe.

The region of Flanders, today part of Belgium, France, and the Netherlands, gained importance during the 1100s. It was the meeting point of trade routes that led across France, down the Rhine River from Germany, across the English Channel from England,

Tolls

Toll roads are not modern inventions. The first record of a toll being collected was along a military route in Persia in 2000 B.C. In Europe in the Middle Ages, tolls were used to support the construction of bridges. The chapel on the Pont d'Avignon, in fact, doubled as a toll station. A horse and rider paid two deniers (similar to pennies) and a wagon paid twice as much.

Turnpikes were named because at one time travelers on such roads had to stop at a gate made of poles or pikes to pay a toll. The pike was turned open after the toll was paid. Early in the development of the North American colonies, private companies built turnpikes and charged travelers tolls to use them. Now the states build roads and bridges, either with money from the federal government or with tolls collected from users of those roads and bridges (See the photograph at the bottom right.)

Rivers and canals have also provided natural opportunities for toll stations. By the year 1300, there were more than 35 sites along the Rhine River in Germany where fees were collected. In England travelers were charged for passage both over and under London Bridge. Today ships pay tolls to go through Canada's Welland Canal and through the Suez and Panama Canals.

A 1400s illustration of a toll being paid on crossing a bridge (top). Modern toll station (bottom right).

and south from the coasts of the Baltic Sea. Moreover, people throughout Europe eagerly sought the fine woolen cloth that was the chief product of Flanders. During the 1100s, Flanders became the textile headquarters of Europe. Cities such as Ghent and Bruges became thriving centers of population and wealth.

Hamburg, Lübeck, and Bremen became the most important commercial cities on the North and Baltic Seas. Because Germany lacked a strong central government, these trading cities formed an alliance called the Hanseatic League. Eventually, the league had about 100 member cities. It became a powerful influence on the commerce of northwestern Europe during the 1300s and 1400s.

The Hanseatic cities set up permanent trading posts in Flanders, Scandinavia, England, and Russia. Any member that failed to abide by league agreements lost its trading privileges. If a ruler revoked the privileges of any Hanseatic traders, the league stopped all shipments of goods to that country. Sometimes the league members waged small-scale wars in an effort to regain trading rights.

Articles of Trade

By far the most profitable trade for medieval merchants was in luxury or "exotic" goods from eastern and Southwest Asia. The Crusades caused a great increase in demand for spices, medicines, perfumes, dyes, and precious gems from Asia. Manufactured goods included silk, cotton, and linen fabrics, as well as gold, silver, and ivory art objects. Southwest Asia also supplied textiles, rugs, grain, and fruit.

Europe offered various products in exchange for Asian goods. The Baltic region supplied fur, timber,

Trade Fairs of the Middle Ages

Imagine the excitement of a medieval European fair. Merchants from throughout Europe as well as parts of Asia and Africa arrive in town, setting up colorful tents and stalls to display their goods: fragrant spices from the East, silk from China, fine woolens from Flanders, cheese, oil, wine, leather goods, jewelry, and precious metals. Entertainers arrive as well—jugglers, acrobats, musicians, and exotic animals with their trainers.

Medieval fairs were colorful events, but they were also an important economic institution. During the Middle Ages, trade increased and merchants began to sell their goods when people gathered in towns for religious festivals. As the fairs grew larger and more elaborate, new systems were developed to make trade easier. Because people came from all over Europe, a standard system of weights and measures was needed for the goods sold by weight or length. The troy weight—named for the town of Troyes, France—was established to weigh silver and gold and is still in use today. The trade fairs inspired the growth of new financial practices as well. For example, Italian merchants developed the bill of

Manuscript illumination showing the annual fair at Lendit in France

exchange, a written promise to pay a sum of money at a later time.

The trade fairs of the Champagne region of France are some of the best known, but there were also fairs in Italy, Germany, and England. These fairs created ties between regions and brought economic prosperity and liveliness to medieval Europe.

---

fish, and grain. From Spain came wine, oil, leather, and weapons and armor. Other European products included metal goods and glassware from Venice, fine woolen cloth from England and Flanders, and wine from France.

Markets and Fairs

As trade grew, merchants needed places where they could exchange goods. Many villages had weekly market days, but these local markets did not attract large crowds. Some merchants began to sell goods during religious festivals. Then some local rulers established fairs for the sale of imported goods. They realized that they could become wealthy by charging fees, or taxes, on the merchandise sold. Local rulers guaranteed special services to merchants who held a fair, such as protection from assault, theft, or arrest. Armed guards were often provided on the roads leading to the fair and also within the fairgrounds, helping to ensure the safety of all participants.

Champagne, a region in northeastern France that lay directly along the trade route between Italy and northern Europe, held the most important and best-known fairs. Six fairs, each lasting 49 days, were held annually at four towns in the region. Held at different times, the fairs provided a central marketplace for all of Europe during most of the year.

A simple **barter economy**—that is, one in which goods and services are exchanged for other goods and services without the use of money—could not meet the needs of fairs as large and elaborate as those of Champagne. Even though little money might actually change hands at a fair, the value of goods had to be fixed in terms of a common medium of exchange. Because many different kinds of coins existed, money changers at the fairs estimated the value of the currency of one region in relation to the currency of another. In this way the money changers helped in the exchange of goods.

Fairs also became an important social function where people met and shared news. They helped create ties between regions and broadened people's outlook. Travelers came from great distances to attend large fairs, which offered entertainment such as jugglers, clowns, and musicians in addition to the opportunity to buy and sell.

Manufacturing, Banking, and Investment

There were three important developments that resulted from the revival of European trade: a manufacturing system, a banking system, and the practice of investing capital.

Manufacturing grew out of trade. In a new method of production called the **domestic system**, manufacturing took place in workers' homes rather than in a shop or factory. A good example of the domestic system was the woolen industry. In this system an individual would buy wool and then distribute it to several workers. For an agreed price, each worker performed a particular job, such as spinning, weaving, or dyeing. The individual who owned the wool then collected the spun wool or the finished cloth and sold it for the highest price possible. The domestic system began in towns, but by the end of the Middle Ages, it had spread to the countryside.

Banking—in a form in which we recognize it— also developed in the later Middle Ages. In addition to evaluating and exchanging various currencies, money changers now began to provide other services. The word *bank* comes from an old Italian word, *banca*, meaning the "money changer's bench."

Lending money was the most important service early bankers performed. Rulers, nobles, and merchants often needed to borrow funds to finance their activities. During the early Middle Ages, Jews had done much of the moneylending because the Christian church prohibited **usury** (YOO·zhuh·ree), the charging of interest on loans. By the late Middle Ages, however, Christians became more involved in moneylending. While restrictions on charging interest on lent money remained, most legal codes related to business transactions and the repayment of debt allowed interest to be collected.

Moneylenders also eased the transfer of funds from one place to another by developing special notes, called letters of credit, to be used instead of money. A person could take a letter of credit issued by a banker in Ghent and cash it with another banker in Venice. This somewhat resembled our modern-day checking accounts.

With the growth of trade also came **capital**, which is wealth earned, saved, and invested to produce profits.

Investors sometimes formed partnerships, pooling their capital to finance new businesses. In this way, each party contributed part of the cost and received a share of the profits.

These three developments—manufacturing, banking, and investing of capital—laid the foundation for the emergence of a **market economy**, an economy in which land, labor, and capital are controlled by individuals. It was the market economy that formed the basis of the modern capitalist system. (See Chapter 19.)

Section 2 Review

1. **Define** barter economy, domestic system, usury, capital, market economy
2. **Locate and Explain the Significance** English Channel, Flanders
3. **Understanding Ideas** Describe areas that experienced a revival of trade in the later Middle Ages.
4. **Summarizing Ideas** Why were fairs important in medieval society?
5. **Determining Cause and Effect** How did the revival of European trade bring about the development of a manufacturing system, a banking system, and the practice of investing capital?

Section 3

The Growth of Towns

Focus Questions

- **What rights did medieval townspeople have?**
- **How did merchant and craft guilds contribute to the communities in which they existed?**
- **What factors led to the decline of serfdom?**

The growth of towns and cities accompanied the revival of trade in the Middle Ages. In fact, trade and cities always grow together. In a town or city, we find all the conditions needed for exchanging goods and services.

Beginning in the late 900s, existing towns began to grow larger. New towns grew up at locations important for trade—natural harbors, the mouths of rivers, and cargo transfer points.

Guilds monitored the quality of products and educated their members. This is the sign of the Venetian Pharmacists' Guild.

The Rights of Townspeople

As towns grew, it became clear that the town dweller did not fit into the manorial system. Townspeople made their living by manufacturing and trade. They played little part in the villages' agricultural economy.

Townspeople wanted to control their own governments. Under feudalism, however, lords controlled the town and would give up control only in exchange for something. Sometimes townspeople won rights of self-government by peaceful means. In other cases, however, they resorted to violence and even war.

Some lords granted political liberties to towns to encourage their development. Sometimes towns bought charters of liberties—written statements of their rights—from their lords.

Town and city charters differed widely from place to place. In time, though, those who lived in towns in Europe were assured of at least four basic rights: (1) *Freedom.* No matter what their birth or origin, people who lived in a town had a chance to become free. If officials did not challenge them for a year and a day, they became free. This broke all ties to a manor or manor lord. A serf who escaped to a town could thus become free. (2) *Exempt status.* Inhabitants of towns were also exempt, or free, from having to perform any services on the manor. (3) *Town justice.* Towns had their own courts, made up of prominent citizens familiar with local customs, which tried cases involving townspeople. (4) *Commercial privileges.* Townspeople had the right to sell goods freely in the town market and to charge tolls to all outsiders trading there.

Guilds

As trade increased and towns grew larger and wealthier, medieval merchants began to unite in associations. Because of the dangers of travel, traders often assembled convoys—groups that travel together for safety. Arranging such convoys, however, took much planning and money. Gradually, merchants founded associations called guilds.

In each town, an association called a **merchant guild** gained a monopoly—the sole right to trade there. Merchants from other towns or foreign nations could not trade in that town unless they paid a fee. In addition, guilds acted as charitable organizations. They made loans to members and looked after those who were in any kind of trouble. For example, they supported the widows and children of deceased members.

In time the skilled workers who were engaged in manufacturing formed **craft guilds**. Each of these guilds included all the people engaged in one particular craft, such as shoemaking or weaving. These guilds regulated wages and set hours and conditions of labor. They also set standards of quality for manufactured goods, disciplined workers, looked after ill or disabled members, and supervised the training of skilled workers. A master worker, or fully accepted member of the guild, had to be a man.

A candidate for membership in a craft guild went through two preliminary stages of training, which took years to complete. In the first stage, he served as an **apprentice**. A boy's parents usually apprenticed, or bound by legal agreement, their son, often paying a hefty fee to a master worker to learn a trade. The boy lived at the home of the master, who gave the apprentice food, clothing, and training. The period of apprenticeship varied from five to nine years.

After completing his apprenticeship, a young man became a journeyman. A **journeyman** was a skilled artisan who worked for a master for daily wages. After working for wages for some time, he could become a master by submitting proof of his skill—a "masterpiece," or piece of work judged worthy of a master. If the guild masters approved his work, the journeyman could open a shop of his own.

Toward the end of the Middle Ages, the line between masters and journeymen became much more distinct and much harder to cross. Journeymen usually remained wage earners all their lives. Often the master's son inherited the business and position without performing the required apprenticeship.

The Rise of the Middle Class

A new class of merchants, master workers, and skilled workers emerged in medieval society. The members of this class were called burgesses in England, bourgeoisie (boorzh·wah·ZEE) in France, and burghers in Germany—all from the word *burg*, or *borough*, meaning town.

The rise to prominence of this class during the later Middle Ages transformed European society. Townspeople tended to want stable and uniform governments that would protect trade and property, so they usually favored kings over nobles. To gain their support, kings began to consult them and to employ them in government positions.

Life in Medieval Towns

Medieval towns and cities were small by modern standards. About 9 out of 10 cities in northern Europe had fewer than 2,000 inhabitants. According to some estimates, Paris in the 1200s had a population of about 150,000. London, with about 40,000, was far above average, as was Lübeck, Germany, with its 10,000 inhabitants.

Physically compact, the medieval city often stood on top of a hill or at the bend of a river so that it could be defended easily. Because city land was scarce and valuable, houses were built five or six stories high. To increase the space inside a building, each story projected out a little farther than the one below. Thus, at the top the houses almost met over the middle of the street. Each city had some particularly fine buildings, such as a cathedral, a town hall, and the guild halls.

A medieval city would have offended the eyes and noses of people today. Sewage littered dark, filthy streets and was dumped into open gutters that were cleared only when it rained. Epidemics ran rampant. There were no streetlights. Servants accompanied law-abiding people who ventured out at night to protect them from robbers, for there were no police. Despite the uncomfortable conditions, however, life in the medieval city was not completely unpleasant. The medieval city was a busy and interesting place, alive with activity and people—peddlers, lawyers, merchants, strolling actors, musicians, and jugglers.

The Decline of Serfdom

As the number of townspeople increased, the number of serfs declined. The growing towns offered serfs a chance to improve their hard lives. They might escape to the town and become free. Even if they did not, the town changed their way of living. Because the town needed food, serfs could sell their produce for money. Thus they could pay for the use of their lands in money rather than in labor.

Changes in agricultural methods also caused the number of serfs to decline. In England, for example, some landowners fenced off part of their land for sheep pastures, eliminating the need for shepherds. This action left some serfs without work and forced them into the cities. A devastating epidemic in the mid-1300s also contributed to the decline of serfdom.

The Black Death

In 1347 a plague, which Europeans came to call the Black Death, swept into Europe. The disease originated in Asia. It spread to the Mediterranean ports of Europe by way of trading vessels, which carried infected rats on board. The plague was transmitted to humans in two forms, the bubonic plague and the pneumonic plague. The bubonic plague erupted when rats infected with a bacterium were in close contact with people. The inevitable fleas that lived on the rats transmitted the disease to people. A person bitten by a disease-carrying flea soon showed symptoms of the plague—infected lymph glands accompanied by painful swelling and high fever. The pneumonic plague, which was caused by the same disease-carrying rat fleas, attacked the lungs. Unlike bubonic plague, however, a person sick with pneumonic plague became contagious and could transmit the disease to other people through coughing and sneezing. Pneumonic plague was—and still is—almost always fatal.

It is difficult to estimate the total number of plague deaths throughout Europe. They happened so rapidly that often the survivors could not keep up with burying the dead. Bodies were loaded on carts and dumped in common graves outside the town. Entire villages and towns were emptied. England lost one third of its population. According to some estimates, as many as 25 million people died throughout Europe, which would account for about one third of the population. Europe was left with a population decline from which it did not begin to recover for more than 100 years.

These devastating losses disrupted Europe's religious, social, and economic institutions. The church lost some of its power and prestige. People's faith had been shaken. Relationships between the upper and lower classes began to change as workers, now in short supply, could demand higher wages. Conflicts between the classes led to peasant revolts, which broke out in several European countries by the end of the 1300s.

Section 3 Review

1. **Define** merchant guild, craft guilds, apprentice, journeyman
2. **Understanding Ideas (a)** How did townspeople gain rights of self-government? **(b)** What were the most important of these rights?
3. **Comparing Ideas (a)** What were the differences between merchant guilds and craft guilds? **(b)** How did these guilds contribute to medieval communities?
4. **Determining Cause and Effect (a)** How did the growth of towns contribute to the decline in the numbers of serfs? **(b)** What other factors contributed to the decline of serfdom?

Section 4

Life and Culture in the Middle Ages

Focus Questions

- **What were the important developments in literature during the later Middle Ages?**
- **How did Abelard and Aquinas contribute to medieval thought?**
- **What were the most important types of architecture during the Middle Ages?**

Civilization developed only after early humans had settled in towns and cities. In a similar way, the culture of the Middle Ages did not flourish until city life revived.

Language and Literature

After the Roman Empire collapsed, Latin continued to be the written and spoken language of educated people in western Europe. During the Middle Ages, however, common people, with little education, began to speak **vernacular languages**, or "everyday" speech that varied from place to place. These languages included early forms of English, Italian, French, German, and Spanish.

Vernacular literature. In time, writers also began to use vernacular languages. The troubadours' songs were one of the first forms of vernacular literature. **Troubadours**, or traveling singers, wrote lyrical poems of love and chivalry, which they sang in the castles and courts of feudal lords, as well as in towns.

Another form of vernacular literature was the national epic. France had *The Song of Roland*, which was set during the time of Charlemagne. Germany had the *Nibelungenlied*, a legend of the hero Siegfried and a war between the Huns and the Burgundians in the A.D. 400s. Romances, or works of prose fiction, were also popular with medieval audiences. The most popular romances were the adventures of King Arthur and his Knights of the Round Table. One of the greatest French romances is *Romance of the Rose*, a story about love, written in part by Guillaume de Lorris.

The growth of towns created an audience for a new kind of literature that the French called *fabliaux* (FA·blee·oh), which were short comic stories in rhymed verse. These stories mocked the lofty ideals of chivalry, ridiculed human foolishness, and criticized the clergy in particular. Animal stories or fables such as that of Reynard the Fox also grew increasingly popular during this period.

Another form of vernacular literature that developed during the Middle Ages was drama. Miracle plays, mystery plays, and morality plays were short dramas with religious or biblical subjects as their theme. These plays often enhanced church services at Easter and Christmas. Later, as towns grew, the plays were presented to audiences in town marketplaces. One very popular play was *Noye's Fludde*, "Noah's Flood." It told how Noah built his ark, collected pairs of all creatures, and kept them and his family safe during the flood.

Dante and Chaucer. Two writers, Dante and Chaucer, represent the flowering of medieval vernacular literature. Dante Alighieri was born in Florence, Italy, in 1265. He used Latin when writing scholarly works. When writing poetry, however, he preferred the Italian dialect of his native Tuscany. Because Dante used the Tuscan dialect in his most famous works, which were widely read throughout Italy, it became the written language of all Italy. Thus Dante is considered the father of modern Italian.

Dante's greatest work is *The Divine Comedy*. It tells of a pilgrimage to the three realms where Christian souls could go after death—hell, purgatory, and paradise. Dante is guided through hell and purgatory by the Roman poet Virgil. He is guided through heaven by Beatrice, a young woman of Florence who became his

The Canterbury Tales

The pilgrims in *The Canterbury Tales* by Geoffrey Chaucer represent almost every social class in English society. In the Prologue, Chaucer parades a colorful cast of characters, each with an interesting story to tell, before the reader. The rhyming poetry and subtle satire of *The Canterbury Tales* make the work fun to read even today. The following verses from the Prologue show Chaucer's mastery of description and satire.

"
There was a Knight, a most distinguished man,
Who from the day on which he first began
To ride abroad had followed chivalry,
Truth, honour, generousness and courtesy.
. . . .
There also was a Nun, a Prioress,
Her way of smiling very simple and coy.
Her greatest oath was only 'By St. Loy!'
And she was known as Madam Eglantyne.
And well she sang a service, with a fine
Intoning through her nose, as was most seemly,
And she spoke daintily in French, extremely.
. . . .
A Monk there was, one of the finest sort
Who rode the country; hunting was his sport.
A manly man, to be an Abbot able;
Many a dainty horse he had in stable.
. . . .
There was a Merchant with a forking beard
And motley dress; high on his horse he sat,
Upon his head a Flemish beaver hat
And on his feet daintily buckled boots.
He told of his opinions and pursuits.
. . . .
They had a Cook with them who stood alone
for boiling chicken with a marrow-bone...
But what a pity—so it seemed to me,
That he should have an ulcer on his knee.

Scene from *The Canterbury Tales*

. . . .
A Doctor too emerged as we proceeded;
No one alive could talk as well as he did
On points of medicine and of surgery.
. . . .
This Pardoner had hair as yellow as wax,
Hanging down smoothly like a hank of flax.
In driblets fell his locks behind his head
Down to his shoulders which they overspread;
Thinly they fell, like rat-tails, one by one.
He wore no hood upon his head, for fun.
. . . .
Now I have told you shortly, in a clause,
The rank, the array, the number and the cause
Of our assembly in this company
In Southwark, at that high-class hostelry..."

literary inspiration. They meet the souls of famous people, both good and evil. A work of this sort gave Dante the opportunity to criticize the society of his own time. He mentioned the names of his enemies in Florence, placing them in hell. He placed his allies in heaven.

Geoffrey Chaucer was born in England around 1340. He wrote his most famous work, *The Canterbury Tales*, in the form of a series of stories told by a group of pilgrims on their way to Thomas Becket's shrine in Canterbury. His poem pokes good-natured fun at

In his narrative poem, *The Divine Comedy*, Dante reflects on the fate of his soul in the earthly and spiritual worlds. This scene from the poem shows Dante and his beloved Beatrice in Paradise.

English society and satirizes the clergy. All Chaucer's works are written in a dialect of Middle English, a forerunner of modern English. By writing his popular works in English, Chaucer added to its literary prestige and set an example that was followed by poets after him.

Education

During the early Middle Ages, only a few nobles and some clergy were educated, mainly at monasteries or by teachers in the church. Gradually, however, schools admitted any males who wanted to study. Located in prosperous towns, these schools had simple beginnings. A teacher could set up a place of instruction and try to attract students to enroll in the school by paying a fee. This educational system resembled that of Athens' when Plato and Aristotle taught.

As teachers and students increased in number, they united to form guilds for both protection and privileges. Such a guild was called a *universitas*, a Latin word meaning "an association of people." Gradually, the word *university* came to mean an association of people organized for the purpose of teaching and learning.

Four outstanding universities developed between the late 1000s and the end of the 1200s. Those at Paris and at Oxford, in England, specialized in theology, or the study of religious doctrine, and the liberal arts, which included Latin grammar, logic, rhetoric, arithmetic, geometry, astronomy, and music. The University of Bologna, in Italy, taught civil law and canon, or church, law. The University at Salerno, also in Italy, specialized in medicine. During the next two centuries, numerous universities were formed throughout central and northern Europe.

Eventually, medieval universities established standard courses of study, with uniform requirements for the various stages of progress. These stages were represented by academic degrees. The degree of bachelor of arts showed that a student had finished the apprenticeship. After further study and examination, the student qualified for the degree of master of arts and could then teach. The student was admitted to the guild of teachers at a ceremony called commencement because it signified the beginning of work as a teacher. Only then could the student study one of the specialties offered at medieval universities—theology, law, or medicine.

Philosophy

During the Middle Ages, the classic works of the ancient Greek and Roman philosophers came to the attention of western Europe through the Muslims in Spain and Sicily, places where Christian and Muslim cultures mingled during periods of relative peace. Deeply impressed by the intellectual achievements of the Hellenistic world, European scholars spent quite a bit of time trying to reconcile Aristotle's ideas with those of early church writers. Aristotle emphasized human reason. The church writers, however, emphasized faith. The attempt of medieval philosophers to reconcile Christian faith with Aristotle's philosophy is often called **scholasticism**. The aim of the scholastic philosophers was to discover how people could improve themselves in this life by reason and also ensure salvation in the life to come.

Peter Abelard, who taught in Paris in the 1100s, was an important scholastic philosopher. In his book *Sic et Non*, "Yes and No," he raised many questions about church doctrine. The book was a collection of statements showing inconsistencies of teaching by the church. After each statement, Abelard placed quotations of scripture from the Bible, decrees of the popes, and the writings of church philosophers. Many of these documents conflicted with each other.

Probably the greatest of all medieval philosophers was Thomas Aquinas, a Dominican friar. His principal work, *Summa Theologiae*, written in the

Building History Study Skills

READ
WRITE
INTERPRET
CONNECT
THINK

Making Connections with History: Linking Literature to History

The literature of a society as found in novels, poems, and stories gives us information about the values and culture of a people. The content is fictional, but the ideas often indicate what the people of that society believed and what they felt was important. Literature helps us understand the intangible or underlying values and beliefs of a society.

How to Link Literature to History

To link literature to history, follow these steps.

1. Identify the source. Is the selection a novel, a poem, or a story? When was it written? Why was it written?
2. Explain the contents. What is the selection about? What is the main theme? Who are the characters in the selection?
3. Identify the values or beliefs being expressed.
4. Connect the literature to history. Does the literature represent an ideal, or is it the story of a real event? Does it support or contradict the historical facts?

Developing the Skill

The troubadours' love songs focused on courtship. In the following poem, the troubadour, who was named Cercamon, sings of his lady. Read the poem and then attempt to explain the historical link.

❝Now that the air is fresher
and the world turned
   green,
I shall sing once more
of the one I love and
   desire,
but we are so far apart
that I cannot go and witness
how my words might please her.
. . . .
I sing of her, yet her beauty
is greater than I can tell,
with her fresh color, lovely eyes,
and white skin, untanned

and untainted by rouge.
She is so pure and noble
that no one can speak ill of her.
But above all, one must praise,
it seems to me, her truthfulness,
her manners and her gracious speech,
for she never would betray a friend;
and I was mad to believe
what I heard tell of her
and thus cause her to be angry.
. . . .
I never intended to complain;
and even now, if she so desires,
she could bring me happiness
by granting what I seek.
I cannot go on like this much longer,
for since she's been so far away
I've scarcely slept or eaten.❞

An English knight

Written in the 1100s, the poem is about romantic love. The young man has lost his love because he believed lies about her. He is devastated by their separation.

The poem reflects the age in which it was written, with the woman represented as an ideal —pure, noble, gracious, and loyal, with "lovely eyes and white skin, untanned and untainted by rouge." It demonstrates the attitude of men toward women during the age of chivalry. Women were regarded as the weaker sex and, according to the code of chivalry, had to be protected and defended. Along with describing the woman in idealistic terms, the poem places her on a pedestal.

Practicing the Skill

Using the information on linking literature to history, choose a poem or novel written by a twentieth-century author and find characteristics in the work that reflect modern times.

To apply this skill, see Applying History Study Skills on page 275.

The flying buttresses of Notre Dame in Paris, shown in this photograph, support the church's high walls at points where extra support is necessary to maintain its height. The interior view of Reims Cathedral (inset) provides an interior glimpse of beautiful Gothic architecture.

late 1200s, summarized Christian thought at that time. In it Aquinas examined each point of Church doctrine and tried to show that it could be arrived at by logic or reason as well as by faith. Today the *Summa* forms one of the bases for the teaching of theology in Roman Catholic schools.

Science

Medieval thinking was deductive, leaving little room for scientific progress. In other words, an idea was taken from an authority, usually the Bible, accepted as true, and used as a basis for reasoning. Classical writings, such as those of Galen and Ptolemy, formed the basis of much medieval science.

While the Arabs preserved the great accomplishments of Hellenistic science, only two subjects received serious attention in Europe: mathematics and optics (the study of light). Europeans regarded mathematics as important because of its use in counting, calendars, trade, and measuring. They considered optics important because of their belief that God's influence was carried by light. Some important

work was done, beginning in the 1000s in mathematics and during the 1100s and 1200s in optics. It was not until the 1500s, however, that major interest in science reappeared and led to vast changes in the understanding of the physical aspects of the world.

Europeans did make some technical advances based on practical know-how rather than science. These included improved winches and pulleys, iron plows, and better yokes for oxen. Windmills and waterwheels, invented in Asia, spread to Europe.

Art and Architecture

During the Middle Ages, most artists dedicated themselves to glorifying God. Church architecture became the primary art form, and the other arts embellished or beautified it.

Between 1000 and 1150, most architects used the vaults, arches, domes, and low horizontal lines characteristic of Roman architecture. This style later came to be called Romanesque, meaning "similar to the Roman." Because of the enormous weight of the domed stone roof, the walls of a Romanesque church generally had only a few small windows. This resulted in very dark interiors. Romanesque churches had relief sculpture on both the inside and the outside. Frescoes also adorned the walls.

During the mid-1100s, master builders in western Europe modified elements of Romanesque architecture to develop a different style of church architecture. Critics ridiculed this new style because it did not conform to the standards of classical architecture. These critics called the new style Gothic, after the barbarian Goths. Despite the origin of the name, Gothic has come to be considered one of the most beautiful styles of architecture ever developed.

In contrast to the low, heavy Romanesque churches, the spires of Gothic churches soared delicately above the roofs of the surrounding town. Outside the walls, builders used rows of supporting ribbed vaults, called flying buttresses, which they connected to the church with arches. Because the buttress carried part of the weight of the roof, the walls could be high and thin, with large windows. Everything in Gothic churches— pointed arches, tall spires, and high walls—reached toward heaven.

The inside of the Gothic church also differed from that of the Romanesque church. Statues of the holy family, saints, and rulers lined the interior, sculpture in relief adorned the walls, and stained-glass windows let in shafts of sunlight.

In many ways the Gothic church exemplified the changing world of the late Middle Ages. The tall structure rose above the growing town around and below it. Marketplaces in the shadows of its walls teemed with traders. Religious pageants and miracle plays were performed both within the church and outside its carved doors. All the skills of the medieval world went into the building of this monument to God.

Section 4 Review

1. **Define** vernacular languages, troubadours, scholasticism
2. **Identify** Dante, Chaucer, Abelard, Aquinas
3. **Summarizing Ideas** Briefly describe the major works of Dante and Chaucer.
4. **Analyzing Ideas** How do Abelard and Aquinas exemplify scholastic thought?
5. **Evaluating Ideas** "The design of the Gothic cathedrals drew people's attention upward to God." Use information from this section to support this statement.

Wars and the Growth of Nations

Focus Questions

- **What was the Hundred Years' War?**
- **What factors strengthened the monarchies of England, France, and Spain?**
- **During the 1300s and 1400s, what was happening to the Holy Roman Empire?**

Under feudalism in the early Middle Ages, the people of a country did not look to a central government for defense or help; neither did they feel any loyalty toward the country as a whole. Instead, the loyalty of the people of a country lay with a local feudal lord, a manor village, or a town.

Gradually, however, with the decline of feudalism, states began to form. Kings began to build their kingdoms into organized nations. The development of a nation usually coincided with the growth of patriotism among its people. **Patriotism**, the feeling of loyalty to a country as a whole, gives the feeling of belonging to a large society rather than to only a small community.

England

The authority of the English king, although partially restricted by Parliament, increased in various ways. These included the development of a single system of law and courts and an increase in revenue as the country grew more prosperous. Moreover, the military strength of a professional army and the support of the townspeople strengthened the king's position against the feudal lords.

Therefore, as a result of the authority of the English King increasing, the power of feudal lords decreased. The number of serfs declined. Increasingly, villages and farms of free peasants dotted the English countryside.

The Hundred Years' War. English prosperity and the development of a strong national government suffered a setback during a long war with France. The Hundred Years' War, the collective name for a series of conflicts lasting from 1337 until 1453, had several causes. The English king Edward III held the provinces of Aquitaine and Gascony in France. This made him a vassal of the French king. However, when the last male member of

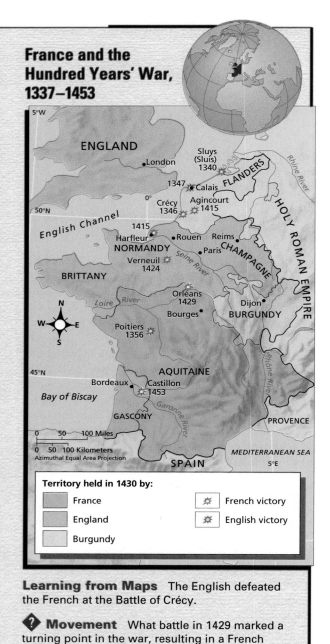

France and the Hundred Years' War, 1337–1453

Territory held in 1430 by:

- France
- England
- Burgundy

☼ French victory
☼ English victory

Learning from Maps The English defeated the French at the Battle of Crécy.

Movement What battle in 1429 marked a turning point in the war, resulting in a French victory?

The Hundred Years' War brought death and destruction to both England and France. It also led to two key developments.

The use of new weapons. The use of new weapons—particularly the longbow, gunpowder, and the cannon—weakened feudalism. The English longbow was five or six feet long, with an effective range of 200 yards. English foot soldiers armed with longbows soundly defeated a French feudal cavalry at Agincourt (AJ·uhn·kohrt) in 1415. Knights on horseback were no match for foot soldiers with longbows.

Both French and English troops began to use gunpowder and cannons during the Hundred Years' War. At first cannons were only crude tubes of wood and metal out of which exploding gunpowder hurled stones or chunks of metal. They were difficult to aim properly. More effective cannons and smaller, hand-held guns developed from these rather simple weapons. As a result, castles no longer provided strong protection for the feudal lord and his soldiers because one powerful blast from a cannon could break through a castle's thick walls.

The growing power of the English Parliament. Parliament, especially the House of Commons, gained more power over the king. To finance the war, the English king needed tax revenue, and to collect these taxes, the king needed the consent of Parliament. In April 1376, members of the House of Commons, angry at the course of the war and concerned about problems at home, first met separately from the lords and then confronted them with their demands. Among the concessions they gained were a special council to advise the king and the right to consider tax legislation before it was discussed by the lords. By the end of the 1300s, Parliament's consent was required for all extraordinary taxation.

Despite many English victories, when the Hundred Years' War ended in 1453, England had lost all its lands in France except Calais. (See map on this page.) Almost exactly 100 years later, this too was relinquished.

The Wars of the Roses. A struggle for the throne between the York and Lancaster families began in 1455 and delayed the emergence of a strong centralized government in England. In this civil strife—the Wars of the Roses—the Yorkists used a white rose as their badge, and the Lancastrians used a red rose. Small bands of nobles and their private armies did most of the fighting.

In 1485 Henry Tudor, a member of the House of Lancaster, ended the wars by defeating the Yorkist king Richard III. Henry seized the throne of England, married a daughter of the House of York, and became

the Capetian dynasty died, Edward laid claim to the French throne. The French assembly chose Philip VI instead. In 1337 Edward renewed his claim and brought an army to Flanders, a commercially rich area that England and France had competed for control of for some time. The conflict had begun.

Henry VII, founder of the Tudor dynasty. The English people, tired of war and disorder, willingly accepted the strong government that Henry VII established.

France

Many of the same factors at work in England during the 1300s and 1400s were also at work in France. The Capetian kings had developed a strong monarchy, although the Hundred Years' War with England caused French kings to lose some of their power. France suffered more than England during that war because the fighting took place on French soil. Bands of pillaging English soldiers devastated the French countryside. Even during the periods of relative peace, starvation plagued the citizens. The following excerpt describes the misery of the people in 1421.

> ❝And in truth when good weather came, in April, those who in the winter had made their beverages from apples and sloe plums emptied the residue of their apples and their plums into the street with the intention that the pigs of St. Antoine would eat them. But the pigs did not get to them in time, for as soon as they were thrown out, they were seized by poor folk, women and children, who ate them with great relish, which was a great pity, each for himself; for they ate what the pigs scorned to eat, they ate the cores of cabbages without bread or without cooking, grasses of the fields without bread or salt. ❞

Joan of Arc. During the Hundred Years' War, rivalry broke out between branches of the royal family—Burgundy and Orléans—making it difficult for the French to fight the English. Defeat followed defeat. However, French fortunes in the war were revived by a 16-year-old peasant girl, Joan of Arc. Joan said she had heard the voices of three saints—Michael, Catherine, and Margaret—telling her to leave her small village and help defend the city of Orléans, which was under English attack. She persuaded the French authorities to allow her into the city. In 1429, inspired to greater efforts by Joan's presence, the weary French troops rallied and saved the city. That same year Joan helped the heir to the French throne take the crown as Charles VII.

Burgundian forces, who were allied with England, captured Joan in May 1430. She was turned over to the church to be tried as a heretic. Convicted, she was burned at the stake in 1431.

Joan of Arc's courage as well as her martyrdom created strong patriotic feeling among the French. By 1453 they had driven the English out of France except for the port of Calais. As in England, a stronger monarchy had also been reestablished.

The Estates General. In 1302 Philip IV (the Fair) established the Estates General, a representative assembly resembling the English Parliament. It took its name from the groups that attended the meetings: members of the clergy (First Estate), nobles (Second Estate), and common people (Third Estate). During the Hundred Years' War, when France lacked a strong king, the Estates General controlled finances and passed laws. After the war, however, with a stronger monarchy, it became clear that the Estates General was too unwieldy a body to govern the country. It never gained the right to approve taxes, which was so important for the English Parliament. In France the king could levy taxes on his own authority.

Louis XI. Louis XI further strengthened the French monarchy during his reign, from 1461 to 1483. Louis avoided war except as a last resort, preferring to use diplomacy, at which he was a master. In fact, his opponents called him the Universal Spider because of his skills at conspiracy and intrigue. Domestically, his rule was characterized by a harsh but efficient administration and high taxes.

Louis XI used diplomacy to build an alliance against the powerful Duke of Burgundy, Charles the Bold. He did so by persuading the leaders of Switzerland, an independent nation, that a strong Burgundy would threaten Swiss freedom. The Swiss then did Louis's fighting for him. In 1477 the Duke of Burgundy was killed in battle, and Louis seized much of the territory of Burgundy.

The French king continued to solidify his power, recovering French fiefs that had been part of the Burgundian state. He gained Brittany by marriage. France gradually became unified under the monarchy.

As the power of French kings increased, the power of French feudal lords declined. However, French nobles had many privileges and remained rich and influential until the mid-1700s.

As feudalism declined, French peasants did not gain as much personal freedom as the English did. Also unlike the English, they still had to pay many dues and owed services to the manor and its lord.

Spain

By 1400 four principal Christian kingdoms—Portugal, Castile, Navarre, and Aragon—had emerged on the Iberian Peninsula. (See map on page 270.) Granada also shared the peninsula.

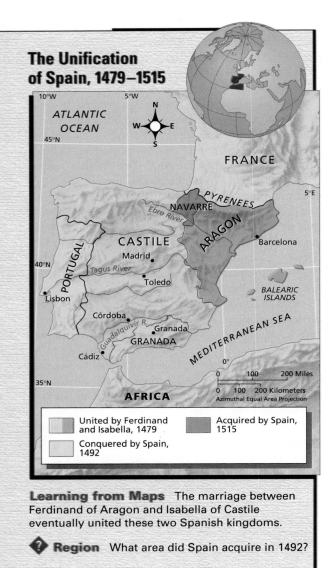

The Unification of Spain, 1479–1515

ATLANTIC OCEAN

FRANCE

PYRENEES

NAVARRE

Ebro River

ARAGON

PORTUGAL

CASTILE

Madrid

Barcelona

Tagus River

Toledo

BALEARIC ISLANDS

Lisbon

Córdoba

Guadalquivir R.

Granada

GRANADA

MEDITERRANEAN SEA

Cádiz

AFRICA

0   100   200 Miles
0   100   200 Kilometers
Azimuthal Equal Area Projection

Legend:
- United by Ferdinand and Isabella, 1479
- Conquered by Spain, 1492
- Acquired by Spain, 1515

Learning from Maps The marriage between Ferdinand of Aragon and Isabella of Castile eventually united these two Spanish kingdoms.

? Region What area did Spain acquire in 1492?

The first real step toward unification of the peninsula came in 1469, when Isabella of Castile married Ferdinand of Aragon. The two kingdoms remained separate, but their rulers joined forces in a war against the Moors in 1492, capturing Granada. Granada had been the last stronghold of the Moors in Spain. In the late 1400s and early 1500s, Ferdinand and Isabella united Castile and Aragon to form the new nation of Spain and added the kingdom of Navarre to its territories.

Ferdinand and Isabella made Spain a strong monarchy, taking powers away from the church courts and the nobles. Ardent Catholics, they looked with displeasure at the non-Christians in their kingdoms. Moors had been in the southern part of Spain since the 700s. Jews had been there from the time of the Roman Empire.

In 1492 Ferdinand and Isabella ordered all Jews within their two kingdoms to become Christians or leave. Several years later, they required the Moors to make the same choice. Most people in both groups chose to leave. This policy acted to weaken Spain because both the Moors and the Jews had been valuable leaders in industrial and commercial activity.

The Holy Roman Empire

England, France, and Spain had each formed powerful nations after 1100. However, Germany and Italy—the regions that made up the Holy Roman Empire—did not become unified nations until the 1800s. The Holy Roman emperor lacked the power he needed to exercise complete control.

In the early days, the rulers of many German states elected the Holy Roman emperor. Gradually, the number who could vote for emperor decreased. Finally, by a decree issued in 1356, Emperor Charles IV ruled that only seven electors would choose the emperor.

The electors feared giving too much power to one of their own group or to any other powerful prince. As a result, for many years they elected only princes who had little land or power. The Holy Roman emperor had no real authority, but he did have prestige. For this reason, the election became an occasion for bribery and the trading of political favors.

In 1273 a member of the Habsburg family, which ruled a small state in what is now Switzerland, was elected emperor. The Habsburgs, although weak princes with little land, used the prestige of the title Holy Roman emperor to arrange marriages with powerful families. In this way, the Habsburg family gained control of the duchy of Austria and nearby lands. Many other well-planned marriages eventually gave them control of vast amounts of territory in the empire. (See map on page 271.)

After 1437 the Habsburgs maneuvered cleverly enough to ensure that the Holy Roman emperor was nearly always a Habsburg. Although they became the most powerful family in Europe, they could not unify the Holy Roman Empire, or even the regions within it. For example, Germany, though dominated by the Habsburgs, was ruled primarily by territorial princes. Nor was Italy unified. A major barrier to its unification lay in the fact that the country was divided, as by a belt across the middle, by the Papal States ruled by the pope.

Map of Europe, c. 1500

Learning from Maps In 1500 the Holy Roman Empire included lands in Italy as well as some in Germany, Switzerland, Austria, and Czechoslovakia.

 Place What countries bordered the Holy Roman Empire?

Section 5 Review

1. **Define** patriotism
2. **Identify** Joan of Arc, Charles VII, Estates General, Ferdinand, Isabella, Habsburgs
3. **Summarizing Ideas** Describe the causes for the Hundred Years' War.
4. **Analyzing Ideas** What factors led to the strengthening of central government in England, France, and Spain after the Hundred Years' War?
5. **Interpreting Ideas** Why did Italy and Germany fail to become unified nations during the later Middle Ages?

Section 6

Challenges to Church Power

Focus Questions

- **What events challenged the power of the church beginning in the 1300s?**
- **What criticisms came from within the church?**

Innocent III was pope from 1198 to 1216. Under him the medieval papacy reached the height of its power. After his time, however, the temporal, or worldly, power of the church began to weaken. This occurred for two main reasons.

First, Europe was changing. Kings developed strong national governments with rich treasuries. The importance of townspeople grew, and they often felt that the restrictions of church laws hindered trade and industry.

Second, the wisdom of the Muslims and the pagan Greeks appeared in Europe, and much of it conflicted with the teachings of the church. As a result, a spirit of skepticism, or questioning, began to develop. People criticized the church because of its great wealth, its methods of raising money, and the worldly lives of some members of the clergy.

Boniface VIII and Philip IV

A serious clash between the church and secular authority erupted over the issue of whether the clergy had to obey national laws or pay taxes. In 1294 Philip IV of France demanded that the clergy pay taxes to the national treasury. His demand angered Pope Boniface VIII. The pope was an intelligent and cultured man, but he was also proud, impulsive, and harsh in his policies. Boniface argued that the clergy

did not have to pay taxes. In a decree called the *Unam Sanctam*, Boniface declared his own supremacy over temporal rulers.

As the struggle wore on, Philip summoned the first meeting of the Estates General in 1302. He accused the pope of simony and heresy. He also demanded that a general council of the church bring Boniface to trial. The French king then had his envoy in Italy seize the pope and hold him prisoner. Although quickly released, Boniface died soon afterward. Following his death, the political power of the papacy lessened.

The Babylonian Captivity

Shortly after Boniface's death, Philip IV managed to have one of his French advisers elected pope. The new pope, Clement V, moved the headquarters of the papacy from Rome to Avignon, in southern France. The next six popes were also French, and Avignon remained the papal capital for nearly 70 years.

This period of papal history—from 1309 to 1377—is known as the **Babylonian Captivity**, named after the period of Hebrew exile in Babylon more than 18 centuries before. For 1,000 years, Rome had been the center of the church in the west. With the pope

The papal palace at Avignon was home to seven popes between 1309 and 1377. The impressive structure was built on land 190 feet above the town and inside three miles of ramparts for protection.

living in France, people in other countries became suspicious of the French monarch's control of the church. Rome fell into lawlessness and impoverishment in the pope's absence.

The Great Schism

The 1370s continued to be a difficult time for the papacy. The French pope Gregory XI returned the papacy to Rome in 1377. The cardinals in Rome elected an Italian pope, Urban VI, but in 1378 the French cardinals elected a French pope, Clement VII, who remained at Avignon. The Italian pope excommunicated the French pope and cardinals; the French pope excommunicated the Italian pope and cardinals.

The period from 1378 to 1417 is known as the **Great Schism** (SI·zuhm), meaning a division into hostile groups. For political reasons, each pope had the support of certain national rulers. Generally, the people and clergy of a country followed the choice of their ruler.

In 1414 a church council met at Constance in an attempt to heal the schism and to consider reforms of all the weaknesses of the church. The council quickly dealt with the schism by deposing both the Italian and French popes. It agreed that a new pope should be elected but not until a program of reforms had been adopted.

The Council of Constance had more difficulty agreeing on a program of reforms. Everyone agreed that corruption in the church and immorality among the clergy must end. However, whenever a definite plan was proposed to deal with a problem, the delegates disagreed so strongly that no conclusion could be reached.

After long and bitter debate, the council decided that church councils should be called regularly to deal with problems, including needed reforms. The council drew up a statement of reforms and the cardinals then elected a new pope.

Continued Criticism of the Church

The Babylonian Captivity and the Great Schism weakened the authority and prestige of the papacy and increased criticism of the church. Some of this criticism came from within the church itself.

In 1324 two scholars and philosophers, Marsilius of Padua and John of Jandun, wrote an influential work entitled *Defender of the Peace*. According to the writers, the pope was the elected head of the church only and had no other temporal power. The authors believed that the church's power belonged with a general council that fairly represented both the clergy and the laity. This departed from Pope Boniface VIII's concept of papal power in the *Unam Sanctam*.

John Wycliffe. John Wycliffe was a member of the clergy and a teacher at Oxford University in England in the late 1300s. He attacked the wealth of the church, immorality among the clergy, and the pope's claim to absolute authority. He seemed driven to replace the authority of the church, which he felt had been discredited, with that of the Bible. To allow this to occur, in about 1382 Wycliffe promoted the first translation of the entire Bible from Latin into English. This enabled people to read and interpret scripture for themselves.

Jan Hus. Wycliffe's books were widely read both in England and in Europe. His writings influenced Jan Hus of Bohemia, a rector at the University of Prague. Hus became popular with the people of Bohemia by denouncing abuses in the church, but he angered the clergy and was excommunicated in 1411. Hus appeared before the Council of Constance to answer charges of heresy. In 1415 the council tried and condemned him as a heretic and ordered him burned at the stake.

By the end of the 1400s, the church seemed to have weathered the worst of its troubles. The demand for councils had died away, and the popes still held authority over the church. Yet, ideas had taken hold among the laity that would later reappear to challenge the spiritual and moral authority of the church.

Section 6 Review

1. **Define** Babylonian Captivity, Great Schism
2. **Identify** Boniface VIII, John Wycliffe, Jan Hus
3. **Locate and Explain the Significance** Avignon, Prague
4. **Analyzing Ideas** What caused the decline of the church's temporal power after the reign of Innocent III?
5. **Summarizing Ideas (a)** What were the Babylonian Captivity and the Great Schism? **(b)** How did they weaken the church?
6. **Understanding Ideas** What ideas arose in the 1300s and early 1400s among the laity that challenged the spiritual and moral authority of the church?

Chapter 11 Review

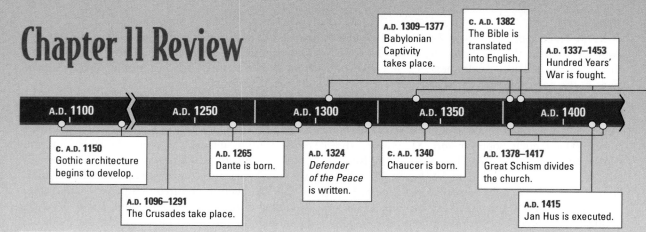

A.D. 1309–1377
Babylonian Captivity takes place.

C. A.D. 1382
The Bible is translated into English.

A.D. 1337–1453
Hundred Years' War is fought.

A.D. 1100   A.D. 1250   A.D. 1300   A.D. 1350   A.D. 1400

C. A.D. 1150
Gothic architecture begins to develop.

A.D. 1265
Dante is born.

A.D. 1324
Defender of the Peace is written.

C. A.D. 1340
Chaucer is born.

A.D. 1378–1417
Great Schism divides the church.

A.D. 1096–1291
The Crusades take place.

A.D. 1415
Jan Hus is executed.

Chapter Summary

The following list contains the key concepts you have learned about the Crusades, the revival of trade, and the beginnings of nations in the High Middle Ages.

1. The Crusades were organized by Christians chiefly to regain the Holy Land from the Turks. The Crusades had several important effects on Europe: the introduction of new weapons, increased royal power, the weakening of feudal lords, and intellectual and commercial stimulation.

2. Even before the Crusades, trade had begun to revive in Europe. Italians acted as distributors for traders from Asia and from central and northern Europe. Flanders had great commercial importance, as did the trading cities of the Hanseatic League. Trade was aided by fairs and led to the development of a monetary and banking system.

3. Towns grew as trade revived. Townspeople gained important rights, including freedom, town justice, and commercial privileges. Merchants and craft workers organized guilds.

4. Medieval culture flourished with the revival of towns. Vernacular languages developed and were used by such writers as Dante and Chaucer. At great universities, scholastic philosophers, including Abelard and Aquinas, sought to reconcile faith and reason. In this period, Romanesque church architecture gave way to the Gothic style.

5. National governments continued to grow stronger. After the Hundred Years' War and the Wars of the Roses, England's government was centralized under Henry VII, founder of the Tudor dynasty.

6. In France, the martyrdom of Joan of Arc and the French victory over the English in the Hundred Years' War spurred patriotism. Louis XI added much land to the royal territory and helped unify France.

7. In Spain, Ferdinand and Isabella created a strong monarchy but weakened the country by driving out the Moors and Jews. Germany and Italy remained disunited until the 1800s.

8. The Babylonian Captivity and the Great Schism weakened papal authority. Criticism came from individuals within the church, including John Wycliffe and Jan Hus.

Reviewing Important Terms

On a separate sheet of paper, supply the term that correctly completes each statement.

1. _____ _____ is the term used to describe everyday speech that varies from place to place.

2. _____ was the attempt of medieval philosophers to reconcile faith and reason.

3. A method of production in which the workers performed their jobs in their homes was called the _____ _____.

4. The _____ were expeditions by Christians to regain the Holy Land from the Turks.

5. In a(n) _____ _____, goods are exchanged for other goods without the use of money.

6. A skilled artisan who worked for a master for daily wages was a(n) _____.

7. In a(n) _____ _____, land, labor, and capital are controlled by individuals.

8. In the Middle Ages, the church prohibited _____, or the charging of interest on loans.

9. In medieval towns, the organization that gained a monopoly, the sole right to trade there, was called a(n) _____ _____.

10. In the late Middle Ages, the skilled workers who were engaged in manufacturing formed _____ _____.

11. ___ is a feeling of loyalty to one's country as a whole.

12. Being a(n) ___ was the first stage of training in a craft.

Developing Critical Thinking Skills

1. **Summarizing Ideas** What was the original purpose of the Crusades? What were their actual effects?

2. **Analyzing Ideas** How did the teachings of Peter Abelard and Thomas Aquinas build on those of Aristotle?

3. **Comparing Ideas** Describe the Romanesque and Gothic styles of church architecture.

4. **Understanding Cause and Effect** What caused trade to increase in Europe in the late Middle Ages, and how did this affect the economy of Europe?

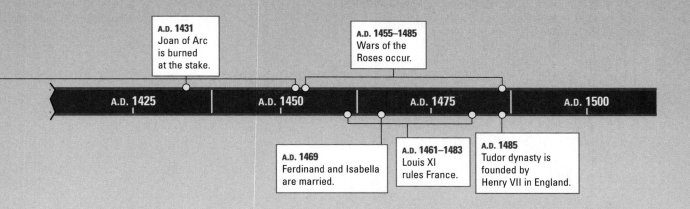

Relating Geography to History

Use the map of the Crusades on page 252 to complete the following exercises.

1. Examine the bodies of water, cities, and islands that crusaders passed through during the Crusades. Write a summary statement about the areas that were affected.
2. Speculate about the positive and negative consequences that these areas experienced during the time of the Crusades.

Relating Past to Present

1. In the late Middle Ages, the longbow, the cannon, and the pike changed the nature of warfare and contributed to the decline of feudalism. Do library research to find out more about medieval weapons and also research the weapons developed in the 1900s. What effects have these weapons developed in the 1900s had on the modern world?
2. Consult your village, town, or city planning agency to answer the following questions. **(a)** What are some of the major building code regulations for housing? How are sewage, clean water, and garbage disposal provided for or regulated? **(b)** Compare your information with what you have learned about towns and cities in the Middle Ages.

Applying History Study Skills

Before completing this activity, review Building History Study Skills on page 265. Read the following excerpt from a poem written by a French noble in the 1100s. Then answer the questions.

> "I love the springtide of the year
> When leaves and blossoms do abound,
> And well it pleases me to hear
> The birds that make the woods resound
> With their exulting voices.
> And very well it pleases me
> Tents and pavilions pitched to see,
> And oh, my heart rejoices
> To see armed knights in panoply [full armor]
> Of war on meadow and on lea [pasture].
> . . . .

> And well I like a noble lord
> When boldly the attack he leads,
> For he, whene'er he wields his sword,
> Inspires his men by his brave deeds,
> Their hearts with courage filling.
> When tide of battle's at the flood,
> Each soldier then, in fighting mood,
> To follow should be willing,
> For no man is accounted good
> Till blows he's given and withstood."

1. Why does the poet long for the springtime?
2. How does he feel about the fighting lord?
3. What is the theme of the poem, and which sentences help you identify the theme?
4. How is the poem similar to the troubadour's love song on page 265? How is it different?

Search the Internet through the HRW Web site for information on the Black Death in Europe in the 1300s. Find as many details as you can about the course of the disease and its effects on communities and individuals. Then write a newspaper article about the plague as if you were living at the time.

HRW
GO TO: go.hrw.com
KEYWORD: SCØ Black Death

Building Your Portfolio

1. **Writing a Report** Using encyclopedias or books on the Middle Ages, collect additional information about one of the Crusades. Then imagine you are a crusader and write an imaginary diary entry about your experiences on your journey to the Holy Land. Place your diary entry in your portfolio.
2. **Presenting an Oral Report** Find one or more books on medieval knighthood. Read about the values of chivalry and the love of battle. Present an oral report on your findings to the class. Place your notes and other research material in your portfolio.

The Civilizations of East Asia

TIME

A.D. 552–1573

| 3.7 million B.C. | 4000 B.C. | A.D. 2100 |

A.D. 552–1573

PLACE

China, Japan, Korea, and mainland Southeast Asia

Japan

Mainland Southeast Asia

China

Korea

Tang dynasty silk painting

Significance

From about A.D. 552 to 1573, great civilizations flourished in East Asia. The Chinese and Japanese established complex patterns of government, society, and culture.

The Chinese developed a remarkably inventive civilization. Chinese culture extended far beyond the country's borders. Korea felt China's strong influence, although it managed to maintain its own political and cultural identities.

A different civilization emerged on the islands of Japan. Although the Japanese too were enormously influenced by Chinese culture, they also developed their own distinct culture and created long-lasting traditions. Although influenced by India and China, mainland Southeast Asia developed its own distinct cultures.

Terms to Define

Zen	shogun
Diamond Sutra	samurai
kami	Bushido
Shinto	seppuku
The Tale of Genji	daimyo

People to Identify

Li Bai	Marco Polo
Du Fu	Rabban Bar Sauma
Empress Wu	Fujiwara
Genghis Khan	Minamoto
Kublai Khan	Ashikaga
Batu	Yi
Golden Horde	Sejong

Places to Locate

Grand Canal	Kyoto
Changan	Kamakura
Kaifeng	Korea
Beijing	Vietnam
Hangzhou	Cambodia
Karakorum	

Chapter Theme Questions

- **Politics and Law** How might a stable government promote social, cultural, and economic growth?
- **War and Diplomacy** What might occur when conquerors are very different from the people they conquer?
- **Cross-cultural Interaction** How might cultures mix yet remain unique?

D eveloped in about the 1200s and written down several centuries later, a strict code of chivalry and conduct called Bushido acted as a guide for the Japanese samurai, or warriors. Reminiscent of the standards expected of the knights during the medieval period in Europe, one part of the code stated:

❝One who is a samurai must before all things keep constantly in mind, by day and by night, from the morning when he takes up his chopsticks to eat his New Year's breakfast to Old Year's night when he pays his yearly bills, the fact that he has to die. That is his chief business. If he is always mindful of this, he will be able to live in accordance with the paths of Loyalty and Filial Duty, will avoid myriads of evils and adversities, keep himself free from disease and calamity and moreover enjoy a long life. He will also be a fine personality with many admirable qualities.❞

Section 1

China Under the Sui, Tang, and Song Dynasties

Focus Questions

- **What important changes occurred during the Tang and Song dynasties?**
- **What were the great accomplishments of Chinese culture in this period?**
- **How did the Chinese people live during this time?**

In Europe the Western Roman Empire never recovered after its collapse in the late 400s. In China, the Han dynasty collapsed at about the same time. However, the Huns and other nomadic invaders from Tibet and Mongolia eventually settled down, established kingdoms, and adopted Chinese customs. In the late 500s, a unified empire was established in China. By the mid-600s, China was being ruled by

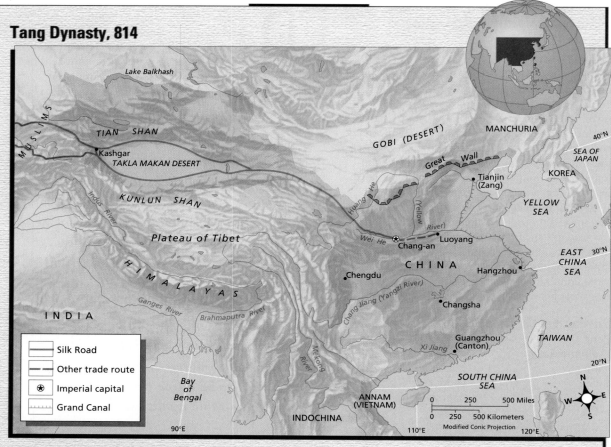

Tang Dynasty, 814

Learning from Maps The Tang rulers extended their empire westward into Central Asia and southward into Indochina.

❓ **Human-Environment Interaction** Along what waterway could Tang people travel between the cities of Tianjin and Hangzhou?

a dynasty that was stronger, wealthier, and grander than the Han dynasty.

The Sui and Tang Dynasties

The short-lived Sui dynasty succeeded in reuniting China in 589. In their brief period of power, Sui rulers began working on one of the engineering marvels of the ancient world—the Grand Canal. By skillfully using existing waterways in east-central China and also by digging new ones, the builders of the Grand Canal linked northern and southern China for the first time in history.

The Sui rulers proved overambitious in administration, trying to do too much at once. They tried unsuccessfully to conquer southern Manchuria and northern Korea and were defeated by invading Turks in

615. An uprising in 618 ended the Sui dynasty and ushered in a new dynasty—the Tang.

Expansion under the Tang. The early Tang rulers defeated the invading Turks to the north and west and extended China's frontiers farther west than ever before. (See map on this page.) Tang rulers made contact with India and the Muslim Empire, and Chinese ideas greatly influenced China's eastern neighbors, Korea and Japan. This contact with other peoples also influenced and enhanced the culture of China.

The Tang established their capital at Chang-an. During the 700s and 800s, a total of about 2 million people lived in and around Chang-an, making it the largest city in the world at that time. The city served not only as the center of government but also as a center of culture. People from many parts of the

Tang Camel

This lively ceramic figure of a two-humped camel was used as a tomb figure during the Tang dynasty (617–907). The practice of burying pottery replicas of servants and favorite animals was widespread in ancient times. It replaced the older, more primitive custom of killing slaves and cattle to provide the dead person with company and food in the afterworld.

In addition to servants and animals, the Chinese also buried figures of musicians, dancers, bodyguards, and grooms. Although tomb figures had been made even long before the Han dynasty (202 B.C.–A.D. 220), the realistic horses and camels of the Tang period are regarded as the finest.

The brilliant colors, the sense of drama, and the joyous pose of this camel are typical of the rebirth in art that took place under Hsüan Tsung (SHOO·AHN·ZOONG), the sixth Tang emperor. During his reign, China experienced great prosperity. Ceramists began to borrow colors and motifs from Persia, India, and Syria, becoming more international in style.

world made Chang-an their home. In its marketplaces, Arabs, Persians, Jews, Greeks, and native Chinese shopped side by side.

Like the Han dynasty centuries earlier, the Tang dynasty also gave China a golden age. Although the Tang dynasty itself lasted only until 907, it began a much longer period during which China became the most powerful, the most sophisticated, and the wealthiest country in the world.

Literature under the Tang. During the Tang dynasty, numerous Chinese poets created an abundance of fine literature. Later Chinese anthologies, or literary collections, include more than 48,900 poems by almost 2,300 Tang poets. Although exact opposites in personality, two writers of the 700s represent the best of these poets.

Li Bo (Li Po), a Daoist, spent a great deal of his life seeking pleasure. His writings—happy, light, and elegant—describe the delights of life. His approach to life, however, may have been his undoing. According to Chinese legend, Li Bo became tipsy and drowned while reaching from a boat for the moon's reflection in the water.

Du Fu, on the other hand, possessed a serious, even solemn nature and devoutly followed the teachings of Confucius. His carefully written verses showed his deep concern for the suffering and tragedy of human life.

Religion in Tang China. Missionaries from India had introduced Buddhism into China during the Han dynasty. Under the Tang dynasty, however, Buddhism reached its peak in China. The Empress Wu, who ruled China from 690 to 705, was a zealous supporter of Buddhism. The only woman to hold the Chinese throne in her own right, Empress Wu was a strong leader and an able administrator.

During this time period, Buddhism was also strengthened by wealthy Buddhist believers, who donated land for monasteries. Many different sects developed, the most famous of which is known by its

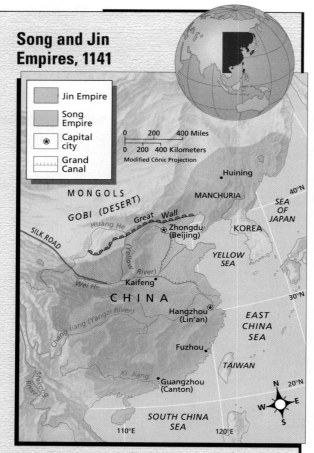

Song and Jin Empires, 1141

Legend:
- Jin Empire
- Song Empire
- ⊛ Capital city
- Grand Canal

0   200   400 Miles
0   200   400 Kilometers
Modified Conic Projection

MONGOLS
GOBI (DESERT)
MANCHURIA
Huining
SEA OF JAPAN
Great Wall
Huang He
Zhongdu (Beijing)
KOREA
SILK ROAD
Wei He
(Yellow River)
Kaifeng
YELLOW SEA
CHINA
Chang Jiang (Yangzi River)
Hangzhou (Lin'an)
EAST CHINA SEA
Fuzhou
TAIWAN
Xi Jiang
Mekong River
Guangzhou (Canton)
SOUTH CHINA SEA
110°E   120°E
40°N
30°N
20°N

Learning from Maps Foreigners established the Jin dynasty in the north, dividing China and forcing the Song dynasty into the south.

❓ Place What city became the capital of the Song dynasty?

later Japanese name, **Zen**. Zen Buddhism stressed meditation as a means to enlightenment and had a marked similarity to Daoism. Inspired by the example of Buddhism, Daoists formed sects that appealed to the masses of peasants. In later centuries, the religion of the common people in China contained a complicated blend of Buddhist and Daoist teachings.

In time the growing wealth of Buddhist monasteries began to alarm government officials. They tried to tax the monasteries' lands and sometimes seized their precious art objects for the emperor's treasury. In the

last century of the Tang dynasty, fanatical officials persecuted Buddhists. They destroyed 40,000 shrines and 4,600 monasteries and forced 260,500 monks and nuns to give up their religious duties and return to ordinary life. Buddhism continued to exist as a religion in China, but it was never again so important a force in Chinese life.

A revival of Confucianism occurred during the Tang dynasty. The government revised the civil service examinations to once again stress the Confucian classics. The construction of temples for worshipping Confucius reinforced this emphasis on Confucian philosophy. A form of Confucianism called Neo-Confucianism (*neo* means "new") continued as the main religion of China's governing classes until the early 1900s.

The decline of the Tang dynasty. The Tang dynasty reached its height in about 750 and then gradually declined under the rule of weak emperors. By 900, nomadic peoples had invaded, tax revenues had diminished, and governors in the provinces had challenged the emperor's power. The Tang dynasty was overthrown in 907, when a warlord, after having murdered the emperor several years earlier, seized the throne for himself.

China Under the Song Dynasty

In 960 Zhao Kuangyin (JOW·KWAHNG·yin) established the Song dynasty. Like the Tang, the Song faced foreign invasion and civil wars.

By the mid-900s, the principal foreign pressure came from the north, from Mongols called the Qidan (CHI·DAHN). They had occupied Chinese territory in southern Manchuria and in time invaded as far south as the Huang He. When the Qidan threatened the Song capital at Kaifeng, the Song emperors kept the peace only by paying a huge tribute. By 1042 these tributes cost the Song more than 200,000 ounces of silver annually, a tremendous economic burden.

Another Central Asian people, the Ruzhen, moved into Manchuria and took over northern China in 1126. The Ruzhen established the Jin dynasty in the north, with its capital at what is now Beijing, while Hangzhou (HANG·CHOW) became the capital of the Song dynasty in the south. (See map on page 284.)

Trade and arts. Despite the problems of the Song emperors, Chinese civilization remained at a high level under their rule. Foreign trade expanded. Hangzhou and Guangzhou (GWAHNG·JOH) were key bases for overseas commerce. A thriving caravan trade also brought in goods from Central Asia and India.

Exports included gold, silver, copper, and "cash" (strings of copper coins). At this time, porcelain—a fine, translucent pottery—became one of China's most valuable exports. Song artisans perfected the art of making porcelain, creating delicate vases with sides as thin as eggshell.

Song artists also produced beautiful landscape paintings. Inspired partly by the Daoist love of nature, they painted scenes of natural grandeur, with jagged mountain peaks rising above misty hills and rushing water. Many of these landscapes were painted on silk.

The civil service system. The Chinese further improved their civil service system during the Song dynasty. Examinations took place in the capital every three years. To qualify for these, an individual first had to pass an examination at the local level. The Song eliminated the need for sponsorship, which for years had allowed only those from influential families to take the examinations.

Because of the intense competition for civil service employment, steps had to be taken to prevent cheating and corrupt practices by government officials who might accept bribes or be swayed by friends. Candidates were identified by numbers, not names, and guards watched them take the examination. Clerks then copied the candidates' papers so that no one's handwriting would be recognized. Finally, three judges read each paper.

Great inventions. The Chinese probably developed gunpowder in the A.D. 100s, but even as late as the Tang dynasty, they used it only in firecrackers. They first used gunpowder as an explosive for war under Song rule, around the year 1100.

Printing was another momentous Chinese invention. The Chinese had learned very early how to make ink and paper. They probably took the first step toward printing in the late A.D. 100s, during the Han dynasty, when the Chinese classics were carved in stone. Artisans could copy these writings by carefully fitting damp paper over the stone inscription and patting the flat surface with soot. This resulted in a white-on-black image of the original. The next step probably came with seals of metal or wood on which an inscription was carved in reverse. By the 500s, such seals had become quite large, and the images they created resembled today's block prints.

The world's first printed book was the ***Diamond Sutra***, a Buddhist religious text printed in China in 868, during the Tang dynasty. It was made in the form of a roll of six sheets of paper pasted together. Carved blocks were used to print the words on the roll.

Movable type, which allows separate characters to be arranged freely to form words and sentences, appeared in the 1040s. The characters were made of pottery, tin, wood, or lead. This technique was not widely used in China, however. Because the Chinese language consists of so many characters, printers would have had to make a huge number of separate movable blocks to represent them all. For this reason, the Chinese preferred blocks carved with an entire page of text.

Peasant life. By about 1050, China's population was approximately 100 million people. The great majority of them were peasants, who lived and worked in the countryside. Two important changes took place in peasant life during the Tang and Song dynasties.

One change stemmed from technological improvements in agriculture. Many extensive water control projects had been built in southern China. As a result, the number of irrigated fields where rice could be grown increased. In addition, a new kind of quick-ripening rice from Southeast Asia made it possible to grow two crops of rice each year instead of only one. Also from Southeast Asia came an entirely new crop, tea, which soon became a popular drink throughout China.

Thus agricultural productivity greatly increased, especially in southern China. Peasants had more work to do than ever before, but they also had a greater chance to produce surplus food. That surplus could be sold in the many small market towns.

The second important change in the life of the peasants stemmed from an alteration in the tax system that had taken place during the Tang dynasty. Under the new policy, the government initiated a two-tax system. One tax, paid in money, was levied on family households. The amount varied according to the number of people in the household. The second tax, paid in grain, was levied on land. The effect of the new policy was to increase the tax burden on peasants. Peasants who could not pay their taxes were forced to sell their land and become tenant farmers. As tenant farmers, they paid the landlords high rents, sometimes half the crops they raised. Land became increasingly concentrated in the hands of landlords.

Peasants worked in their fields all day long to keep up with their high rents. They might earn extra money by raising silkworms or gathering herbs. Women in the peasant families sometimes made items such as straw and cloth shoes to help bring in extra income for their families. They also helped in the fields.

One relief from the daily routine was going to market. The markets provided entertainment by storytellers, musicians, and fortune-tellers, as well as the opportunity to meet with trade and craft workers from other parts of the empire. Two or three times a year, peasant families also had a chance to relax at festivals held in the villages. Everyone would gather to enjoy feasting and music. Then the daily routine of hard work would begin again.

City life. During the Song period, a larger share of China's population than ever before came to live in cities and towns. Hangzhou, the capital of the dynasty after 1127, had a population of about 2 million, with another 2 million living near the city. Marco Polo, a merchant and explorer from Venice, visited the city in the late 1200s and recorded his amazement at its size and beauty. In addition to Hangzhou, many other cities and towns, large and small, were scattered throughout the empire. Although outnumbered by rural peasants, the city dwellers dominated Chinese society and culture.

The cities of Song China bustled with activity. Huge shipments of rice, fish, and vegetables arrived daily in the marketplaces. Shops specializing in luxury goods—embroidered silks, pearl necklaces, chess sets, and printed books—lined the main streets. Shops selling noodles, candles, and other articles of everyday use were crowded into the narrow side streets and alleyways. Amusements included puppet shows, plays, and performances by dancers and acrobats on the streets.

Officials and wealthy merchants lived in fine homes surrounded by gardens and artificial lakes. Ordinary people lived in crowded apartments, with only one or two rooms for an entire family. Some people had no homes at all. They begged for food and slept wherever they could find shelter. The government set up hospitals and orphanages to help the poor. It also gave food and money to the needy after disasters. However, poverty remained a serious problem in China's cities. In times of great floods or famines, peasants would crowd into the cities and increase the number of poor people.

During this period, the status of women in Chinese society began to change. In cities their work was less needed than it had been on farms. The custom of footbinding spread among the upper classes. Footbinding was a practice in which a girl's feet were bound tightly with strips of linen, toes tucked underneath, to prevent further growth. During the Song dynasty, girls in upper-class families began to have their feet bound from the age of five. Despite its crippling effect, the custom continued among the wealthy. It was a kind of status symbol because it showed that a man was successful enough to support a woman who could not work.

Chinese food. Many of the foods found on the tables of Chinese homes and restaurants today were also served during the time of the Song dynasty. The development of agriculture in southern China made rice the basic food of the Chinese diet. Ordinary people ate rice three times a day, with small portions of dried fish or pork on the side. Wealthy people enjoyed a healthier diet. They could afford fresh fruits and vegetables and greater quantities of fish and meat.

Meat and vegetables were cut into small pieces and then stir-fried for only a few minutes. The Chinese used chopsticks instead of forks and knives, probably because they served the food already cut into bite-sized pieces. Spices and seasonings such as cinnamon, garlic, ginger, salt, sugar, honey, and soy sauce added flavor. The Chinese believed in the value of contrasting flavors—bitter, salty, sour, hot, and sweet. They tried to achieve a mixture of these flavors in the meals they cooked.

Section 1 Review

1. **Define** Zen, *Diamond Sutra*
2. **Identify** Li Bo, Du Fu, Empress Wu
3. **Locate and Explain the Significance** Grand Canal, Chang-an, Kaifeng, Beijing, Hangzhou
4. **Identifying Ideas** What important changes occurred in government and society during the Tang and Song dynasties?
5. **Summarizing Ideas** Describe two important aspects of Chinese culture.
6. **Analyzing Ideas** (a) How did peasant life change during the Tang and Song dynasties? (b) What was life like in Chinese cities?

Section 2

The Mongol Empire

Focus Questions

- How did the Mongols succeed in conquering and ruling vast areas?
- What effect did the Mongols have on China?

The nomadic peoples who lived in Central Asia, to the north and northwest of China proper, inhabited barren lands not well suited to farming.

Mongol warriors demonstrated amazing horsemanship; they exhibited such skill by shooting arrows while riding at top speeds. This manuscript from the 1200s illustrates a battle between Mongol tribes.

Living in clans, they raised horses and sheep and spent their lives moving their herds from one pasture to another. The hardships of outdoor life made these nomads sturdy and self-reliant. They were also fierce warriors. A strong leader could organize the clans into a disciplined, powerful fighting force.

Genghis Khan and the Mongols

Strong leaders emerged among the Huns and other Central Asian nomadic tribes. Many led invasions into China over the centuries. The fiercest nomadic leader of all time was the Mongol Genghis Khan, who lived from about 1162 to 1227. Originally named Temujin, he was given the title Genghis Khan, meaning "Universal Ruler," in 1206 and went on to create an immense empire. (See map on page 284.)

The Mongols inhabited the area to the north of China, a region now called Mongolia. At its height, the Mongol army consisted of about 100,000 cavalry troops. With their superior military technology and battle tactics, they were able to conquer vast and heavily populated territories.

Before the invention of firearms, warriors on horseback usually had a great advantage over soldiers on foot. Mongol cavalry troops, who took extra horses with them on campaigns, could cover up to 100 miles in a day. Specially designed saddles and iron stirrups enabled them to fire arrows with deadly accuracy while moving at full speed. On the open plains of Central Asia, they learned to make good use of their speed and mobility on horseback.

In open battle, seemingly endless columns of Mongol riders surrounded the enemy in a way similar to that of hunters surrounding wild game. Genghis Khan also successfully led the Mongols in siege warfare, a method of wearing down the enemy through constant attack or threat of attack. The use of such machines as catapults, giant crossbows mounted on stands, and bamboo-tube rockets packed with gunpowder and fired from a longbow helped the Mongols improve their siege methods. Battle provided a test of the soldiers' abilities and a way for them to acquire riches, honor, and personal power.

Mongol conquests. In the early 1200s, Mongols under Genghis Khan swept down from Karakorum, their capital. They captured the city now called Beijing and named it Khanbalik (kahn·buh·LEEK). They then turned westward, conquering Central Asia and most of Persia. Under Kublai (KOO·bluh) Khan, a grandson of Genghis Khan, the Mongols completed their conquest of China. They also conquered the area now called Tibet as well as parts of Southeast Asia. They tried unsuccessfully to conquer Japan and the rest of Southeast Asia.

Another grandson of Genghis Khan, Batu, invaded Europe around 1240, sweeping with his troops across Russia, Poland, and Hungary to the outskirts of Vienna. They plundered city after city, either killing the inhabitants or taking them as slaves. To terrified Europeans, the Mongolian forces became known as the Golden Horde—"golden" for the glittering appearance of their tents in the sun. The Mongols eventually left Poland and Hungary, but they controlled Russia for almost 200 years.

Mongol rule. The Mongol Empire was divided into four parts. These four parts remained united for about a century and then, in the 1300s, slowly began to drift apart.

In 1260 Kublai Khan, who lived from 1215 to 1294, was given the title of Great Khan and recognized as the head of the whole Mongol Empire. He introduced Chinese ceremonies to his court and relied on Chinese officials in the lower and middle ranks of the hierarchy. Kublai Khan maintained two palaces, a summer palace in Mongolia and an especially lavish one near Beijing.

China Under the Mongols

In 1271 Kublai Khan proclaimed the beginning of his own dynasty, the Yuan dynasty in northern China, with Beijing as his capital. Yuan forces defeated the Song dynasty in southern China in 1279 and ruled all of China until 1368.

Under Mongol rule, China prospered in many respects. During more than a century of invasion and warfare, its population had declined from 100 million to only 60 million. With the restoration of peace, however, the population began to increase.

Kublai extended the Grand Canal from the Huang He to Beijing, some 1,000 miles, in order to ship rice from southern China to his expanding capital city. A swift courier service operated between 10,000 stations, each about 25 miles apart and stabling hundreds of horses. Kublai also linked China to India

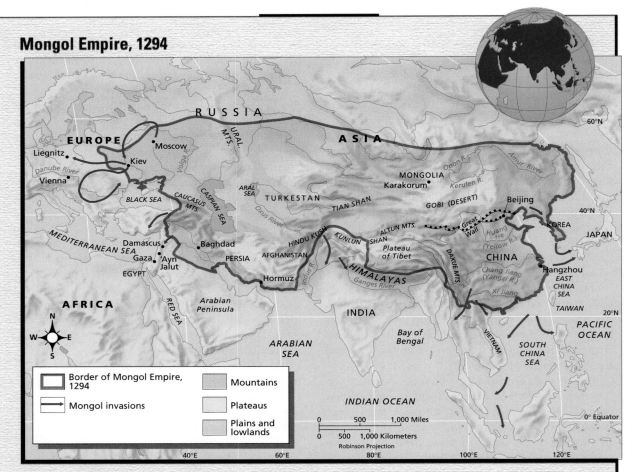

Mongol Empire, 1294

Learning from Maps   Under the leadership of Genghis Khan and his grandson Kublai Khan, Mongol soldiers captured much of Asia.

? Movement   What country did the Mongols unsuccessfully try to invade across the East China Sea?

Travelers East and West

Imagine yourself a medieval traveler, perhaps en route from the Mediterranean to East Asia in search of exotic spices, silks, jewels, and perfumes. On the road, hundreds or thousands of miles from home, you meet your fellow travelers: merchants from the East and the West carrying trade goods, pilgrims on their way to religious shrines, knights in search of employment. You have no road map, and the travel over dirt roads, by foot or on horse or mule, is difficult. If you are fortunate enough to find an inn, you will pass an uncomfortable night curled up on the floor in a corner of a room crowded with other travelers, as well as with rats, mice, and fleas. Despite the difficulties, however, you and many others in the 1300s have a passion for travel and exploration. There is a strong possibility you have heard tales of the two greatest world travelers of your time: Marco Polo and Ibn Battuta.

Illustration from *The Travels of Marco Polo* showing navigators in the Indian Ocean using an astrolabe

Marco Polo began his career of world exploration when he was 17 years old. In 1271 he set out from his home in Venice, Italy, with his father and uncle, who were Venetian merchants. After three years of traveling by ship, then by camel, they arrived in China at the summer palace of the Mongol ruler Kublai Khan. Evidently impressed with Polo's knowledge of four languages, Kublai Khan engaged him as an emissary. For 17 years, Polo traveled throughout China. After 24 years and nearly 15,000 miles, the three Polos returned to Venice. Marco Polo wrote an account of his travels in a book called *Description of the World*, which was widely read throughout Europe.

Ibn Battuta, who was born in 1304 in Morocco, North Africa, began his travels a year after Marco Polo's death and journeyed an even greater distance than Polo. At the age of 21, Ibn Battuta's pilgrimage to the Muslim holy cities of Mecca and Medina (Al-Madīnah) sparked his enthusiasm for travel. During the course of his travels, Ibn Battuta journeyed to Egypt, Syria, Baghdad, East Africa, Asia Minor, the Balkans, southern Russia, Central Asia, Afghanistan, India, and China. Twenty-four years after his departure, Ibn Battuta returned to Morocco by traveling through the East Indies. Once settled in North Africa, he described his impressions and experiences in a book called the *Rihla*.

Kublai Khan giving his golden seal to the Polos

Kublai Khan united China into one vast empire that enjoyed prosperity during his reign. His successors, however, a series of weak governors, witnessed the collapse of the dynasty.

and Persia by roads, which greatly improved trade. However, heavy taxes during the Yuan period also harmed the economy.

Contacts with Europeans. During Mongol rule, contacts between Europe and China increased. King Louis IX of France and the pope in Rome sent ambassadors to China during the 1200s. Christian missionaries, as well as the famous Venetian merchant Marco Polo, also traveled to China. Marco Polo's Chinese counterpart, Rabban Bar Sauma of Beijing, journeyed across Asia to Persia, then to Constantinople, and eventually to Italy, where he talked with the pope. Bar Sauma also went to France, where he met King Philip IV and visited the University of Paris. Representatives of all nations and faiths were received by Kublai, including artisans from France and Italy.

Chinese-Mongol relations. The Yuan dynasty had brought certain benefits to China, but a strong antagonism existed between the conquerors and the conquered. To begin with, their languages differed. Even more important, however, was the discrimination the Mongols practiced. Important positions in the government could be held only by Mongols or other non-Chinese people. Mongol laws provided for more severe punishments for Chinese criminals than

for non-Chinese ones. The Mongols also prohibited marriage between people of different groups.

When Kublai Khan died in 1294, he left China to weak successors. Four Mongol emperors ruled China between 1320 and 1329 alone. During the period after Kublai's death, the country experienced many problems. The Huang He flooded, destroying crops and causing famine to spread throughout the land. Many organizations calling for revolution sprang up. Finally, in 1368, the Yuan dynasty came to an end with the overthrow of the last Mongol emperor.

Nevertheless, the Mongols clearly influenced China in several positive ways. The Mongols brought peace and expanded contact with Europe. They improved communications and made local governments directly responsible to the central government in Beijing. Later Chinese dynasties built on the Mongols' political reforms by concentrating greater power in the hands of the emperor.

Section 2 Review

1. **Identify** Genghis Khan, Kublai Khan, Batu, Golden Horde, Marco Polo, Rabban Bar Sauma
2. **Locate and Explain the Significance** Karakorum
3. **Understanding Ideas** How were the Mongols able to quickly conquer so much land in Asia?
4. **Analyzing Ideas** What were the positive and negative effects of the Mongol rule of China?

Section 3

Japan, Korea, and Southeast Asia

Focus Questions
- **What factors influenced Japan's development?**
- **What was the strongest influence on the culture of Korea?**
- **Which cultures shaped the development of mainland Southeast Asia?**

Japan consists of a chain of islands in the western Pacific Ocean off the east coast of Asia. Most of the country's large population lives on the four main islands: Honshu (HAWN·shoo), Hokkaido (hoh·KY·doh), Kyushu (KYOO·shoo), and Shikoku (shee·KOH·koo).

The Physical Setting

Because Japan is so mountainous, only about one fifth of its area can be used for farming. This farmland, however, produces a great deal of food, thanks to abundant rainfall, plentiful sunlight, long growing seasons, and the diligence of Japanese farmers. An extensive network of rivers provides easy irrigation and, in modern times, a source of electric power. The rains also support heavy forest growth. Nature is not entirely kind to Japan, however. Earthquakes, tidal waves, and typhoons often strike the islands and can cause extensive damage.

Until modern times, the seas surrounding Japan shielded the islands from foreign influences. This protection allowed the Japanese to choose whether they wanted to have contact with other peoples. At times in their history, they have been very interested in the outside world, especially China. At other times, they have preferred to live in isolation.

The Mongols under Kublai Khan unsuccessfully tried twice to conquer Japan. In 1281, for example, an immense Mongol fleet carrying more than 150,000 soldiers assembled to invade Japan. However, an extraordinarily powerful typhoon devastated the invasion fleet, a storm that the grateful Japanese considered the "divine wind," or kamikaze.

Japan's Beginnings

The majority of people in Japan are descendants of migrants from the Asian mainland who first came to the Japanese islands in prehistoric times. By the first centuries A.D., these migrants had organized themselves in clans. The most powerful clans lived on the island of Honshu. Over the past 2000 years, the Japanese people have established a strong and unified cultural identity.

Religion played an important role in the emergence of a unified Japanese society. From earliest times, the Japanese believed in gods or nature spirits called **kami.** These kami, they believed, lived in such natural objects as sand, waterfalls, and great trees. Many Japanese clans trace their origins to a particular kami. Now called **Shinto**, this religion has no established scripture or specific doctrine. Shinto worship involves prayers and rituals to satisfy the kami and to appeal for help, especially for fertility and bountiful crops. Shinto is also concerned with ritual cleanliness.

Shinto also played an important role in the unification of Japan under imperial rule. Early emperors

What If?

The "Divine Wind"
Suppose the wind had been calm on that day in 1281 when the Mongols were set to invade Japan. What might have been the consequences?

apparently acted as chief priests for the Shinto religion. In the entire history of Japan, only one imperial family, the Yamato clan, has ruled. The first Yamato emperor was enthroned in the A.D. 400s, making it the longest unbroken dynasty in the history of the world. According to tradition, the Japanese emperors claimed descent from the sun goddess. This belief was not officially denied until 1946, after Japan's defeat in World War II.

Early History of Japan

Only sketchy records of early Japanese history exist. The Chinese, however, knew about Japan before A.D. 100. Chinese writing was introduced in Japan by way of Korea and adapted in the early 700s. Another Chinese influence was Buddhism, which was formally introduced in 552. At first the emperor's conservative advisers were uncertain about the new religion. One of them even threw a statue of Buddha into a canal after an epidemic that he interpreted as a sign of the Japanese gods' anger over the new religion. Some years later, however, when another epidemic broke out, the advisers interpreted the illness as a sign of the new religion's power, and the emperor allowed Buddhist temples to be rebuilt. Buddhism then won many converts among nobles at the emperor's court.

In later centuries, Buddhism spread among the common people and became an important part of Japanese life. It did not replace Shinto, however. For most of Japanese history, people believed in both religions at the same time. They celebrated important events, such as births and marriages, according to Shinto rituals. They held funerals according to Buddhist rituals.

Chinese influence. Japanese adoption of Chinese writing and Buddhism led to the introduction of other Chinese ideas and ways of life. The Japanese made use of Chinese governmental methods, artistic designs, road engineering, medical knowledge, weights and measures, and styles of clothing.

The Japanese sent their first ambassadors to China in 607. Japanese students returning from China in the 640s believed Japan inferior in various ways and worked to have more aspects of Chinese culture adopted in their country.

In 702 Japan's emperor issued a law code modeled on one from China's Tang dynasty. The code regulated all aspects of life in Japan and established a highly centralized government under the emperor. In 794 the Japanese built a capital named Heian (HAY·ahn), which became the modern city of Kyoto (KYOH·toh). In Heian, members of the ruling class began to develop a distinctive culture less dependent on Chinese models. For example, earlier poetry had been written in Chinese. Japanese poets now began writing in their own language.

Upper-class Japanese women. Women played an important role in the life of the Japanese court in Heian. Their contributions to literature were especially distinctive. Several women wrote diaries. Around the year 1000, Lady Murasaki Shikibu wrote *The Tale of Genji,* the world's first novel. It tells the story of Prince Genji, the perfect courtier. Written in a quiet, sensitive style and filled with poems about the beauties of nature, it became one of the masterpieces of Japanese and world literature.

Feudal Japan

Although emperors continued to reign in Heian, after the early 800s the centralized political system adopted from China gradually fell into decline. In its place, Japan developed a system of local power that in many ways resembled feudalism, the social system that prevailed in Europe at this time.

In Japan the feudal system contained two conflicting sources of power. One was the central government, in which an important family held power in the name of the emperor. The other source of power consisted of powerful local landholders who established and led a class of warriors.

Central government. The first family to gain control over the emperor and to use his power to their advantage were the Fujiwara. By holding important government offices and by marrying into the emperor's family, the Fujiwara successfully gained control of the central government from the mid-800s to the mid-1100s.

In 1156 civil war broke out when the Taira clan challenged the Minamoto clan for power. Eventually, the Minamoto emerged triumphant. In 1192 the emperor granted Minamoto Yoritomo the title of **shogun,** or general. While the emperor remained the theoretical source of legitimate authority in Japan, real power now rested with the shogun. In addition to being the chief military officer of the central government, the shogun controlled finance, law, the courts, and appointments to office. From his own capital at Kamakura, Yoritomo established a military government to rule Japan.

The center of political intrigue now shifted from the imperial court to the new Kamakura shogunate. Not long after Yoritomo's death, power shifted to the Hojo clan, who ruled as regents in the name of puppet Minamoto shoguns. Although the Hojo were able to successfully repel the Mongol invaders, their power, too, soon declined.

In 1331 the Emperor Go-Daigo attempted to restore the power of the imperial court. Though Go-Daigo managed to destroy the Kamakura shogunate, he never regained real power. Instead, one of his generals, Ashikaga Takauji (ah·shee·KAH·gah tah·KOW·jee), claimed the shogunate for his own clan. Ruling from their new capital at Kyoto, the Ashikaga shoguns ruled for nearly two and a half centuries.

Local rule. The leading families and their shoguns wielded power in the central government, but their power did not extend to the local level. There wealthy landlords held power. The landlords hired warriors called **samurai** to protect themselves. In some respects, the samurai were similar to the feudal knights in Europe. A samurai was fiercely devoted to his lord and his clan. His power rested on his skill with the sword.

The samurai followed a code of behavior called **Bushido**—"way of the warrior"—that stressed bravery, loyalty, and honor. Samurai were expected to endure great physical hardship without complaint and to have no fear of death. If they displeased their lords or were defeated in battle, they might practice **seppuku,** ceremonial suicide. Also known as hara-kiri, or "belly slitting," seppuku was a way to avoid the shame and dishonor that would accompany disobedience or defeat.

In time local lords known as **daimyo** (DY·mee·oh)— "great names"—acquired great power. During the Ashikaga shogunate, these lords and their samurai became the most powerful people in Japan. The Ashikaga retained control of the shogunate until 1573 but had no significant power after about 1460. Real power rested with the many daimyo, who then began

Building History Study Skills

READ
WRITE
INTERPRET
CONNECT
THINK

Interpreting History: Reading a Chart

Charts are visual ways of organizing information to show relationships. For example, a time line is a chart for recording the dates and order of events. A classification chart groups pieces of information so that they can be compared easily. An organization chart shows relationships within a system or group, using connecting lines to show who has authority over whom. A flowchart illustrates the steps in a process. A family tree diagrams the structure of a family.

How to Read a Chart
To read a chart, follow these steps.
1. Identify the type of chart and its purpose.
2. Identify the details.
3. Relate the details to each other.

Developing the Skill
The chart to the right is an organization chart. It records the structure of Japanese society under the feudal system. The emperor is at the top of the feudal structure. Under him is the shogun. The daimyo are under the shogun, the samurai under the daimyo, and the merchants, peasants, farmers, and craft workers are at the bottom of the structure.

The chart's dotted lines show weak or formal rule. The solid lines show real power. The relationship of the samurai to the daimyo can be seen, as can the relationship of the daimyo to the shogun and that of the shogun to the emperor. By reading the chart, you can see clearly that the daimyo possessed great power in feudal Japan.

Practicing the Skill
Using the information chart in this feature, draw an organization chart that shows the structure of the United States government. You may need to use an American government textbook to find the information necessary to practice this skill.

To apply this skill, see Applying History Study Skills on page 293.

A samurai warrior on horseback

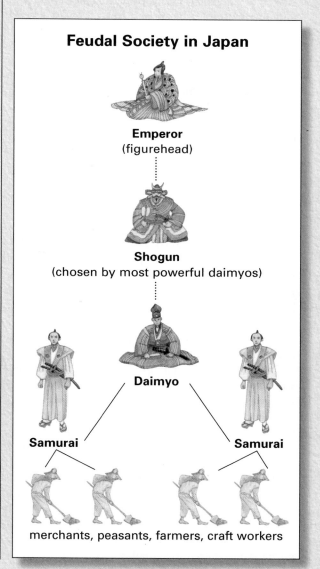

Feudal Society in Japan

Emperor
(figurehead)

Shogun
(chosen by most powerful daimyos)

Daimyo

Samurai   **Samurai**

merchants, peasants, farmers, craft workers

to fight among themselves for supremacy. For about a century, Japan had no effective central government.

Life in Feudal Japan

As a consequence of the struggles for power, warfare was a frequent occurrence in feudal Japan. Nevertheless, considerable economic and cultural growth took place during the feudal period.

The daimyo encouraged peasants to grow more crops because larger yields meant more taxes for the daimyo. They also promoted and taxed trade, financing their military campaigns with the money they received.

For people of lower status, the instability and frequent warfare offered a chance to rise in the world. Any man who could use a sword or a lance could join a daimyo's army. If he proved himself to be a good fighter and leader, he might be promoted to a higher rank. Smaller landholders in one region might join together to put pressure on the daimyo or even gain control of the local government.

The spread of Buddhism. A religious awakening also occurred during the feudal period in Japan. Buddhists established new sects, including several that taught that salvation could come through faith alone. According to the older Buddhist sects, a person had to make contributions to monasteries and study Buddhist scriptures to achieve salvation. Because only wealthy people could afford to do that, the new sects appealed to ordinary people.

Zen Buddhism, a sect introduced from China in the late 1100s, particularly interested warriors. Zen stressed salvation through enlightenment, not through faith, and taught that the life of the body was not important. To achieve enlightenment, a person had to engage in long hours of meditation and rigorous self-discipline. Warriors found that practicing Zen helped give them the courage and determination they needed to fight.

Zen and Japanese culture. The Ashikaga shoguns strongly supported Zen Buddhism. They built Zen monasteries throughout the country and encouraged the artistic efforts of Zen monks. Several new art forms inspired by Zen developed during the late 1300s and early 1400s, at the height of Ashikaga power. One was landscape architecture, the art of designing gardens. By the careful arrangement of rocks, trees, and water, Zen believers tried to represent the essential beauty of nature.

Another new art form was the tea ceremony, a ritual designed to produce spiritual calm. A few people would gather in a small, simply furnished room that overlooked a garden. One would make tea with slow, choreographed movements, while the others sat quietly. Then they all drank the tea, admired the pottery bowls in which it was served, and enjoyed the beauties of nature in the garden outside.

Yet another artistic expression of Zen was the Noh play. First performed in the 1300s, Noh plays were highly stylized dance dramas. They might be on religious, historical, or romantic themes. Like Greek plays, Noh plays were performed on a bare stage by male actors wearing masks while a chorus chanted the story.

Civilization in Korea

Korea occupies the rugged, mountainous peninsula south of Manchuria on the east coast of Asia, across a sea channel from Japan. (See map on opposite page.) China controlled the peninsula for much of Korea's history and, as a result, greatly influenced Korea's political and cultural development. As early as 300 B.C., Chinese migrants began bringing their culture to Korea.

China conquered Korea in 109 B.C. to 108 B.C., during the Han dynasty. After the fall of the Han dynasty, three independent Korean kingdoms, with shifting boundaries, controlled the peninsula. The kingdom of Silla eventually emerged as the strongest and unified the country by about A.D. 670. During the rule of the Chinese Tang dynasty, Korea maintained much of its independence but acknowledged China's dominance. Korea then became part of the Mongol Empire, and when the Mongols were expelled, a new Korean dynasty, the Yi, was founded in 1392. This dynasty survived for centuries, until Japan annexed Korea in 1910.

Buddhism had been introduced to Korea in the A.D. 300s and had a great influence on the country. Buddhist teachings can be seen in Korea's culture, philosophy, and morality. During the period of the three kingdoms, Buddhism was regarded as the state religion. Zen, which was introduced in the 700s, became the dominant form of Buddhism.

Scholars studied the Confucian classics, and the government adopted the Chinese civil service system, based on the teachings of Confucius. The Koreans did not, however, copy the Chinese in all respects. They retained both their native dress and their own language. Sejong, a Yi emperor who ruled in the mid-1400s, directed the development of a Korean alphabet. In fact, the Koreans invented a method of printing using movable metal type that the Chinese later adopted.

Korea and Japan

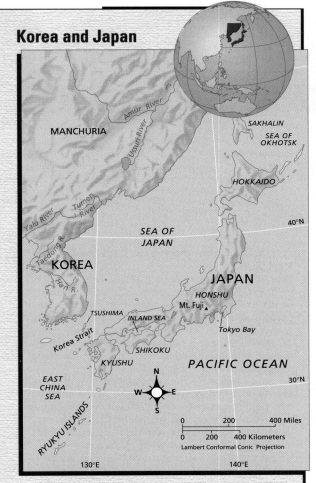

Learning from Maps Zen Buddhism spread from China to both Korea and Japan.

? Location Approximately how much distance across the Korea Strait separates Korea and Japan?

Civilization in Mainland Southeast Asia

Mainland Southeast Asia consists of the modern-day countries of Cambodia, Laos, Vietnam, Myanmar, Malaysia, and Thailand (formerly Siam). China is to the north of this region, and India borders it on the northwest. As a result, the region shows the influences of both of these cultures.

China controlled the northern part of Vietnam, called Nam Viet, during much of its history. The Vietnamese tried several times to gain independence, finally succeeding in 939. Not long after this, however, Vietnam fell into chaos. Local warlords struggled for power until several dynasties were established that stabilized and developed the nation.

China heavily influenced the culture of Vietnam. Vietnam adopted Mahayana Buddhism from the Chinese, which ultimately became the guiding element of the Vietnamese culture. Daoism and Confucianism also contributed to the development of the Vietnamese culture and society. In addition, Vietnam used the writing system and political structure of the Chinese.

Much of the rest of mainland Southeast Asia was influenced by Indian culture. Early in the history of Southeast Asia, people from India began to settle in the region, many of them Hindu and Buddhist missionaries. The Sanskrit language came into wide use, helping to spread Indian literature. Evidence of the Indian cultural impact can still be found in the southern part of the Malay Peninsula. In present-day Cambodia, ruins of the city of Angkor Thom and the huge temple of Angkor Wat offer reminders of Indian influence. Reliefs with scenes from the Hindu epics adorn Angkor Wat, one of the architectural wonders of the Far East.

Centered in modern-day Cambodia, the Khmer Empire grew to control much of Southeast Asia during its height, from about 850 to 1250. The Khmers embraced the Indian principle of a god-king for many years but eventually rebelled against these god-kings. Instead, the Khmers adopted a sect of Theraveda Buddhism, which had no use for elaborate ceremonies and temples such as Angkor Wat. Theraveda Buddhism became the predominant form of Buddhism in Southeast Asia.

Section 3 Review

1. **Define** kami, Shinto, *The Tale of Genji*, shogun, samurai, Bushido, seppuku, daimyo
2. **Identify** Fujiwara, Minamoto, Ashikaga, Yi, Sejong
3. **Locate and Explain the Significance** Kyoto, Kamakura, Korea, Vietnam, Cambodia
4. **Understanding Ideas** **(a)** What were China's major contributions to and influences on Japan? **(b)** What other factors influenced the development of Japanese society?
5. **Identifying Cause and Effect** What effect did years of Chinese domination have on Korean culture?
6. **Summarizing Ideas** Describe the influences of China and India on the countries of mainland Southeast Asia.

Chapter 12 Review

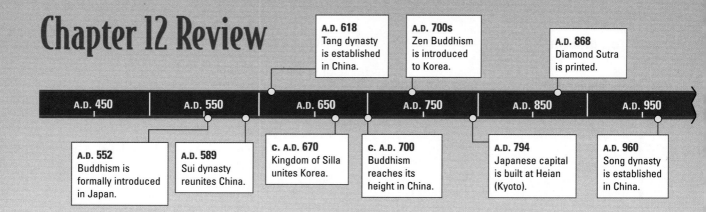

A.D. 618
Tang dynasty is established in China.

A.D. 700s
Zen Buddhism is introduced to Korea.

A.D. 868
Diamond Sutra is printed.

A.D. 552
Buddhism is formally introduced in Japan.

A.D. 589
Sui dynasty reunites China.

C. A.D. 670
Kingdom of Silla unites Korea.

C. A.D. 700
Buddhism reaches its height in China.

A.D. 794
Japanese capital is built at Heian (Kyoto).

A.D. 960
Song dynasty is established in China.

Chapter Summary

The following list contains the key concepts you have learned about the civilizations of China, Japan, Korea, and mainland Southeast Asia.

1. A unified empire was reestablished in China in 589 by the Sui dynasty. The Sui's greatest accomplishment was the beginning of the Grand Canal, which linked northern and southern China for the first time in history.
2. During the Tang and Song dynasties, the Chinese civil service system was perfected. Important innovations in the use of gunpowder and printing were made during these dynasties.
3. In the 1200s, the nomadic Mongols of Central Asia were united into a powerful fighting force under Genghis Khan and later his grandsons Kublai Khan and Batu. They conquered China, Persia, and much of eastern Europe.
4. Mongol rule brought economic growth to China. Also under the Mongols, population increased, roads and canals were built, and trade developed with other peoples. Though the Chinese resented the Mongols, Chinese dynasties adopted the Mongols' political method of concentrating greater power in the hands of the emperor.
5. Japan was influenced by China but created its own distinct culture. Its island location made it safe from foreign invasion. Japan developed a political

system in which there was both central and local power.
6. The Shinto religion played an important role in helping unite Japanese society. Shinto lacks established scripture and doctrine but relies on the performance of prayers and rituals to satisfy numerous gods or nature spirits called kami. Japanese emperors claimed divine descent from the sun goddess. In all its history, Japan has been ruled by only one imperial family.
7. Japan developed a feudal political system. The central government was controlled by the shogun, who held power in the name of the emperor. At the local level, power was in the hands of daimyo, local landlords, and the warrior samurai. At times the daimyo fought each other for power.
8. Korea, although dominated by China for most of its history, managed to develop its own culture. The Koreans had their own native dress as well as their own language and developed their own alphabet. Movable type was invented in Korea.
9. The countries of mainland Southeast Asia were strongly influenced by China and India. Northern Vietnam was controlled by China for much of its history. Cambodia and the other countries of Southeast Asia were more influenced by the religions and cultures of India.

Reviewing Important Terms

On a separate sheet of paper, supply the term that correctly completes each statement.

1. _____ was a ceremonial suicide in Japan.
2. The chief officer of a Japanese emperor who became the agent of the ruling family was the _____ .
3. _____ were warriors in Japan.
4. The _____ were local rulers in Japan who commanded samurai and gradually acquired great power.

Developing Critical Thinking Skills

1. **Analyzing Ideas (a)** What agricultural improvements took place in China during the Tang and Song

dynasties? **(b)** What part of China was most affected by these changes?
2. **Comparing Ideas** How was the role of emperor in Japan different from the role of emperor in China?
3. **Analyzing Ideas** In what ways did the Chinese influence the culture of Korea?

Relating Geography to History

Using the map of China on page 70 and the map of the Tang Dynasty on page 278, list the physical obstacles a merchant would have had to overcome in his travels along the Silk Road.

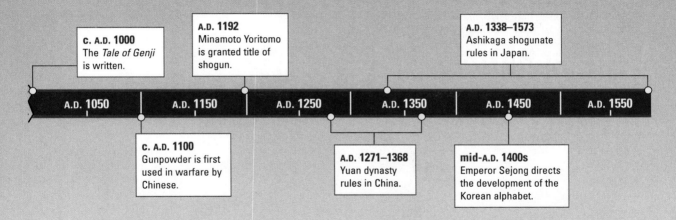

c. A.D. 1000
The *Tale of Genji* is written.

A.D. 1192
Minamoto Yoritomo is granted title of shogun.

A.D. 1338–1573
Ashikaga shogunate rules in Japan.

A.D. 1050 | **A.D. 1150** | **A.D. 1250** | **A.D. 1350** | **A.D. 1450** | **A.D. 1550**

c. A.D. 1100
Gunpowder is first used in warfare by Chinese.

A.D. 1271–1368
Yuan dynasty rules in China.

mid-A.D. 1400s
Emperor Sejong directs the development of the Korean alphabet.

Relating Past to Present

1. Consult an American history textbook to learn how and why the United States government introduced civil service examinations in the late 1800s. Review Chapter 4, and compare the beginnings of the American civil service examinations with the civil service examinations in China.
2. Describe the development of printing in early China. Where did the technique of movable type come from? What impact do mass-produced paperback books have on our society today?

Applying History Study Skills

Before completing this activity, review Building History Study Skills on page 289.

Look again at the steps for reading a chart. Then complete the following exercise.

Study the chart in the next column. It shows the Confucian Five Relationships and how they operate. Then answer the following questions.

1. What type of chart is it?
2. (a) According to the chart, what does a son owe to his father? (b) What does a father owe to a son? (c) What is the obligation of a younger brother to an older brother? (d) What is the obligation of a wife to a husband? (e) What is the obligation of a husband to a wife?
3. Would you characterize the relationships shown on the chart as unequal or as complementary? Explain.
4. How many of the five relationships relate to the family? Why?

internetconnect

Search the Internet through the HRW Web site for more information on Genghis Khan. Prepare a presentation for your class that describes the history of his empire, its artifacts, and the legacies that survive today.

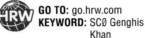 **GO TO:** go.hrw.com
KEYWORD: SC0 Genghis Khan

Building Your Portfolio

1. **Writing a Report** Read poems by the Chinese poets Li Bai and Du Fu. Write a report on what life was like in China during the Tang dynasty. Use the poems as your source. Place the report in your portfolio.
2. **Presenting an Oral Report** Find out more about Marco Polo's impressions of the Chinese people. You might want to read selections from Ronald Latham's *The Travels of Marco Polo* (Penguin). Report your findings to the class. Place your notes and other research material in your portfolio.

Confucian Five Relationships

The Five Relationships and the attitudes they involve can be set out as follows:

Father	**Son**
Is kind	Shows respect
Gives protection	Accepts father's guidance
Provides education	Cares for him in old age and performs the customary burial ceremonies

Elder Brother	**Younger Brother**
Sets an example of refinement and good behavior	Respects the character and experience of the elder

Husband	**Wife**
Carries out his family duties	Looks after the home
	Is obedient
Is honorable and faithful	Diligently meets the needs of her husband and children
Provides for his wife and family	

Elder	**Junior**
Gives encouragement	Shows respect
Shows consideration toward younger people	Defers to the advice of those with more experience
Sets a good example	Is eager to learn

Ruler	**Subjects**
Acts justly	Are loyal
Strives to improve the welfare of his people	Serve their ruler
Is worthy of loyalty	Honor their ruler because of his position and character

Africa and the Americas

TIME

1800 B.C.–A.D. 1500

1800 B.C.–A.D. 1500

3.7 million B.C.   4000 B.C.   A.D. 2100

PLACE

Africa and the Americas

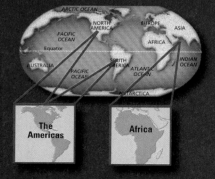

ARCTIC OCEAN

NORTH AMERICA   EUROPE   ASIA

PACIFIC OCEAN   AFRICA

Equator

AUSTRALIA   SOUTH AMERICA   ATLANTIC OCEAN   INDIAN OCEAN

PACIFIC OCEAN

ANTARCTICA

The Americas   Africa

Timbuktu, northern Mali

Significance

Civilizations developed in unique ways on the continent of Africa and in the Americas. From early times, African peoples formed societies that were reflections of the physical resources that surrounded them. Trade was an important factor in how various kingdoms and empires developed in Africa.

Civilizations of the Americas, on the other hand, were isolated from contact with other parts of the world. Complex civilizations grew up in the Andes and Mesoamerica. Empires rose, grew, and fell as stronger peoples conquered weaker ones.

Terms to Define

savannas	matrilineal
tropical rain forests	adobe
jungle	tepees
linguists	*chinampas*
oral traditions	*quipu*

People to Identify

Mansa Musa	Maya
Sunni Ali	Toltec
Pueblo people	Quetzalcóatl
Hopewell culture	Aztec
Olmec	Inca
Chavín	

Places to Locate

Niger River	Mali
Congo River	Songhay
Zambezi River	Timbuktu
Sahara	Gao
Kalahari Desert	Rocky Mountains
Kerma	Andes
Napata	Tula
Meroë	Yucatán Peninsula
Kilwa	Chichén Itzá
Lake Chad	Tenochtitlán
Ghana	Cuzco

Chapter Theme Questions

- **Cross-Cultural Interaction** How might trade influence the spread of culture?
- **Geography** How might the cultures and traditions of people be influenced by the geographical area in which they live?
- **War and Diplomacy** What factors might lead to the rise and decline of civilizations?

On July 24, 1911, in the Peruvian Andes, the American archaeologist Hiram Bingham made a discovery. He uncovered the fabled lost city of the Inca—one of the greatest civilizations of the Americas. Bingham marveled at what he saw:

❝ Suddenly I found myself confronted with the walls of ruined houses built of the finest quality of Inca stone work. It was hard to see them for they were partly covered with trees and moss, the growth of centuries, but in the dense shadow, hiding in bamboo thickets and tangled vines, appeared here and there walls of white granite . . . carefully cut and exquisitely fitted together. . . .

Surprise followed surprise in bewildering succession. . . . Suddenly we found ourselves standing in front of the ruins of two of the finest and most interesting structures in ancient America. Made of beautiful white granite, the walls contained blocks of Cyclopean size, higher than a man. The sight held me spellbound. . . . ❞

Bingham's discovery, called Machu Picchu, was only one of many glorious cities built by the peoples of the Americas. African peoples created equally spectacular civilizations.

Section 1

Africa's Early History

Focus Questions

- **What major geological and climatic characteristics affected Africa's early history?**
- **How do historians learn about people who left few, if any, written records?**
- **What were the predominant patterns of life in many early African societies?**

Written records, surviving monuments, and ruins help to provide evidence of the great civilizations that thrived in North Africa before A.D. 1500. Equally important developments had been taking place in the rest of Africa—the vast portion of the continent south of the Sahara known as Sub-Saharan Africa.

The Physical Setting

Most of the vast expanse of Sub-Saharan Africa rests on a plateau. Here and there, however, basins and deep valleys form depressions in this plateau.

The plateau. The great plateau of Sub-Saharan Africa straddles the equator like a giant inverted bowl, uplifted in the center and then dropping sharply to the coastal plain.

The steep shoreline contains few harbors. Most rivers, including the important Niger, Congo, and the Zambezi, are navigable only for relatively short distances into the interior because of numerous rapids. Although these rivers limited trade, they also protected many parts of Africa from invasion. The absence of good natural harbors and navigable rivers also hindered long-distance communication and contact among the peoples of Africa.

Along the northern coast of Africa, rainfall patterns produce a Mediterranean climate. Below this region, however, lies the enormous Sahara, covering more than one fourth of the continent. The southern edge of the Sahara is a region known as the Sahel, where sparse, unpredictable rainfall often results in severe droughts. South of the Sahel is a vast area of relatively dry grasslands called **savannas**, dotted with a few trees and thorny bushes. The Kalahari and Namib Deserts also cover part of southern Africa. (See map on opposite page.)

Some areas of western and central Africa south of the savanna receive more than 100 inches of rain each year. There vast forests called **tropical rain forests** thrive. People often mistakenly call these forests jungles. However, a **jungle** is a thick growth of plants found in a tropical rain forest wherever sunlight penetrates the dense umbrella of tall trees and reaches the forest floor.

The wet climate of the rain forests provides fertile breeding grounds for insects that carry deadly diseases. For example, mosquitoes transmit malaria and yellow fever, and the tsetse fly carries sleeping sickness. Although modern medicine can treat these diseases, many Africans perished from them in earlier centuries.

Other geographical features. Six depressions appear in the plateau. These basins, formed around Lake Chad and Africa's five major rivers, are Sub-Saharan Africa's drainage basins.

Perhaps the most remarkable geographic feature of Sub-Saharan Africa is the Great Rift Valley. Formed thousands of years ago when a part of the plateau sank because of movements of Earth's crust, this steep-sided structural crack runs north and south near the plateau's eastern edge. Today many long, narrow lakes lie in the rift valley.

Isolated mountain peaks dot the eastern part of the African plateau. Some, such as Mount Kenya and Mount Kilimanjaro, jut thousands of feet above the plateau. Important highland regions include the Ethiopian Plateau in the northeast, the Atlas Mountains in the northwest, and the Drakensberg Mountains in the southeast. Some ranges even have active volcanoes.

Rediscovering the African Past

Scholars rely on a variety of methods to understand the African past prior to the development of writing there. For example, **linguists**—scholars who study languages—have used computers and mathematics to compare the roots of words and common vocabulary. This technique—lexicostatistics—has helped solve the mystery of how Bantu, a family of closely related languages spoken in many parts of Africa, spread. The study suggests that for centuries peoples have migrated throughout Sub-Saharan Africa.

An original "cradle land" of the Bantu language lay in the region that is today the Nigeria-Cameroon border. From there, beginning perhaps 2,000 years ago, Bantu-speaking people began to migrate eastward as well as southward into what is today the country of Gabon. These migrations continued for about 1,000 years. Over time Bantu languages spread throughout the continent south of the Cameroon bend and became one of the largest language groups on the continent.

The study of **oral traditions**—poems, songs, or stories passed by word of mouth from one generation to another—has been another source of information about specific African clans, villages, and dynasties. Africans have always had a strong sense of their own history. Individual families or villages preserved the memory of important events by incorporating them into poetry or song. People then passed these stories on from one generation to the next, with each generation adding to the tradition. Anthropologists and historians have now written down much of this oral tradition of Africans.

Other fields of scholarship have also helped unlock the secrets of Africa's past. For example,

Africa

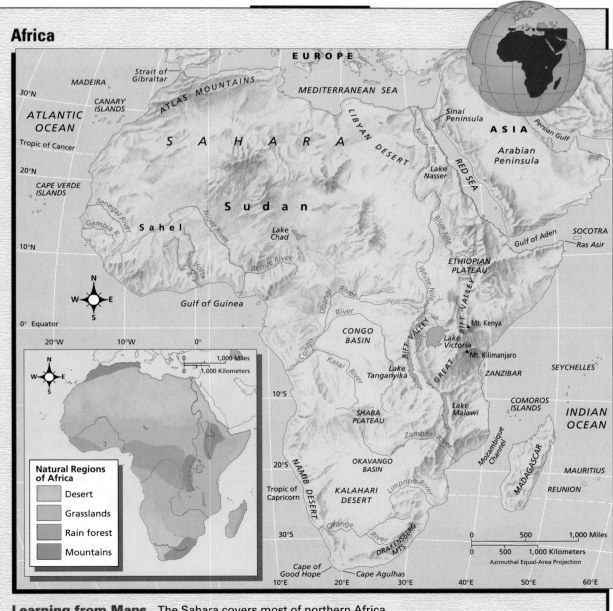

Learning from Maps The Sahara covers most of northern Africa.

? Location Through what physical features does the Tropic of Capricorn run?

scholars who study music have discovered similarities in the design and tuning of xylophones in East Africa and Indonesia, in Southeast Asia. These similarities suggest that at some early date there was some sort of cultural exchange between Asia and Africa. The prevalence in Africa of the banana—a crop native to Asia—supports this suggestion.

Certain languages also provide evidence of an exchange. The Malagasy language, which is spoken on the island of Madagascar in the Indian Ocean off the east coast of Africa, has many words in common with languages spoken on the islands of Indonesia. Through study of musical instruments, plants, and language, scholars have determined that this

Trumpets

The sound of trumpets has been echoing around the world for centuries. The first trumpets were made from hollow branches or reeds. They were used to frighten away evil spirits, to make mournful sounds at funerals, and in the evening to appeal to the Sun to return the next day. In some parts of Switzerland, the alpenhorn still sounds for daily ceremonies and festivals.

Early Africans used horns to send messages over long distances. In present-day Nigeria, horns are still sounded at celebrations. In the Americas, the Inca used trumpets made of shell and ceramics in their ceremonies. (See bronze Benin, c. 1550, royal horn player at right.)

Both the Egyptians and the Hebrews used metal trumpets. The Bible says that when Joshua fought the battle at Jericho, the blast of seven trumpets made the walls fall down. Today, at the ceremony to celebrate the Jewish New Year, the *shofar* is sounded. Carved from a ram's horn as in ancient times, the sounding of the horn reminds Jewish worshippers of their ancient origins.

Trumpets as we know them are shaped like those used in Europe in the 1500s. Some musicians feel that the peak of trumpet performance has come only recently from the contributions of America's great jazz musicians, such as Wynton Marsalis (below) and Chuck Mangione (below right).

cultural exchange between Asia and Africa took place in perhaps the A.D. 300s or 400s.

Scholars have also discovered that the people of Sub-Saharan Africa were particularly adept at coping with their often harsh environment. Although wheat and barley could not be cultivated south of the Sahara near sea level, people there were able to domesticate a variety of crops. For example, the early people of the Sahel domesticated millet and sorghum, grains that grow well in harsh conditions. In later centuries, these grains became the staple crops of the people of Sub-Saharan Africa.

Although the people of Sub-Saharan Africa domesticated various crops, changes in the climate of the Sahel soon altered patterns of agriculture. As the region became much drier, people either migrated farther south or came to rely increasingly on herding.

Archaeology has also added much to our understanding of African history. Excavation sites throughout the continent have revealed details on daily life in early Africa.

Patterns of Life

Based on scholarly studies of the African past, experts have drawn several conclusions about patterns of life in early Africa. They believe that most Africans lived in small, independent villages and were farmers, herders, or fishers. Relationships established by kinship and age provided the ties that bound the different societies together. Within this system, women played a crucial role. Unlike Europe and Asia, in Africa women were the primary farmers, although some agricultural tasks were performed by men. It is believed by scholars that societies in many parts of Sub-Saharan Africa were **matrilineal**. People trace their ancestors and inherit property through their mothers rather than through their fathers in matrilineal societies.

Religion was an important part of life in many African cultures. In most of these societies, people believed that spirits populated the world. Most religious systems included a supreme creator god and other gods associated with certain aspects of nature or human activities, such as farming.

Elders usually exercised authority over the village. Life in the villages of Africa was closely bound to the agricultural cycles of planting and harvesting. Through the rise and fall of numerous kingdoms, the village survived as the basic unit of society and the economy. Its persistence makes it a vital part of the African heritage.

Section 1 Review

1. **Define** savannas, tropical rain forests, jungle, linguists, oral traditions, matrilineal
2. **Locate and Explain the Significance** Niger River, Congo River, Zambezi River, Sahara, Kalahari Desert
3. **Identifying Ideas** What geographic factors made contact difficult among peoples in Africa's interior?
4. **Summarizing Ideas** What nonwritten evidence has been used to identify early African cultures?
5. **Synthesizing Ideas** What conclusions have scholars reached about patterns of life in early Africa?

Section 2

African City-States and Kingdoms

Focus Questions

- What were some distinguishing characteristics of the kingdoms of Kush and Aksum?
- What part did trade and trade routes play in the rise and fall of East and central Africa's early kingdoms?
- For what are the early kingdoms of West Africa noted?

While some African peoples lived happily without developing state structures, others came together to establish small city-states, kingdoms, and even empires before A.D. 1500. These states were as diverse as the African geography.

Kush

Along the Nile River, south of the major centers of ancient Egypt, lay an area known as Nubia. Nubia thrived as an important corridor of trade for gold, ivory, ebony, and ostrich feathers. Here caravans hauled goods from the Red Sea to barges on the Nile. Here, too, arose a powerful kingdom known as Kush.

Kush (See map on page 300) traces its roots to the city of Kerma, a trading center of southern Nubia that emerged about 1800 B.C. Recent archaeological

Above: Aerial view of ruins of the kingdom of Kush.
Below: Lion temple in the kingdom of Kush.

not know why, many believe that the land's loss of fertility due to overuse contributed to the decline. In addition, Kush may have lost control over the trade routes. Some scholars look to a rival state, Aksum, as the cause for this loss of control.

Aksum

Situated in the Ethiopian Highlands south of Kush, Aksum straddled the trade routes from the Red Sea into Egypt and the interior of Africa. (See map on this page.) As Kush declined, Aksum became a major competitor for control of this trade and sent war elephants, rhinoceros horns, tortoise shells, incense, and spices to the Mediterranean world by way of Egypt.

discoveries indicate that interaction between this region and Egypt resulted in a rich cultural exchange.

Over the next centuries, Kush became a distinct kingdom. It had its own dynasty and a capital at Napata, which was a city upstream from Kerma. However, Kush maintained close cultural and economic ties with Egypt. Nevertheless, beginning in the 1300s B.C., Kush started to become more independent; by about 1000 B.C., it was quite isolated from Egypt's culture. Three hundred years later, in about 710 B.C., Kush conquered Upper Egypt. For about 40 years a Kush dynasty ruled a unified Egypt. Then the Assyrians, who were armed with iron weapons, invaded in 671 B.C.

With the Assyrian invasion, the kingdom of Kush weakened. Following the Assyrian sack of Napata in about 592 B.C., the kingdom reorganized itself around a new capital at Meroë and began a new period of growth and cultural achievements. Meroë was one of the earliest centers of ironworking in Africa—in fact, in the ancient world.

The kingdom of Kush also controlled trade routes from the Red Sea to the Nile. Caravans brought Hellenistic, Persian, and Indian influences that the people of Meroë adapted to their own culture.

The brilliant Kush civilization was at its height from 250 B.C. to A.D. 150. The people erected impressive pyramids and temples and crafted exquisite pottery and ornaments. Then the Kush civilization mysteriously declined. Although scholars do

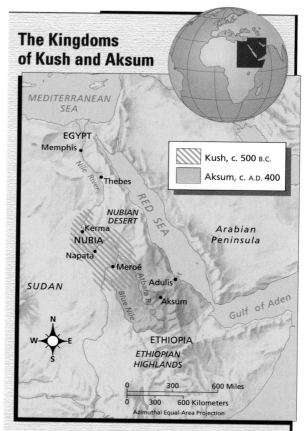

The Kingdoms of Kush and Aksum

Kush, c. 500 B.C.
Aksum, c. A.D. 400

MEDITERRANEAN SEA
EGYPT
Memphis
Thebes
Nile River
RED SEA
NUBIAN DESERT
Kerma
NUBIA
Napata
Meroë
Atbara R.
Adulis
SUDAN
Blue Nile
Aksum
Arabian Peninsula
Gulf of Aden
ETHIOPIA
ETHIOPIAN HIGHLANDS

0   300   600 Miles
0   300   600 Kilometers
Azimuthal Equal-Area Projection

Learning from Maps Although the kingdom of Kush was a thriving center of trade between 250 B.C. and A.D. 150, the kingdom of Aksum defeated Kush and later controlled trade along the African side of the Red Sea.

? Place What cities within these two kingdoms are located along bodies of water?

Building History Study Skills

READ
WRITE
INTERPRET
CONNECT
THINK

Writing About History: Paraphrasing Information

As you study world history and perfect your writing skills, you will use many primary and secondary sources. You might either quote or paraphrase these sources. Quoting means to repeat exactly the words of the author or speaker. Paraphrasing is restating something in your own words. Putting something into your own words often helps you think about what you have read and makes it easier to understand and remember, especially for tests. If you are writing a report, paraphrasing will help you avoid plagiarizing, or copying the words and ideas of others without acknowledging the source.

How to Paraphrase Information

To paraphrase, follow these steps.
1. Define the main idea of the selection.
2. Indicate the details—bits and pieces of information related to the main idea.
3. Put the main idea and details in your own words.
4. Compare your statement with the original selection by asking questions:
   - Have you written a complete thought?
   - Does it make sense?
   - Does it have new information that focuses on meaning?

Developing the Skill

The following document describes how the king of the African state of Kilwa learned of gold in Sofala and secured a trading monopoly. Read the document. Then define the main idea and paraphrase the document in a few sentences.

❝However it happened, we learn from the Chronicle of the Kings of Kilwa . . . that the first people on this coast who came to the land of Sofala in search of gold were inhabitants of the city of Mogadishu. How the kings of Kilwa came into possession was in this manner. A man was fishing in a canoe outside the bar of Kilwa near an island called Miza. He caught a fish on the hook of the line he had cast into the sea. Feeling from the struggles of the fish that it was very large and not wishing to lose it, he weighed anchor and left himself at the will of the fish. Sometimes the vessel went where the fish took it and sometimes where the currents, which are very strong there, so that when the fisherman wished to return to the port whence he had come, he could not reach it. At last, more dead than alive from hunger and thirst, he came to the port of Sofala, where he found a ship of Mogadishu, which had come there to trade. In this vessel he returned to Kilwa and related what had occurred and what he had seen of the gold trade.

It was part of the agreement between these Gentiles and the Moors of Mogadishu that every year they should send some young Moors so that there should be some of this race there. When the King of Kilwa learnt this part of the contract and its conditions from the fisherman, he sent a ship there to arrange commerce with the Kafirs. With regard to the young Moors for whom they asked, he offered to give so many cloths a head in lieu of those they asked, or, if they wanted them so as to have a race of them there, he said some of the inhabitants of Kilwa would go and settle there . . . and that they would be glad to take their daughters as wives, by which means the people would multiply. By means of this entry the Moors of Kilwa got possession of the trade.❞

The topic of the selection is how the king of Kilwa created a trading monopoly on the gold found in Sofala. The details focus on how the existence of gold in Sofala was discovered and related to the king, and how the king negotiated a trade agreement. The following is a paraphrased statement of the selection.

The people of Mogadishu were the first to go to Sofala in search of gold. The king of Kilwa learned of this from a fisherman from Kilwa who had gotten lost at sea. This man ended up at the port of Sofala, where he found a trading ship from Mogadishu. The king learned of a condition of the trade agreement between Sofala and Mogadishu in which a number of Moors were to be sent to Sofala each year. The king offered to send people from his own country and bettered the offer by having those people marry women from Sofala in order to multiply the race. This offer gave the kingdom of Kilwa control of the gold trade.

Practicing the Skill

Reread the selection by Hiram Bingham on page 295, and put it in your own words.

To apply this skill, see Applying History Study Skills on page 313.

Finally, around A.D. 330 King Ezana of Aksum inflicted a crushing defeat on Kush and established a thriving kingdom. During his reign, Ezana converted to Christianity, and the religion, which incorporated many elements of the people's traditional beliefs, has remained an important influence in the region.

For the next 400 years, Aksum controlled the African side of the Red Sea trade. Its influence beyond this region, however, ended with the rise of Islam. By the early 700s, Muslim forces controlled both the Arabian and the African sides of the Red Sea.

East Africa and Trade

No large kingdoms such as Kush and Aksum emerged on the coast of East Africa. Instead, a series of city-states arose and dominated coastal trade in the Indian Ocean. The seasonal monsoon winds provided a reliable means of travel. Sailors explored the seas and developed trade routes linking all shores of the Indian Ocean. Africans exported gold, slaves, ivory, hides, and tortoise shells and imported porcelain and weapons.

The spread of Islam to northeastern Africa also created favorable conditions for trade. Along the East African coast, a golden age began in the 700s and lasted through the 1300s. The opportunity to make money in Africa attracted merchant families, adventurers, and refugees fleeing the Shi'ah-Sunni conflicts in Arabia and Persia. They settled on islands and easily defensible spits of land, where they soon established many thriving trading centers.

Over several generations, a unique African culture—Swahili—developed on the East African coast. The people of this culture spoke Swahili, a Bantu language with Arabic and Persian influences. Although the Swahili speakers were not a unified ethnic group, their common pursuits—especially trade—and language bound them together.

The earliest of the city-states—Mogadishu (moh·guh·DEE·shoo), Pate, and Malindi—lay in the north. Gradually, commercial activity shifted southward. By the 1100s Kilwa, the most famous city-state, was one of the leading ports along the African coast.

Under Kilwa's leadership, coastal civilization flourished. Ibn Battuta, a famous Muslim traveler of the 1300s, described Kilwa as one of the most beautiful and well-constructed towns in the world. Recent archaeological excavations have uncovered a massive trade center and a large mosque that reveal the city's wealth and achievements.

This ritual implement was discovered in the present-day nation of the Democratic Republic of the Congo (formerly known as Zaire) in central Africa.

Central Africa and Great Zimbabwe

Kilwa grew as a port for the shipment of gold mined along the Zambezi River in central Africa. For centuries, gold and other goods had moved from inland Africa to the coast, passing eastward through small-scale trade networks based on the exchange of essential items such as salt, tools, or cloth.

The growth of Indian Ocean trade after the 900s dramatically increased the demand for gold. Kingdoms vied for control over the mining of gold and its shipment to the coast. Within the next several centuries, the Shona people, who immigrated onto the plateau land of what is today Zimbabwe, asserted control over local peoples and mining activities.

Scholars believe that the Shona built fortified enclosures and probably attained great wealth and power. Great Zimbabwe, the largest and most famous of these fortresses, became the center of the Shona state. A 60-acre site boasted a hilltop fortification with many rooms and a pattern of passageways that was mazelike. Below the hill was a thick stone-block wall, a tower, and the foundations of other stone buildings. All the large stones were cut to fit and stay in place without mortar.

History Through the Arts

Royal Figure from West Africa

The people of Ife, in what is now southwestern Nigeria, began making life-sized bronze and naturalistic terra-cotta heads more than 700 years ago. Ife was the largest and probably the oldest town that was founded by the inhabitants of the region—the Yoruba people.

Bronze is a difficult metal to cast. The Yorubas' technique of casting bronze reached a level of excellence that was not equaled in West Africa from that time on.

The magnificent example of bronze casting shown here depicts a Yoruban king. The beaded crown tells us that the head is that of a very important king. The vertical lines represent ritual scarring—a practice still followed by people in some parts of Africa. A beard and a mustache were attached to the holes around the mouth.

Art historians believe that the bronze figure was probably made while the ruler was alive. After death, however, it became a "trap" for his spirit—and therefore his power—in that his own hair was added to the figure.

Excavation of the site revealed a rapid and seemingly mysterious decline in the 1400s. Scientists now believe that the area may have experienced an ecological disaster. One theory is that the population grew so quickly that it outpaced dwindling water and food resources. Without enough food and water, people starved, and the brilliant civilization declined.

Kingdoms and Cultures of West Africa

In West Africa, between Lake Chad and the Atlantic Ocean, several important African societies flourished. They included Ghana, Mali, and Songhay. (See map on page 304.) Knowledge of these kingdoms comes largely from oral tradition and from the writings of African scholars and Muslim traders.

The wealth and strength of these kingdoms depended on control of the trade routes across the Sahara. At the desert's edge, traders exchanged gold (extracted from the forest zone south of the Sahel) for salt (mined in the Sahara). The people of the Sahel needed the salt to flavor and preserve their food. The traders from the north wanted the gold for coins and for buying goods from Europe. At the sites where this gold-for-salt exchange took place, important commercial cities grew and flourished. Indeed, West Africa produced most of the world's gold until 1500. In time traders in these cities also exchanged ivory and slaves in return for textiles, jewels, and copper.

In these civilizations, monarchs ruled, assisted by officials. Often adorned with gold, these monarchs presided over elaborate ceremonies and administered justice. According to the Muslim historian Al-Bakri, trial by wood was common:

"When a man is accused of denying a debt or having shed blood or some other crime, a headman takes a thin piece of wood, which is sour and bitter to taste, and pours upon it some water which he then gives to the defendant to drink. If the man vomits, his innocence is recognized

Trading Kingdoms of Africa, c. 1230–1591

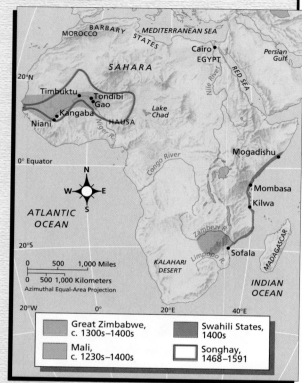

Learning from Maps Eastern and central Africa became centers of trade during a 300-year period.

? Region Through what kingdoms does the Niger River flow?

and he is congratulated. If he does not vomit and the drink remains in his stomach, the accusation is accepted as justified."

Below the royal family and government officials on the social scale came merchants, farmers, fishers, and cattle breeders. Slaves, whose numbers remained small, ranked at the bottom of the scale.

Ghana. Ghana, the earliest of these kingdoms, traces its origin to Kumbi (or Kumbi Saleh), a long-established trading village situated in the southeastern part of modern Mauritania. Ghana was at its peak in the A.D. 1000s, but its period of prosperity was short-lived. In the late 1000s, a Muslim religious revival

and the preaching of a holy war stirred up Berber tribes, who had once controlled trade in the Sahara. They invaded Ghana. The kingdom never recovered from this attack and around 1235 ceased to exist.

Mali. The rise of a successor kingdom—Mali—followed the fall of Ghana. This new kingdom came to power in the region that had been Ghana, as well as in vast areas to the north and west and along the upper Niger River. Under Mansa Musa, who ruled in the early 1300s, Mali's power reached its peak. When Mansa Musa made his pilgrimage to Mecca, as many as 80,000 other pilgrims, including 500 slaves each carrying a four-pound bar of gold, accompanied him. Upon his return, Musa supported education, the arts, and building. Under his rule, Timbuktu became an important center of Muslim learning, with a large university that attracted scholars from Egypt and Arabia.

When Ibn Battuta visited Mali shortly after Mansa Musa's death, the wealth and peace of the kingdom astounded him. He wrote:

"They [the people of Mali] are seldom unjust and have a greater abhorrence of injustice than any other people. Their Sultan shows no mercy to any one guilty of the least act of it. There is complete security in their country. Neither traveler nor inhabitant in it has anything to fear from robbers or men of violence. They do not confiscate the property of any white man who dies in their country, even if it be uncounted wealth. On the contrary, they give it into the charge of some trust-worthy person among the whites, until the rightful heir takes possession of it."

Although disputes over dynastic succession weakened Mali, it managed to maintain control over the desert trade routes until the 1400s. Then in 1468 Sunni Ali, leader of a region that had broken away from Mali's authority, captured Timbuktu, ushering in the age of the third kingdom—Songhay.

Songhay. The kingdom of Songhay was centered on the important trading city of Gao. From there it controlled a kingdom larger than that of Mali. Sunni Ali, founder of the kingdom, was an excellent soldier and an able administrator. He established a government designed to ensure tighter control over his subjects. He divided the kingdom into provinces, each with a governor and officials who reported directly to the king in his capital at Gao. He also built a fleet of warships to enforce peace along the Niger River, which had become a major route of African commerce. His policies and those of his successor,

Askia the Great, caused Songhay to thrive until the Moroccans invaded in 1591.

Section 2 Review

1. **Identify** Mansa Musa, Sunni Ali
2. **Locate and Explain the Significance** Kerma, Napata, Meroë, Kilwa, Lake Chad, Ghana, Mali, Songhay, Timbuktu, Gao
3. **Understanding Ideas** Describe the kingdoms of Kush and Aksum.
4. **Summarizing Ideas** What factors helped make East Africa and central Africa centers for trade?
5. **Analyzing Ideas** Provide evidence to support the idea that Mali and Songhay were powerful, wealthy kingdoms.

Section 3

The Earliest Americans

Focus Questions

- What might have motivated early humans to migrate to the Americas?
- How did life change for early hunters and gatherers who learned how to cultivate food?
- What distinguished the early American cultures in the West and Southwest, the Pacific Coast, the Great Plains, and the Eastern Woodlands?

From the beginning of history until about 500 years ago, the peoples of the Eastern and Western Hemispheres had virtually no contact with each other. Although Vikings landed at several places in the Americas around A.D. 1000, the accounts of their voyages remain largely unknown. Old European maps show a vast blank space or fanciful islands where what we now call the Western Hemisphere lies. Europeans were unaware that millions of people already inhabited that vast region of the world.

The Physical Setting

The Americas stretch more than 9,000 miles from Greenland in the north to Cape Horn at the southern tip of South America. Not surprisingly, geographic contrasts typify this enormous expanse of land.

Almost every type of climate and terrain can be found somewhere in the Americas. Jagged mountains curve like a rugged backbone near the western coast of the Americas. Known as the Rocky Mountains in North America, they extend through Mexico and into South America, where they are called the Andes. To the east of the mountains on both continents are flatter lands dotted here and there by mountains.

The Americas also include two of the world's great river systems. In North America, the Mississippi River drains much of the continent and provides a major transportation route. In South America, the Amazon River, second only to the Nile in length, flows about 4,000 miles from the Andes through dense rain forests before emptying into the Atlantic Ocean.

The Great Migrations

Between 50,000 and 14,000 years ago, while the Ice Age still gripped Earth, people migrated from Asia to the Americas across what is now the Bering Strait, off the coast of Alaska. During periods in the past, a "bridge" of land stood there. Even when water covered that bridge of land, the strait spanned only about 50 miles, and people in boats could have crossed it easily.

Neither a single large migration nor a continuous flow of people from Asia populated the Americas. Rather, over the centuries, a series of waves of different peoples crossed to the Americas. Changes in Asia's climate may from time to time have forced people northeastward and across the strait. From there they drifted toward warmer climates.

Some people moved into the eastern and central areas of North America. Others migrated farther south, through Mexico and Central America and across the narrow Isthmus of Panama. From there the South American continent spread out before them.

What If?

The Bering Strait
Prehistoric peoples migrated across a land bridge linking Asia and North America. How do you think the course of world history would have been different if this land bridge still existed?

Peoples of North America, 2500 B.C.–A.D. 1500

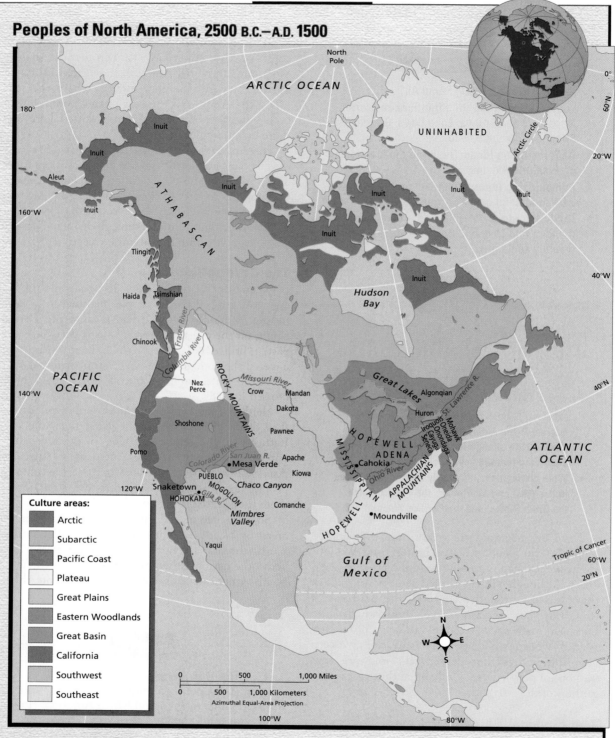

Culture areas:
- Arctic
- Subarctic
- Pacific Coast
- Plateau
- Great Plains
- Eastern Woodlands
- Great Basin
- California
- Southwest
- Southeast

0   500   1,000 Miles
0   500   1,000 Kilometers
Azimuthal Equal-Area Projection

Learning from Maps Various groups of people settled across the North American continent from the Southwest to the Arctic.

? Region What cultures are enclosed on all sides by land?

Evidence from a 1997 study of a site in Chile called Monte Verde, however, suggests that the people who crossed the land bridge may have done so earlier than scientists had once thought. In fact, this evidence seems to indicate the existence of humans in South America as early as 10,500 B.C.

The Development of Agriculture

The first people in the Americas were nomads who lived by hunting and gathering. About 11,000 years ago, massive changes in climate led to the melting of the glaciers, the submersion of the land bridge, and the extinction of many large animals. Increasingly, people began to rely on plants as a source of food in order to survive. Gradually, a new way of life emerged—farming. The earliest traces of farming in the Western Hemisphere, dating from around 7000 B.C., have been found in south-central and northeastern Mexico. From Mexico, farming spread both north and south. Scholars believe that the first farmers planted corn, beans, squash, and a variety of other crops. In South America and on the islands of the Caribbean, farmers raised avocados, beans, corn, peanuts, pineapples, and various root crops, such as sweet potatoes. In the highlands of Peru, the potato was the most important food.

Farming began at about the same time in both hemispheres but developed more gradually in the Americas. The plow was not invented in the Americas, partly because animals large enough to pull it, such as horses, were not available there. For the same reason, the ancient people of the region did not use wheeled implements in agriculture, although ancient toys unearthed in Mexico show that the people did know of the wheel. In the highlands, farmers used digging sticks to plant rows of seeds. They also used dead fish as fertilizer.

Agriculture produced enough to support village life and the beginnings of towns. By the time of Columbus's voyage in 1492, people as far north as the northeastern United States and Canada and as far south as Argentina depended on farming for their food supply. In Mexico and in the Andes, agriculture and sophisticated systems of food storage formed the basis of highly advanced civilizations.

The North Americans

In what is today the United States and Canada, many different cultures and societies thrived. (See map on opposite page.) The cultures of these peoples in many cases depended on the geography of the region that they inhabited.

The West and Southwest. The Pueblo people created a well-developed culture in what is now the southwestern United States. These farmers lived in permanent settlements and used **adobe**—a sun-dried brick—to build communal houses, ancient versions of our apartment houses. They erected many multi-storied houses, some with as many as 800 rooms, and clustered others together beneath overhanging cliffs so they could be better defended.

The Pacific Coast. Several tribes with economies based largely on fishing lived on the northwest coast of North America. Expert woodworkers and weavers, these people crafted majestic totem poles—great wooden carvings of people and beasts that symbolized tribal history.

The Great Plains. An entirely different culture flourished in the Great Plains, an area that stretches between the Rocky Mountains and the Mississippi River. Here tribal peoples lived by hunting the huge herds of wild buffalo that roamed the land. The Plains peoples ate the meat of the buffalo and used its hide to make clothing and to build their cone-shaped tents, called **tepees**.

The Eastern Woodlands. The Eastern Woodlands stretch from what is now Canada to the Gulf of Mexico

Artifacts from different groups of North American Indians. Above: bird mask. Below: painted hide.

This group of dwellings, built under the protection of a cliff, is only one of the many prehistoric ruins found at Mesa Verde National Park in southwestern Colorado.

and from the Atlantic Ocean to the Mississippi River. In the Eastern Woodlands some of North America's most sophisticated cultures flourished. One group in the region, the Hopewell culture, settled in the Ohio Valley sometime around 300 B.C. to 200 B.C. The Hopewell left many earthen mounds, presumed to be burial mounds, as well as foundations for buildings.

The tools, jewelry, and weapons found in mounds built as burial places reveal that the Hopewell had highly developed artistic skills. Some of the mounds are in the shapes of animals. One such mound in Ohio, which may have been built by the Hopewell, is called the Great Serpent Mound. This mound is about 1,300 feet long. Mound excavations have also revealed objects such as grizzly-bear teeth and obsidian from the Rocky Mountains, mica from the Appalachian Mountains, and shark teeth and turtle shells from the Gulf Coast. These objects are

evidence of an extensive trading network connecting diverse peoples over a vast area of North America.

Section 3 Review

1. **Define** adobe, tepees
2. **Identify** Pueblo people, Hopewell culture
3. **Locate and Explain the Significance** Rocky Mountains, Andes
4. **Understanding Ideas** Why did early peoples migrate to the Americas?
5. **Summarizing Ideas** (a) List the important crops grown in the Americas. (b) What factors limited farmers' productivity?
6. **Contrasting Ideas** In what ways did the various cultures of early North America differ from each other?

The Empires of Mexico and Peru

Focus Questions

- What were the characteristics of the Olmec, Maya, and Toltec cultures?
- What means did the Aztec use to build their strong civilization?
- How did Inca methods for strengthening their empire differ from those of the Aztec rulers?

By about 1500 B.C., the peoples along the coast of Peru and in central Mexico lived in villages. In another 500 years, ceremonial and trading centers, made possible by the food surplus of many villages, began to appear. The central areas of these cities were occupied by priests and high officials. The common people lived in nearby farming villages. The societies of some of these cities remain mysterious because scholars have not fully deciphered most of their hieroglyphic writings.

The Olmec and the Chavín

The earliest of these cultures in Mexico, the Olmec civilization flourished for approximately eight centuries, starting in about 1200 B.C. The Olmec left eight giant stone heads and many objects made of jade. Carved from basalt that had to be transported from quarries 50 miles away, the stone heads weigh up to 40 tons. Although scholars are unsure about how the Olmec moved the giant stones, they believe that only a highly sophisticated society could have developed the technology to do so. Olmec society seems to have been divided into a large class of farmers and a small elite that held political, military, and religious power. Their art suggests that they worshipped a god that was part jaguar and part human.

In the highlands of Peru and along its coast, a culture called Chavín developed at about the same time. Chavín artists created ceramic religious vessels and decorated seashells with images of cats. The Olmec and Chavín cultures mysteriously disappeared between 400 B.C. and 200 B.C.

The Maya

Perhaps the most advanced culture of the Americas was that of the Maya, who occupied most of the

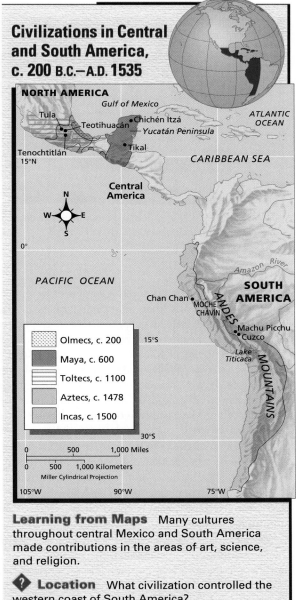

Civilizations in Central and South America, c. 200 B.C.–A.D. 1535

Legend:
- Olmecs, c. 200
- Maya, c. 600
- Toltecs, c. 1100
- Aztecs, c. 1478
- Incas, c. 1500

0 500 1,000 Miles
0 500 1,000 Kilometers
Miller Cylindrical Projection

Learning from Maps Many cultures throughout central Mexico and South America made contributions in the areas of art, science, and religion.

? Location What civilization controlled the western coast of South America?

Yucatán Peninsula, and extended as far south as present-day El Salvador. (See map on this page.) Skilled architects and engineers, the Maya built many steep, pyramid-shaped temples several stories tall. They also developed the only complete writing system in the Americas. It used hieroglyphs, or glyphs. Archaeologists have begun to translate some of the glyphs, which have given us a whole new understanding of Maya society.

This Maya observatory is located in Chichén Itzá on the Yucatán Peninsula.

The Maya farmers produced a surplus of food, perhaps more efficiently than European farmers of the time. This food helped support noble and priestly classes, whose members did not perform any manual labor. At the heart of Maya society lay their religion. Maya religion was complex and involved the worship of many gods. It was also closely bound up with their dependence on agriculture for their survival. One of the most important Maya gods was the rain god. Sometimes in periods of crisis, such as droughts, Maya priests offered human sacrifices to the gods, hoping for rain.

The Maya also studied astronomy. They learned to predict solar eclipses and devised an extremely accurate agricultural calendar. The Maya developed a counting system that was based on the number 20 and included zero (0).

About A.D. 900 a mysterious catastrophe struck the Maya civilization. The population declined sharply and people fled the ceremonial centers. Scholars can only speculate, but any number of disasters could have caused the decline. Maya farming methods may have worn out the soil, warfare between the Maya city-states may have intensified, or possibly the peasants revolted and overthrew the nobles and priests.

The Toltec

Around A.D. 800 a people called the Toltec invaded central Mexico from the north. Ruled by a military class, the Toltec built a capital city called Tula and within several centuries had spread their influence as far south as the Yucatán Peninsula. (See map on page 309.) In the process, they encountered the crumbling Maya Empire. The influence of Toltec religion and

designs is noticeable in the ruins of Chichén Itzá (chee·CHEN eet·sah), the chief Maya city of this era.

Like the Maya, the Toltec erected pyramid-shaped buildings. However, they never produced art as elaborate as that of the Maya. The Toltec extended their empire much farther than had the Maya and introduced the working of gold and silver. The Toltec also spread the worship of their god, Quetzalcoatl (kwet·suhl·koh·AH·tl), represented by a feathered serpent, and practiced human sacrifice. In the late A.D. 1100s, however, Tula was destroyed, effectively ending the domination of the Toltec.

The Aztec

Around A.D. 1200 peoples from the north launched further invasions of central Mexico. A number of these groups fought one another in central Mexico. Out of these struggles emerged the strongest group—the Aztec (See map on page 309.)

The Aztec had been wandering warriors. According to legend, the Aztec priests had instructed them to settle where they saw a sign—an eagle sitting on a cactus and devouring a serpent. They finally saw the sign on one of a pair of islands in Lake Texcoco in Mexico. It was there that they built their city of Tenochtitlán (tay·NAWCH·teht·LAHN).

From the mid-1300s on, the Aztec increased their power until they dominated central Mexico. Conquered tribes paid tribute or taxes to Aztec rulers.

By building causeways, the Aztec expanded Tenochtitlán to make room for great pyramid-temples, marketplaces, and palaces for the nobles and wealthy families. The city may have had as many as 250,000 inhabitants at its period of greatest power and prestige in the 1400s.

The Aztec incorporated into their culture the inventions of peoples they conquered or with whom they traded. They soon learned techniques of working with gold and silver, weaving, and pottery-making and acquired the use of the calendar and mathematics. Their artisans produced finely finished pieces of art.

The Aztec perfected farming on **chinampas**, raised fields formed from mud scooped up from the bottoms of shallow lakes. The use of *chinampas* gave the Aztec huge crop yields and are still used for farming today.

The military dominated Aztec society. Warfare carried great prestige and led to wealth and power. The Aztec believed that the sun god was in a constant struggle against the forces of darkness. To keep up his strength and to ensure that he would succeed in bringing a new day each morning, they fed him with

The gold earrings (left) and the tapestry (right) are examples of Inca art and crafts.

human sacrifices. In this way, the world would be preserved from destruction. Warfare was therefore important because it was through capture that victims were obtained to be sacrificed on the temple altars.

Just as the great Aztec civilization had grown rapidly, so it was to fall in a very short time. By the end of the 1400s, surrounding peoples who had been paying tribute to the Aztec revolted. However, the final blow to the Aztec Empire came from foreign conquerors—the Spanish explorers of the early 1500s.

The Inca

At about the same period that the Aztec civilization in Mexico was at its height, another civilization in the Andes Mountains of South America was expanding. (See map on page 309.) These people—the Inca—based their religion on worship of the Sun and moon. Their name meant "children of the Sun."

The Inca Empire expanded steadily. By the latter part of the 1400s, it extended along most of the west coast of South America and far into the Andes, covering much of the present-day nations of Peru, Ecuador, Bolivia, and Chile. Its capital was Cuzco.

In Inca society, the emperor ruled as an autocrat but used his power to improve the empire. The Inca built fortresses and irrigation systems and laid roads, many of them paved. Pack animals called llamas carried goods, and swift runners brought news to the Inca capital. The rulers of the empire prevented local famines by maintaining storehouses and distributing food supplies when crops failed.

After conquering their neighbors, the Inca rulers sought to eliminate regional diversity. To pacify and colonize newly conquered lands, they sometimes moved entire villages to the new lands. They established an educational system, particularly for the children of the nobility, that taught the imperial language, Inca religion, and history. Even today millions of native people in the five South American countries of Peru, Ecuador, Bolivia, Chile, and Argentina speak the Inca language—Quechua (KE·chuh·wuh). The excellent Inca road system also served to unify the empire.

Although the Inca did not have a system of writing, they did keep records by means of the *quipu* (KEE·poo)—a kind of knotted string used to assist the memory. They were quite advanced in the practice of medicine, using anesthetics and even performing operations on the brain.

Just as with the Aztec, the Spaniards conquered the Inca in the 1500s. Yet many aspects of this great civilization lived on in the isolated highland valleys of the Andes.

Section 4 Review

1. **Define** *chinampas, quipu*
2. **Identify** Olmec, Chavín, Maya, Toltec, Quetzalcóatl, Aztec, Inca
3. **Locate and Explain the Significance** Tula, Yucatán Peninsula, Chichén Itzá, Tenochtitlán, Cuzco
4. **Summarizing Ideas** What were the earliest civilizations in the Americas like?
5. **Analyzing Ideas** Why did the Aztec succeed in building a strong civilization?
6. **Comparing Ideas** (a) How were the civilizations of the Aztec and Inca similar? (b) How were they different?

Chapter 13 Review

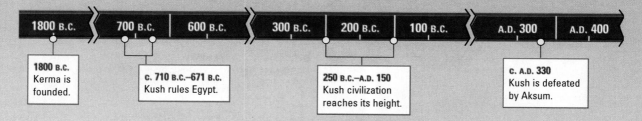

| 1800 B.C. | 700 B.C. | 600 B.C. | 300 B.C. | 200 B.C. | 100 B.C. | A.D. 300 | A.D. 400 |

1800 B.C.
Kerma is founded.

c. 710 B.C.–671 B.C.
Kush rules Egypt.

250 B.C.–A.D. 150
Kush civilization reaches its height.

c. A.D. 330
Kush is defeated by Aksum.

Chapter Summary

The following list contains the key concepts you have learned about civilizations in Africa and the Americas.

1. Sub-Saharan Africa lies on a great plateau, broken here and there by basins and the Great Rift Valley.
2. Scholars have used linguistics, oral traditions, music, and archaeology to unlock the African past.
3. Africans lived primarily in small villages, where families were very important.
4. The great kingdoms of Kush and Aksum dominated the interior of eastern Africa.
5. Independent city-states, noted for their trading activity, were established on Africa's eastern coast. The region experienced a golden age that lasted from the 700s through the 1300s.
6. In central Africa, the Shona controlled a large area of land.
7. To the west, large kingdoms such as Ghana, Mali, and Songhay developed. These kingdoms controlled the vital gold-for-salt trade.
8. Successive waves of immigrants from Asia settled the Americas. Many crossed the land bridge that linked Asia and the Americas. New evidence suggests that these migrations may have occurred earlier than scientists once thought.
9. North American tribes included the Pueblo farmers of the West and Southwest, the fishers of the Pacific Coast, the hunters of the Great Plains, and the Hopewell of the Eastern Woodlands.
10. As agriculture and small towns developed, several great cultures arose—the Olmec, Maya, Toltec, and Aztec of Mexico and Central America, and the Chavín and Inca of South America.

Reviewing Important Terms

On a separate sheet of paper, match each of the following terms with the correct definition below.

a. savannas
b. linguists
c. oral traditions
d. *chinampas*
e. *quipu*
f. adobe
g. tepees
h. tropical rain forests
i. jungle
j. matrilineal

_____ 1. Scholars who study languages
_____ 2. Kind of knotted string developed by the Inca to assist the memory
_____ 3. A vast area of relatively dry grasslands
_____ 4. Raised fields that the Aztec created for agriculture
_____ 5. Poems, songs, or stories passed by word of mouth from one generation to another
_____ 6. Cone-shaped tents made of buffalo hide
_____ 7. Sun-dried brick
_____ 8. Society in which people trace their ancestors and inherit property through their mothers rather than their fathers
_____ 9. Forests where annual rainfall exceeds 100 inches
_____10. A thick growth of plants found in a tropical rain forest wherever sunlight penetrates the dense umbrella of tall trees and reaches the forest floor

Developing Critical Thinking Skills

1. **Summarizing Ideas** (a) What types of trade developed across the Sahara and along the eastern coast of Africa? (b) What similarities or differences in trade do you notice among different civilizations?
2. **Interpreting Ideas** (a) What evidence supports the claim that the Maya were one of the most advanced cultures of the Americas? (b) In what ways were the Maya as advanced as Europeans of the same period?
3. **Classifying Ideas** Supply the name of the area or culture that completes each statement.
   (a) The _____ developed a counting system based on 20.
   (b) _____ was an early East African center of iron-working.
   (c) The first West African kingdom to build up gold-for-salt trade was _____.
   (d) Timbuktu, the capital of _____, was a center of Muslim learning.
   (e) _____ became the most famous city-state for East African trade.
   (f) The _____ of Mexico farmed on raised fields.
4. **Evaluating Ideas** How do architecture and the use of metals reflect the accomplishments of a civilization? Give an example from one African and one American civilization to support your answer.

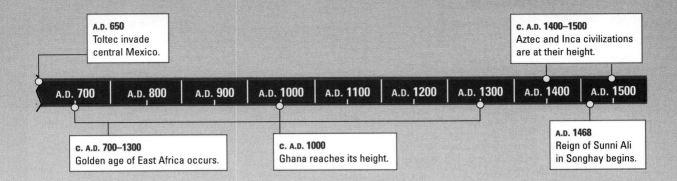

A.D. 650
Toltec invade central Mexico.

C. A.D. 1400–1500
Aztec and Inca civilizations are at their height.

A.D. 700 | **A.D. 800** | **A.D. 900** | **A.D. 1000** | **A.D. 1100** | **A.D. 1200** | **A.D. 1300** | **A.D. 1400** | **A.D. 1500**

C. A.D. 700–1300
Golden age of East Africa occurs.

C. A.D. 1000
Ghana reaches its height.

A.D. 1468
Reign of Sunni Ali in Songhay begins.

Relating Geography to History

(a) Using information in this chapter, trace on maps of Africa and the Americas the migration routes of the peoples who established great civilizations. (b) What climatic and geographical obstacles did they have to overcome? (c) What approximate dates are given for these migrations?

Relating Past to Present

1. There are three major families of languages south of the Sahara: Niger-Kordofanian, Nilo-Saharan, and Khoisan. Niger-Kordofanian includes about 300 Bantu languages, which you read about in the text. Find out more about these language families and their roots in the past.

2. Many English words have roots in Latin American cultures. Use a dictionary to find the origin of these words: chocolate, hammock, potato, quinine, tapioca, tobacco, tomato, avocado.

Applying History Study Skills

Before completing this activity, review Building History Study Skills on page 301.

Read the following excerpt in which Olaudah Equiano describes his Nigerian home.

"In our buildings we study convenience rather than ornament. Each master of a family has a large square piece of ground, surrounded with a moat or a fence. . . . Within this, are his houses to accommodate his family and slaves, which if numerous, frequently present the appearance of a village. In the middle, stands the principal building, appropriated to the sole use of the master and consisting of two apartments; in one of which he sits in the day with his family, the other is left apart for the reception of his friends. . . . On each side are the apartments of his wives, who also have their separate day and night houses. The habitations of the slaves and their families are distributed throughout the rest of the enclosure. These houses never exceed one story in height; they are always built of wood . . . crossed with wattles and neatly plastered within and without."

1. What is the main idea of Equiano's description?
2. In two complete sentences, paraphrase the main idea of the excerpt.

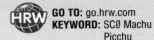
📡 internet**connect**

Search the Internet through the HRW Web site for more information on the Inca city of Machu Picchu. Using the information, create an Internet scavenger hunt for your classmates. Make a list of 10 questions and let them hunt for answers. When possible, include images as clues.

HRW **GO TO:** go.hrw.com
KEYWORD: SCØ Machu Picchu

Building Your Portfolio

1. **Preparing an Oral Report** Form study groups to prepare oral reports on the Native Americans of North America. Each group should choose one Native American culture to research. Assign each member of the group a particular area of study, such as clothing, shelter, transportation, or religious beliefs. One source for your research might be Alvin Josephy's *The Indian Heritage of America* (Knopf). Another source might be scholars at a local college or university. Place your notes and other research materials in your portfolio.

2. **Constructing a Chart** Use resources in your school or public library to locate more information on the decline of the kingdoms of Africa and the Americas discussed in this chapter. Then prepare a chart that lists the reasons for the decline of these kingdoms in three categories: political, economic, and social. Place the chart in your portfolio.

3. **Writing a Report** In January 1997, several archaeologists and anthropologists visited the site of Monte Verde in Chile. These scientists now believe that this site pushes back the date of the migrations to the Americas. Research (using magazines, the Internet, etc.) the excavation and studies of Monte Verde. Then write a report on the findings of the scientists. Place the report in your portfolio.

Unit Summary

The following list contains the key concepts you have learned about the world in transition.

1. A brilliant and sophisticated civilization, the Byzantine Empire survived for 1,000 years and helped preserve the heritage of Greece and Rome. After the split of the Christian church in 1054, the empire became the seat of the Eastern Orthodox Church. Later, Kievan Russia and Moscow adopted many Byzantine traditions.
2. The rise of Islam transformed much of Asia and parts of Africa and Europe. Its early believers spread the Islamic faith widely.
3. The great Frankish king, Charlemagne, created an empire that included much of western Europe.
4. Two important medieval institutions were feudalism and the manorial system.
5. During the Middle Ages the church in western Europe performed many of the same functions as modern governments.
6. Kings in France and England gradually extended their authority in the late Middle Ages.
7. The Crusades were organized chiefly to regain the Holy Land from the Muslims, but they produced a number of other effects.
8. Towns grew and medieval culture flourished as trade revived. Townspeople gained important rights—freedom from service to the manor, town justice, and commercial rights.
9. Under the Sui, Tang, and Song dynasties the Chinese made notable achievements. Their important inventions included gunpowder and printing.
10. In the 1200s the nomadic Mongols of Central Asia were united into a powerful fighting force under Genghis Khan.
11. Japan was influenced by China but created its own distinct culture.
12. From ancient times through the 1500s a remarkable variety of societies arose on the African continent. The great kingdoms included Kush, Aksum, Zimbabwe, Ghana, Mali, and Songhay.
13. In the Americas complex civilizations developed, especially in various regions of North America and in Mexico and Peru.

Reviewing Concepts

On a separate sheet of paper, name the individuals who might have made the following statements.

1. "I used my native Italian language to describe a journey through hell, purgatory, and heaven."
2. "I brought the papacy to the height of its power and influence."
3. "I was crowned Emperor of the Romans in 800."
4. "I led the political, economic, intellectual and artistic revival of the Byzantine Empire."
5. "I led my Mongol army into China, conquering Central Asia and most of Persia."
6. "I asked my followers to believe in one God, Allah, and accept me as his prophet."
7. "I defended my French city of Orléans against the English, but I was eventually burned as a heretic."
8. "I conquered England in 1066 but also retained control over large territories of France."
9. "I was forced by my nobles to sign a charter protecting their rights and limiting my power."
10. "I was the first ruler of the independent state called Russia, and the first czar."

Applying Critical Thinking Skills

1. **Classifying Ideas** Name the culture that each of the following phrases describes.
   (a) Artistic expression represented by the tea ceremony and Noh plays
   (b) Spread from Arabia with a new religion claiming one God for all peoples
   (c) Continued the Roman Empire in the East and helped Christianity spread into Russia
   (d) Built steep pyramids as temples, had a counting system based on 20, and predicted solar eclipses
   (e) Perfected civil service examinations
2. **Analyzing Ideas** Both the Christian Church and Islam split into two or more branches. Why do you think such splits occur?
3. **Synthesizing Ideas** Trade and city life are considered essential to civilization. Defend or oppose this idea as it would apply to any three of the following: western Europe, China, Russia, western Africa.
4. **Comparing Ideas** Compare the western European culture of the Middle Ages to Islamic culture of the same period with regard to scientific accomplishments, language and literature, and concepts of law and justice.

Relating Geography to History

Study the maps of Africa and the Americas on pages 297 and 306 and the map of the world on pages R2 and R3.
(a) What geographic factors isolated the peoples of Sub–Saharan Africa from people in the rest of the world?
(b) What geographic factors isolated the peoples of North and South America from people in the rest of the world?

Writing About History

1. Work with other members of your class to write a scene from a play in which a representative from Mali, one of Charlemagne's lords, a Muslim mullah, a Song emperor, the Tokugawa shogun, and an Inca ruler debate the merits of their civilizations.
2. Use recent issues of periodicals such as *National Geographic* and Internet research through the HRW

Web site to write a report on recent archaeological excavations in the Americas and Africa.

Further Readings

Baudez, Claude-François, and Sydney Picasso. *Lost Cities of the Maya.* Harry Abrams, 1992. Fascinating account of the Maya civilization.

Gruzinski, Serge. *The Aztecs: Rise and Fall of an Empire.* Harry Abrams, 1992. Lavishly illustrated history of the Aztec.

Hollister, Warren C. *Medieval Europe: A Short Sourcebook.* Mc-Graw, 1996. Readings about medieval Europe.

Holmes, George, ed. *The Oxford Illustrated History of Medieval Europe.* Oxford University Press, 1990. Shows territorial changes in Europe between A.D. 400 and 1500.

Time-Life, eds. *The Mongol Conquests.* Time-Life, 1989. Illustrated history of the Mongol Empire in 1200 to 1300 as well as other empires of the period.

Tuchman, Barbara. *A Distant Mirror. The Calamitous 14th Century.* Ballantine Books, 1987. Analyzes life in Europe during the 1300s.

UNIT 3 CHRONOLOGY

Date	Politics	Science and Technology	Society and Culture
750 B.C.—A.D. 500	Height of Kush kingdom 13* Kush defeated by Aksum 13 Mayan civilization 13 Angles and Saxons in England 10		Saint Patrick of Ireland 10
A.D. 500–700	Justinian's empire 8 Sui and Tang dynasties in China 12 Muslim invasion of Spain 9 Battle of Tours 9	Beginning of golden age in East Africa 13	Hagia Sophia 8 Buddhism in Japan 12 Muhammad 9 Tang ceramics 12 Islam in East Africa 13
700–1000	Charlemagne 10 Viking invasions 8 Alfred the Great 10 Height of Maya civilization 13 Song Dynasty 12 Ghana civilization 13 Feudalism begins in Europe 10	Viking navigational techniques 10 Manorialism 10	Illuminated manuscript 10 Cyrillic alphabet 8 *Diamond Sutra* 12 *Anglo-Saxon Chronicle* 10 *The Tale of Genji* 12
1000–1250	Toltec 13 Norman Conquest 10 Yaroslav the Wise 8 Frederick Barbarossa 10 Innocent III 10 Magna Carta 10 Chinese gunpowder used in warfare 12	Optics in Europe 11 Flying buttress 11	Development of universities 11 Division of Christian church 8 Domesday Book 10 Crusades begin 11 Concordat of Worms 10 Nigerian bronze sculpture 13 Gothic cathedrals 11
1250–1500	Mongols in Russia 8 Yuan dynasty 12 Marco Polo 12 Mali and Songhay 13 Hundred Years' War 11 Timur destroys Delhi 9 Fall of Constantinople 8 Joan of Arc 11 Height of Aztec and Inca civilizations 13	Inca irrigation and roads 13 Inca *quipu* 13 Aztec pyramids 13	*The Divine Comedy* 11 Babylonian Captivity 11 Great Schism 11 Defender of the Peace 11 Black Death 11 Wycliffe's English Bible 11 *The Canterbury Tales* 11 Jan Hus executed 11

*Indicates chapter in which development is discussed

The World in Transition

The Byzantine Empire, Kievan Russia, and the Mongols

The collapse of the Roman Empire in the West resulted in the disappearance of strong governments. However, the Roman Empire in the East—the Byzantine Empire—maintained its traditions and kept out barbarian invaders.

The Byzantine Empire

By the early A.D. 500s the Western Roman Empire had broken down into a group of Germanic tribal kingdoms. The Eastern Roman Empire, on the other hand, had defeated the barbarians and was primed for a great political, economic, intellectual, and artistic revival under the leadership of Emperor Justinian. Although many problems plagued the Byzantine Empire after Justinian's death, its political, military, and economic strengths helped it survive for many years.

The Christian church. A debate arose in the East about the role of icons, or holy pictures, in church services. The controversy drastically affected the Byzantine Empire's relations with Rome. After years of controversy, the Christian church officially split in 1054. In the West, it became known as the Roman Catholic Church with the pope in Rome as its head. In the East, it became known as the Eastern Orthodox Church with the patriarch in Constantinople as its head. The two churches remain separate today.

Byzantine culture and the preservation of Roman law. The Byzantine Empire preserved and passed on the classical learning of ancient Greece, Rome, and the East. Of particular importance was the preservation of Roman law. Emperor Justinian had his scholars collect and organize all the laws of the Roman Empire. The entire collection is known as the *Corpus juris civilis*, Latin for "body of civil law." It contains the original laws compiled by Justinian, often called the Justinianic Code. This code was used as the basis of many European legal systems during the Middle Ages, and its influence continues today.

The Rise of Russia

A vast plain stretches across eastern Europe and Central Asia. In the southwestern portion of the plain, where it is known as the steppe, a military ruler of a people called the Rus took control. The word *Russia* is probably derived from this name.

Kiev, which served as the capital of the region, prospered because of its strategic location along rich trade routes. In time, Kiev became the most powerful principality in Kievan Russia, an area that included many semi-independent cities.

The Byzantine church became increasingly important in Kievan Russia. Although authors wrote epic poems and chronicles about wars, religious hymns and sermons constituted the bulk of Kievan literature. Icon painting became the most distinctive Kievan art form. Agriculture and trade were the most important economic activities in Kievan society.

The Rise of the Mongols

After the rule of Yaroslav the Wise ended in 1054, Kiev declined in power and wealth. By 1240 Mongol invaders from the plains west of the Ural Mountains had conquered and burned almost every city in Kievan Russia.

In time Mongol rule grew weaker, and the princes of the region became more independent. During the 1300s, Moscow became the strongest principality. By the late 1400s, Moscow had overthrown Mongol rule and become the center of the independent state called Russia.

The Islamic Empire

In the A.D. 600s the prophet Muhammad began preaching Islam, today the world's second-largest religion.

The Rise and Spread of Islam

The central belief of Islam is that there is only one God. The holy book of Islam is the Qur'an (kuh·RAN).

According to Muslims, the Qur'an presents God's ordinances and teachings as revealed to Muhammad.

According to the Qur'an, a Muslim must meet five important obligations known as the Five Pillars of Islam: (1) Recite the profession of faith: ". . . there is no deity except Allah [God] and that Muhammad is His Servant and Messenger." (2) Pray five times a day facing Mecca, the holy city of Islam. (3) Give alms—money or food—to the poor. (4) Fast from first light to sunset during the month of Ramadan. (5) If possible, make a pilgrimage to Mecca at least once in a lifetime.

Muhammad also emphasized the importance of the jihad (ji·HAHD), or struggle to defend the faith. Anyone who died in this struggle, Muhammad said, was a martyr who would receive the blessings of God and rewards in heaven. After Muhammad's death, Islam spread widely, but it also experienced divisions.

Islamic Civilization
Islamic government allowed its rulers to wield great authority. Within the stable society that developed, both economic and cultural activity flourished. The Islamic culture adopted the best ideas, customs, and institutions they found. They combined the scientific and philosophical ideas of Greece, Rome, and Asia.

Islamic and Mughal Rulers in India
In 997 the Turks began raiding northern India. These raids led to conquest. Over time the small states of the Rajput princes fell to the Turks. In 1193 the Muslims occupied Delhi, and by the early 1200s they

The Alhambra, Granada, Spain

controlled most of northern India in what was called the Delhi sultanate.

Civil wars and the devastating onslaught of the Turko-Mongol leader Timur interrupted Muslim rule. Despite these setbacks, the first period of Muslim rule in India had important and lasting consequences. The Muslims introduced a new and important language—Urdu—and the religion of Islam.

As the Delhi sultanate grew weaker, Rajput princes again struggled for control of India. Thus, as in the time of Timur, India was vulnerable to Mongol attack. In 1526 Babur the Tiger, a descendant of Timur, occupied Delhi and founded the Mughal Empire.

CHAPTER 10

The Rise of the Middle Ages
The period in western European history following the collapse of the Roman Empire, from about A.D. 500 to about 1500, is called the Middle Ages.

The Rise of the Franks
After the Roman Empire collapsed, many Germanic tribes, including the Visigoths, the Vandals, the Burgundians, and the Ostrogoths, plundered Europe, and some established kingdoms. Of all the Germanic tribes, the Franks played the greatest role in European history. The greatest Frankish ruler was Charlemagne, who assumed the throne in A.D. 768 and ruled until 814.

Although Charlemagne was a powerful ruler who organized an efficient government, his empire crumbled soon after his death. This decline occurred not only because of internal feuds but also because invaders—Muslims, Slavs, Vikings, and Magyars—swarmed into the empire from every direction.

Feudalism and the Manorial System
We call the political structure that evolved in Europe after the death of Charlemagne feudalism. Feudalism was a system in which kings and powerful nobles granted land to other nobles in return for loyalty, military assistance, and other services. By the 1000s this structure was firmly established throughout most of western Europe.

Feudalism was essentially a governmental and military system. The manor, a large estate that included

The Bayeux tapestry

a village, became the economic unit of the early Middle Ages.

The lord and several peasants shared the land of a manor. Most of the peasants on a manor were serfs, people who were bound to the land. Serfs were not slaves, however, for they could not be sold away from the land. This system was called the manorial system.

The Church
Central governments in medieval Europe were weak or did not exist at all. Therefore, the church performed many of the functions of modern governments.

Members of the clergy were organized in ranks according to their power and responsibilities. The levels of this hierarchy, starting at the bottom, were the parish priest, the bishop, the archbishop, and the pope and his curia. A second group of clergy was the monastics—monks and nuns. Problems of the church in medieval Europe included lay investiture, the worldly lives of the clergy, simony, and heresy.

The Struggle for Power in England and France
Before the A.D. 1000s, kings and lords often struggled for power. From this struggle gradually emerged such kingdoms as England and France, where the king's authority grew stronger than that of the lords.

England. In 1066 Duke William of Normandy invaded and conquered England. Kings after William strengthened the central government. One of William's successors, King John, brought on a revolt among the nobles by forcing them to pay taxes that they considered unjust. In 1215 the nobles forced John to accept a document known as Magna Carta (Latin for "great charter"), which protected the liberties of the nobles. Although the charter was not considered significant at the time, later political thinkers regarded many of its clauses as important precedents.

In the century that followed the signing of Magna Carta, the two most important developments in English history were the evolution of Parliament—the legislative body of England—and the growth of common law—the type of law based on judges' decisions.

France. In 987 an assembly of nobles chose Hugh Capet, a French noble, as king. Capet and his descendants, called the Capetians, ruled France for over 300 years and steadily increased royal power by adding to the royal lands and developing a strong central government.

The Clash over Germany and Italy
During the A.D. 1000s the Holy Roman emperors who ruled what are now Germany and northern Italy often clashed with the papacy because the emperors claimed the right to appoint bishops. The issue was finally settled in 1122 when an assembly of church leaders, nobles, and representatives of the Holy Roman Empire reached an agreement known as the Concordat of Worms. The Concordat provided that only church officials could elect bishops.

CHAPTER 11

The High Middle Ages
During the Middle Ages cities became powerful centers of social and political change. Trade revived as people began to look outward, away from Europe.

The Crusades
During the A.D. 1000s the Saljuq Turks conquered Palestine. Christian pilgrims to Palestine came home with reports of persecutions at the hands of the Turks. Pope Urban II called for a war to recover the Holy

Land for Christians. The expeditions to regain the Holy Land are called the Crusades.

From a military standpoint, all the Crusades except the first failed. However, Europeans learned about many things of military importance, including the crossbow and perhaps the use of gunpowder. The Crusades hastened the decline of feudalism and helped strengthen the authority of kings.

The Revival of Trade

Trade nearly died out in western Europe after the A.D. 400s. Trade first began to revive in Italy, where neither trade nor towns had declined as much as elsewhere. Trade also revived in northern Europe. Important developments resulted, including a manufacturing system, a banking system, and the investment of capital. These developments laid the foundation for the emergence of a market economy, one in which individuals control land, labor, and capital.

The Growth of Towns

The growth of towns accompanied the resurgence in trade. As the number of towns increased and their populations grew, a new class of merchants, master workers, and skilled workers emerged in medieval society. Since townspeople wanted stable and uniform governments that would protect trade and property, they usually favored kings over nobles.

Life and Culture in the Middle Ages

Two writers, Dante and Chaucer, represent the flowering of medieval literature. Dante Alighieri was born in Florence, Italy, in 1265. Dante's greatest work is *The Divine Comedy*. Geoffrey Chaucer of England wrote *The Canterbury Tales* in the form of a series of stories told by a group of religious pilgrims.

The later Middle Ages witnessed the growth of universities. By the 1300s universities could be found in towns throughout central and northern Europe. Church architecture was the primary art form. Cathedrals were built in the soaring Gothic style instead of the earlier Romanesque style based on Roman architecture.

Wars and the Growth of Nations

As a result of the decline of feudalism, states began to form. Kings began to build their kingdoms into organized nations.

Crusader siege of Jerusalem

The authority of the English king, although partially restricted by Parliament, increased in various ways. A single system of law and courts developed, and increased revenue as the country grew more prosperous.

During the Hundred Years' War, Joan of Arc's help in the defense of Orléans and her later martyrdom created strong feelings of patriotism among the French. As in England, a stronger monarchy was reestablished.

Spain had been divided into four kingdoms during the early Middle Ages. In the 1500s, however, Ferdinand and Isabella united Castile and Aragon to form the new nation of Spain. They added the kingdom of Navarre to its territories and made Spain a powerful monarchy.

Unlike England, France, and Spain, Germany and Italy—the regions that made up the Holy Roman Empire—did not become unified nations until the 1800s.

Challenges to Church Power

The late Middle Ages also witnessed changes in the status of the church. By the early 1300s, French kings named the popes, who ruled the church from Avignon in southern France rather than from Rome. This period of papal history—from 1309 to 1377—is known as the Babylonian Captivity.

The situation for the church worsened after 1378 when two popes, one French and one Italian, claimed power during a period called the Great Schism. The Babylonian Captivity and the Great Schism weakened the authority and prestige of the papacy and increased criticism of the church.

CHAPTER 12

The Civilizations of East Asia

From about A.D. 552 to 1573 great civilizations flourished in East Asia.

China

The Sui dynasty succeeded in uniting China in A.D. 589. In their brief period of power, Sui rulers oversaw the building of one of the engineering marvels of the ancient world—the Grand Canal—linking northern and southern China for the first time. However, an uprising in 618 ended the Sui dynasty, which was replaced by the Tang dynasty.

Although the Tang dynasty itself lasted less than 300 years, it began a 1,000-year period during which China became the most powerful, the most sophisticated, and the wealthiest country in the world.

The next dynasty, the Song, faced both foreign invasion and civil wars. Nevertheless, during Song rule, Chinese civilization remained at a high level, and trade expanded.

The Mongol Empire

In the 1200s the Mongols under the leadership of Genghis Khan captured the city now called Beijing and named it Khanbalik (kahn·buh·LEEK). They then turned westward, conquering Central Asia and most of Persia. Under Kublai Khan, the Mongols conquered the area now called Tibet and parts of Southeast Asia.

Japan, Korea, and Southeast Asia

Only sketchy records of early Japanese history exist. We do know that China influenced Japan, and that the centralized political system adopted from China

gradually fell into decline after the early 800s. In its place Japan developed a system of local power that in many ways resembled feudalism, the social system that prevailed in Europe at that time.

In Japan the feudal system contained two conflicting sources of power. One was the central government, in which an important family held power in the name of the emperor. The other source consisted of powerful landholders who established and led a class of warriors.

In 1192 the Minamoto clan emerged triumphant from a civil war, and the emperor gave Minamoto Yoritomo the title of shogun. Real power now rested with the shogun, who was the chief military officer and also controlled finance, law, and the courts.

The leading families and their shoguns had power in the central government, but at the local level landlords hired warriors called samurai to protect themselves.

For much of Korea's history China controlled the peninsula and greatly influenced its political and cultural development. Mainland Southeast Asia, which borders China on the north and India on the northwest, shows the influence of both of those cultures.

Tang dynasty silk painting

CHAPTER 13

Africa and the Americas

Civilizations developed in unique ways in Africa and in the Americas. Trade was an important factor in how various kingdoms and empires developed in Africa south of the Sahara. In isolation from contact with other parts of the world, complex civilizations grew up in the Andes and Mesoamerica.

Africa's Early History

Scholars rely on many methods to understand the history of Africa. Experts believe that most Africans lived in small, independent villages ruled by elders. Relationships established by kinship and age bound the different areas together. Within this system, women played a crucial role. Through the rise and fall of numerous kingdoms, the village survived as the basic unit of society and the economy.

African City-States and Kingdoms

Along the Nile River, south of the major centers of ancient Egypt, arose a powerful kingdom known as Kush. At first, Kush maintained close cultural and economic ties with Egypt. When it became more independent, it conquered Upper Egypt in about 710 B.C. Later, the kingdom of Aksum arose in the Ethiopian Highlands.

No large kingdoms such as Kush and Aksum emerged on the coast of East Africa. Instead, a series of city-states emerged and dominated coastal trade in the Indian Ocean.

The growth of Indian Ocean trade after the A.D. 900s dramatically increased the demand for gold. The Shona people, who immigrated onto the plateau land of what is today Zimbabwe, achieved control over local peoples and mining activities.

In West Africa, between Lake Chad and the Atlantic Ocean, several important African societies developed. The most powerful included Ghana, Mali, and Songhay.

The Earliest Americans

The first people in the Americas lived by hunting and gathering. Gradually a new way of life emerged— farming. In what are now the United States and Canada, many different cultures and societies thrived. The cultures of these peoples often depended on the geography of the region they inhabited.

The Empires of Mexico and Peru

Several cultures developed in Central and South America. Early cultures included the Olmec and the Toltec in Mexico and the Maya in the Yucatán Peninsula. Around A.D. 1200, peoples from the north invaded central Mexico. One of these groups, the Aztec, soon emerged as the strongest. The Aztec incorporated into their culture the inventions of peoples they conquered or with whom they traded. They soon learned metalworking, weaving, and pottery. They also made and acquired the use of the calendar and mathematics.

At about the same time that the Aztec civilization in Mexico was at its height, another civilization in the Andes Mountains of South America was expanding. These people—the Inca—based their religion on worship of the Sun and moon. Their name meant "children of the sun."

By the late 1400s the Inca Empire extended along most of the west coast of South America and far into the Andes, covering much of the present-day nations of Peru, Ecuador, Bolivia, and Chile.

Synthesis Review

1. **Understanding Ideas** What were the greatest Byzantine contributions to civilization?

2. **Explaining Ideas** Why was the jihad of great importance to Muslims?

3. **Summarizing Ideas** What were the basic principles of feudalism and the manorial system?

4. **Analyzing Ideas** How did the growth of towns in the Middle Ages affect the growth of national states?

5. **Comparing Ideas** How did the governmental system of Japan resemble feudalism as it existed in Europe?

6. **Classifying Ideas** How did different types of cultures develop in different parts of Africa?

7. **Synthesizing Ideas** Explain why you think the Byzantines and the Muslims were able to control large empires when Europe was fragmented.

UNIT 4

The Emergence of Modern Nations

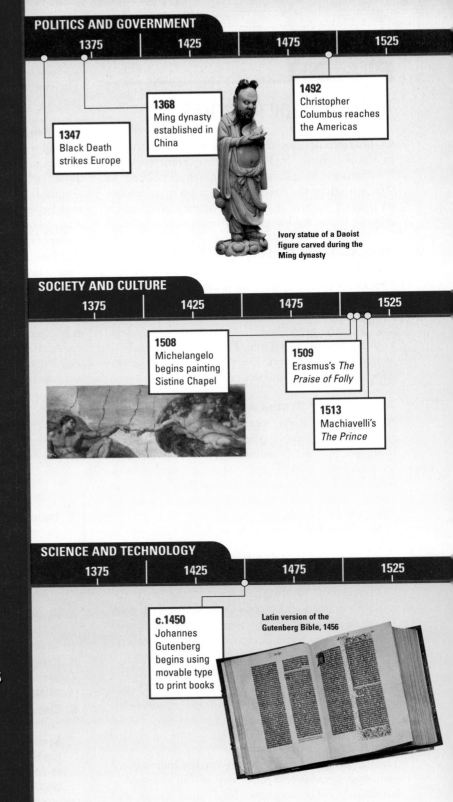

POLITICS AND GOVERNMENT

1375　1425　1475　1525

1347
Black Death strikes Europe

1368
Ming dynasty established in China

1492
Christopher Columbus reaches the Americas

Ivory statue of a Daoist figure carved during the Ming dynasty

SOCIETY AND CULTURE

1375　1425　1475　1525

1508
Michelangelo begins painting Sistine Chapel

1509
Erasmus's *The Praise of Folly*

1513
Machiavelli's *The Prince*

SCIENCE AND TECHNOLOGY

1375　1425　1475　1525

c.1450
Johannes Gutenberg begins using movable type to print books

Latin version of the Gutenberg Bible, 1456

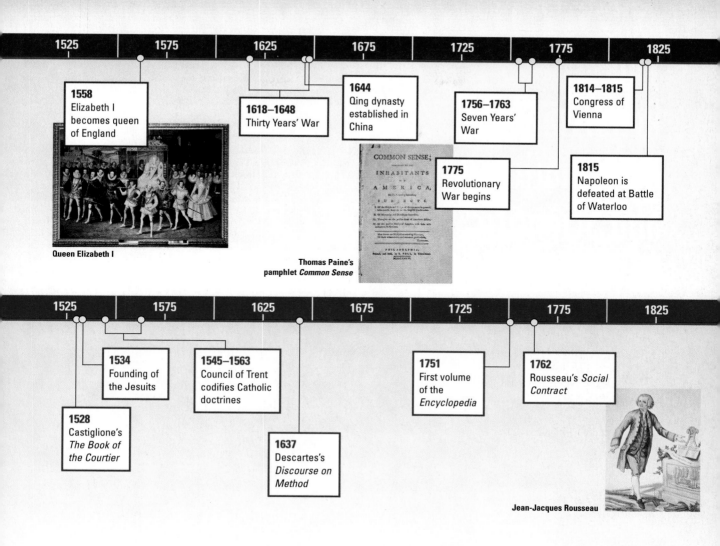

1558
Elizabeth I becomes queen of England

Queen Elizabeth I

1618–1648
Thirty Years' War

1644
Qing dynasty established in China

1775
Revolutionary War begins

1756–1763
Seven Years' War

1814–1815
Congress of Vienna

1815
Napoleon is defeated at Battle of Waterloo

Thomas Paine's pamphlet *Common Sense*

1528
Castiglione's *The Book of the Courtier*

1534
Founding of the Jesuits

1545–1563
Council of Trent codifies Catholic doctrines

1637
Descartes's *Discourse on Method*

1751
First volume of the *Encyclopedia*

1762
Rousseau's *Social Contract*

Jean-Jacques Rousseau

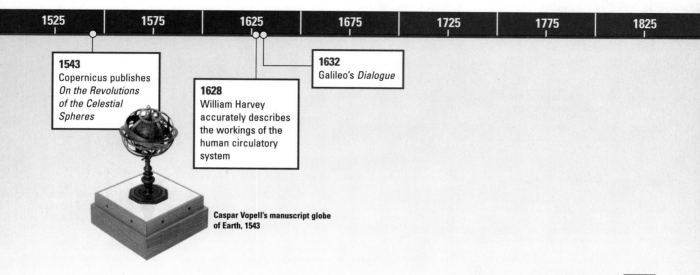

1543
Copernicus publishes *On the Revolutions of the Celestial Spheres*

1628
William Harvey accurately describes the workings of the human circulatory system

1632
Galileo's *Dialogue*

Caspar Vopell's manuscript globe of Earth, 1543

The Renaissance, Reformation, and Scientific Revolution

TIME

A.D. 1350–1700

A.D. 1350–1700

3.7 million B.C. | 4000 B.C. | A.D. 2100

PLACE

Europe

Europe

ARCTIC OCEAN

NORTH AMERICA

EUROPE

ASIA

PACIFIC OCEAN

AFRICA

Equator

SOUTH AMERICA

ATLANTIC OCEAN

INDIAN OCEAN

AUSTRALIA

PACIFIC OCEAN

ANTARCTICA

The Medici Family Palazzo, Florence

Significance

If you were to think about the differences between medieval and modern times, you would probably think first of the great difference in the material goods available. Today we have CD players, microwave ovens, and conveniences that medieval people never dreamed of. However, another and perhaps even greater difference exists: a difference in attitudes. Beginning in the 1300s, people gradually began to look for new ways to explain why and how things happened in the world.

Many historians believe that the changes in attitude that altered how people viewed themselves and their world grew out of a philosophical and artistic movement that began in Italy in the early 1300s. Because it centered on a revival of interest in the classical learning of Greece and Rome, we call this movement the **Renaissance** (REN·uh·sahnts), a French word meaning "rebirth."

Terms to Define

Renaissance	Counter-Reformation
humanists	broadsides
perspective	almanacs
Reformation	standard of living
indulgences	inflation
95 theses	Scientific Revolution
sects	scientific method
predestination	geocentric theory
theocracy	heliocentric theory

People to Identify

Niccolò Machiavelli	Martin Luther
Leonardo da Vinci	John Calvin
Michelangelo	Ignatius de Loyola
Johannes Gutenberg	Nicolaus Copernicus
William Shakespeare	Galileo

Places to Locate

Florence	Zurich
Venice	Geneva
Wittenberg	

Chapter Theme Questions

- **The Arts** How might the influx of new ideas affect the arts?
- **Religion** What factors might have led to major shifts in religious thought?
- **Science** How might a change in methods of investigation lead to an entirely new way of viewing the world?

On November 4, 1966, newscasts across the world carried reports of a staggering natural disaster. In northern Italy the Arno River had burst over its banks, sending torrents of swirling floodwaters cascading through the museums, cathedrals, and libraries of Florence. When the waters receded, they left layer upon layer of sewage and muck. Within days, hundreds of people converged on the waterlogged city to help with the massive cleanup.

Why would news of a flood in northern Italy electrify people across the world? Quite simply because that city contained the world's greatest store of Renaissance art and literature. One reporter noted:

❝It is fair to say that much of what we know today of painting and sculpture, of architecture and political science, of scientific method and economic theory, we owe to the artists, politicians, statesmen, bankers, and merchants of the Renaissance—that explosion of intellectual and artistic energy in Italy between 1300 and 1600. And Florentines stood at the turbulent center of the Renaissance.❞

The outpouring of creativity that was the Renaissance changed the course of Western civilization.

Renaissance Writers and Artists

Focus Questions

- **What led to the Italian Renaissance?**
- **What were the characteristics of Italian Renaissance art?**
- **What were the characteristics of the Northern Renaissance in terms of humanist thought, literature, and art?**

Scholars use the term *Renaissance* to refer not only to a philosophical and artistic movement but also to the period during which it flourished. The

Renaissance was a time of many developments, including the invention of the printing press, advances in science, and a new emphasis on reason.

The Origins of the Italian Renaissance

A renewed interest in Greek and Roman literature and life characterized the Renaissance. In many ways it was natural that this interest would reawaken in Italy. Ruins of the mighty Roman Empire served as constant reminders of Roman glory. The tradition of Rome as the capital city of a vast empire lived on in the popes, who made Rome the seat of the Roman Catholic Church. The Crusades and trade with Africa and Southwest Asia introduced new ideas and brought Italians into contact with the Byzantine

civilization, whose scholars had preserved much learning from classical Greece and Rome. Arab and African developments in such disciplines as medicine and science fired the curiosity of many Italian scholars.

Italian cities such as Florence, Rome, Venice, Milan, and Naples had grown rich through trade and industry. Their citizens included many educated, wealthy merchants. In Florence, for example, the Medici (MED·ee·chee) family grew wealthy first as bankers and then as rulers of the city-state. As leader of Florence, Lorenzo Medici became a great patron of the arts and influenced Florence's artistic awakening.

The Humanities

Beginning in the 1300s, a number of Italian scholars developed a lively interest in classical Greek and Roman literature. Medieval scholars who had studied ancient history had tried to bring everything they learned into harmony with Christian doctrine. By contrast, the Italian scholars studied the ancient world to explore its great achievements.

These Italian scholars stressed the study of grammar, rhetoric, history, and poetry, using classical texts. We call these studies the *humanities*; people who specialized in the humanities were called **humanists.** Humanists searched out manuscripts written in Greek and Latin. Often they would find more than one copy of a work. If the copies differed, humanists compared the different versions to try to determine which was most authentic. In doing so they displayed a critical approach to learning that had been lacking.

As humanists studied classical manuscripts, they came to believe that it was important to know how things worked. This belief led them to emphasize education. However, they also felt that a person should lead a meaningful life. Humanists became convinced that a person had to become actively involved in practical affairs such as patronage of the arts.

Humanists viewed existence not only as a preparation for life after death but also as a joy in itself. Along with a belief in individual dignity came an admiration for individual achievement. Many individuals of this period displayed a variety of talents, such as being both poet and scientist.

Writers of the Italian Renaissance

One of the first humanists, the Italian Francesco Petrarch (PEE·trahrk), lived from 1304 to 1374. Like many of the humanists, Petrarch became famous as a scholar and as a teacher. He also wrote poetry, and his sonnets to Laura, an imaginary ideal

Renaissance Italy, c. 1500

Learning from Maps During the Renaissance, Italy was a patchwork of small states.

? Place To what republic did the island of Corsica belong?

Machiavelli: Lessons in Statecraft

Niccolò Machiavelli is considered one of the most influential political writers of the Renaissance. While the political theorists of the Middle Ages wrote about politics in an idealistic way, Machiavelli strived to present the realistic side of politics in his work. His ideas were based on his perception of human nature from a historical context.

According to Machiavelli, an essential link existed between the condition of the state and the condition of the people. The state, he wrote, must be unified and efficient. If the state were divided and inefficient, drastic measures might be required to regain control.

Machiavelli's most well-known work, *The Prince*, was essentially a handbook on how to be a great ruler. Machiavelli believed that a ruler did not have to abide by traditional customs and morals but instead should be concerned only with power and success in political ventures. As an example of this new type of ruler, Machiavelli cited Cesare Borgia, who achieved political power through cruel and ruthless means. *The Prince* has often been considered a justification of the type of tyrannical leadership practiced by rulers such as Borgia.

In his essay, Machiavelli advised rulers to maintain the safety of their states by whatever means they thought necessary and not to let considerations of honesty, justice, or honor hamper them. Today we use the word Machiavellian to describe people who use deceit and who have little regard for morality in their effort to get what they want. In this excerpt from *The Prince,* Machiavelli discusses power and the need to inspire fear in one's subjects: "A controversy has arisen about this: whether it is better to be loved than feared, or vice versa. My view is that it is desirable to be both loved and feared; but it is difficult to achieve both and, if one of them has to be lacking, it is much safer to be feared than loved.

"For this may be said of men generally: they are ungrateful, fickle, feigners [liars] and dissemblers [deceivers], avoiders of danger, eager for gain. While you benefit them they are all devoted to you: they would shed their blood for you; they offer their possessions, their lives, and their sons . . . when the need to do so is far off. But when you are hard pressed, they turn away. A ruler who has relied completely on their promises and has neglected to prepare other defences, will be ruined, because friendships that are acquired with money, and not through greatness and nobility of character, are paid for but not secured, and prove unreliable just when they are needed.

"Men are less hesitant about offending or harming a ruler who makes himself less loved than one who inspires fear. For love is sustained by a bond of gratitude which, because men are excessively self-interested, is broken whenever they see a chance to benefit themselves. But fear is sustained by a dread of punishment that is always effective."

Machiavelli

Title page from *The Prince*

woman, are considered some of the greatest love poems in literature.

Petrarch's main influence, however, grew out of his desire for continuity with classical writers, whom he believed were committed to virtue in both public and private life. Petrarch thought these individuals could best be imitated if one studied their writings. The study of the writings of the ancient Greeks and Romans came to be called *classical education.* A command of classical languages, as they had been used by the ancient Greeks and Romans, became the mark of an educated person.

The humanists remained deeply committed to Christian teachings. For that reason, they sometimes felt a tension between their commitment to the study of the ancients and their commitment to Christianity. Petrarch, for instance, agonized over his lust for fame (a common Roman ambition) because he feared it would hurt his chances for salvation. Like most Italian humanists, Petrarch thought it important to lead a full and active life here on earth, even if that meant devoting less time to spiritual concerns.

Niccolò Machiavelli (mahk·yah·VEL·lee) of Florence, a diplomat and historian who lived from 1469 to 1527, ranks as one of the most illustrious of the many Renaissance writers. In 1513 he wrote a famous essay, *The Prince,* which described government not in terms of lofty ideals but as Machiavelli felt government actually worked.

Machiavelli can be considered a humanist because he looked to the ancient Romans for models and because such matters as the workings of politics interested him. However, the lack of concern for morality that he wrote about in *The Prince* set him apart from other humanists, who considered virtue their main aim.

Baldassare Castiglione (kahs·teel·YOH·nay) was an Italian diplomat and writer who lived from 1478 to 1529. In 1528 he published what was probably the most famous book of the Renaissance, *The Book of the Courtier.* Castiglione's work is a book on courtesy as well as an explanation of the role of the refined courtier as opposed to that of the coarse knight of the Middle Ages. As nobles lost their military role, Castiglione gave them a new idea of refined behavior. The setting for the book is the court at Urbino, an Italian city-state where the author lived many happy years. Castiglione's characters are real people who reflect in fictional conversations on how gentlemen and gentlewomen ought to act in polite society.

The Italian writer Baldassare Castiglione used the literary device of a dialogue between friends to discuss proper manners for ladies and gentlemen at Renaissance courts.

Italian Renaissance Artists

Art in addition to literature flourished in Italy during the Renaissance. In an outburst of creativity, Italian artists produced some of the world's most exquisite masterpieces.

Medieval paintings stressed the world beyond everyday life—a world associated with religious subjects—and depicted formal and stylized figures. The most noticeable characteristic of Renaissance painting, on the other hand, is its realism. Renaissance painters depicted realistic and lifelike human figures in their paintings. Even the backgrounds of these paintings differed from those of medieval paintings. Earlier artists had portrayed the Holy Land. Renaissance painters showed the rugged countryside that they knew.

The success of many female Renaissance artists, such as Sofonisba Anguissola, was accepted only as a pursuit of "womanly virtue." Anguissola is best known for her self-portraits and for her portrait of Philip II.

Realism and Perspective

In the Middle Ages, paintings did not look particularly realistic. Almost all art was religious, and artists were not interested in drawing attention to the human nature of, for example, Jesus and Mary. Instead, artists tried to visually represent spiritual aspects of their subjects. For example, the relative size of figures or objects often showed their importance in a spiritual hierarchy.

With the Renaissance came a new interest in accurately depicting the beauty of the human form and the natural world. To be realistic, a painting had to create the illusion of distance and depth on a flat surface. In the early 1400s, a Renaissance architect named Filippo Brunelleschi performed a series of optical experiments to devise mathematical formulas for achieving perspective. Brunelleschi discovered the laws of linear perspective, which explain how the human eye perceives distant objects as

smaller than close ones. Renaissance painters soon began to use Brunelleschi's rules of perspective in their works.

In *The School of Athens* (above), Raphael used precise mathematical measurements and perspective techniques to render the architectural setting and the people within it. In this scene, which appears on a wall in the Vatican Palace in Rome, Plato and Aristotle are surrounded by other famous Greek philosophers.

Renaissance painters could make their works lifelike because they had learned a very important technique of painting called **perspective.** By making distant objects smaller than those in the foreground, and by arranging objects in certain ways, an artist could create the illusion of depth on a flat canvas.

Giotto (JAWT·oh), who lived from 1276 to 1337, and Masaccio (mah·ZAHT·choh), who lived from 1401 to 1428, were important realist painters. According to legend, a fly in one of Giotto's paintings looked so lifelike that an observer tried to brush it off. Masaccio used light and shadows to give the effect of depth to objects.

The late 1400s and early 1500s are often referred to as the High Renaissance. Among the many great painters of this period, four made particularly outstanding contributions to the arts.

Leonardo da Vinci (dah·VEEN·chee)—painter, sculptor, engineer, architect, and scientist—lived from 1452 to 1519. Da Vinci used his experiments in

science to enhance his painting. Studies of anatomy helped him draw the human figure, and mathematics helped him organize the space in his paintings. People throughout the world still marvel at his mural *The Last Supper*. Probably his most famous painting is the portrait called *Mona Lisa*.

Another master of Renaissance art, Michelangelo Buonarroti (mee·kay·LAHN·jay·loh bwaw·nahr·RAW·tee), lived from 1475 to 1564. Millions of people have visited the Sistine Chapel of the Vatican, the residence of the pope in Rome, and looked with wonder at the frescoes Michelangelo painted on the ceiling.

Although he was a brilliant painter, Michelangelo preferred sculpture. Both his paintings and his stone carvings of such biblical figures as David and Moses suggest a massive dignity. Almost as versatile as da Vinci, Michelangelo also wrote poetry and worked as an architect, helping design St. Peter's Basilica in Rome.

Raphael (RAF·ee·el), who lived from 1483 to 1520, became so popular in Florence that the pope hired him to help beautify the Vatican by painting frescoes in the papal chambers. Raphael also painted exquisite madonnas, representations of the Virgin Mary.

Titian (TISH·uhn), who lived from about 1488 to 1576, spent most of his life in his native Venice. His works, such as *The Assumption of the Virgin,* portray a vivid sense of drama and are noted for their rich colors. The Holy Roman Emperor sponsored many of Titian's works, and he became one of the first painters to obtain wealth for his paintings.

Dozens of other artists prospered in Italy in the 1400s and 1500s. Princes supported many of these artists. The princes thought they would achieve lasting fame if they became patrons of the arts. Thus the patrons helped foster the enormous creativity of the period.

The Northern Renaissance

Humanist thought spread beyond Italy. Numerous mountain passes, such as the Brenner and the Great Saint Bernard, pierced the rugged Alps and allowed people—and ideas—to pass from Italy to northern Europe. The Danube, Rhône, and Rhine rivers provided even easier routes. New ideas, often carried by northern European students who had studied in Italy, soon traveled to Germany, the Netherlands, France, and England.

Printing. A remarkable new process—printing—also helped ideas spread. Hundreds of years earlier, the Chinese had learned how to create a wooden block into which writing or pictures could be etched. Printers applied ink to the block and pressed the block onto paper. Then the block was reinked. In this way the writing or pictures could be reproduced many times. The Chinese had also learned how to assemble the block from separate pieces, or type, that could be used again and again—movable type. The European invention of printing, however, appears to have been completely independent of the Chinese process.

Scholars believe that in about 1450, Johannes Gutenberg of Mainz, Germany, became the first European to use movable type to print books.

Michelangelo was commissioned to create his sculpture *David* in 1501. Standing in front of the Palazzo Vecchio, Florence, it embodies the power and beauty of Michelangelo's style.

Building History Study Skills

READ
WRITE
INTERPRET
CONNECT
THINK

Making Connections with History: Using Art to Understand Values

In 1508 Pope Julius II commissioned Michelangelo to paint the ceiling of the Sistine Chapel in Rome. Perched atop a new type of scaffolding that he had designed for the project, Michelangelo worked until 1512 to complete the commission. The result of his work has often been called the best example of Renaissance art in the world.

By studying the works of art produced during a specific period in history, we can learn much about the values of the people who created the art. Much of the art of the Middle Ages in western Europe, for example, reflects the religious nature of the society. The backgrounds of paintings focus not on real scenery but on heavenly backdrops, symbols, or gold reflections. People's faces reflect piety rather than individuality, and the figures themselves do not appear three-dimensional. Renaissance art retains religious themes while reflecting the humanistic and secular values of the time.

How to Use Art to Understand Values

To use art for understanding values, follow these steps.

1. Identify when the artwork was produced. What historical period does the artwork represent?
2. Explain what major theme the artist is attempting to illustrate. Does the artwork depict a religious theme? Does it show daily life?
3. Identify the subject of the work of art and note the details.
4. Use the theme and the subject to help explain the values of the historical period in which the work was created.

Developing the Skill

The illustration at the top of this page shows a detail from Michelangelo's *The Creation of Adam* on the ceiling of the Sistine Chapel in Rome. The painting reflects the values of the southern Renaissance.

The painting has a religious theme, similar to paintings of the Middle Ages. The subject is God's creation of Adam; however, the focus is on the humanity of Adam. Michelangelo captures Adam at the very moment that God holds out his hand to give life to his creation. Michelangelo portrays Adam as weak—barely able to lift his arm to receive the gift of life from God. God, on the other hand, appears supremely powerful.

Based on the painting, what conclusions can you draw about values during the Renaissance? The painting shows the concern with religious themes, as does medieval art. Michelangelo, however, depicts figures as intensely human and realistic. The painting captures the beauty of Adam's face, his reflection of God's power and glory, and the heroic individualism at the beginning of life. The painting shows that during the Renaissance people were intensely religious. At the same time, they believed in the dignity of human beings.

Practicing the Skill

Find and study an illustration of a modern work of art. Explain how this artwork reflects the values of modern society.

To apply this skill, see Applying History Study Skills on page 353.

Gutenberg developed a printing press on which he printed a number of copies of the Bible between 1453 and 1455. Other publishers adopted the printing press, and books soon helped spread new ideas to a large audience.

The most influential humanist of northern Europe was Desiderius Erasmus (i·RAZ·muhs), who was a Dutch scholar. He learned about the ideas of the Italian humanists from printed books. Erasmus, who lived from around 1466 to 1536, entered a monastery as a young man. After his ordination into the priesthood, though, he left the monastery so that he could pursue his studies of the classics.

Unlike the Italian humanists, Erasmus and other northern humanists were interested in the early Christian period as well as in early Roman and Greek culture. Erasmus believed that in its early years, Christianity had existed in harmony with classical civilization. He applied to his study of the Bible the critical method that the Italian humanists had developed, and he argued for a return to the original, simple message of Jesus. Erasmus was saddened that the medieval scholars had made Christian faith less spiritual and more complicated and ceremonial. He published stinging criticisms of the church's lack of spirituality, as did other northern humanists.

Erasmus's most famous book, *The Praise of Folly*, ridiculed ignorance, superstition, and vice among Christians. Erasmus criticized fasting, pilgrimages to religious shrines, and even the church's interpretation of parts of the Bible.

Erasmus's friend Thomas More, the English humanist, took a similar view. In 1516 More published *Utopia*, a book in which he criticized the society of his day by describing an imaginary, ideal society. Here citizens lived together harmoniously. All citizens were equal, and everyone worked to support the society. More's Utopia became so popular that today *utopia* means "an ideal place or society."

English literature. Renaissance literature in England reached its peak in the late 1500s and early 1600s. William Shakespeare (1564–1616) stands out as the most prominent English literary figure of this period. Like many other playwrights, Shakespeare used familiar plots, but he built masterpieces of poetic drama around them.

Shakespeare portrayed personality and human emotions with a skill that few writers have ever matched. The moody Hamlet, the young lovers Romeo and Juliet, and the tragic Macbeth seem as real today as when Shakespeare first created them.

Northern Renaissance Artists

The dynamic new painting techniques of Italian artists inspired artists outside of Italy. Northern European merchants carried Italian paintings home, and painters from northern Europe studied with Italian masters.

In Flanders, a group of painters developed their own distinct style. The painters became known as the Flemish School. They are credited with perfecting the technique of painting in oils on canvas. The brothers Hubert and Jan van Eyck, who lived in Flanders until the mid-1400s, paid great attention to detail in works such as *The Adoration of the Lamb*, the altarpiece of the cathedral at Ghent.

One of the most famous Flemish artists, Pieter Brueghel (BROO·guhl) the Elder, painted in the mid-1500s. Brueghel loved the countryside and the peasants of his native Flanders and painted lively scenes of village festivals and dances. He also used his paintings as a means to criticize the intolerance and cruelty he saw around him.

The German artist Albrecht Dürer (DYUR·uhr), who lived from 1471 to 1528, was famous for his

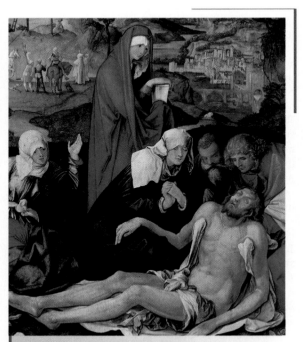

Albrecht Dürer, a renowned German printmaker and painter of the Renaissance, depicted various biblical scenes in his works. This image shows the deposition, or removal, of Christ from the cross.

copper engravings and woodcuts. Advances in printing technology had already made mass production of books possible. Dürer became one of the first to see the possibilities of printed illustrations in books.

Although a German, Hans Holbein the Younger (c.1497-1543), did most of his work in other countries. Holbein traveled throughout Europe to paint portraits of famous people such as Erasmus, Thomas More, and King Henry VIII of England. This emphasis on portrait painting reflected the Renaissance interest in the individual.

Section 1 Review

1. **Define** Renaissance, humanists, perspective
2. **Identify** Niccolò Machiavelli, Leonardo da Vinci, Michelangelo, Johannes Gutenberg, William Shakespeare, Pieter Brueghel, Albrecht Dürer, Hans Holbein the Younger
3. **Locate and Explain the Significance** Florence, Venice
4. **Analyzing Ideas** What impact did humanist ideas have on the Italian Renaissance?
5. **Understanding Ideas** Describe the realism of Italian Renaissance art as related to the work of one Italian Renaissance artist.
6. **Contrasting Ideas** Contrast the Northern Renaissance with the Italian Renaissance in terms of humanist thought, literature, and art.

Section 2

The Protestant Reformation

Focus Questions

- **What circumstances made Germany vulnerable to major religious change?**
- **Who was Martin Luther and what were the reforms that he proposed?**
- **How and why did Protestantism spread beyond the country of Germany?**

In about 1500, several northern humanists suggested that the Roman Catholic Church had lost sight of the spiritual mission proclaimed by Jesus. Instead of setting an example of moral leadership, they said, popes acted as political leaders and warriors. Instead of encouraging inner piety, priests engaged in vice and misconduct. The humanists claimed that the church as a whole seemed more interested in its income than in saving souls. The northern humanists sought a new emphasis on personal faith and spirituality. When the Catholic Church ignored their concerns, a new generation of reformers urged believers who were unhappy with traditional religion to withdraw from the church and gather together with like-minded people. This religious revolution, which split the church in western Europe and created several new churches, is called the **Reformation.**

The Origins of the Reformation

The first break with the Roman Catholic Church occurred in Germany, where the political situation of the time helped lay the foundation for the Reformation. Unlike some countries during the early 1500s, Germany lacked a strong central government. Although Germany formed the core of the Holy Roman Empire, the empire included about 300 independent states. The weak emperor could not control independent ideas about religion within the German states or prevent abuses of power by the pope.

Pope Leo X continued the rebuilding of St. Peter's Basilica in Rome. An enthusiastic monk named Johann Tetzel was sent to raise funds in northern Germany. Using a technique that had become accepted in the church, Tetzel asked people to buy **indulgences,** or pardons from punishment for sin.

Indulgences, part of the sacrament of penance, had originally been a reward for exceptionally pious deeds, such as helping a poor person go on a Crusade. Renaissance popes, however, sold indulgences simply to raise money.

This misuse of indulgences appalled the northern humanists, who wanted the church to become more spiritual. The concern grew especially strong in Germany, where many political leaders gave sellers of indulgences great freedom of movement. One unhappy observer, Martin Luther, protested Tetzel's behavior in 1517.

Martin Luther's Protest

Martin Luther was born in 1483 to a moderately prosperous peasant family in the small mining community of Eisleben in Saxony. Luther's family made sure he received a good education. Although he planned to become a lawyer, as a young man Luther considered

Although Martin Luther studied law at the University of Erfurt, he subsequently joined the Augustinian order and received a doctorate in theology.

himself a terrible sinner, and he worried desperately about the salvation of his soul. One summer day as he walked home, a sudden storm overtook him. A blinding bolt of lightning struck close by. Luther cried out, "Saint Anne, help! I will become a monk!" He gave up studying law to enter a monastery and spend his life in search of salvation.

Luther found that the church's methods for overcoming sin gave him no comfort. He did all the things required of him, including making a trip to holy places in Rome. Nothing, however, relieved his feeling of damnation.

Through his biblical studies, a revelation, or new understanding, came to Luther. He came to believe that all the ceremonies and good deeds made no difference in saving a sinner. The only thing that counted, Luther felt, was an inner faith in God. As long as people did not rely on their own actions, but believed God would save them, they could receive salvation by God's grace.

On the basis of this new insight, he developed beliefs that later became known as Lutheranism. Luther believed that a simple faith could lead everyone to salvation. He also believed Tetzel committed a grave theological error by asking poor people to give up their money for false promises of forgiveness.

In 1517 Luther challenged Tetzel by posting on the church door at Wittenberg **95 theses,** or statements, about indulgences. Sales of indulgences began to decline. The news quickly spread across Europe that a monk had publicly challenged the selling of indulgences.

Luther clearly considered himself a reformer within the main tradition of the church. He was surprised at the widespread impact of his ideas, and had no wish to break with the church. But because he dared to challenge church practices, church leaders denounced him.

Luther's Break with the Medieval Church

By 1520 Luther openly disagreed with many church doctrines. The sole religious authority, he said, was the Bible. Popes and bishops should not tell a person what to believe. Luther believed that ceremonies did not counteract sins and that priests had no special role in helping people to salvation. He felt that God viewed all people with faith equally. Luther considered his church a "priesthood of all believers."

Taking advantage of the power of the printed word to spread ideas, in 1520 Luther wrote three publications that outlined his doctrines, attacked the pope, and called on all Germans to support his views. In 1521 Pope Leo X declared Luther a heretic and excommunicated him.

To put Luther's punishment into effect, the Holy Roman Emperor Charles V summoned Luther to the Imperial Diet, a special meeting of the rulers of the empire, at the city of Worms (VOHRMZ). Luther was commanded to renounce his ideas. When he refused, the Diet of Worms banished him from the empire and prohibited the sale or printing of his works. Luther was now considered an outlaw. Because Germany lacked a strong government, however, the emperor could not enforce the Diet's ruling. The Elector of Saxony, Frederick the Wise, protected Luther and provided a place for him to hide while the uproar caused by the confrontation at the Diet of Worms died down.

In 1522, while under the protection of Frederick the Wise, Luther translated the New Testament of the Bible into German. By 1534 he had translated the entire Bible from Hebrew and Greek. Now all literate Christians that lived in Germany could read the Bible themselves.

Emperor Charles V continued to oppose Luther's doctrines and did what he could to keep Lutheranism from spreading. The princes who supported Luther protested the emperor's treatment of Lutheranism. Because of the protest, the followers of Luther and all later reformers came to be called "Protestants."

Luther's works continued to circulate, and his ideas continued to spread. In time he established a new church called the Lutheran Church. Luther kept the organization of the new church as simple as possible. Lutheran clergy, called ministers, had no special powers; they served merely to guide their congregations to the true faith. Ministers also had less importance than Catholic priests had, because Luther permitted only the two sacraments mentioned in the Bible—baptism and communion—rather than the seven sacraments practiced in the Roman Catholic Church.

The Spread of Protestantism

Luther had touched a very deep desire among the people of Europe for a simpler, more direct faith. Within a short time after he took his stand, many rulers in the German states established the Lutheran Church within their domains. In addition, dozens of other reformers appeared who were dissatisfied with both the Roman Catholic Church and the Lutheran Church.

Charles V attempted to stop the spread of Protestantism, but for about 10 years he was too busy fighting the Ottoman Turks and the French. Then in 1546 he sent his armies against the Protestant princes in Germany for both religious and political reasons. The emperor won most of his battles with the princes, but in the end he could not defeat them or the Lutheran Church. Charles V finally reached a compromise with the princes with the signing of the Peace of Augsburg in 1555.

One of the provisions of the Peace of Augsburg stated that each German ruler had the right to choose the religion for his state. His subjects had to accept the ruler's decision or move away. Almost all the princes of northern Germany accepted Luther's faith.

The sects. Hundreds of new religious groups emerged throughout Germany and Switzerland in the 1520s and 1530s. These groups, known as **sects,** did not form organized churches with clear-cut rules, authority, discipline, and membership. The sects were societies of a few people gathered together, usually with a preacher as their leader.

Most of the sects later died out. The Anabaptists are somewhat of an exception. This sect believed that infants should not receive baptism because they could not understand the significance of the ceremony. Instead, they believed baptism should be offered only to adults who accepted the Anabaptist faith. The beliefs of this sect survive today in Mennonite and Hutterite religious communities.

The Anglican Church. In England the Protestant Reformation came about by entirely different means than in Germany. True, some Protestant ideas had filtered into England by the 1520s. The English also had a tradition of resistance to the popes that went back to John Wycliffe in the 1300s. However, King Henry VIII caused the break between England and the Roman Catholic Church between 1529 and 1536. The break was a political move that had little to do

This manuscript page illustrates the restoration of a statue of Mary that had been destroyed by violence during the Reformation.

with religious doctrine. In fact, before 1529 Henry VIII had defended the church so well against Martin Luther's ideas that the pope had granted Henry the title of "Defender of the Faith"—a title that the present monarch of England still bears.

England's break with Rome took place because Henry VIII wanted to divorce his wife, Catherine of Aragon, for not producing a male heir to the throne. The king believed that a continuing strong monarchy depended on having a son to succeed him. The royal couple had a daughter, Mary, but England had no tradition of a ruling queen. Furthermore, Henry wanted to be rid of Catherine and to marry Anne Boleyn, a lady-in-waiting at the court.

Although the Catholic Church forbade divorce, the pope could make exceptions. Pope Clement VII, however, refused to dissolve Henry's marriage. Clement made his decision in part because troops led by Catherine of Aragon's nephew, the Holy Roman Emperor Charles V, had captured and sacked Rome in 1527.

Pope Clement's refusal to grant the divorce infuriated Henry, who withdrew England from the Catholic Church and created a new church. In a series of laws, Parliament created the Church of England with the king as its head. Although the Church of England, or Anglican Church, slowly acquired some Protestant doctrines, it kept the organization and many of the ceremonial features of the Catholic Church.

Of course, Henry VIII's church granted his divorce. The king eventually married six times in all. He finally fathered a son, the future Edward VI, although not by Anne Boleyn. More important historically, by creating the Anglican Church he opened the way for the Protestant Reformation in England.

Section 2 Review

1. **Define** Reformation, indulgences, 95 theses, sects
2. **Identify** Martin Luther
3. **Locate and Explain the Significance** Wittenberg
4. **Understanding Ideas** What specific issue sparked the Reformation in Germany?
5. **Contrasting Ideas** What were the main differences between Luther's ideas and those of the Roman Catholic Church?
6. **Summarizing Ideas** Describe how Protestantism spread beyond Germany.

The Catholic Reformation

Focus Questions

- **Who was John Calvin? What role did he play in the Reformation?**
- **What steps did the Catholic Church take to respond to Protestant reform?**
- **What was the approach used by the Jesuits to Catholic reform?**

Although areas of northern Europe became Protestant during the Reformation, millions of Europeans remained faithful to the Roman Catholic Church. Change and challenge continued, however, even in countries such as France, where the Catholic faith remained strong. After 1550 the religious conflict in Europe was dominated by the followers of a French-born reformer named John Calvin and a remarkable Catholic revival known as the Counter-Reformation.

Calvin and Calvinism

Huldrych Zwingli (TSVING·lee), the vicar at the cathedral in Zurich in the early 1500s, was greatly influenced by the humanist writings of Erasmus. Zwingli was stirring up religious reform in Switzerland when he heard about Luther's 95 theses. Zwingli and Luther met and discovered that they agreed, more or less, on doctrine but disagreed about forms of worship and the use of images. Zwingli's supporters, for example, covered up wall decorations in churches.

In 1531 Zwingli died in a battle between Catholics and Protestants, but the French Protestant John Calvin carried on the work of the Reformation in Switzerland. Calvin founded a Protestant church that had a strong following. He formulated a complete and clear set of beliefs, the *Institutes of the Christian Religion*, published in 1536. This work laid down exactly what the faithful ought to believe on every major question of religion. Calvin thus provided his followers—Calvinists—with a code that united them and strengthened them against opposition and persecution.

In 1536 Calvin settled in the city of Geneva, where Calvinism became the official religion. Calvin retained Luther's reliance on faith and on the Bible. He also placed added emphasis on the belief, common among Protestant theologians during the 1500s, that God had decided, at the beginning of time, who would be saved—a belief known as **predestination.** Those predestined (or chosen beforehand) for salvation were called "the elect." They formed a special community of people who were expected to follow the highest moral standards. These standards placed great emphasis on devoutness and self-discipline and frowned on frivolity. The individual was to possess a complete dedication to God's wishes.

Calvin became very influential in Geneva. The city became a **theocracy,** or a government ruled by a clergy claiming God's authority. By attaching such great importance to righteous living, the lives of the citizens were regulated down to the smallest detail. Laws prohibited dancing, card playing, showy dress, and profane language. Violation of these laws resulted in severe punishment.

Calvinism soon spread to France, where its converts became known as Huguenots (HYOO·guh·nahts). Although France remained primarily Catholic, Calvinists controlled nearly one third of the country at

one point. Many high-ranking nobles as well as townspeople adopted the Calvinist doctrines. The Catholic French monarchs considered the Huguenots a threat to national unity.

Beginning in 1562 the Huguenots defended themselves in a series of bloody civil wars with the Catholics. In 1598 King Henry IV issued the Edict of Nantes (NANTS), which gave the Huguenots freedom of worship and some political rights.

Calvinist minorities also existed in Poland and Hungary in eastern Europe. The Calvinists met with the most success, however, in Scotland, in the northern Netherlands, and in some parts of Germany. In these countries the strength of the Calvinists among the people persuaded rulers to change their views. In a form called *Puritanism*, Calvinism would play a vital role in England and in its North American colonies. By 1600 the Calvinist churches were among the strongest of the many Protestant churches established in Europe.

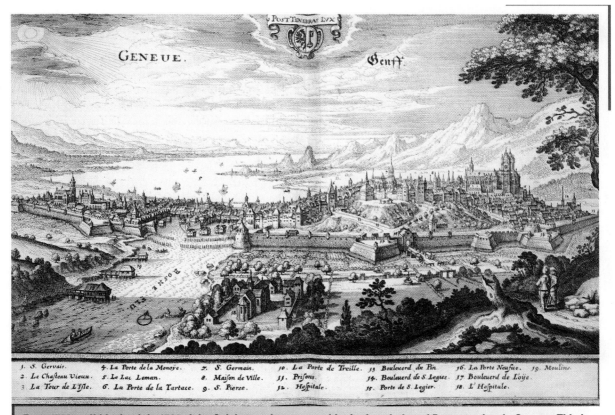

From 1536 until his death in 1564, John Calvin was instrumental in the foundation of Protestantism in Geneva. This is a map of Geneva during the time of Calvin.

The Counter-Reformation

It took some time for the Catholic Church to recognize that Protestantism posed a serious threat. The pope at first dismissed Luther's criticisms. A number of people within the Catholic Church, including Erasmus, had called for internal reforms even before Luther appeared. As the breakup of the church continued, these reformers eventually convinced the pope of the drastic need for change.

In the 1530s a major reform effort known as the **Counter-Reformation,** or the Catholic Reformation, began in the Catholic Church. Initially created to foster a more spiritual outlook in the Catholic Church, the Counter-Reformation also clarified the doctrines of the church and pursued an aggressive campaign against Protestantism.

Pope Paul III commissioned the Venetian painter Titian to record the Council of Trent in session.

Counter-Reformation tactics. Pope Paul III, who reigned as pope from 1534 to 1549, began a deliberate policy of reviving a more spiritual outlook in the Catholic Church. To accomplish this, he appointed devout and learned men as bishops and cardinals.

Pope Paul III also brought the medieval Inquisition to Rome. Spanish authorities had been trying and punishing so-called heretics since 1478. The Inquisition borrowed its cruel punishments, such as burning at the stake, from governments, which had used such methods against the worst criminals and traitors. The leaders of the Inquisition did not see themselves primarily as punishing Protestants but rather as keeping Catholics within the church.

In 1559 Pope Paul IV introduced another method of combating heresy. He established the *Index of Forbidden Books*, which forbade Catholics to read certain books that were considered harmful to faith or morals. The Index was a recognition of the role printing had played in spreading the Reformation. Before the printing press, the church could easily find and burn manuscripts of heretical works. After printing was developed, it became far easier to forbid people to read certain books than to burn the books. The Catholic Church maintained the Index until 1966, when the Second Vatican Council finally abandoned it.

The Council of Trent. Pope Paul III knew that no counterattack against Protestantism would be possible unless Catholic doctrines were well defined. Church authorities often disagreed about complicated doctrines, which made it difficult to take a stand against opposition. In 1545 Paul summoned church leaders to the Italian city of Trent. The Council of Trent, which met in three sessions from 1545 to 1563, defined official church doctrine with the same precision Calvin had used to define his faith.

The Council of Trent banned the sale of indulgences and tightened discipline for the clergy. In most cases, however, the council reaffirmed the importance of those doctrines that Protestants rejected. It emphasized the need for ceremonies, arguing that God ought to be worshiped with pomp and splendor. It noted that people must depend on priests because God granted forgiveness only through the church. The council stressed that although everyone enjoyed free will, a person's fate after death depended not only on his or her faith, as Luther claimed, but on ceremonial church actions as well.

The decisions made at the Council of Trent were effective for the Catholic Church. Many people found Protestantism's simplicity and austerity appealing, but many others took comfort from ancient ceremonies, beautifully decorated churches, the authority of priests, and the idea that one could perform good works to gain salvation.

Soldiers of the Counter-Reformation

A new aggressiveness on the part of the Catholic Church became a major reason for the success of the Counter-Reformation. This aggressiveness took many forms. Better-educated priests worked more forcefully for the church. The old religious orders reformed their rules, while new religious orders such as the Society of Jesus, known as the Jesuits, formed.

Ignatius de Loyola founded the Jesuits in 1534. Loyola was a Spanish soldier whose leg had been shattered fighting for Charles V against the French. Loyola's long period of recovery from his injury gave him time to read about the lives of Jesus and the saints. Like Martin Luther, Loyola wondered how he could attain salvation despite his sins. The answer came to him in a vision that he recorded in his book *Spiritual Exercises*. According to Loyola, salvation could be achieved by self-discipline and by doing good deeds—in other words, by one's own actions. Loyola convinced six fellow students at the University of Paris to take religious vows of poverty, chastity, and obedience to the pope and to follow him. Less than 10 years after Loyola founded his group, Pope Paul III recognized it as an official order of the Catholic Church.

Loyola organized the Jesuits like a military body, with discipline and strict obedience. He was the general of the order; the members were his soldiers. The Jesuits quickly became the most effective agents in spreading Catholicism. By 1556 the order had about 1,000 members. Their missions took them as far away as China and Japan. In Europe their preaching and their hearing of confessions slowed the spread of Protestantism in Poland, Germany, and France.

The Jesuits stressed education. They founded some of the best colleges in Europe, combining humanist values with theology to turn out learned, fervent supporters of the church.

Although some people had cherished hopes that the Reformation would bring about a new spirit of tolerance, the period from the 1530s through the mid-1600s was a time of devastating religious wars, sometimes interrupted by long truces, in Germany, Switzerland, France, and the Netherlands. Not until the mid-1600s, when the wars ended, could the

Ignatius de Loyola received approval from Pope Paul III to found a new Catholic order, that of the Society of Jesus, or Jesuits, through which he organized a system of schools and universities.

results of the Reformation and the Counter-Reformation be fully seen.

Results of the Religious Upheaval

The most striking result of the religious struggle of the 1500s was the emergence of many different churches in western Europe. In Italy, although Protestantism never made much headway, interest in church reform remained strong. Most of the people of southern and eastern Europe and the native population of Ireland remained firmly Catholic. France and the Netherlands had large numbers of Protestants. In Switzerland, northern Germany, England, Scotland, Norway, Denmark, and Sweden, various Protestant faiths became the established church, backed by the central government (see map on page 340).

Another far-reaching result of the Reformation and Counter-Reformation was a new interest in education. Many new universities had appeared in the 1400s and 1500s because of the humanists' concern for learning. After the mid-1500s enrollments in

European Religions, 1600

	Lutheran		Roman Catholic
	Calvinist		Orthodox
	Anglican		Muslim
	Roman Catholic with Protestant minorities		Boundary of Holy Roman Empire

Learning from Maps Although the Reformation gained many converts in northern Europe, southern Italy remained predominantly Catholic.

? Region What religions were dominant in Scotland? Norway? England?

these universities increased dramatically; religious reformers supported this trend.

Protestants believed that people could find their way to Christian faith by studying the Bible. As a result, reading became increasingly important. In their schools the Jesuits and other new religious orders worked to strengthen the faith of the Catholics. Education did not mean tolerance of new ideas, however. Neither the Protestant nor the Catholic authorities permitted views that differed from their own.

The Reformation led to an increase in power of national governments and a decrease in power of the pope. In Protestant regions each government took responsibility for the leadership of the official church. In Catholic areas, rulers loyal to the pope often obtained considerable control over their churches.

Section 3 Review

1. **Define** predestination, theocracy, Counter-Reformation
2. **Identify** John Calvin, Ignatius de Loyola
3. **Locate and Explain the Significance** Zurich, Geneva
4. **Understanding Ideas** What were the main ideas of John Calvin and how were they expressed in the government of Geneva?
5. **Summarizing Ideas** Describe how the Catholic Church responded to the Reformation, including the role of the Council of Trent.
6. **Analyzing Ideas** Why were Ignatius de Loyola's efforts to strengthen the Catholic Church successful?

Section 4

Culture and Daily Life

Focus Questions

- **What were the characteristics of village life in Europe during the period of time known as the Renaissance and Reformation?**
- **How did villagers learn about the world outside their villages?**
- **What changes in daily life occurred in the 1500s and 1600s?**

The ideas that shaped the Renaissance, the Reformation, and the Counter-Reformation involved relatively few people. Ordinary people had their own views about themselves and the world around them.

Magic and Witchcraft

Most Europeans lived in or near small villages and spent their entire lives combating nature to raise food. People close to the land could never predict what life would bring. They never knew when a cow might suddenly fall ill, when lightning might burn down a cottage, or when churning would fail to turn milk into butter.

The world of spirits. Since people considered God to be a distant, unknowable force, they thought spirits populated the world. Although good spirits abounded, demons, or devils, made life difficult. Because of this belief in spirits, nothing was considered an accident.

If lightning struck a house, a demon had caused it. If a pitcher of milk spilled, the evil work of a demon was the cause. Many "superstitions," such as the belief that walking under a ladder might bring bad luck, began during this period.

Village priests usually accepted these beliefs or at least pretended to ignore them. To the ordinary villager, the priest's explanation that the misfortune was God's will or God's punishment for sin was not very satisfying. Nevertheless, villagers believed that the priest's actions could have positive effects. For example, every spring in a special ceremony, the priest would go out to the fields to bless the earth and pray for good crops. His blessing of a husband and wife at a wedding supposedly gave the couple a good start in life, and baptism was thought to safeguard a newborn child.

The priest, however, was not the only person to whom the villagers turned in times of trouble. They also looked to a so-called "wise" or "cunning" man or woman. This person, usually an older village member, was thought to have a special understanding of the way the world operated. Ordinary people would explain their problem—a lost ring, a cruel husband, a sick pig, or even an ominous sign—to these "wise" folk. Since people believed nothing happened by accident, anything unusual, such as a frog jumping into a fishing boat, was taken as a warning. The wise man or woman would explain what the warning meant and would sometimes recommend a remedy to ward off evil. The remedy might include wearing a good-luck charm, chanting a strange spell, or drinking a special potion.

The belief in witchcraft. Wise people were often called "good witches." However, if their relationship with their neighbors turned sour, wise people might be accused of being "bad witches." In many cases the person accused of witchcraft would be an elderly widow. Perhaps too weak to work, with no husband or family to support her, she would be the most defenseless person in the community and an easy target for attack.

Stories about witches became more sensational as they spread throughout the countryside. Outrageous accusations were made. A person might be accused of flying on a broomstick, sticking pins into dolls, or dancing with the devil in the woods at night. If the majority of people believed an accusation, a priest might be asked to hold a ceremony to exorcise, or drive out, a demon that was thought to have taken over the witch's body. In other cases, the accused person might be dragged to a bonfire, tied to a stake, and burned, perhaps with the approval of the local lord.

An enormous outburst of "witch hunting" occurred in Europe in the mid-1500s and lasted for more than 100 years. Both religious and secular leaders were ready to see the existence of witches as an acceptable explanation for the problems in the world around them. Eventually, however, as the religious wars came to an end and people experienced greater security in their lives, fewer cases of witchcraft were reported.

Forms of Recreation

For most people, daylight meant work and night meant sleep. Because manual farming methods were slow, people needed all their daylight hours for raising food. Evening activities were limited because the farmers were exhausted from working all day and because they could not afford the candles needed for light. Still, they did find time for relaxation.

Every village had a gathering place where people came together to drink, sew, do simple chores, and tell stories. Some people played games such as skittles (a form of bowling). Occasionally, traveling companies of actors passed through a village and put on a simple show. The year contained many special days. The church decreed some holidays. Others honored a local saint or tradition. During some holidays, the villagers donned costumes and would often put on their own ceremonies.

A favorite ceremony poked fun at the familiar sights and scenes of village life. In different parts of Europe, this ceremony had different names. Whether it was called "rough music," "charivari," or "abbeys of misrule," the basic ceremony was much the same. The young men of the village formed a procession and marched along, ridiculing accepted customs or the foolish people of the village. For example, two young men might impersonate a couple known to everyone because the wife beat the husband. The impersonators would be pulled along in a cart and, as they passed by, the other villagers would jeer and hoot at them.

Sometimes the marchers had more serious targets; they might want to show how things would look if the poor or the weak had power. They would dress a fool like a bishop, or they would put the poorest man on a throne. At this point, the jokes lost their lightheartedness and symbolized the resentment the villagers felt about the privileges of those who ruled them.

Pieter Brueghel the Elder is known for his depictions of peasant life. *The Peasant Wedding,* painted in the 1560s, shows a group of guests seated at a table as food is being prepared.

Games

People throughout the ages have played games for amusement and diversion. In some cultures, games were a way for children to learn skills that would be useful to them in later life. In addition, games provided relief and relaxation from the routine of hard work in the home or the fields.

Dice have been found in Egyptian tombs. The modern game of backgammon developed from a board game played in Mesopotamia, and chess probably was first played in India.

More than 400 years ago, the Flemish artist Pieter Brueghel painted the large picture shown here (above). The picture is almost an encyclopedia of the games played by children of Brueghel's time. Brueghel loved to show the activities of peasants and working people. This painting depicts at least 80 games, including everything from marbles to hockey to ring-around-the-rosy and hoop rolling.

Many games are played by adults as well as by children. Baseball, for example, can be a pickup game in a neighborhood park or a schoolyard, or a competition among professional athletes. In recent years people of all ages have been fascinated by the new games and twists on old games that electronics and the computer have made possible.

The wide appeal of games to people of all ages may account for a feature of Brueghel's painting that has never been explained. Some people think that all the people playing games in his paintings look like adults. Perhaps Brueghel wanted to suggest that adult activities are no different from the games that children play. However, we cannot know for sure. What we do know is that many of these games and activities are still amusements today (center), for children as well as for grownups throughout the world.

Violence and Protest in the Village

Villagers lived in close-knit communities. Anyone who seemed to upset their traditions or their sense of proper behavior was treated harshly. The strain of hardship or famine could cause villagers to respond, sometimes violently.

The women of the village often led these protests. Because women were responsible for feeding their families, they especially felt the impact of taxes or food shortages. If the women suspected, for example, that a baker hoarded bread or sent it elsewhere for higher profits, they might ransack the baker's shop.

On the other hand, people of this time tended to identify closely with other members of their community. In large communities, such as towns, this might mean members of one's profession. In smaller villages, whole communities tended to work and make decisions together.

Printing and the Spread of Knowledge

In the 1500s the world beyond the village began to affect village life. Printed works and, in some areas, traveling preachers, inspired the changes.

Few ordinary villagers could read. Often even the village priest could not read. Nevertheless, soon after the invention of movable type, publishers started selling popular works. Single printed sheets known as **broadsides** began to appear. A broadside might include a royal decree or news of some sensational crime or other event. Books and broadsides arrived in the village, carried by peddlers who brought goods from the outside world. When the villagers gathered together, they might enjoy listening to someone read the latest broadside.

While romances and epics of the classical age appealed to the nobility, publishers quickly found subjects that appealed to country folk and produced cheap books for this new market. The most common books were **almanacs,** the ancestors of *The Old Farmer's Almanac* of today. In the almanacs were predictions about the weather and the prospects for growing crops. Almanacs also contained calendars, maps, and medical advice. The books were best-sellers because they spoke to the beliefs and concerns of the ordinary people.

Soon after Luther's break with the church in 1521, new religious ideas reached the villages. Sometimes preachers came to visit. Books might come out of the peddlers' packs. Perhaps people heard stories that attacked the church read in the village gathering place. Certainly the messages of Luther and Calvin traveled in this way, as did translations of the Bible.

This photograph shows the printing press invented by Johannes Gutenberg.

What If?

Printing
What if Europeans had not developed movable type until about 1600? How might that have affected the course of the Renaissance? The Reformation? The Counter-Reformation?

As Protestants and Catholics battled for the loyalties of ordinary people, leaders of both sides encouraged the founding of primary schools in the villages and towns. Both Protestant and Catholic leaders believed that knowledge would lead a person to support the faith. In spite of this common concern for education, the followers of the differing religions struggled to coexist peacefully. Neither side, unfortunately, included tolerance in its teachings.

Changes in Daily Life

In addition to undergoing religious and political changes, Europeans experienced economic changes as well. The measure of the quality of life of a people or a country is called the **standard of living.** The standard of living is not strictly limited to income or economic output; it also includes working conditions, home life, the environment, health, and leisure.

Population and inflation. After the Black Death of the 1300s cut Europe's population by at least one third, some peasants prospered. There were fewer people to cultivate the land, so their labor was in demand. This often resulted in higher wages.

By 1550, when the religious wars had begun to ravage Europe, conditions changed. The population was growing rapidly. With the growth of the population came **inflation,** a rise in prices for goods. After 1550 wages could not keep up with the rise in prices, especially of farm products.

Diet. During this period, white bread made from wheat was a rarity. Meat was scarce and expensive, and fish only a little less so. Salt, needed to preserve fish and meats, had long been an important item of trade in Europe, but was still costly. Cheese and eggs, cheap sources of protein, were an important part of the diet everywhere. Butter was not widely used outside northern Europe until the 1700s.

The spices that had earlier come to Europe from the East had been largely luxury items. By the 1500s and 1600s, however, the importation of spices had become highly competitive. In the 1500s traders began introducing Europeans not only to new vegetables— asparagus, spinach, lettuce, green beans, tomatoes, and melons—but also to the luxuries of coffee, tea, and chocolate.

Not everyone had access to the new and varied diets. Wealthy people still lived better than most of the peasants and the urban poor, who for the most part ate the same simple meals they had eaten for centuries.

The table settings and customs that we know today were not common in the early Renaissance period. People ate mostly with their fingers, picking what they wanted from a large common dish. In some areas people ate from wooden plates. Guests brought their own knives; individual forks did not come into use until the 1500s, and spoons not until a century after that.

Housing. Brick and stone became more common construction materials in the growing cities of Europe after the 1500s. In the countryside, however, peasants continued to live in thatched-roof cottages as they had in the Middle Ages. Most rural houses were small. Because glass was expensive and sometimes not available even for the wealthy, most houses had shutters rather than glass windows.

Peasants' houses boasted only the necessities of rural life—a large cooking pot, a table, a bench, and a few tools. Those who were fortunate had a bed; others slept on sacks filled with straw. Entrenched in poverty, with little hope of escaping their fate, many peasants sought refuge in the cities.

The Decline of Traditional Culture

The migration from countryside to city further altered traditional popular culture. In the city, food came from a shop rather than directly from a field. Local governments helped out when disaster occurred. If famine struck, authorities distributed bread. If plagues broke out, the government would set up hospitals and quarantines.

Gradually, more sophisticated attitudes began to take hold among the residents of towns and cities. In particular, people's understanding of how things happened in the world began to change. Demons and spirits no longer dominated views of daily life. People sought rational explanations for day-to-day events, and there now seemed less need for magic and "wise" folk. This development has been referred to as the "disenchantment" of the world—the removal of "enchantment," or magic, from nature. One of the most important influences on the growth of this new attitude was the cultivation of modern science.

1. **Define** broadsides, almanacs, standard of living, inflation
2. **Determining Cause and Effect** How did a belief in spirits lead to the witch hunts of the 1600s?
3. **Analyzing Ideas** Describe the importance of printing in the spread of knowledge.
4. **Interpreting Ideas** What economic and cultural changes occurred in the lives of people living in the 1500s and 1600s?

Section 5

The Scientific Revolution

Focus Questions

- **What factors contributed to the birth of the Scientific Revolution?**
- **How did Copernicus, Kepler, and Galileo challenge traditionally held views?**
- **How did Descartes, Bacon, and Newton help to shape the scientific method?**
- **What were some of the discoveries made during the Scientific Revolution?**

Unlikely though it may seem, belief in magic helped create the revolution in thinking that led to modern science. In the 1500s it was not only ordinary people who thought hidden forces controlled the world; the early scientists also hoped to discover what they called the secrets of nature. Alchemists were people who used spells and magic formulas to try to change one substance into another—for example, lead into gold. Astrologers believed that the position of the stars in the sky affected human life.

What made the early scientists more than just alchemists or astrologers was that they had very general interests. They wanted to find out why stones fall, why the stars seem to move, or what function the heart serves. They attempted to uncover the invisible structure of the universe by performing experiments and using mathematics—two methods that proved more effective than chants or spells.

The success of these early investigators in solving ancient problems in astronomy, physics, and anatomy created a new way of thinking that no longer relied on magic. This new way of pursuing knowledge is now called science. Before the 1600s the word science meant "knowledge." After the 1600s the sense of the word evolved into the narrower meaning it has today.

Experiments and Mathematics

The Europeans' ideas about the universe had come to them from the ancient Greeks and Romans. People considered Aristotle and Galen to be absolute authorities who knew the truth. However, as the humanists unearthed more classical manuscripts, they found that even the respected ancient writers did not agree with each other. As people began to examine the world around them, they made observations that did not correspond to ancient beliefs.

As a result, people in the 1500s began to question traditional opinions. They began to observe and experiment for themselves. Most importantly, they described nature without any reference to previous beliefs. The foundation of this approach was the principle of doubt; nothing was to be believed unless it could be proved by experiment or mathematics. The transformation in thinking that occurred during the 1500s and 1600s as a result of this new system of investigation is known as the **Scientific Revolution.**

The new approach relied heavily on the scientists' ability to conduct scientific experiments. Scientists had access to newly invented instruments, such as the barometer, the microscope, and the thermometer, which improved their ability to observe and measure. At the same time, improved mathematical calculations became essential to investigations of nature. The method of inquiry that includes carefully conducted experiments and mathematical calculations—to verify the results of these repeatable experiments—is called the **scientific method.** The scientific method also involves making logical deductions from self-evident principles.

Astronomy, Physics, and Anatomy

New frontiers in science attracted people with interests in different fields of study. Five Europeans in particular—Copernicus, Kepler, Galileo, Vesalius, and Harvey—became pioneers of modern astronomy, physics, and anatomy.

Copernicus. For centuries astronomers had believed in the theory Ptolemy put forth in about A.D. 100: Earth was the center of the universe and the other planets and the Sun moved around it. Ptolemy's theory is called the **geocentric** ("Earth-centered") **theory,** from the Greek words *geo,* meaning "Earth," and *kentron,* meaning "center."

In the early 1500s, a Polish scientist named Nicolaus Copernicus discovered ancient writings arguing that the Sun was the center of the universe. Copernicus's theory developed as the **heliocentric theory,** from the Greek word *helios,* meaning "sun." After a long period of study and observation, Copernicus became convinced that the heliocentric theory best explained all the known facts of astronomy of his time. In 1543 Copernicus published his conclusions in a book titled *On the Revolutions of the Celestial Spheres.*

The book caused little stir at the time. Few people believed in the heliocentric theory because it seemed to contradict the evidence of the senses. Anyone could "see" that the Sun and planets moved around Earth. Anyone could "feel" that solid Earth did not move.

Copernicus could not test and prove the heliocentric theory with the instruments or the mathematics available to him. Proof had to wait for the work of two later scientists, a German named Kepler and an Italian named Galileo.

Kepler and Galileo. Johannes Kepler, who was a brilliant mathematician who lived in the late 1500s and early 1600s, used mathematics to test the heliocentric theory of Copernicus. At first Kepler could not make the theory fit the observed facts. It is said that he calculated the problem many times before he discovered the solution. Copernicus had written that Earth and other planets went around the Sun in orbits, or paths in space, that were exact circles. Kepler discovered that the orbits were not exact circles, they were ovals called ellipses. Now other facts made sense. The heliocentric theory of the universe *could* be supported mathematically.

Because Kepler's proof could not be seen or observed, only mathematicians understood it. An Italian professor of mathematics and astronomer, Galileo Galilei, provided concrete evidence that Earth revolves around the Sun.

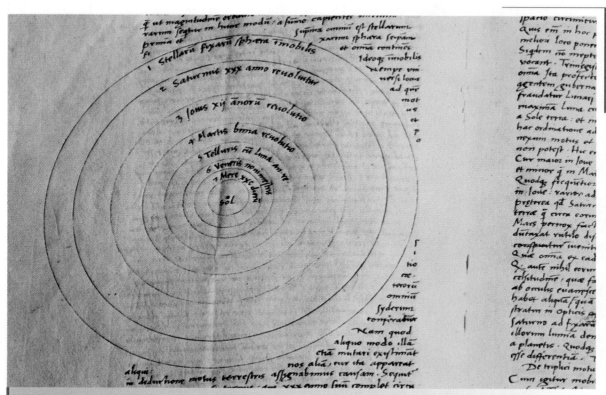

Nicolaus Copernicus published his support of the heliocentric theory of the universe in 1543. This 16th-century manuscript shows the Copernican (heliocentric) system of the universe with the Sun at the center and the planets orbiting the Sun.

Galileo had read of a Dutch eyeglass-maker who put two glass lenses together in a tube to make a telescope. By looking through the telescope, a person could see distant objects more clearly. Galileo made a telescope for himself. By modern standards Galileo's telescope was only a small one, but it allowed him to see more of the heavens than anyone had ever seen. He could see the mountains and valleys of the moon and the rings around the planet Saturn. He observed sunspots. He proved that Earth rotated on its axis. His discovery that the moons of Jupiter revolve around the planet helped disprove the geocentric theory of Ptolemy by showing that not every heavenly body revolves around Earth.

Galileo published his findings in 1632 in a work called *Dialogue on the Two Great Systems of the World.*

His work, unlike that of Copernicus, caused an uproar. Many people now wanted telescopes. Many others believed telescopes to be the devil's work and refused to have anything to do with them. Scholars who accepted the authority of Ptolemy refused to believe the heliocentric theory. The church disapproved because the theory seemed to contradict the Bible. The church further insisted upon its right to condemn any scientific explanations that differed from scripture. In 1633 the Inquisition summoned Galileo to Rome, where it ordered him to renounce his belief that Earth moves around the Sun. Galileo did as he was asked, but legend tells us that as he rose from his knees before the Inquisitors he muttered, "Yet the earth *does* move." The new ideas continued to advance.

The Italian astronomer Galileo was called before the Inquisition and forced to deny his observations.

The Microscope and the Telescope

Repeated experimentation and careful measurement—so vital to the scientific method—were greatly aided by the development of new technology. Two of the technological innovations of the Renaissance—the microscope and the telescope—expanded human sight in amazing ways. One allowed scientists to look inward at the minute structures of the human body. The other opened the door to the universe beyond.

Engravers, workers in fine detail, are thought to have been the first to capture water in glass globes and gaze through it as a magnification aid. Lenses appeared in the late 1200s. It is not surprising therefore that three spectacle-makers, Zacharias Janssen, his father Hans, and Hans Lippershey, have been credited with developing an early microscope with simple lenses in the final decade of the 1500s. Less than 100 years later, in the 1670s, Anton van Leeuwenhoek had devised a microscope that allowed him to see bacteria of only 2 to 3 micrometers in diameter.

Galileo, in 1609, was the first to use the compound lenses of a telescope to view the skies. The telescopes that he built were larger and more powerful than any that had been built before. What he observed with his telescope confirmed Galileo's belief in the heliocentric views of Copernicus. Both these inventions, developed within twenty years of each other, were to open the eyes of science for centuries to come.

Galileo was interested in physics as well as astronomy. Perhaps the most remarkable of his discoveries disproved the popular belief that heavier bodies fall faster than lighter ones. Galileo proved mathematically that, in the absence of air friction, all objects fall at the same speed regardless of their weight. This discovery laid the foundation for the modern science of mechanics, the study of matter in motion.

Vesalius and Harvey. Andreas Vesalius, a Flemish scientist, pioneered the study of anatomy. Vesalius refused to accept the descriptions of human muscles and tissues that Galen had written 1,400 years earlier. Vesalius conducted his own investigations to see how the human body was constructed. In 1543, the same year that Copernicus published his book, Vesalius published a landmark work in the history of medicine called On the Fabric of the Human Body.

Equally important was the work of William Harvey, an English physician. Using laboratory experiments, Harvey described the circulation of the blood through veins and arteries, the working of the body's most important muscle—the heart, and the function of the blood vessels.

The Triumph of Science

The effects of these discoveries were felt throughout Europe. So much had been accomplished. Knowledge had advanced so far that the scientists' methods became examples for everyone.

Just as new religious orders of the Counter-Reformation spread the revived faith in the church, scientific "orders" helped spread developments of the Scientific Revolution. In Rome there was the Accademia dei Lincei, founded in 1603. King Charles II granted a charter to the Royal Society in London in 1662, and Louis XIV established the French Academy of Sciences in 1666. The printing press helped the scientists just as it had the religious reformers. Most societies published journals so that scientists everywhere could read of work being done throughout Europe.

Descartes. One of the most influential advocates of science was René Descartes (day·KAHRT), a French philosopher and scientist who lived from 1596 to 1650. Educated at a Jesuit college, Descartes decided to become a soldier in order to learn more about the world around him. He saw little fighting as a soldier and thus had ample time to think.

Descartes believed that one should question all assumptions before accepting them. He decided to start fresh with a new philosophy based on his own reason. In his *Discourse on Method* (1637), he argued that everything had to be proved, except basic ideas that were true beyond all doubt. For example, Descartes believed that the fact that he could think proved that he existed: "I think, therefore I am," he wrote. This was his first truth. From this basic truth, Descartes established a method of inquiry in which all

René Descartes published his *Discourse on Method* anonymously in 1637.

thoughts would follow the clear, orderly progression of scientific reasoning.

Bacon. Descartes's contemporary, the English philosopher Francis Bacon, took a somewhat stronger line concerning how conclusions should be reached. Bacon rejected deducing knowledge from self-evident principles and instead argued that only through observation and repeatable experiments could theories be built. Bacon thus relied on proofs that could be demonstrated physically, not through deductive logic. He believed that the pursuit of scientific knowledge would enrich human life immeasurably.

Newton. In 1687 Isaac Newton published his *The Mathematical Principles of Natural Philosophy*. It combined and related the contributions of Copernicus, Kepler, and Galileo. These early scientists had shown that the planets, including Earth, revolve around the Sun. But they had not been able to explain *why* the planets moved as they did.

Newton's book contained his laws of motion and universal gravitation, which explained the movements of objects on Earth as well as of the planets. His law of universal gravitation states that all bodies attract each other with a force that can be measured. This force holds the whole system of sun and planets together by keeping them in their orbits.

Newton's work had a tremendous influence on the thinking of his own era and on all later scientific thought. The English poet Alexander Pope described Newton's impact: "Nature and Nature's laws lay hid in night; God said, 'Let Newton be!,' and all was light."

Other scientific discoveries. New discoveries were made elsewhere in Europe. Working independently of each other, both Newton and Gottfried Wilhelm Leibniz (LYP·nits), a German philosopher and mathematician, developed calculus, a branch of mathematics that studies continuously changing quantities. A Dutch scientist, Antoni van Leeuwenhoek (LAY·vuhn·hook), used the microscope, an invention of the late 1500s, to discover bacteria. The microscope enabled him to study a whole new world of life that could not normally be seen by the human eye.

Robert Hooke of England, who lived from 1635 to 1703, also worked with the microscope. The first person to identify cells in living matter, Hooke examined a thin slice of cork and noticed that it consisted of small rectangular "rooms." He called these "rooms" cells because they looked like the *cells* in which bees store their honey.

The Anglo-Irish scientist Robert Boyle is known as the founder of modern chemistry, the study of the

This painting, which hangs in the palace at Versailles, shows the establishment of the French Academy of Sciences in 1666.

composition of materials and the changes they undergo. Another English chemist, Joseph Priestley, discovered the element later called oxygen. (Elements are the fundamental substances that make up matter.)

A French scientist, Antoine Lavoisier (luhv·WAHZ·ee·ay), named oxygen. Lavoisier showed that fire was not an element, as many had believed. He proved that fire was the result of the rapid combination of oxygen with another substance. Lavoisier also demonstrated that matter is indestructible; it can be changed from one form into another, but it cannot be created or destroyed. For example, when water boils, it does not disappear. It forms steam, which combines with the air. The water's form has changed, but the water has not disappeared. Lavoisier's discovery is known as the law of the conservation of matter.

By the time Priestley and Lavoisier made their discoveries, the scientific point of view dominated European thought. The people of the 1700s spoke of their changing times as an "Age of Enlightenment."

Section 5 Review

1. **Define** Scientific Revolution, scientific method, geocentric theory, heliocentric theory

2. **Identify** Nicolaus Copernicus, Galileo

3. **Analyzing Ideas (a)** Define "Scientific Revolution." **(b)** Describe the factors that led to the birth of the Scientific Revolution.

4. **Summarizing Ideas** Explain how Copernicus, Kepler, and Galileo challenged traditionally held views and developed the heliocentric theory.

5. **Interpreting Ideas** Why were the ideas of Descartes, Bacon, and Newton significant to the scientific method?

6. **Evaluating Ideas** Choose three discoveries of the Renaissance and Reformation era and evaluate their importance.

Chapter 14 Review

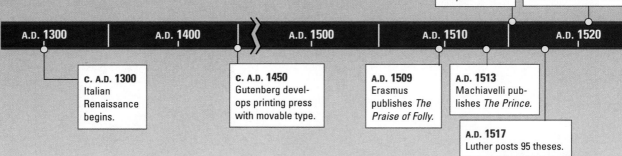
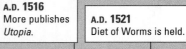

A.D. 1516 More publishes *Utopia*.

A.D. 1521 Diet of Worms is held.

A.D. **1300**   A.D. **1400**   A.D. **1500**   A.D. **1510**   A.D. **1520**

C. A.D. 1300 Italian Renaissance begins.

C. A.D. 1450 Gutenberg develops printing press with movable type.

A.D. 1509 Erasmus publishes *The Praise of Folly*.

A.D. 1513 Machiavelli publishes *The Prince*.

A.D. 1517 Luther posts 95 theses.

Chapter Summary
The following list contains the key concepts you have learned about the Renaissance and the Reformation.
1. Beginning in the early 1300s, a literary and artistic movement known as the Renaissance swept Italy and then spread to northern Europe.
2. The humanists, such as Petrarch, Erasmus, and More, emphasized a renewed interest in classical learning, a critical spirit, and enthusiasm for life in this world.
3. The Renaissance also inspired masterpieces in painting and sculpture.
4. In Germany, Martin Luther broke away from the Roman Catholic Church and began the Protestant Reformation. The doctrines he developed, known today as Lutheranism, spread throughout northern Europe.
5. In England the Anglican Church was founded under Henry VIII.
6. John Calvin's teachings spread from Switzerland to much of Europe.
7. In the 1530s the Roman Catholic Church began the Counter-Reformation. At the Council of Trent, church leaders defined official doctrines. The church used the Inquisition and the *Index of Forbidden Books* to combat heresy. New religious orders, such as the Jesuits, tried to halt the spread of Protestantism.
8. The development of the printing press and the religious changes of the Reformation brought new ideas to the lives of ordinary people. New attitudes toward nature and toward the community took hold.
9. The Scientific Revolution transformed the methods and understanding of astronomy, physics, and anatomy. Europeans made important technological and scientific achievements. The new scientific attitude would dominate future European thought.

Reviewing Important Terms
On a separate sheet of paper, supply the term that correctly completes each statement.
1. The creative movement that began in Italy in the 1300s and included a revival of interest in the classical learning of ancient Greece and Rome is called the _____.
2. People who used classical texts to study grammar, rhetoric, history, and poetry were called _____.
3. The painting technique in which painters make distant objects smaller than those in the foreground and arrange the objects in certain ways to make them appear more realistic is called _____.
4. The religious revolution, which split the church in western Europe and created several new churches, is called the _____.
5. The sale of _____ by the church in Germany sparked the Reformation.
6. Calvin made Geneva a _____ in which the government was ruled by a clergy claiming God's authority.
7. The _____ _____ marked the development of a new way of thinking about the world.
8. Nicolaus Copernicus caused controversy with the _____ _____, which contradicted what most people believed about the relationship between Earth and the Sun.

Developing Critical Thinking Skills
1. **Evaluating Ideas** Identify what each of the following people contributed to the humanist movement. Which person do you think made the greatest contribution? Why? **(a)** Petrarch; **(b)** Machiavelli; **(c)** Erasmus; **(d)** Shakespeare?
2. **Summarizing Ideas** Describe what Martin Luther's ideas were on each of the following: **(a)** salvation; **(b)** the sacraments; **(c)** the clergy.

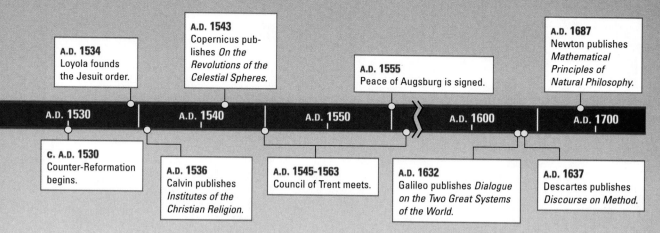

A.D. 1534
Loyola founds the Jesuit order.

A.D. 1543
Copernicus publishes *On the Revolutions of the Celestial Spheres.*

A.D. 1555
Peace of Augsburg is signed.

A.D. 1687
Newton publishes *Mathematical Principles of Natural Philosophy.*

A.D. 1530 — A.D. 1540 — A.D. 1550 — A.D. 1600 — A.D. 1700

C. A.D. 1530
Counter-Reformation begins.

A.D. 1536
Calvin publishes *Institutes of the Christian Religion.*

A.D. 1545-1563
Council of Trent meets.

A.D. 1632
Galileo publishes *Dialogue on the Two Great Systems of the World.*

A.D. 1637
Descartes publishes *Discourse on Method.*

3. **Interpreting Ideas (a)** What was the Counter-Reformation? **(b)** What did it try to accomplish? **(c)** How successful was it?
4. **Understanding Ideas** During the time of the Reformation, most people in Europe lived in small villages. Describe how villagers explained the natural events that occurred in their lives.
5. **Analyzing Ideas** How did the Scientific Revolution change the way people viewed themselves and their world?

Relating Geography to History

Study the map of the world on pages R4 and R5 in the Atlas. **(a)** Why was Italy ideally suited to establish trade with Southwest Asia? **(b)** How did the ideas of the Italian Renaissance spread to northern Europe?

Relating Past to Present

1. A Renaissance person is defined as one who is knowledgeable in both science and art. **(a)** Give an example of someone in today's world who might be called a Renaissance person. **(b)** What are the advantages and disadvantages of this combination of knowledge for an educated person?
2. **(a)** How did the invention of printing revolutionize the spread of knowledge and ideas in Europe during the time of the Reformation? **(b)** Describe how radio and television have changed our understanding of the world.

Applying History Study Skills

Before completing this activity, review Building History Study Skills on page 331.

Look again at Michelangelo's *The Creation of Adam* on page 331. Then look at the statue of Hermes by Praxiteles in column two on this page.

1. How do these works of art show similarities between the values of Greek and Renaissance societies?
2. How do they show differences?

 internetconnect

Search the Internet through the HRW Web site for more information on one of the Renaissance writers that you read about in this chapter. Present an oral report about that person. Be certain that your biography discusses the person's major achievements.

GO TO: go.hrw.com
KEYWORD: SCØ Renaissance

Building Your Portfolio

1. **Writing a Report** Leonardo da Vinci was one of the greatest geniuses of the Renaissance. Prepare a written report on Leonardo's talents and achievements and place a copy in your portfolio. You may use the following sources: "The Scope of Genius" in John Hale's *The Renaissance* (Time-Life Books) and "Leonardo da Vinci" in *Horizon Book of the Renaissance* (American Heritage).
2. **Writing a Monologue** Do research to find out additional information about what it was like to be a European villager during some part of the period from 1300 to 1700. Write a monologue about a typical day or week in your life, or about a special occasion such as a holiday or feast. Begin with a description of the time and place when you lived. Place a copy of the monologue in your portfolio.

European Exploration, Expansion, and Absolutism

TIME

A.D. **1400–1800**

A.D. **1400–1800**

| 3.7 million B.C. | 4000 B.C. | A.D. 2100 |

PLACE

Europe, Asia, North and South America

Europe

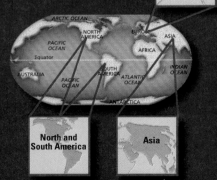

North and South America

Asia

King Louis XIV of France

Significance

European expansion between 1400 and 1800 occurred only after technological, economic, and political changes had taken place in Europe. By the 1600s, a system of government called **absolute monarchy** (where the ruler has total control of the state without needing to consult other leaders or representatives of the people) had become dominant in Europe.

Terms to Define

absolute monarchy	subsidies
compass	Treaty of Tordesillas
astrolabe	triangular trade
latitude	Middle Passage
galleys	viceroys
Commercial Revolution	guerrilla warfare
joint-stock company	tax farming
mercantilism	intendants
favorable balance of trade	divine right of kings
tariffs	balance of power

People to Identify

Prince Henry the Navigator	Marie de Medici
Bartholomeu Dias	Cardinal Richelieu
Vasco da Gama	Cardinal Mazarin
Amerigo Vespucci	Jean-Baptiste Colbert
Vasco Núñez de Balboa	Jacques Cartier
Ferdinand Magellan	René-Robert de La Salle
Juan Sebastián de Elcano	Peter the Great
Juan Ponce de Léon	Catherine the Great
Hernán Cortés	Maria Theresa
Moctezuma	the Great Elector
Francisco Pizarro	Frederick William I
Charles V	Frederick the Great
Philip II	

Places to Locate

Cape of Good Hope	Moscow
Brazil	Sea of Azov
Isthmus of Panama	Black Sea
Philippine Islands	St. Petersburg
Tenochtitlán	
Versailles	

Chapter Theme Questions

- **Economic Organization** What factors might lead nations to venture into the unknown?
- **Politics and Government** How might a vast colonial empire affect a nation's health at home?
- **War and Diplomacy** What might happen when countries expand their borders rather than seek colonies overseas?

Archaeologists believe recently discovered ruins on Haiti's north shore may be those of the first Spanish settlement in North America—Christopher Columbus's lost colony, La Navidad. Archaeologist Kathleen A. Deagan, confident that her search for the colony had ended, wrote:

❝ *Just before midnight on Christmas Eve, 1492, a sleepy helmsman gave the tiller of Christopher Columbus's flagship, Santa María, to the ship's boy. . . . The hapless lad promptly ran the ship onto a coral reef off the north coast of Haiti . . . Attempts to free the vessel failed, the planking opened, and the Admiral abandoned her for Niña. . . .*

Columbus appealed for help to Guacanagari, the Indian . . . chief, whose village was about four miles from the wreck. The Indians helped unload supplies, . . . dismantle the ship's timbers and boards, and carry them . . . to the village. . . . Thus the tiny settlement—named for the infant child of Christmas, La Navidad— was established. . . .

We can only speculate upon what happened next. When Columbus returned 11 months later, he found the settlement burned and all his men dead. . . .

The site was forgotten for nearly 500 years. Now . . . our team . . . believes we have found it again. ❞

Christopher Columbus was only one of many Europeans who spread Western civilization throughout the world.

Section 1

The Foundations of European Exploration

Focus Questions

- **What technological advances helped make the great European explorations possible?**
- **What was the Commercial Revolution?**
- **What was mercantilism, and what role did colonies play in it?**

Before the 1400s, Europeans had little contact with other parts of the world. Marco Polo traveled to

China, the Crusaders tried to capture the Holy Land from the Arabs, and Europeans engaged in the spice trade. Nevertheless, in general Europeans had neither the interest nor the ability to explore foreign lands. By the late 1400s, however, technology, economics, politics, and society as a whole had changed significantly. These changes sparked European interest in the world beyond Europe and provided the opportunity to explore it. Soon adventurous Europeans discovered new routes to many foreign places. These discoveries opened up an era of exploration that lasted for the next 400 years.

Technological Advances

Since the time of the Crusades, Europeans had known about the riches of Asia—spices, silks, and jewels. Early European explorers sought to acquire these goods, which were very valuable trading items, even in small amounts. Spices, silks, and jewels came mainly from India, China, and the islands of Southeast Asia. To reach these distant places safely and to compete successfully with powerful Arab and local traders, Europeans began to focus on finding new sea routes to the East. To do this, Europeans needed better maps, navigation instruments, ships, and guns—in short, Europeans needed more advanced technology.

Mapmaking. Mapmaking improved during the Renaissance because of the Europeans' growing interest in the writings of ancient geographers and their desire for pictorial accuracy. Most scholars knew—as Ptolemy's maps had shown—that the world was round. Renaissance mapmakers added information about Africa and Asia but not yet, of course, about North and South America. It seemed possible that the distance from Europe to Asia would be shorter going west—across the Atlantic Ocean—than going east. Inspired by the new maps, daring sea captains soon set out on their travels, opening up new worlds scarcely dreamed of before.

Navigation instruments. Just as important as maps were the navigation instruments that helped make it possible for ships to sail out of the sight of land without losing their bearings. One such navigation instrument was the **compass**. As early as the 1100s, European navigators had learned that an iron needle rubbed against a piece of lodestone—a kind of magnetic rock—would become magnetized and turn toward the north if they floated it in water on a stick or through a straw. In the 1300s, by fixing the needle to a card marked with directions, these European navigators created a true compass.

Another important navigation instrument, the **astrolabe**, applied astronomy and geometry to navigation and allowed sailors to determine the relative apparent height of stars and planets. Using this information, they could calculate a ship's **latitude**, its distance north or south of the equator.

New ships. Long-distance exploration also required improvements in ships. Before and even during the 1400s, long ships called **galleys** carried most European coastal trade. Slaves or prisoners of war strained at the 50 or 60 oars that propelled the galley. In deep ocean waters, traders used sailing ships. Until the late 1400s, these clumsy sailing vessels could travel only in the direction in which the wind blew.

In the late 1400s, ship designers in Portugal and Spain made important improvements. They reduced the width of ships in proportion to their length, made smaller and different-shaped sails, and moved the location of the rudder—a device used for steering—from the side to the rear, or stern, of the ship.

In his paintings, Jan Vermeer frequently gives the viewer a glimpse of a figure in the midst of an activity. "The Astronomer" illustrates research and work related to mapmaking.

A Mariner's Astrolabe

The process of determining a vehicle's position and directing its movement is called navigation. The word *navigation* comes from two Latin words—*navis,* meaning "ship," and *agere,* meaning "to drive."

The explorers of the 1500s sailed with only a few simple technological aids to guide them. However, with these, along with the stars and the Sun, they navigated the oceans of the world. They could plot and hold a course, measure their progress, and estimate their position in relation to land.

Astrolabes, usually made of brass or iron, were widely used in the Middle Ages by astronomers to plot the position of the Sun and other celestial bodies. In the 1400s, sailors began using the technology of astrolabes to determine the latitude of their ships.

A sailor would sight a star along the bar shown in the photograph. Then, by aligning the bar with markings engraved on the disk of the astrolabe, he could determine the latitude.

The astrolabe became obsolete with the invention of the sextant, an instrument navigators use to measure the angular distance between two points such as the horizon and the Sun.

These improvements allowed ships to sail against the wind, to travel quickly, and to be steered with reasonable accuracy.

The cannon. Europeans first used cannons in war during the 1400s. Until then naval warfare had consisted of ramming and boarding an enemy vessel. Shipboard cannons and the handguns carried by sailors now helped Europeans defeat the navies of their enemies.

Economic Changes

The development of improved ways of doing business also played an important part in the new exploration. In some cases, developments that had already begun, such as the use of money and the services provided by banks, simply changed to accommodate the needs of exploration. In other cases, the old methods of doing business became inadequate, and Europeans worked out new ones. The changes in the European economy were so extensive that some historians have referred to the period from 1400 to 1750 as the **Commercial Revolution**.

Standardized money. Before the 1400s, the value of money had not been standardized. That is, the value of certain coins might change, depending on the amount of precious metal used to make them. The scarcity of precious metals from which coins were made, the great variety of coins in use, and the lack of a fixed value for money handicapped Europeans.

During the 1400s, however, Europeans developed standard systems of money. The Italian cities led the way in minting coins that had a fixed value. The value of the gold florin of Florence and the ducat (DUHK·uht) of Venice became very dependable. Later the Spanish kings used silver and gold shipped from the New World to pay debts owed their bankers. These payments helped relieve the shortage of precious metals in Europe.

The standardization of money made economic transactions much more reliable. Anyone who accepted a florin in payment for goods or services knew that the money was worth a certain amount and could be used to buy other goods or services. This in turn encouraged the growth of international trade and banking. The large sums that banks now accumulated made it possible for them to lend money to governments and major trading companies who financed large overseas expeditions.

Joint-stock companies. Individual merchants often combined their resources in a new type of business organization called a **joint-stock company**. Such a company raised money by selling stock, or shares, in the company to investors. These shareholders became co-owners. Shareholders divided profits according to the numbers of shares of stock they owned. Joint-stock companies raised large amounts of money from people willing to invest in their activities.

With the standardization of money, monarchs financed overseas trade and the settlement of colonies.

Political Changes

Technological and commercial advances alone could not have made successful explorations possible. Money provided by the stronger and more ambitious monarchies that emerged in Europe in the 1400s and 1500s financed these expeditions. By then dynastic ambitions and rivalries between countries often made the central governments enthusiastic supporters of new exploration and colonization. Gaining riches from overseas exploration was one way a country could become more powerful than its rivals.

Despite the contributions of the Italian city-states to the Commercial Revolution and the growth of capitalism, they had not financed explorations or established overseas colonies. As the age of exploration began, trade that previously had been concentrated in the Mediterranean area and southern Germany now moved to the Atlantic nations. In Portugal, Spain, and France, monarchs and their advisers not only financed voyages but also controlled exploration and the building of overseas empires.

Mercantilism

The economic and political changes associated with overseas expansion also contributed to a new economic theory called **mercantilism**. According to this theory, a country's government should do all it could to increase the country's wealth. A country's wealth was measured by how much gold and silver it possessed. Because according to this belief the world contained only a fixed amount of such wealth, to increase its own wealth, a country had to take wealth away from another country.

Balance of trade. Mercantilists thought a nation could gain wealth by mining gold and silver at home or by acquiring colonies that were rich in those precious metals. It could also get wealth by selling more goods than it bought in foreign countries, thus creating a **favorable balance of trade**. By bringing money into a country, a favorable balance of trade strengthened the country itself and weakened its foreign rivals, who ultimately paid in gold and silver for the goods they bought, thus depleting their supplies of those metals.

To gain a favorable balance of trade, a nation could take several measures. It could reduce the amount of goods imported into the country by imposing **tariffs**, or import taxes, on foreign goods. The importer paid the tax and added that amount to the selling price of the goods. The higher price discouraged people from buying foreign goods. A nation could also try to

The Growth of Banking Families

One of the outgrowths of the Commercial Revolution was the formation of powerful families in Europe that handled trading and banking concerns. Such families thrived as the economic life of the Middle Ages began to change and long-distance trade became more common.

Although a local guild leader could handle trade in his area, he did not have the capital, the time, or the knowledge to run a worldwide operation. A new kind of businessman emerged to fill the gap. Usually such a man began as a merchant of a specific type and ended as a banker. The Medici family of Italy followed this path. So did the Fuggers (FOOG´uhrz) in the area that is now Germany.

The Fuggers began their rise in the early 1400s, when Hans (or Johann) Fugger gained control of the weaver's guild in Augsburg. He began to deal in a new type of cloth, thereby extending his base of trade. As family members traveled to Venice, the business began to encompass spices, silks, and other Eastern goods. The Fuggers invested their profits in non-textile concerns, including mining. By the 1500s, they had enough extra capital to lend money to the popes, to Charles V (who spent it to gain the title Holy Roman emperor), and later to both the German and Spanish ruling families. Jakob II (called the Rich) Fugger, grandson of Hans, is shown above with his chief accountant.

The Fuggers continued to be a force through the end of the 1500s, declining only after 1600 as trade in the Atlantic became more important and the Dutch took control of the mouth of the Rhine River for their own profit.

increase the value of its exports. Manufactured goods were the most valuable kind of exports because they sold for more money than raw materials; woolen cloth, for instance, brought more than raw wool. Therefore, mercantilist nations encouraged manufacturers, exporters of manufactured goods, and shipbuilders. In many cases, governments made grants of money called **subsidies** to help establish new industries and build ships. A nation could also try to make itself self-sufficient by producing everything it needed, plus a surplus of goods for export. The self-sufficient nation did not have to depend on foreign countries, which were always rivals and might at any time become active enemies. The desire for self-sufficiency helped stimulate the race to acquire overseas colonies.

The role of colonies. Colonies played an important part in mercantilism. Those that produced gold and silver were the most desirable. Next best were those that produced raw materials that could not be produced at home. By buying these materials in its colonies, a nation could avoid buying from a foreign rival. Thus money did not leave the nation or empire, which maintained complete control over its wealth.

Finally, mercantilist theory put a high value on colonies as markets for the manufactured goods of the home country. Governments passed strict laws to prevent colonists from buying foreign manufactured goods or selling their raw materials anywhere except the home country. In this way, the home country kept strict economic control of its colonies. In addition, home countries might ban colonies from manufacturing their own goods, forcing the colonists to buy such goods from the home country.

Social Change

Government policies by themselves did not create a willingness to explore and settle overseas. Certain changes in society also made exploration and resettlement abroad attractive to many people.

After 1500 Europe experienced a population increase. Some urban areas became very crowded. Adventurous people hoped that despite harsh living conditions in the colonies, settling overseas would give them a fresh start and a better life.

Some people went to the colonies hoping to reap quick profits. Tales of gold and jewels, of fabulous cities such as the legendary El Dorado in South America, as well as of fertile soil persuaded thousands that easy wealth lay overseas.

Others—such as the French Huguenots and the English Puritans—went overseas to escape religious or political persecution at home. Some went to spread Christianity. Often a combination of reasons caused people to resettle in new lands.

Section 1 Review

1. **Define** absolute monarchy, compass, astrolabe, latitude, galleys, Commercial Revolution, joint-stock company, mercantilism, favorable balance of trade, tariffs, subsidies
2. **Summarizing Ideas** Describe the improvements in navigational aids and ship construction that made long-range exploration possible.
3. **Understanding Ideas** Explain the importance of the Commercial Revolution.
4. **Interpreting Ideas** What role did colonies play in mercantilism?

Section 2

Voyages of Portugal and Spain

Focus Questions

- **What were the accomplishments of Prince Henry the Navigator, Bartholomeu Dias, and Vasco da Gama?**
- **What was the impact of the voyages of Christopher Columbus?**
- **What were the characteristics of the Atlantic slave trade, and why did it prosper?**

Explorers sailing under the flags of Portugal and Spain made the first European voyages into unknown waters. These explorers were driven by curiosity and by religious and economic aims and backed by their governments. The voyages of these courageous men served as the foundation for future empires.

Portugal and Prince Henry

Perched at the southwestern corner of Europe, the small nation of Portugal was one of the first to become strongly interested in exploration. Prince Henry (often called the Navigator), a member of the Portuguese royal family, was largely responsible for this interest. Henry hoped to acquire gold for Portugal. He also hoped to start a Crusade against the Muslims in Africa, where he thought he might even find and join forces with a legendary priest and king known as Prester John.

To help accomplish his goals, Prince Henry is thought to have founded a school of sailing and navigation at Sagres. (Some historians dispute the existence of this school.) By 1418 his navigators began a series of explorations westward into the Atlantic and southward along the west coast of Africa. Henry's explorers claimed for Portugal several islands, including the Azores in the Atlantic Ocean. On the African coast, the Portuguese began to trade for slaves, gold, and ivory.

Further explorations brought the Portuguese even greater gains. In 1488 Bartholomeu Dias sailed around the Cape of Good Hope at the southern tip of Africa. Although Dias had to turn back, he had found the route to the Indian Ocean. Building on this knowledge in 1497, Vasco da Gama sailed beyond the Cape of Good Hope eastward across the Indian Ocean, landing in India in 1498. (See map on pages 362 and 363.) From a second voyage a few years later, he returned home with a fabulous cargo of spices and jewels.

Da Gama's successful voyages represented a tremendous stroke of good fortune for the Portuguese. Their ships could now sail to India and the East Indies and bring back rich cargoes of Asian goods. The direct ocean route saved the Portuguese money because they could buy goods directly from Asia rather than from Arab traders or Italian merchants, who charged very high prices. Ships could carry goods for long distances more cheaply than could wagons or animals traveling overland. In addition, ships did not have to pay the tolls that frequently were levied on overland transportation.

Christopher Columbus

Spain, too, became interested in the search for new trade routes. Its rulers, King Ferdinand and Queen Isabella, decided to finance a voyage by Christopher Columbus, a Genoan navigator. Inspired by the writings of Marco Polo and influenced by Ptolemy's description of the round Earth, Columbus believed he could reach Asia quickly by sailing westward instead of making the long trip around the tip of Africa.

In August 1492, Columbus set sail from Palos, Spain, with three small ships—the *Niña* the *Pinta*,

Pictured is a woodcut illustration of Columbus's flagship *Santa Maria*.

and the *Santa Maria*—across the Atlantic. On October 12, 1492, his small fleet landed at a tiny island that Columbus named San Salvador. (See map on pages 362 and 363.)

After exploring other islands in the area, he returned triumphantly to Spain early in 1493 to report his discoveries. Because he believed the islands lay off the east coast of India, Columbus called them the Indies and their inhabitants Indians. In fact, he had discovered the islands in the Americas that were later to be known as the West Indies. Columbus made three more voyages to the "Indies" between 1493 and 1504. For the rest of his life he believed he had landed off the coast of Asia.

The Impact of Columbus's Voyages

In the years after Columbus's voyages, a massive interaction between the so-called New World and the Old World took place. This interaction, often referred to as the Columbian Exchange, involved the movement of products, plants, animals, and even diseases between the Western and Eastern Hemispheres. For example, gold and silver mined in South America were shipped eastward to Spain. American precious metals helped Spain become a world power.

The interchange between the Americas and the Old World affected the way people lived. The diet of Europeans changed markedly after American foods such as potatoes, tomatoes, beans, and corn were introduced in Europe. Horses and cattle, brought to the Americas by the Spanish, greatly altered the lives of Native Americans, especially in what today is Mexico and the southwestern United States. Other exchanges were less beneficial.

European Explorations, 1487–1682

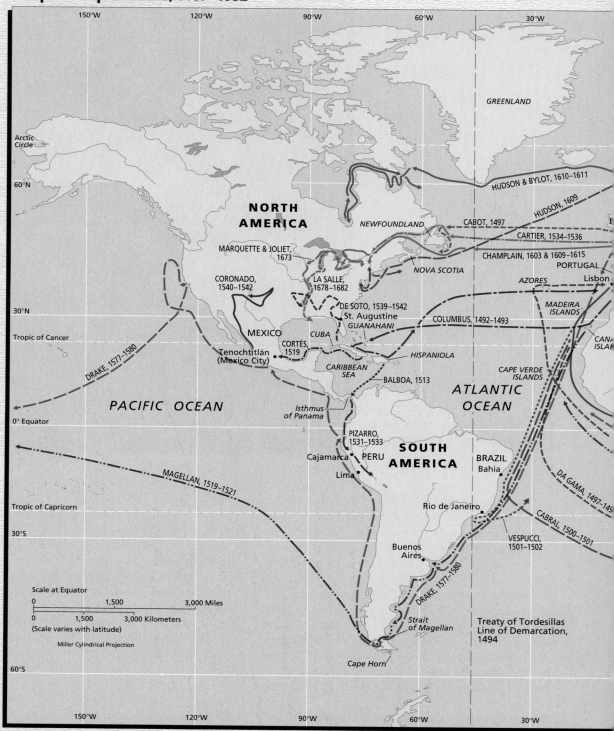

150°W 120°W 90°W 60°W 30°W

GREENLAND

Arctic Circle

60°N

HUDSON & BYLOT, 1610–1611

NORTH AMERICA

NEWFOUNDLAND

HUDSON, 1609

CABOT, 1497

CARTIER, 1534–1536

MARQUETTE & JOLIET, 1673

CHAMPLAIN, 1603 & 1609–1615

PORTUGAL

CORONADO, 1540–1542

LA SALLE, 1678–1682

NOVA SCOTIA

AZORES

Lisbon

DRAKE, 1577–1580

30°N

DE SOTO, 1539–1542

St. Augustine

GUANAHANI

MADEIRA ISLANDS

Tropic of Cancer

MEXICO

CUBA

COLUMBUS, 1492–1493

CANA ISLAN

Tenochtitlán (Mexico City)

CORTÉS, 1519

HISPANIOLA

CARIBBEAN SEA

BALBOA, 1513

CAPE VERDE ISLANDS

ATLANTIC OCEAN

PACIFIC OCEAN

0° Equator

Isthmus of Panama

PIZARRO, 1531–1533

SOUTH AMERICA

BRAZIL

Bahia

Cajamarca

PERU

DA GAMA, 1497–149

Lima

MAGELLAN, 1519–1521

Rio de Janeiro

CABRAL, 1500–1501

Tropic of Capricorn

VESPUCCI, 1501–1502

30°S

Buenos Aires

DRAKE, 1577–1580

Scale at Equator

0   1,500   3,000 Miles

0   1,500   3,000 Kilometers
(Scale varies with latitude)

Miller Cylindrical Projection

Strait of Magellan

Treaty of Tordesillas Line of Demarcation, 1494

60°S

Cape Horn

150°W 120°W 90°W 60°W 30°W

Learning from Maps European explorers set out to the east and west to discover new lands.

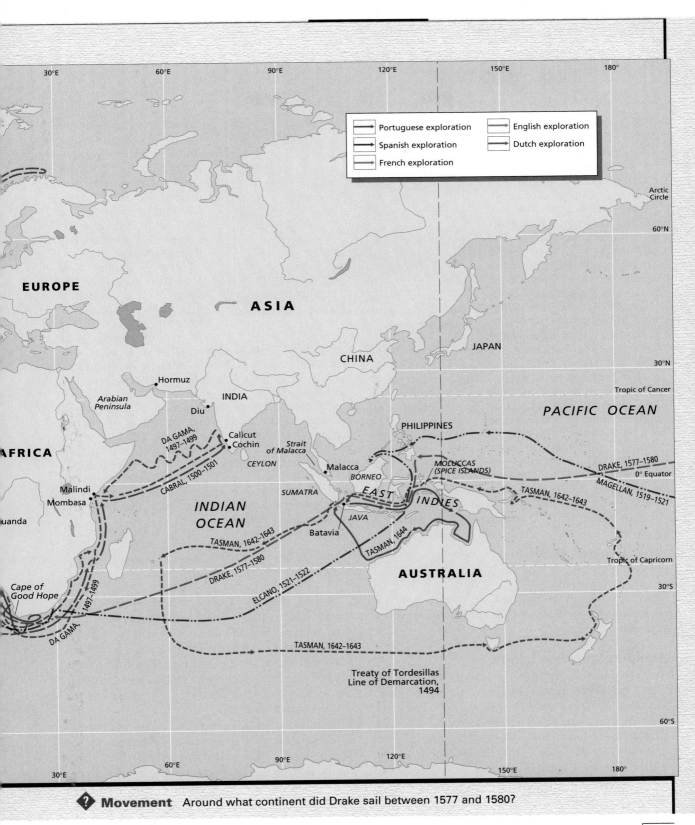

Portuguese exploration	English exploration
Spanish exploration	Dutch exploration
French exploration	

EUROPE

ASIA

Arctic Circle

60°N

JAPAN

CHINA

30°N

Tropic of Cancer

PACIFIC OCEAN

Hormuz

INDIA

Arabian Peninsula

Diu

PHILIPPINES

DA GAMA, 1497–1499

Calicut

Cochin

Strait of Malacca

AFRICA

CEYLON

Malacca

BORNEO

MOLUCCAS (SPICE ISLANDS)

DRAKE, 1577–1580

0° Equator

CABRAL, 1500–1501

MAGELLAN, 1519–1521

Malindi

Mombasa

SUMATRA

INDIAN OCEAN

EAST INDIES

TASMAN, 1642–1643

uanda

JAVA

TASMAN, 1642–1643

Batavia

TASMAN, 1644

1497–1499

DRAKE, 1577–1580

Tropic of Capricorn

Cape of Good Hope

ELCANO, 1521–1522

AUSTRALIA

30°S

DA GAMA,

TASMAN, 1642–1643

Treaty of Tordesillas Line of Demarcation, 1494

60°S

30°E   60°E   90°E   120°E   150°E   180°

❓ **Movement**   Around what continent did Drake sail between 1577 and 1580?

The Columbian Exchange

Today computer and communication technologies enable people all over the world to exchange information and goods and services, making the world seem a smaller place. What we call the Columbian Exchange, an equally important kind of exchange between the Americas and the rest of the world, began in 1492, when Columbus sailed from Spain across the Atlantic Ocean. With their arrival in the Americas, Columbus and the Europeans

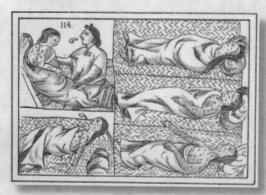

This Aztec drawing shows the stages of smallpox, ending with death.

who came after him initiated contact between peoples and civilizations that had not been in contact for 9,000 years. Along with the exchange of people came a variety of other exchanges. We are still experiencing today both the positive and negative impacts of this contact.

The exchange of crops across the Atlantic caused landscapes to change and populations to grow. White potatoes, originally grown and domesticated in the Andes, today feed millions of people in northern Europe, Russia, and China. Wheat, on the other hand, was not grown in the Americas until it was brought there by

Europeans. American corn, or maize, first domesticated by Native Americans, is now an essential crop in many nations, including Romania, Egypt, South Africa, and China. The tomato originated not in Italy but in the Americas.

Many animals were also introduced to the Americas by Columbus and other Europeans. Horses, cattle, goats, sheep, chickens, and house cats crossed the Atlantic Ocean with European travelers. North America, in exchange, gave Europe and Asia the turkey, gray squirrel, and muskrat.

Of course, there were also negative consequences of the Columbian Exchange. The most devastating imports from Europe and elsewhere to the Americas were diseases: measles, typhus, plague, and smallpox. Native American populations had never experienced these diseases before and had no immunity to them. They were thus extremely vulnerable to such diseases, and millions died from them.

Smallpox and other diseases carried westward by Europeans nearly destroyed the native population of Spanish America.

Dividing the New Lands

In the late 1400s, Spain and Portugal often claimed the same newly discovered lands. To resolve their conflicts, in 1493 Pope Alexander VI issued an edict that drew on a world map a line of demarcation down the middle of the Atlantic Ocean. He granted Spain the rights to all newly discovered lands west of the line. Portugal could claim all those to the east of the line. Neither country, however, was to occupy lands already claimed by a Christian ruler.

A year later, the **Treaty of Tordesillas** between Spain and Portugal moved the line farther west. (See map on pages 362 and 363.) A Portuguese captain, Pedro Cabral, reached the east coast of South America by accident in 1500. He had sailed for India but had been blown off course and reached Brazil. He was able to claim this region for Portugal under the Treaty of Tordesillas.

Eventually, Spain took control of most of Central and South America, along with the Philippines. (See map on pages 370 and 371.) Portugal had the territory on the Brazilian coast as well as territory on both the eastern and western coasts of Africa and in Asia and the East Indies.

Vespucci, Balboa, and Magellan

Other explorers followed Columbus westward. Between 1497 and 1503, Amerigo Vespucci, a navigator from Florence, took part in several Spanish and Portuguese expeditions across the Atlantic. Unlike other explorers, Vespucci was convinced that the land he saw was not part of Asia but was instead what he called a New World. After reading Vespucci's writings describing this new land, a German mapmaker called it America after Vespucci, whose first name, in Latin, is *Americus*.

In 1513 a Spaniard named Vasco Núñez de Balboa crossed the Isthmus of Panama and reached a vast ocean. Balboa called it the South Sea and claimed it for Spain. It now seemed clear that the so-called New World really was a distinct landmass, separate from Asia.

Ferdinand Magellan, a Portuguese navigator sailing for Spain, proved it. In 1519, with five ships, Magellan set out from Spain, crossed the Atlantic to South America, and sailed along its eastern shore until he reached the southernmost tip. After passing through the strait now named for him, Magellan found himself in a great ocean. Because it appeared to be very calm, he named it the Pacific Ocean, from the Latin word *pacificus*, meaning "peaceful." This was the same ocean Balboa had named the South Sea.

Magellan sailed westward across the Pacific and reached the Philippine Islands, claiming them for Spain. There in 1521 he died in a fight with the islanders. His crew, led by Juan Sebastián de Elcano, sailed on. Eventually, one ship and 18 crew members made it back to Spain in 1522, completing this first round-the-world voyage.

Portuguese Expansion

After the voyages of Dias and da Gama, the Portuguese pursued the dream of dominating trade with Asia.

Around 1510 the Portuguese conquered part of the southwest coast of India, making the port of

Magellan (shown here) and Elcano's circumnavigation of the globe between 1519 and 1522 provided the first indisputable proof that Earth was round.

Goa (GOH·uh) their administrative center. From India they moved on to the East Indies. (See map on pages 362 and 363.) They conquered Malacca (muh·LAK·uh), on the southwest coast of the Malay Peninsula. Then they moved east to take the Moluccas (muh·LUKH·uhz), a group of islands. Europeans called them the Spice Islands because spices grew there in abundance.

The Portuguese then turned their attention to the island of Ceylon (now Sri Lanka), off the southeast coast of India, adding it to their chain of trading bases. With its key location between Goa and Malacca and its tea and spices, Ceylon helped the Portuguese dominate trade with the East Indies. The Portuguese also gained footholds in China and Japan, and established several fortified trading posts on the East African coast.

Portugal's colonies in Asia and around the Indian Ocean, though important, were small trading bases. In the Americas, however, the Portuguese founded a much larger colony in Brazil. There they established enormous agricultural estates on which they grew sugar for export.

The Slave Trade

As they did in Asia, the Portuguese went to Africa to trade. At first the Portuguese, largely at the request of Christian missionaries who wanted to convert the continent's inhabitants, maintained friendly relations with the Africans. The Portuguese treated the monarch of the African kingdom of Kongo as a legitimate and "brother" king to the Portuguese ruler. In turn, the king of the Kongo welcomed the newcomers and accepted baptism. Envoys from the Kongo traveled to Europe. The cordial relations, however, soon collapsed when the economic interests of Portuguese traders became evident.

Portuguese economic interests in Africa centered largely on slavery, which had been practiced for thousands of years. Europeans themselves had been slaves in the Byzantine Empire and in the Arab and Turkish Empires. During the 1500s, however, the new European overseas empires began to require slave labor.

The slave trade grew very gradually, beginning in earnest when the Portuguese set up sugar plantations on the islands of Príncipe and São Tomé off the coast of west-central Africa. To operate efficiently and profitably, these plantations required large numbers of slaves. Plantation owners acquired their slaves from the African mainland. As plantation agriculture spread to Brazil and the Caribbean islands, the demand for slaves increased. By the early 1600s, the slave trade served as the chief purpose of European relations with Africa.

Spain annexed Portugal in 1580. At around the same time, the Dutch emerged as the leading naval power and became active in the slave trade. The Dutch also took over some of Portugal's colonies, most notably the East Indies. Later the English and the French also became involved in the slave trade.

Triangular trade. The Atlantic slave trade was one aspect of a system known as the **triangular trade**. In the first stage of the system, merchants shipped cotton goods, weapons, and liquor to Africa in exchange for slaves or gold. The second stage—called the **Middle Passage**—was the shipment of slaves across the Atlantic to the Americas. There the traders sold the slaves for produce from the plantations. To complete the triangle, merchants sent the plantations' products to Europe, where they were used to buy manufactured products to be sold in the Americas. Some products from plantations, such as tobacco, were traded in Africa for more slaves.

Middle Passage. The Middle Passage had a brutal and dehumanizing effect on all involved. The traders chained the slaves in the overcrowded hold of the ship to prevent them from jumping overboard or organizing a rebellion aboard ship. In the hold, slaves had little food or water and no provision for sanitation. Many died before they ever reached their destination.

At the height of the trade, between 1741 and 1810, European slave ships carried an average of about 60,000 slaves each year. Recent estimates indicate that between 1451 and 1870 some 10 million Africans survived the horrendous journey to become slaves in the Americas. Perhaps another 1.5 million died during the Middle Passage. Many others died even earlier, during the process of enslavement by fellow Africans and on the hard trip from the interior of Africa to the coast. This tragic loss meant that Africa's population did not increase between 1650 and 1800, when Europe's population was growing rapidly.

African kingdoms and slavery. Beginning in the 1400s and 1500s, strong states began to emerge in West Africa. Over the next centuries, groups such as the Asante and kingdoms such as Benin and Dahomey became powerful. Many of these states profited from the slave trade.

Although not all Africans participated in the slave trade with Europeans, many African societies had practiced slavery well before the arrival of the Europeans. Slaves were usually obtained through war or in raids.

This 1800s sketch shows the horribly crowded conditions aboard a slave ship.

African slavery differed in some respects from that in the Americas, however. African slave owners preferred women and children for labor and sometimes killed males because they were likely to cause trouble or try to escape. Europeans, on the other hand, were more interested in male slaves to do manual work on colonial plantations. African societies generally allowed slaves to buy back their freedom, and they treated slaves as people with a role in society. Europeans, on the other hand, generally considered slaves as property to be bought or sold for profit.

Because Europeans rarely ventured beyond Africa's coast, they needed the help of Africans in gathering and transporting slaves. Some African societies and individuals willingly joined in the slave trade to obtain arms and other goods from Europe. In turn neighboring groups either had to participate in the trade or become its victims. The demand for slaves led to increased slave raiding, which had a disastrous effect on the future of the continent.

Weaknesses of the Portuguese Empire

Portugal rapidly acquired wealth and a vast empire, but that empire declined almost as swiftly as it rose. Several factors hastened the decline. First, the Portuguese government, with a shaky financial base, had overextended its empire.

Second, the sea voyages to the distant colonies, and the governing of them, proved to be a drain on Portugal's population. Many Portuguese men went to sea, never to return. Thousands of soldiers and sailors were needed to sustain the overseas empire. While Portuguese ships made enormous profits in trade, frequent mishaps from shipwrecks and encounters with enemies reduced both monetary gains and the number of men who were able to return home.

Because Portugal had a small population to begin with, the losses could not easily be replaced.

Third, Spain annexed Portugal in 1580, and Portugal did not regain its independence until 1640. In the meantime, Spain limited Portuguese trade and also neglected the colonies that the Portuguese had established overseas.

Taking advantage of these weaknesses, the Dutch and English captured much of the Asian trade from the Portuguese during the 1600s. However, small Portuguese colonies survived in Africa, India, and China, but they no longer served as sources of great wealth. Only Brazil and Angola continued to serve as major Portuguese colonies.

Section 2 Review

1. **Define** Treaty of Tordesillas, triangular trade, Middle Passage
2. **Identify** Prince Henry the Navigator, Bartholomeu Dias, Vasco da Gama, Amerigo Vespucci, Vasco Núñez de Balboa, Ferdinand Magellan, Juan Sebastián de Elcano
3. **Locate and Explain the Significance** Cape of Good Hope, Brazil, Isthmus of Panama, Philippine Islands
4. **Summarizing Ideas** Briefly state the major accomplishments of each of the following people: Prince Henry the Navigator, Bartholomeu Dias, and Vasco da Gama.
5. **Evaluating Ideas** Why were the voyages of Christopher Columbus important?
6. **Understanding Ideas** Describe how the Atlantic slave trade worked and what led to its success.

The Spanish and Dutch Empires

Focus Questions

- **How did Spain extend its power abroad and at home?**
- **Why were the Dutch successful in the 1600s?**
- **Why did the Spanish Empire decline?**

Throughout the 1500s, Spain was the most powerful nation in Europe and had the largest overseas empire. Within just 150 years, however, Spain's power declined. The reasons for the rise and rapid decline of the Spanish Empire are woven through an intricate network of historical events.

Spain's Colonial Empire

Portugal's main interests, with the exception of Brazil, lay in Africa and Asia. Spain, on the other hand, turned most of its energies to the Americas. In Asia only the Philippine Islands held great interest to Spain as a colony.

Beginning with the expeditions of Columbus, Spaniards explored the West Indies, Central America, and parts of the mainland of North and South America. (See map on pages 362 and 363.) They failed to find the spices they sought and soon learned that the land they explored was not the East Indies. However, America's abundant natural resources offered them other opportunities.

Starting in the Caribbean, Spanish exploration and colonization moved to the American mainland. Leaving Puerto Rico, Juan Ponce de León sailed northward in 1513 and explored what today is the state of Florida. A later expedition to Florida, under Pánfilo de Narváez, ended in disaster in 1528. A handful of survivors, led by Alvar Núñez Cabeza de Vaca, traveled through what is now the southwestern United States and Mexico for seven years.

Conquests. Other explorers went to the Yucatán in Mexico and learned of the great Maya and Aztec civilizations. In 1519, with 11 ships and about 600 men, Hernán Cortés invaded Mexico. After seizing the Aztec ruler Moctezuma (MAWK·tay·soo·muh), Cortés captured and destroyed the great Aztec city of Tenochtitlán—on the ruins of which the Spanish built Mexico City—and eventually conquered the entire Aztec Empire. Horses and guns, unknown in the Americas, helped the small Spanish force overcome the Aztec armies.

The Spaniards also heard of a great and rich civilization in South America. In early 1530, Francisco Pizarro led an expedition of 180 men and 37 horses from the Isthmus of Panama to the Inca Empire in what is now Peru and in 1532 seized it for Spain.

In time Spain controlled a vast empire in the West Indies, Central America, southern and western North America, and much of South America. (See map on pages 370 and 371.) The Spaniards became colonizers in the true sense of the word. Unlike the Europeans in Africa and Asia, who became mainly traders, the Spaniards in the Americas established settlements.

Government and society. Spain developed a centralized form of government for its colonies. **Viceroys**, representatives of the monarch, reported to the Council of the Indies in Spain. The council planned and directed the development of Spain's empire.

For a time, Spain grew enormously rich from its colonies' valuable silver mines in the regions that are now Bolivia and northern Mexico. Although agriculture and trade remained important, mineral resources became the Spanish Empire's main asset.

The native inhabitants had no immunity to diseases that the Spanish brought with them. The societies conquered by Cortés and Pizarro had already been weakened by European diseases. Massive epidemics of smallpox, typhus, and measles killed millions. In an area covering Mexico, the southwestern United States, and much of Central America, the native population is estimated to have declined from between 11 and 25 million in 1492 to 1.25 million by 1625. Because the Spaniards needed workers for mines and farms, they imported slaves from Africa to compensate for the loss of Indian labor.

Spain's Colonial Rivals

The Spanish government made every effort to keep the wealth of the Americas for Spain alone. It kept foreigners out of the Spanish colonies and decreed that silver and gold from the Americas could be carried only in Spanish ships and only to the Spanish port of Seville.

Making rules, however, proved easier than enforcing them. Spain's colonial rivals—the French, Dutch, and English—envied Spain's American wealth and used various means to capture a share of it. They traded in Spain's American ports and encouraged pirates to attack Spanish ships.

Shortly after arriving in Peru, Francisco Pizarro's group met the Inca emperor Atahualpa (shown kneeling). When he refused to acquiesce to either Christianity or the Spanish Crown, they captured and killed him.

Spain's rivals also attempted to establish colonies in the Americas, paying no attention to the pope's line of demarcation. Some inroads were made on Spanish territory; for example, England, Holland, and France acquired islands in the West Indies. However, the Spanish Empire in the Americas remained otherwise largely intact until the early 1800s.

Charles V

While Spanish explorers were creating a great empire outside Europe, Spanish kings expanded their authority in Spain itself. One of the greatest of these kings was Charles V, a member of the Habsburg family.

The Habsburgs were an old German family that often succeeded in increasing its land and power through marriages. A series of such marriages brought Charles to the Spanish throne in 1516. Three years later, he was elected Holy Roman emperor. Although he was the first king named Charles to rule Spain, he was the fifth Charles with the title Holy Roman emperor and is known in history as Charles V.

With Charles's titles and power came great responsibilities and conflicts. Born in Flanders, Charles, according to one historian, "spoke Flemish by choice, Spanish, French, and Italian to his officials, and German to his horse." As king of Spain, he needed to acquire a Spanish viewpoint. As Holy Roman emperor, however, he would be expected to support German aims. Charles was embroiled in religious conflicts in Germany; it was he who called Martin Luther to Worms in 1521. Moreover, as the secular leader of Christian Europe, Charles had to assume responsibility for defending Europe against the Ottoman Turks. The Ottoman Turks were invading central Europe and attacking European ships as they sailed in the Mediterranean.

Charles V halted the Turkish penetration of central Europe by driving the Turks away from Vienna in 1529. Religious wars between Catholics and Lutherans in Germany were temporarily settled by the 1555 Peace of Augsburg. Yet the nearly continuous wars drained Spain's human and financial resources.

European Overseas Empires, 1700

Learning from Maps European countries governed territories across the globe.

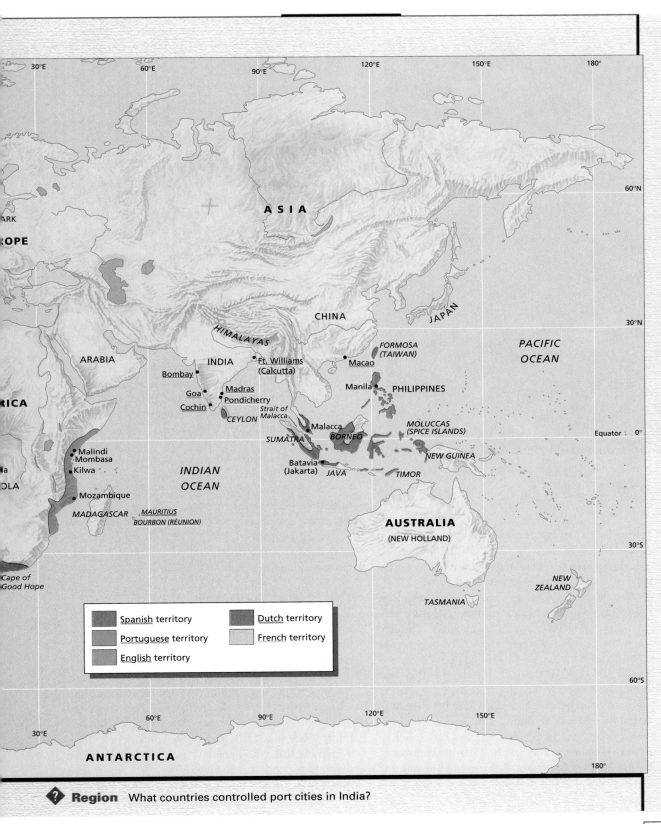

ASIA

CHINA

HIMALAYAS

ARABIA

INDIA

Bombay

Goa
Cochin

Madras
Pondicherry

Ft. Williams
(Calcutta)

CEYLON

Strait of
Malacca

Macao

Manila

FORMOSA
(TAIWAN)

PHILIPPINES

PACIFIC
OCEAN

JAPAN

SUMATRA

Malacca

BORNEO

MOLUCCAS
(SPICE ISLANDS)

Equator   0°

Malindi
Mombasa
Kilwa

Batavia
(Jakarta)

JAVA

TIMOR

NEW GUINEA

INDIAN
OCEAN

Mozambique

MADAGASCAR

MAURITIUS
BOURBON (RÉUNION)

AUSTRALIA
(NEW HOLLAND)

30°N

60°N

30°S

NEW
ZEALAND

Cape of
Good Hope

TASMANIA

60°S

Spanish territory

Portuguese territory

English territory

Dutch territory

French territory

ANTARCTICA

30°E   60°E   90°E   120°E   150°E   180°

❓ **Region** What countries controlled port cities in India?

In this scene, Charles V observes the ladies taking their turn at the hunt.

Spain lacked industries, and the government did little to encourage them. It also had difficulty feeding its people because so much land was devoted to raising sheep for wool. Food prices quintupled between 1500 and the mid-1600s. Charles's government, although tightly controlled by him, could not operate efficiently over a realm that included lands scattered throughout Europe as well as colonies overseas in the Americas.

Charles V realized that this scattered empire had become too large for any one monarch to rule. In 1556 he gave up his throne and divided his vast lands between members of his family. Charles's son Philip II received Spain and its possessions, and his branch of the family became known as the Spanish Habsburgs. Charles's brother Ferdinand I, king of Hungary and Bohemia, became Holy Roman emperor and head of the Austrian branch of the Habsburg family.

Charles V himself retired to a monastery, where he continued to take an interest in political affairs. He died in 1558.

Philip II

Unlike his father Charles V, Philip II was born and educated in Spain. He ruled until his death in 1598. Philip had such a dedicated sense of responsibility that he had almost no private life and worked long hours at the business of being king. He wanted to make Spain stronger at home so that it might continue as Europe's leading power. He made the central government responsible only to the king.

Philip built a new royal residence, El Escorial, 25 miles from Madrid. From there, surrounded by mounds of government papers, he drew the reins of the government so tightly that he almost paralyzed the administration. Philip II also saw himself as the leader of the Counter-Reformation. A very devout Catholic, he ordered the Spanish Inquisition to redouble its efforts to find and stamp out heresy at home. Abroad Philip became involved in wars to defend Catholicism and advance Spain's glory. These wars further drained the Spanish treasury. As taxes never kept up with expenses and bankers charged more and more interest on loans they made to Spain, the government's financial problems grew worse.

Philip found it impossible to subdue all the enemies of Spanish power and of Catholicism. He defeated the Ottoman Empire in the Mediterranean, but an attempted invasion of England in 1588 by a huge fleet, the Spanish Armada, ended in disaster. An attempt to invade France to prevent a Protestant from becoming king also proved an expensive failure. The most costly disaster of all resulted from Philip's policy toward the Netherlands.

The Rise of the Dutch

The provinces of the Netherlands that Philip II inherited had been a great trading center and one of Europe's richest areas since the Middle Ages. The people of these provinces had a proud tradition of independence. By the 1550s, Calvinism was already making headway in the area. Philip II's harsh treatment of his subjects in the Netherlands led to catastrophe for Spain.

The people of the Netherlands strongly distrusted Philip, who turned this distrust into outright rebellion by making three fundamental errors. First, he ignored the long tradition of self-rule in the Netherlands and insisted that he, not the local nobles, held all authority. Second, he taxed the Netherlands' trade heavily

History Through the Arts

PAINTING

Young Woman with a Water Jug

What does this young woman see as she gazes through the window? On the wall behind her is a map, and perhaps it has led her thoughts to faraway places. The window lets light in on her starched linen headdress, and the Sun sparkles on the metal pitcher and tray, defining the pattern on the Asian tablecloth. The cloth is an example of the varied goods that overseas trade brought to the Dutch people after they had won their independence from Spain.

In the 1600s, Dutch merchants grew rich enough to buy handsome silks and linens for their wives and to commission artists to paint for them. Artists flourished in the prosperous economy of the Netherlands, and Jan Vermeer, who painted this picture, was one of the finest. His painting gives us a close look at daily Dutch life.

The Metropolitan Museum of Art, Marquand Collection, Gift of Henry G. Marquand, 1889. (89.15.21). Photograph © 1993 The Metropolitan Museum of Art.

Vermeer's *Young Woman with a Water Jug*

to finance Spanish wars. Third, he persecuted the Calvinists.

In 1568 a revolt led by William the Silent, the prince of Orange, grew so strong that Philip could not stop it. The people of the Calvinist northern provinces lived on land that was below sea level, protected by large dikes. They opened the dikes, flooding the countryside and leaving Philip's army helpless. William relied on swift raids by bands of soldiers to keep the Spanish army off balance. Today we call this military technique **guerrilla warfare**.

In 1579, under William the Silent's leadership, the northern provinces declared their independence from Spain and became known as the United Provinces of the Netherlands. Today we refer to this area as simply the Netherlands.

William was assassinated in 1584, but his sons continued the struggle against Spain. The war continued, interrupted by a 12-year truce from 1609 to 1621, until 1648, when the northern provinces won their independence. Spain did manage to win back the loyalty of the heavily Catholic southern provinces of the Netherlands, partly because Philip

promised them greater self-rule. The southern region remained under the rule of Spain and was known as the Spanish Netherlands. (See map on page 386.) In 1713, when the Austrian Habsburgs took possession, it became known as the Austrian Netherlands. Since 1830 it has been the independent country of Belgium.

Dutch society. The people of the northern provinces of the Netherlands—the Dutch—created one of Europe's most remarkable societies. The Netherlands lay on the North Sea, and the Dutch, a seafaring people, built very efficient ships and became excellent sailors. Primarily traders, they dominated European commerce throughout the 1600s. Their ships carried most of Europe's trade. The city of Amsterdam became a world financial center. Dutch banks, trading companies, manufacturing enterprises—especially shipbuilding—and overseas colonies became models of efficiency.

The Dutch had a relatively open society. Calvinists did become the dominant religious group, and only Calvinists could hold political offices. The Dutch generally, however, moved toward a policy of religious toleration.

EUROPEAN EXPLORATION, EXPANSION, AND ABSOLUTISM | **373**

Amsterdam also became a lively cultural center. The philosopher René Descartes, the scholar of international law and freedom of the seas Hugo Grotius, and the painter Rembrandt thrived in this comfortable and inspiring setting.

The Dutch colonial empire. In the age of exploration, Dutch merchants set up a number of companies to trade in various parts of the world. In 1602 the Dutch combined several of their trading companies into one powerful organization, the Dutch East India Company. The Dutch government gave this company the sole right to carry on trade between the Netherlands and Africa and the East Indies.

The Dutch established their first colony in Asia in 1619 on the island of Java. From Java they expanded westward to take the island of Sumatra and eastward to seize the valuable Spice Islands from the Portuguese. Next came Malacca and the island of Ceylon, as well as Cochin on the southwest coast of India. In 1652 the Dutch founded a colony at the Cape of Good Hope, which helped them supply and protect their trade routes to Asia and along the African coast.

The Portuguese had held only strategic points along the coasts in order to control the sea-lanes. The Dutch, however, realized that a successful empire required much more extensive control, both on the land and over the people. They did not stop with establishing a trading post at Batavia (now Jakarta) on the island of Java, for example, but instead took over the entire island with its crops of sugar, tea, coffee, and spices.

The Dutch even gained some commercial influence in Japan. Because they had not come as missionaries, the shogun—the Japanese military ruler—allowed the Dutch to trade in Japan and to operate a trading post at Nagasaki.

In the Western Hemisphere, the Dutch founded colonies in three areas—the West Indies, South America, and North America. In 1626 they purchased Manhattan Island from the Indians. There they founded New Amsterdam, which later became known as New York City.

The colonial empire that the Dutch established differed significantly from that of the Spanish. At no time did the Dutch try to convert the people they conquered to Christianity or force them to speak Dutch or to live under the laws of the Netherlands. The Dutch came as traders, with the intention of making money. In this sense, the overseas empire of the Netherlands reflected the businesslike society of the home country.

Decline of the Spanish Empire

The revolt of the Netherlands against Spanish rule in 1579 marked the beginning of the decline of the mighty Spanish Empire. A number of factors led to this decline. One factor was a steadily growing population—more people needed to be fed, clothed, and housed. At the same time, gold and silver flowed into Spain from the colonies. As a result of this gold and silver flowing into Spain, the increase in the amount of money drove up prices in Spain. Because it cost more to produce goods in Spain than in other countries, Spanish industry declined.

An enterprising middle class might have helped Spanish industries develop despite these obstacles. Many Spanish nobles, however, preferred military careers. Some of the ablest individuals chose careers in the church rather than in secular life. In addition, Spain expelled first the Jews and later the Moriscos—Moorish converts to Christianity who were suspected of secretly practicing Islam. Unfortunately for the Spanish economy, many Moriscos were skilled farmers and able artisans. The expulsion of the Jews and the Moriscos may have contributed to the weakening of Spain's economy.

Much of the wealth from its empire simply passed through Spain because it was used to buy goods from other nations. In contrast, with the gold and silver they received for goods they sold to Spain, Spain's enemies—France, England, and the Netherlands—developed their own industries and grew strong at Spain's expense.

At home, high taxation and inflation brought on economic discontent. This discontent, along with agricultural failures, caused many country people to leave their homes and eventually led to their emigration from Spain.

Section 3 Review

1. **Define** viceroys, guerrilla warfare
2. **Identify** Juan Ponce de Léon, Hernán Cortés, Moctezuma, Francisco Pizarro, Charles V, Philip II
3. **Locate and Explain the Significance** Tenochtitlán
4. **Understanding Ideas** Describe the growth of the Spanish colonial empire.
5. **Contrasting Ideas** How did the Dutch colonial empire differ from the Spanish colonial empire?
6. **Interpreting Ideas** Why did Spanish power decline in the late 1500s?

France in the Age of Absolutism

Focus Questions
- **How did Henry IV and Cardinal Richelieu strengthen France?**
- **What was the Thirty Years' War?**
- **How was central authority strengthened during the reign of Louis XIV?**

Following Spain's slow decline, France, under King Louis XIV, emerged as the leading European power. It had recovered rapidly from the religious wars of the 1500s, thanks to the policies of Henry IV, the first monarch of a new royal house in France, the Bourbons. Assisted by two shrewd Roman Catholic cardinals, the Bourbons would make the monarchy absolute in France.

Henry IV

Henry IV was from Navarre—a tiny kingdom that straddled the Pyrenees between France and Spain. He ruled France from 1589 to 1610. Henry had been a Huguenot, but he realized he could not rule France successfully as a member of a religious minority. Wanting to rule a strong, united, and peaceful kingdom, he converted to Catholicism, reportedly remarking, "Paris is well worth a mass!" To protect the Huguenots, however, he issued a special order, the Edict of Nantes, which guaranteed freedom of worship and political rights. The edict defused the religious conflict and ended the civil wars.

Henry also attempted to resolve other major problems. Powerful nobles had undermined royal authority in the 1500s, and Henry worked to restore the power of the central government. He also attempted to discipline the army and rebuild the infrastructure of the country. France's financial difficulties, however, defied easy solutions. The French system of taxation was inefficient, corrupt, and unjust. As in the Roman Empire, **tax farming**, selling the right to collect taxes to private individuals called tax farmers, was common. These tax farmers paid the government a fixed sum, collected all they could, and kept any surplus. Many became rich. Furthermore, because the nobles and clergy did not pay the direct tax, called the taille (TY),

and had few other taxes to pay, the tax burden fell most heavily on the peasants.

Henry chose the able Duke of Sully as minister in charge of finances. Even Sully, however, could not make the system truly fair. Nobles and clergy continued to be largely free from taxation. Nevertheless, Sully abolished some unnecessary public offices and stopped certain tax collection abuses. As a result, the treasury showed a sizable surplus, which provided funds to finance trade and industry.

Cardinal Richelieu's Program for France

Henry IV's son and successor, Louis XIII, was only eight years old when a fanatical monk stabbed his father to death in 1610. The boy's mother, Marie de Medici, became regent—the ruler of France until Louis came of age.

Louis XIII came of age in 1614, but his mother continued to rule for three years thereafter. Louis's health was poor and he suffered from a lack of concentration, but he quickly learned to select good advisers who provided firm leadership. Louis chose as his chief

In addition to supporting the arts and the University of Paris, Cardinal Richelieu founded the French Academy, which continues to reflect literary standards today.

minister Cardinal Richelieu (RISH·uhl·oo), who ran the government of France from 1624 until 1642.

A political genius, Richelieu had a keen understanding of the possibilities of politics and diplomacy. He wanted to make the king supreme in France, and France supreme in Europe. To accomplish the first aim, he set out to destroy the power of the nobles and the remaining political independence of the Huguenots, which had been protected by the Edict of Nantes. In addition, he wanted to strengthen France economically by continuing Sully's policy of encouraging trade and industry. To make France supreme in Europe, Richelieu planned to reduce the power of the Spanish and Austrian Habsburgs.

Huguenots. Richelieu believed that the provisions of the Edict of Nantes allowing the Huguenots to control fortified cities were politically dangerous. The Huguenot cities, which were like states within a state, made strong centralized government impossible. In 1627 Richelieu himself, temporarily trading his cardinal's hat for a military helmet, directed the attacks on the Huguenot seaport of La Rochelle and other fortified towns. The next year, after stubborn but futile resistance, the Huguenots asked for peace. Richelieu took away their special rights in fortified cities, but he allowed the Huguenots to continue to worship freely, hold public office, and attend schools and colleges.

Nobles. The cardinal next turned to the problem of the nobles to finish the work that Henry IV had begun. To crush the nobles' military power, he ordered that any of their fortified castles not necessary for the defense of France be leveled. Then he reduced their political power. With the king's consent, the cardinal appointed as governors of provinces only well-educated professionals who favored a strong monarchy. He also strengthened the power of the regional administrators known as **intendants**. To hold these positions, he chose middle-class people who had no interest in advancing the power of the nobles. Richelieu gave the intendants strong administrative powers and made them directly responsible to the king, who appointed them and could remove them.

The Thirty Years' War

Richelieu's foreign policy was as determined and calculating as his policy at home. He did not allow his position as a Catholic cardinal to interfere with his primary goal of strengthening France at the expense of the Habsburgs. The Thirty Years' War (1618–1648) offered a golden opportunity to achieve this goal.

The Thirty Years' War actually consisted of stretches of fighting interrupted by intervals of peace. It began because the religious conflicts between Protestants and Catholics in Germany had never completely died down following the Peace of Augsburg in 1555. Constant rivalry continued among the more than 300 German princes, who also wanted to be independent of the Holy Roman emperor. In addition, France, Denmark, and Sweden were all looking for opportunities to diminish the power of the Habsburgs and the Holy Roman Empire.

The war began in 1618 in Prague, when Protestant rebels threw two emissaries of the Holy Roman emperor from a castle window. The incident erupted into a rebellion, which the emperor sent troops to suppress. Protestant German princes and Protestant Danes went to war against him. The emperor defeated the king of Denmark, who had to promise not to interfere in German affairs. Sweden then took up arms.

Cardinal Richelieu favored the Swedes over the Catholic Habsburgs, but he believed that it was in France's interest to prolong the war without involving France directly. The other nations would become weak from fighting, while France remained strong. Most of the battles of the Thirty Years' War took place in Germany, much of which became a wasteland through fire, disease, and plundering by soldiers. France eventually joined the war against the Habsburgs. By 1648 the French and their allies had achieved many of their aims.

The participants in the Thirty Years' War, many exhausted after the years of fighting, signed the Treaty of Westphalia in 1648. (See map on page 379.) France was strengthened by receiving Alsace, a valuable territory along the Rhine River. The Treaty of Westphalia recognized the Netherlands and Switzerland as independent nations, which weakened the Habsburgs. The Habsburgs suffered further blows because the peace made the princes in Germany virtually independent of the Holy Roman emperor.

Because the Austrian Habsburgs no longer exercised any real authority in Germany, they began to look eastward rather than westward. They paid more attention to their own possessions—Austria, Bohemia, and Hungary—and eventually created a new empire centered along the Danube River instead of in Germany.

The Fronde. Although France emerged more powerful from the Peace of Westphalia, a series of rebellions erupted in the country between 1648 and 1652. These rebellions were known as the Fronde, from the French word for "sling." The term compared the rebels—Frondeurs—to mischievous schoolboys who use slingshots when the teacher looks away. Nobles led the rebellions, but many peasants and the citizens of Paris also supported them. The Fronde threatened the centralized royal power that Richelieu and Cardinal Mazarin, his successor, had built up. The Frondeurs wanted to revive the independence of localities and the power of the nobility. Mazarin crushed the Fronde, although with some difficulty, and no major attempts to restrict the French royal power were made for more than 135 years.

The Sun King

Louis XIV, whose 72-year reign from 1643 to 1715 was the longest in French history, benefited from the strengthening of central authority. While a boy, Louis had witnessed the rebellion of the Fronde in Paris. It may have been the dangers and humiliation he faced during that time that made him determined to allow no opposition and to make his power absolute.

Versailles. As a way to help accomplish these goals, Louis built an enormous palace at Versailles (ver·SY), a few miles outside of Paris. There he established his court and moved the French government. The elaborate palace cost an immense sum that strained the French economy. Louis was denounced as being too extravagant and was even accused of trying to ruin the nation financially.

The palace emphasized the grandeur and power of Louis XIV and France. Louis believed in the **divine right of kings**, meaning that God had ordained him to govern France. "L'état, c'est moi" ("I am the state"), he proclaimed.

To increase royal authority over the nobility, Louis insisted that the most important nobles of France live at Versailles. There they had to serve him, helping him dress in the morning, joining him in the hunt—a passion with the Bourbons—performing the ceremonies of the court, and handing him his nightshirt when he went to bed. In this way, Louis could keep his eye on them. Instead of trying to gain power by fighting the monarchy, the nobility now could advance only by getting royal favors and offices.

Versailles and its absolute monarch became the ideal of European royalty. European nobility adopted the language and customs of France. Louis XIV adopted as his personal emblem the Sun, whose rays symbolized the extent of his power and influence. He looked like a king, lived like a king, and behaved like a king.

The policies of Louis XIV. Louis chose competent advisers, although he made most important decisions himself. One of his most outstanding advisers was

Louis XIV (shown on the horse above the crowd in this painting) encouraged improvements in most realms of French society, from art and literature to transportation.

Jean-Baptiste Colbert (kawl·BAIR), an expert in finance. Colbert, a member of the middle class, followed Sully's ideas in promoting economic development. He tried to bolster French industry at home and French trade abroad. He granted government subsidies to private companies to build new industries or strengthen existing ones. He placed high tariffs on foreign imports and improved transportation. Colbert encouraged French companies to establish colonies and carry on trade with Canada, the West Indies, and East Asia.

Like Sully, Colbert also tried to eliminate corruption and waste in the tax-farming system. His efforts resulted for a time in the accumulation of enough money to pay for economic improvements, a large army, and exploration abroad.

Louis XIV was concerned about religious disunity in France. The Huguenots, he believed, disturbed the unity of the country and weakened the central authority. Consequently, in 1685 he revoked the Edict of Nantes, ending the policy of toleration for Protestants.

More than 200,000 productive Protestant citizens fled France rather than become Catholics, a development that weakened France in the long run.

The Wars of Louis XIV

Louis chose as his secretary of state for war the Marquis de Louvois (loov·WAH), a military genius who completely reorganized the army. Officers and soldiers received extensive training and followed strict discipline. The officer responsible for this training, General Jean Martinet, furnished a word to the language: anyone who is a strict disciplinarian is called a martinet. By the early 1700s, the French had a force of 400,000 well-trained soldiers, an army larger and more powerful than Europe had ever seen.

Why did Louis XIV need such a large army? He had territorial ambitions and was convinced that France's security depended on the country having natural frontiers. The Alps, the Mediterranean Sea, the Pyrenees, the Atlantic Ocean, and the English Channel already protected France in the southeast, south, southwest, and northwest. Like Richelieu, Louis wanted to make France even safer by extending its territory to the Rhine River, its natural frontier on the northeast and east. To gain his ends, Louis fought four wars between 1667 and 1713. (See map on opposite page.)

Louis's goals alarmed the other European countries, which united to counteract the great power of France. At various times, the Netherlands, England, and Spain, as well as Austria, Brandenburg, and other German states, formed alliances to amass enough power to equal or surpass that of France. The maintenance of an equilibrium in international politics is known as the **balance of power**.

The wars took a tremendous toll on France's resources. By the end of Louis's third war, in 1697, France was under tremendous financial strain. Louis even melted down the royal silver to help pay for his wars.

War of the Spanish Succession. The War of the Spanish Succession was Louis XIV's last war. It was fought over the question of who should succeed to the throne of Spain. The last Spanish Habsburg king died in 1700, leaving the throne to a French prince, Philip of Anjou, Louis's grandson.

The other European nations feared the prospect of Bourbon rulers in both Spain and France. Dreading the possibility of the two nations under one monarch, the nations of Europe went to war with Louis. Battles raged throughout Europe, on the high seas, and in America.

French armies and fleets met defeats everywhere, and Louis finally agreed to a settlement in 1713.

The European settlement in 1713. The Treaty of Utrecht, which ended the War of the Spanish Succession, became important in the history of both Europe and America. It recognized Louis XIV's grandson as King Philip V of Spain but provided that the French and Spanish crowns were never to be united. Great Britain became France's chief enemy because the treaty gave it lands in North America at the expense of France.

The French Colonial Empire

The empire that France began to lose after the War of the Spanish Succession had begun in the early 1500s. French explorers such as Jacques Cartier (kahr·TYAY) made several voyages to North America. Cartier's voyage up the St. Lawrence River as far as Montreal in 1535 to 1536 gave the French a claim to much of eastern Canada. Not until 1608, however, when Samuel de Champlain founded Quebec, did they make a permanent settlement.

France then established several other settlements in the St. Lawrence Valley and in the Great Lakes region. The French developed a profitable fur trade with the Indians and engaged in fishing cod off Newfoundland and Nova Scotia.

Between 1679 and 1682, René-Robert de La Salle sailed down the Mississippi River to the Gulf of Mexico and claimed the entire inland region of North America for France. He named the region Louisiana in honor of Louis XIV. French settlement in North America grew very slowly, however. Elsewhere in the Americas, the French occupied Haiti and the sugar producing islands of Guadeloupe and Martinique in the West Indies.

The French also established colonies in Asia. On the southeast coast of India, the French East India Company established a trading post at Pondicherry in 1674 and controlled part of India through the 1700s.

The Legacy of Louis XIV

Louis XIV died in 1715. His endless wars in which so many lives were lost and so much money was spent had exhausted the French people. Nevertheless, despite his defeats, the Sun King had in fact made France a very powerful nation. While Great Britain became the strongest colonial power, within Europe France remained the largest, the richest, and the most influential nation.

After Louis's death, the nobles won back many of the powers they had been deprived of under his rule. For the next 50 years, the French government seemed stable. Beneath this appearance of stability, however, lay a decline in royal authority that led to revolution. Louis XIV's great-grandson and successor, Louis XV, proved to be an ineffectual ruler partly because of his lack of self-confidence. During his reign (1715–1774), a succession of ministers ran the country.

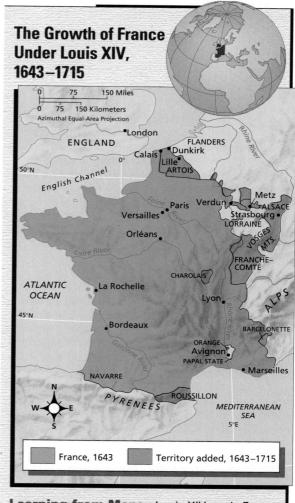

The Growth of France Under Louis XIV, 1643–1715

0   75   150 Miles
0   75   150 Kilometers
Azimuthal Equal-Area Projection

London
ENGLAND
Calais   Dunkirk   FLANDERS
50°N   Lille   ARTOIS
English Channel
Rhine River
Seine River   Paris   Verdun   Metz   ALSACE
Versailles   Strasbourg
LORRAINE
Orléans   VOSGES MTS.
Loire River
FRANCHE-COMTÉ
CHAROLAIS
ATLANTIC OCEAN   La Rochelle
Lyon   ALPS
45°N   Rhône River
Bordeaux   BARCELONETTE
Garonne River   ORANGE
Avignon
PAPAL STATE
NAVARRE   Marseilles
N   ROUSSILLON
W   E   PYRENEES   MEDITERRANEAN SEA
S   5°E

| France, 1643 | Territory added, 1643–1715 |

Learning from Maps Louis XIV made France a large and powerful nation, extending its territory in three directions.

? Place What city in southeastern France remained outside Louis XIV's control?

Section 4 Review

1. **Define** tax farming, intendants, divine right of kings, balance of power
2. **Identify** Marie de Medici, Cardinal Richelieu, Cardinal Mazarin, Jean-Baptiste Colbert, Jacques Cartier, René-Robert de La Salle
3. **Locate and Explain the Significance** Versailles
4. **Understanding Ideas** List and discuss two ways in which Henry IV and Cardinal Richelieu strengthened France.
5. **Contrasting Ideas** Describe the different effects of the Thirty Years' War on Germany and on France.
6. **Interpreting Ideas** How did Louis XIV effectively increase the power of the French monarchy?

Section 5

Eastern and Central Europe in the Age of Absolutism

Focus Questions

- Why was Russia isolated from western Europe?
- What changes did Peter the Great and Catherine the Great bring to Russia?
- What problems faced the Habsburgs and the Hohenzollerns in eastern Europe, and what conflicts resulted from them?

While in the countries of western Europe national governments were strengthened at the expense of local authorities and the nobility, the new empires of Russia, Prussia, and Austria developed in eastern and central Europe.

Russian Isolation

After more than 200 years of Mongol rule, Russia became an independent country in 1480. By this time, the rulers of Moscow had become the most important in Russia, and they continued to expand their power and territory by conquests, marriages, and alliances.

Reading About History: Making Inferences

As you study history, you often read a source to understand the facts of an event or events the author is explaining. For example, read the following description of Versailles.

"The palace of Versailles cost 5 million livres out of a total state budget of 120 million livres. . . . In 1682, 22,000 workers were laboring on it; the next year, there were 36,000. In 230 acres of gardens, 1,400 fountains were installed, and 25,000 full-grown trees were transplanted in one year so that Louis XIV would not have to wait for saplings to grow."

The facts of the quotation are obvious. Thousands of people worked on the palace at Versailles (shown in photo), and the construction cost a great deal of money. By "reading between the lines," however, you can find information that is only implied—for example, that Louis XIV possessed great power.

When you read between the lines, you are using your reasoning ability to discover new meanings. In this way, you can identify something that the writer does not actually state. Your identifications are called inferences.

How to Make Inferences
To make inferences, follow these steps.
1. Select the main idea or literal interpretation.
2. Look for clues that suggest, or imply, additional meaning, such as key phrases or emotional words.
3. Add the clues to the original interpretation.
4. Create a revised meaning based on the connection between the stated ideas and the implied ideas.

Developing the Skill
In the following selection from *A Description of East India Company,* Peter Van Dam, an officer of the company, describes how the Dutch government stimulated and promoted trade by establishing the Dutch East India Company. What inferences can you make about the key to the company's success?

"The Company's charter authorized it to make alliances with princes and potentates east of the Cape of Good Hope and beyond the Straits of Magellan, to make contracts, build fortresses and strongholds, name governors, raise troops, appoint officers of justice, and perform other necessary services for the advancement of trade. . . .The Company after the date of this charter has made great progress in the Indies. It has captured a number of fortresses from the Spaniards and the Portuguese...and has established trading posts at several places. It was decided as a consequence that it was desirable to establish a formal government in the Indies."

The selection states that the company could make treaties and set up governments. The key phrases "made great progress" and "as a consequence" are clues that can help you "read between the lines." These phrases indicate that although the company was set up for trade, it had many political successes. One inference that you can make is that the company owed its economic success to the political powers that it enjoyed. Control of certain political rights was linked to the development of trade. The Dutch East India Company was a political as well as an economic organization.

Practicing the Skill
Read a political article in the newspaper or listen to a televised news program that focuses on a political issue. Then list several facts and any inferences you can make from the article or program.

To apply this skill, see Applying History Study Skills on page 391.

Moscow's rulers differed widely in their abilities, but a few had the qualities needed to build a large and powerful state.

Several factors—both cultural and physical—tended to separate Russia from western Europe. One factor was an Asian influence resulting from Mongol domination. Another factor was that Western civilization had reached Russia from Constantinople and the Byzantine Empire, not from western Europe. Russia's religion was Eastern Orthodox rather than Roman Catholic or Protestant. Russia's use of the Cyrillic alphabet posed a barrier to communication for Russia with the rest of Europe, which used the Roman alphabet.

Most importantly, Russia's geography isolated the country from the rest of Europe. The country was almost entirely landlocked. The stronger kingdoms of Sweden and Poland blocked Russia from the Baltic Sea. To the south, the Ottoman Turks held the coast of the Black Sea. To the west, the vast plains of Poland and eastern Europe hindered commercial contacts. Russia's many navigable rivers did not flow into the great oceans and seas of commerce.

A new dynasty. Some 20 years after the death of Ivan the Terrible in 1584, Russia underwent a period of unrest. Nobles fought for power, various claimants sought the throne, and Russia's neighbors invaded. Then in 1613 a national assembly elected as czar Michael Romanov, the first of the Romanov dynasty, which would rule Russia for 300 years.

In the mid-1600s, the response of the Romanov rulers to events in Russia strengthened the monarchy. Representative institutions were restrained. The government repressed religious dissenters called Old Believers, who opposed reforms decreed by the patriarch of Moscow. It established mutually beneficial relations with Cossacks, peasants who had fled from Polish serfdom and settled on Russia's southern frontier. Moreover, the Romanovs established serfdom more firmly during this time.

In this way, the czars continued and reinforced the Russian form of absolutism created by Ivan the Terrible. In 1682 Peter I became czar at the age of 10, co-ruling with his half brother and half sister. He became the sole ruler of Russia in 1689. A leader of remarkable vision, Czar Peter I used his power to change Russia in important ways.

Peter the Great

Czar Peter I ruled Russia until 1725. An energetic giant of a man—more than six and a half feet tall—he had dark hair and eyes, a swarthy complexion, and a prominent nose. Peter also had a violent temper and was capable of great cruelty. His suspicions that his son Alexis was disloyal led to Alexis's death in prison. This strong-willed and ruthless czar decided that Russia's future lay toward Europe.

One of Peter's major goals was to enable Russia to end its landlocked situation and acquire warm-water ports on the Sea of Azov and the Black Sea. The Ottoman Empire, which controlled all the land between the Black Sea and the Mediterranean Sea, blocked that ambition. Peter realized that to defeat the Turks he would need two things: help from western Europe and a stronger, more efficient Russia.

Peter's foreign mission. In 1697 Peter, who often disguised himself as a private citizen, went with a Russian delegation to several countries in western Europe to negotiate an alliance against the Turks. The mission failed in that purpose, but it was of great importance because the czar learned about the West. He met leaders in many fields of activity and learned from scientists and artisans. He even worked as a carpenter in a Dutch East India Company shipyard to learn ship construction.

Westernization. Peter decided to remodel Russia along western European lines. Influenced by the example of France, he reorganized his army and equipped it with better weapons. He then engaged the army in a long war (1700–1721) with Sweden, which resulted in Russia gaining territory with access to the Baltic Sea. The war also ended Sweden's short-lived role as a great power in Europe.

In this new territory on the eastern coast of the Gulf of Finland, Peter built a completely new city, St. Petersburg. (See map on page 383.) In 1703 he moved the capital from Moscow to St. Petersburg, bringing the center of Russian government closer to the nations of western Europe. As Russia's "window to the West," St. Petersburg came to symbolize the new Russian policy of westernization.

Westernization meant many things. Women abandoned some of their former isolation and took a greater part in community life. The czar forced the nobles to give up their long robes—suitable for Russia's long, bitterly cold winters—and wear European-style short coats. Peter also forced men to shave off their long beards.

Much more important, however, were Peter's changes in Russian trade, finance, industry, and government. Armies and navies cost money to operate; to obtain this money, Peter imposed taxes on nearly everything. He also encouraged the development of foreign trade and manufacturing.

In government Peter followed the absolutist ideas of Louis XIV of France. The czar had complete control of a highly centralized administration, and the nobles were merely his agents. As in France, the monarchy controlled local governments. The Orthodox Church, too, fell under Peter's control.

The nobility. Peter created a new service nobility, whose rank and privileges depended on the amount of government service performed rather than on family status. In return for government service, Peter granted the nobles large estates with thousands of serfs. His changes not only increased the number of serfs but also worsened their condition. At a time when serfdom was declining rapidly throughout western Europe, the czar began a policy of binding the Russian serfs to their lords as well as to the land. When the serfs rebelled, they were brutally crushed.

Although Peter failed to westernize Russian society completely, under his leadership Russia became a great power. Few individuals in history have made so strong a personal mark on their time.

Catherine the Great

Peter was succeeded by his second wife, Catherine I, who ruled for two years. She was followed by several other Romanov rulers. Peter's daughter Elizabeth

Peter the Great built the city of St. Petersburg to be the capital of his empire.

This painting shows Peter the Great disguised as a Dutch shipbuilder. He toured western Europe to familiarize himself with advances in European technology.

then ruled from 1741 to 1762 and paved the way for Catherine II, later known as Catherine the Great.

A princess from a small German state, Catherine had married the heir to the Russian throne, Elizabeth's nephew and Peter the Great's grandson. However, her unpopular husband, who became Peter III, preferred Prussians and Prussia to anything Russian. Peter III ruled for only six months in 1762 and then was murdered by powerful nobles who supported Catherine. She ruled from that time until 1796.

Domestic and foreign policy. Catherine II did not earn her title "the Great" from her domestic policy. Her support of art, science, literature, and the theater had little meaning or value to most Russians, who lived in deep ignorance and poverty. She extended serfdom into the new lands she acquired, and the masses—the common people—lived much as they had before. Under Catherine II, the nobility, however, became more westernized. They spoke French and lost touch with most of the Russian people. The vast gap between rulers and ruled helps explain the

undercurrent of discontent that finally exploded in revolution in Russia in the 1900s.

It was Catherine's foreign policy—a continuation of the expansionist policies of Peter the Great—that made her great. Russia still sought warm-water ports through the control of the Sea of Azov and the Black Sea. In a successful war against the Turks, Catherine won control of most of the northern shore of the Black Sea and a protectorate over the Crimea.

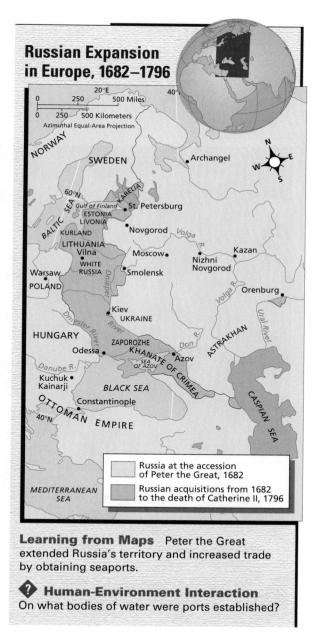

Russian Expansion in Europe, 1682–1796

Russia at the accession of Peter the Great, 1682

Russian acquisitions from 1682 to the death of Catherine II, 1796

Learning from Maps Peter the Great extended Russia's territory and increased trade by obtaining seaports.

❓ **Human-Environment Interaction** On what bodies of water were ports established?

The Polish question. Catherine also made great territorial gains to the west. There the kingdom of Poland was large but weak. Its kings were elected by the nobles. The election campaigns to determine who would be king invited domestic and international troubles. Prussia, Austria, France, and Russia each repeatedly plotted to put its favorite on the Polish throne.

In Poland's legislature, only nobles were represented. The legislature rarely accomplished anything because any one member could veto any legislation being considered.

Poland contained large minority groups of various nationalities and religions. Most Poles were Roman Catholic, and they and their leaders often discriminated against and oppressed minority groups. Sometimes the oppressed groups appealed to Prussia, Austria, or Russia for help.

In 1772 these three powers decided to take advantage of Poland's weak condition and seize slices of Polish territory for themselves. This action is known as the First Partition of Poland. (See map on opposite page.)

The Poles were unable to resist the partition. In 1791 they tried to reform and strengthen their nation by adopting a new constitution. This constitution would have established a hereditary monarchy and abolished the veto privileges in the legislature. However, in 1793 Russia and Prussia took another helping of Polish lands with the Second Partition. In the Third Partition by Austria, Prussia, and Russia in 1795, Poland disappeared from the map of Europe until 1919.

Catherine the Great had not only wrested control of the Black Sea from the Turks but had also acquired the largest share of Poland. She had added more than

Catherine the Great supported art and literature, favored the education of women, and built hospitals.

The Partitions of Poland, 1772–1795

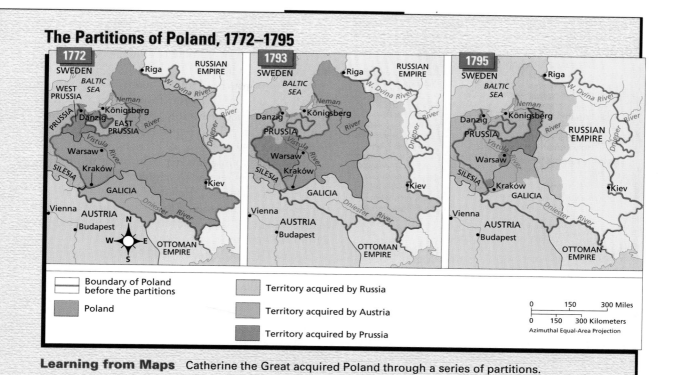

Learning from Maps Catherine the Great acquired Poland through a series of partitions.

? Region By 1795 what countries had received sections of territory previously held by Poland?

200,000 square miles of territory to her empire. Russia's borders now extended well into central Europe, and Russia became a force to consider in the European balance of power.

Russian Expansion

Russia's expansion differed from that of the western European countries. Instead of expanding overseas, Russia expanded overland. In addition to the political expansion south and west, Russian settlers, spear-

headed by the freedom-loving Cossacks, moved eastward. In 1581 the Cossacks conquered the remnants of the Mongol Golden Horde and captured their capital city of Sibir. With that, the way lay open to the vast, sparsely populated region east of the Urals known as Siberia.

This region's rich fur trade drew many people. Much like the pioneers of the American West, the early Russian settlers built small posts for trade and defense. These grew into the towns and cities of Siberia. At the Amur River, Russians came in contact with the Chinese, who resisted Russian expansion into their country. In 1689 the Russians and Chinese signed a treaty that fixed the boundary between them north of the Amur River and provided for Chinese-Russian trade. By 1741 the Russians had crossed the Bering Strait and established a colony in Alaska in North America. Later Russian trading posts expanded southward.

Habsburg Austria

The Austrian Habsburgs lost much territory in the Thirty Years' War. In the 100 years after the war,

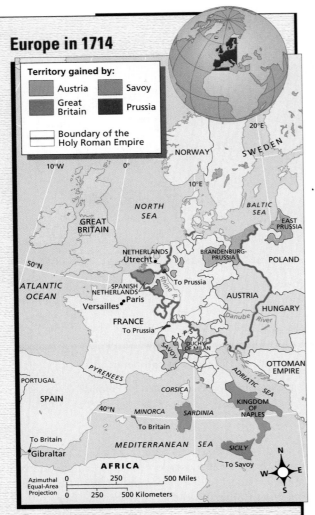

Europe in 1714

Territory gained by:
- Austria
- Savoy
- Great Britain
- Prussia

Boundary of the Holy Roman Empire

NORWAY
SWEDEN
NORTH SEA
BALTIC SEA
GREAT BRITAIN
EAST PRUSSIA
NETHERLANDS
Utrecht
BRANDENBURG-PRUSSIA
POLAND
ATLANTIC OCEAN
SPANISH NETHERLANDS
To Prussia
Versailles
Paris
AUSTRIA
Rhine R.
FRANCE
HUNGARY
Danube River
To Prussia
ALPS
DUCHY OF MILAN
SAVOY
OTTOMAN EMPIRE
PYRENEES
ADRIATIC SEA
PORTUGAL
CORSICA
SPAIN
KINGDOM OF NAPLES
MINORCA
SARDINIA
To Britain
MEDITERRANEAN SEA
SICILY
To Britain
Gibraltar
To Savoy
AFRICA
Azimuthal Equal-Area Projection
0   250   500 Miles
0   250   500 Kilometers

Learning from Maps The governance of many European territories was redistributed by 1714.

? Region What four areas did Austria acquire?

By it, the rulers of Europe would promise to allow Maria Theresa to inherit the Habsburg lands intact, even though the law in some lands required that the inheritance go to a male.

The laws of the Holy Roman Empire also prevented Maria Theresa from being elected empress. She became Holy Roman empress in 1745, however, when her husband Francis was elected emperor.

Maria Theresa inherited a patchwork of territories and peoples: Germans, Hungarians, Italians, Belgians, Romanians, Poles, Bohemians, Serbs, Croatians, and Slovenes. This great variety led to many conflicts of language, religion, and nationality within the empire.

Several German states envied Habsburg power. For example, Bavaria, which is located in southern Germany, jealously guarded its lands and independence. They did this sometimes by forming alliances with France against the Habsburgs. Austria's chief rival was Brandenburg-Prussia, a small north German state that in 1740 did not even have a common boundary with Austria.

The Rise of the Hohenzollerns

During the Middle Ages, the Hohenzollerns had ruled only a small territory in southern Germany. The ambitious family wanted to increase its power, influence, and landholdings. Near the end of the Middle Ages, one branch of the family settled in Brandenburg, in northern Germany. The ruler of Brandenburg eventually became an elector of the Holy Roman Empire.

During the Reformation, the Protestant Hohenzollerns seized lands belonging to the Catholic Church in their territories. By the end of the Thirty Years' War in 1648, they ruled several widely scattered territories in Germany, including Prussia, which bordered the Baltic Sea.

---

however, Austria won new lands. These gains came in central Europe and the Balkans at the expense of the Turks and in territories received as a result of the Treaty of Utrecht. The Habsburgs now had an empire that extended into Hungary, the Balkans, and the Italian Peninsula.

In 1740 Holy Roman Emperor Charles VI died, leaving no sons and only his 23-year-old daughter, Maria Theresa, to inherit Austria and the other Habsburg lands. Charles had spent most of his reign (1711–1740) trying to persuade other European rulers to accept a statement called the Pragmatic Sanction.

The Hohenzollerns

1640–1688	Frederick William, the Great Elector
1688–1713	Frederick I
1713–1740	Frederick William I
1740–1786	Frederick II (the Great)

Maria Theresa (standing next to her husband, Francis) made improvements in education, medicine, and military affairs. Among her 16 children was Marie Antoinette, the future queen of France.

One of the greatest of the Hohenzollerns, Frederick William, called the Great Elector, guided his state through the difficult last years of the Thirty Years' War. After the Thirty Years' War ended, he then turned to the rebuilding and further strengthening of Brandenburg-Prussia. The Great Elector reorganized the armies of all his lands into one strong force. In addition to reorganizing his armies, he also improved the tax collection system and encouraged agriculture, industry, and transportation.

All the Hohenzollern possessions in northern Germany were called Prussia beginning with the reign of Frederick I (1688–1713), the Great Elector's successor and the first king of Prussia.* The original duchy of Prussia became known as East Prussia. (See map on opposite page.)

---

*As a reward for supporting the Habsburgs in the War of the Spanish Succession, the Holy Roman emperor granted Frederick I the title King of Prussia in 1701.

Frederick William I. Frederick I, one of the many European rulers who tried to imitate Louis XIV of France, maintained a large, lavish court. His son and successor, Frederick William I, disliked French ways intensely and got rid of much of this luxury when he became king in 1713.

Frederick William used the money he saved to strengthen Prussia. He doubled the size of the Prussian army and made it the most efficient fighting force in Europe. One of Frederick William's few extravagances was going to great expense to obtain tall soldiers, men between six and seven feet in height, from countries all over Europe, to form a regiment of giants.

In addition to strengthening the army, Frederick William created an efficient governmental bureaucracy. Tax collecting and government spending were carefully planned. Frederick William also encouraged trade and the development of new industries. Convinced that all children should have a primary education, he required that all parents send their children to school.

Europe in 1786

Legend:
- Possessions of the Austrian Habsburgs
- Possessions of the Hohenzollerns
- Boundary of Holy Roman Empire

0 250 500 Miles
0 250 500 Kilometers
Azimuthal Equal-Area Projection

SWEDEN
St. Petersburg
KINGDOM OF DENMARK AND NORWAY
Stockholm
RUSSIA
KINGDOM OF GREAT BRITAIN AND IRELAND
NORTH SEA
BALTIC SEA
EAST PRUSSIA
London
PRUSSIA
Berlin
POLAND
Warsaw
Vistula River
ATLANTIC OCEAN
English Channel
UNITED NETHERLANDS
HANOVER
AUSTRIAN NETHERLANDS
SAXONY
SILESIA
LESSER GERMAN STATES
Paris
FRANCE
LORRAINE
BOHEMIA
BAVARIA
Vienna
Buda Pest
HUNGARY
Bay of Biscay
SWITZERLAND
AUSTRIA
Danube River
BLACK SEA
Avignon
SAVOY
MILAN
PARMA
MODENA
VENETIAN REPUBLIC
ADRIATIC SEA
OTTOMAN EMPIRE
Constantinople
LUCCA
GENOA
TUSCANY
PAPAL STATES
MONTENEGRO
KINGDOM OF SARDINIA
CORSICA
Rome
AEGEAN SEA
PORTUGAL
Madrid
SPAIN
MINORCA (British)
BALEARIC ISLANDS (Spanish)
SARDINIA
KINGDOM OF NAPLES
Gibraltar (British)
MEDITERRANEAN SEA
SICILY
CRETE
AFRICA

60°N
50°N
40°N
10°W
0°
10°E
20°E

Learning from Maps By 1763 the Habsburgs and Hohenzollerns both controlled vast lands in Europe.

Location What two cities stand on opposite sides of the Danube River?

Frederick the Great. Frederick William I worried that his son and successor, Frederick, showed little interest in either military life or government service. Instead, the youth wrote poetry, played the flute, and read philosophy. The king used the harshest methods, even imprisonment, to force his heir to become the kind of son he desired. Frederick and a companion tried to escape the country, but they were both caught. King Frederick William I forced his son to watch as his friend was executed.

Frederick William I need not have worried about his son's ability to lead his country. Frederick II—or Frederick the Great—proved to be an even stronger ruler than his father. He became king in

1740, the same year that Maria Theresa became ruler of Austria. Frederick II was highly intelligent, and he was also dedicated to expanding the territory and prestige of Prussia.

Conflict Between Prussia and Austria

Frederick William I had signed the Pragmatic Sanction guaranteeing Maria Theresa her Habsburg possessions. Shortly after becoming king, however, Frederick II marched the strong army his father had created into Silesia, one of Maria Theresa's most valuable provinces. Prussia had no legal claim to Silesia; the province had rich farmlands and iron deposits, however, and possessing it would add greatly to Prussia. Frederick seized it easily.

The conquest of Silesia marked the beginning of the first of two major European wars—the War of the Austrian Succession, which lasted from 1740 to 1748. In this war, Austria, Great Britain, the Netherlands, and eventually Russia were allied against Prussia, Bavaria, Spain, and France. Austria and its allies lost the war, and Silesia was ceded to Prussia.

The Diplomatic Revolution and the Seven Years' War. Several years after the War of the Austrian Succession there was a major "reversal of alliances," known as the Diplomatic Revolution, in Europe. Austria and Great Britain had since the time of Louis XIV been allied against the French. In 1756, however, Great Britain allied itself with powerful Prussia in an attempt to gain greater security; France, in an attempt to curb Prussia's power, allied itself with Austria and Russia. For many years afterward, France and Austria continued steadfastly to oppose Great Britain and Prussia.

These rivalries led to the Seven Years' War, which lasted from 1756 to 1763. Like the War of the Austrian Succession, the Seven Years' War involved almost all of Europe at one time or another. Because European countries had colonies overseas, the fighting was not limited to Europe. Battles were also fought between Great Britain and France in India and North America. In America the Seven Years' War is known as the French and Indian War. In fact, the fighting of the Seven Years' War actually began in North America.

At one point in the Seven Years' War, Prussia was opposed by virtually all the European powers except Britain and seemed on the brink of total defeat. Fighting against great odds, Frederick dashed from one front to another to direct his troops in holding off the invaders. Prussia was aided by the death of Empress Elizabeth of Russia, a bitter opponent. Her successor, Czar Peter III of Russia, admired Frederick and made peace with Prussia.

By the Treaty of Hubertusburg in 1763, Prussia kept Silesia. By the Treaty of Paris, which was signed in the same year, France lost most of its colonies in North America. The British gained control of Canada and of Louisiana east of the Mississippi River, and they remained dominant in India. The Seven Years' War ended, however, with no clear victor.

The years of peace. Frederick the Great spent the first 23 years of his reign at war. He spent the last 23 years of his reign showing that he also had a genius for organization and administration. He expanded and further improved public education and the already excellent Prussian civil service system. He made legal and court reforms and encouraged trade and manufacturing. He was committed to religious tolerance, although he had no interest in granting self-government to national or ethnic minorities under Prussian rule. Through Frederick's hard work and wise direction, the expanded state of Prussia recovered the prosperity it had lost during the long years of war. (See map on opposite page.)

Prussia also continued to make territorial gains. Frederick the Great helped to bring about the First Partition of Poland in 1772. By taking Polish territory along the Baltic coast, he linked Prussia and East Prussia. When he died in 1786, Frederick left a greatly enlarged and prosperous nation. Prussia had become a formidable rival of Austria for control of the German states and a first-class power in Europe.

Section 5 Review

1. **Identify** Peter the Great, Catherine the Great, Maria Theresa, the Great Elector, Frederick William I, Frederick the Great
2. **Locate and Explain the Significance** Moscow, Sea of Azov, Black Sea, St. Petersburg
3. **Understanding Ideas** What factors separated Russia from western Europe?
4. **Interpreting Ideas (a)** Describe how Peter the Great tried to westernize Russia both culturally and politically. **(b)** How did Catherine the Great continue Peter's foreign policy?
5. **Analyzing Ideas** How did Frederick the Great contribute to the growth of Prussia?

Chapter 15 Review

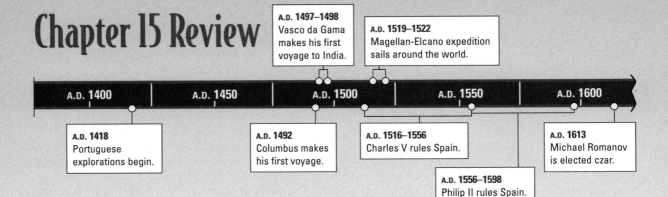

A.D. **1497–1498**
Vasco da Gama makes his first voyage to India.

A.D. **1519–1522**
Magellan-Elcano expedition sails around the world.

A.D. **1400**   A.D. **1450**   A.D. **1500**   A.D. **1550**   A.D. **1600**

A.D. **1418**
Portuguese explorations begin.

A.D. **1492**
Columbus makes his first voyage.

A.D. **1516–1556**
Charles V rules Spain.

A.D. **1613**
Michael Romanov is elected czar.

A.D. **1556–1598**
Philip II rules Spain.

Chapter Summary

The following list contains the key concepts you have learned about European expansion and the formation of strong, centralized monarchies in Europe from about 1400 to about 1800.

1. Europeans were able to expand overseas because they developed or improved techniques to be used in mapmaking, navigation, ship design, and weaponry.
2. The development of new economic policies and the Commercial Revolution that began in 1400 also enabled Europeans to begin large-scale overseas expansion.
3. The political and economic changes associated with overseas expansion contributed to a new economic theory called mercantilism.
4. Portuguese and Spanish explorers took the lead in discovering new lands and trade routes. Sometimes these countries came into conflict over their possessions.
5. Beginning with Portugal, European countries became involved in the slave trade in Africa.
6. Spain established a vast colonial empire and became the greatest power on the European continent until the mid-1600s. It lost this superiority, however, because of its foreign and domestic policies.
7. After the Dutch declared their independence from Spain, they created a large overseas empire. They dominated European commerce throughout the 1600s.
8. Cardinal Richelieu and Louis XIV weakened the Habsburgs and made France an absolute monarchy. Their ambition to expand to France's natural frontiers, territory reaching the Rhine River, brought France into a series of wars.
9. During the 1700s Peter the Great and Catherine the Great extended both the powers of the central government and the boundaries of Russia.
10. Conflict between the rising power of Hohenzollern Prussia and the Habsburgs of Austria brought most of Europe into wars fought in Europe, North America, and India.

Reviewing Important Terms

On a separate sheet of paper, supply the term that correctly completes each statement.

1. In a(n) _____ _____, the ruler determines policy without needing to consult other authorities or the people's representatives and has complete power.
2. The captain of a ship at sea can determine latitude by means of an instrument called the ____.
3. The changes in the European economy were so considerable that some historians have referred to the period from 1400 to 1750 as the ____ ____.
4. A(n) ____ ____ ____ raised money by selling shares in the company to investors.
5. An economic theory called _____ maintained that governments should try to increase their nations' wealth and that the world contained only a fixed amount of wealth.
6. By selling more goods in foreign countries than it buys, a country creates a(n) ____ ____ ____ ____.
7. A(n) ____ is an import tax on foreign goods.
8. Government grants of money called _____ helped establish new industries and build ships.
9. ____ ____ was a term for selling the right to collect taxes to private individuals.
10. In France Cardinal Richelieu strengthened the power of regional administrators known as ____.
11. The _____ _____ was the shipment of slaves across the Atlantic Ocean to the West Indies or the southern colonies of British North America.
12. The principle of maintaining an equilibrium in international politics is known as the ____ ____ ____.

Developing Critical Thinking Skills

1. **Interpreting Ideas** What were the changes in technology that made it possible for Europeans to explore foreign lands?
2. **Summarizing Ideas** What social changes in Europe created a willingness to explore and settle overseas?
3. **Evaluating Ideas** Why was Dutch society considered one of Europe's most remarkable societies?
4. **Comparing Ideas** How was Spanish and Dutch colonization different from Portuguese colonization?
5. **Understanding Ideas (a)** How did the Thirty Years' War weaken the Austrian Habsburgs? **(b)** How did

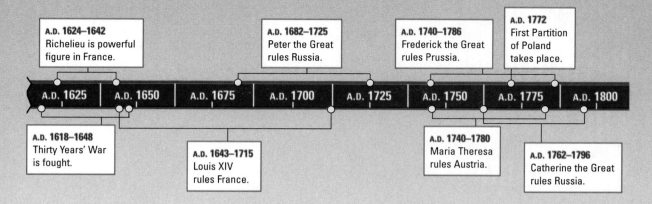

A.D. 1624–1642
Richelieu is powerful figure in France.

A.D. 1682–1725
Peter the Great rules Russia.

A.D. 1740–1786
Frederick the Great rules Prussia.

A.D. 1772
First Partition of Poland takes place.

A.D. 1625   A.D. 1650   A.D. 1675   A.D. 1700   A.D. 1725   A.D. 1750   A.D. 1775   A.D. 1800

A.D. 1618–1648
Thirty Years' War is fought.

A.D. 1643–1715
Louis XIV rules France.

A.D. 1740–1780
Maria Theresa rules Austria.

A.D. 1762–1796
Catherine the Great rules Russia.

Austria benefit in the 100 years after the war? **(c)** What country benefited most from the Thirty Years' War?

6. **Contrasting Ideas** Compare the reigns of Peter the Great and Catherine the Great. **(a)** How were they different? **(b)** What were the important accomplishments of each?

7. **Synthesizing Ideas** Explain how Cardinal Richelieu and Louis XIV strengthened the central government in France over local, religious, and class interests.

8. **Analyzing Ideas** What factors enabled Prussia to create a strong, centralized government and become a great European power by the mid-1700s?

Relating Geography to History

During the period of the great European overseas explorations, certain geographical areas were important to navigation, exploration, and trade routes. Using the map on pages 362 and 363 and information in your textbook, explain the geographical importance of the following: **(a)** Cape of Good Hope; **(b)** Strait of Magellan; **(c)** African coast.

Relating Past to Present

1. It has been said that Louis XIV's control of a large and well-trained army gave him the desire to use it. Does the existence of great armies today lead to the same result? Explain your answer.

2. The 1600s are often called the French century. Is there a nation you think the 1900s will be named after? Give reasons for your answer.

Applying History Study Skills

Before completing this activity, review Building History Study Skills on page 380.

Queen Elizabeth I of England addressed her military forces on August 9, 1588, as they prepared to fight the Spanish Armada sent by Philip II. From the following selection, what inferences can you make about Queen Elizabeth?

"Let tyrants fear; I have always so behaved myself that, under God, I have placed my chiefest strength and safeguard in the loyal hearts and good will of my subjects. And therefore I am come amongst you at this time, not for my recreation or sport, but being resolved, in the

midst and heat of the battle, to live or die amongst you all; to lay down, for my God, and for my kingdom, and for my people, my honour and my blood...

I know I have but the body of a weak and feeble woman; but I have the heart of a king, and of a king of England too; and think foul scorn that Parma or Spain, or any prince of Europe, should dare to invade the borders of my realms: to which, rather that my dishonour should grow by me, I myself will take up arms."

1. Why is Elizabeth making the speech?
2. What does the speech tell you about Elizabeth's relationship to her people?
3. What does Elizabeth mean by "I have the body of a weak and feeble woman; but I have the heart of a king"?
4. What inferences can you make about Elizabeth's role as a ruler? About Elizabeth as a person?

📰 internet**connect**

Search the Internet through the HRW Web site to find information on the Atlantic slave trade. Prepare an oral report that includes information that you researched from these Web sites.

 **GO TO:** go.hrw.com
KEYWORD: SCØ Slave Trade

Building Your Portfolio

1. **Relating Literature to History** The novels of Alexander Dumas deal with France during the reign of Louis XIV. Read one of these novels to discover more about life in France during this period. *The Three Musketeers* or *The Man in the Iron Mask* might be especially appropriate. Write a brief book report. Place your report in your portfolio.

2. **Conducting Research** St. Petersburg (for many years known as Leningrad), founded by Peter the Great, became a symbol of the new Russian policy of westernization. Using books in your library, prepare a short report on St. Petersburg, concentrating mainly on its founding. Place your report in your portfolio.

Revolution and Change in England

TIME

A.D. 1485–1760

| 3.7 million B.C. | 4000 B.C. | A.D. 1485–1760 | A.D. 2100 |

PLACE

The British Isles, North America, India

British Isles

North America

ARCTIC OCEAN
NORTH AMERICA
EUROPE
ASIA
PACIFIC OCEAN
AFRICA
Equator
AUSTRALIA
SOUTH AMERICA
ATLANTIC OCEAN
INDIAN OCEAN
ANTARCTICA

India

English victory over the Spanish Armada in 1588

Significance

England experienced religious and political turmoil from the end of the 1400s to the middle of the 1700s. In addition to problems at home, rebellions in Ireland and Scotland also troubled English rulers. England, however, moved toward a stronger parliamentary government and emerged with one of the world's most powerful empires.

Terms to Define

revolution
gentry
burgesses
covenant
Long Parliament
constitution
habeas corpus

Toleration Act
cabinet
prime minister
limited constitutional
  monarchy
sea dogs

People to Identify

Mary I
Philip II
Elizabeth I
Mary Queen of Scots
James I
Charles I
Cavaliers
Roundheads
Oliver Cromwell
New Model Army
Rump Parliament

Charles II
Tories
Whigs
James II
William III
Mary II
Thomas Hobbes
John Locke
John Cabot
Sir Francis Drake
Henry Hudson

Places to Locate

English Channel
Ulster
Bombay
Hudson Bay

Jamestown
Plymouth
Barbados

Chapter Theme Questions

- **Religion** How might religious conflict lead to political conflict?
- **Politics and Law** What kinds of struggles might occur as a nation moves toward a representative form of government?
- **Geography** How might an island nation expand its empire?

I n the following passage, the author Lytton Strachey gives us a glimpse of Queen Elizabeth I, who ruled England from 1558 to 1603.

“ *While the Spanish ambassador declared that ten thousand devils possessed her, the ordinary Englishman saw in King Hal's full-blooded daughter a Queen after his own heart. She swore; she spat; she struck with her fist when she was angry; she roared with laughter when she was amused. And she was often amused. A radiant atmosphere of humour coloured and softened the harsh lines of her destiny, and buoyed her up along the zigzags of her dreadful path. Her response to every stimulus was immediate and rich: to the folly of the moment, to the clash and horror of great events, her soul leapt out with a vivacity, an abandonment, a complete awareness of the situation, which made her, which makes her still, a fascinating spectacle.* ”

Elizabeth I, one of England's strongest monarchs, led her country successfully through a very turbulent time in its history.

Section 1

The Tudors and the Stuarts

Focus Questions

- **How did Tudor and Stuart rulers handle conflicts between central government and local authority in their monarchies?**
- **What role did religious intolerance play in the growing struggle between Parliament and royalty?**
- **How did financial pressures become the source of conflict between monarchs and Parliament?**

Chapter 15 described the struggle between central governments and local authorities for control in

European countries. In these countries, the central governments usually won, and the most extreme form of central government—absolute monarchy—became common in most of these European countries. Of all the revolts in the mid-1600s, the most severe took place in England. The clash there led in the 1640s and 1650s to civil war and **revolution**—a radical attempt to change the very structure of a country's government. Although a more limited monarchy was eventually restored, this period of conflict influenced both English history and political ideas throughout Europe.

The Reign of Mary Tudor

In the late 1400s, a new royal family, the Tudors, became England's rulers. The Tudors made efforts to strengthen their powers as rulers in a way similar to those made by rulers of France and Spain. Following the turbulence of the Wars of the Roses, the first Tudor king, Henry VII, brought stability and prosperity to England. Of the five Tudor monarchs, Henry VIII, who reigned from 1509 to 1547, and his daughter Elizabeth I, who reigned from 1558 to 1603, had the greatest success as rulers over England. During his reign, Henry VIII established a new official English church, the Anglican Church.

Elizabeth I's life was full of conflict; her half sister Mary I imprisoned her in the Tower of London for two months for what Mary deemed suspicious activity.

After the short reign of sickly Edward VI, Mary I, the oldest daughter of Henry VIII, ascended the throne in 1553 to become the first reigning queen of England. Her personal unhappiness and her devotion to Catholicism shaped her reign. Though she did not lack courage or kindness, she had a fierce determination to make England a Catholic nation again. Mary's unpopular marriage to Philip II of Spain, a leader of the Counter-Reformation, outraged her Protestant subjects. Determined to rid England of clergy who would not conform to the laws of the Catholic Church, Mary had nearly 300 people burned at the stake, including Thomas Cranmer, archbishop of Canterbury. These persecutions earned her the nickname "Bloody Mary" and provoked rebellion, but they completely failed to destroy Protestantism.

The Reign of Elizabeth I

When Mary I died in 1558, her Protestant half sister Elizabeth became queen. Adept at politics, Elizabeth used parliamentary acts to prevent conflict and strengthen Protestantism. For example, people who did not attend the Anglican Church had to pay fines.

Mary Queen of Scots. Religion also entered into the question of who should succeed Elizabeth. In a monarchy, the oldest child usually inherits the throne. Elizabeth did not marry, however, and had no children. Her closest relative and heir—Mary Stuart, queen of Scotland, or Mary Queen of Scots as she is more commonly known—was Catholic.

The prospect of Mary Queen of Scots becoming queen of England horrified English Protestants. However, it also delayed the plans of Philip II of Spain to invade England and force a Catholic ruler on the English people.

In 1568, to escape problems in Scotland, the headstrong Mary fled to England, only to be imprisoned by Elizabeth. Later Mary foolishly plotted with Philip II's ambassadors in England to kill Elizabeth and seize the English throne. After some hesitation, Elizabeth signed the Scottish queen's death warrant, and in 1587 Mary was beheaded. King Philip II, angered by English raiders at sea and Elizabeth's aid to Protestants in his realm, planned an invasion of England.

The Spanish Armada. In 1588 Philip sent a fleet of 130 ships, called the Invincible Armada, north toward the English Channel. The English summoned all their ships to intercept the Spanish Armada. The smaller English ships were swifter and more maneuverable, and their guns fired faster and from a longer range than the guns on the Spanish ships.

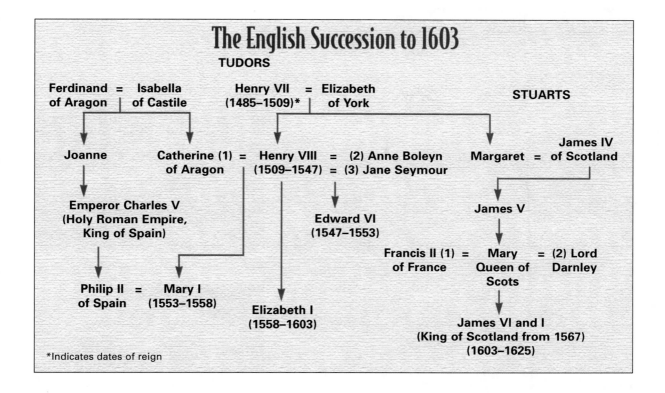

The English Succession to 1603

TUDORS

Ferdinand = Isabella
of Aragon   of Castile

Henry VII = Elizabeth
(1485–1509)* | of York

STUARTS

Joanne

Catherine (1) = Henry VIII = (2) Anne Boleyn
of Aragon   (1509–1547) = (3) Jane Seymour

Margaret = James IV
of Scotland

Emperor Charles V
(Holy Roman Empire,
King of Spain)

Edward VI
(1547–1553)

James V

Philip II = Mary I
of Spain   (1553–1558)

Elizabeth I
(1558–1603)

Francis II (1) = Mary = (2) Lord
of France   Queen of   Darnley
               Scots

James VI and I
(King of Scotland from 1567)
(1603–1625)

*Indicates dates of reign

The English broke the huge Spanish formation, then damaged and sank some of the lumbering vessels. The Spaniards attempted to escape to the North Sea and then northwest around all the British Isles. Autumn storms, navigation errors, and lack of supplies proved deadly. Some of the Spanish ships reached the open sea and limped home, but many foundered on the rocky, desolate coasts of Scotland and Ireland. Only about half of the Invincible Armada straggled back to Spain. The combination of skilled English seafaring and bad weather had been disastrous for King Philip's enormous fleet and his overseas ambitions. Even with Spain's external threat destroyed and Elizabeth's Protestant rule secure, Elizabeth's government still faced two major problems at home.

The religious problem. Religious issues in England were unsettled. The monarchy under Henry VIII had broken with the pope and established Anglicanism as England's religion, but many people believed that the change had not gone far enough. They wanted to "purify" the English church even more. These people, called Puritans, objected to the continuation of many Catholic practices. Although the Anglican Church had abolished the Mass, it still had bishops. Priests still dressed in elaborate robes for religious services, and the congregation still knelt during services.

The Puritans thought these customs too Catholic and wanted to abolish them.

Like many monarchs, the Protestant Tudors thought religious disunity threatened stability. They wanted to unite their subjects in the Anglican faith. Therefore, they persecuted both remaining Catholics and non-Anglican Protestants such as Puritans. Not only did they fail to end dissent, but they made dangerous enemies of non-Anglican Protestants.

The Puritans became increasingly unhappy about the Anglican Church and the quality of the clergy. Queen Elizabeth, however, refused to allow further changes in the church. Her religious policies were tolerant compared to those of other rulers, but they were objectionable to Catholics on one side and Puritans on the other. Eventually, these same objections would contribute to rebellion against the monarchy itself.

Elizabeth I and Parliament. In England, Parliament, the body of representatives from the whole country, had the right to approve all taxes and pass laws. Parliament gained power and prestige in the 1530s, when Henry VIII used it to pass laws that made England a Protestant nation. Moreover, people looked to Parliament as a restraint on the monarchy because it represented the wishes of people outside the central government.

Theater

Ruins of a Roman theater with a 3,500 seating capacity

New Shakespeare Globe Theater in London

Interior of the new Shakespeare Globe Theater

People have enjoyed going to see plays as a form of entertainment since the earliest times. In ancient Greece and Rome, performances were given in great open-air arenas (above). In ancient Japan, the Noh plays were popular forms of entertainment.

During the Middle Ages, sacred stories and plays with Christian themes, called morality plays, were performed in or near churches. By the time of the Renaissance, special buildings were built for dramatic performances. These buildings came to be known as theaters.

Perhaps the most famous theater in history was the Globe. This octagon-shaped theater was built in the late 1500s on the south bank of the Thames River, across from London. Most of William Shakespeare's plays had their earliest performances in the Globe. A reconstructed Globe Theater now stands near the site of the original theater.

Londoners flocked to see the latest comedies and tragedies of writers such as Shakespeare, Christopher Marlowe, and Ben Jonson. Often drawing on the models of classical Greece and Rome, these writers created dramas beyond mere morality plays; they were works full of romance, humor, violence, and despair.

Plays were performed in the daytime, when there was enough natural light to illuminate the stage. The center of the theater was open to the sky. Ordinary tradespeople sat or stood in this open area, ready to be rained upon if the weather turned bad. Nobles and rich merchants sat in boxes around the sides of the theater. The stage itself was covered by an overhanging roof.

The human emotions explored by the plays of the Elizabethan and Restoration periods are so universal that many of the plays continue to be performed. Love, ambition, madness, and revenge have been themes of drama since ancient times. The same themes are still used by modern playwrights. Our enjoyment of the theater is one way in which we are linked with our ancestors.

Parliament had two houses. The House of Lords consisted of nobles and higher clergy. The House of Commons represented two classes: gentry and burgesses. The **gentry**, though without titles, had social position and owned land. Occasionally, younger sons of nobles, who could not inherit their fathers' titles or positions, settled into the gentry. Merchants and professional people from towns and cities made up the **burgesses**.

Although England maintained distinct classes, lines between the gentry and burgesses could and sometimes did become blurred. Class lines, for example, might be crossed for economic reasons. Rich merchants who owned land might be considered gentry. Younger sons of nobles might enter professions and come to be regarded as burgesses. Together the two groups had considerable power that commanded the respect of the monarch.

Elizabeth I summoned Parliaments often during her reign and gave the appearance of heeding them. She managed Parliament cleverly, obtaining the taxes she needed without letting members influence her policy too directly. Although annoyed at petitions urging her to marry, Elizabeth generally refrained from curtailing freedom of speech in Parliament. Despite her skill at managing Parliament, Elizabeth found it increasingly difficult to prevent its members, particularly Puritans, from questioning government policies. During the reigns of her successors, Parliament's questions became ever more challenging. In time members of Parliament would begin a revolution when a monarch refused to hear their views.

The Roots of the English Revolution

Between 1603, when Elizabeth died, and 1640, relations between the monarchy and its subjects deteriorated. The main stages in that deterioration suggest how and why it happened.

James I. The first problem arose almost immediately. Elizabeth I had never married and left no heir. King James VI of Scotland, a member of the Stuart family and the son of Mary Queen of Scots, succeeded Elizabeth to the English throne as James I of England.* At age 39, he had thin brown hair, a straggly beard, and spindly legs. The gangly king also had rough manners, at least according to his English political opponents. However, James had a taste for learning and was a man of considerable intelligence. A writer in his youth, he was an experienced ruler when he came south to

---

*From this time on, England and Scotland were ruled by the same monarch.

England. Even so, he lacked common sense in financial matters and in diplomacy. According to Henry IV of France, he was "the wisest fool in Christendom."

James had managed to rule Scotland by balancing one faction with another and keeping the church in Scotland under control. His English subjects, however, suspected that, as a foreigner, he did not really understand how their parliamentary system worked. At his first Parliament, James, who strongly believed in the divine right of kings, intervened in a House of Commons matter over membership. A few insulted members drew up a document called *The Form of Apology and Satisfaction* to define the role of the House of Commons for the king.

Finance and foreign policy occupied James's attention during much of his reign. He was a strong supporter of the Anglican Church and had little tolerance for the Puritans' demands for reform. Although James did agree to a new translation of the Bible into English, the King James Version, he refused other changes to church doctrine. (This Bible, also known as the Authorized Version, is still one of the most widely used English translations.) It was during James's reign that some Puritans began to leave England, including one group that fled to Holland and later sailed to America in the *Mayflower*.

The main opposition to James I came from Parliament, in which the Puritans were strongly represented. His reign saw rising inflation and growing government activity. James could never collect enough money in taxes to finance his policies. When taxes passed by Parliament proved insufficient, he raised money by selling titles of nobility, granting monopoly rights to private companies, and increasing customs duties. Parliament objected to these methods. It also objected to James's attempt to create an alliance with England's old enemy, Spain. The negotiations finally broke down, and the two nations went to war.

Charles I. At the time of his death in 1625, James I and his subjects had an uneasy relationship. The tension between the monarchy and the people exploded during the reign of his son Charles I, who ruled from 1625 to 1649. Brave but personally shy, Charles believed in the divine right of kings as firmly as his father had. These qualities kept him out of touch with people and political realities. Charles married a French Catholic princess, Henrietta Maria, an unpopular choice that further isolated him from the people.

When Charles I could not get funds from the Puritan-dominated Parliament, he tried to force people to lend him money and imprisoned some who

The Authorized Version of the Bible (The King James Bible)

In January 1604, James I of England held the Hampton Court Conference near London. At this conference, James responded to demands of the Puritans that included reforms to church government and changes in *The Book of Common Prayer*. The king rejected many of the Puritans' demands but agreed to one that had a powerful effect on religious practice as well as English literature and speech for centuries to come: a new translation of the Bible.

James approved a committee of 54 scholars for the translation task, but the finished work was that of only 47 of these scholars. They worked in six groups at three locations—Westminster, Oxford, and Cambridge—with each group assigned a section of the text. The labor took seven years to

complete, and the new translation was published in 1611. The scholars worked with both existing English translations and texts available in the original languages of Hebrew and Greek. The result was a translation that became the standard Bible in English for nearly three centuries. It quickly became the most popular book in English.

Although later translators had access to more accurate texts as well as a better understanding of Greek and Hebrew, the King James Version of the Bible is a masterpiece of the English language of the time—the language of great English writers such as Shakespeare, Ben Jonson, and John Donne. Its grandeur and simplicity had an influence on English prose and poetic style for many years to come.

---

refused. Confrontation with Parliament during 1628 led members to present Charles with the Petition of Right, which reasserted four ancient liberties. Charles signed the Petition of Right, hoping Parliament would release funds. He agreed not to levy taxes without consent of Parliament, not to declare martial law, not to quarter soldiers in private homes in peacetime, and not to imprison people without specific charge. Charles did, however, continue to levy taxes. When members of the House of Commons vehemently objected, he dissolved Parliament.

For the next 11 years, Charles refused to call Parliament into session, hoping to govern without opposition. During these years, he used drastic means to collect money and revived long-ignored royal fees and fines. The economy improved, but resentment grew.

Charles took his title as head of the Anglican Church seriously. He favored a formal and ceremonial faith, which seemed Catholic and offensive to Puritans. Many left the country for a new life in America during the 1630s, following those who had been leaving since the early 1600s. Those who stayed became determined opponents of the king.

These Puritans increasingly dominated the House of Commons, joining others in Parliament who thought the king's rule was growing tyrannical. Charles began to use royal courts against his enemies. The once popular royal courts, though, did not guarantee civil liberties, a fact exploited by the king. Decisions were made in secret by judges, not by juries. Lawyers of common-law courts resented these rivals to their system, especially because they believed the king controlled the judges. One court, the Court of Star Chamber—named for the wall and ceiling designs in the room where it met—severely prosecuted Puritans and critics of government. Members of the gentry, who would have been exempt from corporal punishment in civil courts, and other commoners who opposed Charles hated the Star Chamber. It seemed to many English people that Charles was increasingly imposing an absolute rule.

The Scots. When Charles tried to impose a liturgy, or prescribed form of ritual, based on the Anglican *Book of Common Prayer*, on Scotland, rebellion broke out. The state religion of Scotland was Presbyterianism, a Protestant denomination modeled on Calvinism.

Anthony Van Dyck, Charles I's court painter from 1632 to 1641, painted this hunting portrait of the king in 1635.

Elders known as presbyters, rather than bishops, ruled the Presbyterian Church, and Presbyterians had their own liturgy. Moreover, the changes appeared to Scots to move toward hated Catholicism. In 1638 many responded to Charles's attempt to Anglicanize the Presbyterian service by signing a National Covenant. In this **covenant**, or solemn agreement, Scots swore that changes in the church in Scotland violated both their religion and acts of the Scottish Parliament. To Scottish Presbyterians, loyalty to their church—the Kirk—came before loyalty to the king. The Scots raised an army, and Charles took troops to Scotland, but he was easily outmaneuvered. Seeking more funds to put down the rebellion, he called Parliament into session, then dismissed it when it insisted on airing its grievances first. A second defeat—this time in England itself—gravely disturbed Charles. Realizing he could not defend England without new taxation, he again called Parliament into session in November 1640.

Section 1 Review

1. **Define** revolution, gentry, burgesses, covenant
2. **Identify** Mary I, Philip II, Elizabeth I, Mary Queen of Scots, James I, Charles I
3. **Locate and Explain the Significance** English Channel
4. **Summarizing Ideas** How did Elizabeth I, James I, and Charles I deal with conflicts with Parliament during their reigns as the monarch of England?
5. **Analyzing Ideas** How did religious differences influence English politics during the reigns of James I and Charles I?
6. **Evaluating Ideas** How did financial issues eventually become the breaking point for the struggle between Parliament and the Stuart kings?

Civil War and Revolution

Focus Questions

- **How did rebellion in Ireland trigger the English Civil War?**
- **What was Cromwell's commonwealth, and how did it govern after the war?**
- **Why was the monarchy restored in England?**

The Parliament of 1640—known as the **Long Parliament**—reconvened periodically for 20 years. The Puritans who controlled the House of Commons took actions to limit the monarchy. They abolished the king's power to dissolve Parliament and passed a law requiring that Parliament meet at least once every three years. They declared illegal or amended many of the king's tax levies. Parliament abolished the Court of Star Chamber and forced the execution of two of the king's advisers for treason. When radical Puritans in Parliament tried to effect sweeping changes in the church, public support began to move toward the king.

The Irish Problem

While the Long Parliament worked at reducing the king's authority, trouble broke out in Ireland. England had ruled parts of Ireland since the late 1100s but had never brought the Irish completely under control. The English conquerors historically had seized land belonging to Irish owners and given it to English settlers. Under James I, the English settlers who went to Ireland were mostly Anglican. These landowning Anglo-Irish became the upper class and controlled most of the country's wealth. Later, Scottish Presbyterians settled in the northern region called Ulster. Mostly farmers and merchants, they became the middle class. The majority of native Irish remained Roman Catholic and worked as tenant farmers and laborers. They formed the lowest social and economic class and were often brutally repressed. In 1641 a bloody rebellion led primarily by Irish Catholics began against England, heightening Protestant fears of Catholics.

The rebellion in Ireland brought crisis. Parliament knew it needed a huge army to put down the Irish rebellion, but it did not trust Charles to control it. A complete list of grievances against the king, the Grand Remonstrance, was passed. Bills were proposed to put the military under Parliament's control.

"By God, not for an hour," replied Charles. Charles heard rumors that the queen might be impeached and led troops to the House of Commons to arrest some of his opponents. Neither side compromised, and a civil war began in 1642.

English Civil War

The citizenry was divided. Generally, the king's supporters, called royalists or Cavaliers, after the king's cavalry, included Anglicans, Roman Catholics, nobles, and those who opposed the changes that Parliament wanted. Those citizens who believed that royal power should be curbed, including Puritans and other non-Anglican Protestants, supported the parliamentary opposition. They were sometimes called Roundheads, after the close haircuts that the Puritan soldiers wore.

Oliver Cromwell, a rising Puritan leader, organized his troops into a powerful army that had great success against the royalists. Cromwell's New Model Army, which was formed in 1645, was drilled, disciplined, and zealous. After a defeat at Naseby in 1645, Charles fled to the Scots. Oxford, the Royalist headquarters, surrendered to the New Model Army in June 1646, bringing an end to the first stage of the civil war. After negotiations failed between Charles and the Scots, they turned him over to Parliament.

Various political and religious groups struggled for control. Chief among these groups were the Presbyterians, a majority in Parliament, and the Independents, supported by the army. Cromwell conducted negotiations with the king, hoping he would agree to become a figurehead. Then, in November 1647, Charles escaped and organized his Scottish supporters to fight again. Cromwell's army crushed them and hardened its attitude. Troops moved on the House of Commons, preventing Anglican and Presbyterian members from entering, leaving approximately 60 Independents loyal to the army. This remnant of the Long Parliament became known as the Rump Parliament.

Death of the king. The Rump Parliament abolished both the monarchy and the House of Lords. It proclaimed England a commonwealth, a term used at the time to mean a republic, and appointed a special court to try Charles for treason and other crimes. Charles refused to plead to a court he considered illegal. The court condemned Charles, and he was beheaded in front of the palace at Whitehall in 1649. Charles I faced death bravely and was regarded by many people as a martyr. His courage and the citizens' desire for stability would make it easier for his son, who fled to France after his father's death, to return later as king. Meanwhile, Oliver Cromwell took control of England.

Cromwell's Commonwealth

Oliver Cromwell was a pious and honest Puritan who possessed the qualities of a powerful orator and skilled leader. However, he also believed that he had been placed in power by divine providence. Therefore, when he felt moved to suppress dissent, such as in Ireland, he could be harsh. He was privately tolerant in religious matters, though fervent Puritan followers sometimes forced his hand.

Although Cromwell held considerable power, he was a reluctant dictator. He preferred a parliamentary, republican government and made several attempts to create one amid the chaos. He tried twice to establish a **constitution**—a document outlining the fundamental laws and principles that govern a nation. The Instrument of Government in 1653 was the first written constitution of a major European nation. It gave Cromwell the title lord protector and provided that landowners would elect members of Parliament. Cromwell was lord protector until 1658, an era often called the Protectorate.

Discontent never subsided. Cromwell's government might have been overthrown except for three factors: (1) It had enough money from taxes and the sale of confiscated royalist lands to support itself and its army. (2) Its army was disciplined and powerful, discouraging other groups from making attempts against it. (3) Its enemies, the Irish and the royalists, had no organized army. Cromwell repressed the Irish so brutally that his name inspires hatred even today, and the royalists never posed a serious threat.

Cromwell's foreign policy related to his domestic policy, that of encouraging manufacturing and trade. During the civil war in England, Dutch merchants and shipowners had established a profitable trade

Oliver Cromwell led parliamentary forces in battles at Naseby and Oxford. Following the execution of Charles I in 1649, Cromwell ruled England as lord protector from 1653 to 1658.

What If?

English Civil War
Neither Charles I nor Parliament expected their differences to end in war. What if Charles and Parliament had been able to compromise on control of the army in 1640? Do you think the civil war and revolution would have happened anyway?

Section 2 Review

1. **Define** Long Parliament, constitution
2. **Identify** Cavaliers, Roundheads, Oliver Cromwell, New Model Army, Rump Parliament
3. **Locate and Explain the Significance** Ulster
4. **Understanding Ideas** How did the rebellion in Ireland influence the civil war in England?
5. **Summarizing Ideas** Describe the role of Oliver Cromwell after the death of Charles I.
6. **Synthesizing Ideas** Why was Oliver Cromwell unable to establish a permanent republic in England?

transporting goods. Cromwell challenged the Dutch by having Parliament pass the Navigation Act of 1651, requiring that all imports be shipped in English ships or ships of the country producing the goods.

Cromwell's policies led to a war with the Dutch from 1652 to 1654. Because the Dutch transported so much of the world's trade, they realized that the freedom of the seas was at stake. Although the war ended indecisively, the English navy gained prestige, and Cromwell demonstrated that the English government would use its growing power to aid English commerce.

The End of the Revolution
The experiment with republican government failed. Cromwell quarreled almost as much with Parliament as had the Stuart kings, and parliamentary resentment of central power resurfaced. Before his death in 1658, Cromwell, like Charles I whom he had replaced as king, dissolved Parliament and ruled alone. After Cromwell's death, his son Richard was named lord protector, but his weak leadership lost the support of the army.

By 1660 the English people, too, had undergone a change of feelings. Though some had favored the execution of Charles I, Cromwell's commonwealth had neither settled the nation nor solved its problems. After some hesitation, the Parliament of 1660, with the support of the army, invited Charles II, the son of Charles I, to return to England. Wildly cheering crowds greeted him in London. Some historians call the period from 1642 to 1660 the English Revolution. This includes the years of civil war from 1642 to 1649, together with the changes in society and government that continued until the return of a monarch in 1660. Although the country seemed to have weathered its troubles, another 30 years would pass before the monarchy and Parliament would achieve a workable balance.

Section 3

England's Constitutional Monarchy

Focus Questions
- **What happened during the Restoration?**
- **What was the Glorious Revolution?**
- **How did a constitutional monarchy come into being in England?**

The struggles between king and Parliament did not end in 1660. An echo of the crisis occurred in the 1680s. After that uncertainty passed, however, the English created a more stable government that linked monarch and Parliament in a workable partnership.

Charles II and the Restoration
The reign of Charles II is called the Restoration because monarchy was restored in England. Literature and music of the time are referred to as Restoration works, and the arts prospered under Charles II.

Unlike his father, this Charles was a tall, striking figure. He had dark brown hair and eyes, and he resembled his Medici and Bourbon ancestors. Charles was well-mannered, but because he also loved entertainment and pleasure, people dubbed him the "Merry Monarch." Charles removed restrictions on the theater and other forms of entertainment that the stern Puritans of the commonwealth era had legislated.

The period following the fall of Cromwell's commonwealth in 1660 is known as the Restoration because the monarchy was restored to England with Charles II (shown here as a small boy).

Contrary to his nickname, the "Merry Monarch," however, Charles II had learned much from his years in exile after his father's death. Cynical and cautious, he deferred to Parliament when his policies met opposition, although he often used roundabout methods to gain his ends. Charles continued Cromwell's commercial policy, which eventually led to wars with the Dutch. During these wars, England seized the Dutch settlement of New Amsterdam in North America and renamed it New York. Charles also explored an alliance with France, partly in secret, but public protest forced him away from close relations with that nation. Charles's decision not to ally his country with France marked the beginning of 150 years of rivalry between England and France for mastery of the sea and for colonial power.

Charles II tolerated Catholicism and hoped to lift some of the legal restrictions on the faith during his reign. However, attempts to do so met with such strong parliamentary opposition that he abandoned the effort.

Political Parties Develop

Because Charles II and his Portuguese queen, Catherine of Braganza, had no children, it seemed clear that Charles's younger brother James, a Roman Catholic, would succeed him. The two political parties that were developing at this time held opposing ideas about royal succession.

The two groups, of almost equal strength—Tories and Whigs—had begun to develop in Parliament. Like the terms *Cavalier* and *Roundhead*, the terms *Tory* and *Whig* were originally unflattering nicknames. *Tory* was an Irish word that suggested a Catholic outlaw. It was applied to people who supported the hereditary right of James to rule. Although Tories strongly supported the Anglican Church, they were willing to accept a Roman Catholic ruler. The term *Whig* originally meant "horse thief" and later was applied to Scottish Presbyterians. It suggested a group that was rebellious. The Whigs claimed the right to deny the throne to James and wanted a strong Parliament. They vigorously opposed the idea of a Catholic ruler.

James II and the Glorious Revolution

Charles II died in 1685, and his younger brother did come to the throne, as James II. The humorless James was less flexible than his older brother. As a Catholic and an ardent believer in royal absolutism, James antagonized both Whigs and Tories. Many of his actions, intended to ease life for Catholics, frightened and roused Protestants to greater resistance.

One of the issues of James's reign once again involved succession to the throne. James's daughters, Mary and Anne, were both raised as Protestants at Charles II's insistence, and both married Protestant princes. However, James's first wife died, and he married again, this time to a Catholic princess, Mary of Modena. In 1688 she gave birth to a son, who would by law succeed his father before his older half sisters. Because the boy was a Catholic like his parents, English Protestants feared a whole line of Catholic rulers on the throne of England.

Now all the groups who opposed James combined to bring about the event known as the Glorious Revolution. Whigs and Tories, united in fear of Catholicism, agreed that James must abdicate. A number of leading nobles invited James's daughter Mary and her Dutch husband William of Orange to take the throne of England. Although William landed in England with an army in 1688, armed force was hardly necessary. James, unable to rally anyone to his support and fearful of assassination, fled to France. Parliament gave the crown to William and Mary as the joint rulers William III and Mary II.

New Ideas About Government

The English civil war and the events that followed led not only to changes in government but also to new ideas about government. The English philosopher Thomas Hobbes lived through the civil war and was disturbed by the chaos it created. He set forth his political philosophy in a book called *Leviathan*, published in 1651.

Hobbes explained that groups of people first lived in anarchy, what he considered a state of nature.

Although Mary II's parents were Catholic, they raised their daughter as a Protestant. Mary II's marriage to her Protestant cousin William III led to five years of joint Protestant rule.

John Locke, an English writer of philosophy and political thought, believed that people have certain rights that the state should protect.

Life was violent and dangerous under these circumstances, so people chose a leader to rule them. To maintain a stable society, people made an unwritten social contract or "covenant." Under this contract, argued Hobbes, people must give the monarch absolute power, or anarchy results. The people retain only the right to protect their own lives.

John Locke, another English philosopher, considered these ideas but interpreted them differently. Locke supported Parliament in the struggles with James II. He articulated the principles on which supporters of the Glorious Revolution acted in 1688, publishing them in his *Two Treatises of Government* in 1690.

Like Hobbes, Locke believed that people had first lived individually and then made a social contract. However, he believed that people had given up only some of their individual rights and had kept others. The rights they kept included the right to live, to enjoy liberty, and to own property, and they could expect rulers to preserve these rights.

According to Locke, a ruler who violated these rights violated natural law and broke the unwritten social contract. The people had the right to overthrow such a ruler and replace him with one who pledged to observe and protect their rights. Locke thus defended the actions of those who had forced James II to leave the throne, and provided a justification for offering the crown to William and Mary. Locke's ideas would influence later revolutions in America and France as well.

Safeguards Against Absolute Rule

Parliament passed laws attempting to safeguard against arbitrary rule as early as the reign of Charles II. In 1679 it passed an important measure, the Habeas Corpus Act. This act provided that anyone who was arrested could obtain a writ, or order, demanding to be brought before a judge within a specified period of time. The judge would decide whether the prisoner should be released or charged and tried for a crime. The writ itself was called **habeas corpus**, Latin for "you shall have the body." The Habeas Corpus Act protected individuals against arbitrary arrest and imprisonment.

A document called the Declaration of Rights was read to William and Mary before their ascent to the throne in 1689. That year, Parliament formalized the Declaration of Rights as the Bill of Rights. The Bill of Rights declared that Parliament would choose the ruler, who as an official would be subject to parliamentary laws. The ruler could not proclaim or suspend any law.

Building History Study Skills

READ
WRITE
INTERPRET
CONNECT
THINK

Reading About History: Identifying a Point of View

A point of view presents a person's outlook on a subject or an event. It is important to know the author's point of view in order to determine the accuracy of the information presented. By understanding the author's viewpoint, you can tell what facts have been ignored or what data have been exaggerated. You can also evaluate how reliable the information is.

How to Identify a Point of View
Follow these guidelines to identify a point of view.
1. State the author's topic.
2. Identify the main idea.
3. Determine how and why emphasis has been placed on the main idea.
4. Select words and phrases that signal an opinion, emotion, or exaggeration.
5. Indicate ideas or facts about the subject that the author did not include.
6. State the author's point of view.

Developing the Skill
The issue of how and why government is organized was an integral part of the English civil war and the Glorious Revolution. Thomas Hobbes in *Leviathan* and John Locke in *Two Treatises of Government* contributed their thoughts to the discussion. Read the selections from their works. What are their points of view? How are their ideas similar? How are they different?

"In the first place, I put for a general inclination of all mankind, a perpetual and restless desire of power after power, that ceaseth only in death. . . .

During the time men live without a common power to keep them all in awe, they are in that condition which is called war; . . . as is of every man, against every man. . . .

In such condition, there is no place for industry . . . and consequently no culture of the earth; no navigation; . . . no commodious building; . . . no arts; no letters; no society; and which is worst of all, continual fear, and danger of violent death; and the life of man, solitary, poor, nasty, brutish, and short. . . .

The only way . . . they may nourish themselves and live contentedly is to confer all their power and strength upon one man, or upon one assembly of men, that may reduce all their wills . . .

unto one will. . . . This is more than consent, or concord; it is a real unity of them all, in one and the same person, made by covenant of every man with every man. . . . This done, the multitude so united in one person, is called a commonwealth."

(Thomas Hobbes, *Leviathan*)

"Political power is that power which every man having in the state of nature has given up into the hands of the society. . . . And this power has its original only from compact and agreement, and the mutual consent of those who make up the community. . . .

The reason why men enter into society is the preservation of their property; and the end why they choose and authorize a legislative is that there may be laws made and rules set as guards and fences to the properties of all the members of the society. . . . Whenever the legislators endeavor to take away and destroy the property of the people, or to reduce them to slavery under arbitrary power, they put themselves into a state of war with the people who are thereupon absolved from any further obedience."

(John Locke, *The Second Treatise of Government*)

Both men discuss how governments are formed. Hobbes claims that man in a state of nature is in constant disorder. He forms a government to ensure protection, prosperity, and order for himself. Man gives up his individual will to a ruler. Revolution is not justified because the ruler protects the common good. The signal words are fear, danger, brutish, concord, unity, and consent.

Locke believes that man in a state of nature has political power and forms a society to protect property. Government is a contract between the ruler and the governed. The government's purpose is to protect individual rights. Locke says that the contract can be broken if the ruler does not protect property. The signal words are arbitrary and slavery.

Practicing the Skill
Choose a current political article from a periodical and identify the point of view.

To apply this skill, see Applying History Study Skills on page 413.

The ruler could not impose any tax or maintain an army in peacetime without Parliament's consent. Parliament had to meet frequently, and the monarch could not interfere with the elections of its members. The Bill of Rights guaranteed the right of the members of Parliament to express themselves freely.

The Bill of Rights also protected private citizens. All citizens had the right to petition the government for relief of injustice. In addition, no one could be required to pay excessive bail or be subjected to cruel and unusual punishment.

In 1689 Parliament also passed the **Toleration Act**. This act granted freedom of conscience and the right of public worship to those Protestants (now called Dissenters) who were not members of the Anglican Church. It did not, however, bring about complete religious freedom. For example, Roman Catholics and Jews lived under heavy restrictions, and Dissenters could not hold public office.

In 1701 Parliament passed the Act of Settlement, designed to keep Catholics from the English throne. The act provided that if William III should die with no heir, Mary's sister, Anne, would inherit the throne. If Anne had no children, the throne would go to another Protestant granddaughter of James I, Sophia, the electress of Hanover in Germany.

Parliament Rules England

The Bill of Rights and the Act of Settlement marked the end of the long struggle between monarch and Parliament to determine who would rule the country. By 1700, although England remained a monarchy, Parliament held the power. However, Parliament did not represent all the people. Hereditary nobles and higher clergy made up the House of Lords. Even the House of Commons, which was gradually becoming the more powerful of the two houses, was not particularly representative. Only the male gentry who were landowners and the powerful commercial people had the right to vote for members of the House of Commons.

In the 50 years following 1689, Parliament continued to gain importance as the real power in the governing of England. During this time, the organization and institutions characteristic of today's British government gradually emerged.

For centuries English monarchs had met with advisers to discuss government problems. After the revolution and Restoration, parliamentary leaders had the power to accomplish goals, and William III chose his officers of state from among them. These ministers, or heads of government departments, became known as the **cabinet**.

At first the cabinet included both Whigs and Tories. However, during the reign of William III, it became clear that the government ran more smoothly when most of the cabinet ministers belonged to the majority party in the House of Commons. Sometimes rulers accepted those whom they did not prefer merely to make working with Parliament possible. Additional changes increased parliamentary control of the English government during and following the reign of William III. Among these changes, Parliament gained the right to declare war, and the monarch stopped vetoing acts of Parliament.

Act of Union

In 1707 the parliaments of England and Scotland passed the Act of Union, uniting England and Scotland. At the end of William's reign, impending war with France made the union a strategic and political asset. Scottish resentment of wealthy England might otherwise have led the Scots to take the side of France again. The Act of Union merged the two countries into one kingdom, known as Great Britain. (See map on page 408.) The act abolished Scotland's parliament and gave the Scots seats in the English House of Lords and House of Commons.

Some people opposed the union at first, particularly some in Scotland, but the union proved beneficial. By removing trade barriers, it encouraged commerce and brought prosperity to both England and Scotland. The Scottish city of Glasgow grew from a fishing village into a great port. The Universities of Edinburgh and Glasgow became major centers of learning in Europe during the 1700s.

Queen Anne, who ruled from 1702 to 1714, had 17 children, but none survived her. When she died, her designated successor, Sophia, electress of Hanover, had already died. Thus Sophia's son George became George I, the first of the Hanoverian dynasty of Great Britain. Both he and his son George II were born in Germany and were unfamiliar with British government and customs. George I, who ruled until 1727, spoke no English. George II, who was king until 1760, spoke fluent English but depended on ministers such as Sir Robert Walpole to manage the administration. Although the details of British government interested both kings, neither understood the larger issues. As a result, the cabinet became increasingly important in the British system of government.

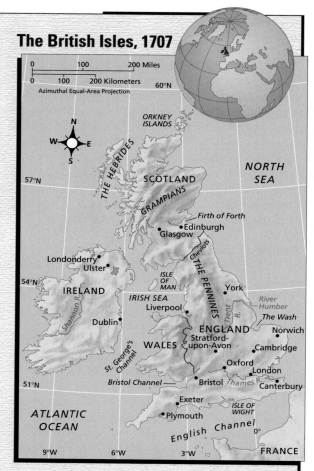

The British Isles, 1707

0 100 200 Miles
0 100 200 Kilometers
Azimuthal Equal-Area Projection

60°N

ORKNEY ISLANDS

NORTH SEA

THE HEBRIDES

57°N

SCOTLAND

GRAMPIANS

Firth of Forth
Edinburgh
Glasgow

Cheviots

Londonderry
Ulster

ISLE OF MAN

THE PENNINES

York

54°N

IRELAND

IRISH SEA

Liverpool

River Humber

The Wash

Trent R.

Dublin

ENGLAND

Norwich

Shannon R.

WALES

Stratford-upon-Avon

Cambridge

St. George's Channel

Oxford

London

51°N

Bristol Channel

Bristol

Thames R.

Canterbury

Exeter

ISLE OF WIGHT

ATLANTIC OCEAN

Plymouth

English Channel

0°

9°W 6°W 3°W

FRANCE

Learning from Maps In 1707 Parliament united Scotland and England as the Kingdom of Great Britain.

? Place What islands lie off the coast of Scotland?

head of state. The monarchy was limited, however, in that a constitution restricted the monarch's powers and the monarch was required to consult Parliament.

The British constitution is not a single written document such as that of the United States. It consists partly of great documents that include among others Magna Carta, the Petition of Right, the Habeas Corpus Act, the Bill of Rights, and the Act of Settlement. It also includes acts of Parliament, which any succeeding Parliament may change. Several features of the British governmental system have never been written down; for example, the powers of the prime minister and the functions of the cabinet are based largely on tradition. The prime minister rather than the monarch selects the other members of the cabinet. Together the prime minister and the cabinet plan and carry out policies of the government.

Great Britain is one of the world's oldest constitutional governments. Its limited monarchy became a model for governments of other nations that wanted to end absolute monarchies.

Section 3 Review

1. **Define** habeas corpus, Toleration Act, cabinet, prime minister, limited constitutional monarchy
2. **Identify** Charles II, Tories, Whigs, James II, William III, Mary II, Thomas Hobbes, John Locke
3. **Understanding Ideas** How did the Restoration renew religious discord within Parliament?
4. **Analyzing Ideas** What role did attitudes toward Catholicism play in the Glorious Revolution?
5. **Interpreting Ideas** (a) How did the English Bill of Rights limit the powers of the monarch? (b) How did it protect private citizens?

A Constitutional Monarchy

For more than 20 years—from 1721 to 1742—the Whigs controlled the House of Commons. Their recognized leader, Sir Robert Walpole, was a minister under two kings. Walpole had strong leadership capabilities and was regarded as the **prime minister**, the first minister, although early prime ministers usually carried the title of first lord of the treasury. Under the rule of the Hanoverians, the prime minister became the real head of the government, and Great Britain became a **limited constitutional monarchy**. It was a monarchy in that a king or queen was the

Section 4

English Colonial Expansion

Focus Questions

- How did British naval exploits strengthen the empire?
- How did mercantilism affect colonial policy?

Spain and Portugal established vast overseas empires during the 1500s, while England remained preoccupied with problems at home. Even though these problems persisted during the 1600s, English mariners began explorations that allowed the English to claim lands in the Americas and Asia. English merchants founded companies to trade in these new lands, in addition to the English companies that traded in Russia and in the Baltic. By the mid-1600s, English naval power had become a major force, and in the 1700s, Europe began to recognize British naval supremacy on the high seas. At the same time, the British merchant shipping fleet had replaced the Dutch fleet as leader in mercantile shipping. By the 1760s, Great Britain's colonial empire had no serious mercantile competition in North America or India.

Explorers and Sea Dogs

Shortly after Columbus landed in the Western Hemisphere in 1492, King Henry VII commissioned a Venetian captain named John Cabot to sail to North America. In 1497 and 1498, Cabot explored the coasts of Newfoundland, Nova Scotia, and possibly New England. Although Cabot's voyages gave the English a claim in North America, it was not until almost a century later that the English took steps to develop this territory in North America.

During the reign of Queen Elizabeth I, in the second half of the 1500s, an adventurous group of sea captains appeared in England. The English called this group of traders and pirates **sea dogs**. These men—Sir John Hawkins, Sir Francis Drake, and Sir Walter Raleigh, among others—challenged Portuguese and Spanish monopolies of overseas trade. They also made important voyages of exploration. Sir Francis Drake, for example, sailed westward from North America across the Pacific Ocean, around the southern tip of Africa, and north to England. In 1580 he became the first English sea captain to sail around the globe.

However, the English sea dogs were better known for plundering foreign shipping. They stole from Spanish ships not protected by convoys, and they seized slaves that were being shipped from Africa and sold them in Spanish colonies. These repeated raids greatly angered King Philip II of Spain. He protested to Queen Elizabeth, who claimed that she was helpless in the matter. Secretly though, Queen Elizabeth supported the sea dogs and shared what they had stolen. Pirates and patriots, the sea dogs played a part in England's defeat of the Spanish Armada in 1588, and they strengthened the seafaring tradition of the island nation.

Upon Francis Drake's return from his three-year circumnavigation of the world, Queen Elizabeth I knighted him for his discoveries.

The English in India

The defeat of the Spanish Armada encouraged the English to establish colonies overseas. In 1600 Queen Elizabeth I granted a charter to a trading company called the British East India Company.

This company set up trading posts at Bombay, Calcutta, and Madras in India. The company dealt mainly with local rulers because the Mughal Empire had declined in power. To gain the support of these rulers, the company helped those who were weak, used force without hesitation against those who opposed the company, and extended generous gifts to those who might be swayed by bribery.

The English East India Company eventually set up a few trading posts in Malaya and the East Indies, but India remained its headquarters and chief source of trade and wealth. The company became extremely wealthy and powerful and virtually ruled India into the 1800s.

This is a painted wood model from the first half of the nineteenth century depicting an Indian court (called the Cutchery) which was presided over by an English East India Company officer.

The English in the Americas

England was slow to establish colonies in North America. Initially, the English explored the continent in order to find the so-called Northwest Passage to Asia—a non-existent water route through the Americas to the north and west. The Spanish dominated the southern route around Cape Horn in South America.

Henry Hudson searched extensively and unsuccessfully for the Northwest Passage. In 1609, on a voyage for the Dutch, he charted much of the coast of eastern North America and explored the river that now carries his name. On a voyage for the English one year later, he explored Hudson Bay in northern Canada.

As the search for a Northwest Passage to India continued, the English began to establish colonies along North America's eastern coast. The first of these colonies were founded by private companies or individuals. The English established the first permanent settlement at Jamestown, Virginia, in 1607. In 1620 they founded the second settlement, Plymouth, in what is now the state of Massachusetts.

Many of the settlements were founded for commercial purposes. Investors hoped that the settlers would raise products that would make the home country more self-sufficient. However, the first North American colonies proved to be an economic disappointment. Few of the original investors made a profit or even got their money back. Many colonists had reasons other than profit for settling in North America. These people hoped to find greater political and religious freedom and to make better lives for their families.

As in other colonial empires, the English used slavery in their colonies, especially those in southern North America and the West Indies. Settlements on the Caribbean islands, such as Barbados, were commercially successful largely because of slave labor.

Self-government set England's empire apart from other European colonial empires. Most English colonies had some form of representative assembly, or governing body, although official control remained firmly in the hands of the home country.

In his expeditions for the Dutch and the English, Henry Hudson explored a river and a bay that were later given his name. This image shows the landing of Henry Hudson on Manhattan Island.

Mercantilism and the British Colonies

The British government did intervene in colonial economies in attempts to make them more profitable. The policy of mercantilism maintained that colonies existed for the benefit of the home country. Colonies supplied needed raw materials and furnished a market for Britain's manufactured products.

The British government passed a number of mercantilist regulations that affected its North American colonies, beginning in the 1650s. One regulation required that certain colonial products could be sold only in Britain, even though higher prices might be obtainable in another country. Other regulations discouraged colonists from manufacturing. For example, the British government forbade colonists to ship woolen cloth that they had manufactured to places outside their own colony.

These trade regulations aroused resentment, and colonists found many ways to evade them. Colonists avoided paying taxes whenever and however they could. Smuggling became a respectable occupation and was difficult to prevent because the long American coastline had many harbors and inlets. Until the mid-1700s, however, the British government only loosely enforced its trade restrictions.

Section 4 Review

1. **Define** sea dogs
2. **Identify** John Cabot, Sir Francis Drake, Henry Hudson
3. **Locate and Explain the Significance** Bombay, Hudson Bay, Jamestown, Plymouth, Barbados
4. **Understanding Ideas** What was the significance of the English sea dogs?
5. **Analyzing Ideas** What were the results of British mercantilist policy?

Chapter 16 Review

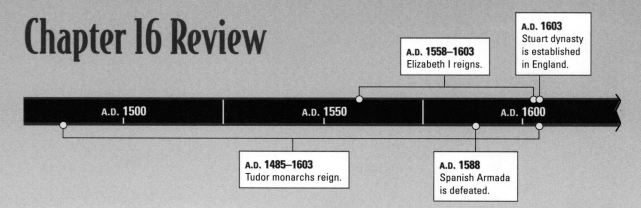

A.D. 1558–1603 Elizabeth I reigns.

A.D. 1603 Stuart dynasty is established in England.

A.D. 1500

A.D. 1550

A.D. 1600

A.D. 1485–1603 Tudor monarchs reign.

A.D. 1588 Spanish Armada is defeated.

Chapter Summary
The following list contains the key concepts you have learned about England, the evolution of its monarchy, and the growth of its empire.

1. Elizabeth I faced threats from Spain abroad and from Catholics and Puritans at home. She established a strong central government while respecting the rights of members of Parliament.
2. The Stuarts believed in the divine right of kings. Their reigns were characterized by quarrels with Parliament over taxation and a wide variety of other issues.
3. Oliver Cromwell and the Puritans executed King Charles I and established a republic called a commonwealth. Cromwell made England strong, but his experiment in republican government failed. After his death, the English restored the monarchy under Charles II.
4. Under the later Stuarts, England feared the prospect of Catholic succession to the throne. Developing political parties called Whigs and Tories united to create a permanent Protestant succession. Parliament passed the Act of Settlement, which was designed to keep Catholics from the English throne.
5. Thomas Hobbes and John Locke each formed a theory of government based on a social contract between rulers and ruled. Locke's idea that the people had the right to overthrow a ruler who violated the contract expressed the English and later American and French justification for revolution.
6. In the first half of the 1700s, Britain established an empire in North America and India that was largely unchallenged. Mercantilism, the idea that colonies exist for the benefit of the home country, was the governing philosophy of the empire.

Reviewing Important Terms
On a separate sheet of paper, supply the term that correctly completes each statement.

1. Members of the House of Commons came from the _____, who represented the landowning classes, and the _____, who represented the urban merchants and professional people.
2. A(n) _____ is a document outlining the fundamental laws and principles that govern a nation.
3. The _____ _____ protected individuals against arbitrary arrest and imprisonment.
4. The _____ is a small group of advisers or ministers who deal with government policy and issues.
5. English traders and pirates who challenged overseas trade monopolies were called _____ _____.
6. A radical attempt to change the very structure of a country's government is called a(n) _____.
7. England developed a(n) _____ _____ _____, or government in which a constitution limits the powers of the monarch and a prime minister is the real head of the government.

Developing Critical Thinking Skills
1. **Understanding Ideas (a)** Why did James I and Charles I quarrel with Parliament? **(b)** What issues led to a civil war in the 1640s?
2. **Explaining Ideas (a)** Why did Catholicism cause fear among many English people during the 1500s and 1600s? **(b)** What did Parliament do in 1701 to prevent Catholics from becoming kings and queens of England?
3. **Comparing Ideas** Compare the strengths and weaknesses of Parliament and monarchs during the reigns of Elizabeth I, Charles I, and William and Mary.
4. **Applying Ideas (a)** How did the view of English monarchs differ from the view of members of Parliament on the role and succession of royalty? **(b)** What other issues lay behind the divisions among people, Parliament, and rulers as they struggled to govern their country?
5. **Evaluating Ideas** Do you think the conflict between the monarchy and Parliament was more about control of government or more about religious issues? Explain.

Relating Geography to History
Use the map of the British Isles on page 408 to answer the following questions. **(a)** What geographical advantages did the Scots have over Charles I in the rebellion over the imposition of Anglican liturgy? **(b)** How did geography contribute to the difference between English attitudes toward the Scots and toward the Irish?

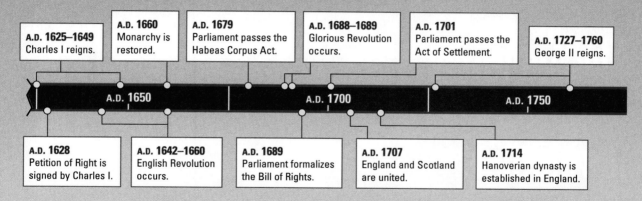

A.D. 1625–1649 Charles I reigns.

A.D. 1660 Monarchy is restored.

A.D. 1679 Parliament passes the Habeas Corpus Act.

A.D. 1688–1689 Glorious Revolution occurs.

A.D. 1701 Parliament passes the Act of Settlement.

A.D. 1727–1760 George II reigns.

A.D. 1650   A.D. 1700   A.D. 1750

A.D. 1628 Petition of Right is signed by Charles I.

A.D. 1642–1660 English Revolution occurs.

A.D. 1689 Parliament formalizes the Bill of Rights.

A.D. 1707 England and Scotland are united.

A.D. 1714 Hanoverian dynasty is established in England.

Relating Past to Present

1. The Petition of Right, the Habeas Corpus Act, the English Bill of Rights, and the Toleration Act covered many important rights of individual citizens. List the rights protected by these measures. Use American civics or government books to find out how many of these rights are protected today by the United States Constitution.

2. The British monarchy today has little power, yet the monarchy as an institution is generally respected and supported in Great Britain. The monarch still serves certain functions in Great Britain and what is today known as the Commonwealth of Nations. Examine textbooks that discuss comparative government or articles about British life today, and list some important functions that the monarch still performs. You might want to compare the political role of Queen Elizabeth II with that of Elizabeth I, listing the powers that belonged to the earlier queen that do not belong to the current queen.

Applying History Study Skills

Before completing this activity, review Building History Study Skills on page 406.

During the English Civil War, the victorious Parliamentarians and their generals sought to devise a new government for England. A small party of radicals, called the Levelers, demanded a radical change for the government of England. Their point of view is represented in the Putney Debates, from which the following selection is taken. Read the excerpt below, and try to identify the point of view presented.

"I do hear nothing at all that can convince me why any man that is born in England ought not to have his voice in election of burgesses. It is said that if a man have not a permanent interest, he can have no claim; and we must be no freer than the laws will let us to be . . . and I do think that the main cause why Almighty God gave men reason, it was that they should make use of that reason, and that they should improve it for that end and purpose that God gave it [to] them. . . . I do not find anything in the law of God, that a lord shall choose twenty burgesses, and a gentleman but two, or a poor man shall choose none: I find no such thing in the law of

nature, nor in the law of nations . . . and am still of the same opinion, that every man born in England cannot, ought not, neither by the law of God nor the law of nature, to be exempted from the choice of those who are to make laws and for him to live under, and for him (for aught I know) to lose his life under."

1. (a) What is the main idea? (b) How is the main idea repeated and emphasized?
2. What are the signal words?
3. Which ideas has the speaker neglected to mention?
4. Why are the speaker's ideas considered radical?
5. What is the speaker's point of view about men and their relationship to their government?

internet connect

Sir Walter Raleigh did not limit his activities to the high seas. In addition to being a favorite of Elizabeth I, he was also a prolific writer. Search the Internet through the HRW Web site to find and print out examples of his writing. Discuss what you have found in class.

HRW GO TO: go.hrw.com KEYWORD: SCØ Sir Walter Raleigh

Building Your Portfolio

1. **Writing a Report** Prepare a report about the Spanish Armada. Answer the following questions in your report. (a) What was the background of the Spanish-English conflict? (b) Why did Philip II want to conquer England? (c) How was religion a factor? (d) How was Elizabeth I regarded by other European monarchs? (e) How was the Spanish fleet defeated? (f) What was the significance of the English victory? You might use encyclopedias and Garrett Mattingly's *Armada* (Houghton Mifflin). Place your report in your portfolio.

2. **Presenting an Oral Report** Rulers such as Queen Isabella of Spain and Queen Elizabeth I of England supported voyages of exploration. Find out more about these rulers and why they supported these adventures. Include examples of voyages of exploration in your research. Present an oral report to the class. Place your notes in your portfolio.

CHAPTER 17

The American and French Revolutions

TIME
A.D. 1715–1829

A.D. 1715–1829

3.7 million B.C.   4000 B.C.   A.D. 2100

PLACE

North America, France, and the rest of Europe

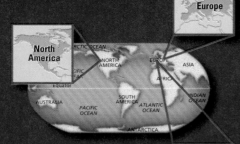

A 1789 painting illustrating the day after the storming of the Bastille

Significance

The idea that people should have a voice in government greatly influenced French political writers of the 1700s. In addition, the American Revolution, with its central theme of the freedom and dignity of human beings, helped inspire the French people to overthrow the existing government and establish a government based on these ideas.

Terms to Define

Enlightenment	conservatives
rationalism	radicals
philosophes	moderates
salons	universal manhood
popular sovereignty	suffrage
enlightened despotism	conscription
Patriots	counterrevolution
Loyalists	coup d'état
federal system of	plebiscite
government	Concordat
executive branch	nationalism
legislative branch	scorched-earth policy
judicial branch	legitimacy
Bill of Rights	indemnity
bourgeoisie	reaction
tithe	reactionaries
émigrés	liberalism
departments	

People to Identify

Denis Diderot	Maximilien
Baron de Montesquieu	Robespierre
Voltaire	Napoleon Bonaparte
Jean-Jacques Rousseau	Horatio Nelson
Lord North	Duke of Wellington
Louis XV	Czar Alexander I
Louis XVI	Louis XVIII
Emmanuel Joseph Sieyès	Castlereagh
Olympe de Gouges	Talleyrand
Georges-Jacques Danton	Metternich

Places to Locate

Concord	Kingdom of the
Yorktown	Netherlands
Elba	Saxony
Waterloo	Grand Duchy of
St. Helena	Warsaw

Chapter Theme Questions

- **Philosophy** How might applying logic and reason to politics change people's political views?
- **War and Diplomacy** How might a colonial society react to mistreatment by the home country?
- **Politics and Law** What conditions might lead to revolution, and how might revolution open the door to new political systems?

Although Baroness Emmuska Orczy wrote the novel *The Scarlet Pimpernel* years after the French Revolution, in it she captured the spirit of an age that transformed the social order, as this excerpt shows.

❝ During the greater part of the day, the guillotine had been kept busy at its ghastly work; all that France had boasted of in the past centuries of ancient names and blue blood had paid toll to her desire for liberty and for fraternity. . . .

But this was as it should be. Were not the people now the rulers of France? Every aristocrat was a traitor; . . . for two hundred years now, the people had sweated and toiled and starved to keep a lustful court in lavish extravagance. Now the descendants of those who had helped to make those courts brilliant had to hide for their lives—to fly, if they wished to avoid the tardy vengeance of the people. ❞

Like many revolutions, the French Revolution traced its roots to early political writers.

Section 1

The Enlightenment

Focus Questions

- **What changing worldviews characterized the Age of Enlightenment?**
- **What qualities of government did philosophes praise and promote?**
- **How were the ideas of Diderot, Montesquieu, Voltaire, and Rousseau similar? How were their ideas different?**

Some people who lived during the 1700s thought of their century as an Age of Enlightenment. Spurred by Descartes's methodology for understanding the truth and by Newton's explanation of the working of the universe, researchers had made great advances in the physical sciences. During the **Enlightenment** philosophers believed they could apply the scientific method and use reason to logically explain human nature.

Characteristics of the Enlightenment

During the 1700s, an increasing number of people began to believe that every natural phenomenon had both a cause and an effect. The thinkers of the Enlightenment attempted to test everything by observation and to determine the cause-and-effect relationships between natural events.

Another characteristic of the Enlightenment was **rationalism**, the belief that truth can be arrived at solely by reason, or rational, logical thinking. Because of this central belief, historians also refer to the Age of Enlightenment as the Age of Reason.

Thinkers during the Enlightenment also believed in natural law—that objects in nature behaved in ways that humans could understand and predict. The discoveries of Newton and other scientists seemed to support the idea of an orderly universe. Many individuals came to feel that laws of nature governed the universe and all its creatures. These beliefs formed the foundation of modern natural sciences.

God, they believed, had created the world and made rules for all living things. Just as the law of gravity governed the physical movement of planets, so other laws governed human behavior. To live in harmony, people had to live according to this natural law. Thus the thinkers of the Enlightenment became convinced that progress could always take place.

Crusaders of the Enlightenment

Their contemporaries called the thinkers of the Enlightenment **philosophes** (fee·luh·ZAWFS); *philosophe* is the French word for "philosopher." The philosophes were not only philosophers, however, but also critics of society. They wrote to one another, and they published their ideas in books, plays, pamphlets, newspapers, and "encyclopedias." Before and during the Reformation, the humanists and religious reformers had used the printing press effectively. Now the philosophes used the printed word to spread the ideas of the Enlightenment.

The *Encyclopedia*. Although Britain and its allies curbed Louis XIV's expansion of French rule and maintained the balance of power, France remained both the strongest political power and the dominant cultural influence in Europe. Educated people throughout Europe spoke and wrote French. They read the *Encyclopedia,* a handbook or reference book on the Enlightenment, which became the most famous publication of the period.

The philosophe Denis Diderot (dee·DROH) edited the *Encyclopedia.* He and his co-editor, Jean d'Alembert, published the first edition of the *Encyclopedia* in 28 volumes between 1751 and 1772.

The leading philosophes all contributed articles to the *Encyclopedia.* Their writings criticized the church, the government, the slave trade, torture, taxes, and war. They covered nearly every subject—many of them technical in nature—in the rational, questioning style of the Enlightenment.

The French authorities frowned on critical writings, however, and they imprisoned Diderot and several other philosophes. Nevertheless, people throughout Europe purchased editions of the *Encyclopedia,* read it, and adopted its ideas.

Salons. Philosophes gravitated to France, particularly to Paris. There famous hostesses set up **salons**, or gatherings of the social, political, and cultural elite. One such hostess, Marie-Thérèse Geoffrin, subsidized the *Encyclopedia.* Amid lavish entertainment and witty and intelligent conversation, the philosophes could meet and discuss their ideas.

Political Criticism

The philosophes critically examined the political and social institutions of their day. They tried to learn how these institutions had developed. They analyzed the power of kings, the special position of the church, and the privileges of clergy and nobles. Several philosophes attacked the idea of privileged classes. They thought that political and social institutions should be changed to benefit everyone instead of just certain groups.

Montesquieu. A number of French philosophes adopted the ideas of John Locke, about whom you read in Chapter 16. In 1748 Baron de Montesquieu (MOHN·tes·kyoo) published *The Spirit of the Laws,* in which he tried to describe what he considered a perfect government. After studying all existing governments, Montesquieu concluded that the British had the most nearly perfect form. He wrote that its greatest strength lay in the fact that power was divided equally among the three branches of government: the legislative, which made the laws; the executive, which administered them; and the judicial, which interpreted and applied them. Each branch balanced and checked the power of the others.

Montesquieu's high opinion of the British form of government was based on a misunderstanding of it. As you know from reading Chapter 16, the legislative and executive powers were largely combined in the House of Commons rather than organized into

Marie-Thérèse Geoffrin's salon in the Hôtel Rambouillet provided an opportunity for others to meet artists on Mondays and writers on Wednesdays.

separate branches of government. Nevertheless, Montesquieu's ideas carried great weight in the formation of limited monarchies in Europe. In the United States, his concept of checks and balances influenced the framers of the Constitution in 1787.

Voltaire. The French writer François-Marie Arouet, known as Voltaire, exemplified the spirit of the Enlightenment. After serving two sentences in the Bastille (Paris's prison), Voltaire fled for a time to Britain. He commented on the political system of Britain and British customs in *Philosophical Letters* (1734), which helped popularize British ideas in France.

When he returned to France, Voltaire attacked everything he considered sham or superstition. He wrote a variety of works, including plays, histories, essays, poems, and books. His novel *Candide* is a satire that ridicules everything from oppressive government to prejudice and bigotry. Voltaire was a prominent public figure, and he fought against intolerance and injustice, particularly in cases involving religious prejudice. He is credited with a famous statement on freedom of speech: "I disapprove of what you say, but I will defend to the death your right to say it."

Rousseau. Jean-Jacques Rousseau (roo·SOH) first gained attention in 1749 by writing that history repeats itself in cycles of decay and that we have only to look at Egypt, Greece, Rome, and Byzantium for examples. In his most famous book, *The Social Contract*, published in 1762, Rousseau wrote that people are born good but that environment, education, and laws corrupt them. The free and good state into which people are born can be preserved only if they live under a government that they have chosen and can control. In other words, just laws and wise governments must be based on **popular sovereignty**—that is, created by and subject to the will of the people. This idea of Rousseau's had enormous influence, extending even to the colonial revolutionaries in North America.

In some ways, Rousseau belongs outside the Enlightenment. In an age of reason, he distrusted reason, believing that it brought corruption and misery. Rousseau preferred a kind of pastoral state, free of complicated institutions. By the 1780s, many people who had tired of rationalism accepted Rousseau's philosophy. His influence was greatest in the later years of the Enlightenment.

His work foreshadows romanticism, which became significant during the first half of the 1800s.

Enlightened Despotism

The philosophes argued and worked to make a better world based on reason. They did not criticize religion and people's faith, as it might have appeared. Rather, they fought superstition, the institution of the church, and the ignorance of some of the clergy. They recognized the role of monarchy, but they disliked absolute monarchy. Most philosophes favored **enlightened despotism**—a system of government in which absolute monarchs ruled according to the principles of the Enlightenment.

In countries with absolute monarchies and strong censorship, rulers and clergy fought the ideas of the philosophes. They prohibited the publishing of books by philosophes, or they censored the books, removing any material unflattering to public officials or the church. The clergy preached against the philosophes, whom they accused of undermining the church.

Faced with this unfavorable attention, the philosophes became cautious. Some, such as Voltaire, moved to other countries, out of the reach of the French authorities. Later, other people not content merely to discuss such ideas preferred instead to act on them. By the late 1700s, both North America and France, the home of the Enlightenment, were settings for major political and social revolutions.

Section 1 Review

1. **Define** Enlightenment, rationalism, philosophes, salons, popular sovereignty, enlightened despotism
2. **Identify** Denis Diderot, Baron de Montesquieu, Voltaire, Jean-Jacques Rousseau
3. **Understanding Ideas** What were the main characteristics of Enlightenment thinking?
4. **Summarizing Ideas** Describe three examples of systems of government that philosophes found to be praiseworthy.
5. **Contrasting Ideas** Compare and contrast the ideas of the following philosophes: Diderot, Montesquieu, Voltaire, and Rousseau.

The American Revolution

Focus Questions

- How did the colonists' attitudes toward Britain change during the early and mid-1700s?
- Why were the Articles of Confederation considered to be inadequate?
- What system of government did the Constitution establish?

New ideas were not confined to Europe in the 1700s. In North America, the British colonists' new way of life and their distance from Britain began to create new attitudes about their relationship with the home country. Their immediate concerns had to do with British trade regulations and how they affected the colonists' quality of life. The colonists also disliked the French along their borders. After defeating the French, however, the North American colonists struggled increasingly with the British and finally declared their independence.

British-French Rivalry

While the British established colonies along the Atlantic coast of North America, the French developed settlements to the north and west in what was called New France. In the 1700s, as American settlers moved westward across the Appalachian Mountains, conflict with the French was inevitable.

The French and British governments had struggled for decades for dominance in Europe. The conflicts between these two powers were also acted out in North America, mostly in the form of frontier skirmishes. The colonies counted on British assistance for defense against the French, and both sides recruited Native Americans to fight with them.

The decisive conflict that settled the British-French imperial rivalry in North America was the French and Indian War (1754–1763), known in Europe as the Seven Years' War. The Treaty of Paris in 1763 confirmed the sweeping British victories not only in North America but in many other parts of the world as well. The British now controlled land from the Atlantic Ocean to the Mississippi River and from the Gulf of Mexico almost to the Arctic Ocean. British power and worldwide prestige had reached a new height.

Increased Control over the Colonies

The British built up a large debt while waging war against the French on three continents between 1754 and 1763. Because the British had helped the colonists, they felt justified in asking the colonists to help repay this debt.

At the same time, British governments during the 1760s lacked a consistent policy toward their greatly expanded North American empire. In 1763, following an American Indian uprising, the British forbade any colonists to settle in the land west of the Appalachian Mountains. Great Britain also attempted to bring its colonies under closer economic control by enforcing mercantilist trade regulations. The Sugar Act of 1764 imposed new taxes on sugar and many other items imported into North America from non-British colonies. The colonists came to believe that the British intended to curb their liberties.

In 1765 Parliament passed the Stamp Act. This law required that the colonists pay a tax—in the form of special stamps—on wills, mortgages, contracts, newspapers, pamphlets, calendars, playing cards, and almanacs. The colonists unified in opposition to the Stamp Act. They began to think as a single people instead of as people from 13 separate colonies. They boycotted British products. Their refusal to buy British goods exerted economic pressure on British merchants, who complained to Parliament. As a result, the British repealed the Stamp Act in 1766.

With each new law, the colonists increased their resistance. Some laws were repealed; others were not. The colonists argued that they had no representatives in the British Parliament and that "taxation without representation" constituted tyranny. Between 1763 and 1775, relations between the British government and the American colonies grew steadily worse.

Intensified Conflict

King George III, who reigned from 1760 to 1820, was the first Hanoverian monarch to be born in England and the first to place England's interests over those of his German possession of Hanover.

George believed that Parliament had too much power in the constitutional system governing Great Britain. He was determined to select his own ministers from the "King's Friends" in Parliament. The political world became extremely unsettled. Six prime ministers came to power during an eight-year period. Against this confusion, the crises leading to the final break with the American colonies unfolded. As the

The Stamp Act required stamps such as this one to be placed on all the colonists' commercial and legal papers.

colonists hardened their resistance to British policy, George III became equally determined to coerce them. By 1770 he found a prime minister who was willing to carry out this objective—Lord North.

The colonists were by no means united for independence. However, more and more came to believe that breaking away from British rule was the only way to guarantee their rights. About one third of the colonists were **Patriots**, who actively favored independence. Another third were **Loyalists** (also known as Tories), who strongly opposed independence. The remainder of the colonists did not take sides.

In 1773 Lord North's government allowed the British East India Company to ship tea directly to the colonies. Angry colonists, upset at the prospect of a monopoly, threw the tea into the Boston harbor (the "Boston Tea Party"). The British government responded to the Boston Tea Party by closing the port of Boston to all shipping. Colonists called this act and a series of other laws passed in 1774 the Intolerable Acts.

The Patriots took action. In the fall of 1774, delegates from 12 of the 13 colonies—Georgia did not attend—met in Philadelphia in the First Continental Congress. The delegates demanded that the colonists be granted the full rights of British citizens. The delegates also pledged to support each other in the future and agreed to meet the following year if Great Britain did not repeal the Intolerable Acts.

The Battles of Lexington and Concord (shown above) marked the beginning of the American Revolution.

In April 1775, British troops, feeling threatened, marched from Boston to seize colonial guns and gunpowder stored nearby. At the towns of Lexington and Concord, the British fought skirmishes with groups of armed colonists, who forced them to retreat to Boston. The American Revolution had begun.

The Declaration of Independence
When delegates to a Second Continental Congress met in Philadelphia in May 1775, many still hoped for reconciliation. Then news of the fighting at Lexington spread, and attitudes changed. The delegates took steps to prepare for war. A little more than a year later, the delegates voted to declare their freedom from Great Britain. On July 4, 1776, they adopted the Declaration of Independence, which established the United States of America as an independent nation. Thomas Jefferson, the declaration's principal author, expressed American sentiments with nobility and grandeur.

The Declaration of Independence shows the influence of Enlightenment philosophers such as John Locke. It states that all men are created equal and have certain "unalienable Rights." Among these rights are "Life, Liberty, and the pursuit of Happiness." This idea—the right to equal opportunity and equal justice—is the foundation of our democratic ideal. Although the ideal was not stated to include women or slaves, the demand for a broader equality and justice concerned many people.

The declaration also stated that all powers of government come from the people. No government can exist without the consent of its citizens because citizens create governments to protect individual rights. If a government fails to protect or attempts to destroy rights, the people have the right "to alter or to abolish" the government and to set up a new government that will safeguard their rights.

These were extreme ideas. It is one thing to reject absolute monarchy. It is quite another to give people the right to abolish a government that does not uphold the rights of the citizens.

The War for Independence
Each side had advantages and weaknesses as the American Revolutionary War began. The Americans were defending their own homes in well-known territory. The British had to cross an ocean, bringing with them most of their military supplies and equipment.

The war against the colonists was not popular in Great Britain. Some British even sympathized with the Americans. The British had not favored large standing armies since the English civil war in the late 1600s. In addition, Britain had no allies against the colonists. Therefore, King George III had to hire mercenaries, many of them German. Nevertheless, Great Britain's strength lay in the organization of its army and navy. British troops were well trained, and the British fleet was the strongest in the world.

The lack of unity among the colonies helped the British. The colonies voluntarily sent representatives to the Continental Congress, but progress was slow because the proposals of the Continental Congress had to be almost unanimously passed. Moreover, to meet the immediate need of financing the war, the Continental Congress borrowed money and printed its own paper money. However, because it had no way of paying its debts, its credit was poor.

The weaknesses of the American government made it difficult to build a strong army. At first the American forces were mostly poorly trained and undisciplined volunteers. The American troops could seldom successfully oppose the well-trained British army in large-scale battle. Nevertheless, the Americans had good leaders, including General George Washington, who served as commander of the American forces. In addition, other nations offered military officers, troops, ships, and money to the colonists' cause.

The fighting. Most of the fighting took place between 1776 and 1781. (See map on this page.) A major turning point came when the Americans defeated a British force under General John Burgoyne at Saratoga, New York, in October 1777. Now the colonists seemed to have a chance of winning. The French government, eager to weaken the British empire, agreed to an alliance with the United States. Spain and the Netherlands also joined the colonists' efforts. In 1781 the Americans and their French allies trapped the main British army at Yorktown, Virginia. (See map on page 422.) With this victory, the Americans had effectively won the war.

Ending the war. In 1783, after two years of negotiation, with Benjamin Franklin as the shrewd and persuasive chief American negotiator, the British and the Americans and their allies signed the Treaty of Paris. The Americans won not only independence but also a territory much larger than the original thirteen colonies. (See map on page 423.)

Military Campaigns of the American Revolution, 1775–1783

3 Captured by Americans, Nov. 12, 1775.

1 War begins, April 19, 1775.

4 First great American victory, Oct. 17, 1777.

2 British defeat Americans, June 17, 1775.

6 George Rogers Clark defeats British along Ohio River, 1778–1779.

5 Campaign of Sept. 1777 to June 1778. Washington spends terrible winter at Valley Forge.

10 French blockade, Sept. 1781.

11 General Cornwallis surrenders to Washington, Oct. 19, 1781.

9 French forces join Washington's army, July 1781–Sept. 1781.

7 Controlled by British, Feb. 1781–Nov. 1781.

8 Occupied by British, May 12, 1780. Recaptured by American general Nathanael Greene, Dec. 14, 1782.

Ft. Ticonderoga May 10–12, 1775
Saratoga
Lexington and Concord
Bunker Hill
Boston
Germantown, Oct. 4, 1777
Valley Forge
Brandywine, Sept. 11, 1777
Philadelphia
New York
Vincennes Feb. 25, 1779
Guilford Courthouse March 15, 1781
Yorktown
Kings Mountain Oct. 7, 1780
Camden Aug. 16, 1780
Charleston
Wilmington
Montreal

QUEBEC
ME (MA)
NH
MA
NY
CT
RI
PA
NJ
MD
DE
VA
NC
SC
GA

SPANISH LOUISIANA
ATLANTIC OCEAN
Gulf of Mexico

Lake Superior
Lake Michigan
Lake Huron
Lake Erie
St. Lawrence River
Ohio River
Mississippi River
APPALACHIAN MOUNTAINS

60° W
40° N
30° N
90° W
80° W
70° W

0   125   250 Miles
0   125   250 Kilometers
Albers Equal-Area Projection

American campaign
British campaign
American victory
British victory
Blockade

Learning from Maps   Saratoga marked the first great American victory.

? Place   In what state was the Battle of Saratoga fought?

The Articles of Confederation

In 1781 the American states ratified, or accepted, the Articles of Confederation, a plan of government the Second Continental Congress had adopted in 1777. The Articles of Confederation provided for a central government, with a one-house Congress in which each state had a single vote. Congress had the authority to declare war, make peace, conduct foreign relations, and settle disputes between the states.

The government under the Articles of Confederation lasted from 1781 to 1789. The great weakness of the Articles was that Congress had no power to enforce its measures. The government had no power to tax, to coin money, or to regulate trade with foreign countries or among the states. Laws required the approval of at least nine of the states. The Articles provided for no chief executive officer, and the only courts were state courts.

The Constitution

Americans soon realized that the Articles of Confederation provided inadequate government. In 1787 delegates from the states met again in Philadelphia to revise the Articles. It soon became apparent, however, that what was needed was more than just a revision of the Articles; the delegates needed to write a constitution that would provide the framework for a new, stronger government.

After unanimously electing George Washington as the presiding officer, the delegates to the Constitutional Convention turned to the issue at hand—to create a central government strong enough to act on matters that concerned all the states. At the same time, they wanted to leave the states *some* freedom to act for themselves. To solve this problem, the delegates decided to adopt the **federal system of government.** The resulting Constitution divided governmental powers between the central, or federal, government and the individual states. It gave the federal government the power to declare war, make treaties, coin money, raise armies, and regulate trade with foreign countries. All other powers belonged to or were shared by the states and the people.

The framers of the Constitution created three branches of the federal government. The **executive branch** (the president) enforced the laws, the **legislative branch** (Congress) made the laws, and the **judicial branch** (the federal courts) interpreted and applied the laws. The framers gave each branch certain powers and specified in the Constitution how each branch of government acted as a check on the others.

Some Americans were concerned that the Constitution did not offer enough protection and freedom to individuals. They wanted to be sure of what rights they did or did not have. The first 10 amendments of the Constitution, added in 1791, are known collectively as the **Bill of Rights.** They specifically guarantee certain basic rights of every United States citizen. These rights include freedom of religion, speech, press, assembly, and petition. The Bill of Rights also guarantees freedom from illegal search and seizure and the right to a jury trial.

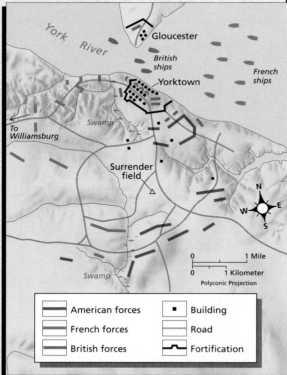

The Siege of Yorktown, September 28–October 19, 1781

York River

Gloucester

British ships

French ships

Yorktown

Swamp

To Williamsburg

Surrender field

Swamp

N
W
E
S

0   1 Mile
0   1 Kilometer
Polyconic Projection

American forces	■ Building
French forces	Road
British forces	Fortification

Learning from Maps The British were trapped with their backs to the sea during the siege of Yorktown.

❓ **Movement** What country provided the Americans with aid at sea?

The United States in 1783

Original 13 states

Territory ceded by Great Britain, 1783

British territory

Spanish territory

BRITISH NORTH AMERICA

Claimed by Great Britain until 1842

Lake Superior

Lake Michigan

Lake Huron

L. Ontario

Lake Erie

St. Lawrence R.

ME (MA)

NH

Disputed

MA • Boston

CT RI

40°N

NY

Fort Detroit ■

PA

NJ

• New York

• Philadelphia

MD

DE

VA

• Richmond

APPALACHIAN MOUNTAINS

Ohio River

St. Louis

Mississippi River

SPANISH LOUISIANA

NC

ATLANTIC OCEAN

SC

GA

• Charleston

Savannah

30°N

Claimed by Spain until 1795

• New Orleans

SPANISH FLORIDA

Gulf of Mexico

BAHAMAS

0   200   400 Miles

0   200   400 Kilometers

Azimuthal Equal-Area Projection

90°W

80°W

N W E S

Learning from Maps The Treaty of Paris gave the United States additional territory to the west of the original 13 colonies.

? Region What was the western border of the new nation?

Effects of American Independence

The American Revolution put into practice the ideas of John Locke and other political philosophers of the Enlightenment. The American experience gave encouragement to people everywhere who opposed domination by absolute monarchy and privileged classes. The adoption of democratic ideals of government was a landmark in world history.

The democracy that the Americans achieved in 1789, however, was very different from democracy today. In 1789, the states restricted voting to adult, free, property-owning males. Also in 1789, women could not vote, and the large black slave population had no political rights at all.

Clearly, many liberties still had to be won. Nonetheless, from the American Revolution, there emerged a new kind of government and a new relationship among citizens. Its final form may not have been what most American patriots intended when the Revolution began. However, their common beliefs and the economic and political needs of the new nation created a country that inspired loyalty.

Section 2 Review

1. **Define** Patriots, Loyalists, federal system of government, executive branch, legislative branch, judicial branch, Bill of Rights
2. **Identify** Lord North
3. **Locate and Explain the Significance** Concord, Yorktown
4. **Interpreting Ideas** How did mercantilism affect the British colonies in North America?
5. **Analyzing Ideas** Why were the Articles of Confederation ineffective?
6. **Summarizing Ideas** Describe the government created by the Constitution.

Section 3

The French Revolution

Focus Questions

- **What conditions in France in the early and mid-1700s contributed to the movement there toward revolution?**
- **What did the National Assembly accomplish?**
- **What type of government did the Constitution of 1791 establish?**
- **What occurred after the Constitution of 1791 went into effect?**

At almost the same time that revolution was brewing in the British colonies, disturbing events were also occurring in France. When the French Revolution began in 1789, the rest of Europe watched in horrified astonishment. For more than 100 years, France had been the largest and most powerful European nation. Within a few months, however, the king lost his power to make laws, and eventually

While paintings such as this one seem to idealize peasant life, in reality members of the Third Estate lived under harsh and oppressive conditions that were anything but idyllic.

The First and Second Estates had the fewest people, but these estates also had the most wealth, power, and privilege.

First Estate. The First Estate consisted of the clergy of the Roman Catholic Church and constituted less than 1 percent of the population. The church retained many of the privileges it had held since the Middle Ages. Only church courts could try priests and bishops. The clergy did not have to pay taxes. The church owned about one tenth of all French land and received enormous amounts of money from rents, taxes, and fees. The higher clergy—archbishops, bishops, and abbots—held most of this wealth. As a result, some of these people had become lazy, worldly, and neglectful of their spiritual duties.

In contrast, the lower clergy—the parish priests—performed most of the work and received very little pay. In addition to giving religious guidance, these parish priests tended to the problems of and educated their parishioners.

Second Estate. The nobility, the Second Estate, represented less than 2 percent of the population. They still had special privileges and customs that had originated in feudal times: the right to wear a sword; primogeniture, or the right of the eldest son to inherit titles and lands; and the right to function as "lord of the manor." The nobles paid few taxes, if any, and they still collected feudal dues from peasants. Only nobles held the highest positions in the army and government. Although some cared about the welfare of France, as a class the nobility were thoughtless, irresponsible, and extravagant.

Third Estate. The rest of the people of France—approximately 97 percent—belonged to the Third Estate. This Third Estate was itself subdivided into three groups.

At the top stood the **bourgeoisie**—the city-dwelling middle class—made up of merchants, manufacturers, and professional people such as doctors and lawyers. Many of them possessed wealth and education. Below the bourgeoisie came the laborers and artisans of the cities. The peasants ranked at the bottom of the Third Estate and often led miserable lives. By the 1700s, most peasants still owed feudal dues and services such as working on roads. They paid rent for the land they worked, the heaviest taxes, and one tenth of their income—the **tithe**—to the church. They worked long and hard, but they had no voice in making or changing the laws that kept them under the absolute control of their landlords and the king.

the people's elected representatives voted for his execution. These new rulers wrote a constitution and reformed many laws. The radical change made people feel that they were living in a new era. They began to refer to the period before 1789 as the Old Regime.

The Old Regime

How did the French Revolution happen? To answer that question, we must look first at the Old Regime. You will recall from earlier chapters that the French kings constructed an absolute monarchy in which the king's will was law. You will remember, too, that the French organized their society into three estates. Great inequality existed among these estates.

Growing Discontent

Around the mid-1700s, discontent in France began to grow. Several factors explain this discontent. The first resulted from the growth of the French population. Families had more children to support, and they needed more food and money.

Changing economic conditions in France also spurred discontent. The nobles, clergy, and some of the bourgeoisie who owned land pressed the peasants for higher rents. In the cities, laborers found food prices rising higher and higher, but wages were not going up as quickly. The artisans and peasants resented the rich, who collected their rents, lived in big houses, and had plenty to eat. The poor blamed the king for allowing prices to get so high. They loathed having to pay taxes when the nobles and clergy did not. Sometimes the poor took to the streets and rioted against these higher prices and taxes. The worsening economic conditions also reinforced the determination of the first two estates to protect their most important privilege: freedom from taxation.

Although the bourgeoisie prospered during the 1700s, they too experienced discontent. They wanted political power equal to their economic strength. Rich merchants and manufacturers resented paying taxes when the nobles and clergy did not. The bourgeoisie wanted to be able to conduct business without any interference from government. They also wanted their sons to have important positions in the church, army, and government. However, only nobles could hold such positions.

Discontent simmered among the First and Second Estates too. For a century or more, the nobility and upper clergy had disliked the increasing concentration of power in the hands of French kings. France became larger and its kings more powerful, with larger armies at their disposal. The nobles did not profit from this trend; instead, they lost much of their influence.

Mutual discontent. The various groups in French society had different kinds of grievances, but they shared the same ideas and used the same words to express them. They all talked of "liberty" and "equality" as their natural rights. Even though they meant different things to different people, these ideas of liberty and equality more or less unified France's various groups in a major challenge to the king's power in 1789.

The Financial Crisis

The crisis that now paralyzed France stemmed from many years of conflict. The wars of Louis XIV had left France saddled with a huge debt. In 1715 a new king, Louis XV, had begun his reign, and for nearly two decades France had enjoyed peace. However, the national debt had continued to grow. Wise rulers might have averted this financial crisis, which ultimately toppled the monarchy, but the Bourbons had apparently lacked that wisdom.

Louis XV. King Louis XV's reign, one of the longest in French history, lasted 59 years—from 1715 to 1774. Only 5 years old when he came to the throne, he began his reign backed by the goodwill of the French people, who called him Louis the Well-Beloved. The intelligent Louis XV might have become a great king, but in later years his laziness, personal vices, and intrigues exhausted the country's goodwill.

When taxes did not produce enough money to meet expenses, Louis borrowed more and more from the bankers. He refused to economize. Warned that his actions endangered France, he supposedly remarked, "It will survive for my time. After me, the deluge."

Louis XVI. In 1774 Louis XVI succeeded Louis XV as the ruler of France. His wife, Marie Antoinette, the daughter of the Austrian empress Maria Theresa, served as the target for all people determined to undermine the monarchy. To begin with, her marriage to Louis was part of an unpopular alliance between Austria and France. She had beauty, grace, and charm, but she chose her friends unwisely and allowed their ideas to influence her unwelcome involvement with politics. In time the French people came to hate her.

King at the age of 19, Louis XVI cared more for hunting than governing his country. However, France's worsening debt, which had grown rapidly because of French assistance to the United States during the American Revolution, forced him to tackle his governmental tasks.

Louis sought help from financial experts. They all gave him the same advice: tax the first two estates. Each time new taxes were proposed, however, the nobles protested and refused to cooperate. Sometimes they led riots that the king found difficult to put down. By 1787 the country had exhausted its credit, and bankers refused to lend the government more money. France faced financial disaster.

Reluctantly, Louis XVI decided to convene the Estates General at Versailles in May 1789. He hoped that by calling together the representatives of all three estates, not just of the nobility, he could get approval for his plan to tax the wealthy.

The Meeting of the Estates General

At the time the king called the meeting of the Estates General, France was suffering from crippling inflation in addition to the government's financial crisis. Moreover, the harvest of 1788 had been poor; because food was in short supply, it was extremely expensive. Peasants and urban laborers found they had to spend half their income just for bread.

The planned meeting of the Estates General created feelings of excitement and expectation among the people. Emmanuel Joseph Sieyès (syay·YES), a clergyman who would become a leading revolutionary, expressed the grievances of the Third Estate:

"What then is the Third Estate? All. But an 'all' that is fettered [chained] and oppressed. What would it be without the privileged order? It would be all; but free and flourishing. Nothing will go well without the Third Estate; everything would go considerably better without the two others."

The French people hoped the meeting of the Estates General would solve their problems. However, no one knew exactly what powers and rules the Estates General had, because it had not met for 175 years. Many people felt that if it had power only to advise the king and not to make and carry out laws, the meeting would be useless. They also argued about the rules. In the past, the three estates had met separately, and each estate had cast one vote. This procedure had always allowed the clergy and nobles of the First and Second Estates to outvote the Third Estate.

Some representatives of the Third Estate were acquainted with the ideas of Montesquieu and Voltaire. A few nobles, such as Count de Mirabeau, also consented to represent the Third Estate. As the representatives of the majority of the people, they insisted on having a real voice in decisions without being automatically outvoted by the other two estates. The Third Estate had as many representatives as the First and Second Estates combined. Therefore, the Third Estate wanted the three estates to meet together, with representatives voting as individuals.

The Estates General assembled first in a combined meeting on May 5, 1789. Louis XVI then instructed the delegates to follow the old custom of each estate meeting separately and voting as one body. The representatives of the Third Estate refused to meet separately. They claimed that the Estates General represented the French people, not the three classes. Therefore, all the representatives should meet together and vote as individuals.

Always hesitant, Louis failed to take action. As a result, on June 17, 1789, the Third Estate proclaimed itself the National Assembly. The French Revolution had begun. The rebellious representatives then invited the delegates of the other two estates to join them in working for the welfare of France. When the king had the representatives of the Third Estate locked out of their meeting place, they met at a nearby indoor tennis court. There, on June 20, they made a pledge called the Tennis Court Oath. The representatives declared that they would not stop meeting until they had written a constitution for France and had seen it adopted. Finally, the king gave in and ordered the three estates to meet together.

The Spread of the Revolution

Now Louis XVI tried to do secretly what he had dared not do openly. He began to bring troops to Paris and to Versailles, where the representatives were meeting. Fearing that he planned to drive out the National Assembly by force, the people of Paris took action. On July 14, 1789, they stormed and captured the Bastille, the hated prison-fortress, in search of weapons. They planned to use the weapons to defend the National Assembly against the royal troops.

The outbreak of violence by the people of Paris led to the formation of a new government for the city.

The Third Estate stood relentless in its desire for all the estates to meet together. Locked out of their usual meeting hall, they gathered at a nearby tennis court, pledging to continue their efforts until France adopted a constitution.

Independence Days

Most modern nations celebrate a day in honor of their heritage each year. For many this takes the form of an independence day, marking the date when the nation became a distinct political unit.

Perhaps the oldest independence day is August 1 in Switzerland. It marks the day in 1291 when three Swiss cantons, or states, agreed to form a union. Switzerland has now grown to 26 cantons, and they all celebrate independence on August 1.

After World War II, many colonies of European nations gained independence. Each year some hold festivals celebrating their freedom, such as the ones in India (below left) and in Mexico (below right).

Even nations so ancient that they cannot record an independence date have established a national festive day. For example, in England there are fireworks on Guy Fawkes Day, November 5, to commemorate the day in 1605 when the British government uncovered and foiled a plot to blow up Parliament.

A number of nations consider themselves to be creations of revolutions. The French observe

Bastille Day every July 14. It marks the day in 1789 on which a Paris mob stormed the dreaded royal prison, the Bastille. The French people regard this event as the beginning of their freedom.

In the United States, Americans observe a holiday on July 4, the day in 1776 on which the Declaration of Independence was adopted. Americans celebrate the day with parades, speeches, and fireworks (above).

During the War of 1812 between the United States and Great Britain, the British attacked coastal strongholds from the sea with cannons and rockets. After the British bombarded Fort McHenry, in Baltimore, Maryland, in this way, an American lawyer named Francis Scott Key wrote a poem describing the battle that he had witnessed. Later his poem, set to music, became the American national anthem. Today, as Americans watch "the rockets' red glare" during Independence Day fireworks displays, they are reminded of the link between the beauty of the celebration and the seriousness of battle.

Under General Lafayette, the French hero who had fought in the American Revolution, a people's army, the National Guard, was formed. The tricolor—a flag bearing vertical red, white, and blue stripes, which has remained the flag of France—replaced the white flag of the Bourbons with its fleur-de-lis (lily) symbols.

The events in Paris were repeated throughout France. In July and August, a "Great Fear" swept across the land. The peasants believed rumors that the nobles planned to send bandits into the countryside to crush them and the French Revolution. They feared that the nobles would hoard grain and starve the peasants into submission. Eager to take revenge for old wrongs, the peasants attacked and often destroyed monasteries and manor houses. They burned the hated documents that recorded rents, feudal dues, and other obligations. These actions showed how widespread people's hatred of the social system of the Old Regime had become.

The End of the Old Regime

Many members of the National Assembly felt that they could deal with revolutionary violence only by removing the oppression and injustice that produced it. In a little more than a month, they took several important steps in this direction.

As of August 4, 1789, the National Assembly abolished the last remnants of feudalism in France. Delegates repealed the tithe and canceled all feudal dues and services owed by the peasants. They also did away with the special privileges of the First and Second Estates.

Following these reforms, on August 27, 1789, the assembly adopted the Declaration of the Rights of Man and of the Citizen. The English Bill of Rights, the writings of Rousseau and other philosophes, and the American Declaration of Independence strongly influenced this document.

The Declaration of the Rights of Man stated that men are born equal and remain equal before the law. It proclaimed freedom of speech, of the press, and of religion. It guaranteed men the right to take part in their government and to resist oppression and declared that all citizens had an equal right to hold public office. It also assured the right to personal liberty, which men could lose only after a fair trial and conviction. The declaration stated and defined the principles that became the slogan of the French Revolution: "liberty, equality, fraternity."

These rights, however, were not extended to women. During the French Revolution a group of women led by a Parisian playwright, Olympe de Gouges, wrote the *Declaration of the Rights of Women and Citizenesses*, but the National Assembly rejected it. The leaders of the Revolution believed in equality for men, but they did not believe that women were the equals of men.

Although the National Assembly swept away the remains of feudalism in France, the Old Regime died hard. Many nobles fled to Great Britain, to Italy, and to Germany. There they plotted continuously to overturn the Revolution. These **émigrés**—French for "emigrants"—became a constant source of trouble for France in the years to come.

Some nobles remained at Versailles with the king. Their opposition to some of his policies had helped start the Revolution. Now they sided with the king in favor of a return to the Old Regime. This was made clear at a banquet at which the king and queen were greeted with loud applause, royalist tunes were played, and insults were shouted at the National Assembly. When news of this banquet reached the people several days later, a crowd led by women stormed into the palace and forced Louis XVI, Marie Antoinette, and their family to return to Paris with them. The National Assembly accompanied the royal family to Paris.

Reforms in Government

The abolition of feudalism and the issuing of the Declaration of the Rights of Man established the guiding principles of the French Revolution. The National Assembly then began to work out the details. Between 1789 and 1791, it passed many laws aimed at correcting abuses and setting up a new government.

The National Assembly reformed France's administrative structure, abolished the old provinces, and divided France into 83 equal districts called **departments.** It also called for the election of all local officials.

The National Assembly, in addition, assumed the burden of the national debt. In 1789 the assembly seized land that belonged to the Catholic Church and offered it for sale to the public. The proceeds from the sale would then be used to pay off the national debt. The wealthier peasants, who had been renting this land, bought a good portion of it.

In 1790 the assembly issued the Civil Constitution of the Clergy. This law stated that people in the parishes and dioceses would elect their clergy. The government—as a compensation for seizing church lands—would pay the salaries of priests and bishops. The pope refused to allow the clergy to accept this arrangement, and most obeyed him.

This engraving depicts a mob of angry Parisian women on October 5, 1789, marching to Versailles. They blamed Louis XVI for the nationwide food shortage.

The Constitution of 1791

In 1791 the National Assembly finally finished writing a constitution for France. This constitution limited the authority of the king and set up a government that was divided into three branches—executive, legislative, and judicial.

The constitution greatly reduced the powers of the king. He could not proclaim laws or block laws passed by the legislature. Tax-paying male voters elected the members of the one-house legislature, the Legislative Assembly. The National Assembly was dissolved, and no one who had been a member could run for election to the Legislative Assembly. Despite the guarantees of equal rights and powers, wealthy men held most of the political power under France's new constitution.

Louis XVI reluctantly consented to the limitations imposed on him. At the same time, he secretly encouraged the émigrés to plot with foreign governments. The king hoped that such plots would lead to the overthrow of the new government and a return to the Old Regime.

Some of the king's advisers urged him to flee and seek help directly from nations friendly to the monarchy. On June 20–21, 1791, Louis XVI and his family did attempt to escape to the country. In spite of a disguise, Louis was recognized. The revolutionaries arrested him and his family and sent them back to Paris.

People hoped that under the new constitutional monarchy, France could recover without further revolutionary disturbances. Instead, the king's attempted escape marked a fatal turning point. People no longer trusted Louis, and they publicly discussed creating a republic.

The Legislative Assembly and War

The new government provided for by the Constitution of 1791 went into effect in October, but it lasted less than a year. The revolutionaries had not

Two Declarations of Freedom

In the last decades of the 1700s, revolutions shook both sides of the Atlantic. In 1776 the 13 British colonies of North America declared their independence. In 1789 the French people overturned the absolute power of King Louis XVI and established a limited monarchy.

In both of these revolutions, important documents marked political change: the Declaration of Independence in the United States in 1776 and the Declaration of the Rights of Man and of the Citizen in France in 1789. The two share many features and ideas.

The French undoubtedly were inspired by the American example. However, the common elements are not just due to imitation. The documents resemble each other because both drew on similar ideas.

It was the time of the Enlightenment, also called the Age of Reason. People were beginning to question old institutions.

They no longer accepted, for example, that monarchies were the natural order of things. In this climate of critical evaluation, the two declarations were born. Both claimed the sanction of God. The Americans wrote in 1776 that men "are endowed by their Creator with certain unalienable Rights." The French in 1789 proclaimed the rights of man "under the auspices of the Supreme Being."

Both documents drew on the political ideas of John Locke, who had brilliantly defended the Glorious Revolution of 1688. Locke had maintained that men are "by nature, all free, equal, and independent." Governments, he said, were established by people and could be changed by people—if necessary by force.

There are two other striking parallels between the American and French declarations. First, each presented ideas in general terms; *all* mankind, in *all* societies, had the same rights the Americans and the French claimed. Second, each carefully avoided a clear statement on the issue of slavery. Neither explained how slavery could or should be reconciled with universal freedom.

There were also major differences between the two documents; the documents came out of different societies. The Declaration

of Independence was written when the American colonies were at war. The government in London refused to negotiate with the colonies in a state of rebellion. Early battles such as Bunker Hill resolved little except to strengthen the determination of the American patriots. State assemblies were setting up governments to replace British officials who had fled or been thrown out. Many nations, including France, sympathized with the colonies.

Thus certain features of the Declaration of Independence can be placed in perspective. Written largely by Thomas Jefferson, the Declaration of Independence was carefully composed and elegantly written. It took pains to explain American actions to the outside world. It went from general principles to a lengthy set of charges against George III. The king, it said, had proved himself a tyrant "unfit to be the ruler of a free people." The document vividly invited other oppressed peoples to follow the American lead. When governments become despotic, people must respond: "It is their right, it is their duty, to throw off such Government."

In contrast, the Declaration of the Rights of Man was written when France was experiencing a time of relative—though also uneasy—peace. The French had just recently overcome an unjust division into three estates: the clergy, the nobles, and the

commoners. The commoners had chafed under the injustice of this division. They were the most numerous and the most heavily taxed. Why, then, should they have so little voice in the government? They had successfully rebelled and formed a national assembly. Now they prepared to write a constitution. The Declaration of the Rights of Man was composed to guide those who were drafting the constitution.

The Declaration of the Rights of Man lacked the organization and the brilliant force of its American counterpart, but its purpose was clear: to remind France's citizens of "the natural, unalienable and sacred rights of man."

Starting with a statement of general principles, the Declaration of the Rights of Man followed with the listing of 17 specific claims. In this document, there was no direct attack on the king, nor was there a direct call for other peoples to follow the French in overturning an unjust government.

Instead, the document took aim at specific abuses of the Old Regime. No one, it said, should

be persecuted for religious beliefs. Those who are taxed should have a say in its proportion, collection, and duration. Public offices should be open to all.

While the American Declaration of Independence was a war cry for a society under attack, the French Declaration of the Rights of Man was intended to stabilize the new order. Yet it failed. The turmoil in France was not over. The king balked at his diminished role. Some revolutionaries wanted to spread the new order beyond the borders of France, plunging the nation into war with its neighbors. France then fell under a dictatorship that limited some of the very rights the document so eloquently guaranteed. Thus, to some extent, the Declaration of the Rights of Man was overwhelmed by events, whereas the Declaration of Independence led Americans to victory and freedom.

Page 430: Thomas Jefferson (top), Signing the Declaration of Independence (bottom). Page 431: Revolution in Paris (top), John Locke (middle), Declaration of the Rights of Man (below).

Paris, 1789

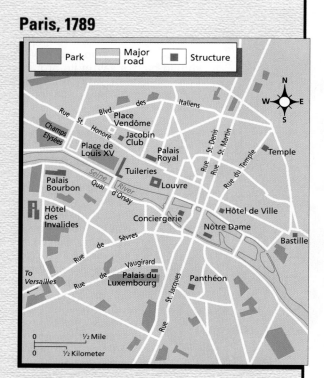

Park Major road Structure

Learning from Maps Louis XVI and his family were imprisoned in the Temple.

Location In which direction is the Temple from the Tuileries?

Revolution, the terms *right, center,* and *left* have referred to conservative, moderate, and radical political opinions, respectively.

The Legislative Assembly frequently deadlocked on domestic issues, but it united in facing a foreign threat. Before the Legislative Assembly first met, Marie Antoinette's brother Emperor Leopold II of Austria and King Frederick William II of Prussia had issued the Declaration of Pillnitz. This declaration invited European rulers to help Louis XVI restore the French monarchy.

The fear of foreign invasion electrified the Legislative Assembly. Each group in the assembly hoped that a successful foreign war would increase its own influence. Louis XVI favored war because he hoped that foreign armies would defeat the French army and restore his authority. Only a few people feared that war would lead to dictatorship. With only a few members opposed, in April 1792, the Legislative Assembly voted to declare war on Austria. It hoped to keep Prussia and the other German states out of the war, but it failed in that objective. Soon afterward an army of Austrian and Prussian troops invaded France.

The End of the Monarchy

The invasion of France by Austrian and Prussian armies touched off mass uprisings in Paris. A group of radicals seized control of the city government and set up an organization called the Commune.*

When the Prussian commander, the Duke of Brunswick, vowed to destroy Paris and punish the revolutionaries if any harm came to the royal family, members of the Commune threatened the Legislative Assembly with violence unless it abolished the monarchy. The Commune accurately accused Louis XVI of plotting with foreign monarchs to overthrow the Constitution of 1791. Revolutionary troops arrived from Marseilles to defend Paris, singing their marching song—"La Marseillaise"—which became France's national anthem.

---

*People called *sans-culottes* offered the greatest support to the Commune. The term *sans-culottes* means "without knee breeches"—the craftworkers, artisans, apprentices, and small shopkeepers of Paris who belonged to the *sans-culottes* wore long pants, while the nobility and rich bourgeoisie wore knee breeches. It became unfashionable to dress like the nobles and the wealthy, so in this way, revolution and social class influenced fashion. In the 1800s and 1900s, all men in the West began wearing long pants.

created a sound government to replace the Old Regime. They had set up a weak executive and a powerful but inexperienced legislature elected by a minority of the population.

Three factions, or groups of people with differing attitudes, sat in the Legislative Assembly. One group believed that the Revolution had gone far enough. They considered the ideal form of government to be one in which the king had limited authority. They were the **conservatives**—that is, they did not want to change existing conditions. Another group, called the **radicals**, wanted to get rid of the king, set up a republic, and institute far-reaching changes. A third group, the **moderates**, had no extreme views. They sided with either conservatives or radicals depending on the issues at hand.

In the hall where the Legislative Assembly met, conservatives sat on the right, moderates in the center, and radicals on the left. Since the French

Building History Study Skills

READ
WRITE
INTERPRET
CONNECT
THINK

Thinking About History:
Examining How Perspective Influences Viewpoints

A person's perspective often influences how he or she views events. Many factors, including education, social class, religion, age, gender, ethnic group, and personality, shape a person's perspective and influence his or her viewpoint. For example, a wealthy man might feel that only people who own property should be allowed to vote because they have a material stake in the society. In this case, the man's social class influences his viewpoint on voting rights. You can understand events in history more clearly if you can determine the way different groups of people interpret the meanings of these events.

How to Examine
How Perspective Influences Viewpoints
To examine how perspective influences viewpoints, follow these steps.
1. Identify the goal or purpose of your analysis.
2. Determine what factors help to shape the person's perspective.
3. Identify how the person views specific events in history.
4. Determine how the person's perspective influences his or her viewpoint.

Developing the Skill
Olympe de Gouges was from the lower middle class in Paris during the French Revolution. The following excerpt is from her Declaration of the Rights of Women and Citizenesses. Determine how her perspective would influence her viewpoint on the Declaration of the Rights of Man and of the Citizen and on the Constitution of 1791.

❝Woman is born free and her rights are the same as those of man. Social distinctions can be based only on the common good . . . The law must be an expression of the general will; all citizens, men and women alike . . . must be equally eligible for all public offices, positions, and jobs, according to their capacity and without any other criteria than those of their virtues and talents. [Women] . . . have the right to go to the scaffold; they must also have the right to go to parliament. . . .

Women, wake up . . . recognize your rights. Man, the slave, has multiplied his strength. . . .

A patriotic women's club at the time of the French Revolution

What advantages have you got from the Revolution?❞

The goal is to determine whether Olympe de Gouges would view the events of the French Revolution as steps toward liberty. Her words show her concern for political justice and rights for women. She believes that if women can fight and die for the Revolution, they are entitled to its benefits. Her perspective as a woman influences her viewpoint.

The Declaration of the Rights of Man made no mention of women. Olympe de Gouges wrote her declaration in response to this omission. She asserts that people who "go to the scaffold" (the platform on which beheadings took place) also have the right "to go to parliament."

Olympe de Gouges would condemn the Constitution of 1791 as a denial of liberty. It reinforced property rights for upper-class men. People had to own property to have the right to vote. Women could not own property, so they could not vote. Olympe de Gouges's perspective leads her to the view that the French Revolution was not over because it had not gone far enough in guaranteeing liberty for all people.

Practicing the Skill
How might the perspective of a wealthy factory owner and that of an unemployed laborer influence their viewpoints on a new law lowering taxes and canceling unemployment insurance?

To apply this skill, see Applying History Study Skills on page 451.

On August 10, 1792, the Legislative Assembly, coerced by the Commune, suspended the office of king. Armed Parisians marched on the Tuileries Palace, massacred many of the king's guards, and imprisoned Louis and his family in the Temple. (See map on page 432.) The Commune now ruled Paris, and the Legislative Assembly tried to govern France.

With the monarchy suspended, France needed a new constitution. The Legislative Assembly voted itself out of existence and set a date for the election of delegates to a National Convention to draw up another constitution for France. In late 1792, in the midst of great danger, with a foreign war and political turmoil at home, France faced both a national election and a complete change of government.

Section 3 Review

1. **Define** bourgeoisie, tithe, émigrés, departments, conservatives, radicals, moderates
2. **Identify** Louis XV, Louis XVI, Emmanuel Joseph Sieyès, Olympe de Gouges
3. **Explaining Ideas** Describe the social structure of France during the Old Regime.
4. **Interpreting Ideas** Why did discontent grow in France during the mid-1700s?
5. **Understanding Ideas** Describe the accomplishments of the National Assembly.
6. **Summarizing Ideas** For what kind of government did the Constitution of 1791 provide?
7. **Analyzing Ideas** Why did the Legislative Assembly exist for so short a period of time?

Section 4

The French Republic

Focus Questions

- **How did the National Convention govern France from 1792 to 1793?**
- **Why did the Reign of Terror occur, and what did its supporters hope to accomplish?**
- **In what ways did Napoleon Bonaparte distinguish himself prior to 1799?**

The delegates to the National Convention were elected by **universal manhood suffrage**. This meant that every adult male could vote, whether he owned property or not.

The National Convention

The National Convention held its first meeting in September 1792. The delegates, like those in the Legislative Assembly, were divided into three main groups. This time, however, no one supported the king. The Girondists, so called because many of them came from the department of the Gironde in southwestern France, were republicans who represented the middle class and feared the domination of France by Paris. The Jacobins, members of a radical political club of that name, were republicans who favored domination by Paris. Among the most powerful Jacobins were Georges-Jacques Danton and Maximilien Robespierre. The third group consisted of delegates who had no definite views. Later most of these delegates came to favor the Jacobins. The National Convention also included some Jacobins who were extreme radicals and wanted reforms that would benefit all classes in society, including the *sans-culottes*. Jean-Paul Marat, a doctor from Paris, led these radicals.

The National Convention governed France for three years. As soon as it met, it proclaimed the end of the monarchy and the beginning of a republic. Besides drawing up a new constitution, it had to suppress disorder and revolt at home and fight a war against foreign invaders.

The National Convention tried Louis XVI on charges of plotting against the security of the nation. The National Convention found Louis XVI guilty and sentenced him to death. On January 21, 1793, Louis was beheaded by the guillotine, a new device believed by its inventor to allow for quick and more humane executions. The trial and execution of a monarch was shocking to the rest of Europe. Even in the United States, many people were disturbed by the increasing radicalism of the French government.

What If?

Louis XVI
Louis XVI was a weak monarch who was more interested in hunting than in governing France. How do you think world history would have been different if Louis XVI had been a strong king such as Louis XIV?

The National Convention sentenced Louis XVI to death. He was beheaded on January 21, 1793, by the guillotine, a device that had been introduced in France the year before. Shown here is a museum photo of a restored guillotine.

Exporting the Revolution

Even before Louis XVI's execution, the National Convention had heard encouraging news. They were told that the French army had defeated the Austrian and Prussian forces and stopped the invasion. The French followed up their military victories by invading the Austrian Netherlands.

The decision to export the ideas of the French Revolution by force of arms alarmed the monarchs of Europe. Great Britain, the Netherlands, Spain, and the kingdom of Sardinia joined Austria and Prussia to form an alliance (later called the First Coalition) against France. For a time, the enemies of France succeeded in driving French troops out of the Austrian Netherlands, and they invaded France again.

In 1793 the National Convention took extreme steps to meet these challenges from outside France. It set up the Committee of Public Safety, one of whose jobs was to direct the army in crushing foreign invaders. It also established a court called the Revolutionary Tribunal to try "enemies of the Revolution."

To meet the danger of invasion, the Committee of Public Safety adopted **conscription**—the draft. All unmarried, able-bodied men between 18 and 25 were liable for military service. As a force of loyal, patriotic young men, the French army took on a new, nationalistic spirit. In this "new" army, men of all classes who proved their ability and daring could serve as officers. For the first time, a country called upon the talents and abilities of its entire population to fight a war. During the 1800s conscription became common in Europe.

There were armed uprisings against the revolutionary government. In western France, particularly in the department of the Vendée, the "Royal and Catholic army" fought against the French revolutionary army. The term that describes their activities is **counterrevolution**, because it was aimed counter to, or against, the Revolution. In short, counterrevolutionaries supported the Old Regime.

Jacobins, including Danton and Robespierre, controlled the National Convention. They arrested many Girondist delegates who opposed their policies.

Charlotte Corday, a young woman from Normandy influenced by Girondist propaganda, journeyed to Paris and assassinated Marat. The Revolutionary Tribunal sent her to the guillotine for her crime.

The Reign of Terror

To meet the danger of opposition and revolt within France, the National Convention started systematically suppressing all opposition. The Reign of Terror, as it became known, lasted from September 1793 to July 1794. Robespierre wrote: "It is necessary to annihilate both the internal and external enemies of the republic or perish with its fall."

The Revolutionary Tribunal arrested, tried, and executed many people on mere suspicion. Marie Antoinette became an early victim of the Reign of Terror. The Jacobins directed the Reign of Terror not only against the nobility, however. The guillotine was used to behead people suspected of disloyalty regardless of their class. The revolutionaries executed twice as many people from the bourgeoisie as nobles and clergy, and nearly three times as many peasants and laborers as people from all other classes. Danton and Robespierre sent their Girondist opponents and Olympe de Gouges to the scaffold.

In the spring of 1794, Danton made it known that he felt the Reign of Terror had accomplished its purpose and should be relaxed. In contrast Robespierre became even more fanatical and accused Danton of disloyalty to the Revolution. He had Danton and his followers put to death.

For several months, Robespierre carried out a policy of extreme suppression, convinced that only he could protect the Revolution from its enemies.

Bust of Robespierre. Jacobins, including Danton and Robespierre, controlled the French National Convention.

The Death of Marat

It is hardly surprising that the art of France reflected the shattering changes brought about by the French Revolution. In subject, in mood, and in technique, these changes are evident in this work by Jacques-Louis David. His painting illustrates the Jacobin leader Jean-Paul Marat who was stabbed to death by Charlotte Corday as he was bathing. (Marat suffered from a painful skin disease caught while he was hiding in the sewers, and he could only find relief by sitting in a warm bath.) Corday sympathized with the Girondists, who felt that Marat was a cruel tyrant.

Because of its bizarre circumstances, Marat's assassination was not a conventional subject for a painting. But David—himself a revolutionary who at one time presided over the National Convention—was a celebrated artist and succeeded in creating a moving and forceful painting. In Marat's hand is a letter from his assassin. The knife that she plunged into his chest lies on the floor. The painting's stark drama is highlighted by David's simple inscription, "To Marat."

Finally, a few members of the National Convention called a halt. In July 1794, they arrested Robespierre and guillotined him. The Reign of Terror was over.

Work of the National Convention

Despite the dangers and difficulties of the time, the National Convention made many reforms, affecting every level of French society. It provided for a national system of public education, and it abolished slavery in the French colonies.

In addition, the National Convention adopted the metric system of weights and measures. Today most parts of the world use the metric system. The National Convention also adopted a new calendar with colorful names that reflected the seasons, such as

Thermidor for the time of heat (roughly July) and *Ventôse* for the time of wind (roughly March). This calendar did not survive, however, perhaps because it also increased the number of days in a week from 7 to 10—an arrangement that met with little support among working people!

Meanwhile, the citizen army swept to victory. By 1795 the French had driven invaders from French soil and conquered territory as far as the Rhine River in Germany. Even more important, the First Coalition began to break up. A new militaristic spirit swept the country. The National Convention used the army to quell opposition even at home. It crushed an uprising in Paris in October 1795, demonstrating that the new government would not accept any opposition.

The Directory

In 1795 the National Convention drafted another constitution. Universal manhood suffrage disappeared and only male property owners could vote. The wealthy controlled the government, as they had under the rule of the National Assembly. The new constitution established an executive branch of five directors. The directors gave their name to the government that was created by the Constitution of 1795: the Directory.

Although the Directory governed France for four years, it pleased neither the radicals nor the conservatives. Prices skyrocketed out of control, and the peasants, *sans-culottes,* and all the poor people suffered. Weak, corrupt, and selfish, the five directors quarreled among themselves and were ineffective problem solvers. The economic situation got worse. When crowds protested, the directors used the army to put down the unrest. A worker in Paris summed up his feelings this way:

"Under Robespierre blood was spilled and we had bread. Now blood is no longer spilled, and we have no bread. Perhaps we must spill some blood in order to have bread.**"**

The Directory soon became as unpopular as the Old Regime. It repeated history by going bankrupt, and it paved the way for military dictatorship.

Napoleon Bonaparte

Under the guidance of the Directory, the continuing war with Great Britain, Austria, and Sardinia provided opportunities for able military leaders. During this period, from 1795 to 1799, a relatively unknown general named Napoleon Bonaparte came to the public's attention. As a general at age 26, he had suppressed the uprising in Paris aimed at preventing the establishment of the Directory.

Born in 1769 on the French island of Corsica, Napoleon Bonaparte attended military school in France and graduated as an artillery officer. He might have remained there had the Revolution not given him the opportunity to rise to the rank of general.

Napoleon bundled extraordinary energy into a five-foot-two-inch frame. He combined overwhelming ambition with a vain and domineering personality. He also proved to be a superb organizer and administrator in both political and military affairs. Above all, Napoleon had military genius.

Napoleon Bonaparte is considered to rank among the great generals of all time. Because of the dominant

Napoleon attended three different military academies during his youth.

role that he played beginning in 1796, the wars that the French fought from then until 1815 are generally known as the Napoleonic Wars.

Napoleon's genius lay in his ability to move troops rapidly and to mass forces at critical points on the battlefield. These techniques gave him an advantage over his opponents' older, slower tactics.

In Italy Napoleon quickly showed his ability. He took a small, weak, and poorly equipped French army and within weeks so organized and inspired it that he forced the Sardinians to make peace. Napoleon defeated the Austrians four times, and in 1797 he forced them to sign a humiliating peace treaty that gave France control of all of northern Italy.

The Directory worried that the popular Napoleon might seize power. Napoleon, on the other hand, continually sought new conquests to keep his name before the French people. He proposed to weaken the British in a military campaign in Egypt that would cut off their trade with India. The Directory quickly agreed because such a campaign would keep him out of Paris.

In 1798 Napoleon launched the military campaign in Egypt. It ended in disaster. The British destroyed the French fleet near Alexandria, thus cutting the French army's supply lines. Napoleon left his army to its fate and returned to France. He concealed the true situation in Egypt and made exaggerated claims of victories.

Although Napoleon became the popular hero of the time, France faced a truly dangerous situation. The British had organized a Second Coalition against France that included Austria and Russia. Coalition forces drove French armies out of Italy, and French control over the other conquered states slipped.

Napoleon's Seizure of Power

As conditions worsened, Napoleon's supporters believed that only he could win victory abroad and restore order at home. Fearing that royalists might seize control, these supporters organized a plot to overthrow the government and place Napoleon in power. The plotters wanted stability in France to ensure that they could keep the nationalized property they had bought and the power they had acquired. In 1799 the legislature ousted four of the directors, leaving the way open for change. Troops with bayonets surrounded the legislature and forced most of its members to leave. Those who remained turned the government over to Napoleon and his fellow plotters.

A seizure of power by force is called a **coup d'état** (koo day·TAH), meaning literally a "stroke of state." Napoleon himself said later, "I found the crown of France lying on the ground, and I picked it up with my sword."

Section 4 Review

1. **Define** universal manhood suffrage, conscription, counterrevolution, coup d'état
2. **Identify** Georges-Jacques Danton, Maximilien Robespierre, Napoleon Bonaparte
3. **Understanding Ideas** Describe the three main groups that made up the National Convention.
4. **Summarizing Ideas (a)** What was the Reign of Terror? **(b)** What kinds of people were among its victims?
5. **Analyzing Ideas** Explain the circumstances that made Napoleon's coup d'état possible.

The Napoleonic Era

Focus Questions

- **What course did Napoleon's career take between 1799 and 1804? What powers did he hold?**
- **What effect did Napoleon have on the rest of Europe, and what conflicts emerged?**
- **How was Napoleon defeated?**

Although Napoleon's government kept the form of a republic, the coup d'état of 1799 had made him dictator of France. From 1799 until 1814, Napoleon influenced events in France and the rest of Europe to such a great extent that this period is known as the Napoleonic Era, or the Age of Napoleon.

The people of France accepted Napoleon's dictatorship. Some, weary of the long period of chaos, wanted stability. Others were afraid to protest because they feared arrest. Instead of trying to abolish the changes brought on by the Revolution, Napoleon supported many of them. He respected most of the ideals of the Declaration of the Rights of Man and did not restore serfdom and feudal privileges. He reassured the peasants that the land they owned would remain theirs.

However, liberty under Napoleon meant only freedom of opportunity. It was not liberty from control because Napoleon believed that the people should obey orders given by a leader.

Napoleon and the Consulate

Napoleon reorganized and centralized the administration of France to give himself unlimited power. The executive branch, made up of three consuls, gave its name to the first five years of Napoleon's rule—the Consulate. Napoleon took the title First Consul, the title used in the Roman Republic.

As First Consul, Napoleon commanded the army and navy. He also had the right to appoint and dismiss all officials and to propose all new laws. None of the Consulate's legislative bodies had any real power; they merely rubber-stamped Napoleon's decrees.

Napoleon submitted the constitution of his new government to the people for a vote, a procedure known as a **plebiscite**. Under this procedure, people could vote only yes or no and could not make any changes. Even with these limitations, a vast majority of French voters approved the new constitution.

People usually remember Napoleon for his military leadership. However, his work in government had more importance and a more lasting effect. Under Napoleon's direction, scholars completed the revision and organization of all French law into a system called the Napoleonic Code.

Napoleon established the Bank of France, a central financial institution. His government also established the public education system planned by the National Convention. This system included elementary schools, high schools, universities, and technical schools. A central agency called the University of France supervised and directed the nation's schools.

The Civil Constitution of the Clergy of 1790 had ruptured relations between the Roman Catholic Church and the French government. Napoleon ended the conflict by reaching an agreement called the **Concordat** with the pope in 1801. The Concordat acknowledged Catholicism as the religion of most French citizens, but it did not abolish the religious toleration guaranteed by the Declaration of the Rights of Man. Most important, the church gave up claims to the property the government had seized and sold during the Revolution.

In a display of shrewd and skillful diplomacy, Napoleon destroyed the Second Coalition. Russia deserted the coalition in 1799. By 1801 Austria asked France for peace, and in 1802 Great Britain and France signed a peace treaty. For a time, it looked as though Napoleon would keep his promise to the French people: peace won by military victory, firm and steady government, and economic prosperity.

Napoleon as Emperor

In France Napoleon's supporters moved to increase his power by making it permanent and hereditary. In another plebiscite in 1804, the French people voted to declare France an empire. First Consul Napoleon Bonaparte became Emperor Napoleon I.

The coronation of Napoleon in the Cathedral of Notre Dame in Paris inaugurated the empire. One part of the elaborate ceremony was especially significant. The pope had come to Paris to crown the new emperor. However, when the time came for him to place the crown on Napoleon's head, Napoleon seized the crown and placed it on his head himself. Thus he demonstrated that the power and authority that he held were not given to him by anyone but himself.

The empire expanded far beyond France's old boundaries. Throughout Europe, however, people wanted to destroy Napoleon's empire. The British became his most determined adversaries once they realized that his ambition threatened their commerce, their empire, and their control of the seas. Great Britain renewed the war against France and in 1805 organized the Third Coalition. Austria, Russia, and Sweden allied themselves with Great Britain; Spain was allied with France. Napoleon planned to defeat the British navy and then invade Great Britain.

However, in 1805 a British fleet led by Admiral Horatio Nelson defeated a combined French and Spanish fleet near Trafalgar off the southern coast of Spain. Nelson was killed in the battle, but not before he had destroyed the French and Spanish fleet. Britain was no longer in danger of invasion. Napoleon succeeded spectacularly, however, in land battles against Austria and Russia.

The Continental System

Napoleon had nothing but contempt for the British, calling them "a nation of shopkeepers." He believed that if the British lost their foreign trade and its profits, they would be willing to make peace on his terms. Therefore, he ordered a blockade of the British Isles and forbade anyone in the French Empire or its allied states to trade with the British. This blockade was called the Continental System because Napoleon controlled so much of the continent of Europe.

The British responded with a blockade of their own against the French. They ordered ships of neutral countries to stop at British ports to get a license before trading with France or its allies. Napoleon in turn ordered the French navy to seize any neutral ship that obeyed the British order.

This conflict placed neutral nations in an awkward position. The Continental System and the British blockade hit the United States especially hard. Both France and Great Britain stopped American ships, but British ships did the most damage to American trade. This conflict helped bring about the War of 1812 between Great Britain and the United States.

Although the British blockade hurt France, Napoleon continued to win battles against the powers in the Third Coalition. In December 1805, he smashed the combined forces of Russia and Austria at Austerlitz, a town north of Vienna. Shortly thereafter, the Third Coalition collapsed.

The Reorganization of Europe

By 1808 Napoleon completely dominated Europe. (See map on page 442.) He forced Austria and Prussia to sign humiliating peace treaties, and Czar

As emperor, Napoleon established several institutions similar to those of the old monarchy. For example, this painting by Jacques-Louis David shows Napoleon crowning his wife, Josephine, empress on December 2, 1804, in Notre Dame Cathedral.

Alexander I allied Russia with France. Napoleon ruled the Austrian and Dutch Netherlands and Spain and forced Denmark and the Papal States into alliances.

Napoleon organized the most important of the German states into the Confederation of the Rhine, with himself as protector. He abolished the Holy Roman Empire in 1806, with its emperor taking the lesser title of emperor of Austria. He unified all the small northern Italian states into the kingdom of Italy and made them dependencies of France. He also placed members of his large family on the thrones of the countries he had conquered.

Napoleon did not limit the changes he made in Europe to enlarging his empire and reorganizing the conquered territories. On the contrary, he instituted far-reaching changes. Wherever the French army went, it put the Napoleonic Code into effect, abolished feudalism and serfdom, and introduced its modern military techniques.

Without intending to, the French also helped awaken in the people they conquered a spirit of **nationalism**, or love of one's country rather than of one's native region. In France the events of the Revolution and the stirring words of the Declaration of the Rights of Man had made people think of themselves as French, with a country and ideals worth

fighting for. Now these same feelings of loyalty and patriotism for their homelands appeared among the conquered peoples, and they wanted to rid themselves of French rule.

In 1808 Napoleon ruled Europe, but time worked on the side of his enemies. The coalitions reassembled, and his opponents' armies grew stronger. The military leaders who opposed him copied his methods of moving and massing troops quickly.

The Peninsular War

To the south of France, on the Iberian Peninsula, lay Spain and Portugal. In 1807 Portugal refused to observe the Continental System because the nation's prosperity depended on trade with Great Britain. In retaliation the French army occupied Portugal and drove its king into exile.

Napoleon then decided to conquer Spain. After forcing the Spanish king to abdicate, Napoleon made his brother Joseph the king of Spain. Resenting a foreign king, the Spanish people revolted in 1808. The British sent an army under Arthur Wellesley, the future Duke of Wellington, to help the Spanish and Portuguese drive out the French. In spite of Napoleon's attempts, he failed to suppress the Spanish uprising and defeat the British.

The Peninsular War, as this war was called, lasted from 1808 to 1814. Napoleon continued to control Spain's government, but the campaign drained French military resources.

In 1814 the Spanish, with British help, drove out Joseph Bonaparte. They then drew up a new constitution that provided for a limited monarchy. The Spanish revolt and the new constitution illustrated the tremendous influence of the ideals of the French Revolution. It also showed the rising spirit of nationalism as well as general opposition to Napoleon.

Catastrophe in Russia

Czar Alexander I of Russia, who reigned from 1801 to 1825, viewed Napoleon's domination of Europe with alarm and distrust. The French Continental System had disrupted a long-established exchange of Russian raw materials for British manufactured goods. Gradually, the czar relaxed his enforcement of the Continental System in Russia, and in 1812 he announced the resumption of trade with Great Britain.

Inefficient as it was, the blockade continued to be Napoleon's only way of striking at the British.

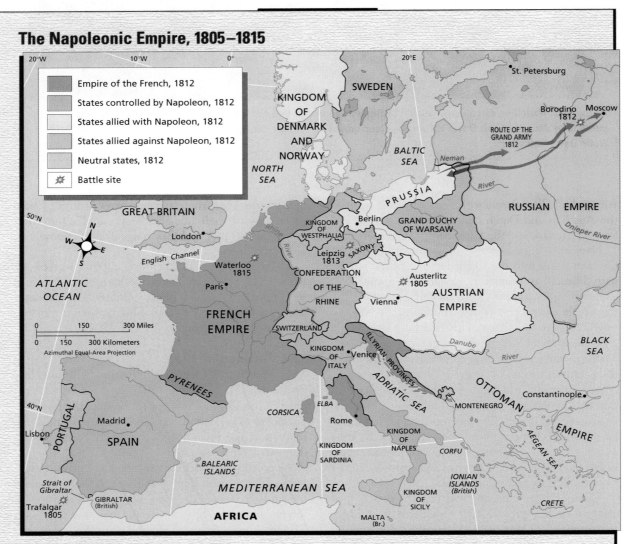

The Napoleonic Empire, 1805–1815

Legend:
- Empire of the French, 1812
- States controlled by Napoleon, 1812
- States allied with Napoleon, 1812
- States allied against Napoleon, 1812
- Neutral states, 1812
- Battle site

Learning from Maps Napoleon gained control over most of western Europe through a series of conquests and alliances.

 Region What area was neutral in 1812?

He found it intolerable for Russia, a French ally, to openly ignore it. Napoleon decided to invade Russia, and he exerted pressure on all parts of his empire to supply soldiers.

When finally assembled, Napoleon's Grand Army totaled 600,000 soldiers. However, this huge force differed greatly from the enthusiastic, loyal, and patriotic armies of the early French Empire. Fewer than half the soldiers were French. The majority of the Grand Army consisted of soldiers from Napoleon's conquered states or from countries he forced to be his allies. The soldiers had little heart for this war.

In the spring of 1812, Napoleon's army began its march eastward toward Russia. (See map on opposite page.) Instead of battling the French on the vast plains of western Russia, the Russian army retreated slowly, drawing Napoleon's army deeper into the country. As the Russians retreated, they practiced a **scorched-earth policy**, the tactic of burning or destroying crops and everything else that might be of value to the invaders.

In autumn the French captured Moscow, but it was a hollow victory. As soon as the French entered the city, the Russians set it afire so that nothing would be left for their enemies. The fire destroyed so many buildings that the French troops had no housing. To make matters worse, the harsh Russian winter lay ahead, and Russian troops lurked in the countryside, endangering the Grand Army's long supply line from France. Napoleon had already lost many soldiers to disease, cold, and hunger, in addition to those killed in battle. Faced with further hardships, he ordered a retreat to France on October 19, 1812.

Napoleon's retreat from Moscow ranks as one of the greatest military disasters of all time. In addition to the snow and bitter cold, the French troops had to pass through devastated countryside, constantly under attack from Russians. Napoleon left his army to fend for itself and hurried to France to raise new forces to defend his empire. When the Grand Army reached Prussia in December, it had lost more than two thirds of its troops. The Russian army followed the retreating French and invaded Napoleon's empire.

Final Defeat

Everywhere in western Europe, monarchs broke their alliances with Napoleon. Prussia, Austria, and Great Britain joined Russia in a new and final alliance to crush France. Napoleon faced overwhelming odds.

Napoleon tried his old strategy of striking before his enemies could unite, but this time he was too late.

In October 1813, Napoleon's forces and the army of the new alliance met at Leipzig, in Saxony. The allies beat the French decisively, and Napoleon retreated into France. A series of brilliant military maneuvers by Napoleon did not prevent the allies from capturing Paris in March 1814.

Napoleon agreed to give up all claims to the throne for himself and his family. The allies granted him a pension and allowed him to retire to the small island of Elba off the west coast of Italy.

The victorious allies wanted to make peace with France and to make sure the country could never again disrupt European affairs. They agreed that France could keep the boundaries of 1792. They also restored the Bourbon monarchy to the throne in the person of Louis XVIII, brother of executed Louis XVI.*

The Hundred Days

During 1814 and early 1815, the restored Bourbons made many enemies among the French people. Learning of the discontent in France, Napoleon plotted his return. He escaped from Elba and landed in France on March 1, 1815.

When Louis XVIII sent troops to capture Napoleon, Napoleon faced the soldiers, saying, "If there be one among you who wishes to kill his Emperor, he can. I come to offer myself to your assaults." Resistance quickly crumbled, and Napoleon led a triumphant army into Paris on March 20, beginning a period called the Hundred Days. A frightened Louis XVIII had fled into exile; Napoleon once again ruled France.

Napoleon hoped that disputes among his opponents over the division of territory in Europe would keep them from opposing his return, but he was mistaken. The combined armies of Prussia, Great Britain, and the Netherlands moved toward France. Napoleon once more assembled a French army to battle them.

On June 18, 1815, the allied and French armies met in battle at Waterloo, where the British, under the command of the Duke of Wellington, and their Prussian allies dealt Napoleon a final defeat. Napoleon abdicated again, and the Bourbons returned once more.

Napoleon surrendered to the British, asking at first to be allowed to go to the United States. Instead, the British sent the defeated emperor to live under constant guard on the lonely, dismal island of St. Helena in the South Atlantic. There Napoleon died in 1821.

---

*Royalists referred to the young son of Louis XVI and Marie Antoinette as King Louis XVII. He is believed to have died in prison in 1795.

Government of France, 1774–1814

1774	Louis XVI became king.
1789	Third Estate, as National Assembly, assumed power.
1791	Legislative Assembly, with Louis XVI as constitutional monarch, began rule.
1792	Monarchy was suspended and National Convention began governing.
1795	Directory took control.
1799	Consulate was established, with Napoleon as First Consul.
1804	Napoleon was crowned emperor.
1814	Napoleon was overthrown and Bourbon monarchy was restored.

As the years passed, Napoleon's legend grew. People forgot the war and his failures and remembered only his glories and achievements. Literature and art celebrating Napoleon and his achievements multiplied. In 1840 the British allowed the French to take his remains back to Paris, where they lie to this day under the dome of the Invalides, the magnificent home for disabled soldiers.

Section 5 Review

1. **Define** plebiscite, Concordat, nationalism, scorched-earth policy
2. **Identify** Horatio Nelson, Duke of Wellington, Czar Alexander I, Louis XVIII
3. **Locate and Explain the Significance** Elba, Waterloo, St. Helena
4. **Summarizing Ideas** Describe Napoleon's career from the coup d'etat through 1804.
5. **Analyzing Ideas** How did Napoleon's actions affect other parts of Europe?
6. **Synthesizing Ideas** Explain the circumstances that led to Napoleon's defeat.

A Return to Peace

Focus Questions

- **What were the guiding principles at the Congress of Vienna?**
- **What steps did European powers take to maintain order and stability in the years following the Congress of Vienna?**
- **What effect did Metternich and liberalism have on Europe?**

With the final defeat of Napoleon in 1815, Europe reached an important turning point. For more than 25 years, the most powerful political influence on the continent had been the French Revolution. Even though Napoleon did not always uphold the ideals of the Revolution—liberty, equality, and fraternity—he did carry its influence throughout Europe.

As long as Napoleon ruled France, the governments of other nations feared that France would export political unrest or rebellion and challenge their authority. Once they defeated Napoleon, the major European powers were determined to restore order, keep peace, and squelch the ideas of the Revolution. After 1815 they followed policies designed to maintain stability and to suppress any danger of political upheaval.

The Congress of Vienna

Stability could be achieved only by settling political and territorial questions arising from the Napoleonic Wars. The Congress of Vienna, a conference held in the Austrian capital, undertook the settling of these questions. The congress began in September 1814, while Napoleon was in exile on Elba. Napoleon's return from exile interrupted the congress in 1815, but after his final defeat at Waterloo, it resumed its work.

Despite the presence of hundreds of statesmen and diplomats, only a few people made the real decisions at the Congress of Vienna. Great Britain, Austria, Russia, and Prussia had done the most to defeat Napoleon. Their four representatives were Viscount Castlereagh, foreign secretary of Great Britain; Prince Klemens von Metternich, foreign minister of Austria and chairman of the conference; Czar Alexander I of Russia; and King Frederick William III of Prussia.

Two of the most influential diplomats at the Congress of Vienna were Talleyrand of France and Metternich of Austria. This painting by Jean-Baptiste Isabey shows the Congress of Vienna in session.

Surprisingly, the representative of defeated France, Charles-Maurice de Talleyrand, played an important part at the Congress of Vienna. A shrewd negotiator, Talleyrand wielded great influence as the representative of Louis XVIII.

The Principles of the Congress of Vienna

Three principles guided the decisions of the Congress of Vienna. (1) The countries that suffered most at the hands of Napoleon—especially the four great powers—had to be compensated for their losses. (2) The balance of power had to be restored in Europe. This meant that the nations of Europe had to keep any one nation from becoming too powerful. (3) All decisions would follow the rule of **legitimacy**, which meant that all former ruling families should be restored to their thrones.

Compensation. The Netherlands, one of Napoleon's early conquests, received the Austrian Netherlands and became the single Kingdom of the Netherlands. As compensation for this loss, the

Austrians gained the northern Italian states of Venetia and Lombardy. Austrian Habsburgs also became rulers of the northern Italian states of Parma, Modena, and Tuscany.

Because Sweden had fought against Napoleon, it received Norway, formerly a Danish possession. This territorial adjustment punished Denmark for cooperating with Napoleon. Prussia received an area along the Rhine River.

Although Great Britain did not receive any territory in continental Europe, it did gain possessions overseas—several islands in the French West Indies and the Mediterranean island of Malta. From the Danish, the British gained Helgoland, an island in the North Sea. British possession of Cape Colony in Africa was also confirmed.

However, the winning powers soon quarreled over the division of spoils. The two most difficult problems concerned Poland and the German state of Saxony. From Prussia's Polish territory, Napoleon had created the Grand Duchy of Warsaw, which he had given to his faithful ally, the king of Saxony. Russia now demanded this territory. Prussia agreed to this provided that it gain possession of Saxony.

Balance of power. The proposed arrangement between Prussia and Russia for the territories of Saxony and the Grand Duchy of Warsaw also threatened the balance of power that the Congress of Vienna was trying to create. Both Great Britain and Austria opposed the arrangement. Great Britain did not want to see Russia become too strong. Austria feared that the addition of Saxony might make Prussia too powerful in German affairs. For a time, the threat of war loomed. Then Talleyrand suggested a compromise that settled the argument. Most of what had been the Grand Duchy of Warsaw went to Russia. Prussia got the rest of it, along with part of Saxony. (See map on this page.)

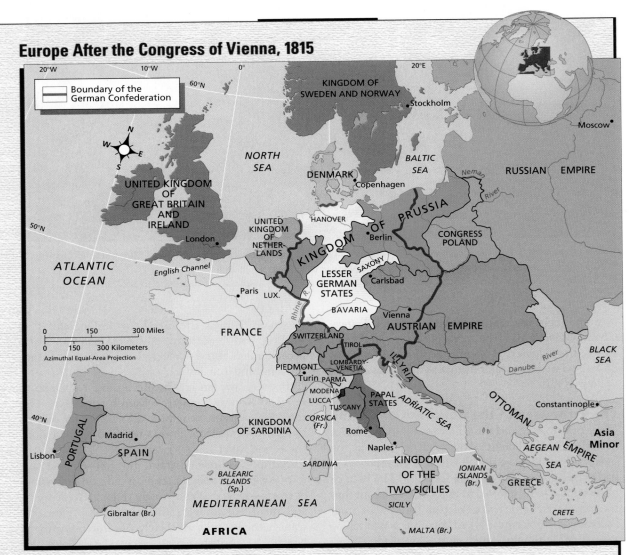

Europe After the Congress of Vienna, 1815

Learning from Maps The Congress of Vienna attempted to settle political and territorial questions arising from the Napoleonic Wars.

? Place France's territory was greatly reduced after the Congress of Vienna; what island remained under the French crown?

All of this territorial reshuffling set up a ring of strong states around France so that it could not again threaten the peace of Europe. France was stripped of its conquests, and its boundaries were returned to where they had been in 1792. In addition, it had to pay a large **indemnity**—a compensation to other nations for damages it had inflicted on them. France also had to pay for forts that the victorious nations now maintained on the French borders.

However, consideration for the balance of power prevented a much harsher punishment, which some delegates wanted to impose on France. Most European leaders realized that, for example, dividing France up among the victorious powers would cause instability in the future. Besides, Britain and Austria, concerned about the rising military strength of Prussia and Russia, wanted France to serve as a counterbalance.

Legitimacy. At Talleyrand's urging, the Congress of Vienna made settlements based on the principle of legitimacy. The Bourbon monarchy, already restored in France, also returned to power in Spain and in the kingdom of the Two Sicilies. This principle was not followed everywhere, however. The Austrian Habsburgs, for example, now dominated Italy through their new Italian territorial gains.

Reaction, Absolutism, and Nationalism

A time of **reaction** followed the first few years after the Napoleonic Era. In other words, those in authority wanted to return to the conditions of an earlier period. **Reactionaries** are extremists who not only oppose change but generally would like to turn the clock back to the time before certain changes occurred. After 1815 the victors in Europe attempted to restore a balance of power, or stability, and to emphasize a conservative view toward all things political.

In Spain and the Two Sicilies, the reinstated rulers abolished the constitutions that had been adopted during Napoleon's rule. They returned to absolutism almost as if nothing had ever happened. Switzerland alone retained its constitutional government but had to promise to remain neutral in European wars. The European powers guaranteed this neutrality.

Napoleon's conquests had resulted in the spread of new political ideas and the rise of nationalism. Groups that shared a common language, history, and culture now wanted to be united under their own governments. The reactionary powers considered this movement dangerous and tried to stamp it out. For a while they succeeded, and the Congress of Vienna left nationalist groups disappointed. Some Italians, for example, had hoped for a united Italy. Their hope went unfulfilled. To make matters worse, many Italian states were placed under a hated foreign rule. The major powers also blocked the desire of the Polish people for national independence.

The German desire for national unity came closer to fulfillment. Napoleon had consolidated many of the German states into the Confederation of the Rhine. Now more states, including Prussia, formed the German Confederation, which had 39 members. Austria dominated this confederation because an Austrian delegate always presided over its assembly.

Alliances Among the Great Powers

The idea of revolution still haunted the governments of Europe. As a result, they believed that a special watch had to be kept for the lurking dangers that might upset the peace they had so painstakingly created.

The Quadruple Alliance. The four allies that had finally defeated Napoleon—Great Britain, Austria, Russia, and Prussia—agreed in 1815 to continue their alliance. The chief purpose of the Quadruple Alliance was to discuss common interests and help maintain peace. Members of the alliance agreed to hold periodic conferences to keep the major powers in agreement on matters that concerned them all.

The Holy Alliance. Czar Alexander I of Russia held strong religious ideals. He believed that Christian moral principles and a strong sense of duty should guide monarchs. He also firmly believed in absolute monarchy. Shortly before joining the Quadruple Alliance, he urged that all rulers pledge themselves to rule as Christian princes by signing an agreement called the Holy Alliance. All the rulers of Europe signed it except the British king; the Turkish sultan, who was not a Christian; and the pope, who refused to be instructed in Christian principles by the Orthodox czar. Historians view the document as a major symbol of the conservatism that existed during this period. Metternich and Castlereagh personally viewed the agreement as an insignificant document and a meaningless event.

The Concert of Europe. Out of the more practical Quadruple Alliance grew what was called the Concert of Europe—a form of international government by concert, or agreement. It was aimed at maintaining peace and the status quo (a Latin phrase meaning roughly "the condition in which things exist"). In this case, the status quo meant maintaining the balance of power established by the Congress of Vienna.

The first of the periodic conferences provided for by the Quadruple Alliance met in 1818. France, having fulfilled the terms of the peace settlements, returned to the European family of nations and was admitted to the Quadruple Alliance, making it the Quintuple Alliance. The Concert of Europe succeeded in peacefully solving several international disputes, setting a precedent for future international organizations. The Concert of Europe continued to be effective until 1848.

The Age of Metternich

For 30 years after the Congress of Vienna, Prince Metternich influenced Europe so strongly that the period is sometimes known as the Age of Metternich.

---

* Today, liberalism is identified with government programs that seek to protect the individual, such as Social Security.

A reactionary, Metternich believed strongly in absolute monarchy. He looked with fear and horror at liberalism. The movement known as **liberalism*** extended the principles of the American and French Revolutions with their ideals of individual rights and the rule of law. Metternich believed in suppressing such ideas as freedom of speech and of the press.

Metternich aimed to prevent war or revolution and to preserve absolutism. He had little difficulty achieving these goals in Austria. To meet these ends, he set up an efficient secret police system to spy on revolutionary organizations and individuals.

Because Austria controlled the German Confederation, Metternich persuaded the rulers of most German states to adopt the same methods. In France, King Louis XVIII moved cautiously in domestic affairs. However, he willingly joined in suppressing revolutions elsewhere.

Metternich (shown in painting) was instrumental in the reorganization of Europe after the Napoleonic Era.

Political Liberalism

The ideas of liberals greatly influenced politics during the 1800s. These ideas could be seen in the internal political conflicts of Great Britain, France, Italy, Germany, and the United States. Liberalism took many different forms in these countries, but certain key ideas remained identical. These included a belief in the importance of individual liberties, such as freedom of thought, religion, and economic opportunity. Above all, liberals hated the tyranny of absolute rule. Thus they worked to secure constitutions and other legal safeguards to limit governmental authority and protect civil liberties. On the other hand, most liberals during this period did not believe that all people should have the right to vote. Instead, most liberals believed that voting should be limited to men with property.

Reaction to Metternich

Liberals reacted strongly to the decisions of the Congress of Vienna and to Metternich's actions. A number of uprisings occurred in Europe, and Metternich turned the Concert of Europe into an instrument of suppression. Whenever a threat to the status quo arose, representatives of the five powers gathered to discuss ways of handling it. Austria, Russia, and Prussia, in particular, were zealous in their efforts to thwart revolutions.

Great Britain, however, had no desire to intervene in other nations' affairs. It opposed interfering in the attempts of liberal popular movements to overthrow absolute rulers. Great Britain itself had a representative government. The British people as a whole sympathized with liberal popular movements in their struggles to institute similar governments. Furthermore, Great Britain had national interests that were different from those of other European nations. Great Britain withdrew from the Quintuple Alliance in 1822, and under the influence of a new foreign secretary, George Canning, increasingly turned away from the autocratic states of the continent.

The Metternich System in Operation

For a time, the Metternich system operated successfully. When discontent flared up among German university students in 1819, Metternich called together the leaders of the larger states of the German Confederation at Carlsbad in Bohemia. At his insistence, they adopted measures known as the Carlsbad Decrees. The decrees placed students and faculty members under strict watch. They censored newspapers and periodicals and authorized an organization to search for secret revolutionary activities. These measures prohibited political reforms that conflicted with absolute monarchy.

As repression increased, several underground movements that opposed the status quo were initiated. In 1820 a revolt in Spain forced King Ferdinand VII to restore the constitution he had abolished. This alarmed the four continental members of the Quintuple Alliance. Despite British protests, they sent a French army to Spain. In 1823 they restored Ferdinand to power, brutally crushing the revolt and its leaders.

The Spanish revolt inspired other uprisings in the 1820s. In the kingdom of the Two Sicilies, revolutionaries forced the ruler to grant a constitution. An Austrian army put down this revolt.

In 1821 nationalism upset the international order when the Greeks revolted against the Ottoman Turks. Influenced by Metternich, European rulers ignored Greek pleas for aid. However, many individuals supported the Greeks, either as volunteers or by sending arms. One volunteer was Lord Byron, the British poet, who died of a fever in Greece in 1824.

Finally, Russia, Great Britain, and France brought pressure on the Ottoman sultan. By the Treaty of Adrianople in 1829, Greece became an independent state. Greek independence demonstrated the first real failure of the Metternich system in Europe. This successful attempt at independence showed that the sense of nationalism encouraged by the French Revolution could not be suppressed forever.

Section 6 Review

1. **Define** legitimacy, indemnity, reaction, reactionaries, liberalism
2. **Identify** Castlereagh, Talleyrand, Metternich
3. **Locate and Explain the Significance** Kingdom of the Netherlands, Saxony, Grand Duchy of Warsaw
4. **Understanding Ideas** Describe the guiding principles at the Congress of Vienna.
5. **Summarizing Ideas** Describe the alliances made by the European powers in the years after Napoleon.
6. **Synthesizing Ideas** Explain the interplay between Metternich and liberalism in Europe.

Chapter 17 Review

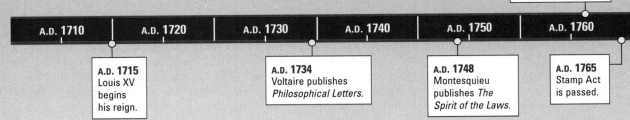

A.D. **1762**
Rousseau publishes
The Social Contract.

A.D. **1710** A.D. **1720** A.D. **1730** A.D. **1740** A.D. **1750** A.D. **1760**

A.D. **1715**
Louis XV
begins
his reign.

A.D. **1734**
Voltaire publishes
Philosophical Letters.

A.D. **1748**
Montesquieu
publishes *The
Spirit of the Laws*.

A.D. **1765**
Stamp Act
is passed.

Chapter Summary

The following list contains the key concepts you have learned about the American Revolution, the French Revolution, and the Napoleonic Era.

1. During the Enlightenment, thinkers began to criticize the established political institutions.
2. The philosophes included Diderot, Montesquieu, Voltaire, and Rousseau.
3. Great Britain had been involved in worldwide conflicts from 1754 to 1763. This left the British heavily in debt. However, when they attempted to tax their North American colonies, they met opposition.
4. The American colonists disagreed with the way the British governed them. Unable to change British policy, the thirteen colonies chose independence.
5. Discontent that existed in France and Louis XVI's failure to solve the government's continuing financial crisis were the direct causes of the French Revolution.
6. In 1789 Louis XVI summoned a meeting of the Estates General in an attempt to solve the financial crisis of the monarchy. When he insisted on following old procedures, the Third Estate met separately and proclaimed itself the National Assembly.
7. The National Assembly wrote the Constitution of 1791, creating a limited constitutional

monarchy. Invasion by Austrian and Prussian troops touched off riots that led to the end of the monarchy in 1792.

8. The National Convention proclaimed a republic and executed the king. Threatened by new invasions, an army was drafted to defend the nation while the Reign of Terror suppressed opposition at home.
9. The inefficient and corrupt Directory followed the National Convention.
10. In 1799 Napoleon Bonaparte took over the government in a coup d'état. Napoleon ruled France as a military dictator and expanded French control throughout Europe.
11. Napoleon became emperor. In response to French invasion, feelings of nationalism were ignited through most of Europe.
12. After several military defeats, Napoleon abdicated and went into exile on Elba in 1814. Napoleon soon escaped, only to be defeated again at Waterloo.
13. The Congress of Vienna and alliances that were established later attempted to restore the status quo in Europe.
14. The ideals of liberalism and nationalism could not be suppressed. In the 1820s, rebellions against reactionary policies broke out in several European countries.

Reviewing Important Terms

On a separate sheet of paper, match each of the following terms with the correct definition below.

a. Enlightenment
b. scorched-earth policy
c. federal system of government
d. popular sovereignty
e. department
f. conscription
g. coup d'état
h. conservatives
i. bourgeoisie
j. executive branch

_____ 1. Movement stressing the use of reason to explain human nature logically
_____ 2. City-dwelling middle class in France
_____ 3. One of 83 administrative districts in France
_____ 4. People who do not want to change conditions as they exist
_____ 5. Government in which power is divided between the central government and states
_____ 6. Government policy requiring people to serve in the army
_____ 7. Burning or destroying crops and everything else that might be of value to the enemy

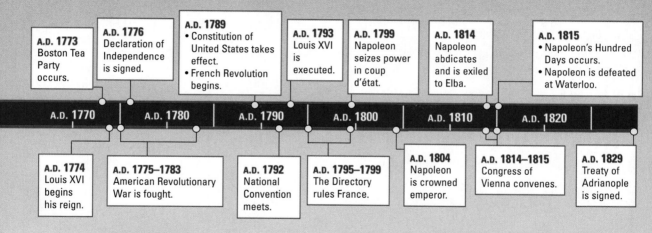

A.D. 1773 Boston Tea Party occurs.

A.D. 1776 Declaration of Independence is signed.

A.D. 1789
• Constitution of United States takes effect.
• French Revolution begins.

A.D. 1793 Louis XVI is executed.

A.D. 1799 Napoleon seizes power in coup d'état.

A.D. 1814 Napoleon abdicates and is exiled to Elba.

A.D. 1815
• Napoleon's Hundred Days occurs.
• Napoleon is defeated at Waterloo.

A.D. 1770 A.D. 1780 A.D. 1790 A.D. 1800 A.D. 1810 A.D. 1820

A.D. 1774 Louis XVI begins his reign.

A.D. 1775–1783 American Revolutionary War is fought.

A.D. 1792 National Convention meets.

A.D. 1795–1799 The Directory rules France.

A.D. 1804 Napoleon is crowned emperor.

A.D. 1814–1815 Congress of Vienna convenes.

A.D. 1829 Treaty of Adrianople is signed.

_____ 8. Seizure of power by force
_____ 9. Government by free choice of the people
_____ 10. Division of American government that enforces the laws

Developing Critical Thinking Skills

1. **Understanding Ideas** (a) What were the major ideas of the Enlightenment? (b) How did Diderot help spread these ideas?
2. **Evaluating Ideas** The Declaration of Independence and the U.S. Constitution have been called documents for the ages. Do you agree with this description? Explain.
3. **Analyzing Ideas** (a) What were the lasting social, political, and cultural effects of the French Revolution? (b) Given these effects, do you think the French Revolution was successful? Why or why not?
4. **Synthesizing Ideas** Who do you think had a greater impact on Europe in the 1800s—Metternich or Napoleon? Supply evidence from this chapter.

Relating Geography to History

Compare the map of Napoleonic Europe on page 442 with the map of Europe after the Congress of Vienna on page 446. Then write a paragraph describing the resulting boundary changes.

Relating Past to Present

1. The French Revolution completely altered the political structure of Europe. (a) What effects are revolutions having on life in today's world? (b) Where are revolutions currently taking place?
2. Compared to the disciplined methods of the British soldiers, the North American colonists' techniques were guerrilla warfare. (a) How is guerrilla warfare conducted? (b) Why has this type of warfare often been effective against trained, disciplined armies?

Applying History Study Skills

Before completing this activity, review Building History Study Skills on page 433.

Edmund Burke was a member of the British Parliament during the American and French Revolutions. During the unrest leading up to the American Revolution, he urged Parliament to compromise with the colonists' demands. In 1790 he published his *Reflections on the Revolution in France.* Read the excerpt below and explain how his perspective influences the way in which he views the events of the French Revolution.

"The fresh ruins of France, which shock our feelings wherever we can turn our eyes, are not the devastation of civil war; they are the sad but instructive monuments of rash and ignorant counsel in time of profound peace...Whilst they are possessed of these notions, it is vain to talk to them of the practice of their ancestors, the fundamental laws of their country, the fixed form of a constitution, whose merits are confirmed by the solid test of long experience...

They have the 'rights of men.'...But to form a free government; that is, to temper together these opposite elements of liberty and restraint in one consistent work, requires much thought, deep reflection, . . . [a] powerful and combining mind. This I do not find in those who take the lead in the National Assembly."

internet connect

Search the Internet through the HRW Web site for information on one of the major battles of the American Revolution. (There are several military history sites on the Internet.) Describe the battle's significance.

GO TO: go.hrw.com
KEYWORD: SC0
American Revolution

Building Your Portfolio

1. **Preparing a Book Report** Read *A Tale of Two Cities* by Charles Dickens. Describe how the French Revolution affected the lives of the main characters. Place the book report in your portfolio.
2. **Writing an Essay** Describe how the ideas of Montesquieu and Rousseau were reflected in the Declaration of the Rights of Man and the French constitutional monarchy set up by the National Assembly in 1791. Place the essay in your portfolio.

Asia in Transition

TIME

A.D. **1368–1868**

A.D. **1368–1868**

3.7 million B.C. | 4000 B.C. | A.D. 2100

PLACE

China, Japan, Southwest Asia, and India

China

ARCTIC OCEAN

NORTH
AMERICA

EUROPE

ASIA

PACIFIC
OCEAN

AFRICA

Equator

SOUTH
AMERICA

ATLANTIC
OCEAN

INDIAN
OCEAN

AUSTRALIA

PACIFIC
OCEAN

ANTARCTICA

Japan

Southwest Asia

India

The Imperial Palace in the Forbidden City (Beijing, China)

Significance

Between 1400 and the mid-1800s, many of the major countries in Asia reached a political and cultural peak and then began to decline. In China and Japan, following centuries of remarkable political and technological achievement, rulers attempted to keep their countries stable and orderly and to prevent change by limiting contact with the outside world. This policy, however, had a price. Although China and Japan had built civilizations at least as sophisticated as those in Europe, these civilizations gradually slowed their courses of progress without ideas and innovations from other countries.

The Ottoman, Mughal, and Persian Safavid Empires reached the zenith of their political and cultural power in the 1500s and 1600s. Then decline also overtook these three empires.

Terms to Define

junks	extraterritoriality
queue	consulates
philology	sepoys
free trade	

People to Identify

Nurhachi	Selim III
Kangxi	Mahmud II
Oda Nobunaga	Safavids
Toyotomi Hideyoshi	Shah 'Abbas I
Tokugawa Ieyasu	Nadir Shah
Matthew Perry	Robert Clive
Süleyman the Magnificent	Charles Cornwallis

Places to Locate

Beijing	Nagasaki
Manchuria	Lepanto
Guangzhou	Black Sea
Shanghai	Sea of Azov
Macao	Isfahan
Hong Kong	Tehran
Kyoto	Delhi
Edo	Bengal

Chapter Theme Questions

- **Cross-Cultural Interaction** Why might a country want to limit its contacts with other countries?
- **Politics and Law** What are possible advantages of centralized power?
- **Religion** What might be the positive and negative effects of close ties between the religion and government of a country?

One of the greatest contributions of the Japanese to the literary world is a form of poetry called haiku, which means "comic" or "lighthearted." A highly popular form of poetry, haiku are very short verses—usually 17 syllables—that convey ideas and achieve subtle effects. The following examples of these charming verses are from the Japanese poet Matsuo Basho, who wrote in the 1600s.

" *There goes my best hat*
as down comes rain on my bald
pate, plop! plop! Oh well. . ."

"Low clouds are shattered
into small distant fragments
of moonlit mountains."

"Swallows, spare those bees
humming westward at evening
laden with honey."

"Scattered on the sand
like jewels, seashells tangled
in kelp and rubbish. . ."

"The best I have to
offer you is the small size
of the mosquitoes."

"On a journey, ill,
and over fields all withered, dreams
go wandering still. **"**

Asian civilizations had long fascinated Europeans. Asian rulers, however, did not always consider contact with Europeans desirable.

Section 1

The Ming and Qing Dynasties

Focus Questions

- **How did the Ming relate to the outside world?**
- **What were the achievements and problems of the Qing?**
- **How was Chinese culture affected by the arrival of Europeans?**

In 1368 Zhu Yuanzhang (joo yoo·en·jahng), who was a former Buddhist monk, overthrew the Mongol

Yuan dynasty of China. Calling himself the Hongwu, or "Vastly Martial," emperor, he established the Ming, or "Brilliant," dynasty, which remained in power until 1636, when the Qing (ching), or "Pure," dynasty replaced it.

Ming Policy Toward the Outside World

During the early Ming period, the Chinese were probably the most skillful sailors in the world. They built large, sturdy ships known as **junks**, some of which were over 400 feet long. Since the early 1100s, the Chinese had used the compass—which they probably invented—in navigation. Under the Ming dynasty, in 1405, the emperor financed a Chinese fleet that sailed all the way around Southeast Asia to India. Another Chinese fleet crossed the Indian Ocean and reached Aden, on the southern coast of the Arabian Peninsula, in 1415.

These and other voyages occurred almost 100 years before Vasco da Gama sailed from Portugal to India by going around the tip of Africa. The Chinese clearly had the ability to become a great seafaring power, as several European countries later did. However, the naval expeditions of the early Ming period did not continue for very long. The later Ming emperors—unlike, for example, Prince Henry the Navigator in Portugal or Queen Elizabeth I in England—had little interest in sea power or in foreign trade. They stopped financing naval expeditions and for a time outlawed overseas trade. Both Confucian attitudes toward trade and concern for the security of the land frontier between China and Central Asia prompted this policy.

Confucian Attitudes Toward Trade

After defeating the Mongols in 1368, the Ming emperors tried to rid China of all Mongol influences. They looked to the great ages in China's past for inspiration and tried to re-create the grandeur of the Han, Tang, and Song dynasties. As part of that effort, the Ming emperors restored Confucianism—to which the Mongols had paid only lip service—as the official philosophy of the government.

Confucian philosophy divided society into four classes. First in order of importance were the scholar-gentry, who governed the country for the emperor. Next came the peasants, who produced food and paid the taxes that supported the empire. Artisans, who made useful and beautiful objects, came third. At the bottom of the social order were the merchants. The Chinese tended to regard merchants as parasites who made profits from selling goods that the peasants and artisans had produced. The Chinese saw trade as a necessary evil, not as a desirable pursuit.

As followers of Confucius, the Ming emperors tried to keep trade with other countries to a minimum. Unlike European monarchs, who were influenced by mercantilism, the emperors of China did not believe that foreign trade benefited the country, which they saw as self-sufficient. Trade, therefore, was seen as beneficial to the other party, not to China. Government revenue came from land taxes, not taxes on trade. The emperors received tribute from governments in Korea, Japan, and Tibet. In return they gave the rulers of these nations lavish presents. The emperors did not intend these exchanges to increase China's wealth—they designed the tribute system to enhance China's prestige and security.

The Ming Empire, 1424

Capital city

0   250   500 Miles
0   250 500 Kilometers
Modified Conic Projection

N
W   E
S

GOBI (DESERT)   MANCHURIA   40°N

SEA OF JAPAN

Great Wall   Beijing   CHOSŎN (KOREA)

Yalu R.

Amur River

Wei He   Huang He   Grand Canal   YELLOW SEA   130°E
(Yellow R.)

CHINA   Nanjing   30°N

Chang Jiang (Yangzi R.)   Hangzhou   EAST CHINA SEA

Chongqing

Guangzhou (Canton)   TAIWAN   20°N

Xi Jiang

ANNAM (VIETNAM)   SOUTH CHINA SEA

Mekong R.

110°E   120°E

Learning from Maps Ming rulers moved the imperial capital from Nanjing to Beijing.

? Movement Along which waterway could a traveler journey from Hangzhou to Beijing?

The Northern Frontier

After their victory over the Mongols, the Ming emperors wanted to make sure that no Central Asian people ever again conquered China. They therefore concentrated their efforts on securing the long northern land frontier. Defense of the frontier required constant attention, and it cost a great deal of money.

To protect that frontier, the Ming strengthened the Great Wall of China. They encouraged soldiers to move with their families into the frontier zone, offering the soldiers free land there in exchange for protection of the strategic mountain passes. Peasants and city dwellers were also encouraged to move. In 1421 the Ming moved the imperial capital from Nanjing, in central China, to Beijing, in the north. (See map on opposite page.) Beijing was only 40 miles south of the Great Wall.

The Ming emperors tried to prevent the nomadic tribes of the north from uniting to create a powerful fighting force. Individual tribes that submitted to the Ming sent yearly tribute to Beijing and exchanged gifts with the emperor. In return for their loyalty, the Ming rulers gave the nomadic chiefs titles, money, and honors. In addition, the emperors had to entertain and present lavish gifts to the hundreds of nomads who came to Beijing on yearly tribute missions.

The overseas expeditions had been extremely expensive. The Ming emperors did not have the financial resources to encourage overseas expeditions in addition to financing their domestic expenses. To save money for frontier defense, among other reasons, the Ming emperors ended the long-range overseas expeditions of the early 1400s.

The Founding of the Qing Dynasty

Throughout most of the Ming period, the northern frontier remained secure. Occasionally, small bands of nomads seeking greater riches than they could obtain through the tribute system crossed the frontier, but the Chinese always succeeded in driving them away.

In the early 1600s, however, a new and very serious threat emerged in Manchuria, to the northeast of China. (See map on page 456.) There a chieftain named Nurhachi unified the many tribes into a single people—the Manchu. After taking over Korea and Inner Mongolia, Nurhachi's son and successor, Abahai, proclaimed the Qing dynasty. The Manchu captured Beijing in 1644 with the help of a Chinese general. The Qing dynasty ruled China from this time until 1911. Once again, despite all the efforts of the

Ming, barbarians (outsiders) had conquered China and established their own dynasty.

Even though the Qing dynasty was non-Chinese, it actually became one of the most characteristically Chinese in outlook. The Qing emperors adopted the culture of the Chinese and governed the country with traditional Chinese techniques.

One such ruler was Emperor Kangxi (KAHNG·SHEE), who ruled from 1661 to 1722. Kangxi knew the Chinese classics well and sponsored many important literary and educational projects. He actively presided over the civil service examination system. He supervised efforts to control flooding on China's major rivers and to build grain storehouses in case of famine. He reduced expenditures at his court and exempted many people from taxes. Kangxi ruled in accordance with the teachings of Confucius, just as the Ming emperors had done.

At the same time, Kangxi and the other Qing emperors tried to preserve distinctions between the Manchu—who were a minority in the empire—and the Chinese people. All Manchu had to study the Manchu language and Manchu cultural traditions. The Qing forbade the Chinese people to marry Manchu or to settle in Manchuria. The dynasty maintained this region as a tribal homeland for the Manchu. Finally, the Qing required all Chinese men to wear their hair in a single braid, called a **queue** (tail). The queue distinguished the Chinese from the Manchu and signified Chinese submission to Manchu rule.

The Ming and Qing Economies

The Qing emperors, like the Ming, considered agriculture to be the basis of China's wealth. They maintained traditional political institutions and generally supported traditional Chinese ideas and values. Neither the Ming nor the Qing emperors showed great interest in change. Nevertheless, change occurred.

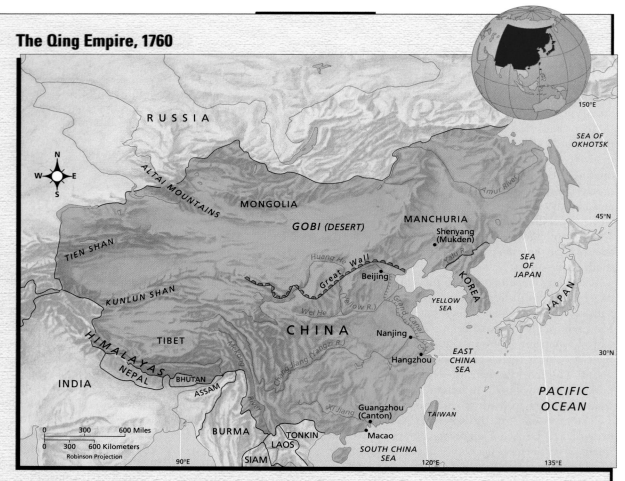

The Qing Empire, 1760

RUSSIA

SEA OF
OKHOTSK

150°E

ALTAI MOUNTAINS

MONGOLIA

GOBI (DESERT)

MANCHURIA

Shenyang
(Mukden)

45°N

TIEN SHAN

Huang He

Great Wall

Beijing

Yalu R.

KOREA

SEA
OF
JAPAN

JAPAN

KUNLUN SHAN

Wei He

(Yellow R.)

Grand Canal

YELLOW
SEA

HIMALAYAS

TIBET

CHINA

Nanjing

Chang Jiang (Yangzi R.)

Mekong

EAST
CHINA
SEA

30°N

Hangzhou

NEPAL

BHUTAN

INDIA

ASSAM

River

Xi Jiang

Guangzhou
(Canton)

TAIWAN

PACIFIC
OCEAN

0   300   600 Miles
0   300   600 Kilometers
Robinson Projection

BURMA

TONKIN
LAOS

Macao

SOUTH CHINA
SEA

SIAM

90°E

120°E

135°E

Learning from Maps   Under the Qing dynasty, China's borders expanded
to the north and to the west.

 Place   Which mountain range lies on China's southwest border?

New patterns of commerce and trade began to appear. The growth of cities begun during the Song dynasty continued under the rule of the Ming and Qing emperors. Peace and urban growth contributed to the expansion of trade within China. While the Chinese looked down on merchants in theory, in practice they needed them to supply the urban population with food, textiles for clothing, and other essential goods.

Certain regions of the country began to specialize in the production of particular products. For example, Guangzhou (GWANG·JOH) in the south, formerly called Canton by English-speakers, became a center for the manufacture of woks—the shallow iron cooking pans that the Chinese still use today. The region

inland from Shanghai, in central China, became a center for the weaving of cotton cloth. Traders transported goods from these manufacturing centers by barge and junk along the rivers, canals, and coastal waters. The goods came to Beijing, the new and growing capital city, and to other large urban centers such as Guangzhou and Shanghai.

Father Matteo Ricci, who was an Italian missionary to China in the late 1500s, gives a fascinating description of the Grand Canal and the hazards of traveling on it.

❝So great is the number of boats that frequently many days are lost in transit by crowding each other, particularly when water is low in the canals. To prevent this, the water is held back at stated places by wooden locks, which also serve as bridges. . . . At times it happens that the rush of water is so high and strong, at the exit from one lock or at the entrance to another, that the boats are capsized and the whole crew is drowned. The boats of the Magistrates and of other Government dignitaries are drawn up the stream, against the current, by wooden devices on the shore, and the expense for such hauling is paid by the Government. **"**

The Chinese shipped such goods as tea and silk by caravan to Central Asia and Russia. In addition, some Chinese ships continued to sail to Southeast Asia and India to trade, despite the government's disapproval of such voyages.

While cities grew, the vast majority of China's people continued to live in the countryside, where they increased the amount of land under cultivation. New crops—such as sweet potatoes, peanuts, and tobacco—were introduced from the Americas. The sweet potato became known as "the poor man's food" in southern China because it thrived in soils unsuited to the growing of rice. It also provided more basic nutritional value than most other food crops.

The Growth of Popular Culture

As in Europe, the growth of cities and the increasing wealth of urban merchants and artisans in China encouraged the rise of popular culture. As early as the Yuan dynasty in the 1300s, city people read novels and plays in the common everyday language rather than in the literary language. During the Ming and Qing dynasties, these popular novels and plays increased in number. Old tales about bandits and corrupt officials, which had once been recited by storytellers in the streets, now appeared in novels written by professional authors. The writings of this period realistically portrayed Chinese society and family life.

Scholarship also flourished under the rule of the Ming and Qing emperors. Under Kangxi especially, Chinese scholars wrote long and detailed histories of earlier dynasties as well as essays on Confucian ethics. As the humanists had done in Europe during the Renaissance, Chinese scholars applied intensive study to ancient writings. In the 1700s, Chinese scholars began to compile a great manuscript library that included rare works of the past. Eventually the library contained 36,000 volumes. During the Qing dynasty also, scholars studied **philology**, the history of literature and language. A few scholars, mostly Daoists, conducted studies of plants and animals.

This picture scroll shows a street scene during the Ming dynasty.

Qing Society

Qing society continued to be based on the family—a unit of people related to each other by blood, marriage, or adoption. Daughters, when they married, would go to live with their new husbands' families. The wives of a family's sons would join the sons' household.

The male head of the family had considerable power to direct the activities of each member for the good of the family as a whole. The family, like the state, reflected the hierarchies of Confucian thought.

The Decline of the Qing Dynasty

By about 1800 the Qing dynasty had begun to decline. After more than a century of peace, the soldiers of the Manchu army had lost much of their discipline and skill as warriors.

Under the rule of the Qing, government services for the people also deteriorated. China's population had grown rapidly. Between 1750 and 1850, for example, the population more than doubled, increasing to 430 million people. Peace and increases in agricultural output contributed significantly to this population growth. Chinese peasants raised larger crops, making it possible to feed more people. The increase in population, however, was not matched by growth in either the number or the efficiency of government officials.

As in the past, local officials relied on powerful local rural families, the gentry, to make the political system work. These local officials collected taxes from the peasants, sending the revenue to the government.

These Chinese silk weavers are working on a manual loom during the Qing dynasty.

In return, the emperor permitted them to keep a small portion of the taxes they collected.

This system functioned fairly smoothly for many years and made it possible for a relatively small number of officials to administer the affairs of a large country. During the late Qing period, however, corruption among government officials caused serious problems. High-ranking bureaucrats began to use their positions in the emperor's service to acquire great personal fortunes. They pressured local officials throughout China to give them money and expensive gifts.

Those local officials, forced to pay bribes or lose their jobs, pressured the gentry for more tax revenues. The gentry in turn demanded more taxes from the peasants. Less and less of the money collected went to provide necessary services such as flood control and road repairs. Instead, the money ended up in the hands of the emperor's officials.

Discontent and Rebellion

In 1796, discontent over increased taxes and decreased services erupted into a great peasant rebellion, the White Lotus Rebellion. Members of the White Lotus Society, a Buddhist cult that had been active in the late Yuan and Ming periods, led the revolt. The government succeeded in restoring peace in 1804, after a difficult struggle. The dynasty had been seriously weakened, however, and in subsequent years it weakened further. The basic causes of discontent remained, and other uprisings and rebellions occurred frequently after 1850.

The Qing dynasty seemed to be following in the footsteps of previous Chinese dynasties. It had claimed the Mandate of Heaven after victories in battle and had achieved great heights. Now a discontented people challenged the dynasty. If the pattern of past Chinese history had repeated itself, eventually a powerful rival to the Qing emperor would have emerged, defeated the Qing army in battle, and claimed the Mandate of Heaven for himself. The new emperor would then have established a new and more vigorous dynasty.

Chinese history did not follow that traditional pattern now, however, because new influences appeared from abroad. Just as the Qing dynasty started its decline, new peoples appeared in China—the Europeans. Before very long, an unprecedented series of crises developed in China.

The Portuguese in China

Around 1514, the first Portuguese ships reached the southeastern coast of China. After years of negotiation, the Chinese allowed the Portuguese to establish a trading station at Macao in 1557.

Portugal's impact, however, was not limited to trade. The Jesuit missionaries who arrived on Portuguese ships enjoyed considerable success in China. They used their knowledge of astronomy to gain admission to the emperor's circle. By helping to revise the Chinese calendar, they proved themselves useful to the emperor, whose duties still included predicting eclipses and the timing of the seasons. The emperor appointed the Jesuit missionaries to official positions in his palace, giving them the opportunity to convert a number of high-ranking Chinese officials to Christianity.

In the 1700s, however, the Qing emperors turned against the Jesuits, claiming that they had become too much involved in Chinese politics. The emperors denounced Christianity as a subversive, anti-Confucian sect. After that, the number of converts to Christianity dwindled.

The British in China

In the early 1700s, British ships began arriving frequently at Guangzhou, where the British had established a trading post in the late 1600s. The British came to China to buy silk and tea, which the Dutch had introduced to Europe in the 1600s. Great Britain was rapidly becoming a land of tea drinkers, and the British regarded Chinese teas as the best in the world.

The British East India Company monopolized the new trade in Chinese teas. The company agreed to accept Chinese restrictions on its activities in order to get adequate supplies of tea. The Chinese allowed company ships to dock only at Guangzhou and to trade only with a small number of officially licensed Chinese merchants. These Chinese merchants in turn paid large fees to the Chinese government. Only a few representatives of the British East India Company were permitted to stay in Guangzhou,

This early map of Nanking, China, indicates the location of Jesuit missions there.

where they lived in a special foreign settlement outside the city walls.

For a time the Chinese government succeeded in isolating the British with these trading and housing restrictions. They kept contact between the British and the Chinese to a minimum. In the late 1700s, however, two new developments led to a deterioration in British-Chinese relations and eventually resulted in war between these two countries.

Free trade ideas. The first development was the spread of **free trade** ideas from the West. The concept of free trade, which developed as a reaction against mercantilism, meant that government should not restrict or interfere in international trade. Not all British traders worked for the British East India Company. Those who tried to operate independently in Asia resented the monopolies enjoyed by the British company.

The British government also wanted to secure additional overseas markets for the products of British industry. It sent official missions to Beijing in 1793 and again in 1816 to request that the Chinese open several more ports to British ships. Both missions failed.

In 1834 the British government took a decisive step in initiating a free trade policy. It abolished the British East India Company's monopoly on trade with China. The British government sent an official to Guangzhou for trade talks, but the Chinese rebuffed this official's efforts.

The opium trade. The other development that led to war between China and Great Britain involved the steady expansion of the tea trade. The British East India Company had paid for its purchases of Chinese tea with cotton from India, which was used to supply the many weavers in central China. There was a limit to the Chinese demand for this cotton, however, and the Chinese showed little interest in other European trade goods. The British demand for tea, on the other hand, continued to increase. The company had to find some new product to exchange for tea. The product they chose was opium, an addictive narcotic.

British India produced opium and exported it to China in increasing quantities from the late 1700s onward. Opium addiction spread among the Chinese people, and the Chinese government grew alarmed—especially since much of China's silver supply was being used to help pay for the ever-growing volume of imported opium. Chinese authorities demanded that opium sales be stopped and that all opium cargoes be turned over to them.

One Chinese product prized by Europeans was porcelain like this decorative plate.

The Opium War. When the Chinese tried to suppress the opium traffic in South China and insisted on maintaining the traditional merchant tribute system, a war broke out between China and Great Britain. This conflict, known as the Opium War, lasted from 1839 to 1842.

During the Opium War, the Chinese army and naval forces proved to be no match for the better-armed and better-trained British. A small British naval force, which included iron-hulled steamships, moved up the coast from Guangzhou, defeating Chinese resistance with relative ease. In 1842 the British secured control of a region near Nanjing, a population center strategically located close to the Grand Canal. At that point the Qing officials agreed to negotiate on British terms.

The 1842 Treaty of Nanjing ended the Opium War. This treaty compelled China to give the island of Hong Kong to the British and to open five ports to British trade. These ports became the first Chinese treaty ports. Only a fixed, low tariff could be charged on British goods entering the country by these ports. A further provision of the treaty stated that British subjects in these ports would be governed by British, not Chinese, laws and would be tried in British courts. This exemption of foreigners from the laws of the country in which they live or do business is called **extraterritoriality**.

The Opium War broke out when the Chinese government tried to control the British opium trade between India and China. This painting from Britain's National Maritime Museum illustrates the British merchant steamer *Nemesis* attacking and destroying 11 Chinese junks at Chuenpez Canton, China.

Great Britain could not hold its privileged trade monopoly in China for long. France and other Western powers, including the United States, soon demanded and received similar trade treaties with provisions for extraterritoriality. Forced to sign them, the Chinese called them "unequal" treaties. They were unequal in that the Chinese received no benefits from them; all gains were made by the other countries who insisted on the treaties.

The Taiping and Other Rebellions

An event that occurred within China made the intrusion of the Western powers easier. In the mid-1800s, southern and central China were torn by a great rebellion that threatened to overthrow the Qing. The leader of this revolt was a southern Chinese man named Hong Xiuquan (hoohng shee·oo·choo·ahn), who had been influenced by Christian teachings. He claimed to be the younger brother of Jesus and that his mission was to establish a new dynasty—the Taiping, meaning "Heavenly Peace." His ideas attracted many followers among the Chinese.

The Taiping Rebellion lasted from 1850 to 1864 and caused terrible destruction in southern China and the Chang Jiang valley. Millions of people were killed, and cities and agricultural resources were destroyed. At the same time, the Qing faced rebellions by Muslims in central and western China who wanted to create their own independent states. After a long struggle, the Qing finally put down these rebellions in the late 1870s.

The Taiping Rebellion and the other revolts seriously weakened both the Qing dynasty and China as a whole. To raise money, the government established a system of internal tariffs. Administered locally, the tariffs tended to weaken the central government even more. Then foreigners took over the collection of customs duties in Chinese ports, weakening China's control over its revenues still further.

More "unequal" treaties. In 1856, war with Great Britain again broke out over a trade dispute. British forces, with French aid, again defeated the Chinese. The Chinese were forced to sign another "unequal" treaty, which opened additional treaty ports on the coast and along the Chang Jiang. The Chinese had to allow the British to open an embassy in Beijing, the Qing capital. Other foreign powers soon followed Great Britain's example by opening their embassies in Beijing.

Building History Study Skills

READ
WRITE
INTERPRET
CONNECT
THINK

Thinking About History: Analyzing Consequences

Every human action and decision produces a consequence, or result. For example, if you stayed up last night until about 2:00 A.M. and had to get up at 6:00 A.M. today, the consequence would be that you are tired today. If you decided to work very hard to prepare for a test, the result would probably be a good grade on the test. Since history deals with human actions, analyzing the consequences of these actions will help you gain new insight into historic events. Knowing the consequences helps you understand the impact of historic changes. Consequences can be immediate or long-range, positive or negative.

How to Analyze Consequences

To analyze consequences, follow these steps.
1. Identify the purpose or goal of the action or decision that you are studying. Ask: What did the person or persons hope to achieve?
2. Identify the immediate and long-range consequences of the action or decision.
3. State the positive and/or negative consequences of the action or decision.
4. Draw a conclusion by asking: Did the action or decision help to achieve the purpose or goal?

Developing the Skill

The excerpt below describes the civil service examinations in China. As you read, consider what consequences the examinations had for the government of China.

"A much-debated issue about Chinese history is the extent to which the examination system was vigorously applied and whether it brought a significant flow of new blood into Chinese ruling circles. . . .

. . . The system was on the whole highly competitive, and it certainly succeeded in impressing upon most people the idea that they were being ruled by their . . . superiors. . . . In traditional China the sons of mandarins obviously had . . . advantages because they were brought up in a home environment in which education and the achievement of official status were stressed. . . .

However, few families had more than two generations in office. . . . On balance, it would seem that there was more mobility throughout most of Chinese history than in even eighteenth- and nineteenth-century England."

The purpose of your study is to analyze the consequences of the civil service examination system for Chinese government and society. The statement discusses the positive outcomes of the system. The examinations contributed to social mobility. Anyone could take them, and the examinations had a performance requirement rather than a class requirement. People from all classes could be chosen for positions by scoring well. Therefore, the system provided for competent leadership by the ablest people. Other positive consequences included an emphasis on education, since education was the best means of securing a position in the civil service. It was also a movement away from the traditional pattern of heredity determining ability.

What were the overall consequences of the civil service examination system for Chinese government and society? The civil service examination system rewarded talent, not birth, and promoted education and efficient government.

Practicing the Skill

In a local newspaper, read an article that deals with a government decision or policy. Then analyze the consequences that this decision or policy might have.

To apply this skill, see Applying History Study Skills on page 477.

Chinese scholars collating classic texts

In addition, Great Britain took possession of a small section of the Chinese mainland that was located opposite of Hong Kong, and the Chinese government had to pledge to protect Christian missionaries and their converts.

In separate treaties, Russia gained even more than trade privileges and extraterritoriality. It received territory north of the Amur River and east of the Ussuri River, bordering on the Sea of Japan. In the southern part of this newly gained territory, the Russians founded the port of Vladivostok.

Section 1 Review

1. **Define** junks, queue, philology, free trade, extraterritoriality
2. **Identify** Nurhachi, Kangxi, Hong Xiuquan
3. **Locate and Explain the Significance** Beijing, Manchuria, Guangzhou, Macao
4. **Understanding Ideas** Why did foreign trade and overseas explorations decline during the Ming dynasty?
5. **Interpreting Ideas** (a) What cultural developments took place during the Ming and Qing dynasties? (b) What led to the decline of the Qing dynasty?
6. **Analyzing Ideas** Analyze the impact that contact with Europeans had on China.

Section 2

The Tokugawa Shoguns in Japan

Focus Questions

- **What were the strengths of the Tokugawa shoguns in Japan?**
- **What was society like under the rule of the Tokugawa shoguns?**
- **How did Japan's isolation end?**

China's culture influenced that of early Japan. Until the late 1500s, however, feudal Japan followed a course of political development more like that of Europe than of China.

In the late 1400s, the Japanese local lords—daimyo—began to fight among themselves for survival and supremacy. The struggle among the daimyo resulted in the creation of a political system that was a cross between feudalism and centralized monarchy. The Japanese established this hybrid system during the Tokugawa (TOH·KOOHG·AH·WAH) shogunate, in 1603. It survived until 1868.

Founding of the Tokugawa Shogunate

In 1467, rival branches of the Ashikaga family in Japan became involved in a dispute over the selection of the next shogun. This conflict marked the beginning of 100 years of almost constant warfare in Japan. A number of local daimyo, sensing the weakness of the Ashikaga, fought for control of the country. A series of three daimyo emerged in the late 1500s as victors in this long struggle. They succeeded in establishing themselves as overlords of the other daimyo, and they created a centralized feudal system.

Oda Nobunaga. The first of these overlords, Oda Nobunaga (ohd·ah noh·boo·NAH·gah), began his career as a minor daimyo. He succeeded, by means of conquest and alliances, in capturing the city of Kyoto in 1568. Nobunaga ended the Ashikaga shogunate in 1573 and then started to consolidate his power in central Japan. Before he could defeat his remaining rivals, however, one of his own vassals killed him in 1582.

Toyotomi Hideyoshi. Another vassal, Toyotomi (toh·yoh·toh·mee) Hideyoshi, leader of Nobunaga's army, assumed Nobunaga's position as overlord after he was murdered. Born in 1536 to a humble peasant family, Hideyoshi had risen to a high position—from warrior to general—in Nobunaga's army. In the 1580s Hideyoshi defeated several powerful daimyo in battle, and by threats and diplomacy he forced the others to pledge their loyalty to him.

Hideyoshi did not totally destroy the defeated daimyo, but he weakened them by reducing the size of their territories so that they could not threaten him again. He also carried out a "sword hunt" to disarm the peasants. Thereafter, peasants could no longer rise to become warriors. Only men born into warrior families could become warriors.

In 1592, and again in 1597, the ambitious Hideyoshi sent his army to invade Korea. He wanted to build an extensive empire and give Japanese warriors an opportunity to do battle. At first the Japanese invasion force succeeded. As the battles continued, however, a Chinese army that was aiding the Koreans pushed the Japanese invaders back to the coast.

Japanese warriors regularly exercised and meditated to keep fit for battle.

When Hideyoshi died in 1598, the Japanese withdrew to their homeland.

Tokugawa Ieyasu. Hideyoshi's most powerful vassal, Tokugawa Ieyasu, succeeded him as overlord. Ieyasu established his capital at Edo (AY·doh), the city that is now Tokyo. (See map on page 465.) Other daimyo resisted Ieyasu, but he defeated them in 1600. Then, in 1603, he became shogun. The Tokugawa family retained the title of shogun for more than 250 years, establishing a government known as the Tokugawa shogunate.

Tokugawa Ieyasu crushed his defeated rivals. He took away much of their land and made them swear oaths of loyalty to him and his family. He allowed other daimyo, who then numbered about 260, to keep possession of their private domains. However, he reserved for himself the right to expand or reduce the size of their territories in the future.

Within his own domain, each daimyo governed almost as an absolute ruler. The local peasants paid taxes that the daimyo used to support both himself and those in his service, such as the samurai. The Tokugawa family had its own very large domain, which comprised about one fourth of the productive land in Japan. Thus, the Tokugawa did not rule the entire country directly, nor did they personally tax the entire population. In this way Japan maintained a degree of political and economic decentralization.

Tokugawa Power

As overlords the Tokugawa did have considerable influence over the behavior of the daimyo. Behind this influence lay the Tokugawa wealth and military power. The Tokugawa shoguns prohibited daimyo alliances. Most daimyo had to spend every other year in Edo, the shogun's capital, and they left their families there as hostages when they returned to their own domains. The expense of maintaining two grand residences—one in Edo and one in the provinces—and of traveling to and from Edo in elaborate processions drained the financial resources of the daimyo. Living in Edo also tended to transform them from warriors into courtiers. In this manner the Tokugawa shoguns maintained control over the daimyo.

The Tokugawa shogunate shaped Japanese life in several ways. By establishing a strong central government, the shoguns brought more than two centuries of stability to Japan. Their control of the daimyo helped to keep peace in the countryside. In addition, by setting trade restrictions and limiting contact with foreigners, they achieved almost complete isolation from Europe by 1650. This was a response to the growing contact with foreigners that had occurred over the previous centuries.

Japan and Foreign Contacts

Japanese sailors and traders had traveled overseas since the 1000s. In the early 1400s, during the Ashikaga shogunate, Japanese ships had sailed to Korea and China, seeking profitable trade. Sometimes the Japanese had resorted to piracy, seizing whatever they could from the local inhabitants.

These Japanese traders sailed mostly from those ports in western Japan that were closest to the Asian mainland. They carried sulfur, copper-painted folding fans, scrolls, and swords as exports, and they imported silks, porcelain, books, paintings, and copper coins.

The Portuguese in Japan. In the mid-1500s, the daimyo found another source of wealth: trade with the Portuguese, whose ships began to appear in Japanese waters. Portuguese traders introduced two influences in Japan that the Tokugawa shoguns later considered undesirable: the musket and Christianity. Oda Nobunaga had used troops armed with muskets during his military campaigns. However, the Tokugawa shoguns considered the musket an unwelcome invention. This new weapon went against the traditional samurai ethic, an ethic based on skill. With strict limits placed on their manufacture, the technology of firearms in Japan made no advances and may have even declined after 1650. Christianity was undesirable because it taught loyalty to a power other than the Tokugawa shogun.

Christian missionaries. In the wake of Portuguese traders came Christian missionaries. Chief among them were the Jesuits, who had achieved notable success during the Counter-Reformation in Europe. The Jesuits concentrated their efforts on converting the daimyo to Christianity. They had discovered that it was easier to convert a daimyo first and then build churches and seek converts in the domain that he controlled. By the early 1600s, the missionaries had converted as many as 500,000 Japanese to Christianity.

Closing the country. The success of the Jesuits alarmed the Tokugawa shoguns. They saw Christianity as a subversive force that might undermine their authority. They also feared that the missionaries might bring European armies to conquer Japan. Early in the 1600s, the shoguns forced Portuguese traders and missionaries to leave Japan.

By this time the Portuguese faced stiff competition from the Dutch, both in Japan and in the spice trade in the islands off the coast of Southeast Asia. The Dutch had accepted a strictly controlled trading relationship with the Tokugawa shogunate. The shoguns allowed only a few Dutch merchants to live near Nagasaki, a port city on the Japanese island of Kyushu. In addition, the shoguns themselves controlled the small amount of trade Japan conducted with the Dutch.

These Dutch merchants were the only Europeans allowed to trade in Japan after the Tokugawa closed the country in the 1630s. The Tokugawa prohibited the building of oceangoing ships, banned travel abroad by Japanese, and killed foreign sailors who had been shipwrecked in Japan. Like China, Japan now concentrated on domestic affairs and tried to ignore the outside world. As an island country without any land frontiers across which people might slip unnoticed, Japan achieved more complete isolation than did China.

Society Under the Tokugawa

The Tokugawa shoguns, like most of the emperors of China, did not promote change. Stability was a much more important ideal. Confucian ideas and institutions borrowed from China supported this ideal.

First, the Tokugawa shoguns adopted—with some modifications—the Confucian ideal of social classes.

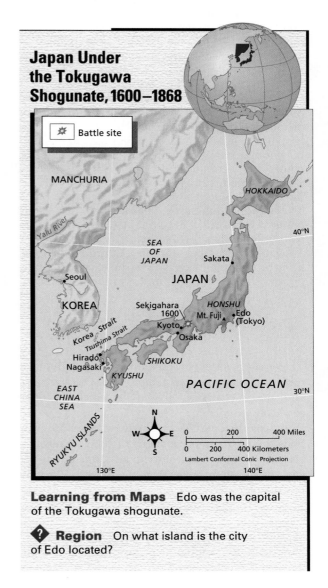

Japan Under the Tokugawa Shogunate, 1600–1868

☼ Battle site

MANCHURIA

HOKKAIDO

Yalu River

SEA OF JAPAN

Sakata

40°N

Seoul

JAPAN

KOREA

Sekigahara 1600

HONSHU

Mt. Fuji

Edo (Tokyo)

Korea Strait

Kyoto

Tsushima Strait

Osaka

Hirado

Nagasaki

SHIKOKU

KYUSHU

PACIFIC OCEAN

30°N

EAST CHINA SEA

RYUKYU ISLANDS

N W E S

0   200   400 Miles

0   200   400 Kilometers

Lambert Conformal Conic Projection

130°E   140°E

Learning from Maps Edo was the capital of the Tokugawa shogunate.

❓ Region On what island is the city of Edo located?

Evening Squall at Ohashi

The emergence of popular culture in Tokugawa Japan was reflected in the subjects of woodblock prints. Recreational and theatrical scenes, as well as scenes of such commonplace activities as fishing and farming, were captured by the gifted artists and printmakers of the 1600s, 1700s, and 1800s.

In this woodblock print by Ando Hiroshige, people are opening umbrellas over their heads to protect themselves from the rain as they hurry over a wooden bridge. The artist shows a single moment caught in time. As we look at the picture, we can almost sense the suddenness of the storm and feel the sensation of the rain on our skin.

Prints such as this were the result of a collaboration of skilled artists and craftspeople. A publisher suggested the subject and directed the production of the print. The artist then made the first drawing, which the engraver cut into a series of wooden blocks. Finally, the printer chose the colors and applied one color to each block. Specially made papers were pressed onto each of the blocks in succession, and the accumulation of color produced the total picture. The blocks could be used repeatedly, and the resulting prints were sold in the publisher's shop.

Woodblock prints were first utilized as illustrations in popular books. However, when many people showed interest in the prints themselves, publishers began producing them separately. As the technique became more popular, it began to reflect the tastes of people in the growing middle class. They were the chief buyers of the prints, which they used for decoration in place of more expensive paintings.

They ranked warriors, who fulfilled roughly the same role as scholar-gentry in China, first. Peasants, artisans, and merchants followed in descending order of importance.

In Japan, people belonged to these classes by birth. Sons followed the occupations of their fathers. For example, a person born into an artisan family in the city of Osaka remained a member of the artisan class in Osaka for life.

Second, the Tokugawa shoguns encouraged education in the Confucian classics for members of the warrior class. The shoguns established schools in the various domains to prepare young warriors for their new peacetime role as government officials. The shoguns, however, did not adopt the Chinese civil service examination system. In Japan, warriors became officials by heredity alone. Males born into low-ranking warrior families worked as low-ranking officials in their domains. Those born into high-ranking families served as high-ranking officials.

As a further means of maintaining control, the shoguns usually required a warrior to live in the castle town of his daimyo. Instead of living on the income of their own estates in the countryside, warriors now received salaries. This policy deprived them of the opportunity to develop independent sources of wealth or power. It also eliminated any opportunity to revolt against their lords.

Change and Culture in Tokugawa Japan

As in China, the rulers of Japan could not prevent social, economic, and political change within their country. Much of the change that took place in Japan resembled that which occurred in China. Cities grew in both size and importance. Internal trade expanded, and various regions of the country began to specialize in certain crops and handicrafts. The growth of cities and the increasing wealth of merchants and artisans led to the rise of a popular culture. By the early 1700s, new forms of literature, theater, and art had taken root. Many of these new forms catered to the tastes and lifestyles of ordinary city residents.

The End of Japan's Isolation

As part of the Tokugawa plan for keeping Japan isolated, the government refused to give shelter to ships of other nations during storms and, in fact, treated shipwrecked sailors harshly. Such treatment of American whaling and merchant ships angered westerners. Western nations wanted Japan to follow China's lead and end its isolation.

At last, in 1853, United States President Millard Fillmore sent a naval force to Japan under Commodore Matthew Perry. Commodore Perry had orders to negotiate a diplomatic and commercial treaty that would guarantee the safety of American sailors and also open Japanese ports to American trade. He presented a letter from President Fillmore—a letter strongly urging the Japanese to agree to such a treaty—and promised to return for an answer the following year.

The American visit to Japan sparked controversy within Japan. Some powerful leaders favored military resistance and continued isolation. Others, however, believed that Japan could not hold out, and the views of this group prevailed. The shogun, influenced by the threat of naval bombardment by the Americans, reluctantly agreed to negotiate when Commodore Perry returned in 1854.

The negotiations between Commodore Perry and the shogun led to the Treaty of Kanagawa (kah·NAH·gah·wah) in 1854, which was a turning point in Japanese history. The Japanese opened two ports to let Americans obtain shelter, fuel, and supplies, opening the door to trade. Within two years Japan signed similar treaties with Great Britain, Russia, and the Netherlands. As part of the

Typical instrumentation of a trio from the Tokugawa period included a singer, a lute player, and a flutist.

agreements with these countries, the foreign nations were allowed to establish **consulates**—diplomatic offices headed by consuls.

Japanese opponents of the Tokugawa shogunate criticized the government for agreeing to the treaties that had been signed with these foreign nations. Nevertheless, in 1858 the governments of Japan and the United States agreed to exchange ministers. The new treaty between these two countries also allowed foreign residence in Edo and Osaka, international trade, and extraterritorial privileges. In addition, the Japanese now opened more treaty ports to the United States. Similar agreements with other nations soon followed.

The Decision to Modernize

As Japan confronted challenges from the outside world, the Japanese recognized the need to modernize their country if they were to maintain their independence. The question was, on what basis would the modernization take place?

The Tokugawa shoguns hoped to maintain their own position by preserving the traditional political institutions of the shogunate. Their inability to resist Western demands, however, undermined their right to rule in the minds of many samurai. A growing number of opponents of the shogunate began to complain about its weakness abroad and autocracy at home. In the 1860s, civil war broke out between the Tokugawa and anti-Tokugawa forces in Japan. Calling for major political reforms, the anti-Tokugawa forces overthrew the shogunate in 1868. Restoring the power of the emperor, they moved Japan toward a more centralized government. The emperor, a teenager, named his reign Meiji, meaning "Enlightened Rule."

Section 2 Review

1. **Define** consulates
2. **Identify** Oda Nobunaga, Toyotomi Hideyoshi, Tokugawa Ieyasu, Matthew Perry
3. **Locate and Explain the Significance** Kyoto, Edo, Nagasaki
4. **Understanding Ideas** What benefits did the Tokugawa shoguns bring to Japan?
5. **Summarizing Ideas** What was society like under the Tokugawa shogunate?
6. **Analyzing Ideas** How did the isolation of Japan end?

The Islamic Empires of Asia

Focus Questions

- **What problems did the Ottoman and Safavid empires face?**
- **What factors weakened the Mughal Empire?**
- **How did the British expand their control over the country of India?**

In the 1500s, Islam was the dominant religion from the Iberian Peninsula to the East Indies. Three large Islamic empires existed in that vast area: the Ottoman, the Persian, and the Mughal.

The rulers of these Muslim states set up strong central governments. They also faced religious divisions among their people with continuing quarrels between the Shi'ah and the Sunnis.

During the Tokugawa period, artists made miniature sculptures called netsukes. These small figures were often inlaid with shells and ivory and worn as jewelry.

This painting illustrates the Turkish sultan Süleyman the Magnificent at the Battle of Mohács in Hungary.

The Ottoman Empire

After the Ottoman Turks conquered Constantinople in 1453, they continued to expand overland while European nations expanded overseas. Led by Süleyman the Magnificent (called by his people Süleyman the Lawgiver), the Turks conquered Hungary and nearly captured the Habsburg capital of Vienna in 1529. By the middle of the 1500s, the Ottomans ruled most of eastern Europe, western Asia, and North Africa. (See map on page 470.)

Later in the century, however, the Ottomans began to suffer reverses. In 1571 a fleet composed of ships from several European powers, led by Philip II of Spain, defeated the Turks at the Battle of Lepanto, near Greece. In 1683, troops led by the Polish king John Sobieski again halted them outside Vienna.

The Ottoman Empire's capital was Constantinople. From there the sultans and their grand viziers (vuh·ZIRZ)—whose duties were similar to a prime minister's—ruled the empire's diverse population. Turks lived in the heart of the empire in Asia Minor. Christians of various ethnic groups inhabited the Balkans, and Muslim Arabs lived in the Fertile Crescent and along the Mediterranean shore of North Africa.

Decline begins. Süleyman the Magnificent died in 1566. In the 1600s the empire began its slow decline. The economy suffered because the empire had lost its control of both the silk and the spice trades when the new sea routes to Asia were opened up by Europeans. The empire was weakened by poor government, conflicts over the succession to the sultanate, corruption, an enormous bureaucracy, and rebellions among the Janissaries, the elite slave troops. The Ottomans lost the Crimean Peninsula and lands around the Black Sea and the Sea of Azov to the Russians in the late 1700s. Napoleon invaded Egypt, an Ottoman possession, in 1798. Later, territories in the Balkans were also lost.

Attempts at reform. Sultan Selim III, who ruled the empire from 1789 to 1807, attempted reforms in administration, taxation, and the military. However, conservatives and Janissaries who were opposed to change overthrew him.

Another ruler, Mahmud II, had more success with reform. Mahmud ruled from 1808 to 1839. Although Great Britain, France, and Russia forced him to recognize Greece's independence in 1829, Mahmud destroyed the Janissaries and modernized the government through autocratic reforms. The Ottoman Empire continued to decline, however. A constitution that provided for representative government was adopted in 1876 but then ignored. In the late 1800s, more lands in the Balkans, the Mediterranean, and North Africa were lost. Rebellions, such as one attempted by the Armenians, were harshly suppressed. By the early 1900s, the Ottoman Empire had become so weak that it was known as the "Sick Man of Europe." The empire finally came to an end in 1923, when a republic was established in Turkey.

Persia

The peoples of Persia, the land lying between the Ottoman Empire and the Mughal Empire of India, had become Muslim early in Islamic history, in the 600s. In 1501 a Turkic dynasty called the Safavids (sah·FAH·vidz) established a very strong central government, with its first capital city at Tabriz, in northwestern Persia.

The Safavids, especially under the rule of Shah 'Abbas I (from 1588 to 1629), brought Persian society to great heights in the 1500s and early 1600s. Isfahan,

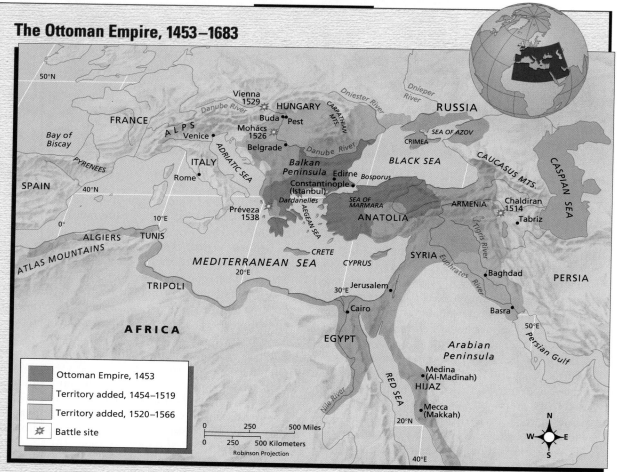

The Ottoman Empire, 1453–1683

Ottoman Empire, 1453

Territory added, 1454–1519

Territory added, 1520–1566

Battle site

Learning from Maps At its zenith under Suleyman, the Ottoman Empire included parts of eastern Europe, western Asia, and northern Africa.

Location Which two battle sites are found around the 38°N parallel?

Shah 'Abbas I strengthened the Safavid dynasty by forcing Uzbek and Ottoman forces out of Persia.

which became the new capital in 1598, had a brilliant court and was considered one of the great cities of the Muslim world. Shah 'Abbas's reign saw a flowering of literature—especially poetry—and the arts. Persian calligraphy, textiles, and carpet weaving became renowned. The economy thrived.

The Safavids followed the Shi'ah element of Islam, and they ruthlessly forced Shi'ism upon the Persian population as the state religion. Shi'ism made a very important contribution to later Iranian nationalism. Shi'ah helped give the Persians—today's Iranians—a separate identity from the greater number of Sunnis—Turks and Arabs—who lived around them. This nationalism would have important consequences for Iran in the 1900s.

The rulers who succeeded 'Abbas proved increasingly inept, and in 1736 the Safavid dynasty ended. The Persian nobles then chose a brilliant military leader, Nadir Shah, as their new monarch. Nadir Shah began a campaign of conquest that brought the lands as far west as Delhi under Persian control. He also seized part of the Ottoman Empire. After Nadir Shah's assassination in 1747, however, Persia lost those lands. Persia then split into a number of small states. At the end of the 1700s, the Qajar—another Turkic people—established a Persian dynasty with its capital at Tehran.

The Mughal Empire in India

The wealth and resources of India and its position along the sea routes to Southeast Asia attracted European traders. India had impressive quantities of jewels and gold. European travelers observed that India's rulers enjoyed luxurious lives, unmatched by those of any European monarchs. India's great cities, such as Agra and Delhi, seemed much larger than any in Europe. Agriculture flourished on the subcontinent, where the monsoon season allowed more than one harvest a year.

Nevertheless, the Mughal Empire had become the weakest of the three Muslim empires by the 1700s. Since the mid-1600s, Mughal rulers had faced financial difficulties that weakened the central government. The Mughals maintained huge and expensive armies which they believed were necessary to hold their empire together. In addition, the court became increasingly luxurious and expensive to support. To pay for these expenses, the Mughal emperors increased taxes.

The Mercator Projection: A Map for Navigators

When people look at a map, they usually have no idea of which projection cartographers used to construct that map. However, almost everyone has heard of or seen the most frequently used projection—the Mercator—developed by Gerardus Mercator in 1569. It was the map projection used by European navigators in their voyages of exploration and empire building in the years that followed.

In his projection Mercator drew the lines of latitude and longitude as straight lines that crossed each other at right angles so that navigators could draw straight lines to plot their courses. This meant that the distance between parallels, or lines of latitude, increased as latitude increased. If Mercator had drawn the parallels with even spacing, as they are shown on a globe, straight lines plotted on them would not represent true compass bearings.

The actual mathematical computations that Mercator used to develop his projection were complex, but the idea behind his projection was quite simple. Picture a spherical balloon inside a hollow cylinder. Then, imagine that the balloon has lines of latitude and longitude marked on it and that the line marking the equator just touches the wall of the cylinder. Now imagine blowing up the balloon. As the balloon stretches, the lines of longitude lie as straight lines along the walls of the cylinder and the lines of latitude are stretched apart in proportion. As a result, the farther away from the equator and towards the poles you look, the greater the distortion in scale. Also, although land shapes appear correct, the areas of the landmasses are greatly distorted. Nevertheless, for every point on the map, the angles shown are uniform in every direction. This allows a navigator to plot a straight line course, because a line connecting any two points follows a single compass direction.

The Mercator projection is a valuable navigational tool. It is convenient to use because the shapes of the continents are correct and are easily recognized. But as a result of frequently seeing the Mercator projection, many people have no idea of the proper size of the continents in relation to one another.

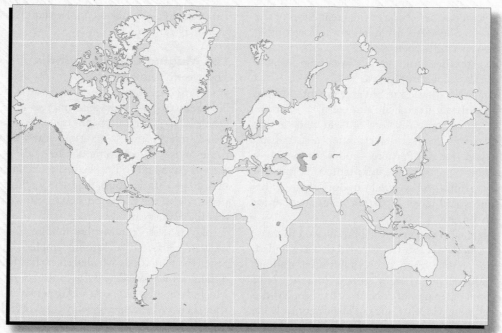

On the Mercator projection, landmasses retain their true shape, although their scale becomes more distorted as distance from the equator increases.

As a result of his two governorships in Bengal, Robert Clive laid the foundation for the expansion of the British Empire in India.

Sometimes one third or more of the crops that the peasants raised had to be paid as taxes. As a result, the peasants' levels of production and prosperity declined, reducing the revenue base.

With the empire weakened, the powerful new Persian ruler Nadir Shah delivered the final blow to Mughal power in India. In 1739 Nadir Shah sacked Delhi and confiscated the jewel-encrusted Peacock Throne of the Mughals. The Mughals lost their wealth, their prestige, their army, and much of their territory. Although an emperor remained on the throne in Delhi until the 1850s, during the remainder of the 1700s the Marathas, Sikhs from the Punjab, and Afghan Muslim invaders fought for control of the country. An India torn by dissension was much easier for Europeans to conquer.

Europeans in India

The Mughal Empire was the least successful of the major Muslim empires in confronting European power. To the east, the Chinese and Japanese managed to keep Europeans out altogether for a long time. In India, however, the Mughal emperors could not dislodge the Portuguese in the 1500s. Nor could they resist the English, who by the 1600s had begun to replace the Portuguese as the major European presence in India. Over the years this presence grew.

The British East India Company, founded in 1600, controlled England's trade with India. By the 1700s the company's chief rival was the French East India Company. Both the English and the French trading companies desired commercial profits, not Indian colonies, since few of their citizens lived there.

In 1756 the Seven Years' War began in Europe, with England and France on opposing sides. Hostilities between the two countries occurred in India as well as elsewhere around the world. At this time the Mughal Empire lacked a strong central power, and local leaders struggled for advantage. Taking advantage of the chaos, the British and the French formed alliances with rival Indian rulers.

The British trading post at Calcutta lay within the important Indian state of Bengal, whose ruler was allied with the French. In 1756, Bengali troops captured Calcutta and imprisoned many British citizens, locking them up overnight in a small jail cell that became known as the Black Hole of Calcutta. By morning, dozens of the prisoners had suffocated.

The British East India Company and its Indian allies, who were under military leader Robert Clive,

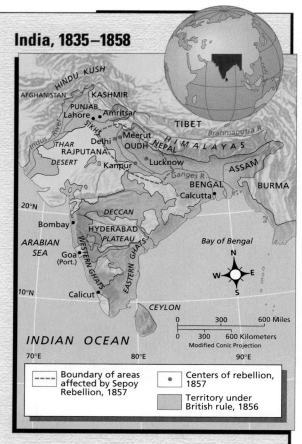

India, 1835–1858

Learning from Maps The British acquired a large amount of territory in India during the early to mid-1800s.

❓ Human-Environment Interaction
Around which physical features did the British settle by 1856?

fought back vigorously. In a series of decisive victories, Clive crushed the French and their Indian allies. The Treaty of Paris in 1763, which ended the Seven Years' War and its related conflicts around the world, left the French with only a few tiny footholds in India along the coast and gave the British a free hand in the rest of the subcontinent.

Expansion of British Authority

The British East India Company now governed a huge realm. The responsibility soon strained the company's resources, and some of its officials engaged in corrupt practices. As a result the British government began to regulate the company's activities. In the late 1700s,

the British government assumed the right to appoint the company's highest official, the governor-general. However, the company remained free to earn profits and to use its officials and troops as it chose.

In the late 1780s, the British government named Charles Cornwallis—the same General Cornwallis who had surrendered to George Washington at Yorktown in 1781—governor-general of the British East India Company in India. One of his first actions was to clean up the widespread corruption among company officials. Blaming some of the corruption on Indian employees, Cornwallis ordered them excluded from all important company positions. Indian resentment over this discrimination lasted for years.

Rivalries and even warfare continued among various Indian states. The British took advantage of these conflicts to expand their control over additional Indian territory. Religious hatred between Hindus and Muslims helped the British, as did the caste system (which was discussed in Chapter 3), which prevented Indians from uniting against the foreigners. The British did not even always need to employ their own troops in actual fighting. Often they could make use of local Indian troops—called **sepoys** (SEE·poyz)—who were trained and led by British officers.

By 1857 the British East India Company ruled about three fifths of the Indian subcontinent directly. This company ruled most of the rest of the Indian subcontinent indirectly through its control of local princes. Great Britain also controlled the island of Ceylon (now named Sri Lanka), which it had seized from the Dutch between 1795 and 1796.

Until about 1825 the British made no attempt to impose their own way of life on India. In the 1830s, however, English became the language of instruction in Indian schools, and Indian pupils studied Western literature, history, and science.

Like their Mughal predecessors, the British in India tried to prohibit slavery, the killing of infant girls, and the ritual suicide of widows (which is known as suttee). The British also tried to suppress thuggee, which involved ritual murders and robberies committed by members of a secret religious cult. From this practice we get our word *thug*.

The Indian Revolt

India in the mid-1800s was a huge piece of land, with millions of people and an ancient civilization, controlled by a foreign commercial corporation. The British population in India had grown rapidly and now included the wives and families of British men.

Indians resented the British and their increasing tendency to impose Western ways of life upon India. The sepoys were particularly dissatisfied because they had been forced to fight for the British in numerous campaigns in Afghanistan and Burma. In 1857 they revolted.

The immediate cause of the Indian Mutiny, or Sepoy Rebellion, involved a new kind of rifle that the British East India Company had issued in 1857. In order to load his rifle, the sepoy had to bite off part of the cartridge. A false rumor spread that these cartridges had been greased with the fat of cows and pigs to make the bullets slide more easily through the barrel. The sepoys included both Hindus and Muslims; Hindus regard cows as sacred, and Muslims are forbidden to eat pork. This rumor, therefore, struck at the religious sensibilities of both groups.

Agitators whipped up existing resentments by claiming that the company had purposely insulted the two religions. With help from Indian civilians, the sepoys staged a widespread and violent mutiny against their British masters. (See map on opposite page.)

The Indian Mutiny nearly drove the British out of India, but troops sent from Great Britain finally suppressed the rebellion. To discourage future uprisings, the British took several steps. Leading sepoys were executed. In 1858 the British Parliament, concerned over the administration of India by the British East India Company, dissolved the company and transferred its power in India to the British government.

In 1876 Britain's Queen Victoria was proclaimed empress of India. Great Britain now formally filled the void left by the passing of the Mughals.

Section 3 Review

1. **Define** sepoys
2. **Identify** Süleyman the Magnificent, Selim III, Mahmud II, Safavids, Shah 'Abbas I, Nadir Shah, Robert Clive, Charles Cornwallis
3. **Locate and Explain the Significance** Black Sea, Sea of Azov, Delhi, Bengal
4. **Contrasting Ideas** In what ways were the problems of the Ottoman and Safavid Empires similar and different?
5. **Summarizing Ideas** What weaknesses led to the end of the Mughal Empire?
6. **Analyzing Ideas** How did the British expand their authority over India?

During the 1857 massacre at Cawnpore (Kanpur), a town in northern India, rebelling sepoys killed British women and children.

Chapter 18 Review

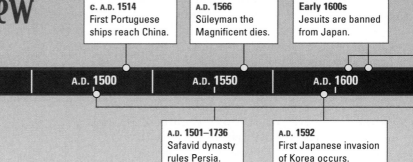

c. A.D. 1514
First Portuguese ships reach China.

A.D. 1566
Süleyman the Magnificent dies.

Early 1600s
Jesuits are banned from Japan.

A.D. 1400 | A.D. 1450 | A.D. 1500 | A.D. 1550 | A.D. 1600

A.D. 1368
Ming dynasty is established in China.

A.D. 1501–1736
Safavid dynasty rules Persia.

A.D. 1592
First Japanese invasion of Korea occurs.

Chapter Summary

The following list contains the key concepts you have learned about China, Japan, Southwest Asia, and India in the era of European expansion.

1. The rulers of the Ming and Qing dynasties tried to isolate China by prohibiting Chinese merchants from trading overseas and by restricting foreign merchants to special settlements inside China.

2. The Ming and Qing emperors brought peace to China, but by the late 1700s, corruption among officials, increased taxes, and decreased services led to discontent and rebellion. China's defeat by Great Britain in the Opium War forced the nation to deal with the outside world. Chinese weakness enabled foreigners to obtain special privileges in China.

3. The Japanese struggled over who was to be supreme—the central government run by the shoguns or the local lords called daimyo.

4. The Tokugawa shoguns established internal peace and in the 1630s closed Japan to foreign missionaries and merchants. In 1853 the United States sent a naval force to Japan to negotiate a diplomatic and commercial treaty to guarantee the safety of American sailors. These negotiations led to the Treaty of Kanagawa in 1854, which opened Japan. Similar agreements followed.

5. The Ottoman Empire remained a threat to central and eastern Europe until the late 1600s, after which it began a gradual decline. In the early 1800s, Mahmud II introduced reforms, but the Ottoman Empire continued to decline until it was replaced by a Turkish republic in 1923.

6. The Safavid dynasty brought Persia to great cultural and political heights. After the Safavid dynasty fell, Nadir Shah assumed power. Through a campaign of military conquest, Nadir Shah greatly extended Persia's boundaries. After his assassination, however, Persia lost these lands and split into smaller states.

7. The Mughal emperors could not keep European traders out of India. The Seven Years' War between Great Britain and France helped to cement British domination in India.

8. India was governed by the British East India Company. In 1857 the Indians rebelled against the British in what is known as the Sepoy Rebellion. The British put down the rebellion and dissolved the British East India Company. They transferred the rule of India to the British government. Some years later, Queen Victoria was proclaimed Empress of India.

Reviewing Important Terms

On a separate sheet of paper, supply the term that correctly completes each statement.

1. Early Chinese ships were called _____.
2. The Manchu emperors forced Chinese men to wear a long braid called a _____ to symbolize submission.
3. Chinese scholars during the Qing dynasty became interested in _____, the study of the history of literature and language.
4. Under _____ _____, the government does not restrict or interfere in international trade.
5. Diplomatic offices headed by consuls are called _____.
6. _____ were native Indian troops trained by British officers.
7. _____ exempts foreigners from the laws of the country in which they live or do business.

Developing Critical Thinking Skills

1. **Summarizing Ideas** List the actions taken by the Ming dynasty to protect China's northern frontier.
2. **Explaining Ideas** How did the Tokugawa shogunate maintain a long period of peace within Japan?
3. **Analyzing Ideas** What issues were of concern to the Japanese in deciding whether to modernize their country, and what was the outcome?
4. **Interpreting Ideas** Explain the ways in which the decline of the Ottoman Empire and the decline of the Persian Safavid Empire were similar.
5. **Comparing Ideas** Compare the way the British established trade in China with the way in which they established it in India.
6. **Understanding Relationships** Describe the results of European contact with each of the following: (a) China; (b) Japan; (c) India.

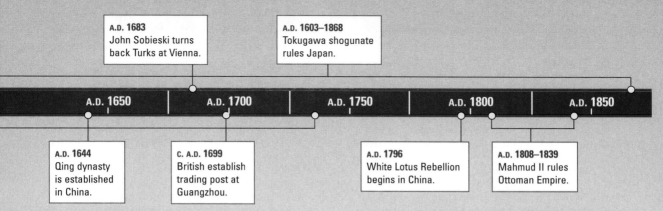

A.D. **1683**
John Sobieski turns back Turks at Vienna.

A.D. **1603–1868**
Tokugawa shogunate rules Japan.

A.D. **1650**   A.D. **1700**   A.D. **1750**   A.D. **1800**   A.D. **1850**

A.D. **1644**
Qing dynasty is established in China.

C. A.D. **1699**
British establish trading post at Guangzhou.

A.D. **1796**
White Lotus Rebellion begins in China.

A.D. **1808–1839**
Mahmud II rules Ottoman Empire.

Relating Geography to History

Turn to the map of India on page 474, and answer the following questions: **(a)** Why did British control of India begin along the coast and move gradually inland? **(b)** When you look at British acquisitions from 1835 to 1858, what geographic pattern do they seem to follow? **(c)** Why might the British have had more difficulty controlling some areas than others?

Relating Past to Present

1. Review the military problems that the Ming dynasty had along its land borders with central and northern Asia. Then ask your librarian to help you find source materials on the tensions between China and the former Soviet Union, China and India, or China and Vietnam, since the 1950s. What are the reasons for the tensions between these countries?
2. Europeans transmitted their culture to the areas of the world that came under their domination. Choose an area of the world today that is experiencing the influence of Western ideas and culture. Describe some of these influences. What impact might they have on the traditional way of life in that area?
3. The British excluded the Indians from any important positions in the British East India Company. Naturally, the Indians developed a deep resentment of this policy of exclusion. How do you think this superior attitude that colonial rulers had over their subjected people has affected the relationship between the former colonial power and its former colonies?

Applying History Study Skills

Before completing this activity, review Building History Study Skills on page 462.

Read the following selection from a 1636 Tokugawa edict banning contact with foreigners. Then answer the questions that follow.

"No Japanese ships may leave for foreign countries. . . . No Japanese may go abroad secretly. If anyone tries to do this, he will be killed, and the ship and owner(s) will be placed under arrest while higher authority is informed. . . . No offspring of Southern Barbarians [Europeans] will be allowed to remain. Anyone

violating this order will be killed and all his relatives punished according to the gravity of the offense."

1. What consequences did people face if they ignored the decree?
2. What do you think were the positive and negative long-term consequences of the decree?

Building Your Portfolio

1. **Writing a Report** As you have read, the art form of woodblock printing became popular in Japan during the Tokugawa period. Use books in your library to write a report in which you answer the following questions: Why was this art form popular? What was its subject matter? How did Japanese woodblock prints change in the 1800s? One source for your research might be Seiichiro Takahashi's *Traditional Woodblock Prints of Japan* (Weatherhill). Place the report in your portfolio.
2. **Writing an Essay** The opium trade became a major source of conflict between Great Britain and China. Write an essay describing the dilemma of the Chinese officials in attempting to stop the opium traffic. Also, describe how the British used the Opium War to place demands on the Chinese. Place the essay in your portfolio.
3. **Presenting an Oral Report** Prepare an oral report to describe how the Indians reacted to British rule. Be sure to include details of the Sepoy Rebellion. Place the notes and research materials for your report in your portfolio.

Unit Summary

The following list contains the key concepts you have learned about the emergence of modern nations.

1. Beginning in the 1300s a revival of interest in the classical learning of Greece and Rome, known as the Renaissance, swept Italy and later the rest of Europe.

2. In Germany, Martin Luther began a reform movement within the Roman Catholic Church but ended by breaking with the church. The result was the Protestant Reformation. The doctrines he developed, known today as Lutheranism, spread throughout northern Europe. Later, churches in many parts of Europe broke away from the Roman Catholic Church.

3. The Scientific Revolution of the 1500s and 1600s transformed the methods and the understanding of astronomy, physics, and anatomy.

4. In the 1400s and 1500s, Europeans expanded overseas. Portuguese and Spanish explorers took the lead in discovering new lands and trade routes that paved the way for Europe's domination of most of the world.

5. The rulers of Europe centralized government in their own hands, and by the mid-1600s they had established absolute monarchies in France, Russia, Prussia, and Austria.

6. In England monarchs and Parliament clashed throughout the 1600s. Finally, Parliament emerged the winner and launched Great Britain on the road to democratic government.

7. During the Enlightenment, thinkers began to criticize the established political institutions.

8. In the 1700s the British colonists in what is today the United States won their independence.

9. Growing discontent in France, and Louis XVI's failure to solve the government's continuing financial crisis, led to the French Revolution in 1789.

10. Through a series of steps France became first a republic and then an empire under Napoleon Bonaparte. When Napoleon was defeated in 1815, the European powers attempted to restore the old regimes, but the principles of the revolution could not be suppressed.

11. China and Japan tried to protect their cultures from outside influences. However, they were unsuccessful as European powers made major inroads into both of these countries by the 1800s.

12. The Ottoman, Persian, and Mughal Empires declined in the 1700s. India then became a target for European colonialism. Great Britain began taking control of the Indian subcontinent in the late 1700s.

Reviewing Concepts

On a separate sheet of paper, match each of the following people with the appropriate description from the list that follows:

a. Leonardo da Vinci
b. Peter I
c. Prince Henry
d. Louis XVI
e. Bartholomeu Dias
f. Michelangelo
g. Tokugawa Ieyasu
h. Machiavelli
i. Petrarch
j. Charles V
k. Oliver Cromwell
l. Catherine II
m. Henry VIII
n. Copernicus

_____1. Built a new capital in Russia that would be a "window to the West"

_____2. Painter, sculptor, engineer, architect, and scientist who painted the *Mona Lisa*

_____3. Polish scientist who concluded that the Sun was the center of the universe

_____4. English king who broke with the Roman Catholic Church

_____5. Powerful overlord who established a long-lasting shogunate

_____6. Sailed around the southern tip of Africa

_____7. Italian poet who was one of the first humanists

_____8. Led the revolt against Charles I in England

_____9. Russian ruler whose expansionism gained control of the northern shore of the Black Sea

_____10. Supported Portugal's interest in exploration

_____11. King of France, who was executed

_____12. Artist who painted the frescoes on the ceiling of the Sistine Chapel

_____13. Italian Renaissance thinker who wrote about politics and government

_____14. Habsburg who was king of Spain and Holy Roman emperor

Applying Critical Thinking Skills

1. **Interpreting Ideas** In what ways did European art of the 1500s and 1600s reflect the new ideas and attitudes of the Renaissance?

2. **Analyzing Ideas** How did the ideas of humanism and the Scientific Revolution change Europe?

3. **Understanding Ideas (a)** According to the theory of mercantilism, what benefits did European nations hope to gain from colonial empires? **(b)** How did the building of empires affect the people of the colonies?

4. **Classifying Ideas** List the powers that Parliament gained at the expense of the English monarch between 1603 and 1714.

5. **Describing Ideas (a)** Describe the changes that occurred in China during the Ming and Qing dynasties. **(b)** How were they similar to the changes that took place under the Tokugawa shogunate?

6. **Comparing Ideas** Compare the goals and achievements of the French and American Revolutions.

Relating Geography to History

How did the relative locations of China and Japan make it easier for the governments in those countries to shun contact with foreigners, while the relative location of the Ottoman Empire made such isolation more difficult?

Writing About History

1. Use resources in your school or public library to find information on Japanese and Chinese painting in the 1700s and 1800s. Then find sources that explain how Japanese and Chinese artists influenced European and American artists. Present your findings in a written report.
2. Work with two or three of your classmates to develop a comparative essay explaining the unique features of Japanese, Chinese, European, Indian, Persian, and Ottoman cultures in the 1700s and 1800s.

Further Readings

Bainton, Roland H. *Here I Stand: A Life of Martin Luther.* NAL/Dutton, 1995. Recounts major events of Luther's life.

Dickens, Charles. *A Tale of Two Cities.* Bantam, 1989. Fictional account of events in London and Paris at the time of the French Revolution.

Ferguson, Wallace K. *The Renaissance.* Paperbook Press, Inc., 1991. Analyzes the causes of the Renaissance and compares the Italian Renaissance with the Northern Renaissance.

UNIT 4 CHRONOLOGY

Date	Politics	Science and Technology	Society and Culture
1300–1450	Ming Dynasty established **18** Growth of Italian cities **14***	Prince Henry the Navigator **15** Printing press **14**	Humanism **14** Italian Renaissance **14**
1450–1550	Columbus **15** Treaty of Tordesillas **15** Da Gama **15** Cortés **15** Magellan **15** Beginnings of Safavid dynasty **18** Henry VIII **14**	Copernicus **14** Vesalius **14**	Northern Renaissance **14** Da Vinci **14** *The Prince* **14** *Utopia* **14** Michelangelo **14** Luther **14** Diet of Worms **14** Counter-Reformation **14** Council of Trent **14**
1550–1650	Peace of Augsburg **14** Süleyman the Magnificent **18** Spanish Armada **15** Elizabeth I **16** Edict of Nantes **14** Tokugawa shogunate established **18** Michael Romanov **15** Richelieu **15** Thirty Years' War **15** Qing dynasty established **18**	European shipbuilding **15** Microscope **14** Kepler **14** Galileo **14** Telescope **14**	Shakespeare **14** King James Version of the Bible **16** Rembrandt **15**
1650–1750	Louis XIV **15** Glorious Revolution **16** Peter I **15** Act of Union **16** Maria Theresa **15** Frederick the Great **15**	Versailles **15** Newton **14**	*Leviathan* **16** *Two Treatises of Government* **16** Enlightenment **17** Voltaire **17** Rousseau **17**
1750–1850	Catherine II **15** Partitioning of Poland **15** American Revolution **17** French Revolution **17** Napoleon **17** Congress of Vienna **17**		*Encyclopedia* **17** *The Social Contract* **17**

*Indicates chapter in which development is discussed

The Emergence of Modern Nations

CHAPTER 14

The Renaissance, Reformation, and Scientific Revolution

A great burst of creativity began in Italy in the early 1300s. Because this movement centered on a revival of interest in the classical learning of Greece and Rome, we call it the Renaissance, a French word meaning "rebirth."

Renaissance Writers and Artists

Beginning around the 1300s, a number of Italian scholars, such as Francesco Petrarch (PEE·trahrk) and Baldassare Castiglione (kahs·teel·YOH·nay), developed a lively interest in classical Greek and Roman literature. Using classical texts, these Italian scholars stressed the study of grammar, rhetoric, history, and poetry. These studies were called the humanities, and people who specialized in the humanities were called humanists. A Renaissance diplomat and historian, Niccolò Machiavelli (mahk·yah·VEL·lee), wrote his famous book *The Prince,* in which he described government not in terms of lofty ideas but as he believed that government actually worked.

Art as well as literature flourished during the Renaissance. The most noticeable characteristic of Renaissance painting is realism, as shown in the works of Giotto (JAWT·oh), Masaccio, Leonardo da Vinci, Michelangelo Buonarroti (mee·kay·LAHN·jay·loh bwaw·nahr·RAW·tee), Raphael, and Titian (TISH·uhn).

Over time, humanist thought spread beyond Italy into northern Europe. Northern humanist writers, such as Erasmus and Thomas More, were interested in the early Christian period as well as in Greek and Roman culture. Expanding trade and the invention of the printing press helped ideas to spread during the Renaissance.

The Protestant Reformation

In about 1500, several northern humanists suggested that the Roman Catholic Church had lost sight of its spiritual mission. When the Catholic Church ignored their concerns, a new generation of reformers spurred a religious revolution. This revolution, which split the church and created several new churches, is called the Reformation.

The first break with the Roman Catholic Church occurred in Germany, where many humanists opposed the church's policy of selling indulgences, or pardons from punishment for sin. One of these critics was Martin Luther, a German monk. Although his original intent was to bring reforms to the Roman Catholic Church, Luther was denounced, and his actions resulted in the founding of the Lutheran Church. Other religious groups, called Protestant because their founders protested Catholic Church policies, also sprang up.

The Catholic Reformation

Although areas of northern Europe became Protestant during the Reformation, millions of Europeans remained faithful to the Roman Catholic Church. After 1550, religious conflicts arose between followers of the reformer John Calvin and supporters of a Catholic revival known as the Counter-Reformation.

John Calvin founded a theocracy—a government ruled by clergy claiming God's authority—in Geneva, Switzerland. Calvinism spread to France and to other parts of Europe. The Calvinists and other reform groups posed a threat to the Catholic Church. In

The Medici Family Palazzo, Florence

response, the papacy initiated reforms to foster a more spiritual outlook, to clarify doctrines, and to lead an aggressive campaign against heresy. During this time Ignatius de Loyola founded the Society of Jesus, or the Jesuits.

The religious struggles of the 1500s had a number of results, including the emergence of many different churches in western Europe, a new interest in education, an increase in the power of national governments, and a decrease in the power of the pope.

Culture and Daily Life

At the time of the Renaissance and the Reformation, most Europeans lived in small villages. Over time, people left the countryside in search of a better life in growing towns and cities. Gradually, more sophisticated attitudes began to take hold among these urban residents, and people's understanding of the world began to change. People sought rational explanations for day-to-day events through science.

The Scientific Revolution

Science changed as early investigators began to question traditional opinions and to perform new experiments. Most important, they described nature without any reference to previous beliefs. The foundation of this approach was the principle of doubt; nothing was to be believed unless it could be proved by observation, experiment, or mathematics. The transformation in thinking that occurred during the 1500s and 1600s as a result of these new attitudes and methods is known as the Scientific Revolution. Advances occurred in the fields of astronomy, physics, anatomy, biology, and chemistry. Five Europeans in particular—Copernicus, Kepler, Galileo, Vesalius, and Harvey—became pioneers of modern science. Descartes, Bacon, and Newton advanced the philosophical and scientific thinking of the time.

CHAPTER 15

European Exploration, Expansion, and Absolutism

In 1400 Europe's monarchs lacked the wealth and power of the strongest rulers of China, India, Africa, the Americas, and Europe's neighbor, the Ottoman Empire. Less than 400 years later, however, Europe had become the dominant civilization on Earth, and European nations had colonies all around the world.

Foundations of Exploration

Several factors encouraged Europeans to explore the world. First, technological advances—such as improved mapmaking, better navigation instruments, advanced ship design, and new weapons—made long voyages possible. Second, the development of new economic policies and improved ways of doing business, including the standardization of money and the creation of joint-stock companies, played an important part in exploration. Third, strong and ambitious monarchies supported exploration and colonization. Finally, social changes such as overcrowding in Europe and religious zeal stimulated exploration.

Voyages of Portugal and Spain

Explorers sailing under the flags of Portugal and Spain made the first European voyages into unknown waters. The Portuguese sailed along the west coast of Africa, around the Cape of Good Hope, and across the Indian Ocean to India. Likewise, the Spanish became interested in the search for new trade routes; they sent expeditions across the Atlantic to the Americas. A tragic aspect of the building of these empires was the slave trade. As Spain and Portugal established colonies across the globe, they imported African slaves to work the lands.

Although Portugal rapidly acquired wealth and a vast empire, that empire declined almost as swiftly as it rose. Three main factors hastened the decline. First, the Portuguese government, with an insecure financial base, had overextended its empire. Second, the empire proved to be a drain on Portugal's population. Third, Spain annexed Portugal in 1580, and until Portugal won independence in 1640, Spain limited Portuguese trade and neglected its colonies.

The Spanish and Dutch Empires

Spain turned most of its colonial energies toward the Americas—the West Indies, Central America, North America, and South America. Spain developed a centralized form of government for its colonies. Representatives of the monarch, called viceroys, reported to the Council of the Indies in Spain.

While explorers were creating a great empire outside Europe, kings expanded the authority of Spain itself. Such a king was Charles V, who was also the Holy Roman emperor. He halted the Turkish penetration of central Europe and, with the Peace of Augsburg, for a time settled religious wars between the Catholics and the Lutherans in Germany. Continuous war, however, drained Spain's human and financial resources. Spain also lacked industries, and land was not used efficiently for food production.

Charles V realized that this scattered empire had become too large for any one monarch to rule. In 1556 he gave up his throne and divided his vast lands between his son, who became Philip II of Spain, and his brother, who became Holy Roman emperor Ferdinand I.

The people of the Dutch provinces that were inherited by Philip II, however, strongly distrusted the Spanish crown. Philip had ignored the authority of the local nobles, taxed Dutch trade heavily, and persecuted the Calvinists. In 1579 the Dutch declared their independence from Spain.

Throughout the 1600s, the Dutch dominated European commerce. They built efficient ships and were excellent sailors. The city of Amsterdam became a world financial center. Dutch banks, trading companies, manufacturing enterprises, and overseas colonies became models of efficiency.

After the Dutch revolt, the Spanish Empire declined. Population growth, inflation, the lack of an enterprising middle class, and undeveloped industry were all contributing factors. Discontent caused many people to emigrate from Spain.

France

After Spain's decline, France emerged as a leading European power under Louis XIV. It had recovered rapidly from the religious wars of the 1500s, thanks to the policies of Henry IV, the first Bourbon monarch. The Bourbon kings would make the monarchy absolute in France.

The Thirty Years' War strengthened France and weakened the Habsburgs' rule in Austria. Louis XIV increased royal authority and engaged in wars that extended France's territory. Besides claiming territory to the northeast, Louis XIV claimed Canadian territory in North America.

Eastern and Central Europe

The empires of Russia, Prussia, and Austria developed in eastern and central Europe. In the 1600s, Russian czars dealt successfully with many internal problems and created a form of absolutism. Peter I, called Peter the Great, acquired ports on the Black Sea, claimed new territories, and established closer ties with the West. Catherine I, called Catherine the Great, further strengthened Russian culture and foreign policy. Russia's expansion differed from that of the western European countries; instead of expanding overseas, Russia expanded overland.

CHAPTER 16

Revolution and Change in England

While nations of the continent of Europe were establishing absolute monarchies, England was developing a constitutional form of government.

The Tudors and the Stuarts

In the late 1400s a new royal family, the Tudors, became rulers in England. They brought stability and prosperity to England. Parliament gained power and prestige during the reign of Elizabeth I. However, when the throne passed to the Stuarts, the relationship between Parliament and the monarchs deteriorated. The reign of James I was characterized by financial difficulties. Although Charles I, his successor, tried to rule without calling Parliament, he assembled the legislative body in 1640 because he was in need of funds.

Civil War and Revolution

The Parliament of 1640, controlled by the Puritans, took actions to limit the monarchy. A rebellion in Ireland sent the monarchy into crisis and provoked a violent civil war in 1642. As a result of this conflict the Puritan Oliver Cromwell came to power, establishing a republican form of government. Charles I was executed.

The experiment with republican government failed, however; Parliament and Cromwell quarreled nearly as much as the legislature had with previous rulers. By 1660 the English people had undergone a

English (shown in photo) victory over the Spanish Armada in 1588

change of sentiment. Although some had favored the execution of Charles I, Cromwell's commonwealth had neither settled the nation nor solved its problems. After some hesitation, the Parliament of 1660 invited Charles II, the son of Charles I, to return to England.

England's Constitutional Monarchy

Having learned from his years in exile, Charles II cooperated with Parliament. However, the next king was his brother, James II, who clashed with the legislative body. When James's Catholic wife gave birth to a son, both of England's political parties opposed the idea of a Catholic ruler and forced James to abdicate. A number of leading nobles invited James's Protestant daughter, Mary, and her husband, William of Orange, to take the throne of England. Thus Parliament gave the crown to William and Mary as joint rulers.

Over time, many safeguards were instituted against absolute monarchy in England. For example, in 1679 Parliament passed the Habeas Corpus Act, which made provisions for arrested people to appear before a judge. Before granting the throne to William and Mary, Parliament required them to accept the Bill of Rights. This document declared that Parliament would choose the ruler, who would be subject to parliamentary laws. In addition, the ruler could not proclaim or suspend

laws, impose taxes, maintain an army in peacetime without Parliament's consent, or interfere with the elections of Parliament's members.

Although England remained a monarchy in 1700, Parliament held the power. In 1707 the parliaments of England and Scotland passed the Act of Union, uniting the two countries into one kingdom known as Great Britain.

English Colonial Expansion

While Spain and Portugal established vast overseas empires during the 1500s, England remained preoccupied with problems at home. Even though these problems persisted during the 1600s, English mariners began explorations that allowed England to claim lands in the Americas and Asia. By the 1760s the British empire had no real mercantile competition in North America or in India. The English East India Company set up trading posts in India, Malaya, and the East Indies. In search of a Northwest Passage to India, the English also established colonies along North America's eastern coast.

CHAPTER 17

The American and French Revolutions

The idea that the people should have a voice in government greatly influenced French politics of the 1700s. The American Revolution, with its central theme of freedom and dignity of human beings, helped to inspire the French Revolution.

The Enlightenment

Some people of the 1700s thought of their century as an Age of Enlightenment. Thinkers of the Enlightenment believed that they could apply the scientific method and logically explain human nature. The philosophes, such as Denis Diderot (dee·DROH), Baron de Montesquieu (MOHN·tes·kyoo), Voltaire, and Jean-Jacques Rousseau (roo·SOH) were not only philosophers, however, but also critics of society and politics.

The American Revolution

New ideas were not confined to Europe in the 1700s. The British colonists' new way of life in North

America and their distance from Britain began to create new attitudes about their relationship with the home country. Their immediate concerns were British trade regulations and the presence of the French along their borders. Colonists struggled increasingly with the British and finally declared their independence.

The new nation attempted government under the Articles of Confederation. However, when it became evident that the articles did not give the central government enough power, the nation adopted the Constitution with provisions for a stronger federal government. To guarantee the rights of American citizens, the Bill of Rights was added to the Constitution.

The French Revolution

Simultaneous with revolution in the British colonies, disturbing events were occurring in France. The French rulers had constructed an absolute monarchy based upon the division of society into three groups, or estates. The First and Second Estates, including the clergy and the nobility, had the fewest people but the most wealth, power, and privilege. The Third Estate, which included more than 90 percent of the people, consisted mostly of peasants and had very little power.

Discontent in France began to grow in the mid-1700s. Several factors explain this dissatisfaction. The population was growing, and French families needed more food and money. The middle and poorer classes

A 1789 painting illustrating the day after the storming of the Bastille

loathed having to pay taxes when the nobles and clergy did not. Finally, both the nobles and the clergy disliked the increasing concentration of power in the hands of the king.

When Louis XVI called a meeting of the Estates-General in 1789, discontented groups throughout France hoped for reforms. The people did not want to follow the old custom of each estate meeting separately and voting as one body. They claimed that all the estates should meet and vote. When Louis failed to take action, members of the Third Estate boldly proclaimed themselves the National Assembly, thus beginning the French Revolution.

Hearing that the king had ordered troops to Paris and Versailles, the French people took action. On July 14, 1789, they stormed and captured the prison-fortress known as the Bastille in search of weapons to defend themselves.

Quite rapidly, the National Assembly became the government of France and enacted reforms to abolish the last remnants of feudalism in France. The assembly adopted the Declaration of the Rights of Man and of the Citizen, guaranteeing basic human rights. Likewise, the assembly passed laws aimed at correcting abuses and organizing a new government. In 1791 the assembly finished writing a constitution that limited the powers of the king and established a constitutional monarchy.

When Austria and Prussia invaded France, a group of radicals seized control of the Paris government and established the Commune. The Commune accused Louis XVI of plotting with foreign monarchs to overthrow the Constitution of 1791. Subsequently, the Legislative Assembly voted to suspend the French monarchy.

The French Republic

A new legislative body, the National Convention, met in 1792 to proclaim the end of the monarchy and the beginning of a republic. The convention also tried Louis XIV on charges of plotting against the security of the nation and ordered his execution.

In spite of the dangers and difficulties of the time, the National Convention made many reforms in France. It provided for a national system of public education, and it abolished slavery in the French colonies.

In 1795 the directors of the National Convention drafted another constitution, under which an executive body called the Directory controlled France. Although the Directory governed for four years, it pleased neither the radicals nor the conservatives. Finally, in 1799, Napoleon Bonaparte took over the government.

The Napoleonic Era

Although Napoleon's government kept the form of a republic, he became dictator and emperor of France. The French army conquered most of Europe under his rule. However, Great Britain, Austria, Prussia, and Russia soon united against the French. Napoleon was decisively defeated at the Battle of Waterloo in 1815 and exiled to the island of St. Helena, where he died in 1821.

A Return to Peace

After the final defeat of Napoleon in 1815, European leaders met at the Congress of Vienna to redraw the map of Europe. Three principles guided the decisions of the Congress of Vienna. First, the countries that suffered most at the hands of Napoleon—especially the four great powers—had to be compensated for their losses. Second, the balance of power had to be restored in Europe. This meant that the nations of Europe had to keep any one nation from becoming too powerful. Third, legitimacy, which meant that all former ruling families should be restored to their thrones, had to be upheld.

CHAPTER 18

Asia in Transition

Between 1400 and the mid-1800s, many of the countries in Asia reached a political and cultural peak and then began to decline.

China

During the Ming and Qing dynasties, peace and urban growth contributed to the expansion of trade in China. The growth of cities and the increasing wealth of urban merchants and artisans in China encouraged the rise of popular culture. Scholarship also flourished under the rule of the Ming and Qing emperors.

Just as the Qing dynasty started its decline, Europeans appeared in China. The Portuguese, the British, and the Russians claimed trading privileges in China—often with disastrous effects for the Chinese people.

Japan

In the late 1400s the Japanese daimyo began to fight among themselves for survival and supremacy. The struggle among the daimyo resulted in the creation of a political system that was a cross between feudalism and centralized monarchy. The Japanese established this hybrid system, known as the Tokugawa (TOH·KOOHG·AH·WAH) shogunate, in 1603.

The Tokugawa shogunate shaped Japanese life in several ways. By establishing a strong central government, the shoguns brought more than two centuries of stability to Japan. In setting trade restrictions and limiting contact with foreigners, they achieved almost complete isolation from Europe by 1650. Internal trade expanded, and various regions began to specialize in particular crops and handicrafts.

The Islamic Empires

In the 1500s three large Islamic empires existed: the Ottoman, the Persian, and the Mughal. The rulers of these Muslim states set up strong central governments. However, the Mughal Empire in India, financially weak, had little success when it confronted a European power. The British East India Company steadily increased its control until India became an official part of the British Empire in 1876.

Synthesis Review

1. **Understanding Ideas** Why did Martin Luther and John Calvin criticize the Roman Catholic Church?
2. **Summarizing Ideas** What factors encouraged European exploration and expansion?
3. **Determining Cause and Effect** In what ways did wars and revolutions in England encourage the growth of constitutional government?
4. **Seeing Relationships** How did discontent in France and America lead to the French and American Revolutions?
5. **Analyzing Ideas** How did Britain gain power and influence throughout India?
6. **Synthesizing Ideas** In what ways did revolutions in England and America influence the French Revolution?

5

Industrialism and Nationalism

POLITICS AND GOVERNMENT

1700	1725	1750	1775

1789
French Revolution topples monarchy

1791
Revolution breaks out in Haiti against France

SOCIETY AND CULTURE

1700	1725	1750	1775

c. 1700
Enclosure movement continues in England

1770
Composer Ludwig van Beethoven born in Germany

1776
Adam Smith publishes *The Wealth of Nations*

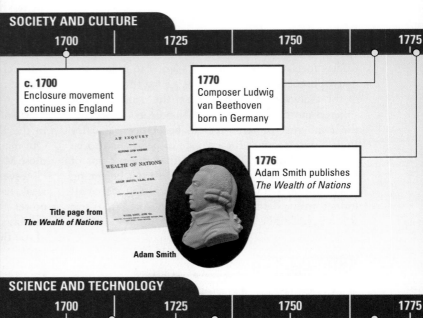

Title page from
The Wealth of Nations

Adam Smith

SCIENCE AND TECHNOLOGY

1700	1725	1750	1775

1712
Thomas Newcomen devises first successful steam engine

1769
James Watt patents modern steam engine

1733
Flying shuttle rapidly increases weaving rate

1793
American Eli Whitney invents the cotton gin

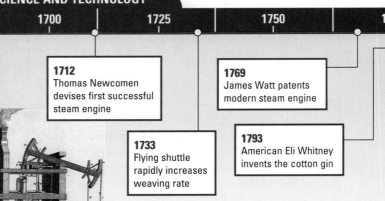

Thomas Newcomen's steam engine

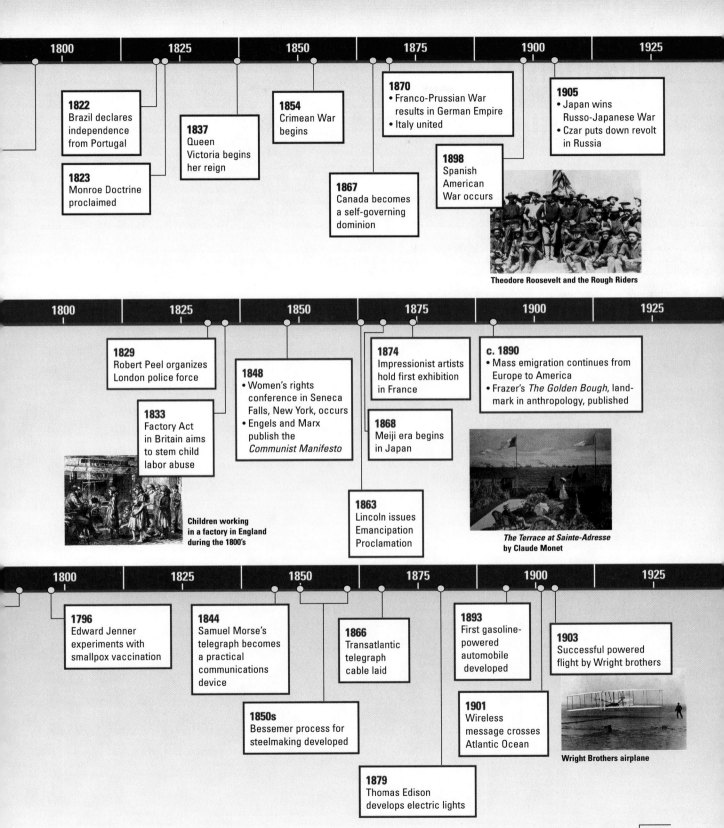

1800 — 1825 — 1850 — 1875 — 1900 — 1925

1822
Brazil declares independence from Portugal

1823
Monroe Doctrine proclaimed

1837
Queen Victoria begins her reign

1854
Crimean War begins

1870
• Franco-Prussian War results in German Empire
• Italy united

1867
Canada becomes a self-governing dominion

1898
Spanish American War occurs

1905
• Japan wins Russo-Japanese War
• Czar puts down revolt in Russia

Theodore Roosevelt and the Rough Riders

1800 — 1825 — 1850 — 1875 — 1900 — 1925

1829
Robert Peel organizes London police force

1833
Factory Act in Britain aims to stem child labor abuse

1848
• Women's rights conference in Seneca Falls, New York, occurs
• Engels and Marx publish the *Communist Manifesto*

1874
Impressionist artists hold first exhibition in France

1868
Meiji era begins in Japan

1863
Lincoln issues Emancipation Proclamation

c. 1890
• Mass emigration continues from Europe to America
• Frazer's *The Golden Bough*, landmark in anthropology, published

Children working in a factory in England during the 1800's

The Terrace at Sainte-Adresse by Claude Monet

1800 — 1825 — 1850 — 1875 — 1900 — 1925

1796
Edward Jenner experiments with smallpox vaccination

1844
Samuel Morse's telegraph becomes a practical communications device

1866
Transatlantic telegraph cable laid

1850s
Bessemer process for steelmaking developed

1893
First gasoline-powered automobile developed

1901
Wireless message crosses Atlantic Ocean

1879
Thomas Edison develops electric lights

1903
Successful powered flight by Wright brothers

Wright Brothers airplane

The Industrial Revolution

TIME
A.D. 1600–1901

A.D. 1600–1901

3.7 million B.C.   4000 B.C.   A.D. 2100

PLACE
Great Britain, the United States, France, and Germany

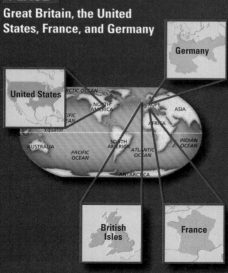

Germany

United States

ARCTIC OCEAN

NORTH AMERICA

EUROPE

ASIA

PACIFIC OCEAN

Equator

AFRICA

AUSTRALIA

SOUTH AMERICA

ATLANTIC OCEAN

INDIAN OCEAN

PACIFIC OCEAN

ANTARCTICA

British Isles

France

Steam locomotive

Significance

A revolution began in the 1700s, when power-driven machines began to perform much of the work that people had done before. This shift is referred to as the **Industrial Revolution**. It led to so many significant changes in the way goods were produced and in the way people lived that it completely transformed the world.

Terms to Define

Industrial Revolution	monopoly
enclosure movement	cartels
crop rotation	business cycle
factors of production	depression
mechanization	free enterprise
domestic system	laissez-faire
factory system	utilitarianism
Bessemer process	strike
capitalism	unions
commercial capitalism	collective bargaining
industrial capitalism	socialism
division of labor	utopian socialists
interchangeable parts	bourgeoisie
mass production	proletariat
sole proprietorship	authoritarian socialism
partnership	communism
corporation	democratic socialism

People to Identify

James Hargreaves	Adam Smith
Richard Arkwright	Thomas Malthus
Eli Whitney	David Ricardo
James Watt	Charles Dickens
Henry Bessemer	Jeremy Bentham
John McAdam	John Stuart Mill
Robert Fulton	Sir Thomas More
Samuel Morse	Robert Owen
Cyrus Field	Karl Marx

Places to Locate

Manchester	Silesia
Lyons	

Chapter Theme Questions

- **Technology** What effect might new machines and inventions have on how people work and how they view their work?
- **Social Relations** How might the shift from an agricultural society to an industrial society change people's social relationships?
- **Economic Organization** What new ideas about working and business might arise from worker discontent and rapid industrial growth?

I magine an American farmer of English and German heritage talking to his granddaughter about his life. He sits on a porch looking out over land that he and his ancestors have tilled for three generations. The old man tells his granddaughter about the stories he heard when he was a boy in the 1890s—stories of how his ancestors had left the old country and migrated to America.

They farmed and ranched, making a hard living from the land. They had no tractors, planters, or harvesters. They traveled by horse and buggy and planned parties for nights when the moon was full so that travelers could find their way back to their homes over unlit roads. They wore handstitched clothes, which they washed by hand and hung on a line to dry. They could not watch television, go to the movies, surf the Internet, or drive a car on paved roads to buy frozen foods at supermarkets.

As a young man at the turn of the century, the grandfather saw more changes within a few years than generations of old folks had seen in a lifetime. Now he speaks to his granddaughter about seeing the promise of modern technology fulfilled, making a better life for the generations to come.

The rapid changes the old man began witnessing in the early part of the twentieth century were the product of the Industrial Revolution, which changed the way goods were produced and the way people lived.

The Origins of the Industrial Revolution

Focus Questions

- **Why did the Industrial Revolution originate in Great Britain?**
- **How did new inventions in the textile industry spur the development of other new inventions?**
- **What developments in transportation and communication helped speed and spread the Industrial Revolution?**

Significant changes in agricultural methods, though gradual, preceded and made possible the

Industrial Revolution. These changes, known as the Agricultural Revolution, began with farming changes made in the Netherlands, which were then copied and developed by the British. The Agricultural Revolution's results helped bring about the Industrial Revolution that originated in Great Britain.

The Agricultural Revolution

Before the 1600s, most European villagers were allotted a plot or strip of land for cultivating their own food. In addition to this land for individual use, there were open, common lands used jointly by the villagers for grazing sheep and cattle. In the 1600s, English farmers accelerated the process of fencing off, or enclosing, common lands into individual holdings, largely for the benefit of the already wealthy landholders. This **enclosure movement** continued into the 1700s. Farmers combined small strips of land to form larger holdings that were more efficient for large-scale farming. The enclosure movement reached its height in the early 1800s in Great Britain, when a growing population increased demand and raised prices for agricultural products. The need to feed its own people during the Napoleonic Wars also made it necessary for Britain to increase its food production.

The enclosure movement had significant consequences. As large landowners added to their holdings, they forced owners of small plots to either become tenant farmers or give up farming and move to the cities. Also, because land did not have to be farmed in common, farmers could experiment with their new methods of farming without having to seek the consent of the other villagers.

Among the first who experimented in the early 1700s were so-called gentlemen farmers such as Jethro Tull. Concerned about the wasteful practice of scattering seeds by hand over a wide area, Tull invented a seed drill, which made it possible to plant seeds in the soil in regular rows.

While visiting France and Italy, Tull saw that grape farmers had good results from uprooting the weeds between the rows and breaking up the soil. Tull developed a horse-drawn hoe to do this work on his own fields in England.

Another English gentleman farmer, Viscount Charles "Turnip" Townshend, a former British ambassador to the Netherlands, began to use a Dutch technique to avoid another wasteful practice. Traditionally, farmers left some of their fields unplanted, or fallow, each year to allow nutrients to replenish the soil. By means of repeated experiments,

Townshend learned that alternating different kinds of crops would preserve soil fertility. For example, he would plant grain crops such as wheat and barley one year and root crops such as turnips the next. This system, called **crop rotation**, has become a basic principle of modern farming.

Additional improvements in machinery increased production and made farm labor easier. For example, iron plows replaced wooden ones. An American inventor, Jethro Wood, invented an iron plow with standard parts so that a farmer could replace a broken part at low cost rather than having to buy a whole new plow every time one part broke.

Some of the new agricultural techniques and machines were expensive. Farmers who could afford them made large profits, but many farmers with small holdings could not afford additional equipment.

By the 1800s, improvements in agriculture had decreased the demand for farm laborers. People who might have worked on farms chose instead to look for work in the cities, where they created a large labor force.

Factors of Production

The more intense phase of technological development known as the Industrial Revolution that followed the Agricultural Revolution began in Great Britain because a certain combination of conditions existed there. Great Britain had what economists call the **factors of production**, or the basic resources necessary for industrialization: land, capital, and labor. When economists speak of land, they are referring to all natural resources, of which Great Britain had an abundant supply—particularly of coal and iron ore. Furthermore, Britain's excellent harbors facilitated trade, and its many rivers provided waterpower and inland transportation.

Great Britain also had access to capital. Capital includes money and goods such as tools, machinery, equipment, and inventory that are used in the production process. Many Britons had grown rich in the 1700s and now wanted to invest in new businesses.

In addition to land and capital, Great Britain had an abundant supply of labor, in this case, industrial workers. A growing population and migration into the cities fueled this supply.

Several other conditions help explain why the Industrial Revolution began in Great Britain. The British Isles and overseas colonies represented huge markets that created a large demand for British goods. Additional trade opportunities also existed in many other parts of the world, which could be reached by the British navy and merchant fleet, the best in the world. Equally important was the British government's concern for commercial interests. Parliament passed laws that protected businesses and helped them expand.

The Textile Industry

The cotton textile industry was the first industry in Great Britain to undergo **mechanization**, the use of automatic machinery to increase production. England had imported cotton cloth since the late Middle Ages, but in the 1600s, businesses began importing raw cotton and employing spinners and weavers to make it into cloth. This industry was an example of the **domestic system**, a system in which men and women work in their homes. The work was done by hand, and England could not produce enough cotton cloth to meet demand.

New inventions. The first step toward mechanization came with the improvement of the loom for weaving cloth. A loom is set up with a series of threads, called the warp, strung from top to bottom. The loom operator pushes a shuttle containing the woof (now called the weft), or the thread running crosswise to the warp, back and forth across the loom in a very time-consuming process. In 1733 an engineer named John Kay invented the flying shuttle, a cord mechanism that moved the woof thread more rapidly through the loom. Now weavers could weave faster than the spinners could produce thread on their simple spinning wheels. The demand for thread rose dramatically—a better spinning machine was needed.

James Hargreaves, a poor English weaver, came up with a machine in the 1760s that he named the spinning "jenny," probably for a member of his family. This machine could produce eight times as much thread as a single spinning wheel. Several years later, Richard Arkwright made further improvements with a machine called the water frame, which was a machine driven by waterpower.

Workers could use the jenny and the small, hand-operated, and relatively inexpensive flying shuttle in their homes. However, most people who worked at home could not make use of the expensive water frame, which required waterpower and a good deal of space. For this reason, Arkwright opened a spinning mill, bringing workers and machines together in one place to make goods. Employees worked a set number of hours for a certain amount of money. By 1784 Arkwright employed several hundred workers. This spinning mill marked the beginning of the modern **factory system**.

In 1779 Samuel Crompton combined the best features of the spinning jenny and the water frame in another machine, the spinning mule. Now weavers could get plenty of fine-quality thread. However, even with the flying shuttle, the weavers failed to meet the demand for cloth.

In 1785 an English minister, Edmund Cartwright, met the need for a faster weaving process with his invention of a loom which was powered by using water.

This print published circa 1835 illustrates a carding engine (left) delivering the cotton in a single sliver. The machines are driven by belts from the overhead shafts, which could be powered by water or steam.

The Story Behind the Industrial Revolution

Historians consider the Industrial Revolution to be one of the two most important changes that have taken place in the history of the world. Just as the start of agriculture did 10,000 years ago, the Industrial Revolution marks a turning point in history.

The Industrial Revolution is, of course, a more recent change. Just 300 years ago, people could do work or produce goods only by using their own muscles, the muscles of animals, or unreliable sources of power such as wind (in windmills) or water (in water mills). As a result, production was limited.

The Industrial Revolution made it possible to do more work and produce goods in abundance. Now people could use machines driven by fuels such as coal and oil, and the supply of these fuels seemed unlimited.

This remarkable change in production began at a particular time, the late 1700s, and in a particular country, Great Britain. Why did this change in production start then and there? Historians suggest that all of the pieces of the puzzle, as it were, happened to exist in Britain, and only in Britain.

For one thing, after the mid-1700s, the demand for manufactured goods such as cloth grew rapidly and outran the capacity of individual, rural spinners and weavers, who often worked in their own homes. In addition, the population grew faster than the

Top: Trade Emblem of the Amalgamated Society of Engineers, Machinists, Millwrights, Smiths and Pattern Makers
Bottom: James Ward painting of a farm family before the Industrial Revolution

American chemical plant, 1920

supply of goods. Moreover, if Britain could produce goods quickly and cheaply, it had existing markets, both at home and overseas. Britain's empire included parts of North and South America, Asia, and Africa. The demand was there. The problem was how to satisfy it. Here Britain had an advantage over its European neighbors. Because of advances in agriculture, Britain had better farm machinery and more scientific methods of cultivation than most of Europe. The process of consolidating small landholdings into larger, more productive farms was already well under way. This paved the way for industry because fewer farmworkers were needed, and more workers were available for other jobs.

If labor is one necessary resource, raw materials are equally important resources. As it happened, Britain's plentiful underground supplies of coal became the key to Britain being able to support its own new industries. Another piece of the puzzle fell into place.

Already wealthy because of trade with the outside world, Britain could afford to invest in new ventures. In addition, the British government safeguarded property against seizure by the government. Both these facts provided a perfect climate for individual and industrial innovation. Thus, a talented inventor such as James Watt, who devised an efficient steam engine, found himself richly rewarded—in a country where such wealth was secure.

The other wealthy countries of western Europe could not match Britain's advantages—they did not have all the pieces of the puzzle. For example, France, by 1763, had lost much of its empire to Britain.

Lacking an empire, there were no instant markets that would create demand for French-made products.

Britain was a country with limited government, enthusiasm for change, and stimulating contact with the outside world. By the 1780s, the Industrial Revolution had begun to transform the textile industry. Developments in that industry spurred other advances.

More than any other invention, the steam engine drove the Industrial Revolution forward by providing a source of power that did not depend on human muscle or the power of the wind or moving water. The increase in power now available to produce goods was remarkable.

Industrial change spread in two important ways. First, new industries sprang up as people applied the steam engine to new uses. Second, the Industrial Revolution crossed from Britain to other countries. Between 1815 and the 1850s, steam engines, factories, and railroads began to appear in parts of France, Belgium, the Netherlands, Germany, and northern Italy.

After 1870 the Industrial Revolution entered still another phase. It is the period that extends to the present; some historians call it the Second Industrial Revolution. Electric power and the internal combustion engine joined the steam engine. Many products of industry—telephones, automobiles, radios, and television sets—became available to most citizens of industrialized countries. The great industrial transformation that had begun in the special conditions of Great Britain soon encircled the globe.

First auto show, Madison Square Garden, 1900

Using this power loom, one person could weave as much cloth as 200 hand-loom operators.

This series of spinning and weaving innovations illustrates the cascading effect of invention. The flying shuttle created a need for more thread. The resulting faster method of spinning caused the price of cloth to go down, and the demand went up, creating a need for improved weaving machines. The power loom filled that need. Each invention went on to create a new need, and human ingenuity filled each new gap with a new invention.

Effects of mechanization. With all these improvements, cotton cloth became cheaper to produce and sell. As the price went down, the demand increased and so did the need for more raw cotton. In 1761 England imported 4 million pounds of cotton. In 1815 it imported 100 million pounds.

Most of the imported raw cotton came from the southern United States. At first, cotton cultivation had not been profitable there because it was difficult to remove the seeds from the cotton fibers to prepare the cotton for market. Cleaning the cotton was slow manual work. In 1793 Eli Whitney invented the cotton gin, a machine that could do this job much more quickly and efficiently than by hand. Equipped with Whitney's invention, the southern United States met the demands of the British textile manufacturers and became the cotton-producing center of the world. At the same time, by making cotton production more profitable, the cotton gin helped perpetuate slavery in the United States.

Steam Engines

Waterpower drove the early machines of the Industrial Revolution. Although waterpower represented a great improvement over human, animal, and wind power, it did have drawbacks. A factory had to be located beside a stream or river, preferably near a natural waterfall or a place where a dam could be built. Often this location was not near transportation, raw materials, a labor supply, or markets. A second drawback was that the water flow could vary greatly with the seasons. People began to look for a continuous, dependable, and portable power source; they found it in steam.

People had observed the power contained in steam since ancient times. It was not until 1712, however, that Thomas Newcomen, who was an English engineer, produced the first successful steam engine. Initially, workers used Newcomen engines to pump water from mines. These crude machines were more

What If?

The Cotton Gin
What if the cotton gin had not been invented? How might the history of the American South have been different?

powerful and dependable than water wheels, however, they were expensive to operate.

In the 1760s, James Watt, a Scottish instrument maker and engineer, studied the Newcomen engine. He invented several improvements and in 1769 patented the modern steam engine. Industry quickly adapted the Watt engine to drive the new spinning and weaving machines. As a result of Watt's invention, steam replaced water as industry's major power source.

Iron and Steel

The invention and availability of more and more machines produced a great demand for iron to make them. From early times, people in the British Isles had produced iron, using wood or charcoal to fuel the forges needed to separate the element from its ore. Then it was discovered that coal worked even better than wood or charcoal. As the Industrial Revolution continued, iron and coal became the two major raw materials of modern industry. Great Britain had an enormous advantage over other countries because it had large amounts of these two resources.

Many early steam engines exploded because the iron used to build them could not withstand the high pressure of steam. Industry needed a stronger, harder metal. Suppliers met this need with steel, which is iron with certain impurities removed. In the 1800s, the process for making steel was slow and expensive. However, during the 1850s, an American, William Kelly, and an Englishman, Henry Bessemer, developed a cheap and efficient method of making steel. It involved forcing air through the molten metal to burn out carbon and other impurities that made the metal brittle. This procedure is known today as the **Bessemer process**.

Industrialization in Other Fields

Using steam engines and iron and steel, British manufacturers quickly introduced power-driven machinery in many industries. The production of shoes, clothing, ammunition, and furniture became mechanized, as did printing and papermaking. People used machines to cut and finish lumber, to process foods, and to make other machines.

Some new inventions and innovative processes had important by-products. These by-products often developed into separate industries. For example, iron smelteries used coke, a by-product of coal, to improve the smelting process. Then someone discovered that the gases that coal released during the coke-making process could be burned to give light. During the 1810s, London became one of the first cities to pipe in gas to burn in street lamps. By the 1850s, hundreds of cities throughout the Western world used gas to light streets and homes.

Improvements in the production of rubber expanded the use of this raw material during the 1800s. Rubber was first used to make waterproof shoes and coats, but they became sticky in warm weather. In 1839, after years of experimenting, Charles Goodyear of the United States discovered a process of "curing" rubber to make it more elastic and usable. He mixed raw rubber with sulfur and then heated the mixture. Goodyear's method, called vulcanizing, became the basis of the modern rubber industry.

The oil industry developed around the mid-1800s, when people discovered how to use crude oil, or petroleum, to produce paraffin for candles, lubricating oil for machinery, and kerosene for lighting and heating.

Transportation

The Industrial Revolution also transformed transportation. When the revolution first began, land transportation was almost the same as it had been during the Middle Ages. Roads were little more than trails blurred with thick dust in dry weather and buried in deep, slippery mud when it rained.

A passenger in a stagecoach could travel perhaps 50 miles in one long day, barring unforeseen delays. Pack horses and clumsy wagons carrying heavy goods made even less progress in a day's journey.

Roads and canals. Industrialization made improved transportation necessary. Factories required delivery of raw materials, and finished products had to be transported to markets as quickly as possible. A Scottish engineer, John McAdam, worked out a new way of building roads that improved travel conditions. Layers of carefully selected smaller stones topped a roadbed of large stones. These roads, called macadam roads, served as a model for engineers in

This photo, taken in a steel works plant in Homestead, Pennsylvania, shows a huge Bessemer converter that converts iron into steel in 15 minutes.

later times. Today road builders use asphalt to bind the smaller stones together.

Great Britain and other countries of western Europe also had extensive networks of rivers that served as water highways. Some canals connected them, but workers constructed many more canals after engineers began using locks—gates that regulate the level and flow of water. Many canals were built between 1760 and 1850. However, although canals were cheaper and slightly faster than roads, new forms of transportation soon began to compete with the canals.

Railroads and steamboats. Watt's steam engine offered many possibilities for new means of transportation. In 1814 George Stephenson, an English engineer, perfected a steam-propelled moving engine, or locomotive, that ran on rails. In 1829 Stephenson's famous locomotive, the *Rocket*, pulled a line of cars from Liverpool to Manchester, reaching for a short time the amazing speed of 30 miles per hour. Networks of railroads soon connected much of the Western world. Continuous improvements, such as steel rails, air brakes, and comfortable coaches made railroad transportation fast, safe, and affordable.

Many people tried adapting the steam engine for use on ships. Robert Fulton, an American engineer and inventor, was the first to succeed at this.

This scene of steamboats on the Mississippi River was prepared by the nineteenth-century lithograph firm Currier & Ives. Their hand-colored prints recorded local social history.

He established the first regular inland steamboat service that produced a profit. His boat, the *Clermont*, was launched on the Hudson River in 1807. One year later, after improvements to the boat, the *Clermont* began regular trips between New York City and Albany. Steamboats soon appeared on many of the rivers and lakes of the world.

In 1838 the *Great Western*, a ship operated only by steam, crossed the Atlantic Ocean in 15 days, less than half the time it took a sailing ship. Samuel Cunard of Great Britain, who founded the Cunard Line shipping company in 1839, provided regular steamboat service across the Atlantic. Soon ships built of iron and steel instead of wood moved goods all over the world in less time and for less money than ever before.

The Communications Revolution

Scientific research played only a small role in the invention of textile machinery, the steam engine, the locomotive, and the steamship. All of these inventions represented the work of amateur inventors and engineers. These inventions did not come from scientists' laboratories. In communications, however, scientific research played a more significant role in the development of technology.

For centuries people had observed electricity and its connection with magnetism, but they had put their knowledge to little practical use. For one thing, no one had found a way to provide a steady flow of electric current. Around 1800 an Italian, Alessandro Volta, built the first battery, a device that provided a steady current of electricity. In the 1820s, André Ampère of France worked out principles governing the magnetic effect of an electric current.

Samuel Morse of the United States put the work of Volta and Ampère to practical use. Morse sent an electrical current over a wire to a machine at the other end of the wire. Each time electricity passed along the wire, the machine clicked. By 1838 Morse had worked out a system of dots and dashes—the Morse code—by which these clicks could be translated into letters of the alphabet. By 1844 Morse's invention, the telegraph, had become a practical communication instrument. Soon telegraph wires, stretched across continents, transmitted ideas at the speed of electricity.

People also found a way to carry electricity under the sea by using cables—heavily insulated telegraph wires. Early in the 1850s, a cable across the English Channel connected Great Britain with the European continent.

However, spanning the great distance of the Atlantic Ocean presented enormous difficulties. Not until 1866 did Cyrus Field and a group of Americans lay a cable across the Atlantic Ocean. Soon afterward cables connected all continents of the world.

The Spread of Industry

For various reasons, the rapid changes in agriculture, industry, transportation, and communications had little effect on the European continent for several years. Many European countries did not have raw materials or large, accessible markets for their products. In addition, the wars of the French Revolution and the Napoleonic Era slowed Europe's industrial development.

France, however, did develop some industry, especially textiles, iron, and mining. The French government helped this development in two ways. First, it imposed high tariffs to keep out foreign manufactured goods. Second, it encouraged the construction of railroads. However, in the 1800s France remained largely an agricultural country. Most of France's working population at this time was still made up of farmers and peasants.

Industry grew more slowly in the German states than in Great Britain because Germany had no efficient central government to aid industrial growth. Still, Germany held its own as an industrial power. By the time the German states were unified in the 1870s, the pace of Germany's industrialization was approaching that of Great Britain.

The United States eagerly adopted British inventions and methods. The United States had everything it needed for industrial development—national unity and a vast country with rich natural resources. It also had a rapidly increasing population, inventive genius, and a willingness to adopt, to adapt, and to take the risks involved in business.

A network of canals and railroads crept across the United States during the 1800s, and industry moved west as transportation developed. The steel industry grew in Pittsburgh and the Great Lakes region, and machinery was manufactured in Chicago. By 1869 a railroad connected the East Coast with the West Coast of the United States. Before the end of the century, the United States had surpassed Great Britain in the production of iron and steel.

Along with the growth of American industry came significant changes in farming. Eli Whitney's cotton gin enabled the southern states to supply cotton to the British textile industry. Another invention was a machine for harvesting grain, patented by Cyrus McCormick in 1834. The McCormick reaper, which was drawn by horses, freed many farmers from the slow, backbreaking work of cutting grain with sickles or scythes. Other inventions, such as the mechanical thresher for separating the grains of wheat from their stalks and hulls, followed.

Section 1 Review

1. **Define** Industrial Revolution, enclosure movement, crop rotation, factors of production, mechanization, domestic system, factory system, Bessemer process
2. **Identify** James Hargreaves, Richard Arkwright, Eli Whitney, James Watt, Henry Bessemer, John McAdam, Robert Fulton, Samuel Morse, Cyrus Field
3. **Determining Cause and Effect** (a) What was the enclosure movement, and how did this movement lead to changes in agriculture? (b) What were the principal effects of the Agricultural Revolution?
4. **Analyzing Ideas** Why did the Industrial Revolution begin in Great Britain?
5. **Synthesizing Ideas** Describe the importance and results of inventions in the textile industry.
6. **Evaluating Ideas** What were four important developments in transportation and communication during the Industrial Revolution?

Section 2

The Factory System

Focus Questions

- In what ways did the increased use of machinery affect workers and working conditions?
- What caused the middle class to expand, and in what ways was the middle class distinct from the working class?
- How did the lives of women change during the Industrial Revolution?

For centuries skilled artisans produced goods of all kinds in their homes or in small shops. The artisan controlled the training of apprentices, the quality and price of goods, and the pace of each workday. During the 1700s, the opportunity for a higher standard of living lured thousands of English farm workers to the city to work in the factories spawned by the Industrial Revolution. The emergence of these factories was only one of the many changes the Industrial Revolution created.

The Effect of Machines on Work

The introduction of steam-powered machinery made work easier to do. Instead of spending several years as an apprentice learning a trade, a person could learn to perform a task or operate a machine in a few days.

Employers wanted people who could learn a few simple tasks and soon discovered that women and children could operate machines as efficiently as men. Employers preferred to hire young men and women rather than older, skilled people. Young people did not have set working habits and did not expect high wages. Women and children would work for lower wages than men. Consequently, the early textile factories employed mainly children and young women.

As machines became more widely used, older, skilled workers often found themselves unemployed. Factories no longer needed their abilities as weavers or spinners and would not hire them for simpler work. To make up for their lost income, many of these people sent their children to work in textile factories while they looked for odd jobs in cities or on farms.

The Wage System

The factory system differed significantly from the domestic system. Under the domestic system, workers usually worked unsupervised in their homes. They turned over finished products, such as thread or cloth, perhaps once a week, and were paid for the number of items completed. In factories, instead of working on a product from beginning to end, each worker performed only a small part of the entire job. Under the factory system, dozens or hundreds of workers toiled in the same room under the watchful eyes of supervisors. Everyone was employed by the factory owners. Factory owners paid their workers wages based on the number of hours worked or the amount of goods produced.

Several factors determined factory workers' wages. First, employers wanted to produce goods as cheaply as possible. Thus, factory owners set wages in relation to other costs of production. For example, if the cost of land or capital increased, the owners lowered wages.

Second, an oversupply of workers lowered wages. On the other hand, wages rose when there were not enough workers to do a particular job.

Third, wages often depended on what people could earn at other kinds of work. For example, early employers in textile factories wanted to attract young women as workers. The employers therefore paid young women more than they could earn as household servants.

Fourth, wages were higher for men than for women. For example, in cotton mills and the London clothing trades in Great Britain, men earned as much as twice what women earned. Women were thought to be adding "a little something" to a family's income, even if in reality a woman was the only wage earner for her family.

Factory workers acquired skills and were paid accordingly, but they had little else to show for their work. They did not own their tools or equipment, as domestic workers had, and there were few opportunities for advancement within the factory.

Factory Rules and Regulations

Factory work changed working people's work habits. Workers had many rules to follow. They had to arrive at the factory for work promptly. They could eat meals and take breaks only at set times, and they could leave only with permission. They worked whether it was hot or cold, winter or summer, day or night. Breaking the rules or missing work for any reason could result in heavy fines, pay cuts, or job loss.

In the early factories, workers spent 14 hours a day, six days a week, on the job. Instead of the work being adjusted to the seasons, as it was under the domestic system or on farms, factory workers had to adjust their lives to the demands of machines, and the machines never needed to rest. Some workers even complained that people in authority expected them to become machines themselves.

Factories were uncomfortable places; they were noisy, dirty, and poorly ventilated. The air was hot and steamy in summer and cold and damp in winter. Sanitary facilities were primitive. Early machines had no safety devices, and serious injuries occurred frequently. Employers provided no accident insurance or other form of compensation for injury.

One of the most alarming features of early industrialization—in light of twentieth-century attitudes—was child labor. Five-year-old children were commonly employed in cotton mills and in mines. Conditions were particularly bad in coal mines, where women and children pulled carts through tunnels that were too low to allow a donkey or a grown man to pass through.

Thonet Rocker

Some inventions, such as the steam engine, affected people the world over. Others were less universal in their impact, though no less significant in terms of their ingenuity. Michael Thonet, a German cabinetmaker living in Austria, invented a process that revolutionized furniture making. He used this process in the mid-1860s to craft the bentwood rocker shown here. Thonet's patent consisted of bending solid wood by steaming it and then clamping a thin strip of steel along one side. The process eliminated complex jointing and carving. The simple process allowed Thonet to hire local people rather than expensive artisans for his European factories.

Many years before the Industrial Revolution had any impact on the rest of the furniture industry, Thonet's chairs, hat stands, and other pieces were being mass-produced. By 1870 Thonet's company was making about 1,300 pieces of furniture a day. In other words, with a six-day workweek, his factory produced 400,000 pieces annually—an early triumph in mass production.

Abusive situations in factories soon scandalized Great Britain. In 1832 a parliamentary committee investigated working conditions of children in textile mills. As a result of this investigation, Parliament passed the Factory Act of 1833, which allowed for factory inspection and enforcement of child labor laws. The following exchange between the parliamentary committee and 23-year-old Elizabeth Bently, who began to work in a flax mill when she was 6 years old, illustrates the committee's findings:

"What were your hours of labor?—From five in the morning till nine at night, when they were thronged. . . .
Suppose you flagged a little, or were too late, what would they do?—Strap us.
Girls as well as boys?—Yes.
Have you ever been strapped?—Yes, severely. . . .

You are considerably deformed in your person in consequence of this labor?—Yes, I am.
At what time did it come on?—I was about thirteen years old when it began coming, and it has got worse since.**"**

Living Conditions of Workers

Life in the mines and factories was hard and monotonous, and life in the workers' homes was not much better. Working people lived in cramped and poorly maintained apartment houses called tenements. As many as a dozen people might dwell in a single room. One bed might have been shared by half a dozen children at one time. As late as 1840, 40,000 to 50,000 working-class people in Manchester, England, lived in cellars. The illness, death, or unemployment of a working father or mother could send a family to the brink of starvation.

Although the working classes suffered during the Industrial Revolution, their living standard improved considerably when inexpensive consumer goods produced in the factories became available to them. In time, workers' wages increased somewhat, increasing the buying power of the large working sector of the population.

Conditions in industrial cities during the Industrial Revolution were shocking when evaluated by today's standards. However, the lower economic classes, whether peasants or artisans, had always worked long and hard. They had always suffered from periodic famines and epidemics. Moreover, women and children had always worked hard, especially in rural areas.

The Development of the Middle Class

During the Industrial Revolution, the balance of economic and political power shifted from agriculture to manufacturing. As the two trends of industrialization and urbanization continued and the industrial society expanded and became more complicated, a middle class grew. It consisted of bankers, manufacturers, merchants, lawyers, doctors, engineers, professors, and their families.

The life of the middle and upper tiers of the middle class contrasted markedly with that of the working class. The groups lived apart, workers in crowded slums and middle-class people in larger houses in more spacious neighborhoods. The two groups dressed differently. Workers wore work shirts; lawyers and merchants wore suits. Working-class women dressed in plain skirts and blouses; most women of the middle class wore lace and frills. The lower tier of the middle class, however, would have been largely indistinguishable from the working-class people.

The laboring poor who worked on farms or in factories continued to struggle economically as had their parents and grandparents. The middle class, however, gained prestige and political recognition. Members of the middle and upper tiers of the middle class could afford to own property, hire servants, eat well, and enjoy some comfort. Affluent middle-class parents sent their children to school to receive training for good jobs. Often the younger generation inherited money and social position from their parents.

Aristocratic government leaders sought the advice of middle-class economists. Soon government leaders became as concerned about the future of industry as they were about the future of agriculture.

The Effect of Industrialization on Women's Lives

The Industrial Revolution affected women of different classes in different ways. In the past, in addition to working in the fields, women had spun yarn, woven cloth, made clothing, and prepared meals. They manufactured goods for sale and assisted their husbands in craft shops or small family businesses. However, the Industrial Revolution moved most manufacturing into factories and many working families into the cities. All classes of city-dwelling people purchased food and clothing at large markets instead of making these products at home. As city dwellers, many women no longer had the resources or the need to do the important work of growing food or making cloth for clothing.

Working-class women. The early textile mills hired women to tend machines that spun cotton into thread. Women could perform this task efficiently and were paid less than men. Thus industrialization changed the location of work for working-class women, but it did not raise their status.

While some working-class women took factory jobs, many others continued to work at what was a traditional job for women, domestic service. For centuries young, single women had been hired as maids, cooks, and nannies in other people's homes. Many men had worked as grooms, gardeners, footmen, valets, and butlers. After industrialization more middle-class families could afford to hire servants. As a result, more jobs for servants became available.

As the number of farms declined during the Industrial Revolution, rural areas offered fewer jobs. Daughters of farm families now took jobs as servants in the city. For many country women, domestic service represented a first step into city life. Working as a servant called for the skills that most girls would have been taught anyway, such as cleaning, cooking, and caring for young children. Servants lived with the families for whom they worked. Thus a girl moving from the country had a place to live and food to eat. After living for a while in the city as a servant, a young woman might take a job in a shop or factory.

Middle-class women. The Industrial Revolution brought new wealth and greater luxury to middle-class women, who could hire servants to assist them in cooking, cleaning, and taking care of their children. While their husbands went to work each day, middle-class wives stayed home. Middle-class people placed increasing emphasis on the idea that women belonged at home and men belonged in the working

During the Industrial Revolution, many young girls, such as those seen here, took jobs in garment factories.

and Great Britain, the need for teachers increased. Women began to enter the teaching field. By the end of the 1800s, elementary school teaching had become largely a female profession.

Section 2 Review

1. **Locate and Explain the Significance** Manchester
2. **Understanding Ideas** How did machines change the way work was done?
3. **Summarizing Ideas** What four factors determined the wages of a factory worker?
4. **Analyzing Ideas** Tell how the middle class expanded and gained in importance.
5. **Synthesizing Ideas** (a) What jobs were open to women in the 1800s? (b) How did these jobs affect their lives?

world. According to some writers of the day, woman's nature equipped her only for raising children and caring for the home. More and more people considered earning money as a corruption of "true womanhood." Some women accepted and enjoyed this role, but others began to express a very different attitude.

In the mid-1800s, some middle-class women began voicing their need for roles outside the home. For some, a life outside the home meant a measure of freedom. For others, especially those who were single, this meant paid work, which was a financial necessity, not just charity work. The issue of a woman's right to work was hotly debated throughout the 1800s. Gradually, the idea gained some acceptance.

During the late 1800s, more jobs became available and acceptable for women. The demand for public health care created a need for nurses and social workers, greatly increasing opportunities for women. In addition, the call for secretaries and telephone and telegraph operators opened up other avenues for women who needed or wanted to work.

Demands also arose for improvements in education. College courses were opened to women, and special women's colleges were established. As public education spread in the 1870s and 1880s in France

Section 3

New Methods and Business Organizations

Focus Questions

- How did methods of production change during the Industrial Revolution?
- Why did corporations emerge, and how did they affect the way business was done?
- What is the business cycle, and how does it affect society?

Throughout the 1800s, inventions, new sales methods, and new methods of production and distribution of goods caused rapid growth in industry. This growth brought many changes to the factory system and to the organization of businesses. Some of these changes date to the early Industrial Revolution. Other changes came after about 1870 as a result of scientific developments.

The factory system also introduced a new phase in the development of **capitalism**—the economic system in which individuals rather than governments control the factors of production. Before the Industrial Revolution, most capitalists were merchants who bought, sold, and exchanged goods. We refer to this type of capitalism as **commercial capitalism**. However, the capitalists of the Industrial Revolution became more involved in producing and manufacturing goods themselves. Furthermore, the methods used for production were largely mechanized and industrialized. For these reasons, this type of capitalism is referred to as **industrial capitalism**.

Division of Labor

As we have seen, industrialization changed the methods of production. Factory owners hired large numbers of unskilled laborers, divided the manufacturing process into a series of steps, and then assigned a step to each worker. This was a form of **division of labor**. Because a large number of items could be produced in a given length of time, the cost of the items diminished. The use of machinery helped the division of labor because machines performed many of the steps.

Interchangeable Parts

The American inventor Eli Whitney used division of labor and **interchangeable parts** to make muskets in the late 1700s. In Whitney's factory, some people worked on musket barrels, others on trigger mecha-

nisms, and still others on the wooden stocks or handles.

The use of interchangeable parts for his firearms became an essential part of Whitney's system. Previously, firearms had been handmade by skilled artisans. Each gun was slightly different. Whitney designed machinery that unskilled workers could operate. This machinery turned out identical, interchangeable parts. This development made division of labor possible in a product composed of several parts that had to fit together. Whitney's system resulted in the speedy production of a large number of inexpensive muskets that could be easily repaired. Other manufacturers, realizing the usefulness of interchangeable parts, quickly adopted the idea.

The Assembly Line

Division of labor and the use of interchangeable parts are two essential elements of mass production. **Mass production** is the system of manufacturing large numbers of identical items.

A third element of mass production is the assembly line. Until the late 1800s, each of the various parts of a manufactured object was transported to a central point, where workers assembled the object. Then

In 1913 Henry Ford's main plant was located in the Detroit suburb of Highland Park.

manufacturers devised the assembly line. A conveyor belt carried unfinished products from worker to worker. As each item passed, each worker performed a certain task. The assembly line saved time and energy and increased the number of times per hour a worker could perform his or her assigned task.

Henry Ford saw great potential in the mass-production system. By applying it to the production of automobiles, he founded one of the largest industries in the United States. A conveyor belt carried the automobile frame from one worker to the next. Each worker made a small contribution by adding one or more of the thousands of interchangeable parts that composed the Model T Ford. Mass production lowered the price of automobiles, making them accessible to most American families.

American and European industrialists began to mass-produce clothing, furniture, and machinery. Because mass production usually lowered the cost of an item, more people could buy more and more goods and enjoy a higher standard of living.

Rise of the Corporation

Before the Industrial Revolution, most businesses were either sole proprietorships or partnerships. A business owned and controlled by one person is a **sole proprietorship**; a **partnership** is a business owned and controlled by two or more people. Although both types of businesses give their owners considerable freedom to make economic decisions, both types have disadvantages. For example, both sole proprietors and partners are responsible for all debts even if the debts exceed the original amount of investment. In addition, sole proprietorships and partnerships usually remain small. Small companies with few workers typically cannot afford mass-production methods or the machinery necessary for large-scale production.

As the scale of business grew during the 1800s, so too did the **corporation**. A corporation is a business organization in which individuals buy shares of stock, elect directors to decide policies and hire managers, and receive dividends according to the number of shares they own. Unlike sole proprietors and partners, a shareholder's financial responsibility is limited to the amount that he or she invests. For this reason, corporations are attractive to investors.

In the late 1800s, corporations increased greatly in terms of the amount of capital invested and in terms of size. In 1901 American financier J. P. Morgan and his associates formed the United States Steel Company, the first of many billion-dollar corporations.

Banks and other financial institutions played an increasingly important role in forming and operating these large corporations.

Increasing the size of a corporation did not always increase its profits. A large manufacturing enterprise could generally produce goods at a lower cost than a small one. To get lower costs, however, the factory had to operate at full capacity, turning out as many goods as possible. Sometimes a factory produced so many goods that selling them all became a problem.

When a number of corporations were producing the same products, competition became very keen. The smaller and less efficient businesses suffered if they tried to sell their products by cutting prices. Often these smaller firms had to sell out to larger firms.

As a result, although the size of individual corporations increased steadily, the number of individual corporations in some industries decreased. Sometimes a corporation would buy so many smaller companies that it would create a **monopoly**. A monopoly is the complete control of the production or sale of a good or service by a single firm. In the United States, corporations such as Standard Oil and United States Steel created monopolies.

By 1900 a number of giant corporations in Germany had combined to control entire industries. These combinations of corporations were known as **cartels**. For example, a cartel might own coal and iron mines, steel mills, and factories that used steel to build machines, thus controlling all aspects of an industry.

Business Cycles

As industrial production became more and more important, it influenced a country's entire economy. The Industrial Revolution brought alternating periods of prosperity and decline—a pattern known as the **business cycle**.

When one industry did well, other industries also prospered. If, for example, there was a great demand for machines, there would also be a demand for the coal and iron needed to make them. If, on the other hand, a large firm reduced its orders of iron and laid off workers, other companies would also be affected. The iron suppliers might have to cut down production and lay off workers as well. The laid-off workers would not be able to pay their rent or buy food. These workers would have to apply for other jobs. When there were many workers available for just a few jobs, employers reduced wages, knowing that they could find workers who would agree to low pay. In some cases, the effects would go on spreading to other industries, until the entire economy was in a **depression**, the lowest point of a business cycle.

These economic fluctuations affected the lives of all the people in an industrialized country, even those people who did not work in factories. In addition, events in one country could affect the economy of another country. During the American Civil War, for example, the Confederacy could not ship cotton to Great Britain. The shortage of cotton contributed to a depression in the British textile industry.

Section 3 Review

1. **Define** capitalism, commercial capitalism, industrial capitalism, division of labor, interchangeable parts, mass production, sole proprietorship, partnership, corporation, monopoly, cartels, business cycle, depression
2. **Evaluating Ideas** (a) What is the chief advantage of mass production? (b) What three elements are needed to make mass production possible?
3. **Comparing Ideas** What advantages did corporations have over sole proprietorships and partnerships?
4. **Analyzing Ideas** Why might monopolies and cartels be harmful to a nation's economy?
5. **Synthesizing Ideas** How did the Industrial Revolution bring about the business cycle?

Section 4

Living and Working Conditions

Focus Questions
- **What were Adam Smith's ideas, and how did they affect people's views of industrialism?**
- **Why did reform movements arise, and what issues did reformers take on?**
- **How did workers themselves try to improve their situations?**

As the Industrial Revolution progressed, the interests of employers often conflicted with the interests of workers. Employers needed workers who would come to work on time, do their jobs quickly and well, follow factory rules, and accept relatively low wages.

Workers, on the other hand, needed wages high enough to support their families even through difficulties. They wanted some control over their work hours, the conditions in the factories, and the conditions in the towns where they lived. However, society in general was influenced by certain economic theories that had become widespread as the Industrial Revolution progressed, and workers' demands went unanswered.

Adam Smith

During the Enlightenment of the 1700s, a group of economists, called Physiocrats, attacked the ideas of mercantilism. Mercantilism was the economic theory based on the belief that the world contained only a fixed amount of wealth, and, in order to increase its wealth, a country had to take some wealth from another country. These economists believed that natural laws should be left to govern economic life. Any attempt to interfere with these natural economic laws was certain to bring disaster. Adam Smith, a Scot who accepted some of the ideas of the Physiocrats, stated his views in his book *The Wealth of Nations*, which was published in 1776.

Smith reasoned that two natural laws—the law of supply and demand and the law of competition—regulate all business and economic activity. In any business, Smith believed, prices—and therefore profits—will be fixed by the relationship of supply to demand. If an article is scarce and in great demand, people will pay a high price for it. Thus profits from its sales will rise. The makers of the product will then invest their money to produce more of the scarce article. Soon the supply of the article will exceed the demand for it.

Now each manufacturer will face competition. To get people to buy a product, the manufacturer will have to reduce the price or improve the quality or both. If too many manufacturers produce the same article, the price of the item will go down so far that some manufacturers will not make enough money to cover their costs. The least efficient businesses may be forced out of business. When such manufacturers quit producing the article, the supply of the article will decrease and the price will go up. Then the capable, efficient, and well-organized producers will make a reasonable profit.

Adam Smith wrote that every person should have the freedom to start any business of their choice.

Building History Study Skills

READ
WRITE
INTERPRET
CONNECT
THINK

Interpreting Visuals: Determining Cause and Effect

Understanding history requires that you identify the causes of historical events and determine their effect on history. A cause is the reason that something else happened. An effect is the result or consequence of an action or a situation. Usually an event, an idea, or a situation results from several causes. In history causes can be divided into two types. Underlying causes are long term. Immediate causes lead directly to an event. For example, practicing a sport may lead to a championship. The immediate cause of that victory, however, is the winning game.

How to Determine Cause and Effect
To determine cause and effect, follow these steps.
1. Identify the focal point of your study.
2. Determine the underlying causes. For example, did new ideas cause people to act in a certain way?
3. Identify the immediate cause. For example, did a political candidate seeking an office win or lose the election because bad weather resulted in a low voter turnout?
4. Formulate a conclusion about the significance of the causes and effects of a historical event.

Developing the Skill
Economists often wonder why industrialization suddenly "takes off" at a certain time in a particular place. Walter Rostow, a twentieth-century economic historian, has advanced the theory that every society develops according to a dynamic production pattern that consists of five stages. The chart below explains the five stages of Rostow's theory.

The chart shows that in stage one, the economy is based on agriculture. Traditional values prevail. The underlying causes for the Industrial Revolution are economic, political, social, and intellectual. Economically, there needs to be an agricultural surplus that generates capital. The traditional social structure declines with the rise of a commercial class. A centralized national government encourages economic modernization. Ideas about the benefits of profit are praised rather than degraded. The immediate cause originates from a surge of production and the rapid expansion in one industry, which serves as the basis for modernization. The significance of the process is that in order for the Industrial Revolution to occur, a social, political, and intellectual change must take place. The economic system is intertwined with the culture and the value system.

Practicing the Skill
Use the characteristics of society on the chart as the basis for your own chart on the development of the space industry.

To apply this skill, see Applying History Study Skills on page 513.

Rostow's Theory of Industrial Development

Characteristics	Stage One: *Traditional Society*	Stage Two: *Preconditions for Take-Off*	Stage Three: *Take-Off*	Stage Four: *Drive to Maturity*	Stage Five: *Age of Mass Consumption*
Economy	• agricultural • limited production	• agricultural surplus • surplus capital • expansion of trade	• surge of technology • rapid expansion of industry	• technology extended to all sectors	• increased production and use of durable goods
Society	• hierarchical social structure	• beginning of a commercial class	• entrepreneurial class more dominant	• urbanization • increase in skilled and professional workers	• rise of a new middle class • shift to suburbs
Political Power	• regionally based power in the hands of landowners	• centralized national government	• groups in power encourage economic modernization	• industrial leaders highly influential	• social welfare • more resources for military
Values	• belief that change will not occur	• spirit of progress	• investment of capital for profit becomes important	• emphasis on technology • expectation of progress	• acquisition of consumer goods important

He also believed that a person's business should be operated for the greatest advantage. The result, Smith said, would benefit everyone. Laborers would have jobs, investors and owners would make profits, and buyers would receive better goods at lower prices. Smith's system was one of complete **free enterprise**.

Smith's ideas appealed to industrialists because the forces he outlined supposedly worked automatically. Smith argued that if anything interfered with the absolutely free working of supply and demand and competition, the system could not work well. Laws and regulations, such as those imposed under mercantilism, were thought of as interfering with the workings of natural law or natural economic forces.

Thomas Malthus and David Ricardo

Smith's ideas received strong support from Thomas Malthus and David Ricardo. Malthus was an Anglican clergyman who became a professor of economics. In his book *An Essay on the Principle of Population*, published in 1798, he wrote that population increases present the greatest obstacle to human progress. People, he said, multiply more rapidly than the food supply increases, despite such checks as famines, epidemics, and wars. He believed that human misery and poverty are inevitable.

David Ricardo was an English businessman who amassed a large fortune early in life and then was elected to the House of Commons. He, too, wrote that working-class poverty is inevitable. In his book *Principles of Political Economy and Taxation*, published in 1817, Ricardo stated that supply and demand determine wages. When labor is plentiful, wages remain low. When labor is scarce, wages soar. As population grows, Ricardo wrote, more and more workers become available, and wages inevitably drop. Ricardo's idea became known as the iron law of wages.

Malthus and Ricardo painted a grim picture of workers as inevitably poor and suffering. Understandably, the new social science of economics became known as the "dismal science."

Laissez-Faire

The writings of economists such as Smith, Malthus, and Ricardo supported industrialists who wanted to buy labor, like any other commodity, as cheaply as possible. Their economic theories also indicated that governments should not interfere with the operations of business. This attitude was summed up in the French phrase **laissez-faire** (le·say-FAR), meaning "let do" or leave things alone.

The British put the theory of laissez-faire into practice. Formerly, either the government or the guilds had regulated the quantity and quality of goods and the hours and wages of workers. Starting in the 1840s, most regulations were discontinued. Tariffs, which had regulated foreign trade, were abolished. Trade was almost completely unregulated. Other European countries and the United States adopted features of laissez-faire economics, although not as completely as did Britain.

Growing Interest in Reform

At the same time, more and more people were realizing that things could not be left entirely alone. Humanitarians—people who work to improve the conditions of others—urged reforms. Ministers preached against what they considered the unchristian selfishness of businesspeople.

Influential writers made the public aware of the terrible conditions in mines and factories. The great English writer Charles Dickens used his novels *Dombey and Son* and *Hard Times* to attack selfish business leaders. In *David Copperfield*, Dickens drew on his own wretched childhood experiences as a worker in a warehouse. Essayists and critics such as Thomas Carlyle and John Ruskin denounced the materialism—the obsession with money and the neglect of spiritual values—of their times.

Many people began to feel that government needed to regulate work hours and set minimal standards for wages and working conditions. These people argued that such laws would not interfere with the natural workings of the economy.

In Great Britain, some reformers adopted the ideas of philosopher Jeremy Bentham. In his 1789 book, *An Introduction to the Principles of Morals and Legislation*, Bentham argued that every act of a society should be judged in terms of its utility, or usefulness. His theory was thus known as **utilitarianism**. A law was useful, and therefore good, said Bentham, if it led to "the greatest happiness of the greatest number" of people. Bentham believed that people needed education so they could better determine what things were good for them or made them happy.

Bentham and his followers advocated reform of the prison system; they advocated education as well as legal reform. They thought that government should create conditions to enable as many people as possible to find happiness.

History Through the Arts

Hard Times

English novelist Charles Dickens (1812–1870) achieved lasting fame for his portrayal of British society during the early Industrial Revolution. These excerpts from the novel *Hard Times* describe Coketown, a town spawned by the Industrial Revolution.*

"It was a town of red brick, or of brick that would have been red if the smoke and ashes had allowed it; but as matters stood it was a town of unnatural red and black like the painted face of a savage. It was a town of machinery and tall chimneys, out of which interminable serpents of smoke trailed themselves for ever and ever, and never got uncoiled. It had a black canal in it, and a river that ran purple with ill-smelling dye, and vast piles of buildings full of windows where there was a rattling and a trembling all day long, and where the piston of the steam-engine worked monotonously up and down like the head of an elephant in a state of melancholy madness. It contained several large streets all very like one another, and many small streets still more like one another, inhabited by people equally like one another, who all went in and out at the same hours, with the same sound upon the same pavements, to do the same work, and to whom every day was the same as yesterday and tomorrow, and every year the counterpart of the last and the next. . . .

Seen from a distance . . . Coketown lay shrouded in a haze of its own, which appeared impervious to the sun's rays. You only knew the town was there, because you knew there could have been no such sulky blotch upon the prospect without a town. A blur of soot and smoke, now confusedly tending this way, now that way, now aspiring to the vault of Heaven, now murkily creeping along

The Bessemer works at Sheffield, England

the earth, as the wind rose and fell, or changed its quarter: a dense formless jumble, with sheets of cross light in it, that showed nothing but masses of darkness:—Coketown in the distance was suggestive of itself, though not a brick of it could be seen. . . .

The streets were hot and dusty on the summer day. . . . Stokers emerged from low underground doorways into factory yards, and sat on steps, and posts, and palings, wiping their swarthy visages, and contemplating coals. The whole town seemed to be frying in oil. There was a stifling smell of hot oil everywhere. The steam-engines shone with it, the dresses of the Hands were soiled with it, the mills throughout their many stories oozed and trickled it."

*Coke is the residue left after distillation of coal or other materials such as petroleum. Coke was often used as fuel.

John Stuart Mill

Philosopher John Stuart Mill, although a believer in laissez-faire, criticized what he considered the economic injustices and inequalities of British society. Mill's father had taught his son Bentham's principles of utilitarianism. Mill also believed government should work for the well-being of all its citizens. He could not accept an economic system that left the working classes trapped in miserable poverty. Mill believed government should intervene to protect working children and improve housing and factory conditions. He advocated not only full democracy but also complete equality in all respects between men and women. In 1861 he wrote, "All human beings have the same interest in good government; the welfare of all is alike affected by it, and they have equal need of a voice in it to secure their share of its benefits."

In Mill's view individual liberty, which included the liberty to think as one pleased and to express one's views, was a basic human right. Mill believed governments should guarantee that liberty.

Early Reform Laws

Great Britain made early attempts to improve working conditions through legislation. Britain's initial laws dealt with the employment of women and children. Working conditions for these two groups in particular scandalized many people.

Beginning in 1819, Parliament attempted to legislate hours and conditions for children working in cotton mills. The first of these laws, the Factory Act of 1819, proved ineffective because it included no means of enforcement. The Factory Act of 1833 allowed for investigation and enforcement of the previous act's measures and extended them to all textile factories. Under the terms of these laws, textile mills were prohibited from employing children under 9 years of age. Children between the ages of 9 and 13 could work no more than 8 hours daily, six days a week. Children between ages 13 and 18 could work no more than 12 hours a day.

Nine years later another law prohibited the employment in coal mines of all women and of children under 10. A great advance came in 1847 with the passage of the Ten Hours Act. This law established a 10-hour working day for women and for children under the age of 18 in textile factories. Because it was not profitable to keep the factories running when the women and children were gone, textile factories adopted the 10-hour workday for all workers.

Despite these reform laws, the conditions under which many workers labored remained harsh. Factory reform laws often were not strictly enforced, and these laws did not solve all of the workers' problems. For example, the factory reform laws did not deal with wages. Eventually, workers would achieve improved working conditions through better organization and government legislation.

Worker Strikes

One way that workers could protest working conditions and low wages was for a group of them to refuse to work. A group of miners, for example, who believed they were being paid too little for their work would refuse to enter the mines. When an entire group of workers refused to work, they were said to be on **strike**. Workers often made a list of their demands and told the employer they would not work until these demands were met. Employers sometimes

Young people made up a considerable portion of the American labor force. Strikes became common throughout the late 1800s and into the 1900s.

agreed to give the strikers what they wanted. At other times, the employers either fired all the strikers and hired new workers or simply waited until the strikers returned to work.

Hundreds of strikes took place in industrial countries during the 1800s. The strikers usually made two kinds of demands—higher wages for workers and more control over working conditions. Sometimes strikes began as demands for higher wages but became protests against general working and living conditions of the working class. Strike leaders demanded a reorganization of society to end the differences between rich and poor, employers and workers.

Large protest movements occurred in northern England in 1811 and 1812; in the silk-weaving city of Lyons, France, in 1831, and in the mining towns of Silesia, in eastern Europe, in 1844. These demonstrations ended when the governments sent troops to arrest protesting workers.

The Union Movement

To strengthen their position, workers sought ways to organize permanently. They felt their efforts would be more successful if they belonged to associations of workers. These associations would collect dues and use the money to pay workers while they were on strike. The associations could plan actions and coordinate the demands of different types of workers in the same factory. These associations came to be called **unions**.

Organizing unions was not easy. British, French, and German law, for instance, regarded workers' associations as illegal. When British workers tried to unite anyway, employers persuaded Parliament to pass laws against them. The Combination Acts of 1799 and 1800 stated that people who united with others to demand higher wages, shorter hours, or better working conditions could be imprisoned.

Eventually, however, the workers began to make some progress. In 1824 Parliament repealed the Combination Acts, permitting laborers to meet to agree on wages and hours. Finally, in the 1870s Parliament passed laws legalizing strikes.

When workers gained the legal rights to form unions and to strike, they gained power. Gradually, factory owners recognized unions as a single voice of all the member workers. Union and management representatives met to negotiate wages, hours, and working conditions. If the bargainers could agree, they wrote their agreements into a contract that would last for a fixed period of time. This process of negotiation is called **collective bargaining**.

Section 4 Review

1. **Define** free enterprise, laissez-faire, utilitarianism, strike, unions, collective bargaining
2. **Identify** Adam Smith, Thomas Malthus, David Ricardo, Charles Dickens, Jeremy Bentham, John Stuart Mill
3. **Locate and Explain the Significance** Lyons, Silesia
4. **Understanding Ideas** (a) According to Adam Smith, how did the law of supply and demand and the law of competition work? (b) What conclusion did Smith draw from these laws?
5. **Interpreting Ideas** How was the theory of utilitarianism applied to social reform?
6. **Evaluating Ideas** Were unions necessary, or could workers have found other ways to protect themselves? Explain your answer.

Section 5

Calls for Reform

Focus Questions

- **What type of society did early socialists want to establish?**
- **How did Robert Owen put his socialist beliefs into action?**
- **What did Karl Marx believe would happen to the capitalist world of the 1800s?**

In the economy that resulted from the Industrial Revolution, a few people became enormously rich, while most remained poor. The uneven distribution of wealth disturbed many people. Some reformers became convinced that laissez-faire capitalism was not the best economic system. They argued that laws could not do enough to remedy inequalities. The only way to distribute wealth more evenly, they thought, was to change the ownership and operation of the means of production. The means of production include the capital and equipment used to produce and exchange goods—for example, land, railroads, mines, factories, stores, banks, and machines.

Socialism

Some reformers of the 1800s advocated a political and economic system called **socialism.** In this system, governments own the means of production and operate them for the welfare of all people.

Socialists wanted to establish an economic system that would abolish the profit motive and competition. They believed everyone, not just capitalists and owners, had a right to share in the profits.

The early socialists believed that people could live at peace with each other if they lived in small cooperative settlements, owning all the means of production in common and sharing the products. The socialists tried to work out detailed plans for model communities and then tried to persuade people to set up the communities. Sir Thomas More, an English humanist, described such a model community in 1516 in his *Utopia*. Thus these early socialists were sometimes called **utopian socialists**.

In Great Britain, the most influential utopian socialist was Robert Owen, who lived from 1771 to 1858. Owen quit school at age 10 and went to work. By the age of 19, he managed a large cotton mill. In just a year or so, he was able to purchase, along with his partners, a spinning mill in New Lanark, Scotland. Owen ran the mill for decades, in spite of switching partners. In 1814 Owen entered into partnership with Jeremy Bentham.

Owen believed that if people lived in a good environment, they would cease to act selfishly. As a factory owner, Owen felt responsible for his workers and devoted much time and money to making their lives happier and more secure. He built good homes for them, established a store where they could buy inexpensive food and clothing, and set up schools for their children.

Owen believed, however, that workers should not be completely dependent on their employers. He encouraged workers to form unions. He also established cooperative communities in Great Britain and in the United States.

The Theories of Karl Marx

Some thinkers grew impatient with early socialism, which they regarded as impractical. They felt the entire capitalist system should be changed. Karl Marx, a journalist and the most important of these critics, was born in Prussia in 1818. Marx's radical political views made him unpopular in his own country. Forced to leave, he eventually settled in London, where he lived until his death in 1883.

Marx believed that all the great changes in history came from changes in economic conditions. In 1848, with a fellow German, Friedrich Engels, Marx published the *Communist Manifesto*, a pamphlet outlining his ideas. Marx and Engels summed up their view of human history in one sentence: "The history of all hitherto existing society is the history of class struggles." They then went on to support their view.

"Free man and slave, patrician and plebeian, lord and serf, guild master and journeyman, in a word, oppressor and oppressed, stood in constant opposition to one another, carried on an uninterrupted, now hidden, now open fight, a fight that each time ended either in a revolutionary reconstitution of society at large or in the common ruin of the contending classes."

Marx stated that each stage of history involved inequality, and therefore struggle, between those who owned property and those who did not. In the capitalist stage of the 1800s, for example, the struggle existed between the owners, or **bourgeoisie**, and the working class, or **proletariat**.

Marx argued that all wealth is created by labor. Under capitalism, he said, labor receives only a small fraction of the wealth it creates. Most of the wealth goes to the owners in the form of profits, which Marx called surplus value. As a result of this unequal distribution of wealth, he thought the time would soon come when capitalist society would divide into two classes—a few capitalists and a vast mass of workers, or proletariat. The proletariat, concentrated in cities, would suffer poverty and unemployment.

Marx predicted that the capitalists would continue to amass wealth while driving the proletariat deeper and deeper into poverty. In these circumstances, the proletariat in the most advanced and industrialized nations would unite, seize power in a revolution, and establish socialism. Because many people would not readily accept socialism, initially the workers would have to control the government. Marx referred to this phase as the "dictatorship of the proletariat." After a period of education, people would become experienced in working together cooperatively. Force would no longer be needed, and the state would "wither away." This last stage, characterized by a truly classless society, Marx called *pure communism*.

Marx believed that pure communism was the inevitable outcome of human history. Each person, Marx also believed, would contribute what he or she could and would receive what he or she needed. Marx said, "From each according to his abilities, to each according to his needs."

In Marx's time, the terms *communism* and *socialism* were used in many different ways. To Marx and Engels, a communist was one who believed that people would live cooperatively without being forced to do so.

Marx called his variety of socialism "scientific socialism" because he thought he was describing objective laws of historical development—laws that would work inevitably. Marx published many of his ideas in *Das Kapital* (German for "capital"), a book that analyzed capitalism in detail.

Variations of Socialism

In the mid-1800s, socialists in several European countries began forming political parties to put their ideas into practice. The ideas of Marx and Engels influenced many of these parties. Marxist, or radical, socialists generally believed in the necessity of revolution to overthrow the capitalist system. They wanted to establish a system in which government owned almost all means of production and controlled economic planning. Today we call this economic and political system—which ignores basic human rights—**authoritarian socialism**, or **communism**.

Another group of socialists, though influenced by Marx, believed that socialism could develop gradually through education and democratic forms of government. These moderate socialists believed that when enough people became educated about socialism, they would elect socialist representatives to their government. Then government would take over the means of production peacefully. The owners would be paid for their property, and government would operate the means of production in the interest of all people. Today we call this type of socialism **democratic socialism**. Under democratic socialism, unlike under authoritarian socialism, the people retain basic human rights and partial control over economic planning through the election of government officials. Individuals may own private property, but the government controls at least some of the means of production.

Marx believed that workers had to unite in order to fight capitalism successfully. In 1864 he helped establish the International Working Men's Association, called the First International. This organization disbanded, however, in 1876. A Second International was formed in 1889, after Marx's death. Torn by disagreements between moderate and radical socialists, the Second International survived only into the early 1900s. Elsewhere, particularly in Russia, Marx's ideas would have profound effects.

Karl Marx analyzed capitalism in *Das Kapital*. He did not foresee how collective bargaining would result in better working conditions, avoiding a worldwide socialist revolution.

Section 5 Review

1. **Define** socialism, utopian socialists, bourgeoisie, proletariat, authoritarian socialism, communism, democratic socialism
2. **Identify** Sir Thomas More, Robert Owen, Karl Marx
3. **Understanding Ideas** What were the important ideas contained in socialism?
4. **Summarizing Ideas** What kinds of reforms did Robert Owen suggest?
5. **Synthesizing Ideas** (a) According to Karl Marx, what causes conflict within a society? (b) What would inevitably happen within a capitalist society, and how would the conflict be resolved?

Chapter 19 Review

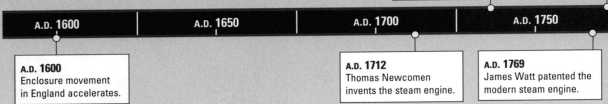

A.D. 1733
John Kay invents the flying shuttle.

A.D. 1776
Adam Smith publishes *The Wealth of Nations.*

A.D. 1600

A.D. 1650

A.D. 1700

A.D. 1750

A.D. 1600
Enclosure movement in England accelerates.

A.D. 1712
Thomas Newcomen invents the steam engine.

A.D. 1769
James Watt patented the modern steam engine.

Chapter Summary

The following list contains the key concepts that you have learned in this chapter about the Industrial Revolution and the resulting changes in political and economic thought.

1. The Industrial Revolution—changes brought about by the introduction of power-driven machinery—originated in Great Britain. In time, the Industrial Revolution transformed the world.
2. The Industrial Revolution was preceded by the Agricultural Revolution.
3. The replacement of waterpower by steam power was basic to the Industrial Revolution. Almost as important was the development of the Bessemer process, a new method of making steel that made steel readily available to the newly founded industries.
4. Transportation improved with better roads, networks of canals and railroads, and the use of steam power in ships. The wireless telegraph made rapid communication possible.
5. By gathering workers together in factories, the Industrial Revolution brought an end to the traditional practices of artisans who had worked in their homes or in small shops.
6. Factory workers became dependent on wages and no longer controlled the pace of their work because they had to do what they were told.
7. Living and working conditions were often poor during the early Industrial Revolution.
8. A series of innovations in business practices accompanied the Industrial Revolution. Mass production—based on the division of labor, interchangeable parts, and the assembly line—transformed several industries and permitted the growth of enormous corporations.
9. Workers began to protest harsh working conditions and low wages. The first labor unions were organized to seek improvements in working conditions and to obtain higher wages.
10. Socialists such as Karl Marx believed that a more fundamental transformation of politics and society was necessary.

Reviewing Important Terms

On a separate sheet of paper, supply the term that correctly completes each statement.

1. The changes industrial technology brought about affected manufacturing so deeply that they are referred to as the _____ _____.
2. The basic resources necessary for industrialization (land, labor, and capital) are called the _____ _____ _____.
3. Alternating crops to replenish nutrients in the soil is called _____ _____.
4. The use of _____ _____ allowed Eli Whitney to speed up the production of muskets.
5. The _____ _____ involved burning impurities such as carbon out of iron with a blast of air forced through molten metal.
6. A(n) _____ occurs at the lowest point in the business cycle.
7. A(n) _____ occurs when a group of workers refuse to work.
8. The idea that government should not interfere with the operation of business is called _____.
9. _____ is an economic system in which individuals control the factors of production.
10. A(n) _____ is the control of the total production or sale of a good or service by a single firm.
11. A(n) _____ is a business organization in which individuals buy shares of stock, elect directors to decide policies and hire managers, and receive dividends according to the number of shares they own.

Developing Critical Thinking Skills

1. **Determining Cause and Effect** How did the Industrial Revolution change the relationship between workers and employers that existed in the Middle Ages?
2. **Using Primary Sources** Laws regulating child labor did not exist in the 1700s. The following excerpt from Elizabeth Barrett Browning's poem "The Cry of the Children" describes the life of working-class children.

"'For oh,' say the children, 'we are weary,
   And we cannot run or leap. . . .
For all day, we drag our burden tiring
   Through the coal-dark, underground;
Or, all day, we drive the wheels of iron
   In the factories, round and round.'"

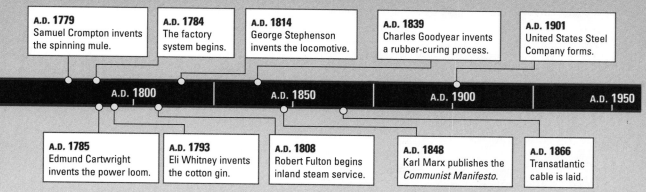

A.D. 1779
Samuel Crompton invents the spinning mule.

A.D. 1784
The factory system begins.

A.D. 1814
George Stephenson invents the locomotive.

A.D. 1839
Charles Goodyear invents a rubber-curing process.

A.D. 1901
United States Steel Company forms.

A.D. 1800   A.D. 1850   A.D. 1900   A.D. 1950

A.D. 1785
Edmund Cartwright invents the power loom.

A.D. 1793
Eli Whitney invents the cotton gin.

A.D. 1808
Robert Fulton begins inland steam service.

A.D. 1848
Karl Marx publishes the Communist Manifesto.

A.D. 1866
Transatlantic cable is laid.

(a) How did Browning view working conditions in Great Britain? (b) What evidence in the poem supports your answer? (c) Based on information in this chapter, how were working conditions gradually improved?

3. **Analyzing Ideas** How did industrialization affect the lives of women?

4. **Summarizing Ideas** (a) What problems did workers face during the Industrial Revolution? (b) What problems did employers encounter?

5. **Understanding Ideas** (a) Why did Adam Smith's ideas appeal to industrialists? (b) Why did industrialists oppose the ideas of Karl Marx?

Relating Geography to History

Using information in this chapter, write a short essay on the relationship between geography and the Industrial Revolution. For example, how might working conditions have been different if the geography of Great Britain and the United States had not been suited to producing coal or growing cotton?

Relating Past to Present

1. During the Industrial Revolution, many countries held exhibitions to showcase the latest technological developments. Investigate some of the important technological achievements of the 1990s. Use this information to design a poster for a similar exposition in the near future.

2. Use resources in your school or public library to construct a chart showing how long it took to travel from New York to California in 1850, 1900, 1930, and 1990. Your chart should include what form of transportation most people used in each of the years listed.

Applying History Study Skills

Before completing this activity, review Building History Study Skills on page 505.

In the following excerpt from *The Stages of Economic Growth*, W. W. Rostow suggests why the Industrial Revolution began in England. Read the excerpt. Then answer the questions that follow.

"Now, why Britain? Why not France? . . . The French . . . were too rough with their Protestants. They were politically and socially too inflexible, caught up . . . in . . . a

caste society. The best minds and spirits of eighteenth-century France . . . had to think about political, social and religious revolution rather than economic revolution. Moreover, the French were committed heavily to ground warfare in Europe; and they cheated on shipping and naval strength . . . when ships mattered greatly. . . .

Britain alone was in a position to weave together cotton manufacture, coal and iron technology, the steam-engine, and ample foreign trade to pull it off."

1. What question is Rostow posing?
2. What were the underlying causes for France's inability to industrialize?
3. What were the underlying causes for Great Britain industrializing first?

internet connect

In 1836, 20-year-old Charlotte Brontë sent Robert Southey, the poet laureate of Great Britain, some of her poems. In return, he replied: "Literature cannot be the business of a woman's life, and it ought not to be." Search the Internet through the HRW Web site to find information on some of the female writers of the Victorian Age. Under what names did they publish? Did they continue to use these names? Why do you think they used these names? Be prepared to discuss your findings in class.

GO TO: go.hrw.com
KEYWORD: SCØ Victorian Age Writers

Building Your Portfolio

1. **Practicing Map Skills** By the 1850s, iron and coal had become the two major raw materials of modern industry. Using an atlas, draw an outline map of the world showing the global distribution of these resources today. Place the map in your portfolio.

2. **Relating Literature to History** Read the chapter entitled "No Way Out" in *Hard Times* by Charles Dickens. As you read, consider the differences between the worker (or "hand") and the owner of the factory. (a) How does Dickens portray industrial society in the 1800s? (b) What aspects of that society does he seem to be criticizing? Explain. Place your answers in your portfolio.

Life in the Industrial Age

TIME

A.D. **1800–1928**

A.D. **1800–1928**

3.7 million B.C. | 4000 B.C. | A.D. 2100

PLACE

The United States and Europe

Europe

United States

ARCTIC OCEAN

NORTH AMERICA

EUROPE

ASIA

PACIFIC OCEAN

AFRICA

EQUATOR

SOUTH AMERICA

ATLANTIC OCEAN

INDIAN OCEAN

AUSTRALIA

PACIFIC OCEAN

ANTARCTICA

Joseph Nash lithograph of Machinery Hall in
British section of Great Exhibition, 1851

Significance

In addition to changing economies and societies, the Industrial Revolution had a profound effect on science, art, music, and literature.

Terms to Define

dynamo	social sciences
aerodynamics	social Darwinism
biological sciences	psychoanalysis
physical sciences	psychiatry
evolution	emigrations
genetics	"bobbies"
pasteurization	suburbs
antisepsis	romanticism
radioactivity	realism
quantum	regionalism
quantum theory	naturalists
special theory of	impressionists
relativity	

People to Identify

Michael Faraday	Ivan Pavlov
Thomas Edison	Sigmund Freud
Alexander Graham Bell	Sir Robert Peel
Guglielmo Marconi	Walter Camp
Wilbur and Orville Wright	Sir Walter Scott
Charles Darwin	the Grimm brothers
Robert Koch	Johann Wolfgang von
Sir Alexander Fleming	Goethe
John Dalton	James Fenimore Cooper
Dmitry Mendeleyev	Ludwig van Beethoven
Wilhelm Röntgen	Pyotr Ilich Tchaikovsky
Pierre and Marie Curie	Giuseppe Verdi
Max Planck	Gustave Flaubert
Albert Einstein	Mark Twain
E. B. Tylor	Émile Zola
James George Frazer	Paul Cézanne
Auguste Comte	Auguste Rodin
Herbert Spencer	

Places to Locate

New York	Berlin
Paris	London

Chapter Theme Questions

- **Science and Technology** What might be the relationship between scientific discoveries and technological breakthroughs?
- **Social Relations** In what ways might industrialization alter society's institutions and change the way people live?
- **The Arts** How might social and economic developments influence artistic expression?

People's lives were altered greatly as a result of the Industrial Revolution. The era produced changes in the way people worked, but it also made changes to the way they lived and thought. The inventions that followed the initial wave of the Industrial Revolution were also significant. One of the greatest transformations of the 1800s and early 1900s was the advent of new ways to communicate.

In 1901 the Italian Guglielmo Marconi sent the first radio transmission across the Atlantic. This is how Marconi later described the event:

❝Shortly before mid-day I placed the single earphone to my ear and started listening. . . . The answer came at 12:30 when I heard, faintly but distinctly, pip-pip-pip. . . . The result meant much more to me than the mere successful realization of an experiment. . . . I now felt for the first time absolutely certain that the day would come when mankind would be able to send messages without wires not only across the Atlantic but between the farthermost ends of the earth.❞

Marconi glimpsed the future in a moment, a future of communication between nations, continents, and even the vast reaches of outer space.

Advances in Technology and Communication

Focus Questions

- **How did the development of new sources of power lead to technological advances?**
- **What inventions improved communications in the late 1800s?**
- **What was the importance of the internal combustion engine?**

Beginning in the early 1800s, manufacturers increasingly applied the findings of science to their businesses, thus generating new industrial growth.

Paris Exposition Poster

In 1889 the French held a spectacular exposition in Paris to celebrate the hundredth anniversary of the French Revolution. In its many buildings, the exposition featured examples of the tremendous industrial progress that had been made during the 1800s. To celebrate the exposition, the French newspaper *Le Figaro* published a special supplement, using this poster as its cover. The famous Eiffel Tower soars in the background. At the time, the tower was the tallest structure in the world. It stands as a monument to the engineering skills and achievements of the 1880s.

The 1889 exposition made extensive use of electric lighting, then a great novelty. At night the lower part of the Eiffel Tower and the surrounding fountains were lit, creating a spectacular show. People from all over the world traveled to Paris to see the splendor of the exposition.

The exposition contained thousands of exhibits. The Gallery of Machines housed an exhibit of 16,000 machines developed during the Industrial Revolution. The exposition provided a preview of the technology that would be increasingly important in everyday life in the 1900s.

Today people continue to flock to world's fairs and other shows that, like the 1889 exposition, highlight technological advances.

The application of scientific solutions to industrial problems resulted in (1) the development and use of new sources of power, (2) inventions that provided rapid communications over long distances, and (3) the creation of new products and materials and the improvement of old ones.

Electricity

As industry grew during the 1800s, manufacturers continued to search for new and better power sources. In the 1870s, a tremendous new source of power—electricity—was developed.

The English scientist Michael Faraday made key discoveries about electricity in the 1820s and 1830s. From the work of André Ampère and other scientists, Faraday knew that electricity could produce magnetism. He wanted to find out whether magnetism could produce electricity. He found that by moving a magnet through a coil of wire he could generate an electric current in the wire.

Faraday concentrated primarily on exploring the nature of electricity. Others used his discovery to develop the **dynamo,** or electric generator. Driven either by a steam engine or by waterpower, the dynamo transformed mechanical power into electrical energy. This energy in turn could generate power to run machinery in factories.

English and American inventors worked on making practical use of another property of electricity that had been discovered. It was known that a current passing through certain kinds of wire caused the wire to glow. Here was a promising new source of light for streets, homes, and factories. Electric lightbulbs were first produced in the 1840s, but they burned out in a matter of minutes. In 1879 American inventor Thomas Edison made a bulb that glowed for two days before burning out. After further improvements, electric lighting gradually replaced other methods of illumination over the next several decades.

To make electricity practical, it had to be transmitted efficiently from the place it was generated to the place it would be used. After much work on the problem, Edison developed a successful central powerhouse and transmission system that was put into operation in 1882 in New York City and London and soon in a variety of other places.

The electrical industry grew rapidly. Waterfalls, such as Niagara Falls, were used to run huge dynamos, whose hydroelectric power was sent long distances through wires. Dams were built in many countries to provide artificial sources of waterpower.

As the large-scale production and transmission of electricity became a reality in the late 1800s, electric motors replaced steam engines in factories. Where hydroelectric power was either unavailable or too expensive, steam engines turned the generators at central powerhouses.

Communications

The development of electrical power spurred the growth of other inventions. A significant advance in the communications field occurred in the 1870s, when Alexander Graham Bell sent the human voice over a long distance by means of an electrical circuit. Bell, an American, patented his telephone in 1876. Then in 1895 the Italian inventor Guglielmo Marconi developed a way to send messages through space without wires.

Marconi's invention was based on the work of two earlier scientists, James Clerk Maxwell of Great Britain and Heinrich Rudolph Hertz of Germany. Maxwell had made a mathematical study of electricity and magnetism. In 1873 he asserted the existence of invisible electromagnetic waves that travel through space at the speed of light. In the 1880s, Hertz proved that such waves existed by transmitting and receiving them, and he also measured their length and speed.

Marconi invented instruments for sending and receiving these radio waves, as they came to be called. His wireless telegraph soon proved itself valuable for ship-to-ship and ship-to-shore communication. In 1901 he sent the first wireless message across the Atlantic Ocean.

The Internal Combustion Engine

Electricity was not the only type of power that became significant in the 1800s. The electric motor, although useful, had one significant limitation: it had to be connected to its power supply. This made it impractical as a means of moving vehicles.

Automobiles. In the late 1800s, several European inventors worked on engines that used a portable fuel supply of oil or gasoline to propel vehicles. The device was called the internal combustion engine because the combustion, or burning, of fuel took place inside a closed cylinder. (In the steam engine, combustion takes place outside the cylinder.) Pioneers in this field included Gottlieb Daimler and Karl Benz of Germany and Etienne Lenoir of France. In 1893 Charles and Frank Duryea built the first successful gasoline-driven automobile in the United States. Fifteen years later the American inventor Henry Ford produced his first commercially successful automobile, the Model T.

Airplanes. Since the 1700s, people had used balloons filled with gases lighter than air to float above

A French aviator, Louis Blériot, became famous in 1909 for making the first flight across the English Channel.

the ground. Beginning in the 1800s, inventors tried to devise a heavier-than-air machine that would actually fly. The first people to succeed in flying a powered airplane in sustained, controlled flight were Wilbur and Orville Wright of the United States. They achieved this feat at Kitty Hawk, North Carolina, in 1903.

The Wright brothers' achievement was another example of the combination of science and technology. The Wrights succeeded where others had failed because they had studied **aerodynamics**—the principles governing the movement of air around objects—and used the internal combustion engine to propel their plane through the air.

Section 1 Review

1. **Define** dynamo, aerodynamics
2. **Identify** Michael Faraday, Thomas Edison, Alexander Graham Bell, Guglielmo Marconi, Wilbur and Orville Wright
3. **Understanding Ideas** How does developing new sources of power spur the development of other types of inventions?
4. **Summarizing Ideas** Explain the importance of the telephone and the wireless telegraph.
5. **Analyzing Ideas** Why was the internal combustion engine superior to electricity for powering vehicles?

Petroleum and the Industrial Age

Petroleum—crude oil—and its products have been in use for thousands of years. Ancient Egyptians used pitch, a thick, sticky form of petroleum, to coat mummies as they prepared them for burial. Ancient Babylonians used pitch to build walls and pave streets.

Yet it took two inventions of the 1800s—the kerosene lamp and, to a much greater extent, the internal combustion engine—to create the enormous demand that has made petroleum such a crucial commodity today.

The petroleum industry is one of the world's largest. It experienced its first boom in 1859, when a retired train conductor in Pennsylvania powered a well drill with an old steam engine and struck oil. (See early wooden derrick oil field in photo.) The growth of this industry is an excellent example, however, of the interplay between technology and industry. At first kerosene was the chief product of the petroleum industry. Gasoline was seen as a useless by-product of the process and was even dumped in creeks and rivers. Around 1900, however, electric lights began to replace kerosene lamps, reducing the demand for this petroleum product. At the same time, the use of automobiles began to increase. With that development, the petroleum industry expanded rapidly.

Today petroleum powers automobiles, farm equipment, airplanes, trucks, trains, and ships, and it generates heat and electricity. Yet it is used for much more than fuel—petroleum products include detergents, carpeting, cosmetics, plastic, and fabrics.

Advances in Science and Medicine

Focus Questions

- **What progress was made in the area of biological sciences?**
- **How did advances in medicine benefit society?**
- **What advances were made in the study of atomic theory?**

The **biological sciences**—biology and genetics—deal with living organisms, as does medicine. The **physical sciences** are concerned with the properties of energy and inanimate, or nonliving, matter. Physical sciences include astronomy, geology, physics, and chemistry. During the 1800s and early 1900s, significant advances were made in both branches of science and in medicine.

Cell Theory in Biology

Scientists of the 1800s were as interested in explaining the nature of life as they were in exploring the nature of nonliving matter. Biologists had long been familiar with the idea of cells, the tiny units of living matter. Scientists in the 1600s examined living matter under their microscopes and saw what we now know to be plant and animal cells. Those early observers noticed that the cells of different species are of different shapes and sizes, but they did not draw any general conclusions about them.

In the 1850s, the work of the German scientist Rudolf Virchow expanded cell theory. Virchow showed that disease in living organisms was caused by changes in cells, or their destruction, as a result of some outside force or agent. From his study of cells, Virchow also concluded that every new cell must come from some older cell and that only living matter can produce new living matter. Thus by the late 1800s, scientists generally accepted the cell as the basic unit of living matter.

Lamarck's Theory of Inheritance

Cell theory did not account for the rich variety of plants and animals on Earth. Until the mid-1800s, most people believed that all the different kinds of plants and animals had been created at one time. The religious beliefs of many cultures hold divine beings responsible for creating all things on Earth.

One group of scientists, however, offered a different theory. They argued that the thousands of kinds of modern plants and animals had evolved, or developed, from common ancestors long ago. This kind of development through change is called **evolution.**

In science new theories often raise new questions. Those who believed in evolution now had to explain how plants and animals had evolved. In the early 1800s, Jean-Baptiste Lamarck, a French biologist, suggested that living things changed their form in response to their environment. A giraffe, for example, acquired a long neck because it always had to stretch to eat leaves high up in trees. Such changes were then passed on by inheritance to its descendants. Conversely, other characteristics might gradually disappear if they were never used. Lamarck thought that these kinds of change, continuing from generation to generation for millions of years, could have produced present-day plants and animals out of the first bits of living matter.

Lamarck's theory did not become a part of modern biology because it was later largely disproved. However, it influenced other scientists, among them a British biologist named Charles Darwin.

Darwin's Theory of Evolution

Charles Darwin had spent nearly 30 years studying plant and animal life. In 1859 he published his theory of evolution in a book called *On the Origin of Species by Means of Natural Selection.*

Darwin began with a well-known biological fact: no two creatures are exactly alike, not even offspring and their parents. He combined this fact with the ideas of Thomas Malthus. Malthus believed that as a result of natural dangers and constraints, including a limited food supply, there were always more creatures born than could survive. Therefore, Darwin

Charles Darwin gathered most of the material for his theory of evolution during a 5-year surveying expedition off the coast of South America and the Pacific Islands. Upon his return to England, he spent 20 years writing his theory of evolution.

reasoned, in any generation some creatures will survive and some will perish. Those who survive will, in general, be those whose characteristics are best adapted to the existing environment. This idea is often called the survival of the fittest, or natural selection. The strongest survivors will live to produce offspring, who will then repeat the process and tend to possess the advantageous traits of their parents. In this way, Darwin theorized, one could explain the evolution of all forms of life from earlier forms.

Darwin's theory inspired a great deal of scientific activity. It motivated other scientists to gather evidence to try to either prove or disprove it. They looked for evidence in fossils as well as in the study of living organisms. The theory of natural selection was especially controversial, however, for two reasons. First, it stated that human beings developed from other animals, an idea many found offensive. Second, many people thought that it contradicted the story of Creation in the Bible.

Genetics

Darwin left an important question unanswered: Why were the offspring not exactly like their parents? Unknown to Darwin, Gregor Mendel, a monk in Austria, had been gathering evidence that would answer this question. Mendel founded **genetics**—the study of the ways in which the inborn characteristics of plants and animals are inherited by their descendants. He did much of his research in the 1850s and 1860s, although other scientists did not learn about it until later.

Mendel worked in a quiet monastery garden, where he bred pea plants. He mated tall plants with short plants, which produced not medium-sized pea plants but all tall plants. Then Mendel fertilized these tall offspring with their own pollen and was surprised to find that they produced a mixed generation of both short and tall plants. In some way, the characteristic of shortness had been hidden in the tall plants.

From his experiments, Mendel concluded that inborn characteristics were not necessarily blended or mixed together. Instead, he believed, they were all inherited as if they were separate particles. In some cases a trait could be carried but not expressed. For example, tall plants could carry and pass on to the next generation the particles that would cause shortness.

The Fight Against Disease

Remarkable breakthroughs in medicine accompanied the advances in science and helped prolong human life. Until the late 1800s, as many as 50 percent of the people born died within the first five years after birth. Disease killed more people than did wars, famines, or natural disasters. Little was known about the causes of disease. Scientists had seen bacteria under the microscope as early as the 1600s but had not suspected their connection with disease.

Edward Jenner. Smallpox was one of the most dreaded diseases of the time. Periodically, it swept through cities in epidemics. Edward Jenner, an English physician, made a thorough investigation of smallpox in the late 1700s in the hope of finding a way to prevent it. He learned that milkmaids who had once had cowpox (a disease similar to smallpox but much milder) did not get smallpox even during an epidemic. After years of experimenting, Jenner developed a safe technique for vaccinating people to prevent smallpox. (The principle of inoculation was very old—it had been known in India many centuries earlier. However, as practiced in Europe at the time, it involved inoculating people with human smallpox

What If?

Vaccines
In 1796 Edward Jenner developed a vaccine effective against smallpox. If the smallpox vaccine and vaccines effective against other diseases had been available earlier, society might be different in what ways?

bacilli. The procedure was dangerous and sometimes even fatal.) In 1796 Jenner made a vaccine from the fluid in cowpox sores and scratched it into the skin of a boy's arm. The boy developed a mild case of cowpox but quickly recovered. When the boy was later exposed to smallpox, he did not contract it.

Louis Pasteur. Jenner had developed a method of preventing smallpox through vaccination, but he did not know the scientific principle that made it work. This principle came to light in the late 1800s through the work of the French chemist Louis Pasteur. He identified small microorganisms called bacteria.

Louis Pasteur became known for discovering the process called pasteurization, which involves heating liquids and foods to high temperatures to kill bacteria.

Science Fiction

Storytellers since the time of the ancient Greeks have enjoyed imagining that people are capable of breaking the laws of nature and gaining fantastic strength or powers. They have also imagined amazing machines and mythical figures with magical abilities. In a sense, the spirit of discovery expressed in the scientific and industrial ages—and in new theories about the structure of the universe—was reflected as well in a type of literature that we today call science fiction.

Since the time of the Scientific Revolution, literary fantasies have often taken a special form inspired by the achievements of science. A favorite subject of science fiction has been space travel. The great scientist Johannes Kepler, who played a major part in the revolution in astronomy during the 1600s, wrote a book called *The Dream*. In it Kepler imagined his mother flying to the moon on a broomstick. This book created problems for his mother, for it was used as evidence that she was a witch. Although not strictly within the realm of science fiction, Kepler's work is an extremely imaginative description of life in space.

Stories similar to today's science fiction were popular in the 1700s and 1800s. The French philosopher Voltaire imagined a visit to Earth by an enormous native of the star Sirius. The English novelist Mary Wollstonecraft Shelley imagined a medical student named Victor Frankenstein, who created a living monster out of a corpse. In the late 1800s, the French writer Jules Verne wrote a series of stories about incredible journeys—in a balloon, on a rocket, and in a submarine. In the late 1800s, the English novelist H. G. Wells imagined a machine that could stop time. He also imagined Martians invading Earth.

In more recent times, much of science fiction—in films as well as books—has dealt with life on other worlds in space. However, the basic theme has remained the same: fantastic people or creatures who can do things that normally are impossible. By showing us the impossible, science fiction tries to teach us something about the limits of our lives.

Jules Verne illustration: "A Trip From the Earth to the Moon" (1865)

Still from "War of the Worlds"

The Museum of Modern Art/Film Stills Archives

Satellite circling Earth

Until Pasteur's time scientists believed that certain living things, including bacteria, sprang to life out of nonliving matter. This process was called spontaneous generation. Pasteur's experiments showed that bacteria reproduce like other living things and travel from place to place in the air, on people's hands, and in other ways.

Pasteur learned that bacteria are responsible for many phenomena. For example, some bacteria cause fermentation, turning grape juice into wine or making milk sour. In the 1860s, Pasteur developed a process of heating liquids to kill bacteria and prevent fermentation—a process that was named **pasteurization** in his honor. He also determined that some bacteria cause diseases in animals and also in humans. These harmful bacteria are called germs or microbes.

During the 1870s, Pasteur experimented with the germ that causes anthrax, a disease which is often fatal to both animals and humans. He produced a vaccine containing weakened anthrax germs, which he injected into animals. The vaccine prevented them from catching the disease. Pasteur determined that when weakened germs enter the body, the system builds up substances called antibodies to fight them. These antibodies remain in the body and are strong enough to kill the more deadly germs if exposure to them occurs. Thus Pasteur showed why Jenner's smallpox vaccine had been effective.

Pasteur used this same technique in fighting rabies, a fatal disease communicated to humans by dogs or other animals infected with a certain virus (a minute organism smaller than bacteria). In the 1880s, Pasteur found a way to weaken the rabies virus. He injected the vaccine he produced into a boy who had been bitten by a rabid dog, and the boy survived.

The Development of Surgery

Through the centuries, surgery had been a desperate measure, always painful and often fatal. Surgeons usually performed only operations that could be completed in a few minutes, such as tooth extractions and limb amputations. Sometimes more complicated procedures were attempted. Patients had to be forcibly held down or their senses dulled with liquor or opium.

In the 1840s, it was discovered that ether and chloroform would cause unconsciousness or deaden sensation and thus eliminate pain. Such anesthetics both relieved the patients' suffering and made longer operations possible.

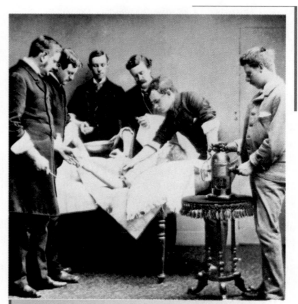

Opium and rum were used for deadening pain until physicians of the 1800s discovered anesthetics such as nitrous oxide, ether, and chloroform.

Even after anesthetics came into use, however, many patients survived the surgeon's knife only to die from infection soon afterward. Pasteur's discoveries about germs helped remedy this situation. Joseph Lister, an English surgeon, studied Pasteur's work and developed **antisepsis**—the process of killing disease-causing germs. Lister used carbolic acid as an antiseptic; milder chemicals later came into use for this purpose. Although the general use of antiseptics was adopted slowly, it eventually helped reduce bacterial infection not only in surgery but also in childbirth and in the treatment of battle wounds.

Other Medical Advances

Robert Koch, a German physician, made discoveries that reinforced those of Pasteur. In 1882 Koch isolated the germ that causes tuberculosis. He also identified the germ responsible for Asiatic cholera and developed sanitary measures, such as water filtration, to prevent disease.

The discoveries of Pasteur, Lister, and Koch were the starting point of an international fight against disease. Knowing the nature and role of bacteria and viruses, scientists could now isolate the causes of many diseases and develop vaccines for inoculation against them.

Scientists traced some epidemic diseases, including malaria and yellow fever, to germs carried in the bodies of mosquitoes and transmitted by their bite. Thus the battle against disease was extended to the mosquitoes that carried it. Bubonic plague, found to be carried by fleas on rats, was brought under control in Western countries through rat-extermination campaigns.

Scientists developed and tested many new medicines. Aspirin, which became available in the 1890s, reduced pain and fever. Insulin, developed in the 1920s, saved diabetics from certain death and enabled them to lead normal lives. Other medicines were used to treat bacterial infections. For example, Sir Alexander Fleming of Great Britain discovered penicillin in 1928. The sulfonamides, or sulfa drugs, were developed in Germany in the 1930s. Neither penicillin nor the sulfas, however, came into wide use until the 1940s.

Atomic Theory

According to modern atomic theory, all matter in the universe consists of very small particles called atoms. The arrangement and structure of these atoms and their chemical combinations with each other account for the different characteristics of the materials that make up our world.

We can trace the beginnings of atomic theory, as we can many other scientific ideas, back to ancient Greek philosophers such as Democritus. For many centuries, however, this was only one of several philosophical theories about physical reality. During the Scientific Revolution of the 1500s and 1600s, people began to accept atomic theory as part of science, although neither experimental proof nor mathematical demonstration yet supported it.

John Dalton, an English chemist and schoolteacher, was the first scientist to obtain convincing experimental data about the atom. In 1803 he outlined a method for "weighing" atoms. After studying the ratios of elements in various gases, Dalton assigned an arbitrary weight of 1 to the lightest element, which is hydrogen. Dalton then expressed the weights of all of the other known elements in proportion to it.

During the 1800s, many scientists explored the paths opened up by Dalton, learning much about the atom. In 1869 the Russian chemist Dmitry Mendeleyev (men·duh·LAY·uhf) produced the first workable classification of the elements. Somewhat modified, Mendeleyev's periodic table is a familiar feature of today's chemistry textbooks.

Modern atomic theory originated in the study of chemistry. However, it soon became part of physics—the science of matter and energy—when scientists studying heat and gases explained their findings with a new theory about atoms in motion. In the 1800s, some scientists began to think of heat as the result of the motion of a substance's atomic particles. In a cold substance—ice, for example—the atoms move relatively slowly. In a hot substance—such as scalding water—the atoms move much more vigorously, even colliding with one another. When water boils, the atoms move extremely fast, and the water turns into a gas—water vapor.

The Structure of the Atom

In 1895 the German physicist Wilhelm C. Röntgen (RENT·guhn) was sending electricity through a vacuum inside a glass tube. He noticed that a fluorescent substance on a table nearby glowed brightly when the electric current was switched on in the tube. Röntgen immediately concluded that the tube was sending out a new form of ray. Soon he discovered that the rays penetrated many substances, including human skin and tissue, and could leave an image on a photographic plate. Because he did not know what caused this powerful penetrating radiation, Röntgen named the rays X rays. X rays became an important diagnostic tool in medicine, and their existence raised new questions about the physical world.

The English physicist J. J. Thomson probed further into the nature of matter. In 1897 he discovered the electron, a tiny particle that has a negative electrical charge. Thomson found that an electron was more than 1,000 times lighter than the smallest known atom, and he theorized that all atoms contained electrons. Therefore, subatomic particles (that is, particles inside atoms), rather than the atoms themselves, must be the true building blocks of all matter in the universe.

While most physicists reluctantly accepted the electron's existence, Pierre and Marie Curie, a French husband-and-wife team of chemists, provided new evidence that atoms were not the simple, indivisible particles pictured by earlier scientists. The Curies experimented with the elements uranium and radium. They found that the atoms of these elements constantly disintegrated and released energy on their own. This process is called **radioactivity.** Elements that disintegrate and release energy in this way are called radioactive elements.

Ernest Rutherford of Great Britain combined Thomson's ideas about electrons with the Curies' discovery of disintegrating atoms in a new theory of the atom. Rutherford maintained that at the center of the atom lay an extremely small and relatively heavy core, or nucleus. Electrons whirled in circular orbits around the nucleus. When Rutherford bombarded the nucleus with heavy particles from radioactive elements, he found that it was made up of positively-charged particles, which he called protons. With the discoveries of Thomson, the Curies, and Rutherford, scientists no longer thought of the atom as a solid piece of matter.

Later scientists modified Rutherford's description of the atom. Rutherford had thought in terms of two subatomic particles—electrons and protons. However, his successors discovered first another particle in the nucleus of atoms, the neutron, and eventually discovered many more elementary sub-atomic particles.

Planck and Einstein

In 1900 the German physicist Max Planck disproved the then-common belief that energy was continuous and that it could be divided into any number of smaller units. Planck proved that energy could be released only in definite "packages," which he called *quanta* (the plural of **quantum,** the Latin word for "how much"). Planck's **quantum theory** formed the basis for a completely new approach to the study of matter and energy.

In 1905 Albert Einstein, an extraordinary young German scientist, published four papers that revolutionized physics. In his first paper, Einstein examined some of the basic concepts of mechanics and tried to prove the existence of atoms. An earlier scientist had observed that pollen dust suspended in water moved in seemingly inexplicable ways. Einstein found that the movement of the pollen dust could be explained as the result of atoms hitting it.

In his second paper, Einstein extended Planck's quantum theory to describe the nature of light. Planck believed that light was a continuous wavelike phenomenon. Einstein used mathematics to show that light can also be described as a cascade of minute particles of energy.

In his third paper, Einstein developed the **special theory of relativity**. He concluded first that no particles of matter can move faster than the speed of light. He also maintained that motion can be measured only relative to some particular observer. From

Albert Einstein, who had been a professor of physics at universities in Switzerland, Prague, and Germany in the early 1900s, was invited to join the Institute for Advanced Study in Princeton, New Jersey, in 1933.

this he claimed it does not make sense to speak of absolute motion, space, or time.

A brief fourth paper by Einstein developed the equation $E = mc^2$. According to this equation, E (energy) equals m (mass) multiplied by c^2 (the speed of light squared). This formula means that a small amount of mass can be transformed into a tremendous amount of energy.

Einstein's theories overturned long-held ideas. Isaac Newton and the scientists who followed him had thought of the universe in terms of three dimensions: length, breadth, and depth. They believed that gravity forced all particles of matter to move toward one another. Now Einstein's theory of relativity declared that all events occur not only in the three dimensions of space but also in a fourth dimension—time. This four-dimensional system Einstein called the space-time continuum. Gravity, he said, is not a property of matter but rather a property of the space-time continuum.

The theories of Max Planck and Albert Einstein paved the way for other important work. For example,

Niels Bohr, a student of J. J. Thomson, applied quantum theory to the study of the structure of atoms. He discovered that the behavior of atoms revealed information about their structure.

Section 2 Review

1. **Define** biological sciences, physical sciences, evolution, genetics, pasteurization, antisepsis, radioactivity, quantum, quantum theory, special theory of relativity
2. **Identify** Charles Darwin, Robert Koch, Sir Alexander Fleming, John Dalton Dmitry Mendeleyev, Wilhelm Röntgen, Pierre and Marie Curie, Max Planck, Albert Einstein
3. **Contrasting Ideas** Explain how Lamarck's theory of evolution differed from that proposed by Darwin.
4. **Evaluating Ideas** In what ways did Gregor Mendel's research strengthen the theories of Charles Darwin?
5. **Analyzing Ideas** How did the research of Edward Jenner, Louis Pasteur, and Joseph Lister benefit society?
6. **Summarizing Ideas** What were Einstein's major contributions to physics?

Section 3

Social Sciences in the Industrial Age

Focus Questions

- **What social sciences developed in the 1800s?**
- **What new ideas were introduced in the study of human behavior?**

During the 1800s, interest in a new field of study, the **social sciences**, grew rapidly. The social sciences are those branches of knowledge that scientifically study people as members of society. The social sciences deal with many subjects—economics, political institutions, history, and relations among people. The idea of making the study of these subjects objective and factual—of treating them like sciences—was new in the 1800s.

Political Science and Economics

The study of politics dates back to the Greek philosophers Plato and Aristotle. Later it was the subject of such thinkers as Machiavelli, Locke, and Rousseau. In the 1800s, the study of politics became known as political science, and writers tried to study law and government in the scientific manner of physicists and biologists.

Another social science, economics, had already been well developed in the work of Adam Smith and others. However, not until the later 1800s did economists begin to follow the practice of scientists by collecting and arranging statistics in order to test their theories.

History

Like political science, the study of history dates back to the Greeks. Views of history, however, also underwent change in the 1800s. Influenced by nationalism, many scholars wrote histories detailing the accomplishments and glories of their native countries. In addition, historians increasingly based their writings on the systematic study of original materials and the careful organization of facts. They began a massive search for evidence of the past in documents, diaries, letters, and other sources. New interpretations of history began to emerge.

One new trend in history was the study of all the people in a society. Here a writer of the 1700s proved influential—the French philosopher Voltaire, who was noted for his attention to social and intellectual history. His works inspired many historians to concentrate less on wars and great leaders and more on the study of ordinary people and how they lived. Another trend, influenced by Darwin, was the interpretation of historical events in terms of evolution.

Archaeology and Anthropology

Archaeology, the scientific study of human culture through the artifacts left behind, became a separate field of study in the mid-1800s. It was in the 1800s that scientists learned how old Earth was and how long humans had lived on it. Archaeologists found prehistoric cave paintings in Spain and France. They found remains of Egyptian, Sumerian, and Assyrian cultures and used excavation techniques to determine the sequence of cultural developments in such ancient cities as Troy and Mycenae.

Anthropology is the study of different societies, both of the past and of the present. Anthropologists in the 1800s began to explore the continuities in the attitudes of human societies and in the way people relate to one another. The British anthropologist E. B. Tylor adopted the German term *kultur* to describe the set of beliefs and behaviors that a society shares. Tylor discussed this concept in his book *Primitive Culture* (1871), in which he looked at religion as it evolved in all human cultures.

James George Frazer, another British anthropologist, took this approach further in his book *The Golden Bough* (first published in 1890). Frazer compared the customs of different societies and tried to show links between those societies in magical beliefs, religion, and attitudes toward authority. The study of similarities and differences among various societies has remained a major interest of anthropologists.

Sociology

Sociology—the study of human relationships in society—also first appeared in the 1800s. The writings of the French philosopher Auguste Comte greatly influenced this branch of the social sciences. Comte argued that the study of society should follow scientific methods by using objective facts and avoiding personal interpretations.

Tutankhamen's tomb remained preserved for more than 3,000 years, until Howard Carter excavated it in 1922. A room in the tomb with treasures is shown here.

Photography by Egyptian Expedition, The Metropolitan Museum of Art

In the 1800s, sociologists became particularly interested in adopting the theories of the biological sciences. Herbert Spencer, for example, used the concept of evolution as the basis for studying human communities. As you have read, Darwin claimed that nature "selected" certain individuals—those most fit to survive—and allowed others to die. In his works *Social Statics* (1851) and *Principles of Sociology* (1876, 1882, 1896), Spencer applied this theory of natural selection to society, coining the phrase "survival of the fittest."

Spencer thought that human society, like the plant and animal worlds, had evolved from lower to higher forms through natural selection.

"The individuals best adapted to the conditions of their existence," he wrote, "shall prosper most, and the individuals least adapted to the conditions of their existence shall prosper least. . . . Pervading all Nature we may see at work a stern discipline which is often a little cruel that it may be very kind."

The application of Darwin's theory to society came to be known as **social Darwinism**. It led to the conclusion that those who had acquired wealth and social standing had done so because of their superior abilities. Poverty, on the other hand, supposedly proved that people or groups were unfit. This view came to be seen as simplistic, however, as social problems grew more severe and society became more complex. Consequently, social Darwinism lost much influence.

Psychology

Psychology, another new science of the 1800s, studies the human mind—how it works and how it affects behavior. Psychology's origins can be traced back to the works of Greek thinkers. Because psychology did not involve experimentation, most people considered it a branch of philosophy. However, in the mid-1800s, a number of scientists began to approach psychology as an experimental science like biology.

Pavlov. Darwin's theory of evolution had a strong impact on the new science of psychology. Among other things, it influenced psychologists to study animal behavior and to apply their findings to humans. Perhaps the most famous of these early experimenters was the Russian physiologist Ivan Pavlov.

In the 1890s, Pavlov discovered the conditioned reflex. Psychologists had long known that certain behavior was automatic. A child does not have to be taught to pull his or her hand away from fire but removes it automatically. In the same way, a dog does not have to be taught to salivate, or water at the mouth, when eating food. Psychologists call this kind of involuntary response a reflex action.

By experimenting with dogs, however, Pavlov proved that an animal could be conditioned, or taught, to have certain reflex actions. First, he offered food to a dog. The dog salivated. Second, he rang a bell each time the food was presented to the dog. The animal salivated, evidently associating the sound of the bell with food. After many repetitions, Pavlov offered no food to the dog but rang the bell. The dog salivated. It had been conditioned to salivate when it heard the bell. As a result of his research, Pavlov believed that all habits, even mental activity, constitute a series of connected conditioned reflexes.

Freud. In the early 1900s, Austrian physician Sigmund Freud (FROID) developed a revolutionary explanation of human behavior. Freud introduced the concept of the unconscious—the mental processes of which a person is unaware—as a determining factor in human behavior.

Freud had hypnotized certain mentally disturbed patients. He found that under hypnosis the patients could remember past experiences that they otherwise could not recall. Freud believed that these early experiences had led to their illness. He treated his patients by gradually bringing the disturbing memories, fears, and conflicts back to the level of consciousness. To do this, he studied their dreams and encouraged them to talk about whatever came into their minds. Then he interpreted these dreams and thoughts to show what lay beneath them in the unconscious mind.

Freud believed that troubled patients had unknowingly forced unpleasant experiences into the unconscious. To cure such patients, it was necessary to make them aware of these experiences again. Freud called this process of revealing and analyzing the unconscious **psychoanalysis**. He discussed his theory fully in the book titled *A General Introduction to Psychoanalysis*, published in 1910.

Some psychologists challenged aspects of Freud's theories. However, much of his basic theory and method forms the foundation of modern **psychiatry**—the study and treatment of mental illness.

Freud's concepts were also extremely influential on several of the other social sciences. Sociologists, anthropologists, and political scientists adopted aspects of the Freudian perspective, seeing certain

Sigmund Freud's pioneering work in psychoanalysis had a great influence on art, literature, and education.

social behaviors, cultural attitudes, and structures of authority as generated by unconscious psychological needs and motivations.

Section 3 Review

1. **Define** social sciences, social Darwinism, psychoanalysis, psychiatry
2. **Identify** E. B. Tylor, James George Frazer, Auguste Comte, Herbert Spencer, Ivan Pavlov, Sigmund Freud
3. **Analyzing Ideas** How did the study of politics, economics, and history change in the 1800s?
4. **Summarizing Ideas** What did the studies of anthropologists show?
5. **Understanding Ideas** What contributions did Pavlov and Freud make to the understanding of the human mind?

Society and Culture in the Industrial Age

Focus Questions

- **What factors led to the rapid growth of population in the 1800s?**
- **What were the causes and effects of the growth of public education?**
- **What new leisure and cultural activities developed during the 1800s?**

During the 1800s, improvements in medicine, sanitation, and food storage and distribution led to an increase in population. For example, Europe's population grew from about 200 million in 1800 to double that number by 1900. In the United States and Europe, the rate of population growth was highest in the regions where industrialization advanced most rapidly. At the same time, education became available to more than wealthy and middle-class children, and more people engaged in cultural and leisure activities.

Emigration

As the population in Europe grew, it also became more mobile. Large numbers of people moved across national boundaries and oceans to foreign lands. Such movements of people away from their homelands are called **emigrations.** The largest emigrations were from Europe to North and South America, Africa, Australia, and New Zealand.

Like so many other changes, these movements to other lands intensified after 1870. Between 1870 and 1900, more than 10 million people left Europe for the United States alone. This was one of the greatest mass movements of people in human history.

Many people fled from countries with poor economic conditions, such as Ireland and Italy. Other people, such as Jews, Armenians, and Slavs, fled oppression and discrimination.

Within Europe itself, large numbers of people moved to the areas of greatest industrialization in northern and western Europe, where rapid industrialization had created a great demand for factory labor. Higher wages in these countries attracted people, and steamships and trains made travel safer and more affordable.

The Shift to the Cities

As the population increased, changes in agriculture, industry, and transportation produced another striking result—the rapid growth of cities. While employment opportunities on farms declined, the developing industries located in or near cities offered new jobs. The factory system became the greatest spur to city growth.

Many early factories were located in already established cities, which then grew tremendously. The population of Manchester, England, for example, expanded from 18,000 in 1772 to 303,000 in 1851. When factories were built in rural areas, cities grew up around them. City living became the way of life for more and more people.

Before the Industrial Revolution, the vast majority of people lived in rural areas or in small villages. By 1900, however, in many nations, more people lived in or near cities than in the countryside. In Great Britain, about 10 percent of the population lived in cities in 1800. By 1921 that figure had grown to 80 percent. Similar changes took place in other countries. In 1800 not a single city in the Western world had a population of 1 million. Yet only 100 years later, cities such as New York, Paris, Berlin, and London each had more than a million inhabitants.

Sanitation and Public Order

European and American cities of the 1800s differed significantly from cities today. People got their daily water supply from public fountains because houses did not have running water inside. The water in fountains came from polluted rivers, which no one knew how to purify.

Until very late in the century, cities did not have sewers. Neither public nor private garbage collection companies existed, so people dumped garbage on the streets. In cities, smoke from the factories added to the bad smells from sewage and garbage. Thus large cities were foul-smelling, disease-ridden places.

After the 1870s, the situation began to change. Technological advances made possible many improvements such as iron pipes, flush toilets, and water systems. Cities installed closed public sewers and piped water into homes. City governments passed laws requiring better heating systems and better construction of buildings. Governments also installed street lights and paved roads.

The governments of the growing cities also found they needed a new kind of law enforcement. Police officers had to patrol streets to prevent robberies,

Ellis Island in New York Harbor served as a major immigration station, receiving approximately 17 million people into the United States between 1892 and 1943.

direct crowds safely, and protect the lives and property of city dwellers.

In 1829 Sir Robert Peel, a leader of the House of Commons, organized a permanent police force for the city of London. This force was responsible for maintaining order and making sure that people obeyed the law. The London police were nicknamed **"bobbies"** after Peel's first name, Robert, and are still called that today. Other major cities soon followed London's lead and established police forces.

The Development of Suburbs

As cities grew and became more crowded, their boundaries expanded to include surrounding areas. In addition, people moved outside cities to new areas called **suburbs**—residential areas on the outskirts of cities. In the United States, suburbs connected to the city by streetcar and ferry transportation began to develop in the early 1800s. Later in the century, suburbs developed along railroad and horse-drawn bus lines. Families lived in the suburbs, where there was less crowding, noise, and dirt, but their working members journeyed each day to jobs in the city.

Suburbs began to spread quickly during the mid-to-late 1800s, as more and more cities established public transportation systems. At first ordinary working people could not afford the fares of trains and horse-drawn buses. Only employers, managers, merchants, and professionals enjoyed these transportation luxuries. They could afford to live fairly long distances from work, in the new suburbs, while factory workers had to live within walking distance of their jobs. In time, however, lower fares made it possible for more people to ride trolleys or other public transportation to work.

Improvements in Diet and Food Storage

Science and technology combined to produce better methods of preserving and transporting food. Pasteurization was one important step. So was refrigeration, which also retards the growth of bacteria. Refrigerators appeared in the late 1800s. They later became an indispensable household feature in many industrialized countries. Refrigerated railroad cars were first used around 1850 to transport meats, fruits, and vegetables. These developments helped make a balanced diet available year-round.

Scientists also learned more about the relationship of food to health. In the early 1900s, biologists discovered the importance of vitamins and minerals in the diet. Diseases resulting from vitamin deficiencies, such as beriberi and rickets, were soon wiped out in the more industrialized regions of the world. Life expectancy as well as population increased.

Growth of Public Education

To many people, the ideas of the American and French Revolutions about liberty, equality, and representative government made it important to provide education for all citizens. In the years following these events, both France and the United States took steps to establish public school systems.

There was some resistance to this idea from people who believed that the cost of education would result in increased taxes. As the years went by, however, other factors encouraged the development of free public education, schooling free of charge for all, regardless of social class. Industrialists wanted literate workers as well as more engineers, scientists, and skilled technicians. Other people believed that state-sponsored schools, rather than private ones, were necessary to develop patriotic citizens. Military leaders wanted educated soldiers for their armies. Many ordinary people believed that education would improve their children's chances for a better life.

After 1870 governments in western Europe and the United States began to pass laws making some form of education both universal—available to all children—and compulsory. In some countries, the government provided only elementary education. In others the government also funded secondary, or high school public education. In the United States, many public school systems were expanded to include kindergarten for young children and state universities for advanced study. New subjects, especially the sciences, were added to the existing curricula, and vocational and technical training were also introduced. Teachers had to take special courses that prepared them to teach new subjects.

In European nations, the central governments established and controlled schools. In the United States, where local governments were stronger, the individual states established schools and set standards. Local school districts administered schools and levied taxes to support them.

For the most part, children of the lower classes attended school only as long as the law required them to attend. Then they went to work to earn money to help support their families. Middle-class children, on the other hand, went on to secondary school and often went on to college.

Education for Women

During the 1800s, a great deal of debate focused on education for women. Some people argued that most educational courses were either unsuitable or unnecessary for women. Others insisted that education for women was important because it made them better wives and mothers. Still others said that women should have equal opportunity in every area of life, including training for careers outside the home.

Toward the end of the 1800s, elementary education for girls was included in the provisions many countries passed guaranteeing education for all. However, opportunities for secondary education were limited. In the United States, Great Britain, and France, high schools for girls emphasized foreign languages, literature, history, and home economics. Boys, on the other hand, studied sciences, mathematics, and philosophy as well as classics, history, and literature.

Some people objected to these differences. The Englishwoman Emily Davies, for example, urged her government to improve women's education sufficiently to allow women to attend the universities. In 1865 she said:

❝We are not encumbered [burdened] by theories about equality and inequality of mental power in the sexes. All we claim is that the intelligence of women, be it great or small, shall have full and free development. And we claim it not specially in the interest of women, but as essential to the growth of the human race.**❞**

Few colleges admitted women as students during the 1800s. Consequently, people who believed that women should have the opportunity to receive a university education opened colleges for women. In the United States, Mary Lyon founded the Mount Holyoke Female Seminary in 1837. This school later became Mount Holyoke College. In Great Britain, Girton College opened in 1869, and Newnham College opened in 1871. Today these colleges are part of Cambridge University.

The Effects of Education

The spread of education had many positive results. People became better informed about current issues and took an active interest in a variety of government activities. Because more people could read, greater quantities of newspapers, magazines, and books were published for people of all ages.

Newspapers, which were not widely read before 1800, became especially popular and important. During the 1800s, they expanded their coverage to include politics, foreign affairs, and art and science. To attract readers, the editors also included weekly stories by famous authors, such as Émile Zola and Charles Dickens.

Some newspapers advocated a particular political position. They supported or criticized the policies of one political party or one government figure or another and often featured humorous political cartoons.

To expand circulation, newspapers lowered prices. Publishers used advertising as a way of increasing income, attracting readers, and keeping prices low. New technology, such as the linotype, which set type by machine instead of by hand, and the electric-powered rotary press, improved printing processes. The invention of the telegraph made it possible for reporters to convey news quickly. Newspapers could send reporters to distant places and have them transmit stories to their home offices.

As newspapers grew, so did the number of job opportunities for journalists and editors. In the past, writing had been something that people did in addition to other work. It was not a full-time profession. Over time, however, journalism became an accepted and respected occupation. People began to view it as an opportunity for an exciting career.

Leisure and Cultural Activities

Many of today's popular forms of entertainment first developed during the 1800s. Before that time, of course, people also enjoyed concerts, plays, games, and sports. As the populations of cities grew during the industrial age, however, the numbers and variety of these activities increased. Large audiences now paid to hear professional musicians perform or to watch professional athletes compete.

Sports. People had participated in athletic events for many centuries. The rich hunted wild animals and even played a form of tennis. The poor may have organized informal games on the village common. In

Education for women was changing during the 1800s. The women in this classroom are studying subjects such as geography and science.

Winslow Homer painted this scene of a croquet game in the park in 1866. He began his career at the age of 19 as a freelance magazine illustrator.

fact, we can trace the origins of soccer, rugby, and football to a game played by villagers using an inflated pig's bladder as a ball.

During the 1800s, many games became more organized. In Great Britain, "football" (known as soccer in the United States) was among the first games to change from an informal community activity to a professional spectator sport. Rugby and American football evolved from this early kicking game.

According to legend, in 1823 during a "football" game, a young student at Rugby School in England caught a kicked ball and ran toward the goal. Although the boy had violated the rules of the game, the idea of running with the ball eventually won favor and in time led to rugby.

In the 1860s, the London Football Association drew up official rules for games called soccer and rugby, and in 1871 the association established a national competition among football clubs. By the mid-1880s in England, many soccer and rugby players were full-time athletes. Football clubs for working-class

people were created in the 1870s. By that time, in England laws granted factory workers Saturday afternoon and Sunday as rest days.

In the 1880s an American named Walter Camp (the "father of football") adapted rugby into an early form of the game known as football in the United States. Professional football leagues were established in the United States by 1920. Soccer, rugby, and football were now three sports played by amateurs and professionals and watched by paying spectators.

A sport that experienced a great boom in the 1890s in the United States was bicycling. By 1896 there were more than 500 manufacturers of bicycles. These manufacturers, like automobile manufacturers several decades later, had machine technology and assembly-line systems. A traffic code introduced in New York City in 1897 to regulate bicycle and horse traffic also anticipated codes later established for automobiles.

Baseball also became popular in the late 1800s in the United States. English children's games using a bat and ball appear to date back to the 1700s, but it was in 1845 that a written set of rules gave baseball its modern form. The game became a popular pastime for troops in the Civil War, and in the late 1860s the first professional baseball team, the Cincinnati Red Stockings, was formed. Baseball quickly grew in popularity at both the amateur and professional levels.

Concert halls, museums, and libraries. Before the 1800s, individuals and private groups sponsored most cultural activities. Musicians performed concerts in the homes of the rich or as part of religious services. Wealthy individuals and families who wanted to commemorate a family or personal event commissioned paintings and sculptures. Religious or civic organizations also commissioned artworks for display in churches or clubs.

During the 1800s, art and music became available to more people. Popular entertainment had been available in taverns in England for many years. As the urban population grew in the 1800s, however, and there was a greater demand, music and concert halls began to spring up. Music halls offered a combination of musical and comic entertainment. In the latter part of the century in the United States, a type of light entertainment known as vaudeville became popular in frontier settlements as well as urban centers. [Vaudeville, named after a valley town

La Scala, the prominent Milanese opera house, opened in 1778. It can seat more than 2,000 people.

in France where satirical songs were performed, consisted of light, often comical theatrical performances that frequently combined dialogue, dancing, pantomime, and singing.]

During the 1800s, some art collections originally displayed in private homes and churches were moved to public museums. The Louvre museum in Paris, for instance, had contained the art collections of the kings of France. In 1793, as a consequence of the French Revolution, it became a public museum. Later the museum was enlarged and acquired major works of art from all over the world.

Public libraries were opened, including the great Bibliothèque Nationale in Paris and the reading-room of the British Museum in London. In the United States, the wealthy industrialist Andrew Carnegie sponsored free public libraries in many cities.

Public parks and urban planning. Crowded cities had few places for outdoor recreation. When railroads were built, people often rode trains to the countryside. They could spend the day there, away from the congestion, noise, and dirt of city streets. Some people demanded, in addition, that city governments provide parks within cities for recreation.

By the end of the 1800s, many cities had playgrounds for children. Private lands were donated or purchased by city governments and given to the people as public parks. Large areas inside city limits—for example, the Bois de Boulogne (BWA duh boo·LOHN) in Paris and Central Park in New York City—were set aside as public parks.

Section 4 Review

1. **Define** emigrations, "bobbies," suburbs
2. **Identify** Sir Robert Peel, Walter Camp
3. **Locate and Explain the Significance** New York, Paris, Berlin, London
4. **Summarizing Ideas** Explain the improvements in city life that were made possible by new technological advances.
5. **Interpreting Ideas** Describe how changes in diet and food storage helped the population grow.
6. **Analyzing Ideas** (a) List some of the reasons for the growth of public education. (b) What positive results occurred as a result of the spread of education?
7. **Classifying Ideas** What new forms of leisure and cultural activities developed in the 1800s?

Literature, Music, and Art in the Industrial Age

Focus Questions
- **What ideas were part of the romantic movement?**
- **Who were some of the great writers, musicians, and artists of the romantic movement?**
- **How does realism differ from romanticism?**
- **What other artistic movements emerged during this time?**

Literature, music, and art reflected the dramatic social and economic developments of the industrial age. Even in their most personal statements, artists often revealed in their works a sense of the rapidly changing times and the influence of revolutionary scientific ideas.

Romanticism
Many writers of the early 1800s belonged to the artistic movement known as **romanticism,** or the romantic movement. The work of such artists appealed to sentiment and imagination and dealt with the "romance" of life—life as they thought it should be rather than as it actually was. The romantic movement was partly a reaction to the Enlightenment, the movement in the 1700s that had emphasized reason and progress. Romantics glorified emotion and instinct. They idealized nature and the golden past.

The romantic movement was also a product of the revolutions of the 1700s and 1800s. Political revolution in France had overturned the old order of society in the names of liberty and equality. So, too, romanticism overturned the formal structures that had governed literature and art in the 1700s and released a spirit of creativity and individuality.

In Great Britain, the most famous romantics were a group of young poets whose works were filled with emotion and a strong love for beauty and nature. The works of William Wordsworth, Percy Bysshe Shelley, John Keats, Lord Byron, Samuel Taylor Coleridge, and others are among the classics of literature.

Many romantic writers glorified the past, especially the Middle Ages with its castles, ladies, and chivalrous knights. For example, in *Ivanhoe*, the Scottish novelist Sir Walter Scott wrote about the days of knighthood. *The Hunchback of Notre Dame*, by French author Victor Hugo, was also set in medieval times. Alexandre Dumas told the tale of *The Three Musketeers*, who roamed France in the days of Cardinal Richelieu.

Interest in the past was related to the growing nationalism of the times. Many writers turned to folklore, songs, and the history of their own countries for their subject matter. Germany was not yet a unified nation in the early 1800s, but a great national literature arose there. The Grimm brothers collected the famous fairy tales that bear their name. This collection remains a favorite of children even today. Friedrich von Schiller wrote of liberty in *William Tell*, a drama about a Swiss hero. Johann Wolfgang von Goethe (GUHR·tuh), one of the greatest German masters of poetry, drama, and the novel, also wrote during this period. The drama *Faust*, the story of a man's bargain with the devil, is the most famous of Goethe's works.

Romanticism also influenced American writers of the early 1800s. For example, James Fenimore Cooper wrote adventure stories that idealized the American Indian and the frontier. Washington Irving produced romantic stories that were set in New York's Hudson River valley.

Romantic Music

In music, as in literature, the 1800s began with a shift to romanticism. One of the leaders of this transition was the German composer Ludwig van Beethoven (BAYT·hoh·vuhn). Beethoven brought to music some of the same aims that the British poets of his time brought to literature. He expressed his love of nature in the *Pastoral Symphony*. A call for liberty and freedom dominates his one opera, *Fidelio*, as well as the final movement of his ninth, and last, symphony. Beethoven's music arouses powerful and passionate emotions.

The romantic movement produced a great outpouring of musical composition, especially in Austria and Germany. Johannes Brahms composed powerful symphonies and concertos. Although they are classical in form, they surge with rich, intensely emotional music. Franz Schubert, Robert Schumann, and Felix Mendelssohn brought to their music the lyric quality of romantic poetry. Schubert and Schumann are especially remembered for their melodic songs, or *lieder*.

Frédéric François Chopin (SHOH·pan), a Polish-born composer who lived in France, wrote expressive and beautiful piano works. Franz Liszt of Hungary used gypsy songs and dances in some of his compositions. He also developed the tone poem, a symphonic piece based on a literary or philosophical theme that was often taken from romantic literature.

In Russia, Pyotr Ilich Tchaikovsky (chy·KAHF·skee) wrote highly emotional and melodic operas, ballet music, symphonies, and other orchestral works. Often his compositions were built around stories. Examples are the fairy tale ballet *The Sleeping Beauty*, the overture fantasy *Romeo and Juliet*, and the *1812 Overture*, which commemorates Napoleon's defeat in Russia. Tchaikovsky and, even more, other Russian composers, especially Modest Mussorgsky—known for his opera *Boris Godunov*—developed nationalistic music that emphasized Russian folk themes. As in literature, strong national feeling was an essential part of the romantic movement in music.

Perhaps the greatest Italian operatic composer of the 1800s was Giuseppe Verdi. His best works, such as *Othello* and *Aïda*, contain some of the most beautiful and dramatic music ever written for the human voice. In keeping with the spirit of his times, the stories and themes of many of his early operas were highly nationalistic. Verdi's operas inspired a generation of Italians who were not yet politically united.

In Germany the best-known operatic composer of the 1800s was Richard Wagner (VAHG·nuhr). He referred to his operas as music dramas, and in them he combined singing, music, dancing, costumes, and scenery to create intensely dramatic spectacles.

A child prodigy, Frédéric Chopin began playing the piano at the age of six.

Mary Ann Evans wrote realistic novels under the name George Eliot.

romantic interest in nature. Their work had intense color and vitality, partly because they often painted outdoors instead of working in their studios.

Romanticism in architecture expressed itself first in the so-called Gothic revival of the mid-1800s. This was an attempt to re-create the great architectural style of the Middle Ages. The British houses of Parliament as well as many American churches, college buildings, and other public structures of the time were designed in the Gothic style.

Photography
The age of photography was born when Louis-Jacques-Mandé Daguerre introduced his daguerreotype, an early type of photograph, in 1839. Photography subsequently has had a significant impact on society. In the 1800s, photographs brought the world into people's hands and showed it to them in new ways. Photographs taken by William Jackson influenced Congress to vote to make Yellowstone the first national park. Mathew Brady's Civil War photographs depicted war's grim realities. Like the novels of Charles Dickens, the photographs of Jacob Riis and others showed the lives of poor people in dramatic ways. The camera's ability to capture such scenes helped give rise to realism.

The Rise of Realism
The subject matter of much romantic literature and art had little to do with the lives of ordinary people. In the mid-1800s, writers and artists began to take a new approach. Dealing with the realities of everyday life and expressing a keen observation of social settings, this approach is called **realism.** One of the most important realists was Gustave Flaubert (floh·BAIR) of France. His novel *Madame Bovary* (1857) described with extraordinary attention to detail the life of an ordinary woman. In Great Britain, Mary Ann Evans wrote realistic novels under the name George Eliot. In *Middlemarch* (1871–1872), considered her masterpiece, Eliot describes various classes in Victorian society.

Often the realists made social and economic conditions their theme. The Russian Leo Tolstoy in his monumental novel *War and Peace* (published in parts during the latter half of the 1860s) portrayed war not as a romantic adventure but as a vast confusion of misery and death. The Norwegian dramatist Henrik Ibsen brought human problems onto the stage. His play *A Doll's House* (1879) advocated the equality of husband and wife in marriage.

Like his contemporaries, Wagner was an intense nationalist. He based many of his operas on Germanic myths.

Other composers of the late 1800s followed in the general tradition of romantic music. Gustav Mahler of Austria, for example, wrote his lengthy symphonies for huge orchestras and choruses. Other composers, however, developed new styles. Claude Debussy (deb·YOO·see) of France employed unusual harmonies and rhythms in creating musical impressions of clouds, the sea, and other aspects of nature.

Romantic Painting and Architecture
Although Germans, Austrians, Russians, and Italians dominated the music world in the 1800s, many outstanding painters and sculptors were French, Spanish, and British.

In the 1820s and 1830s, romantic painters, like romantic writers, chose subjects from the past and depicted scenes bursting with action and drama. One such painter was Eugène Delacroix (del·uh·KRWAH) of France. Landscape painters John Constable and J. M. W. Turner of Great Britain reflected the

Building History Study Skills

READ
WRITE
INTERPRET
CONNECT
THINK

Interpreting Visuals: Using Art as a Historical Document

Works of art are usually not created in isolation from society. They often reflect not only the values of the artist but those of his or her society as well. The artist may be criticizing social conventions or political practices or reflecting the values of the historical period. In such cases, by paying attention to the details and themes that the artist depicts, you can gain a better understanding of the historical period. Asking questions, such as the ones below, is an important part of viewing a work of art and helps you understand its significance.

- What is the painting telling about the politics, the society, or the people of the historical period?
- To what extent is the artist reflecting or criticizing the society?
- To what extent is the painting a document?

How to Use Art as a Historical Document
To use art as a historical document, follow these steps.
1. Identify the historical period in which the work of art was created.
2. Determine the theme of the painting.
3. Connect the theme to the historical period.
4. Indicate whether the artwork reflects or criticizes the society, and explain how it does so.

Developing the Skill
Study Honoré Daumier's painting, *The Washer-woman* (right). What is it saying about working-class people and the kinds of lives that they lead?

Daumier rebelled against the romantic tradition in art and sympathized with the working class. Instead of imagining the past or musing about nature, Daumier's art reflects social realities. The Industrial Revolution created an urban working class that labored long and hard. The theme of *The Washerwoman* is the dignity and humanity of working people. The painting sensitively portrays poor, working people as having strength and dignity; harsh working or living conditions do not prevent their humanity from showing through.

Is there a message in this painting? Daumier's painting is telling us about the social effects of the Industrial Revolution. Daumier is realistically portraying hardship and struggle by showing the heavy bundle the woman carries and the posture of both figures. These are not people to pity, however. Instead, the artist portrays the individual humanity and strength of his subjects.

Practicing the Skill
Visit a local art museum or look in an art history book to find a modern painting. Study the painting carefully so that you can interpret what the artist is saying. Using the steps above, try to determine how the work of art could be used as a historical document.

To apply this skill, see Applying History Study Skills on page 541.

With *Le Moulin de la Galette*, Pierre-Auguste Renoir gives us a fleeting glimpse of people dancing and talking during a concert at an outdoor café in 1876.

In the United States, one form of realism was **regionalism**—the portrayal of everyday life with attention to how it was lived in particular locales. Examples are Mark Twain's novels *The Adventures of Tom Sawyer* (1876) and *The Adventures of Huckleberry Finn* (1884), with their earthy and humorous depictions of life along the Mississippi River.

Toward the end of the 1800s, a number of writers called **naturalists** carried realism even further. They described the ugly and sordid aspects of everyday life, attempting to screen emotion and opinion from their writings. The French novelist Émile Zola was a leader of this approach. He wrote as if he were a scientist objectively studying and carefully recording all human activities. Although people objected to his frankness, his exposure of shocking conditions of, for example, miners in his novel *Germinal* helped bring reform. Another realist was the British novelist Charles Dickens, who often wrote about the poor people of London.

In painting, the kind of realism that portrayed people and everyday life in the industrial age characterized the works of the French artists Gustave Courbet (koor·BAY) and Honoré Daumier (dohm·YAY). Another kind of "realism" was attempted by a group of painters who are known as **impressionists**.

Impressionist painting flourished first during the 1860s and 1870s in France. Impressionist painters tried to give vivid impressions of people and places as they appeared at a particular moment and in a particular light. To do this, the impressionists carefully studied light and color. They stopped motion and showed subjects from unusual, new perspectives. They experimented with small patches of different colors placed side by side to create shimmering effects. Claude Monet (moh·NAY) and Pierre-Auguste Renoir (ren·WAHR) were leading impressionist painters. Schools of impressionism also flourished in the United States and England.

The Metropolitan Museum of Art, H. O. Havemeyer Collection, Bequest of Mrs. H. O. Havemeyer, 1929. (29.100.370) Photograph © 1981 The Metropolitan Museum of Art

Edgar Degas, best known for his works of dancers, admired the human form and produced faithful renderings of it in oils, pastels, and bronze. Shown is Degas' "Little Fourteen-Year-Old Dancer."

Experiments in Art Forms

Like writers and musicians, painters and sculptors often rebelled against the materialism and mechanization of an industrial world. There was less nationalism in art than in literature or music. In painting and sculpture, there was much intensely individualistic experimentation. In the late 1800s, for example, there was the aesthetic movement in England. With a belief in "art for art's sake," this movement did not require art to be religious, political, or educational.

Paul Cézanne's landscapes and still lifes emphasized the forms and shapes of his subjects. He began to move beyond surface appearances to explore the abstract qualities of color and design. This shift away from showing recognizable, realistic scenes, introduced by Cézanne, influenced other artists who are often collectively termed postimpressionists.

One such artist was Paul Gauguin (goh·GAN). Gauguin, who left Europe to live in Tahiti, stressed color and simple, flat shapes in his paintings. Henri Matisse painted many decorative scenes of southern France. He, too, emphasized color design at the expense of realism. The Dutch painter Vincent van Gogh (van GOH) expressed intense emotions in his work by means of thick brush strokes of pure color and distorted perspectives. Edgar Degas (deh·GAH), Henri Toulouse-Lautrec (too·LOOZ·loh·TREK), and Édouard Manet (ma·NAY) all painted scenes of Parisian life in highly personal styles.

The French sculptor Auguste Rodin (roh·DAN) also broke with tradition. Some of his statues included unworked portions of the marble from which they were carved, giving his work a deliberately unfinished quality. Like many of the artists of the time, Rodin rejected expectations that art should show people, objects, and scenes as they appear in real life. The growing interest of many artists in abstract forms marked the end of the emotional strivings of romanticism and pointed the way toward the new artistic interests of the 1900s.

Section 5 Review

1. **Define** romanticism, realism, regionalism, naturalists, impressionists
2. **Identify** Sir Walter Scott, the Grimm brothers, Johann Wolfgang von Goethe, James Fenimore Cooper, Ludwig van Beethoven, Pyotr Ilich Tchaikovsky, Giuseppe Verdi, Gustave Flaubert, Mark Twain, Émile Zola, Paul Cézanne, Auguste Rodin
3. **Summarizing Ideas** Briefly explain the romantic movement of the early 1800s and give examples of romanticism in each of the following: literature, music, art, and architecture.
4. **Contrasting Ideas** How did the ideas and works of realists differ from those of the romantics?
5. **Analyzing Ideas** How did the work of Cézanne, Gauguin, and Rodin show individualism?

Chapter 20 Review

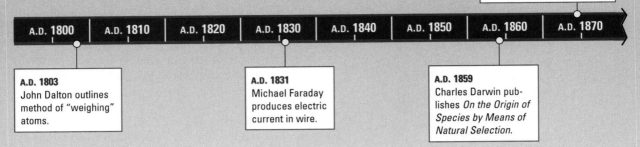

A.D. 1869
Dmitry Mendeleyev develops first workable classification of the elements.

A.D. 1800 | A.D. 1810 | A.D. 1820 | A.D. 1830 | A.D. 1840 | A.D. 1850 | A.D. 1860 | A.D. 1870

A.D. 1803
John Dalton outlines method of "weighing" atoms.

A.D. 1831
Michael Faraday produces electric current in wire.

A.D. 1859
Charles Darwin publishes *On the Origin of Species by Means of Natural Selection*.

Chapter Summary

The following list contains the key concepts you have learned about advances in technology, science, education, and the arts between 1800 and 1928.

1. In the late 1800s, the use of electricity became widespread. New inventions, such as the telephone and wireless telegraph, made rapid communication possible, and the development of the internal combustion engine helped to improve transportation.
2. Science developed rapidly during this period. In the biological sciences, knowledge of the cell, the basic unit of living matter, deepened. The theory of evolution proposed by Darwin had an enormous impact. The new science of genetics, founded by Mendel, answered many questions about biological inheritance.
3. Significant progress also was made in the physical sciences. Atomic theory became the basis for understanding matter. The brilliant work of Albert Einstein revolutionized the study of energy and matter.
4. Pasteur, Lister, Koch, and Fleming made advances in medicine. New drugs and medical techniques, such as surgery with anesthesia, were developed.
5. Those who studied the behavior of people as members of societies began to use scientific methods. Their fields of study came to be known as the social sciences and included new techniques for understanding history, politics, and economics. New social sciences included anthropology, sociology, and psychology.
6. Improvements in diet and food storage improved people's lives, while immigration to the cities changed population patterns.
7. Public education won gradual acceptance in western Europe and the United States in the late 1800s. More and more people learned to read and write. This educated audience spawned the publication of books, magazines, and newspapers.
8. The arts reflected the social and economic changes of the industrial age. In the early 1800s, many writers, musicians, and artists were caught up in the romantic movement, which emphasized emotion, nature, and often nationalism.
9. In the late 1800s, romanticism gradually gave way to realism. In painting and sculpture, romanticism and realism were followed by experimental, highly personal styles.

Reviewing Important Terms

On a separate sheet of paper, match each of the following terms with the correct definition below.

a. physical sciences
b. special theory of relativity
c. social science
d. romanticism
e. biological science
f. realism
g. regionalism
h. impressionists

_____ 1. The portrayal of everyday life with special attention to how it was lived in different locales
_____ 2. Artists who painted people and places as they appeared at a particular moment and who experimented with light and color
_____ 3. Art movement dealing with the realities of everyday life
_____ 4. Area of study dealing with living organisms
_____ 5. Area of study dealing with people as members of society
_____ 6. Artistic movement that emphasized sentiment and imagination
_____ 7. Theory that motion could be measured only relative to a particular observer
_____ 8. Area of study dealing with the properties of energy and nonliving aspects of nature

Developing Critical Thinking Skills

1. **Summarizing Ideas** List and describe four of the technological advances made during the last half of the 1800s.
2. **Understanding Ideas** What medical advances saved lives in the late 1800s and early 1900s?
3. **Determining Cause and Effect** What effects did population growth have on the growth of cities, and what effects did urbanization in turn have on people's lives?

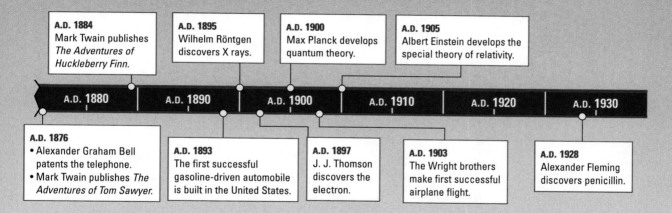

A.D. 1884 Mark Twain publishes *The Adventures of Huckleberry Finn.*

A.D. 1895 Wilhelm Röntgen discovers X rays.

A.D. 1900 Max Planck develops quantum theory.

A.D. 1905 Albert Einstein develops the special theory of relativity.

A.D. 1880 A.D. 1890 A.D. 1900 A.D. 1910 A.D. 1920 A.D. 1930

A.D. 1876
• Alexander Graham Bell patents the telephone.
• Mark Twain publishes *The Adventures of Tom Sawyer.*

A.D. 1893 The first successful gasoline-driven automobile is built in the United States.

A.D. 1897 J. J. Thomson discovers the electron.

A.D. 1903 The Wright brothers make first successful airplane flight.

A.D. 1928 Alexander Fleming discovers penicillin.

4. **Classifying Ideas** Identify the name of the author or composer of each of the following literary or musical works: **(a)** *Madame Bovary;* **(b)** *Middlemarch;* **(c)** *A Doll's House;* **(d)** *The Adventures of Tom Sawyer;* **(e)** *Fidelio;* **(f)** *War and Peace;* **(g)** *Aïda.*

5. **Analyzing Ideas** How might each of the following be considered a response to industrialization: **(a)** romanticism; **(b)** realism; **(c)** compulsory education.

Relating Geography to History

Select a particular author, composer, or artist discussed in this chapter. Use encyclopedias or other references to find out about the area where this person lived and whether he or she traveled extensively. Then write a short summary explaining how that person's environment and the extent of his or her travel may have affected his or her contributions to literature, music, or art.

Relating Past to Present

1. To investigate medical progress during the 1900s, interview a physician, nurse, pharmacist, or public health official in your community. You may wish to include the following questions. **(a)** In your field, how have medical advances made during the 1800s been improved upon? **(b)** What do you feel has been the most significant medical breakthrough in recent years? Share the responses you receive with your classmates in a class discussion.

2. Newspapers and magazines experienced great growth during the late 1800s. Find two newspapers or magazines existing today that originated before 1928. Ask your librarian about the availability of early issues. Notice the kinds of articles and advertisements that ran when the magazine or newspaper first appeared. How do they compare with those printed today? What do the advertisements suggest about changes in society over a period of time?

Applying History Study Skills

Before completing this activity, review Building History Study Skills on page 537.

Several historical themes of the first half of the 1800s are combined in *Le Moulin de la Galette* by French painter Pierre-Auguste Renoir, shown on page 538. Renoir was an impressionist, and in this painting he shows people at a popular café in a French city. Study the painting and answer the following questions.

1. **(a)** How would you define impressionism? **(b)** How is it portrayed in *Le Moulin de la Galette*?
2. What class of people does the painting show?
3. How does Renoir use light and color in this painting?
4. Compare *Le Moulin de la Galette* to Daumier's *The Washerwoman.* What are similarities? Differences?

Building Your Portfolio

1. **Presenting an Oral Report** Using books on the history of art, such as Helen Gardner's *Art Through the Ages* (Harcourt Brace Jovanovich) or H. W. Janson's *History of Art* (Prentice-Hall), examine paintings from the romantic period. Choose one or more paintings by a particular artist. What is the subject of each painting? What do you think the artist was trying to convey? What techniques did he or she use to create the painting? In what way does this artist represent romanticism? Place your notes from your report in your portfolio.

2. **Preparing a Book Report** Writers of the early 1800s turned to nature and the past for inspiration, and their stories were often filled with adventure, romance, and heroism. Read one of the following novels and explain how it reflects the ideas of the romantic movement: Sir Walter Scott's *Ivanhoe* (Pocket Books); Rafael Sabatini's *Scaramouche* (Houghton Mifflin); Baroness Emmuska Orczy's *The Scarlet Pimpernel* (Macmillan). Place your book report in your portfolio.

CHAPTER 21

The Age of Reform

TIME
A.D. **1791–1911**

A.D. **1791–1911**

3.7 million B.C. | 4000 B.C. | A.D. **2100**

PLACE
The British Empire, the United States, France, and Latin America

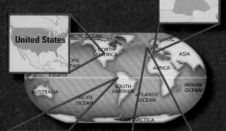

France

United States

Latin America

British Empire

Detail of painting by Everett Shinn, "The Eviction" (1904)

Significance

As the Industrial Revolution swept through Europe and the United States, an upper middle class emerged. Many members of this class believed in **liberalism***, a political philosophy grounded in the Enlightenment and the French Revolution. This philosophy advocated representative government to protect individual freedoms.

Terms to Define

liberalism	anarchists
suffrage	coalitions
Chartists	*haciendas*
home rule	*peninsulares*
suffragettes	*creoles*
Northwest Ordinance	*mestizos*
sectionalism	*mulattoes*
secede	Monroe Doctrine
total war	*caudillos*

People to Identify

Queen Victoria	Louis XVIII
Benjamin Disraeli	Charles X
William Gladstone	Louis Philippe
Fabian Society	Florence Nightingale
Lord Durham	Archduke Maximilian
Aborigines	Alfred Dreyfus
Maori	Toussaint-Louverture
the Grimké sisters	José de San Martín
Elizabeth Cady Stanton	Simón Bolívar
Lucretia Mott	Bernardo O'Higgins

Places to Locate

Ontario	Rio de Janeiro
Quebec	Haiti
Australia	Gran Colombia
New Zealand	

Chapter Theme Questions

- **Politics and Law** What might motivate people to reform society?
- **War and Diplomacy** What might happen when a nation experiences a civil war?
- **Social Relations** What factors might lead people to strive for independence?

---

*Liberalism in the 1800s differed greatly from liberalism today. For example, in the 1800s, a liberal policy might extend the vote only to educated male property owners.

F lorence Nightingale was a heroic Englishwoman who fought long-standing prejudices to make nursing more professional. During the Crimean War, under terrible conditions, she reorganized inept military hospitals into efficient, sanitary places for saving lives. The following excerpt from Cecil Woodham Smith's biography *Florence Nightingale* describes the admiration and respect she earned from the doctors and fighting men who observed her during the war.

❝*In January, 1855 there were 12,000 men in hospital and only 11,000 in the camp before Sebastopol; and still the shiploads came pouring down. It was, Miss Nightingale wrote, 'calamity unparalleled in the history of calamity.'*

In this emergency she became supreme. She was the rock to which everyone clung...

Her calmness, her resource, her power to take action raised her to the position of a goddess. The men adored her...The doctors came to be absolutely dependent on her.❞

The voices of women struggling for recognition of their rights through political reform began to be heard in the 1800s.

Section 1

Liberal Reforms in Great Britain and Its Empire

Focus Questions

- **What types of reforms were instituted in Great Britain in the 1800s and 1900s?**
- **What were the achievements of Benjamin Disraeli and William Gladstone?**
- **How did Great Britain respond to the desire of its colonies for greater self-government?**

During the 1800s, individuals who believed in liberalism were very active in politics. In Great Britain and in other parts of the British Empire, for example, liberals helped enact a number of reforms aimed at protecting political and civil liberties. Some reforms extended the right to vote to working men and eventually to women. Another abolished slavery, which had denied human and civil rights to people of African descent.

British Reforms of the 1800s

Great Britain was one of the first European nations to sharply limit the power of the monarchy. The Glorious Revolution of 1688 made Parliament the real ruler of the country. (See Chapter 16.) Great Britain became a limited constitutional monarchy with executive power vested in a cabinet headed by the prime minister.

Voting restrictions. Theoretically, the House of Commons represented all British people. The voters of each borough, or local district, elected members of the House of Commons. However, the right to vote and the right to hold public office were severely restricted in several ways: (1) Only property owners and a few other privileged men could vote. (2) People voted in the open rather than in private. Unscrupulous people could ensure "cooperation" by bribing or intimidating voters. (3) In some boroughs, nobles, already members of the House of Lords, controlled the choice of a representative. (4) Antiquated boundaries of boroughs, or election districts, did not reflect population distribution at all. (5) Only men who owned substantial property could be elected to the House of Commons. (6) Catholics, Jews, and Dissenters (non-Anglican Protestants) could not hold political office.

The Reform Bill of 1832. As time went on, the middle class and the workers began to demand reforms. At first the upper classes resisted, not only because they wanted to retain power but also because they feared political change might bring about a reign of terror as it had during the French Revolution. Then, from 1793 to 1815, British involvement in wars with France delayed action on reform.

After Napoleon's defeat, Britain, like continental Europe, experienced a period of reaction that threatened even long-established civil liberties such as the right of *habeas corpus*. Reformers who once might have tried to gain the king's support could find no help because of George III's instability and George IV's inattention. However, in 1829, near the end of George IV's reign, one piece of reform legislation passed. The Catholic Emancipation Act permitted the election of Roman Catholics to Parliament if they recognized the Protestant monarch as the legitimate ruler of Great Britain.

By 1830 the middle class and laborers demanded more extensive reforms. Several times the House of Commons passed bills that gave more people the right to vote and reapportioned election districts more fairly. Each time, the House of Lords refused to pass the bill. When the Whigs came to power in 1830, Prime Minister Charles Grey recommended to William IV that he create as many new lords as necessary to give the bill a majority in the House of Lords. William at first refused, but he gave in when governmental chaos loomed. To avoid the threat of a new majority of lords with reformist intentions, the House of Lords grudgingly passed the bill in 1832.

The Reform Bill of 1832 took seats in the House of Commons away from the less populated boroughs and gave seats to the new industrial cities. It also lowered property qualifications for voting. Although no real change in the composition of the House of Commons resulted, the middle class created by the Industrial Revolution now had a voice in government, and this new class gained parliamentary power.

The Whig Party, which had forced passage of the Reform Bill of 1832, had the support of these new voters. Joining with some Radicals and more liberal members of the Tories, the party became the Liberal Party. The Tory Party of the large landowners, who had opposed the reforms of 1832 and hesitated to go farther, became known as the Conservative Party.

Social and economic change. Vital social and economic developments took place after 1832. In 1833 Parliament passed an act that provided for the abolition of slavery in British colonies. Now freedom from slavery was law throughout the British Empire.

The Liberal Party soon forced the adoption of other reforms. A modest first step toward free public education was taken in 1833, giving financial support to private and church schools.

The Liberal Party also helped repeal the unpopular Corn Laws. For many years, the Corn Laws had set high tariffs on imported grain. By raising prices on imports, the Corn Laws protected expensive British grain against competition from cheaper foreign crops. British landowners benefited because they could sell their grain at high prices. High prices, however, harmed British workers, who had to buy grain products or starve. In 1846, after a bitter fight, Parliament repealed the Corn Laws. Grain could be imported into Britain free of tax. The repeal of the Corn Laws represented Britain's first step toward free trade.

Chartism. Beginning in the 1830s, a group known as the London Workingmen's Association began its

Building History Study Skills

READ
WRITE
INTERPRET
CONNECT
THINK

Reading About History: Understanding Ideology

An ideology is a body of ideas on which a particular system is based. In the 1800s in Europe, the two conflicting ideologies were liberalism and conservatism. Liberalism was based on the political philosophy of the French Revolution and the Enlightenment. Those who followed the ideology of political liberalism believed in a constitution that protected individual rights. The role of the government was to protect these rights. An economic liberal believed in the freedom of the individual to pursue economic gain without government interference.

On the other hand, conservatism was the ideology of the old order that was hostile to the French Revolution and the Enlightenment. Those who followed the ideology of political conservatism believed in a traditional government system that upheld the privileges of the upper classes. Economic conservatives believed in the government's role to manage the economy so that the state would prosper.

Understanding an ideology helps you determine the extent to which a person's position is based on his or her belief in an ideology rather than specific facts. For example, to what extent is a newspaper's support for a presidential candidate determined by ideology?

How to Understand Ideology

To understand an ideology, follow these steps.
1. Define the ideology. Find out what a person's ideology is by determining how he or she views change and the role of government.
2. Make connections. How does the ideology affect the person's viewpoint or the development of the person's argument?
3. Categorize the ideology. Is it economic or is it political?

Developing the Skill

The cartoons on the right were printed during the debate over the extension of suffrage to the workingman in 1867 in Great Britain. The argument sharply divided liberals and conservatives. Study the cartoons to determine the ideology of each of the cartoonists.

The political cartoon at the top reflected the liberal ideology. The cartoonist depicted the workingman as an angel carrying his tools, while

drinking holy water from a font in a church. The cartoonist probably favored change and supported the government's extension of the right to vote because he drew the worker in such a positive way.

The political cartoon at the bottom expressed the conservative ideology. In this cartoon, the workingman was portrayed as a slovenly drunkard. This cartoonist's sympathy with the conservative ideology is apparent by the negative way in which he depicted the workingman. The cartoonist apparently opposed change because he would not have wanted the government to extend voting rights to the undeserving worker.

Practicing the Skill

Find a political cartoon in your local newspaper. By using the skills listed above, attempt to determine the political ideology of the cartoonist.

To apply this skill, see Applying History Study Skills on page 571.

Queen Victoria's reign, the longest in British history, was marked by industrial progress at home and colonial expansion abroad.

reform work. Reforms such as universal male **suffrage**, or voting rights; the secret ballot; and payment for members of Parliament, so that even workingmen could afford to enter politics, were proposed by this group in a document called the People's Charter. Those who advocated these reforms became known as **Chartists**.

The Chartists presented petitions to Parliament in 1839, 1842, and 1848. The Chartists' popularity was based on very real grievances from the working class, but Chartists could not agree on aims and tactics. Many people believed such movements threatened the very foundations of society, and in 1848 British authorities worried that revolution might occur in Great Britain, as it had elsewhere. The economy improved, however, and unrest subsided.

Despite the failure of the Chartist movement, Parliament eventually adopted most of the reforms its members advocated. Workers continued to seek voting rights, and more and more who favored an increasingly democratic government joined them.

In 1867 Parliament passed a second reform bill with more sweeping reforms than the first. It almost doubled the number of those who could vote. By lowering property qualifications, the second reform bill extended the vote to most urban industrial workers. However, vast numbers of people in the lower classes, such as agricultural workers, could not yet vote, nor could women.

Disraeli and Gladstone

King William IV died in 1837 with no male heirs, so his 18-year-old niece, Victoria, became queen. She was interested in government but interfered little, allowing her prime ministers a free hand. Victoria reigned from June 1837 until January 1901, a 63-year period so distinguished in British history that it is known as the Victorian Age.

Two notable prime ministers—Benjamin Disraeli and William Gladstone—dominated the political arena between 1868 and 1894. Disraeli led the Conservative Party and served twice as prime minister. In addition to enthusiasm and a mastery of politics, Disraeli had an intense interest in foreign affairs and expansion of the British Empire.

Disraeli's first term as prime minister lasted only a few months. He first became prime minister when the Earl of Derby resigned in February 1868, but his party was defeated by the Liberals in a general election that was held that year. During his second ministry, from 1874 to 1880, Britain gained control of the Suez Canal, and Queen Victoria became the empress of India.

William Gladstone led the Liberal Party and served four terms as prime minister. He was devout, cautious, and formal. Gladstone concerned himself first with British domestic and financial matters. Under his leadership, Parliament attempted additional reforms, many of which went into effect.

Benjamin Disraeli, Queen Victoria's favorite prime minister, served two terms, the first in 1868 and the second from 1874 to 1880.

Gladstone became prime minister in 1868. One of his achievements as prime minister was the passage of the Education Act of 1870, which created a national elementary education system. This act allowed children of the working classes to receive an elementary education for a small fee. Elementary education became free in England in 1891.

In 1872, under Gladstone's leadership, Britain adopted the secret ballot. Now a man could vote as he chose without fearing consequences because someone disapproved of his politics. The secret ballot also reduced bribery, which had been common, and protected workers in cities from intimidation by bosses.

In 1884 Gladstone and the Liberals pushed through Parliament the third reform bill, which gave the vote to most agricultural workers. In the following year, 1885, the Redistribution Bill divided Britain into electoral districts approximately equal in population. Although the bill did not achieve complete equality in representation, it was an important step in this direction.

The Irish Question

One area in which Liberals proved unsuccessful concerned the "Irish question," whether Ireland should rule itself or be ruled by England. Liberals favored **home rule** for Ireland. Conservatives were determined not to yield power. In 1801 the Act of Union had joined Ireland and Great Britain to form the United Kingdom of Great Britain and Ireland. The Act of Union disbanded Ireland's Parliament, leaving the Irish with little representation in the British Parliament. In addition to resenting scant parliamentary representation, the Irish people—mostly Catholic—resented their taxes supporting the Anglican Church.

The Irish hated British rule, especially absentee landlords, who owned much of the land. Policies designed to help British industry hurt Irish agriculture, and the poor suffered. In the mid-1800s, the potato crop failed and famine swept Ireland. Those who could fled to the United States. Gladstone tried unsuccessfully to get home rule bills passed. After much turbulence, Conservatives, in order to "kill Home Rule with kindness," agreed to some land reforms in the 1890s, and tension temporarily eased.

British Reforms of the Early 1900s

Social reform accompanied political reform. During the late 1800s and early 1900s, the labor union movement grew stronger in Great Britain. Socialism, too, attracted many followers.

Social reforms. In 1884 a group of intellectuals founded the Fabian Society, an organization aimed at improving society through socialist ideas and education. The Fabians, whose members included playwright George Bernard Shaw, began working through established political parties. In 1906 they helped workers, frustrated by both Liberals and Conservatives, found the British Labour Party.

In 1905 the Liberal Party returned to power. Under Herbert Asquith, who was the prime minister from 1908 to 1916, Liberals adopted extensive social welfare legislation. Laws provided for old-age pensions, health and unemployment insurance, and efforts to reduce unemployment. To pay for these benefits, Parliament raised taxes.

Changes within Parliament. The budget of 1909 increased taxes for the wealthy. The enraged House of Lords opposed the budget, and Liberals took steps to decrease the power of the lords. The Parliament Act of 1911 took away the lords' powers to veto tax and appropriation bills and allowed them only to delay

---

Reforming the British Parliamentary System

1829	Catholic Emancipation Act permitted Roman Catholics to be elected to Parliament.
1832	Reform Bill of 1832 redistributed seats in Parliament and lowered property qualifications for voting.
1867	Reform Bill of 1867 further lowered property qualifications, almost doubling electorate.
1872	Secret ballot was adopted.
1884	Reform Bill of 1884 gave vote to most farmworkers.
1885	Redistribution Bill divided Britain into approximately equal electoral districts.
1911	Parliament Act of 1911 took away power of House of Lords to veto parliamentary bills
1928	All British women over age of 21 were granted voting rights.

Hunger and Despair: The Irish Potato Famine

One of the most wrenching changes of the 1800s was not the result of a reform movement. A terrible famine devastated Ireland in the 1840s. Millions left the country, an emigration that changed the social fabric of Ireland and the United States forever.

In 1845 a previously unknown fungus struck the potato crop, the mainstay of Irish agriculture. Plants that looked fine one day wilted the next or yielded potatoes that quickly rotted. The blight returned, year after year, and in the wretchedly poor country, hunger led to weakness, which led to epidemic and starvation. Unable to work or to pay their landlords, thousands of Irish families were evicted from their homes to die in the streets and countryside. Children, as in all famines, suffered most: "their limbs fleshless...their faces bloated yet wrinkled and of a pale greenish hue." Famine and disease probably killed between 1.1 and 1.5 million people.

Few in the British government cared. Some charitable efforts were made, and Sir Robert Peel urged policies to help the Irish, but relief was often too late. Distrust was so deep that some Irish refused British corn, fearing that the unknown food was poisonous.

Those who were able to do so left Ireland. More than 2 million people left between 1845 and

Irish immigrants sail to the United States, c.1848

1855, doing anything they could to raise the money needed for passage.

In America life was hard. Starving, often without skills, and facing both religious and cultural prejudice, the Irish were treated poorly. Exploited by employers and slumlords, women often became servants, and men became laborers.

Nevertheless, the Irish eventually became a potent force in American labor and politics. Many saw themselves as involuntary exiles and vowed to return to Ireland someday. Though they had left their native country they never abandoned their love of it, and pride in the ancestral homeland endures today.

---

passage of other bills. Many nobles bitterly opposed the act, and the House of Lords passed it only after George V, who had become king in 1910, threatened to create enough new Liberal lords to pass it.

Within a month after the passage of the Parliament Act of 1911 a law was passed that gave members of the House of Commons a salary of 400 pounds a year, which was a good salary for the time. It meant that a person without an independent income could afford to serve in Parliament.

Women's voting rights. Since the late 1880s, many women in Great Britain had demanded the right to vote. Led by energetic and outspoken women such as Emmeline Pankhurst and her daughter, Christabel, they were called **suffragettes** because they wanted suffrage for women. Suffragettes petitioned Parliament

and demonstrated, becoming increasingly disruptive and determined. Many people thought that compromise might be reached earlier, but women's suffrage was delayed until after World War I.*

Changes Within the British Empire

As Great Britain instituted social and political reforms, changes occurred within other parts of the British Empire as well. Settlers in the British colonies of Canada, Australia, and New Zealand benefited from the liberal policies being enacted in Great Britain.

---

*In 1918 a bill gave the right to vote to women over the age of 30 if they or their husbands owned property. In 1928 another bill granted all British women over the age of 21 the right to vote.

Canada

Canadians were dissatisfied with British rule in the early 1800s. British settlers in Upper Canada (part of what is now Ontario) wanted more self-government, and French Canadians in Lower Canada (part of what is now Quebec) resented British control.

During the 1830s, a business depression, unemployment, and crop failures led to uprisings in both Lower and Upper Canada. French Canadians tried to establish an independent French republic, and British Canadians sought greater freedom from British officials. Both revolts failed.

The Durham Report. In 1838 the British government sent a new governor-general, Lord Durham, to Canada to try to settle disagreements between English- and French-speaking Canadians. A member of the Liberal Party, Durham was given broad powers to reform Canada's government.

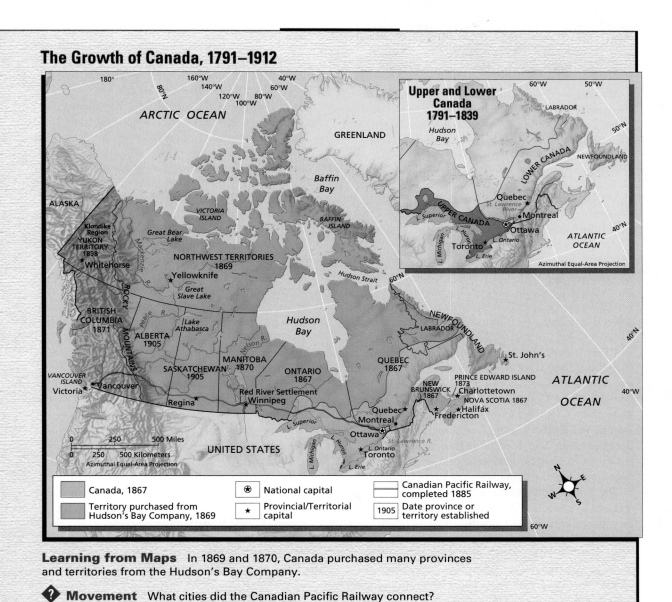

The Growth of Canada, 1791–1912

Learning from Maps In 1869 and 1870, Canada purchased many provinces and territories from the Hudson's Bay Company.

Movement What cities did the Canadian Pacific Railway connect?

This photograph shows Victoria, the capital of British Columbia. Founded in 1843, the territory was named after Queen Victoria and has remained quite British in character.

What If?

Great Britain and the American Revolution
What if Great Britain had not experienced the American Revolution? How might its policies have been different with regard to governing other colonies?

In 1839 Lord Durham submitted a report to Parliament with basic recommendations that governed later British colonial policy. Britain was anxious not to repeat in Canada the mistake that had cost it the American colonies. Remote government had failed to treat colonists as full citizens and was too far away to grasp unique circumstances or enforce central authority. Lord Durham suggested that if Great Britain granted self-government to colonies such as Canada, the colonies would remain in the empire.

Lord Durham also recommended that Canada be united. In 1840 the British Parliament did this with the passage of the Act of Union. Effective in 1841, British Upper Canada and French Lower Canada were united. A parliament was created in which French and British regions had equal representation. Between 1846 and 1848, the British expanded the power of Canada's Parliament and granted self-government to the Canadian people.

The British North America Act. The union of Upper and Lower Canada did not work well in any respect. Each region was suspicious of the other, and their equal strength in Parliament resulted in deadlock. A solution came in 1864, however, when the eastern colonies of New Brunswick, Nova Scotia, and Prince Edward Island considered forming a federal union. Delegates from Canada and the colonies met in the city of Quebec. They recommended a plan of federation, which the British Parliament approved as the British North America Act of 1867. The act created the Dominion of Canada with the provinces of Ontario, Quebec, Nova Scotia, and New Brunswick.

By the terms of the British North America Act, each province had a legislature to deal with local affairs. The federal Parliament, which dealt with national issues, met at the Dominion capital, Ottawa, Ontario. This government, far more powerful than the provincial legislatures, was a parliamentary democracy with a cabinet based on the British model. Liberal and Conservative political parties in Canada resembled those in Great Britain. The party in power appointed the prime minister, who had much the same role as the British counterpart.

In 1869 and 1870, Canada purchased huge areas of land, including the present Northwest Territories, from the Hudson's Bay Company, a private trading company. Some residents, a multiracial group called métis, resisted, arguing that the Hudson's Bay Company did not own the land to sell. As a concession to the métis, Canada created the province of Manitoba in the southeast portion of the area. This also served to strengthen Canadian control of the area, reducing the worry that the United States might attempt to annex the region. British Columbia and Prince Edward Island also became provinces during the 1870s, bringing the total number of provinces in the Dominion to seven.

Canada continued to expand westward, much as the United States was doing. The completion of the Canadian Pacific Railway opened western Canada to immigration. (See map on page 549.) As a result, two more provinces—Alberta and Saskatchewan—joined the Dominion in 1905.*

---

*In 1949 Newfoundland and its dependency, Labrador, became the tenth province of the Dominion of Canada.

The discovery of gold in the Klondike region led to the development of northwestern Canada. During the late 1890s, thousands of prospectors rushed to the area. The Klondike gold rush brought so many people that the Yukon Territory was organized in 1898.

Australia

Australia is a huge island, a continent in itself. Yet for centuries it remained unknown to the Western world. European explorers who sailed into the Pacific Ocean in the 1500s missed it entirely. The Dutch sighted the continent in the early 1600s and named it New Holland but considered it too poor to colonize. Captain James Cook, a British sailor on a scientific expedition for the navy, sailed along Australia's eastern shore in 1770. He named the region New South Wales, because of its resemblance to southern Wales, and claimed it for Great Britain.

Before the American Revolution, Great Britain often sent prisoners to North America. After the loss of the American colonies, the British began sending convicts to Australia. The first shiploads arrived in New South Wales in 1788, and soon the convicts founded the town of Sydney on the southeast coast. Free settlers with land grants arrived shortly afterward. Convicts who served their sentences and gained freedom could stay in Australia and own land. However, these two groups did not always get along.

The early 1800s became a lawless period in Australia. Clashes among immigrants, ex-convicts, and gangs of escaped convicts called bushrangers occurred often. The original Australian people, the Aborigines, were pushed into the interior.

In 1829 the British claimed the entire continent of Australia. By 1836 the colonies of Tasmania, Western Australia, and South Australia had been organized.

Kapunda Coppermine in South Australia

Australia and New Zealand, c. 1800s

Learning from Maps Britain established colonies across the Australian continent.

? Place What island did the British settle off one part of the southern coast of Australia between the 140°E and 160°E lines of longitude?

The colony of Victoria was formed in 1851, and the discovery of gold that year brought a flood of immigrants. Queensland was formed in 1859. (See map on this page.)

The Australian colonies developed independently of each other. They modeled their legislatures after the British Parliament, except that members of both the upper and lower houses were elected. (In New South Wales, members of the upper house were appointed.) In the 1890s, the colonies began to consider forming a federal union to protect against territorial expansion by European nations. The colonies united in 1901 to create the Commonwealth of Australia, a self-governing part of the British Empire.

The native Aborigine population was dramatically reduced by the settlement of Europeans. Many Aborigines died as the result of new diseases introduced to the area. Ideas of racial superiority also led to brutal violence against native peoples, and many whites wanted the Aborigines to simply die out. Similar attitudes shaped immigration policy, which prohibited immigration by non-Europeans. This "white Australia policy" antagonized many nations, particularly those in Asia.

As Australia's economy grew, trade unions and the Labor Party influenced Parliament to adopt social legislation. Parliament passed bills establishing old-age pensions, compulsory arbitration of labor disputes, and wage-fixing boards, among others.

New Zealand

Dutch sailors, and later Captain Cook, sighted the islands of New Zealand, southeast of Australia. Private companies developed the islands in the 1820s and 1830s. In 1840 a treaty with Maori (MOW·ree) chieftains, the native rulers of the islands, established British control. In 1852 Britain's Parliament gave New Zealand a constitution, and the islands became a self-governing colony.

Disputes over land brought British settlers into conflict with native inhabitants, and several Maori wars took place in the 1860s and early 1870s. In other respects, the development of New Zealand resembled that of Australia. The settlement of Europeans caused a decline in the Maori population—from both disease and warfare—as it had in the Australian Aborigine population. Gold was discovered in 1861, bringing new waves of immigrants. In 1893 New Zealand became the first country in the world to grant the vote to women. In 1907 New Zealand joined the British Empire as a dominion.

Section 1 Review

1. **Define** liberalism, suffrage, Chartists, home rule, suffragettes
2. **Identify** Queen Victoria, Benjamin Disraeli, William Gladstone, Fabian Society, Lord Durham, Aborigines, Maori
3. **Locate and Explain the Significance** Ontario, Quebec, Australia, New Zealand
4. **Understanding Cause and Effect (a)** Why was the Reform Bill of 1832 necessary in Great Britain? **(b)** How did the bill affect the British government?
5. **Comparing Ideas** Compare the views and achievements of British prime ministers Benjamin Disraeli and William Gladstone.
6. **Analyzing Ideas** In what ways did Great Britain influence the reform movement in its colonies?

Expansion and Reform in the United States

Focus Questions

- How did the United States expand its territory across the North American continent?
- What issues contributed to the Civil War, and what were its effects?
- How did the United States change in the period after the Civil War?

When the United States ratified its Constitution in 1788, the new nation consisted of 13 states along the Atlantic coast and additional territories that extended to the Mississippi River. The country's population was about 4 million people, most of whom lived in farming communities in the eastern part of the nation.

The nation was born during a time of European turmoil, and most Americans wanted to avoid European affairs and develop their country. They did this so successfully that, during the next 100 years, the territory of the United States grew to almost four times its original size, and its population increased to about 60 million. By 1900 the United States took its place among the great nations of the world.

Territorial Growth

By the mid-1800s, the United States had completed its territorial expansion across the North American continent to the Pacific Ocean. By the end of the century, it had also become an imperial power, acquiring territory in the Pacific and Caribbean regions.

The Northwest Territory. The land bounded by the Appalachian Mountains, the Ohio and Mississippi Rivers, and the Great Lakes was known as the Northwest Territory. States that had originally claimed this area turned the land over to the United States when they ratified the Articles of Confederation. Once the nation had won independence, hundreds of settlers pushed across the mountains into the Northwest Territory. In 1787 Congress passed the **Northwest Ordinance** to provide some form of government for the settlers.

The Northwest Ordinance of 1787 guaranteed that people who lived in territories would have rights equal to those who lived in the original 13 states. It

---

provided that the Northwest Territory would be divided into states and admitted into the Union on an equal basis with existing states. When a territory had 5,000 adult males, it could form a legislature to govern the territory. Then, when a territory had 60,000 inhabitants, it could adopt a constitution and apply for statehood.

Many people left their homes on the Atlantic seaboard to settle the Northwest Territory. These settlers knew that the territories would be admitted to the Union as states. Of the 10 new states that were added to the United States between 1791 and 1836, 6 were part of the Northwest Territory.

Completing the expansion. Many of the principles of the Northwest Ordinance were applied to new lands as the nation continued to expand. In 1803 Napoleon sold the vast territory of Louisiana (which Spain had ceded to France) to the United States. Extending westward from the Mississippi River roughly to the Rocky Mountains, the Louisiana

U.S. Territorial Expansion, 1785–1898

Alaska Purchase, 1867
Azimuthal Equal-Area Projection

Northwest Territory, 1787
Louisiana Purchase, 1803
Oregon Country, 1818
Florida Cession, 1819
Texas Annexation, 1845
Mexican Cession, 1848
Gadsden Purchase, 1853
Disputed area
Present-day boundary

Boundary set by Oregon Treaty, 1846
Boundaries set by Webster-Ashburton Treaty, 1842
Ceded by Great Britain, 1818
CANADA
Claimed by Great Britain until 1842
St. Lawrence River
Columbia River
ROCKY MOUNTAINS
Missouri River
Great Plains
Missouri Compromise Line
Colorado River
Ohio River
Mississippi River
UNITED STATES Before 1785
Arkansas River
PACIFIC OCEAN
ATLANTIC OCEAN
Gila River
Rio Grande

Annexation of Hawaii, 1898
Albers Equal-Area Projection

Ceded by Spain, 1819
Gulf of Mexico
MEXICO

0   250   500 Miles
0   250   500 Kilometers
Azimuthal Equal-Area Projection

50°N
40°N
30°N
70°W
80°W
90°W
110°W
120°W

Learning from Maps Throughout the 1800s people moved westward across the United States in search of new land.

? Region What region was purchased from France in 1803? What region was acquired from Mexico in 1853?

Purchase almost doubled the territory of the United States. The United States also purchased Florida from Spain in 1819. (See map on page 553.)

In 1836 American settlers in Mexican territory south of the Louisiana Purchase declared themselves independent and established the Republic of Texas. The United States annexed Texas by treaty in 1845, and war with Mexico resulted. American victory in the Mexican War gained the Mexican Cession, a huge region that eventually became the states of Utah, Nevada, California, and parts of Arizona, Colorado, New Mexico, and Wyoming.

In 1846 a treaty with Great Britain gave the United States the Oregon Country. The states of Oregon, Washington, Idaho, and parts of Montana and Wyoming were created from this land. In 1853 the United States made the Gadsden Purchase, buying from Mexico a strip of land in what is now southern New Mexico and Arizona.

Thus by the 1850s, the young nation stretched from coast to coast and from Mexico to Canada. During the next 50 years, settlement caught up with territorial acquisition. Discovery of gold in California in 1848 led to the California gold rush and great westward migration. Cattle ranchers, farmers, and miners settled in the plains and mountains of the western United States.

Political Growth

In the early days of the United States, some states had allowed only white male property owners to vote. New states farther west imposed few property requirements. In time eastern states dropped property qualifications for male voters.

In the 1820s and 1830s, many other changes occurred. Public education became more widespread. An increasing number of political offices became elective instead of being appointive. Political candidates came to be chosen by party conventions rather than by small groups of legislators. Although voters had little say in who was nominated, more voters than ever before decided elections.

The Issue of Slavery

Although the United States had a unified federal government, **sectionalism**—rivalry among various sections of the country—plagued the young nation. During the early 1800s, three major sections emerged: the Northeast, a region of growing cities and industry; the South, an agricultural area with many farms, including large cotton and tobacco plantations;

and the West, a frontier region of small, independent farms that were located between the Appalachians and the Mississippi River.

With such different ways of life, it is not surprising that people from these sections held differing views on such subjects as federal financing of improvements, tariffs, banking and currency, and public lands. However, the issue of slavery soon became the greatest issue dividing the country.

Slavery had existed in the American colonies almost from the beginning. The United States Constitution accepted slavery but left its regulation up to the states. Each state had the power to preserve or abolish the institution of slavery.

Some people in the South believed they needed slaves to harvest cotton and tobacco, which grew well in the climate of the southern states and required intensive labor to cultivate. Thus slavery grew in the South, especially after the invention of the cotton gin made cotton a profitable crop.

A question soon arose: Should slavery be permitted in new territories? Southerners argued that Congress did not have the power to prohibit slavery in the new territories; Northerners argued that Congress did have this power. A growing number of people came to advocate the abolition of slavery altogether. Southerners were determined to preserve enough votes in the Senate to block abolition at the federal level.

Secession and Civil War

Arguments about slavery, as well as about states' rights versus the rights of the federal government, led to bitter sectional quarrels throughout the early 1800s. Southern states threatened many times to **secede**, or withdraw from the Union. Each time, compromises staved off secession. Then in 1860 Abraham Lincoln was elected president. Lincoln headed the newly formed Republican Party, which had pledged to prevent the spread of slavery into the territories.

Shortly after the election, South Carolina seceded from the Union and other southern states followed. They formed the Confederate States of America, with Jefferson Davis as president. Eventually 11 southern states joined the Confederacy.

President Lincoln, arguing that states had no constitutional right to secede, declared that the Southerners had rebelled. The United States government, he proclaimed, had a duty to suppress this rebellion. Efforts at compromise failed, and in 1861 the Union and the Confederacy began a bloody war that would last four years.

Major Civil War Battles

Map legend:

- → Union forces
- → Confederate forces
- ✶ Union victory
- ✶ Confederate victory
- ▮ Union free states
- ▮ Confederate states
- ▮ Union slave states
- ⊛ Capital city

Learning from Maps The North and the South lost more than 600,000 lives during the Civil War.

❓ **Location** What battle was fought the farthest north?

The Civil War was the most costly conflict in which the United States has ever been involved. In many ways, it was also the first modern war. It introduced new and lethal devices such as the explosive shell and the Gatling gun. New strategies such as **total war**—targeting the enemy's military *and* civilian resources—were used. (See map on page 555.)

Many European nations favored the Confederacy. Industrial and commercial interests hoped the war would weaken their business competitors in the Northeast. The British needed cotton from the South and frequently aided Confederate ships by letting them use British ports. Napoleon III of France took advantage of the conflict to intervene in Mexico.

As time went on, it became clear that the agricultural South lacked the manpower, industries, and railroads necessary to defeat the North's armies. The end finally came in April 1865, when the Confederacy surrendered. The Union was preserved.

In January 1863 President Lincoln had issued the Emancipation Proclamation, freeing slaves in those parts of the country still "in rebellion against the United States." Although it had little immediate effect, it signaled that slavery would end everywhere at the end of the Civil War. Following the war, Congress passed three amendments to the Constitution. The Thirteenth Amendment abolished slavery, the Fourteenth Amendment gave former slaves citizenship and equal protection under the law, and the Fifteenth Amendment provided that the right to vote would not be denied "on account of race, color, or previous condition of servitude." Although in some areas of the country these laws were not well observed, the amendments strengthened the principle of equality before the law.

The price of preserving the Union was tragically high. The North and South together lost more than 600,000 people. Families were torn apart and the ideals of the republic damaged. Nor did freedom ease the lives of former slaves. Bitterness endured, for the war left wounds that the nation felt well into the 1900s.

A Changing Nation

The United States experienced phenomenal growth from 1865 to 1900 primarily as a result of industrialization. Cities doubled and tripled in size, and a network of railroads crisscrossed the country.

Immigration. Another important factor in this growth was immigration. For many decades people had come to the United States from England and Scotland. In the mid-1800s, a heavy wave of immigration came from two other regions: Ireland, which suffered severe potato famines, and Germany, where many people fled from revolutions in 1848.

In the late 1800s, immigration increased from southern and eastern Europe, especially Italy, Russia, and Austria-Hungary. Another great wave of immigration including people from Latin America occurred at the turn of the century.

At the Seneca Falls Convention in 1848, Elizabeth Cady Stanton (shown holding child in photo) and Lucretia Mott asked women to organize themselves and assert their rights. Their efforts launched the suffrage movement that won women the right to vote in 1920.

Women's suffrage. Many women campaigned for the abolition of slavery. Some of these abolitionists, such as the sisters Sarah Moore Grimké and Angelina Emily Grimké, began publicly to address the status of women. They insisted that equality be extended to women as well as men.

In 1848 a women's rights conference, organized by Elizabeth Cady Stanton and Lucretia Mott, was held in Seneca Falls, New York. Delegates drew up a list of demands, including suffrage for women.

In the 1890s and early 1900s, many women renewed the campaign for suffrage, skillfully employing both public opinion and the political system. In 1920, with the ratification of the Nineteenth Amendment to the Constitution, women won the right to vote.

Section 2 Review

1. **Define** Northwest Ordinance, sectionalism, secede, total war
2. **Identify** the Grimké sisters, Elizabeth Cady Stanton, Lucretia Mott
3. **Organizing Ideas** List the steps in the territorial expansion of the United States from 1787 to 1853.
4. **Analyzing Ideas** What were the issues that led up to the Civil War?
5. **Interpreting Ideas** How did immigration and the struggle for voting rights change life in the United States after the Civil War?

Section 3

Revolution and Reform in France

Focus Questions

- In what ways did governmental change in France differ from reform in Great Britain during the 1800s and early 1900s?
- Who was Louis Napoleon, and how did he increase his own power in France?
- What problems faced republican France after the reign of Louis Napoleon?

The Congress of Vienna restored the Bourbon monarch, King Louis XVIII, to the throne of France following Napoleon's exiles in 1814 and 1815. Louis, who was glad to be king and unwilling to upset the situation, carried on many of the reforms established between 1789 and 1815. He accepted a constitution that limited his power, and he also established a legislature to assist in governing the country. Louis spent the nine years of his reign balancing between extremists who were determined to restore an absolute monarchy and reformers who were equally determined to further transform France into a true republic.

Charles X

When Louis XVIII died in 1824, his brother, Charles X—an ardent believer in absolute monarchy—succeeded him. As soon as Charles became king, he antagonized his subjects. First, he pledged that the government would reimburse the émigrés whose estates had been seized and sold to the peasants. This unpopular policy meant taxing all the people for the benefit of emigrant nobles, who had opposed reform or democracy in France. Second, Charles abolished most of the liberal provisions of the weak constitution his brother had accepted and tried to restore many features of the Old Regime.

Had Charles or his advisers shown any flexibility, revolution might have been avoided. However, they did not, and in July 1830, revolt spread throughout the country. Surprised by the growing hostility and unprepared to defend his regime, Charles X was forced to abdicate the throne.

The successful rebellion inspired revolutions elsewhere. In December 1830, for example, Belgians declared independence from their Dutch rulers.

Louis Philippe, the "Citizen King"

Leaders of the French revolution of 1830 wanted to be rid of Charles X, but they could not agree on the nature of government after his departure. Those favoring a republic lacked the strength to create one. Finally, all groups agreed on the choice of another king. They selected Louis Philippe, duke of Orléans, who belonged to a branch of the Bourbon family but had a record of liberal beliefs.

Louis Philippe was in a delicate position. He was a king, but an elected king. Having seen the fate of Charles X, Louis Philippe knew that he needed the support of the majority of the French people. He tried to please the people and called himself the citizen king, though he wanted more than merely a symbolic role.

The upper middle class benefited more than any other class during the reign of Louis Philippe. After the revolt of 1830, the voting population was expanded from 90,000 to 200,000 by lowering the voting age and the tax that qualified one to vote. Nevertheless, control was still firmly in the hands of the class of merchants and industrialists. Workers could not organize, and the government outlawed labor unions. High tariffs placed on imported goods benefited owners of industries because they kept foreign-made goods out of France. However, tariffs resulted in higher prices for domestic goods.

While the upper middle class generally favored Louis Philippe, he faced opposition from both monarchists and republicans. One group of monarchists wanted a direct descendant of Charles X to be king, while another group, the Bonapartists, wanted to revive Napoleon's empire. Napoleon's nephew attempted twice to take power, failed, and was sentenced to prison for life. He escaped to England.

At the other end of the political spectrum stood the republicans, who believed that France should become a republic, institute political rights, and make changes to benefit all the people. Most French workers agreed. Their lot had improved little, and they were increasingly attracted to the wealth of socialist ideas circulating at the time. Food shortages and widespread unemployment heightened discontent between 1846 and 1848.

The Revolutions of 1848

In 1848 opposition to the regime of Louis Philippe erupted into violence. Trouble began over the principle of free speech. In February opponents of the government organized "banquets" to criticize official policy (political meetings were forbidden). Louis Philippe issued a decree prohibiting the final "banquet" in Paris.

The decree sparked rioting. The disorder did not seem serious until the National Guard, summoned to restore order, joined the rioters. Although still in control of the army, Louis Philippe had a choice between violence or abdication. He, too, abdicated and left for England.

The people of Paris established a temporary government and proclaimed the Second French Republic in 1848. (The First Republic had lasted from 1792 until 1804, when Napoleon became emperor.) The most active group in the new government consisted of the urban working class, whose leaders believed in socialism. Because economic depression and widespread unemployment paralyzed France, socialist members of the government established "national workshops" to give people work.

This action marked an early instance of a modern government taking responsibility to remedy chronic unemployment in their country.

Adopting universal manhood suffrage, the Second Republic held elections for a National Assembly to write a constitution for a permanent government. When the new National Assembly met in June, conservative members in the majority voted to end the program of national workshops.

This action led to violent rioting in Paris. Fearing a widespread revolution, the National Assembly allowed army officers to assume power. For three days, Paris became a battlefield. The army crushed the rebellion and imprisoned, exiled, or executed its socialist leaders. Karl Marx, the founder of modern socialism, was among those expelled from France.

Louis Napoleon

The new constitution written by the National Assembly provided for a republican form of government, with an elected president. The president would serve a four-year term and would not be eligible for a second term. The National Assembly would be a single legislative body, consisting of representatives elected by universal manhood suffrage.

In December 1848, the Republic held its first elections. Instead of electing as president someone who had helped create the Second Republic, however, the voters overwhelmingly chose Louis Napoleon Bonaparte, Napoleon's nephew.

Louis Napoleon wanted to be more than president. He began to work for the support of various groups in France. Like his uncle, he did everything he could to gain the backing of the army. To win support from French Catholics, he helped the pope suppress an attempt in Italy to set up a republic in Rome. He assisted the Catholic Church in gaining more control over education.

The constitution of the Second Republic, however, limited the president to a single four-year term. Louis Napoleon hoped that an amendment could be passed that would allow him to run for a second term. When it became clear in 1851 that he lacked sufficient votes in the National Assembly to get the amendment, he acted on his second choice, a coup d'état. In December, 70 members of the National Assembly were arrested. Street rioting followed. Promising a vote and a new constitution, Louis Napoleon represented himself as a defender of order. He followed through with the plebiscite, a yes-or-no vote on his actions, which his uncle had employed so successfully.

The Gleaners

Artists convey messages through their choice of subject as well as their artistic style. Jean-François Millet not only rejected the popular romanticized style of his day—the 1850s and 1860s—but also used peasants and workers as his subjects.

Millet, a peasant himself, worked on the land until the age of 20, when he began studying with another artist. Understandably, then, he identified heavily with the peasant class.

Gleaners are the poorest peasants, who gather the leavings from a field after reaping. In this painting, Millet makes them appear graceful and dignified. That *The Gleaners* seems sentimental and idealized today is evidence of constantly changing tastes and values in art.

Believing in Louis Napoleon's famous name and that he actually stood for order, the people voted almost 12 to 1 in his favor.

The Second French Empire

The new constitution extended Louis Napoleon's term as president to 10 years. Although this gave him greater power, his real ambition appears to have been to restore the empire of his uncle Napoleon I.

In 1852 there was another plebiscite for yet another constitution. Following a Senate resolution to restore the empire, Louis Napoleon was elected Emperor Napoleon III. (Napoleon I had a son, who would have been Napoleon II, but he never reigned and died in 1832.)

Though Napoleon III posed as a champion of democratic rights, he limited criticism of his actions through strict censorship and exile of his critics. On the surface, the Second French Empire looked like a democracy. It allowed for a constitution and a legislature elected by universal manhood suffrage. In practice, however, the early reign of Napoleon III was a new style of absolutism. The legislature could pass only those laws proposed by the emperor. Civil liberties were reduced. Political opposition was stifled. Newspapers were censored. The government warned that any paper criticizing the emperor or his government would be warned twice, then shut down. Freedom of speech did not exist. Some liberal professors in universities lost their jobs. For years it was impossible to organize opposition to the government.

As Napoleon III, Louis Napoleon tried to develop his empire through modernization. He helped the middle class by encouraging the development of manufacturing and railroads. At the same time, he tried to keep the favor of lower classes by setting up programs of public works that gave jobs to many people. Domestic affairs stabilized.

Problems in the Crimea and Mexico

To achieve recognition from other European rulers and to improve relations with Britain, Napoleon III involved France in a dispute with the Ottoman Empire.

Because of earlier agreements, Russia claimed the right to protect Orthodox Christians living under the rule of the Ottoman Turks. Similarly, France protected Catholics. In the 1850s, both Russia and France claimed jurisdiction over certain holy places in Palestine, then part of the Ottoman Empire. The Ottomans granted privileges to Catholics but did not do the same for Orthodox Christians. The czar demanded the same privileges for Orthodox

Florence Nightingale organized professional nursing of the wounded during the Crimean War. After the war, she was instrumental in the foundation of the Army Medical School and the Nightingale School for Nurses.

Into the valley of Death
  Rode the six hundred. . .
Cannon to right of them,
Cannon to left of them,
Cannon in front of them
  Volley'd and thunder'd;
Storm'd at with shot and shell,
Boldly they rode and well,
Into the jaws of Death,
Into the mouth of hell,
  Rode the six hundred. **"**

It took two years of fighting, with huge losses on both sides from battle and disease, for the allies to defeat Russia. France won glory but little else. Despite the dreadful carnage, the war had two constructive results. First, modern field hospitals to care for the wounded came into use. Second, Florence Nightingale established professional nursing of the wounded.

Napoleon III now turned to building the French colonial empire. In North Africa, he took advantage of a native revolt to strengthen French rule over Algeria, which had begun in 1830. In 1859 French engineers began constructing the Suez Canal in Egypt. In Asia Napoleon established French control over Cambodia, thus beginning a move into Indochina. He also tried unsuccessfully to intervene in Mexico. Beginning in 1863, French troops supported the regime of Archduke Maximilian of Austria, whom Napoleon III had installed as Mexico's emperor. Mexicans, led by Benito Juárez, overthrew and executed Maximilian in 1867.

Shortly thereafter Napoleon faced mounting pressure in France. Although he had relaxed controls on the press and the public in 1859 (over the objections of his advisers), and had undertaken other reforms, elections in 1869 showed the growing strength of the government's opponents.

Christians. Napoleon III opposed the Russian demand, forming an alliance with Great Britain, which feared Russian expansion toward the Mediterranean Sea.

The Ottoman Turks, backed by France and Great Britain, resisted Russian claims in the Palestine dispute. The three allies declared war in March 1854, and full-scale fighting began six months later, mostly in the Crimea, a peninsula of southern Russia.

The Crimean War has been called the most unnecessary war in history. The hostilities were marked by inefficiency and waste. The famous poem "The Charge of the Light Brigade" by Alfred, Lord Tennyson described one tragic event of the war. Some 600 English horsemen stormed needlessly across a valley and were cut to pieces by enemy fire. The following are two verses from the poem.

"Half a league, half a league,
  Half a league onward,
    All in the valley of Death
      Rode the six hundred.
  'Forward the Light Brigade!
  Charge for the guns!' he said.

The Franco-Prussian War

Napoleon III had to choose between more liberalization or more authoritarianism. He tried to liberalize, and voters approved. Meanwhile, a crisis with Prussia loomed. Prussia was working to unite all German states under its leadership. (See Chapter 22.) Napoleon opposed this unification, as did nearly all the French people, because they distrusted Prussian ambition.

Napoleon tried to prepare for a war by proposing to draft troops, but he was unsuccessful. Otto von Bismarck, head of the Prussian government, had decided that war with France would help achieve

German unification under Prussian leadership. To this end, Bismarck made a series of clever diplomatic maneuvers that insulted the French. In July 1870 France declared war on Prussia just as Bismarck had hoped that they would.

French defeat. From the start of the Franco-Prussian War, the French suffered disastrous defeats. Napoleon III took command of the army and was captured at Sedan. His regime could not survive.

Immediately after Napoleon's capture, the Legislative Assembly proclaimed the fall of the Second French Empire and the establishment of the Third Republic. The new government tried to defend the nation, but after a siege, Paris fell to the Prussians in January 1871, signaling the end of the war.

France Under German Domination

Bismarck drew up the Treaty of Frankfurt, dictating harsh terms to France. The treaty forced France to give up Alsace and the eastern part of Lorraine on the French-German border. France also had to pay a huge indemnity to Germany, and German troops were to occupy northern France until the indemnity was paid.

A provision of the armistice permitted the election of a National Assembly to decide whether France wanted to sign the peace treaty or to resume the war. The republicans urged renewal of the war. The monarchists took the position that France had already suffered defeat and should negotiate with the conquerors. Most of the elected delegates were monarchists—not because the French people favored monarchy but because they overwhelmingly wanted peace. The National Assembly voted to surrender.

As in the revolution of 1848, the people of Paris were strongly republican. They had fought almost alone to defend the besieged city against the Prussians and were angered by the peace terms.

In March socialists and radical republicans in Paris, supported by the National Guard, set up a municipal council to govern the city. It was called the Commune, like the Paris government established in 1792 during the French Revolution. The Communards, members of the Commune, proposed to change France. Their plans included decentralization—the shift of power from the central government to regional and local governments—separation of church and state, and other ideas consistent with socialist reform.

The French government, now in Versailles, thought it wise to disarm the Parisians. Troops sent by the National Assembly entered Paris and fought street to street against the Communards, finally destroying them in May 1871. Retreating Communards executed hostages, and government troops eventually killed or executed almost 20,000 of the Communards. The French government borrowed the money to pay the indemnity specified in the treaty, and the German soldiers left France in 1873.

Many famous buildings, such as the Tuileries royal palace shown in this photo burning, were destroyed by the Communards in the fighting of 1871 in Paris.

The Third Republic

After the fall of Napoleon III, quarreling factions in the National Assembly were unable to agree on a constitution until 1875. Finally, the assembly passed a group of laws known as the Constitution of 1875, which officially made France a republic.

The Third Republic included a president, elected by the legislature for a term of seven years. The legislature consisted of the Senate and the Chamber of Deputies. Members of the Senate were elected by an indirect system, whereas members of the Chamber of Deputies were elected by universal manhood suffrage. In many ways, the government functioned as a limited constitutional monarchy, with the legislature and a cabinet responsible for policy. Although there were many changes of government, the Constitution of 1875 stood for nearly 70 years.

During the late 1800s, France faced problems aggravated by the strongly held opinions of various factions in the legislature. One group wanted to make war on Germany in revenge for the Franco-Prussian War. Another group was hostile to Catholics. Still another backed French expansion overseas, along the lines begun by Napoleon III. The conservative republicans managed to steer a course that avoided extremes. Legislation encouraged education and legalized trade unions, but it did not really move the country toward socialism.

In the 1890s, a financial scandal rocked France. The crisis stemmed from the failure of the Panama Company, which had been formed to build a canal across the Isthmus of Panama. Ferdinand de Lesseps, the man responsible for building the Suez Canal, had been president of the company, and thousands of French people had invested in the venture. The effort failed because of misjudgment of the difficulty involved in building the canal, disease, and improper financing. Accusations of bribery against a number of legislators endangered the government.

Another threat to the Third Republic came from extremists of the labor movement; boycotts, sabotage, and strikes disrupted the economy. **Anarchists**, who believed in the abolition of all governments, waged a terrorist campaign in France and throughout Europe.

The Dreyfus case. Another serious danger to the Third Republic arose in 1894. An attempt to betray French military secrets to Germany was uncovered. A court accused and convicted Captain Alfred Dreyfus, a Jewish officer, of the crime and sentenced him to life imprisonment. However, evidence soon came to light indicating that Dreyfus had been falsely convicted.

Even so, the French army command would permit no criticism of its actions. Monarchists, many Catholics, and anti-Semites—people who dislike Jews—supported the army.

The real traitor was discovered, but the army cleared him. Then Émile Zola, a famous French novelist, wrote an open letter, "J'accuse" (I accuse), which was published in a newspaper. In the letter, Zola blamed the army command and its supporters for covering up the truth. Although many individuals responsible for the false charges against Dreyfus confessed, his name was not cleared until 1906.

The Dreyfus case led to alienation between those who had condemned Dreyfus and supported the army, and those who had supported Dreyfus's cause. The result of this case was widespread cynicism about the Third Republic.

Reform and coalition. After the Dreyfus case, French republicans planned several reforms. They took steps to end the favored position that Napoleon I had given the Catholic Church in France in 1801. The church and the state were officially separated in 1905, and France had complete religious freedom.

Rivalries among the many different political factions caused a great deal of political friction during this era. Groups ranged from monarchists on the far right to radical socialists on the far left. Major parties contained a number of "splinter groups," or smaller divisions. No one party ever completely controlled the French government. In order to get anything done, parties temporarily united to form **coalitions**, or political groups organized in support of a common cause. These coalitions, shifting and varying, nevertheless gave France a period of relative political stability between 1899 and 1905.

Section 3 Review

1. **Define** anarchist, coalition
2. **Identify** Louis XVIII, Charles X, Louis Philippe, Florence Nightingale, Archduke Maximilian, Alfred Dreyfus
3. **Contrasting Ideas** Compare the changes that took place in Great Britain and in France during the first half of the 1800s.
4. **Analyzing Ideas** How did the power of Louis Napoleon grow during his rule?
5. **Explaining Ideas** Describe France's internal political problems in the late 1800s and early 1900s.

Independence Movements in Latin America

Focus Questions

- What was the relationship of Spain and Portugal to their colonies before 1800?
- How did class distinctions contribute to revolutions in Latin America?
- What difficulties did new countries in Latin America face after winning their independence?

By the early 1800s, the ideologies behind the American and French Revolutions affected the political and social thinking of many Europeans. People in the Latin American colonies of Spain and Portugal were also influenced by these upheavals. In time strong movements for independence swept the whole region, from Mexico to the tip of South America.

Colonial Economy

Both the Spanish and Portuguese followed mercantilist principles in organizing their colonies. They believed they gained wealth and power at the expense of other countries and by amassing gold and silver, which they would then use to buy other goods they needed. Spain and Portugal took gold and silver from their colonies and used the colonies as markets for their own goods, cutting them off from trade with other countries. (See map on page 565.)

A system called *encomienda* (en·koh·mee·EN·dah) was introduced in Spanish colonies. Monarchs granted enormous estates to some colonists, or *encomenderos*—conquistadors, or conquerors, and court favorites. Huge land grants dotted Spanish-controlled America, from what today is California in the north to the modern-day nations of Chile and Argentina in the south. On the land, colonists formed large, self-sufficient farming estates, called **haciendas** (hah·see·EN·duhz) in Spanish America and *fazendas* in Brazil. A variety of goods were produced on these estates, such as cattle ranches, where meat and hides were produced, and sugar plantations.

As part of the *encomienda* system, American Indians were used as farm laborers, miners, or servants. The system had disastrous effects on the Indians, who were overworked and mistreated. European diseases also

Africans were imported by the Spanish and Portuguese to work as slaves on their estates, such as on this sugar plantation.

wiped out whole Indian settlements and led to a population decline of more than 90 percent in some areas. As a result of this decline and the increasing demand for labor, the Spanish and Portuguese began to import thousands of Africans as slaves.

Spanish wealth grew in the colonies. Mexico City, Lima, and other cities became centers of commerce, with imposing public buildings, cathedrals, and palaces. The colonial governments built immense fortresses, such as San Cristóbal guarding San Juan in Puerto Rico, to protect the cities from pirates and sea dogs.

Colonial Society

Social classes based on privilege marked colonial society. The highest ranks of society consisted of royal officials, owners of large estates, and mine owners, many of whom were titled nobility. An enormous social gap existed between these classes and town workers, peasants, and slaves.

Racial discrimination was always a fact of colonial life. Europeans, called **peninsulares** because they were born in Spain or Portugal on the Iberian Peninsula, ruled colonial society. Whites born in the colonies—called **creoles**—suffered social snobbery and job discrimination from the *peninsulares*, though some enjoyed great wealth and privilege. American Indians and African slaves shared the bottom of the social pyramid. Furthermore, laws upheld racial distinctions.

By the 1700s, people of mixed ancestry became a majority in Latin American society. **Mestizos** were of American Indian and European background, and **mulattoes** were of African and European ancestry. *Mestizos* and mulattoes usually faced social and racial barriers but had more opportunities than Africans or Indians. *Mestizos* and mulattoes lived and worked everywhere in Latin America, although more *mestizos* lived in Mexico than in Brazil, where mulattoes played a larger role. In the Andes, southern Mexico, and parts of Central America, American Indians remained the largest group.

The Catholic Church. The Catholic Church wielded great power and enormous influence in the Spanish and Portuguese colonies. Missionaries who accompanied explorers and conquistadors to Latin America immediately began converting American Indians to Catholicism. Contributions were made by some missionaries to the exploitation of Indians. Others took an interest in the native culture and tried to prevent the government and individual colonists from abusing the Indians. Bartolomé de Las Casas was an outspoken advocate for the Indians. He spent his life writing books, letters, and petitions decrying the oppression of the Indians.

Social life. A code of honor brought from Spain to Latin America governed all social interactions and served to maintain distance between social classes. For example, unruly or rebellious servants or slaves brought a man dishonor and could therefore be punished. Individual and family honor had to be protected. To accomplish this, women were secluded, chaperoned, and restricted. They could, however, inherit, bequeath, or own property.

In Indian cultures, women had a high status because they controlled food production and gave birth to and cared for children. However, the ruling classes considered all Indians, women and men, subordinate.

Growing Discontent

During the 1600s and 1700s, Spain had relaxed its control over its colonies. This allowed creoles to become more powerful. They began to fill many upper-level positions in the colonial government and owned and operated mines and *haciendas*. In the mid-1700s, in an effort to reassert control, King Charles III of Spain instituted certain changes. Some of these changes that were introduced by King Charles were viewed unfavorably by the colonists.

For example, Charles sent *peninsulares* to take over the top jobs and tightened control over the Catholic Church in the colonies. The Jesuits had become extremely powerful and rich through the ownership of *haciendas*, town property, mines, and thousands of slaves. During the mid-1700s, both the Spanish and Portuguese kings dissolved the Jesuit order in their kingdoms and seized all their colonial property.

Spain's economic policies also angered creoles. Charles III began to relax stiff mercantilist restrictions, and open trade had the potential to harm the interests of creole merchants. In addition, the colonists increasingly resented paying taxes to finance Spain's European wars.

Other factors that led to independence movements were growing feelings of nationalism and interest in the revolutionary events in British North America and France. Patriotism led the creole revolutionary Simón Bolívar (boh·LEE·vahr) to say in 1815, "The hatred that the Peninsula has inspired in us is greater than the ocean between us."

Haiti's Slave Revolution

By the early 1800s, Spain's American colonies were ripe for revolution. The first successful revolt, however, took place in the French colony of Saint Domingue, which is located on the western half of the island of Hispaniola in the West Indies.

In Saint Domingue, a small number of French planters owned plantations tended by African slaves. When the French Revolution broke out, the free mulattoes demanded the same rights as French settlers. In 1791 the slave population rebelled. Mulattoes and blacks united under the leadership of Toussaint-Louverture (TOO·san·LOO·ver·toor), a freed slave, and won control of Saint Domingue in the only successful revolution led by slaves anywhere in the world.

Napoleon I sent an army to try to reestablish slavery and French authority. The French captured Toussaint-Louverture, who died a prisoner in France. However, in 1804 a rebel army defeated the French, and Saint Domingue proclaimed its independence under the ancient name of Haiti, becoming the first independent country in Latin America.

Mexico and Central America

Napoleon's conquest of Spain in 1808 and the Spanish revolt that followed gave colonists in the New World a golden opportunity to declare their

Latin America, 1784

DISPUTED TERRITORY
(Spain vs. Russia)

Monterey

**VICEROYALTY
OF
NEW SPAIN**

UNITED
STATES

Missouri River

Mississippi

Rio Grande

Monterrey

Gulf of Mexico

WEST
FLORIDA

FLORIDA

BAHAMAS
(British)

**ATLANTIC
OCEAN**

Mérida

Havana

**CAPTAINCY-GENERAL
OF CUBA**

CUBA

Guadalajara

Veracruz

JAMAICA

W E S T

HISPANIOLA

PUERTO
RICO

Mexico City

BRITISH
HONDURAS

SAINT
DOMINGUE
(HAITI)

Santo Domingo

I N D I E S

**CAPTAINCY-GENERAL
OF GUATEMALA**

CARIBBEAN SEA

Cartagena

Cumaná

Caracas

**CAPTAINCY-GENERAL
OF VENEZUELA**

*Isthmus
of Panama*

Bogotá

GUIANAS

Popayán

Quito

Guayaquil

**VICEROYALTY OF
NEW GRANADA**

Amazon River

0°

**PACIFIC
OCEAN**

Trujillo

A N D E S

B R A Z I L

Lima

Cuzco

15°S

La Paz

*BRAZILIAN
HIGHLANDS*

Arequipa

**VICEROYALTY
OF PERU**

VICEROYALTY OF

Salta

Asunción

Tucumán

Corrientes

RÍO DE LA PLATA

30°S

Santiago

Montevideo

Concepción

Buenos Aires

Rio de la Plata

A N D E S

PAMPAS

N
W E
S

	Spanish territory
	Portuguese territory
	British territory
	French territory
	Dutch territory

45°S

0   500   1,000 Miles
0 500 1,000 Kilometers
Miller Cylindrical Projection

*Strait of
Magellan*

FALKLAND ISLANDS
(ISLA MALVINAS)

Cape Horn

120°W   105°W   90°W   75°W   60°W   45°W

45°N

30°N

15°N

Learning from Maps By 1784 Spain controlled most of Latin America.

? Region What mountain range runs along the west coast of South America?

independence. In Mexico, creoles, *mestizos*, and American Indians all participated in revolutionary activities. In 1810 a priest named Miguel Hidalgo y Costilla initiated an independence movement in Mexico. He led an army of Indian peasants against Spanish *peninsulares* and creoles.

After Hidalgo's forces achieved some early victories, the Spanish captured and executed him and dispersed his peasant army in 1811. Another priest, José María Morelos y Pavón, who wanted independence, land reform, and the abolition of slavery, assumed leadership of the rebels. Upper-class Mexican creoles feared Morelos and remained loyal to Spain. In 1815 authorities captured and shot him.

In 1814 the absolutist Ferdinand VII regained the throne of Spain. Mexican creoles looked favorably on Ferdinand. However, in 1820 liberal army rebels in Spain stripped the king of some of his powers. The rebellion caused upper-class Mexicans to fear that the new Spanish government would apply liberal reforms in the colonies. Therefore, in 1821 they carried out an independence movement of their own. A militia general named Agustín de Iturbide (ee·toor·BEE·day) proclaimed himself Emperor Agustín I, but his unpopular dictatorial rule did not last long. In 1823 Mexican generals overthrew him, and Mexico became a republic.

José de San Martín (left), an Argentine general, led independence movements in Argentina, Chile, and Peru between 1812 and 1821.

Central America was briefly part of Iturbide's Mexican empire. In 1823, however, representatives from Guatemala, El Salvador, Honduras, Nicaragua, and Costa Rica met to form a federal union called the United Provinces of Central America.

Spanish South America

Three great South American leaders—Simón Bolívar, José de San Martín, and Bernardo O'Higgins—had traveled or studied in North America or Europe. They knew well the ideas of the Enlightenment and the French Revolution. One of the first revolts against Spain took place in 1810 in the southernmost viceroyalty of La Plata. Creole rebels deposed the Spanish viceroy and seized control of the government. Six years later, they declared the independence of the United Provinces of the Río de la Plata, later named Argentina. Meanwhile, Paraguay, another part of the viceroyalty of La Plata, achieved its independence from Spain in a bloodless rebellion in 1811.

In the rest of South America, the struggle turned into a long and bloody civil war led by Simón Bolívar, "the Liberator." Bolívar started the revolt in his native city of Caracas in 1810. He did not succeed in destroying Spain's power in Venezuela until 1821 at the battle of Carabobo. In the meantime, he raised

Toussaint-Louverture led the Haitian independence movement against Napoleon.

another army and defeated the Spanish in New Granada in 1819 at the battle of Boyacá.

Bolívar became president, with almost absolute power, of a new nation called Gran Colombia. The new nation included the present-day countries of Colombia, Venezuela, Ecuador, and Panama.

Meanwhile, Argentine general San Martín gathered another army and made a difficult crossing of the Andes into the region known as Chile. He joined forces with Chileans led by Bernardo O'Higgins and overcame Spanish resistance there in 1818.

From Chile, San Martín's forces sailed north to capture the city of Lima in Peru. The Spanish government fled, and San Martín declared the independence of Peru in 1821. Royalist forces, however, remained in parts of Peru. Internal squabbling among the independence leaders led some Peruvians to invite Bolívar to help them defeat the Spanish. San Martín then withdrew, turning leadership over to the ambitious Bolívar.

In August 1824 Bolívar won a major victory over Spanish forces at Junín (hoo·NEEN) in Peru. By December of that year, the revolutionaries gained their final victory in Peru at Ayacucho (eye·ah·KOO·choh). Peru was free from Spanish rule. In 1825 the northern territory of Upper Peru became a separate republic, named Bolivia in honor of Bolívar.

Brazil

When Napoleon's army invaded Portugal in 1807, the prince regent Dom João, his royal court, and his family fled to Brazil. There the prince regent's rule benefited Brazil, as he opened ports to trade, founded a national bank, and encouraged industry. After the overthrow of Napoleon, Dom João—now King John VI, a dual monarch of Brazil and Portugal—remained in Brazil. In 1820, however, a revolt broke out in Portugal, and the Portuguese insisted that Dom João return home.

The Portuguese then tried to reassert control over Brazil from overseas. Angered Brazilians urged Dom Pedro, Dom João's son who had stayed in Brazil, to declare independence, which he did in 1822. Dom Pedro ruled as emperor until 1831, when he was forced to abdicate. His son, Dom Pedro II, became emperor in 1831 and ruled until 1889.

The new nations of Brazil and Argentina struggled over territory that lay between them. Patriots in this disputed territory gained independence in 1825, calling their country Uruguay.

Almost all of Latin America had thus become independent by 1825. Portugal lost its entire Latin American empire. The Spanish lost all their colonies

Simón Bolívar, nicknamed the Liberator, led revolutions against the Spanish in Venezuela, Colombia, Ecuador, Peru, and Bolivia.

except Cuba and Puerto Rico. Elsewhere in the region, only a few Caribbean islands, parts of Central America, the Guianas, and the Falkland Islands remained under colonial rule. (See map on page 568.)

Foreign Reactions to Independence

Independence opened Latin American markets to trade with countries other than Spain and Portugal. The British hoped to benefit. They were eager to increase commerce with the region, and they viewed the Latin Americans as potential allies against continental Europe, which was growing more conservative.

Preoccupied first with the War of 1812 against Britain and then expansionism, including difficult negotiations with Spain over Florida, the United States paid little attention to Latin America. Even after Spain ceded Florida in 1819, the United States had no established Latin American policy until late in the administration of President James Monroe. Like the British, however, Americans saw Latin America as a new market and were concerned when Spain tried to regain its colonies in the 1820s.

In 1823 President James Monroe sent a dramatic message to Congress. This message is known as the **Monroe Doctrine**. It declared that the United

States would not intervene in Europe's affairs or interfere in any of Europe's remaining colonies in the Western Hemisphere. At the same time, the United States would oppose any attempt by European nations to reestablish their lost colonies, to form new colonies, or to interfere with any government in the Western Hemisphere.

Although European leaders denounced the Monroe Doctrine, no nation seriously tested it. The United States was too weak to enforce the doctrine at the time, but British naval might and political unrest in many nations on the European continent prevented much involvement by European powers in Latin American affairs.

Latin American Unity

Enormous distances, geographical barriers, and regional rivalries prevented unity among the new Latin American countries. Of the former Spanish and Portuguese territories, only Brazil managed to maintain

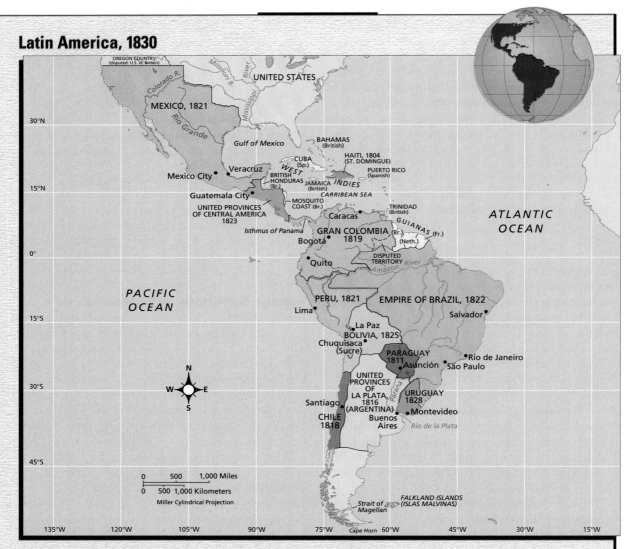

Latin America, 1830

Learning from Maps Within 50 years, the huge Spanish empire in Latin America broke into many independent nations.

? Place What islands remained under Spanish or British rule in 1830?

national unity. Ecuador and Venezuela broke away from Gran Colombia. The United Provinces of Central America crumbled into five separate countries, and Argentina was threatened with divisions within its own country.

In 1826 Bolívar called a congress of Latin American nations to meet in Panama to promote unification. Only Colombia, Peru, Central America, and Mexico attended the Panama Congress. Although the Panama Congress failed, many Latin Americans cherished the ideal of unity.

Internal Problems

Despite problems in the new countries of Latin America, the removal of European authority did have some positive consequences for these countries. For example, some groups began to enjoy greater social mobility. *Mestizos*, in particular, found they were more able to advance socially. International trade also expanded once it was freed from the restrictions of the former colonial powers. In addition, tribute payments by Indians were abolished, and slavery was abolished in most countries by the 1850s, and throughout Latin America by 1888.

Although creoles eventually abolished slavery everywhere, it remained an unresolved issue in some Latin American countries. For example, the slave economy was integral in Brazil throughout the early and middle 1800s. In general though, the creoles attempted to take over the positions of power in the new Latin American nations. Creoles also battled to take over communal lands belonging to the American Indian population, claiming that they needed the lands for economic progress. Moreover, the *haciendas* continued to grow.

Conflict between liberals and conservatives kept many countries in a state of turmoil. The conflict tended to follow class lines, with upper-class creoles espousing conservative values and *mestizos* embracing a liberal philosophy. Conservatives favored retaining as much as possible from their European heritage. They wanted a strong Catholic Church, a monarchy or powerful executive, and government control of the economy. Liberals advocated the separation of church and state, the formation of democratic republics, and a laissez-faire economy.

These internal disagreements prevented the establishment of governments based on an orderly rule of law. Latin American governments came to power as often by rebellion as they did by election. During colonial times, strong central governments merged

with upper-class economic interests to hold the countries together. Brazil, in fact, retained an emperor until 1889, working in concert with an assembly, and was comparatively stable. However, in many countries, creoles retreated to their *haciendas*, while **caudillos**, ambitious *mestizo* military leaders who ruled by personal power, became presidents. These governments headed by the **caudillos** often provided stability but not freedom and tended to last only as long as the dictator did.

Liberals and conservatives also battled over the role of the Catholic Church. Republican governments often took positions against the church. However, educational systems that had been run by the church were neglected, and there was scant public education to replace them. Conservatives, who still constituted the upper class, opposed the loss of church power, and the lower classes remained staunchly Catholic in faith. The result was a jumble of disunity.

With all these conflicts, the first 50 or 60 years of independence proved difficult in many of the Latin American countries. However, in the latter part of the 1800s, growing industry and expanding trade began to bring a somewhat broader distribution of wealth to these countries. Development was rapid, and cities grew, thus bringing social change. Political unrest was frequent; however, many Latin American countries began to achieve stability and economic growth.

Section 4 Review

1. **Define** *haciendas, peninsulares,* creoles, *mestizos,* mulattoes, Monroe Doctrine, *caudillos*

2. **Identify** Toussaint-Louverture, José de San Martín, Simón Bolívar, Bernardo O'Higgins

3. **Locate and Explain the Significance** Rio de Janeiro, Haiti, Gran Colombia

4. **Explaining Ideas** What aspects of Spanish and Portuguese rule in Latin America led to discontent?

5. **Summarizing Ideas (a)** What were the goals of the revolutions that took place in Mexico and Central America? **(b)** What were the results of these revolutions?

6. **Relating Ideas (a)** What economic and social problems faced the creoles in Latin America on the eve of their independence? **(b)** What problems were evident for the creoles after their independence?

Chapter 21 Review

A.D. 1818
Spanish rule ends in Chile.

A.D. 1823
Monroe Doctrine is proclaimed.

A.D. 1854–1856
Crimean War occurs.

A.D. 1790 | A.D. 1800 | A.D. 1810 | A.D. 1820 | A.D. 1830 | A.D. 1850

A.D. 1791
Haiti revolts.

A.D. 1801
British Parliament passes the Act of Union.

A.D. 1804
Haiti proclaims independence.

A.D. 1810
La Plata (Argentina) revolts against Spain.

A.D. 1819
Bolívar becomes president of Gran Colombia.

A.D. 1832
Great Britain enacts Reform Bill of 1832.

A.D. 1852
Napoleon III founds Second French Empire.

Chapter Summary

The following list contains the key concepts you have learned about political changes in the British Empire, the United States, France, and Latin America during the 1800s and early 1900s.

1. Many reforms occurred in Great Britain in the 1800s and early 1900s. With the Reform Bill of 1832 and agitation from people such as the Chartists, voting rights were greatly broadened in Britain. In the early 1900s, women finally gained the right to vote.

2. Queen Victoria gave her prime ministers a great deal of power. Two dominant prime ministers of the Victorian Era were Benjamin Disraeli, leader of the Conservative Party, and William Gladstone, leader of the Liberal Party.

3. The labor union movement and socialism grew in Great Britain in the late 1800s and early 1900s. This movement led to the rise of the Labour Party. When the Liberal Party came to power in 1905, Great Britain adopted extensive welfare legislation.

4. Britain's social and political reforms also extended to colonies within the British Empire, such as Canada, Australia, and New Zealand, which were allowed self-government.

5. Territorial growth and sectionalism in the United States led to war over the issue of slavery.

6. Following the Civil War, Congress passed the Thirteenth, Fourteenth, and Fifteenth Amend- ments to the Constitution. These amendments abolished slavery, made former slaves citizens, and gave African American men the right to vote. Women in the United States were given the right to vote in 1920, by the Nineteenth Amendment.

7. France experienced a series of upheavals in 1830, 1848, and 1871 that rekindled the revolutionary spirit of the 1790s. Each time, politics soon returned to a more stable form. The monarchy was eventually abolished, as was the position of emperor that Napoleon III created for himself. By the early 1900s, France was a republic, governed by coalitions of parties that represented monar- chist, liberal, and socialist beliefs.

8. In the early part of the 1800s, revolutions took place throughout Latin America. Following their independence from Spain, most Latin American countries set up democratic governments.

9. The peoples of Latin America had many regional, economic, ethnic, and social differences. For these reasons, they did not unite but split into many nations after their wars for independence in the early 1800s. Only Brazil managed to maintain stability.

Reviewing Important Terms

On a separate sheet of paper, supply the term that correctly completes each statement.

1. _____ was a movement whose followers believed that people ought to be free to think and work as they please.
2. _____ _____ is a term for self-government.
3. _____ were women who wanted voting rights for all women.
4. _____ is a rivalry among the parts of a country.
5. A(n) _____ believes in the abolition of all government.
6. A(n) _____ is formed by political groups organized in support of a common cause.

Developing Critical Thinking Skills

1. **Analyzing Ideas** (a) What were the aims of the Chartists? (b) How did they contribute to the growth of democracy in Great Britain?
2. **Explaining Ideas** Why did Great Britain allow Canada, Australia, and New Zealand to develop their own governments?
3. **Interpreting Ideas** Describe the actions of Louis Napoleon Bonaparte as liberal or reactionary.
4. **Summarizing Ideas** (a) What was the Monroe Doctrine? (b) Why was it issued?
5. **Explaining Ideas** How did the geography of Latin America prevent unity among its countries?

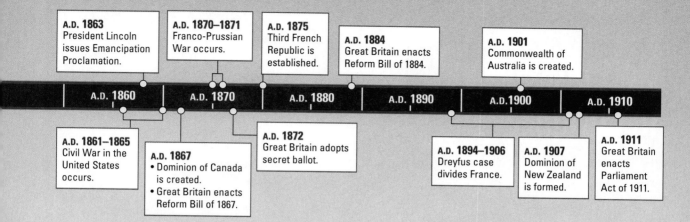

A.D. 1863
President Lincoln issues Emancipation Proclamation.

A.D. 1870–1871
Franco-Prussian War occurs.

A.D. 1875
Third French Republic is established.

A.D. 1884
Great Britain enacts Reform Bill of 1884.

A.D. 1901
Commonwealth of Australia is created.

A.D. 1860   A.D. 1870   A.D. 1880   A.D. 1890   A.D. 1900   A.D. 1910

A.D. 1861–1865
Civil War in the United States occurs.

A.D. 1867
• Dominion of Canada is created.
• Great Britain enacts Reform Bill of 1867.

A.D. 1872
Great Britain adopts secret ballot.

A.D. 1894–1906
Dreyfus case divides France.

A.D. 1907
Dominion of New Zealand is formed.

A.D. 1911
Great Britain enacts Parliament Act of 1911.

Relating Geography to History

Turn to the map on page 553 and answer the following questions. **(a)** After 1783, how did the United States acquire most of its territory? **(b)** Was the land in your state part of the United States before the 1800s? **(c)** If not, when was it acquired? **(d)** How long did it take for the United States to expand its borders from the Mississippi River to the Pacific Ocean? **(e)** Why might such rapid growth encourage the development of liberalism and nationalism?

Relating Past to Present

1. Before taking office, William Gladstone pledged, "My mission is to pacify Ireland." Review the events that prompted Gladstone to make this remark. Then investigate the situation in Ireland today. Which of the problems faced in the 1880s have lingered into the present? How has the British government dealt with the problems in the 1990s?
2. How did the spread of liberalism inspire the start of the women's suffrage movement in Great Britain and the United States? Even though women now have the vote, some people are still working to extend the rights of women. What are some of the reforms that women have called for during the last decade?

Applying History Study Skills

Before completing this activity, review Building History Study Skills on page 545.

Read the following selection from William Gladstone's speech to Parliament on April 8, 1886, supporting home rule for Ireland.

"Our intention is, Sir, to propose to the House of Commons that which, as we think,…will liberate Parliament from the restraints under which of late years it has ineffectually struggled to perform the Business of the country; [that is, to] obtain an answer…to the question whether it is or is not possible to establish good and harmonious relations between Great Britain and Ireland on the footing of those free institutions to which Englishmen, Scotchmen, and Irishmen are alike unalterably attached…

…in point of fact, law is discredited…in Ireland upon this ground especially—that it comes to the people of that country with a foreign aspect, and in a foreign garb. These Coercion Bills of ours…are stiffly resisted by the Members who represent Ireland in Parliament. The English mind…is estranged from the Irish people and the Irish mind is estranged from the people of England and Scotland."

1. How does Gladstone defend his view of home rule for Ireland?
2. Does Gladstone's position, as represented in this selection, represent a liberal or conservative ideology? Explain how you know this.
3. Is Gladstone's ideology economic or political? Write a response to Gladstone from another ideology. How did you determine what would be included in your response?

internetconnect

Search the Internet through the HRW Web site for letters and diary entries from soldiers who served in the U.S. Civil War. Use the documents to explain how the people who served felt about the war and its goals. Be sure to note for which side each of the soldiers fought, and examine how this may have affected his views.

GO TO: go.hrw.com
KEYWORD: SCØ
Civil War

Building Your Portfolio

1. **Presenting an Oral Report** Use encyclopedias to learn more about the ministries in Great Britain of Benjamin Disraeli and William Gladstone. Give an oral report on the types of programs each prime minister supported and how they influenced the direction of Great Britain's domestic and foreign policy. Place your notes in your portfolio.
2. **Writing a Report** During the revolutions of 1848, the people of Paris set up a provisional government and proclaimed the Second French Republic. Using available sources, prepare a report explaining the form that this republic was to take. Place the report in your portfolio.

Nationalism in Europe

A.D. 1806–1913

3.7 million B.C. | 4000 B.C. | A.D. 2100

PLACE

Europe

Europe

ARCTIC OCEAN

NORTH AMERICA EUROPE ASIA

PACIFIC OCEAN AFRICA

Equator

SOUTH AMERICA INDIAN OCEAN

AUSTRALIA ATLANTIC OCEAN

PACIFIC OCEAN

ANTARCTICA

Portrait of Giuseppe Garibaldi in 1849

Significance

In the 1800s, growing nationalism created political change in Europe. Drives to unify peoples and states transformed the continent. These changes brought forward forces that would also have profound impact in the twentieth century.

Terms to Define

risorgimento	Pan-Slavism
Young Italy movement	Emancipation Edict
Zollverein	People's Will
Treaty of Prague	terrorism
kaiser	pogroms
Bundesrat	Social Democratic
Reichstag	Labor Party
Kulturkampf	Duma
Social Democratic Party	Treaty of San Stefano
autocrat	Balkan League
Russification	

People to Identify

Carbonari	William I
Giuseppe Mazzini	Iron Chancellor
Victor Emmanuel II	William II
Camillo Benso di Cavour	nihilists
Napoleon III	Magyars
Junkers	Francis Joseph I

Places to Locate

Lombardy	Holstein
Venetia	Bavaria
the kingdom	Württemberg
of Sardinia	Romania
kingdom of the	Budapest
Two Sicilies	Serbia
Tuscany	Montenegro
Modena	Bulgaria
Parma	Bosnia
Papal States	Herzegovina
Saxony	Cyprus
Schleswig	Rhodes

Chapter Theme Questions

- **Politics and Law** What factors might contribute to a desire for national unification?
- **War and Diplomacy** How can war be a force in unifying a country?
- **Social Relations** What might happen when there is great resistance to reform movements by countries?

Giuseppe Mazzini, who lived from 1805 to 1872, was one of the three rulers of a republic set up in Rome during the ill-fated revolution of 1848–1849. He expresses his anger and sadness at the worsening military situation in the following excerpt from a letter he wrote to an English friend in 1849.

❝*Terror now reigns in Rome; the prisons are choked with men who have been arrested and detained without trial; . . . the citizens best known for their moderation are exiled; the army is almost entirely dissolved, the city disarmed, and the 'factious' sent away even to the last man; and yet France dares not consult in a legal manner the will of the population, but re-establishes the papal authority by military decree. I do not believe that since the dismemberment of Poland there has been committed a more atrocious injustice, a more gross violation of the eternal right which God has implanted in the peoples, that of appreciating and defining for themselves their own life, and governing themselves in accordance with their own appreciation of it. And I cannot believe that it is well for you or for Europe that such things can be accomplished in the eyes of the world, without one nation arising out of its immobility to protest in the name of universal justice.* ❞

The upheaval in Rome was only one of many that erupted in Europe in the mid-1800s.

Section 1

The Unification of Italy

Focus Questions

- **What events led to nationalistic movements for unification in Italy?**
- **Who were the important leaders in the fight for the unification of Italy?**
- **What problems did Italy face after unification?**

Many Italians had been inspired by the liberal and nationalistic ideals of the French Revolution in the

1790s, and revolutionary movements formed against several rulers of the Italian states. Then, conquest by Napoleon I gave the Italian Peninsula something resembling unity for a few years. However, following Napoleon's defeat and the Congress of Vienna in 1815, Italy was again divided. Austria annexed the rich territories of Lombardy and Venetia. The rest of Italy was fragmented into several large and small states. These states were either dominated by Austria or ruled by reactionary monarchs who tried to undo any advances made during Napoleon's time. (See map on page 577.)

Early Movements Toward Unification

Italian nationalism became a strong force in the early 1800s when many thinkers and writers tried to revive interest in Italy's traditions. This nationalistic movement, with its goal of liberation and unification, became known as the **risorgimento**—the Italian word for "resurgence." Because nationalists could not support their cause openly, they formed secret societies. An early group of this sort was the *Carbonari*, Italian for "charcoal-burners."

One of its most famous members, Giuseppe Mazzini, envisioned a united Italy, and he devoted his entire life to this goal. Born in 1805, Mazzini was both imprisoned and exiled for his revolutionary activities. In 1831 he called for all Italian patriots to join a new movement, known as the **Young Italy movement**, to spread the ideals of the risorgimento. The first Italian democratic movement open to all classes, Young Italy insisted that "neither pope nor king," but rather a republic, should rule Italy.

In 1848 liberals and nationalists led revolts in several Italian states. These rebellions overthrew Austrian rule in Lombardy and Venetia, and forced the rulers of the kingdom of Sardinia, the kingdom of the Two Sicilies, and Tuscany to grant constitutions to their subjects. Revolutionaries seized Rome in 1849 and set up a republic that Mazzini and two other leaders governed. However, all but one of these revolutionary movements soon failed. The Austrian army succeeded in recapturing some of its former possessions in northern Italy during the summer of 1849. Former rulers returned to power, revoking constitutions and filling prisons. Only the kingdom of Sardinia, with its mainland capital of Turin, remained an independent kingdom.

After the failure of the revolts of 1848 and 1849, Italian liberals continued their efforts with little success. Disagreeing among themselves, and with the church opposed to them, liberals began to see their movement fall apart. Many Italians, especially the Catholic clergy, wanted a federation of Italian states headed by the pope. Liberals, however, wanted a republic. They opposed federation, partly because the papacy had withdrawn support from the revolt in 1849. Still others wanted a constitutional monarchy under King Victor Emmanuel II of the kingdom of Sardinia.

Only in the kingdom of Sardinia was there hope for progress. Although King Victor Emmanuel II was not especially sympathetic to the liberals and was motivated mainly by a wish to expand Sardinian territory, his parliament and his chief minister, Camillo Benso di Cavour (kahv·OOHR), a liberal and an Italian patriot, supported the goals of the liberals.

Cavour in Sardinia

The chief minister or premier, Count Camillo Benso di Cavour, and not Victor Emmanuel, actually governed the kingdom of Sardinia. Born in 1810, Cavour was a well-educated and widely traveled aristocrat. He edited a nationalist newspaper, *Il Risorgimento*, in 1847, took part in the revolutions of 1848, and in 1852 became premier of the kingdom of Sardinia.

Cavour disliked absolutism and admired the British system of parliamentary government. He wanted Italy to be both united and industrialized under Sardinia's leadership.

Cavour reorganized and strengthened the army. He helped to establish banks, factories, and railroads, encouraged shipbuilding, and negotiated treaties with other countries to increase trade. Believing in the separation of church and state, he tried to reduce the political influence of the church, and he attempted to expel the politically powerful Jesuit order from the country. He also brought the kingdom of Sardinia to prominence through alliance with France and Great Britain in the Crimean War and in the peace conference at Paris in 1856 that ended that war.

Napoleon III and War with Austria

Cavour saw Austria as the greatest obstacle to Italian unification because of its control of part of northern Italy. He proposed an alliance of France and Sardinia against Austria. Napoleon III sought ways to increase French influence, and he hoped that with Austria driven out of Italy, France could dominate a weak confederation of Italian states. Cavour, on the other hand, believed that with Austria out of Italy, other Italian states would join the kingdom of Sardinia in a strong alliance against both France and Austria.

Cavour sought an alliance with Napoleon III in 1858 to evict the Austrians and to unify Italy under the kingdom of Sardinia.

In 1858 Cavour and Napoleon III met secretly to plan strategy against Austria. Napoleon III agreed that if Austria could be provoked into declaring war on the kingdom of Sardinia, France would send troops to help drive the Austrians out of Lombardy and Venetia. In return for this help, Cavour promised to give the French-speaking regions of Nice and Savoy—then Sardinia's possessions—to France. In 1859 Cavour began military preparations for war. Austria demanded that the military buildup in the kingdom of Sardinia be stopped within three days. When this ultimatum was rejected, Austria, as Cavour had hoped, declared war.

At first the war went according to Cavour's plan. Combined forces from the kingdom of Sardinia and France quickly drove the Austrians out of Lombardy and marched on into Venetia. Italian patriots in Tuscany, Modena, and Parma overthrew their Austrian rulers and asked to be annexed to the kingdom of Sardinia.

Napoleon III had not expected Italians to consolidate in this way. He did not want a strong, united Italy, and feared that Prussia, in its own interest, might help Austria. Napoleon III had no desire to get involved in a war against both Austria and Prussia and wished to do nothing to unite the two. In July 1859, only three months after the war began,

Napoleon III signed a secret armistice with Austria. According to its terms, the kingdom of Sardinia received Lombardy, but Austria kept Venetia. The agreement also returned Austrian rulers to Tuscany, Modena, and Parma.

This armistice marked a severe setback for Cavour and the Italian nationalists. Napoleon III had delivered only half of his side of the bargain—control of Lombardy to the kingdom of Sardinia. However, he insisted on collecting his full price—Nice and Savoy. Afraid of losing even the partial victory, King Victor Emmanuel II agreed to the French terms.

The Italian people, however, refused to abandon the idea of unity. Popular feeling ran far ahead of governmental caution. Rebellions in Parma, Modena, and Tuscany again expelled the Austrian rulers and set up temporary governments. The people of Romagna, a province in the Papal States, also revolted. When each of these areas held a plebiscite, or direct vote on the issue, voters overwhelmingly favored joining the kingdom of Sardinia.

Garibaldi and the Thousand

The southern half of the Italian Peninsula, together with the island of Sicily, made up the kingdom of the Two Sicilies. Earlier revolts against harsh Bourbon rule of the kingdom had failed, but it now became the target of the Italian nationalists. Giuseppe Garibaldi, a man devoted to Italian freedom, led the way.

Born in Nice in 1807, Garibaldi joined Mazzini's Young Italy movement when he was in his twenties. In 1834, after being involved in a revolutionary plot in Piedmont, Garibaldi fled for his life to Latin America. Returning to Italy, he fought in the revolutions of 1848. Forced to flee again, he lived in North Africa, the United States, and Peru, before Cavour arranged his return to Italy in 1854.

With Cavour's approval, Garibaldi recruited an army of nearly 1,100 soldiers. They were called Red Shirts because of the colorful uniforms they wore into battle. In the spring of 1860, Garibaldi and his "Expedition of the Thousand" invaded and took Sicily. Crossing to Italy's mainland, Garibaldi and his growing forces seized Naples, the capital city, and drove Francis II and his troops north to the border of the Papal States. Celebrated as a patriot and military genius, Garibaldi became a national and international hero.

Garibaldi planned to continue north to capture Rome and then Venetia. But Cavour, afraid that Garibaldi might set up a republic or that his fame might displace Victor Emmanuel II as Italy's leader, sent an army south to stop Garibaldi's advance. In the process, the kingdom of Sardinia annexed most of the territory of the Papal States.

In the fall of 1860, Garibaldi and Cavour met in Naples. Garibaldi agreed to support the establishment of the kingdom of Italy, with Victor Emmanuel II as king. Garibaldi asked only to serve as governor of Naples. The king and Cavour, fearing his huge popularity, refused his request.

Unification

During 1860 plebiscites were held everywhere in Italy except in Venetia and Rome. The people voted overwhelmingly for national unity under the king of the kingdom of Sardinia. Representatives of the various states met in Turin, the capital of the kingdom of Sardinia, in February 1861, where they confirmed Victor Emmanuel II as king of Italy, and proclaimed his inauguration on March 17.

The new kingdom included nearly all of Italy except Venetia, which still belonged to Austria, and the western part of the Papal States around the city of Rome, ruled by the pope. (See map on opposite page.)

European governments were left with two choices—either recognize the new state or fight it. Outmaneuvered by Cavour, Napoleon III stopped short of war with Italy but did send French troops to protect the papacy and to prevent Italian nationalists from seizing Rome.

Unification was furthered when Italy gained Venetia in the Seven Weeks' War of 1866. When the Franco-Prussian War broke out in 1870, Napoleon III recalled his troops from Rome. The Italians entered the city, over the objections of the pope. The citizens of Rome voted for union with Italy, and later that year Rome was proclaimed the capital of the kingdom of Italy.

Problems of a United Italy

Although politically united, Italy still faced many problems. Few Italians had experience with self-government, and scandals frequently rocked the young nation. The various regions of the country remained divided by cultural traditions and independence. Tensions grew between the industrialized north and the agricultural south. In Sicily local

Giuseppe Garibaldi and his supporters, known as Red Shirts, conquered the Kingdom of the Two Sicilies in 1860, adding this area to the kingdom of Italy.

Kingdom of Sardinia, 1858

Austrian territory annexed by Sardinia, 1859

Territory annexed by Sardinia to form kingdom of Italy, 1860

Austrian territory annexed by Italy, 1866

Territory annexed by Italy, 1870

FRANCE

Vienna

SWITZERLAND

AUSTRIA-HUNGARY

Danube River

SAVOY (to France in 1860)

LOMBARDY · Milan

VENETIA

Turin · Po R.

Venice

NICE (to France in 1860)

Genoa ·

PARMA

MODENA

MONACO

Florence ·

TUSCANY

SAN MARINO

PAPAL STATES

OTTOMAN EMPIRE

KINGDOM

Tiber R.

KINGDOM OF SARDINIA

CORSICA (French)

OF

PAPAL STATES

Rome ·

ADRIATIC SEA

40°N

ITALY

SARDINIA

Naples ·

KINGDOM OF THE TWO SICILIES

TYRRHENIAN SEA

MEDITERRANEAN SEA

10°E

0   100   200 Miles
0   100   200 Kilometers
Azimuthal Equal-Area Projection

SICILY

15°E

N W E S

Learning from Maps Italy was united into a single kingdom over a 12-year period.

? Region What territories did Italy cede to France in 1860?

leaders organized a secret society known as the Mafia, a kind of state within the state that the central government was powerless to control.

Modernization was slow after a brief period of expansion, impeded by political crises and changing government policies. The standard of living remained low for most Italians, and labor problems arose.

Some of Italy's leaders admired the military strength of Germany and hoped to follow a similar course. Attempting to build a colonial empire, Italy engaged in several ventures in Africa in the 1870s and 1880s. A brief, expensive war against the

Ottoman Empire in 1911 brought little material return. The conquest of Libya in 1912 strengthened Italy's position in the Mediterranean region but divided the nation. Although geographically unified, Italy had not achieved political stability.

Section 1 Review

1. **Define** risorgimento, Young Italy movement
2. **Identify** *Carbonari*, Giuseppe Mazzini, Victor Emmanuel II, Camillo Benso di Cavour, Napoleon III
3. **Locate and Explain the Significance** Lombardy, Venetia, the kingdom of Sardinia, kingdom of the Two Sicilies, Tuscany, Modena, Parma, Papal States
4. **Explaining Ideas** Describe the early nationalistic movements toward unification in Italy.
5. **Summarizing Ideas** Explain the contributions of Mazzini, Garibaldi, and Cavour in the Italian unification process.
6. **Analyzing Ideas** Were the problems that Italy faced after its unification in 1870 the result of earlier disunity? Explain your answer.

Section 2

The Unification of Germany

Focus Questions

- How did Prussia replace Austria as the leading German state in Europe?
- In what ways did German unification differ from Italian unification?
- What changes in German government occurred as a result of unification?

That the German people did not form an enduring union before the late 1800s is somewhat surprising. Germans shared a common language and history. Several times, vigorous, intelligent rulers nearly achieved a strong central government, but all of them failed. In the mid-1800s Germany remained what it had been for centuries—a patchwork of independent states. Each one had its own laws, currency, and rulers. In the late 1800s, Prussia led the fight for unification of these states.

Prussia as Leader

Prussia built a strong and prosperous state in the 1700s during the reigns of Frederick William I and his son Frederick the Great. But Napoleon I defeated Prussian armies in 1806 and dominated Prussia for seven years. He seized Prussian lands to form new states and gave them to relatives and allies. To prevent a military threat, he limited the size of Prussia's army and levied a large indemnity. He forced Prussia to support an occupation army within its territory and to contribute soldiers to French armies.

The Prussians, however, found ways around Napoleon's restrictions. For example, Prussia's strength had been based on its army, which the French had now restricted in size. But the Prussians drafted all able-bodied men and required them to serve only short terms, during which they received intensive military training. They then went into the reserves, and a new group of men was drafted into the regular army. Thus trained men, not counted as part of the regular army, could be called into active service when needed. Technically Prussia observed the limits that the French had placed on its standing army but still kept available a large force of trained men.

The revived Prussian state played a major part in the final struggle against Napoleon. Prussian armies defeated the French at Leipzig in 1813 and fought at Waterloo in 1815. Prussia was one of the four great powers represented at the Congress of Vienna. It also joined the Quadruple Alliance.

In 1815 the Congress of Vienna turned Napoleon's Confederation of the Rhine into the German Confederation with additional members that included Prussia. The Congress of Vienna gave Prussia much important territory, including two thirds of Saxony and an area along the lower Rhine River. Prussian lands now stretched almost unbroken from Russia to the Rhine and beyond. Prussia integrated these territories into its efficient government and strong economy.

These territorial changes worked in Prussia's favor. Austria was Prussia's strongest rival for leadership of the German states. An Austrian Habsburg had held the position of Holy Roman emperor since the 1400s, thus giving Austria a vague claim over German states. Napoleon abolished the Holy Roman Empire, and it was not restored by the Congress of Vienna.

In addition, Napoleon's rule had stimulated nationalism in the German states as it had throughout Europe. Some of Germany's greatest thinkers and writers were active during the period of the French Revolution. Although Frederick the Great despised the German language and had usually written and spoken French, Germans now began to appreciate their language, their past, and their traditions.

German nationalism favored Prussia more than Austria. The population of Prussia was mostly German. In Austria, although Germans ruled, there were many other nationalities, including Hungarians, Romanians, Italians, and Slavs. Territorial shifts after the Congress of Vienna moved the focus of Austrian attention south and east, toward Italy and the Balkans.

The *Zollverein*

The first major step toward German unity after the Congress of Vienna concerned the economy. Tariffs levied by each German state made movement of goods from one state to another costly, increasing the price of goods and reducing the amount sold. Prussians even placed tariffs on items shipped from one Prussian possession to another.

The Junkers (YOOHNG·kuhrz), a class of aristocratic landowners, complained that tariffs were hurting sales of farm products. Tradespeople, intellectuals, financiers, and manufacturers began a campaign for freer movement of goods. In 1818 they persuaded the king of Prussia to abolish tariffs within his territories. Beginning in 1820 German states began to make treaties that in 1834 resulted in a customs union called the *Zollverein* (TSOHL·fer·yn). By 1854, the *Zollverein* included most of the German states, except, most notably, Austria.

The *Zollverein* benefited its members by making prices both lower and more uniform. It also led to the spread of industrialization in the German states by providing wide, free markets for German goods and by offering tariff protection against foreign competition. The German states adopted uniform systems of weights, measures, and currency. Manufacturers produced and sold more goods, and the German economy moved toward unification.

The establishment of the *Zollverein* did not bring about immediate political unity. Each of the various states in the German Confederation continued to act independently of the other states. However, by making member states economically dependent on one another, the *Zollverein* paved the way for later political unification.

In the years after the Congress of Vienna, strong nationalistic and democratic movements emerged within the states of the German Confederation. In

1848 uprisings broke out in France. Within weeks, demands for liberal reforms had brought revolutions to almost all the German states. Agitation was intense for a while, and elections were held for representatives to a National Assembly in Frankfurt to try to unify Germany. The constitution drafted by the National Assembly provided for a hereditary monarch, with powers limited by a popularly elected legislature. However, the demands of liberals for representative government were eventually thwarted, leaving an essentially absolutist system in place. German unification was to be accomplished instead by a king and the plans of his powerful chancellor.

Bismarck and Prussian Strength

William I became king of Prussia in 1861. The next year he appointed Otto von Bismarck, who was a conservative Junker politician, to head the Prussian cabinet. Bismarck built the Prussian army into a powerful war machine.

Bismarck opposed democracy and the idea of a parliament. His vision of a state that maintained authority by rewarding the obedient left little room at first for compromise or reform. Bismarck had great contempt for idealists, regarding them as mere talkers, not people of action. He also believed strongly in Prussian destiny to lead the German people to unification. Realizing that unification would come one way or another, his goal was to ensure Prussian dominance of the future German state. He once said that Prussian policy could be carried out "not . . . by speeches and majority decisions . . . but by iron and blood."

Bismarck and William I wanted to strengthen central authority and the Prussian military, but they faced a challenge from the Prussian parliament.

When the parliament refused to approve money for a military expansion program, Bismarck simply collected the taxes without parliamentary authorization. He claimed that the government had to keep functioning

Otto von Bismarck's effective diplomatic alliances and military policies became assets during his unification of Germany into a single empire.

Nationalism

King William I of Prussia

In the early 1800s, Germans began to take a new interest in their national traditions, language, and customs. This nationalistic spirit, inspired in part by the French Revolution, began to be expressed in art, literature, and music in the form of the romantic movement. Romanticism, in turn, helped inspire the political steps toward the unification of Germany.

Inspired by thinkers such as Giuseppe Mazzini, many Germans believed that nationalism was inseparable from liberalism, and that representative government and individual freedoms would advance together with the principles of nationality. However, German unification took a very different direction. Under the direction of Otto von Bismarck and his king, William I of Prussia, Germany's nationalism was conservative and authoritarian. For these leaders, German nationalism was primarily a tool to help advance Prussian control over the rest of Germany.

An obstacle to Prussian ambition appeared to be the liberals in parliament, who were reluctant to fund the expanding Prussian military. Bismarck had no desire to make concessions to liberals and the lower classes. However, he knew that he had no choice but to make some compromises with the liberals dominating parliament.

However, Bismarck also realized that successful military campaigns, appealing to nationalist enthusiasm, could win support from liberals in Germany. The military victories in 1864, 1866, and 1871 helped to convince many liberals to support the Prussian state.

even without agreement. In so doing, he ignored the constitution and the outrage of the liberals. As protests grew, Bismarck hoped that successful foreign policy would calm an increasingly hostile people.

Unification Through War

To increase the power and size of Prussia, Bismarck had to overcome two major obstacles. First, Prussia had to drive Austria from its position of leadership in the German Confederation. Second, Prussia had to overcome Austria's influence over the southern German states, which opposed Prussian leadership. He accomplished these objectives in three wars—the Danish War, the Seven Weeks' War, and the Franco-Prussian War.

The Danish War. On the border between Denmark and Germany lay two small states—the duchies of Schleswig and Holstein. (See map on page 584.) The population of Holstein, which had been part of the German Confederation since 1815, was entirely German. Schleswig's population included a mix of Germans and Danes. The Danish king ruled the two duchies under a constitution that provided separation from Denmark. In 1863 King Christian IX came to the Danish throne. At the insistence of many Danes, he proclaimed a new constitution under which he tried to annex Schleswig to Denmark.

Both Prussia and Austria protested the new Danish constitution. Together they demanded that it be revoked. When Denmark refused, Prussia and Austria declared war on Denmark. Denmark hoped for help from France and Great Britain; however, neither country acted. In 1864, after three months of fighting, Denmark surrendered.

The peace treaty gave the two duchies to Prussia and Austria jointly. That arrangement brought conflict between Austria and Prussia. Austria wanted the two duchies to form a single independent state within the German Confederation. Prussia opposed the idea. After a bitter quarrel, Prussian and Austrian leaders decided that Prussia would administer Schleswig, and Austria would administer Holstein.

The Seven Weeks' War. As Prussian influence expanded, Bismarck moved to confront Austria. He prepared for conflict by means of skillful diplomatic actions, ensuring that no one would aid Austria. First, he persuaded Napoleon III of France to remain neutral if war broke out between Prussia and Austria. In return for neutrality, France expected territory from the German Confederation. Bismarck left Napoleon III with the mistaken idea he might gain some territory on the Rhine, although none was ever ceded.

Bismarck next formed an alliance with the new nation of Italy. In return for support against Austria, Italy would receive the Austrian territory of Venetia. Then, using the ongoing dispute over Schleswig and Holstein, Bismarck provoked Austria into declaring war on Prussia in 1866.

Austria did not anticipate the superb training and preparation of the Prussian army. In fact, Prussia's efficient conduct of the war startled the whole world. Prussian forces took advantage of technology—moving by train, communicating via the telegraph, and using modern weaponry. They defeated the once-powerful Austrians in only seven weeks. The balance of European power dramatically changed.

The **Treaty of Prague** ended the so-called Seven Weeks' War in the summer of 1866. Under its lenient terms Austria approved the dissolution of the German Confederation and surrendered Holstein to Prussia. The Italians gained Venetia.

In 1867 several north German states united with Prussia to form the North German Confederation. Each state had self-government, but the king of Prussia was hereditary president of the Confederation. As the largest state, with the most powerful industry and army, and with the greatest number of representatives, Prussia dominated the legislature of the new confederation.

Only the three southern states of Bavaria, Baden, and Württemberg and the southern part of Hesse-Darmstadt remained outside Prussia's influence. If they could be persuaded to join Prussia, German unity would be complete.

The Franco-Prussian War. Bismarck decided that the way to unite the southern states with the rest of Germany was to provoke a war with France. His opportunity came in 1870 when Spain sought a new ruler. Spain offered the throne to Prince Leopold, cousin of the king of Prussia. France objected to the appointment because it meant that the Hohenzollern family would rule both Prussia and Spain, encircling France. Alarmed by Prussian ambition and angered that Bismarck had "tried to cheat" him after the Seven Weeks' War, Napoleon III demanded of Prussia and Spain that Leopold turn down the offer.

Leopold did withdraw, but the French also insisted that King William I of Prussia pledge publicly that no member of the Hohenzollern family would ever be a candidate for the Spanish throne.

The French ambassador delivered the French demand to King William at a resort known as Ems. The king replied vaguely but politely and declined to discuss such a pledge further at Ems.

Bismarck received a detailed dispatch from the king, summarizing the meeting with the French ambassador. Bismarck edited the dispatch, altering and omitting details. He made it seem as though the French had tried to humiliate the Prussian king, and that William had dismissed the ambassador offensively and contemptuously. Then Bismarck released the so-called Ems telegram to the newspapers.

Outraged at the Ems telegram, France declared war on Prussia in July 1870. Bismarck reasoned correctly that the southern German states would unite against a perceived French threat. He thus converted the states from rivals into allies against France.

The Franco-Prussian War was short but decisive. No outside nation came to the aid of France. Well trained, well equipped, and ably led, the Prussian army defeated the French in hard fighting within a few months. Napoleon III himself surrendered in September, and his government fell. Guerrilla fighting continued until Paris surrendered in January 1871 after a bitter siege. A treaty was concluded in May.

Bismarck had been lenient with Austria following its defeat because he did not want its large German population as enemies, nor did he wish to invite French intervention. He had no such reservations after the Franco-Prussian war, however. France was occupied by German troops, lost Alsace and part of Lorraine, and had to pay a huge indemnity.

Formation of the German Empire

For Germany the peace was not as important as an event that took place before the signing of the treaty. On January 18, 1871, representatives of the allied German states met in the Hall of Mirrors of the palace of Versailles near Paris. There they issued a proclamation declaring the formation of the German Empire, which included all German states except Austria. (See map on page 584.) Berlin, the Prussian capital, became the capital of the empire. King William I of Prussia was proclaimed German emperor. The position of chancellor—or chief minister—was created for Bismarck, who retained his post of prime minister of Prussia as well.

As much as he disliked constitutions, Bismarck, who was nicknamed the "Iron Chancellor" for his policy of "iron and blood," accepted a constitution that united the 25 German states in a federal form of government. This constitution, though it reflected Bismarck's tendency toward authoritarian government, also allowed for rights for individual states because of the rural nature of the region. Each state had its own ruler as well as the right to handle its own domestic matters, including education, law enforcement, and local taxation. Southern states had some special rights, such as Bavaria's right to control its military.

The federal government controlled all common matters, such as national defense, foreign affairs, and commerce. The emperor, called the **kaiser**, headed the government. The kaiser held tremendous power. He appointed the chancellor, and he commanded the army and navy. The kaiser could declare a defensive war on his own, and he could order an offensive war with the agreement of the upper house of the legislature.

The legislative branch of the government consisted of two houses. The **Bundesrat**, or upper house, was a federal council, which consisted of 58 appointed members. The **Reichstag**, or legislative assembly, made up the German legislature's lower house. Its nearly 400 members were elected by universal male suffrage. Theoretically a representative body, the Reichstag, however, had limited powers. It could approve military budgets only once every seven years and saw only those bills that the Bundesrat had already approved. This combination of restrictions made it almost impossible for the Reichstag to effect any liberal democratic change that the Bundesrat or emperor might not support.

The German constitution strongly favored the interests of Prussia. The king of Prussia was also the kaiser of Germany. Prussia had the most delegates in the Bundesrat and, because it was the most populous German state, it also had the largest representation in the Reichstag.

This painting depicts the ceremony in which King William I of Prussia was crowned emperor of Germany.

Building History Study Skills

READ
WRITE
INTERPRET
CONNECT
THINK

Writing About History: Writing a Comparison Essay

To make comparisons is to identify both similarities and differences. Writing a comparison essay helps us to see relationships, make connections between conflicting ideas, and analyze the similarities and differences between these ideas.

How to Write a Comparison Essay

To write a comparison essay, follow these steps.
1. State the topic for comparison.
2. On a separate sheet of paper, write the categories for comparison. The categories should be broad points under which similarities and differences on the topic can be listed.
3. List the similarities and differences under each category. Then begin writing the essay, further explaining these similarities and differences that have been listed under each category.
4. In the last paragraph, form a conclusion that synthesizes the information in your essay. The conclusion should be more than a summary. It should be an analytical statement of comparison, using the categories that you have already developed in the body of the essay.

Developing the Skill

If you were to write an essay comparing Italian and German unification, you might establish the categories of comparison as leadership, methods, and results. Study the following essay and identify the categories.

A caricature of Bismarck

❝A renewed spirit of nationalism marked the late 1800s in Europe. Nationalism triumphed in both Italy and Germany. The unification of these nations was accomplished because of the leadership of Cavour and Garibaldi in Italy, and of Bismarck in Germany.

Cavour's skill lay in his ability to direct political events to his own grand scheme. After he started a war with Austria in 1859, France entered on the side of Italy. Cavour also succeeded in getting Lombardy and some of the central states annexed to Italy.

Garibaldi led his republican army in rebellion in the kingdom of Two Sicilies and, in a compromise with Cavour, made them part of the kingdom of Italy.

German unification did not have the multiple leadership and republican elements that existed in Italian unification. However, the manipulation of Austria and the provoking of war were similar characteristics. Bismarck manipulated events and took advantage of opportunities. He united the southern part of Germany with the rest of the country when he stirred up nationalistic and emotional feelings against France after provoking a war with that nation. Republicanism and liberalism were not part of the German unification process.

Italian unification, although it did involve war, incorporated the ideals of republicanism and nationalism and had two leaders, Cavour and Garibaldi. The unification of Germany included nationalism but came about through Bismarck's policies of 'iron and blood'.❞

Notice that the first paragraph identified the topic and stated the categories. The second, third, and fourth paragraphs developed the categories of leadership, methods, and results. The concluding paragraph synthesized the categories of comparison by showing the different methods of unification.

Practicing the Skill

After reading current newspaper or magazine articles, write a comparison essay on the views of any two political candidates.

To apply this skill, see Applying History Study Skills on page 597.

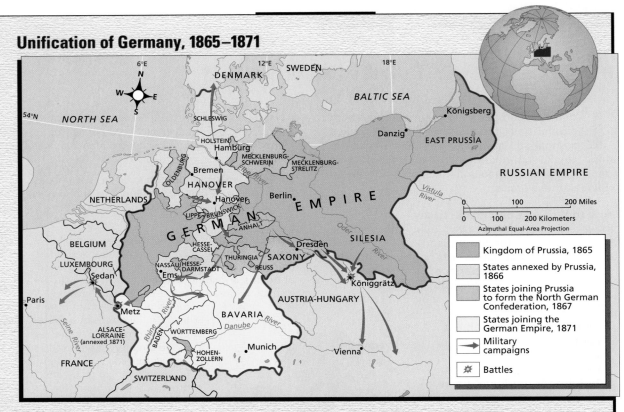

Unification of Germany, 1865–1871

DENMARK
SWEDEN
BALTIC SEA
Königsberg
NORTH SEA
SCHLESWIG
Danzig
EAST PRUSSIA
HOLSTEIN
Hamburg
RUSSIAN EMPIRE
MECKLENBURG-SCHWERIN
MECKLENBURG-STRELITZ
Bremen
OLDENBURG
HANOVER
Berlin
NETHERLANDS
Hanover
E M P I R E
Vistula River
LIPPE BRUNSWICK
G E R M A N
ANHALT
Oder River
BELGIUM
HESSE-CASSEL
Dresden
SILESIA
LUXEMBOURG
THURINGIA
SAXONY
NASSAU HESSE-DARMSTADT
REUSS
Sedan
Ems
Königgrätz
Paris
AUSTRIA-HUNGARY
Metz
BAVARIA
Danube River
ALSACE-LORRAINE (annexed 1871)
WÜRTTEMBERG
Seine River
Rhine River
BADEN
HOHEN-ZOLLERN
Munich
Vienna
FRANCE
SWITZERLAND

Scale: 0 — 100 — 200 Miles / 0 — 100 — 200 Kilometers
Azimuthal Equal-Area Projection

Legend:
- Kingdom of Prussia, 1865
- States annexed by Prussia, 1866
- States joining Prussia to form the North German Confederation, 1867
- States joining the German Empire, 1871
- Military campaigns
- Battles

Learning from Maps As a result of Germany's three wars against Denmark, Austria, and France, Bismarck completed the unification of Germany in 1871.

? Place Identify the battle(s) fought within the boundary of the German Empire? outside the empire?

Section 2 Review

1. **Define** *Zollverein*, Treaty of Prague, kaiser, Bundesrat, Reichstag
2. **Identify** Junkers, William I, Iron Chancellor
3. **Locate and Explain the Significance** Saxony, Schleswig, Holstein, Bavaria, Württemberg
4. **Analyzing Ideas** Explain how the Seven Weeks' War served to display Prussia's superiority over Austria.
5. **Contrasting Ideas** Compare and contrast the different roads that were taken to unification by Italy and Germany.
6. **Summarizing Ideas** Describe the type of government that Germany had after the unification of the German states.

Section 3

Opposition to Bismarck

Focus Questions

- What problems did Bismarck face as chancellor of the German Empire?
- How did Germany become industrialized under Bismarck's leadership?
- What factors led to the waning of Bismarck's power as chancellor?

Because the constitution did not give Bismarck the absolute monarchy he wanted, he tried to achieve it in other ways. However, in the years after formation of the German Empire, he had to accept compromises to make the political system work. Although the constitution gave the people little voice, the government was increasingly forced to attend to their demands.

Problems for the Empire

In spite of rigid control by aristocratic Prussians, the new German federal government soon encountered problems. Dissatisfied groups formed political parties that opposed Bismarck's policies. Some wanted the government to be more liberal and democratic and to enact social reforms. Others feared Bismarck's military policy and the ever-growing army.

Representatives in the legislative assemblies from Prussia were conservative, elected by a special system that gave more representation to voters from the upper class, but politicians from other areas of the empire were more likely to oppose Bismarck. Increasing power of other political groups in the rest of the empire thus increased tension between Prussia and the other German states.

Relations with the Catholic Church presented special problems for Bismarck. He was a Protestant and did not trust the church. A doctrine of papal infallibility announced by the Vatican Council in 1870 added to his distrust of Catholic loyalty to the empire. Many Catholics were also members of the Centre Party, a party he regarded as an enemy.

Bismarck initiated the anti-Catholic program of **Kulturkampf**—German for "culture struggle"—in which Germany passed strict laws to control Catholic clergy and Catholic schools. The laws expelled Jesuits, forbade political expression from the pulpit, and required that all Catholic clergy be Germans who had been educated in German schools. Diplomatic relations with the Vatican were broken as part of *Kulturkampf,* and even more restrictive laws went into effect, establishing civil marriage and eventually confiscating church property.

These policies stirred opposition. The Centre Party doubled in size. Many non-Catholic liberals also joined the opposition. By 1878 Bismarck began to modify the *Kulturkampf* because he needed the support of the Centre Party against a growing socialist presence. He reestablished diplomatic relations with the papacy and had laws against Catholics eased or repealed. The *Kulturkampf* ended in failure by 1887.

Industrial Development Under Bismarck

Bismarck transformed Prussia into an industrial giant. Germany contained a rich store of natural resources, including great coal and iron deposits in the Ruhr Valley and Silesia. The German government managed railroads to promote industrial development, and a system of canals provided cheaper transportation.

Industrialization came later in Germany than in Great Britain and France, which proved to be an advantage for Germany. German industries could use the best methods and most advanced machinery that had been developed elsewhere. German scientists then worked out further changes and improvements.

As chancellor of the German Empire, Bismarck initiated several industrial reforms such as the standardization of money and the centralization of transportation. This photo shows the German industrial city of Dresden in 1875.

Under Bismarck's leadership, the government helped industry in many ways. It standardized money and banking laws throughout the empire. Postal and telegraph services—the means of communication by which so much business was conducted—were centralized. The government encouraged German industrialists to form cartels to control prices, and adopted a high-tariff policy to protect industries from foreign competition. Germany rapidly became an industrial power rivaling Great Britain and France.

Socialism in Germany

With the growth of German industry, cities grew rapidly, and a class of factory workers appeared. German laborers, like those in other nations, wanted decent working conditions. Some people believed that the action of the cartels led to lower wages for workers and higher prices for consumers. Many people thought that these problems required government action. They wanted the government to pass laws that would benefit workers and regulate industry.

As in other European nations, socialist reformers went further, advocating government ownership of major industries. German socialists banded together in 1869 to form what would become the **Social Democratic Party** (SDP). The party grew quickly, with most of its members coming from the ranks of urban workers. By 1877 the Social Democratic Party had elected 12 members to the Reichstag.

Even if the SDP had gained a much greater representation, it would have accomplished very little. The Reichstag could not pass any laws that the Bundesrat opposed. Because the Bundesrat represented aristocratic hereditary rulers, there was little chance that it would propose or pass the laws that socialists wanted. The Reichstag, however, served as a limited public forum in which socialist members could express grievances and make proposals of what they would do if they were given the power.

Bismarck's Antisocialist Campaign

Every gain in socialist voting strength—and every new demand for reform—alarmed Bismarck. When the Social Democrats won more than 490,000 votes in an election in 1877, the chancellor decided to use all of his power to fight them. His opportunity came in 1878, when two attempts to assassinate the emperor occurred. Neither of the would-be assassins had any connection with socialism, and Bismarck knew this. However, he took advantage of public concern to accuse the Social Democrats of plotting

the assassination attempts. The emperor and the Bundesrat dissolved the Reichstag and then called for new elections. A widespread campaign against socialists and their ideas followed.

The election did not change the strength of the Social Democrats in the Reichstag. Bismarck, however, pushed through a number of laws aimed at repressing the socialists. The new laws prohibited newspapers, books, or pamphlets from spreading socialist ideas and banned public meetings of socialists.

Despite such restrictive laws, socialists continued their efforts and the Social Democrats increased their support with each election. As he had done in the *Kulturkampf*, Bismarck changed his tactics to try to retain control against growing opposition.

Since repression had failed, the Iron Chancellor was forced to try another approach. He decided to grant many of the reforms the socialists proposed. If the government granted reforms, Bismarck believed, fewer people would have reason to support the socialists, and the party would lose strength.

Beginning in 1883, he endorsed several far-reaching reforms. First came insurance against sickness, then insurance against accidents—both paid for by employers. Other laws limited working hours, provided for certain holidays from work, and guaranteed pensions for disabled and retired workers.

Germany thus adopted a pioneering program of government-directed social reforms. The reforms did not end socialism in Germany, but they did diminish some of the workers' grievances. Many other industrial nations later adopted similar programs of government-directed social reforms.

The Resignation of Bismarck

Emperor William I died in 1888. His son, Frederick III, reigned for only a few months before he, too, died and was succeeded by his son, William II.

What If?

Bismarck
What if Bismarck had not initiated a program of social reform in Germany in the 1880s? How might the history of Germany and other industrial nations have been different?

The young monarch and the old chancellor soon disagreed deeply. William II felt that Bismarck was too powerful. Bismarck resented the way that the young emperor reduced powers the chancellor had wielded effectively for years. When the socialists scored huge gains in the 1890 elections, Bismarck considered convening the aristocrats to come up with a new constitution.

William II realized that this would create governmental havoc at the outset of his reign. He asked Bismarck to resign, which Bismarck did with a great deal of bitterness. Bismarck criticized his successors for the rest of his life, and though elected to the Reichstag, he refused to serve.

With Bismarck gone, William II set out to expand Germany's influence in the world. He increased the size and strength of the German army even further and began to expand the German navy. This move brought Germany into competition with Great Britain, at that time the world's leading naval power. William signed new agreements with neighboring nations, and by the early 1900s Germany was stronger than ever before.

Shortly after his ascent to Germany's throne, William II (left) forced Bismarck to resign as chancellor.

Section 3 Review

1. **Define** *Kulturkampf,* Social Democratic Party
2. **Identify** William II
3. **Understanding Ideas** What were two problems faced by the German Empire in the 1870s and 1880s?
4. **Analyzing Ideas** What were the major factors responsible for Germany's rapid industrial development under Bismarck?
5. **Interpreting Ideas** What factors combined to decrease Bismarck's power?

Section 4

Reform and Revolution in Russia

Focus Questions

- **What geographical and cultural factors made Russia different from the rest of Europe?**
- **What were the characteristics of Russian domestic and foreign policies?**
- **What types of reform movements occurred in Russia, and what were their results?**

By the mid-1800s Russia had the largest territory and population of any European nation. Yet industrial development, which so strengthened the West, lagged in Russia. Most of the country's extensive natural resources lay undeveloped. Ports were blocked by ice for much of the year, or exits from the seas were controlled by other countries, leaving Russia virtually landlocked. This situation had led to many Russian attempts to win access to the Mediterranean, past Constantinople and the Ottoman-controlled Dardanelles. However, these efforts led to conflicts with the Ottoman Empire.

Unlike Great Britain or France, Russia lacked a homogeneous population. The huge Russian Empire included a great variety of peoples and national groups. Although the largest ethnic groups in the European part of Russia—the Belorussian or White Russian group in the west, the Ukrainians in the agricultural south, and the Great Russians in north and central Russia—were related groups descended from Slavic ancestors, each had its own language, customs, and history. These main Slavic groups were also divided by vast geography. Scattered throughout the empire were numerous racial, national, and religious minorities speaking many languages. Many of these groups, such as the Poles and Finns, had been conquered by the Russians and disliked Russian rule.

Russian Domestic and Foreign Policies

The liberal movement that influenced other European nations so strongly in the 1800s made little progress in Russia. The czar ruled the huge Russian Empire as an **autocrat**, one who holds absolute power. Although the czars tried to maintain autocracy, liberal political developments in Europe affected Russia.

Russia had struggled with the influence of the West from before the time of Peter the Great a century earlier. Nationalistic ideas appealed to the Russian minorities, especially to the strongly patriotic Poles and Finns. By the early 1800s, liberalism began to attract some of the educated members of the Russian aristocracy.

Faced with problems caused by liberal ideas and restless nationalities, the czars took harsh measures. To counteract liberalism the government strictly censored speech and the press and rejected all demands for a constitution. In the 1830s Czar Nicholas I began a program of "**Russification**." This program forced non-Russian peoples in the empire to use the Russian language, accept the Orthodox religion, and adopt Russian customs.

Russian foreign policy had two primary features. (1) In the Balkans, Russia promoted **Pan-Slavism**—the union of all Slavic peoples under Russian leadership. (2) Elsewhere, Russia sought to continue expansion, begun under the first czars, east into Asia and south toward the Ottoman Empire. Expansion southward, however, was halted with a defeat in the Crimean War in the 1850s. Russia lost crucial border territory.

Alexander II and Reforms

Alexander II became czar in 1855. Although basically conservative and autocratic, Alexander cared about public opinion, and he responded, though cautiously, to the movement for freedom for all serfs. His actions were the first steps toward modernization for a country that realized its backwardness with its defeat in the Crimea.

Serfdom had taken a different form in Russia than it had in the rest of Europe. After the time of Peter the Great, serfs were bound to persons and not to the land. They could not leave their villages or masters' homes unless permitted to do so by their owners or ordered to do so by government officials. Although unable to move freely, and largely under the control of their masters, serfs still held a few civil rights such as the right to sue in court.

Toward the middle of the 1800s, reform of serfdom became clearly necessary. Serfdom obstructed development by restricting the labor pool. Factory owners would benefit if the serfs were freed. The industrialists did not believe in liberal ideas; they simply needed workers for their factories. Some nobles who felt a great nation should not sanction the ownership of people also began to support a campaign against serfdom. Another group of government officials, most notably in the ministry of the interior, sought reform for the serfs and convinced Alexander II to consider abolishing this institution.

In 1861 Alexander II issued the **Emancipation Edict,** which freed all serfs. The czar had concluded "it is better to abolish serfdom from above than to wait until the serfs begin to liberate themselves from below." The terms of the edict compensated nobles for land, which peasants could buy in small tracts from the government.

Emancipation did not really improve conditions for the former serfs. Some of the land they had previously farmed was sold to them in tiny plots at high prices. Most freed serfs could not afford to buy enough land to earn the payments for the land, pay taxes, and still make a living. Therefore, they had to rent more land from their former owners—and rents were high. Some former serfs, unable to either buy or rent land, moved to growing towns and cities, where they became cheap sources of labor for factories.

Alexander II attempted other liberal reforms, looking to modernize his nation. Beginning in 1864 he allowed rural districts to elect *zemstvos*. These were councils, at the provincial and county levels, which were elected by all classes, including peasants. *Zemstvos* could levy taxes and controlled programs such as public health, education, assistance for the poor, local crafts, and some public works programs.

Alexander also reformed the courts. Civil and criminal courts were modeled after their European counterparts, and appeals courts were instituted, as were local justices of the peace. Delay and corruption declined in the court system. However, the ministry of the interior still had power beyond the reach of the courts in political cases.

Fabergé Egg

This unusual piece of art is an enameled gold egg containing a completely accurate model of the Gatchina Palace near St. Petersburg. Only five inches high, it even includes a tiny flag flying from the palace tower. It is decorated with pearls and diamonds. Historians think this egg was given to the mother of Czar Nicholas II on Easter morning, 1902. It was customary for the Russian royal family to exchange eggs like this one every Easter. An egg is an ancient symbol of rebirth or renewed life, expressed in Christianity as the resurrection of Jesus at Easter.

The Gatchina egg, as it is called, was created in the jewelry firm of Carl Fabergé in St. Petersburg. Founded in 1842, this company employed the finest jewelers and goldsmiths in all of Europe. These artisans also designed magnificent boxes, clocks, tableware, and jewelry. It was the series of eggs, however, that secured Fabergé's reputation. Most of the eggs were signed by Michael Perchin, who was one of the few native Russians employed by Fabergé.

The famed House of Fabergé was closed in 1918 by officials of the new government. In order to raise money, the government sold all but 10 of the eggs. Today, many of these priceless eggs are housed in private collections and museums.

The policies of reform did not please everyone. Conservatives opposed them and tried to convince the czar that such actions endangered the position of the ruler and the nobles, and thus the stability of the nation. Liberals considered Alexander's reforms to be mere first steps and pointed out the need for further changes. Radicals criticized Alexander even more strongly.

Radicals and Government Reaction

Several groups carried on radical political activity in Russia. Many middle and upper-class intellectuals became nihilists—from the Latin word *nihil*, meaning "nothing"—in the 1860s. They believed a just society could be created only by abolishing the existing political, economic, and social structures and building a completely new Russia.

In the 1870s another group, the Populists, urged their followers to live among peasants as teachers and doctors. Some believed that the large estates of the nobles should be seized and the land divided among the peasants. After the government arrested many Populists, some Russian radicals turned to violent action, splitting off to a movement called **People's Will**. These radicals used **terrorism**—bombings and assassinations by political groups—to try to force the government to grant their demands.

Radical activity gradually made Alexander II more conservative. The first attempt on his life was made in 1866, and after this attempt, he turned to repressive measures. Still, reforms continued. In 1870, major cities were granted limited elected government and in 1874 military reforms were instituted. After repeated assassination attempts, which Alexander faced with great courage, he was killed by a bomb attack by People's Will in 1881.

The assassination of Alexander II ended liberal reform and led to an era of intensive repression. Alexander III and his successor, Nicholas II, used every available means to stamp out liberalism—censorship, control of the church and of education, spies and informers, even imprisonment and exile. They revived and intensified Russification in heavy-handed discrimination against minority groups, and sponsored massacres of Jews in riots called **pogroms** (POH·gruhmz). Many of the reforms of Alexander II were overturned, and Nicholas labeled liberal goals "senseless dreams."

The attempt to preserve the old order met with much opposition—both overt and covert. The development of industry in Russia had produced a class of city workers who wanted the right to form unions and to strike. Liberals and radicals, more determined than ever to gain reforms, found an audience in these often-exploited workers.

The attempts of the Russian government to block all change produced an explosive situation. Terrorism increased. Socialists, who in 1898 had founded the **Social Democratic Labor Party** in imitation of the German Social Democratic Party, grew increasingly radical. The government's repression backfired.

The Revolution of 1905

In 1904 and 1905, Russia went to war with Japan over territories in China and Korea. To the surprise of the world, the Japanese dealt the Russians a humiliating defeat. Russia's loss exposed a government that was corrupt and inefficient, as well as autocratic and oppressive. The defeat spurred discontented groups in the country to action.

On January 22, 1905, "Bloody Sunday," the czar's troops shot at a group of unarmed strikers on their way to deliver a petition to him. The incident triggered the Revolution of 1905. Workers struck and held demonstrations. The street fighting that broke out was especially violent in non-Russian areas, and there were mutinies in the army and navy. Czar

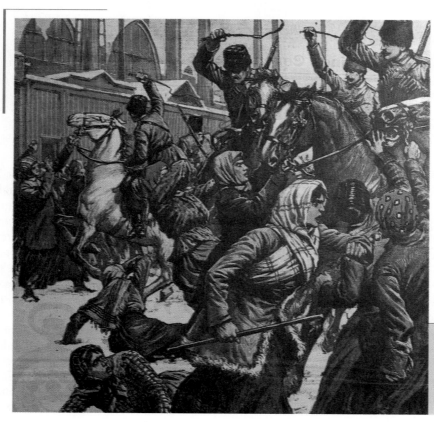

On Bloody Sunday, January 22, 1905, Russian troops fired shots at a group of peaceful demonstrators, thus beginning the Revolution of 1905.

Nicholas II faced a crisis. Russian autocracy had to yield or perish. He reluctantly decided to yield.

The czar issued a decree called the October Manifesto, which promised individual liberties and provided for the election of a parliament called the **Duma**. After more bloody fighting, severe repression and executions stilled the revolution.

Because of its weakness after the Russo-Japanese War, the government had to confront its critics. But autocracy continued. The czar dismissed two sessions of the Duma because members insisted that the czar's ministers be responsible to the Duma. A 1907 electoral law increased the representation of large landowners and restricted the voting of others. The result was a more conservative Duma and one more cooperative with the czar.

The revolutionary movement of 1905 failed to overthrow the czar for three main reasons: (1) The army remained loyal and thus would not end the czar's regime. (2) The French, bound to Russia by military alliance, lent money to the government. (3) The many revolutionary groups were divided in their goals. Moderates feared radical demands and radicals disagreed among themselves.

The reactionaries learned nothing from the Revolution of 1905. The government often treated people with contempt, and bureaucrats openly broke laws that they were supposed to enforce. Using extreme repressive measures as before, the autocracy tried vainly to resist change and to preserve the thousand-year-old monarchy.

Section 4 Review

1. **Define** autocrat, Russification, Pan-Slavism, Emancipation Edict, People's Will, terrorism, pogroms, Social Democratic Labor Party, Duma
2. **Identify** nihilists
3. **Interpreting Ideas** How did Russia's geography and culture make its situation different from Britain and France?
4. **Summarizing Ideas** (a) Explain how liberalism affected Russia's domestic policy. (b) Describe the two features of Russia's foreign policy.
5. **Organizing Ideas** (a) List the liberal reforms that Alexander II accomplished in Russia. (b) What did he do with regard to the serfs?
6. **Analyzing Ideas** (a) Why did the Revolution of 1905 fail to overthrow the monarchy? (b) How did Nicholas II respond to the Revolution of 1905?

Unrest in Austria-Hungary

Focus Questions

- **What led to the formation of the Dual Monarchy, and what problems did it face?**
- **How did the decline of the Ottoman Empire affect European politics?**
- **How did ethnic clashes in southern Europe set the stage for a showdown among major powers?**

"When France sneezes, all Europe catches cold," the Austrian minister Metternich said in 1848. He was referring to the fact that uprisings in France had set off revolts in almost every other European nation. The Austrian Empire proved no exception.

In Vienna demonstrators and the army clashed. A frightened Emperor Ferdinand ordered Metternich, his chief minister, to resign. After having dominated European affairs for over 30 years, Metternich fled the country. Later in 1848 Ferdinand himself abdicated, and the throne went to 18-year-old Francis Joseph I.

Uprisings also occurred in Hungary. The people of this region—one of the largest parts of the Austrian Empire—chafed under Austrian rule. Most of them were Magyars—descendants of a nomadic warrior group that had migrated to Hungary from Russia and Romania in the 900s. The Magyars spoke a language unlike other European languages and maintained a distinct culture. A strong nationalist movement centered on making the Magyars dominant in Hungary and freeing the region from Austrian domination.

Hungarian patriot Lajos Kossuth led a revolt in 1848. For a time it looked as though Hungary would gain independence, and in 1849 Kossuth was elected "responsible governor president" by the Hungarian Diet. However, Austria, with Russia's assistance, soon ousted the revolutionaries. Czar Nicholas I sent troops because he feared that revolution might spread to Russian-controlled Poland. Kossuth fled to Turkey, temporarily ending Hungarian attempts at independence.

Formation of the Dual Monarchy

For almost 20 years after the Revolution of 1848, Austria managed to keep liberalism and nationalism

Ethnic Groups in Austria-Hungary, 1867

PRUSSIA

RUSSIAN EMPIRE

Elbe River

Oder River

BOHEMIA
Prague
CZECHS

MORAVIA
Brno

Vistula River

Kraków

GALICIA

BAVARIA

SLOVAKS

Danube River

Salzburg

Vienna

AUSTRIA-HUNGARY

Buda Pest

Tisza River

Innsbruck

TIROL

Drava River

CARNIOLA

TRANSYLVANIA

LOMBARDY

Trieste

CROATS

CROATIA-SLAVONIA

ROMANIA

Po River

CROATS

SERBS

SERBS

KINGDOM
OF
ITALY

ADRIATIC SEA

DALMATIA

BOSNIA

Sarajevo

SERBIA

OTTOMAN EMPIRE

HERZE-
GOVINA

MONTENEGRO

42°N

0   100   200 Miles
0   100   200 Kilometers
Lambert Conformal Conic Projection

12°E   18°E

Slavs:
- Croats and Serbs
- Czechs and Slovaks
- Poles
- Slovenes
- Ukrainians

Others:
- Germans
- Magyars
- Romanians
- Italians

Learning from Maps   While Austria and Hungary joined together under the Dual Monarchy, they retained separate parliaments and languages.

? Human-Environment Interaction   Which non-Slavic peoples settled throughout Austria-Hungary?

from wrecking its empire. However, after Austria's defeat by Prussia in 1866, Hungarians demanded more freedom. Austria responded in 1867 by forming the Dual Monarchy—also called Austria-Hungary—in which Hungarians shared power with Austrians.

The Dual Monarchy had a common ruler, Francis Joseph I, whose title was Emperor of Austria and King of Hungary. Although three ministries—war, finance, and foreign affairs—conducted government business for the whole empire, Austria and Hungary each had its own parliament. The Austrian parliament met

in Vienna; the Hungarian one met in what became the city of Budapest.

The Dual Monarchy proved to be a practical economic arrangement. Hungary, chiefly agricultural, furnished raw materials and food. Austria, strongly industrial, produced manufactured goods. Each provided markets for the other.

Many problems existed, however. Because of its manufacturing interests, Austria wanted high protective tariffs. As a farming region, Hungary favored low tariffs and freer trade.

Moreover, the formation of the Dual Monarchy did not solve the problem of nationalities. The Austrian Germans and the Hungarian Magyars dominated the population in each of their separate national states. The Austrians spoke German. The Hungarians spoke Magyar, or Hungarian, which had been declared the official language of Hungary. National minorities—the Czechs, Serbs, Croats, Romanians, Poles, Slovenes, Ukrainians, and Italians—existed in both Austria and Hungary. (See map on opposite page.) These people benefited very little from the Dual Monarchy and continued to agitate for self-government.

A disastrous and stunning defeat by Prussia in the Seven Weeks' War in 1866 forced Austria from positions of power in Germany and Italy and its leadership of Europe. To compensate for this setback, and hoping to gain influence and territory, the Dual Monarchy turned toward the Balkans, a region to the southeast controlled chiefly by the Ottoman Empire.

The Ottoman Empire

By the 1800s the Ottoman Empire had declined substantially. At its peak in the 1500s, the empire had stretched around the Mediterranean Sea from Algeria through Egypt and the Arabian Peninsula, through Asia Minor, Mesopotamia, Greece, and into southern Europe as far as Austria. But economic problems and the vast size of the empire made it hard to govern. Military defeats in the 1700s diminished the empire's size, and the rise of local rulers weakened central authority. A rising population was difficult to feed on poor lands. Slow modernization, for economic and cultural reasons, also contributed to the decline of the once-strong and disciplined empire.

Economic and social problems. The subject peoples of the Ottoman Turks did not regard their rulers favorably. Ottoman rulers in the 1800s could not afford many improvements in agriculture or public works projects such as roads and hospitals. The tax system often favored foreign interests at the expense of Ottoman subjects. Many of the people living in the empire were Christians or Jews. In religious and cultural matters, the Turks granted toleration and self-control to non-Muslims under their own religious leaders. However, there was no pretense of equality in Ottoman society or governmental affairs.

Discontent in the Balkans

In the early 1800s, the rise of nationalism increased discontent in the Balkan area of the Ottoman Empire. The Balkan region contained several different peoples—Serbs, Bulgarians, Romanians, Albanians, and Greeks, for example—all of whom wanted to govern themselves.

The Turks tried to suppress nationalistic movements. During the 1820s Greeks and Serbs revolted. Aided by outside powers, Greece gained independence in 1829, and Serbia achieved a degree of self-rule. Encouraged by these successes and by the evident weakness of the Turks, Serbia and Greece tried to gain more territory.

Foreign countries intervened to promote their own interests in struggles between the Turks and these nationalist groups. Russia supported Balkan nationalists for several reasons. The Russians were Slavs like the Bulgarians and Serbs. In addition, like many of the discontented Balkan groups, the Russians were Orthodox Christians. Strategically, if the Ottoman Empire collapsed, Russia might be able to control the water route from the Black Sea to the Mediterranean Sea.

The Russian drive toward the eastern Mediterranean caused the British to support the crumbling Ottoman Empire. Great Britain did not want the Russians in the Mediterranean, where they might challenge British sea power.

It was a curious alignment of nations. The autocratic Russian government promoted the independence of the Balkan peoples. Democratic Great Britain supported the Turks in suppressing self-rule.

The Congress of Berlin and the Balkan Wars

In 1875 revolts broke out in several Turkish provinces in the Balkans. Two years later Russia chose to support the rebels and declared war on the Ottoman Empire. The Turks were defeated and forced to sign the **Treaty of San Stefano** in 1878. The treaty granted independence to Romania, Serbia, and Montenegro. It also created an autonomous Bulgaria, which Russian troops then occupied for some years. The new boundaries of Bulgaria extended to the Aegean Sea in the eastern Mediterranean.

The sudden increase of Russian influence in the Balkans alarmed other European powers. Before the Treaty of San Stefano went into effect, a group of nations led by Great Britain and Austria forced Russia to consent to an international conference.

All the major European powers met at the Congress of Berlin in 1878. The Congress dealt with several territorial issues. Serbia, Montenegro, and Romania retained their independence. Bulgaria was granted self-government, but its area was divided and reduced in size, and it was kept within the Ottoman Empire—thus removing Russia's access to the Aegean Sea. Austria continued to govern Bosnia and Herzegovina but was not permitted to annex them.

The British were given the right to occupy and administer the island of Cyprus, long held by the Turks. The Turkish sultan still officially ruled the island, but Great Britain actually took over. The use of Cyprus as a naval base increased Great Britain's power in the eastern Mediterranean and kept Russia out of the region.

Other nations continued to reduce the size and power of the Ottoman Empire. France, Great Britain, and Italy each seized parts of its African territory. In 1908 Bulgaria became completely independent. In the same year, Austria broke the agreement of the Congress of Berlin by annexing Bosnia and Herzegovina outright. In 1912 Italy seized several islands in the southeastern Aegean Sea, including Rhodes. The island of Crete revolted in 1896 and 1905, resulting first in a degree of self-government and then annexation by Greece in 1913.

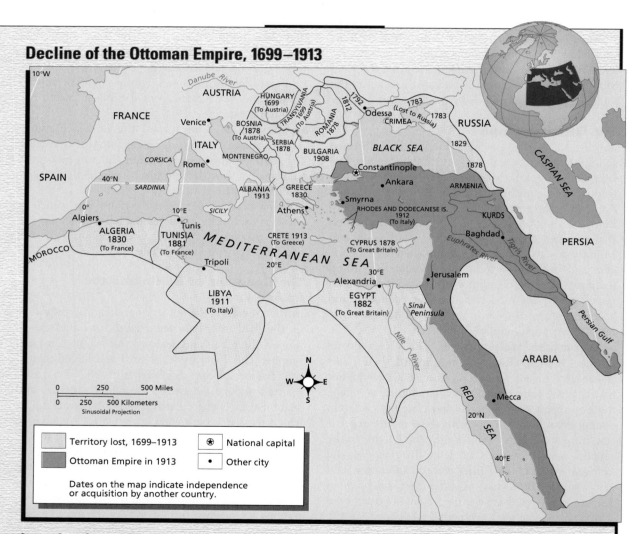

Decline of the Ottoman Empire, 1699–1913

Learning from Maps Throughout the 1800s and early 1900s many territories of the Ottoman Empire became independent or were annexed by other countries.

? Location What are the approximate latitude and longitude coordinates for the capital of the Ottoman Empire?

As a result of the two Balkan Wars, the Ottoman Empire lost a considerable amount of territory. This Balkan Wars illustration is taken from the cover of a 1913 *Le Petit Journal* supplement.

In 1912 and 1913, two wars between independent Balkan nations and the Ottomans further altered national boundaries and increased international tensions. Bulgaria, Serbia, Greece, and Montenegro, known as the **Balkan League**, declared war on the Ottoman Empire and won. The Balkan League wanted to divide among themselves the Balkan territories of the Ottoman Empire. However, they could not agree on the partition of the Turkish territories, and hostilities broke out again in 1913. This time, Serbia, Greece, Montenegro, Romania, and the Ottoman Empire fought against and defeated Bulgaria.

As a result of the first war, Serbia gained a seaport on the Adriatic, and Albania became independent. Bulgaria claimed considerable territory in the central Balkans and along the Aegean Sea. As a result of the second war, however, Bulgaria suffered humiliating territorial losses and was left with only a small outlet on the Aegean.

By the end of 1913, the territory of the Ottoman Empire in Europe had shrunk dramatically. It included only the city of Constantinople and a small region that gave it control of the vital water route from the Black Sea to the Mediterranean. (See map on opposite page.)

Everywhere in Europe, tension, aggression, and expansion marked the behavior of new nations and old in the early 1900s. Internal and international hostilities began to rise to dangerous levels. War clouds gathered on the horizons of major imperial European powers.

Section 5 Review

1. **Define** Treaty of San Stefano, Balkan League
2. **Identify** Magyars, Francis Joseph I
3. **Locate and Explain the Significance** Romania, Budapest, Serbia, Montenegro, Bulgaria, Bosnia, Herzegovina, Cyprus, Rhodes
4. **Summarizing Ideas (a)** When was the Dual Monarchy formed? **(b)** What were its strengths and weaknesses?
5. **Organizing Ideas (a)** How was the Ottoman Empire reduced in size between 1878 and 1913? **(b)** How did this decline of the Ottoman Empire affect European politics?
6. **Interpreting Ideas (a)** Why did the Western nations fear Russian influence in the Balkans? **(b)** What prompted the Congress of Berlin?

Chapter 22 Review

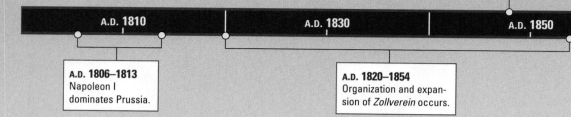

A.D. 1848
Revolts take place in Italy, Germany, and the Austrian Empire.

A.D. 1810

A.D. 1830

A.D. 1850

A.D. 1806–1813
Napoleon I dominates Prussia.

A.D. 1820–1854
Organization and expansion of *Zollverein* occurs.

Chapter Summary

The following list contains the key concepts you have learned about the unification of Italy and Germany and about conflicts that arose in other European nations in the late 1800s and early 1900s.

1. Italy was unified in 1870 due to the efforts of Mazzini, Garibaldi, and Cavour. A kingdom was established, and the capital of this kingdom was Rome.
2. The kingdom of Prussia led the German unification under the leadership of Otto von Bismarck.
3. In Germany, aggressive behavior brought about unification. The Germans used three victorious wars to crush their rivals and to strengthen German nationalism.
4. Bismarck ran into opposition from various political groups. He at first tried to repress the socialists and then endorsed certain reforms. A clash with the new emperor, William II, forced Bismarck's resignation in 1890.
5. Under Bismarck's leadership, Germany industrialized rapidly and became one of the strongest powers in Europe.
6. In Russia the czar maintained autocratic control over the country, despite such reforms as the emancipation of the serfs.
7. Discontent and rebellion continued to occur in the Austrian Empire even after the Dual Monarchy, also called Austria-Hungary, was created. Holding its various nationalities together in unity was a major problem of the Dual Monarchy.
8. As the Ottoman Empire declined, discontent in its Balkan territories led to two Balkan Wars in 1912 and 1913. International tensions increased as a result.

Reviewing Important Terms

On a separate sheet of paper, supply the term that correctly completes each statement.

1. The nationalistic movement in Italy, with its goals of liberation and unification, was called the _____.
2. The emperor of united Germany was called the _____.
3. A(n) _____ is someone who holds absolute power.
4. Bombings and assassinations of high officials by political groups are called _____.
5. The massacres of the Jews in czarist Russia were called _____.

Reviewing Critical Thinking Skills

1. **Comparing Ideas** What were the similarities and differences between the processes of unification in Italy and Germany?
2. **Analyzing Ideas** Otto von Bismarck once remarked, "Politics is the art of the possible." How did Bismarck's actions in forming the German Empire demonstrate his belief in this statement?
3. **Interpreting Ideas** (a) Why did the liberal movement make little progress in Russia during the 1800s? (b) Explain how Russian radicals attempted to bring about change.
4. **Understanding Relationships** Why might each of the following events be considered a response to the rise of nationalism? (a) Unification of Italy and Germany; (b) Start of the Russification program; (c) Establishment of the Dual Monarchy; (d) Further decline of the Ottoman Empire.

Relating Geography to History

In Chapter 15 you read about the rivalry between Prussia and Austria to dominate central Europe. To study the outcome of this struggle for domination, compare the two maps on pages 388 and 584. How did the balance of power change during the period from 1786 to 1871? Using the information in this chapter and in Chapter 15, briefly explain how Prussia came to rule the German Empire.

Relating Past to Present

1. The *Zollverein* was a major step toward German unity. (a) Who belonged to this customs union? (b) How did the various member states benefit from economic cooperation? (c) Using American history or civics books, find out about the laws regulating

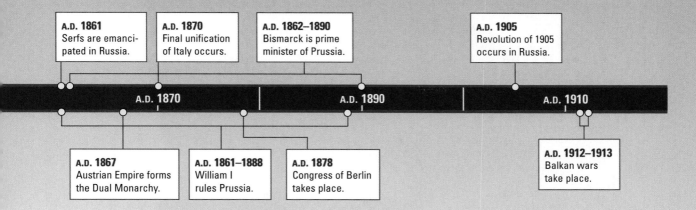

A.D. 1861
Serfs are emancipated in Russia.

A.D. 1870
Final unification of Italy occurs.

A.D. 1862–1890
Bismarck is prime minister of Prussia.

A.D. 1905
Revolution of 1905 occurs in Russia.

A.D. 1870

A.D. 1890

A.D. 1910

A.D. 1867
Austrian Empire forms the Dual Monarchy.

A.D. 1861–1888
William I rules Prussia.

A.D. 1878
Congress of Berlin takes place.

A.D. 1912–1913
Balkan wars take place.

trade among the states in the United States. Can the states impose or collect tariffs? **(d)** Can the federal government grant special trade concessions to any one state or region? **(e)** What evidence of trade among the states can you find in your home?

2. Review the problems facing Russia's economic development during the 1800s. Then clip newspaper and magazine articles that illustrate economic issues facing the region today. Compare the issues of the 1800s with those of the present day. What seem to be the similarities and differences?

Applying History Study Skills

Before completing this activity, review Building History Study Skills on page 583.

Read the following statements. The first is from a speech by Otto von Bismarck on his view of the unification of Germany. The other is from a letter by Giuseppe Garibaldi on his conquest of Naples. How are their views of unification different? How are they similar?

"Germany does not look to Prussia's liberalism, but to its power. Bavaria, Württemburg, and Baden [the south German states] would like to turn to liberalism, but they shall not assume Prussia's role. Prussia must collect its forces for the favorable occasion, which has several times been neglected; Prussia's borders are not favorable to a healthy national life. Not by speeches and decisions of majorities will the greatest problems of the time be decided—that was the mistake of 1848–1849—but by iron and blood."
(Speech to the Prussian Diet, September 1862)

"Having reached the strait, it became necessary to cross it. To have reinstated Sicily in the great Italian family was certainly a glorious achievement. But what then? Were we, in compliance with diplomacy, to leave our country incomplete and maimed? What of the two Calabrias, and Naples, awaiting us with open arms? And the rest of Italy still enslaved by the foreigner and the priest? . . .

I entered Naples with the whole of the southern army as yet a long way off in the direction of the Straits of Messina, the King of Naples having, on the previous day, quitted his palace to retire to Capua.

At Naples, as in all places we had passed through since crossing the strait, the populace were sublime in

their enthusiastic patriotism, and the resolute tone assumed by them certainly had no small share in the brilliant results obtained."
(Garibaldi's Report on the Conquest of Naples)

1. How did Bismarck feel about liberalism?
2. **(a)** How did Garibaldi feel about the role of the people in uniting Italy? **(b)** How did his opinion differ from Bismarck's?
3. What does Bismarck mean by the expression "iron and blood"?
4. **(a)** How was Garibaldi greeted in Naples? **(b)** What might Bismarck have said about this greeting?
5. What was the primary difference between Garibaldi's and Bismarck's approaches to unification?

🖅 internet**connect**

Search the Internet through the HRW Web site for information on the emancipation of the serfs in Russia in 1861. You might, for example, locate a copy of the Emancipation Manifesto of March 3, 1861, or find information about Alexander II. Print out what you find and be prepared to give an oral report.  **GO TO:** go.hrw.com
KEYWORD: SC0
Alexander II

Building Your Portfolio

1. **Presenting an Oral Report** Read Garibaldi's "Proclamation to the Italians," and Bismarck's "iron and blood" speech. Present an oral report explaining why each of these documents might be considered an expression of nationalism. Discuss which one is more idealistic than the other and explain why you feel this way. Place your notes in your portfolio.

2. **Writing a Report** Garibaldi and his comparatively small army succeeded in conquering the Kingdom of the Two Sicilies, which later became part of a united Italy. Prepare a written report on Garibaldi's exploits in Sicily. Place the report in your portfolio.

The Age of Imperialism

TIME

A.D. **1830–1917**

3.7 million B.C. | 4000 B.C. | A.D. 2100

A.D. 1830–1917

PLACE

Africa, Asia, the Pacific, and Latin America

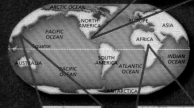

Latin America

ARCTIC OCEAN

PACIFIC OCEAN

NORTH AMERICA

EUROPE

ASIA

AFRICA

Equator

INDIAN OCEAN

AUSTRALIA

PACIFIC OCEAN

SOUTH AMERICA

ATLANTIC OCEAN

ANTARCTICA

Asia and the Pacific

Africa

The first voyage through the Suez Canal on November 17, 1869

Significance

By the early 1800s, European expansion continued as waves of immigrants flowed into the new nations of the Americas or established new settlement colonies in Africa and the Pacific.

Where once they had exercised informal influence over other peoples, after 1870 the empire-builders began to establish new **dependent colonies**, in which non-European majorities were ruled by relatively few European colonial officials. By 1914 the great industrial powers of Europe, the United States, and Japan controlled practically the entire world.

Terms to Define

dependent colonies	paternalism
imperialism	assimilation
"White Man's Burden"	Muslim League
colony	Treaty of Shimonoseki
protectorate	Chinese Eastern Railway
condominium	*Maine*
sphere of influence	Platt Amendment
Fashoda crisis	Roosevelt Corollary

People to Identify

Henry Stanley	Porfirio Díaz
Leopold II	Victoriano Huerta
Cecil Rhodes	Venustiano Carranza
Emilio Aguinaldo	Pancho Villa

Places to Locate

Algiers	Singapore
Tunis	Samoa Islands
Suez Canal	British Guiana
Formosa	Puerto Rico
Liaodong Peninsula	Panama Canal

Chapter Theme Questions

- **Economic Organization** What economic factors might lead a nation to seek relationships with overseas nations or establish overseas colonies?
- **Cross-Cultural Interaction** How might imperialism affect the flow of ideas among peoples?
- **Politics and Law** How might domination by an imperialist nation affect the government and organization of a state, both during foreign dominance and after regaining independence?

I n 1869 the *New York Herald* hired journalist Henry Stanley to locate Dr. David Livingstone, who had disappeared in Africa. In 1871 Stanley finally located Livingstone and wrote of their meeting.

❝**So I did that which I thought was most dignified. I pushed back the crowds, and, passing from the rear, walked down a living avenue of people, until I came in front of the semicircle of Arabs, in front of which stood the white man with the gray beard. As I advanced slowly toward him I noticed he was pale, looked wearied…I would have run to him, only I was a coward in the presence of such a mob… So I did what cowardice and false pride suggested was the best thing—walked deliberately to him, took off my hat, and said, 'Dr. Livingstone, I presume?'**

'Yes,' said he, with a kind smile, lifting his cap slightly.❞

Stanley's highly publicized trip did much to spark European interest in Africa.

Section 1

The Roots of Imperialism

Focus Questions

- **Why did Europeans look outside their own countries for raw materials and markets?**
- **What reasons, other than industrialization, led Europeans to establish colonies and expand their empires?**
- **How did imperialism develop, and what different types of colonial relationships existed?**

Imperialism—the ambition of a powerful nation to dominate the political, economic, and cultural affairs of another nation or region—arose out of a complex mixture of political, economic, and social forces. Historians do not agree on which influences were most important.

Desire for Self-Sufficiency

After 1850 the Industrial Revolution accelerated as new sources of power, new machinery, and new industries were developed. Increased industrial production spurred the demand for traditional raw materials such as iron and coal. In addition, the new industries needed other raw materials, such as manganese and tungsten for making steel alloys, copper for the electrical industry, and rubber for a variety of uses. Industrialization also brought rising standards of living in Europe and the United States and increased the demand for products such as coffee, tea, and spices.

None of the industrialized nations wanted to depend on other nations for raw materials. Government leaders feared that in the event of war their countries would be at the mercy of an enemy. Thus the leaders of the industrial nations sought ways to become self-sufficient by gaining control of the sources of the raw materials they needed.

Need for New Markets

After 1870 new technology made it possible to produce goods in enormous quantities. When the new and expensive industrial machinery was used to full capacity, it could pay for itself and generate profits for its owners. If the machinery was not used to full capacity, owners lost money.

Even with their rising standards of living, people in Europe and the United States could not buy all the goods on the market. To market their goods and to continue to increase their profits, industrialists began to look for new markets in nonindustrialized regions, especially in Asia, Africa, and Latin America.

Imperialists believed that if people in nonindustrialized areas were aware of manufactured goods and if the goods were available, they would buy them. Imperialists even argued that the customs of these people might be remolded to create new markets. Advocates of imperialism wrote articles describing how busy European and American factories would be and how much profit they could earn if only the people of central Africa could be persuaded to wear shirts and ties.

Many Europeans believed that industrialized nations should control their new markets abroad, just as they controlled the colonial sources of their raw materials. Industrialists wanted their governments to guarantee them exclusive rights to sell in these markets. At the same time, they demanded protective tariffs to ensure that they would not lose their home markets to foreign competition.

Nationalism

Nationalism, a strong force throughout the 1800s, became particularly powerful between 1870 and 1914. Many nationalists now argued that having colonies added to their nations' strength and prestige. The recently unified nations of Germany and Italy felt that they had to build up colonial empires to compete with longtime colonial powers such as Great Britain, France, and the Netherlands. However, it is notable that the British, who already had a large empire, entered the imperialistic race for colonies as enthusiastically as did the Germans or Italians.

Imperialists also viewed colonies as sources of troops for the rapidly growing armies of the day. Gurkhas, soldiers from Nepal, joined Australians and New Zealanders to strengthen British armies. Senegalese troops from West Africa fought for the French.

A large navy was even more necessary than a large army to protect widely scattered colonies and far-ranging merchant ships. For many years, steam-powered ships burned coal, and the range of a steamship was "from coal to coal." Thus the coaling station, a place where warships and merchant ships could refuel, became highly important for military and commercial purposes. Tiny islands with nothing to offer except their strategic locations became coaling stations or naval bases. Often these islands became objects of fierce competition among naval powers.

Outlets for Population

Rapid population growth accompanied industrialization. Some historians estimate that the world's population doubled between 1800 and 1900. Industrial development created many jobs, but in Europe there was not enough work to employ all the new job seekers. Displaced farmers and farm laborers, in particular, found it either preferable or necessary to go elsewhere. As a result, Europeans left their home countries in record numbers in the 1880s.

For some countries, such as Britain, Germany, and France, overseas migration was not a new phenomenon. However, for other countries, such as Italy, Spain, and Austria-Hungary, the wave of emigration in the 1880s marked the first mass movement of their peoples. The populations of North America, South America, and Australia swelled as the Europeans established themselves within their borders.

Missionary Motives

The urge to spread the Christian religion influenced colonial expansion during the 1500s and 1600s.

Although Roman Catholic missionaries had continued their work since that time, they increased their activities during the period of imperialism. Growing numbers of Protestant missionaries also attempted to convert people in the colonies to Christianity.

Missionaries did other work as well. Education became a regular missionary activity. Trained medical missionaries went out from Europe and the United States. Consequently, knowledge of medicine, hygiene, and sanitation spread with Christianity.

Cultural Motives

Closely related to the missionary motive was the idea that the people of industrialized Western nations had a duty to transmit Western ideas and knowledge across the globe. People were considered lacking if their religion or their culture differed from that of the West.

The idea of Western superiority was expressed by British poet Rudyard Kipling. The phrase Kipling used as the title of the poem **"The White Man's Burden"** has often been used to identify the attitude that Europeans had toward people in non-Western, nonindustrialized nations. Many Europeans felt an obligation to carry Western civilization to those that they considered less fortunate than themselves. These judgments, however inaccurate, motivated Europeans to alter the way of life of countless peoples, all under the guise of "helping" or "improving" them. Europeans also used the idea of their "burden" to justify imposing their own values and cultural ideas on other peoples.

The British were not the only Europeans who had these attitudes. The French also spoke of their "civilizing mission." The people of each industrial nation considered their civilization and culture to be the highest and therefore the one most suited for enlightening other, less industrialized peoples on Earth.

Opponents of imperialism claimed that the only burden the white man wanted to take up was the burden of colonial wealth, which he wanted to carry back home as fast as possible. Such opponents, however, formed a minority with little influence in their countries.

The Nature of Imperialism

Imperialism created bitter rivalries among the imperial powers and hatred among the colonized peoples. Rivalries led to the building of larger armies and navies and eventually to world conflict.

In the beginning, European governments did not actively plan imperialism. Often it began with the work of individuals such as merchants, explorers, or missionaries. Sometimes these Europeans met with resistance or violence from the local inhabitants. Then European soldiers appeared, followed by government officials to protect the interests of their citizens. Builders, engineers, and technicians who opened mines, built roads, and improved other means of transportation often followed the soldiers and officials. Then the

This photo shows a missionary classroom in the Philippines. In addition to establishing Christianity during the age of imperialism, missionaries also spread their knowledge of education and medicine.

The Voice of Rudyard Kipling

Rudyard Kipling, who lived from 1865 to 1936, is often considered the poet of British imperialism. One of his best-known poems, "The White Man's Burden," was actually written to address the United States's involvement in the Philippines. The first stanza of the poem follows.

> "Take up the White Man's burden—
> Send forth the best ye breed—
> Go bind your sons to exile
> To serve your captives' need;
> To wait in heavy harness,
> On fluttered folk and wild—
> Your new-caught, sullen peoples,
> Half devil and half child."

This poem supplied the phrase "The White Man's Burden," which is often used to sum up the imperialist motive to protect and civilize groups of people who were considered by Europeans to be "primitive"—in Kipling's words, "half devil and half child." Of course, those groups often had rich and highly complex cultures, and coming under European "protection" usually meant conquest and exploitation for them.

Kipling's work reflects many of the troubling and conflicting impulses of imperialism. He did believe that British civilization should be the model for everyone. Yet he was not the shallow racist he is often misunderstood to be. In fact, he strongly believed in the moral worth of all human beings. The words of "The White Man's Burden" dwell on the responsibilities and costs of imperialism, and some of his other

poems criticize a failure to live up to the ideals of imperialism.

Kipling was born in Bombay, India, where he learned the Hindi language from Indian servants. At the age of five or six, he was sent to England and spent much of the rest of his life in England and the United States. He did return to India as a journalist in 1882, spending seven years there. In 1900 he went to South Africa to report on the Boer War. In 1901 he completed his first major novel, *Kim,* which is set in India, as are many of his other novels and stories. In 1907 he won the Nobel Prize for literature.

---

region would be developed for the benefit of the developers. The local population had very little, if any, say in this process.

One of the things that prompted imperialism was the fact that the newly industrialized Europeans had surplus cash. They were looking for new ideas and new places in which to invest. Loans to local rulers often provided the initial wedge of imperialism. Economic involvement in a country often led to political involvement and eventually to control.

Europeans often used this process as a means of gaining control of an area or region.

Several terms used in connection with imperialism need explanation. Originally, a colony was a settlement established in another region by citizens of a country. Early examples of colonies include the Greek colonies throughout the Mediterranean and the British colonies in North America. During the imperialistic era, however, a **colony** was an area in which a foreign nation gained complete control over a given region and its local population. A colony was first gained by settlement or conquest and then annexed, becoming a part of the foreign nation's empire.

In a **protectorate**, the local ruler kept his title, but officials of the foreign power actually controlled the region. The "protecting" power kept out other foreign nations. In a **condominium**, two nations ruled a region as partners. A concession was the grant of economic rights and privileges in a given area. Concessions were given by local rulers to foreign merchants or capitalists who wanted to trade, to build railroads, or to develop mineral deposits and other natural resources. A **sphere of influence** was a region in which one nation had special, sometimes exclusive, economic and political privileges that were recognized by other nations.

Section 1 Review

1. **Define** dependent colonies, imperialism, "White Man's Burden," colony, protectorate, condominium, sphere of influence

2. **Understanding Ideas** Why did European countries seek raw materials and markets outside their own countries?

3. **Summarizing Ideas** Describe four motives behind imperialism that are not related to raw materials or markets.

4. **Comparing Ideas** How might life have differed under the different types of imperialism?

Section 2

European Claims in North Africa and the Sudan

Focus Questions

- What motives did European nations have for establishing colonies or spheres of influence in North Africa?
- What type of control did France exercise over Algiers and Tunis?
- What interests did Britain have in Egypt and in the Sudan?
- How did Italy gain control of Libya?

Throughout history many conquerors, including the Romans, the Byzantines, and the Arabs, imposed their rule on North Africa. In the 1800s, most of the region belonged to the Ottoman Empire, although Ottoman control was weak.

The French in North Africa

For a long time, expert Muslim seafarers known as the Barbary pirates operated off the coast of North Africa, preying on Mediterranean shipping. The term *Barbary* means "of the Berbers"—a people of North Africa who had converted to Islam during the 600s. Four Muslim states—Morocco, Algiers, Tunis, and Tripoli—made up the so-called Barbary States. The countries of Morocco, Algeria, Tunisia, and Libya now occupy the area of the former Barbary States.

The operations of the Barbary pirates gave the French an excuse to intervene in North Africa. A French representative went to the governor of Algiers to discuss the Barbary pirates in 1827. The governor allegedly insulted the French representative by striking him with a flyswatter. By 1830 a French force occupied the city of Algiers. For more than 40 years, the French fought against almost continuous local rebellions.

Economically, however, Algiers was worth the trouble. Many French people and other Europeans moved in. The French officials appropriated, or claimed ownership of, land on which to settle colonists.

Seizure of Tunis. East of Algiers lay the small state of Tunis. Tunis belonged to the Ottoman Empire, though in fact it operated independently. Tunisians were relieved by the French takeover of Algiers in 1830; Algiers had long sought to assert its influence over Tunis. The bey (the Turkish provincial governor) of Tunis at that time was open to Western ideas. He accepted military advice from French advisers and allowed economic assistance to flow from French banks.

The bey imposed higher taxes to pay back the French banks. This was too much of a burden for the still poor population to bear, and there was widespread unrest. By 1869 Tunis was bankrupt. A financial commission was established to restore order and to reorganize Tunis's finances. The commission included British, French, and Italian representatives.

In a complicated series of negotiations, France and Great Britain reached an agreement that was announced in 1878 at the Congress of Berlin. The French were to have a free hand in Tunis, and the British could occupy the island of Cyprus. Italy—which also had aspirations for Tunis—was new, poor, and inexperienced at the diplomatic game and as a result was ignored.

In 1881 France completed the process of exerting its control over Tunis by finding a weak excuse to stage a military action. The result was a protectorate in which the bey remained ruler in name, but the senior French official in Tunis wielded the power. Under the protectorate, public order was maintained, schools and industries were developed, and Tunis's finances were stabilized. However, religious differences and a rising spirit of nationalism inspired many Tunisians to work for independence.

Rivalry over Morocco. After acquiring Algiers and Tunis, it seemed only natural to the French that they continue to expand their influence. Morocco's strategic location along the Strait of Gibraltar made it an appealing prize. Many other European countries also recognized Morocco's importance. France, Spain, Britain, Italy, and Germany all had hopes of acquiring at least some interest in Morocco.

In 1904 France took advantage of Morocco's internal instability by making agreements with Britain, Spain, and Italy. France assumed control of Morocco and promised not to hinder Britain's plans for Egypt or Italy's plans for Libya. Moreover, Spain was allowed to maintain a sphere of influence (for trading purposes) in northern Morocco. Whatever claims Germany made for involvement in North Africa were ignored.

For eight years, the French allowed Morocco's sultans to remain on the throne. The sultan who assumed the title in 1908 proved unable to balance the various factions and European influences in the country. Threatened with utter disorder, he had to resort to asking the French to rescue him. In return, they forced him to sign a treaty by which Morocco became a protectorate in 1912.

The British in Egypt

Egypt had been part of the Ottoman Empire for centuries. However, by the mid-1800s, this empire was crumbling. The Ottoman viceroy in Egypt, called the khedive (kuh·DEEV), had become nearly independent. The khedive still paid some tribute to the Ottoman sultan, but he ruled Egypt with absolute authority.

France held Tunis (now Tunisia) as a protectorate from 1881 until granting it independence in 1956. This illustration shows the French troops storming Tunis in 1881.

In 1854 a French company headed by Ferdinand de Lesseps gained a concession to build a canal through the Isthmus of Suez. The Egyptian government bought almost half of the stock in the company. Individual French citizens bought most of the remaining shares.

Isma'il, the khedive when the canal was completed in 1869, not only inherited a significant debt but was also extravagant and unwise in his own decisions about spending money. Between 1869 and 1879, he increased the foreign debt of his government by more than 2,000 percent.

One of Isma'il's attempts to avoid bankruptcy was to sell Egypt's stock in the Suez Canal. This action provided an opportunity for the British, who wanted to control the canal because it was a vital link in the trade and communication route between Great Britain and India, Australia, and New Zealand. In 1875 the British government bought the Egyptian stock and became the largest single stockholder. Because the British now owned so much of the stock and the rest was so widely scattered among private investors, the British gained virtual control of the canal.

Near the end of Isma'il's reign, an international committee had been established to manage Egypt's huge debt. Having lost favor, Isma'il was deposed in 1879. His successor was challenged by a nationalist group whose members resented increased European control. The nationalists mounted a rebellion in 1882. A British fleet bombarded Alexandria to put down the rioting. Britain then sent troops to suppress another pocket of rebellion near the Suez Canal and then to occupy Cairo. The Egyptian government remained outwardly independent during this period of British occupation, but the British actually ruled Egypt.

Anglo-Egyptian Sudan

The Sudan, a vast region of savannas south of the Sahara, stretches from the Atlantic Ocean to the Nile River valley and beyond. In the imperialistic era, the term *Sudan* also referred to a specific eastern part of this region south of Egypt. Arabs and various local groups inhabited the area, which Egypt claimed.

After Great Britain established control over Egypt in 1882, the Sudan became important to the British. Because the upper Nile flows through the Sudan, control of the region would afford a chance to build dams to store water for irrigation and to control the flow of water in the lower Nile. France also wanted the Sudan; it held possessions farther west, and it already had a toehold on the Red Sea (French Somaliland) and wanted to extend its territory inland.

In 1881 Muhammed Ahmad, proclaiming himself the Mahdi, a title meaning "expected one," became a leader of Muslims discontented with the Sudan's religious and administrative state. Revolutionary forces, inspired by the Mahdi, gained control of several major cities. In early 1885, they captured Khartoum and ruled from there until 1898. In that year, Great Britain invaded the Sudan, intending to prevent the French from gaining control. Under General Herbert Kitchener, British troops quickly and soundly defeated a large Mahdist army.

In June 1896, the French had sent an expedition to Africa under Captain Jean-Baptiste Marchand. The goal was to gain control of the upper Nile at Fashoda. Starting from the French Congo, Marchand and his small force of Senegalese soldiers made a daring, 3,000-mile journey through tropical Africa. In July 1898, Marchand reached Fashoda. British forces arrived two months later. Marchand and Kitchener waited for orders from their respective rulers, while both countries prepared for war. Recognizing that neither its army nor its navy could dominate, France yielded Fashoda to Britain.

The outcome of the **Fashoda crisis** was that France recognized the British as masters of the Sudan. In return, Britain recognized France's claims in French West Africa. Great Britain and Egypt established a condominium in the area, which became known as the Anglo-Egyptian Sudan. The arrangement was an unequal partnership, to say the least, and Britain held the upper hand in all matters.

The Italians in Tripoli

Desert covered most of Tripoli, the Barbary state to the west of Egypt. It, too, was Ottoman. Though Tripoli had little economic value, Italy pursued its imperial interests there. Italy was unable to compete with the larger European imperialist powers, so it had to settle for the crumbs, as it were, of those nations.

In 1911 Italy invaded Tripoli, claiming that some previous trade agreements had been violated. Although the local Turks showed surprisingly strong resistance, the Italians defeated them.

Italy took Tripoli as a colony and renamed it Libya. It was a profitless victory. Except for a narrow strip along the coast, the land was barren. The small population violently opposed Italian rule, and the expense of maintaining troops in Libya proved a drain on the Italian economy.

1. **Define** Fashoda crisis
2. **Locate and Explain the Significance** Algiers, Tunis, Suez Canal
3. **Understanding Ideas** How did imperialism in North Africa threaten world peace?
4. **Summarizing Ideas** Describe the French presence in North Africa.
5. **Integrating Ideas** Why did the British want to take control of Egypt and the Sudan?
6. **Interpreting Ideas** What does the statement "Italy ate the crumbs of imperialism" mean?

Section 3

European Claims in Sub-Saharan Africa

Focus Questions

- **What features of West Africa particularly appealed to French and British imperialists?**
- **What European claims were made in Central and East Africa?**
- **Why was South Africa so valuable?**
- **How did European imperialism affect Africa?**

In the 1500s and 1600s, considered to be the first great period of European colonization, several nations established trading posts on the east and west coasts of Sub-Saharan Africa. Interest in this vast portion of Africa was rekindled during the imperialism of the late 1800s.

Competition for West Africa

West Africa had been a major center of the slave trade. First the Portuguese and Dutch and later the British and French had established trading posts along the coast. When most European countries abolished the slave trade in the early 1800s, these former slaving centers turned to other types of commerce. They traded in palm oil, feathers, ivory, rubber, and other products from the interior. Eager to control this trade, Europeans began to push inland.

European countries sought to link their coastal possessions with new inland holdings. In the bulge of western Africa, the French claimed the ancient city of Timbuktu. They also increased the number of commercial settlements in the coastal areas of Senegal, French Guinea, the Ivory Coast (present-day Côte d'Ivoire), and Dahomey. By 1900 France had claimed a vast area called French West Africa. (See map on page 607.)

In many cases, the French as well as other Europeans met with fierce resistance in their drive to colonize Africa. In what is today Senegal, for example, Samory Touré fought the French on and off from 1883 until he was captured in 1898. In another instance of heroic resistance, the king of Dahomey resisted the French until 1893.

The British competed with the French throughout West Africa. They, too, sought to connect their coastal settlements by means of interior expansion. The Gold Coast (modern Ghana) particularly interested them. Moving inland from coastal bases there, the British came up against the powerful African kingdom of Ashanti. By 1901, however, Britain had annexed all the territory of Ashanti and made the Gold Coast a colony.

The British also expanded into Nigeria, a territory to the east of the Gold Coast that took its name from the Niger, one of the great rivers of Africa. Control of the Niger River ensured control of a huge region rich in resources. In 1861 the British annexed the port city of Lagos and then pushed steadily inland. The Africans resisted the British, but British military forces crushed all resistance and brought Nigeria under colonial rule.

By the early 1900s, France, Britain, Germany, Spain, and Portugal had claimed all of West Africa except Liberia. (See map on page 607.) Settled by freed slaves from the United States, Liberia had become an independent republic in 1847.

Although economically and militarily weak, Liberia maintained its independence. It no doubt would have become the protectorate of an ambitious European power if not for its special relationship to the United States. American diplomatic pressure discouraged European attempts to take over the small republic.

Competition for Central Africa

Henry Stanley's successful search for Dr. David Livingstone did much to publicize the possibilities for imperialistic development in central Africa. Stanley tried but failed to interest the British government in the vast area that he had explored. He then turned to King Leopold II of Belgium, who did want the region.

Africa in 1914

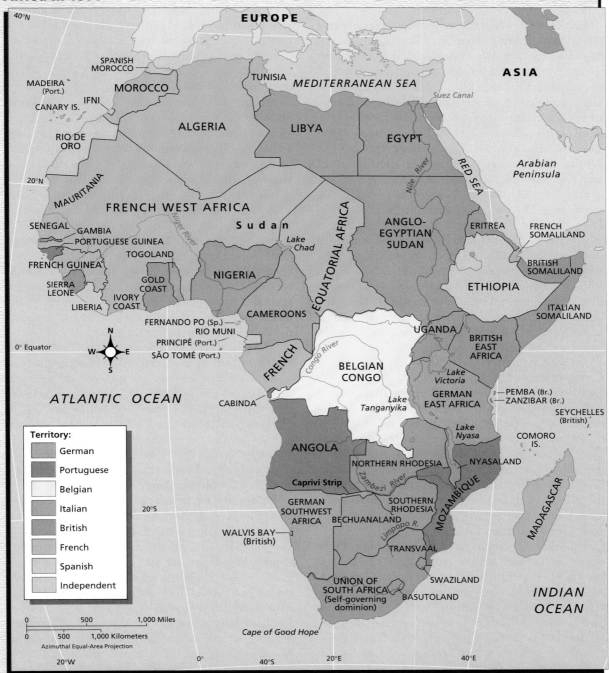

40°N

EUROPE

ASIA

SPANISH
MOROCCO

TUNISIA   MEDITERRANEAN SEA

MADEIRA
(Port.)

MOROCCO

Suez Canal

CANARY IS. IFNI

ALGERIA   LIBYA   EGYPT

RED SEA

Arabian
Peninsula

RIO DE
ORO

20°N

MAURITANIA

FRENCH WEST AFRICA

Nile River

SENEGAL   GAMBIA

Sudan

ANGLO-
EGYPTIAN
SUDAN

ERITREA   FRENCH
SOMALILAND

Niger River

PORTUGUESE GUINEA

Lake
Chad

FRENCH GUINEA   TOGOLAND

EQUATORIAL AFRICA

BRITISH
SOMALILAND

SIERRA
LEONE

GOLD
COAST

NIGERIA

ETHIOPIA

IVORY
COAST

LIBERIA

FERNANDO PO (Sp.)

CAMEROONS

ITALIAN
SOMALILAND

RIO MUNI

UGANDA

0° Equator

PRINCIPÉ (Port.)

SÃO TOMÉ (Port.)

N

W   E

S

FRENCH

Congo River

BELGIAN
CONGO

BRITISH
EAST
AFRICA

Lake
Victoria

ATLANTIC OCEAN

CABINDA

Lake
Tanganyika

GERMAN
EAST AFRICA

PEMBA (Br.)

ZANZIBAR (Br.)

SEYCHELLES
(British)

Lake
Nyasa

COMORO
IS.

Territory:

German

Portuguese

Belgian

Italian

British

French

Spanish

Independent

20°S

ANGOLA

NORTHERN RHODESIA   NYASALAND

Caprivi Strip

Zambezi River

MOZAMBIQUE

MADAGASCAR

GERMAN
SOUTHWEST
AFRICA

BECHUANALAND

SOUTHERN
RHODESIA

WALVIS BAY
(British)

Limpopo R.

TRANSVAAL

0   500   1,000 Miles

0   500   1,000 Kilometers

Azimuthal Equal-Area Projection

SWAZILAND

UNION OF
SOUTH AFRICA
(Self-governing
dominion)

BASUTOLAND

INDIAN
OCEAN

20°W

Cape of Good Hope

0°

40°S

20°E

40°E

Learning from Maps By 1914, most of the major European countries
had established colonies throughout Africa.

❓ **Region** What two African nations remained independent?

After much national and international maneuvering, Leopold, acting as a private citizen, carved out a personal empire of 900,000 square miles.

Leopold's rule of the Congo provides an example of the worst aspects of imperialism. His only interest was in extracting as much wealth as possible from the colony. Forming a corporation, he sold concessions to speculators who shared his interest in a quick profit. Their exploitation of the Congo's supply of natural rubber became an international scandal. Leopold, who never visited Africa, established trading monopolies and introduced a system of forced labor. Thousands of Africans died in Leopold's "service." Finally, faced with international criticism of conditions in the Congo, Leopold transferred ownership of his private colony to the Belgian government in 1908.

North of Leopold's Congo, Pierre de Brazza traveled to the lower Congo River in 1880 and signed treaties establishing a French protectorate. The affected region officially became the French Congo in 1891. The French extended their claims to the northeast, gaining control of a large region north of the Congo and adjoining French West Africa. Combined with the French Congo, this region formed French Equatorial Africa. (See map on page 607.)

Competition for East Africa

On the east coast of Africa, Portugal strengthened and extended its control over Mozambique. To the north of Mozambique, Great Britain and Germany competed for territorial domination. The slave trade had been only marginally active in East Africa before the late 1700s, but it began to increase after about 1780. During this period of more active slave trading, the efforts of missionaries to end the slave trade focused public attention on the area and helped justify European intervention in the area.

The European nations rapidly carved the rest of East Africa into colonies. (See map on page 607.) The only exception was the ancient empire of Ethiopia. Although Italy invaded Ethiopia, the Ethiopian army defeated the Italians at Adowa in 1896, thus ensuring their country's freedom from foreign domination.

Another factor that made it easier for Europeans to colonize East Africa was an ecological disaster in the 1890s. Domestic cattle, introduced to Africa by Europeans, carried a fatal disease known as rinderpest. Rinderpest decimated the East African herds, leading to widespread starvation. The people, thus weakened and besieged by troubles, lacked the ability to resist European colonization.

Competition for Southern Africa

European settlement in South Africa began in 1652, when Dutch settlers founded Cape Town as a resupplying station for ships sailing to the East Indies. The Dutch settlement grew into a large colony called Cape Colony. During the Napoleonic Wars of the early 1800s, the British seized Cape Colony, which then became a British possession.

As British administration became established, many people left the colony and moved to the north and east in a mass migration known as the Great Trek. These people—descendants of the original Dutch settlers—were Boers, and they spoke their own language, known as Afrikaans. In the new territories, the Boers carved out three colonies—Natal (nuh·TAHL), on the southeast coast, the Orange Free State to the west, and the Transvaal to the north.

As the Boers moved into the new territories, they came in contact with the Zulu who lived in the region. Under the great leader Shaka, the Zulu had created a thriving empire with a strong army. For years this army fought the Boers for control of the region. In 1879 the British joined in the war, defeating the Zulu and destroying their empire.

The discovery of diamonds in the Orange Free State and gold in the Transvaal soon intensified the competition in southern Africa. Germany, hoping to find rich mineral reserves, declared a protectorate over the territory of South-West Africa in 1884. In the same year, Great Britain began moving into the interior section of Africa from the south, greatly increasing its holdings. Closely associated with these territorial acquisitions was one individual, Cecil Rhodes, a British speculator.

Rhodes and his influence. Rhodes, a sickly young man who hoped that the climate would improve his health, arrived in Cape Colony in 1870. Moving to the diamond fields in the Boer-controlled Orange Free State, he soon demonstrated a talent for business and a genius for organization. Within 20 years of his arrival, he completely controlled South African diamond production.

Rhodes later organized the colonization of a huge territory farther north. This territory was named Rhodesia after him. Throughout his career, Rhodes displayed creative ideas with regard to both politics and business. One of his greatest hopes was to see British possessions extending from the Cape Colony in the southern part of Africa to Cairo in the north.

In 1895 a colleague of Rhodes tried to topple the Transvaal government, which had resisted European

The Berlin Conference: Making a New Map of Africa

In the mid-1800s, much of the continent of Africa was still completely unknown to Europeans. Despite a history of European contact and involvement in Africa that dated back to Roman times and even earlier, European maps showed the interior of Africa as a blank space—unexplored territory. Trading posts and a few colonies located on the coasts were the extent of Europe's presence in Africa.

However, before the end of the century Europeans had explored and then conquered nearly the entire continent. This remarkable rush to seize territory is often called "The Scramble for Africa." No single event exemplifies this phenomenon as well as the Berlin Conference in 1884.

Otto von Bismarck, the German imperial chancellor, called the Berlin Conference at a time of tension between the nations that were vying for African territory: Portugal, France, Great Britain, Spain, Italy, Belgium, and Germany. Representatives of each of these powers attended the conference, along with delegates from the United States and the Ottoman Empire. No African leaders were invited to attend this conference.

The purpose of the conference was to resolve potential conflicts over colonies. As European leaders' claims to pieces of territories began to overlap, it seemed very possible that the scramble might set off a war in Europe. The conference was called to head off such a war by establishing boundaries that all European powers would respect.

At the time of the Berlin Conference, many Africans were still living under their own governments. With absolutely no regard for those local boundaries, the representatives carved up the continent among themselves. These representatives argued over, drew, erased, and redrew the boundary lines of their new

Victoria Falls, on the Zambia-Zimbabwe border

colonies. Huge parcels of land changed hands, sometimes simply at the whim of one representative. Often people from the same ethnic group found themselves separated and ruled by different colonial powers. Conversely, the new boundaries frequently threw together ethnic groups hostile to one another. Also, in drawing boundary lines the representatives ignored such natural boundaries as rivers and mountain ranges. Ignorant of the continent's geography, the representatives had no idea of the location of such natural dividing lines. (See photo above.)

The decisions made at the Berlin Conference still plague Africa today. Much of Africa secured independence after 1950, but the colonial boundaries established by the Berlin Conference had acquired the legitimacy of time. Even though many of these boundaries were arbitrary and a possible cause of future trouble, the leaders of the new African nations feared that drawing new boundaries might result in complete chaos. Yet at the same time these leaders found it almost impossible to make the old boundary lines function. For many Africans, loyalty to their ethnic group still had far greater meaning than national identity. Conflicting loyalties had disastrous consequences in many countries.

attempts to establish mining operations. The attempt failed, but Great Britain's apparent support of it made relations between the Boers and the British openly hostile. In 1899 war broke out. After three years of costly fighting, the British defeated the Boers and imposed a settlement that favored mining interests.

To ensure Boer support of the peace, the British allowed the Boers to continue using the Afrikaans language in their schools and courts. The British also provided funds for Boers—though not for Africans—to rebuild their destroyed farms. In 1910 a federal constitution united the Cape Colony, Natal, the Transvaal, and the Orange Free State into the Union of South Africa, which was a British dominion. The constitution made it virtually impossible for nonwhites to be given voting rights. The settlement of the South African War, or Boer War, thus laid the basis for the later development of a system of complete racial segregation.

European Government in Africa

The European powers that established empires in Africa generally used one of two forms of government in their territories. France, Germany, Belgium, and Portugal practiced direct rule. Great Britain practiced indirect rule.

The British fought the Boers for three years to gain control of South Africa. This photo shows Boer guerrillas in South Africa.

Direct rule. In colonies with direct rule, the imperial power controlled all levels of government and appointed its own officials to govern the colonies. The Europeans based this type of government on their belief that the Africans were not capable of ruling themselves. As a result of this belief, the Europeans practiced what we refer to as **paternalism**, the system of governing colonies in much the same way that parents guide their children.

European nations practiced various forms of direct rule. For example, the French encouraged **assimilation**, in which the people of the colonies abandoned their local cultures and adopted all aspects of French culture.

Indirect rule. Under the British system of indirect rule, a British governor and a council of advisers made colonial laws, but local rulers exerted some authority. The British chose indirect rule largely because they lacked enough workers to staff all the governments of the vast British Empire, which by then covered almost one fourth of the earth's land surface.

Costs and Benefits of Imperialism

Imperialism was a harsh experience for the entire continent of Africa. The costs and benefits resulting from European expansion were unevenly distributed across the continent.

Some individuals and groups in African society did benefit. New agricultural techniques were introduced in many areas. For example, in Uganda, British support of cotton cultivation gave rise to a relatively stable economy in which cotton still plays an important part. Europeans introduced medicines to help people live longer and healthier lives. They also constructed roads and railroads. These means of transportation were used mostly to connect areas of European settlement with the coast and to move goods to and from European industries. They also served to make African products available for the world market. In the long run, however, the world did not clamor for African products, much to the disappointment of the imperialists.

In spite of decades of intervention or control, most Africans would not and did not adopt European customs or culture. Perhaps this is not so surprising because the European industries and institutions were established largely for the benefit of the Europeans, not for the Africans, who were deemed unworthy of the same treatment as Europeans. The majority of Africans continued to live largely by traditional means, as subsistence farmers or migrant workers.

Building History Study Skills

READ
WRITE
INTERPRET
CONNECT
THINK

Thinking About History: Determining Relevancy

As you do historical research, you often must sift through mountains of information to find what you need. As you do so, you need to be able to distinguish between relevant and irrelevant information. Relevant information includes facts that apply to your topic. For example, if you are researching how the Japanese resisted European imperialism, the shogun's response to Commodore Perry's ultimatum would be relevant. A description of the beauty of Kyoto, which is the emperor's residence, would not be relevant information because it would not help you explain the resistance to imperialism.

How to Determine Relevancy

To determine relevancy, follow these steps.

1. State the topic that you are researching.
2. Identify categories that will help you organize the research topic.
3. Look for definitions, descriptions, details, and evidence on your topic.
4. Examine each piece of information and relate it to the topic. Use the categories you have devised, and discard all information that has no bearing on them.

Developing the Skill

If you were researching the impact that imperialism had on European economies, you might use two categories: costs and benefits. Read the following two selections and determine whether either would be relevant in your research. The first excerpt is from a speech by the British member of parliament Joseph Chamberlain. The second is from the writings of Lord Frederick Lugard, a longtime British colonial administrator.

[1] "We have suffered much in this country from depression of trade. We know how many of our fellow-subjects are at this moment unemployed. Is there any man in his senses who believes that the crowded population of these islands [the British Isles] could exist for a single day if we were to cut adrift from us the great dependencies which now look to us for protection and assistance, and which are the natural markets for our trade?...If tomorrow it were possible, as some people apparently desire, to reduce by a stroke of the pen the British Empire to the dimensions of the United Kingdom, half at least of our population would be starved."

[2] "By railways and roads, by reclamation of swamps and irrigation of deserts, and by a system of fair trade and competition, we have added to the prosperity and wealth of these lands [in Africa], and checked famine and disease...We are endeavouring to teach the native races to conduct their own affairs with justice and humanity, and to educate them alike in letters and in industry."

Political cartoon of Cecil Rhodes astride Africa

In the first excerpt, Chamberlain discusses one of the major benefits of imperialism. It provides trade outlets and also helps feed the many people of Great Britain. It would be relevant in your research of the costs and benefits of imperialism.

The second excerpt, however, would not be relevant to your topic. This excerpt describes the author's view of the benefits of imperialism for the *colonized* nation, not for the *imperial* nation which you are researching.

Practicing the Skill

Read the Rudyard Kipling excerpt on page 602. Then determine whether it would provide relevant information about the costs and benefits of imperialism.

To apply this skill, see Applying History Study Skills on page 627.

1. **Define** paternalism, assimilation
2. **Identify** Henry Stanley, Leopold II, Cecil Rhodes
3. **Summarizing Ideas** Describe the differing European interests in West, Central, and East Africa.
4. **Determining Cause and Effect (a)** What were the reasons for the competition between the British and Boer? **(b)** What were the results of the Boer War?
5. **Evaluating Ideas** What were some of the costs and benefits of imperialism in Africa?

Section 4

European Expansion in South and East Asia

Focus Questions

- **How did Britain's rule of India contribute to the growth of Indian nationalism?**
- **What happened in Japan under the Meiji government, and how did Japan respond to Western imperialism?**
- **Why did Western nations compete for lands in East Asia, and what lands did they claim as their own?**

The strong forces of imperialism that swept Africa in the 1800s also brought important and fateful changes to South and East Asia. In these regions, however, the changes were not as abrupt as they were in so many parts of Africa.

British Imperialism in India

As you read earlier, the British government ruled India directly after the Sepoy Rebellion in 1857. However, British control of the subcontinent remained essentially the same as it had been under the British East India Company. British India still made up about three fifths of the subcontinent. The rest consisted of more than 550 states, headed by local princes. The British government, through its viceroy, controlled the local princes' rights to make treaties and declare war, either with foreign countries or with one another. Great Britain

also regulated Indian internal affairs when it seemed necessary.

To control both British India and Indian states, the British government used the old Roman method of divide and rule. It granted favors to those princes who cooperated with British rule and dealt harshly with those who did not. It treated Hindus and Muslims equally but did little to ease religious hatred between them.

The British were interested chiefly in profitable trade in India. To achieve it, they maintained public order by ending the many local wars and massacres. They set up an efficient governmental administration that built roads, bridges, railroads, factories, hospitals, and schools. They tried to improve agricultural methods, public health, and sanitation.

Many of these improvements helped the Indians, but other effects of British rule were harmful. The Indian handicraft industry almost disappeared. British cotton mills made cloth so cheaply that it could be transported to India and sold for less than handwoven Indian products. Local artisans thus found themselves without a means of support.

During the late 1800s and early 1900s, British rule in India had created a situation in which the peoples of two very different cultures lived side by side with almost no contact. The British had imposed themselves above Indian society as a superior race, a sort of supercaste. The British formed exclusive social circles, open to any European but closed to any Indian, no matter how distinguished. For generations Indians were treated with contempt regardless of their social status, education, or abilities.

The Rise of Indian Nationalism

Although the British did not mingle socially with the Indians, Western civilization had a powerful impact on India. For one thing, it led to a serious conflict of values.

Both Hinduism and Islam stressed age-old customs and respect for tradition. Western culture, on the other hand, emphasized material progress and political change. Indians regarded Europeans as materialists who cared little for the higher values of mind, soul, and spirit. To many Indians, it was impossible to separate religious values and ideas from other parts of their lives. Their religion dictated how they behaved in public, how they conducted business, and so on. The Europeans' ability to separate religion from other aspects of their lives was incomprehensible to traditional Hindus and Muslims.

British education had a profound effect on India. Under the guidance of Viceroy Curzon, who assumed his post in 1899, the British administration actively pursued widespread establishment of schools of all levels. British-provided education was usually in English to further westernize these subjects of the British Crown. In the schools, students also learned about Western ideas such as democracy. Many Indians also came to learn about and believe in the ideas of socialism.

A movement for Indian self-rule began in the late 1800s. Not all Indian nationalists supported the same approach. Some, especially those who had been educated in British schools and universities, wanted to advance toward independence gradually and by democratic methods. They also wanted to keep certain aspects of Western culture and industry that they thought could benefit India. The Indian National Congress, a political party founded in 1885, advocated this moderate approach.

Other people wanted to break all ties with Great Britain in an effort to sweep away all Western influence. The Hindus, particularly, wished to revolt not only against Western culture but also against Islam. The views of this second group alarmed Indian Muslims, who were a minority in the land. British rule protected them from violence, and they feared that if British rule were removed, their future might be in danger. The Muslims were therefore much less enthusiastic about driving out the British than were the Hindus. In 1906 Muslims formed the **Muslim League** to protect their interests. The independence movement in India gathered strength very slowly, and the British kept the country under a tight rein.

The Meiji Restoration in Japan

While imperialism remained firmly entrenched in India, it took a different course in Japan. Although European influence in Japan became strong after the overthrow of the Tokugawa shogunate in 1868, Europeans did not dominate Japan as they did India. Rather, the Japanese under the rule of the Meiji emperor controlled their own affairs and began to industrialize their country.

Real power in the Meiji government was exercised not by the emperor but by samurai from several domains in western Japan. These samurai had grown impatient under the strict, hereditary system of the Tokugawa period, in which birth, not ability, counted. They persuaded the emperor that Japan must take the road toward modernization. Even though the samurai were members of Japan's traditional ruling class, they advocated and carried out radical changes in Japan.

This cartoon shows the residents of Bombay welcoming Prince Edward during his 1875 tour of India. When his mother, Queen Victoria, died in 1901, he became Edward VII, king of Great Britain and emperor of India.

The Meiji Restoration, as the change in 1868 from the Tokugawa shogunate to imperial government is called, was really a social, political, and economic revolution. It corresponded in scope to the revolutions in Western nations during the 1700s.

The old system of social classes was abolished, and all Japanese became free to choose the occupations they wished to pursue. The government established universal compulsory education and almost wiped out illiteracy.

A centralized government replaced the political system of the Tokugawa period. The city of Edo, renamed Tokyo, became the new imperial capital, and the domains came under the control of government officials. The central government encouraged feelings of nationalism and unity by forming a national army and adopting universal conscription.

During the 1880s, an appointed commission wrote a constitution, which the emperor accepted and proclaimed in 1889. The constitution had two major purposes: to impress Western governments with Japan's progress and to provide the Japanese people with a voice, though limited, in national affairs.

The leaders of the Meiji government were monarchists who did not believe in democracy. However, they knew from their study of Western cultures that political absolutism led to popular discontent. Although the new constitution gave the emperor supreme power, he did not exercise it. The constitution established a two-house national assembly, called the Diet, one house of which was elected. Initially, only those Japanese who owned a substantial amount of property had the right to vote, and the elected house of the Diet had very limited powers. In practice, a small group of leaders, acting in the name of the emperor, held the real power in Japan.

The new constitution and the Diet satisfied most Japanese. The government, for its part, was able to concentrate its energies and resources on promoting industrialization and economic development. Japanese leaders believed that their nation had to either catch up with Western nations in technology and wealth or face the humiliation of foreign domination.

Industrialization

Fortunately, Japan was in a position to make rapid economic and industrial progress. Its traditional agricultural economy had created surpluses that could be used to finance industrialization. The government also used factory machinery purchased from several Western countries and enacted a new commercial policy to encourage private investment in industrial enterprises.

By 1900 Japan had acquired the foundations of an industrial economy. Railroads, the telegraph, and telephones linked Japanese cities. Light manufacturing, especially of textiles, was well developed, and Japan had begun exporting machine-made cotton cloth and silk to other countries. The money that these exports earned helped pay for imports of industrial raw materials such as iron ore and petroleum, of which Japan had only limited quantities. The Japanese then used these raw materials in steel production and shipbuilding. Although Japan's economy remained smaller and weaker than that of Western nations, the gap between these nations gradually narrowed as Japan became the first country in Asia to industrialize.

Nevertheless, Japan's leaders continued to feel threatened by imperialist expansion in Asia. This fear motivated the Japanese to embark on a course of imperialist expansion themselves.

The Sino-Japanese War

The territory that most interested Japan was the nearby Korean Peninsula, long a dependency of China. Korean authorities had to refer all matters involving foreign relations to the Chinese emperor. No foreigners were allowed into the country. However, Russia, France, and the United States were all interested in gaining trading privileges there. Fearing that a Western-controlled Korea might threaten its safety, Japan began to demand privileges on the Korean peninsula.

Japan maintained that Korea was independent, while China still claimed Korea as a dependency. In 1876, out of this confusion, Japan secured a treaty that opened three Korean ports to Japanese trade. China then allowed the Koreans to sign treaties of trade and friendship with five Western nations.

In 1894 a rebellion calling for popular liberation broke out in Korea. Both Japan and China sent armed forces to end it. It was a turbulent situation that exploded into the brief Sino-Japanese War, in which Japan defeated China. (*Sino* means "Chinese.")

In addition to trade privileges, the Japanese wanted territory. The **Treaty of Shimonoseki** in 1895 forced China to recognize the complete independence of Korea. China also had to give to Japan the island of Formosa and the nearby islands, the Pescadores. In another provision, China gave Japan the strategic Liaodong Peninsula on the southern coast of Manchuria. At the tip of the Liaodong Peninsula,

This was the scene at Yokohama in 1871 as Prince Iwakura left on Japan's foreign mission to learn about Western countries.

which juts into the Yellow Sea, lay the excellent harbor of Port Arthur. (See map on page 616.) Finally, China also had to pay Japan an indemnity equivalent to $150 million.

Russia and the East Asian Mainland

The Treaty of Shimonoseki displeased the Russians, who had long yearned to expand to the south. Russia had wanted to build a railroad across Manchuria and the Liaodong Peninsula to Port Arthur.

With these plans in the process of development, Russia was more than willing to help China keep Japan away from the Asian mainland. France, which had recently signed an alliance with Russia, was also willing to assist its ally. Germany, which was eager to improve its relationship with Russia, also offered its services. Thus, in a joint note, Russia, France, and Germany advised the Japanese government to withdraw from the Liaodong Peninsula.

The Japanese were furious, but they were not able to resist such powerful forces. They gave the Liaodong Peninsula back to China in return for a larger indemnity. The peninsula was regained by Japan in 1905 and annexed in 1910.

The Price of European Aid

China had to pay a price for the help it received. Its indebtedness to foreign powers led to a flurry of foreign demands. France demanded and received special trading privileges and the right to develop mineral resources in southern China. It also leased the territory of Kwangchowan and acquired permission to build a railroad linking southern China with the French protectorate in Indochina.

Germany leased Qingdao (CHING·DOW) port and surrounding territory on the south shore of the Shandong Peninsula. Germany also received mining rights and permission to build a railway in Shandong.

Great Britain would not be left out. It negotiated for more trading privileges in the Chang Jiang valley and the right to build a naval base at Weihai on the north shore of the Shandong Peninsula to balance the German base at Qingdao.

Russia demanded and received the right to build a railroad across Manchuria—to be called the **Chinese Eastern Railway**. It also received permission to police the Manchurian route as well as certain other extraterritorial privileges.

These privileges greatly angered the Japanese. Western powers had forced them to give up the spoils of their victory. Both China and Japan recalled these events during the next 50 years as they strove for power in East Asia.

Section 4 Review

1. **Define** Muslim League, Treaty of Shimonoseki, Chinese Eastern Railway
2. **Locate and Explain the Significance** Formosa, Liaodong Peninsula
3. **Evaluating Ideas** What were the British methods of government and control in India, and how did they affect the rise of nationalism?
4. **Analyzing Ideas (a)** What governmental and social changes did the Meiji Restoration bring about? **(b)** What role did Western ideas play in these changes?
5. **Determining Cause and Effect** Describe the causes and results of the Sino-Japanese War.

Imperialism in East Asia to 1914

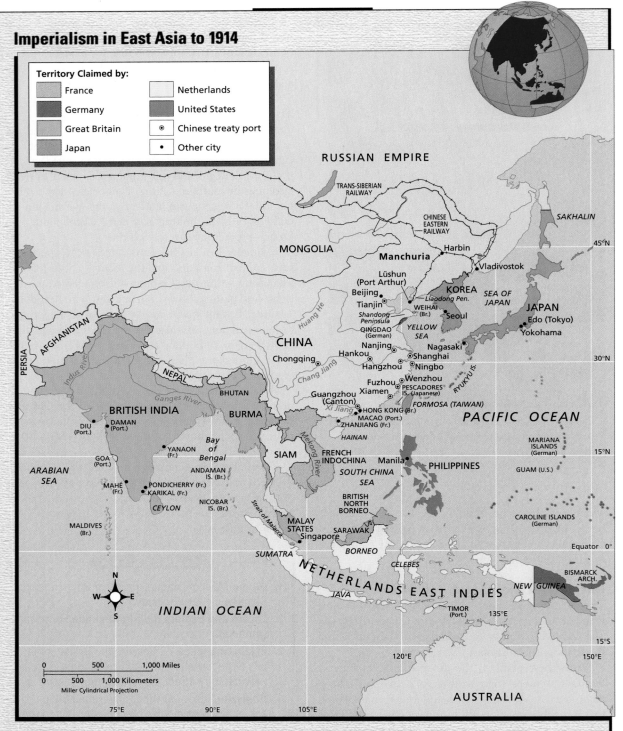

Territory Claimed by:

France	Netherlands
Germany	United States
Great Britain	⊙ Chinese treaty port
Japan	• Other city

RUSSIAN EMPIRE

TRANS-SIBERIAN RAILWAY

CHINESE EASTERN RAILWAY

SAKHALIN

45°N

MONGOLIA

Manchuria

Harbin

Vladivostok

Lüshun (Port Arthur)

Beijing

KOREA

SEA OF JAPAN

JAPAN
Edo (Tokyo)
Yokohama

Tianjin

Liaodong Pen.

WEIHAI (Br.)

Seoul

Shandong Peninsula

AFGHANISTAN

PERSIA

Huang He

CHINA

QINGDAO (German)

YELLOW SEA

Nagasaki

30°N

Chongqing

Hankou

Nanjing

Shanghai

NEPAL

Chang Jiang

Hangzhou

Ningbo

BHUTAN

Indus River

Ganges River

BRITISH INDIA

BURMA

Fuzhou

Wenzhou

PESCADORES IS. (Japanese)

RYUKYU IS.

Guangzhou (Canton)

Xiamen

Xi Jiang

HONG KONG (Br.)

FORMOSA (TAIWAN)

PACIFIC OCEAN

DIU (Port.)

DAMAN (Port.)

MACAO (Port.)

ZHANJIANG (Fr.)

YANAON (Fr.)

Bay of Bengal

ANDAMAN IS. (Br.)

HAINAN

SIAM

FRENCH INDOCHINA

Manila

MARIANA ISLANDS (German)

15°N

GOA (Port.)

ARABIAN SEA

MAHÉ (Fr.)

PONDICHERRY (Fr.)

KARIKAL (Fr.)

CEYLON

NICOBAR IS. (Br.)

Mekong River

SOUTH CHINA SEA

PHILIPPINES

GUAM (U.S.)

MALDIVES (Br.)

Strait of Malacca

BRITISH NORTH BORNEO

CAROLINE ISLANDS (German)

MALAY STATES

Singapore

SARAWAK

Equator 0°

SUMATRA

BORNEO

CELEBES

NETHERLANDS EAST INDIES

NEW GUINEA

BISMARCK ARCH.

INDIAN OCEAN

JAVA

TIMOR (Port.)

135°E

15°S

N
W E
S

0   500   1,000 Miles
0   500   1,000 Kilometers
Miller Cylindrical Projection

120°E

150°E

75°E

90°E

105°E

AUSTRALIA

Learning from Maps By 1914, much of East Asia was controlled by various foreign powers.

? Place Although the British government ruled India, which other European countries controlled Indian cities?

The Metropolitan Museum of Art. The Helena Woolworth McCann Collection. Winfield Foundation Gift, 1968. (58.52) Photograph © 1980 The Metropolitan Museum of Art

Chinese porcelain was imported to Europe where it was considered quite valuable. This punch bowl design depicts trading centers at Canton.

Foreign Influence in Southeast Asia and the Pacific

Focus Questions
- Where in Southeast Asia did each of the major imperial nations extend its influence?
- Why were European nations interested in the Pacific islands?
- Which nations ended up acquiring or controlling the Pacific islands?

The tide of imperialism did not stop in South Asia and East Asia. It affected Southeast Asia and the islands of the Pacific.

Imperialism in Southeast Asia
In the late 1400s and early 1500s, European traders explored the East Indies. In the seaports of these islands and on the nearby mainland, Portuguese and Dutch merchants enjoyed a rich and active trade until the early 1800s.

In the 1800s and early 1900s, European imperialism made its way to Southeast Asia as it did to nearby India and China. The area became an important source not only of spices but also of the world's tea. Later valuable products such as tin and oil came from this area.

British successes. It was natural that the British should take an interest in the kingdom of Burma, on the eastern border of India. By 1886 all of Burma had come under British control.

The island of Singapore, on the tip of the Malay Peninsula, guards the entrance to the Strait of Malacca—one of the most vital trade routes in the world. Britain's first recorded contact with Singapore was by a representative of the East India Company. In 1819 a company ship landed at Singapore. Informed that there were only a few residents and no Dutch among them, the company decided to purchase land for a factory site. It created a city at Singapore, which became an important naval base in the British Empire.

French gains. The eastern part of the mainland of Southeast Asia contained several small nations that struggled with internal instability and were at times also under the influence of Siam. In the late 1800s, French imperialists, by means of assertive economic measures and military intervention, laid claims to the area, and the French became the dominant power in what became known as French Indochina. The original three nations eventually regained their independence and today are the nations of Laos, Cambodia, and Vietnam.

Siam. The kingdom of Siam was better organized than were other parts of Southeast Asia. The British on the Malay Peninsula and the French in Indochina nibbled at the borders of Siam. To maintain their independence, Siamese rulers skillfully maneuvered British interests against French interests. The British and French finally agreed that an independent Siam was a useful buffer state between their possessions. A buffer state, located between two hostile powers, is a small country that serves to decrease the possibility of conflict between them.

The Dutch East Indies. The Dutch East India Company, formed in 1602 to protect Dutch trading interests in the Indian Ocean, succeeded for many years.

By the late 1700s, however, it had become corrupt and inefficient. In 1799 the government of the Netherlands revoked the company's charter and took over the administration of the Netherlands East Indies. By the late 1800s, several local revolts convinced the government of the Netherlands to make basic reforms in the administration of its richest imperial possession.

Interest in the Pacific Islands

Only a few of the islands and island groups in the Pacific were economically attractive to imperialist powers. Europeans were at first interested in acquiring valuable raw materials, such as sandalwood or pearl shell, from the islands. Some of the areas had fertile soil that could support rich plantations. Other islands had minerals to be mined. Imperialism in most of the Pacific islands, however, was based on another motive—the need for coaling stations and naval bases. Because the imperialist powers competed in the Pacific, as elsewhere, none was willing to trust the others for its coal supplies and naval repairs. Each of the powers therefore sought out its own Pacific islands. By 1900 imperialist nations controlled almost all the islands. (See map on page 619.)

The Samoa Islands. In the late 1800s, a serious rivalry over territory in the Pacific involved the Samoa Islands. Here the United States played a major role. American interests in the area had been developing for a number of years. During the 1870s Americans gained the right to use the harbor city of Pago Pago (PAHNG·oh PAHNG·oh) on the island of Tutuila (too·too·WEE·luh), as a trading post, coaling station, and naval base. Great Britain and Germany secured similar rights in other parts of the Samoa Islands.

For a number of years, rivalry among the three foreign nations for control of the Samoa Islands simmered until they teetered on the brink of war. To prevent further trouble, the three nations set up a system of joint control, but it was not to last.

In 1899 the rivals signed a treaty ending the dispute. Great Britain, preoccupied with the South African War, withdrew its interests. The United States established firm control over Tutuila and six other small islands whose combined area was only about 75 square miles. Together these possessions became known as American Samoa. Germany gained control of all the other islands in the Samoan group, which eventually became known as Western Samoa.

The Hawaiian Islands. Far more important to the United States than its Samoan possessions were the Hawaiian Islands. (See map on page 619.) This group of islands had fertile soil, good rainfall, and a mild climate. Foreign traders and missionaries, including Americans, had begun settling there in the 1820s but interfered little with the government and economy of the local people. After 1865, however, businesses from the United States and other foreign nations began to develop sugarcane and pineapple plantations on the islands.

The queen of the Hawaiian Islands resented foreign influence and tried to overturn or bring an end to treaties created by the previous two rulers. Her antiforeign feelings were in turn resented by the resident foreign business leaders. A combination of influential businessmen and their political supporters brought an end to the queen's reign. After several years of turmoil, the queen officially abdicated in 1895 to avoid bloodshed between her supporters and her opponents. The United States annexed the islands in 1898.

The Philippines, Guam, and Wake Island. Since the 1500s and 1600s, the Philippine Islands and Guam in the western Pacific Ocean had been parts of Spain's far-flung empire. In 1898 the United States and Spain went to war. Most of the fighting occurred in Cuba and Puerto Rico, but the first United States military action against Spain took place in the Pacific.

When war erupted, United States naval forces were ordered into action. A squadron of six ships under the command of Commodore George Dewey steamed from the British port of Hong Kong and moved quickly into the harbor of Manila, the capital of the Philippine Islands. Early on the morning of May 1, Dewey's forces attacked the decrepit Spanish fleet. By noon the Spanish ships were completely destroyed, and the city of Manila was at Dewey's mercy. Not a single American sailor was killed in the battle. Within a few months, American land forces, supported by local revolutionaries, defeated the Spanish forces in Manila. With the collapse of

What If?

Imperialism
In the late 1800s and early 1900s, European countries carved out empires in Africa, Asia, and the Pacific. How do you think world history would have been different if the Europeans had not established these empires?

Spanish power at Manila, the entire Philippine Islands came under the control of the United States. At about this time, American forces also occupied Guam, which was a small Spanish-held island east of the Philippines.

Some Filipinos welcomed the Americans and even fought with them against the Spaniards. Most of the local population had suffered under Spanish rule for centuries. Yet many saw little advantage in changing one foreign master for another. Led by Emilio Aguinaldo, Filipino locals fought for independence for three years against American troops. The Filipinos used guerrilla warfare against the better-equipped United States army but were finally defeated in 1901.

Besides acquiring the Philippine Islands and Guam, the United States also took possession of Wake Island in the central Pacific. Thus the United States acquired another link in a chain of island possessions running from its west coast across the vast distances of the Pacific Ocean all the way to East Asia.

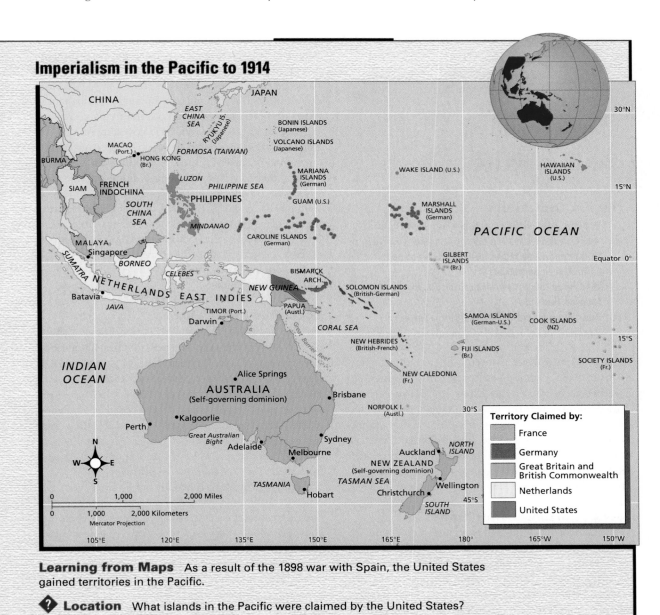

Imperialism in the Pacific to 1914

Territory Claimed by:
- France
- Germany
- Great Britain and British Commonwealth
- Netherlands
- United States

Learning from Maps As a result of the 1898 war with Spain, the United States gained territories in the Pacific.

? Location What islands in the Pacific were claimed by the United States?

1. **Identify** Emilio Aguinaldo
2. **Locate and Explain the Significance** Singapore, Samoan Islands
3. **Analyzing Maps** Using the map on page 619, list the Southeast Asian possessions that colonial powers had acquired by 1914.
4. **Analyzing Ideas** Why were the Pacific islands important possessions?
5. **Summarizing Ideas** Which Pacific islands did the United States control?

Section 6

Imperialism in Latin America

Focus Questions

- **In what ways was imperialism different in Latin America than it was in other parts of the world?**
- **What conditions led to foreign intervention in Latin American nations?**
- **What was the Roosevelt Corollary to the Monroe Doctrine?**
- **How and why did the United States further intervene in Latin America through the 1930s?**

Imperialism in Latin America differed from imperialism in the Pacific. Although Latin American countries were weak, the Monroe Doctrine of the United States, Great Britain's commercial interests and powerful navy, and European attention to other matters prevented attempts to recolonize Latin America. Nevertheless, economic interference in Latin American nations became common as they increasingly attracted European and American investments.

New Opportunities for Trade

As the pace of the Industrial Revolution quickened in Europe and the United States, more agricultural products and raw materials came from Latin American countries. Americans, for example, acquired a taste for bananas, which were imported largely from Central America, and for coffee, which came mostly from Brazil. They bought sugar which was made from sugarcane grown in Cuba, and they smoked cigars made from Cuban tobacco.

The British purchased large quantities of wool, which their factories needed, as well as wheat, beef, and mutton from Argentina and Uruguay. Chile mined nitrates from natural deposits in its northern deserts and sold them to industrial countries for production of fertilizers and explosives. Brazil exported natural rubber from its vast Amazon forests.

Railroads were built to bring these goods to Latin American port cities. The ports were also improved to ease loading of newly perfected steamships. All these developments brought more prosperity to those countries of Latin America that had the opportunity to engage in trade. Argentina especially benefited from these developments. However, some Latin American countries, such as Bolivia and Paraguay, hardly participated in this trade at all. Ruinous internal and external military struggles and ineffective government administration and policy limited their economic growth.

As had occurred in the United States, a few of the Latin American countries—most notably Argentina, Brazil, and Uruguay—attracted a large number of immigrants from Europe. In those countries with successful export trade, industries also began to develop. Foreign investors built factories such as sugar mills to process export goods. Other new factories—textile mills, flour mills, and metalworking shops—produced goods for local markets.

Economic Imperialism

Foreign investors, particularly from Great Britain, owned many of the new railroads, ranches, plantations, and mines in Latin America. Foreign banks financed large-scale commercial agriculture. Central governments allowed foreign capital to enter their countries without much regulation in the hope that foreigners would develop the economy by establishing new businesses there. However, investors usually sent profits from these businesses and interest payments from loans back to their own countries.

Foreign banks lent funds for public improvements. Some of this money went to strengthening armies and navies, making it easier to suppress internal rebellions. However, revolutions sometimes toppled governments that had borrowed money, and new governments would refuse to pay the old debts or pay for foreign property. In addition, most of the development was concentrated in the hands of a few people in cities, so distribution of wealth was uneven, leading to further instability.

Unpaid loans led to intervention by foreign powers. European banking and business leaders persuaded their governments to pressure Latin American governments for payment. Sometimes ships and troops were sent to compel payment. For example, to secure repayment of a debt that the Mexican government under Juarez had refused to pay, France attacked Mexico, set up a government in Mexico City, and made a Habsburg prince, Maximilian, emperor from 1864 to 1867.

American Intervention

Late in the nineteenth century, as the United States became an industrial power, it began to challenge Great Britain, its main rival for dominance of the Western Hemisphere. In the early 1800s, a weak United States made no attempt to enforce the Monroe Doctrine when the offender was Great Britain. For example, the British ousted Argentina from the Falkland Islands (Islas Malvinas), near the tip of South America, in 1833. Although Argentina protested, the United States did not oppose the British action, having had its own difficulties several years before with the Argentines over detainment of shipping in the area.

In 1895, however, the United States did intervene in a dispute between Great Britain and Venezuela. Great Britain had acquired British Guiana (gee·AH·nuh), on the northern coast of South America early in the 1800s. On a number of occasions, Great Britain had tried to extend the boundary of British Guiana westward into territory claimed by Venezuela. The discovery of gold in the disputed area made the crisis more urgent.

Great Britain refused Venezuela's requests to submit the border dispute to arbitration—negotiation for a settlement of the dispute by a party agreed upon by all sides. Venezuela appealed for American help, and President Grover Cleveland pressed Britain. Finally, preoccupied with the South African War, Great Britain submitted the dispute to arbitration for settlement. The United States had successfully championed the cause of a weak Latin American nation against powerful European interests. Perhaps, however, the United States had its own motives for helping Venezuela—the gold in the region was now more accessible to American investors.

The Spanish-American War

In 1898 the United States became even more deeply involved in Latin American affairs. Its involvement grew out of disputes with Spain.

Many railroads in Latin America were funded by Britain and the United States. This railroad runs through a banana plantation in Costa Rica.

The main cause of tension between Spain and the United States was Cuba, a Spanish colony in the Caribbean. (See map on page 624.) For many years, Cubans had been unhappy under Spanish rule. Nationalists, such as the poet-lawyer José Martí, attempted to overthrow the government in the Ten Years' War (1868–1878). However, this military stalemate, and a later failed rebellion in 1895—in which Martí was killed—elevated tension to a high level. The unrest alarmed Americans who had growing investments in Cuba.

Concern for American property was only one reason for tension between the United States and Spain. Many Americans felt sympathy toward Cuba's desire for independence. Anti-Spanish speeches and writings by Cubans who lived in the United States and sensational stories in American newspapers of Spanish atrocities in Cuba stirred hostile feelings.

Anger boiled in 1898 when an American battleship, the *Maine*, exploded in Havana harbor, killing 260 Americans. The *Maine* had been sent to Cuba to protect American citizens and their property. No one knew the cause of the explosion, but many in the United States assumed that Spaniards were to blame. American newspapers played on this assumption, encouraging rising popular sentiment in the United States for war with Spain.

Spain was willing to make concessions to avoid war, but it would not withdraw from Cuba or grant it independence. President McKinley, like his predecessor Cleveland, did not want war. American leaders felt unable to resist mounting popular demand, however, and declared war in April 1898. To pacify members who opposed growing American imperialism, Congress declared that the United States was fighting only on behalf of Cuban independence and had no intention of taking the island for itself.

The war, which had begun with the defeat of the Spanish in the Philippines (see pages 618–619), was a lopsided victory for the United States. In Cuba, American troops, including Theodore Roosevelt and his Rough Riders, landed east of Santiago in June. With Cuban help, American troops pushed to the city. Trying to flee Santiago Harbor, Spanish ships came under heavy fire. All ships were damaged or set ablaze and run aground. After these defeats, Spain sought peace. The Treaty of Paris was signed in December 1898.

By the terms of the peace treaty, Spain surrendered its claim to Cuba. It also ceded its colony Puerto Rico in the Caribbean and the Pacific island of Guam to the United States. In addition, Spain sold the Philippines to the United States for $20 million.

Following the war, United States troops occupied Cuba. The American military disbanded the Cuban army and at first sought to keep Cubans from governing, but it also established schools, built roads, provided sanitation, and worked to wipe out yellow fever. Finally, the United States recognized Cuba's independence, and an elected government led by President Tomás Estrada Palma took office in 1902. Although the United States permitted a Cuban assembly to draw up a constitution, it insisted that the Cuban constitution include the so-called **Platt Amendment**. This amendment forbade any transfer of land except to the United States and gave the United States the right to intervene in Cuba whenever it thought orderly government was endangered. The United States also insisted on having a permanent naval base in Cuba at Guantánamo Bay.

The Panama Canal

In addition to governing its new and far-flung possessions, the United States suddenly had to prepare to defend them. An example of the problem of defense occurred during the Spanish-American War.

Before the war, the American battleship *Oregon* had been stationed on the Pacific coast of the United States. When war became likely, the *Oregon* was summoned to the Caribbean Sea. The battleship had to race around the entire South American continent, a distance of almost 13,000 miles, to reach the Caribbean. The United States realized that it would either have to build two complete navies or find an easier and quicker way to move warships between the Atlantic and Pacific Oceans.

A canal across the Isthmus of Panama had long been considered. The French company that built the Suez Canal had tried unsuccessfully to build a canal across Panama. In the late 1800s, the United States began negotiating for permission and a right-of-way to build a canal. It asked Colombia for a lease to a strip of land across the Isthmus of Panama, then a Colombian province. (See map on page 624.)

Theodore Roosevelt and his regiment of cavalry volunteers known as the Rough Riders fought against the Spanish in Cuba.

After negotiations the Colombian senate rejected the request, a move that angered people in the United States and some in the province of Panama who wanted the canal because it would create great benefits for them. When negotiations seemingly broke down, some Panamanian business leaders and American residents of Panama proclaimed a revolution to gain independence from Colombia.

American warships stationed at Panama prevented Colombian troops from moving in reinforcements to suppress the revolt. The revolution succeeded, and the United States recognized the independence of Panama. In 1903 the new government gave the United States all rights necessary to build a canal across Panama.

The Panama Canal, one of the world's great engineering achievements, opened in 1914. It might have been impossible to build without newly invented power shovels and other new machines. Medical science, too, played a vital part. A Cuban doctor, Carlos Juan Finlay, discovered that mosquitoes carry yellow fever, a disease that had decimated workers attempting to build the canal. By destroying the mosquitoes, scientists controlled the spread of the disease, thus enabling construction crews to work in the Panamanian jungles.

The new canal shortened the sea route from New York to San Francisco by about 8,000 miles. Fleets in the Atlantic and Pacific Oceans could be shifted quickly. Merchant ships of all nations paid a toll to use the canal, but the vastly shortened route saved time and operating costs.

The Panama Canal also had an important effect on the countries of Central and South America that bordered the Caribbean Sea. Formerly a poor and unsettled region in frequent chaos, Central America became a crossroads of trade.

Passing through a series of locks and lakes over a 15- to 20-hour period, ships move from the Atlantic Ocean to the Pacific Ocean through the Panama Canal.

The Roosevelt Corollary

Long before the completion of the Panama Canal, the United States recognized that any strong European power with a foothold in the Caribbean region could threaten the canal or the sea-lanes leading to it. Therefore, the United States adopted a new policy regarding foreign influence in Latin America.

In 1904 President Theodore Roosevelt extended the ideas of the Monroe Doctrine. Roosevelt said that if any situation threatened the independence of any country in the Western Hemisphere, the United States would act as an international police power to prevent a foreign country from intervening. Further, the United States guaranteed that Latin American nations would meet their international obligations. This policy became known as the **Roosevelt Corollary** to the Monroe Doctrine. It was regarded as a natural consequence of the earlier policy, and it would be called into use several times in the coming years.

Although European and American investors stood to benefit from the Roosevelt Corollary, Latin Americans were enraged at the implication that they could not manage their own affairs. Latin American nations supported a statement made by Luis Drago, foreign minister of Argentina. He vehemently denied the European or American right to use military intervention to collect foreign debts—a declaration known as the Drago Doctrine.

Further United States Expansion

Because of political disturbances and defaults on loans, the United States continued to expand its influence in Central America and the Caribbean. The United States created military governments in Nicaragua from 1912 to 1933, Haiti from 1915 to 1934, and the Dominican Republic from 1916 to 1924. Cuba once again was subjected to an occupation government from 1906 to 1909, and United States troops intervened in Cuba again in 1912.

The United States intervened in these countries for several reasons. During the early 1900s, the economies of several nations in the area almost collapsed. The United States feared that its sizeable investments would be destroyed by anarchy or that governments might fall into the hands of leaders who would refuse to pay debts owed to foreign banks. European nations might have used a refusal to pay debts as a pretext for large-scale intervention in the region.

In 1917 the United States purchased from Denmark three of the Virgin Islands east of Puerto Rico. With this purchase, the United States added another base to ensure control over the Caribbean. At the same time, Puerto Ricans became United States citizens and received the right of self-government to guarantee their loyalty in dangerous times.

Mexico's Revolution

The greatest upheaval in Latin America during the age of imperialism was the Mexican Revolution. For 35 years, one dictator, Porfirio Díaz, had dominated Mexico. He had permitted foreign companies to develop many of Mexico's natural resources and had allowed major landowners to buy much of the country's land from poor peasants. In 1910, when the aging Díaz jailed Francisco Madero, his opponent for the presidency, rebellion broke out.

Madero escaped and hoped for a general uprising that did not materialize. A guerrilla war broadened, though, and eventually put Madero in power in 1911. Counterrevolution followed, and in 1913 Victoriano Huerta, a government general, betrayed Madero and seized control of the government. Madero was taken prisoner and shot. A rebellion led by constitutionalist Venustiano Carranza against Huerta began and eventually developed into intense and prolonged civil war among various factions. Warfare dragged on for a decade and approximately 1 million lives were lost.

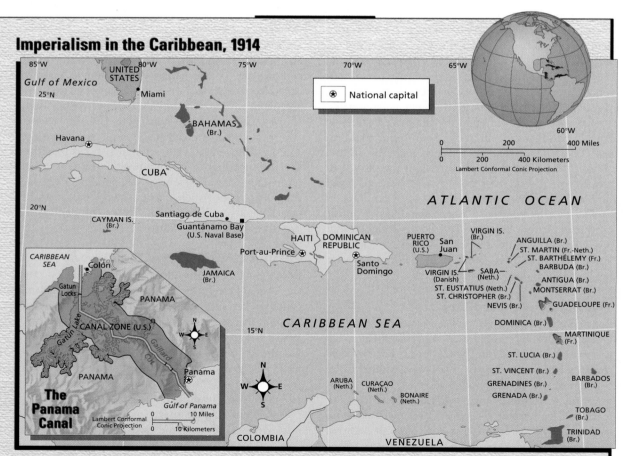

Imperialism in the Caribbean, 1914

Learning from Maps The Caribbean islands, like other countries and territories in East Asia and in the Pacific, were dominated by foreign nations.

? Movement How many miles would a person travel between Miami and San Juan?

Pancho Villa (shown seated in the Presidential Chair) and Emiliano Zapata (seated to Villa's left) were both Mexican revolutionary and guerrilla leaders.

Underlying these struggles were widespread calls for rights to the land. The peasant leader Emiliano Zapata (sah·PAH·tah) voiced these demands.

The violence and unrest frightened American investors and the thousands of Americans who lived in Mexico. President Woodrow Wilson refused to recognize Huerta's government and openly supported Carranza. The idealistic Wilson opposed the Huerta regime because it had deposed Madero, whose movement Wilson had admired. However, Wilson was at first reluctant to send troops into Mexico to protect American lives and property, deciding instead to wait and see what developed. In 1914, though, after the arrest of American soldiers, United States marines occupied the port at Veracruz, cutting off supplies and money to Huerta. Carranza's revolt succeeded, but Pancho Villa (VEE·yah), another revolutionary leader and rival, continued skirmishes with Carranza's government. Two years later, the United States sent troops into Mexico to capture Villa, who had raided a border town in New Mexico, killing several Americans. As American troops went deeper into Mexico, Carranza's government became more upset. Tensions mounted, and for a time there was a threat of war. In 1917 the United States withdrew its troops from Mexico and focused on the world war that was taking place in Europe.

Section 6 Review

1. **Define** *Maine*, Platt Amendment, Roosevelt Corollary

2. **Identify** Porfirio Díaz, Victoriano Huerta, Venustiano Carranza, Pancho Villa

3. **Locate and Explain the Significance** Puerto Rico, Panama Canal

4. **Summarizing Ideas** Describe the nature of imperialism in Latin America.

5. **Analyzing Ideas** For what reasons did foreign powers intervene in Latin American nations?

6. **Understanding Ideas (a)** Explain how the United States applied the Monroe Doctrine in the 1890s. **(b)** What was the Roosevelt Corollary to the Monroe Doctrine?

7. **Analyzing Ideas** Why did the United States intervene in several Latin American countries, including Mexico, in the early decades of the 1900s?

Chapter 23 Review

A.D. 1882 British occupy Egypt.

A.D. 1885 Indian National Congress is founded.

A.D. 1894–1895 Sino-Japanese War is fought.

A.D. 1899 Agreement over Samoa is reached.

| A.D. 1830 | A.D. 1850 | A.D. 1870 | A.D. 1880 | A.D. 1890 | A.D. 1900 |

A.D. 1830 France occupies Algiers.

A.D. 1847 Liberia becomes independent.

A.D. 1869 Suez Canal is completed.

A.D. 1881 Tunisia becomes French protectorate.

A.D. 1898
• Spanish-American War occurs.
• Fashoda incident occurs.
• United States annexes Hawaii.

Chapter Summary

The following list contains the key concepts you have learned about imperialism in the late 1800s and early 1900s.

1. In the late 1800s, European nations became involved in a new kind of empire building, imperialism, that arose from the need for self-sufficiency, new markets, and places in which an ever-growing population could settle.
2. European nations divided up almost all of Africa in the late 1800s. Communication and transportation improved, and the slave trade was abolished. For the most part, Africa and Africans were exploited, and tensions developed that would lead to further struggles later in the 1900s.
3. In India the British government assumed direct control. The British established themselves as a caste superior to the native population.
4. After a civil war in Japan, the emperor was restored to power in 1868. The Japanese then began a successful process of industrialization.

5. Although foreign powers helped China resist the Japanese, the Chinese had to make concessions for receiving this European assistance.
6. Imperialism was also a strong force in Southeast Asia and in the Pacific. By the late 1800s, the kingdom of Siam was the only area of Southeast Asia that remained free from foreign rule.
7. The Pacific islands became valuable as coaling stations and naval bases.
8. The countries of Latin America were weak and vulnerable to economic imperialism. The United States sought to extend its influence and to protect Latin America from the influence of powerful European nations.
9. The relatively easy American victory in the Spanish-American War dramatized the growing strength of the United States. In the early 1900s, the United States became increasingly involved in Latin American affairs, often invoking the Roosevelt Corollary.

Reviewing Important Terms

On a separate sheet of paper, match each of the following terms with the correct definition below.

a. paternalism
b. assimilation
c. arbitration
d. direct rule
e. protectorate
f. sphere of influence
g. buffer state
h. colony
i. concession
j. indirect rule
k. condominium

____ 1. System of colonial government in which the local ruler kept his title but officials of the foreign power actually controlled the region
____ 2. System in which the people of the colonies abandoned their local cultures and adopted all aspects of the colonial power's culture
____ 3. Settlement of a dispute by a party agreed upon by all sides
____ 4. System of colonial government in which the imperialist power controlled all levels of government and appointed its own officials to govern the colony

____ 5. Small country located between two hostile powers and whose presence decreased the possibility of conflict between them
____ 6. Region in which one foreign nation had special, sometimes exclusive, economic and political privileges that were recognized by other nations
____ 7. System of governing colonies just as parents guide their children
____ 8. A system of colonial government under which the governor and a council of advisers developed laws for the colony but local rulers were given the opportunity to exert some degree of authority
____ 9. Grant of economic rights and privileges in a particular area usually given to foreign merchants or capitalists
____ 10. System whereby two nations ruled a region as partners
____ 11. Area in which a foreign nation gained complete control over a given region and the region's local population

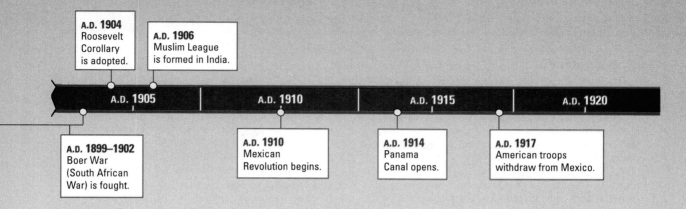

A.D. 1904
Roosevelt Corollary is adopted.

A.D. 1906
Muslim League is formed in India.

A.D. 1905

A.D. 1910

A.D. 1915

A.D. 1920

A.D. 1899–1902
Boer War (South African War) is fought.

A.D. 1910
Mexican Revolution begins.

A.D. 1914
Panama Canal opens.

A.D. 1917
American troops withdraw from Mexico.

Developing Critical Thinking Skills

1. **Classifying Ideas** Name the imperialist nation that claimed each of the following territories: (a) Libya; (b) Nigeria; (c) Algeria; (d) Gold Coast; (e) Morocco.
2. **Contrasting Ideas** (a) How does economic imperialism differ from political imperialism? (b) Why did one often lead to the other during the late 1800s?
3. **Summarizing Ideas** Tell how each of the following nations was able to preserve its independence: (a) Liberia; (b) Ethiopia; (c) Japan; (d) Siam.
4. **Contrasting Ideas** In what ways did the colonial policy of the United States differ from that of other nations?
5. **Evaluating Ideas** What were the positive and negative effects of imperialism in Africa and in India?
6. **Analyzing Primary Sources** Reread the lines from the Rudyard Kipling poem "The White Man's Burden" on page 602. (a) What does Kipling mean by the phrase "white man's burden"? (b) How does he characterize the people who must be "served"? (c) Based on what you have learned about early African, Asian, and Indian civilizations, what arguments might you use to prove Kipling wrong?

Relating Geography to History

Use the maps in the Atlas section of your textbook to answer the following questions: (a) If the Suez Canal did not exist, what would be the shortest water route between London and Bombay? (b) If the Panama Canal did not exist, what would be the shortest water route between New York and Hawaii?

Relating Past to Present

1. Using a world atlas, prepare a map showing the distribution of natural resources in Africa. Compare this map with the map on page 607. (a) What resources did each imperialist nation stand to gain through its possession of African colonies? (b) Which of these resources are most important to industrial nations today?
2. Review the reasons for the United States government's decision to build a canal across the Isthmus of Panama. Then research what has occurred with the canal during the past decade and its status today.

Applying History Study Skills

Before completing this activity, review Building History Study Skills on page 611.

Your topic is "How did the Meiji Restoration speed the industrialization of Japan?" Which of the following items would be relevant to your topic?

1. A new government was located in Tokyo.
2. A system of universal education was set up in Japan.
3. Treaties that gave foreign powers economic advantages were revised.
4. One of the first acts of the new government was to form a national army.
5. Former feudal class privileges were eliminated during the Meiji Restoration.
6. Government policy was primarily decided by a group of young samurai.

Building Your Portfolio

1. **Conducting a Debate** Work with several of your classmates to find information on European imperialism in Africa. Then prepare a debate on the following topic: Resolved: The Europeans exploited Africa and severely damaged indigenous cultures. Place your notes and other research in your portfolio.
2. **Writing a Report** Imperialism arose out of a complex mixture of political, economic, and social forces. One of these was the missionary motive. Using books in your library, prepare a report on missionary activities in colonial areas. Place the report in your portfolio.

Unit Summary

The following list contains the key concepts you have learned about the development of industrial society.

1. The Industrial Revolution—the production of goods by power-driven machinery in factories—began in Great Britain and changed the world. Both steam power and the Bessemer process were extremely important to the early Industrial Revolution.

2. Workers began to protest harsh working conditions and low wages. The first labor unions were organized to seek improvements in working conditions.

3. Socialists such as Karl Marx believed that a more fundamental transformation of politics and society was necessary and would resolve human problems.

4. In the 1800s and early 1900s new inventions, scientific discoveries, compulsory public education, and an interest in the arts improved the quality of life.

5. Many social and political reforms occurred in Great Britain and the British Empire in the 1800s and early 1900s.

6. Territorial growth and sectionalism in the United States eventually led to conflict over the issue of slavery. Eventually the North and South fought a bitter civil war.

7. France experienced political instability in the 1800s. By the early 1900s, France was a republic governed by coalitions of parties that represented monarchist, liberal, and socialist beliefs.

8. The peoples of Latin America gained their independence in the 1800s but did not unite.

9. Due to the efforts of Mazzini, Garibaldi, and Cavour, Italy was unified by 1870. In Germany, Prussia led the movement toward unification.

10. In Russia the czar maintained autocratic control, while discontent and rebellion in the Austrian Empire led to the formation of the Dual Monarchy.

11. In the late 1800s, European nations became involved in a new kind of empire building—imperialism. Europeans established colonies in Africa, Asia, and the Pacific. In most of Latin America, imperialism was economic rather than political.

Reviewing Concepts

On a separate sheet of paper, match each of the following individuals with the correct concept in column two.

a. Mazzini
b. Bismarck
c. Spencer
d. Smith
e. Marx
f. Daumier
g. Beethoven
h. Pankhurst
i. Bentham
j. Monet
k. Einstein
l. Owen
m. Kipling
n. Freud

1. romanticism in music
2. psychoanalysis
3. utilitarianism
4. relativity
5. utopian socialism
6. impressionism
7. risorgimento
8. "White Man's Burden"
9. pure communism
10. *Kulturkampf*
11. realism in art
12. social Darwinism
13. laissez–faire
14. women's suffrage

Applying Critical Thinking Skills

1. **Interpreting Ideas (a)** How did the agricultural revolution help to create a large labor force in the cities? **(b)** Why was this necessary for the development of an industrial economy?

2. **Determining Cause and Effect** What effect did the Industrial Revolution have on each of the following: **(a)** living conditions; **(b)** women's lives; **(c)** family size; **(d)** use of leisure time.

3. **Classifying Ideas** Identify the accomplishments of each of the following: **(a)** John Dalton; **(b)** Marie Curie; **(c)** Albert Einstein; **(d)** Charles Darwin; **(e)** Edward Jenner; **(f)** Louis Pasteur; **(g)** Joseph Lister; **(h)** Sigmund Freud

4. **Understanding Ideas** During the 1800s liberalism emerged as a vital force in Europe. **(a)** What were some of the political ideas associated with liberalism? **(b)** In what nations did liberalism make the greatest progress? **(c)** the least progress?

5. **Analyzing Primary Sources** Metternich once commented, "When France sneezes, all Europe catches cold." **(a)** What do you think he meant by this remark? **(b)** In light of the actions taken by Napoleon III, would you agree or disagree with Metternich? Why or why not?

6. **Evaluating Ideas (a)** What conditions encouraged the growth of nationalism in Europe? **(b)** How did the spirit of nationalism affect the development of Italy? **(c)** of Germany? **(d)** of Austria-Hungary? **(e)** of Russia?

7. **Synthesizing Ideas (a)** How did the Industrial Revolution and the rise of nationalism rekindle the desire for colonies? **(b)** What other factors promoted the renewed interest in empire building? **(c)** How did the imperialism of the late 1800s differ from the colonization of the 1500s and 1600s?

Relating Geography to History

Turn to the map of Africa on page R16. **(a)** How many independent nations exist in present-day Africa? **(b)** How does this number compare with the number of nations shown on the map on page 607? **(c)** Which imperialist power gave up the most territory? **(d)** the least territory?

Writing About History

1. Choose one of the scientists discussed in Chapter 20. Then use resources in your school or public library to find what recent discoveries have advanced the work of this scientist. Write a report detailing your findings.

2. Write a newspaper article dated October 25, 1876, that is written to convince readers that European countries should establish colonies.

Further Readings

Cary, Joyce. *Mister Johnson*. New Directions, 1989. Account of the author's experiences in the British colonial service in Nigeria from 1913–1919.

Morris, James. *Pax Britannica: The Climax of an Empire*. HarBrace, 1980. Well-written and colorful account of the British Empire at its height, at the time of Queen Victoria's Diamond Jubilee.

Mosse, W.E. *Alexander II and the Modernization of Russia*. St. Martin, 1992. Comprehensive biography of Alexander II of Russia that analyzes his impact on Russian society, particularly the peasant classes.

Sinclair, Upton. *The Jungle*. NAL-Dutton, 1960. Reprint of famous social critique of the Industrial Revolution in the United States, including graphic descriptions of abuses of workers.

Twain, Mark. *The Adventures of Huckleberry Finn*. NAL-Dutton, 1997. One of many reprintings of the famous American novel about life on the Mississippi during the early nineteenth century.

UNIT 5 CHRONOLOGY

Date	Politics	Science and Technology	Society and Culture
1750–1800	French and British anti-union laws 19* Haiti revolt 21 Commercial capitalism 19	Watt's steam engine 19 Factory system 19 Cartwright's power loom 19 Whitney's cotton gin 19 Jenner and smallpox 20	*The Wealth of Nations* 19 Beethoven 20 *An Essay on the Principle of Population* 19
1800–1850	British industrial reform 19 Latin American independence 21 Chartist movement 21 *Zollverein* 22 Laissez-faire economics 19 Continuous decline of Ottoman Empire 22 Revolutions of 1848 21, 22 Imperialism in China 23	Fulton's *Clermont* 19 Stephenson's locomotive 19 McCormick's reaper 19 Goodyear's vulcanized rubber 19 Morse's telegraph 19	Romanticism 20 Tchaikovsky, Wagner, and Verdi 20 Brothers Grimm, Goethe, Cooper, and Irving 20 *Communist Manifesto* 19 Victorian Age 21 Utopians 19
1850–1920	Third French Republic 21 Second and third reform bills in Great Britain 21 Meiji Restoration 23 European imperialism 23 U.S. Civil War 21 Establishment of Germany, Italy, and Austria-Hungary 22 Franco-Prussian War 21 Spanish-American War 23 Boer War 23 Russo-Japanese War 22	Bessemer steel process 19 Darwin 20 Pasteur 20 Transatlantic cable 19 Bell's telephone 20 Suez Canal 21, 23 Edison's light bulb 20 Wright brothers 20 Planck and Einstein 20 Panama Canal 23	Realism 20 Dickens 19 Impressionism 20 Nationalism 22, 23 Nihilism 22 Universal education 20 *Principles of Sociology* 20 *Kulturkampf* 22 Socialism 19 Social Darwinism 20 American football 20 Freud 20

*Indicates chapter in which development is discussed

Industrialism and Nationalism

CHAPTER 19

The Industrial Revolution

A revolution quite different from the Scientific Revolution of the 1500s or the political revolutions of the 1600s, 1700s, and 1800s began in Great Britain in the 1700s. This revolution—the Industrial Revolution—transformed the ways goods were produced and completely transformed the world.

The Origins of the Industrial Revolution

Before the Industrial Revolution began, Great Britain experienced a revolution in agriculture. This revolution started when British farmers began to fence off, or enclose, common lands into individual holdings efficient for large-scale farming. By the 1800s, because of improvements in agriculture, farmers needed fewer farm laborers. Many unemployed farmworkers moved to the cities, where they created a large labor force.

The Industrial Revolution began in Great Britain because of a combination of conditions. Great Britain

had what economists call the factors of production, or the basic resources necessary for industrialization: land, capital, and labor.

The cotton textile industry was the first industry in Great Britain to undergo mechanization—the use of automatic machinery to increase production. Other developments there included the steam engine, which improved transportation, and electricity, which revolutionized communications.

The Factory System

The steam engine could be used to power machinery as well as boats and trains. Steam-powered machinery made work easier to do and made it possible to produce a wide array of products in a relatively short time. Most of these goods were manufactured in factories rather than in people's homes.

Life in the mines and factories of the early Industrial Revolution was hard and monotonous, and life in the workers' homes was not much better. Working people lived in cramped and poorly maintained apartment houses called tenements. At the same time, the middle class grew and enjoyed many luxuries unknown before the industrial age. For middle-class women, this meant expanded opportunities for education and employment.

New Methods and Business Organizations

The factory system introduced a new phase in the development of capitalism—the economic system in which individuals rather than governments control the factors of production. Before the Industrial Revolution, most capitalists were merchants who bought, sold, and exchanged goods. This is called commercial capitalism. The capitalists of the Industrial Revolution, however, became more involved in producing and manufacturing goods using mechanization and industrialization. Thus the capitalism of this period is often referred to as industrial capitalism.

Industrialization changed the methods of production and depended on division of labor, interchangeable parts, and the assembly line. It gave rise to a different form of business organization—the corporation.

Living and Working Conditions

During the Enlightenment of the 1700s, a group of economists attacked the ideas of mercantilism. These economists believed that natural laws governed

James Ward painting of a farm family before the Industrial Revolution

economic life, and that any attempt to interfere with these natural economic laws was certain to bring disaster. Adam Smith best stated the views of these economists. Smith wrote that every person should be free to go into any business and to operate it for the greatest advantage. The result, Smith said, would benefit everyone. This system of complete free enterprise became known as laissez-faire.

As time went on, more people realized that things could not be left entirely alone. Many people, such as John Stuart Mill, felt that government needed to intervene to protect working children and improve housing and factory conditions. These people argued that laws regulating working conditions would not interfere with the natural workings of the economy. Over time, governments began to agree with these social reformers.

Many workers, however, felt that governments were not moving fast enough. Sometimes these workers called a strike and refused to work until demands were met.

In order to strengthen their position, workers sought ways to organize permanently into associations called unions. These organizations gradually became legal.

Calls for Reform

Some reformers of the 1800s advocated a political and economic system called socialism. In this system, the government owns the means of production and operates them for the good of all the people.

Some thinkers grew impatient with early socialism, which advocated peaceful methods to attain goals. Karl Marx, the most important of these critics, believed that all the great changes in history came from changes in economic conditions. Under capitalism, he said, labor receives only a small fraction of the wealth it creates. Most of the wealth goes to the owners in the form of profits. This unequal distribution of wealth would ultimately lead to a revolution led by the working class, or proletariat.

Marxist, or radical, socialists generally believed in the necessity of revolution to overthrow the capitalist system. They wanted to establish a system in which the government owned almost all the means of production and controlled economic planning. Two forms of Marxism that later developed are communism and democratic socialism. Marx's ideas had profound effects in Russia.

Life in the Industrial Age

In addition to changing the economy and society, the Industrial Revolution had a profound effect on science, art, music, and literature.

Advances in Technology and Communication

Beginning in the early 1800s, manufacturers increasingly applied the findings of pure science to their businesses, generating a new wave of industrial growth. Electricity, a tremendous new source of power, was developed and used to run generators, lights, the telephone, and the telegraph. The invention of the internal combustion engine led to the development of both the automobile and the airplane.

Advances in Science and Medicine

Scientists during the 1800s and early 1900s investigated the biological sciences—those dealing with living organisms. Many explored the structure of cells, the tiny units of living matter, in an attempt to better understand organic matter and thereby improve human life. Disease prevention was one of the breakthroughs accomplished by this knowledge.

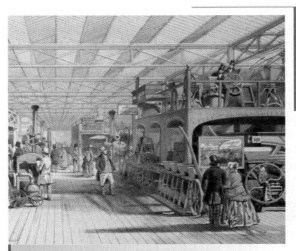

Joseph Nash lithograph of Machinery Hall in British section of Great Exhibition, 1851

The most significant developments in the physical sciences—those that deal with the properties of energy and nonliving matter—centered on atomic theory. This theory states that all matter in the universe consists of very small particles called atoms. The arrangement and structure of these atoms and their chemical combinations with each other account for the different characteristics of the materials that make up our world.

Social Sciences in the Industrial Age

During the 1800s, interest in the social sciences, those branches of knowledge that scientifically study people as members of society, grew rapidly. These subjects include political science, economics, history, archaeology, anthropology, sociology, and psychology.

Society and Culture in the Industrial Age

The progress made possible by science and technology helped produce rapid population growth in industrialized countries. As the population grew, it became more mobile. Large numbers of people emigrated to other countries. Others moved to cities to find jobs in factories. Education became more accessible to a larger part of the population. The number and availability of leisure activities grew along with the population.

Literature, Music, and Art in the Industrial Age

Literature, music, and art reflected the social and economic developments of the industrial age. Artists portrayed a sense of the rapidly changing times and the influences of scientific ideas in their works.

Many writers, musicians, and other artists of the early 1800s belonged to the artistic movement known as romanticism. Their work appealed to sentiment and imagination and dealt with the "romance" of life—life as they thought it should be rather than as it actually was. In the mid-1800s, writers and artists began to abandon romanticism and turn to realism, which emphasized the realities of everyday life.

CHAPTER 21

The Age of Reform

During the late 1800s, people throughout the world clamored for reform. These appeals, based on the philosophy of liberalism, met with varying degrees of success.

Liberal Reforms in Great Britain and Its Empire

Although Great Britain was a limited constitutional monarchy with executive power vested in a cabinet headed by the prime minister, not everyone had a voice in government. In the 1800s, however, a series of reforms extended rights to more of the population. At the same time, vital social and economic reforms took place. Two notable prime ministers—Benjamin Disraeli and William Gladstone—helped promote many of these reforms.

As Great Britain instituted social and political reforms, other changes occurred within the British Empire. The British colonies of Canada, Australia, and New Zealand won self-government. Nevertheless, each maintained close ties with Great Britain.

Expansion and Reform in the United States

The United States expanded across North America, creating a number of new states from these lands. It also acquired foreign territories, especially in the Caribbean region and the Pacific Ocean.

Despite tremendous growth, the United States had one significant problem—the unresolved issue of slavery. This issue, along with the issue of states' rights, led to a brutal civil war that raged between 1861 and 1865 and left much of the nation—particularly the South—in ruins. Nevertheless, the Union was preserved and slavery was abolished. After the Civil War, the United States experienced phenomenal growth primarily as a result of industrialization and immigration.

Revolution and Reform in France

For many years after the Congress of Vienna, the Bourbons continued to rule France. Then in 1830, a revolt forced King Charles X to abdicate. The leaders of the French revolt chose a new king—Louis Philippe, duke of Orléans, who belonged to a branch of the Bourbon family but had a record of liberal beliefs.

In 1848, however, opposition to the regime of Louis Philippe erupted in violence. A new government—a republic—under the leadership of Louis Napoleon was soon proclaimed. Louis Napoleon, however, had imperial ambitions similar to those of his illustrious uncle, Napoleon Bonaparte, and soon established the Second French Empire. The Second Empire lasted until a humiliating defeat by Prussia toppled it in 1871. France was once again proclaimed a republic.

Independence Movements in Latin America

Originally, the Spanish and Portuguese colonies in Latin America were organized primarily by mercantilist principles. Nevertheless, the revolutionary events in British North America and France in the late 1700s aroused interest, particularly among discontented creoles, as upper-class Latin Americans were known. By the mid-1800s this discontent had become full-scale revolution, and the nations of Latin America had won their independence. Leaders such as Simón Bolívar, Toussaint-Louverture, and Miguel Hidalgo y Costilla led these movements.

Portrait of Giuseppe Garibaldi in 1849

Nationalism in Europe

In the late 1800s, the political situation in Europe changed significantly. Nationalism fueled successful efforts to make Italy and Germany unified nations. Russia remained a rigid autocracy, and Austria and Hungary formed the Dual Monarchy.

The Unification of Italy

Italian nationalism became a strong force in the 1800s. Under the leadership of fiery patriots such as Giuseppe Mazzini, people in many parts of Italy clamored for national unity. Although the nationalists made some gains, they could not agree on what type of government the united Italy should have.

One group favored union under the leadership of Sardinia. There, the chief minister or premier, Count Camillo Benso di Cavour, provided the major impetus for Italian unification. Throughout the 1850s and the 1860s, Cavour used diplomacy, war, and persuasion to achieve unity. Finally, in 1870 unification was completed when the Italians claimed Rome.

The Unification of Germany

Like Italy, Germany remained fragmented in the early 1800s. But during the 1860s and 1870s, the long-delayed process of centralization and consolidation under the leadership of Prussia began to pick up speed.

Prussian prime minister Otto von Bismarck used clever diplomacy and wars against Denmark, Austria, and France to achieve unification in 1871. The new German Empire was a federal union under the leadership of the Prussian kaiser, or emperor. The federal government controlled all common matters, such as national defense, foreign affairs, and commerce.

Opposition to Bismarck

In spite of rigid control by the aristocratic Prussians, the new German federal government soon ran into problems. Dissatisfied groups formed political parties that opposed Bismarck's policies. Relations with the Roman Catholic Church proved difficult, and socialists clamored for government ownership of businesses. Despite this opposition, however, Bismarck was able to transform Germany into an industrial power.

Bismarck resigned under the reign of William II. William worked to build up Germany's military strength to an even greater degree and signed new agreements with neighboring nations.

Reform and Revolution in Russia

Ruled by autocratic czars, Russia steadfastly opposed reform. Nevertheless, liberal ideals became popular among discontented Russians—particularly among intellectuals. Faced with problems caused by liberal ideas and restless nationalities, the czars took harsh measures.

Although the late 1800s witnessed reforms such as the freeing of the serfs during the reign of Alexander II, most reform efforts failed. The czars continued to use repression to combat any erosion of their powers. Then in 1904 and 1905 the Russians fought a disastrous war with Japan. Defeat at the hands of the Japanese spurred discontented groups in the country to action and led to revolution. Although Czar Nicholas II granted a few reforms, he later reneged on his promises and resumed his policies of repression.

Unrest in Austria-Hungary

The Habsburgs in Austria also had to confront the rising tide of liberalism in the late 1800s. To combat nationalist demands in the empire, the Austrians formed the Dual Monarchy, in which both Austrians and Hungarians played a vital role in the policies and functions of government.

The formation of the Dual Monarchy failed, however, to solve the problem of nationalities. The Austrians and Hungarians dominated the population in each of their separate national states but national minorities—the Czechs, Serbs, Croats, Romanians, Poles, and Italians—existed in both Austria and Hungary. These people benefited very little from the Dual Monarchy and continued to agitate for self-government.

In addition to internal problems, the Dual Monarchy also faced problems abroad. In the late 1800s, the Habsburgs clashed with the autocratic government of the Ottoman Empire over the Balkans. Although the Ottomans had ruled the Balkans for centuries, their influence steadily weakened as the power of their empire declined. Many parts of the empire were claimed by different European powers.

CHAPTER 23

The Age of Imperialism

Beginning in about 1870, several factors rekindled interest in establishing colonies. During the next 40 years, many nations became involved in imperialism—the domination of a powerful nation over the political, economic, and cultural affairs of another nation or region.

The Roots of Imperialism

Imperialism arose out of a complex mixture of political, economic, and social forces. These forces included a desire for self-sufficiency, the need for new markets, the search for national pride and prestige, the need for places where people could settle and still remain loyal to the home country, the desire to convert people to Christianity, and the desire to transmit Western culture and ideas.

Imperialism created bitter rivalries among the imperial powers and hatred among the colonized peoples. As European powers took over more and more of the world, these rivalries and hatreds intensified.

European Claims in North Africa and the Sudan

In the 1800s most of North Africa belonged to the Ottoman Empire. Because Turkish control in many areas was weak, the Europeans scrambled to claim new colonies. The French claimed Algiers, Tunis, and Morocco. The British established dominance in Egypt and the Sudan, and the Italians took Tripoli, renaming it Libya.

European Claims in Sub-Saharan Africa

The Europeans repeated their colonial ambitions in Sub-Saharan Africa. During the empire building of the 1500s and the 1600s, the Europeans had established settlements on the coasts. In the late 1800s, however, the Europeans moved inland. By 1900 Europeans claimed all land in Sub-Saharan Africa except Liberia and Ethiopia.

Imperialism was a harsh experience for all of Africa. The costs and the benefits resulting from European expansion were unevenly distributed across the continent.

The first voyage through the Suez Canal on November 17, 1869

European Expansion in South and East Asia

The strong forces of imperialism that swept Africa in the 1800s brought important and fateful changes to South and East Asia, although the changes were not as abrupt as they were in so many parts of Africa. In India, for example, the British expanded their imperial rule.

Although European influence in Japan became strong after the overthrow of the Tokugawa shogunate in 1868, Europeans did not dominate Japan as they did India. Rather, the Japanese under the rule of the Meiji emperors managed to keep control of their own affairs and promoted industrialization. At the same time, China came increasingly under European domination, though it remained nominally independent.

Foreign Influence in Southeast Asia and the Pacific

The tide of imperialism did not stop in South and East Asia. It affected Southeast Asia and the islands of the Pacific as well. The British, French, and Dutch claimed parts of Southeast Asia and several islands in the Pacific. The United States claimed part of Samoa, Hawaii, the Philippines, Guam, and Wake Island.

Imperialism in Latin America

Imperialism in Latin America differed from that in the Pacific. The Monroe Doctrine of the United States, along with European attention to other matters, prevented Latin American nations from being recolonized. Nevertheless, the countries of Latin America experienced economic interference as they attracted European and American investment.

In two areas, Cuba and Puerto Rico, however, a foreign government took political control. These islands had been a part of the Spanish Empire for centuries. But in 1898 the United States defeated Spain in the Spanish-American War and claimed the islands. Cuba later became independent, while Puerto Rico became a commonwealth of the United States. And in Panama, the United States built a canal and controlled the territory known as the Canal Zone.

The greatest upheaval in Latin America during the age of imperialism was the Mexican Revolution. A civil war dragged on for a decade among various factions. The United States, which had sent troops in 1914, withdrew in 1917 to focus on the world war in Europe.

Synthesis Review

1. **Understanding Ideas** Why did the Industrial Revolution begin in Great Britain?
2. **Determining Cause and Effect** How did the Industrial Revolution alter population patterns?
3. **Comparing Ideas** How did political developments in France and Great Britain differ in the late 1800s?
4. **Interpreting Ideas** How did Bismarck deal with the socialists?
5. **Analyzing Ideas** What factors led Europeans to found colonies in the late 1800s?
6. **Synthesizing Ideas** Why do you think democracy triumphed in Great Britain and the United States but failed in Russia?

POLITICS AND GOVERNMENT

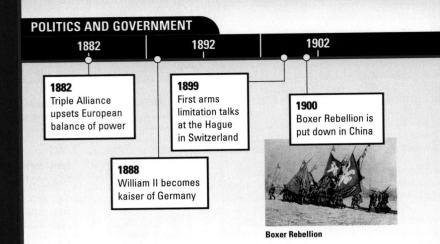

1882   1892   1902

1882
Triple Alliance upsets European balance of power

1888
William II becomes kaiser of Germany

1899
First arms limitation talks at the Hague in Switzerland

1900
Boxer Rebellion is put down in China

Boxer Rebellion

SOCIETY AND CULTURE

1882   1892   1902

1886
American Federation of Labor (AFL) founded

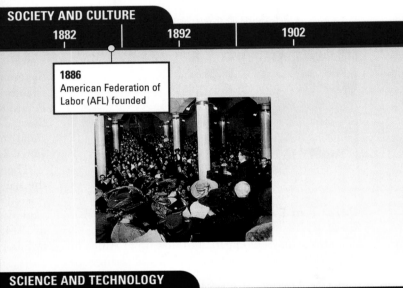

SCIENCE AND TECHNOLOGY

1882   1892   1902

1884
Modern machine gun invented

1895
Röntgen discovers X rays

1903
Marie and Pierre Curie share Nobel Prize for discovery of radioactivity

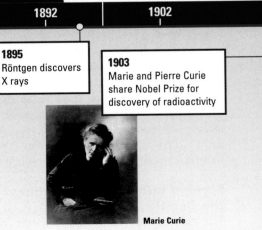

Marie Curie

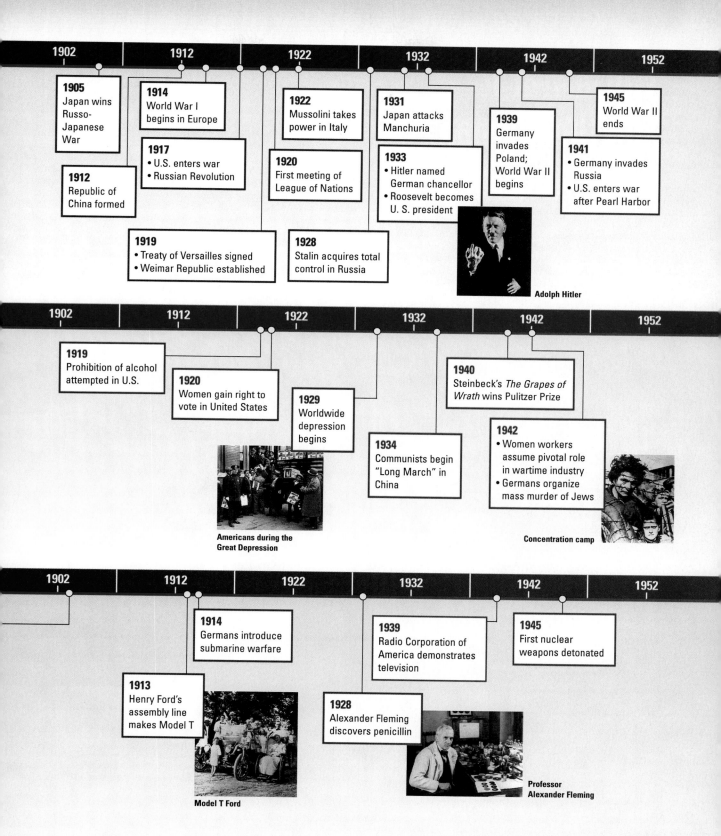

Timeline 1

1902　1912　1922　1932　1942　1952

1905
Japan wins Russo-Japanese War

1914
World War I begins in Europe

1912
Republic of China formed

1917
• U.S. enters war
• Russian Revolution

1922
Mussolini takes power in Italy

1931
Japan attacks Manchuria

1939
Germany invades Poland; World War II begins

1945
World War II ends

1920
First meeting of League of Nations

1933
• Hitler named German chancellor
• Roosevelt becomes U. S. president

1941
• Germany invades Russia
• U.S. enters war after Pearl Harbor

1919
• Treaty of Versailles signed
• Weimar Republic established

1928
Stalin acquires total control in Russia

Adolph Hitler

Timeline 2

1902　1912　1922　1932　1942　1952

1919
Prohibition of alcohol attempted in U.S.

1920
Women gain right to vote in United States

1929
Worldwide depression begins

1940
Steinbeck's *The Grapes of Wrath* wins Pulitzer Prize

1934
Communists begin "Long March" in China

1942
• Women workers assume pivotal role in wartime industry
• Germans organize mass murder of Jews

Americans during the Great Depression

Concentration camp

Timeline 3

1902　1912　1922　1932　1942　1952

1914
Germans introduce submarine warfare

1939
Radio Corporation of America demonstrates television

1945
First nuclear weapons detonated

1913
Henry Ford's assembly line makes Model T

1928
Alexander Fleming discovers penicillin

Model T Ford

Professor Alexander Fleming

World War I and the Russian Revolution

TIME

A.D. **1882–1920**

A.D. **1882–1920**

3.7 million B.C.	4000 B.C.	A.D. 2100

PLACE

Europe, Africa, and the Middle East

Europe

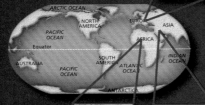

ARCTIC OCEAN

NORTH AMERICA

EUROPE

ASIA

PACIFIC OCEAN

AFRICA

Equator

AUSTRALIA

PACIFIC OCEAN

SOUTH AMERICA

ATLANTIC OCEAN

INDIAN OCEAN

ANTARCTICA

Africa

Middle East

A Letter from the German Trenches, plate 30 from *The Great War: A Neutral's Indictment*

Significance

In 1899 and again in 1907 in an effort to limit armaments and establish rules of war, representatives of several nations met at The Hague, in the Netherlands. Even as these nations discussed peace, however, some of them prepared for war. In the summer of 1914, a war began that involved nearly all the major nations of the world and was so destructive that people of the time called it the Great War. Today we call it World War I.

Terms to Define

militarism	war of attrition
mobilized	contraband
Triple Alliance	atrocities
Triple Entente	Fourteen Points
Pan-Slavism	armistice
Balkan "powder keg"	Paris Peace Conference
ultimatum	reparations
belligerents	League of Nations
Central Powers	Treaty of Versailles
Allied Powers	World Court
U-boats	economic sanctions
propaganda	mandate

People to Identify

Archduke Francis Ferdinand	V. I. Lenin
Woodrow Wilson	Communists
Arthur Zimmermann	Ferdinand Foch
Mensheviks	Big Four
Bolsheviks	Sudeten Germans

Places to Locate

Serbia	Soviet Union
Bosnia	Château-Thierry
Sarajevo	Saint-Mihiel
Marne River	Rhineland
Danzig	Saar River valley
Gallipoli Peninsula	Polish Corridor
Verdun	Czechoslovakia
Brest-Litovsk	Yugoslavia

Chapter Theme Questions

- **War and Diplomacy** How might the conflicting interests of nations help set the stage for war?
- **Technology** In what ways might technology affect warfare?
- **Politics and Law** What might be the effects of a war on a country's internal political system?

The soldiers of World War I came to realize that terror and death stalk both sides. The following excerpt from Erich Maria Remarque's novel *All Quiet on the Western Front* describes a German soldier's feelings upon the death of an enemy soldier.

" The rattle of machine-guns becomes an unbroken chain. Just as I am about to turn around a little, something heavy stumbles, and with a crash a body falls over me into the shell-hole, slips down, and lies across me. . . .

The silence spreads. I talk and must talk. So I speak to him and say to him: 'Comrade, I did not want to kill you. . . . You were only an idea to me before. . . . But now, for the first time, I see you are a man like me. . . . Forgive me, comrade. We always see it too late. Why do they never tell us that you are . . . like us, that your mothers are just as anxious as ours, and that we have the same fear of death, and the same dying and the same agony— Forgive me, comrade; how could you be my enemy? If we threw away these rifles and this uniform you could be my brother.' "

The events that ended in the horror soldiers experienced on battlefields during World War I began with conflicting national interests among European nations.

Section 1

Setting the Stage for War

Focus Questions

- **What factors led to World War I?**
- **Why were the Balkans called a powder keg?**
- **How were the countries of Europe aligned at the beginning of the war?**

In the decades before 1914, many European nations pursued interests and policies without regard for the wishes or interests of their neighbors. These conflicting interests set the stage for war.

For a time after the Congress of Vienna in 1815, relations among European powers had been more or less harmonious. Beginning in the late 1800s, however, cooperation among the European nations broke down and rivalries increased. These rivalries grew both within Europe, especially in the Balkan region, and overseas as a result of imperialism.

In her book *The Guns of August*, Barbara Tuchman describes an event in England that temporarily brought the European nations together and marked the transition between an old and a new historical era.

"So gorgeous was the spectacle on the May morning of 1910 when nine kings rode in the funeral of Edward VII of England that the crowd, waiting in hushed and black-clad awe, could not keep back gasps of admiration. In scarlet and blue and green and purple, three by three the sovereigns rode through the palace gates, with plumed helmets, gold braid, crimson sashes, and jeweled orders [military decorations] flashing in the sun. After them came . . . heirs . . . queens . . . and a scattering of special ambassadors from uncrowned countries. Together they represented seventy nations in the greatest assemblage of royalty and rank ever gathered in one place and, of its kind, the last. The muffled tongue of Big Ben tolled nine by the clock as the cortege left the palace, but on history's clock it was sunset, and the sun of the old world was setting in a dying blaze of splendor never to be seen again."

As rivalries intensified in the early 1900s, the great powers plunged toward war, pressed forward by at least four factors: nationalism, imperialism, militarism, and the system of alliances.

Nationalism and Imperialism

Spurred by the nationalism that developed after the French Revolution and the Napoleonic Wars, throughout the 1800s, nationalities tried to unite under governments controlled by their own people. This desire to unite all the people of a nation under a single government, however, had explosive possibilities in a Europe where a single government often ruled many national groups.

The European imperialist states came to the brink of war several times as they scrambled to partition Africa, Asia, and the rest of the world. Germany and France, for example, narrowly avoided war over their rival claims to Morocco on two occasions, in 1905 and 1911. They managed to settle the incidents with makeshift compromises that failed to resolve the overall problem.

Militarism

The glorification of armed strength, or **militarism**, dominated the thinking of many European leaders before World War I. These leaders believed that only the use of force could solve problems among nations. It seemed to them that a militarily strong nation usually got what it wanted, as Prussia had proved in its wars with Austria and France. Weaker nations lost out, as Italy had learned from its imperialistic ventures in Africa.

In the late 1800s, European nations built large armies of men who were drafted and given military training. If one nation **mobilized**, or readied its army and other resources for combat, other nations would also mobilize to protect themselves. In a chain reaction, this would force all nations in Europe to mobilize, or else risk being caught unprepared.

As international rivalries intensified, each European nation believed that it was necessary to keep its armed forces stronger than those of any potential enemy. Armies grew larger as spending for such things as new weapons and for the fortification of national boundaries multiplied. In the 1890s, Germany began to build a large navy to rival that of Great Britain. Great Britain, especially dependent on sea power, responded by expanding the size of its navy. In 1906 Great Britain launched the *Dreadnought*, the world's first modern battleship. Germany rushed to build similar ships.

The System of Alliances

In the period from 1864 to 1871, the unification of Germany and that of Italy had changed the balance of power in Europe. The unification of Germany, especially, created an entirely new situation. In place of a group of relatively weak states, a powerful German Empire, under the leadership of Prussia, emerged. Otto von Bismarck, the skillful and strong-willed German chancellor, shaped its ambitious foreign policy.

Three Emperors' League and the Triple Alliance. Bismarck feared that France would seek revenge for its 1871 defeat in the Franco-Prussian War by trying to regain Alsace-Lorraine, the region it had lost to Germany. He therefore set his foreign policy to keeping France diplomatically isolated and without allies. Bismarck particularly wanted to prevent a

In the image labels:
Lord Fisher's design: 1,000 feet long. Six 20 in. guns.

Stern by stern "Dreadnought's bows would reach this point

H.M.S. Dread. 526 Ton

Broadside of Fisher design (A) 26,000 lbs.
"Dreadnought" 6,880 lbs. (B)

In 1906 the British launched the *Dreadnought,* a new type of battleship that featured turbine power and rotating batteries of guns.

Franco-Russian alliance because it would isolate Germany diplomatically and, at worst, mean that Germany would have to fight a war on both its eastern and western borders.

In 1879 Bismarck formed a defensive alliance with Austria-Hungary. Then in 1881 the chancellor set up the Three Emperors' League, a secret agreement among the emperors of Germany, Russia, and Austria-Hungary, who agreed to remain neutral if any of the others went to war with another country.

In 1882 Bismarck persuaded Italy to join in the alliance he had made with Austria-Hungary, thereby creating the **Triple Alliance**. Although Bismarck considered Italy a weak link, the formation of the Triple Alliance had isolated France, accomplishing his primary foreign policy goal. The Triple Alliance completely upset the balance of power in Europe.

The Reinsurance Treaty. In 1887 the Three Emperors' League ended. Russia and Austria-Hungary were rivals in the Balkans, where the Ottoman Empire had lost control over several territories. Russia resented Germany's support of Austria-Hungary in the region, but Bismarck made a new agreement with Russia, the Reinsurance Treaty of 1887. This treaty provided that each nation would be neutral if the other became involved in a defensive war.

The Triple Entente. In 1888 the unstable William II became kaiser of Germany. Before very long, he dismissed Bismarck as chancellor and abandoned Bismarck's careful policies.

France, meanwhile, had been trying to gain allies to break out of the diplomatic isolation in which Bismarck had placed it. The opportunity arose after William II allowed the Reinsurance Treaty to lapse. Because of an economic crisis in Russia, the czar sought a loan. France hurried to lend the money and took other steps to win Russia's friendship. In 1894 Russia and France formed an alliance, making a reality of Bismarck's fear that Germany would face enemies to the east and the west.

As the second-greatest industrial power in Europe, Germany increasingly competed with Britain economically. After 1888 Germany energetically entered the race for overseas territories, demanding its "place in the sun" as a great power. William II also began Germany's naval buildup. The rapid growth of the German navy troubled the British.

Great Britain started its own search for allies. In 1904 the British and the French settled their differences in Africa and reached an agreement, the Entente Cordiale—French for "friendly understanding." In 1907 Great Britain and Russia tried to come to an agreement as well. Reaching such an agreement proved difficult because of the two nations' rivalry from the Middle East to the Pacific. Nevertheless, they now agreed to recognize each other's spheres of influence in Asia. The resulting alignment of France, Russia, and Great Britain was called the **Triple Entente**. Both France and Russia also had secret understandings with Italy, which meant that the Italians had a foot in both camps.

Dangers of the alliance system. By 1907 the rival alliances threatened world peace because they divided Europe into two armed camps. Should hostilities develop between any two rival powers, all six nations might become involved in the fighting, regardless of whether the original dispute concerned all of them. A minor quarrel had the potential to lead to serious consequences, as events in 1914 would prove.

The Balkan "Powder Keg"

Nationalists in Serbia, whose independence from the Ottoman Empire had been recognized by the Congress of Berlin in 1878, hoped to make their country the center of a large Slavic state. The Serbian nationalists especially wanted the provinces of Bosnia and Herzegovina because Serbia was landlocked and these two provinces would provide an outlet on the Adriatic Sea.

The decision of the Congress of Berlin in 1878 to make the two provinces protectorates of Austria-Hungary (see Chapter 22) severely disappointed the Serbs. After Austria-Hungary annexed Bosnia and Herzegovina in 1908, infuriated Serbian nationalists increased their agitation against Austria-Hungary.

Russia, the largest Slavic country, saw itself as the protector of the Balkan Slavs and supported Serbia's goals. The nationalist movement that pressed for the political and cultural unity of all Slavs under Russian leadership was called **Pan-Slavism**. The British distrusted Russian influence in the Balkans, however. They were very concerned with Russian access to the Mediterranean, and the Ottoman Empire seemed too weak to block Russian aggression.

Instead of taking advantage of the Anglo-Russian rivalry, Germany's Kaiser William II pursued policies that created shared interests between the British and the Russians. To reinforce the Triple Alliance and make up for the weakness of Italy, the kaiser began negotiating to bring the Ottoman Empire, an old enemy of Russia, into the Triple Alliance and thereby extend German influence into the Balkans.

Germany also planned to build a railroad from Berlin through the Balkans to Constantinople and on to Baghdad, near the Persian Gulf. This plan aroused many fears. The British regarded the proposed railroad as a threat to the sea route through the Suez Canal, their Mediterranean-Red Sea "lifeline" to India. It also seemed to endanger British interests in the Persian Gulf. The Russians feared that Germany would become a strong protector of the Ottoman Empire. This would diminish Russia's chances of securing access to the Mediterranean through the Dardanelles.

Germany's actions in the Balkans worsened an already dangerous situation. They resulted in what Bismarck had tried to avoid—the strengthening of ties between Great Britain and Russia. Both countries wanted to resist German expansion in the Balkans. Austria-Hungary, on the other hand, feared Pan-Slavism and gained Germany's support in its opposition to Slavic nationalism.

Assassination at Sarajevo

The spark that touched off the explosion of the **Balkan "powder keg"** and led to war came on June 28, 1914. The heir to the Austro-Hungarian throne, Archduke Francis Ferdinand, and his wife were visiting Sarajevo, the capital of Bosnia and Herzegovina. As they rode in an open automobile, a young man fired a revolver at them, killing both the archduke and his wife.

The assassin, Gavrilo Princip, belonged to the Black Hand, one of the many secret societies of Serbian nationalists opposed to Austro-Hungarian rule. Although Princip had acted without the authority of the Serbian government, some Serbian leaders were aware of his plans and had furnished arms and ammunition to Serbian terrorists.

The assassination brought to a head the bitterness between Serbia and Austria-Hungary. The Austro-Hungarian government was determined to use it as a reason to punish the Serbs. Before Austria-Hungary acted, however, it wanted to make sure of German support in case the Russians should try to help Serbia. Germany promised to back Austria-Hungary in anything the nation did. Encouraged by this so-called blank check, the Austro-Hungarians presented an **ultimatum** to the Serbian government. In an ultimatum, one party threatens harmful action to another if the other party rejects its proposals.

War Between Austria-Hungary and Serbia

In its ultimatum, Austria-Hungary made the following demands: (1) The Serbian government would

Gavrilo Princip, a Serbian terrorist, assassinated Archduke Francis Ferdinand. Here he is being taken to prison by police and soldiers.

condemn all propaganda against Austria-Hungary and suppress publications and societies that opposed Austria-Hungary. (2) Serbia would ban from its schools books and teachers who did not favor Austria-Hungary. (3) Serbia would dismiss any officials who had promoted propaganda against Austria-Hungary. (4) Austro-Hungarian officials would participate in the proceedings against those accused of the crime at Sarajevo. If Serbia did not agree to these terms, Austria-Hungary would resort to military action.

The Serbian government replied by accepting the first three terms and rejecting the last, but it offered to submit the fourth point to the International Court at The Hague. Assuming, however, that Austria-Hungary would not accept this offer, the Serbian government ordered mobilization of its troops. Ignoring the positive aspects of Serbia's reply, Austria-Hungary, assuming that it could quickly achieve victory, declared war on Serbia on July 28, after the time limit of the ultimatum had expired.

Mobilization of Europe

Attempts to persuade Austria-Hungary to continue negotiations proved futile. Germany continued to support Austria-Hungary. Russia prepared to defend Serbia by mobilizing troops along the Russian-Austro-Hungarian border. Expecting Germany to join Austria-Hungary, Russia also sent troops to the German border.

Germany immediately demanded that Russia cancel its mobilization or face war. When Russia ignored this ultimatum, on August 1, 1914, Germany declared war on Russia. Convinced that France was prepared to side with Russia and hoping to gain a military advantage by swift action, Germany declared war on France two days later.

Great Britain Enters the War

The great powers had guaranteed Belgian neutrality in 1839, shortly after Belgium gained its independence. Under the terms of this guarantee, Belgium agreed to stay out of any European war and not to help any **belligerents**, or warring nations. In turn, the other powers agreed not to attack Belgium. However, Belgium's location and flat terrain was of great importance to Germany's military plans. The German strategy called for the German army to mobilize, strike, and knock France out of the war before the Russians could attack from the east. Because the Franco-German border was hilly and well fortified, the Germans planned to attack through Belgium on the coastal plain between France and Germany. This attack through Belgium by Germany was in direct defiance of the 1839 guarantee. (See map on page 644.)

After the German government declared war on France, it sent an ultimatum to Belgium, demanding that German troops be allowed to cross Belgian territory. The British protested, insisting that Germany observe Belgian neutrality. The German foreign minister, referring to the 1839 guarantee, replied that surely Great Britain would not fight over "a scrap of paper." German soldiers marched into Belgium on August 4, 1914. The kaiser had promised them, "You will be home before the leaves have fallen from the trees." As a result of the invasion of Belgium, Great Britain declared war on Germany later that day.

The War Expands

Later in August, Japan entered the war on the side of Great Britain and France. Japan hoped to gain German possessions in China and the Pacific.

In Europe all the nations of the Triple Alliance and the Triple Entente except Italy were now at war. The Italian government took the position that the

Europe on the Eve of World War I, 1914

Triple Alliance
Triple Entente
Neutral countries
National capital
70° N
10°E
20°E
30°E
40°E
20° W
10° W
0°
60° N
50° N
40° N
NORWAY
SWEDEN
FINLAND
Petrograd
RUSSIA
ATLANTIC OCEAN
NORTH SEA
DENMARK
BALTIC SEA
GREAT BRITAIN
NETHERLANDS
London
Berlin
GERMAN EMPIRE
Vistula River
Volga River
Dnieper R.
English Channel
BELGIUM
Rhine R.
LUXEMBOURG
Paris
ALSACE-LORRAINE
Danube R.
Vienna
CASPIAN SEA
FRANCE
SWITZERLAND
AUSTRIA-HUNGARY
Bay of Biscay
ROMANIA
BLACK SEA
BOSNIA AND HERZEGOVINA
Sarajevo
SERBIA
BULGARIA
ITALY
ADRIATIC SEA
PORTUGAL
SPAIN
CORSICA (French)
Rome
MONTENEGRO
Balkan Peninsula
Constantinople
ALBANIA
OTTOMAN EMPIRE
Tigris R.
BALEARIC ISLANDS (Spanish)
SARDINIA (Italian)
GREECE
Euphrates R.
Baghdad
SICILY (Italian)
CYPRUS (British)
MEDITERRANEAN SEA
CRETE (Greek)
0 200 400 Miles
0 200 400 Kilometers
Azimuthal Equal-Area Projection
AFRICA

Learning from Maps Defensive alliances polarized Europe into two armed camps before the fighting actually began.

Region What nations belonged to the Triple Entente?

Austro-Hungarians had acted as aggressors when they declared war on Serbia. Thus, the Triple Alliance, which was a defensive treaty, did not require Italy to give aid to its allies.

Italy remained neutral for nine months. Finally, it signed secret treaties with Great Britain, France, and Russia that guaranteed Italy a share of the spoils after the defeat of Germany and Austria-Hungary. In May 1915, Italy entered the war against Germany and Austria-Hungary, which had been its former allies under the Triple Alliance.

In the meantime, Germany had been trying to gain other allies. In November 1914 the Ottoman Empire entered the war on the side of Germany and Austria-Hungary. The Turks, although not a strong military power, occupied a strategic position. Their control of Constantinople and the Dardanelles bottled up Russia's Black Sea fleet. It also prevented Russia's allies from sending supplies to Russia through the Mediterranean and Black Seas. Germany also persuaded Bulgaria, a rival of Serbia, to enter the war in October 1915.

1. **Define** militarism, mobilized, Triple Alliance, Triple Entente, Pan-Slavism, Balkan "powder keg", ultimatum, belligerents
2. **Identify** Archduke Francis Ferdinand
3. **Locate and Explain the Significance** Serbia, Bosnia, Sarajevo
4. **Understanding Ideas** List the factors that contributed to World War I.
5. **Summarizing Ideas (a)** What event can be said to have "lit the fuse" in 1914? **(b)** What made the area involved so important?
6. **Evaluating Ideas** How did the events that took place on June 28, 1914, develop into full-scale war, and how did the nations involved in these events align themselves?

Section 2

World War I: A New Kind of War

Focus Questions

- Who was involved in the war by the beginning of 1916?
- What innovations were introduced into warfare during World War I?
- What course did the war take from the beginning through 1916?
- How did the war affect the United States?

The soldiers who marched enthusiastically off to war in the summer of 1914 thought they would win a quick and decisive victory and come home as heroes in time to celebrate the New Year. They were wrong—tragically wrong. This war would in fact go on to last for four years.

The Belligerents

Germany, Austria-Hungary, Bulgaria, and the Ottoman Empire became known as the **Central Powers**. Notice on the map on this page that the Central Powers formed an almost solid block of territory extending from the North Sea to the Middle East. This geographical proximity gave the Central Powers the advantages of easy communication and

Europe in 1916–1917

Learning from Maps While Britain set up a naval blockade in the North Sea to cut off Germany's sea routes, Germany organized a counterblockade of U-boats off the west coast of Britain.

? Place What North Sea battle was fought in 1916 to break through the blockades?

rapid troop movements. Another advantage that the Central Powers enjoyed was Germany's very well-trained and well-equipped army.

Great Britain, France, Russia, and their partners in the war became known as the **Allied Powers**, or the Allies. Although they did not have the geographic unity of the Central Powers, they had more soldiers and a greater industrial potential. The British also had the world's largest navy. Therefore, the Allies could obtain food and raw materials more easily and could blockade and attempt to starve the Central Powers.

As a result of diplomatic maneuvers, Greece and Romania joined the Allies in 1916. Eventually, 32 countries made up the Allied side. Many of them, however, joined late in the war and made only token contributions to the war effort.

Weapons That Changed History

Wars have been fought throughout history. What has determined the outcomes of these wars? One answer is the bravery—or cowardice—of the individual soldier. Another factor that determines the outcomes of these wars is the skill of the commander.

The outcomes of battles and wars, however, have often been decided by the kinds of weapons used by one side or the other. On some occasions, weapons have given an advantage to the attacker. At other times, the advantage has rested with the defensive side.

The first weapons were muscle powered—from rocks or spears thrown from the hands of Cro-Magnon men to swords in the hands of Roman legionnaires to lances and longbows in the hands of medieval knights and archers. Innovative generals added mechanical devices. The ancient Assyrians and Egyptians, for example, put sharp blades on the wheels of their chariots. Many ancient and medieval civilizations used catapults to hurl pieces of rock or metal over city or castle walls.

Animal power augmented human power. For instance, in 217 B.C. Hannibal invaded Italy with elephants.

Trojan horse

The Romans learned the value of cavalry when fierce Goth invaders on horseback crushed the Roman infantry at Adrianople in A.D. 378.

Horses were effective, however, only in the open field. They were useless against the last line of defense—the wall. Cities became self-contained fortresses when surrounded by high walls. Ramparts allowed defenders to fight from above. The Byzantines, for example, sprayed "Greek fire"—an early form of the burning liquid of the flame-thrower—on attackers from the walls of Constantinople and also used it in naval battles.

Gunpowder made war even more destructive. Gunpowder was first used in the West in about 1320, although it had been invented in China centuries earlier. By 1500 any army worth its salt had muskets and cannons. At first, the cannon seemed to be the ideal offensive weapon. Kings such as Louis XI of France used cannons to destroy the castles of upstart nobles and to help create powerful and centralized national states. But, cannons could also be put to defensive use, such as to

Medieval catapult

English longbows

German tank corps

destroy attacking armies as easily as they were able to destroy fortifications.

At the start of the 1800s, Napoleon Bonaparte used combinations of attacking artillery, infantry, and cavalry with dazzling success. He battered the enemy lines with heavy guns, sent his infantry charging in to break the foe, then crushed the retreating troops with his cavalry.

Later in the 1800s, railroads, though not weapons, became a powerful factor in how war was fought. First used extensively in the American Civil War (1861–1865), fought between the North (Union) and the South (Confederacy), railroads made it possible for reinforcements and supplies to reach battling armies quickly. At the Battle of Bull Run (July 1861), for example, reinforcements brought by rail enabled the Confederates to turn defeat into victory.

The American Civil War was one of the first great conflicts fought in the Industrial Age. Factories mass-produced guns, bullets, and other necessary goods such as uniforms, shoes, and blankets. The

Atomic explosion

Union's greater industrial capacity was an important factor in its 1865 victory.

World War I was directed by generals who at first tried to imitate Napoleon. There were long artillery barrages to soften up the enemy, followed by mass infantry charges. However, the machine gun, combined with barbed wire barriers and trenches, gave the advantage to the defenders. Huge infantry attacks resulted in unprecedented slaughter. World War I ended only when one side collapsed from exhaustion.

World War II (1939–1945) brought a shift back to the offensive. Using large numbers of tanks and airplanes, Hitler's German war machine quickly crushed Poland (September 1939) and France (May–June 1940). The tide of war turned against Germany not so much because of new defenses against the tank and the plane, although radar did help. The Allies won the war in large part because they were able to produce more offensive firepower than the Germans. Against such force, the Axis Powers were doomed.

World War II in the Pacific ended with the use of the most fearsome weapon ever developed—the atomic bomb. In August 1945, the United States dropped atomic bombs on two Japanese cities, Hiroshima and Nagasaki. For a few years, only the United States had the atomic bomb. Today a number of other nations have also developed nuclear arms.

The existence of nuclear weapons throughout the world is an unsettling development. Their destructive power would seem to give the ultimate advantage to the attacking side. Yet, as history since 1945 has shown us, nuclear weapons have become the ultimate defense by deterring either side from attacking. By their potential to kill, these weapons have helped keep peace.

American aircraft carrier

F-16 fighters

Innovations in Warfare

World War I was an industrialized war. Industry produced weapons with the same efficient mass production methods that it had applied to other products.

One of the most important new weapons of World War I was the machine gun. Its sweeping, rapid-fire spray of bullets was deadly and often made infantry advances terribly costly. To protect themselves from the machine gun's raking fire and from artillery bombardments, soldiers dug systems of trenches.

Both sides used weapons that had never been tried before. In 1916 the British introduced the tank, an armored vehicle on which guns were mounted. Tanks enabled troops to tear through barbed wire and cross enemy lines.

Another new weapon was the recently invented airplane. Airplanes were primarily used for observing troop movements. Although early military airplanes were not very maneuverable or fast, they sometimes engaged in air battles called dogfights and dropped bombs.

Germany became the first nation to make effective use of submarines. Its **U-boats** (from the German word *Unterseebooten*, meaning "underwater boats") caused extensive losses to Allied shipping. The Germans also introduced poison gas.

Previously in Europe, most wars were fought by professional soldiers whose only source of income was their military pay and rations. In contrast, armies of drafted civilians fought the battles of World War I. Those who could not fight worked at home to help the war effort. Many women participated by working in factories. A war in which nations turn all their resources to the war effort became known as "total war."

To stir the patriotism of their people and support for the war effort, governments made wide use of **propaganda**—ideas, facts, or rumors spread deliberately to further one's cause or to damage an opposing cause. Governments set up agencies to handle the flow of information about the war. Newspapers and popular magazines, especially those of the Allies, portrayed the enemy as brutal and subhuman, while praising their own national aims and achievements.

The War from 1914 to 1916

Germany's attack on France was launched across neutral Belgium. By September 1914, German troops had reached the Marne River near Paris. However, the French and British armies managed to hold the line, and Paris was saved.

France's success in the Battle of the Marne changed the entire nature of the war. Germany's hope of swift victory ended. Both sides now dug trenches on the western front, which stretched from Switzerland to the shores of the North Sea.

On the eastern front, the Russians were still completing mobilization. Responding to a plea by the French to divert German forces from the western front, the Russian army launched an attack toward the important German seaport of Danzig.

In late August, the Russians met a German force in the Battle of Tannenberg, which is located in East Prussia. (See map on this page.) The Russians suffered a

The Eastern Front, 1914–1918

Learning from Maps With Russian forces threatening the German port of Danzig, the Germans retaliated by driving the Russians back eastward.

? Movment What battle on the Baltic Sea did the Germans win in 1917?

humiliating defeat. Soon afterward the Germans launched an offensive in the east and crossed into Russian Poland.

The war was fought outside of Europe also. Fighting took place in the Middle East, Africa, and in the Pacific.

Fighting on Gallipoli. Although Russia had a huge army, it lacked enough guns and ammunition to equip its soldiers properly. In 1915 Great Britain and France decided to attempt to force their way through the Dardanelles so that they could capture Constantinople. They had hoped that this would remove the Ottoman Empire from the war and allow supplies to reach the Russians.

The British and French had hoped that bombardment from their heavily armed battleships alone would destroy the Ottoman artillery on the Gallipoli Peninsula.

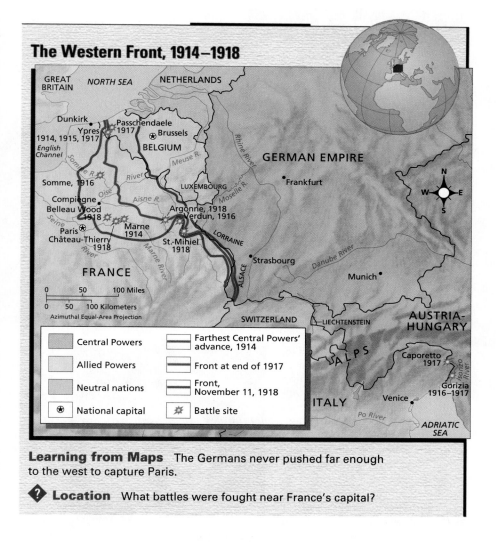

The Western Front, 1914–1918

Legend:
- Central Powers
- Allied Powers
- Neutral nations
- ⊛ National capital
- Farthest Central Powers' advance, 1914
- Front at end of 1917
- Front, November 11, 1918
- ✳ Battle site

Learning from Maps The Germans never pushed far enough to the west to capture Paris.

? Location What battles were fought near France's capital?

When the bombardment failed after several days, however, they decided to land troops on the Gallipoli Peninsula. The Turks resisted stubbornly and the fighting became a stalemate. After eight months of fighting and the loss of hundreds of thousands of lives on both sides, the Allies abandoned their plans to capture Constantinople and withdrew from Gallipoli.

Naval warfare. The British decided to blockade the North Sea to keep merchant ships from reaching Germany. Originally, they set up the blockade to prevent the Germans from getting raw materials to manufacture war equipment. Gradually, however, the blockade became an attempt to ruin the German economy and starve the German people.

Germany also set up a blockade. Employing its fleet of U-boats, it attempted to win the war by sinking ships carrying food and munitions to the British.

In May 1915, without warning, a German submarine sank the British passenger liner *Lusitania* off the coast of Ireland. The sinking of the *Lusitania,* which was carrying passengers as well as a cargo of war materials to England, killed nearly 1,200 people, including more than 100 Americans. Woodrow Wilson, the U.S. president, warned Germany that the United States would not tolerate another such incident. For the next year and a half, Germany used submarine warfare only sparingly. It did not wish to provoke the neutral Americans into entering the war.

In May 1916, the only large naval battle of the war was fought by Germany and Britain in the North Sea off the coast of Jutland, Denmark. Although both sides claimed they had won a victory, the German navy did, however, retire to port, where it remained for the rest of the war.

Women in Wartime

In August 1914, Europe plunged into World War I. European countries found themselves in desperate need of war matériel (equipment and supplies). Many of their former factory workers, however, were men who were now serving as soldiers. In Europe and the United States (which entered the war in 1917), women took on jobs formerly held almost exclusively by men. Women's participation in the war effort would have dramatic social consequences.

With men off at war, women augmented or gave up their traditional roles as homemakers and domestic workers to manage farms or stores or to become factory workers (see top photo), mail carriers, and bank tellers. They served in medical positions on the front lines.

After the war ended in 1918, many women left their jobs to make way for the men returning home from war. In the meanwhile, however, women had gained a new sense of independence that they did not want to lose. This economic independence often led to independence in other areas. For example, some women began to cut their hair short and wear shorter skirts, breaking centuries-old traditions. (See center photo.) Women gained the right to vote and so had a voice in the

political process. Aviator Amelia Earhart symbolized the new attitude of many women in the 1920s and 1930s—strong, independent, willing to take the same risks that men took.

When World War II began in 1939, women once again made important contributions to the war effort. As members of the armed forces, women served as nurses and clerical workers. They entered the workforce in record numbers, with some 4 million women working in defense plants. These women were exemplified by "Rosie the Riveter," often seen on posters—the prototype of the able, independent young woman who worked in a factory building tanks, airplanes, or guns. (See bottom photo.)

At the close of the war in 1945, women once again were expected to return to the home. By now, however, their role had permanently taken a new direction. Today women are an established part of the workforce. Female soldiers now train in boot camp alongside men. Although women do not serve as front line infantry, they serve in almost every other military role, including as fighter pilots.

The Stalemate

By 1916 the war in the west had become a stalemate on land as well as on sea. However, military leaders on both sides were slow to realize they could not break through the other's line of trenches. As both armies continued to launch attacks, small areas of land changed hands again and again, costing each side thousands of lives. The conflict had become a **war of attrition**—a slow wearing-down process in which each side tries to outlast the other.

One horrifying example of such warfare occurred in northeastern France. (See map on page 649.) The Germans massed their forces and attacked Verdun in February 1916, hoping to bleed the French army to death. After months of fighting and bombardment, the Germans finally gave up in December. At Verdun each side lost more than 400,000 soldiers.

The United States and World War I

When World War I began in 1914, President Wilson said the United States would be neutral. Most Americans viewed the war as a European affair in which the United States should not become involved.

Trade with the belligerents. Nevertheless, the war soon affected the United States. As the most highly industrialized neutral nation, the United States became a supplier of food, raw materials, and munitions to both sides. The U.S. government insisted on the right of American businesses to trade freely with either side. According to international law, however, if a ship carried **contraband**—war materials supplied by a neutral to a belligerent nation—the goods could be seized. The United States also insisted on the right of its citizens to travel safely on ships of any nation.

The United States government also permitted banks, corporations, and private citizens to buy bonds of foreign governments and sell them goods on credit. At the beginning of the war, American investors and businesspeople dealt with both sides. As the British blockade of Germany tightened, however, American trade became more one-sided toward the Allies.

America enters the war. Britain's propaganda impressed Americans far more than did Germany's. Graphic stories spread by the British of German **atrocities**—brutal crimes of war, often said to have been committed against defenseless civilians—angered Americans, although many of these stories were exaggerated or untrue.

Early in 1917, circumstances pushed the United States into the war. In January the German foreign minister, Arthur Zimmermann, sent a secret telegram

to the German ambassador in Mexico. It instructed him to draw Mexico into the war on Germany's side. In exchange, Germany promised Mexico the return of parts of the southwestern United States that Mexico had lost in 1848. The British intercepted the telegram, decoded it, and had it published in American newspapers. Americans were enraged.

Faced with serious food and munitions shortages, the Germans decided to resume unrestricted submarine warfare. They realized this might bring the United States into the conflict, but they hoped the submarine war would force Britain to give up before that could happen. German submarines began attacking any ship found in what Germany declared a "war zone" around Britain. Once again, Americans were killed in some of these attacks. The costly renewed submarine attacks did not force Britain to ask for peace.

Meanwhile, in March 1917, revolutionaries overthrew the autocratic czarist government of Russia. Now all the major Allied countries had democratic governments while none of the Central Powers did. Americans could more readily participate in a war between democratic and nondemocratic countries.

On April 2, 1917, President Wilson addressed Congress. Proclaiming that "the world must be made safe for democracy," he asked for a declaration of war against Germany. On April 6, Congress voted to comply with that request. The United States now joined the war on the side of the Allies.

Section 2 Review

1. **Define** Central Powers, Allied Powers, U-boats, propaganda, war of attrition, contraband, atrocities
2. **Identify** Woodrow Wilson, Arthur Zimmermann
3. **Locate and Explain the Significance** Marne River, Danzig, Gallipoli Peninsula, Verdun
4. **Analyzing Ideas** What countries belonged to the Central Powers and the Allied Powers by the beginning of 1916?
5. **Understanding Ideas** Name some important new weapons and military techniques introduced in World War I.
6. **Summarizing Ideas** Describe the progress of the war from 1914 through 1916.
7. **Analyzing Ideas** (a) How was the United States as a neutral power affected by World War I? (b) What factors led to the United States entry into the war?

The Russian Revolution

Focus Questions

- **What internal problems did Russia face during World War I, and how did they lead to the Russian Revolution?**
- **How did Lenin come to power in Russia?**
- **What steps did the Communists take to cement their control of the Russian government?**

Russia, torn by revolutionary disturbances throughout the 1800s, faced continuing problems in the early 1900s. Russians had long been denied democratic rights and civil liberties, but the Revolution of 1905 had brought about no real changes. The elected legislative body, the Duma, had little power. The czar, Nicholas II, did not trust the Duma and remained a nearly absolute ruler. Some Russians, especially university students, joined secret societies that committed assassinations of government officials.

Grave economic problems also confronted the country. Although Russia had been industrializing rapidly in recent decades, it still was the most backward of the major European powers. Debts, taxes, and rents still kept most Russian peasants in poverty even though serfdom had been abolished in 1861.

Czar Nicholas II was the last Russian emperor. Unable to maintain his people's support, he abdicated in March 1917. He and his family were imprisoned and executed in July 1918.

Russia in World War I

World War I exposed Russia's weaknesses. The country lacked enough railroads and good roads, and its industry could not adequately equip or supply its army. The Ottoman Empire's entrance into the war on the side of the Central Powers helped cut Russia off from outside supplies.

The Allies had counted on the great number of soldiers in the Russian army. When war came, however, Russian troops proved to be poorly equipped and badly led. The inefficient and corrupt government was unfit to deal with the problems of modern warfare. Russian losses in the war were enormous: 1.7 million soldiers were killed, nearly 5 million were wounded or disabled, and some 2 million civilians died.

The spring of 1917 found the Russian people weary of hardships and disheartened by the appalling casualties their army had suffered in the war. They had lost faith in their government and in Czar Nicholas II. Strikes and street demonstrations broke out in Petrograd, as St. Petersburg had been called since 1914. When the Duma demanded reforms in the government, Nicholas dissolved it.

In the past, the government had always been able to use the army against disturbances such as those in Petrograd. Now, however, the soldiers joined the rioters. The Duma, encouraged by the army's disobedience, refused the czar's order to disband.

In March 1917, unable to control either his subjects or his army, Nicholas II abdicated. He and his family were arrested and the next year they were murdered by the Bolsheviks, who were ruling Russia at that time. The monarchy and the Romanov dynasty that had maintained Russian autocracy for 300 years were both ended.

Lenin and the Bolsheviks

A liberal provisional government was set up to rule Russia until a constitutional assembly could be elected to establish a new permanent system of government. While the provisional government tried to restore order, however, another body worked for more radical change in Russia.

This body, known as the Petrograd Soviet of Workers' and Soldiers' Deputies (*soviet* is the Russian word for council), had been quickly organized when disorders began in Russia. The Petrograd Soviet's leaders modeled it on similar organizations that had participated in the Revolution of 1905. Some members of the Petrograd Soviet were socialists called

Mensheviks. The organization also contained a group of more radical socialists, known as Bolsheviks.

Other soviets similar to the one in Petrograd sprang up elsewhere in Russia. Many people throughout the country supported their program. The soviets called for immediate peace, land reforms, and the turning over of factories to the workers. The provisional government, in contrast, pledged to continue the war and was much more cautious about reforms.

The leader of the Bolsheviks was V. I. Lenin. He was born Vladimir Ilyich Ulyanov in 1870, but after becoming a revolutionary he assumed the name Lenin. Lenin was an intelligent and forceful man. He came from the middle class and had studied law. After his older brother was executed by the czarist police as a revolutionary terrorist, Lenin became a revolutionary himself.

On April 16, 1917, Lenin, with German help, returned to Russia from Switzerland, where he had been living, and urged that all governing power be turned over to the soviets. He called for "peace, land and bread," a slogan with great popular appeal.

Lenin was a Marxist. Partly because of the conditions existing in Russia, however, he developed his own version of Marxism. Lenin believed that because Russia had comparatively little industry and only a small working class, the forces of history in the country might not move precisely as Marx had predicted. Therefore, he said, it was necessary for a small group of devoted Marxists to train the workers to become a revolutionary force. Lenin's adaptation of Marxism formed the basis of what became communism.

On November 7, 1917, the Bolsheviks overthrew the provisional government under Alexander Kerensky and seized control of Russia. This revolution is sometimes called the October Revolution (for the month in which it occurred, according to the calendar then used in Russia), or the Bolshevik Revolution, to differentiate it from the March Revolution that ousted Nicholas. In 1918, the Bolsheviks renamed themselves the Communist Party.

Peace and Civil War

Despite the losses Russia had suffered, the provisional government had kept Russia in the war. Now at Lenin's direction, a peace treaty was signed with the Central Powers in March 1918 at the city of Brest-Litovsk, taking Russia out of the war. Desperate for peace, the Communists accepted the very harsh terms dictated by Germany and agreed to give up a sizable amount of territory.

Vladimir Ilyich Lenin, founder of the Communist Party in Russia, led the Bolshevik Revolution.

The new regime then turned its attention to internal problems. The Communists faced much opposition within Russia. Their opponents included liberals, Mensheviks and other socialist factions, and right-wing groups that wanted to restore the monarchy. A civil war broke out in Russia.

The Communists had adopted red, the symbolic color of European revolutionary socialism, as their color. For this reason, they became known as Reds. Right-wing opponents of the Communists were called Whites. The Red Army—as the forces of the new government were called—fought many battles with the White forces, leaving an appalling trail of destruction. The civil war, which began in early 1918, lasted almost three years, adding to the devastation begun by World War I.

The Allies had been angered by the new Russian government's signing of a separate peace with the Central Powers. They wanted to prevent aid they had sent Russia from falling into the hands of the Germans. They also feared that if the Communists gained control of Russia, revolution would spread to their countries. The Communists had been calling for such a revolution. Thus the Allies aided some of the White forces with arms and money. Several nations, including Britain, France, and the United States, even sent small numbers of troops to oppose the communist government. These efforts were half-hearted, however, and had little effect. By 1921 the Communists had completely defeated the White forces. In 1922 the Communists renamed the lands they ruled the Union of Soviet Socialist Republics, or the Soviet Union.

Section 3 Review

1. **Identify** Mensheviks, Bolsheviks, V. I. Lenin, Communists
2. **Locate and Explain the Significance** Brest-Litovsk
3. **Understanding Cause and Effect** How did internal problems in Russia during World War I affect the course of the revolution in Russia in 1917?
4. **Explaining Ideas** How did Lenin and the Bolsheviks come to power in Russia?
5. **Analyzing Ideas** (a) How did the signing of the peace treaty by the Communists in 1918 help the new regime maintain power? (b) Why did it anger the Allied Powers?

Section 4

The Terms of Peace

Focus Questions
- What were the Fourteen Points?
- How did World War I come to an end?
- What problems faced the leaders at the Paris Peace Conference?

President Woodrow Wilson's statement of America's aim in entering the war—to make the world "safe for democracy"—established an idealistic reason for the war. But the Bolshevik Revolution in Russia and Russia's signing of a separate peace treaty with the Central Powers at Brest-Litovsk dampened Allied morale. The bloody stalemate on the western front continued. To many people, the war seemed likely to last years longer.

The Fourteen Points

In January 1918, about 10 months before World War I ended, President Wilson, in a speech to Congress, set forth a set of ideas for a just world after the war.

Wilson's plan became known as the **Fourteen Points**. Six of the points (points 1–5 and 14) contained plans of a general nature. The eight remaining points dealt with specific countries and regions, such as Russia, Belgium, Alsace-Lorraine, and the Balkans.

The six general points may be summarized as follows: (1) no secret treaties; (2) freedom of the seas for all nations; (3) removal of all economic barriers or tariffs; (4) reduction of national armaments; (5) fair adjustment of all colonial claims, with equal consideration given to the interests of the colonial powers and the people of the colonies; and (14) establishment of "a general association of nations" to guarantee political independence and protection to large and small states alike.

The Fourteen Points caught the imagination of people everywhere. Even in Germany, where the population was tired of the hardships of the war, people were impressed by Wilson's proposals.

Defeat of the Central Powers

The Treaty of Brest-Litovsk with Russia allowed the Germans to withdraw troops from the eastern front and concentrate their efforts on a huge offensive in the west during the spring and summer of 1918. This offensive, which lasted until mid-July, represented a last attempt to break through the Allied lines, capture Paris, and end the war before the Americans could arrive in strength and turn the tide.

At the end of May, the Germans again reached the Marne River, only 37 miles from Paris. By this time, however, thousands of American troops were landing in France every month.

Under a newly organized joint command, headed by the French marshal Ferdinand Foch (FAWSH), the Allied forces stopped the Germans in June at Château-Thierry. In July the Allies began to counterattack. A major Allied offensive in September at Saint-Mihiel and in the Argonne Forest forced the German armies back to the borders of Germany. (See map on page 649.)

At the same time, conditions worsened for the Central Powers elsewhere in the war. Bulgaria, seeing little hope for victory or for help from its allies, surrendered on September 30, 1918. The Turks soon asked for peace. By October a revolution in Austria-Hungary had brought the old Habsburg Empire to an end. Austria and Hungary then formed separate governments and stopped fighting.

In Germany the government of Kaiser William II soon collapsed. President Wilson had told German

These victorious American soldiers are marching through the Arc de Triomphe (Arch of Triumph), where today an eternal flame burns to honor France's World War I Tomb of the Unknown Soldier.

Costs of the War

The costs of World War I stagger the imagination. Each of the belligerent nations suffered enormous losses that had lasting consequences. It is estimated that the war left some 10 million soldiers dead and around 20 million more wounded—many of them crippled for life.

Militarily, Germany suffered most severely, losing more than 1.8 million soldiers. Russia lost almost as many, and France and its colonies lost nearly 1.4 million. Austria and Hungary counted nearly 1 million dead in the war, and Great Britain lost almost 1 million. The United States lost some 50,000 in battle.

Civilian casualties were also very high. Naval blockades, artillery and aerial bombardments, famine, disease, and political violence all took their toll. The destruction of property was appalling. One historian has estimated that the total cost was more than $300 billion, an enormous figure for the time.

The Paris Peace Conference

After the armistice in November 1918, the Allies faced the task of arranging peace terms. President Wilson had written and spoken of a peace conference that would write a treaty that was fair to all. However, the war had caused so much bitterness and had cost so much in terms of human lives and property that the European Allied governments were determined to dictate the terms of peace.

Delegates of the victorious nations met in Paris in January 1919. This meeting is referred to as the **Paris Peace Conference** or the Versailles Conference. Almost all the Allied Powers sent representatives. Russia, having left the war and now in the midst of a civil war, was not invited.

Representatives of the defeated Central Powers played no role in writing the terms of the treaties. The conference was dominated by the leaders of the four most powerful Allies—Great Britain, France, the

leaders he would deal only with a government that truly represented the German people. Many Germans, wishing to end the war, looked upon the kaiser as an obstacle to peace. On November 9, the kaiser's abdication was announced, and the German Republic was proclaimed.

In November 1918, the new German leaders signed an **armistice**, an agreement to stop fighting. The armistice provided that at the eleventh hour on the eleventh day of 1918 all fighting would cease. The Germans grimly signed the armistice in a railroad car in the forest of Compiègne in France.

According to the severe terms of the armistice, the Treaty of Brest-Litovsk was canceled. Germany also had to surrender its submarines and a large part of its surface fleet. In addition, it had to release all war prisoners and turn over munitions that might make additional fighting possible. The Allies reserved the right to occupy all German territory west of the Rhine River.

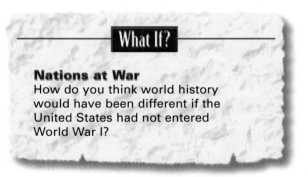

What If?

Nations at War
How do you think world history would have been different if the United States had not entered World War I?

Duchamp and the Dadaists

World War I raged violently for four years. When it ended, more than 10 million soldiers and millions more civilians had lost their lives. Such devastation did not go unnoticed in the art world. Artists expressed their anger and bitterness over the war by producing anti-art, works that mocked the values of a society that could have produced such a war. This school of art was called Dada.* Dada art showed objects and ideas that seemed to have no relation to each other. Some critics refer to Dadaist works as nonart.

Man Ray was one of the most famous of the Dada artists. Born in Philadelphia, he moved to Paris in 1921. Ray worked in a wide variety of media,

including painting, photography, and motion pictures. He experimented endlessly with techniques such as superimposing shapes onto photographs to create strange, nonsensical images. The piece shown to the right, "Aviary," combines paint, pencil, and ink on cardboard.

United States, and Italy. Known as the Big Four, these leaders were Prime Minister David Lloyd George of Great Britain, Premier Georges Clemenceau (kle·mahn·SOH) of France, President Woodrow Wilson of the United States, and Premier Vittorio Orlando of Italy.

Problems Facing the Peacemakers

After the end of World War I, Europe faced a confusing political situation. Republics had replaced hereditary monarchies in the three great former empires of Germany, Austria-Hungary, and Russia. A fourth empire, that of the Ottoman Turks, tottered on the brink of collapse. Ethnic groups in Russia and the defeated empires pressed their claims for independence. These groups wanted independence, self-government, and unity within the borders of a single nation. The spirit of nationalism also began to grow in overseas colonies as well.

Territorial claims. The victorious nations had many conflicting territorial demands that they found difficult to reconcile. France wanted, above all, security against

---

Dada is a French word for wooden horse or hobbyhorse. A sculptor and a German writer accidentally discovered the word in a dictionary. They liked the sound of the word and its whimsical, nonsensical quality. To them, of course, the violence of World War I made no sense either.

another German attack. It insisted on the return of the former provinces of Alsace and Lorraine. This had been guaranteed in the Fourteen Points. In addition, France demanded that its border be moved eastward to the Rhine River so that France would possess the more militarily defensible Rhineland, the German territory located on the west bank of the Rhine River. France also demanded the Saar River valley, with its valuable deposits of coal, as reparation.

Italy claimed the Tirol region and the city of Trieste in accordance with the secret treaties it had made in 1915. It also claimed the port city of Fiume, although Fiume had not been promised in the secret treaties. Lloyd George, Wilson, and Clemenceau agreed to the Tirol region. However, they steadfastly opposed giving Fiume to Italy. The controversy became so bitter that Orlando for a time left the conference and went home in disgust.

Belgium, which had suffered under wartime German occupation, requested two small portions of German territory along the border. Great Britain wanted Germany's African colonies. It also insisted that the German navy be destroyed and that Germany be prohibited from building warships.

During the war, Japan had occupied the previously German-held Marshall, Caroline, and Mariana Islands, as well as Qingdao and most of the

Shandong Peninsula. Now that the war was over, Japan wanted to keep all these regions. Another bitter quarrel followed.

Reparations and peacekeeping. The destruction caused by the war prompted the question of **reparations**—payment for war damages. Who should pay for the damages and how much?

Finally, the conference considered the question of a world organization to maintain peace, an idea dear to Wilson's heart. The formation of a **League of Nations** had widespread appeal, but many European leaders doubted its practical usefulness.

The Peace: Justice or Vengeance?

Early in the conference, two conflicting viewpoints had surfaced. The British, French, and Italian governments claimed to support the Fourteen Points. Yet they had never really given up the aims stated in the secret treaties—to divide the territories taken from the Central Powers among themselves after the war. The Fourteen Points represented a "peace of justice," whereas the terms of the secret treaties represented a "peace of vengeance."

Wilson believed that the conference must write a "peace of justice," as the Fourteen Points outlined, so that the settlement would be fair and lasting and not create a basis for new wars. However, the war had left bitterness, hatred, and a longing for revenge. Many of the victors believed the Central Powers, and especially Germany, had been responsible for the war. They demanded that the defeated be taught a stern lesson.

Section 4 Review

1. **Define** Fourteen Points, armistice, Paris Peace Conference, reparations, League of Nations
2. **Identify** Ferdinand Foch, Big Four
3. **Locate and Explain the Significance** Château-Thierry, Saint-Mihiel, Rhineland, Saar River valley
4. **Summarizing Ideas (a)** What were the six general proposals of Wilson's Fourteen Points? **(b)** What effect did the Fourteen Points have?
5. **Understanding Ideas** What events led to the end of World War I?
6. **Evaluating Ideas (a)** Why did Wilson believe in a "peace of justice"? **(b)** Why did others oppose this belief?

Creating a "New Europe"

Focus Questions
- **What were the specific provisions of the Treaty of Versailles?**
- **What issues emerged as the victors dealt with various nations and national minorities?**
- **What were the aims of the League of Nations?**

The victorious Allied Powers made separate treaties with each of the five Central Powers. Because Austria and Hungary now had separate governments, five treaties had to be drawn up—with Germany, Austria, Hungary, Bulgaria, and the Ottoman Empire. The treaty with Germany is called the **Treaty of Versailles** because it was signed at the Palace of Versailles, outside Paris.

The Versailles Treaty

In May 1919 representatives of the new German Republic were called in, presented with a peace treaty, and told to sign it. The Germans complained bitterly that the treaty did not follow the Fourteen Points. They objected especially to two parts. First, the treaty made Germany, the sole surviving Central Power, admit that it alone was guilty of starting the war and therefore must pay reparations. Second, the treaty did not specify the total amount of the reparations. Nevertheless, the Germans had no choice but to sign the treaty. In late June 1919, Germany, still bitterly protesting, signed the treaty.

The Versailles Treaty provided for the formation of the League of Nations, which will be discussed later in this section. It also made numerous territorial adjustments and placed various restrictions on Germany.

Germany lost considerable land along its northern, western, and eastern borders (see map on page 659) as well as its overseas colonies. Alsace-Lorraine was returned to France. Belgium gained some small territories along its border. Germany agreed not to fortify the Rhineland, which Allied troops would occupy for an unspecified period of time. The Saar Valley would fall under the administration of the League of Nations for 15 years. During that time, all the coal mined in the area would go to France in partial payment of reparations. At the end of 15 years, the people of the Saar Valley region would go to the polls to vote.

Building History Study Skills

READ
WRITE
INTERPRET
CONNECT
THINK

Interpreting Visuals: Using a Map as a Historical Document

The Congress of Vienna in 1815 resulted in border changes in Europe (see maps entitled "Napoleonic Empire, 1805–1815," and "Europe After the Congress of Vienna, 1815," in Chapter 17). Studying changes in the map of Europe before and after the Congress of Vienna helps you understand the political and historical development of Europe before World War I.

A major goal of the participants at the Congress of Vienna was to prevent France from again acting aggressively as Napoleon had acted. Consequently, the Austrian Netherlands (Belgium) was united with Holland (the Dutch Netherlands) to act as a buffer state against France. The Rhineland became the border of Prussia. Savoy and Genoa were added to Sardinia to make Sardinia a larger state along the border of France. The changes made by the Congress of Vienna did not allow for self-determination; the overall principle of the changes focused on the balance of power. Do you notice any other balance-of-power provisions indicated by the changes shown on the two maps? What consequences did they have for the historical development of Europe?

How to Use a Map as a Historical Document

To use a map as a historical document, follow these steps.
1. Identify the subject of the map.
2. Identify the historical context of the map.
3. Explain the information about the subject included on the map.
4. Connect the information on the map to the historical context of the subject.
5. Compare the map with other maps.

Developing the Skill

World War I created new borders in Europe. The Treaty of Versailles and the other peace agreements changed the nature of Europe's geography, economy, and politics. Studying maps of Europe before and after World War I, just as you have studied maps of Europe before and after the Congress of Vienna, helps you understand the political and historical development of Europe. Look at the maps entitled "Europe on the Eve of World War I, 1914," on page 644 and "Europe After the Versailles Settlements, 1919–1920," on page 659. How did Europe change? How did these changes affect European history?

The historical context is the impact that World War I had on Europe. The maps give information about the consequences of World War I for European history. Large empires broke up, and a number of smaller countries were created. Germany lost Alsace-Lorraine to France; Serbia became part of Yugoslavia; Austria-Hungary was divided into Austria, Hungary, Czechoslovakia, and Yugoslavia. Poland reappeared, and Russia became the Soviet Union. The Polish Corridor was created out of part of Germany. There were other changes as well. As the Congress of Vienna attempted to prevent French aggression, the World War I settlements attempted to prevent German aggression. The loss of Alsace-Lorraine and the Polish Corridor, for example, weakened Germany. However, the changes also contained the seeds of a future war because of German resentment to the loss of this land and new and continuing nationality problems.

Practicing the Skill

Look at a map that shows the European colonies that are located in Africa in the early 1900s. Then look at a recent map of Africa. What generalizations can you make about shifts in power in Africa since the early 1900s?

To apply this skill, see Applying History Study Skills on page 663.

The Big Four at Versailles

Europe After the Versailles Settlements, 1919–1920

Learning from Maps Many new countries were added to the continent of Europe after World War I.

? Place What city became the capital of Yugoslavia? Of Czechoslovakia? Of Finland? Of Poland?

They could choose to remain under League control, to become part of France, or to rejoin Germany.

Poland was restored as an independent nation and received a large area of formerly German land. This region included the so-called Polish Corridor, which cut off East Prussia from the rest of Germany and gave Poland an outlet to the Baltic Sea. The port of Danzig became a free city administered by the League of Nations.

Germany had to abolish conscription and could not maintain an army of more than 100,000 men. It was not allowed to manufacture heavy artillery, tanks, military airplanes, or poison gas. In addition, Germany could have no submarines and only a small number of warships. These measures were intended to ensure that Germany would not be able to wage aggressive war, but the Allies lacked effective means for enforcing them.

Former Austro-Hungarian Territories

Austria-Hungary's Dual Monarchy had split in two as the war ended. The victors wrote one treaty with Austria in September 1919 and a separate treaty with Hungary in June 1920. Austria, now an independent republic, lost the southern Tirol and the city of Trieste to Italy. The new republic could not grow enough food for its people or supply its industries with adequate raw materials. As a result, Austria soon sank into financial crisis and poverty.

Hungary lost a great deal of the territory it had governed under the Dual Monarchy to the newly created nation of Czechoslovakia, which included Czech, Slovak, and Ruthenian peoples. In the western Balkans, the new nation of Yugoslavia united the former independent kingdoms of Serbia and Montenegro, the former Habsburg provinces of Bosnia and Herzogovina, and a section of the Adriatic coast.

Bulgaria and the Ottoman Empire

The victors also penalized Bulgaria. In its treaty, signed in 1919, Bulgaria lost territory, including its outlet to the Aegean Sea, which went to Greece.

The Ottoman Empire paid an even higher price for being on the losing side. Its treaty, which was signed in 1920, resulted in a great loss of territory. The Dardanelles and Bosporus remained in Turkish hands; however, these areas had to be kept unfortified and controlled by an international commission.

Several new states—Palestine, Transjordan, and Syria (including present-day Lebanon)—emerged from former Turkish territory in the eastern Mediterranean area. Turkish territory farther east became the country of Iraq. These territories were administered by Great Britain or France under the supervision of the League of Nations.

Former Russian Territories

In 1918 four new nations—Finland, Estonia, Latvia, and Lithuania—along the Baltic Sea had declared their independence from Russia. The victorious Allies recognized their independent sovereignty. Much of the territory of restored Poland also came from Russia, as well as from Germany and Austria-Hungary. In addition, Russia lost the province of Bessarabia, in the southwest, to a greatly enlarged Romania.

Dissatisfied Minorities

The peace treaties solved many problems but also created new ones. One of the most difficult problems was that of national self-determination.

President Wilson had held out the promise of independent nationhood for all national or ethnic groups, most of whom had belonged to one or another of the great empires that disappeared at the end of the war. However, not every ethnic group could be united under its own government. For example, there were thousands of German-speaking Austrians in the Tirol, which came partly under Italian rule. Germans lived in Danzig and the Polish Corridor. Some 3 million German-speaking former Austrian subjects—known as Sudeten Germans—now lived in Czechoslovakia.

These national minorities—people of one nationality living under a government controlled by another nationality—were unhappy. Some minorities, such as the Armenians and Kurds, many of whom lived in the Ottoman Empire, were brutally oppressed. Although each minority group was guaranteed certain rights that were to be protected by the League of Nations, the nationalities problem remained.

The League of Nations

During the negotiations among the Allied leaders over the peace settlements, President Wilson made several compromises with the ideals of his Fourteen Points. He realized that the treaties failed in many respects to provide a "peace of justice." He consoled himself, however, with the thought that the new League of Nations would be able to remedy any injustices caused by the treaties.

A special commission, which included Wilson, wrote the Covenant of the League of Nations. This Covenant, adopted by the Paris Peace Conference, became part of the Versailles Treaty, which the United States did not ratify.

Organization. According to the Covenant, the League of Nations had two main aims: (1) to promote international cooperation and (2) to maintain peace by settling disputes among nations and by reducing armaments. The League was to include all independent European sovereign nations. Three main agencies—an assembly, a council, and a secretariat—would conduct League business. The League was to work closely with a related but independent body, the Permanent Court of International Justice, or **World Court**, which is located at The Hague in the Netherlands.

The Assembly would be composed of representatives of all member nations. Regardless of size, each nation was to have one vote. The Council, the main peacekeeping body, was to be composed of 9 member nations (later increased to 14). It would consist of 5 permanent members—Great Britain, France, Italy,

Despite a lack of support from the United States, 42 member countries established the League of Nations in January 1920. This photograph was taken later in 1920 at the League's first public session.

Japan, and the United States—the victorious powers of the war. The remaining seats on the Council were to be filled by rotation from among the other nations.

Maintaining the peace. The members of the League of Nations agreed not to resort to war and promised to submit their disputes to the World Court or specially convened commissions for arbitration. The League of Nations Covenant provided that if a member nation broke this agreement, the League could impose penalties. Possible penalties included breaking diplomatic relations, imposing **economic sanctions**—the refusal to trade with the offending member nation—or blockades. Military force would be considered only as a last resort.

Mandates. The League of Nations provided a way to deal with the colonies of the defeated Central Powers. Until the people of such a colony were considered ready for independence, the League agreed to hold the area in trust and to assume responsibility for it. The League designated the area a **mandate** to be administered by the government of an "advanced" nation. The administering nation pledged that it would prepare the people of the area for self-government and make annual reports to the League concerning the area's progress. German possessions in Africa and the Pacific and Ottoman territories in the Middle East were assigned as mandates either to Britain, France, Australia, New Zealand, or Japan. The mandate for South-West Africa was assigned to South Africa.

The Start of the League. Although the League of Nations had been a favorite idea of Wilson's, the United States itself never became a member of the organization. Some Americans disapproved of the League's powers, while others wanted changes in the Versailles Treaty, which included the League Covenant. After fighting in a bloody European war, Americans were fearful of being dragged into another war by commitments to League peacekeeping. As a result of this opposition, the U.S. Senate refused to ratify the Versailles Treaty. Instead, the United States eventually signed a separate peace treaty with Germany.

Despite the absence of the United States, the 42 member nations represented at the League of Nations' first meeting in Geneva in November 1920 held an optimistic view of the future. Germany could not join the League until 1926, and Russia did not become a member until 1934. Ultimately, however, 59 countries became members of the League of Nations.

Section 5 Review

1. **Define** Treaty of Versailles, World Court, economic sanctions, mandate
2. **Identify** Sudeten Germans
3. **Locate and Explain the Significance** Polish Corridor, Czechoslovakia, Yugoslavia
4. **Understanding Ideas** Explain the provisions of the Treaty of Versailles concerning **(a)** reparations; **(b)** Germany's colonies; **(c)** German military power.
5. **Analyzing Ideas** How did the Treaty of Versailles create problems with regard to national minorities?
6. **Summarizing Ideas** What was the League of Nations, and what were its aims?
7. **Evaluating Ideas** Do you consider World War I a major turning point in world history? Why?

Chapter 24 Review

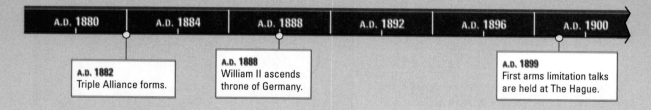

| A.D. 1880 | A.D. 1884 | A.D. 1888 | A.D. 1892 | A.D. 1896 | A.D. 1900 |

A.D. 1882
Triple Alliance forms.

A.D. 1888
William II ascends throne of Germany.

A.D. 1899
First arms limitation talks are held at The Hague.

Chapter Summary
The following list contains the key concepts that you have learned about World War I and the Russian Revolution.

1. Suspicions and rivalries among European nations intensified beginning in the late 1800s. This was caused by strong national feelings, the spread of imperialism, military buildups, and a system of rival alliances.
2. The 1914 assassination of Archduke Francis Ferdinand in Sarajevo sparked World War I.
3. Within a few months, almost all the nations of Europe, plus Japan, were at war.
4. Most people expected the conflict to be over quickly and decisively. Instead, the struggle dragged on for four terribly bloody years.
5. In Russia a revolution toppled the 300-year rule of the Romanov dynasty and ended in a Communist-ruled state.
6. In 1917 the United States entered the world war, providing the fresh troops and new resources that helped defeat the Central Powers.
7. In early 1918, Russia signed a peace treaty with the Central Powers that took it out of the war. Germany mounted an offensive to break the military deadlock on the western front but failed.
8. Although the war ended in 1918, it left problems that continued to plague governments for years. Many lives had been lost, much property had been destroyed, and great bitterness remained. Many problems remained unresolved.
9. Woodrow Wilson's Fourteen Points offered idealistic goals that might have created a lasting framework for peace after World War I. At the Paris Peace Conference, however, many of these goals were forgotten as the Allies sought to punish the losers and collect reparations for their wartime losses.
10. After the war, national groups demanded recognition, especially in eastern Europe.
11. Many hoped the League of Nations would help keep the peace and settle disputes among countries. The United States did not join the League.

Reviewing Important Terms
On a separate sheet of paper, match each of the following terms with the correct definition below.

a. mobilize
b. contraband
c. militarism
d. belligerent
e. atrocities
f. reparations
g. armistice
h. ultimatum
i. propaganda

_____ 1. Brutal crimes of war
_____ 2. Payment for war damages
_____ 3. To ready an army and other resources for combat
_____ 4. Threat by one side of harmful action if the other side rejects its proposals
_____ 5. Agreement to stop fighting
_____ 6. War materials supplied by a neutral nation to a belligerent nation
_____ 7. Ideas, facts, or rumors deliberately spread to further a cause
_____ 8. Warring nation
_____ 9. Glorification of armed strength

Developing Critical Thinking Skills
1. **Classifying Ideas** (a) What was the immediate cause of World War I? (b) What were the underlying causes?
2. **Contrasting Ideas** President Wilson believed the war could be settled with a "peace of justice." (a) What ideals in the Fourteen Points worked toward this goal? (b) What obstacles blocked Wilson's efforts to carry out his plan?
3. **Interpreting Ideas** How did the Allies view the Russian Revolution and civil war?
4. **Evaluating Ideas** (a) How did the peace settlements after World War I readjust the balance of power in the world? (b) Did the peace settlements correct the causes of World War I or ignore them? Explain.
5. **Using Maps** Study the maps on pages 644 and 659. (a) What happened to the Central Powers as a result of World War I? (b) What happened to the Russian Empire?
6. **Using Pictures** As you learned in this chapter, governments used propaganda to encourage citizens to support the war effort. Locate a copy of a propaganda

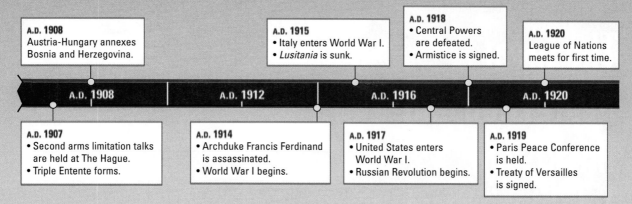

A.D. 1908
Austria-Hungary annexes
Bosnia and Herzegovina.

A.D. 1915
• Italy enters World War I.
• *Lusitania* is sunk.

A.D. 1918
• Central Powers
  are defeated.
• Armistice is signed.

A.D. 1920
League of Nations
meets for first time.

A.D. 1908   A.D. 1912   A.D. 1916   A.D. 1920

A.D. 1907
• Second arms limitation talks
  are held at The Hague.
• Triple Entente forms.

A.D. 1914
• Archduke Francis Ferdinand
  is assassinated.
• World War I begins.

A.D. 1917
• United States enters
  World War I.
• Russian Revolution begins.

A.D. 1919
• Paris Peace Conference
  is held.
• Treaty of Versailles
  is signed.

poster from the era. **(a)** What techniques or symbols used in the poster might arouse a sense of patriotism? **(b)** To what emotions does this poster seem to appeal?

Relating Geography to History

Using information from this chapter and Chapters 21 and 23, answer the following questions. **(a)** Why did Britain's geographical situation make it very concerned around 1900 about Germany's decision to build a large fleet? **(b)** How did geography work both to keep the United States out of World War I and to contribute a reason for it to enter the war?

Relating Past to Present

1. Review the following causes of World War I: nationalism, militarism, imperialism, and international alliances. Which of these forces are still present in the world? Clip newspaper or magazine articles that support your answer.
2. Before World War I, the Balkan region was known as a "powder keg." **(a)** Why was it given this name? **(b)** Are there any similarities between the Balkans in the early 1900s and the Balkans today? **(c)** If so, what actions might be taken to prevent the start of a war there?
3. In 1899 and again in 1907, several nations participated in arms limitation and laws of war conferences held at The Hague. Using library resources, locate books and articles about disarmament efforts in recent years. You might consider efforts to control nuclear weapons, chemical and biological warfare, and land mines. Are any of the obstacles to disarmament today the same as those faced in the late 1800s and early 1900s? Are any unique to the present? Explain.

Applying History Study Skills

Before completing this activity, review Building History Study Skills on page 658.

Study the maps titled "Europe in 1916–1917" on page 645; "The Eastern Front, 1914–1918," on page 648; and "The Western Front, 1914–1918," on page 649, in conjunction with the text of the chapter. Then answer the following questions to help you use the maps as historical documents.

1. Where did most of the fighting on the western front take place?
2. Describe the location of the Brest-Litovsk line. What did it mean for the war on the eastern front?
3. Which side do you think had the greater strategic advantage? Why?
4. At the time of the armistice on the western front, had Germany lost much territory?
5. What may have been a reason why Switzerland was a neutral country?
6. Explain why these referenced maps can be described as historical documents.

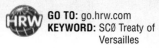
internet**connect**

Search the Internet through the HRW Web site for additional information on the Treaty of Versailles. Then list three of the most important decisions made in the treaty.

HRW **GO TO:** go.hrw.com
KEYWORD: SCØ Treaty of Versailles

Building Your Portfolio

1. **Writing a Report** While troops bogged down in the muddy trenches of Europe, other battles were taking place in the skies. Using your school or public library as a source for information, write a short report on developments in air warfare during World War I. Also investigate the pilots who flew these missions, such as Baron von Richthofen (the "Red Baron"), Eddie Rickenbacker, or members of the Lafayette Escadrille. Place your report in your portfolio.
2. **Preparing a Book Report** Read one of the following novels, and present a book report to the class: Ernest Hemingway's *A Farewell to Arms* (Scribner's); Erich Maria Remarque's *All Quiet on the Western Front* (Fawcett); or Willa Cather's *One of Ours* (Random House). Note the author's point of view on war. How does it compare with the idealism expressed by President Wilson at the start of World War I? Place your book report in your portfolio.

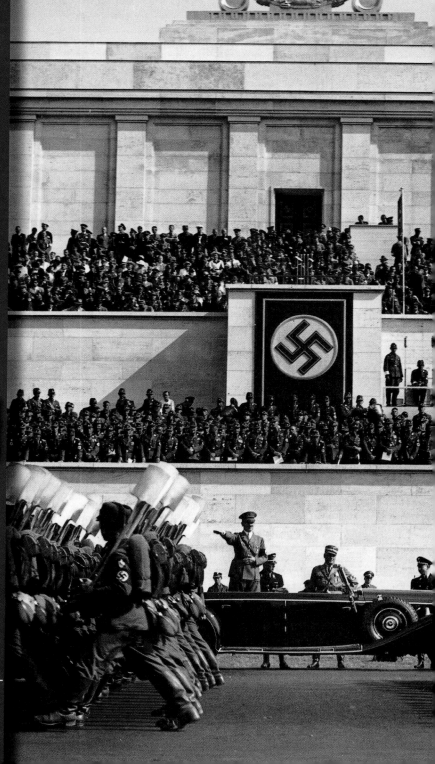

The Great Depression and the Rise of Totalitarianism

TIME

A.D. 1919–1936

A.D. 1919–1936

3.7 million B.C. | 4000 B.C. | A.D. 2100

PLACE

Europe and
the United States

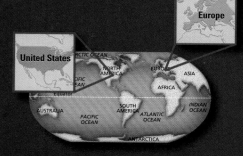

Europe

United States

ARCTIC OCEAN

NORTH
AMERICA

EUROPE

ASIA

AFRICA

Equator

PACIFIC
OCEAN

SOUTH
AMERICA

ATLANTIC
OCEAN

INDIAN
OCEAN

AUSTRALIA

PACIFIC
OCEAN

ANTARCTICA

Hitler rally, 1935, Nuremberg

Significance

Disgusted by the death and waste in World War I, writers and painters began reacting against traditional forms of literature and art. The tremendous economic prosperity that appeared immediately after the war soon crumbled into a terrible economic depression.

Totalitarian regimes—highly centralized governments that allowed no opposition and held total control—claimed to offer Europeans security amid the instability and uncertainty of the period. Tragically, this era served only as a prelude to an even more devastating war.

Terms to Define

totalitarian regimes	Maginot Line
surrealism	Locarno Pact
The Waste Land	general strike
cubism	Popular Front
functionalism	nationalized
international style	Easter Rising
economic boom	fascism
Roaring Twenties	corporatist state
Prohibition	Mein Kampf
economic nationalism	Third Reich
market speculations	Rome-Berlin Axis
on margin	Union of Soviet Socialist
Great Depression	Republics
Social Security Act	collective farms
Tennessee Valley	command economy
Authority	Politburo
Johnson Act	purge
planned economy	Comintern

People to Identify

Thomas Mann	Éamon De Valera
James Joyce	Józef Pilsudski
Ernest Hemingway	Black Shirts
Igor Stravinsky	il Duce
Pablo Picasso	storm troopers
Frank Lloyd Wright	der Führer
Herbert Hoover	Gestapo
Ramsay MacDonald	Leon Trotsky

Chapter Theme Questions

- **The Arts** In what ways might the questioning of traditional values and beliefs be reflected in the arts?
- **Economic Organization** How might worldwide depression lead to changes in government?
- **Politics and Law** What conditions might help to encourage the formation of authoritarian forms of government?

During the 1930s a natural disaster overtook the American farmer as a prolonged drought destroyed farmland from Texas to the Dakotas. As the drought continued, wind blew the dry topsoil into swirling dust clouds, turning the region into what became known as the Dust Bowl. These conditions forced many farm families to leave their homes. In this excerpt from his novel *The Grapes of Wrath*, John Steinbeck describes the hardships of Dust Bowl families as they prepare to leave Oklahoma for California.

❝In the little houses the tenant people sifted their belongings and the belongings of their fathers and of their grandfathers. Picked over their possessions for the journey to the west. The men were ruthless because the past had been spoiled, but the women knew how the past would cry to them in the coming days. . . . How can we live without our lives? How will we know it's us without our past? No. Leave it. Burn it. . . . And they piled up the goods in the yards and set fire to them. They stood and watched them burning, and then frantically they loaded up the cars and drove away, drove in the dust. The dust hung in the air for a long time after the loaded cars had passed.❞

Just as these families experienced hardships, so, too, did many millions struggle during the years between the two world wars.

Section 1

The Postwar Era

Focus Questions

- In what ways did Europeans change their way of thinking about society after World War I?
- What developments in sciences and arts contributed to or demonstrated these changes?

World War I profoundly disrupted European and American society. Ideas about nations and people were changed by the mass destruction. A journalist writing in 1938 offered an impression of these times:

> "Marx, Freud, Einstein all conveyed the same message to the 1920s: the world was not what it seemed. The senses, whose . . . perceptions shaped our ideas of time and distance, right and wrong, law and justice, and the nature of man's behaviour in society, were not to be trusted. . . .
>
> The impression people derived from Einstein, of a universe in which all measurements of value were relative, served to confirm this vision."

The work of leading thinkers, writers, and artists of the time reflected and heightened this sense of disquiet and uncertainty.

The Effects of New Scientific Ideas

Following World War I, many people rejected the belief in continual human progress first expressed during the Enlightenment. Instead they felt a sense of alienation and cynicism. Scientists, who since the 1600s had been proving that human beings could solve almost any problem, began to suggest something else in the early 1900s. Some people interpreted the ideas of psychologist Sigmund Freud, for example, to mean that people could no longer be quite so confident about the powers of rational thought.

Freudian psychology. Sigmund Freud had developed theories of the unconscious (see Chapter 20). He believed that the unconscious mind governs human behavior. In Freud's opinion people are generally unaware of the mental processes of the unconscious. Freud had begun writing in the early 1900s, but his ideas about the unconscious mind and irrationality did not gain popularity until after World War I. If people believed that the unconscious and not the rational mind were controlling people's actions, then much that seemed bewildering could be explained. These ideas seemed to help people understand why the dreadful devastation of World War I had taken place, why things had not turned out as they had hoped, and why uneasiness in human life continued.

Einstein's physics. The theory of relativity made Albert Einstein famous (see Chapter 20). In this theory he had argued that even such seemingly absolute and definite concepts as space, motion, and time had to be seen as relative, or dependent on one another. This concept encouraged those who had come to believe that social standards, whether of morality or of artistic taste, were not absolute. The philosophy of ethical relativism argues that values are relative to societies, and that there is no objective way of justifying one set of principles for all groups. The work of Werner Heisenberg made certainty in basic scientific measurements no longer seem possible, and Einstein's physics seemed to support the relativist's view, though Einstein himself had a "passionate sense of social justice and social responsibility."

After World War I, science itself thus seemed to intensify rather than to relieve doubts about the basic nature of human beings and society. These shifts in understanding caused some people to doubt that science would solve humanity's problems. Distrust in human progress added to uncertainty and lack of confidence in the future.

New Directions in Literature

The major writings of World War I and the postwar years revealed dissatisfaction with traditional ideas, and tried to assert a new vision. The German historian and philosopher, Oswald Spengler, expressed a mood for the era with *The Decline of the West*. Spengler believed that civilizations pass from youth to maturity, and from maturity to old age and death. In his book Spengler predicted that European civilization would disintegrate, a view matching the disillusionment of the era. In literature, writers experimented with form, and influenced by Freud, began to probe unconscious motivations.

Novels. The French novelist Marcel Proust rejected the idea of literature as a pursuit of intellect. Proust believed that reality is a world of memory and sensation lost in daily life. In a minutely-detailed account of a man's search for meaning, Proust vividly brought to life the sensory impressions of a disappeared past. The first part of *Remembrance of Things Past*, a multi-volume novel, appeared in 1913, but most of it was published after World War I. Proust became world famous, and respect for his work continued beyond his death in 1922.

Among the themes of Thomas Mann, Proust's German contemporary, were the constant presence of death amid life and the alienation of the writer from society. An atmosphere of decadence and sadness pervades many of his novels—reflecting moods of the 1920s and 1930s. The somber atmosphere is notable in *The Magic Mountain* (1924), which, set in a hospital, deals symbolically with the moral state of Europe.

The works of Franz Kafka, a Czech writer, pleased those who liked **surrealism** in literature after World War I. Surrealism attempts to merge conscious and unconscious ideas to portray and interpret life in a dreamlike way.

Charlie Chaplin in *Modern Times*

Mechanization created feelings of uneasiness in many people. One of these people was the brilliant comedian Charlie Chaplin. Characterizing the human spirit in its loneliness and humor, he used the new invention, the movie, as the vehicle for his satire. One of his most famous films was *Modern Times,* which was released in 1936. The movie depicts him, in his usual role as a gentle tramp, at work in a huge factory. Here he is shown tightening bolts on an endless assembly line. In pursuit of one neglected bolt, he knocks other workers over, upsets the entire factory routine, and ends as a captive of the machinery.

The Museum of Modern Art/Film Stills Archives

Most of Kafka's works were unknown before his death in 1924, but a friend refused to follow a request to destroy them. In *The Trial* (1925), the main character is tried in a hostile atmosphere for a crime about which he knows nothing. In *The Castle* (1926), a man seeks an authority in a castle, but never finds the official, despite searching through endless corridors and dealing with many other people. These stories of struggle to find meaning and Kafka's unique way of telling them later influenced many writers.

Ireland's James Joyce caused a great stir during this period. In his sometimes bewildering masterpiece, *Ulysses* (1922), Joyce tried to convey everything that happened to a man and everything the man thought, both consciously and unconsciously, in a single day. Joyce used a technique called "stream of consciousness." Influenced by psychoanalysis, the technique attempts to record everything that comes into a character's mind in all experience. *Ulysses* is difficult to understand because it lacks normal punctuation and skips about seemingly at random. *Ulysses* was a revolutionary work that broke away from many of the traditions of the novel. Joyce's

experimentation with language and form was characteristic of post-World War I artists.

American Ernest Hemingway wrote in clear, simple prose. His aim, apparent in *A Farewell to Arms* (1929), was to express the stark disillusionment with life so common in the years after World War I.

Poetry. The American-born poet T. S. Eliot, who spent most of his life in England, expressed the deep pessimism of the postwar years through poetry that altered traditional forms. In his famous poem **The Waste Land** (1922), Eliot gives a despairing description of a world without faith, incapable of restoring spiritual and moral values. Many poets of this period also abandoned traditional rhyme and meter. Instead they wrote poetry without rhyme that had lines of varying lengths. They also experimented with punctuation and even with the physical appearance of their poems.

New Directions in Music and Painting

Musicians and painters cast aside traditional forms and styles with the same creativity as did writers of this period. Some new ideas of musicians and painters originated before World War I, but did not take hold until the unsettled postwar years.

Music. One of the pioneers of a new direction in music was Igor Stravinsky. Born in Russia, he lived most of his life in western Europe and the United States. Stravinsky's ballet *The Rite of Spring* (1913) caused a major uproar at its first performance because it broke so completely with traditional music composition. This composition featured different instruments playing in different keys at the same time, creating a sound that many people found distressing.

Three Austrians, Arnold Schoenberg and his students Alban Berg and Anton von Webern, were even more revolutionary. They wrote what is called atonal music. In Schoenberg's atonal compositions, he abandoned the conventional eight-tone musical scale and instead used a twelve-tone scale. Schoenberg and his followers avoided such traditional forms as the symphony and the concerto. They wrote pieces for unusual collaborations of instruments, such as Webern's *Quartet for Violin, Clarinet, Tenor Saxophone, and Piano*. Their melodies were not developed in a traditional way, and their music sounded strange and unfamiliar to audiences.

Painting. Similar experimentation with forms and styles occurred in the field of painting. Artists of the early 1900s sought new ways to portray the world around them, and dramatically altered traditional representations of humanity and nature.

Pioneers of a new style of art were Spain's Pablo Picasso and the French artist Georges Braque, who worked in Paris. They created a new style called **cubism**, which emphasized geometric forms, shapes, and designs. Using shapes such as cones, cylinders, spheres, flat planes, and especially cubes, they showed the abstract structures of the objects they painted, not their surface appearances. In fact, Picasso and Braque often depicted objects from several different perspectives at the same time. Thus, for example, one might see half a face in profile and half from the front.

Picasso explained nontraditional depictions of reality in his artwork by saying that painting is "a mediator between this strange hostile world and us, a way of seizing the power by giving form to our terrors as well as our desires." Thus Picasso suggested that although he knew his work disturbed people, doing so was part of his purpose. He expressed the anxiety of the era in unsettling forms.

Other painters moved beyond traditional forms in various ways. Surrealistic painters attempted to symbolize the unconscious. Their works featured perfectly painted objects that did not seem to relate to one another. The Spanish surrealist Salvador Dali painted *The Persistence of Memory* (1931), which depicts a dreamlike landscape with what looks like liquid clocks draped over a tree branch and the edge of a shelf. Other artists, notably Russian Wassily Kandinsky and Dutch Piet Mondrian, painted purely abstract designs.

Writers, musicians, and painters of the post-World War I era broke dramatically with the attitudes and styles of the past. They created works reflecting apprehension and cynicism in their views of modern life in the late 1920s and the 1930s—views shared by many people.

Popular Culture

Novelists such as Franz Kafka and composers such as Arnold Schoenberg appealed only to a small audience. Many people found entertainment and escape in other new forms of entertainment.

Popular music. One favorite diversion of many people was listening to music on phonograph records or on the radio. More and more households had radios in the 1920s and 1930s, and music aimed at a mass audience filled the air waves. This was the dawn of the era of the "Big Bands." These "Big Bands" played dance music with catchy melodies written by composers such as Cole Porter and Hoagy Carmichael. In addition, the musical, a type of play featuring song and dance, became a major attraction in the theater. Irving Berlin and George Gershwin composed songs for a golden age of musical theater.

Gershwin and Berlin were also composers of jazz, an innovative popular music borrowed from African Americans. Jazz began in the southern United States in the late 1800s. Performed primarily by African American musicians, jazz developed especially in New Orleans, a city of many cultures. Using African as well as American music as inspiration, jazz emphasizes individual experimentation. One of its major forms, the blues, centers on themes of heartache and sadness, popular during the depressed 1930s.

Film. The chief entertainment for popular audiences of the 1920s and 1930s came from another new art form, the film, or motion picture. Invented around the year 1900, motion pictures swept through Europe and the United States. The first public showings occurred around 1910, and by the 1920s millions of moviegoers routinely waited in long lines to see their favorite films.

The Development of Radio

Up to the end of World War I, radio had been used mainly to send messages by Morse code. David Sarnoff, who became general manager of Radio Corporation of America (RCA), first had the idea of broadcasting music over the radio. RCA began manufacturing "radio music boxes" in 1920. Almost overnight, the radio became a wildly popular consumer item. In just two years, more than 2 million families owned radios.

As radios became popular, the number of broadcasting stations increased dramatically. The first commercial broadcasting station, KDKA in Pittsburgh, went on the air on November 2, 1920, to broadcast the results of the presidential election. Exactly two years later, 564 stations were operating. Soon networks of radio stations were formed: NBC in 1926, CBS in 1927.

Radio became an important source of information and entertainment. News events were broadcast almost as they happened. "Soap operas" (so named because they were often sponsored by soap companies) were popular with homemakers. Shows such as "The Lone Ranger" and "Superman" were aimed at children. In the evening, families listened to the situation comedy "Amos 'n' Andy," a show so popular that many movie theaters interrupted their film to turn on radios so that the audience could hear it. The radio had clearly become an important part of American life.

Films, too, reflected the feelings of the postwar era. Although slapstick comedies were a prevalent form in early movies, some also carried disturbing messages. The greatest film directors—D. W. Griffith in the United States and Sergei Eisenstein in the Soviet Union—made powerful films about human intolerance and cruelty. Most movies, however, offered viewers escape and entertainment.

Architecture

Architecture also underwent great change during the postwar years. New technical advances, such as the use of structural steel, made a remarkable transformation in this area possible.

American Louis Sullivan pioneered the new architecture. Not only did he help to develop the skyscraper, but he also developed a style called **functionalism**. The fundamental principle of functionalism is that a building should be designed for its specific use rather than according to any predetermined style.

Louis Sullivan's pupil Frank Lloyd Wright adopted Sullivan's ideas and added his own. One of Wright's major theories stressed that buildings should be appropriate to their environment. For example, Wright's prairie houses in the Midwest were low buildings with long horizontal lines. In the 1920s Wright built the Imperial Hotel in Tokyo. Adapting the hotel to its location, he floated the foundation on a cushion of mud instead of anchoring it rigidly to rock. Because of this adaptive construction, it was the only large structure in Tokyo to survive the severe earthquake of 1923.

European architects also developed a new style of architecture. Influenced by American architects Sullivan and Wright, a group of architects including the Frenchman Le Corbusier and the German Walter Gropius developed a functional architecture called the **international style**. This style made use of uninterrupted expanses of steel and glass.

The new art forms showed a radical change—a break as dramatic as the one between medieval and Renaissance styles. It was as if nothing—neither music, books, paintings, nor architecture—could be the same again after World War I.

Between 1900 and 1910, Frank Lloyd Wright designed many prairie houses in the Midwest that blended with the flat landscape around them. Subsequent commissions included the Imperial Hotel in Tokyo and the Guggenheim Museum in New York City. Shown above are examples of exterior and interior views of Wright's prairie house design.

Section 1 Review

1. **Define** totalitarian regimes, surrealism, *The Waste Land*, cubism, functionalism, international style
2. **Identify** Thomas Mann, James Joyce, Ernest Hemingway, Igor Stravinsky, Pablo Picasso, Frank Lloyd Wright
3. **Analyzing Ideas** Describe the ways in which the arts and popular entertainment reflected an atmosphere of social uncertainty after World War I in Europe.
4. **Interpreting Ideas** The 1920s and 1930s witnessed much experimentation in art forms. Give an example of this experimentation in each of the following categories: **(a)** literature, **(b)** music, **(c)** painting, **(d)** film, and **(e)** architecture.
5. **Explaining Ideas** Describe how the theories of Freud and Einstein related to the new scientific ideas of the postwar period.

Section 2

Postwar Prosperity Crumbles

Focus Questions

- How did social life change in the United States after World War I?
- What were the causes of the worldwide Great Depression that began in 1929?
- What were the effects of the Great Depression in Europe and the United States?
- What was the New Deal, and how was it a dramatic change for the government of the United States?

Like France and Great Britain, the United States had fought on the victorious Allied side in World War I. Unlike the Europeans, however, the Americans had fought in the war for less than a year. The Atlantic Ocean had separated the United States from the battlefields, and no American land had been devastated. The United States emerged much stronger economically at the end of the war. By 1918 the economy had expanded tremendously, resulting in an **economic boom**, or sudden increase in prosperity.

Postwar Prosperity

The United States emerged from the war as an apparent successor to Great Britain in world leadership. American involvement in the war had been decisive in the Allied victory, and the United States had also played a strong role in the peace settlement.

The United States' financial status most dramatically indicated its potential leadership. The economy of Europe was badly weakened by the devastation of war, forcing Europeans to purchase many products from the United States. Profits for American businesses resulted in a huge increase in overseas investment after 1914. Meanwhile, Europeans struggled to pay their debts to each other and to the United States after the war.

However, the refusal of the United States to join the League of Nations indicated that the United States did not want the responsibility of world leadership. Americans seemed to want to enjoy their newfound prosperity and avoid further entanglement in European affairs.

The Roaring Twenties

Historians have dubbed the decade of the 1920s the **Roaring Twenties** because of the booming economy that brought a fast pace of life and a sometimes frantic pursuit of pleasure to the era. Some have attributed that atmosphere to American exposure to European attitudes during World War I, or to a disillusioned rebellion against traditions that had failed. Other factors also contributed to social change.

During the 1920s many changes affected people's lives. Automobiles became a popular means of transportation. Commercial airlines began carrying mail (regular passenger service did not begin until the 1930s, and even then remained uncommon). Telephones linked millions of homes, and movies became a favorite form of entertainment. Jazz became popular, new fast dances like the Charleston gained acceptance, and movie stars became public idols. Charles Lindbergh gained immediate worldwide fame for his 1927 solo flight across the Atlantic Ocean, a feat that had never before been accomplished.

This era of enormous confidence also prompted a revolt against traditional morality and standards. Women gained more freedom as they won the right to vote and joined the work force in greater numbers than ever before. **Prohibition**—the Eighteenth Amendment—forbidding the manufacture, sale, and transportation of alcoholic beverages was widely evaded. Smuggling and bootlegging—the illegal manufacture and sale of liquor—made Prohibition ineffective, and the amendment was repealed in 1933.

The Economy

Although the United States prospered during this period, some economic flaws existed. For example, wages paid to laborers did not keep pace with inflation. In other words, not enough money ended up in the hands of consumers so that they could buy all the goods being produced. Instead, profits went either to stockholders or toward reinvestment in new machinery and additional factories. Increased use of labor-saving machinery stimulated production but at the same time increased unemployment, as fewer employees were needed to produce more and more goods.

Agriculture suffered as well. During the war, European demand for grain had driven prices up, and many American farmers had taken out loans to buy modern machinery and cultivate new land. In the 1920s European demand fell, and world grain prices dropped. Farmers were forced to produce as much as they could to try to pay off their debts. Serious overproduction was the result.

Another problem occurred because of **economic nationalism**. This is the policy a nation uses to improve its economic well-being by establishing protective tariffs and similar restrictions on the import and export of goods. In the 1920s many countries set up tariffs to protect their own expanding industries from foreign competition. However, the home markets of each country could not consume what was produced, and high tariffs made it difficult to market the surplus abroad.

High American tariffs made it hard for European countries to sell their goods in the United States. Because they could not sell goods *to* the United States, they could not acquire dollars to purchase goods *from* the United States, or to pay off their war debts. Banks and businesspeople in the United States willingly lent money to Europeans so that they could buy American goods. But this practice merely created more indebtedness.

Speculation, Panic, and Crash

Throughout the 1920s millions of Americans made **market speculations**, or risky investments, in the stock market, hoping for quick, high profits. The stock market is the organization through which stock certificates are bought and sold. A company issues shares of stock to raise capital for its business. Investors buy shares to earn income from the company's earnings called dividends, or to resell the shares for profit if their value rises. During the 1920s prices of stocks sold on the New York Stock Exchange soared, and many investors did make large profits. Everyone expected stock prices to rise indefinitely.

Trouble loomed, however, with the growing practice of buying **on margin**. Investors borrowed money to buy stock using only the value of the stock or its expected profit as security. They often put down as little as 10 percent of the full price. When the stock's value rose, the stock could be sold at the higher value, and profit made to cover the cost. If the value of the stock fell, however, the investor had no means to repay the original amount borrowed, and the lender had no way to recover the money.

On October 29, 1929, panic swept investors in the New York Stock Exchange. Stock prices sank to an all-time low when more than 16 million shares of stock were suddenly dumped on the market. With prices falling, no one would buy. As a result, most of the stocks on the exchange became virtually worthless. Vast fortunes vanished. Banks called in loans, which could not be repaid, and thousands of banks and their customers—businesses, factories, farms, mining companies, and individuals—went bankrupt.

The Great Depression

The collapse of the New York Stock Exchange marked the beginning of a worldwide depression called the **Great Depression**. Some of the effects of this economic crisis included falling wages and prices, a slowdown of business activity, and a high rate of unemployment. Many of the most reliable European banks closed their doors. By 1932 more than 30 million workers in countries throughout the industrialized world could not find jobs. Germany stopped paying reparations, and the Allied nations ceased payments of war debts to the United States.

Strangely, poverty during the Depression occurred in the midst of abundant productivity. Prices fell to very low levels, but goods could not be sold because people simply did not have the money to buy them. Some countries tried to force prices to rise by

What If?

The Great Depression
What if the crash of 1929 had not occurred? Would there have been a Great Depression? Explain.

destroying agricultural surpluses—Brazil burned excess coffee for a decade. The world economy sank. By 1932, the total value of international trade had fallen by more than half.

Responses to the Great Depression

The United States responded to the Great Depression by continuing its policy of economic nationalism. It raised tariffs even higher and cut off American loans to Europe. Germany and Austria had wanted to establish a customs union to aid their economies. However, several European nations opposed the project, and the World Court banned it. In many cases, it appeared, the immediate response to the Great Depression made recovery more difficult.

In 1933 a world economic conference met in London, but it failed to promote greater financial cooperation among the industrial nations. Most of these countries had already decided upon economic nationalism to protect themselves in the Great Depression.

Great Britain tried to induce full employment and stimulate production by granting low-interest loans to its industries. In addition to raising its tariffs against foreign goods in 1931, Great Britain formed a system for economic cooperation within its empire. In 1932 at a conference in Ottawa, Canada, Great Britain devised a system of imperial preference. Through this system the dominions and possessions within the British Empire agreed to levy low tariffs on one another's products. In a period of international economic uncertainty, they were attempting to become economically self-sufficient.

France, less industrialized than Great Britain, did not suffer as badly during the Great Depression. However, French trade declined, unemployment increased, and industrial production dropped sharply. The uncertainty of the Depression years caused greater political instability in France than troubles following the war had created. In 1933 alone there were three changes of government.

Elsewhere in the world, the Great Depression caused unrest and violence. In Germany it helped destroy the Weimar Republic established at the end of the war. The representative governments that did survive the severe shock of the Great Depression had strong democratic traditions.

The New Deal

The United States was behind most other industrial nations in creating social legislation. Unemployment insurance and government relief programs did not exist. As a result, when the Great Depression hit, American workers had to rely on their savings, if any, and on charity provided by private organizations. People stood in breadlines in America to receive a bowl of soup or a plate of stew. Some earned money by selling apples in the streets.

Under President Herbert Hoover, the federal government tried to remedy these severe conditions, but the measures adopted were not extensive. Hoover believed that prosperity was "just around the corner." Americans in great numbers disagreed with Hoover, and elected a new president, Franklin D. Roosevelt, who took office in 1933.

Roosevelt immediately embarked upon a program of relief and reform called the New Deal. Under the provisions of the New Deal program, the government granted money to each state for food, shelter, and clothing for the needy. The government also began a program of public works to provide employment through the construction of various public buildings, roads, and other projects.

Following Roosevelt's emergency relief program, Congress enacted sweeping reform of the economic system. Banks and stock exchanges were placed under stricter regulation. The **Social Security Act** of 1935 provided for unemployment and old-age benefits. A 40-hour workweek and minimum wage levels were established. The federal government guaranteed workers the long fought-for right to form unions.

The federal government also tried to relieve the desperate situation of farmers by paying them to take land out of production and to plant crops that would revitalize the soil. Later the government adopted a program of buying surplus farm crops to prevent the prices of farm goods from plunging.

Another federal program of far-reaching economic and social significance established the **Tennessee Valley Authority**, or TVA, in the valley of the Tennessee River and its tributaries. The TVA built a series of multipurpose dams in this area to generate cheap electricity, help prevent floods and soil erosion, and improve navigation along the river. The project proved remarkably successful.

Occupied primarily with domestic problems, the administration made some effort to revive world trade.

In this scene from the Great Depression, women and children receive food from the New Hope Mission in New York City.

During his nearly four full terms as president of the United States, Franklin Roosevelt developed many government agencies to provide farmers and the unemployed with financial assistance.

Specific efforts were made by the Roosevelt administration to revive trade in Latin America. A series of treaties and laws called the Good Neighbor policy both helped Western economies and at the same time enhanced the image of the United States. However, the United States also passed the **Johnson Act** of 1934, which prohibited loans, even private ones, to countries that had not paid their war debts. Many European nations could not pay their debts, and this act of economic nationalism further hurt foreign trade and European economies.

Under the New Deal, the United States government became more deeply involved than ever before in the welfare of its own citizens. The government attempted in many ways to restore prosperity. However, the impact of the Great Depression was too great to be cured completely by programs, even those as ambitious as the New Deal. Only when the United States mobilized its industrial sector for war did the Great Depression end.

Political Tensions After World War I

Focus Questions

- **What were conditions like in France after World War I?**
- **Why were times difficult in Great Britain after World War I?**
- **How did the countries created from the former Austria-Hungary fare in postwar Europe?**

The events of the postwar years strained older and more experienced European democracies such as France and Great Britain. The economies of these nations had been harmed by the war, and recovery was made difficult by debt and the lack of good markets in the weakened nations. Unemployment rose because production had expanded to fill wartime needs, and now an overabundance existed.

Many Europeans believed that governments needed to take a more active role in economic matters. Before World War I, many people had believed that governments should not interfere in business matters.

However, wartime needs had led several nations to adopt a **planned economy**—an economy in which government directs the use of national resources and regulates the economy to achieve both goals and stability. As the system had worked in wartime, why not use it to solve peacetime economic problems?

In some European nations, such as Poland and Austria, different problems arose. These countries set up republics after World War I. Their societies lacked experienced leaders, as well as a history of democratic institutions solving problems. When problems arose, such as the crisis of the Great Depression, political and social unrest rose rapidly, and serious signs of governmental weakness appeared.

France's Postwar Difficulties

During the four years of World War I, northern France had been a major battleground. At war's end, farmland and even entire cities lay in ruins, and trenches and shell holes scarred the land. The most modern parts of France's agriculture and industry had been destroyed. Most tragic of all, a high percentage of the young men of France had been killed.

Thus France emerged from World War I victorious but unstable. It still owed money that it had borrowed from its citizens and from the United States during and after the war. Its industry was weak and production had declined. Inflation also took its toll. The burden of higher prices fell mostly on industrial workers and the lower middle class—those least able to pay.

The expenses of the French government soared for several reasons. The government embarked on a massive reconstruction of war-damaged areas. Inflation soared and France still had its heavy debt, as well as interest on that debt, for war material. But most important, perhaps, it had to pay for military security.

The Maginot Line. Twice in less than 50 years, Germany had invaded France. To prevent invasion from happening again, France rebuilt its army. It also constructed a series of steel and concrete fortifications called the **Maginot** (MA·zhuh·noh) **Line**. Named after its planner, this extensive defense system stretched nearly 200 miles (320 kilometers) along the borders of Germany and Luxembourg.

Construction of the Maginot Line cost enormous sums of money. Haunted by the experience of World War I, the French planned to make their defenses so strong that the country could never again be invaded overland from the east.

International affairs. In the beginning of 1923, struggling Germany informed the Allies that it could not continue to pay war reparations on schedule. Despite British objections, France and Belgium marched troops into Germany's coal- and iron-rich Ruhr Valley in January 1923. France intended to force payment, even seizing industry, until it collected the money Germany owed. German workers resisted by halting production, and the French withdrew after a renegotiated payment schedule was agreed upon.

By 1925 the political situation in Europe seemed to be improving. In that year, representatives from Great Britain, France, Germany, Belgium, Italy, Czechoslovakia, and Poland met at Locarno, Switzerland. There they signed a number of treaties known together as the **Locarno Pact**. Delegates to the conference pledged that their countries would peacefully settle all future disputes, guaranteed the existing Franco-German boundaries, and negotiated outstanding issues. In addition, France signed mutual assistance treaties with Poland and Czechoslovakia.

However, France's protective alliances began to weaken. By the mid-1930s Belgium canceled its defensive alliance with France and declared itself neutral in any future war. France formed a shaky alliance with its prewar ally Russia, now under a Communist government. Wartime ally Italy, now under the rule of a militaristic dictatorship, resumed its old opposition to France. In keeping with its aim of encircling Germany, France developed postwar alliances with Yugoslavia and Romania as well as the alliances already made with Poland and Czechoslovakia. However, these nations, although they shared France's mistrust of Germany, were relatively weak allies.

Political unrest. In early 1934 a scandal occurred in the French government that touched off huge riots in Paris. Anti-parliamentary rioters demanded an end to the republican form of government. Some advocated fascist regimes that they felt would protect the nation and combat instability.

Trade unions responded to the threat from the right-wing conservatives by calling a **general strike**—a refusal by laborers in various industries to work until demands are met. Shortly thereafter, parties of the left-wing organized a coalition government called the **Popular Front**. Its leader, Léon Blum, a socialist, became premier of France in 1936. United for the moment against the threat of a coup d'état (seizure of power by force), Blum's government carried out reforms.

The Popular Front first persuaded leaders of industry to grant pay increases to end the strike. The government then established a 40-hour workweek and granted workers the right to paid vacations. It also set up a system for the arbitration of labor disputes. The Bank of France came under government control and the armaments industry was partially **nationalized**— put under government control or ownership.

Prices, however, continued to rise to such levels that increased wages did little to help. Industrialists refused to cooperate. Continuing hostility from the right wing, who believed "Better Hitler than Blum," and divisions in his own Popular Front ended Blum's ministry after only one year. Through his leadership in this brief period, however, France's government enacted important reforms.

After the fall of the Popular Front, French workers suffered severe setbacks. Most of the pro-labor reforms of Blum's ministry were canceled, and the working class came to oppose the government harshly. Many political and social groups, some with extreme approaches, developed. Traditional French systems of government and society were questioned.

France remained a democracy, but bitter divisions existed among the people. France also feared German military power, which began recovering strength at an alarming rate.

Great Britain After World War I

Like France, Great Britain faced grave economic difficulties after World War I. Great Britain had become a debtor nation, and the capital it had used to finance industrial expansion was gone.

British industry and trade suffered. As in other countries, disarmament had left many factory workers unemployed. Coal, long a mainstay of British industry, was being surpassed by other forms of power. The United States and Japan had taken many of Great Britain's world markets during the war. After the war Britain's outdated factories and machinery made competition with newer American or Japanese technology difficult. In addition, the high tariffs of economic nationalism damaged British trade because Great Britain needed to sell abroad in order to pay for imports of food and raw materials.

Labor troubles. By 1921, nearly a quarter of Great Britain's work force was unemployed. This high unemployment rate meant labor unrest. Labor unions fought to maintain the high wages and full employment rate of the war years, while industrialists fought to resist the unions' demands. Meanwhile, government had to pay unemployment benefits.

World War I brought death and destruction to millions of people across the world. Here a café in postwar Paris bustles as the French try to regain a sense of normalcy in their lives.

In the Easter Rising, a Citizen Army parades outside Liberty Hall.

In 1926 coal miners called a strike. Workers in iron and steel, transportation, building, and printing industries left their jobs as well, creating one of the largest general strikes in British history. The general strike ended after nine days, and the miners returned to work months later in defeat. Later the government passed legislation that controlled unions and outlawed general strikes.

A spokesman for workers was Ramsay MacDonald, leader of the Labour Party. Although the Labour Party grew stronger, it lacked a majority in the House of Commons. Therefore, MacDonald formed a coalition with the Liberal Party, which had declined in strength because it could not attract working-class members. Coalition government determined British policy for all of the 1930s, with MacDonald, Stanley Baldwin, and then Neville Chamberlain at its head. Through strict government economy, protectionist policies, and help for the construction industry, the British economy slowly recovered. Thus Great Britain avoided the deep social unrest that toppled democratic governments elsewhere in Europe.

Ireland. In the 1920s Great Britain faced more problems in a country it had ruled for centuries. During the 1800s the British government and Irish nationalists struggled over the issue of home rule for

Ireland. The matter of limited self-government was unresolved by 1914, and most Irish people still yearned for complete independence.

During World War I, Irish nationalists revolted in the **Easter Rising** on Easter Monday, April 24, 1916. The British harshly suppressed the rebellion and executed its leaders. Fighting broke out again in 1918. For years the Irish Republican Army and British troops were engaged in a series of violent and bitter struggles.

The British lost what support of the Irish people it had, and with Ireland virtually ungovernable, Great Britain was pressed for settlement. A treaty divided Ireland in 1922, with Catholic southern Ireland becoming the Irish Free State, a self-governing dominion with loose ties to Great Britain. Six northern counties with a Protestant majority chose to remain in the United Kingdom, with representatives in British Parliament, as Northern Ireland.

Many Irish nationalists refused to accept the arrangement, and civil war raged again in 1922. Eventually, Irish nationalists came to power politically. In 1937 the Irish Free State adopted a new constitution and the name Éire (AR·uh). Éamon De Valera (dev·uh·LER·uh) was elected its first prime minister. In 1949 Eire became completely independent, calling itself the Republic of Ireland.

Many of the issues that divided the island for centuries trouble it still. Religious and political factions in Northern Ireland and the Republic of Ireland remain hostile to each other, and the relations between Great Britain and Ireland are still troubled.

Eastern Europe

As western European powers struggled politically and economically to recover in the aftermath of World War I, new nations in eastern Europe struggled to form governments and identities. Instability in eastern Europe had led to the outbreak of World War I, and after the Treaty of Versailles, boundaries had been redrawn. The cultural tensions that sparked the first world war had not disappeared, however. These problems resurfaced in the political situations that existed in eastern European nations, both internally and externally.

As nations with little democratic experience struggled to maintain governments, economic problems added to their difficulties. The breakup of the Russian and Austro-Hungarian empires disrupted old patterns of trade. With the Great Depression devastating economies throughout the industrialized world, policies of economic nationalism offered little prospect of help to the countries of eastern Europe.

Finland, Czechoslovakia, and the Baltic countries of Latvia, Estonia, and Lithuania managed to sustain democratic regimes, but few other nations in eastern Europe succeeded in doing so. Three examples help illustrate what happened.

Austria. The Austria created after the war was a small poverty-stricken nation. Many Austrians would have preferred *Anschluss* (union) with Germany, but peace treaties forbade it. Austria's economic weakness and a continuing struggle between urban socialists and rural conservatives weakened the attempt at democracy. A third of the country's population lived in Vienna, once the capital of a large empire, and they contended for control against the rest of the country, who saw the nation's needs differently. The result was paralysis. Factions set up private armies in the streets, and the desire for order made authoritarian rule more appealing. The country became progressively less democratic.

Hungary. Hungary was declared a republic in November 1918. In March 1919, Béla Kun, a Hungarian Communist who had participated in the Russian Revolution, replaced a weak republic and tried to establish a system modeled on Russia's new government. He succeeded in ousting most of the Romanian troops that were then occupying Hungary, but he also nationalized the land, which antagonized the people. The distribution of food failed. Russia did not help as promised, Kun's government fell, and Romanians entered Budapest in August that same year.

By 1920 the Allies had persuaded Romania to withdraw and Hungarian Admiral Miklós Horthy, a representative of the military class, ruled. Under Admiral Horthy's reactionary rule, postwar reconstruction was impossible. Parts of Hungary's prewar territory had been given to Austria, Romania, Poland, and Italy, and new boundaries cut off factories from supplies and markets. As the wheat market collapsed and the Great Depression deepened, Hungary sought help first from the League of Nations, then Italy and Germany. Thus the nation found itself with less and less control of its destiny.

Poland. The new Polish democratic constitution of 1921 was closely modeled on that of France's Third Republic (see Chapter 21). However, bitter opposition from many groups prevented the new government from operating effectively. High German tariffs crippled the Polish economy, and the country became more and more unstable. In 1926 Marshal Józef Pilsudski (peel·soot·skee) installed a military dictatorship. Economically distressed and located between Germany and Russia, democracy in Poland had little chance.

Section 3 Review

1. **Define** planned economy, Maginot Line, Locarno Pact, general strike, Popular Front, nationalized, Easter Rising
2. **Identify** Ramsay MacDonald, Éamon De Valera, Józef Pilsudski
3. **Organizing Ideas** What internal problems did France experience during the period after World War I?
4. **Analyzing Ideas** In many European countries democracy was replaced by authoritarian rule in the years following World War I. Great Britain, however, avoided this fate. Explain why this was possible.
5. **Explaining Ideas** Why were the eastern European countries less able than their western counterparts to deal with the problems resulting from the Great Depression?

Fascist Dictatorships in Italy and Germany

Focus Questions

- **What common conditions did totalitarian regimes in Europe seek to address?**
- **What were the characteristics of Mussolini's rise to power?**
- **How did provisions of the Treaty of Versailles lead to Hitler's rise to power?**

As it did elsewhere, the war and its aftermath took their toll in Italy and Germany. Heavy loss of life, a crushing burden of debt, high unemployment, and runaway inflation plagued these countries. In Italy labor troubles resulted in violent strikes. The Italian government, a constitutional monarchy, seemed unable to respond effectively to these problems.

The Rise of Fascism in Italy

One person who did offer a clear response was Benito Mussolini. The son of a blacksmith, he had been a socialist as a young man and had edited a socialist newspaper. His writing had brought him several terms in jail and a period in exile. During World War I his views changed. Mussolini became an extreme nationalist, and the Italian Socialist Party expelled him. After Italy joined the Allies, he enlisted in the army and was wounded in battle.

When Mussolini returned from the war, he began to organize his own political party. He called it the Fascist Party and called its doctrine **fascism** (FASH·iz·uhm). The words *fascist* and *fascism* come from the Latin word *fasces*. In ancient Rome a *fasces* was a bundle of rods bound tightly around an ax, symbolizing governmental authority. Mussolini adopted this symbol, referring to a *Fasci di Combattimento*, fighters bound as tightly as the rods around the ax. Thus his nationalist movement gained a name.

In his book *Delivered from Evil*, Robert Leckie describes Benito Mussolini's physical features and the imposing personality that brought him and the Fascist Party to power in Italy in the 1920s:

"At . . . his full height . . . [he was] . . . remarkable for his commanding head and his broad low brow, piercing black eyes, wide mouth and jutting square jaw. Because of his great head, he gave the impression of physical strength. Yet, if he were to remove his outer garments, it would be seen that his shoulders were thin, his arching chest a pouting pigeon's breast and his arms and legs spindly. However, like Napoleon, he could strike fear into men twice his size with a direct glance from those astonishing eyes.**"**

Fascism, like communism, relies on dictatorial rule and a totalitarian regime, in which the state maintains rigid control of the people through force and censorship. All authority belongs to the state, with individual rights subordinate to it. However, important differences exist between communism and fascism. Communism seeks a socialist economy and international revolution. It appeals to workers and promises a classless society. Fascism, on the other hand, is extremely nationalistic, and appeals to the middle class while promising to preserve existing social classes. Fascism defends ownership of private property. Each system violently opposes the other.

Mussolini Gains Power

Mussolini found his first followers among demobilized soldiers and discontented nationalists. Gradually, however, the Fascists attracted professionals, wealthy landowners, and businesspeople, especially large manufacturers who were interested in blocking communist gains among workers. These new supporters provided financial assistance to the Fascists. Fascists also developed strong support among the lower middle classes, who had been severely hurt by inflation, and among the unemployed.

Recognizing the appeal of anticommunism, Mussolini emphasized it in his program. He promised to prevent a proletarian revolution. Fascism began to stand for the protection of private property and the middle class. At the same time, he proposed a collaboration between labor and management to restore and protect the economy. He also stressed national prestige, pledging that Italy would return to the military glories of the Roman Empire.

The Fascists began a violent campaign against opponents, especially socialists and communists. Rowdy groups broke up strikes and political meetings and drove properly elected socialist officials from office. Fascists became known as the Black Shirts for the shirt they wore as a uniform.

In October 1922 Black Shirt groups from all over Italy converged on Rome, claiming they were coming to defend Italy against a communist revolution.

Liberal members of the Italian parliament insisted that the king declare martial law. When he refused, the cabinet resigned. Conservative advisers then persuaded the king to appoint Mussolini premier and to ask him to head a coalition government.

Mussolini had often criticized democracy as a weak and ineffective form of government. Once in office, he began to destroy democracy in Italy and set up a dictatorship. He appointed Fascists to all official positions both in the central government and in the provinces. He pushed through parliament a new election law providing that the party receiving the most votes would automatically gain two thirds of the seats in the Chamber of Deputies, the lower house of parliament. The Fascists won the election in 1924, and in 1925, Mussolini was made "head of the government," accountable to no one. He took the title *il Duce* (DOO·chay), Italian for "the leader."

Italy as a Police State

Now all of the outward signs of a dictatorship appeared. Opposition parties were disbanded. The government suspended freedom of speech, freedom of the press, freedom of assembly, and trial by jury. Labor unions came under government control, and strikes were outlawed. Uniformed and secret police spied on everyone.

Mussolini became commander in chief of the army, navy, and air force and head of the police.

Although he allowed the king to reign as a figurehead, real power lay in the hands of the Grand Council of the Fascist Party. Mussolini headed the Council.

The Corporatist State

Mussolini argued that in a modern industrial society, representation according to geographic location was outdated. Instead, he introduced a new and complicated system of government called corporatism in which representation was according to profession or occupation. The country's major economic activities, such as agriculture, transportation, manufacturing, and commerce, were formed into syndicates that resembled corporations. Thus Italy became known as a **corporatist state**.

By the 1930s, Italy had 22 of these "corporations." In each corporation representatives of government, management, and labor met to establish wages and prices and to agree upon working conditions. Private property remained in the hands of its owners, and profits were allowed. Labor unions and capitalists alike had to submit to the will of Mussolini's government. All parts of society had to cooperate with one another for the goals of the state.

In addition to reshaping the government, Mussolini strengthened the army and navy and increased armaments. These two additional changes

Mussolini's "Sons of the Wolf"

in Italy had a double purpose: to reduce unemployment and to increase military strength. Thus a new form of linkage between public and private sectors appeared in Italian government. The Fascist dictator, Mussolini, sat at the top of the entire system.

The Weimar Republic

As in Italy, difficulties in Germany gave rise to political change after World War I. In November 1918 Germany was declared a republic. The following year, an assembly met in the city of Weimar (VY·mahr) and drafted a constitution that made Germany a federal republic, known as the Weimar Republic.

Germany's new government had a president and a two-house parliament elected by universal suffrage. The parliament included the Reichsrat (RYKS·raht) and the Reichstag. The president appointed the chancellor, Germany's prime minister.

The Weimar Republic was not popular with the German people. The republic had been born in the desire to end the war and to avoid a revolution in Germany as had occurred in Russia. Many Germans opposed republican government, and because Weimar representatives signed the humiliating Versailles Treaty, the German people came to see the Weimar Republic as a traitorous government.

Many of the difficulties of the Weimar Republic reflected the economic, social, and political problems that faced all of Europe after the war. Unemployment was high and inflation soared, ruining German currency. In 1923 it took more than 1 trillion marks to equal 25 cents, and money devalued so rapidly printers quit putting numbers on bills.

Within its first year, two attempted revolutions threatened the Weimar Republic. In Berlin, a right-wing group tried to overthrow the republic and briefly controlled the city. The attempted overthrow in Berlin was defeated by a general strike. Socialist and communist workers paralyzed Berlin and made it impossible for the right-wing rebels to set up their own government. In 1923, a Communist government took over Munich, the capital of the state of Bavaria, and attempted to withdraw from the federal union. The revolt was crushed by army units and private right-wing armies that began a reign of right-wing terror of their own. Though the rebellions failed, they demonstrated the extreme weakness of the Weimar Republic.

The Nazis and Hitler

One of the many political parties that formed in Germany after World War I was the German Workers'

Inflation soared in Germany during the early 1920s. The value of the mark fell so low that people could get more value out of the marks by baling and selling them by weight as waste paper than they could by using marks as currency.

Party. In 1920 the German Workers' Party, attempting to broaden its appeal, changed its name to the National Socialist German Workers' Party, or Nazi Party. The party did not represent the working class, as its name might indicate. The Nazi Party was extremely nationalistic and violently anticommunist. Promising to protect Germany from communism, the party eventually attracted the support of wealthy business leaders and landowners in Germany.

One of the first Nazi recruits, an ex-soldier named Adolf Hitler, was born in Austria in 1889. He was the son of a minor government official. As a young man, Hitler had gone to Vienna, where he failed as an artist and was therefore forced to work at various odd jobs. It was there in Vienna, where Jews contributed to the city's rich cultural life and also had risen to respected positions, that Hitler became resentful of the Jews and violently anti-Semitic.

Hitler served in the German army in World War I and later moved to the city of Munich in the state of Bavaria, where he joined the German Workers Party. Head of the Nazis by 1921, he took part in the uprising in Munich in 1923. The uprising failed, and Hitler was sentenced to prison. While there, he wrote **Mein Kampf** (*My Struggle*), a rambling book that expressed the spirit of the Nazi movement. In

Hitler (left) and Mussolini (right) review German troops in Berlin on one of Mussolini's many state visits to Germany.

Mein Kampf, Hitler left no doubt about his goals for the German nation. He wrote:

> ❝If the National Socialist [Nazi] movement really wants to be consecrated [honored] by history with a great mission for our nation . . . it must find the courage to gather our people and their strength for an advance along the road that will lead this people from its present restricted living space to new land and soil.❞

Hitler possessed hypnotic talent as an orator, and after his release from prison, he took advantage of radio to spread his message. In the confused situation of the postwar years, his emotional speeches attracted enthusiastic listeners. The frustration, bitterness, and patriotism Hitler expressed reflected the feelings of many Germans who felt humiliated by the Treaty of Versailles. The unfair war reparations and loss of territory made some eager to follow a leader that might restore Germany's lost glory.

Hitler's program found appeal in Germany. Facing economic and social disaster, Germans responded to the charismatic speaker, and Nazi popularity rose in each election. Hitler promised to repeal the Versailles Treaty, especially the "war-guilt" clause. He said that he would restore Germany to equality in armaments and regain all its lost territory and colonies to build a "Greater Germany." Like Mussolini, he promised protection against communism.

To these promises Hitler added his garbled racial doctrine. According to this doctrine, the Germans, as "Aryans" (a misapplied use of the word), were a "master race." All other races were inferior. As Hitler's power increased, his personal traits of intolerance, hatred, and contempt for non-Germanic people became the policies of the government.

Hitler's Rise to Power

The Nazis had few followers* until the Great Depression. In the election of 1930, however, many middle-class voters turned to the Nazi Party. These voters had experienced economic hardships and had lost their savings because of inflation. In addition, many of them feared a Communist revolution. Two years later the Nazi Party won 230 seats in the Reichstag. Although their party was the largest single party there, the Nazis still did not have enough votes to form a government.

In January 1933, when it appeared that no other party could successfully form a government, the president of the republic, Paul von Hindenburg, appointed Hitler as chancellor.

Because the Nazis still lacked a majority, Hitler used the Nazis' private army—the storm troopers, or Brown Shirts—to intimidate the Reichstag. When someone set fire to the Reichstag building in February 1933, Hitler was granted emergency powers to deal with this alleged Communist revolt. Hitler expertly used these powers to make himself a dictator.

The Nazi Program in Action

Once in power, Hitler, who regarded Mussolini's totalitarian state to be a natural ally, took the title *der Führer* (FYOOR·ur), German for "the leader." Quickly turning Germany into a police state, Hitler banned opposition parties, labor unions, and opposition newspapers. To enforce these policies, Hitler gave the Gestapo, a secret-police force, wide-ranging powers. Former allies in the march to power were executed.

Liberals, socialists, and Communists often ended up dead or in large prisons that were called concentration camps. Members of the so-called inferior races increasingly suffered severe persecutions. Jews became particular targets of the Nazi attacks. They were deprived of their civil rights, publicly humiliated, and murdered by storm troopers. In some places the Nazis forced the Jews to live in segregated neighborhoods called ghettos.

---

*In 1925 the growing Nazi Party had 25,000 members; four years later it had 180,000 members.

Building History Study Skills

READ
WRITE
INTERPRET
CONNECT
THINK

Thinking About History: Analyzing Documents

Documents are basic sources for historians. They are used to answer a question, to develop a theory, or to support a view of a historical event. Documents can be any information written on a particular subject and may consist of essays, books, charts, and graphs, to name a few. Reading and analyzing documents helps you to formulate your own view of events based on the evidence and your analysis. Using documents helps you to integrate information and form conclusions.

How to Analyze Documents
To analyze documents, follow these steps.
1. Explain the question, theory, or point of view being researched in the documents.
2. Classify the documents. Determine whether they deal with political, economic, or social issues.
3. Identify the source of the documents.
4. Determine the validity and bias of the documents being analyzed.
5. Connect the documents to each other.
6. Formulate a thesis statement based on the connection found in the documents.

Developing the Skill
The following documents deal with Hitler's rise to power in Germany. The question the documents focus on is "How did Hitler destroy parliamentary democracy in Germany?"

The Election Results		
	November 1932	March 1933
National Socialists	196	233
Nationalists	51	53
People's Party & Bavarian Peoples Party	31	21
Catholic Center	70	73
Socialists	121	120
Communists	100	81

"The following is decreed as a defensive measure against Communist acts of violence, endangering the state: Sections 114, 115, 117, 118, 123, 124, and 153 of the Constitution of the German Reich are suspended until further notice. Thus, restrictions on personal liberty, on the right of free expression of opinion, including freedom of the press, on the right of assembly . . . association, . . . warrants for house-searches, . . . are also permissible beyond the legal limits otherwise prescribed.**"**

The documents should be classified as political because the subject of each is government. The source of the documents is Tony Edwards' *History Broadsheets, Hitler & Germany 1919–1939*. The documents are unbiased because they merely state facts.

The chart of the election results tells us that there was a multiparty system in Germany's Weimar Republic after World War I. The parties are listed from extreme right-wing National Socialists (Nazis) to extreme left-wing Communists. In order to rule, a party had to have most of the seats, or a majority, in the Reichstag. No party was ever strong enough to have a majority without combining their votes with those of at least one other party. As the chart indicates, the Nazis won the most seats in the Reichstag in the election of 1932, but did not have a majority. Their major competitors were the Communists and the Socialists at the other end of the political spectrum. However, following the election of 1933 the Nationalists formed a coalition with the Nazis, giving them a majority in the Reichstag.

The second document helps explain how the Nazis were able to consolidate their power by destroying the opposition. The Emergency Decree was based on the burning of the Reichstag, which the Nazis unjustly blamed on the Communists. This decree played on the fear of disorder and revolution that people believed was caused by the Communists. The Emergency Decree also put restrictions on the Communists, who were the Nazis' biggest rivals and to whom they had lost seats in the Reichstag in the election of 1933.

Practicing the Skill
Read the excerpt from *Mein Kampf* on page 682. What bias does the document show? What can you learn about Hitler's plans for Germany by studying the document?

To apply this skill, see Applying History Study Skills on page 689.

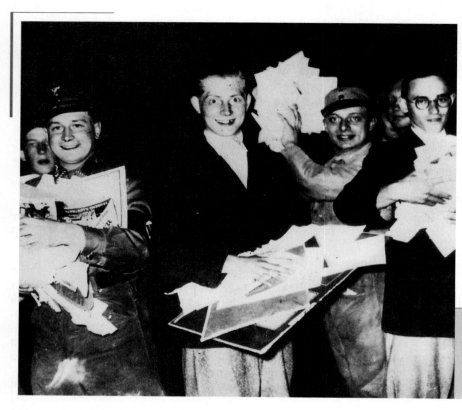

Nazis and German students here carry books and pamphlets to be burned during a demonstration against un-Germanic literature.

Some Jews were forced to wear yellow Stars of David, the six-pointed star that is a symbol of Judaism, on their clothing. Hitler later carried this policy to monstrous extremes resulting in the extermination of millions of Jews. (See Chapter 27.)

Like Mussolini, Hitler promised to restore the glories of Germany's past and to bring Germany to full economic recovery. He called his regime the **Third Reich** and promised the Germans that it would last 1,000 years. *Reich* is the German word for "empire." (The first empire in Germany had been the Holy Roman Empire, and the second was the German Empire of the Hohenzollerns.)

Hitler claimed that German racial superiority justified taking land from the Slavs of eastern Europe in order to provide living space for Germany's expanding population. Such expansion would necessitate a large, well-equipped army. Germany began secretly rearming in the early 1930s, and then in 1935 openly defied the terms of the Versailles Treaty.

According to the Versailles Treaty, the Rhineland was to be left unfortified. However, in the spring of 1936, Hitler ordered troops into the area. Due to the fact that France underestimated Hitler's force and

Great Britain felt that the event was not worth going to war, neither country acted.

Encouraged by his easy success in the Rhineland, Hitler sought alliance with Mussolini, isolated from the rest of Europe because of his invasion of Abyssinia. In the fall of 1936, the two dictators signed a treaty forming the **Rome-Berlin Axis**.

Section 4 Review

1. **Define** fascism, corporatist state, *Mein Kampf*, Third Reich, Rome-Berlin Axis
2. **Identify** Black Shirts, *il Duce*, storm troopers, *der Führer*, Gestapo
3. **Summarizing Ideas** Describe the common conditions that Italian and German forms of fascism sought to address.
4. **Understanding Ideas** How did Mussolini gain and maintain power?
5. **Analyzing Ideas** "The Treaty of Versailles created the atmosphere that made nazism possible." Do you agree or disagree? Give reasons for your answer.

Dictatorship in the Soviet Union

Focus Questions

- **How did Lenin deal with the grave problems that were facing the Soviet Union following the successful revolution?**
- **What was collectivization, and how was it instituted under Lenin and Stalin?**
- **How did Stalin bring the Soviet Union to a state of totalitarianism?**

As soon as the Communists seized power in 1917, they reorganized Russia's government. They sought a settlement of the war. They moved the capital from Petrograd to Moscow, and they tried to resolve internal disagreements. Lenin became the head of the cabinet, the Council of People's Commissars. The Congress of Soviets was established, a national legislative body made up of more than 1,000 representatives. Real power, however, rested with the People's Commissars.

Russia Under Lenin

In 1922 the Communist leaders gave Russia a new name, the **Union of Soviet Socialist Republics** (USSR). This change indicated that power had been transferred to the soviets, or revolutionary councils. After 1922 the people of Russia became known as the Soviet people.

Politically the country was divided into separate republics joined in a federal union. Eventually the USSR was composed of 15 of these republics.

Between 1918 and 1921, Soviet leaders had followed a policy known as War Communism. They nationalized Russian industries. However, social and economic measures were not based on a long-range plan. Communist leaders had to develop a program to build their new society in Russia.

Faced with economic collapse in 1921, Lenin announced the New Economic Policy (NEP) that allowed some free enterprise. The NEP permitted individuals to buy, sell, and trade farm products. The major industries—oil, mining, steel, and the railroads—remained under government ownership and management. Smaller businesses and home industries could be privately owned and operated for profit. A new class of small businessmen, the Nepmen, arose, and the economy made gains.

Soviet agriculture remained a problem. The government tried to persuade the peasants to form **collective farms**—land pooled into large farms on which people could work together as a group. During the revolution farmlands had been seized from the wealthy landlords and divided among the peasants. On a collective farm, peasants could share the scarce modern farm machinery. The policy eventually became mandatory.

A Power Struggle

When Lenin died in 1924, a power struggle erupted in the Communist Party. The main contenders were Leon Trotsky and Joseph Stalin. Trotsky, a talented party organizer, had almost single-handedly created the Red Army that defended the Bolshevik Revolution. Stalin was general secretary, or leader, of the party.

One issue in the power struggle concerned the future of the revolution. Trotsky followed the strict Marxist belief that revolution should take place all over the world. Stalin, however, broke with the doctrine and advocated "socialism in one country." Stalin argued that after socialism succeeded in the Soviet Union, revolution would spread to the rest of the world.

A bitter, savage, and merciless struggle between the two factions began. By 1928, however, Stalin emerged securely as leader. Trotsky went into exile and was later murdered in Mexico, reportedly on Stalin's orders.

The Five-Year Plan

In 1928 Stalin ended the NEP and returned to a controlled **command economy**, in which government planners make all economic decisions. Economic controls from 1918 to 1921 had been emergency measures. Now Stalin's goal was to make the planned economy a permanent feature in the Soviet Union.

A plan for economic growth, the first Five-Year Plan, was published in 1928. It set industrial, agricultural, and social goals for the next five years. Stalin insisted on ambitious targets for the plan.

The Five-Year Plan stretched the resources of the Soviet Union to the breaking point in an attempt to turn the country into a modern, industrialized society. Expansion of heavy industries occurred at the expense of industries producing consumer goods.

After Lenin's death, Stalin gained political power in the Soviet Union, ruling as dictator from 1929 until 1953.

The planners hoped that collective farming would produce enough food for the Soviet people as well as a surplus for export. Money received from farm exports would help pay for modern machinery, which would in turn advance the drive toward industrialization. Efforts to encourage voluntary collectivism had produced inadequate results. Therefore, collectivism was mandated, and all farms were to be merged into collectives. Peasants had to join or suffer severe consequences. Those who attempted to retain their lands faced execution, imprisonment, or exile. Collectivization went poorly, and famine resulted. Millions of people died.

The first Five-Year Plan actually succeeded in most industries. The government turned about 90 percent of the productive farmland into collective farms. A second Five-Year Plan, even more comprehensive than the first, went into effect in 1933. This second program called for production increases in heavy industries, with a particular emphasis on military production. Those who expected an increase in consumer goods or food supply as a reward for hard work and sacrifice were disappointed. In fact, production of consumer goods decreased as the Soviet government placed all of its efforts on the expansion of heavy industry. Rather than receiving a reward, the Soviet people faced harder times as consumer goods and food became more scarce.

Stalin's Dictatorship

Stalin's control of the Communist Party had been his most effective means of blocking his rival Trotsky. Now, as control of government centralized, more control than ever was applied to society at large.

A police state. The czars had used secret police and spies to maintain their absolute rule. Stalin began to use similar tactics. Under Stalin the Soviet people still experienced rule by fear. People had to conform without dissent to the dictates of the Communist Party or face punishment such as imprisonment.

The Soviets disestablished the Orthodox Church and seized its property. They discouraged religious worship and taught atheism in schools. Artists, writers, and musicians were ordered to produce "socialist realism" as an indication of their service to the state, with their works subject to rigid control and censorship by the government.

Government under Stalin. In 1936 Stalin proclaimed a new constitution for the Soviet Union. The Stalin Constitution, as it was called, preserved the essential framework within the Soviet government that had existed under Lenin. The parliamentary body, which was called the Supreme Soviet, met twice a year. The Council of People's Commissars, which was later renamed the Council of Ministers, held executive and administrative authority.

On paper the Soviet government appeared to be democratic. In reality, however, most power lay in the hands of the **Politburo** (Political Bureau) of the Communist Party, which was a small committee that was elected by the Supreme Soviet. As head of the Communist Party, Stalin controlled the Politburo. In other words, he held dictatorial power, with virtually complete authority.

The Soviet Union's totalitarian dictatorship under Stalin grew harsher. In 1934, following the assassination of a high party official, Stalin began a **purge** of party members supposedly disloyal to him. Through intimidation, brutality, and public trials which were staged for show, Stalin began to rid the party of all members who might not submit to his will. This practice of purging extended into the general population, and often occurred without a trial for the accused. Scholars estimate that by 1939 more than 5 million people had been arrested, deported, imprisoned in forced labor camps, or executed.

The Comintern

The Soviet Union's foreign policy during the 1920s and 1930s contained contradictions. On the one

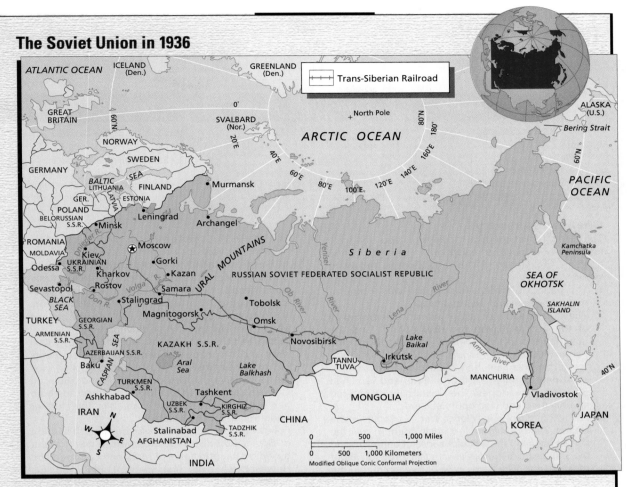

The Soviet Union in 1936

Trans-Siberian Railroad

Learning from Maps During his rule, Stalin deported many people to labor camps and killed those who posed a threat to him.

 Place What city is located at the eastern end of the Trans-Siberian Railroad?

---

hand, the new Communist government wanted to be accepted by the established nations of the world. On the other hand, however, its support of the Third International, also called the Communist International or the **Comintern**, alienated many countries. Lenin had founded this organization in 1919 to help spread the revolution throughout the world. The Comintern continued to agitate for the overthrow of capitalist democracies.

Communist parties existed in many countries outside Russia. The Comintern worked through these parties to arouse workers and urge rebellion. These open calls for revolution caused fear, suspicion, and hostility in the outside world.

Section 5 Review

1. **Define** Union of Soviet Socialist Republics, collective farms, command economy, Politburo, purge, Comintern
2. **Identify** Leon Trotsky
3. **Explaining Ideas** Describe the New Economic Policy of Russia.
4. **Comparing Ideas** (a) How was the idea of a collective farm different from previous agricultural policy? (b) How was collectivization instituted under Lenin and Stalin?
5. **Summarizing Ideas** Describe the growth of totalitarianism under Stalin in the Soviet Union.

Chapter 25 Review

1923
France occupies Ruhr Valley.

1925
Locarno Pact is signed.

A.D. 1918   A.D. 1920   A.D. 1922   A.D. 1924   A.D. 1926   A.D. 1928

1919
• Weimar Republic is established.
• Comintern is founded.

1922
• Mussolini begins rule in Italy.
• Irish Free State is founded.

1928
• Stalin assumes full power in the Soviet Union.
• First Soviet Five-Year Plan begins.

Chapter Summary

The following list contains the key concepts you have learned about political, social, and economic conditions in the United States and Europe following World War I.

1. The period following World War I was a time of major stresses and uncertainties.

2. The literature, music, art, architecture, and science of the time reflected the new outlook and the uncertainties of the period. James Joyce and Pablo Picasso abandoned traditional forms and created works that had disturbing implications. Even new popular art forms, films and jazz, had pessimistic overtones. The Western world entered an unsettled and less optimistic era.

3. Following victory in World War I, people in the United States realized that their country was the richest nation in the world. A sense of optimism and the influence of European contact brought about rapid change. The pace of life quickened during the decade appropriately called the Roaring Twenties.

4. The economic bubble burst with the stock market crash and the beginning of the Great Depression

in 1929. In 1933 President Roosevelt enacted policies for recovery known as the New Deal.

5. In Europe instability was widespread. The British and the French maintained their democratic traditions despite labor unrest and the problems of unemployment caused by the Great Depression. In eastern Europe, a number of the new nations abandoned democracy for dictatorships.

6. In Italy and Germany, dissatisfaction with the weakness and hesitations of democratic governments led to an extreme form of dictatorship that was called fascism. Mussolini in Italy and Hitler in Germany established totalitarian regimes, and both had expansionist foreign ambitions that further undermined Europe's stability.

7. Following its civil war, Russia became the Union of Soviet Socialist Republics, with a government based on the principles of Marx and communism. However, when its first leader, Lenin, died, his successor, Stalin, maintained control of the country only by brutally crushing his opponents and setting up a totalitarian dictatorship.

Reviewing Important Terms

On a separate sheet of paper, supply the term that correctly completes each statement.

1. _____ _____ are formed when land is pooled into large farms on which people can work together.

2. Governmental regulation and direction of national resources to achieve economic stability occurs in a(n) _____ _____.

3. A(n) _____ _____ occurs when workers in several industries refuse to continue working until their demands are met.

4. When a country tries to improve its own economic well-being through protective tariffs and similar restrictions, it is adopting the policy of _____ _____.

5. _____ was the doctrine of Mussolini.

6. A sudden increase in prosperity is called a(n) _____ _____.

7. When people make _____ _____, they are investing in stocks in the hope of attaining quick, huge profits.

Developing Critical Thinking Skills

1. **Interpreting Ideas** How did the arts and popular culture reflect the disillusionment of the postwar era?

2. **Analyzing Ideas** (a) Why did the demobilization of troops put economic pressures on the nations of Europe? (b) Why were Great Britain and France better able to deal with these problems than the new nations of eastern Europe?

3. **Organizing Ideas** Explain how each of the following contributed to the rise of nazism in Germany: (a) creation of the Weimar Republic; (b) signing of the Versailles Treaty; (c) high unemployment and soaring inflation.

4. **Summarizing Ideas** (a) What was War Communism? (b) What was Russia's New Economic Policy? (c) How did each program attempt to stimulate the Russian economy?

5. **Explaining Ideas** Explain the similarities and differences between fascism and communism.

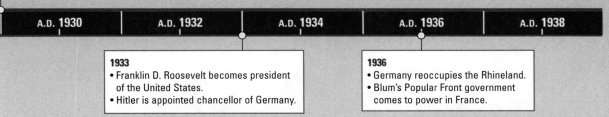

1929
Great Depression
begins.

A.D. **1930**   A.D. **1932**   A.D. **1934**   A.D. **1936**   A.D. **1938**

1933
• Franklin D. Roosevelt becomes president
  of the United States.
• Hitler is appointed chancellor of Germany.

1936
• Germany reoccupies the Rhineland.
• Blum's Popular Front government
  comes to power in France.

Relating Geography to History

Turn to the map of the Soviet Union on page 687 and to the map of Europe after the Congress of Vienna in Chapter 17, page 446. Then complete the following. **(a)** List the republics in the Soviet Union in 1936. **(b)** List the countries bordering the Soviet Union that were part of Russia in 1815. **(c)** Why did the Soviet Union lose a sizable amount of its territory after pulling out of World War I?

Relating Past to Present

1. **(a)** What did the leaders of the Easter Rising in 1916 hope to accomplish? **(b)** Based on what you know about events in Northern Ireland today, have these goals been achieved? **(c)** Explain the goals of the citizens of Northern Ireland today. **(d)** Are these goals the same as those of the Easter Rising?
2. **(a)** List the programs that President Roosevelt instituted during the New Deal. **(b)** Which of these programs are still in existence? **(c)** Choose one of these and find out why this program has continued. **(d)** What is its main purpose? **(e)** Do any groups of people think the program should be discontinued? If so, why?

Applying History Study Skills

Before completing this activity, review Building History Study Skills on page 683.

Study the following documents. The first document gives Stalin's justification of his methods in industrializing the Soviet Union. The second document is a chart summarizing the results of the Five-Year Plans. Decide how each document helps answer the question "How was Stalin able to industrialize the Soviet Union?"

"It is sometimes asked whether it is not possible to slow down the tempo a bit, to put a check on the movement. No, comrades, it is not possible! The tempo must not be reduced! On the contrary, we must increase it as much as is within our powers and possibilities. . . .

To slacken the tempo would mean falling behind. And those who fall behind get beaten. . . . No, we refuse to be beaten! One feature of the history of old Russia was the continual beatings she suffered for falling behind, for her backwardness. She was beaten by the Mongol Khans. She was beaten by the Turkish beys. She was beaten by the Swedish feudal lords. She was beaten by the Polish and Lithuanian gentry. She was beaten by the British and French capitalists. . . . All beat her—for her backwardness."

The Five-Year Plans and Beyond

Economic Growth Rates in the Soviet Union (in percent)		
	First Five-Year Plan, 1928–1932	Second Five-Year Plan, 1932–1937
Industrial Output	10.6	10.1
Electric Power	26.3	21.8
Ferrous Metals	11.0	22.0
Agricultural Output	−5.5	1.0
Crops	2.1	6.5
Livestock	−11.4	−2.1

Search the Internet through the HRW Web site for information about the Great Depression. Then write several journal entries as if you were a teenager living then.

GO TO: go.hrw.com
KEYWORD: SCØ Great Depression

Building Your Portfolio

1. **Writing a Report** Using resource books for your research, prepare a brief biographical sketch of Benito Mussolini. Place the report in your portfolio.
2. **Presenting an Oral Report** Prepare a report on the response of the United States and European nations to the Great Depression, explaining why the policy of economic nationalism created more problems than it solved. Place your notes and other research materials in your portfolio.

New Political Forces in Africa, Asia, and Latin America

TIME

A.D. 1898–1938

A.D. 1898–1938

3.7 million B.C. | 4000 B.C. | A.D. 2100

PLACE

Africa, Asia, and Latin America

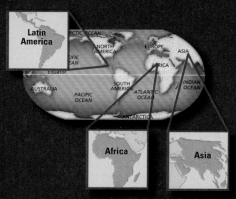

Diego Rivera mural

CHAPTER FOCUS

Significance

Europe and the United States faced social, political, and economic challenges during the early decades of the 1900s. In other parts of the world, however, people's main concern was political change. Of the countries of the British Empire, India set out on a path toward independence, and other countries developed new relationships with Great Britain. The two major independent countries of the Middle East, Turkey and Persia, also began rapid political transformation, and new political forces stirred throughout Africa.

Profound changes transformed the great civilizations of China and Japan. In China the ancient dynastic cycle was broken, and the long and difficult process of creating new political structures began. Neighboring Japan set its course for economic growth and foreign expansion.

The countries of Latin America faced economic and social change as well as an uncertain relationship with the United States. Many Latin American countries, like others in the 1920s and 1930s, developed governments with strong centralized power.

Terms to Define

Zionism
passive resistance
Statute of Westminster
Open Door Policy
Guomindang
Long March
Treaty of Portsmouth
Good Neighbor Policy

People to Identify

Arthur Balfour
Mohandas Gandhi
Kemal Atatürk
Reza Shah Pahlavi
Nnamdi Azikiwe
Jomo Kenyatta
Leopold Senghor
Sun Yixian
warlords
Chiang Kaishek
Mao Zedong

Places to Locate

Egypt
Iraq
India
Ankara
Iran
Jiangxi
Shaanxi
Mexico City
Buenos Aires

Chapter Theme Questions

- **Social Relations** What changes might nationalist groups demand?
- **Politics and Law** What might happen when the military takes an active role in government?
- **Economic Organization** How might economic crises sometimes lead to political crises?

In the early 1900s, dynastic rule in China came to an end. A large nationalistic movement spread across China, led by Sun Yixian, who described the necessity of nationalism to his fellow Chinese.

❝Considering the law of survival of ancient and modern races, if we want to save China and to preserve the Chinese race, we must certainly promote nationalism. . . .

In comparison with other nations we have the greatest population and the oldest culture, of four thousand years' duration. . . . But the Chinese people have only family and clan groups; there is no national spirit. Consequently, . . . we are the poorest and weakest state in the world, occupying the lowest position in international affairs; the rest of mankind is the carving knife and the serving dish, while we are the fish and the meat. . . . If we do not earnestly promote nationalism and weld together . . . we face a tragedy—the loss of our country and the destruction of our race.❞

China was only one area of the world convulsed in change after World War I.

Section 1

The British Empire in the Postwar Era

Focus Questions

- Why did British rule in Egypt and the Middle East come to an end?
- How did the people of India pursue their desire for self-rule?
- How did the British respond to calls for change in other parts of their empire?

Although the British Empire had grown larger as a result of the Paris peace conference, its continued existence was nonetheless threatened. People in all parts of this vast British empire voiced demands for more freedom, for self-government, and even for their complete independence.

Independence for Egypt

Officially, the Ottoman Empire ruled Egypt, but since 1882 the British had controlled the country. In 1914, when the Ottomans joined the Central Powers, the British declared Egypt a protectorate. Although the protectorate formally ended in 1922, Britain reserved the right to defend Egypt and the Suez Canal and administered part of the country to protect its interests.

During the 1920s and early 1930s, a strong independence movement grew in Egypt. In 1935 Italy invaded Egypt's neighbor Ethiopia. To ward off further Italian aggression, Egypt and Britain signed the Anglo-Egyptian Treaty of 1936. Reached after intense negotiation, the treaty gave Egypt independence and Britain military control of the Suez Canal for 20 years. The two nations pledged to support each other in the event of war in the Middle East, and Britain sponsored Egypt's membership in the League of Nations. Many Egyptians were unsatisfied, however, for British troops remained garrisoned throughout Egypt. Genuine independence did not come until after World War II.

The Palestine Issue

Peace settlements after World War I gave Great Britain mandates for what would become Transjordan, Iraq, and Palestine. These lands were all formerly part of the Ottoman Empire.

A spirit of nationalism had arisen among Arabs during the last years of the Ottoman Empire. In that spirit, Arabs had helped the British against the Ottoman Empire during World War I. When, after the war, France and Britain imposed their control in the Middle East, many Arabs felt betrayed. Some rebelled. To placate angry Arabs, a section of Palestine called Transjordan was separated from the Palestinian mandate in 1921. Although the British recognized Transjordan as an independent state in 1928, they retained considerable control through a strong military presence. In 1932 Great Britain also recognized Iraq as an independent kingdom but again retained authority in military and financial matters.

Of the three Middle Eastern mandates, only Palestine remained under complete British control. Palestine was important because of its strategic location and because a vital oil pipeline from Iraq ended at the port of Haifa. However, the British faced a difficult problem in Palestine.

Since the late 1800s, Jews from Europe had been establishing small colonies in Palestine. These colonists supported a nationalist movement called **Zionism**, which aimed to build a Palestinian homeland for Jews.* In 1917 the British foreign secretary, Arthur Balfour, eager for Jewish support in the Allies' war effort, told Zionist leaders that the British would "view with favour" the creation of a Jewish "national home" in Palestine. The Balfour Declaration, as it came to be called, also stated that the establishment of such a homeland should not threaten civil and religious rights of non-Jews, who made up almost all of Palestine's population.

Earlier, however, the British also had promised to help form an independent Arab state that might include parts of Palestine. After World War I, both Jews and Arabs wanted Great Britain to fulfill its promises. Arabs viewed the number of Jews settling in Palestine as especially alarming. While Britain sought a solution to the problem, tensions between Arabs and Jews intensified, and violence occurred.

Hoping to calm the fears of Arabs, the British placed limitations on the number of Jews allowed to immigrate to Palestine. Jewish settlers bitterly resented this policy, especially when Nazi persecution of European Jews increased. During the 1930s, many Jews fled Europe to avoid Nazi persecution. Immigration to Palestine increased. Arabs demanded that immigration cease and rebelled in 1936. The Peel Commission in 1937 declared the Zionist desire for a homeland and the Arab desire for independence irreconcilable and recommended dividing the area. World War II stalled further action on the controversial plan.

Independence Movements in India

As Great Britain's largest colony, India commanded more British attention than did the Middle Eastern mandates. India had contributed both troops and money to the Allies in World War I. In return Great Britain had promised India more self-government.

Some in Britain felt that giving up control of the colonies would render Britain a "third-rate power." Others believed that the principles of self-rule applied to other parts of the British Empire should govern Indian policy. Indian society itself was split many ways. Some Western-educated Indians remained in favor of continued rule of their country by Great Britain.

---

*Theodor Herzl, an Austrian Jew, is considered the founder of the Zionist movement. Zion, one of the hills of ancient Jerusalem, came to be a synonym for the Jewish people of their dream for a homeland.

Building History Study Skills

READ
WRITE
INTERPRET
CONNECT
THINK

Writing About History: Writing a Problem-Solution Essay

Writing a problem-solution essay includes analyzing a problem in order to provide a solution to the problem. For example, assume that a city's crime rates are increasing. Consequently, a problem can be identified—it is not safe to walk alone on city streets at night. The problem also has a logical solution—the mayor of the city and the city council could approve more funds so that the police could patrol the high-crime areas more frequently at night.

How to Write a Problem-Solution Essay

To write a problem-solution essay, follow these three steps.

1. Identify the problem.
2. Describe the problem.
3. State a solution and relate it to the problem.

Developing the Skill

Mohandas Gandhi lived for a time in South Africa, where he formulated many of his theories about nonviolence. Gandhi believed that practicing satyagraha would help end the injustice he witnessed in South Africa. *Satya* means truth. *Agraha* means firmness or force. Satyagraha is therefore translated as "truth force," a firm devotion to truth in a spirit of peace and love. If you were to write an essay on the problem of injustice that Gandhi first faced in South Africa and the solution that he formulated, it might appear as follows.

❝In 1906 the Transvaal government of South Africa published an ordinance requiring the official registration of its Indian population. The Indians held a mass protest meeting in September 1906 in Johannesburg. Gandhi, speaking to the large crowd, told the people to pledge defiance of the ordinance and go to jail if necessary. Gandhi believed the people should protest rather than forfeit their right to free movement.

Gandhi's solution to the problem was to develop the idea of satyagraha, which he said is 'the vindication of truth, not by the infliction of suffering on the opponent, but on one's self.' According to Gandhi, 'the opponent must be weaned from error by patience and sympathy.' Satyagraha reverses the 'eye for an eye' policy, which ends in making everyone blind. It returns good for evil until the evildoer tires of evil. This was Gandhi's plan for dealing with South African injustice.❞

The first paragraph identifies and defines the problem—the injustice of the South African government, which requires the Indian people to submit to official registration that monitors their movement and creates racial distinctions. The solution that Gandhi developed was satyagraha, or truth force. That is, if a person resists the law nonviolently and is willing to suffer the consequences, ultimately that person will change the opposition. Gandhi's method, which was not to allow the protester to adopt the method of the oppressor, was designed to appeal to the conscience of the opposition.

Practicing the Skill

Research the effects of Gandhi's solution and explain how they might be incorporated into the model problem-solution essay.

To apply this skill, see Applying History Study Skills on page 709.

Mohandas Gandhi (left), 1930

In contrast, Indian nationalists wanted complete independence, though they did not agree on how to achieve it. Any settlement in India had to accommodate the diversity and tension present in Indian society. Regional interests varied widely, as did religious thought. An uneasy truce reigned between Hindus and Muslims, and large gulfs existed between upper-caste and lower-caste Hindus.

The leading advocate of Indian nationalism was Mohandas K. Gandhi, who became leader of the Indian National Congress—India's most important political party. Many Indians revered Gandhi as a spiritual force as well as a political leader, calling him Mahatma, or "Great Soul." Educated in England, Gandhi sought complete independence for India. He urged Indians to give up Western ways and return to their ancient culture and religions.

Gandhi opposed any use of force or violence. In 1920 he explained his reasons for favoring nonviolence as a means of achieving independence.

"As soon as India accepts the doctrine of the sword, my life as an Indian is finished. . . . I tell you that whilst my friend . . . has adopted the doctrine of non-violence as a weapon of the weak, I believe in the doctrine of non-violence as a weapon of the strongest. I believe that a man is the strongest soldier for daring to die unarmed with his breast bare before the enemy."

Drawing on ideas from Hindu scriptures and the New Testament, Gandhi developed a political approach known as nonviolent noncooperation. This technique of **passive resistance**, a form of civil disobedience, called for citizens to peacefully refuse to cooperate with the government in order to win concessions from it.

Gandhi's program of nonviolent noncooperation included a boycott of British goods and a refusal to pay taxes. Gandhi and his followers were imprisoned numerous times. Trying to control the nationalist movement, British authorities restricted the civil liberties of many leaders, and British soldiers repeatedly used force to break up nationalist political gatherings. Many moderate Indians turned against British rule.

In 1935, after years of reports and conferences, Great Britain granted India a new constitution that provided for elected representation. However, the British still controlled India's defense, revenue, and foreign policy and could veto legislation. Committed to total self-government, the nationalists opposed the new constitution, but agreed to work within it, and gained greater power after the elections. Efforts for complete independence continued.

The Statute of Westminster

Even in those parts of the British Empire where a degree of self-government already existed, people sought greater independence. In Canada, Australia, New Zealand, and the Union of South Africa, Great Britain still appointed a governor-general, who could veto laws (though they did so rarely). Great Britain also controlled the foreign policy of these areas.

After World War I, these dominions wanted complete self-government. Showing readiness to accommodate, Great Britain agreed without a struggle.

In 1931 an act of Parliament, the **Statute of Westminster**, recognized Canada, Australia, New Zealand, and South Africa as completely independent. The four nations joined with Great Britain as equal partners in a loose organization called the British Commonwealth of Nations. The British Parliament had no power either to make laws for or interfere with Great Britain's Commonwealth partners. However, each member agreed to declare loyalty to the British monarch.

Over the years, other British colonies became independent and joined the Commonwealth. Like other nations, Britain faced economic depression after World War I and needed increased trade to stimulate its economy. British trade abroad was hurt by nationalism, and favorable trade arrangements among Commonwealth nations made membership attractive. The Commonwealth worked well economically for both Great Britain and its former colonies.

Politically, however, the vast British empire had proved burdensome. In the Middle East and India especially, more colonies demanded independence.

Section 1 Review

1. **Define** Zionism, passive resistance, Statute of Westminster
2. **Identify** Arthur Balfour, Mohandas Gandhi
3. **Locate and Explain the Significance** Egypt, Iraq, India
4. **Understanding Ideas** How were Egypt and the Middle East mandates given independence from Great Britain?
5. **Analyzing Ideas** What methods did Gandhi use to gain independence for India?
6. **Evaluating Ideas** How did the Commonwealth of Nations benefit both Great Britain and its former colonies?

Turkey, Persia, and Africa

Focus Questions

- How did ideas about modern nationalism manifest themselves in Turkey and Persia?
- In what way did World War I change the attitude of Africans toward colonial governments?

The nationalist ideas that swept the Middle East after World War I also affected Turkey and Persia in Southwest Asia and the whole of Africa. As a result, new political forces began to stir.

Turkey Under Mustafa Kemal

The Treaty of Sèvres stripped the Ottoman Empire of all its territories except Turkey. In 1919 Greek troops arrived to impose those terms on Turkey and began expanding their control. Pockets of Turkish resistance, officially opposed by the weak Ottoman government, grew.

Under the able and energetic leader Mustafa Kemal, a hero of the fighting at Gallipoli, young nationalists pressed the government to respond and eventually took control of the assembly. Declaring the sultan to be under the control of the nation's enemies, the assembly appointed an executive council, headed by Kemal, to run the country. Defeating the Greeks near Ankara in 1921, Kemal's forces drove them from Turkey in 1922. That same year, the assembly abolished the sultanate and in 1923 established the Republic of Turkey. The nationalists then moved the capital from Constantinople to Ankara.

Initially, the assembly included various factions, but later assemblies seated few who opposed the first president, Mustafa Kemal. The government became a one-party system led by the chief executive.

Kemal sought to modernize and westernize Turkey because he believed that the war had shown the superiority of Western technology. He viewed Islam as a roadblock to modernization and drew up a new constitution that ended the long unity of Islam and the government. He abolished the position of caliph and attacked Islam's influence by shifting the weekly holiday from Friday to Sunday and abandoning the Islamic calendar.

Kemal ordered the Turkish people to adopt Western ways. He prohibited the wearing of traditional clothing such as the fez, the traditional Turkish hat. In addition, he insisted that all Turks adopt family surnames, as Europeans did. He himself took the name Atatürk, meaning "father of the Turks." He also supported laws that gave women the right to vote and hold office, and he abolished polygamy—the practice of having more than one wife.

In further efforts to modernize, Atatürk's country adopted a secular court system, metric weights and measures, and the Roman alphabet. Atatürk also instituted a program of economic development, including state-run industry and subsidized farming.

Modernizing Persia

Turkey's neighbor Persia had never come under Ottoman control. Since the late 1700s, it had been ruled by shahs of the Qajar dynasty. In the early 1900s, however, both Great Britain and Russia established spheres of influence in Persia and increasingly influenced the Persian government.

In 1921 Reza Khan, a Persian army officer with strong nationalist sentiments, seized control of the government in a coup d'état. Some four years later, he deposed the ruling shah and assumed the throne,

The Shah of Persia (right) and Kemal Atatürk (left) met in 1934 in the city of Ankara, Turkey.

taking the title Reza Shah Pahlavi. Like Kemal Atatürk, Reza Shah wanted to modernize his country and free it from foreign domination. He therefore embarked on a massive reform program. He strengthened the army, broke the power of contentious tribes, built roads and hospitals, established a university, and gave women more rights. Reza Shah also introduced an ambitious economic development plan that improved transportation and communication systems and established new industries. In 1935 he announced that the country would be called officially what its people called it—Iran.

Although Iran's constitution called for a limited monarchy, most of the power remained in Reza Shah's hands. He strictly controlled the press and suppressed political parties. The Shah's secret police force ruthlessly put down any opposition to his government. His foreign policy of balancing British and Russian interests led him to seek closer ties to Germany, which would eventually cause his downfall.

Africa After World War I

The many Africans who fought in the armies of Great Britain and France during World War I expected to be rewarded with greater political freedom after the war. Like the Indians, they were disappointed.

Increased political activity. The years after World War I saw an increase in political activity among Africans. The war itself had served as a broadening experience for many. Military service took them away from their homes. For the first time, they experienced the world beyond their immediate villages and families. When these former soldiers returned home, they brought with them new ideas about freedom and nationalism. In time they put these ideas to work organizing anticolonial protest movements.

Colonial education also influenced many Africans to become politically involved. Missionary and government schools taught African students the Western ideals of equality and self-improvement. Yet colonial governments denied these same Africans opportunities for self-determination and economic advancement. As more and more Africans personally experienced the contradiction between Western teaching and the reality of colonialism as it existed in Africa, they became determined that change must come. Racism and political repression awakened in many Africans a desire to work for reform and even independence.

New political associations. Alarmed at the growing spirit of dissent among Africans, many colonial governments considered reform. However, Africans had begun to organize. In Tanganyika, a former German colony whose mandate had been assigned to Great Britain, Africans from the lower ranks of the civil service formed a civil servants' association. Because the association was open to all Africans, it overcame traditional ethnic barriers and was soon at the center of anticolonial protest in Tanganyika. Similarly, other labor unions and workers' associations became important forums for the expression of African grievances.

In response to the formation of these new political associations, colonial governments strengthened the authority of tribal chiefs who favored colonial rule. At the same time, the colonial authorities agreed to institute some reforms. A few cooperative chiefs and piecemeal reform, however, could not stem the rising tide of the opposition of Africans to colonialism and the desire for independence.

New leaders. By the 1930s, Africans increasingly were calling for independence rather than reform. The most insistent of these calls came from the group of young, Western-educated men—among them Nnamdi Azikiwe (ah·ZEEK·wah) of Nigeria, Jomo Kenyatta of Kenya, and Leopold Senghor of Senegal—who had assumed the leadership of the anticolonial movement. Following Gandhi's example, they organized demonstrations, strikes, and boycotts against their colonial rulers. They also employed Western methods of political organization to attract more support for their cause. By the end of the 1930s, these men led a growing movement dedicated to ending colonial rule.

Section 2 Review

1. **Identify** Kemal Atatürk, Reza Shah Pahlavi, Nnamdi Azikiwe, Jomo Kenyatta, Leopold Senghor

2. **Locate and Explain the Significance** Ankara, Iran

3. **Understanding Ideas** Why did the Ottoman Empire finally end after World War I?

4. **Comparing Ideas** (a) How were the reform programs of Kemal Atatürk and Reza Shah alike? (b) How were the reform programs of both different?

5. **Analyzing Ideas** Why did participation in World War I increase Africans' hopes and expectations for independence?

Unrest in China

Focus Questions

- **How did resentment of foreign interests lead to the downfall of the Qing dynasty?**
- **How did the nationalist movement grow and change under the leadership of both Sun Yixian and Chiang Kaishek?**
- **How did communism develop in China?**

Some historians believe that changes occurring in China in the 1920s were rooted in events that took place around 1900. Until then the imperialist powers of France, Germany, Great Britain, Japan, and Russia had maintained spheres of influence mainly along the Chinese coast and up the Chang Jiang. At the turn of the century, however, they began to move into China's interior, pursuing wealth there as well.

The United States, a new world power, watched these developments with some concern. It did not want American merchants excluded from Chinese trade. In 1899 the American government therefore appealed to nations with interests in China to recognize what it called the **Open Door Policy**. Under this policy, all nations would have equal rights to trade anywhere in China. Nations contacted by the United States responded evasively. The United States interpreted the responses as agreement. In practice the scramble for trade and privileges continued as before.

The Boxer Rebellion

By the end of the 1800s, China's fate as a subordinate nation seemed sealed. Foreign powers had won numerous concessions and privileges from the Chinese. Traders and missionaries traveled the country at will. Foreign interests dominated the economy and government through Chinese intermediaries.

In 1898, hoping to stem foreign interference by revitalizing his government, the young Qing emperor attempted a series of reforms to modernize administration, education, law, military affairs, and technology. The drastic cultural changes called for by these reforms offended China's conservative leaders, and the emperor's aunt, the aging empress dowager (widow of an earlier ruler) Cixi (TSOO·SHEE), took action. The emperor was imprisoned, and for the next 10 years Cixi ruled China.

The empress dowager's officials encouraged antiforeign movements breaking out in the provinces. A growing group called the Society of the Harmonious Fists began to attack Chinese converts to Christianity, then foreign missionaries. In English the members of this society were called simply Boxers. In what became known as the Boxer Rebellion, the Boxers attacked foreigners throughout China, destroying churches, railways, and mines—anything connected with outsiders. Seeking protection, many foreigners fled to embassies in Beijing. There they came under siege by an army of angry Boxers.

Despite rivalries, the imperialist nations were determined to protect their common interests in China. They acted jointly against the Boxers, sending to Beijing an army comprising soldiers from Great Britain, France, Germany, Russia, Japan, and the United States. This army relieved the besieged embassies and put down the rebellion in 1900. The foreign powers then imposed heavy penalties on the Chinese, including a demand for payment of a large indemnity. In addition, the foreign powers claimed the right to maintain troops at Beijing and along the Chinese Eastern Railway to the coast.

The crushing of the Boxer Rebellion brought China completely under foreign domination. Partition of China into colonies was avoided because other powers realized that Russia and Japan, because of their location, would benefit most from any division of China. To protect its interests, the United States reasserted the Open Door Policy to include maintaining China's territorial integrity. Still, foreign armies were stationed in the northern provinces of China.

Overthrow of the Qing Dynasty

The Boxer Rebellion failed to fulfill its major aim—to drive foreigners from Chinese soil. However, it did foster nationalistic sentiment among the Chinese people, especially the young and well educated. These nationalists advocated true reform of China itself. A new political party, the **Guomindang**, or Chinese Nationalist Party, grew out of this reform movement. The party's director, Sun Yixian (also known as Sun Yatsen), lived for many years in the United States, attended school in Hawaii, and studied medicine at a British college in Hong Kong.

Influenced by Western ideas gathered by Sun Yixian and others, the nationalists wanted a constitutional government with civil liberties guaranteed by a bill of rights. They also wanted industrialization to defend China economically against imperialist powers. In the nationalists' view, China could protect itself against foreign domination only if it became a modern nation.

The Qing rulers, under pressure from the nationalists, tried to carry out reforms, including outlining a constitution in 1908 and promising its implementation in nine years. Nationalists, merchants, and gentry, however, wanted a complete break with the "Old China" and an end to the Qing dynasty.

In 1911 a series of revolts, led mostly by army officers who supported Sun Yixian, spread throughout southern China. Yuan Shikai, the leader of an imperial army, did not respond with force but negotiated, hoping for a smooth transition to a new dynasty, with himself in a position of power. No agreement was reached, however, and the 268-year Qing dynasty ended.

Forming the Chinese Republic

In February 1912, the Guomindang forced the last Qing emperor, a young boy, to abdicate. The Guomindang then proclaimed China a republic. Sun Yixian had described the Guomindang philosophy as the "Three Principles of the People": the people's government, the people's rights, and the people's livelihood. These principles called for (1) political unification and the end of foreign influence; (2) a gradual change to

Sun Yixian (Sun Yatsen), pictured here with his wife, worked to unite China under one government.

democratic government, with full personal liberties and rights for all Chinese people; and (3) economic improvements, including industrialization and the provision of more equitable distribution of land.

Problems with the warlords. Proclaiming revolutionary change proved to be easier than accomplishing it. At first the Republic of China hardly existed, as revolution and assassination marked its early years. Yuan Shikai became president, and Sun Yixian fled to Japan. Yuan attempted to restart an imperial dynasty with himself on the throne. His effort failed, but the country was in turmoil. Warlords, who had acquired power during the last years of the Qing dynasty, ruled most of the country and refused to surrender power.

The Nationalists—as members of the Guomindang called themselves—hoped to defeat the warlords and establish the Republic of China with a strong central government. To fulfill this aim, they asked for help from foreign powers. Only the Soviet Union responded. In the early 1920s, the Soviets sent technical, political, and military advisers to help reorganize the Guomindang and build a modern Chinese army.

A split in the Guomindang. When Sun Yixian died in 1925, Chiang Kaishek (chang ky·SHEK), a military commander who had studied the Soviet Red Army in Moscow, assumed leadership of the Nationalists. Under Chiang's command the Nationalist army grew stronger. In 1926 Chiang began a military campaign—called the Northern Expedition—against the warlords of the north. Warlord resistance collapsed when confronted by the efficient, highly motivated Nationalist troops. In quick succession, the Nationalists gained control of Hunan province and the cities of Wuhan (which include Hankou and Wuchang).

Disagreements, however, divided the membership of the Guomindang. The left wing of the party, composed of socialists and Communists, wanted to put more power into the hands of peasants and workers. The conservative right wing opposed such radical change, especially any reforms designed to redistribute land and give it to peasants. Chiang Kaishek became the leader of this right wing.

In 1927, before the Guomindang completed the Northern Expedition, Chiang expelled all Soviet advisers from the country and moved against the party's left-wing members. Troops loyal to Chiang attacked the communist stronghold of Shanghai, arresting thousands of Communists and executing them on the spot. Secure in the belief that the Communists no longer

P'u-i, the Last Emperor of China

For thousands of years, the Chinese people were ruled by emperors. Imperial rule came to an end in 1912, when the last emperor, a boy of six, gave up the ancient throne.

Ironically, the last emperor of China was not Chinese but Manchu. In the 1600s, the Manchu people invaded and conquered China, establishing the Qing dynasty. Two hundred years later, the Manchu government had become weak and corrupt. During the 1800s, Europeans forced China to open its ports to European trade, and China was in danger of being divided among foreign powers. The Chinese blamed the Manchus for their humiliating situation. In 1911 Nationalist revolutionaries overthrew the Qing dynasty, establishing the Republic of China. The boy Henry P'u-i (also known as Pu Yi), the last Qing emperor, formally abdicated on February 12, 1912.

Former Emperor P'u-i was imprisoned for 14 years by the Chinese as a war criminal. He is shown signing his confession before being released from prison.

The end of imperial rule did not bring peace and prosperity as the revolutionaries had hoped, however. Instead, the country was left weak and disunited. For nearly four decades following the fall of the Qing, China suffered the effects of instability.

posed a threat to his leadership, Chiang established a Nationalist government in Nanjing.

The Nanjing Government

Chiang and his followers wanted a strong, efficient government, but not a democratic one. Eventually, they set up a one-party system with Chiang as virtual dictator.

Chiang tried to promote economic development, but a lack of capital hindered his efforts to industrialize. Defense expenditures took much government revenue that could have been used for industrialization. Foreign control of many of China's natural resources also slowed economic development.

Even so, the areas of China under Nationalist control made notable progress. The Nationalists began a massive road construction program and started to repair, rebuild, and extend the railroad system. In addition, they strengthened the financial system by establishing a national bank. All levels of the educational system also improved.

However, the Nationalists failed to deal with two crucial problems. Because they needed the support of landowners and merchants, they made no changes in the oppressive system of land ownership, nor did they change methods of tax collection in the countryside.

In short, they did little to eliminate the causes of suffering and discontent among Chinese peasants—the country's vast majority.

The Growth of Chinese Communism

In July 1921, a small group of Chinese intellectuals met in Shanghai and founded the Chinese Communist Party. Inspired by the example of the Russian Revolution and the ideologies of Marx and Lenin, the founders of Chinese communism hoped to free their country from foreign domination and economic backwardness. They first set about building strong party organizations and labor unions in the cities. They also cooperated with the Guomindang in efforts to defeat the regional warlords.

At first, when the Guomindang was weak and in need of support, the Nationalists welcomed Communists. As the Communist Party grew stronger, however, conservative Nationalists became alarmed. Chiang Kaishek purged the Communists from the Guomindang in 1927 and executed many of them. In the early 1930s, when Chiang realized that he had failed to destroy the Communist Party, he undertook several large-scale military campaigns to "annihilate" communism once and for all.

Civil War in China, 1925–1935

Area controlled by Guomindang, 1925

The Long March, 1934–1935

Guomindang victories over the warlords

Guomindang strikes against the Communists

Japanese territory

Learning from Maps It took Communists more than a year to march from the southeastern province of Jiangxi to the northwestern province of Shaanxi.

Place What river did the group cross in the middle of their journey?

The Long March. Those Communists who escaped the purge of 1927 fled first to Jiangxi province in southeastern China. There they set up their own government—modeled after the Russian communist regime—called the Chinese Soviet Republic. Nationalist forces repeatedly attacked, then besieged the soviet in 1934. A few months later, Communists broke through the siege lines and evacuated Jiangxi.

In the famous **Long March**, which lasted more than a year, about 100,000 Communists made their way on foot to Shaanxi province in northwestern China.

Pursued by Nationalist troops and strafed by aircraft, they crossed 18 mountain ranges and 24 rivers, a distance of about 6,000 miles, under incredibly arduous conditions. A few deserted, but many more died on the journey. Those who survived, along with Communists already in Shaanxi, established their headquarters in the isolated mountain town of Yenan. (See map on this page.) On the march, a charismatic young man named Mao Zedong (MAOOH ZUH·DUHNG) had established himself as a leader.

Mao Zedong. Born in the countryside of southeastern Hunan province, Mao had long argued that Chinese peasants, not the urban proletariat, could provide the best basis for a communist revolution in China. In a rural province far from the major cities of China, he had a chance to prove his argument.

In Shaanxi province, Mao and his followers practiced the programs of land and tax reform always advocated by the Communists. To ensure success, they met with the peasants and listened to their problems. The Communists also explained China's problems to the peasants and urged them to support the revolution.

Suspicious of outsiders, the peasants of Shaanxi did not trust the Communists at first. However, when they found that the Communists were trying to understand and help them solve their problems, the peasants rallied to the cause. Many volunteered to

Throughout the Long March, Mao Zedong (shown on horseback) and his group fought Chiang Kaishek's army in a series of military engagements.

serve in the communist army, called the Red Army. Others provided useful information about the location and movement of Nationalist troops.

With the aid of the local peasant population, the Communists managed to rebuild their strength and resist efforts of the Nationalists to destroy them. The Nationalists, under Chiang Kaishek, had chosen to attack communism rather than face the growing threat from Japanese militarism. Many Chinese disliked this policy, believing that "Chinese don't fight Chinese" and that Japan was the true enemy. Support for the Communists grew.

Section 3 Review

1. **Define** Open Door Policy, Guomindang, Long March
2. **Identify** Sun Yixian, warlords, Chiang Kaishek, Mao Zedong
3. **Locate and Explain the Significance** Jiangxi, Shaanxi
4. **Analyzing Ideas (a)** What was the Boxer Rebellion? **(b)** What were its results?
5. **Classifying Ideas (a)** Describe Sun Yixian's three goals for the Chinese republic. **(b)** With what problems did the Nanjing government fail to deal?
6. **Evaluating Ideas** What factors helped communism take hold in China?

Section 4

Japan Between the Wars

Focus Questions
- **How and why did Japan pursue a policy of expansionism in the late 1800s?**
- **What caused the Russo-Japanese War, and what were its results?**
- **What changes in Japanese life were caused by rapid modernization?**

Japan had begun to modernize in the late 1800s. However, the economic, social, and political reforms achieved during that time created problems. Japan's desire for territory on the Asian continent intensified these problems.

Japanese Expansion

The reforms introduced by the leaders of the Meiji Restoration transformed Japan into a modern industrial and military power. This newly acquired status enabled Japan to embark on a policy of expansionism in the late 1800s. Extending Japanese influence would serve two purposes. First, it would provide both new sources of raw materials for the country's growing industries and new markets for the products of those industries. Second, it would show the nations of the West just how far Japan had progressed. Other parts of Asia, especially weak China, seemed to provide opportunity for expansion.

Korea and Manchuria. Korea had long interested Japan. The Treaty of Shimonoseki that ended the Sino-Japanese War in 1895 forced China to cede Taiwan and the Pescadores to Japan and provided for Korean independence. Soon, however, Japan dominated the Korean government.

Japan's relationship to China indirectly caused another Japanese conflict, this conflict with Russia. After the Boxer Rebellion, most foreign powers withdrew their troops from China. However, a force of 100,000 Russian soldiers lingered in Manchuria. Despite protests by the Japanese government, Russia maintained the troops and had forced a lease from China for a railway line to extend across Manchuria. The Russians now had a port leased from China in 1898, and they looked set to dominate Manchuria.

Believing that war with Russia was likely, in 1902 Japan signed an alliance with Great Britain. Each nation agreed that the other had the right to defend special interests in China, Manchuria, and Korea against any third power. The two nations agreed that if either one became involved in a war with a single power, the other would remain neutral. If a third power joined the conflict, they would aid each other. The obvious target of the alliance was Russia.

The Anglo-Japanese alliance meant great prestige for Japan. The nation no longer stood alone but now had the support of one of the most powerful countries in the world. The alliance also increased pressure on Russia to withdraw from Manchuria. Diplomatic attempts failed, and finally in January 1904, Japan issued an ultimatum to Russia. Russia refused to answer Japan's demands.

The Russo-Japanese War. In February 1904, without a declaration of war, the Japanese attacked and badly damaged the Russian fleet at Port Arthur in Manchuria. In March Japanese troops overran Korea and pushed the Russians back through Manchuria in a series of battles throughout the summer. Another

Japanese force landed on the Liaodong Peninsula in Manchuria and, with the help of the navy, lay siege to Port Arthur. In February and March of 1905, 330,000 Russian and 270,000 Japanese troops fought a great battle at Mukden. Losses were heavy on both sides, and the Russians pulled back. Then in May 1905, the Japanese navy stunned the world at the Battle of Tsushima with the complete destruction of the Russian Baltic fleet.

Shorter supply lines and a better-prepared military helped Japan in the war against Russia. However, the Japanese army suffered heavy casualties, and the cost of the war strained the Japanese economy. As a result, the Japanese asked United States president Theodore Roosevelt to mediate the conflict. Roosevelt reluctantly agreed, and in 1905 invited representatives from Japan and Russia to negotiations at Portsmouth, New Hampshire. Later that year an agreement ended the Russo-Japanese War.

The Treaty of Portsmouth. Under the agreement known as the **Treaty of Portsmouth**, Russia ceded to Japan its lease on the Liaodong Peninsula, including Port Arthur, and the southern half of the Russian island of Sakhalin, north of Japan. Russia also gave up control of the southern branch of the Chinese Eastern Railway and recognized Japan as the dominant power in Korea. In addition, Russia agreed to withdraw all troops, except for railway guards, from Manchuria.

In this painting, the Japanese navy attacks Russian forces at Port Arthur. The Treaty of Portsmouth ended the Russo-Japanese War with the cession of Port Arthur to Japan.

The Treaty of Portsmouth—which won Roosevelt the Nobel Peace Prize in 1906—eliminated any competition in Manchuria. It also signaled that other countries respected Japan's growing strength. When Japan proclaimed the annexation of Korea in 1910, none of the other imperialist powers protested.

Problems of Modernization

In less than 50 years, Japan had advanced from a feudal agrarian nation to one of the world's leading industrial nations. Victories over China and Russia had established Japan as a military power. However, these considerable achievements also created new problems for the island nation.

Industrialization and scientific development brought higher standards of living and improved medical care to Japan, spurring population growth. Cities grew rapidly, and every inch of suitable land was placed under cultivation. Even so, the increased food supply could not match the rapid population growth.

Japanese people began to emigrate to Korea and Taiwan, as well as to Hawaii and other islands of the Pacific. Thousands more left for the United States. In time the United States prohibited the immigration of Asians while still admitting Europeans. The Japanese deeply resented such discrimination.

Japanese industrialization created yet another problem. Japan had to import raw materials because it lacked almost all those needed in modern industry. To pay for these raw materials, it had to sell goods abroad. As purchasers of both food and raw materials, Japan had to export effectively to survive.

In trying to export its goods, Japan met with restrictions in the rough world of international trade. Many countries passed tariff laws to protect their home markets against Japanese competition. These countries argued that Japanese goods had an unfair advantage because cheap labor enabled Japanese manufacturers to

What If?

The Russo-Japanese War
Japan's startling victory in the Russo-Japanese War made it the equal of other imperialist powers competing in the Pacific. How might the course of history have been different if Russia, not Japan, had won the Russo-Japanese War in 1905?

charge lower prices. For the island nation, a modernizing economy had to expand or collapse.

Social Tensions in the 1920s

Social and political stability had marked the Meiji era. During that time, there was a gradual movement toward constitutionalism, but customs and law allowed for little dissent. By the 1920s, however, the situation had changed. Economic development, universal education, and new ideas from the West all contributed to changes in attitudes among the Japanese people. Many believed that the time had come for the people to benefit from Japan's economic advances.

Industrial workers organized labor unions and called strikes for higher wages and better working conditions. Tenant farmers organized unions, too, and demanded lower agricultural rents. Urban intellectuals and university students, inspired by the victory of the Western democracies over Germany in World War I, argued that democracy was the wave of the future. They organized a movement for universal manhood suffrage, which they saw as an essential first step toward promoting democracy in Japan. Women, however, were not given the right to vote until 1945. Other Japanese became interested in socialism and communism. These people protested the government's expansionist policies and tried to organize a revolutionary political movement in Japan.

Some young Japanese also began to question the traditional values of their society. As an educated class grew, its tastes changed from purely Japanese pursuits. New ideas and arts entered Japan from the West along with economic prosperity. The center of Japanese society, formerly an agricultural one, became the modern city. After World War I, Japanese enthusiastically greeted new forms of entertainment. They enjoyed Western dance, listened to jazz, and played baseball. The first modern Japanese novel had appeared in 1889, and the decade after the Russo-Japanese War produced a number of important Japanese writers. Many of their novels dealt with the struggles of individuals in a changing society.

Factories found a source of labor from farm villages, and women took jobs in manufacturing and textile work. Women also began to participate in office work, and a feminist movement, though unsuccessful, began.

These changes did not come without reaction. When markets collapsed in the worldwide depression of 1929, many felt that the country had been subverted economically and morally by focusing on international rather than traditional Japanese interests.

Growing Influence of the Military

Japanese political leaders of the 1920s had difficulty finding answers to all the concerns of the Japanese people. They granted universal manhood suffrage in 1925, yet they could not agree on what to do about other demands. In addition, there seemed to be no clear remedy to the country's precarious economic position. Furthermore, some groups vehemently

Kabuki, a form of Japanese theater incorporating song, dance, and mime, portrays historical and contemporary events during performances that can last an entire day. This is an exterior view of a Japanese Kabuki theater.

opposed increasing westernization. In this atmosphere of discord and dissatisfaction, the influence of the Japanese military grew steadily stronger.

The constitution of 1889 had charged top-ranking officers with carrying out the emperor's commands and recommending to him what those commands should be. Senior officers, who were subject to no civilian control, recommended who should serve as the government's minister of war and minister of the navy. Because only members of the military could hold these two posts, civilian authorities had almost no control over military affairs.

Until the late 1920s, military ministers generally cooperated with civilian members of the government. After that, however, military leaders began to assert their powers in order to influence government policy. They had seen in World War I a new kind of war in which victory had depended on total mobilization, not only of troops but also of the entire spiritual and material resources of the nation. Believing that victory in any future war would require the same kind of mobilization, the military ministers saw discontent in Japan as a serious problem. Dissatisfaction indicated weakness in Japanese society and constituted a threat to the nation's security in the event that there was war. To preserve the nation, the military ministers felt that they must do everything in their power to eliminate this discontent.

The economic problems that Japan faced in the late 1920s also influenced military officers to take a more active role in government. Officers in the army and navy believed that the Western nations would never treat Japan as an equal. As proof of this, they pointed to the restrictions many Western countries had imposed on Japanese immigration and exports. Young officers, particularly, were influenced by groups that believed in the "purity" of Japanese culture and expansionism. Japan should pursue a more independent course, they argued, especially in Asia.

In time the military began to insist that the Japanese people pay greater attention to traditional values. Military leaders also called for a larger army and a stronger navy. In addition, they advocated a Japanese "Monroe Doctrine" that would reserve special powers in East Asia similar to those exercised by the United States in the Western Hemisphere. In particular, military leaders saw Manchuria as a target for future expansion. The growing influence of the military ultimately would have far-reaching consequences for all of Japanese society and for the rest of the world as well.

Section 4 Review

1. **Define** Treaty of Portsmouth
2. **Understanding Ideas** Why did the Japanese want to expand their influence during the late 1800s?
3. **Determining Cause and Effect** Why were the Japanese able to defeat Russia in the Russo-Japanese War?
4. **Summarizing Ideas** What new economic and social problems were created by Japanese modernization?

Section 5

Latin America Between the Wars

Focus Questions

- How did the economies of Latin American nations change after World War I?
- Why did authoritarian regimes come to power in many Latin American nations?
- What kind of relationship did Latin America have with the United States?

As the 1920s began, Latin America appeared to be headed for prosperity. However, the region soon would suffer the effects of the worldwide economic crisis of the 1930s.

Economic Developments

Agricultural products such as beef, wheat, sugar, coffee, and fruits continued to dominate the economies of Latin American nations. However, during the early 1900s, Mexico became a leading exporter of oil. Oil was also discovered in Venezuela, Peru, Bolivia, and Colombia. The mining of other resources, such as copper in Chile and Peru, tin in Bolivia, and bauxite in Guiana, also grew rapidly during this period. For the most part, British and American companies owned the oil and mining operations.

In addition, the 1920s saw a great expansion in the generation of electric and hydroelectric power, financed mainly by foreign investors. The energy that was produced enabled many Latin American countries

Rivera's *Fruits of Labor*

After World War I, life in Mexico changed dramatically. Diego Rivera, one of Mexico's finest artists, recorded these changes. As a youth, Rivera studied in Spain and France and was befriended by Pablo Picasso. He settled in Paris and later traveled extensively throughout Europe. In Italy Rivera studied fresco painting. In 1921, he returned to Mexico where the clamor for social reform changed the direction of his work.

As a member of the art movement known as social realism, Rivera produced many paintings that dealt with current problems. Of particular interest are his works that show the plight of the peasants of Mexico. The Mexican government liked Rivera's art and commissioned him to paint murals for many schools and government buildings in Mexico. On the left is a detail from his fresco *Fruits of Labor,* commissioned by the Ministry of Education in Mexico City. In it he honors working people and their children. This impressive fresco took Rivera and a crew of assistants from 1923 to 1929 to complete.

to industrialize during the 1920s. For example, the larger countries in the region began to produce textiles, construction materials, machinery, and automobiles. Oil refining and food processing also became important industries at this time. Heavy industrialization in Latin America, however, would come after World War II.

Changes in Society

Industrialization contributed to the growth of cities. By 1935 Mexico City, Rio de Janeiro, São Paulo, and Buenos Aires all had 1 million or more inhabitants. These and other major cities in the region extended their transportation, sewer, and utilities systems to accommodate the influx of people and industries.

Industrialization also contributed to a change in Latin America's social structure. To provide labor for growing industries, many countries—particularly Argentina, Brazil, and Chile—had encouraged immigration from Europe since the late 1800s. New arrivals from across the Atlantic swelled the ranks of Latin America's working classes.

With growth came an increase in labor union activity. Although Latin American workers first began to organize in the late 1800s, the 1920s saw a surge in labor union membership. Latin American unions, which were largely socialist or anarchist in outlook, employed the strike as the primary way to achieve

their ends. As a result, by the late 1920s, practically every major city in Latin America had been hit by general strikes. Many governments mobilized police and troops to put down these strikes violently. Some governments outlawed both strikes and labor unions.

The middle class also began to grow as new jobs opened up in the professions, government service, and commerce. The increasing numbers of merchants, shopkeepers, and small-business owners added to this growth. The military was professionalized as the sons of the middle class became its officers. Moreover, changes in university programs created opportunities for middle-class youth in engineering, business, and public administration. Such developments gave the middle class potential access to greater power.

Political Changes

Political life in Latin America underwent sweeping change in the early 1900s. In Chile, Argentina, Peru, and Brazil, for example, political parties backed by the middle class emerged. Mexico, wracked by regional factionalism, went to a single-party political system. Mexico's leaders hoped to guarantee stability and solidify the changes that had taken place after the revolution, in spite of assassinations and divisions. In Uruguay reformers led by President José Batlle y Ordóñez (BAHT·yay ee awr·THOHN·yays) enacted a broad reform program that included free elections, a social security system, and nationalization of railroads and public utilities.

Democracy still eluded most Latin American governments. The nature of the groups in power, though, shifted. As countries industrialized, the concerns of the growing number of workers could not be ignored, and urban political movements made these concerns their agenda. Middle-class politicians, struggling for control with the upper-class landowners, turned also to the new working class for support in elections. Elections did not necessarily transfer power smoothly, however. In some countries, forcible overthrow remained the method of changing governments.

The Effects of the Great Depression

As the 1920s drew to a close, prices for Latin America's major agricultural exports, such as sugar and coffee, began to fall. Chile's export economy suffered a crippling blow when German scientists developed a process for making synthetic nitrates which are used in fertilizers and explosives. As a result of this new process, the market plunged for Chile's major export, nitrates.

The worldwide economic depression caused the prices of Latin America's exports to fall even farther. Because they received such a small return on their exports, many Latin American nations found it impossible to import any but the most essential goods. Some countries stopped making payments on foreign debts. As the region's economies continued to falter, unemployment spread, causing worker unrest.

Authoritarian Regimes

Economic crisis soon led to political crisis. Coups d'état overthrew many Latin American governments in the 1930s. In some cases, these coups toppled constitutional systems that had existed for 30 to 40 years. Only Uruguay, which experienced a minor crisis between 1933 and 1935, and Mexico, which had undergone a revolution from 1911 to 1917, avoided major political upheaval.

Planters and exporters, whose fortunes had been wiped out during the Great Depression, lost much of their power as middle classes rebelled. The military strongly influenced or controlled many new governments. In some countries, American-trained military leaders sought to rule. In Nicaragua, for example, General Anastasio Somoza seized power in 1936, two years after assassinating his chief rival, nationalist guerrilla leader Augusto César Sandino. In the Dominican Republic, General Rafael Trujillo

Molina (troo·HEE·yoh moh·LEE·nah) began a 31-year dictatorship in 1930.

In some countries, the new military officers considered upper-class landowners and exporters corrupt, accusing them of having conducted dishonest elections and of allowing foreigners to take control of national resources. Consequently, the military leaders limited the landowners' political influence. At the same time, some new governments broke the power of labor unions and other worker and peasant organizations. Many governments simply abolished these groups and jailed their leaders. In Brazil power became increasingly concentrated in the hands of President Getúlio Vargas, who suppressed any expression of dissent and dismantled any framework of democracy. Sometimes the military governments reacted more violently. In El Salvador, for example, the army massacred more than 10,000 peasants in an effort to destroy a popular movement led by Agustín Farabundo Martí, a one-time follower of Sandino in Nicaragua.

Some military leaders, however, saw that they could curb popular movements through persuasion rather than terror. A number of governments controlled the labor movements by recognizing and giving favors only to those unions loyal to the military. At the same time, many military governments tried to limit the appeal of left-wing movements by responding to some of the needs of ordinary people. These governments enacted some land reforms and passed laws giving workers benefits such as pensions and minimum wages.

Relations with the United States

In U.S. relations with Latin America, President Franklin D. Roosevelt's administration tried to undo the ill will and suspicion created by the earlier United States policy of intervention. During the 1930s, Roosevelt fostered a program he called the **Good Neighbor Policy**. This policy stressed cooperation among the American nations and noninterference by the United States in Latin American affairs.

In 1933 the United States joined other American nations at the Pan American Conference in Montevideo, pledging not to intervene in the internal or external affairs of Latin American nations. As proof of its intentions, the United States recalled the army units that had occupied Haiti since 1915. It also surrendered its right to interfere in the affairs of Panama in the Hull-Alfaro Treaty of 1936.

A situation in Cuba, however, sorely tested the Roosevelt administration's commitment to the Montevideo agreement. In 1933 a group of radical

Disorder was widespread in Cuba in 1933. Here police open fire on Cubans in Havana as they are celebrating the rumor that President Machado has resigned.

reformers overthrew the Cuban dictator Gerardo Machado. The new government immediately declared a socialist revolution and nationalized a number of companies owned by investors from the United States. In response the Roosevelt administration refused to grant diplomatic recognition to the new government. Once again it appeared that the United States would intervene, as was its privilege under the Platt Amendment. (See Chapter 23.)

The United States did not interfere directly, but when Cuban army sergeant Fulgencio Batista decided to overthrow the reformers, Roosevelt's envoy to Cuba encouraged him. Even though the United States no longer intervened directly in Latin American affairs, it still had considerable influence over Latin American nations such as Cuba. Batista remained the power in the background while a series of civilian governments nominally ruled Cuba. In recognition of the stability that Batista brought to Cuba, the United States canceled the Platt Amendment in 1934.

Economic Nationalism

During the 1930s, most governments of industrialized Latin American nations followed a policy of economic nationalism. They reacted to the decline in markets for their exports by encouraging industry. In this way, they hoped to become more self-sufficient. The Vargas regime in Brazil achieved considerable

success in this effort. By the time the army ousted Vargas in 1945, Brazil was producing many of its own consumer goods.

In some ways, economic nationalism was a product of the world's Great Depression. With international markets gone and exchange rates unfavorable for what little was imported, many Latin American nations had no choice but to develop their own industries for manufactured goods. The necessity of economic nationalism coincided with growing feelings of political nationalism, encouraged by the middle class, who wanted to be dependent on neither Europe nor the United States.

The most significant act of economic nationalism occurred in Mexico in 1938. American- and British-owned oil companies in Mexico became involved in a wage dispute with their workers. When the Mexican Supreme Court ruled in favor of the workers, the foreign-owned oil companies refused to accept the decision of the court. As a result, President Lázaro Cárdenas intervened and nationalized the oil industry.

The British angrily broke diplomatic relations. The Americans hesitated, then took a more subtle approach, attempting to preserve the Good Neighbor Policy. The Roosevelt administration applied various indirect pressures, trying to force the Mexican government to pay the oil companies what they claimed their holdings were worth. Finally, the two governments reached a compromise. Mexicans regard March 13, 1938, when President Cárdenas nationalized the oil companies, as the birth date of Mexican economic independence.

Section 5 Review

1. **Define** Good Neighbor Policy
2. **Locate and Explain the Significance** Mexico City, Buenos Aires
3. **Analyzing Ideas (a)** What economic problems did Latin America experience during the late 1920s and the 1930s? **(b)** What impact did these economic problems have on political life in Latin America?
4. **Understanding Ideas** Why did authoritarian governments come to power in many parts of Latin America?
5. **Evaluating Ideas** How did the Good Neighbor Policy affect the relationship between Latin America and the United States?

Chapter 26 Review

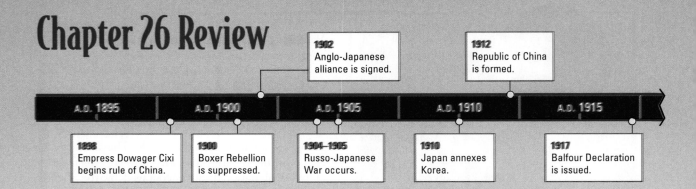

1902
Anglo-Japanese alliance is signed.

1912
Republic of China is formed.

A.D. 1895   A.D. 1900   A.D. 1905   A.D. 1910   A.D. 1915

1898
Empress Dowager Cixi begins rule of China.

1900
Boxer Rebellion is suppressed.

1904–1905
Russo-Japanese War occurs.

1910
Japan annexes Korea.

1917
Balfour Declaration is issued.

Chapter Summary
The following list contains the key concepts you have learned about the political forces that emerged in Africa, Asia, and Latin America in the early 1900s.

1. During the 1920s and 1930s, Egypt, Transjordan, and Iraq appeared to become independent countries. However, Great Britain continued to exert control in these countries. At the same time, Palestine's future remained in doubt, but India moved toward independence.
2. Great Britain and its former colonies organized the Commonwealth of Nations.
3. Political and social reforms were attempted in Turkey and in Persia. Africa witnessed the stirrings of political activity that were to lead to major transformations in the years ahead.
4. The Chinese began the long and difficult process of making adjustments to the modern world.

Revolution brought imperial rule to an end in China; however, the Guomindang had trouble establishing its power in the new republic.
5. Dramatic change took place in Japan. This change was witnessed as Japan defeated first China and then Russia at the turn of the century. The Japanese faced economic and social pressures after the end of World War I.
6. Developments in Latin America reflected the worldwide economic crisis. The 1920s and 1930s were also a time of rapid social change, and, in a number of countries, governments became more authoritarian in nature.
7. Latin American relations with the United States improved as a result of the Good Neighbor Policy; however, economic nationalism led to a degree of tension between the countries.

Reviewing Important Terms
On a separate sheet of paper, supply the term that correctly completes each statement.

1. Many Jews supported _____, which aimed to build a Palestinian homeland for the Jews.
2. Gandhi's technique of _____ _____ called for citizens to peacefully refuse to cooperate with their government in order to win concessions from it.

Developing Critical Thinking Skills
1. **Analyzing a Primary Source** The verse below is from a poem entitled "Reproach" by Muhammad Iqbal, an Indian poet and a fervent nationalist who wanted independence for India. Read these lines, and answer the questions that follow.

"Your fate, poor hapless India, there's no telling—
Always the brightest jewel in someone's crown;
Mortgaged to the alien, soul and body too,
Alas—the dweller vanished with the dwelling—,
Enslaved to Britain you have kissed the rod:
It is not Britain I reproach, but you."

(a) What does Iqbal think India's fate will be?
(b) Whom does he blame for this situation? (c) Why?

(d) What actions do you think Iqbal might want the Indian people to take?
2. **Comparing Ideas** After World War I, many colonies wanted independence. Compare the British reaction to demands for Indian independence with the reaction to similar demands from Canada, Australia, New Zealand, and the Union of South Africa.
3. **Interpreting Ideas** (a) How did Sun Yixian hope to bring democracy to China? (b) What obstacles prevented him from succeeding?
4. **Summarizing Ideas** (a) What changes did the Nationalists initiate in China? (b) What problems did they fail to solve?
5. **Determining Cause and Effect** What economic and social problems did Japan face as a result of its rapid modernization and industrialization?
6. **Analyzing Ideas** Why did President Roosevelt introduce the Good Neighbor Policy during his administration as president?
7. **Classifying Ideas** Name the country in which each of the following people played vital leadership roles:
(a) Anastasio Somoza; (b) Kemal Atatürk; (c) Chiang Kaishek; (d) Mohandas Gandhi; (e) Fulgencio Batista; (f) Reza Shah Pahlavi.

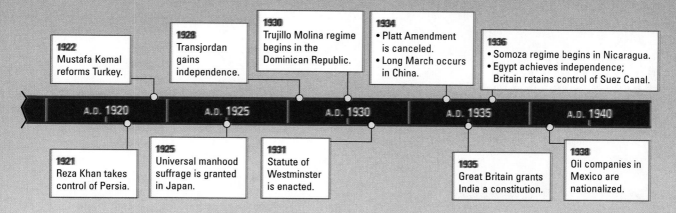

1922
Mustafa Kemal reforms Turkey.

1928
Transjordan gains independence.

1930
Trujillo Molina regime begins in the Dominican Republic.

1934
• Platt Amendment is canceled.
• Long March occurs in China.

1936
• Somoza regime begins in Nicaragua.
• Egypt achieves independence; Britain retains control of Suez Canal.

A.D. 1920   A.D. 1925   A.D. 1930   A.D. 1935   A.D. 1940

1921
Reza Khan takes control of Persia.

1925
Universal manhood suffrage is granted in Japan.

1931
Statute of Westminster is enacted.

1935
Great Britain grants India a constitution.

1938
Oil companies in Mexico are nationalized.

Relating Geography to History

Study the map of the Guomindang military operations on page 700. (a) Near what cities did the Guomindang victories over the warlords take place? (b) Near what cities did the Guomindang strikes against the Communists take place?

Relating Past to Present

1. Examine a historical atlas containing a map of the Middle East in the 1930s. (a) How does this map compare with a map of the Middle East today? (b) What recent problems in the Middle East date to the days of the British and French mandates? Explain how the mandates contributed to these problems.
2. (a) What issue strained relations between the United States and Mexico in the 1930s? (b) Does this issue still cause difficulties between the two nations? Explain.
3. Review the information in this chapter on the importance of the military in Japan, Persia (Iran), and Latin America. Choose one of these areas. Use newspapers and magazines to determine what role the military plays in this area today. Is the military stronger or weaker than it was in the 1920s and 1930s?

Applying History Study Skills

Before completing this activity, review Building History Study Skills on page 693.

Mohandas Gandhi organized the "Salt March" in India in 1930 to protest the British tax on salt. Read the following excerpt on the march from *I Found No Peace* by journalist Webb Miller.

"The salt deposits were surrounded by ditches filled with water and guarded by four hundred native Surat police. . . . Half a dozen British officials commanded them. The police carried lathis—five-foot clubs tipped with steel. Inside the stockade twenty-five native riflemen were drawn up.

In complete silence the Gandhi men drew up and halted a hundred yards from the stockade. A picked column advanced from the crowd, waded the ditches, and approached the barbed-wire stockade, which the Surat police surrounded, holding their clubs at the ready. Police officials ordered the marchers to disperse under a recently imposed regulation which prohibited gatherings of more than five persons in any one place.

The column silently ignored the warning and slowly walked forward. . . .

Suddenly, at a word of command, scores of native police rushed upon the advancing marchers and rained blows on their heads with their steel-shod lathis. Not one of the marchers even raised an arm to fend off the blows. They went down like tenpins. . . .

The survivors without breaking ranks silently and doggedly marched on until struck down."

1. What problem does the excerpt describe?
2. What is the solution to the problem?
3. How is the solution related to satyagraha?
4. (a) How would you evaluate the method? (b) Can non-violence triumph over violence? (c) Why or why not?
5. Write a conclusion analyzing the method of nonviolence in response to the salt tax. Use your answers to question 4 to support your conclusion.

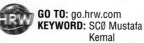

internet connect

Search the Internet through the HRW Web site for information on Mustafa Kemal and the reforms that occurred in Turkey under his rule. Be sure to include specifics on such reforms as women's rights and the separation of church and state. Be prepared to discuss your findings with the class.

GO TO: go.hrw.com
KEYWORD: SC0 Mustafa Kemal

Building Your Portfolio

1. **Preparing an Oral Presentation** Empress Dowager Cixi was a power in China from 1861 until her death in 1908. Using research materials, prepare a brief report on the life of this leader. In your report, note reasons why her policies might have helped bring about the end of the Qing dynasty. Place your research materials in your portfolio.
2. **Constructing a Chart** Make a list of the major changes that took place in Latin America during the 1920s and 1930s. Then prepare a chart in which you classify each of the items on your list under one of the following headings: economic, social, or political. Place the chart in your portfolio.

CHAPTER 27

World War II

TIME

A.D. **1921–1945**

| 3.7 million B.C. | 4000 B.C. | A.D. 2100 |

A.D. **1921–1945**

PLACE

Asia and the Pacific, Europe and the Mediterranean

Europe and the Mediterranean

Asia and the Pacific

U.S. troops land on Normandy Beach, June 10, 1944

Significance

By the mid-1930s, most European nations once more claimed loyalty to one of two opposing camps. One group included those nations generally satisfied with the World War I peace settlement. The other group consisted of dissatisfied nations. International relations between the two groups grew strained. In 1939 Japanese aggression in Asia and German aggression in Europe erupted into World War II.

Terms to Define

Kellogg-Briand Pact	Neutrality Acts
Lytton Commission	isolationists
Falange	Lend-Lease Act
Axis Powers	Atlantic Charter
Anti-Comintern Treaty	"New Order"
Munich Conference	"Final Solution"
appeasement	Auschwitz
German-Soviet	Holocaust
nonaggression pact	"soft underbelly of the
blitzkrieg	Axis"
"phony war"	island hopping
collaborators	Operation Overlord
Luftwaffe	V-E Day
Battle of Britain	V-J Day

People to Identify

Yuko Hamaguchi	Charles de Gaulle
Francisco Franco	Franklin D. Roosevelt
Neville Chamberlain	Erwin Rommel
Edouard Daladier	Hideki Tojo
Winston Churchill	Dwight Eisenhower
Philippe Pétain	Douglas MacArthur

Places to Locate

Beijing	El Alamein
Ethiopia	Munich
Italian Somaliland	Stalingrad
Sudetenland	Pearl Harbor
Albania	Guadalcanal
Tinian	Normandy
Iwo Jima	Okinawa
Dunkirk	Hiroshima

Chapter Theme Questions

- **War and Diplomacy** How might regional conflicts grow to involve many nations?
- **Social Relations** How might racial prejudice be used as a political weapon?
- **Technology** When technology is developed in response to war, how can it be both beneficial and destructive?

A colonel in the American Thirty-ninth Infantry Regiment wrote a longing letter to his fiancée from Germany on October 12, 1944. A portion of his letter read:

❝Well darling, I am growing older as the days go by, why in two more days I'll be twenty-five. Bet I'll be an old grey-headed man by the time all of this is over and the countries have decided to do away with the Army of Occupation. Every now and then I get to see an American paper and it seems to me that everybody is so worried about what is to happen after the War that they do not give very much thought to the fact that there is a long road ahead of us before the War is over.❞

It would indeed be seven months before the Allies would declare victory in Europe. It would be nearly a year until the Japanese surrendered unconditionally and World War II was over. The Allied victory came about 6 years after the beginning of World War II, but concern about world peace had arisen as much as 20 years earlier, during the 1920s.

Section 1

Threats to World Peace

Focus Questions

- **What aggressive territorial policies did Japan and Italy carry out beginning in the early 1920s?**
- **Why was the League of Nations ineffective in trying to stop aggression in Asia and Europe during this period?**
- **How did civil war in Spain lead to a fascist dictatorship there?**

The League of Nations had limited effectiveness, and the major powers held diplomatic conferences outside the organization. The first of these conferences was held in 1921 and 1922 in Washington, D.C. Nine powers that had interests in East Asia (excluding the Soviet Union, which was not invited to the meeting) attended the Washington Conference.

Several treaties resulted from the conference. The Five-Power Treaty, for example, provided for a 10-year "naval holiday," during which no major warships would be built. The participating nations also signed the Nine-Power Pact, agreeing to take no additional territory from China and to maintain the existing Open Door Policy. As a result of the Washington Naval Conference and other diplomatic settlements, peace was preserved throughout the 1920s.

The most optimistic of the international conferences took place in 1928 in Paris. The American secretary of state, Frank B. Kellogg, and the French foreign minister, Aristide Briand, drafted a treaty condemning war. Eventually, 62 nations signed the **Kellogg-Briand Pact**, which made war "illegal," though it did not specify how to prevent war. In the 1930s, it became clear that such imprecise and unenforceable measures would no longer be adequate.

Japanese Aggression in Asia

Beginning in the late 1920s, the military gained increasing power in Japan. In 1930 Japan's liberal prime minister, Yuko Hamaguchi, was fatally shot. Political disorder followed. Within two years, militarists controlled the Japanese government.

Attack on Manchuria. In September 1931 a group of Japanese soldiers set off an explosion on a Japanese-controlled railroad near the city of Mukden, Manchuria. The Japanese government blamed China, as the soldiers had hoped. Japanese troops occupied Mukden and, within several months, all of Manchuria. The Republic of China appealed to the League of Nations for help. This incident sparked a conflict between Japan and China that was to continue, intermittently, until 1945.

The League of Nations sent an investigating commission, headed by Lord Lytton of Great Britain, to Manchuria. At the same time, Japan continued its conquest. In 1932 Japan declared Manchuria to be an independent nation, under the name Manchukuo (MAN·CHOO·KWOH), and installed a puppet government.

The **Lytton Commission** advised the League not to recognize Manchukuo's independence and recommended that the region be restored to China. When the League voted on this recommendation, only Japan opposed it. The recommendation was thus defeated, but Japan withdrew from the League of Nations in protest of what it called unfair treatment.

Although the major nations joined in condemning Japan's aggression, no nation was willing to take military action on China's behalf. Japanese aggression unleashed a chain reaction that led to the collapse of peace in the West and in the East.

War in China. Confidently, Japan made further demands on China. It announced its intention to extend its influence not only to all of China but also throughout East and Southeast Asia and the western Pacific. In July 1937, Japanese and Chinese troops clashed near Beijing. Japanese armies captured the city and at once began to move southward. Though the Chinese armies engaged Japanese forces in a costly and damaging war, the Chinese gradually lost ground to Japan.

By 1939 the Japanese occupied about one fourth of China, including all its seaports, the Chang Jiang Valley as far as Hankou, and many cities in the interior. (See map on opposite page.) Still the Chinese stubbornly resisted. This resistance proved an enormous strain on the resources of both nations.

Italy's Conquest of Ethiopia

Italy was a one-party state under the fascist premier Benito Mussolini, who had assumed power in 1922. Mussolini focused on improving the nation's economy through increased taxation, reduced government spending, and suppression of strikes. Mussolini also sought to solve his country's economic problems by overseas expansion. Ethiopia, one of the few independent nations in Africa, became the object of his ambitions.

A border incident provided the pretext for aggression. In December 1934 an Italian border patrol in Italian Somaliland clashed with an Ethiopian border patrol. Ethiopia, unprepared to resist aggression from a power such as Italy, asked the League of Nations for protection. The League could not help in a military sense; it maintained no armed forces. It did bring the dispute to arbitration, but the results were inconclusive. After nearly a year of tension, Mussolini, using Italian forces from Eritrea and Italian Somaliland, invaded Ethiopia. (See map on page 717.) The poorly equipped Ethiopian army was no match for the Italians.

The League then declared Italy an aggressor and applied economic sanctions—a boycott on trade with Italy. The sanctions, however, were too weak to undermine Italy. For example, they did not include oil, iron, or steel. Italians triumphantly entered the Ethiopian capital, Addis Ababa (AHD·dis AH·bah·bah), in spring 1936. Mussolini declared Ethiopia a part of the Italian

The Expansion of Japan, 1928–1941

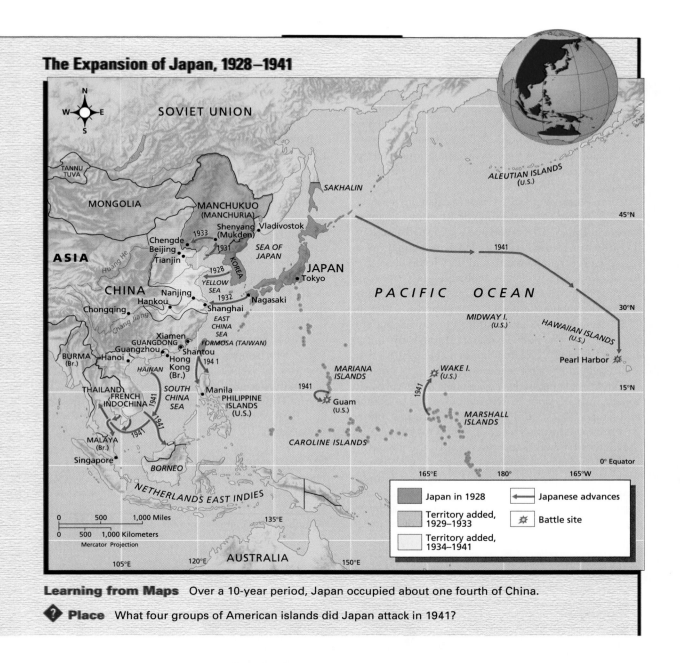

Learning from Maps Over a 10-year period, Japan occupied about one fourth of China.

? Place What four groups of American islands did Japan attack in 1941?

Empire and proclaimed the Italian king, Victor Emmanuel III, emperor of Ethiopia.

Despite almost universal disapproval of Italy's actions, no major power was willing to use force to uphold the League's sanctions. In Great Britain and the United States, people still remembered the horror of World War I. They did not want to risk another war. France, where the loss of men in the war had been great, adopted a defensive policy and built elaborate fortifications along the Maginot (MA·zhuh·noh) Line.

In addition, many nations were preoccupied with the effects of the Great Depression. In 1937 Italy withdrew from the League. In light of the world's failure to act, it was easy for Japan and Italy to conclude that they could continue their acts of aggression unopposed.

Civil War in Spain

Economically, Spain lagged far behind the rest of western Europe during the 1800s. Although some industry existed, the economy remained primarily agricultural. The nobility owned large estates that included much of the nation's land. The educational system was controlled by the church.

In 1876 the Spanish government had become a constitutional monarchy. An elected parliament called the Cortes limited the king's power. Politically, the country was unstable. Throughout the early 1900s, violent strikes, political assassinations, military plots, and separatist movements in the provinces plagued the nation.

After World War I, the chaos in Spain grew worse. In 1923 General Miguel Primo de Rivera y Orbaneja, known as Primo, led a revolt and established a military dictatorship. King Alfonso XIII remained as a figurehead and supported the military leader insofar as he allowed him to enact political and economic reforms. Primo, backed by the army, held power until he lost the support of both the army and the king in 1930. King Alfonso forced Primo to resign, but the king had lost the public's respect through his initial support of Primo's dictatorship. In 1931 King Alfonso abdicated, and Spain became a republic.

The Spanish Republic. Spain's new leaders planned to establish freedom of religion, to separate church and state issues, and to place education under government control. The government took land from the Catholic Church and the nobility and gave it to landless peasants. Members of the clergy were barred from teaching in schools, and the Catholic Church now had to pay its clergy. Workers received many benefits—shorter hours, better wages, the right to organize, and a voice in the management of business.

These sweeping reforms antagonized Spanish conservatives, who quickly lent their support to a fascist party called the **Falange**.* The Falange was determined to preserve the power of the army, landowners, and the church, regardless of whom the voters might elect to office.

Nationalists versus Loyalists. In February 1936, a Popular Front government that included Socialists and Communists won a major election. The Spanish Popular Front, like the Popular Front in France, represented a coalition of left-wing working-class parties united in their opposition to fascism. Prominent fascists were jailed, and the Falange responded with terrorist acts. In July a Falange leader was assassinated. Following his murder, army uprisings, led by Falangists, erupted in the Canary Islands and in Spain itself. The bitter civil war that followed lasted for almost three years.

The Falangist rebels, who were led by General Francisco Franco, called themselves Nationalists. Those who supported the republic were known as Loyalists, or Republicans. By the end of 1936, the Nationalists controlled most of northern and western Spain. The Loyalists controlled the east and southeast, most of the northern coastline, and the capital city of Madrid.

Foreign Assistance to Spain

The Spanish Civil War soon became a small European war. Germany and Italy saw a fascist Spain as a part of

Falange is the Spanish word for "phalanx."

This Spanish woman is assembling a fuselage in an airplane factory during the Spanish Civil War.

Guernica by Pablo Picasso

Although Pablo Picasso lived in France, he was born in Spain and was keenly sympathetic to the Loyalist cause during the Spanish Civil War. His painting *Guernica* expressed his outrage over the bombing of the town of Guernica, which had no strategic value. Using only blacks, grays, and whites, Picasso evoked anguish and horror with his distorted figures writhing in agony under a stark electric light. The painting was on tour in New York City in 1939 when World War II began. Picasso directed that it stay in the United States until democracy had returned to Spain. *Guernica* was returned to Spain in 1981 and was placed in a museum in Madrid.

their plan to surround France with unfriendly powers and threaten Great Britain. They sent fully equipped military units to bolster Nationalist forces.

Sympathetic to the republican government, the Soviet Union sent planes, technicians, and military advisers. Soviet help to the Loyalists, however, was not nearly as extensive as the support Franco received from his fascist allies.

Volunteers from France, Great Britain, the United States, and other nations also clamored to help the Spanish Republic. These antifascist volunteers became known as the International Brigades. The number of brigade volunteers may have been as high as 70,000, though there were only about 20,000 on the field at any given time. On the other hand, Italy sent more than 50,000 trained troops to assist the Nationalists.

The Spanish Civil War brought into the open the seething struggle between fascism and socialism in Europe during the 1930s. It also became a testing ground for new weapons and tactics such as improved aircraft and strategic bombing missions.

The French and the British feared that the Spanish Civil War might spread to the rest of Europe. In September 1936, at the suggestion of the French government, a nonintervention committee representing the major European nations was established. These nations unanimously agreed to a policy of nonintervention in Spain that included a blockade intended to halt the flow of volunteers and supplies to both sides. The blockade cut off most aid to the Loyalists, but it did not hinder German and Italian assistance to Franco.

Spain Under Franco

By the spring of 1938, the Nationalist forces in Spain had grown strong enough for a large-scale offensive. They defeated the Loyalist troops in March 1939, with the capture of Barcelona and Madrid. During the Madrid campaign, one of Franco's generals claimed he had four columns—long, narrow lines of troops—marching on the city and a fifth column within Madrid that would rise against the defenders at the appropriate time. The term *fifth column* has come to mean traitors within a country who assist its enemies.

Franco then set up a fascist government modeled loosely on Mussolini's dictatorship in Italy and became head of the state with unlimited power. He assumed the title *el Caudillo* (cow·THEE·yoh)—Spanish for "the leader." Franco's political party, the Falange, was the only one permitted. Its national council, chosen by Franco, advised him on legislation, though the council held no real power.

The economic organization of Spain resembled that of fascist Italy, with syndicates, or corporations, organized according to occupations and economic activities. In other respects, however, Spain was clearly under the domination of a militaristic leader. The government abolished free elections and most civil rights. Under Franco's regime, the old ruling groups—the army, the landowners, and the Roman Catholic Church—continued to hold positions of power.

Although Spain had become a fascist dictatorship, Franco did not join the Rome-Berlin Axis. The civil war had devastated the country, and many years were to pass before economic recovery took place and hatred among Spaniards waned.

Section 1 Review

1. **Define** Kellogg-Briand Pact, Lytton Commission, Falange
2. **Identify** Yuko Hamaguchi, Francisco Franco, Nationalist, Loyalist, International Brigades
3. **Locate and Explain the Significance** Mukden, Manchukuo, Beijing, Chang Jiang Valley, Ethiopia, Italian Somaliland
4. **Summarizing Ideas** Describe the aggression of Japan and Italy that began in the early 1920s.
5. **Analyzing Ideas** What factors contributed to the ineffectiveness of the League of Nations in dealing with the aggression of Japan and Italy?
6. **Determining Cause and Effect** How did a fascist dictatorship develop in Spain?

Section 2

Hitler's Aggressions

Focus Questions

- How was Hitler able to acquire Austria and Czechoslovakia?
- In what ways did Great Britain and France try to avoid war, and how did they prepare for war when it became inevitable?
- How did the major powers of Europe respond to the Nazi-Soviet Pact, and how did they respond to Hitler's invasion of Poland?

As Germany grew stronger, Adolf Hitler's foreign policy became more aggressive. In 1933 he had taken Germany out of the League of Nations and announced his intention to rearm the country. In March 1936, German troops marched into the Rhineland, violating the Treaty of Versailles. In October 1936, following the outbreak of the Spanish Civil War, Hitler and Mussolini formed a military alliance called the Rome-Berlin Axis and began referring to themselves as the **Axis Powers**.* Shortly afterward Japan and Germany pledged to work together to prevent the spread of Russian communism. They signed an agreement called the **Anti-Comintern Treaty**, which Italy soon endorsed. Thus by the end of 1936, the nations that would eventually enter World War II as the Axis Powers—Germany, Italy, and Japan—had camouflaged their aggressive intentions under the pretense of resisting communism. Hitler became convinced that he could do as he pleased, and for a time he seemed right. The democratic nations had done very little to halt the spread of fascism in Ethiopia and Spain.

Annexing Austria

A Nazi Party had been formed in Austria in the late 1920s. By the early 1930s, the extremely conservative Austrian government was doing little to resist Nazi inroads. By 1938 threats from both Hitler and Mussolini forced the Austrian government to include Nazi members in its cabinet.

Though the Austrian chancellor had made an agreement with Hitler on *Anschluss* (union) with Germany, he regretted the agreement and suggested that the Austrian people be allowed to vote on the issue. Hitler refused to permit it, preferring instead to overcome Austria with a show of strength. The chancellor resigned, and a German army marched into Austria unopposed. In March 1938, Hitler proclaimed Austria a part of the Third Reich. (See map on opposite page.) Even though *Anschluss* was specifically forbidden by the Treaty of Versailles, Great Britain and France did nothing more than send protests to Hitler, which he ignored. The League of Nations took no action.

The addition of Austria enlarged Germany's population, territory, and resources. It also increased Hitler's influence in Europe. Strategically, Germany had now penetrated the heart of central Europe and reached a common border with its ally Italy. The annexation of Austria threatened Czechoslovakia,

---

*Mussolini originated the term *Axis Powers*. He claimed that an imaginary line drawn from Rome to Berlin formed the "axis" on which the world would turn from that time forward.

which Hitler had designated as the next objective in his expansion program. Germany now almost completely encircled Czechoslovakia. Nazi propaganda, however, claimed that Czechoslovakia had become a "dagger pointed at the heart of Germany."

Czechoslovakia and the Sudeten Crisis

Around the western rim of Czechoslovakia, in a region known as the Sudetenland (soo·DAYT·uhn·land), lived more than 3 million Germans. This territory, once part of the huge Habsburg Empire, had been included in Czechoslovakia after World War I. A chain of mountains, which gave the new state a natural and defensible frontier, separated the Sudetenland from Germany and Austria. Czechoslovakia had fortified these mountains heavily. Now they had become a defensive line—second in importance in Europe only to France's Maginot Line.

German and Italian Expansion, 1935–1941

Legend:
- Germany, 1935
- Acquired by Germany, 1935–1939
- German protectorates and Vichy France
- Italy and possessions, 1935
- Acquired by Italy, 1935–1939
- Minor Axis powers, 1941
- Axis advances
- Controlled by Axis, December 1941
- Controlled by Allies, December 1941
- Area of the Battle of Britain
- Neutral countries
- Farthest Soviet advance, 1940

Ethiopia, 1935–1941

Learning from Maps Within six years of expansion, the Axis Powers controlled much of Europe and North Africa.

Region What countries remained neutral during this period?

The Czech government tried to protect the rights of the Sudeten Germans. It allowed the people to use the German language in their schools and to be represented according to population in the parliament, civil service, and army. Still, many Sudeten Germans wanted union with Germany. Also, a strong Nazi Party grew in the Sudetenland.

After Germany's annexation of Austria, Sudeten Nazis demanded a completely self-governing Sudetenland. Hitler took up their cause. Riots broke out in the Sudetenland, and in September 1938, the situation became so critical that the Czech government placed the country under martial law.

Hitler, representing his actions as protective of fellow Germans, announced that Germany would invade and then annex the Sudetenland. This would mean disaster for Czechoslovakia. The loss of its heavily fortified mountain region would leave the country defenseless against Germany. When Germany sent troops to the frontier, the world waited tensely to see what action Czechoslovakia's allies would take.

The Czechs had defensive alliances with both France and the Soviet Union. The Soviet alliance provided for assistance to the Czechs only if France did likewise. France turned to Great Britain for support. Great Britain, however, urged France to be patient and advised the Czechs to make every possible concession to avoid war. The Czech government then granted increased independence for the Sudetens.

Still dissatisfied, Hitler began to increase Germany's military preparations. On September 22, 1938, he demanded that the Sudetenland be turned over to Germany. If it were not, he said, he would invade it and take it by force.

Appeasement at Munich

As tensions mounted in Europe, Hitler invited the British prime minister, Neville Chamberlain, and

German soldiers enter Prague as residents of the city stand somberly on the sidewalks.

Edouard Daladier (dah·lahd·yay), the premier of France, to attend a meeting in Munich (referred to as the **Munich Conference**). Also in attendance would be Italy's Mussolini. The conference was to begin on September 29, and the four participants would attempt to settle the Czech problem peaceably. Conspicuously not invited to send representatives were the Soviet Union, which, along with France, had pledged to defend Czechoslovakia, and Czechoslovakia itself.

Fearful of German military might and knowing how ill-prepared their own countries were, Chamberlain and Daladier accepted Hitler's demand that the Sudetenland be annexed to Germany. The policy they followed—attempting to preserve peace by yielding to the demands of the aggressor—is known as **appeasement**. Upon his return to London, Chamberlain triumphantly addressed a cheering crowd, announcing that he believed he had achieved "peace in our time."

Soon after the Munich Conference, France announced that it would neither honor its alliance with Czechoslovakia nor provide any assistance. Germany began to occupy the Sudetenland. The small country of Czechoslovakia, deserted by its allies, was now rendered defenseless. The rule of force in international affairs marked yet another victory.

In speaking of the Sudetenland, Hitler stated that it was the last territorial claim he would make in Europe. In March 1939, however, Hitler sent his

---

What If?

The League of Nations
If the League of Nations had taken stronger actions against Hitler and protected the independence of European countries such as Czechoslovakia, how might the course of world history have been different?

troops throughout the Czech area of Czechoslovakia and made it a German protectorate. He then declared the remainder of the country an independent state called Slovakia, which he soon seized.

Czechoslovakia had been the last democracy in Central Europe. Yet within six months, this independent republic was erased completely from the map. Once again the League of Nations had failed to be effective; its complete helplessness was now obvious. In the meantime, the political situation in Europe headed rapidly toward chaos.

Unchecked Fascist Aggression

Not satisfied with Czechoslovakia, Hitler next moved toward Lithuania. His quarrel with that nation involved the former East Prussian port city of Memel. (See map on page 717.) Germany had surrendered Memel to the Allies under the Versailles Treaty. In 1923 Lithuania took the city.

After Hitler came to power, a Nazi Party formed by the Germans in Memel demanded that Germany annex the city. Hitler echoed these demands. By March 1939, Lithuania could not withstand the pressure and ceded Memel and adjacent territory to Germany.

Still another nation lost its independence in the spring of 1939. Mussolini, once a model for other dictators, had by now become Hitler's imitator. In April 1939, Mussolini invaded Albania, on the east coast of the Adriatic Sea. (See map on page 717.) The Italians took the country in only a few days. King Zog and Queen Geraldine fled the country, and the king of Italy, who had recently become emperor of Ethiopia, gained an additional title—king of Albania.

Preparations for War

After Hitler took over Czechoslovakia, British and French leaders could no longer maintain their illusions about the intentions of the fascist dictators. Britain and France therefore began to prepare for war. In Great Britain, Neville Chamberlain ordered that Britain's rearmament program be stepped up and rushed a draft law through Parliament. France already had a defensive alliance with Poland. Great Britain announced that it, too, would help Poland if Germany attacked.

France also had a nonaggression treaty with the Soviet Union. Now Great Britain and France approached the Soviet leader, Joseph Stalin, suggesting a mutual alliance against Germany. Even though the Soviet Union had joined the League of Nations, while Japan, Germany, and Italy had dropped out, Soviet leaders remained suspicious of the Western

democracies. Until this time, the Western nations—fearful of communism—had excluded the Soviet Union from all major decisions affecting Europe and the rest of the world. The Soviet leaders in turn feared that the Western powers would welcome a chance to turn Hitler loose on them.

The Soviets insisted that any mutual assistance pact they might sign with Great Britain and France guarantee the independence of Poland, Finland, and the Baltic countries of Estonia, Latvia, and Lithuania. The Soviets also wanted a military alliance with all of these countries to ensure immediate response in the event of a German attack. This suggestion brought instant protests from the nations involved. All but Lithuania had common borders with the Soviet Union. A military agreement would mean that, in case of a German attack, Soviet armies would have the right to move into their countries to meet the Germans. The negotiations dragged on, resulting in a stalemate.

The Nazi-Soviet Pact

At the same time that Stalin was negotiating with Great Britain and France, he was carrying on secret negotiations with Germany. In August 1939, the Western democracies received a tremendous shock. Hitler proudly announced a **German-Soviet nonaggression pact**. Soviet leaders in Moscow soon confirmed the announcement.

This cartoon satirizes Stalin's pact with Hitler; together they agreed to carve eastern Europe into new territory for the Soviet Union and Germany.

The reasons for such an agreement between openly declared enemies were not immediately apparent. However, many historians believe that neither the Germans nor the Soviets expected the treaty to be a lasting one. Both Hitler and Stalin may simply have been playing for time. Hitler wanted to assure himself of Soviet neutrality in the event that Britain and France took action against Germany. Stalin apparently hoped that Hitler would find himself bogged down in the West. This would give the Soviet Union adequate time to prepare for its eventual, inevitable encounter with Germany.

Publicly the German-Soviet nonaggression pact, also called the Nazi-Soviet Pact, pledged that Germany and the Soviet Union would never attack each other. Each would remain neutral if the other became involved in war. Secretly, however, the two dictators agreed to divide eastern Europe into spheres of influence. Germany was to take western Poland. The Soviet Union was to have a free hand in the Baltic countries, in eastern Poland, and in the province of Bessarabia, which it had lost to Romania in 1918.

Little doubt existed as to the meaning of the pact. The Western nations had lost a possible ally in the East, and Germany had secured a pledge of the Soviet Union's neutrality, a tremendous military advantage.

Danzig and the Polish Corridor

The crisis that finally touched off World War II began in Poland. Hitler's dispute with that country involved the Polish Corridor, the strip of territory cut through Germany to allow Poland access to the seaport of Danzig. (See map on page 717.) Danzig was a free city, protected by the League of Nations. Both Germany and Poland had rights to use the port.

Because Danzig had a large German population, Hitler claimed it for Germany. A strong Nazi Party, encouraged by propaganda and financial help from Berlin, developed in Danzig. By 1937 it controlled the city government. It took actions and issued demands that made relations with Poland increasingly difficult. The city commissioner appointed by the League was powerless to do anything.

After securing Austria and Czechoslovakia, Hitler intensified his campaign against Poland. Within a week after signing the nonaggression pact with the Soviet Union, Hitler demanded that Danzig be returned to Germany and that the Germans be allowed to occupy a strip running through the Polish Corridor.

On the morning of September 1, 1939, Hitler declared the annexation of Danzig to the Reich.

At the same time, without warning, his air force launched a massive attack on Poland. Nazi troops, led by tank columns, penetrated the border. Two days later Great Britain and France decided that they would not tolerate any further Nazi aggression. They kept their promises to Poland and declared war on Germany. Within 48 hours the unannounced attack on Poland had become the beginning of World War II.

Section 2 Review

1. **Define** Axis Powers, Anti-Comintern Treaty, Munich Conference, appeasement, German-Soviet nonaggression pact
2. **Identify** Neville Chamberlain, Edouard Daladier
3. **Locate and Explain the Significance** Sudetenland, Munich, Memel, Albania, Polish Corridor, Danzig
4. **Evaluating Ideas** How did Hitler's annexation of Austria benefit Germany?
5. **Sequencing Ideas** Describe the steps by which Hitler took over Czechoslovakia.
6. **Understanding Ideas** (a) How and why did Great Britain and France try to appease Hitler? (b) What preparations did these two countries make for war when Hitler's intentions became clear to them?
7. **Summarizing Ideas** How did the German-Soviet pact and Hitler's aggression in Poland lead to World War II?

Section 3

Axis Gains

Focus Questions

- How did control of Norway, Denmark, and the Low Countries benefit Hitler?
- What success did Hitler have in France?
- What was the Battle of Britain, and why were the Germans unable to prevail?
- What role did the United States play at the outset of the war, and how did that role change?

Hitler's invasion of Poland introduced the world to a new kind of warfare. The attack was a **blitzkrieg**

(German for "lightning war"); that is, it was conducted with great speed and force. Dive-bombers screamed from the skies, dropping explosives on cities. Panzer* units—tanks and armored trucks—advanced swiftly. Poland was unprepared for this kind of mechanized warfare. After a month of resistance, Poland surrendered to Hitler.

The "Phony War"

While Germany attacked Poland, France moved its army up to the Maginot Line, the chain of fortifications guarding France's eastern frontier. British forces landed on the northern coast of France. The British navy blockaded Germany's ports. The Germans massed troops behind the Siegfried Line, the system of fortifications they had built in the Rhineland. Although German submarines had begun to sink merchant ships, there was little action on the western front. Despite the increase in mobilization and arms production, newspapers began to speak of the **"phony war"** in western Europe. Many people referred to this war as a "sitzkrieg," or sitting war, instead of a blitzkrieg. Some still hoped that an all-out war could be avoided.

As the Germans marched into Poland from the west, the Soviet army massed on the Soviet-Polish border. Then, in accordance with the secret provisions of the Nazi-Soviet Pact, the Soviets invaded eastern Poland on September 17. Once again Poland disappeared from the map of Europe. The Soviets also seized control of Estonia, Latvia, and Lithuania.

On November 30, 1939, the Soviet Union attacked Finland. The Finns appealed to the League of Nations, which did little but expel the Soviet Union for its aggression against a fellow member nation. Although the Finns fought bravely, their resistance crumbled in March 1940.

Scandinavia and the Low Countries

On April 9, 1940, the "phony war" ended with a sudden German invasion of Denmark and Norway. The Germans could sometimes rely on help from **collaborators**, people who were willing to assist their country's enemies. In Norway a critical collaborator was a Norwegian Fascist Party leader named Quisling, whose name is now used as a synonym for the word *traitor*. He gave significant aid to the occupying forces, even providing information prior to the invasion. In a single day, German troops seized several of Norway's strategic North Sea ports. Both Denmark and Norway fell to German control.

*Panzer comes from the German word for armor.

The reasons for Hitler's invasion of these countries soon became clear. By seizing them, Germany had secured an outlet to the Atlantic. Thus Hitler made certain that his country's navy would not be bottled up in the Baltic Sea as it had in World War I. The long, irregular Scandinavian coastline gave Germany excellent submarine bases. The terrain also provided many good sites for airfields. Thus shipping to France and Great Britain was put in grave danger.

The British realized that Hitler now posed an immediate threat to their safety. Neville Chamberlain, who symbolized the policy of appeasement, was forced to resign as prime minister in May 1940. He was succeeded by Winston Churchill, one of the few prominent politicians to attack appeasement and to warn against the Nazi menace in the 1930s.

Hitler, meanwhile, continued to attack. On May 10, 1940, German armored units invaded the Low Countries—the Netherlands, Belgium, and Luxembourg. Luxembourg fell in one day, the Netherlands in five. When the Dutch city of Rotterdam resisted the German army, Hitler ordered his air force to attack it. Even while a surrender was being negotiated, Nazi bombers leveled the heart of the city. At the end of May, Belgium also surrendered.

Hitler's forces were now in a position to outflank France's Maginot Line. German panzers drove westward toward the English Channel. Reaching the coast, they cut off a large number of British,

A blitzkrieg or "lightning war," such as the one Germany used against Poland, included military tactics of speed and surprise. Germany's motorized army is shown speeding into Poland.

Belgian, and French troops from the main French force to the south. Outnumbered and with no room to maneuver, the encircled Allied troops attempted to evacuate from the French seaport of Dunkirk.

Evacuation of Dunkirk. The British air force, badly outnumbered, struggled to assist the trapped forces in Dunkirk. Fortunately, the German ground forces stopped their advance. Every available ship and boat—even fishing craft and rowboats—in Britain was ordered to Dunkirk. They were subject to attacks by aircraft, submarines, and artillery as they picked up troops from the beaches. Between May 27 and June 4, about 338,000 men were safely transported across the channel to England, although all their heavy equipment was lost.

The reason why Hitler did not attack the retreating Allies is not known for certain. For three days, he held back his tanks, probably believing his air force could finish off the Allied forces. This decision would later be considered a costly mistake because it allowed Britain to rally.

Although Dunkirk represented a military defeat for the Allies, the success of the rescue operation helped raise British morale considerably. On June 4, Prime Minister Churchill addressed the British people in one of his most stirring speeches. His forceful and engaging voice boomed over the airwaves:

66We shall go on to the end, we shall fight in France, we shall fight on the seas and oceans, we shall fight with growing confidence and growing strength in the air, we shall defend our island, whatever the cost may be, we shall fight on the beaches, we shall fight on the landing grounds, we shall fight in the fields and in the streets, we shall fight in the hills; we shall never surrender, and even if, which I do not for a moment believe, this island or a large part of it were subjugated and starving, then our Empire beyond the seas, armed and guarded by the British fleet, would carry on the struggle, until, in God's good time, the New World, with all its power and might, steps forth to the rescue and the liberation of the old.99

The Fall of France

After the evacuation of Dunkirk, the French were left to fight alone on the European continent. The Maginot Line was useless. Having taken Belgium, the Germans were in a position to attack France from the north, where few fortifications existed.

Germany turned southward to attack the heart of France early in June 1940. The French fought a

desperate, losing battle. Their army, anticipating the static fighting of World War I, was neither trained nor equipped for this new kind of war. Northern France was a scene of utter confusion. Civilians, carrying whatever possessions they could, blocked roads in their attempt to flee southward. German planes bombed and machine-gunned the refugees, causing further panic and disorder.

Mussolini, taking advantage of France's weakness, declared war on France and Great Britain on June 10, and Italian forces attacked southern France. On June 14, the Germans entered Paris, and the French armed resistance in the north collapsed. Rather than surrender, the French cabinet resigned.

Some French leaders, however, were willing to surrender. The aged Marshal Philippe Pétain (PAY·tan), a hero of World War I, formed a government and assumed dictatorial powers. Late in June, Hitler forced the Pétain government to sign an armistice with Germany and Italy. Hitler insisted it be signed in the same railroad car where the Germans had signed the armistice to end World War I in November 1918.

The terms of the armistice were severe. German troops were to occupy northern France, including Paris, and a strip of territory along the Atlantic coast southward to Spain. France had to pay the costs of this occupation. The French navy was to be disarmed and confined to French ports. Pétain's government moved to the city of Vichy (VISH·ee), in the south. Thus France was divided into occupied France, administered by the Germans, and Vichy France, which collaborated with the Germans. The Vichy government also controlled most French possessions in North Africa and the Middle East.

The French Resistance. Some of the French who wanted to continue to fight against Germany escaped to Africa or to Britain. Under the leadership of General Charles de Gaulle (duh GOHL), they formed the Free French government, with its headquarters in London. As the war went on, the Free French army, equipped by the Americans and British, played a part in several campaigns.

Within France itself, an underground movement, the resistance, flourished. Its members worked secretly to oppose the occupying German forces. Similar resistance movements developed in other German-occupied countries as well. Members of some of these resistance groups were called *maquis* (mah·KEE)—a French term for scrubby undergrowth, common in the areas where resistance fighters hid.

Resistance to Nazi Occupation

Tens of thousands of ordinary people chose to act with extraordinary courage and resist Nazi domination in Europe by forming underground resistance organizations. In many countries, small bands of guerrilla fighters lived in the countryside, harassing German troops and destroying military trains and communication lines. In urban areas, resistance members published underground newspapers, passed information about the Nazis on to the Allied forces, provided safe houses for people hunted by the Nazis, and performed acts of sabotage.

No group in Europe was more at risk from Nazi tyranny than the Jews. Many European

U.S. Postal Stamp honoring Raoul Wallenberg

citizens risked their lives to protect their Jewish neighbors from being deported to the Nazi camps, where death was almost certain. Jews were hidden in secret rooms, in attics, and in barns. Many individuals also helped Jews escape Nazi-occupied Europe to other countries.

One such person was the Swedish diplomat Raoul Wallenberg, who helped save as many as 100,000 Hungarian Jews. He issued Swedish passports to Jews, which allowed them to claim protection from neutral Sweden. He hid many in houses he had bought or rented himself, and toward the end of the war, he persuaded the Nazis to spare the lives of 70,000 Jews living in a ghetto in Budapest.

To cripple the Germans, the *maquis* engaged in sabotage. They blew up bridges, wrecked trains, and cut telephone and telegraph lines.

The Battle of Britain

After France fell, French generals predicted that Britain, which they considered a weaker country, would "in three weeks . . . have her neck wrung like a chicken." (Churchill later commented: "Some chicken! Some neck!")

Hitler began scattered bombing raids on Great Britain, gradually increasing them in intensity. He then offered to negotiate a peace settlement, but Churchill rebuffed him.

At the end of June 1940, Churchill braced the British people for the dangerous battle that he was certain would soon come.

> ❝Hitler knows that he will have to break us in this island or lose the war. If we can stand up to him, all Europe may be free and the life of the world may move forward into broad, sunlit uplands. But if we fail, then the whole

world, including the United States, including all that we have known and cared for, will sink into the abyss of a new Dark Age. . . . Let us therefore brace ourselves to our duties, and so bear ourselves that, if the British Empire and its Commonwealth last for a thousand years, men will say, 'This was their finest hour.'❞

Hitler ordered his air force, the **Luftwaffe**, to soften up Britain for invasion. He shifted the *Luftwaffe* squadrons to airfields closer to Britain, in occupied France and Belgium. Germany first focused its devastating air attacks on British military targets. Later the Germans struck at railroads and civilian and industrial targets. This period of Germany's air raids on Britain is known as the **Battle of Britain**.

German bombers blasted British cities with explosives and firebombs. The *Luftwaffe* bombed London continually during September and October. In November the city of Coventry burned almost to the ground. The Germans wanted to lower morale and destroy the people's will to fight, but the undaunted British resolutely dug out of the ruins and carried on. Essential to their resistance was the more and more

The Battle of Britain, lasting 10 months, involved a series of German air attacks against Great Britain. Here a mother and daughter prepare homemade wooden shutters for protection.

successful defense by fighter planes of the Royal Air Force, or the RAF.

British planes, though fewer in number, were more maneuverable than the German planes. British pilots flew combat missions day after day, night after night. The RAF also had radar, a new electronic tracking device that helped detect the approach of enemy aircraft or ships. This prevented the Germans from making surprise attacks. Without the element of surprise, the *Luftwaffe* was not able to dominate. The RAF's control of the air prevented German invasion across the English Channel. Of the British fighter pilots, Churchill said, "Never in the field of human conflict was so much owed by so many to so few."

The Germans continued their night bombing raids for almost two years. At the same time, British bombers made increasingly heavy raids on German cities. By the middle of 1941, air warfare had leveled off, partly because Germany had begun directing some of its war resources to the east. However, because of Germany's effective blockade of British shipping from European ports, there was a chance that Great Britain could be starved into surrendering. This might have happened had it not been for the United States.

United States Involvement

In a series of **Neutrality Acts** passed between 1935 and 1937, the United States had expressed its determination to remain neutral in future wars. This legislation forbade Americans to sell war equipment to belligerent nations, prohibited loans to belligerents, prohibited Americans from sailing on ships of belligerents, and restricted the entry of American ships into war zones.

When war in Europe broke out in 1939, many people believed that Nazi Germany threatened not only Europe but civilization itself. The majority of Americans, however, believed that Europe's wars were of no concern to the United States. These **isolationists**, as they were called, had risen to power at the end of World War I and were responsible, in part, for keeping the United States out of the League of Nations. Now, however, their power began to fade as fear of a Nazi conquest of the world increased.

In 1939 a revised Neutrality Act allowed American firms to sell munitions to belligerent nations on a cash-and-carry basis. In spite of German submarine attacks, Great Britain still controlled the sea routes between the United States and Great Britain. Thus, in effect this law permitted the sale of arms only to Great Britain.

After the evacuation from Dunkirk and the fall of France, American sympathy for the British increased. President Franklin D. Roosevelt was convinced that Britain was the front line of a war that would involve the United States sooner or later. In September 1940, President Roosevelt, by executive order, transferred 50 old American naval destroyers to Great Britain. In exchange Great Britain gave the United States long-term leases on naval and air bases in Newfoundland, the West Indies, and British Guiana. In that same month, Congress passed the first national draft law ever adopted by the United States during peacetime.

Early in 1941, Churchill appealed to the United States: "Give us the tools, and we will finish the job." In March, Congress passed the **Lend-Lease Act**, authorizing the president to supply war materials to Great Britain on credit. Now the direction of America's involvement became clear.

The Atlantic Charter

To avoid the criticism that the secret treaties of World War I had raised, President Roosevelt and Prime Minister Churchill publicly announced the national policies of the two democracies. In August 1941, they met on board a British battleship off the coast of Newfoundland and drew up a statement that became known as the **Atlantic Charter**.

Among its provisions and in the spirit of Wilson's Fourteen Points, the charter stated that Britain and the United States (1) sought no territorial gain, (2) would allow no territorial changes without the consent of the people concerned, (3) respected the right of all people to choose their own form of government, (4) believed that all nations should have equal rights to trade and to raw materials, (5) wanted nations to cooperate on economic matters to ensure everyone a decent standard of living, (6) believed people everywhere should have the right to security and freedom from want and fear, (7) believed freedom of the seas should be guaranteed, and (8) believed that nations must abolish the use of force and establish a system of general security, implying the formation of an international organization.

By autumn 1941, the United States Navy was waging an undeclared war on German submarines. American warships escorted convoys in the western Atlantic, allowing the British to concentrate in the eastern Atlantic. Isolationist opinion remained strong in the United States, although the bombing of British cities had aroused American sympathy. Now the only remaining restrictions prohibited American merchant ships from being armed or entering war zones. In November 1941, Congress abolished even these restrictions. The United States now gave the British all aid short of joining in the war.

Section 3 Review

1. **Define** blitzkrieg, "phony war," collaborators, *Luftwaffe*, Battle of Britain, Neutrality Acts, isolationists, Lend-Lease Act, Atlantic Charter

2. **Identify** Winston Churchill, Philippe Pétain, Charles de Gaulle, *maquis*, Franklin D. Roosevelt

3. **Locate and Explain the Significance** Maginot Line, Siegfried Line, Rotterdam, Dunkirk, Vichy France, occupied France, Coventry

4. **Summarizing Ideas** Summarize German progress in the war through the first half of 1941.

5. **Evaluating Ideas** How was British airpower able to prevent a German invasion across the English Channel?

6. **Sequencing Ideas** Describe the progression of United States involvement in World War II from the Neutrality Acts to giving Great Britain all aid short of entering the war.

The Soviet Union and the United States

Focus Questions

- **What steps did the Axis Powers take in an effort to control eastern Europe, the Middle East, and the Soviet Union?**
- **What did Hitler hope to accomplish with his "New Order" and his "Final Solution"?**
- **How did Japan's goals in the Pacific lead to war with Britain and the United States?**

In the fall of 1940, Germany held almost all of western Europe. It controlled the Atlantic coastline from the tip of Norway to southern France. (Spain, under Franco's fascist rule, remained neutral but allowed German submarines to use its ports.) Italy and Germany also controlled much of the western Mediterranean coastline, an important advantage.

Great Britain still held Gibraltar, on the southern coast of Spain; the islands of Malta and Cyprus, in the Mediterranean; and Alexandria, in Egypt. British troops were stationed in Palestine and in Egypt, protecting the Suez Canal. In September Japan joined the Rome-Berlin Axis, allying itself with Hitler and Mussolini.

Eastern Europe and the Mediterranean

Mussolini, hoping to build a Mediterranean empire for Italy, sent his troops into Egypt and Greece in the fall of 1940. The decision proved to be unwise. The attack on Greece quickly bogged down. The British stopped the Italian army's advance into Egypt. In their counterattack, the British took Tobruk, a port city of Libya. (See map on page 717.) An Italian invasion of British Somaliland at the same time also failed, and a counterattack by the British drove the Italians out of Ethiopia as well.

When Hitler turned his attention to the Balkans, Axis fortunes in eastern Europe improved. Germany seized Romania, needed for its rich oil fields. In March 1941, pressure on Bulgaria resulted in German occupation. By November, Romania, Bulgaria, and Hungary had allied themselves with Germany.

In April 1941, Hitler invaded Yugoslavia, having failed to persuade its government to allow German

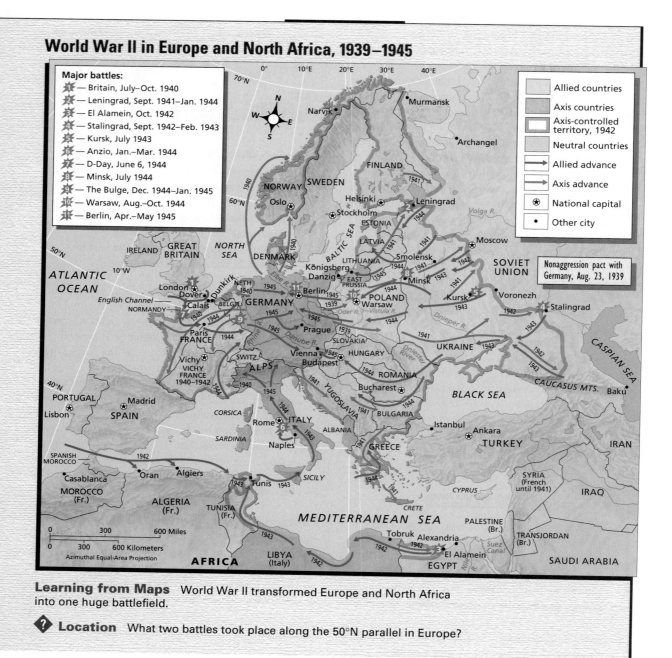

World War II in Europe and North Africa, 1939–1945

Major battles:
- ✳ — Britain, July–Oct. 1940
- ✳ — Leningrad, Sept. 1941–Jan. 1944
- ✳ — El Alamein, Oct. 1942
- ✳ — Stalingrad, Sept. 1942–Feb. 1943
- ✳ — Kursk, July 1943
- ✳ — Anzio, Jan.–Mar. 1944
- ✳ — D-Day, June 6, 1944
- ✳ — Minsk, July 1944
- ✳ — The Bulge, Dec. 1944–Jan. 1945
- ✳ — Warsaw, Aug.–Oct. 1944
- ✳ — Berlin, Apr.–May 1945

Allied countries
Axis countries
Axis-controlled territory, 1942
Neutral countries
Allied advance
Axis advance
National capital
Other city

Nonaggression pact with Germany, Aug. 23, 1939

Learning from Maps World War II transformed Europe and North Africa into one huge battlefield.

❓ **Location** What two battles took place along the 50°N parallel in Europe?

---

troops to march through to Greece. Although the Germans crushed the Yugoslav army in less than two weeks, Yugoslavs waged an effective guerrilla campaign for the rest of the war.

Next came Greece. Despite fierce resistance by the Greeks, assisted by British troops, the German forces quickly prevailed. The British withdrew to the island of Crete, which the Germans captured in May with

a parachute assault. Thus Germany controlled the Balkan Peninsula except for European Turkey. (See map on this page.) In June, Germany and Turkey signed a treaty ensuring Turkish neutrality.

The German victories in the Balkans set the stage for Hitler's more basic goal, the invasion of the Soviet Union. Axis forces were also in a position to threaten the Middle East. The rich oil fields of the region would have given Hitler a considerable advantage, and the loss of the Suez Canal would have endangered the British position in India, Southeast Asia, and the Pacific. The French mandates, Lebanon and Syria, were controlled by the Vichy government, and many citizens of Iraq and Egypt, eager to be rid of their British occupiers, leaned toward the Axis.

A pro-Axis coup d'etat in Iraq in the spring of 1941 sharpened Allied fears. British and Indian troops moved in and crushed the coup in May, while Free French forces drove the Vichy French out of Lebanon and Syria in July. Now the Allies turned their attention to North Africa, where the situation had grown worse.

German troops, commanded by General Erwin Rommel—soon to be nicknamed the Desert Fox—had moved across the Mediterranean to Libya in early 1941. These forces quickly inflicted several defeats on the British, driving them back into Egypt. Fighting raged back and forth through 1941 and 1942.

However, by the summer of 1942 the British were achieving success in the naval and air war in the Mediterranean, allowing them to build up troops and equipment in North Africa while increasingly cutting off Axis supplies. In October, Rommel's forces were soundly beaten at the Battle of El Alamein. (See map on page 726.) Now the Axis forces, unable to make up their losses, retreated to Tunisia.

Germany's Attack on the Soviet Union

The Soviet Union regarded the German victories in the Balkans with alarm and anger. It considered the Balkans, especially Romania and Bulgaria, to be within its own sphere of influence.

At a Soviet-German conference in Berlin in November 1940, the Soviets demanded that Bulgaria, Istanbul, the Dardanelles, and the Bosporus be retained in their sphere of influence. Hitler suggested instead that Germany should have Europe and that the Soviet Union should establish a sphere in Asia. The Soviets rejected this suggestion.

On June 22, 1941, the war entered a new phase. Without declaring war, German armies invaded the Soviet Union. Hitler had opened a massive new front in the east, 2,000 miles long from north to south. Churchill offered aid to the Soviet Union, and the United States also declared its willingness to help.

Sending aid to the Soviets, however, was extremely difficult. Ships could not sail the route across the Mediterranean and through the Dardanelles, the Bosporus, and the Black Sea without risking submarine and air attacks from bases in Italy and the Balkans. The route through the Baltic Sea was impossible. Convoys to two Soviet ports, Murmansk and Archangel in the Arctic, had to pass the long, German-held coast of Norway. To avoid these dangers, the Allies developed a new route from the Persian Gulf across Iran by train and truck to the southern part of the Soviet Union.

The Soviet Defense

The initial thrust of the Nazis into the Soviet Union was devastating. Everywhere the Soviet armies were driven back. Soon Moscow and Leningrad were under siege. There, however, the attack bogged down.

The Soviet defenders used the same scorched-earth tactics against Hitler that their ancestors had used against Napoleon. The retreating soldiers and civilians carried away what they could and destroyed everything else. Thus the territory the Germans gained was more a hindrance than a help. In addition, many Soviet soldiers remained hidden in swamps and forests, making daring guerrilla attacks on railroads, bridges, and trains.

Hitler had expected the Soviet Union to surrender quickly. The long sieges at Leningrad and Moscow disrupted his timetable, however. When the short Russian autumn came, Hitler faced the same decision Napoleon had had to make: Should he retreat or should he stand? Hitler chose to stand.

Soon the Germans had to face a new enemy—the bitterly cold Russian winter. The Soviets chose the winter for a counterattack, which was intended primarily to relieve pressure on Moscow. The Germans were forced to retreat.

The year 1941 ended with the Germans deep inside the Soviet Union. In the spring of 1942 Hitler ordered a new offensive to the south. The strategic objective was the oil-producing area around Baku, on the shore of the Caspian Sea. To protect the flank of that main attack, a part of the German army was to capture the city of Stalingrad on the Volga River. (See map on page 726.) German troops pushed into Stalingrad on September 12, 1942, but there Soviet resistance grew stronger. Hitler now made capture of Stalingrad the main objective of the offensive, while Stalin ordered that the city be held at all costs. The Battle of Stalingrad had begun.

"New Order" and "Final Solution"

The invasion of the Soviet Union was part of Hitler's master plan for a European **"New Order."**

Geopolitics

Early on the morning of September 1, 1939, German tanks, troop carriers, and dive-bombers poured over the Polish border. The Polish army, outnumbered perhaps two to one, fought valiantly, but it was no match for the overwhelming surprise attack. In just a few weeks, Poland was utterly defeated by Hitler's blitzkrieg. World War II had begun.

Theories of geopolitics current at the time helped inspire Hitler's aggressive policies. In the decades before World War II, Englishman Sir Halford J. Mackinder and German Karl Haushofer had attempted to develop geopolitics into a science. Both had developed theories that attempted to "prove" that world domination in the future would be based on the control of Europe, Asia, and Africa. These theories treated these three continents as a single landmass, called the World Island. The World Island held the majority of the world's population and natural resources, so control of it by any single nation would inevitably allow control of the rest of the world. The key to controlling the World Island, according to these theorists, was control of the region Mackinder named the Heartland, which included eastern Europe and the western Soviet Union. A nation that controlled this strategic area would be self-sufficient in food and natural resources, and would be in a position to conquer the rest of the World Island.

Historians are not certain to what extent Hitler was directly influenced by the writings of Mackinder and Haushofer. However, even before the Nazis came to power in Germany their political agenda included the need for *Lebensraum*, "living space" in which the German people could expand. Hitler rejected overseas colonies as the solution to this problem, and insisted that the necessary territory was to be found in eastern Europe. Of course, since this territory was already populated, this would require military invasion.

In Hitler's view, people and nations were locked in a constant struggle for existence. Therefore, the German people were perfectly justified in conquering land that was populated by Slavic peoples, who were, according to Hitler, biologically inferior. This view, in turn, fit perfectly with another of Hitler's motivations, his hatred of communism and the Soviet Union.

Nazi troops in Warsaw, Poland

Hitler's racist ideas helped convince him that the Soviets would be easily defeated by the soldiers of the German "master race."

Germany was not alone in its aggressive expansionism. Japan also had too many people and too few resources, and it was heavily dependent on imports of raw materials. Following the worldwide economic collapse in 1929, Japan developed a policy of expansionism. In 1931 Japan seized the Chinese territory of Manchuria, which had plentiful natural resources. In 1937 the Japanese attacked China, and by 1939 they controlled a large portion of eastern China. Japanese military leaders began plans for a Pacific empire that would include all of eastern Asia.

The struggle for territory by both Germany and Japan ultimately failed, but not before it brought a war in which millions of lives were lost. In the end, expansionist policies brought devastation to Germany and Japan, as well as to much of Europe and Asia.

Geopolitics are still an influence on international relations today. However, they are no longer considered as important as they were in the past. Technological advances such as improved communications and transportation have helped nations overcome geographical factors that once limited them. The ability of bombers and, above all, long-range missiles to attack from one continent to another with nuclear weapons means that no geographical barrier or strategic territory can ensure military security.

Hitler wanted to organize the European continent into a single political and economic system ruled from Berlin and dominated by the "Aryan race." According to this plan, the Soviet Union would supply Germany with food and raw materials. Any problems this would cause the Russians were not of concern to Hitler. According to Nazi ideology, all Slavs were "racially inferior."

Another aspect of Hitler's "New Order" went into effect as the Germans continued their offensives. In 1941 Hitler ordered the annihilation of the entire Jewish population of Europe. The Nazis referred to this program as the **"Final Solution"** of the "Jewish question." This unbelievably barbaric goal was possible in Hitler's Germany because of the zeal of the minority who accepted Nazi theories about Aryan superiority and because of the passivity of the majority of Germans.

Jews were transported to Germany and Poland by the hundreds of thousands. There they were held in "protective custody" in concentration camps. Among the most infamous of these camps were Dachau and Buchenwald in Germany. In Poland there were Treblinka and **Auschwitz**, which were extermination camps. Those Jews who were not shot or murdered by poison gas lived in unspeakable conditions. The combination of forced labor, brutal treatment, starvation, squalor, and disease killed thousands of other camp residents.

In his book *Never to Forget*, Milton Meltzer quotes an SS* officer sent to a Polish death camp to deliver poison gas. There he witnessed the mass extermination of Polish Jews. The following excerpt is from the officer's handwritten account.

"They all walked along the path . . . and entered the death chambers. A sturdy SS man stood in the corner and told the wretched people in a clerical tone of voice: 'Nothing at all is going to happen to you! You must take a deep breath in the chambers. That expands the lungs. This inhalation is necessary because of illness and infection. . . .'

This gave some of these poor people a glimmer of hope that lasted long enough for them to take the few steps into the chambers without resisting. The majority realized—the smell told them—what their fate was to be. So they climbed the steps and then they saw everything. . . . They hesitated, but they went into the gas chambers, pushed on by those behind them, or driven by the leather whips of the SS. . . . Many people were praying. . . .

The SS forced as many in together as was physically possible. The doors closed. . . . After 28 minutes only a few were still alive. At last, after 32 minutes everyone was dead.

Men of the work squad opened the wooden doors from the other side. . . . The dead were standing upright . . . pressed together in the chambers. . . . One could see the families even in death. They were still holding hands. . . . Two dozen dentists opened the mouths with hooks and looked for gold. . . . The . . . corpses were carried in wooden barrows just a few meters away to pits."

During the war, people in some western European countries, especially Denmark, tried to protect Jewish citizens. In eastern Europe, however, a long tradition of anti-Semitism made the Nazi program easier to carry out and its results more devastating.

By the time the Nazi government fell, its leaders and its followers had murdered an estimated 6 million European Jews. This systematic Nazi destruction of almost an entire race is referred to as the **Holocaust**. The Nazis also murdered millions of Slavs, Gypsies, homosexuals, and others who did not fit the perfect "Aryan mold."

Japanese Aggressions in the Pacific

The struggle against the Axis Powers took another important turn in December 1941, when events in the Pacific drew the United States into the war. Japanese militarism and aggression had increased throughout the 1930s. Japanese armies pushed farther and farther into China, although the Chinese continued to resist. Early in 1939, with the situation in Europe growing increasingly tense, Japan saw a chance to extend its control over Southeast Asia. Japan first captured several small islands off the coast of French Indochina. (See map on page 733.) Thus Japan severed the British sea route from Hong Kong to Singapore. Neither France nor Great Britain had a chance to prevent this move.

After both the Netherlands and France fell, Japan made further aggressive moves in East Asia. The Japanese government declared the Netherlands East Indies to be under Japanese "protective custody." The Japanese forced the Vichy government to allow French Indochina to become a Japanese protectorate.

---

*Hitler's SS (*Schutzstaffel*) was the military arm of the Nazi Party, sworn to absolute obedience. Members served as Hitler's bodyguards and later took charge of intelligence, central security, and the extermination of people in concentration camps.

In September 1940, Japan formed an alliance with Germany and Italy. The United States disapproved but did nothing. In April 1941, Japan and the Soviet Union signed a five-year nonaggression treaty. In July Japan, knowing it was taking a risk, moved farther south to occupy lands in French Indochina. The United States responded to this action in three ways: by protesting violations of the Nine-Power Pact of 1922, by providing assistance to the Chinese Nationalists, and by placing an embargo on the sale of oil and scrap iron to Japan. Japan thus became even more intent on securing oil reserves in the Netherlands East Indies. Now only the American-held Philippines and the Hawaiian Islands threatened Japanese supremacy in the Pacific. The United States, meanwhile, had already moved a large part of its Pacific Fleet to Hawaii.

Relations between the United States and Japan steadily deteriorated. An even more militaristic government came to power in Japan under Premier Hideki Tojo. Early in 1941, the Japanese government had decided that war could not be avoided. They began to plan a surprise attack on the U.S. Pacific Fleet. In spite of that plan, the Japanese government sent special "peace" mission representatives to Washington, D.C., in November.

During World War II, the warring nations used posters, cartoons, and radio announcements as propaganda to encourage civilians to take part in the war effort.

American Entry into the War

On December 7, 1941, while Tojo's representatives were still in Washington, the Japanese launched a surprise bombing raid on the American naval base at Pearl Harbor, Hawaii. They intended to strike such a severe blow that the United States would be unable to resist the Japanese in the Pacific. Several American battleships were sunk; others were badly damaged. American dead totaled more than 2,300. By luck, the three American aircraft carriers escaped the attack. These vessels were vital to U.S. efforts later.

In an excerpt from his book *At Dawn We Slept*, historian Gordon Prange relates an eyewitness account of the attack on Pearl Harbor.

❝When the attack began, . . . the explosion of
bombs, the whine of bullets, the roar of planes,
the belching guns of aroused defenders, the
acrid smell of fire and smoke—all blended into
a nerve-racking cacophony [sound] of chaos. . . .
Bombardiers still dropped their torpedoes, while
dive bombers pounced like hawks. . . . Far
above, high-level bombers rained their deadly
missiles as fighters shuttled in and out, weaving
together the fearful tapestry of destruction.❞

On December 8, 1941, Congress declared war on Japan, as did the British Parliament. Three days later, Germany and Italy declared war on the United States, and Congress replied with its own declaration of war. The United States became a full-fledged belligerent in World War II.

The Japanese quickly took advantage of American unreadiness. On the same day as the attack on Pearl Harbor, Japan captured the American island outpost of Guam and began aerial attacks on the Philippines. Soon afterward the Japanese landed on the island of Luzon. In less than three months, mainland areas of Burma, Thailand, and Malaya, including the mighty British fortress of Singapore, fell to Japan. (See map on page 733.)

The Japanese went on to conquer what became a vast island empire: most of the Netherlands East Indies (Indonesia), the Philippines, and the Gilbert Islands. Australia remained the last stronghold of resistance in the southwest Pacific. The landing of the Japanese on New Guinea and the Solomon Islands, however, threatened to cut off Australia's critical supply routes from Hawaii.

1. **Define** "New Order," "Final Solution," Auschwitz, the Holocaust
2. **Identify** Erwin Rommel, Hideki Tojo
3. **Locate and Explain the Significance** El Alamein, Murmansk, Stalingrad, Pearl Harbor, Gilbert Islands, Solomon Islands
4. **Summarizing Ideas** Describe the success of the Axis attacks on eastern Europe, the Middle East, and the Soviet Union.
5. **Interpreting Ideas** (a) What were Hitler's plans for a "New Order" in Europe? (b) How did his "Final Solution" fit into this plan?
6. **Analyzing Ideas** (a) What did the Japanese hope to gain by their attack on Pearl Harbor? (b) Did they succeed? Explain your answer.

Section 5

The End of the War

Focus Questions

- **What success did the Allies experience in North Africa, Italy, and at sea?**
- **How did the Allies achieve victory in Europe?**
- **What steps did the Allies take to end the war with Japan?**

Representatives of 26 nations met in Washington, D.C., in January 1942 to unite in the common purpose of defeating the Axis. Chief among these Allies were Great Britain, the Soviet Union, and the United States. Other nations in Europe, Asia, and the Americas contributed as well. Each nation pledged to use all its resources to defeat the Axis, not to sign any separate peace treaties, and to abide by the provisions of the Atlantic Charter.

Important Offensives

The German offensive in the summer of 1942 had pushed the Soviets back to Stalingrad. (See map on page 726.) There what may have been the most decisive battle of the war went on for six months. The Germans penetrated the city, suffering terrible losses in the process. Instead of retreating, the determined Soviets defended the city street by street and house by house.

In November 1942, the Soviets began a counterattack, encircling the German troops in Stalingrad. Although Hitler ordered his trapped forces to fight to the death, what was left of his army in the city surrendered in January 1943. The Battle of Stalingrad was a crucial point in the war. The Germans never entirely recovered from this defeat.

North Africa. The Allies also made progress in North Africa during 1942. British troops under General Bernard Montgomery were pursuing Rommel's forces westward across Libya into Tunisia. In November 1942, American and British forces under General Dwight Eisenhower of the United States landed in Morocco and Algeria. They pushed eastward into Tunisia as Montgomery's army moved westward. Rommel's army was trapped between the two Allied forces. By the middle of May 1943, the Axis forces in North Africa were forced to surrender.

As a result of Rommel's defeat, North Africa was securely under Allied control. Italy's African empire disappeared, and control of the French colonies in Africa passed to the Free French government. The Allies had maintained control of the Suez Canal and had made the Mediterranean more secure for Allied naval operations.

The Invasion of Italy

Throughout 1942 Stalin demanded that the British and Americans open a second front in Europe to relieve the German pressure on the Soviet Union. The Allies argued that an attack before they were fully prepared would be too risky. Stalin suspected the Allies hoped that Germany and the Soviet Union would destroy each other.

When the Allies secured North Africa, Stalin renewed his demands for a landing in Europe. American leaders proposed an invasion of France, the most direct route to Germany. Churchill, however, insisted on attacking what he called the **"soft underbelly of the Axis"**—through Italy and the Balkans. In July 1943, American and British armies landed on the island of Sicily. The American and British took the island in little more than a month. Then they prepared to invade the Italian mainland.

Many Italian leaders were ready to make peace with the Allies as a result of the Axis defeats in North Africa. With the Allied landing on Sicily, Mussolini was forced to resign, and Marshal Pietro Badoglio (bah·DOHL·yoh) became premier. Badoglio's first act was to dissolve the Fascist Party. His government also began secret negotiations with the Allies. When the

Allied army landed on the southwestern tip of Italy in September 1943, the Italians agreed to cease aggression against the Allies. In fact Italy declared war on Germany. German troops still present in Italy, however, continued to resist Allied troops.

The War at Sea and in the Air

Meanwhile, the Allies were winning the Battle of the Atlantic. This conflict between German and Allied ships had begun in 1939. For a time, German submarines sank an enormous number of Allied ships. In the spring of 1943, however, destroyers and other armed ships effectively escorted convoys of troop and supply ships sailing from the United States. Planes based both on land and on aircraft carriers also protected the convoys. Improved sonar technology located submarines, eliminating much of their advantage.

American and British bombing attacks against Germany and the occupied countries intensified. The Allies bombed strategic military sites as well as industrial areas. The Allies bombed nearly every German city, and many were severely damaged.

The War in the Pacific

The Japanese advance in the Pacific suffered its first setback in May 1942. In the Battle of the Coral Sea, American and Australian air and naval forces defeated a Japanese fleet steaming toward Australia. Soon afterward an American fleet met a larger Japanese fleet pushing eastward to try to capture Midway Island, northwest of Hawaii. (See map on opposite page.) The Americans defeated the Japanese in the crucial Battle of Midway in June. With these two victories, the United States Navy began to turn the tide in the war against Japan.

Early in August 1942, to protect the Australian supply line, American marines landed on the Solomon Islands, seizing the airfield on Guadalcanal. This was the first invasion of Japanese-held territory and an important morale booster for the United States. Four times in the next three months the Japanese launched savage attacks on the American forces. All were repulsed, with horrendous losses on both sides.

In 1943 the Allies took the offensive in the Pacific. Forces from Australia and New Zealand assisted those from the United States. Together they waged a long series of battles aimed at driving the Japanese out of the Solomon Islands. Then they adopted a strategy called **island hopping**. Only certain Japanese-held islands were captured; others were bypassed and left without supplies.

During 1944 the Americans cleared the Japanese from the Marshall Islands, New Guinea, and the Marianas. Saipan and Tinian, in the Marianas, became bases for bombing attacks on Japan. In October 1944, an American army under General Douglas MacArthur landed at Leyte in the central Philippines. Shortly after the landing, the Japanese fleet suffered a crushing defeat in a great air and sea fight, the Battle of Leyte Gulf. After six months, the Allies had secured the Philippine Islands; small, fierce battles continued there, however, until the end of the war.

At the same time, British forces (actually mostly troops from India, West Africa, and other British colonies), with increasing American support, were fighting the Japanese in the jungles and mountains of Burma. The main Allied goal was to open a supply line to the Nationalist Chinese, since the Japanese occupied the Chinese coast. In late 1944 and early 1945 the Allied armies pushed into Burma, although Japanese forces there continued to hold out until the end of the war.

Victory in Europe

As British and American troops slowly fought their way up the Italian Peninsula, the bulk of German forces were still locked in savage battles with the Soviet Union. It was clear that another, larger invasion of Europe was needed to create the hoped-for "second front." Plans were drawn up for **Operation Overlord**, the invasion of northwest France. It would be the largest amphibious invasion in history.

On June 6, 1944—D-Day as the military called it—the long-awaited landing began. Thousands of landing craft brought soldiers to the beaches of a narrow, heavily wooded peninsula on France's Normandy coast. (See map on page 726.) The Germans had expected a landing in France but could not predict the exact location of the assault. When they did find out, German forces rushed to meet the Allied invasion. Allied air power, however, hindered their progress. Within a month, more than 1 million Allied troops had landed.

After heavy fighting, Allied troops broke out of Normandy and into northern France. At the same time, Allied forces landed on the Mediterranean coast of France and fought their way northward. On August 25, 1944, Allied troops entered Paris. By September they faced the strongly fortified Siegfried Line along Germany's western frontier.

World War II in the Pacific, 1941–1945

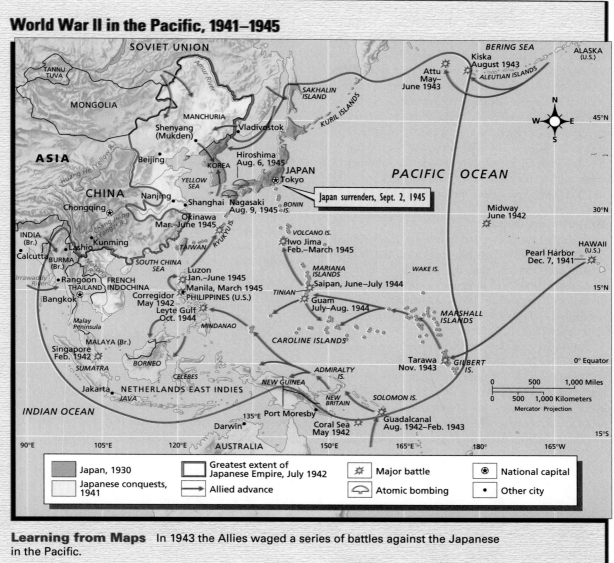

Legend:
- Japan, 1930
- Japanese conquests, 1941
- Greatest extent of Japanese Empire, July 1942
- Allied advance
- Major battle
- Atomic bombing
- National capital
- Other city

Learning from Maps In 1943 the Allies waged a series of battles against the Japanese in the Pacific.

? Place Over what two cities did the Allies drop the atomic bombs just three days apart?

The drive from the east. Several weeks after D-Day, the Soviets began a major drive against Germany from the east. By the end of 1944, the Red Army had taken Finland, Estonia, Lithuania, Latvia, Romania, and Bulgaria. The British assisted in driving the Germans out of Greece. Yugoslavia had been liberated earlier with the help of resistance fighters under Marshal Tito. By July 1944, Soviet troops were approaching the eastern outskirts of Warsaw, Poland.

The drive from the west. The Americans pierced the Siegfried Line in October after five weeks of fighting. The Allies captured port cities in France and Belgium, easing their supply problems. The Allies also cleared Alsace and Lorraine of German troops.

The Germans still had enough strength for one desperate counterattack. Just before Christmas in 1944, they drove a 50-mile wedge into Allied lines in Belgium. After a costly 10-day battle—the Battle of the Bulge—the Allies turned back the German drive.

Finally, in early spring 1945, German defenses collapsed. At the end of April, the German army in Italy surrendered unconditionally. Italian guerrillas pursued and captured Mussolini, shot him, hung his body upside down by the heels, and displayed it in Milan.

The Soviet and American armies made their first contact at Torgau, in eastern Germany, on April 25, 1945. It was agreed that the Soviets would take Berlin. On April 30, as the Soviets closed in, Hitler committed suicide. Two days later, the Soviets captured the devastated city. Within a week the German high command surrendered unconditionally. May 8, 1945 was **V-E Day**, the day of victory in Europe.

Attacks on Japan

Though the war had ended in Europe, it continued in the Pacific. Long-range bombers from the Marianas could now reach the main islands of Japan. Systematic raids on Japanese industrial cities had begun in November 1944. However, the Allies needed still closer islands to use as fighter bases and emergency landing fields.

American marines landed on the small volcanic island of Iwo Jima, about 650 miles southeast of Tokyo, and captured it after a month of the most bitter fighting of the war. (See map on page 733.) The Japanese resisted even more strongly as their home islands were approached. Okinawa, the largest of the Ryukyu Islands, was taken by the Allies after more desperate fighting.

Kamikaze planes frequently dropped from heights of 25,000 feet and achieved speeds of over 600 miles per hour by the time of impact. Ceremonial headbands were given to kamikaze pilots before takeoff.

At Okinawa 263 Allied ships were sunk or damaged by suicide attacks of Japanese pilots who crashed their planes into the ships. These were called kamikaze attacks, meaning "divine wind." The Japanese believed that pilots who pledged to die for the emperor would save the empire, just as the divine wind had saved Japan from Chinese-Mongol attack in 1281.

The kamikaze pilots were young volunteers. Their only mission was to select an appropriate target and dive onto it. An excerpt from a diary kept by a sailor includes a kamikaze pilot's last letter to his girlfriend.

"Do not weep because I am about to die. If I were to live and one of my dear ones to die, I would do all in my power to cheer those who remain behind. I would try to be brave. . . .

I pray for the happiness of you all, and I beg your forgiveness for my lack of piety.

I leave for the attack with a smile on my face. The moon will be full tonight. As I fly over the open sea off Okinawa I will choose the enemy ship that is to be my target.

I will show you that I know how to die bravely."

Despite such determined resistance, the Allies continued their intensive bombing of Japan. Japanese ports were effectively blockaded and the Japanese navy was immobilized. Nevertheless, the Japanese government refused to surrender. The Allies began to prepare for a massive invasion of the Japanese home islands.

Yalta and Potsdam

Roosevelt and Churchill had long hoped to persuade Stalin to enter the war against Japan. Before the defeat of Germany, however, the Soviet Union had been completely occupied in defending itself.

In February 1945, Roosevelt and Churchill met with Stalin at Yalta, in the Soviet Union. The Big Three, as these Allied leaders were called, agreed that, once defeated, Germany would be temporarily divided and occupied by Allied troops, including those of France. The liberated areas of Europe would be allowed to democratically elect their governments. The Soviet Union was to enter the war against Japan. As compensation it was to receive several Japanese territories.

Another conference began on July 17, 1945, at Potsdam, near Berlin. Roosevelt had died in April, and Harry Truman was now president of the United States. He scheduled a meeting with the other members of the Big Three—Churchill and Stalin. But, before the Potsdam meeting ended on August 2, Churchill had been replaced at the conference.

Building History Study Skills

READ
WRITE
INTERPRET
CONNECT
THINK

Reading About History: Understanding a Biographical Account

History is more than the factual study of events and the analysis of important issues. People, and the decisions they make, have a significant impact on history. One way to understand the role of people from a historical perspective is to study biographical accounts—secondary sources about a person's life that are based on primary sources. Biographical accounts help establish a person's place and significance in regard to a historical event.

How to Understand a Biographical Account

To understand a biographical account, follow these steps.

1. Explain the historical context of the subject of the account. For example, what events led up to the events that occurred during the person's life?
2. List the major events of the person's life.
3. Identify the person's beliefs.
4. Explain the person's responses to historical events during his or her life.
5. Identify how other people have tended to view the person.
6. Assess the historical significance of the individual. For example, what role did he or she play in the causes or the effects of certain events?

Developing the Skill

Prime Minister Winston Churchill's leadership abilities in government and his influence as the author of such books as *The Second World War* and *A History of the English-Speaking Peoples* affected not only British history but world history as well.

The following excerpt from the prime minister's speech to the House of Commons in May 1940, as well as the wartime conferences listed in the next column, illustrate Churchill's place in history. What do the excerpt and the list suggest about Churchill's ideas and actions?

"I have nothing to offer but blood, toil, tears, and sweat. . . .

You ask what is our policy? I will say: It is to wage war, by sea, land and air, with all our might and with all the strength that God can give us: to wage war against a monstrous tyranny, never surpassed in the dark, lamentable catalogue of human crime. That is our policy. You ask, What is our aim? I can answer in one word: Victory—victory at all costs, victory in spite of all terror, victory, however long and hard the road may be; for without victory, there is no survival."

The following list contains several of the wartime conferences Churchill attended during World War II.

- August 1941: Churchill and Roosevelt meet on a battleship off the coast of Newfoundland to issue the Atlantic Charter on postwar aims.
- December 1941: Churchill and Roosevelt meet in Washington, D.C., to confirm that the defeat of Germany will take precedence over the defeat of Japan.
- August 1942: Churchill confers with Stalin in Moscow and informs the Soviet leader that there can be no second front in Europe in 1942.
- August 1943: Churchill and Roosevelt meet in Quebec to confirm the Allied landings at Normandy, and they also agree to landings in southern France.
- September 1944: Churchill and Roosevelt meet in Quebec to discuss victory plans.
- October 1944: Churchill and Stalin meet in Moscow to discuss eastern Europe's future.
- July–August 1945: Churchill, Truman, and Stalin meet at Potsdam to hammer out peace treaties.

Churchill became prime minister at a moment of disaster. The German armies occupied Holland, the Belgian king surrendered, and the French army was driven back to Paris. Although the outlook for Europe appeared dim, the inspiring words of Churchill's "blood, sweat, toil, and tears" speech rallied the British people and encouraged them to persevere. His unwavering leadership at the wartime conferences contributed to the Allied victory, thus having an impact on world history.

Practicing the Skill

Locate two of Franklin Roosevelt's speeches to Americans during World War II and identify significant excerpts from each. How do these excerpts help you determine Roosevelt's significance in world history?

To apply this skill, see Applying History Study Skills on page 739.

Clement Attlee of the Labour Party had become Britain's new prime minister. The leaders planned for the control and occupation of Germany and issued an ultimatum to Japan, demanding unconditional surrender. Japan rejected the ultimatum.

However, the Americans now had a secret weapon, an atomic bomb. Scientists from many nations—including refugees from fascist-controlled countries—had worked to harness the enormous energy released by splitting atoms. They had succeeded in creating the most destructive weapon yet known. By using this weapon, the Allies would not need to invade Japan.

Japanese Surrender

When the Japanese government refused to surrender, President Truman made an important decision—to use the atomic bomb against Japan. On August 6, 1945, an American B-29 bomber dropped the deadly weapon on Hiroshima.

The impact of the bomb pulverized everything in the vicinity and generated a spontaneous fire that destroyed the city. At least 80,000 people were killed instantly, with many more injured. Subsequent deaths and illness from radiation sickness are uncounted. In Tokyo, government officials had difficulty comprehending the scale of the damage. On August 9, the Soviet Union declared war on Japan. Soviet armies swept into Manchuria, where they met little resistance. On the same day, an American plane dropped a second atomic bomb on the city of Nagasaki.

On August 14, the Japanese surrendered unconditionally, asking only that the emperor be allowed to retain his title and authority as emperor. The Allies agreed, on the condition that he accept the orders of the supreme allied commander in the Pacific, General Douglas MacArthur. On September 2, 1945 (known as **V-J Day**), representatives of both sides signed the Japanese surrender documents aboard the American battleship *Missouri* anchored in Tokyo Bay.

Costs of the War

World War II, to a much greater extent than World War I, was a war of movement and of machines. These factors helped make it the most destructive war in history. More than 22 million military personnel died, and more than 34 million were wounded. Battle losses of the Soviet Union alone have been estimated at anywhere from 7 million to 11 million lives, although an

The Big Three meet in Yalta to decide the fate of postwar Europe. Seated from left to right: Churchill, Roosevelt, and Stalin.

These Coast Guardsmen on board their ship celebrate V-J Day. Although Japan agreed to end the war on August 14, 1945, the statement of surrender was not signed until September 2, 1945, thus making that date the official V-J Day.

accurate count has never been made. Germany lost about 3.5 million military personnel. Japan's total loss—civilian and military—was nearly 2 million. Great Britain, France, and the United States each lost several hundred thousand in battle. Six million Jews and millions of other people died or were killed in German concentration camps and gas chambers. Upward of 16 million civilians were killed in Europe and Asia. Millions more were uprooted as the war moved across the countryside.

As the war progressed, weapons and tactics became more devastating. More shocking, people even in the Western democracies came to feel that killing civilians was acceptable if it weakened the enemy. By 1943 Allied air attacks on Axis civilian centers were accepted as simply part of modern warfare. The destruction of Hamburg and Dresden and the atomic bombings of Hiroshima and Nagasaki did not immediately bring any great public protest. By 1945 the bombing of cities was seen as a normal practice of war.

Section 5 Review

1. **Define** "soft underbelly of the Axis," island hopping, Operation Overlord, V-E Day, V-J Day

2. **Identify** Dwight Eisenhower, Douglas MacArthur

3. **Locate and Explain the Significance** Guadalcanal, Saipan, Tinian, Normandy, Iwo Jima, Okinawa, Hiroshima

4. **Understanding Ideas** What did the Allies gain as a result of their victories in North Africa, in Italy, and in the Atlantic?

5. **Analyzing Ideas** (a) What was the importance of D-Day? (b) How did Germany try to counterattack Allied forces in France?

6. **Evaluating Ideas** (a) What role did the atomic bomb play in the surrender of Japan? (b) Were the Allies right to use the atom bomb on Japan? Why or why not?

Chapter 27 Review

| A.D. 1920 | A.D. 1922 | A.D. 1931 | A.D. 1933 | A.D. 1935 |

1921–1922
Washington Naval Conference is held.

1931
Japanese attack Manchuria.

1936
Spanish Civil War begins.

Chapter Summary
The following list contains the key concepts you have learned about World War II.

1. In the 1930s, a series of acts of aggression by the Japanese, Italians, and Germans brought about World War II. At first the democracies were reluctant to resist these acts, preferring instead to follow a policy of appeasement.
2. The Japanese made gains in Manchuria and China. Italy captured Ethiopia, fascists took over Spain following the country's civil war, and the Germans seized Austria and Czechoslovakia. The League of Nations proved incapable of halting these advances.
3. Only when Hitler invaded Poland in September 1939 did his principal opponents, Great Britain and France, decide to stand firm. They were at a severe disadvantage because the Soviet Union had signed a nonaggression pact with Germany. Nevertheless, Great Britain and France declared war on Germany in 1939.
4. By the fall of 1940, the Axis Powers had conquered most of Scandinavia, defeated France, and forced British troops off the continent of Europe. They also had formed an alliance with Japan. During the next year, their battle successes reached a peak and then began to decline.
5. Despite isolationist opposition, the United States began to send supplies to Great Britain in 1940.

During the same year, Great Britain's air force turned back German air attacks and prevented an invasion of England.

6. In 1941, after considerable successes in the Balkans, Germany suddenly attacked the Soviet Union. In addition, the Japanese attacked the American fleet at Pearl Harbor in Hawaii. This assault brought the United States into the war.
7. Within German-occupied Europe a vicious and barbaric policy of exterminating all Jews, known as the Holocaust, was put into effect.
8. The Soviets counterattacked, and the German army was forced to engage in heavy fighting on the eastern front.
9. In 1943 the Allies invaded Sicily from North Africa. At the same time, they began an offensive to drive the Japanese out of the Pacific islands.
10. In 1944 the Allies invaded France. Finally, in 1945, they conquered Germany.
11. The dropping of atomic bombs on Hiroshima and Nagasaki forced Japan to surrender.
12. The cost of the war, in terms of suffering and death, was worse by far than that of any other war in history.
13. The end of the war brought hope that the aims proclaimed in the Atlantic Charter of 1941—including an end to wars, self-determination, and decent living conditions for all people—might at last be realized.

Reviewing Important Terms
On a separate sheet of paper, match each of the following terms with the correct definition below.

a. appeasement
b. Holocaust
c. blitzkrieg
d. isolationists
e. collaborators

_____ 1. Those who oppose involvement in the affairs of other nations
_____ 2. Systematic destruction of Jews by the Nazis
_____ 3. People who cooperate with the enemies of their country
_____ 4. Lightning war
_____ 5. Attempt to preserve peace by giving in to an aggressor's demands

Developing Critical Thinking Skills
1. **Analyzing Ideas (a)** Japanese aggression in Asia started a chain reaction that eventually led to war. Why? **(b)** At what point do you think world war became inevitable? Explain.
2. **Evaluating Ideas (a)** In certain respects, the Spanish Civil War was a preview of the global war that was to come. Why? **(b)** What role did Spain play once World War II started?
3. **Classifying Ideas (a)** What nations participated in the conference at Munich? **(b)** What did each of these nations hope to achieve? **(c)** How did the decisions that were reached at Munich affect the future of Czechoslovakia?

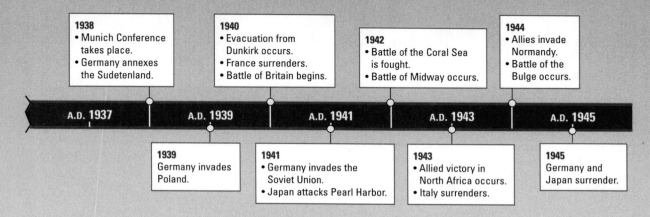

1938
• Munich Conference takes place.
• Germany annexes the Sudetenland.

1940
• Evacuation from Dunkirk occurs.
• France surrenders.
• Battle of Britain begins.

1942
• Battle of the Coral Sea is fought.
• Battle of Midway occurs.

1944
• Allies invade Normandy.
• Battle of the Bulge occurs.

A.D. **1937**   A.D. **1939**   A.D. **1941**   A.D. **1943**   A.D. **1945**

1939
Germany invades Poland.

1941
• Germany invades the Soviet Union.
• Japan attacks Pearl Harbor.

1943
• Allied victory in North Africa occurs.
• Italy surrenders.

1945
Germany and Japan surrender.

Relating Geography to History

Turn to the map on page 726. **(a)** What nations did the Axis Powers hold at the height of their power? **(b)** What nations remained neutral or nonaligned? **(c)** Based on information on this map, why might Churchill have considered Italy the "soft underbelly of the Axis"?

Relating Past to Present

1. "The next World War," declared Albert Einstein after the bombing of Japan, "will be fought with stones." **(a)** What might he have meant by this comment? **(b)** What efforts are being made today to limit the production and sale of nuclear weapons?
2. Prior to American entry into the war, President Roosevelt called the United States the "arsenal of democracy." **(a)** What did he mean by this phrase? **(b)** Does the United States still play this role in world affairs? **(c)** Why or why not? If possible, clip current newspaper or magazine articles that illustrate your answer.
3. Review the failure of the League of Nations to end Italian aggression in Ethiopia during the 1930s. Then find information on Soviet intervention in Afghanistan and Poland during the 1980s. **(a)** What actions did the United Nations take? **(b)** Were any of the problems faced by the United Nations similar to those experienced by the League? Explain.

Applying History Study Skills

Before completing this activity, review Building History Study Skills on page 735.

Read Mussolini's description of the nature of fascism. Then answer the questions that follow his description.

"The foundation of Fascism is the conception of the state—its character, its duty, and its aim. Fascism conceives of the State as an absolute, in comparison with which all individuals or groups are relative, only to be conceived of in their relation to the State. The conception of the Liberal State is not that of a directing force ... but merely a force limited to the function of recording results: on the other hand, the Fascist State is itself conscious and has itself a will and a personality. ...

The [individual] is deprived of all useless and possibly harmful freedom, but retains what is essential; the deciding power in this question cannot be in the individual, but the State alone."

1. How did Mussolini define fascism?
2. **(a)** What do you think Mussolini meant when he said the state was an absolute? **(b)** That freedom could be "useless" or "harmful"?
3. Use information in the chapter to determine whether Mussolini's ideas coincided with his actions.
4. **(a)** What is Mussolini's place in Italian history? **(b)** In world history?

---

internetconnect

Search the Internet through the HRW Web site to gather information on some of the battles of World War II that are not mentioned in the text. Research one land battle, one sea battle, and one air battle. Who was involved in each of these battles? What was the outcome of each?

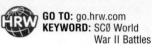

GO TO: go.hrw.com
KEYWORD: SCØ World War II Battles

Building Your Portfolio

1. **Writing a Report** Prepare a report on one of the following books about the Holocaust: Anne Frank's *The Diary of a Young Girl* (Doubleday), John Hersey's *The Wall* (Random House), Ilse Koehn's *Mischling, Second Degree* (Puffin), Arnost Lustig's *Night and Hope* (Northwestern University Press), or Elie Wiesel's *Night* (Bantam). In your report, note whether the story is fiction or nonfiction. Briefly discuss the background of the author. Then describe the way each of the central characters responds to Nazi persecution. Place your report in your portfolio.
2. **Conducting an Interview** Interview a friend or relative who remembers the World War II years. Ask this person to explain the meaning of the following words or phrases: *victory garden, ration books, blackouts, dog tags, Rosie the Riveter, war bonds, C-rations, black market.* During your interview, try to discover other World War II terms that you might add to the list. Place your notes in your portfolio.

Unit Summary

The following list contains the key concepts you have learned about world war in the twentieth century.

1. The rivalries among European nations intensified in the late 1800s and early 1900s.
2. The 1914 assassination of Archduke Ferdinand and his wife in Sarajevo sparked World War I and within a few months almost all the nations of Europe, and Japan, were at war. Italy entered the war in 1915, and the United States entered in 1917, both on the side of the Allies.
3. A dramatic upheaval took place in Russia, where in 1917 a revolution abolished the monarchy. Following the civil war in Russia, a government based on the principles of Karl Marx and communism was created.
4. Although World War I ended in 1918, the problems it caused continued to plague governments.
5. Woodrow Wilson's Fourteen Points offered idealistic goals, but as the Allies sought to collect reparations for their wartime losses and to gain additional territory, many of his goals were forgotten.
6. In 1920, 42 nations founded the League of Nations. The United States, however, did not join.
7. The new outlook and the uncertainties of the stressful period following World War I were reflected by the science, literature, music, and art of the time.
8. In the United States, a sense of optimism and the influence of European contact brought about rapid change during the decade called the Roaring Twenties.
9. The stock market crash in 1929 marked the beginning of the Great Depression. In Europe the depression caused widespread political instability.
10. In Italy and Germany dissatisfaction with the weakness and hesitations of democratic governments led to an extreme form of dictatorship called fascism.
11. In territories controlled by Great Britain, major political changes took place during the 1920s and 1930s. Political and social reforms also took place in Turkey, Persia, China, Japan, and Africa.
12. Developments in Latin America reflected the worldwide economic crisis.
13. In the 1930s the League of Nations failed to halt a series of aggressions by the imperial government of Japan and the Fascists, which brought about World War II. In 1945 the Allies conquered Germany and Japan.

Reviewing Concepts

On a separate sheet of paper, match each item at the left with its description at the right.

a. Kellogg-Briand Pact
b. Balfour Declaration
c. Nazi-Soviet Pact
d. Atlantic Charter
e. Zimmermann telegram
f. Fourteen Points
g. Yalta Conference
h. *Mein Kampf*
i. Treaty of Portsmouth
j. Versailles Treaty

1. Called for "peace of justice"
2. Stated principles underlying Nazi movement
3. Settled Russo-Japanese War
4. Levied heavy reparations on Germany
5. Outlawed war
6. Announced war aims of the democracies
7. Pledged Soviet Union's neutrality
8. Temporarily divided Germany
9. Favored creation of Jewish "national home"
10. Invited Mexico to join the Central Powers

Applying Critical Thinking Skills

1. **Summarizing Ideas** (a) How did World War I help bring about a boom period in the United States? (b) What conditions brought this boom period to an end?

2. **Classifying Ideas** Choose two of the following areas and discuss how they reflected the uncertainties of the period following World War I: (a) literature, (b) music, (c) painting, (d) architecture, (e) film.

3. **Contrasting Ideas** How did Sun Yixian, Chiang Kaishek, and Mao Zedong differ in their plans for China's future? Include the following topics in your answer: (a) the role of the people; (b) foreign interference in China; (c) economic reforms; (d) constitutional government; and (e) the need for modernization.

4. **Evaluating Ideas** (a) What were the foreign policy objectives of Italy, Germany, and Japan in the 1930s? (b) How did these nations achieve their objectives?

5. **Determining Cause and Effect** (a) Compare the causes of World War I with the causes of World War II. (b) Why might the Versailles Treaty be considered a cause of World War II?

6. **Comparing Ideas** (a) Compare the principles expressed in the Atlantic Charter with those presented in the Fourteen Points. (b) How did each of these documents seek to establish "peace of justice"?

7. **Analyzing Ideas** (a) How did the United States assist the Allies before December 1941? (b) Why did the United States move away from its neutral status?

8. **Determining Cause and Effect** (a) How did the bombings of Hiroshima and Nagasaki change the nature of warfare? (b) What other technological developments grew out of World War II?

Relating Geography to History

Refer to maps in Chapter 24 and Chapter 27. How did the map of Europe change after the Treaty of Versailles? How did it change during World War II?

Writing About History

President Truman once declared, "Men make history and not the other way around." Use three of the following leaders as examples to explain Truman's statement: (a) Woodrow Wilson, (b) Sun Yixian, (c) Mustafa Kemal, (d) Mohandas Gandhi, (e) Winston Churchill.

Further Reading

Achebe, Chinua. *Things Fall Apart*. Knopf, 1995. Discusses the effects of Western customs and values on traditional Nigerian culture, set in an Ibo village during the height of European imperialism.

Horne, Alistair. *The Price of Glory: Verdun 1916*. Viking Penguin, 1994. A vivid narrative account of the battle of Verdun.

Remarque, Erich Maria. *All Quiet on the Western Front*. Fawcett, 1987. A reprinting of the famous 1929 novel describing World War I through the eyes of a group of German soldiers.

Richter, Hans P. *I Was There*. Puffin Books, 1987. Gives an eyewitness account of a boy who participated in the Hitler Youth.

Salisbury, Harrison E. *The New Emperors: China in the Era of Mao and Deng*. Avon, 1993. An account of Chinese leadership from the time of Mao forward.

Steinbeck, John. *The Grapes of Wrath*. Viking Penguin, 1992. A reprinting of the classic 1939 novel, recounting the struggle of Dust Bowl families during the Great Depression.

UNIT 6 CHRONOLOGY

Date	Politics	Science and Technology	Society and Culture
1880–1910	Zionism 26* Triple Alliance and Triple Entente 24 Boxer Rebellion 26 Russo-Japanese War 26	Louis Sullivan 25 Einstein 25	Freudian psychology 25 Picasso and cubism 25 Motion pictures 25
1910–1920	Chinese Republic 26 Assassination of Archduke Ferdinand 24 World War I 24 *Lusitania* sunk 24 Russian Revolution 24 Treaties of Brest-Litovsk and Versailles 24 Weimar Republic 25	U-boats 24 Machine guns 24 Military airplanes 24 Tanks 24	Proust 25 Stravinsky, Schoenberg, Berg, Webern 25 Spengler's *The Decline of the West* 25
1920–1930	Mohandas Gandhi 26 Lenin's NEP 25 Chiang Kaishek 26 Mussolini 25 Stalin 25 Atatürk 26 Fascism 25	Frank Lloyd Wright 25 Automobile, telephone, radio 25	Jazz 25 Joyce's *Ulysses* 25 T. S. Eliot 25 Mann 25 Kafka and surrealism 25 Hemingway's *A Farewell to Arms* 25
1930–1939	Great Depression 25 Rise of Hitler 25 Azikiwe, Kenyatta, Senghor 26 FDR's New Deal 25 Soviet purges 25 Long March 26	TVA 25	big band era 25 Steinbeck's *The Grapes of Wrath* 25 Dali 25
1939–1945	Germany invades Poland 27 Pearl Harbor 27 Yalta and Potsdam 27	Hiroshima and Nagasaki 27 Blitzkrieg 27 Panzer units 27 Radar 27	Atomic bomb 27 Meltzer's *Never to Forget* 27

*Indicates chapter in which development is discussed

World War in the Twentieth Century

CHAPTER 24

World War I and the Russian Revolution

In the summer of 1914, a war began that resembled no previous conflict. Industrial technology had produced weapons far more destructive than any used in previous wars. This horrifying war dragged on for more than four years, taking a devastating toll in lives and property.

Setting the Stage for War

In the last half of the 1800s cooperation among nations broke down and rivalries increased. As these rivalries intensified in the early 1900s, the major powers plunged toward war, pressed forward by at least four factors: nationalism, imperialism, militarism, and the system of alliances. By 1907 rival alliances, divided into two armed camps, threatened world peace.

A Letter from the German Trenches, plate 30 from The Great War: A Neutral's Indictment

The incident that provoked Europe to go to war occurred in the Balkans on June 28, 1914, when Archduke Francis Ferdinand and his wife were assassinated. The assassin belonged to a secret society of Serbian nationalists who strongly opposed Austro-Hungarian rule.

The murders brought to a head the bitterness between Serbia and Austria-Hungary. When Serbia did not accept all of the terms of an ultimatum issued by Austria-Hungary, its leaders declared war on Serbia. Then on August 1, 1914, Germany declared war on Russia. Convinced that France was prepared to side with Russia and hoping to gain a military advantage by swift action, Germany declared war on France. When German troops passed through neutral Belgium on their way to France, Great Britain declared war on Germany. Other European and Asian nations soon entered the war.

A New Kind of War

Germany, Austria-Hungary, Bulgaria, and the Ottoman Empire became known as the Central Powers. Great Britain, France, Russia, and their partners in the war joined together as the Allied Powers, or the Allies. Eventually 32 countries made up the Allied forces. Many of them, however, joined late in the war and made only token contributions to the war effort.

Previously in Europe, most wars were fought by professional soldiers whose only source of income was their military pay and rations. In contrast, armies of drafted civilians fought the battles of World War I. Those people who could not fight worked at home to help the war effort. Many women participated by working in factories.

Both sides dug trenches on the western front, which stretched from Switzerland to the North Sea. On the eastern front, the Germans forced the Russians eastward into Poland. By 1916 the war in the west had become a stalemate on land as well as at sea.

As the most highly industrialized neutral nation, the United States became a supplier of food, raw materials, and munitions to both sides. When the Germans began attacking any ship, enemy or neutral, the United States joined the war on the side of the Allies.

The Russian Revolution

The spring of 1917 found the Russian people weary of hardships and disheartened by the appalling casualties that they had been suffering in the war. They had lost faith in the government and Czar Nicholas II. Strikes and street demonstrations broke out in Petrograd, as St. Petersburg had been called since 1914. In March 1917, unable to control either his subjects or his army, Nicholas abdicated. He and his family were arrested, and they were murdered the following year.

A liberal provisional government was set up to rule Russia until a constitutional assembly could be elected to establish a new permanent system of government. While the provisional government tried to restore order, another group worked for more radical change in Russia. By November the Bolsheviks, or Communists, under the leadership of V. I. Lenin, had seized control of the Russian government.

At Lenin's direction, a peace treaty was signed with the Central Powers in March 1918. The new regime then turned its attention to internal problems. Civil war lasted almost three years, with the Communists ultimately gaining control of Russia.

The Terms of Peace

In January 1918, about 10 months before World War I ended, President Wilson of the United States announced his ideas for a just world after the war. His plan became known as the Fourteen Points. After the armistice in November 1918, the Allies faced the task of arranging peace terms. The Paris Peace Conference, or Versailles Conference, considered territorial claims and payments for damage. While the Allies believed that the settlement should be fair and lasting, the war had left a feeling of bitterness and hatred among many of the victors. They thought that the Central Powers, especially Germany, had been responsible for the war.

Creating a "New Europe"

In a series of peace treaties with each of the five Central Powers, the Allies redrew the boundaries of Europe. The Versailles Treaty forced Germany to pay reparations, surrender territory, and limit the number of men in its army. In addition, the Allies made provisions to form the League of Nations. According to its Covenant, the League had two aims: (1) to promote international cooperation and (2) to maintain peace by settling disputes among nations by reducing armaments. Although the League of Nations had

been a favorite idea of Wilson's, the United States itself never became a member of the organization.

CHAPTER 25

The Great Depression and the Rise of Totalitarianism

For a time immediately following World War I, it appeared that the world had indeed been made "safe for democracy." However, the war changed how people viewed the world. Many nations struggled to survive politically and economically.

The Postwar Era

Following World War I, many people rejected the belief in continual human progress first expressed during the Enlightenment. Instead, scientists, writers, and artists expressed a sense of alienation and cynicism.

Many of these intellectuals, however, appealed to a small audience. Most people found escape from the disillusionment of troubled times in new forms of entertainment such as popular music and motion pictures. Architecture also underwent great change during the postwar years. New technical advances, such as the use of structural steel, made skyscrapers and bold new architectural designs possible.

Postwar Prosperity in Ruins

The United States emerged from the war as an apparent successor to Great Britain in world leadership. However, the refusal of the United States to join the League of Nations indicated that the United States did not want this responsibility. Americans preferred to enjoy their newfound prosperity during the Roaring Twenties and avoid further entanglement in European affairs.

This prosperity, however, was short-lived. The collapse of the New York Stock Exchange plunged the United States and the rest of the industrial world into a severe economic recession, known simply as the Great Depression.

In response to the hardships of the Great Depression, voters in the United States elected Franklin D. Roosevelt president. Roosevelt embarked on a program of relief and reform, called the New

Deal, to combat the depression. However, only when the United States mobilized for war once again in the late 1930s, did the economy improve.

Political Tensions After World War I

The events of the postwar years strained the older and more experienced European democracies of France and Great Britain. The economies of these nations had been harmed by the war, and recovery was made difficult by debt and lack of good markets.

France emerged from World War I victorious but unstable. The country still owed money that it had borrowed from French citizens and the United States during and after the war. Its industry was faltering, production was declining, and inflation was soaring. Although a socialist government took power in 1936, bitter divisions still existed.

Like France, Great Britain faced grave economic difficulties after World War I. By 1921 nearly one fourth of Great Britain's work force was unemployed and workers from many industries began striking. The British and Irish governments also struggled over control of Ireland.

As western European powers attempted to recover from World War I, the nations of eastern Europe struggled to form governments and identities. While Finland, Czechoslovakia, and the Baltic countries managed to sustain democratic regimes, other countries, such as Austria, Hungary, and Poland, were less successful.

Fascist Dictatorships in Italy and Germany

The war and its aftermath also took their toll in Italy and Germany. Heavy loss of life, the burden of debt, high unemployment, and runaway inflation plagued these countries. In Italy the problems led to the rise of Benito Mussolini, whose Fascist Party set up a military dictatorship. In Germany Adolf Hitler became dictator and leader of the Nazi Party. The new leaders of both countries established totalitarian regimes.

Dictatorship in The Soviet Union

Similar developments occurred in the Soviet Union. Although Lenin had allowed free enterprise to exist under his New Economic Policy (NEP), his successor Joseph Stalin announced the end of the NEP and the return to a controlled command economy. Through a series of Five-Year Plans, the Soviets tried to create an industrialized nation. These plans, however, con-

Hitler rally, 1935, Nuremberg

centrated on the expansion of heavy industry and defense at the expense of producing consumer goods, creating shortages of basic necessities. Like the Fascists in Italy and the Nazis in Germany, Stalin created a totalitarian regime that deprived the people of human rights.

CHAPTER 26

New Political Forces in Africa, Asia, and Latin America

The postwar years also witnessed profound changes outside Europe. When India set out on a path toward independence, other countries followed suit; Turkey, Persia, and Africa began political transformations. Likewise, the civilizations of China, Japan, and South America faced political, social, and economic change.

The British Empire

Although the British Empire had grown larger as a result of the Paris Peace Conference, its continued existence was nonetheless threatened. People in all parts of the empire voiced demands for more freedom, for self-government, and even for complete independence.

In the Middle East, the British recognized the independence of Transjordan and Iraq. Only Palestine remained under British control. While the British and Egyptian governments agreed that Egypt would be granted independence, Great Britain would control the Suez Canal for 20 years.

As Great Britain's largest colony, India commanded more British attention than did the Middle Eastern mandates. Some Western-educated Indians favored continued rule by Great Britain. In contrast, Indian nationalists wanted complete independence. Mohandas K. Gandhi became a great advocate of Indian nationalism. In 1935, after years of reports and conferences, Great Britain granted India a new constitution with provisions for elected representation. However, the British still controlled India's national defense, revenue, and foreign policy and could veto legislation. Committed to total self-government, the nationalists opposed the new constitution, but they agreed to work within it to gain power after the elections.

Even in those other parts of the British Empire where a degree of self-government already existed, people sought greater independence. In Canada, Australia, New Zealand, and the Union of South Africa, Great Britain still appointed a governor-general who could veto laws. After World War I, these dominions sought complete self-government. Showing remarkable willingness to accommodate and adjust to political reality, Great Britain readily agreed to their demands.

Turkey, Persia, and Africa

The nationalist ideas that swept the Middle East after World War I also affected Turkey, Persia, and Africa. In Turkey, an able and energetic leader, Mustafa Kemal, emerged as president and worked to modernize the nation.

In Persia, Reza Khan, an army officer with strong nationalist sentiments, seized control of the government in a coup d'état. Some four years later, he deposed the ruling shah, took the title Reza Shah Pahlavi and assumed the throne. Like Kemal, Reza Shah wanted to modernize his country and free it from foreign domination.

The years after World War I also saw an increase in political activity among Africans. Many leaders such as Nnamdi Azikiwe (AH·ZEEK·WAH) of Nigeria,

Jomo Kenyatta of Kenya, and Leopold Senghor of Senegal worked for independence in their countries.

China

In the 1800s the Western powers carved out spheres of influence in China. When the Chinese attempted to oust foreigners during the Boxer Rebellion, the imperialist nations crushed the revolt and imposed heavy penalties on the Chinese. Although the rebellion failed to drive foreigners from Chinese soil, it fostered nationalistic sentiment among the Chinese people.

In 1911 a series of revolts, led mostly by army officers who supported Sun Yixian, spread throughout southern China. Although the leader of the imperial army hoped to negotiate with these rebels, no agreement was reached and the Qing dynasty ended. In 1912 the emperor abdicated and a republic was proclaimed.

However, China's problems were far from over; the ruling political party, the Guomindang, soon split into rival factions. On one side were the Nationalists, led by Chiang Kaishek (chang ky·SHEK). Opposing the Nationalists were the Communists, led by Mao Zedong (MAOOH ZUH·DUHNG).

Japan

By the early 1900s, Japan had advanced from a feudal agrarian society to a leading industrial and military power. Although the Japanese economy grew rapidly, it could not provide food for everyone. As a result, many Japanese people began emigrating to Korea, Taiwan, Hawaii, and other islands of the Pacific Ocean. Thousands more left for the United States.

Japan also had to import raw materials, since it lacked much of those needed in modern industry. To pay for these raw materials, it had to sell goods abroad. Many countries, however, placed tariffs on Japanese goods. For the island nation, a modernizing economy had to expand or collapse. Many Japanese, dissatisfied with the economy, began to accept the arguments of military leaders that Japan needed to become an imperialist power in order to survive.

Latin America

The 1920s brought a period of prosperity to Latin America. Industrialization contributed to the growth of cities and the expansion of the middle class. Many Latin American countries became leading exporters of agricultural products and mining resources.

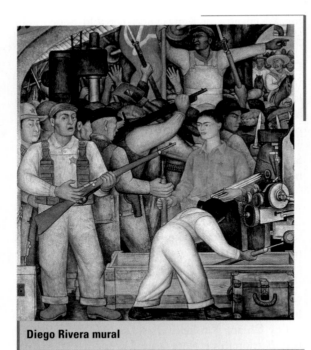

Diego Rivera mural

other group consisted of dissatisfied nations. With each passing year, relations between the two groups grew more strained.

Threats to World Peace

Although many international conferences in the 1920s worked to maintain peace, several local conflicts erupted. The Japanese military, having gained control of the government, invaded Manchuria. Japan soon occupied about one fourth of China. In Africa, Mussolini and his Italian forces waged a campaign to conquer and colonize Ethiopia. In Spain, a bitter civil war resulted in the establishment of a fascist government under the leadership of Francisco Franco.

Hitler's Aggressions

Germany also embarked on a program of conquest in the 1930s. In March 1936 German troops marched into the Rhineland, violating the Treaty of Versailles. Then in October 1936, following the outbreak of the Spanish Civil War, Mussolini and Hitler formed a military alliance called the Rome-Berlin Axis and began referring to themselves as the Axis Powers. Shortly afterward, Japan and Germany pledged to work together to prevent the spread of communism in Russia.

In March 1938 Hitler's troops marched unopposed into Austria and the Sudetenland in Czechoslovakia. In 1939 Germany occupied all of Czechoslovakia, the last democracy in Central Europe. The Axis Powers wanted still more territory, and in the spring of 1939, Hitler took Lithuania, and Mussolini conquered Albania.

Faced with this aggression, Great Britain and France prepared for war. Although the two countries tried to forge a mutual alliance with Joseph Stalin of the Soviet Union, their negotiations failed. Instead, the Western democracies received a tremendous shock when Hitler announced a German-Soviet nonaggression pact. Publicly this pact pledged that Germany and the Soviet Union would never attack each other; each would remain neutral if the other became involved in war. Secretly, however, the two dictators agreed to divide eastern Europe into spheres of influence. Germany was to take western Poland and the Soviet Union was to have eastern Poland and the Baltic countries.

The crisis that finally began World War II was Hitler's attack on Poland. Great Britain and France stood by Poland and declared war on Germany.

However, the Great Depression caused the prices of these exports to fall. Because they received such a small return on their exports, many Latin American nations found it impossible to import any but the most essential goods. Economic crisis soon led to political crisis. Coups d'état overthrew many Latin American governments in the 1930s. In some cases, these coups toppled constitutional systems that had existed for 30 to 40 years.

President Roosevelt fostered a program called the Good Neighbor Policy. This policy stressed mutual cooperation among the American nations and restricted interference by the United States in Latin American affairs.

CHAPTER 27

World War II

During the 1930s most European nations once more claimed loyalty to one of two opposing camps. One group included those nations that were generally satisfied with the World War I peace settlement. The

Axis Gains

Hitler's attack was conducted with great speed and force; Poland was unprepared and after a brief but devastating war, it surrendered to Germany. Next, Hitler invaded Scandinavia, the Netherlands, Belgium, and Luxembourg. By June 1940, the Axis Powers had launched attacks in both northern and southern France. Hitler tried to conquer Great Britain as well, but the British held their own. Although the United States remained officially neutral, it gave assistance to Great Britain in the form of war supplies.

The Soviet Union and the United States

By late 1940 it appeared that the Axis Powers were winning the war. They controlled the Atlantic coastline from the tip of Norway to southern France and also much of the Mediterranean coastline. Hitler also sent forces into the Middle East and North Africa.

On June 22, 1941, the war entered a new phase. Without declaring war, German armies invaded the Soviet Union. British Prime Minister Winston Churchill offered aid to the Soviet Union, and the United States also declared its willingness to help. This assistance helped the Soviets stall the Nazi offensive.

The invasion of the Soviet Union was part of Hitler's master plan for the creation of a "New Order" in Europe. Hitler wanted to organize the entire continent into a single political and economic system ruled by the "Aryan race." To reach this goal, the Nazis mercilessly murdered millions of Jews, Gypsies, Slavs, homosexuals, and other groups whom they considered inferior.

The struggle against the Axis Powers received a major boost in December 1941 when conflict in the Pacific Ocean drew the United States into the war. Japan, having formed an alliance with Germany and Italy, launched a surprise attack on the American naval base at Pearl Harbor, Hawaii. As a result, the United States declared war on the Axis Powers.

The End of the War

Throughout 1942 and 1943 the Axis Powers experienced defeats in Europe and the Pacific. The war reached its final phase with the Allied invasion of France on June 6, 1944.

Before the end of the war, Allied leaders Franklin Roosevelt of the United States, Winston Churchill of Great Britain, and Joseph Stalin of the Soviet Union met at Yalta in February 1945. The Big Three, as these Allied leaders were called, agreed that Germany should be temporarily divided and occupied by Allied troops, including those of France. Germany surrendered on May 8, 1945.

Another conference began on July 17, 1945, at Potsdam, near Berlin. At this conference the leaders planned for the control and occupation of Germany and issued an ultimatum to Japan demanding unconditional surrender. Japan surrendered in August after the United States dropped atomic bombs on Hiroshima and Nagasaki.

U.S. troops land on Normandy Beach, June 10, 1944

Synthesis Review

1. **Comparing Ideas** How did World War I differ from earlier wars?
2. **Interpreting Ideas** Why did the Great Depression lead to political instability in Europe?
3. **Evaluating Ideas** What factors led many countries in Asia, the Middle East, and Africa to seek independence?
4. **Analyzing Ideas** What event precipitated Japan's surrender?
5. **Synthesizing Ideas** How did disillusionment with the World War I peace settlements lead to World War II?

POLITICS AND GOVERNMENT

1945   1953   1961

1945
United Nations is established

1947
India gains independence

1948
Soviet blockade of Berlin and U.S. airlift occur

1949
Communists win control of China

1950
Outbreak of Korean War

1959
Castro overthrows Batista in Cuba

1961
Building of Berlin Wall

Berlin Wall

Fighting the Korean War along the 38th parallel

SOCIETY AND CULTURE

1945   1953   1961

1946
Nuremberg trials end

1948
Marshall Plan goes into effect

1953
The term *rock 'n' roll* gains wide usage in U.S.

1950
Mother Teresa founds religious order in Calcutta

1954
U.S. Supreme Court bans school segregation

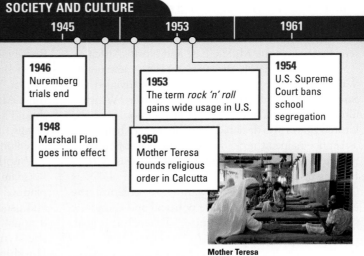

Mother Teresa

SCIENCE AND TECHNOLOGY

1945   1953   1961

1946
ENIAC computer built in U.S.

1949
USSR detonates its first atomic bomb

1957
USSR launches *Sputnik* satellite

1961
Soviets put first human in space

ENIAC computer

1954
Salk polio vaccine released

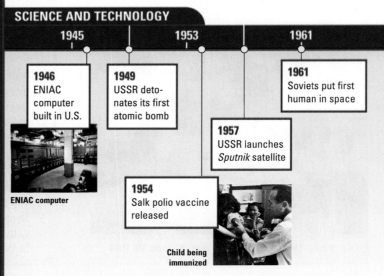

Child being immunized

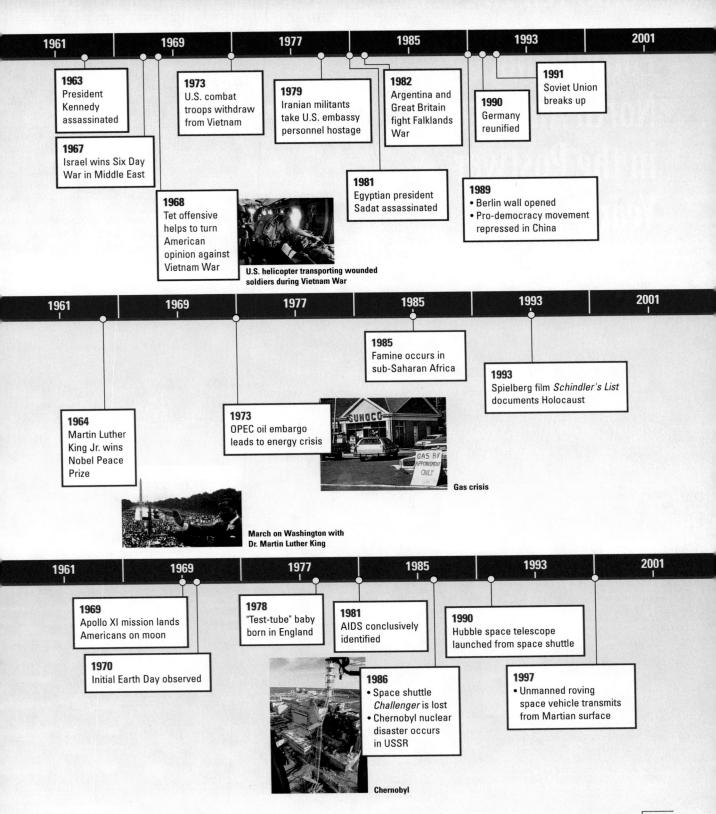

1961   1969   1977   1985   1993   2001

1963
President Kennedy assassinated

1967
Israel wins Six Day War in Middle East

1968
Tet offensive helps to turn American opinion against Vietnam War

1973
U.S. combat troops withdraw from Vietnam

1979
Iranian militants take U.S. embassy personnel hostage

1982
Argentina and Great Britain fight Falklands War

1981
Egyptian president Sadat assassinated

1989
• Berlin wall opened
• Pro-democracy movement repressed in China

1990
Germany reunified

1991
Soviet Union breaks up

U.S. helicopter transporting wounded soldiers during Vietnam War

1961   1969   1977   1985   1993   2001

1985
Famine occurs in sub-Saharan Africa

1993
Spielberg film *Schindler's List* documents Holocaust

1964
Martin Luther King Jr. wins Nobel Peace Prize

1973
OPEC oil embargo leads to energy crisis

Gas crisis

March on Washington with Dr. Martin Luther King

1961   1969   1977   1985   1993   2001

1969
Apollo XI mission lands Americans on moon

1970
Initial Earth Day observed

1978
"Test-tube" baby born in England

1981
AIDS conclusively identified

1990
Hubble space telescope launched from space shuttle

1986
• Space shuttle *Challenger* is lost
• Chernobyl nuclear disaster occurs in USSR

1997
• Unmanned roving space vehicle transmits from Martian surface

Chernobyl

Europe and North America in the Postwar Years

PLACE

Europe, the United States, and Canada

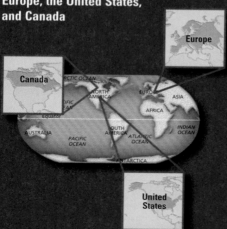

Europe

Canada

United States

United Nations General Assembly in session

Significance

During World War II, Allied leaders met several times to discuss what the future of Europe would be after the war. Once the war ended, however, prewar differences that had divided the Western European democracies from the communism of the Soviet Union re-emerged. The Soviet Union moved to ensure its future security by establishing communist-controlled governments in the countries occupied by its troops. Alarmed by such apparent Soviet expansionism, the Western democratic nations and many other noncommunist countries rallied behind U.S. leadership to contain the threat of communist expansion.

Suspicion and hostility between the communist and Western nations led to the **Cold War**, a conflict waged primarily by economic and political means, as each side sought to extend its influence among the other nations of the world.

Terms to Define

Cold War	welfare state
Nuremberg trials	Great Society
denazification	recessions
veto power	civil rights
containment	NAACP
Cominform	DEW Line
market economy	St. Lawrence Seaway
command economy	

People to Identify

Big Three	Charles de Gaulle
Allied Control Council	Nikita Khrushchev
Council of Foreign Ministers	Alexander Dubcek
	Joseph McCarthy
Security Council	Martin Luther King Jr.
General Assembly	Fidel Castro
Konrad Adenauer	

Places to Locate

Yalta	East Prussia
Oder-Neisse line	

Chapter Theme Questions

- **War and Diplomacy** How might strategic decisions made during a war affect the conduct of diplomacy during peace?
- **Cross-Cultural Interaction** What kinds of groups might nations form in order to solve their common problems?
- **Economic Organization** How might economic organizations affect a country's ability to recover from the devastation of war?

In 1946 Sir Winston Churchill, the former prime minister of Great Britain, visited Westminster College in Fulton, Missouri. His address to an audience of students, faculty, and their distinguished guest, President Harry Truman, became one of the most memorable speeches of his career. The recent takeovers by Soviet-backed communist regimes in Eastern Europe had deeply disturbed the Western nations. The following excerpt from Churchill's speech describes the sense of uncertainty that darkened postwar Europe—and the world.

> **" A shadow has fallen upon the scenes so lately lighted by the Allied victory. . . . From Stettin in the Baltic to Trieste in the Adriatic, an iron curtain has descended across the Continent. Behind that line lie all the capitals of the ancient states of central and eastern Europe. . . . All these famous cities and the populations around them lie in what I must call the Soviet sphere, and all are subject in one form or another, not only to Soviet influence, but to a very high and, in many cases, increasing measure of control from Moscow. . . . I have felt bound to portray the shadow which, alike in the west and in the east, falls upon the world. "**

This standoff between East and West colored world events during the postwar era.

Section 1

Aftermath of the War in Europe

Focus Questions

- **What were the basic provisions of the postwar settlement in Europe?**
- **How did the Allies respond to the Nazi atrocities that became public knowledge after the war?**
- **How and why was the United Nations organization established?**

Victory over the Axis powers brought on a whole new set of problems for Allied leaders. To a certain extent these problems were the result of strategic decisions made during the war. In November and December 1943, for example, the three main leaders of the Allied powers—Roosevelt, Churchill, and Stalin—met at Tehran, the capital of Iran. They decided to defeat Germany by forcing a war on two fronts: Western Allied forces, led by the United States and Britain, would launch an invasion of the European continent across the English Channel and attack Germany from the west, while Soviet forces would attack Germany from the east. This decision was fateful, for it meant that the Western forces would meet their Soviet allies somewhere in the middle of Germany, with Soviet troops occupying most of Eastern Europe.

In February 1945, Roosevelt, Churchill, and Stalin met again in the Black Sea resort town of Yalta. The three leaders reached agreements in several areas. With victory now clearly in sight, they agreed to divide both Germany and Austria into zones of military occupation based on the territories their respective armed forces were liberating from the Nazis. Berlin, which would lie wholly within the Soviet zone, was also to be divided into four parts, with the Soviets in charge of East Berlin and the Western Allies establishing their own zones in West Berlin. Vienna was to be similarly divided. The division of Germany was supposed to be only a temporary measure, however, until a final settlement could be arranged at a general peace conference.

The Allies also seemed to reach an agreement on Poland and the territories the Soviets had already taken in Eastern Europe. Roosevelt and Churchill believed that these countries should be allowed to determine their own futures. Consequently, they obtained promises from Stalin that he would allow free elections and the establishment of democratic governments in accordance with the terms of the Atlantic Charter. In return they agreed with Stalin that the governments in these eastern countries must be friendly to the Soviet Union. Each side left the conference with the impression that its own viewpoint had won the day. For Stalin, however, friendly governments meant governments under Soviet control. Moreover, he believed that free elections and democracy could really only occur after the peoples of Eastern Europe had been properly educated in socialist principles. In short, from a Western perspective, his promise of free elections would eventually prove meaningless.

The three leaders also considered the larger question of how to prevent another war from occurring.

There was considerable disagreement. Both Churchill and Stalin believed that the best way to insure peace was for the victorious Allies to divide the world into spheres of influence. President Roosevelt, however, advocated the internationalist approach that had been the basis of the League of Nations after World War I. He proposed a new United Nations Organization that would succeed (where the old League of Nations had failed) in keeping the peace through collective security arrangements. The initial plans for such an organization had already been worked out in a conference attended by representatives of the United States, Britain, the Soviet Union, and China in the summer of 1944 at Dumbarton Oaks, near Washington, D.C. At Yalta the three leaders discussed the proposed charter and agreed on voting procedures to be followed in the United Nations.

The Occupation of Germany

After Germany's surrender in May 1945, the Allies completed the occupation of their respective zones and established temporary military governments. (See map on opposite page.) In July the Big Three met at Potsdam, outside Berlin, to establish the groundwork for a postwar settlement. The Soviet Union was represented by Stalin and the United States by Truman (who had become president of the United States upon Roosevelt's death in April). Churchill, and later Clement Attlee (who had replaced Churchill as British prime minister), represented Great Britain. The three powers agreed on several basic principles. Germany must be demilitarized; the Nazi Party must be disbanded and outlawed; German political life should be reconstructed on a democratic basis; and those responsible for the atrocities of the war should be brought to trial. The Allied leaders also agreed that Germany should remain a single state though decentralized and under the rule of occupation governments for the moment.

To oversee the various occupation governments, the Allies had established the Allied Control Council. They also agreed at Potsdam that a Council of Foreign Ministers, representing the Soviet Union, Great Britain, the United States, France, and China, should write the peace treaties. As the two councils began their work, however, it soon became clear that the Western democracies and the Soviet Union had very different plans for a postwar settlement. The major disagreements occurred over two questions: reparations and the boundaries of postwar Germany.

Territorial adjustments. Stalin insisted that the Soviet Union would retain the Polish territories and territories on the Baltic Sea gained as a result of the Nazi-Soviet Pact. Poland, he suggested, should be compensated for this loss of its eastern territories with a gift of territory in the west—German territory up to the line of the Oder and Neisse Rivers. At Potsdam, the Western Allies agreed to the Oder-Neisse boundary line. Poland also took part of East Prussia, and the Soviet Union took the rest. This transfer of territory to Poland and the Soviet Union stripped Germany of one fourth of its land.

One of the consequences of these territorial adjustments was a large increase in Germany's postwar population. The Soviets, for example, evicted the Germans from East Prussia and from the Soviet-controlled Baltic countries. Poland followed suit, expelling Germans from the area of prewar Poland as well as from the new territory they had just gained at Potsdam. Czechoslovakia, too, insisted that Sudeten Germans who had supported Hitler's invasion of Czechoslovakia must leave the country. These moves, though not surprising in view of the prewar troubles with ethnically German minorities, created a serious problem. The burden of housing, feeding, and employing these refugees fell on a shrunken and divided postwar Germany.

Demilitarization and reparations. The Allied Control Council solved the immediate problem of keeping Germany peaceful by swiftly disbanding all German land, air, and sea forces. The Allies demanded that all industrial plants and equipment that had been used in the war industry be dismantled. This plan proved difficult to enforce, however, since the Allies first had to answer the complex question of what constituted a war industry. A factory that manufactures tractors, for example, may easily be converted to produce tanks.

In addition, the Allies disagreed on the question of German economic revival. The United States and Britain concluded that a revival of German industry was essential to the general prosperity of postwar Europe as a whole. France initially preferred to keep Germany weak industrially to prevent any possibility of future rearmament. To the Soviets, reparations were more important than a revival of German industrial and economic prosperity. They demanded that Germany pay them the staggering sum of $10 billion in reparations.

Western leaders haggled with the Soviets, but in the end, they agreed that the Soviets might claim

Occupied Germany, 1945–1955

Learning from Maps After the war, the Allies decided to divide Germany into zones of military occupation.

Place How was the city of Berlin divided?

reparations, mostly in the form of industrial equipment, not only from their own zone of occupation but from the Western zones as well. Under this agreement, the Soviets dismantled and moved hundreds of manufacturing and industrial plants from Germany to the Soviet Union. The removal of so many factories and industrial materials severely damaged the prospects for German industrial revival. Eventually, the Western Allies halted the flow of reparations from their zones to the Soviet Union.

Confronted by such controversial issues and disagreements, the Allied Control Council found it increasingly difficult to reach decisions. With the council in almost constant deadlock, the Allied occupation administrations soon began to ignore it altogether and to administer their own zones as they saw fit.

Nuremberg trials and denazification. The military occupation of Germany revealed to the world the full extent of the horrors of German concentration camps and the terrible consequences of the Nazi policy of racial purification. Although Hitler was dead and some of his highest-ranking officers had escaped to Spain and Latin America, many Nazi leaders had been captured. The victorious Allies were determined that those responsible for the war and all of its horrors should be held accountable. In 1945 and 1946, a special international court met at Nuremberg, Germany. The Nuremberg court charged 22 of the principal Nazi leaders with crimes against peace and crimes against humanity as well as conspiracy in the extermination camps, the slave labor camps, and the conquered countries. In a series of trials, referred to as the **Nuremberg trials**, 12 of the defendants were sentenced to death, 7 were sentenced to life imprisonment, and 3 were acquitted. At the same time, the court declared the Nazi Party a criminal organization. Trials of other war criminals continued for many years in postwar Germany.

In addition to trying Nazi leaders, the Allies also pursued a policy of **denazification**, which included removing former Nazis from positions of authority in government, industry, and education. However, difficulties soon developed. The German economy had broken down almost completely. Its rebuilding required technically skilled leaders, many of whom had been Nazis.

Peacemaking Problems

In addition to deciding what to do with the defeated powers, the Allies confronted the daunting task of reconstructing Europe itself. The governments of the United States, the Soviet Union, and Great Britain had survived the test of war. Elsewhere, however, the destruction unleashed by the Nazis had undermined or destroyed many prewar governments. As many of the European states emerged from the shambles of the war, they established new forms of government in place of the old.

This October 1946 photo was taken at the Nuremberg trial of Nazi leaders.

In 1946, for example, a plebiscite, or a direct vote by the people on a national issue, abolished the monarchy in Italy and established a republican form of government. In France a provisional government, headed by General Charles de Gaulle, ran the country until 1946, when a new constitution was adopted and the Fourth Republic was proclaimed.

Much of the rest of Europe also faced major changes. In Eastern Europe, the Soviets had established temporary governments in the countries they had liberated. These governments were heavily dominated—in most cases controlled outright—by Communists, despite the anticommunist feelings of the majority of the population. Greece had a tottering monarchy and was in the throes of a civil war, and the political futures of both Germany and Austria remained uncertain. Allied efforts to achieve a final postwar settlement in all of these areas proved extremely difficult. It soon became clear that the Soviet Union and the Western Allies had fundamentally conflicting goals for postwar Europe.

In February 1947, after nearly a year and a half of heated debate, the Council of Foreign Ministers reached agreement on peace treaties with Italy, Romania, Bulgaria, Hungary, and Finland. Italy renounced all claims to countries that it had invaded during the war. It also lost some territory to France, Yugoslavia, and Greece; its colonies were placed under a trusteeship of the United Nations. Romania, Hungary, Bulgaria, and Finland also had to return territory they had taken and accept changes in their prewar boundaries. Furthermore, they had to reduce their armed forces and pay reparations to nations that their armies had invaded.

The negotiations over the treaties exposed a growing rift between the Soviet Union and the Western Allies. The Soviets were determined to ensure that Communists controlled the governments of the Eastern European countries that were occupied by the Red Army. Only in this way, they insisted, would they be safe from future invasion. The Western Allies objected, insisting that there must be free elections and governments that were generally representative of all democratic elements in the population. In the end, a compromise was reached when the Soviet Union agreed to allow a few representatives of noncommunist political parties to participate in the new governments of Eastern Europe.

The Allies were unable to achieve agreement on the most important treaties. The four-way occupation of Austria, for example, continued for years without any agreement as to peace terms. Finally, in 1955, a treaty with Austria was negotiated and signed. The treaty restored Austria as a sovereign, independent republic within its 1938 boundaries. Austria, however, had to agree to be permanently neutral. It had taken the Allies 10 years to reach an agreement over Austria. In the case of Germany, the Allies never agreed to a final settlement. The division of Germany into eastern and western parts eventually became a formal division into two countries.

The United Nations

Despite their disagreements over the status of Eastern Europe, Germany, and Austria, after the war the Allies continued with their plans for a new international organization to be known as the United Nations, which would replace the old League of Nations.

In April 1945, representatives from 51 nations met in San Francisco. After two months, this General Assembly agreed to a final version of the charter, which was then submitted to the government of each representative for ratification. By October 1945, the required number of nations had ratified the charter, and the United Nations (UN) was established. Its primary purpose was to maintain international peace and security and to act as a deterrent to aggressors. As a part of this mission, it was also designed to foster cooperation among the nations of the world in solving international social, cultural, and economic problems.

In many ways the structure of the United Nations represented a compromise between those who still thought that great powers deserved more influence, and those who preferred a more idealistic approach to maintaining world peace on the basis of collective security. Consequently, the two most important bodies of the UN were the Security Council and the General Assembly.

The Security Council. The Security Council was the body charged primarily with maintaining international peace and security. It was to act as a mediator in international disputes and seek to prevent aggression by any nation. The Council was composed of 10 temporary members, elected from the General Assembly for two-year rotating terms, and 5 permanent members. The permanent members were the five major powers that had formed the core of the Allied powers—the United States, Britain, France, the Soviet Union, and China. Each of these countries could prevent the Council from taking an important action by using its **veto power**—the power to defeat a measure with a single vote. In this way the

Security Council was designed to satisfy those who felt that some nations should have more influence than others.

The General Assembly. The General Assembly, on the other hand, was designed to appeal to those who felt that all nations deserved equal status. Ultimately, any nation that wished to join would be admitted to the General Assembly, including those that had been defeated in the war. Each member nation in the Assembly, regardless of size or power, would have the same rights and voting power as any other. The Assembly was responsible for drawing up the UN budget and assessing each member nation's share of the cost. The General Assembly also elected the secretary-general and the judges of the International Court of Justice.

In addition to these two main bodies, the UN is also composed of four other major organizations. Sustaining and supporting the entire organization is the Secretariat, a staff of clerical and administrative workers, technical experts, and advisers, all working under the secretary-general. The International Court of Justice at The Hague, in the Netherlands, presides over questions of international law. The new Trusteeship Council replaced the old mandate system of the League of Nations. Finally, the Economic and Social Council sponsors a host of specialized agencies including the World Health Organization (WHO), the UN Educational, Scientific and Cultural Organization (UNESCO), the International Bank for Reconstruction and Development (also called the World Bank), and the International Monetary Fund (IMF), among others.

Section 1 Review

1. **Define** Cold War, Nuremberg trials, denazification, veto power
2. **Identify** Big Three, Allied Control Council, Council of Foreign Ministers, Security Council, General Assembly
3. **Locate and Explain the Significance** Yalta, Oder-Neisse line, East Prussia
4. **Understanding Ideas** Describe the principal terms of the postwar settlement of Europe.
5. **Summarizing Ideas** What action did the Allies take to deal with the atrocities committed during the war?
6. **Analyzing Ideas** What are the goals of the United Nations?

What If?

The United Nations
One of the main purposes of the United Nations is to maintain world peace. How might peace have been maintained in the postwar world if the UN General Assembly had had the power to enforce decisions and the Big Five did not have veto power?

Section 2

Origins of the Cold War

Focus Questions

- **How did the Western Allies respond to Soviet policies in Eastern Europe immediately after World War II?**
- **What long-range measures did the United States take to deal with Europe's economic plight and the apparent threat of Soviet expansion?**

With the Red Army occupying all of Eastern and part of Central Europe at the war's end, and the United States in sole possession of the atomic bomb, each side increasingly came to fear the other. Although the struggle between democracy and communism occasionally led to bloody local wars, for the most part the Cold War was a war of ideas and differing worldviews waged by the two great superpowers, as they came to be called. Political and economic means were used instead of weapons, partly because the development of atomic bombs and later nuclear weapons that could destroy the world made another world war unthinkable.

The End of the Alliance

As the Soviet Union and the Western Allies continued to disagree over fundamental questions after the end of World War II, the alliance that had defeated the Axis powers finally dissolved. In its place, a new rivalry emerged between two armed camps supporting the two superpowers. On one side was the Soviet Union, supported by the communist nations of the world. The Soviet Union and its communist allies were sometimes called the Eastern bloc. On the other side was the United

States, supported by the Western democracies and other noncommunist nations. The two sides were distinguished by completely different political and economic systems.

Partly as a consequence of these political and economic differences, after the war the Soviet Union and the Western Allies also came to have vastly different ideas about how to reconstruct Europe. Each side naturally believed that its own system should be the model. In addition, each side was worried about its future security. The Soviet Union was determined to protect itself from any future attack from the West—as the Germans had attacked Russia twice in a generation. With this in mind, as the Red Army rolled across Eastern and Central Europe, Stalin insisted on placing governments that would be friendly to Soviet interests in power in the liberated states. This would create a buffer zone of communist countries along the western frontier of the Soviet Union.

Disagreement over Poland. The first sign of trouble came in Poland, whose invasion by Hitler had been the trigger for the war in the first place. Although a free Polish government-in-exile had been established in London, Stalin refused to recognize it. Instead, he installed a pro-Soviet Polish government that was dominated by Communists. In addition, he insisted that the Soviet Union would retain the territories in Poland and the Baltic states that it had taken at the time of the Nazi-Soviet Pact. To the Americans and British, however, this policy seemed to violate his agreement at Yalta to allow free elections in the countries that had been liberated by the Red Army. The Western Allies became increasingly suspicious that Stalin's real goal was to dominate all of Europe.

Soviet expansion. Other Soviet actions fueled Western fears. In the summer of 1945, for example, Stalin massed troops along the border of Turkey. He demanded the return of territory in Caucasia that had once been annexed by the czars. He also insisted on joint Soviet-Turkish control over the straits connecting the Black Sea to the Aegean and Mediterranean Seas. Such control would guarantee the Soviet Union an outlet for its Black Sea fleet into the Mediterranean. Then, in February 1946, Stalin suddenly announced that the communist struggle for worldwide revolution would continue. In March, Soviet forces that had occupied northern Iran during the war refused to withdraw as scheduled. Instead they supported the establishment of the communist Tudeh Party in Iran.

Winston Churchill delivered his "iron curtain" speech at Fulton, Missouri, in early March 1946.

Under intense pressure from the United States and Britain, the Soviets eventually backed down from their position in Turkey and Iran. Nevertheless, other Soviet actions seemed to indicate a policy of expansionism, not mere self-defense. When a further crisis broke out in Greece in early 1947, the United States finally decided to openly oppose the expansion of communism around the world.

The Truman Doctrine

In 1944, after the Nazis had withdrawn from Greece, civil war broke out between conservative members of the Greek resistance movement, loyal to the monarchy, and the communist partisans. Britain, supporting the royalists, negotiated a truce in 1945. In the summer of 1946, however, the Communists renewed the civil war. They were aided and supplied by the new communist governments of Albania, Bulgaria, and Yugoslavia. The Greek government turned once again to the British for help.

Exhausted and practically bankrupted by the war, the British decided that they could no longer afford to defend states like Iran, Turkey, and Greece against Soviet expansion. In February 1947, the British informed the United States that they were ending financial aid to Greece and Turkey and would withdraw their troops from Greece. They hoped that the United States would provide the necessary assistance to prevent communist domination in the region.

Building History Study Skills

READ
WRITE
INTERPRET
CONNECT
THINK

Reading About History: Identifying an Argument

When we hear the word *argument,* we often think of a disagreement or a dispute. However, when historians use this word, they are speaking of a thesis or main point supported by reasons and examples. Identifying an argument is the first step in determining its validity.

How to Identify an Argument

To identify an argument, follow these steps.

1. Explain the author's thesis or main point. Ask what the author is attempting to prove. You can look for key words and phrases such as *therefore, in conclusion, consequently,* or *I support.*
2. Identify the reasons given to support the main thesis. How does each reason elaborate on the main point?
3. Find the examples that support the reasons.
4. Connect the thesis of the argument with the reasons and examples.

Developing the Skill

Read the following selection from Thomas G. Paterson's *On Every Front: The Making and Unmaking of the Cold War.*

"[T]he Cold War derived from three closely intertwined sources: the conflict-ridden international system; the divergent fundamental needs, ideas, and power of the major antagonists, the United States and the Soviet Union; and the diplomatic conduct . . . —the tactics—of American and Soviet leaders. . . . International, national, and individual elements intersected to produce a world divided into competing spheres of influence. . . . Two nations . . . emerged from the rubble of World War II to claim high rank. . . . The competitive interaction between the United States and the Soviet Union . . . shaped the bipolarism . . . of the immediate postwar years. . . . The major powers, in short, intervened abroad to exploit the political opportunities created by the destructive scythe of World War II. The stakes seemed high. A change in a nation's political orientation might presage [predict] a change in its international alignment. The great powers tended to ignore local conditions . . . which might and often did mitigate against alignment with an outside power. Americans . . . feared that a . . . Communist Greece would look to the East and permit menacing Soviet bases on Greek territory or open the door to a Soviet naval presence in the Mediterranean. Moscow dreaded a conservative

President Truman making his first speech to Congress

anti-Soviet Polish government . . ., for it might prove so weak and so hostile to Moscow as to permit a revived Germany to send storm troopers once again through the Polish corridor into the heart of Russia. . . . A Communist China . . . might align with the Soviet Union; a Nationalist China would remain in the American camp. All in all, the rearranging of political structures within nations drew the major powers into competition, accentuating the conflict inherent in the postwar international system."

The author's main point or thesis is that the origin of the Cold War lies in the goals of the United States and the Soviet Union. Both nations, in their efforts to protect their superpower status and their national security, engaged in tactics that reinforced mutual suspicion. The competing ideologies were a basis for mutual mistrust.

The writer supports his thesis with details about the political situation at the end of World War II. He contends that the Soviet Union and the United States interfered in local conflicts because they saw their power interests at stake. The examples that Paterson cites are the situations in Greece, Poland, and China.

The author's argument is based upon his thesis that both powers, the United States and the Soviet Union, share responsibility for the development of the Cold War.

Practicing the Skill

Read a recent newspaper or magazine article that states a thesis or argument on a political point. Identify the argument, using the skill you have just learned.

To apply this skill, see Applying History Study Skills on page 773.

On March 12, 1947, President Truman, speaking before Congress, announced what came to be called the Truman Doctrine. The United States, he said, considered the continued spread of communism to be a threat to democracy. It must be the policy of the United States, he went on, to support free peoples who are resisting attempted takeovers by armed minorities or by outside pressures. He asked Congress to appropriate $400 million to help defend Greece and Turkey from communist aggression. Congress agreed, and with American financial and technical assistance, the Greek government put down the rebellion.

Over the next several months, Truman's advisers developed a full-scale strategy to carry out the president's new policy. The United States would not try to stamp out communism in countries where it already existed, or in any country that freely chose communism. However, it would use its money, materials, technical knowledge, and influence to help countries that were threatened by communist takeover if they asked for help. In short, the United States would contain, or restrict, the spread of communism wherever possible, a policy known as **containment**.

The Marshall Plan

Disagreement over German economic recovery also contributed to the Cold War. Western leaders interpreted Stalin's reluctance to rebuild the German economy as an effort to keep Western Europe economically weak and depressed. Continuing poverty and economic hardship, they feared, would cause people to turn to local communist parties and communist-dominated labor unions.

In 1947, United States secretary of state George Marshall announced a new plan for massive American economic assistance to help Europe recover from the war. The European Recovery Program, often called the Marshall Plan, stipulated that the United States was prepared to assist Europe on certain terms. For example, European countries were encouraged to work together to determine their needs. They were also to try to remove trade barriers so that goods could flow freely throughout the continent. In this way, prosperity was to be restored. The United States included the Soviet Union and its satellites in its offer of aid, but those nations found the conditions unacceptable and rejected it. Eventually, however, 17 European nations participated in the European Recovery Program.

Between 1948 and 1952, the United States spent over $13 billion on the Marshall Plan with tremendous success. By 1952 both industrial production and agricultural production in Europe had risen considerably above prewar levels, and the continent was once again on the road to prosperity. The United States also benefited from the plan, as it supplied export goods for the recovering European economies.

The Cold War in Central Europe

From the Soviet point of view, both the Truman Doctrine and the Marshall Plan seemed like Western efforts to encircle and undermine the Soviet Union. In September 1947, the Soviet government established the Communist Information Bureau, or **Cominform**, an organization that included all European communist parties. Its purpose was to oppose Marshall Plan aid, which was denounced as an American capitalist effort to dominate Europe economically. The Cominform was unsuccessful in opposing Marshall Plan aid. Its major effect was simply to create tension between communist and noncommunist political parties in Europe.

As the West put its new containment policy into place, the Soviets also tightened their grip on the countries of Eastern and Central Europe. In February 1948, for example, the communist members of Czechoslovakia's still-democratic government staged a coup. Taking complete control of the government, they turned Czechoslovakia into a tightly controlled one-party communist state. Thus, Czechoslovakia joined the Soviet-dominated Communist bloc.

Only one break appeared in the iron curtain that divided East and West. During the spring of 1948, a disagreement developed between Stalin and Marshall Tito of Yugoslavia. Although a devoted Communist, Tito objected to Soviet domination. He announced that Yugoslavia would follow an independent course. By June 1948, the split had become definite, and Yugoslavia was expelled from Cominform.

The Division of Germany

By 1948 it was clear that joint government in Germany by the four former Allies was impossible. In late 1947 and early 1948, anxious to achieve economic recovery, the three Western occupying powers took steps to reunite their zones economically and to revive democratic German political life. It became obvious that they were moving toward the establishment of a unified West German state—a move that the Soviets bitterly opposed.

The Berlin blockade. In response, in June 1948 the Soviets blockaded the East German border to all land and water traffic into Berlin from the west. They refused to allow trucks, barges, or trains to pass the checkpoints at the borders, thus threatening the people of West Berlin with starvation. The Western nations acted swiftly during the Berlin blockade. The United States and Great Britain organized an airlift to supply West Berlin. They flew food and supplies in daily to the inhabitants of the Western sectors of the city. The airlift operated so efficiently that raw materials were also supplied to West Berlin factories. To send the message that the Western Allies would not be intimidated, the United States sent strategic bombers to Great Britain. The Soviets made no serious attempts to stop the airlift, and in May 1949, they lifted the blockade.

East and West Germany. In the long term, the Berlin blockade might be seen as the official beginning of the Cold War. In the short term, it had an immediate and important consequence: the division of Germany. With the approval of the Western Allies, in May 1949 a constitutional assembly proclaimed the

The top photo shows supplies being airlifted into West Berlin by the United States and Great Britain. The bottom photo shows a German airlift worker's wife feeding children. Each child's ration is a slice of dark bread and margarine.

Federal Republic of Germany (popularly known as West Germany), with its capital in Bonn. The Soviet Union followed suit. In October 1949 the German Democratic Republic (popularly known as East Germany) was established in the Soviet zone of Germany. The formal division of Germany became a major symbol of the East-West division that was the Cold War.

Cold War Alliances

The division of Germany was but one of a series of events in 1949 and 1950 that made clear the extent of the split between East and West. As the former Allies divided Europe, the Cold War also seemed to spread to the rest of the world. It also became more dangerous as other powers besides the United States learned the secrets of atomic power. In the summer of 1949, for example, the Soviets detonated their first atomic bomb. In October the West was further alarmed when armies of the Chinese Communist Party defeated the Chinese Nationalist government and forced it off the mainland to the island of Taiwan. Not least, the outbreak of the Korean War in 1950, when the communist forces of North Korea invaded South Korea, reminded many people that the Cold War could all too easily become hot. Perhaps the clearest indication of the split, however, came in the form of new political and military alliances.

The North Atlantic Treaty Organization. In April 1949 a mutual defense pact provided for creation of the North Atlantic Treaty Organization (NATO). Twelve nations originally signed the North Atlantic Treaty: the United States, Great Britain, France, Italy, Portugal, Norway, Denmark, Iceland, Canada, Belgium, the Netherlands, and Luxembourg. Greece and Turkey joined NATO in 1952, and West Germany followed in 1955. (See map on opposite page.) The signers agreed that if one member nation were attacked, all members would take united action against the aggressor. Although a detailed defense plan called for a large standing NATO force drawn from all member nations, eventually the organization came to rely heavily on American nuclear weapons to act as a deterrent to any Soviet invasion of Western Europe.

The Warsaw Pact. The Soviet Union responded to the inclusion of West Germany in NATO by establishing a formal, unified alliance of its own. In May 1955 in Warsaw, Poland, the Soviet government held a meeting of representatives of the European Communist bloc—the Soviet Union,

European Alliances, 1955

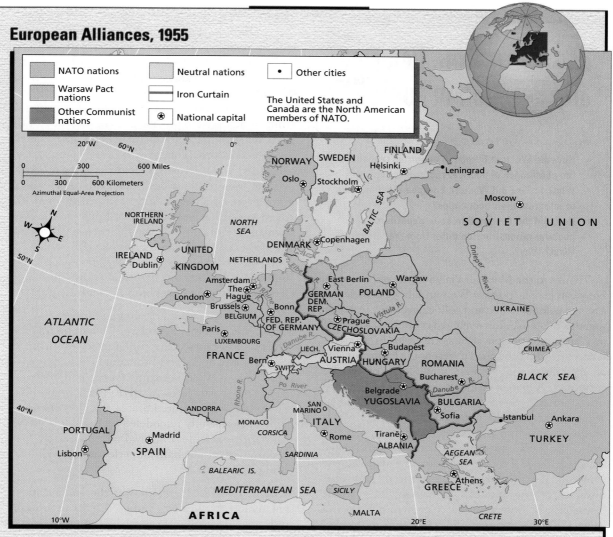

Learning from Maps NATO and the Warsaw Pact divided European allegiances.

❓ **Region** Which countries remained neutral in 1955?

Poland, East Germany, Czechoslovakia, Hungary, Romania, Bulgaria, and Albania. These nations adopted a 20-year mutual defense agreement called the Warsaw Pact. The combined troop strength contributed by member countries along with Soviet troops already stationed throughout the region meant that the Warsaw Pact greatly outnumbered NATO in terms of ground troops. This overwhelming difference in ground troops between NATO and the Warsaw Pact only reinforced the Western reliance on the nuclear deterrent.

Section 2 Review

1. **Define** containment, Cominform
2. **Understanding Ideas** What was the purpose of the Truman Doctrine?
3. **Summarizing Ideas** What were the basic features of the Marshall Plan?
4. **Analyzing Ideas** (a) What were the functions of NATO and the Warsaw Pact? (b) Why were these alliances formed?

Reconstruction, Reform, and Reaction in Europe

Focus Questions

- How did Western European countries respond to the challenges of postwar reconstruction?
- What actions did Western European leaders take to integrate their economies?
- How did the Eastern European experience of postwar reconstruction differ from that of the West? Why?

Thanks to the Marshall Plan and the resolve of the European people, postwar Western Europe experienced a remarkable economic and political recovery. After the war, the Western Allies remained committed to democracy and the principle of majority rule. In economic terms, they also continued to accept the basic principles of capitalism and at least some form of **market economy**. A market economy is one in which competition among private businesses and individuals generally determines what goods and services will be produced, how they will be produced, and what they will cost. The Communist bloc, on the other hand, accepted the Marxist-Leninist doctrine that ordinary people did not always know what was in their own best interests or the interests of society as a whole. Consequently, only the elite Communist Party was believed capable of organizing society properly. In keeping with this principle, communist countries practiced a **command economy**, in which the government made all economic decisions. The market economies of Western Europe helped those nations achieve a higher standard of living than that of Eastern Europe. In a relatively short time, Western Europeans cleared away the rubble of bombed cities and rebuilt roads, rail lines, and bridges. Industries rapidly returned to full production. Eastern Europe also revived after the war, but not nearly as quickly or successfully as the West.

The West German "Miracle"

As the Western Allies encouraged the revival of democratic political parties in West Germany, two main parties emerged that would dominate West German politics in the 1950s and 1960s, the Christian Democrats and the Social Democrats.

The first West German chancellor, Konrad Adenauer, was a Christian Democrat. Under Adenauer's free-market policies, the reconstruction and industrial development of West Germany progressed at a remarkable rate. Many people referred to it as the "German miracle."

During the postwar years, the West German government managed to provide housing and jobs for the many refugees from East Germany and other Eastern European nations. The labor of these refugees contributed to West Germany's rapidly growing economy. German industry flourished, thanks to technological innovation, a commitment to quality, and the absence of strikes and other labor troubles. The West German unit of currency, the *Deutsche mark*, became one of the most stable in the world.

In his book *Germany and the East-West Crisis*, William S. Schlamm describes how one West German built a successful business after the war.

" . . . [A] young friend of mine, a former Sudeten-German, . . . in 1948—when he was thirty-two—crossed the border of the German Soviet Zone and started to manufacture nylon stockings in West Germany. At the end of 1957, nine years later, . . . [H]is plant would be the pride of any United States chamber of commerce. Beautifully remodeled in 1957, it is an authentic example of shrewd rationalization techniques, of mechanical perfection, of tidiness and profitability."

By 1958, West Germany was the leading industrial nation in Western Europe. Under Adenauer's guidance, especially through his commitment to establishing the rule of law as the fundamental principle of the German state, West Germany had also become one of the world's most stable democracies.

Staunchly anticommunist, and especially anti-Soviet, Adenauer also followed a policy of close alignment with the Western Allies. Under his guidance, Germany joined NATO in 1955. He also encouraged Germans in the Soviet bloc to escape to the West. Many did so, particularly in Berlin, where the Western Allies continued to administer the western half of the city. Indeed, so many refugees fled East Germany through Berlin that in 1961 the East German government, almost overnight, erected a wall separating the two halves of the city. Anyone who was caught trying to escape over the wall was shot. The Berlin Wall, with its cap of barbed wire, became a major symbol of the Cold War.

The German government founded the Volkswagen company in 1937, with its headquarters in Wolfsburg. The "Beetle" and "Rabbit" models became very popular in the United States during the 1960s and 1970s.

Although Adenauer retired in 1963, he was followed by a fellow Christian Democrat, Ludwig Erhard, who had been in many ways the architect of the free-market policies that had produced the "miracle." Under Erhard, Germany continued to prosper, although its rate of growth slowed during the 1960s. A mild recession or slowdown in economic activity occurred in 1966. Worries over the economy and the Christian Democrats' foreign policy of complete alignment with the United States eventually caused many Germans to turn to the Social Democrats. Throughout the 1960s the Social Democrats gained ground in local elections and even in the federal parliament. Not until 1969, however, did the Social Democrats win a national majority in the Federal Republic of Germany under their leader, Willy Brandt.

Great Britain After the War

Ironically, perhaps, at the same time that Germany was pursuing free-market policies, Britain was going in the opposite direction. In 1945, British voters rejected Winston Churchill's Conservative Party at the polls. Winning a substantial majority in Parliament, the Labour Party formed Britain's postwar government under Clement Attlee. The Labour Party, a moderate socialist party, made many changes in the British economic and social systems. The government nationalized railroads, utilities, coal mines, and the Bank of England, but did not interfere with four fifths of industry, which remained privately owned. Many welfare measures were passed, including free medical

care for everyone. Great Britain became a **welfare state**—a state in which the government undertakes primary responsibility for the social welfare of its citizens.

Great Britain also faced many severe economic problems after the war. Its industrial equipment was outdated and inefficient. Many workers had been killed in the war. Some scientists and managers had emigrated to Canada, Australia, and the United States. After the war, Great Britain lost valuable colonies and possessions, and the cost of the nation's remaining overseas commitments was a heavy burden. The nation struggled to overcome its nagging economic difficulties.

A new Conservative government was elected in 1951. As prime minister once again, Churchill reversed some of the Labour government's nationalization policies. The government reduced unemployment, raised wages, and allowed industry to thrive. However, the general outlines of the welfare state remained intact even under the Conservatives.

Moreover, Britain continued to lag behind the rest of Europe in economic recovery. Although industrial growth occurred, it was much slower than that of other countries, especially Germany and France. In the 1960s, Great Britain's industrial productivity fell to one of the lowest national levels in the industrialized world. One important reason for this decline was the shift in the world economy from coal as an energy source to oil and nuclear power. Britain's strength traditionally had been its large coal reserves. The Labour Party blamed the Conservatives for the poor economy but did no better when back in office during the 1960s and 1970s.

Inflation began in the late 1960s and escalated in the 1970s. British labor unions fought to maintain high wages, but without also increasing the productivity of British workers. This meant that British goods cost more to make—and to sell—than goods produced by their competitors. Consequently, Britain was unable to develop a favorable balance of trade—in which more goods are exported than imported—and real prosperity remained elusive.

New Republics in France

Postwar France also faced serious problems. After the war, the voters adopted a new constitution and proclaimed the Fourth Republic, but this government was almost as unstable politically as its predecessor. Economically, France had suffered considerable damage during the war, with many towns and cities destroyed and valuable farmlands ravaged. After the war, inflation caused great hardship for the French people. Economic revival began under the policies of French economist Jean Monnet, however, and especially with the help of the Marshall Plan, French agriculture and industry slowly began to recover and even to modernize.

As economic recovery proceeded slowly and painfully at home, France also faced challenges in its overseas empire. Anxious to restore its own prestige as well as France's after the defeat of 1940, the French army conducted bitter and costly wars to re-establish French authority in Indochina and North Africa. In the late 1950s, a crisis over Algeria brought France to the brink of civil war.

Algeria was considered an integral part of France, with more than a million European settlers, many of whose families had been there for a century. In 1954, however, Arab nationalists began a bitter and bloody war for independence. After several years of extreme violence, many people in France were prepared to let Algeria go. Others, including leading elements in the army, violently opposed such a course. In 1958, as crisis engulfed the nation, the French legislature—under pressure from army leaders—turned to General Charles de Gaulle to save the nation from civil war. He was authorized to write a new constitution and to rule by decree until its ratification.

The new constitution created France's Fifth Republic. The constitution gave the president a great deal of power. He appointed the prime minister and could dissolve the legislature and assume dictatorial powers in a national emergency. Through the prime minister, the president could enact laws unless a majority of the National Assembly opposed them.

De Gaulle became the first president of the Fifth Republic. To the surprise of the army, he ended the war in Algeria by accepting Algerian independence. He also moved to peacefully transform the French empire into a voluntary association of self-governing nations known as the French Community.

In foreign policy, de Gaulle was a nationalist. He believed that Europe could prosper only as a close alliance of national states that would retain their individual identity and freedom of action. He opposed British and American influence in Europe because he feared that a rise of imperialism would threaten the individuality of every nation. He feared the Soviet Union less, although he was wary of Soviet expansion into Europe. Balancing these factors, de Gaulle withdrew French forces from NATO command and insisted on developing an independent nuclear force for France, although France remained a political member of NATO.

To further counter Anglo-American influence in Europe, de Gaulle pursued a policy of French and German cooperation. He established close relations with West German Chancellor Adenauer. Together, he believed, the French and Germans could prevent Europe from being dominated too much by Britain and the United States, while at the same time acting as a deterrent to Russian expansion.

In the late 1960s, political conditions within France became unstable. Violent riots shook the nation in 1968. Militant students demanded reforms in the educational system, and strikes for higher wages and better working conditions spread rapidly throughout industrial areas. To meet the crisis, de Gaulle dissolved the National Assembly and called for a general election.

To win a favorable vote, de Gaulle acknowledged the need for social improvements in France. However, soon afterward his popularity declined. In April 1969, in a direct vote, the French people rejected his proposals for reform, and the 79-year-old president resigned.

Other Western European Nations

Recovery in the other nations of Western Europe took many different paths. Denmark, Norway, and Sweden, for example, had experienced relatively little dislocation as a result of the war. Sweden had remained neutral, and although occupied by the Nazis, Norway and Denmark had not been the scenes of any major fighting. After the war, Social Democratic parties that had first been elected in the 1930s remained in power until the 1970s. With strongly entrenched democracies and greater political stability than in other countries in Western Europe,

Chapel by Le Corbusier

World War II, so devastating to people in Europe and elsewhere, also had among its casualties many great works of art. Numerous old and beautiful churches were damaged or destroyed. It was with great joy, then, that Europeans hailed the construction of this new place of worship. Built between 1950 and 1955 by the great architect Le Corbusier, the chapel stands proudly in the green fields of Ronchamp, in France.

Called Notre Dame du Haut, this was one of Le Corbusier's most famous works. The chapel appears large, although it is quite small. It holds only about 200 people. The walls are made of concrete sprayed over metal mesh; the finished walls were then painted white. The roof is also concrete but was left unpainted. Some say that

Le Corbusier's soaring chapel design was inspired by an image of praying hands or the wings of an angel.

throughout the 1950s and 1960s their economies prospered. This prosperity allowed them to establish extensive welfare states, though at the cost of extremely high taxes.

In Italy the Christian Democratic Party dominated the political arena during the 1950s and 1960s. Under Alcide de Gasperi, prime minister from 1945 to 1953, Italy established a capitalist economy, and the country experienced major industrial and agricultural growth.

By the 1960s, the Socialist and Communist Parties had gained considerable strength as labor unrest increased. At the end of the decade, Italy's economic growth declined sharply. This decline contributed to the undermining of political stability.

Economic programs in Greece, Spain, and Portugal met with varying degrees of success. Of all the Western European countries, only Portugal and Spain did not establish full democratic government after the war, but remained authoritarian. All three nations, however, were able to develop free-enterprise systems.

Western European Integration

In the 1950s the French proposed that the nations that produced most of Western Europe's steel and coal unite their facilities. In 1952, France, West Germany, Italy, and the Low Countries (Belgium, the Netherlands, and Luxembourg) formed the European Coal and Steel Community (ECSC). A central authority regulated production and prices, and members did not charge each other tariffs on coal or steel. A remarkable feature of the ECSC was its freedom from national control.

The Common Market. In 1957 the same six nations took another important step toward economic union by establishing the European Economic Community (EEC)—usually called the Common Market. The Treaty of Rome provided for the gradual abolition of tariffs and import quotas among the six member nations. A common tariff would be placed on goods coming into the Common Market from nonmember nations.

The European Community. The Common Market made steady progress toward European economic unity in the 1960s. In 1967 it adopted a five-year plan to provide greater price and wage stability and more uniform tax levels among member countries. Also in 1967, the EEC merged with the European Coal and Steel Community and the Atomic Energy Community, which the six nations had created to share information on the peaceful uses of atomic energy, to form the European Communities, later the European Community, or EC. The European Community set up a single European commission with headquarters in Belgium.

Although Britain could have joined the EEC in the 1950s, British leaders decided against such a course. They still saw their future as tied to the British Commonwealth, rather than to Europe. In the 1960s, however, the EEC prospered economically while Britain lagged behind. Eventually, the British changed their minds and applied for admission. Still worried about undue British influence in Europe, French president Charles de Gaulle vetoed the application. Not until after de Gaulle's retirement and death did Britain finally gain admission to the EEC in 1973.

The Soviet Union After Stalin

In March 1953 Joseph Stalin, who had ruled the Soviet Union with an iron hand for three decades, died. Stalin's death led to a power struggle within the Soviet government. Eventually, Nikita Khrushchev (kroosh·CHAWF), former secretary of the Communist Party in the Ukraine, emerged as Stalin's successor.

After consolidating his position, in February 1956 Khrushchev shocked the leadership of the Soviet Union. In a speech to the 20th Congress of the Communist Party he denounced the policies of his predecessor, condemning Stalin for creating a "cult of personality," for murdering thousands of innocent Soviet citizens and loyal Communist Party members, and for committing a host of other crimes against the Soviet people.

Khrushchev's speech marked the beginning of his new policy of destalinization. Reversing a number of Stalin's policies, Khrushchev lifted restrictions on intellectuals and artists, freed many political prisoners, and ended some of the terrorism of the secret police. He also loosened the central government's tight grip on the economy. Incentives were offered to increase agricultural production. Local factory and farm managers were given more control to help them meet production quotas.

Khrushchev's primary goal was to increase the availability of consumer goods to the Soviet people. Even under his reforms, however, a continuing emphasis on heavy industry, and especially military spending, prevented substantial advances in the production of consumer goods. In addition, although Soviet industry had been rebuilt after the war, it was rebuilt largely with prewar technology. With the limitations imposed

President Dwight D. Eisenhower (left) welcomed Premier Nikita S. Khrushchev to the United States in 1959.

by centralized planning, the only real innovations achieved by the Soviet Union were in military and space technology. To the surprise of the world, the Soviets began the space age when they launched the first orbiting satellite, *Sputnik*, in 1957.

Despite these problems, over the next several decades the Soviet economy did expand, and living standards rose considerably. The Soviet Union gradually became a modern industrial society. By the 1970s, for example, it was producing more coal, steel, cement, cotton, natural gas, and oil than any other country in the world.

For a time, Khrushchev also seemed anxious to improve relations with the Western powers. He adopted a policy known as peaceful coexistence. However, this temporary thaw in East-West relations lasted only until 1960, when an American U-2 spy airplane was shot down over the Soviet Union, leading to the cancellation of a summit talk planned between Khrushchev and U.S. president Dwight Eisenhower. Diplomatic relations further deteriorated with the building of the Berlin Wall in 1961 and a crisis over Cuba in 1962 that brought the Soviet Union and the United States to the brink of nuclear war. After Khrushchev's economic policies also failed to produce the desired results, in 1964 he was forced to resign from office. Under his successor, Leonid Brezhnev, both domestic and foreign policies were tightened once more.

Economic Recovery in Eastern Europe

Like the rest of Europe, the new satellite countries of the Eastern bloc also had to rebuild after the end of World War II. To do so under the thumb of Soviet rule, however, proved difficult. Like the Soviet Union itself, the Eastern European countries lagged behind the West in recovering from the war. Under the new Soviet-controlled governments, efforts were made to collectivize agriculture, with varying results. In Hungary, for example, local resistance resulted in the collectivization of only about a third of the land. Bulgaria, on the other hand, collectivized over half of its available farmland. The Poles resisted collectivization so forcefully that most land remained in private hands. All these efforts at collectivization of agriculture along Soviet lines simply delayed economic recovery in the Eastern European countries.

Under Soviet-style Five-Year Plans and central planning, industrialization of Eastern Europe was more successful. East Germany and Czechoslovakia had industrialized before World War II. Under the new policies these countries expanded their industrial bases. East Germany, which had suffered considerably from having to pay reparations to the Soviet Union in the form of factories and industrial goods, eventually became the major industrial power in Eastern Europe. Hungary and Poland, although still agrarian countries before the war, now also became industrialized. Despite industrialization, however, under Soviet domination consumer goods remained a low priority. Consequently, living standards in Eastern Europe, though they improved, also remained low in comparison with the West.

Upheavals in Eastern Europe

During the early postwar years, the Communist bloc seemed a solid, firmly knit group of nations united by common beliefs, policies, and goals. However, the satellite countries had once been independent nations, some with long-standing antagonisms toward the Soviet Union.

Yugoslavia's growing independence from the Soviet Union after 1948 aroused envy and also inspired some people in the satellite countries. In 1953, Soviet tanks and troops put down a revolt by East German workers. In 1956, Poland threatened to revolt, and as a result, gained a small amount of independence in domestic policy-making. Hungary, too, revolted against Soviet domination in 1956. At first Soviet troops withdrew, but they later returned and violently suppressed the revolt.

Dissatisfaction with communism, and especially with Soviet domination, continued in much of Eastern Europe throughout the 1960s. In 1968, Czechoslovakia, under Alexander Dubcek (DOOB·chek), began a program of reforms. Dubcek promised civil liberties, democratic political reforms, and a more independent political system. This short-lived period of freedom became known as the Prague Spring. Within six months, Warsaw Pact troops, chiefly from the Soviet Union, invaded Czechoslovakia. They seized the reform leaders and replaced them with pro-Soviet people.

Section 3 Review

1. **Define** market economy, command economy, welfare state
2. **Identify** Konrad Adenauer, Charles de Gaulle, Nikita Khrushchev, Alexander Dubcek
3. **Explaining Ideas** (a) Why did the West German economy experience tremendous growth after the war? (b) How did this differ from what happened in Great Britain?
4. **Summarizing Ideas** (a) What changes did the Labour Party bring about in Great Britain? (b) What problems did Great Britain begin to experience in the 1960s?
5. **Analyzing Ideas** What efforts did Western European countries make to integrate their economies after 1945?
6. **Interpreting Ideas** What factors made economic recovery in Eastern Europe different from that in Western Europe?

Section 4

The United States and Canada

Focus Questions

- What kinds of domestic problems did American presidents confront after World War II?
- What were the most pressing foreign-policy issues in the United States after World War II?
- How did Canada develop after World War II?

Despite flourishing economies and powerful roles in world affairs, the United States and Canada faced a number of problems in the postwar years. These difficulties included internal conflicts, political problems, and a gradual realization that economic growth has its limits. Both nations, however, remained committed to maintaining positions of great influence.

Challenges Facing the United States

Between 1945 and 1968, three Democratic presidential administrations and one Republican administration represented the American people. Although these four presidents often had similar goals, they just as often differed on policies for carrying out their goals. Some of the problems that arose during this period proved extremely trying for the men who held the highest office in the land. Their decisions set precedents and shaped the way in which the American people viewed both the world and themselves during a critical period in their country's history.

Domestic policy. At home the United States presidents consistently aimed to resolve social and political problems and maintain a flourishing economy. Following the example of the New Deal, later presidents created new programs to address social problems. Many social programs were launched during the Kennedy and Johnson administrations. President John F. Kennedy introduced a broad program of domestic reforms, highlighted by legislation to reduce social inequalities. He was assassinated in November 1963, however, before Congress had passed much of his proposed legislation.

Vice President Lyndon B. Johnson succeeded Kennedy and attempted to implement an even more sweeping vision of reform. He was determined to create what he called the **Great Society**. His program included major social reform legislation, along with important new civil rights programs.

The economy. Efforts at social reform were underpinned by a booming American economy. After World War II the American economy reached new peaks of productivity, with huge new industries and rapid growth of new construction. Several minor **recessions**—periods of temporary business slowdown and increased unemployment—occurred in the 1940s and 1950s, but the 1960s were a period of continuous growth. Only toward the end of the decade did rising inflation seem to foreshadow problems to come.

McCarthyism. Although economic prosperity led to a rising standard of living, the Cold War contributed to feelings of continuing insecurity for many Americans. In the immediate postwar period, for example, many people did not understand why the

United States had allowed the Soviet Union to spread its sphere of influence throughout Eastern Europe and into other parts of the world. A number of people tried to explain these events by using a conspiracy theory. They believed that Soviet gains had occurred because certain people in the United States government were sympathetic to communism.

Senator Joseph McCarthy of Wisconsin became the most dramatic spokesman for the conspiracy theory. Between 1950 and 1954, he questioned the loyalty of many government officials and built up a large following. In the process he damaged the reputations of many Americans. In 1954 a Senate committee investigated McCarthy's conduct and found his charges groundless, and his influence collapsed. Nevertheless, ongoing crises between East and West, and especially the ever-present threat of nuclear war, left many people feeling uneasy.

The civil rights movement. As the United States grew more affluent, many minorities who had earlier missed out on such opportunities now began to demand equal **civil rights** with the majority of the nation. African Americans, for example, had been freed from slavery during the Civil War and had officially been granted their rights as citizens but, in fact, still lived under many social, political, and economic restrictions. In many regions, in both the North and the South, black people were prevented from voting and from obtaining decent educations, jobs, and housing. Dissatisfaction grew, especially after World War II. Organizations such as the Urban League and the National Association for the Advancement of Colored People (**NAACP**) worked to find employment and to secure civil rights for black Americans.

A turning point in the civil rights movement came in 1954. In the landmark case of *Brown v. Board of Education of Topeka*, the United States Supreme Court unanimously declared that state laws requiring black children to attend separate schools were unconstitutional. States that had such laws were ordered to integrate their schools. This important decision encouraged the growing civil rights movement of the late 1950s and 1960s. In the 1960s, Congress passed several civil rights and voting rights acts that promised political equality for African Americans and other minorities.

The most prominent civil rights leader was Dr. Martin Luther King, Jr., a Baptist minister. He advocated the use of nonviolent methods, such as boycotts, marches, and sit-ins to bring about change. African Americans held peaceful demonstrations and

In an unusual occurrence, four U.S. presidents appear together in this 1961 photograph taken at the funeral of Sam Rayburn. From left to right, they are: John F. Kennedy, Lyndon B. Johnson (who was vice-president at the time this photo was taken but later served as president), Dwight D. Eisenhower, and Harry S Truman.

mass protests against discrimination. For his efforts in furthering the cause of civil rights through nonviolent means, Dr. King was awarded the Nobel Peace Prize in 1964. However, in spite of Dr. King's efforts, many of these protests attracted violent reactions. Dr. King himself died violently at the hands of an assassin. His murder in 1968 dealt a severe blow to the civil rights movement and sparked a wave of riots in cities across the country.

Foreign Policy and the Cold War

For the most part, United States foreign policy during the postwar period revolved around the containment of communism. Following the example of the Truman Doctrine, the Marshall Plan, and NATO, American leaders in the 1950s and 1960s remained determined to prevent Soviet expansion. In Asia, the United States sent troops to South Korea in a "police action" to stop Communists from North Korea from taking over the country. Truman's successor, Dwight D. Eisenhower, brought the Korean War to an end and

created the Southeast Asia Treaty Organization (SEATO) in an attempt to halt further communist advances in that region. He also announced the Eisenhower Doctrine, which provided economic and military assistance to anticommunist countries in the Middle East.

Although there were some efforts to ease Cold War tensions, none lasted. In 1960, for example, a proposed summit between Eisenhower and Khrushchev was scuttled when the Soviets shot down an American U-2 spy plane over the Soviet Union. The following year, the construction of the Berlin Wall made it clear that the Cold War continued in full force.

The Cuban missile crisis. In 1959 the government of Cuba, a corrupt dictatorship, fell to Marxist rebel forces led by Fidel Castro. As Castro began to implement a full communist revolution in Cuba, the Eisenhower administration feared that the island would become a base of Soviet operations. In April 1961, the newly-elected President Kennedy authorized an invasion of Cuba by anti-Castro

Cubans, trained and equipped by the Central Intelligence Agency. The landings, known as the Bay of Pigs invasion, failed to spark the expected anticommunist uprising. American air support was cancelled, and the invaders were killed or captured. Castro now turned to the Soviet Union for support against the United States.

The Bay of Pigs operation convinced Khrushchev that Kennedy was indecisive, and he decided he could strengthen Soviet military power by building nuclear missile sites in Cuba. In October 1962 an American spyplane discovered these missile sites. Alarmed, Kennedy demanded that the Soviet Union withdraw the missiles and blockaded Cuba to prevent any further weapons from entering the island. NATO and Warsaw Pact military forces were placed on full alert. For 13 days the world stood on the brink of nuclear war. Finally, the Soviet Union backed down and agreed to remove the missiles—in exchange for a commitment from the United States not to invade Cuba. Kennedy also indicated privately that he would remove U.S. missiles that had been stationed in Turkey.

The Vietnam War. If the Cuban missile crisis was the most dangerous moment in the Cold War, from an American perspective the Vietnam War was even more damaging internally. American military advisers had been sent to South Vietnam in the 1950s as the French were being forced to withdraw from the country by Vietnamese nationalists. American involvement increased under President Kennedy, and under President Johnson the United States began to commit large numbers of American troops to helping noncommunist South Vietnam defend itself against the communist government of North Vietnam, which was supported by the Soviet Union.

As the war dragged on during the 1960s, however, it soon caused major unrest within the United States. Many antiwar protesters, particularly college students and civil rights supporters, expressed their discontent by staging demonstrations on university campuses. The protesters argued that United States involvement in Vietnam caused needless loss of life. The antiwar protests reached their height in 1968. President Johnson announced that he would not seek re-election, and a violent confrontation broke out between antiwar protesters and the police in the streets of Chicago during the Democratic Party Convention. A shocked nation watched the violence on television. Such scenes did much to undermine the nation's self-confidence.

Canadian Challenges

Active participation in two world wars ended the isolation policy that Canada had maintained for many years. After World War II, Canada became a vigorous supporter of the United Nations and an important member of NATO; loaned billions of dollars to other countries; and welcomed thousands of refugees from Europe.

Economic growth. Canada experienced considerable economic development after World War II. Much of the country remained basically agricultural, producing wheat, corn, and feed grains. Canada's industries also grew after World War II. The large Canadian forest areas provided many wood products. The wood pulp and paper industries expanded. Development of electric power and improvement of transportation stimulated the mining of iron, coal, and uranium, and greater production of oil and gas. Aircraft, electrical, and automobile industries developed in the provinces of Quebec and Ontario. The United States furnished much of the capital for this industrial development.

Relations with the United States. For more than a century, Canada has had a close relationship with the United States. During and after World War II this relationship strengthened, especially with regard to military and economic affairs.

Canadian national defense relied heavily on the United States. Together the two nations built a line of radar installations, called the Distant Early Warning **(DEW) Line**, which extended along the Arctic Circle, to furnish early warnings of air attacks. Together they also established the North American Air Defense Command.

In 1959 the close economic cooperation between Canada and the United States produced the **St. Lawrence Seaway**, a 2,300-mile waterway linking the Great Lakes with the Atlantic Ocean. The seaway enables oceangoing ships to reach every port on the Great Lakes. Another important cooperative venture was the development of the Columbia River basin. This project doubled the water-storage capacity of the Pacific Northwest.

The rise of separatism in Quebec. While Canada prospered in most respects after the war, by the 1960s a new challenge had appeared internally. This new challenge was the growing desire of many French-speaking Canadians, particularly those living in the province of Quebec, to separate from the rest of Canada. Feelings of French nationalism, however, had begun to develop in Canada even before World War II.

Through various lakes, canals, and locks, the St. Lawrence Seaway links the Great Lakes to the Atlantic Ocean.

In the 1960s the desire for separation grew even more intense. In 1967 this movement was fueled by French president Charles de Gaulle. During a visit to Quebec he ended a speech with the slogan of the French nationalists in the province, "Vive le Québec Libre!" which means "Long Live Free Quebec!". By 1970, a new political party, the Parti Quebecois, was able to gain 24 percent of the popular vote in the province of Quebec. Their platform was a call for secession from the Canadian Confederation. Although this was not enough to give them much power, it did serve as an indication that there would be future challenges to Canadian unity by many of its French-speaking citizens.

Section 4 Review

1. **Define** Great Society, recessions, civil rights, NAACP, DEW Line, St. Lawrence Seaway
2. **Identify** Joseph McCarthy, Martin Luther King Jr., Fidel Castro
3. **Understanding Ideas** Describe the domestic policy concerns of the United States from 1945 to 1968.
4. **Explaining Ideas** What foreign-policy issues confronted the United States after World War II?
5. **Interpreting Ideas** What kinds of changes took place in Canada in the postwar years?

Chapter 28 Review

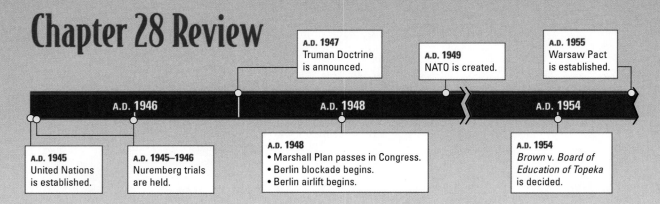

A.D. 1947
Truman Doctrine is announced.

A.D. 1949
NATO is created.

A.D. 1955
Warsaw Pact is established.

A.D. 1946

A.D. 1948

A.D. 1954

A.D. 1945
United Nations is established.

A.D. 1945–1946
Nuremberg trials are held.

A.D. 1948
• Marshall Plan passes in Congress.
• Berlin blockade begins.
• Berlin airlift begins.

A.D. 1954
Brown v. *Board of Education of Topeka* is decided.

Chapter Summary

The following list contains the key concepts you have learned about Europe, the United States, and Canada from 1945 to 1968.

1. After World War II, disagreements between the Soviet Union and the United States resulted in the Cold War. Germany was divided into four zones and occupied by France, Great Britain, the United States, and the Soviet Union. Many Nazi leaders were brought to trial.

2. Following World War II, the United Nations (UN) was established to help maintain world peace. The UN also assumed an important humanitarian role in the promotion of human rights and world health.

3. The creation of satellite nations and establishment of Cominform convinced the West that the Soviet Union planned to spread communism throughout the world. The Truman Doctrine and the Marshall Plan were attempts by the United States to contain communism.

4. The Soviet threat in Europe resulted in the formation of the North American Treaty Organization, which most Western European nations joined. The Soviet Union responded with the Warsaw Pact.

5. West Germany recovered quickly after the war. Great Britain faced difficult economic conditions while maintaining political stability. France experienced economic prosperity despite the political uncertainties of the postwar period.

6. A major source of the growing wealth of Western Europe was the European Economic Community, which was founded in 1957. The organization attempted to eliminate trade barriers that existed between nations.

7. The Communist bloc nations experienced discontent throughout the 1950s and 1960s. In 1956 the Hungarians unsuccessfully revolted, and Czechoslovakia attempted reforms in 1968.

8. When the Soviets placed nuclear missiles in Cuba, the United States blockaded the island. The crisis was the most dangerous moment in the Cold War.

9. The civil rights movement and opposition to the war in Vietnam confronted the United States during the Johnson administration.

10. Canada enjoyed an economic boom after 1945, but it also experienced a separatist movement. Relations with the United States remained close.

Reviewing Important Terms

On a separate sheet of paper, supply the term that correctly completes each statement.

1. The _____ _____ was waged by political and economic means rather than with weapons.

2. The United States policy that attempted to restrict the spread of communism during the postwar era was called _____.

3. A state in which the government undertakes primary responsibility for the social welfare of its citizens is called a(n) _____ _____.

4. A period of slowdown in economic activity is called a(n) _____.

5. _____ was a post-World War II policy of removing Nazis from power in Germany.

Developing Critical Thinking Skills

1. **Explaining Ideas (a)** Why did the Cold War develop?

(b) How did it affect the postwar foreign policies of the major world powers?

2. **Summarizing Ideas** What postwar developments increased tensions between the Soviet Union and Western nations?

3. **Comparing Ideas** Compare the UN General Assembly with the UN Security Council.

4. **Interpreting Ideas** How were the Marshall Plan and the Truman Doctrine designed in an effort to carry out the containment policy?

5. **Organizing Ideas** What were the purposes of the alliance systems set up by the Western nations and by the Communist bloc after 1945?

6. **Understanding Ideas** Why did the countries of Western Europe establish the Common Market?

7. **Synthesizing Ideas** How did the work of civil rights leaders such as Dr. Martin Luther King Jr. lead to changes in United States policy toward equal rights for all citizens?

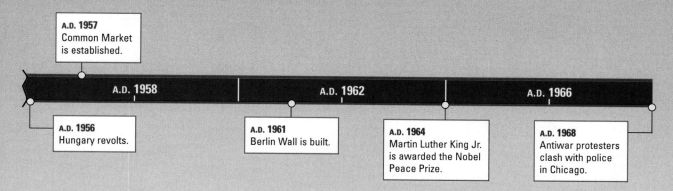

A.D. 1957
Common Market is established.

A.D. 1958

A.D. 1962

A.D. 1966

A.D. 1956
Hungary revolts.

A.D. 1961
Berlin Wall is built.

A.D. 1964
Martin Luther King Jr. is awarded the Nobel Peace Prize.

A.D. 1968
Antiwar protesters clash with police in Chicago.

Relating Geography to History

Turn to the map on page 761. **(a)** Which European nations belonged to NATO? **(b)** Which nations belonged to the Warsaw Pact? **(c)** Which nations remained neutral? **(d)** How was this system of alliances different from the one in operation during the war? **(e)** What accounts for this change?

Relating Past to Present

1. The policies of containment and economic aid were used after World War II to stem the spread of communism. **(a)** What policies has the United States used in recent years to contain communism? **(b)** Did these policies prove successful? **(c)** Are containment policies necessary today? Explain your answer.
2. In the 1950s several Eastern bloc nations tried to free themselves from Soviet control, with little success. In 1989, however, these same nations broke away from the Soviet Union with relative ease. What changes in the communist world made this possible?
3. Cooperation between the United States and Canada has continued since 1945. Using information in the textbook and recent articles in the news, identify some of the ways in which Canada and the United States work together today. What actions might be taken to strengthen our ties with Canada?

Applying History Study Skills

Before completing this activity, review Building History Study Skills on page 758.

On March 12, 1947, President Truman addressed the Congress of the United States with a justification for containment as a basis for American foreign policy. Read the following excerpt from his speech, and then answer the questions to help you identify his argument.

"At the present moment in world history nearly every nation must choose between alternative ways of life. The choice is too often not a free one.

One way of life is based upon the will of the majority, and is distinguished by free institutions, representative government, free elections . . . and freedom from political oppression.

The second way of life is based upon the will of a minority forcibly imposed upon the majority. It relies upon terror and oppression, a controlled press . . . and the suppression of personal freedoms.

I believe that it must be the policy of the United States to support free peoples who are resisting attempted subjugation. . . . I believe that our help should be primarily through economic and financial aid which is essential to economic stability and orderly political processes."

1. How is containment illustrated in this excerpt from President Truman's speech?
2. What reasons does President Truman use to support his main point?
3. How does the president feel about the Soviet Union? Does he give examples to support his position?
4. How would you define the Truman Doctrine?

internet connect

Search the Internet through the HRW Web site for more information about the McCarthy era and its effects on the United States. If possible, locate some first-person accounts of people whose reputations were damaged during this time. Discuss your findings in class.

 GO TO: go.hrw.com
KEYWORD: SCØ
McCarthyism

Building Your Portfolio

1. **Presenting an Oral Report** After Franklin Roosevelt's death, his widow, Eleanor Roosevelt, became the United States ambassador to the United Nations in New York City. Using the *Dictionary of American Biography* or the most recent edition of *Notable American Women,* research Eleanor Roosevelt's public life, beginning with her years as first lady and ending with her career as a diplomat of the United States. Present your findings to the class.
2. **Writing a Report** The position of secretary-general of the United Nations is a demanding and sometimes controversial job. Prepare a written report to find out more about each of the following secretaries-general: Trygve Lie, Dag Hammarskjöld, U Thant, Javier Pérez de Cuéllar, and Boutros Boutros-Ghali.

CHAPTER 29

Asia Since 1945

TIME

A.D. **1945–the present**

A.D. **1945–the present**

3.7 million B.C. | 4000 B.C. | A.D. 2100

PLACE

Asia

Asia

ARCTIC OCEAN

NORTH AMERICA

EUROPE

ASIA

PACIFIC OCEAN

AFRICA

Equator

AUSTRALIA

PACIFIC OCEAN

SOUTH AMERICA

ATLANTIC OCEAN

INDIAN OCEAN

ANTARCTICA

Ho Chi Minh City

CHAPTER FOCUS

Significance

The years after World War II saw major political, economic, and social changes in Asia. The movements for self-rule in Asia that had begun decades earlier came to fulfillment in the postwar period. However, this transition from domination to independence was not always achieved peacefully. A number of newly independent Asian nations became the focus of armed conflicts arising out of the Cold War.

As the 1900s drew to a close, other Asian nations attempted to imitate Japan's "economic miracle." In time, nearly all of these nations began to take an independent, active role in world economic and political affairs.

Terms to Define

nonalignment	Geneva Accords
mixed economy	domino theory
Awami League	Tet Offensive
Great Leap Forward	Paris Peace Accords
Cultural Revolution	ASEAN
"MacArthur Constitution"	"Four Tigers"
Diet	

People to Identify

Jawaharlal Nehru	Toshiki Kaifu
Lord Louis Mountbatten	Ferdinand Marcos
Indira Gandhi	Sukarno
Benazir Bhutto	Viet Minh
Nawaz Sharif	Ho Chi Minh
Mao Zedong	Viet Cong
Deng Xiaoping	Norodom Sihanouk
Syngman Rhee	Khmer Rouge
Park Chung Hee	Pol Pot

Places to Locate

Pakistan	38th parallel
Kashmir	Seoul
Tibet	Phnom Penh
Bangladesh	Hanoi
Taiwan	

Chapter Theme Questions

- **War and Diplomacy** How might conflicting religions and cultures affect the growth of nations?
- **Politics and Law** What problems might nations possibly face as they make the transition from colonial possession to independent statehood?
- **Economic Organization** What factors might aid, and what factors might hinder, the economic development of a country?

The hopes and aspirations of all peoples who seek freedom from colonial rulers were eloquently summed up by Jawaharlal Nehru in a speech announcing Indian independence that he rose to give as midnight approached on August 14, 1947:

"Long years ago we made a tryst [appointment] with destiny, and now the time comes when we shall redeem our pledge, not wholly or in full measure, but very substantially. At the stroke of the midnight hour, when the world sleeps, India will awake to life and freedom. A moment comes, which comes but rarely in history, when we step out from the old to the new, when an age ends, and when the soul of the nation, long suppressed, finds utterance. . . .

At the dawn of history India started on her unending quest, and trackless centuries are filled with her striving and the grandeur of her success and her failures. Through good and ill fortune alike she has never lost sight of that quest or forgotten the ideals which gave her strength. We end today a period of ill fortune and India discovers herself again. The achievement we celebrate today is but a step, an opening of opportunity, to the greater triumphs and achievements that await us."

Within 20 years of this speech made by Nehru, almost every Asian nation had, like India, redeemed the pledge of self-determination.

South Asia After Empire

Focus Questions

- How did differences between Hindus and Muslims lead to a divided India?
- What problems did India face after achieving its independence?
- How did Pakistan and Bangladesh develop after the partition of the Indian subcontinent?

In the years following World War II, the peoples of South Asia moved from colonial rule to independence.

The transition was not an easy one, however. As India and Pakistan emerged from the British Empire to become independent nations, violent clashes between Muslims and Hindus caused turmoil and bloodshed in the region.

The End of British Rule

A movement for independence from Great Britain had developed in India after World War I. Indian nationalists continued to make strong demands for independence throughout World War II. Because of the British government's reluctance to give in to these demands, Indians gave Britain only limited support in the war effort. Furthermore, the Indian National Congress resented the fact that Great Britain had declared India at war with Germany without even consulting with the Congress. Indeed, the government's unilateral action caused the Congress's angry ministers to resign in October 1939 and call for immediate self-government. Subsequent resistance to Great Britain's war effort by leaders of the Congress and others opposed to British rule led to arrest and imprisonment for many Indians.

Wartime developments. With Japan entering the war on the side of Germany, India took on greater importance as an Allied base. Pressure on Britain to reach a settlement with India increased. In March 1942, Britain sent Sir Stafford Cripps on a mission to negotiate terms for India's independence once the war ended. However, the Indian National Congress rejected the government's proposal, as did the Muslim League. Nationalist leader Mohandas Gandhi angrily asked Cripps why he had even come if the British had nothing more to offer.

Soon after the Cripps mission failed, Gandhi launched the "Quit India" movement. Gandhi insisted that Britain's complete separation from India was the only answer to their differences, and he demanded that the British leave India. With Japan posing a growing threat in Southeast Asia, the British government was in no mood for further internal resistance. Britain treated the Quit India campaign as a rebellion and arrested some 60,000 Congress supporters by the end of the year.

While the Indian National Congress continued to resist the British, the Muslim League was more willing to support the war effort. Led by Muhammad 'Ali Jinnah, the Muslim League demanded that a separate Muslim state be formed. The creation of an independent country would ensure that the interests of the Muslim minority would not be lost in a nation with a Hindu majority. As the Indian National Congress pressed its demand that Britain "Quit India", the Muslim League called on Britain to "Divide and Quit."

Despite repeated attempts, talks between Gandhi and Jinnah failed to resolve long-standing differences between Hindus and Muslims. Even after World War II ended, when Great Britain was ready to grant India independence, representatives of the Indian National Congress and the Muslim League could not reach an agreement.

In 1946, Britain's desire to transfer its power to a single Indian administration led to the proposal of a new plan. Under this plan, India would be divided into a federation of provinces. The federation would have a central government, but Muslims would retain control of those provinces in which they formed a majority. This plan also failed, however, when the Indian National Congress and the Muslim League once again could not agree on terms.

After this collapse in negotiations, violence erupted between Muslims and Hindus. Bloody riots first broke out in Calcutta and then spread throughout India. Thousands were killed and injured.

The partition of India. In March 1947, Lord Louis Mountbatten took over as British viceroy. India had by now become such a burden to Britain that the British government had decided to transfer its power to Indian authority no later than June 1948. However, India's raging civil war convinced Mountbatten that even a year was too long to wait to resolve the bloody and dangerous situation. Despite Gandhi's urging to keep India unified, Mountbatten decided to divide India and to do it quickly. The subsequent partitioning of the Indian subcontinent took place along religious lines. (See map on opposite page.)

The process of partition caused tremendous upheaval and resulted in an explosion of violence and bloodshed. As the day of independence approached, millions of Hindus, Muslims, and Sikhs rushed to cross the borders into the newly created nations. Violent clashes left as many as 1 million people dead.

The stroke of midnight on August 15, 1947, marked the official birth of the two nations of India and Pakistan. Their first task involved the integration of the princely states. Over the next two years, these states decided which nation to join. Only Kashmir, which had a Hindu ruler and a predominantly Muslim population, at first joined neither.

Less than six months after the partitioning of India, Mohandas Gandhi, one of the key figures in India's years of struggle for independence, was assassinated.

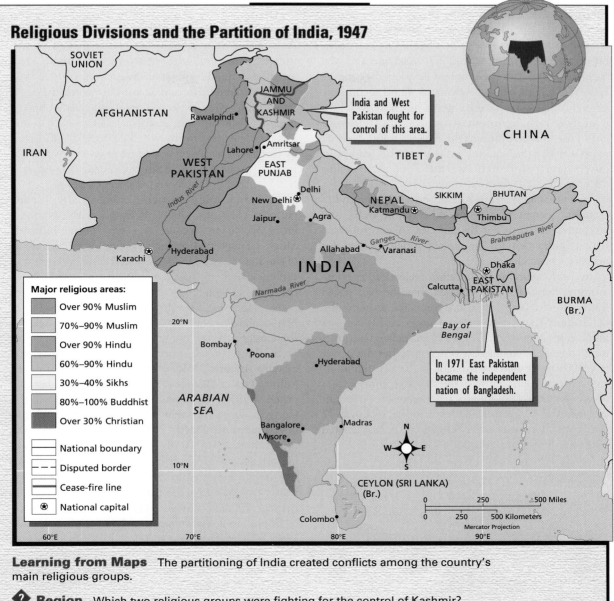

Religious Divisions and the Partition of India, 1947

India and West Pakistan fought for control of this area.

In 1971 East Pakistan became the independent nation of Bangladesh.

Major religious areas:
- Over 90% Muslim
- 70%–90% Muslim
- Over 90% Hindu
- 60%–90% Hindu
- 30%–40% Sikhs
- 80%–100% Buddhist
- Over 30% Christian
- National boundary
- Disputed border
- Cease-fire line
- ⊛ National capital

0 250 500 Miles
0 250 500 Kilometers
Mercator Projection

Learning from Maps The partitioning of India created conflicts among the country's main religious groups.

? Region Which two religious groups were fighting for the control of Kashmir?

The assassin was a Hindu fanatic who resented Gandhi for his tolerant attitude toward Muslims.

Independent India

In 1950 India's new constitution went into effect. It established the Indian government as a federal republic with an elected president and parliament. Although the president is the official head of state, the prime minister and cabinet wield the power.

Government leaders and policies. Jawaharlal Nehru served as India's first prime minister until his death in 1964. Unlike Gandhi, who wanted independent India to return to its traditional way of life, Nehru emphasized modernization.

As prime minister, Nehru had several goals. For one thing, he wanted to unify India by overcoming the dividing forces of religion, language, caste, and regional interests. Having seen religious passions stirred by partition, he wanted India's government to be free of religious interference. He also hoped to strengthen democracy in India. Regarding the economy, Nehru was influenced by Marxism and the socialist model. The government developed a series of Five-Year Plans in an effort to build economic strength. Finally, in foreign affairs he chose to follow a policy of **nonalignment**, refusing to ally India with either the United States or the Soviet Union. Nehru's views on this last matter influenced the leaders of other developing nations, many of whom also adopted a policy of nonalignment.

Two years after Nehru's death, his daughter, Indira Gandhi, became the prime minister of India and attempted to carry out his policies. A controversial figure, Indira Gandhi dominated Indian politics for nearly two decades.

In 1971, after Indira Gandhi's reelection as prime minister, her opponents charged that she had rigged the voting. In 1975, when the courts found her guilty of election fraud, opposition leaders called for her immediate resignation. Gandhi then declared a constitutional state of emergency, which gave her the power to arrest anyone who she thought might threaten internal security. During the state of emergency, which lasted two years, Gandhi enacted a number of unpopular laws. Many Indians turned against her, and in 1977 they voted her out of office. However, she was elected prime minister again in 1980.

This photo shows Indira Gandhi, the only child of Jawaharlal Nehru, campaigning to become prime minister of India. She held office from 1966 to 1977 and from 1980 until 1984.

The most pressing problem that Gandhi faced on her return involved a religious minority, the Sikhs. A group of Sikh separatists, in a campaign to win independence for the province of Punjab, had attacked a number of government officials. In 1984 Gandhi ordered the Indian army to storm the separatists' base, the Golden Temple—the Sikhs' holiest place of worship—in Amritsar. Between 500 and 1,000 people died in the attack. The Sikhs, incensed by this act of sacrilege, vowed revenge. A few months later, two of Gandhi's Sikh bodyguards assassinated her. Her son, Rajiv Gandhi, succeeded her.

In 1989 Gandhi's Indian Congress Party lost the national elections, and V. P. Singh of the National Front Coalition became the new prime minister. Singh championed minority rights, especially rights of the lower castes, but widespread caste and religious violence led to his resignation in 1990. Most observers expected voters to return Rajiv Gandhi to power. However, Gandhi was assassinated, and P. V. Narasimha Rao, who succeeded Gandhi as head of the Congress Party, became prime minister.

In the 1996 elections, the Congress Party was heavily defeated, and Rao resigned. More turmoil followed these elections. H. D. Deve Gowda became prime minister of a coalition government, but the Congress Party withdrew its support of this coalition government in March 1997. I. K. Gujral became prime minister in April. Among the key goals that Gujral set for his coalition government was an improved relationship with Pakistan. Still, with nearly two dozen parties competing for power in parliament, India's political future remained uncertain.

Social and economic problems. Indians speak with great pride of the social and cultural diversity of their country. This very diversity, however, has hindered attempts at unification and thus created problems. India's great variety of languages provides but one example of this. The country has 16 major languages and more than 1,000 minor languages and dialects. In newly independent India, government officials from different regions often found that they could not understand one another. (Although Hindi is the official language of India, English often serves as an auxiliary official language.)

By the end of the 1980s, India's economy had made considerable progress. Under Nehru the country had developed a **mixed economy**, in which private companies owned some industries and the government owned the rest. Through a series of Five-Year Plans, the government charted the way in

Overcrowding has been a major problem in Indian cities, such as Madurai, for many years.

which it wanted the economy to grow. These plans proved quite successful. The country's agricultural output increased, and its textile and steel industries experienced considerable growth. Exports of finished manufactured products, such as clothing and bicycles, showed a marked increase.

Despite such progress, problems remained, many of them stemming from India's ever-growing population. In 1950 the population stood at about 360 million. A little over 30 years later, the population had increased to about 684 million. By the mid-1980s, India had 16 percent of the world's population but only 2 percent of the world's land area. The nation's economic growth could not keep pace with the population increase. Consequently, by the late 1980s, annual per capita income averaged below $300, and the unemployment rate had reached 20 percent. Millions of Indians lived in poverty.

In the 1990s, the government made new efforts to deal with the country's economic problems. With the adoption of a more open policy toward foreign investment and trade, India's economic growth accelerated to an annual rate of almost 7 percent. Nevertheless, serious problems remain. The population continues to grow. Indeed, according to current projections, India—with over 950 million people in 1998—will become the most populous country in the world by 2050, surpassing China.

Foreign relations. In world affairs, India tried to cultivate friendships with both the Communist bloc and the West. As a result, it soon assumed a leadership role in the Non-Aligned Movement among African and Asian nations.

However, India's commitment to nonalignment was strained by tensions with China. In 1950 the Chinese occupied Tibet. Tibetans attempted a rebellion, which the Chinese violently put down. For a long time, India had supported the Dalai Lama, Tibet's religious and political leader. After the Chinese invasion, the Dalai Lama and some of his followers fled to India, where they formed a government in exile. India's relations with China became even more strained in the next few years.

During the 1970s India moved away from its nonaligned stance, establishing close ties with the Soviet Union. Then, in the 1980s, India sought to improve relations with the United States. Even so, the country avoided making a complete commitment to either side in the Cold War. In the 1990s, reforms in India's economic policies led the nation to take a more open approach to foreign affairs and to seek a greater role in the global economy.

The Continuing Problem of Kashmir. Partition in 1947 had left India and Pakistan with a difficult problem in the northern state of Kashmir. (See map on page 777.) Kashmir's ruling prince, a Hindu, at first tried to avoid joining either country. However, Pakistan claimed Kashmir because at least three quarters of its people were Muslim. Jawaharlal Nehru, himself a Kashmiri, supported the Hindu prince with Indian troops.

Clashes between Muslims and Hindus in Kashmir soon led to fighting between Indian and Pakistani soldiers. When the fighting began, the prince declared Kashmir part of India. Sporadic fighting between the two countries continued until 1949. At that time, the United Nations established a cease-fire line. At the point of the establishment of the cease-fire line, India occupied two thirds of Kashmir.

In 1957 India officially annexed part of Kashmir. Pakistan protested, and after sporadic fighting, a full-scale war erupted between the two countries in 1965. Eventually the prime ministers of India and Pakistan agreed to withdraw their troops behind the cease-fire line that had been established in 1949 by the United Nations and to negotiate a settlement. However, the issue of Kashmir nationality remained unsettled, and violence occasionally erupted in the region.

In the late 1980s, Muslim Kashmiris began to demand complete separation from India. Blaming Pakistan for orchestrating these demonstrations, the Indian authorities sent troops to the area. In response, Pakistan put its army on war alert. Border clashes and other violence between warring militant groups became increasingly common. Despite the fact that more than 20,000 people had been killed by 1997, fighting went on. Muslim militants persisted in their demands for independence; insurgents battled against counterinsurgents; and Indian and Pakistani forces continued to exchange gunfire. No immediate prospects for peace in Kashmir were in sight.

The Division of Pakistan

The fate of Kashmir was not the only problem in Indian-Pakistani relations. The issue of independence for Bangladesh also brought India and Pakistan into conflict.

When colonial rule ended, Pakistan was divided into two parts—West Pakistan and East Pakistan— separated by a huge wedge of Indian territory some 1,000 miles wide. The divided nation faced problems similar to those that plagued India—a rapidly growing population, widespread poverty and illiteracy, and cultural and linguistic differences. In addition, a lack of natural resources and its peculiar geographic situation hindered Pakistan's economic development.

At first a dominion of the British Commonwealth, Pakistan became a parliamentary republic in 1956. Soon, however, a succession of military leaders took control of the government.

Independence for Bangladesh. In the elections held in 1970, the **Awami League**—a political party dedicated to independence for East Pakistan—won the majority of the East Pakistani seats in the national assembly. The central government refused to accept the election results. Riots erupted in East Pakistan. The new president of Pakistan, General Agha Muhammad Yahya Khan, sent troops to quell the riots and to arrest the leaders of the Awami League. The situation soon developed into a civil war. Ten million East Pakistanis fled to India. During the civil war, India came to the aid of the East Pakistani rebels, first by sending arms to them and then by providing troops. Late in 1971 the Pakistani troops were defeated. East Pakistan then became the new nation of Bangladesh.

Bangladesh and Pakistan today. Both Bangladesh and Pakistan faced major problems after the division. Bangladesh, ravaged by war, also suffered recurrent famines, floods, and devastating tropical storms. The new government proved unequal to the huge task of rebuilding the country, and in the mid-1970s, it was toppled by a military coup.

In elections held in 1991, the conservative Bangladesh National Party (BNP) won a victory over the left-wing Awami League. BNP leader Khalida Zia became Bangladesh's first woman prime minister. In subsequent years, however, Zia faced mounting attack by Awami League-led opponents, who accused her of mismanagement. Zia was finally forced out in 1996, and new elections brought an Awami League government into power, under Prime Minister Sheikh Hasina Wazed. Although disturbances eased, frequent natural disasters, economic instability, and a legacy of political ill will between the Awami League and the BNP made the future of this desperately poor country very uncertain.

Pakistan, too, faced political instability. For the first half of the 1970s, a civilian government led by Zulfikar Ali Bhutto ruled Pakistan. However, General

When Benazir Bhutto was sworn in as the prime minister of Pakistan, she became the first woman to govern a Muslim country.

Mohammed Zia ul-Haq seized control of the government in 1977 and, two years later, had Bhutto executed. Zia imposed martial law, banned political parties, and reformed the legal system so that it followed Islamic teachings more closely.

Zia answered a growing clamor for a return to democratic rule by promising to hold free elections in 1988. Although Zia was killed in an airplane crash, the elections still took place, and Benazir Bhutto, the daughter of Ali Bhutto, emerged as the winner. She became the first woman to serve as head of state of a Muslim nation. However, charges of corruption and misconduct against members of her administration and growing discontent among the military led to Bhutto's ouster in 1990. She was reelected in 1993, but three years later she was soundly defeated by Nawaz Sharif, after more charges of corruption and incompetence. Like his counterpart in India, Prime Minister Sharif sought to improve relations with his neighbor. However, the history of distrust and violence between India and Pakistan continued to make peace an elusive goal. The development of nuclear weapons by both countries has made the stakes of their rivalry even higher.

Section 1 Review

1. **Define** nonalignment, mixed economy, Awami League
2. **Identify** Jawaharlal Nehru, Lord Louis Mountbatten, Indira Gandhi, Benazir Bhutto, Nawaz Sharif
3. **Locate and Explain the Significance** Pakistan, Kashmir, Tibet, Bangladesh
4. **Determining Cause and Effect** How did differences between Hindus and Muslims lead to a divided India?
5. **Classifying Ideas** List the main political, social, and economic problems faced by India in the last two decades.
6. **Synthesizing Ideas** How did Pakistan and Bangladesh develop after the partition of the Indian subcontinent?

The Rise of Communist China and Taiwan

Focus Questions

- How did Mao Zedong's Communist Chinese government try to rebuild China in the years after World War II?
- What changes occurred in China after the death of Mao?
- What occurred at Tiananmen Square, and what were the consequences for China?
- Why was Korea divided, and how have the two Koreas developed since 1953?

During World War II, the Nationalist and communist Chinese agreed to halt their civil war and form a united front against their common enemy, the Japanese. However, even though both did fight against Japan, conflict between Nationalist and communist forces soon resumed, each side hoping to gain an advantage over the other.

The Communists effectively used the war as an opportunity to expand both their political and military influence in China. By the time World War II ended, the Communists had significantly increased the size of their army as well as the territory under their control. In time, the Communists won the upper hand in the civil war, and by 1949 they had driven the Nationalists from power.

In 1949 Chiang Kaishek, the Nationalist leader, fled with his supporters to the island of Taiwan and established a government there. (See map on opposite page.) On the Chinese mainland the Communists, led by Mao Zedong, established the People's Republic of China. The United States government, which had aided the Nationalists, refused to recognize this new communist government on the mainland.

China Under Mao Zedong

The Communists wanted to create a modern, industrialized nation dominated by the Communist Party. To achieve this goal, the Communists took administrative control. By a combination of elections and appointments, they placed Communist Party members in all the key government and military offices. The

China embarked on its first Five-Year Plan for economic growth in 1953.

new constitution gave executive power to the party's Central Committee and its Political Bureau, headed by Mao Zedong. Zhou Enlai became premier and foreign minister and was a spokesman for China in world affairs.

An overwhelming task faced this new communist government. Years of war had devastated China. Farms lay destroyed, and industry and transportation had almost ceased to function. The Chinese people had fared little better than their country. Miserably poor, they had been decimated by epidemics and famines.

The Communists acted to restore order, bring inflation under control, and eliminate various forms of corruption. They also took violent action against their opponents. About 1 million people lost their lives in Communist Party purges.

In 1953 the Communists began the process of rebuilding China by issuing their first Five-Year Plan for economic growth. The Soviet Union provided part of the capital for this plan—which was modeled

Revolution in China, 1945–1949

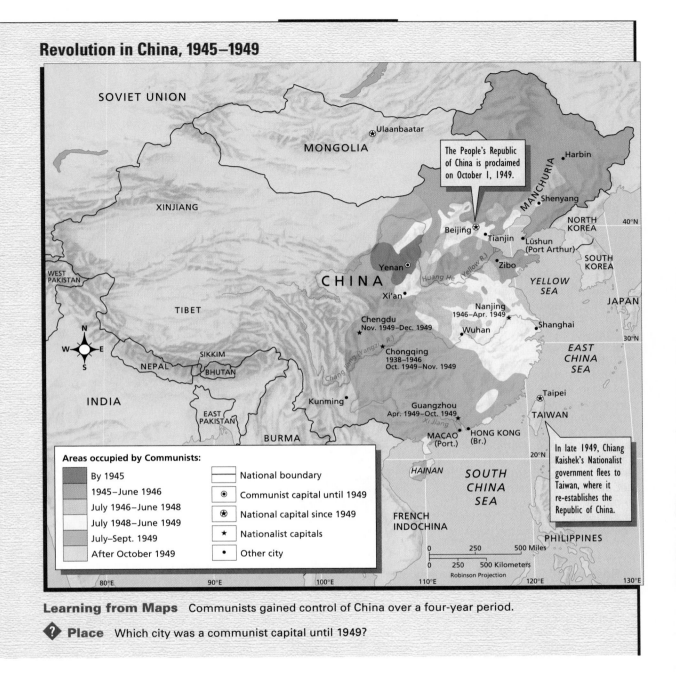

The People's Republic of China is proclaimed on October 1, 1949.

In late 1949, Chiang Kaishek's Nationalist government flees to Taiwan, where it re-establishes the Republic of China.

Areas occupied by Communists:

- By 1945
- 1945–June 1946
- July 1946–June 1948
- July 1948–June 1949
- July–Sept. 1949
- After October 1949

- National boundary
- ⊙ Communist capital until 1949
- ✴ National capital since 1949
- ★ Nationalist capitals
- • Other city

Robinson Projection

Learning from Maps Communists gained control of China over a four-year period.

Place Which city was a communist capital until 1949?

on similar Soviet plans—but most of the financing was Chinese. Although the plan stressed the rapid buildup of heavy industry, it also focused on land reform. The Communists seized farmland from landlords and redistributed it to the peasants. Thousands—some estimates are in the millions—of landlords were killed in the course of this land redistribution program. The peasants organized their newly acquired land into collective farms, while the government operated state farms on much of the land that remained.

Despite periodic droughts and floods, some peasant resistance to collective farming, and inefficient planning by government officials, the first Five-Year Plan was a success. Both agricultural and industrial output increased.

Building History Study Skills

READ
WRITE
INTERPRET
CONNECT
THINK

Reading About History: Identifying Fallacies in Reasoning

In order to prove a point, an author uses logic, or reasoning. Logic is the process of reaching a conclusion based on the available evidence. One way of determining the strength of an argument is to identify fallacies in reasoning. A fallacy is an error in logic.

One type of fallacy in reasoning is to make overgeneralizations, vague or indefinite statements made without supporting evidence. Another example of a fallacy in reasoning would be the stacking of an argument—in other words, carefully choosing only those facts that support one's argument and ignoring others. For example, one might argue for the superiority of the Republican party by pointing out that Republican presidents have negotiated the ends to our wars. While a Republican indeed negotiated the end to both the Korean War and the Vietnam War, Democratic presidents also negotiated the ends to wars. Even if only Republican presidents had negotiated such treaties, this fact alone would not prove one party superior to the other.

How to Identify Fallacies in Reasoning

To identify a fallacy in reasoning, follow these steps.

1. Identify the author's conclusion.
2. Explain the author's reasoning that supports the conclusion.
3. Decide whether the author is making overgeneralizations or stacking the argument.
4. Evaluate the argument. Are the connections valid? Is only one cause identified? Are other causes or issues hidden or ignored? Has a connection between the cause and the effect been proven?

Developing the Skill

Read the following justification of the shooting of landlords from the political writings of Mao Zedong. Can you spot fallacies in Mao's reasoning?

Mao Zedong

"The execution of one such big local bully [landlord] or one member of the evil gentry has its repercussions . . . and is very effective in eradicating any remnant of feudalism. . . . [T]he only effective way of suppressing the reactionaries is to execute at least one or two guilty of the most serious crimes and wrongdoing. . . . When the local bullies and evil gentry were at the height of their power, they killed peasants without batting an eyelid. . . . In view of these atrocities . . . how can one say that the peasant should not now rise and shoot one or two of them . . . ?"

What Mao is seeking to establish is that the shooting of landlords is justified. His main argument is that it is justified because it has a strong effect; in fact, he moves from saying that it has a strong effect to saying that it is the *only* effective means of suppressing reactionaries. Even if it is true that killing has a strong effect, this does not prove that killing is necessary to effect a revolution. He stacks his argument by adding that in the past, landlords shot peasants. Even if landlords did shoot peasants in the past—and he gives no statistical information or proof to support this claim—this does not constitute a justification for such extreme action against a particular landlord now.

Practicing the Skill

Reread the steps in identifying fallacies in reasoning. Then read an editorial in a newspaper and identify any generalizations or fallacies in the editor's reasoning.

To apply this skill, see Applying History Study Skills on page 811.

The Great Leap Forward. Impatient to accelerate progress, Mao's government announced a second Five-Year Plan in 1958. Known as the **Great Leap Forward**, this plan was more ambitious than the first Five-Year Plan. It aimed to speed up economic development while simultaneously developing a completely socialist society.

Under the Great Leap Forward, the Chinese government hoped to increase industrial output to the point where it matched or exceeded that of many Western European countries. To reach this goal, China purchased modern machinery and tried to increase output by running this machinery almost continuously in factories. The government even encouraged the Chinese people to make their own iron and steel in small backyard blast furnaces.

The Great Leap Forward also established huge collective communities, called people's communes, that incorporated agricultural activities and small industries. Life on a commune bore a strong resemblance to life in the military, with dormitories and communal dining halls. Often, children were taken from parents to be raised in separate dormitories. People worked long hours in the fields or factories under strict supervision, and everyone received the same pay, regardless of how much he or she produced.

Many of the changes made under the Great Leap Forward reflected Mao's rejection of individualism. The Communist Party controlled almost every aspect of people's lives on the communes. Furthermore, the Communists stressed loyalty to the Communist Party and to the state, moving away from the Chinese people's traditionally strong ties of family loyalty.

The Great Leap Forward failed dismally. Industrial output decreased, and there were food shortages. In fact, it has been estimated that more than 20 million people starved between 1958 and 1960. The failure of the program also led to disagreements within the Communist Party. Faced with falling productivity and constant criticism from workers and peasants, the government abandoned the Great Leap Forward.

The Cultural Revolution. Since assuming power in 1949, Chinese Communist Party officials have had two basic goals: economic development and creation of a classless society. However, there has often been disagreement within the party on policies to achieve these goals.

In the early 1960s, after the failure of the Great Leap Forward, Mao's prestige within the Communist Party hierarchy was seriously damaged. Liu Shaoqi, Mao's eventual successor as chairman of the People's Republic, implemented his own economic development policies. (Mao had given up the day-to-day administrative tasks of running the country to Liu, but he remained in his position as Communist Party chairman.) For example, although peasants still had to work on the communal farmland, they also had small private plots of land, on which they could raise their own crops. They were also given monetary incentives to raise more crops. Mao was highly critical of these policies.

In 1966 Mao launched the Great Proletarian Cultural Revolution, best known as the **Cultural Revolution**, a violent attempt at social change. Mao aimed to rid China of the "Four Olds"—old customs, old habits, old thoughts, and old culture—replacing them with a new socialist culture. Mao chose China's young people to lead this revolution. These radical high school and college students soon became known as the Red Guards. They went on a rampage throughout China, vandalizing historic buildings, ruining ancient works of art, burning books, and destroying anything they considered part of what they called the "old way." However, they saved their greatest zeal for those people who did not comply fully with Mao's teachings. The Red Guards denounced these people, publicly humiliated them—and sometimes beat, tortured, or even killed them. Those who survived punishment by the Red Guards lost their jobs and their Communist Party membership. Liu himself suffered denunciation and died in jail.

The Cultural Revolution had a disastrous effect on the Chinese economy. Agricultural and industrial production fell dramatically, and the country's economic development plans suffered a severe setback. In 1968 and 1969, Mao and his successor, Lin Biao, tightened the grip of the military over the country, dispersing the Red Guards.

China After Mao

Mao Zedong died in 1976. Upon his death, a struggle began between moderate Communists and a radical group led by Mao's widow, Jiang Qing (jee·AHNG CHING). The moderates wanted to restore order and economic growth, while Jiang Qing's group—later known as the "Gang of Four"—wanted to continue the Cultural Revolution and rid China of all vestiges of the past.

In time, the moderates won control of the major party and government offices, and in an attempt to crush the threat posed by the radicals, they placed the Gang of Four on trial for treason. Found guilty, Jiang

Qing and her three compatriots received life sentences. The moderates then began to reinstate many of those who had been purged from government offices and from the Communist Party during the Cultural Revolution. Over time, the moderates offered some criticism of Mao's radical ideas, denouncing the idea that his policies should invariably be followed.

By the late 1970s, Deng Xiaoping (DUHNG SHOW·PING) had emerged as the leader of the moderates. Although Deng had helped to found the Chinese Communist Party, during the Cultural Revolution his career had been severely damaged. His economic development plan, known as the Four Modernizations, aimed to improve agriculture, industry, science and technology, and national defense. He also fostered greater social openness by encouraging cultural and scientific exchanges with Western countries.

Economic progress and problems. The Four Modernizations plan was intended to improve and update four important areas of the economy. The plan softened the model of state centralized planning, allowing a market economy to develop. In addition, the Four Modernizations encouraged the import of technology from the West.

Through a series of Five-Year Plans, the Chinese government encouraged farmers to increase agricultural production. For example, this merchant sells produce from his own government-allotted farm plot.

Over time, China reformed the areas of banking, finance, city planning, and agriculture. In addition, it encouraged a degree of free enterprise. This new direction in policy led to major economic gains in the mid-1980s and early 1990s. China's economy during this time grew faster than any other major nation's. These gains, however, masked serious economic problems. The rapid growth of the economy fueled inflation, which by 1989 was running at an annual rate of close to 20 percent.

Many Chinese believed that their economic woes were partly the result of government mismanagement and corruption. Their dissatisfaction with the government's handling of the economy helped to create a massive popular movement for political and economic reform in the spring of 1989—a movement that had violent and bloody consequences.

Massacre in Tiananmen Square. In the late 1980s, Deng Xiaoping gave up his government and Communist Party positions, leaving the country in the hands of a younger generation of leaders. The new openness Deng had fostered encouraged many Chinese, especially students, to voice their opinions publicly. Some charged that the government's economic reforms had not brought the promised prosperity, while others called for a "fifth modernization"—democracy. Such views had supporters in high places, including Hu Yaobang, the Communist Party general secretary. Hu was removed from this office in 1987 because of his liberal views.

Hu's views won him a vast following among the reform-minded students of Beijing, however, and when he died in the spring of 1989, thousands took to the streets to mourn his loss. Soon, students were demonstrating daily, calling for the democratic reforms Hu had advocated, such as freedom of the press and free and open elections.

In the spring of 1989, hundreds of thousands of pro-democracy demonstrators occupied Tiananmen Square, Beijing's central gathering place. They demanded an end to corruption in the ruling party, more participation in government, and better conditions at the universities.

Thousands of the students staged a hunger strike. Government orders for them to leave the square were ignored. On May 20 the government imposed martial law. Even so, the demonstrations continued, and large numbers of workers joined the students in Tiananmen Square.

Fearing for the survival of their regime, Chinese leaders ordered the army to use any means necessary

A lone man stands before a line of tanks as Chinese troops move to end student demonstrations in Tiananmen Square on June 3 and 4, 1989.

to end the demonstrations. On June 3 and 4, government troops began to move toward Tiananmen Square, shooting at anyone they saw on the streets. The following morning, soldiers—not students—occupied the square. China's democracy movement had been crushed under the tracks of the army's tanks.

After the crackdown. The exact toll of this brutal suppression remains uncertain, but it is estimated that after several days, up to 500 people were dead and another 3,000 wounded. In addition, thousands of suspected "counterrevolutionaries" were rounded up throughout China. Some were promptly executed, but many remained in jail awaiting trial. Most were eventually sentenced to long prison terms.

World reaction was immediate and stern. The United States, Japan, and the European Community (the European Union since 1993) imposed economic sanctions and demanded that the Chinese government end the crackdown. In response, Chinese officials protested what they called interference in China's internal affairs. Although they eventually lifted martial law, Communist Party leaders maintained a tight hold on Chinese society.

Economic consequences. Stunned by the communist regime's actions, most Western nations and international aid agencies suspended or restricted China's loans. Foreign private investors, too, drastically cut back on their financial activities in China. Tourism, which had become a major source of income

for China, dwindled to almost nothing. With most of its sources of capital now cut off, the already fragile Chinese economy began to founder.

In response, the Chinese government took steps to transform China into a market economy while keeping a communist system. Over time, the government has alternately made greater moves toward market economy reforms and advocated a return to more traditional communist economic policies, including central control.

Despite the fact that many of China's economic and social problems remained unresolved, China's economy grew rapidly in the 1990s. Moreover, the government was able to cut the inflation rate from between 30 and 20 percent in the 1980s to just over 10 percent in 1995, and then to just 7 percent in 1996. Still, unemployment exceeded 30 percent in some cities, labor unrest was widespread, and some 65 million Chinese people lived in poverty.

Jiang Zemin, chosen by Deng Xiaoping as his successor in 1989, became China's president in 1993. In 1997, Jiang proposed a radical new plan to cope with China's persistent socioeconomic problems. Jiang's strategy called for the government to relinquish control of thousands of unprofitable state-owned enterprises. These firms have been experimenting with ways to increase profits, but they have so far been only partially successful in orienting themselves to a market economy.

Foreign Relations Since 1949

While Mao Zedong's government endeavored to reorganize the newly established People's Republic of China, the Chinese Communists were also engaged in worldwide efforts toward an international socialist revolution. In the early 1950s, the Soviet Union and the People's Republic of China were allies, united by political ideology and common economic interests. However, the two nations soon diverged.

Soviet leaders believed that world communism could be achieved through scientific and economic successes rather than through military conquests. Therefore, they felt that they could have "peaceful coexistence" with the West. Chinese leaders, on the other hand, claimed that communist nations had an obligation to support "national wars of liberation." They also argued that nations could never live in peaceful coexistence while capitalism existed. The Chinese insisted that by rejecting revolution as the means of social change, the Soviets had abandoned true Marxism. The Chinese also doubted that the Soviet model of economic development, which stressed heavy industry, would work in China, with its large farming population.

Changing relations. At first the Chinese and the Soviets confined their differences to bitter public speeches as they struggled for leadership in the Communist bloc and in the developing regions of the world. However, during the 1960s both countries began to station troops along their common border. As a result, a number of clashes occurred.

These border skirmishes helped bring about a change in Chinese foreign policy. In the past, Mao Zedong and his advisers had made foreign policy decisions based on which nation they believed posed the greatest threat to China's security. For 20 years no one doubted that that nation was the United States. As Chinese-Soviet relations worsened, however, China became more willing to come to terms with the United States.

The first major sign of change came in 1972, when President Richard Nixon visited China. Soon after, the two nations began to permit the exchange of sports teams, journalists, educators, artists, and business leaders. Finally, in 1979, the United States gave full diplomatic recognition to the People's Republic of China. At about the same time, the United States withdrew its recognition of the Nationalist Chinese government in Taiwan.

Throughout the 1980s China continued to improve its relations with the West. It signed financial aid, technical assistance, and trade agreements with the United States and other Western countries. Further, Chinese leaders negotiated for the return in 1997 of neighboring Hong Kong, which had been a British colony since the 1840s. Over time, Chinese-Soviet relations began to thaw, and Soviet leaders pulled their troops back from the border. Following the dissolution of the Soviet Union, China sought to develop relations with the former Soviet Central Asian republics.

After Tiananmen. Events in Tiananmen Square dramatically changed China's foreign relations. Most Western nations reconsidered their financial and political ties with China. They insisted that they would continue normal relations with China only if the government ended suppression of Chinese citizens' civil and human rights. To bolster their country's tarnished international image, China's leaders turned to the Third World. They forged links with developing countries in Asia and throughout the world. They even developed relations with countries, such as South Korea, that China did not officially recognize.

By 1992, China had largely mended its damaged relationships with most foreign nations except for the United States. By the mid-1990s, however, the two countries enjoyed improved relations. In 1997, President Jiang came to the United States for talks with President Clinton, although China's refusal to meet international standards in regard to human rights continued to cast a shadow over U.S.-Chinese relations.

Korea

Much of the tension between the People's Republic of China and the United States during the 1950s and 1960s grew out of events that took place in Korea after World War II. Agreements made at the end of the war divided Korea at the 38th parallel. The Soviet Union occupied Korea north of this line, while the United States moved troops into the southern part of Korea. The two occupying powers agreed that elections should be held to form a government that

What If?

China and the United States
What if China had not been in conflict with the Soviet Union? Would relations between the United States and China have been different?

The Transfer of Hong Kong

At exactly midnight on June 30, 1997, the Union Jack, Britain's national flag, was lowered for the last time over the territory of Hong Kong. In its place, the red-and-gold flag of China was raised. After 156 years of British control, Hong Kong returned to Chinese rule. For Chinese people around the world, it was a time of great national pride.

For many citizens of Hong Kong, however, the transfer was a time of anxiety. Some were worried that Communist China would try to limit Hong Kong's freedoms, such as freedom of the press or freedom of religion. Others were afraid that Hong Kong's economy, which had been one of the strongest in the region, would falter.

Despite the fears, daily life in Hong Kong remained relatively unchanged for the first several months after the handover. The new government did not interfere with religious freedom or freedom of the press. On the other hand, since the transfer, China has made changes in the Hong Kong legislature that many residents say reduce participation and allow Hong Kong lawmakers less power.

In addition, the widespread problems with Asian economies that occurred at the end of 1997 have affected Hong Kong along with other Asian countries. The effects of this and of decreased tourism—an important industry in Hong Kong—remain to be seen.

would rule the entire country. However, in 1947 the Soviet Union prevented the United Nations commission that was sent to supervise these elections from entering the north.

The Korean War. Elections held in the south resulted in the creation of the Republic of Korea, known as South Korea, with Syngman Rhee as its president and the city of Seoul (SOHL) as its capital. At the same time, the Democratic People's Republic, or North Korea, led by Kim Il Sung, was created in the north. The United Nations recognized South Korea as the legal government, and the Soviet Union recognized only North Korea.

In June 1950 the North Korean army invaded South Korea, quickly taking Seoul. The United Nations Security Council, meeting in emergency session, declared the invasion an unwarranted aggression. It called on UN members to furnish troops and supplies to resist the invasion. (See map on next page.)

Most of the UN troops, as well as their commander, General Douglas MacArthur, came from the United States. In September 1950, MacArthur launched an attack at Inchon, on the coast near Seoul. The North Koreans fell back behind their border, with the UN forces in hot pursuit. As the UN troops approached the Yalu River, the border between Korea and China, several hundred thousand Chinese soldiers joined those of North Korea. This combined force drove MacArthur and his army south of the 38th parallel.

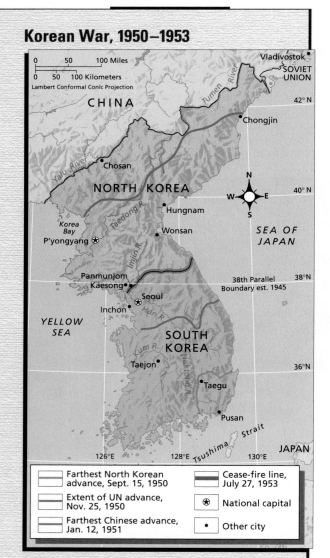

Korean War, 1950–1953

Legend:
- Farthest North Korean advance, Sept. 15, 1950
- Extent of UN advance, Nov. 25, 1950
- Farthest Chinese advance, Jan. 12, 1951
- Cease-fire line, July 27, 1953
- ⊛ National capital
- • Other city

Learning from Maps The Korean War began in June 1950, when North Korea invaded South Korea.

? Location Along which degree of latitude was a cease-fire line established?

A controversy then arose over MacArthur's desire to bomb China's bases in Manchuria and to blockade the Chinese coast. President Harry Truman and the UN General Assembly opposed these actions, fearing that they might lead to a third world war. When MacArthur continued to publicly urge bombing attacks on China, Truman removed him from his post.

Under MacArthur's successor, General Matthew B. Ridgway, the UN forces pushed the Chinese and North Koreans back across the 38th parallel. In July 1951, with the situation at a stalemate, talks to end the hostilities began. After two years of negotiations, the two sides signed an armistice in July 1953 at Panmunjom. It fixed the boundary line between the two Koreas near the 38th parallel. It also established a demilitarized zone of 1.25 miles on either side of the boundary. The armistice also called for a political conference to be held within three months. This conference never took place, however, and no peace treaty was ever signed.

Postwar South Korea. Despite South Korea's small size, various antagonisms divided the country. These conflicts—between provinces, between Buddhists and Christians, between rural and urban people—had existed for years. Despite their differences, however, South Koreans were united in their fear of North Korea. After 1953, President Syngman Rhee used this fear to justify moves that would increase his power and curb criticism of his policies. Therefore, although it had been established as a democracy in 1948, South Korea virtually became a dictatorship.

Violent protests followed Rhee's election to a fourth term as president in 1960, and he resigned. In 1961, army officers led by General Park Chung Hee staged a coup. For the next 18 years, Park ruled with an iron fist, imposing strict censorship on the press and using a powerful secret police force to suppress opposition.

However, President Park also used his power to promote economic development. South Korea's economy expanded very rapidly under his leadership. His government developed industry and increased foreign trade. Although Park's program gave South Korea one of the fastest-growing economies in the world, it was undemocratic and gave South Koreans little political freedom.

Park was assassinated in 1979 by a member of his own Korean Central Intelligence Agency. Almost immediately, a military strongman, Chun Doo Hwan, took control. Chun ruled as an authoritarian, but he continued to support the nation's economic growth. By 1987, however, demonstrations against Chun's govern-

General Douglas MacArthur was commander of the UN forces at the beginning of the Korean War; however, President Truman removed him from his post after MacArthur expressed a desire to bomb Chinese bases in Manchuria.

ment resulted in his resignation. Roh Tae Woo, Chun's handpicked successor, won the election that followed.

Roh promised democratic reforms, some of which he delivered. A new constitution was drafted, allowing the direct election of the president by popular vote. In foreign affairs, Roh promoted contacts with the Soviet Union (later Russia) and China. In 1991 he obtained South Korea's admission to the United Nations and worked to reduce tensions with North Korea. However, both Roh and former president Chun Doo Hwan were tried and convicted in 1996 for having plotted the 1979 government coup through which Chun had come to power. Chun was sentenced to death, and Roh was sentenced to more than 20 years in prison. In sparing him from a death sentence, the court took into account Roh's democratic reforms. These reforms made it possible for Kim Young Sam to succeed Roh as South Korea's next president.

The two Koreas. One of the most notable changes made by Roh's administration was an effort to develop relations with the communist world and to open a dialogue on reunification with North Korea. The idea of reconciliation between North and South Korea gained momentum after the changes in Eastern Europe and the reunification of East and West Germany. (See Chapter 32.) In 1991 the two Koreas signed a pact of reconciliation and nonaggression. However, concern about North Korea's capacity to produce nuclear weapons remained a troubling point.

North Korea's internal problems contributed to continuing unstable relations between North and South Korea. North Korea's centralized, state-owned economy was unable to provide enough food to feed its people. Worsening food shortages plagued the nation so much that many peasants were forced to eat the leaves and bark of trees. The United States and other nations sent millions of dollars in food aid to North Korea. Nevertheless, concerns grew in the mid-1990s that North Korea's famine might possibly cause the government to launch a desperate attack on South Korea. Even though North Korea finally agreed in June 1997 to attend peace talks, the possibility of armed conflict on the Korean peninsula continued to be a cause for great international concern.

Supporters of Roh Tae Woo gathered in Seoul for a campaign rally. He was elected to a five-year term as president of South Korea on February 25, 1988.

The United States had given aid to Chiang Kaishek for many years and had maintained army and navy bases on Taiwan. Agreements reached during President Nixon's visit to the People's Republic, however, led to the renewal of diplomatic ties between the United States and the People's Republic of China. Nevertheless, the United States continued to maintain its social and economic ties with Taiwan. Although it ended diplomatic and military ties, the United States asserted that it would continue to sell defensive arms to Taiwan.

Diplomatic isolation did not prevent Taiwan from developing into a leading economic power in Asia. Even though it had few natural resources, Taiwan developed into one of the world's major producers of manufactured goods. Cheap but skilled labor and efficient management made these goods highly competitive in terms of price and quality. Thus Taiwan soon became a leading exporter, with a large percentage of those exports going to the United States. Over time, the government introduced measures to diversify trade and make the economy less dependent on the export of manufactured goods. Taiwan continued to prosper in the 1990s, achieving one of Asia's highest gross national products.

Moving to democracy. In the political sphere, fundamental changes took place during the 1980s. For the first time, a native Taiwanese held the presidency and the leadership of the Guomindang. Furthermore, Taiwan's leaders encouraged the formation of opposition political parties, promising that future elections would be completely open. In 1989, for the first time, parties other than the Guomindang were able to participate in an election.

Significant political changes continued in the 1990s. Pressure increased for democratic reforms that had been promised in the mid-1980s but were not yet in operation. Finally, in 1996, Taiwan held its first direct presidential election. Incumbent president Lee Teng-hui, the Guomindang candidate, won the election with a landslide victory.

Taiwan and China. Talk of reuniting China and Taiwan has led to little real progress. Although Taiwan has never formally proclaimed its independence, the nation has been self-governing since 1949. In the 1990s the movement for official independence drew increasing support from Taiwan's people. However, while Taiwan demanded to be recognized as China's equal, China insisted that Taiwan was a "renegade province" and warned that a declaration of independence could provoke war. Indeed, in 1995 and 1996, China carried out military exercises and

In February of 1998, former dissident Kim Dae-jung was sworn in as president of South Korea. Once imprisoned and under a death sentence for leading the fight against South Korea's dictatorship, Kim has been described as "Asia's Mandela." He has placed great importance on reviving South Korea's economy and has stated that democracy will go hand in hand with economic growth.

The Nationalists in Taiwan

After the Communists took control of China in 1949, the Chinese Nationalists established themselves on the island of Taiwan, about 100 miles from the Chinese mainland. Their government, called the Republic of China, appeared to be democratic. In reality, however, it operated more like a one-party system, with Chiang Kaishek and other Guomindang (Chinese Nationalist Party) officials holding all the power. Nevertheless, the Republic of China's free enterprise system boosted productivity, and the people enjoyed a relatively high standard of living.

The Republic of China, or Nationalist China, occupied China's permanent seat on the United Nations Security Council until 1971. In that year, the UN expelled the Nationalists and admitted the People's Republic.

Since World War II, Taiwan has become a leading nation in the shipbuilding industry.

missile launches off the coast of Taiwan in an attempt at intimidation. The United States sent aircraft carriers to the area in a show of support for Taiwan.

Section 2 Review

1. **Define** Great Leap Forward, Cultural Revolution
2. **Identify** Mao Zedong, Deng Xiaoping, Syngman Rhee, Park Chung Hee
3. **Locate and Explain the Significance** Taiwan, 38th parallel, Seoul
4. **Understanding Ideas** What methods did the Chinese Communists use to rebuild China after World War II?
5. **Contrasting Ideas** Contrast life in China under Mao with life after his death.
6. **Analyzing Ideas** How did the events that occurred in Tiananmen Square affect China's foreign relations?
7. **Synthesizing Ideas** What problems have troubled the two Koreas?

Section 3

The Japanese Miracle

Focus Questions

- What factors allowed Japan to recover as effectively as it did after World War II?
- How has the relationship between Japan and the United States changed in the years since World War II?
- What political difficulties has Japan faced in the past decade?

After World War II, Japan lost all the territory that it had gained during its period of expansion. Its population, now confined to the home islands, faced very severe shortages of food, clothing, fuel, and other necessities. Japan's economy was ruined. The country desperately needed to increase imports to satisfy its people's needs. Unfortunately, most of the industries that had produced export goods to pay for imports had been damaged or destroyed during World War II.

The devastating effects of the war were apparent throughout the country. Japan's cities lay in ruins. Factories, homes, and the country's infrastructure were damaged or destroyed. The Japanese people were shocked and demoralized.

The Occupation of Japan

After the war, American troops occupied Japan under the command of General Douglas MacArthur. As Supreme Commander of the Allied Powers (SCAP) in Japan, MacArthur became the country's virtual ruler. His first task was to demilitarize Japan. He acted to remove the individuals who had been powerful in the Japanese war machine. Some top war leaders were executed, and more than 5 million troops were disarmed and released from military service. In addition, MacArthur planned to confiscate as reparations the war industries that remained in Japan. By taking factories as reparations, however, he would have created the same difficulties in Japan as were evident in Germany. Unless the Allied Powers wished to support them indefinitely, the Japanese had to be given the opportunity to provide for themselves. To do this, the Japanese needed to keep their factories and convert them to peacetime activities. The United States therefore suggested that the payment of reparations be postponed indefinitely.

MacArthur's second task involved the creation of a nonmilitary and democratic government. Under his supervision the Japanese adopted a new constitution in 1947. The **"MacArthur Constitution"** established Japan as a parliamentary democracy. It called for direct election of the Diet, or parliament, with all adults given the right to vote. The emperor, having renounced his divine status, remained only as a symbol of state. He had little power. Finally, the constitution ended Japan's militarism and included a clause in which the Japanese renounced war as a political tool.

Postwar Developments

Before World War II, Japan had been the most completely industrialized of the Asian nations. Although the destruction of many factories and the loss of its Asian possessions had hurt its economy, Japan made a rapid and impressive recovery after the war.

Economic development. Several postwar SCAP policies aided Japanese economic development. A major program of land reform allowed farmers to own their own land. Mechanization and improved strains of crops also had a positive impact on Japanese agriculture. Farm output increased dramatically.

Before and during the war, powerful industrial and banking firms called *zaibatsu* had controlled industry. The American occupation leaders worked to break up some of these firms, enforce fair trading practices, and prevent the return of monopolies. The large banks were not broken up, however, and they became a positive force in Japan's economic recovery.

In addition, Japan changed the structure of its economy. Instead of concentrating on providing inexpensive textile products, mainly for Asian markets, Japan began to produce advanced technology for a world market. The modern technology that Japan had imported after the war was operated by a skilled and highly motivated workforce. In addition, government cooperation and support for industry fueled Japan's industrial gains.

As a result, by the 1980s, Japan had emerged as Asia's leading economic power. In the 1990s, however, Japan became mired in a stubborn recession, caused partly by financial problems created during the rapid growth of the 1980s and partly by intensifying global competition. Economic growth slowed—to a near standstill from 1992 to 1994—and unemployment rose, reaching a record high 3.5 percent in 1996. As the government came under increasing pressure, its efforts to revive growth met with only limited success.

Japan-U.S. trade. Japan's remarkable economic growth depended on the country finding markets for its rapidly expanding volume of production. For many years the United States was Japan's best customer and its principal supplier of raw materials and agricultural products. In this trade relationship, Japan bought more from the United States than the United States purchased from Japan. Thus the trade balance favored the United States for many years.

Beginning in the late 1960s, however, the balance of trade swung heavily in favor of Japan. Within two decades, Japan's exports to the United States were worth millions of dollars more than the goods the country imported from the United States. In response to this situation, many American politicians pressured their government to limit Japanese imports, such as automobiles. They also wanted Japan to remove controls that restricted the entry of American imports into Japan. The Japanese government agreed to buy more goods from the United States and loosened some restrictions on foreign imports, and by the early 1990s the trade balance between the two countries had improved.

By the mid-1990s, however, the trade imbalance had once again become a significant issue. Talks in April 1997 between President Bill Clinton and Japanese Prime Minister Ryutaro Hashimoto were in part aimed at resolving issues that pertained to this continuing trade imbalance. Other large industrialized countries shared the United States' hope that Japan would increase its imports and take other actions to balance international trade and foster a healthy world economy.

Economic and social changes. Postwar economic growth did not benefit everyone in Japan, but it did bring prosperity to a large part of the population. This prosperity led to an increase in consumerism. For example, many families who had lived more simply before the war acquired labor-saving household appliances and new automobiles.

Economic growth, however, did not necessarily bring an improvement in the quality of life. The Japanese worked longer hours than their Western counterparts, and the cost of living was much higher in Japan than in other industrialized nations. The differences in prices were most marked in land and housing. Rapid industrialization and population growth put land for building at a premium. Consequently, from the 1960s onward, prices for land and housing soared. Industrialization also created another serious problem—environmental pollution. In recent years, many Japanese have called on their government to pay more attention to improving the quality of life and less to promoting further development.

Postwar economic developments brought about far-reaching social changes. As more and more women joined the workforce, their status in Japanese society began to change. In time, they won greater legal, political, and social freedoms. Changing roles within the family and changes in housing arrangements began to cause a decline in the importance of the family, traditionally the center of all Japanese life. As a result, young people began to make decisions and choices for themselves—about marriage partners and work, for example—that their parents would once have made for them.

Foreign Relations and Political Life

The Cold War between the Soviet Union and the West led to a reversal of Japan's international position. The 1947 constitution had limited Japanese armed forces and military production. In addition, the Japanese had signed a treaty agreeing to renounce war as a political tactic. The communist victory in China

Japanese youth during the post-World War II years began to make decisions and choices for themselves.

and the stalemate in Korea changed Western policy toward Japan. The Western nations now felt that Japan should be able to defend itself and also to aid them in case of war in Asia. These nations, therefore, urged Japan to increase its armed forces.

Fearing a return of the militaristic governments of prewar days, the Japanese had little desire to rearm. They preferred to spend their money building peacetime industries, expanding exports, and raising living standards. As a result, Japan's military expenditures remained low. In 1997 the United States and Japan reached an agreement under which Japan would provide the United States with noncombative support and assistance in case of a conflict near Japan.

A more independent stance. Over the past several decades, Japan and the United States have maintained friendly ties. Still, relations between the nations have showed some signs of stress over the years. The Japanese have expressed resentment over the economic and defense pressures put upon them by the United States and other nations during the 1970s and 1980s. The issue of U.S. troops stationed in Japan—especially the forces on the island of Okinawa—has been a sore point since the 1960s. At the same time, many Americans have felt apprehensive about the United States's growing trade deficit with Japan and Japan's increasing stature as a world economic power.

As the 1980s drew to a close, Japan began to pursue a more independent course in international affairs. Japanese leaders moved to consolidate their country's position as an economic and political leader in Asia. They also increased the level of Japan's financial and technical aid to developing countries. By the end of the 1980s, Japan had become the world's leading donor of economic aid. Also, with the growth of democracy in Eastern Europe, Japan's leaders reassessed their country's relations with the nations of the former Soviet Union. For example, in 1996 the leaders of Japan and Russia met for talks. However, relations between the two countries continued to be strained by an ongoing dispute over the Kuril Islands, which the Soviet Union occupied after World

Independent Nations in Southeast Asia, 1945–1984

Learning from Maps Many of the colonies in Southeast Asia became independent countries after World War II.

Place In what year did the Philippines gain their independence?

Toshiki Kaifu and Mikhail Gorbachev signed a joint declaration in April 1991.

Section 3 Review

1. **Define** "MacArthur Constitution," Diet
2. **Identify** Toshiki Kaifu
3. **Evaluating Ideas** What factors allowed Japan to recover as successfully as it did after World War II?
4. **Analyzing Ideas** What role has trade played in the changing relationship between Japan and the United States since 1945?
5. **Summarizing Ideas** Describe Japan's growing independence in world affairs as well as its internal political difficulties.

Section 4

Independence Struggles in Southeast Asia

Focus Questions

- What were the causes and effects of authoritarian rule in the Philippines and Indonesia?
- What types of struggles did nations in Southeast Asia face as they sought stability and prosperity?
- How did the Vietnam War affect Vietnam, Cambodia, and Laos?
- How have events in Thailand followed a different path from that of events in many other Southeast Asian countries?

War II, and which now belong to Russia. Japan still claims several islands in the southern part of the chain of Kuril Islands.

Politics in Japan. Japan's conservative Liberal Democratic Party (LDP) controlled the **Diet**, which is Japan's national legislature and therefore its government. But the Socialists and other opposition parties voiced strong criticism of its policies. These parties especially condemned the ongoing security pact with the United States and the presence of American military bases on Japanese soil.

The ruling party's greatest troubles, however, were self-made. A 1989 financial scandal, involving many top party members, stunned the country. The LDP's image was temporarily rescued by Toshiki Kaifu, who became prime minister some months after the scandal broke. However, Kaifu was forced out of office in 1991, and two years later another political scandal brought down the government of his successor. In the 1993 elections, the LDP lost its majority in the Diet, ending the party's almost 40-year rule. In subsequent years, various coalition governments endeavored to bring about political reforms as well as economic changes for Japan. It was in 1996 that Ryutaro Hashimoto, president of the LDP, became Japan's prime minister.

Southeast Asia consists of 10 countries: the Philippines, Indonesia, Malaysia, Singapore, Brunei, Vietnam, Thailand, Laos, Burma (renamed Myanmar in 1989), and Cambodia (renamed Kampuchea for a time). With the exception of Thailand, all were once colonies. After World War II, these countries gained independence. Some did so peacefully, while others resorted to violent means. After achieving independence each began the long and difficult process of political and economic development. (See map on page 796.)

The Philippines

Spain ceded the Philippines to the United States in 1898. In 1934 the United States Congress passed an act granting autonomy to the Philippines. This legislation also provided for the Philippines to become independent on July 4, 1946, when the country became the Republic of the Philippines. After that date, however, the United States continued to maintain military bases in the Philippines. As compensation, it contributed large sums of money to repair war damage and rebuild the Philippine economy. These close ties to the United States led the Philippine government to adopt a strongly pro-Western foreign policy.

In the 1970s, Marxist guerrillas began to threaten the peace in the Philippines. A revolt by Muslim separatists further strained the country's stability. To deal with this internal disorder, Philippine president Ferdinand Marcos declared martial law and arrested hundreds of his political opponents. In 1973, Marcos extended his power by proclaiming a new constitution that gave him an almost unlimited term in office.

Under the Marcos regime the country made little progress toward democracy, and economic conditions worsened. Opposition to the regime began to grow, however. Then, in 1983, the assassination of opposition leader Benigno Aquino sparked widespread rioting. In 1986 Aquino's widow, Corazon Aquino, ran against Marcos in a special presidential election. Marcos claimed victory, but when it became obvious that he had rigged the election, he was forced to flee the country.

On taking office, Aquino pledged to recover the billions of dollars that she said Marcos and his family had embezzled from the treasury. Aquino did make some gains. She restored constitutional democracy after years of dictatorial rule, and she promoted free enterprise. However, many of the changes she promised—land reform, for instance—were never enacted, and poverty and official corruption persisted.

Fidel Ramos succeeded Aquino as president in 1992. Under Ramos, the economy continued to strengthen. Ramos made an effort to reduce restrictions on business, break up monopolies, and encourage foreign investment in the Philippines. Ramos also made progress in talks with Muslim opposition groups. The economy experienced solid growth in the mid-1990s, but internal problems persisted.

Indonesia

During World War II, the Japanese occupied the East Indies, a group of islands including Sumatra and Java. When the war ended, the Dutch, who had ruled the East Indies since the 1600s, expected to regain control. An Indonesian civil engineer named Sukarno, however, led an independence movement against them. (Many Indonesians have only one

name or are known by only one name.) After a year of bitter fighting, the United Nations intervened to secure a cease-fire. Then, after further struggle and lengthy negotiations, in 1949 the Netherlands granted independence to the East Indies. The East Indies became the Republic of Indonesia, with Sukarno as its first president. West Irian, part of the island of New Guinea, was not included in the Dutch settlement with Indonesia.

Indonesia faced problems similar to those of many other newly independent countries. It had few trained civil servants or administrators and a chaotic political system. However, the country made some significant gains in health and education. Sukarno was also successful in developing a sense of national identity among the Indonesian people.

In the early 1960s, Sukarno's rule became much more authoritarian. In a move that established what he called a guided democracy, Sukarno dissolved the elected parliament and appointed a new one. This appointed legislature proclaimed him President for Life. At about this time, Sukarno also gained control of West Irian from the Dutch.

Sukarno found, however, that Indonesia's problems were multiplying. The economy slowed almost to a standstill. Exports decreased, and inflation and debts rose. Reckless spending brought the nation close to bankruptcy. In 1965, General Suharto, the conservative head of the Indonesian army strategic command, took advantage of a communist insurrection to seize control of the government.

As president, Suharto emphasized economic reforms and worked to build closer ties with the West. Using Western aid, he began an ambitious industrial development program. The slump in oil prices in the early 1980s had a devastating effect on the Indonesian economy, however. As a result, the pace of industrial development in Indonesia again slowed. Suharto continued Sukarno's interest in West Irian. In 1969 he managed to force West Irian to unite with Indonesia. However, opposition to the Indonesian government in this region, today known as Irian Jaya, continued through the 1990s. Unrest also continued in East Timor, an island territory invaded by Indonesia in 1975.

In the late 1980s and through the 1990s, Suharto's authoritarian government came under criticism from people both within and outside the country. Many Indonesians complained about the growing gap between the country's rich and poor, the continued mismanagement, and the corruption of many government officials. Also, a number of Western countries voiced concern

History Through the Arts

WEAVING

Ikat Cloth

The woven cloth shown in this feature, from Bali, Indonesia, was made by an ancient method of dyeing and weaving known as ikat. The ikat method can be found in several parts of Southeast Asia, including Indonesia and Cambodia, and may have originated in India.

Cotton and silk are the most common fibers used for ikat. Before the thread is woven, bundles of threads are tied tightly at carefully calculated points. Then the bundles are dyed. Most of the thread will absorb the dye, but the places where the strands are tied together do not absorb color. Sometimes the process is repeated to include additional colors.

After it is dyed, the yarn is woven on a loom. As the weaving progresses, complex designs

begin to appear. Often only the threads running one way—the threads extended lengthwise on the loom—are pre-dyed. In the southern part of Sumatra, however, the threads going both ways are also dyed. Beautiful designs, with figures such as birds and animals, can be created during this process. Although the process is extremely difficult and laborious, the finished cloths are stunning.

Decorated textiles such as these ikat cloths have been an important part of Indonesian culture for centuries. Ikat cloths are sometimes given as wedding gifts between families. Because of the long time needed to produce them and the high quality of the weaving, however, the cloths were used mostly in ceremonies. Many are considered to represent works of art.

over human rights abuses allegedly committed by the Indonesian military and police forces. Nevertheless, Indonesia continued to make economic progress in the 1990s, and its political and economic importance in the world grew.

President Suharto remained in power until May 1998. After a worsening economic crisis and widespread demonstrations paralyzed the country, Suharto finally resigned, handing over power to his vice-president, B.J. Habibie. People were hopeful that democratizing reforms would follow.

Malaysia, Singapore, and Brunei

In 1963 Malaya (now West Malaysia), Singapore, Sarawak, and Sabah (North Borneo), which had all become independent from Great Britain, united to form the Federation of Malaysia. The new nation faced both external and internal difficulties. To begin with, the Philippines claimed part of Sabah. Also, Indonesia's President Sukarno tried to block the formation of the new federation, saying that it was nothing more than a move by the British to encircle his country. In addition,

Sarawak and Sabah had come under heavy attack from Indonesian communist guerrillas.

Internally, a clash of cultures threatened the federation. The nation's population consisted of Malays, Chinese, and a small percentage of Indians and other ethnic groups. The greatest proportion of the people— about half—were Malays; Singapore, however, had a large majority of Chinese. Most Malays were farmers, while the Chinese were mainly city dwellers, technically trained and experienced in commerce. Malays controlled the government of the federation, but the Chinese controlled most of the business and the wealth.

The Malays forced Singapore to secede from the federation in 1965. Tensions continued to grow between the Malays and the Chinese who remained in Malaysia. Then, in 1969, the tensions exploded in racial riots. As a result, the government declared a state of emergency and suspended parliamentary rule.

After these riots, the government began to seek ways to raise the living standard of the Malay population. By improving the status of the Malay majority, the government hoped to eliminate the educational and economic differences between Malays and other ethnic groups.

Racial tensions erupted once again in 1979 with the arrival of thousands of Vietnamese refugees in Malaysia. Since many of these refugees were ethnically Chinese, the Malays feared that the Chinese faction would gain power. As a result, the Malaysian government denied entry to the refugees. Racial friction continued throughout the 1980s, causing considerable political instability.

In the 1990s, tensions caused by ethnic differences began to ease somewhat. Political difficulties were moderated by Malaysia's impressive economic growth in this period. Indeed, by 1996 Malaysia's economy had become one of the strongest and fastest-growing in the Asia-Pacific region. Still, while sustained economic progress had a positive effect on overall conditions in Malaysia, serious problems remained, such as poor living conditions for many people, pollution, and continued racial and ethnic friction.

The Republic of Singapore. Singapore, a cluster of one major island and more than 50 smaller islands, measures less than 240 square miles in area. For nearly all of the time since it seceded from the Federation of Malaysia in 1965, Singapore has been dominated by one man and one political party—Prime Minister Lee Kuan Yew and his People's Action Party. Throughout his time in office, Lee created a regulated society, imposing strict controls on labor unions, political activity, and the media. When Lee stepped down in November 1990, however, Singapore was one of the world's most politically stable and economically prosperous countries. The People's Action Party remained in control of Singapore's authoritarian government through the mid-1990s, with Lee retaining a role in affairs as Senior Minister.

Singapore began its march to prosperity after it seceded from the Federation of Malaysia. Since the 1970s the economy has grown at an annual rate often reaching 10 percent. This spectacular growth rate was based on a program of industrial development that emphasized, at first, shipbuilding and petroleum refining, and later, electronics and computer software. By the mid-1990s, Singapore had become the center of economic activity in Southeast Asia, and the country's 3 million people enjoyed one of the highest standards of living in Asia.

Brunei. The small sultanate of Brunei on the northern coast of Malaysian Borneo decided against joining the Federation of Malaysia. Its leaders feared that it would be overwhelmed by the larger states of Malaya and Singapore. This oil-rich land remained a protectorate of Great Britain until it achieved full independence in 1984.

Burma (Myanmar)

Since medieval times the area known as Burma has been a strategically important region, an area of important trade routes. During World War II, the country, held by the British, was the starting point of

This view of skyscrapers shows the modernization and the westernization of Singapore.

the Burma Road, over which supplies moved to China for the war against Japan. Japanese armies invaded Burma in 1942 and held it until 1945, when British rule resumed. In 1948, Great Britain recognized Burma's independence.

The new nation faced difficulties that included the lack of a strong central government, a scarcity of trained civil servants, tribal and political dissension, and communist attempts to seize the country. The first premier, U Nu, headed a coalition government that brought the nation some degree of order. However, the coalition soon broke into rival factions, and in 1962 the army, led by General Ne Win, seized control of the government.

Ne Win wanted to make Burma a socialist nation. His repressive government took strict control of the economy, a move that led to economic ruin. Farm production fell, and consumer goods became scarce.

In 1974 a new constitution under Ne Win proclaimed Burma the Socialist Republic of the Union of Burma. In 1988, violent demonstrations forced Ne Win to resign, although the military remained in control. Signaling that they intended to make a fresh start, the leaders of the new military junta renamed the country Myanmar in 1989. They promised to establish a new economic order and enact political reforms, including free elections in 1990. However, when the major opposition party swept the elections, the junta refused to step down. Instead it cracked down on everyone it considered a challenge to its power. One famous dissident, Aung San Suu Kyi, won a Nobel Peace Prize in 1991, while she was under house arrest, for her efforts to bring democratic reform to her country. She was released in 1995. The military's brutal repression added to the nation's unrest. Although antigovernment opposition continued into the mid-1990s, the junta still dominates the country.

Myanmar has had some success in attracting foreign investments, but relationships with the United States and other Western nations have been limited. Myanmar's poor record in human rights as well as its role as a leading producer of illegal narcotics has earned the country growing criticism.

Vietnam

In the late 1800s, the French became the dominant power in the eastern part of the peninsula of Indochina, an area roughly equivalent to the present-day countries of Vietnam, Laos, and Cambodia. However, during World War II, the Japanese took control of the area. When the French tried to return

after the war, the Viet Minh, a communist-led guerrilla group that had fought the Japanese, now began to resist the French. The group's leader, Ho Chi Minh, declared the country independent in September 1945. No major governments recognized Ho's declaration, however, and by the end of 1945 the French had regained control of much of Vietnam.

Ho hoped to negotiate a quick settlement of the independence question. However, the French would agree only to recognize Vietnam as a free state within the French Union, or empire. In 1946 fighting broke out between the French and the Viet Minh in the northern cities of Hanoi and Haiphong. The war dragged on for years. After a major defeat in 1954 at Dien Bien Phu (dyen byen FOO), in which the Viet Minh captured some 13,000 French troops, French leaders were finally ready to negotiate an end to the war.

Vietnam divided. The **Geneva Accords**, signed in 1954, called for the withdrawal of all foreign troops from the area. They also divided Vietnam into two zones at the 17th parallel. (See map on page 803.) For the time being, Ho Chi Minh would remain in control of the north. But an election, set for 1956, would allow the Vietnamese to select a government to reunite the country.

The Geneva Accords left the Viet Minh in a better situation than that of the government in the south. The north began a program of industrialization and collectivization of agriculture, and it experienced steady economic progress for the next decade. With Chinese and Soviet assistance, the Viet Minh began to consolidate their economic and political strength, building a communist state in the north.

In contrast, the south experienced political chaos. Its war-torn economy, a flood of refugees from the north, and fighting among political and religious groups all posed problems for the newly formed government of Ngo Dinh Diem.

Guerrilla war in Vietnam. Under Diem, South Vietnam returned to some semblance of order, but at a price. Diem ruled by totalitarian methods, attempting to suppress all opposition to his government. He showed little interest in reforms or in eliminating government corruption. He refused to hold the proposed elections in 1956.

As Diem's government became increasingly repressive, opposition grew. By the late 1950s the Viet Minh were taking advantage of the situation, forming the National Liberation Front (NLF) with the goal of overthrowing Diem and reuniting Vietnam. The NLF, a mixture of Viet Minh members and dissidents from the south, soon became known as the Viet Cong, or Vietnamese Communists.

With weapons and military expertise from the north, the Viet Cong infiltrated the rural areas of South Vietnam. Their goals were to "neutralize" the south, force the withdrawal of all foreign troops, and finally reunite the two regions under the government of the north. Their tactics, however, included assassination and sabotage as well as more traditional methods of persuasion.

Ngo Dinh Diem responded to both internal dissent and Viet Cong guerrilla activity by becoming increasingly repressive. With conditions in the south growing more and more chaotic, a group of army officers assassinated Diem and took control of the government in 1963. Over the next three years, several different military groups ruled South Vietnam.

American involvement. United States involvement in Vietnam began almost unnoticed. It grew slowly, without either a declaration of war by Congress or an announcement by the government to the American people. President Dwight D. Eisenhower sent financial and military aid as well as a few hundred military advisers to South Vietnam. President John F. Kennedy continued this policy, sending military advisers and supplies to help the South Vietnamese

army. As the guerrilla war increased in intensity, so did the American commitment.

American troop strength began to reach significant numbers in the mid-1960s under President Lyndon Johnson. In March 1965, Marines landed on the beaches near Da Nang, marking the beginning of direct United States military involvement in the war. The Johnson administration explained the increased American military presence in a number of ways. First, communism had to be contained. Second, the administration cited the **domino theory**, the belief that if South Vietnam fell to communism, all of Southeast Asia would follow. Third, the North Vietnamese were aggressors in the conflict and had to be stopped. In January 1965 President Johnson expanded the war by ordering air attacks on North Vietnam.

At the beginning of 1968, North Vietnamese troops and the Viet Cong launched a major offensive. American and South Vietnamese forces drove back the attackers, inflicting heavy casualties. Even so, the Viet Cong considered the **Tet Offensive**—named for the Vietnamese New Year celebration, during which the attack began—a psychological victory. Many Americans, after seeing television pictures of the fierce fighting, openly questioned United States involvement in the war.

The fourth agreement of the Geneva Accords called for independence and presidential elections in Vietnam. Ngo Dinh Diem became president of the Republic of Vietnam.

In March 1968, President Johnson announced a temporary halt to the bombing of North Vietnam. An agreement with North Vietnam to begin negotiating an end to the war soon followed. However, these peace negotiations quickly became deadlocked. During 1969, the first year of Richard Nixon's presidency, there were 540,000 U.S. troops in Vietnam. Nixon announced a policy of "Vietnamization." This involved allowing the South Vietnamese gradually to take over fighting the war while the United States supplied them with arms, equipment, air support, and economic aid. As a first step in this process, he announced the gradual withdrawal of American troops—but at the same time, he escalated the war. In 1970 Nixon ordered an invasion of Cambodia, long used by the Viet Cong as a refuge, and in 1972 he resumed the bombing of North Vietnam.

Ending the war. In 1973 the major parties in the Vietnam War reached a cease-fire agreement. Under this agreement, known as the **Paris Peace Accords**, the United States withdrew its remaining troops from South Vietnam. In return the North Vietnamese were to release American prisoners of war. However, fighting continued in Vietnam in violation of the accords. The South Vietnamese army, without American support, could not hold back the enemy advance, and in April 1975, North Vietnamese troops entered Saigon. Within 24 hours the South Vietnamese government surrendered.

The Vietnam War caused widespread devastation. Estimates of civilian and military casualties for both North and South Vietnam range from 1.3 million to more than 2 million. American combat casualties totaled more than 58,000 killed and some 300,000 wounded. The neighboring countries of Laos and Cambodia also suffered their share of death and destruction. Long-standing rivalries between these two countries and Vietnam complicated efforts to recover and rebuild after the war.

A reunited Vietnam. After the war, North Vietnamese officials controlled and administered all of South Vietnam. Then, in July 1976, the two Vietnams united as one country—the Socialist Republic of Vietnam—with Hanoi, in the north, as the capital. The former southern capital, Saigon, was renamed Ho Chi Minh City, after the North Vietnamese president, who died in 1969.

Even before unification, the North Vietnamese had begun to reform the south along northern lines. Economically, this reform involved nationalizing property, imposing controls on private enterprise, and moving the population from cities to rural areas.

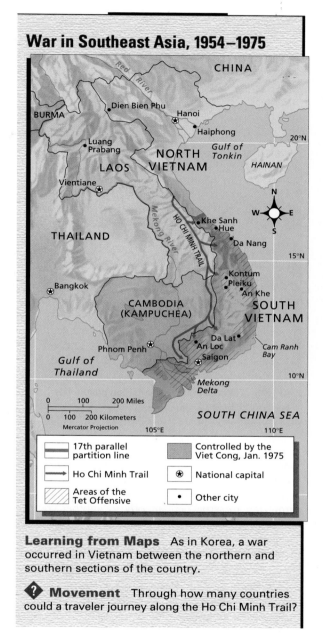

War in Southeast Asia, 1954–1975

Learning from Maps As in Korea, a war occurred in Vietnam between the northern and southern sections of the country.

? Movement Through how many countries could a traveler journey along the Ho Chi Minh Trail?

In the years after the fall of Saigon, more than 1 million South Vietnamese fled their country. Some left because they feared punishment by the North Vietnamese. Others left because of food shortages. However, most people moved on because they did not want to live under a communist government.

Sometimes these refugees had to bribe government officials just to leave Vietnam. Then they faced a dangerous sea voyage to Malaysia, Thailand, or some other

After the Vietnam War, over a million people left Vietnam by boat as refugees.

Southeast Asian country. Many of these "boat people," as the refugees were called, died at sea. Those who survived spent months in crowded camps, waiting for permission to settle permanently in another country. Many eventually made their way to Western countries. The largest number of immigrants came to the United States. In the late 1980s, the troubles of the boat people grew. Some Southeast Asian countries, already overrun with refugees from Indochina, refused to accept any more boat people.

Economic progress. After 1975, Vietnam struggled to make ends meet economically. Burdened by huge debts from fighting the Vietnam War, the country took on more debt in an effort to rebuild after hostilities ended. Military action in Cambodia put further strain on the economy in the 1980s. By the late 1980s, inflation was wildly out of control in Vietnam, and the nation was mired in poverty.

Following the example of other communist countries, Vietnam began to restructure its economy, adding elements of free enterprise. At first, progress under this program of renovation was slow, but, in the 1990s,

Vietnam's economy boomed. Foreign trade expanded, foreign investment in Vietnam increased, inflation was brought under control, and even diplomatic relations with the United States were restored. By 1996, Vietnam's economy was growing at a rate of more than 9 percent.

Cambodia

Cambodia, which had gained independence from France in 1953, attempted to remain neutral in the Vietnam War. The country's leader, Norodom Sihanouk, found neutrality a difficult path to follow, however. North Vietnamese and Viet Cong troops frequently fled into Cambodia to escape capture, and their chief supply route—the Ho Chi Minh Trail—ran through the eastern part of the country.

In 1970, Lon Nol, a pro-American army general, overthrew Sihanouk in a military coup. Lon Nol promised to take a firmer stand against the Vietnamese Communists who used Cambodia as a refuge.

The Khmer Rouge. During the war in Vietnam, the Vietnamese Communists had helped to arm and train a group of Cambodian insurgents called the Khmer Rouge. With this assistance, the Khmer Rouge rapidly grew in strength. Sihanouk, who had gone into exile in China, voiced his support for this group. In 1975, just before Saigon fell, the Khmer Rouge seized Phnom Penh, the Cambodian capital, and established a new Marxist regime under the leadership of Pol Pot.

This new government mounted a brutal campaign to resettle Cambodia's population, sending most city residents into the countryside to create new agricultural villages. Lacking tools and farming experience, many of these former city dwellers died of starvation. The Khmer Rouge also undertook a systematic program to eliminate almost all of Cambodia's government officials, army officers, teachers, and intellectuals. Between 1975 and 1977, well over 1 million Cambodians—about one fifth of the country's people—met their deaths by execution or starvation under Pol Pot's regime. Thousands more fled to makeshift refugee camps in neighboring Thailand.

The Vietnamese invasion. Border disputes and rivalries that were centuries old soon brought the Khmer Rouge into conflict with its Vietnamese neighbors. The Vietnamese invaded Cambodia in 1978. As the Vietnamese advanced toward Phnom Penh, the Chinese threw their support to the Khmer Rouge. Even so, by early 1979 the Vietnamese had overthrown Pol Pot and established a pro-Vietnamese government in Phnom Penh, led by Hun Sen. Throughout the 1980s, fighting between the Chinese-backed Khmer Rouge and Hun Sen's troops with their Vietnamese allies was almost constant. Once again the refugee camps in Thailand became a haven for fearful Cambodians.

In the late 1980s, under pressure from the UN, Vietnam withdrew its troops from Cambodia, and China cut military aid to the Khmer Rouge. The UN sponsored talks on the future of Cambodia to which all affected parties—including Sihanouk's followers, the Khmer Rouge, and the Vietnamese-backed government—were invited. After much discussion, all of these factions agreed in late 1991 to back a UN-sponsored government that would rule until free elections were held.

The UN-sponsored elections finally took place in May 1993 and resulted in a coalition government, with Norodom Sihanouk as king and two co-prime ministers: Norodom Ranariddh, son of Norodom Sihanouk, and Hun Sen. However, conflict between the two prime ministers and their supporters, as well as ongoing Khmer Rouge opposition to the government, left Cambodia's political situation in the mid-1990s increasingly unstable.

Still, there were some positive developments in Cambodia. In 1996 the Khmer Rouge showed clear signs of weakening, and in 1998 the notorious Pol Pot died.

Laos

Like Cambodia, Laos gained independence from France in 1954. Almost immediately, civil war broke out among the country's political factions. This turmoil continued for the next 20 years.

In the meantime Laos, although neutral, became increasingly involved in the Vietnam War. The Ho Chi Minh Trail, the Viet Cong's major supply route, wound through the mountain valleys of eastern Laos into Cambodia and South Vietnam. To break this supply line, the United States began bombing the Laotian countryside, causing heavy damage and many civilian casualties.

By 1975 the internal strife in Laos had ended. The communist faction, the Pathet Lao, had set up a communist regime, the Lao People's Democratic Republic. This new government tried to follow a nonaligned course in the complicated politics of Asia. Ultimately, however, nonalignment proved impossible. Laos had to call on the Vietnamese for help in controlling anticommunist forces in its northern provinces. In return it allowed Vietnam to station 50,000 troops on Laotian soil. As a result, relations between Laos and its neighbors continued to be tense throughout the 1980s.

As the new decade began, this situation gradually changed. Vietnam withdrew its troops from Laos in 1989. Laotian leaders made efforts to improve relations with Thailand and China. They also signed trade and financial aid agreements with the United States, Japan, and the Soviet Union. By the mid-1990s, Laos had attracted a significant amount of foreign investment. Although still one of the world's poorest countries, Laos saw its economy grow at an average annual rate of 6.5 percent between 1990 and 1996.

Thailand

Thailand, formerly called Siam, had never been a European colony. During World War II, however, Thailand became an ally of Japan. Under Japanese pressure Thailand joined the Axis and declared war on Great Britain and the United States.

In the late 1950s, the Thai army took control of the government, establishing a military dictatorship. Strongly pro-Western, this government received military and economic aid from the United States. During the Vietnam War, this close relationship continued. The United States used bases in Thailand as a staging area for bombing raids on North Vietnam, Laos, and Cambodia.

Throughout the 1970s, Thailand was deluged with refugees from war-torn Vietnam, Laos, and Cambodia. The Thai government, along with international relief agencies, set up refugee camps along its border with Cambodia. Communist victories in Vietnam, Laos, and Cambodia during the mid-1970s forced Thailand to reconsider its relationship with the United States. The Thai government began to work to better its ties with its communist neighbors.

Although Thailand has experienced a slow but steady democratization of its political system in recent years, control has shifted back and forth between civilian and military leadership. The nation's various uneasy coalition governments have been unstable and often ineffective. Moreover, political corruption has been all too common.

While Thailand struggled politically, however, the nation developed economically. As foreign investments poured into the country, the Thai economy grew at a rate averaging more than 8 percent annually between 1985 and 1994—one of the world's fastest-growing economies. In 1996, however, the economy weakened. Exports declined, bad debts began to mount, and investors lost confidence.

Thailand also experienced environmental problems, such as erosion caused by the overharvesting of timber. By 1997 the nation was in the grip of a severe financial crisis, and in November of that year, the prime minister (in office less than a year) was forced to resign. The worsening crisis left Thailand's political and economic future uncertain.

Section 4 Review

1. **Define** Geneva Accord, domino theory, Tet Offensive, Paris Peace Accords
2. **Identify** Ferdinand Marcos, Sukarno, Viet Minh, Ho Chi Minh, Viet Cong, Norodom Sihanouk, Khmer Rouge, Pol Pot
3. **Locate and Explain the Significance** Phnom Penh, Hanoi
4. **Comparing Ideas** Compare the causes and aftermaths of authoritarian rule in the Philippines and in Indonesia.
5. **Contrasting Ideas** Describe the differences between the movements toward prosperity in Malaysia and in Singapore.
6. **Summarizing Ideas** How did the struggle in Vietnam affect nations in other parts of the world as well as those in Southeast Asia?
7. **Analyzing Ideas** How has Thailand's history differed from that of its Southeast Asian neighbors since the 1950s?

Section 5

Asian Paths to Prosperity and Security

Focus Questions

- **What factors led to the development of authoritarianism in many parts of Asia?**
- **What problems did Asian countries face as they developed economically, and how did they solve these problems?**
- **In what ways have Asian cultures and economies had an effect on the West?**

Asia is a continent of great diversity, composed of many nations that differ significantly from one another.

However, a closer look at these nations reveals a number of experiences nearly all have shared.

Political Development

Most countries of Asia were once colonies. After achieving independence, most new Asian nations set up representative governments and attempted to build democratic societies. As time passed, however, democracy faded. Violent revolutions established communist governments in China, Vietnam, Cambodia, and Laos. Elsewhere—in the Philippines, Indonesia, and Burma (Myanmar), for example—civil rights came under attack, and authoritarian rule emerged. During the 1980s some Asian countries, such as the Philippines, actually established democratic political systems, while others, like China, flirted with democratization. However, a return to authoritarian rule remained a real and almost constant threat for these fledgling democratic movements.

By and large, three factors gave rise to and helped sustain authoritarianism in Asia. The first factor was the ethnic and cultural diversity within Asian nations. In India, Malaysia, and the Philippines, for example, age-old antagonisms existed among groups with different heritages or religions. From time to time these antagonisms erupted into violence. In such cases government leaders often relied on their military and police forces to maintain domestic peace. To make their work easier, these forces frequently argued for the imposition of strict controls on civil rights. Occasionally, the military forces themselves took over the government when civilian leaders seemed reluctant to impose such controls.

The second factor that helped the development of authoritarianism was fear about national security. For example, because of the communist movements on the Indochina Peninsula, leaders in the Philippines and Indonesia feared the spread of revolutionary ideas to their own countries. As a result, these leaders cracked down on leftist groups and granted sweeping powers to the military whenever the slightest signs of communist influence arose. Similarly, communist countries feared the anticommunist policies of the free world. They also feared each other's intentions. For these communist countries too, fear led to a desire for strong central government and a lack of tolerance for debate and dissent.

The third factor was the desire for economic growth. Many Asian leaders perceived democratic government as wasteful, inefficient, and a hindrance to the speedy development of industrializing policies and programs.

Therefore, the desire of these leaders for rapid economic growth contributed to the emergence of authoritarian regimes. To understand this development, it is necessary to examine economic growth in Asia.

Economic Development

By the 1990s roughly 3 billion people, more than half the world's total population, lived in Asia. A significant number of Asia's people lived in poverty and suffered its consequences—malnutrition, illiteracy, and sharply reduced life expectancy. At the same time, Asia was home to some of the fastest-growing economies in the world.

Attempts at economic development. To help create more prosperous and stable societies, in the 1950s most Asian governments began to foster economic development. The approaches of these governments varied. Some used capitalist means, encouraging private enterprise. Others followed socialist principles, with the central government taking control of the economy. Still others pursued a middle course, combining government planning with private enterprise. Whatever the approach, most governments experienced the same result. With a few exceptions, economic development proceeded slowly, if at all.

Generally, most Asian countries experienced slow economic growth because they had little wealth in the first place. Industrialization required huge investments of money in machinery, factories, and distribution networks. Also, the later a country began the process of industrialization, the greater the investment had to be to bring that country up to the level of the more advanced nations.

In order to get the investment funds they needed, Asian countries depended either on loans or on the export of agricultural goods or natural resources: cocoa, tea, spices, timber, rubber, and copper and other minerals. Throughout most of the 1950s and 1960s, however, the prices of these items in world markets remained relatively low. In addition, periodic economic recessions in the West reduced the demand for these goods.

A shortage of experienced managers and trained workers also slowed economic development in much

Corazon Aquino, elected in 1986, was the first female president of the Philippines.

of Asia. To combat this problem, many Asian governments reformed their educational systems and established vocational schools and industrial training programs. Even so, time was needed for these changes to take effect.

Cooperating for development. In the 1970s, Asian countries began to find ways of dealing with their economic problems. For example, to ensure higher and more stable prices for their exports, many countries combined to form loose economic associations. In addition, Asian countries joined with other developing nations to work for greater concessions from such international loan agencies as the World Bank and the International Monetary Fund (IMF).

Also, Asian countries followed the example of such bodies as the European Union (EU), cooperating to develop common trade and economic policies. For example, the Association of Southeast Asian Nations **(ASEAN)** was organized in 1967 by the governments of Indonesia, Malaysia, the Philippines, Singapore, and Thailand. Its goals were to promote economic growth, social progress, and cultural development in the region as well as to encourage peace and security.

Brunei became a member of ASEAN in 1984 and Vietnam in 1995.

The organization holds regular summit meetings to discuss ways to encourage trade and to handle the problems associated with economic development. In 1996 three more nations—Myanmar, Laos, and Cambodia—joined ASEAN as observer nations. This was a first step toward their full membership in the organization.

Many Asian nations, however, have attempted to spur economic growth through greater government control. Some Asian governments have nationalized certain key industries—oil in Indonesia, for example. By such actions they hoped to ensure the reinvestment of profits in the country's development. Many governments, to prevent interruptions in production, have passed laws limiting the organization of labor unions, or prohibiting strikes and other industrial actions. Such authoritarian measures, in some cases, have led to more rapid economic growth, but at the expense of individual rights and freedoms.

Economic expansion. By the 1990s, Asia's economic situation remained a mixed picture.

The containers stacked on the deck of this Japanese freighter hold just a fraction of the billions of dollars' worth of goods that the United States imports every year from Asian countries.

While some Asian countries had made only limited advances toward economic development, others had made significant progress. Indeed, some countries—most notably those that gave strong support to free enterprise—enjoyed remarkable success. Japan, for example, ranked as one of the world's major economic powers, with Japanese trade and investment contributing significantly to the economic growth of the whole Asian region. South Korea, Taiwan, Singapore, and Hong Kong—known collectively as the **"Four Tigers"**—also played an increasingly important role in the region as well as in the global economy.

In fact, by the mid-1990s, Asia in general had become a region of such powerful economic expansion that observers frequently referred to "the Asian miracle." Many Asian nations were growing at annual rates of 6 to 10 percent. China, an especially dramatic example, has quadrupled its gross national product in the past two decades. Furthermore, although millions of Asia's people still lived in poverty, the number of poor people in East and Southeast Asia had decreased by more than 50 percent between 1975 and 1995.

Nevertheless, there are significant problems in the region, including political instability, overpopulation, and a growing gap between rich and poor. In 1997 the financial crisis in Thailand began to spread to neighboring nations, raising concerns that the Asian miracle was coming to an end.

How quickly Asia will recover from this financial crisis, and how widespread its effects will be, is open to question. However, there seems to be no question about the Pacific region's continuing—and increasingly important—role in the world economy. Indeed, many observers feel that, just as the 1900s were called the American Century, the next 100 years will be the Asian Century. The full impact of Asia's economic growth and development on the global economy is still yet to be seen.

Asian Cultural Diffusion

For hundreds of years, Asia has exercised an incredibly powerful influence on the West. The ancient religions, philosophies, and martial arts of China and Japan have long fascinated many Westerners. Exhibits of Asian porcelain, carpets, manuscripts, and other arts and crafts have drawn huge crowds to Western art galleries. More recently, Asia has exerted an economic influence on Western life by bringing about a change in the buying habits of Western consumers. For example, Asian-made radios, computers, cameras, video equipment, and automobiles, by and large, have dominated world markets over the past decade. Further, many "Western-made" appliances were indeed constructed in the West—but from Asian components.

This economic competition from Asia has both alarmed and intrigued Western business leaders. Since the late 1970s, Western economists have traveled throughout Japan, trying to discover why Japanese goods compete so well in world markets. Many economists have suggested that the answer lies in the cooperative relationship between management and workers. Others have noted that government assistance and low-interest business development loans enable Japanese companies to buy the latest machinery. Still others have pointed out that the Japanese educational system emphasizes the study of science and math. This focus has helped produce a force of scientists and engineers who have been able to develop better, more competitive products. Whatever the answer, most American business schools have deemed that the Japanese approach to management is worthy of extensive study.

Asian thought has also influenced the West, especially since the end of World War II. For example, Mohandas Gandhi's ideas about nonviolent resistance had a powerful impact on the leaders of the civil rights movement in the United States during the 1960s.

At one time, many people believed that because of the significant cultural differences between East and West, mutual understanding was all but impossible. Asians would never understand western society, nor would Westerners ever comprehend the ways of Asian society. However, in the 1980s and 1990s, greater understanding has developed. This understanding certainly will continue to improve as Pacific economic powers such as Japan, South Korea, Singapore, Hong Kong, and Taiwan play an even greater role in the world economy.

Section 5 Review

1. **Define** ASEAN, "Four Tigers"
2. **Classifying Ideas** List three factors that contributed to the development of authoritarian government in Asia.
3. **Analyzing Ideas** What problems have Asian nations faced in bringing about industrial development?
4. **Interpreting Ideas** How have Asian ideas influenced life in the West?

Chapter 29 Review

A.D. 1949
• Communists take over China.
• Indonesia gains independence.

A.D. 1950–1964
Nehru serves as prime minister of India.

A.D. 1942   **A.D. 1946**   **A.D. 1950**   **A.D. 1954**   **A.D. 1958**   **A.D. 1962**

A.D. 1946
The U.S. grants independence to the Philippines.

A.D. 1947
India gains independence.

A.D. 1950–1953
Korean War is fought.

A.D. 1954
Geneva Accords divide Vietnam at the 17th parallel.

A.D. 1958
Great Leap Forward begins.

Chapter Summary

The following list contains the key concepts you have learned about the nations of Asia between the end of World War II and the present.

1. The period following World War II was a time of conflict and tension for many Asian nations.
2. As India became independent of British rule, the subcontinent was partitioned. The nation continued to face internal conflict and economic problems.
3. Pakistan faced problems similar to India's. In addition, Pakistan was divided into two parts. After a civil war, East Pakistan became Bangladesh.
4. The victory of Mao Zedong in 1949 brought the Communist Party to power in China. The Chinese Nationalists, led by Chiang Kaishek, fled to the island of Taiwan, off the coast of China.
5. The Communists implemented several plans to modernize their vast nation, including the Great Leap Forward. After Mao's death, more moderate leaders took over.
6. Korea was divided after World War II. When the communist state of North Korea invaded South Korea in 1950, it was repulsed by UN forces, and an armistice was eventually signed.
7. Japan achieved economic success in the postwar period. Trade imbalances with the United States have caused friction between the two nations.
8. Japan has experienced internal political problems caused by political scandals in the last decade.
9. In the Philippines, Indonesia, Malaysia, and Singapore, economic development was fostered by strong central governments. Despite social problems, these nations began a process of industrialization and economic growth.
10. Decades of conflict in Vietnam involved the United States as well as the Asian nations of Laos and Cambodia. North Vietnam conquered South Vietnam and united the nation in the mid-1970s.
11. Thailand struggled politically and grew economically, but in recent years the country has experienced economic troubles.
12. The difficulties of economic development led many Asian nations to rely on strong central governments. However, in the last decades Asian nations have begun to cooperate for the sake of economic development. Asia has been a continuing economic influence on the West.

Reviewing Important Terms

On a separate sheet of paper, supply the term that correctly completes each statement.

1. A(n) _____ _____ is an economic system in which private companies own some industries while the government owns the rest.
2. India followed a policy of _____, refusing to ally itself with either the United States or the Soviet Union.
3. According to the _____ _____, if South Vietnam fell to communism, other nations of Southeast Asia would follow.

Developing Critical Thinking Skills

1. **Understanding Ideas** What economic and social problems did India face after achieving independence?
2. **Analyzing Primary Sources** Read the selection from the preamble to the Indian Constitution, and answer the questions that follow:

"We, the people of India, having solemnly resolved to constitute India into a sovereign democratic republic and to secure to all its citizens:
JUSTICE—social, economic, and political;
LIBERTY of thought, expression, belief, faith, and worship;
EQUALITY of status and of opportunity; and to promote . . .
FRATERNITY assuring the dignity of the individual and the unity of the Nation,
. . . do HEREBY ADOPT, ENACT AND GIVE TO OUR-SELVES THIS CONSTITUTION."

(a) What type of government does the constitution promise to the Indian people? (b) What ideals does it swear to uphold? (c) How do these ideals compare with those stated in the preamble to the United States Constitution?

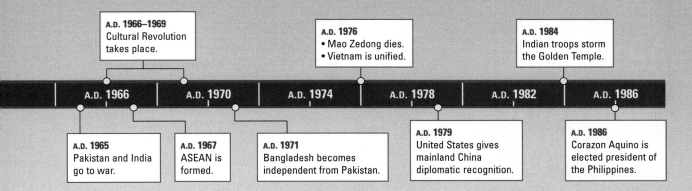

A.D. 1966–1969
Cultural Revolution takes place.

A.D. 1976
• Mao Zedong dies.
• Vietnam is unified.

A.D. 1984
Indian troops storm the Golden Temple.

A.D. 1966 | A.D. 1970 | A.D. 1974 | A.D. 1978 | A.D. 1982 | A.D. 1986

A.D. 1965
Pakistan and India go to war.

A.D. 1967
ASEAN is formed.

A.D. 1971
Bangladesh becomes independent from Pakistan.

A.D. 1979
United States gives mainland China diplomatic recognition.

A.D. 1986
Corazon Aquino is elected president of the Philippines.

3. **Summarizing Ideas** What political and economic policies did the Communists bring about in China after they took over the government?
4. **Analyzing Ideas** How did events in Tiananmen Square affect China's foreign relations?
5. **Evaluating Ideas** (a) Explain how Japan became a powerful industrial nation. (b) What changes and problems came about as a result of this industrialization of Japan?
6. **Determining Cause and Effect** (a) What were the causes of the Vietnam War? (b) How did the United States become involved in the Vietnam War? (c) What were the results, both for Southeast Asian nations and for the United States?
7. **Classifying Ideas** List reasons for past hostilities between the following countries: (a) the Soviet Union and China; (b) India and Pakistan; (c) Pakistan and Bangladesh.
8. **Comparing Ideas** (a) How did the Korean War differ from the Vietnam War in causes and results? (b) How were the two conflicts similar? (c) What roles did the United States and the People's Republic of China play in each of these wars?

Relating Geography to History

Turn to the map of Asia on page 783. (a) How many miles separate Taiwan from the People's Republic of China? (b) How many kilometers? (c) Why is Japan a strategic location for defense of American interests in the Pacific?

Relating Past to Present

1. On a sheet of paper, list evidence that your community has contact with the nations of Asia. For example, observe the cars on a busy street. How many of them are Japanese? Can you buy a shirt made of Indian cotton or a book of Chinese or Japanese poetry? Using this information, write a short essay discussing Asia's influence on the Western world.
2. Use your school or public library to find articles on China today. Then prepare a report that explains how the Communists have changed traditional Chinese society, what economic problems still exist in China, and what modern life is like in China.

Applying History Study Skills

Before completing this activity, review Building History Study Skills on page 784.

Read the following statement from the writings of Mao Zedong. After reading the statement, identify any fallacies in reasoning.

"This leadership of the poor peasants is extremely necessary. Without the poor peasants there can be no revolution. To reject them is to reject the revolution. To attack them is to attack the revolution. From beginning to end, the general direction they have given the revolution has never been wrong. They have hurt the dignity of the local bullies and evil gentry. They have knocked down the big and small local bullies and evil gentry and trampled them underfoot. Many of their deeds in the period of revolution, described as 'going too far,' were in fact dictated by the very needs of the revolution."

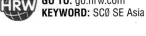

Search the Internet through the HRW Web site for more information on the major urban centers of Southeast Asia. Construct a chart to compare these cities. Include information on population, places of interest, and major economic activities.

GO TO: go.hrw.com
KEYWORD: SCØ SE Asia

Building Your Portfolio

1. **Writing a Report** Conduct research on the Vietnam War and answer the following questions: (a) What were the goals of Ho Chi Minh between 1945 and 1954? (b) Why did the peasants support the Viet Cong? (c) What was the final outcome of the war? Place the report in your portfolio.
2. **Analyzing Literature** One way to gain insight into a culture is to read its literature. Present a short report to the class on a modern novel by a Chinese, Japanese, or Indian author. Tell the class how the book helped you understand the culture of China, Japan, or India. Place your notes or an audiotape of your report in your portfolio.

CHAPTER 30

Africa and the Middle East Since 1945

TIME

A.D. 1945–the present

A.D. 1945–the present

3.7 million B.C.   4000 B.C.   A.D. 2100

PLACE

Africa and the
Middle East

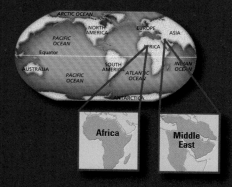

African National Congress rally

Significance

Like World War I, World War II was a watershed in the history of Africa and the Middle East. After the war, nationalism grew at a faster pace than ever. In Africa more radical younger leaders came to the fore, demanding complete self-government and eventually independence from the European colonial powers. The Middle East also saw the emergence of new leaders determined to break free from European domination once and for all. Many of the new nations, however, remained tied economically to the former colonial powers.

Terms to Define

Pan-Africanism	*colons*
CPP	FLN
Mau Mau	kibbutz
apartheid	PLO
MPLA	shuttle diplomacy
UNITA	Camp David Accords
desertification	*intifada*
negritude	petrodollars

People to Identify

Kwame Nkrumah	David Ben-Gurion
Jomo Kenyatta	Chaim Weizmann
Robert Mugabe	King Farouk
Sékou Touré	Gamal Abdel Nasser
Nelson Mandela	Adnan Menderes
F.W. de Klerk	Anwar Sadat
Jerry Rawlings	Ayatollah Khomeini
Ibrahim Babangida	Hafiz Asad
Laurent Kabila	Saddam Hussein
Wole Soyinka	

Places to Locate

Ghana	Persian Gulf
Kenya	Beirut
Zimbabwe	Bahrain
South Africa	Qatar
Horn of Africa	United Arab Emirates
Rwanda	Oman
Aswan High Dam	Tehran

Chapter Theme Questions

- **Politics and Law** How might the process used by a country to achieve its independence affect its subsequent history?
- **Social Relations** How might the presence of different ethnic groups within a country affect the political history of that country?
- **Economics** How might the discovery of an important resource in a region affect that area's history?

During the 1960s, Obafemi Awolowo, a political leader from western Nigeria, reflected on how his newly independent homeland should view human rights:

Every member of any human association has rights, intangible though they are, which are sacred and inalienable, and which must be protected against any invasion, at all costs. In a State, such rights are more carefully and elaborately spelt out, and are termed fundamental human rights. These rights are also regarded as inalienable because they are inherent in, not acquired by, man. Only acquired rights are alienable. . . .

It is, therefore, of exceeding importance that in every written constitution, fundamental human rights should be entrenched, and provisions for their inviolable protection and impartial enforcement should also be clearly set out and entrenched.

Awolowo was only one of many African and Middle Eastern leaders who worked to lead newly independent nations after 1945.

Section 1

African Independence After World War II

Focus Questions

- **What were the characteristics of African nationalism after World War II?**
- **How did colonial rule end in Ghana, Kenya, and British central Africa?**
- **How did the end of colonial rule in the French and Belgian colonies differ from what occurred in the British colonies?**
- **How did South Africa's experience of colonialism and independence differ from that of other nations of Africa?**

World War II was a turning point in the history of Africa. During the war, thousands of Africans served in the armies of the European colonial powers, both inside and outside Africa. The continent itself became a supply route between the Allies and the rest of the world. During the war, the Allied powers also seemed to imply the end of colonial rule in declarations such as the Atlantic Charter. When the war ended, many Africans were no longer satisfied with the status quo, and a new wave of nationalism began to gain strength throughout the continent. Exhausted and nearly bankrupted by the war, most of the old colonial powers soon realized that independence was inevitable. Within a few short decades, the political map of Africa was transformed as colony after colony achieved independence. By the 1990s, all Africa was free from colonial rule.

African Nationalism

Before 1945, talk of nationalism in Africa was largely confined to a few Africans who had been particularly affected by their interaction with Europeans. In the British colonies of West Africa, for example, families of African merchants, along with chiefs from the interior, had long engaged in trade and other business relationships with Europeans. Among these few, many had received an education in Europe or the United States. Some of these individuals worked as missionaries, spreading Christianity in Africa. Others became civil servants. Through such contacts, some became convinced that only by forming modern nations, like those of Europe, could African peoples become free and join in the life of the modern world.

As members of a privileged group, however, many of these Western-educated Africans did not always feel at ease with their own people and did not seek broad popular support. Nor were their demands very great. Generally, they called simply for wider participation in the colonial governments. At the same time, because of their African heritage, they were excluded from European society. Consequently, before the war, these Africans had little influence on colonial policy.

In the 1930s, however, a new brand of African nationalism emerged. During the Great Depression, most colonial governments cut back on wages for African civil servants. This angered many and fueled anticolonial sentiment. The 1936 Italian invasion and conquest of Ethiopia, which had been the last great independent African state, also shocked and angered Africans throughout the continent. A younger, more radical generation of African nationalists began to call for complete self-government, if not yet complete independence.

This second generation of African nationalists was also heavily influenced by the Pan-African movement. **Pan-Africanism** promoted the cultural unity of people of African heritage in their mutual struggle for freedom. The Pan-African movement began among people of African descent in North America and the West Indies. It gained strength particularly in the first half of the 1900s under Marcus Garvey of Jamaica and African American educator W. E. B. Du Bois. Their aim was to win equality for black people in all parts of the world. Ending colonial rule in Africa was central to this aim.

Garvey's cry of "Africa for the Africans at Home and Abroad" alarmed colonial powers. It also drew many young Africans to the cause. For example, delegates to the 1945 Pan-African Congress in Manchester, England, included Kwame Nkrumah (en·KROO·muh) of the Gold Coast, Jomo Kenyatta of Kenya, and Hastings Banda of Nyasaland (now Malawi). They all became leaders of independence movements in their countries.

The events of World War II also contributed to the growth of a more popular African nationalism. During the war, Africa once again became a major supplier of men and matériel for the Allied war effort. Some 80,000 Africans, for example, served in France's armies in Europe, while Great Britain recruited or drafted hundreds of thousands of Africans from its colonies to help the Allies win the war. These Africans, many of whom served outside of Africa, were introduced to a larger world and new ideas. At the same time, declarations such as the Atlantic Charter seemed to promise self-determination for all peoples after the war. Such declarations or statements raised expectations among many Africans that their demands for greater freedom would soon be met.

Despite the expectations of African nationalists immediately after World War II, the colonial powers did not plan to give up their empires in Africa any time soon. Consequently, the struggle for national independence in Africa took many forms. Some colonies followed a sometimes slow constitutional process, with popular elections and a peaceful transfer of power. Other colonies suffered lengthy "wars of national liberation." The specific form of the independence effort depended on the particular experience of imperialism in that part of Africa.

Winds of Change in British Africa

In February 1960, British prime minister Harold Macmillan addressed the South African Parliament.

African Independence, 1946–1993

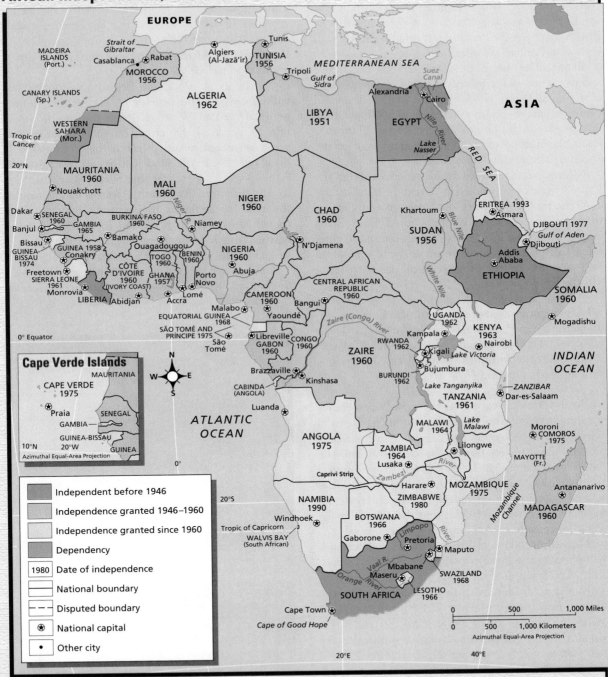

Learning from Maps Many former African colonies have become independent nations since 1946.

❓ **Region** What country remained a dependency in 1993?

Somewhat to the dismay of his listeners who represented both houses of Parliament, he warned that a "wind of change" was sweeping through Africa that would blow away the old days of colonialism. The British had been the first to acknowledge this wind in their own African colonies.

Ghana. The first Sub-Saharan colony to achieve independence under majority rule was Britain's colony of the Gold Coast, in West Africa. In 1957 the Gold Coast became the independent nation of Ghana. (See map on page 815.) Ghana's leader, Kwame Nkrumah, chose the new country's name to commemorate the ancient African kingdom of Ghana.

Nkrumah had received his higher education in the United States and worked in Great Britain. In late 1947, he returned to the Gold Coast upon invitation to be general secretary of the United Gold Coast Convention, a political party of the westernized elite. From this post, Nkrumah began to build a national following. He believed that political unity in Africa was the key to success.

❝African unity is above all a political kingdom, which can only be gained by political means. The social and economic development of Africa will come only within the political kingdom, not the other way around.❞

Soon Nkrumah called on the people to begin a campaign of civil disobedience, including strikes and boycotts of British goods. In this new, more politically charged atmosphere, riots broke out in Accra, the colony's capital city, in 1948. Soon the rioting spread to other towns, and it took the colonial authorities several days to restore order. The Accra riots did much to convince the British that they should make some concessions to African nationalist demands.

Meanwhile, Nkrumah's radical tactics and demands had alarmed the more conservative African leaders, who expelled him from his post. Consequently, in 1949 Nkrumah founded his own political party, the Convention People's Party **(CPP)**, dedicated to achieving immediate self-government. Under his guidance, the CPP became a major political party designed to appeal to the masses.

Under almost constant pressure from the CPP, in 1951 the British colonial authorities agreed to hold a national election in the Gold Coast. Nkrumah's party won a huge victory, but Nkrumah continued to pressure the British for complete independence. Britain finally granted Ghana full sovereignty in 1957.

Kenya. The example of Ghana became an inspiration to African nationalists in other colonies. In some, however, particularly those with significant numbers of white settlers, the movement toward independence was more difficult and complicated. Kenya in East Africa, for example, took a very different road to independence.

By the early 1950s, the British government was willing to give the peoples of East Africa limited political freedom. White settlers in the area, however, rejected any kind of reform. They feared that African self-government would threaten their ownership of huge tracts of fertile land in the central highlands. Rapid population growth after World War II had led to land shortages. As a result, Africans had demanded the right to settle in the central highlands even though they were not allowed to own land there. Further, the Kikuyu, Kenya's largest ethnic group, looked on this area as their ancestral homeland.

Land ownership had an almost mystical quality for the Kikuyu. Kikuyu leader Jomo Kenyatta described the Kikuyu feeling about land this way:

Jomo Kenyatta, who was jailed on charges of leading the Kenyan Mau Mau rebellion of 1952, became the prime minister of Kenya in 1963 and president a year later.

"It is the key to the people's life; it secures them that peaceful tillage [cultivation] of the soil which supplies their material needs and enables them to perform their magic and traditional ceremonies in undisturbed serenity.**"**

The continued exclusion of the Kikuyu from the central highlands soon became a source of tension. Then, in the early 1950s, this tension actually exploded into violence.

In a four-year guerrilla campaign, the "Land and Freedom" army, a secret Kikuyu organization that became popularly known as the **Mau Mau**, caused terror and destruction in the central highlands. During the campaign, the Mau Mau killed about 100 Europeans and some 2,000 Africans loyal to the British government. The British took military actions to suppress the movement. More than 11,500 Kikuyu were killed during or as a result of the war. Thousands were jailed in detention camps. Eventually, the British succeeded in suppressing the Mau Mau and restoring order in Kenya, but they could not put down the drive for Kenyan independence.

In 1961 Kenyatta, who had been jailed as a suspected leader of the Mau Mau, was released. He emerged from prison as the leader of the independence movement. His popularity and forceful leadership helped overcome ethnic rivalries and brought about a shared sense of Kenyan nationalism. Kenyatta won an easy victory in national elections held in May 1963. Later that year, Kenya gained its independence, and Kenyatta became the first prime minister of the new nation. In 1964 he became president, a position he held until his death in 1978.

British central Africa. Developments in Britain's colonies in central Africa—Southern Rhodesia (present-day Zimbabwe), Northern Rhodesia (present-day Zambia), and Nyasaland (present-day Malawi)—also represented an unusual example of both guerrilla warfare and constitutional change. Southern Rhodesia's large white population had achieved internal self-government in the 1920s. The other two territories were governed by Britain.

After World War II, the settlers of Southern Rhodesia combined efforts with the much smaller settler population of Northern Rhodesia to convince the British government to allow the creation of a Central African federation. The British included the small protectorate of Nyasaland, but the Africans who lived there strongly opposed it. As in their other colonies, the British hoped to create a multiracial state. This policy, however, was opposed by the white settlers, who were favored by imperial policies in the 1950s.

Established as a 10-year experiment in 1953, the Federation of Rhodesia and Nyasaland was always bitterly opposed by African nationalist leaders. They saw the Federation as a means by which the white settlers could maintain their control over the black majority populations of the three territories. Throughout the life of the Federation, African nationalism continued to develop. At the end of the 10-year trial period, in 1963, the African majorities in Northern Rhodesia and Nyasaland voted to withdraw from the Federation. In 1964 the two colonies became the independent states of Zambia and Malawi under majority African rule. Britain also tried to force progress toward majority rule on Southern Rhodesia, but the white population led by Prime Minister Ian Smith refused to cooperate.

In 1965 Smith issued the Unilateral Declaration of Independence (UDI) and proclaimed the independent state of Rhodesia. Great Britain and the rest of the world refused to accept Smith's act, insisting that it was illegal, and reduced or cut off trade relations. Although the Smith government was isolated internationally, it still refused to initiate reforms. Consequently, as happened in the neighboring Portuguese colonies, a guerrilla war began.

Little success was achieved in the early years of fighting. However, when Angola and Mozambique became independent from Portugal in 1975, the liberation forces gained a military advantage. They now had countries that were friendly to their cause located in southern Africa. Under the leadership of Robert Mugabe and Joshua Nkomo, the African forces intensified their attacks and succeeded in disrupting the economy of Rhodesia.

As the war became increasingly unpopular among the white population, Smith was forced to seek a solution. Eventually, he worked with moderate African leaders to form a new government under African leadership that would continue to guarantee the privileged status of whites. Even this was not enough to stop the ongoing guerrilla war. Still under enormous pressure, the Rhodesian government finally agreed to hold free elections open to all parties, including the liberation leaders. In these 1980 elections, Robert Mugabe, considered the most radical of the candidates, was the victor.

In April 1980, Rhodesia became the new nation of Zimbabwe—a name taken from the ancient southern African kingdom of Great Zimbabwe. After years of civil war, Zimbabwe's future seemed settled, and the government turned its energies to economic recovery.

The French Colonies

While the British decided to compromise with the demands of African nationalists fairly quickly and easily, in French colonial territories a different pattern emerged. As with other parts of Africa, World War II marked a turning point in France's African colonies.

Before World War II, most of France's African colonies had been organized in two administrative units, French West Africa and French Equatorial Africa. The colonial governors of French West Africa remained loyal to Vichy during the war. French Equatorial Africa, however, led by the governor of Chad, Felix Eboué, the first black man to become a colonial governor, declared its support for the Free French forces of General de Gaulle. In 1944, with de Gaulle's approval, the governors of French Equatorial Africa met in Brazzaville to announce more liberal policies. The Brazzaville Declaration, which outlined these reforms, however, also made it clear that the French Empire would continue and that the colonies could not expect independence.

Following the Allied victory, France itself adopted a new constitution. Under this constitution, the French Empire was transformed into the French Union. The vote was extended to more Africans, who were now eligible to elect some 20 African representatives to the French National Assembly in Paris. Other Africans were also elected to the Assembly of the French Union.

Although this system provided many Africans with political experience, it fell short of real independence. Many Africans felt that their interests were second to those of France. In response, African leaders such as Léopold Senghor of Senegal, Felix Houphouet-Boigny (oo·FWAY BWAH·nyuh) of the Côte d'Ivoire, and Sékou Touré (too·RAY) of Guinea, began to develop the same kind of popular parties that were emerging in British colonies. At first the new political parties only sought self-government within the French Union. As it became increasingly clear that France was not interested in granting anything but limited control over the colonies, however, many African nationalists became more radical in their demands.

In 1958 Charles de Gaulle, the new French president, offered the African colonies a choice. They could remain independent within the French Community (the newly transformed French Union), subject to French control of their foreign affairs, or they could become totally independent. Those colonies that chose to remain within the French Community would continue to receive aid from France. Those that chose independence would be immediately cut off from all aid and contacts with France.

Only Guinea, under Sékou Touré, chose complete independence. The others accepted de Gaulle's new French Community. As de Gaulle had warned, Guinea was immediately isolated from the rest of the French Community, both politically and economically. However, in 1960 those African colonies that accepted membership in the French Community were granted the very independence that Touré had insisted on, but without sacrificing their close economic and political ties to France.

The Belgian Congo

Perhaps the most traumatic transition to independence occurred in the Belgian Congo. (The Belgian Congo later became Zaire, which was renamed the Democratic Republic of the Congo in 1997.) Belgium, which opposed independence because of the colony's great wealth in timber and mineral resources, provided few opportunities for Africans to develop their skills in government.

The Congo was home to many different groups of people, speaking different languages and with different customs. Under Belgian rule, these differences did not diminish but were reinforced. During World War II,

The Congo was a Belgian colony from 1908 until 1960. Violence broke out across the country after independence. Here UN troops arrive in the Congo in 1961.

however, as the local economy worked harder to produce goods for the war effort, many Congolese began to leave their villages and flock to the cities. There they came in contact with other Congolese and began to establish cultural clubs. In the 1950s, events in neighboring British and French colonies finally introduced ideas of nationalism into the Congo. After 1955 the Belgian authorities even allowed the development of new political parties. Most of the new parties remained committed to their local regions, but a few had programs of national unity for all the Congo.

At first the Belgian government resisted nationalist demands. They proposed a gradual 30-year timetable to prepare the Congo for independence. In 1959, however, the pressures of new national ideas and dissatisfaction with Belgian colonial rule resulted in rioting in the capital city of Léopoldville. Alarmed by the violence and aware of developments in the rest of colonial Africa, Belgian authorities reversed their former policy. In January 1960, they announced that the Congo would become independent in six months—on June 30, 1960.

African leaders were not prepared for independence to come so quickly. Many different political parties, all representing different ethnic communities, geographical regions, or political beliefs, participated in the first elections. Patrice Lumumba (luh·MUHM·buh), an outspoken critic of European influence, became premier. Joseph Kasavubu (kah·sah·VOO·boo), the leader of the second-largest party and Lumumba's chief political rival, became president. Fearful of Lumumba's anti-European stance, the vast majority of Belgian technicians and experts left the country almost immediately. With few trained Africans to replace them, the Congo soon descended into chaos.

In July 1960, Congolese soldiers mutinied against their Belgian officers. A period of violence aimed mostly at white people followed. To make matters worse, the copper-rich province of Katanga, led by Moise Tshombe (CHAWM·be), seceded from the Congo. As civil war broke out, first Belgium and then the United Nations intervened. On the invitation of Kasavubu, the Congolese army, under Colonel Joseph Mobutu, overthrew Lumumba, who was assassinated in 1961. Katanga was also brought back into the republic. Fighting wracked the country until 1965, however, when Mobutu himself took full control. Mobutu gradually established a ruthless military dictatorship that lasted into the 1990s. The length of his rule was partly due to the effects of the Cold War, in which Mobutu was supported by the Western powers as a counterbalance to African countries that leaned toward the Eastern bloc. In the 1970s, he pursued a policy of Africanization, changing the name of the country to Zaire and himself taking the African name Mobutu Sese Seko.

The Portuguese Colonies

While many African nations were winning their independence, the Portuguese government continued to oppose independence for its colonies. In desperation, African leaders in Portuguese West Africa, Portuguese Guinea, and Portuguese East Africa organized "liberation armies" to fight for freedom. In a series of long, bloody wars, they gained control of much of the countryside.

These wars continued until 1974, when the military staged a coup in Portugal and announced that Portugal would withdraw from Africa. Within months of the announcement, in 1974 and 1975, Portuguese Guinea, Portuguese West Africa, and Portuguese East Africa—present-day Guinea-Bissau, Angola, and Mozambique, respectively—became independent. The establishment of African nationalist governments in these countries also put enormous pressure on the last holdout of minority white rule in Africa, the Republic of South Africa.

South Africa

South Africa's experience differed from that of any other African nation. In 1910 four territories had come together to form the Union of South Africa: the British territories of Cape Colony and Natal and the former Boer republics of the Transvaal and the Orange Free State, which had been defeated in the recent Boer War and brought under British rule. The new Union of South Africa was a white-ruled nation with dominion status. Although linked to Great Britain in foreign affairs, the dominion ruled itself internally as it saw fit.

Relying on its resources of gold, diamonds, and cheap labor, South Africa experienced an industrial revolution in the early 1900s. Its industrialization was based on the labor of black Africans, who vastly outnumbered whites. Even so, blacks were excluded almost totally from the benefits of South Africa's economic success.

Apartheid. Before World War II, English-speaking whites had dominated the government. By custom, whites and nonwhites were segregated socially. Over time, an unofficial system of separate public facilities for whites and nonwhites developed. Moreover, nonwhites were given few educational opportunities and were kept out of better jobs. Since 1911 employment opportunities for the nonwhite populations had been restricted by law to low-paying manual labor. In addition, the Land Act of 1913 and subsequent amendments restricted Africans, who made up approximately 75 percent of the population, to only 10 percent of the land. Then in 1948, the National Party, which was dominated by the white, Afrikaans-speaking descendants of the original Dutch settlers, came to power in South Africa. The Afrikaners quickly transformed this unofficial system of social segregation and economic exploitation into government policy.

This policy became known as **apartheid**—the Afrikaans word for apartness. It consisted of a number of laws that separated the races in every aspect of life. These laws were a way to legally establish white supremacy in the country. One law called for all people to be classified by race: Bantu (black), Colored (mixed race), Asian, or White. Another law established where each of the four races could live. A third law banned intermarriage between the races. A fourth required all nonwhites to carry an identity pass when traveling outside their designated areas. Other laws established different pay scales for whites and nonwhites.

Apartheid also involved the founding of separate tribal states, known as homelands or Bantustans, for Africans. After a brief period of self-government, these homelands would become completely independent. Afrikaner leaders cited the homelands program to support their claim that the intent of apartheid was that each race would prosper if developed separately. However, the homelands were located in the most barren areas of the country and had few natural resources. Even after independence, the homelands would remain completely dependent on South Africa.

Protests against apartheid. Some organizations had fought racial discrimination in South Africa long before apartheid was established. The African National Congress (ANC)—the best-known antiapartheid group—was founded in 1912. In the 1950s, the ANC launched a campaign of civil disobedience in which ANC members openly violated apartheid laws. The response of the South African government to this campaign of civil disobedience was swift and brutal. In 1960 police opened fire on a peaceful demonstration in the town of Sharpeville, leaving more than 60 dead and hundreds wounded. As world opinion condemned the Sharpeville massacre, in 1961 Prime Minister Hendrik Verwoerd, one of the primary architects of

apartheid, decided to proclaim South Africa a republic and to withdraw from the British Commonwealth.

After Sharpeville some ANC leaders, the black lawyer Nelson Mandela among them, felt that in self-defense they would have to confront violence with violence. In response the government banned the ANC in 1960. Then in 1962, Mandela and other ANC leaders were arrested. Charged with treason and found guilty, they all received life jail terms.

Despite the ban and the loss of its leaders, the ANC continued to operate, primarily from bases outside South Africa. In addition, Desmond Tutu, Steve Biko, and other black leaders continued to speak out against the repressive apartheid laws. Some, such as Biko, paid with their lives. An increasing number of white South Africans, too, became involved in the antiapartheid movement. Helen Suzman, for example, used her position as a member of parliament to criticize the government's policies. However, hers was very much a lone voice in the legislature.

In the meantime, the government proceeded with its policy of repression. In 1976, schoolchildren in Soweto, a black township near Johannesburg, marched peacefully in protest against a new law enforcing the use of Afrikaans in all South African schools. They were met by police who opened fire, killing many. Over the next months, outraged Africans rioted all over the country. About 600 people, most of them black, were killed in the violence. After the Soweto riots, many in South Africa were no longer willing to wait peacefully for change.

In the 1980s, faced with growing protests both inside South Africa and from abroad, the South African government began to retreat from its strict apartheid policies. Constitutional reforms gave some political voice to Colored and Asian South Africans. Black Africans, however, were still denied any political participation, and civil strife continued. Meanwhile, the international community imposed economic sanctions on South Africa, pressuring the country to change its racist policies.

A change of direction. In September 1989, the pace of change in South Africa quickened with the election of F. W. de Klerk as president. De Klerk lifted a 30-year ban on antiapartheid rallies and legalized the ANC and other banned organizations. He also ordered the release of Nelson Mandela in February 1990. In a speech at Capetown celebrating his freedom, Mandela repeated the words he had spoken during his trial:

South Africans stood in long lines as the first all-race South African election took place in April 1994.

"I have fought against white domination, and I have fought against black domination. I have cherished the ideal of a democratic and free society in which all persons live together in harmony and with equal opportunities. It is an ideal which I hope to live for, and to see realized. But . . . if needs be, it is an ideal for which I am prepared to die."

De Klerk expressed the hope that Mandela and other opposition leaders would meet with him to discuss ways to build a new South Africa. The promise of reform, however, did not end the violence and dissension. A fight for leadership of the black population erupted between the ANC and the largely Zulu Inkatha Freedom Party, led by Mangosuthu Gatsha Buthelezi. This fight resulted in the deaths of thousands of black South Africans in the 15 months following the legalization of the ANC. Moreover, not all whites supported de Klerk. Many Afrikaners left de Klerk's National Party and joined the much more right wing Conservatives.

Despite all these challenges, however, in 1994 South Africa held its first all-race elections. Nelson Mandela was elected by an overwhelming majority as the new president of a multiracial South Africa. Pursuing conciliatory policies, Mandela called on people to "heal the wounds of the past." As South Africa moved toward the end of the century, a new era of partnership and cooperation seemed to have replaced the dark era of apartheid.

Section 1 Review

1. **Define** Pan-Africanism, CPP, Mau Mau, apartheid
2. **Identify** Kwame Nkrumah, Jomo Kenyatta, Robert Mugabe, Sékou Touré, Nelson Mandela, F. W. de Klerk
3. **Locate and Explain the Significance** Ghana, Kenya, Zimbabwe, South Africa
4. **Understanding Ideas** Describe how African nationalism began to emerge after World War II.
5. **Summarizing Ideas** Summarize the changes that occurred in Ghana, Kenya, and British central Africa after World War II.
6. **Analyzing Ideas** What factors led to the differing experiences of independence between the British colonies and those of the French and Belgians?
7. **Interpreting Ideas** How did apartheid shape South African history?

Section 2

Africa Since Independence

Focus Questions

- **What challenges did newly independent African countries face?**
- **How did rivalry between the superpowers of the Cold War affect Africa?**
- **How did ethnic diversity contribute to political instability in independent African nations?**
- **In what ways did Africa experience a revival of African culture?**

After gaining independence, the new nations of Africa still faced many serious problems. While specific geographical and historical factors made each nation's problems unique, some common experiences also existed. Practically all the new nations struggled with economic difficulties. Ethnic tensions also racked some of the new countries. In addition, drought, disease, and the Cold War all took their toll on these new nations. Despite these problems, however, the independence that these nations experienced stimulated a revival and development of new cultural expressions throughout much of Africa.

Political and Economic Challenges

Despite the high hopes with which many Africans greeted independence, the years following the end of colonial rule were not easy ones. The new African leaders were inexperienced in politics and in running the new states they had inherited from the colonial rulers. As they failed to improve the lot of their peoples rapidly enough, in many countries, the military began to intervene. Soon most African countries were being ruled by military dictatorships. The case of Ghana provides a good example of the pattern that emerged in many African states after independence.

Ghana. The early years of Kwame Nkrumah's rule coincided with high prices on world markets for Ghana's main cash crop—cocoa. The prosperity that Ghana enjoyed at this time helped make Nkrumah very popular among the people. He exploited this popularity, however, building up a cult of personality around himself. Nkrumah's drive for absolute power resulted in a new constitution in 1964, which established Ghana as a one-party state. Any challenge to Nkrumah was the equivalent of treason. Yet people continued to criticize, especially after the fall of world prices for cocoa. This price drop, combined with government debt and corruption, caused the Ghanaian economy to collapse. Nkrumah responded by becoming more and more ruthless. His popularity declined rapidly, and in 1966, while on a visit to another country, he was ousted in a military coup.

Although few people in Ghana mourned Nkrumah's departure, the situation did not improve. Over the next 12 years, Ghana went back and forth between civilian and military rule. This political instability was matched by fluctuations in the economy, which remained tied to cocoa.

In 1979, just before an election designed to return the government to civilian rule, the military stepped in yet again. This takeover was led by Jerry Rawlings, a young air force pilot. Rawlings stated that the present military leaders were corrupt and inefficient and had to go. After public trials, a number of leading military officers were executed. Rawlings then allowed the elections to take place, and the country returned to civilian rule.

A little over a year later, however, Rawlings stepped in once again. He dissolved the civilian government, claiming that it was worse than the military junta it had replaced. Rawlings felt that Ghana should follow socialist policies. After two years of ever-worsening economic reports, he changed his opinion. In 1983 he put the country's economy on a course

toward free enterprise. By 1990 Ghana's annual rate of economic growth was one of the highest in Africa.

This improvement in the economy, however, came at great cost to the Ghanaian people. They had to endure high taxes on imports, a sales tax, and an income tax. Subsidies on food and fuel were reduced, and the currency was devalued to stimulate exports. Ghanaians grew weary of continued economic measures and Rawlings' rigid government style. Demands for a return to civilian rule increased. In 1992 a new constitution was adopted, and civilian rule was established. Resigning from the military, Rawlings ran for the presidency and won.

Nigeria. While Ghana's experience following independence was similar to that of many African nations, some had to deal with special problems. Many of these problems were left over from the days of colonial rule. For example, new national boundaries often were artificial, drawn by the imperialist powers for their own convenience. In some cases, people of similar racial or cultural backgrounds were separated, while people of different heritages were grouped together. In some places, such as Nigeria, these problems soon led to civil war.

At the time of independence in 1960, Nigeria was a federation of three regions, each of which retained a large degree of local independence. A fourth region was created in 1963. Although this situation resulted in strong ethnic and regional differences in the country, the government hoped that this loose federation would prevent warfare among the various groups. It did not, however, prevent conflict.

In 1966 the military took over the government, but it could not overcome the tensions created by the ethnic and regional distrust. After independence, for example, the federal government's exploitation of major oil deposits, discovered in the late 1950s in the Niger Delta, had increased regional tensions. In 1967 the Eastern Region, home of the Ibo-speaking people, seceded from the federation and declared itself the independent Republic of Biafra. Nigeria plunged into civil war. After more than two years of war and the deaths of as many as several million Biafrans from starvation and disease, Biafra surrendered. Pursuing a policy of conciliation, the Nigerian government gradually restored stability to the country. Nevertheless, ethnicity and regionalism continued to be sensitive issues in Nigeria.

A democratically elected civilian government returned to Nigeria in 1979. At the same time, the country's oil wealth provided Nigerians with the opportunity to escape the poverty that threatened most other African nations. It also appeared that Nigeria might be the first African nation other than South Africa to achieve a high degree of industrialization.

In the 1980s, however, a drop in the international price of oil—the commodity that accounted for 95 percent of Nigeria's export revenues—caused Nigeria's economy to falter. In late 1983, military officers overthrew the civilian government and introduced strict new measures to turn the economy around. In 1983 and again in 1985, the government forced foreigners living illegally in Nigeria, many of them from Ghana, to leave the country.

This government proved very unpopular. In 1985, another military coup, this one led by Major General Ibrahim Babangida, had taken place. Babangida immediately introduced bold new reforms to restore economic and political stability. He renegotiated the country's foreign loans, applying for assistance from international financial organizations.

In 1992 Babangida fulfilled a promise to return the country to civilian rule. In the elections that followed, Moshood Abiola was elected president. Before he

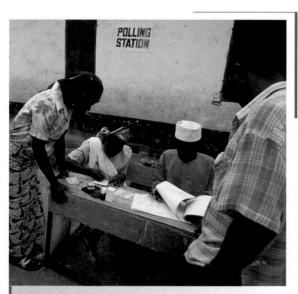

During the late 1980s, the government of President Ibrahim Babangida supported a return to civilian rule in Nigeria, leading to local elections in 1991, national legislative elections in 1992, and presidential elections in 1993. Nigerians are shown above voting in a 1992 election.

could be inaugurated, however, the military again intervened and declared the election results invalid. When Abiola declared himself president anyway, he was imprisoned. Nevertheless, pressures remained strong to return to civilian rule. In 1997 General Sani Abacha, the current military leader, scheduled elections for sometime in 1998. In mid-1998, however, both Abacha and Abiola died of natural causes. A new military strongman, General Abdulsalam Abubakar, took power, pledging to return the country to civilian rule in the near future.

Superpower Rivalries

Superpower rivalry complicated the efforts of new African nations to achieve peace and stability. As these nations sought financial and technical assistance from both the Soviet Union and the United States, they often found themselves caught up in the Cold War.

Angola. When civil war broke out in Angola after independence in 1975, the United States and the Soviet Union rushed arms and support to the rival factions. Soviet military advisers and Cuban troops supported the Marxist Popular Movement for the Liberation of Angola **(MPLA)**. The National Union for the Total Independence of Angola **(UNITA)** received aid from the United States. Fearing that the MPLA might assist Marxist rebels in Namibia, South Africa also supported UNITA. The MPLA eventually gained control, but about 50,000 Cuban troops stayed in Angola to help fight off continued attacks by UNITA.

For the next 12 years, Angola became a battleground for the Cold War between the United States and the Soviet Union. When tensions between the two superpowers eased, moves were made to end the civil war in Angola. A regional agreement that linked independence for Namibia with the withdrawal of Cuban troops from Angola was reached in 1988. In May 1991, the MPLA and UNITA hammered out a peace treaty that also called for free elections late in 1992. The continued hostility between MPLA and UNITA leaders, however, left the success of the treaty in question.

The Horn of Africa. Soviet-American rivalry was even more complex in the Horn of Africa, a strategic area that includes Ethiopia and Somalia. The Horn overlooks the Red Sea as well as the Indian Ocean sea-lanes to the oil-rich Persian Gulf. It is also an area of relative instability, characterized by frequent border disputes and local independence movements.

Although the United States had established a military base in Ethiopia in the 1950s, when the Ethiopian emperor Haile Selassie was overthrown in 1974, a Marxist regime came to power. To support the socialist governments in Ethiopia and in nearby Somalia, the Soviet Union provided military aid and advisers. Cuban troops were stationed in Ethiopia. Although the Soviet Union gained a temporary advantage, it had provided arms to two traditionally hostile neighbors. When Somalia invaded Ethiopia in 1977, the Soviets supported Ethiopia. Somalia was defeated in 1978 by Cuban troops with Soviet weapons, but guerrilla fighting in the region continued until 1988.

The topsy-turvy situation created by superpower rivalry demonstrated that African nations often preferred practical assistance to ideological commitments. This became even clearer in the 1980s and early 1990s, after the end of the Cold War. In 1984 a worldwide relief effort was initiated to help Ethiopia during a severe drought. Somalia, also devastated by drought, called on its Arab neighbors and the United States for aid. Despite financial support, in 1991 the military dictatorships in both Somalia and Ethiopia collapsed. Their overthrow, however, only brought more problems.

Somalia descended into civil war as different clans and rival warlords fought for power. The fighting prevented humanitarian aid from reaching victims of the drought. Consequently, at the urging of the United States, in 1992 an international force, under the authority of the United Nations, intervened in Somalia. Unable to stop the bloodshed, the American-led force withdrew from the country in frustration in 1994.

Meanwhile Eritrea, a northern region of Ethiopia, won its independence after a long guerrilla war against the Ethiopian government.

Ethnic Violence

As Africa moved toward the new millennium, ethnic violence also remained a major problem in many regions. The Nigerian civil war had shown what could happen within a single country. Similar problems existed throughout Africa. In the 1990s, such problems also spilled over national borders, threatening whole regions with conflict.

Rwanda. In Rwanda tensions between the two major ethnic groups, the Tutsi and the Hutu, exploded into violence. In 1994 an estimated 200,000 or more people, mainly Tutsi, had died in massacres.

An estimated 2 million Tutsi and Hutu fled to refugee camps in neighboring Zaire and other countries. Since that time, an additional 100,000 Hutu have been killed by the Tutsi. Many refugees have also died as a result of disease and other natural causes.

Zaire. The presence of so many Rwandan refugees proved a destabilizing factor in Zaire. Partly in response to the problems presented by the refugees, in 1995 the government announced a policy of forced expulsion from the country of the Banyamulenge, ethnic Tutsi who had settled in the eastern Congo as early as the eighteenth century. The Banyamulenge responded by arming to defend themselves and capturing the town of Bukavu. Many observers feared that the Hutu-Tutsi conflict was about to engulf the entire central African lake region. Eventually, however, the Tutsi rebels were joined by other anti-Mobutu forces led by Laurent Kabila. Kabila had been fighting the autocratic and corrupt Mobutu regime for many years. With his new allies, Kabila marched on Kinshasa and in May 1997 forced Mobutu to flee the country. After taking power, Kabila renamed Zaire the Democratic Republic of the Congo and promised to rebuild the country and halt the interference of foreign powers.

Economic and Environmental Challenges

In addition to political challenges, the new African nations faced economic uncertainty. As colonies, they had been part of the economic system of imperialism. In most cases, upon receiving their independence, the new nations lacked the balance between agriculture and industry required for economic growth. Many of them depended on a single crop or mineral resource for most of their income. For example, Ghana depended on cocoa and gold, Zambia on copper, Sudan on cotton, Zaire on cobalt, and Nigeria on oil. All these products were subject to large price swings in world markets.

As they sought to improve their national economies, many African countries turned to international organizations such as the World Bank for loans. However, bad planning, mismanagement, and corruption frequently left them worse off than ever. In addition, African economies were highly vulnerable to changes in the global economy. A worldwide rise in oil prices in the early 1970s, for example, led to huge increases in the prices Africans had to pay for imported goods, which in turn deeply affected their internal economies. Soon most African countries were deeply in debt.

Other problems also plagued Africa. Under colonial rule, improvements in health care, disease control, and nutrition had led to population growth. As the population of Africa continued to expand, however, many farmers overused the land. To grow more food and to produce cash crops for the global economy, farmers planted in dry areas or on hills, where fierce winds often stripped away the topsoil. In addition, people in many parts of Africa cut down trees for firewood. As a result of these practices, **desertification**, or the spread of the desert, became common.

The weather too has not been kind to Africa. Beginning in the late 1960s, a series of droughts struck northeastern Africa, bringing starvation to millions in the Sudan, Somalia, and Ethiopia. International aid in the form of food supplies has helped people survive, but it has not provided a permanent solution to the problem of famine. Further, foreign governments and voluntary agencies have found that providing assistance of any kind is very difficult because of the ongoing civil wars in these countries.

Not the least of Africa's problems has stemmed from the emergence of new diseases. New strains of viruses appeared on the scene in the 1970s and 1980s. AIDS, for example, spread rapidly through many regions of the continent. In 1995 the deadly Ebola virus struck in Zaire, causing the government to close its borders in an effort to halt the disease's spread.

Revival of African Culture

Despite the economic and political disappointments that followed independence, the people of Africa made great strides in one very important area. They experienced a rebirth of cultural self-confidence.

During the colonial era, many Africans lost faith in their own culture as they adopted European attitudes toward Africa. African art and music were considered primitive and crude by Western standards. The literature of Africa—a treasury of oral traditions including myths, proverbs, and folktales—was largely unknown to Europeans, who had no desire to learn about it. Seeing these attitudes, most Africans turned away from their own history and cultural heritage.

Not all Africans, however, followed the European example. In East Africa, Swahili poetry and tales continued to be studied as they had been for hundreds of years. The written records of this Bantu language go back to the 1600s. The language itself has continued to evolve. The acknowledged father of modern Swahili literature is Shaaban Robert, who is best known as a poet but also writes essays and novels.

Miriam Makeba, a prominent South African singer, performs at a concert celebrating Nelson Mandela's 70th birthday.

Many plays and novels have been written in Swahili, the national language of Tanzania and Kenya.

In West Africa, a new literary tradition developed, one using the colonial languages of English and French. Many African authors, especially those from French-speaking areas, first achieved international recognition through works of protest against colonial oppression. In a very intense and personal style, the poems of Léopold Senghor, who later became president of independent Senegal, described the hardships of colonialism. Senghor also celebrated his sense of the deep pride and dignity of being a black African, a concept he called **negritude**, or "blackness." Senghor's works, and the novels of Camara Laye, an exile in Senegal, proudly pointed to the deep, spiritual traditions of Africa and its sense of social community. In 1986 the Nigerian playwright and poet Wole Soyinka won the Nobel Prize in literature, becoming the first African to win the coveted award.

These African writers created a new artistic tradition. The result was a remarkable and varied artistic outpouring. Similar achievements were made in reawakening an interest in African music. In addition, a film industry was begun.

The creativity of Africa's contemporary literature, music, and films was also seen in sculpture. In workshops in Nigeria, Zimbabwe, and elsewhere, African artists employed age-old techniques to give shape to wood and copper. Others were more clearly influenced by Western art. Throughout Africa, this mixture of African and outside influences gave an unusual vitality to the arts. More and more westerners began to appreciate the achievements of African art. Africans themselves found a new pride in their ancient heritage and its unique contribution to world culture.

Section 2 Review

1. **Define** MPLA, UNITA, desertification, negritude
2. **Identify** Jerry Rawlings, Ibrahim Babangida, Laurent Kabila, Wole Soyinka
3. **Locate and Explain the Significance** Horn of Africa, Rwanda
4. **Understanding Ideas** List three problems that African nations faced after independence.
5. **Summarizing Ideas** How did superpower rivalries affect the nations of Angola and Ethiopia?
6. **Determining Cause and Effect** How did ethnic diversity contribute to problems in the independent countries of Africa?
7. **Analyzing Ideas** How has African culture revived in the last half of the 1900's?

Section 3

Nationalism in North Africa and the Middle East

Focus Questions

- How did the rise of Arab nationalism in Algeria affect France's position elsewhere in North Africa and the Middle East after World War II?
- How did conflict in Palestine between Arabs and Zionists affect developments in the Middle East in the postwar period?
- What major issues confronted Turkey and Iran after World War II?

As in Africa below the Sahara, World War II was a turning point for North Africa and the Middle East.

During the war, the British in particular had reestablished their control over strategic countries such as Egypt and Iran. Such control angered many and led to an even more intensive development of nationalism in the region after the war. In addition, the United Nations decision to grant independence to Italy's former colony of Libya raised expectations and demands among the French North African peoples that they, too, should be free from colonial rule. Not least, the discovery of the extent of the Holocaust, which had almost destroyed the Jewish population of Europe, led to renewed conflict in Palestine and eventually the emergence of the new state of Israel.

French North Africa and the Middle East

Like Great Britain, France was exhausted by World War II. Yet also like the British, the French did not immediately expect to have to give up their colonies. The first successful challenge to French colonialism came in the Middle East, in Syria and Lebanon.

Syria and Lebanon. France had first gained control of Syria and Lebanon as a mandate after World War I. In the 1920s, French policy had encouraged the development of a separate state in Lebanon, where there was a slight Christian majority. During World War II, Free French and British troops had taken control of both countries from the Vichy government. After the war, however, despite promises of independence, French troops remained in Syria and Lebanon. Only under British pressure and several brief but bloody battles with Arab nationalists did France finally agree to withdraw. In the mid-1940s both Lebanon and Syria became fully independent republics.

Algeria. The success of Arab nationalism in Syria in particular proved an inspiration to Arab nationalists in French North Africa. The heart of the French colonial empire in North Africa was Algeria. Like South Africa within the British Empire, Algeria had a large European settler community, people known as *colons*, accounting for about 10 percent of the population. These settlers, many of whose families had lived in Algeria since the 1800s, owned most of the colony's industry and its best land. Algeria was not just a colony, however, but had been legally absorbed into France. Algerian voters elected representatives to the French National Assembly in Paris, although voting restrictions limited the participation of the large majority of Muslim Arabs.

As nationalism emerged in other parts of the Middle East after World War II, the Algerians also began to demand independence. When both the *colons* and the French authorities resisted these demands, Algerian nationalists formed an organization in 1954 to fight for independence. The Algerian National Liberation Front, or **FLN** (its French initials), launched its revolution on November 1, 1954.

The Algerian war became extremely brutal as both sides committed atrocities to gain their goals. The FLN waged a terror campaign not only against the French but also against less radical Algerian Arabs who opposed independence. Torture was used by both sides in the conflict. So severe was the war that in 1958 an uprising among the *colons* in Algiers, supported by many army leaders, contributed to the downfall of the French Fourth Republic and the return of General Charles de Gaulle to power in France. The military and the settlers expected de Gaulle to pursue the war against the FLN. Instead, he decided to negotiate a settlement, even if it meant granting Algeria independence. Despite resistance from the army and the settlers, including attempts on his own life, in 1962 de Gaulle did indeed grant Algeria independence.

French police troops occupied streets in Algiers during a 1961 demonstration. The Algerian Revolution ended with the 1962 referendum on independence.

Morocco and Tunisia. The Algerian war had a devastating impact on French colonialism everywhere. The war was an important factor in influencing de Gaulle to offer his terms for independence to the African territories south of the Sahara. It was also partly responsible for independence in Morocco and Tunisia. Neighbors of Algeria, these two Muslim states were French protectorates. French rule in Morocco, in fact, had only been established relatively recently—in the 1920s—and Moroccan resistance remained strong. In 1954 both Moroccan and Tunisian nationalists also launched guerrilla campaigns designed to drive the French from their countries. In 1956, as the war raged in Algeria, France finally gave in. Morocco became a constitutional monarchy under the sultan Sidi Muhammad ben Yusuf, who became King Muhammad V. Tunisia became a republic under Tunisian nationalist leader Habib Bourguiba.

British Withdrawal from the Middle East

Like the French, the British also faced major challenges to their influence and position in the Middle East after World War II. During the war, Britain had stationed huge numbers of troops in Egypt to protect its interests. As in World War I, the British, supported by the United States and the Soviet Union, had also occupied much of Iran in order to keep supply lines to the Soviet Union open. To ensure a pro-Allied government, they had also forced the abdication of Reza Shah and placed his son, Mohammad Reza Shah, on the throne. British troops had occupied Syria along with the Free French government. British troops had also established control over Iraq in order to prevent a pro-German government from seizing power during the war. Not least, the British still held their mandate for Palestine, despite opposition from both Jews and Arabs. In short, at the end of World War II, Britain seemed to be even more firmly in control of the Middle East than ever before. In fact, however, Britain's control over the region was about to slip away.

Creation of Israel. The first major challenge to Britain's position in the Middle East came in Palestine. Once the war in Europe was over, the semi-official Jewish Agency in Palestine withdrew its support for the British mandate in Palestine. The agency conducted an active campaign against the terms of the 1939 White Paper, which had promised an end to Jewish immigration and the establishment of an independent Palestinian state. The Jewish Agency actively supported a massive wave of illegal immigration, as its agents in Europe recruited the displaced Jewish survivors of the Nazi Holocaust for the new Jewish state they hoped to build in Palestine. Meanwhile, extremist Zionist groups, such as the Stern Gang and the Irgun, waged a terrorist campaign against British authorities. In 1946, for example, the Irgun, headed by Menachem Begin (BAY·guhn), blew up the King David Hotel in Jerusalem. Eventually, a virtual state of war existed between the British and the Zionists.

In 1946 the British tried to obtain the help of the United States government to resolve the situation through a joint Anglo-American Committee of Inquiry. The British expected the United States to understand the impossibility of giving the Zionists an independent state of their own in the face of opposition by the Arab majority in Palestine. The committee did recommend against creating a Zionist state. Instead, it recommended continuation of the mandate to give Jews and Arabs a further chance to cooperate economically, as a first step toward creating a binational, bilingual state. Such recommendations were rejected by Arabs and Zionists alike.

Unable to obtain support from the United States or to get the Arabs and Zionists to agree on a settlement, in 1947 Britain announced that it was giving up the mandate and referred the entire problem to the United Nations. In November 1947, the UN voted to partition Palestine into separate Jewish and Arab states, with Jerusalem as an international city. When the last British troops left Palestine in May 1948, Zionist leaders proclaimed the Republic of Israel. Chaim Weizmann became its first president and David Ben-Gurion its first prime minister.

The establishment of a Jewish nation infuriated the Palestinian Arabs. As soon as British troops withdrew from the area, armies from neighboring Arab countries moved against Israel. Although outnumbered by the Arabs, the determined Israelis triumphed. When the war ended in early 1949, Israel had won more territory than it had been allotted in the UN partition plan. The Arab nations accepted a cease-fire, but UN-sponsored efforts to negotiate permanent peace failed. Moreover, hundreds of thousands of Palestinians had been uprooted by the conflict and were living as refugees in neighboring Arab lands. Attempts to work out either the return or the resettlement of these Palestinian refugees also failed.

From 1948 to 1970, Israel absorbed about 1.3 million immigrants, almost tripling the Jewish population of the new country. Impressive social and economic programs were also developed. Collective farms (the best-known form of which is called the **kibbutz**) proved successful in turning former desert areas into productive land.

Among the Arab nations, one emerged from the 1948 war with territorial gains. What remained of the proposed Palestinian state was officially annexed by Transjordan in 1950. (Around the same time, Transjordan changed its name to Jordan.) Other Arabs, including many Palestinians, bitterly opposed this action.

Egypt. At the same time that the British were grappling with the problem of Palestine, they also faced challenges from the growth of nationalism in Egypt. During World War II, British troops had used Egypt as a base of operations. After the war, the continuing presence of large numbers of troops, especially in the vast Suez base, angered many Egyptian nationalists. So too did Britain's continuing control of the Sudan, which many Egyptians considered an Egyptian province. After 1945 Egyptian nationalists expressed their desire for the complete evacuation of the British troops and the ending of British control. Between 1945 and 1952, however, all efforts to negotiate a settlement on either issue failed.

Meanwhile, the corrupt and inefficient government of King Farouk was also coming under fire from both nationalists and reformers. After Egypt's defeat by Israel and partly due to the diversion of funds from the war effort to enrich some of the king's relatives, a group of army leaders decided to overthrow the government. In 1952 the Free Officers Movement led a coup that toppled the monarchy and transformed Egypt into a republic. Eventually, a young charismatic colonel, Gamal Abdel Nasser, emerged as Egypt's new leader.

In foreign affairs, Nasser decided to rid Egypt of foreign domination once and for all. In 1954, after intense negotiations, Great Britain had agreed to evacuate the Suez base and to allow free elections in the Sudan. Despite Egyptian expectations, the Sudan chose independence rather than union with Egypt.

Meanwhile, in domestic affairs, Nasser emphasized land reform, industrialization, greater government control over the economy, and expanded rights for women. He also sought to modernize Egypt through major development projects. His ambitious plans were expensive, however, and he soon decided to seek aid from both East and West. In 1956 these efforts led to a crisis in the Middle East over the Suez Canal.

Windows in Jerusalem

At the beginning of World War II, almost 9.5 million Jews lived in Europe. Then, during the Nazi terrorism that engulfed Europe, as many as 6 million Jews, about two-thirds of all European Jews, lost their lives. In 1948, when the state of Israel was proclaimed, many Jews went to live there to join earlier settlers in developing land.

During the early years when Israel experienced tremendous growth, the Israelis constructed houses, schools, and other facilities for the growing population. One of these was a hospital in Jerusalem. Shown in the photo to the right are brilliantly colored stained-glass windows from the hospital's chapel, or synagogue. These are six of a series of 12 windows, each devoted to one of Jacob's 12 sons, believed to be the founders of the tribes of ancient Israel.

The windows were designed by Marc Chagall, a Russian Jewish artist who spent much of his time in France, settling there permanently in the 1920s. There are no figures of human beings in any of these windows because, by Jewish law, images of people are not permitted to appear in synagogues. The artist cleverly used symbols and abstractions of animals, birds, plants, and fish to tell the stories of the Old Testament. An intensely devout man, Chagall conveyed his love for his faith as well as his sense of history in these beautiful windows.

The Suez Crisis

In 1955 Nasser had announced the signing of an arms agreement between Egypt and Czechoslovakia (acting for the Soviet Union). Alarmed by the possibility of an alliance between Egypt and the Eastern bloc, the United States and Britain offered to help fund the most ambitious of Nasser's development projects for Egypt, the construction of a new dam at Aswan on the Nile. The Aswan High Dam would irrigate new lands for agricultural expansion and produce hydroelectric power. American and British leaders hoped this would keep Egypt from slipping further into the sphere of Soviet influence. Nasser hesitated, however, hoping for a better offer of aid from the Soviets. He also recognized the communist government of the People's Republic of China. When he did finally accept the Western offer to finance the dam, he was told abruptly that the offer had been withdrawn.

Viewing the withdrawal as an insult to Egyptian national dignity, Nasser suddenly nationalized the Suez Canal, which was still controlled primarily by British and French shareholders. The revenues from the canal would help pay for the Aswan High Dam. Nationalizing the canal was also a public way of asserting Egypt's independence from continuing efforts at European domination of the country.

For Arabs and anticolonial nationalists everywhere, Nasser became a great hero. To the West and especially to Britain, however, he became a demon. His nationalization of the Suez Canal eventually led to confrontation with the old colonial powers.

The countries that felt most directly threatened by the move were Britain, France, and Israel. Israel was

What If?

The Birth of Israel
What if the Holocaust had not occurred? Do you think the United Nations would have supported the creation of Israel?

especially alarmed because the Egyptians refused to allow Israeli ships to pass through the canal. Britain and France also were outraged by the maneuver because they both had a stake in the company that had built the canal. The British in particular worried about the strategic implications of an independent Egypt, friendly to the Soviet Union, controlling such a strategic waterway, through which much of the world's trade passed. The French were also angry that Nasser was encouraging anti-French movements in North Africa.

With careful, secret planning, Israel, Britain, and France conspired to overthrow Nasser and take control of the canal. They agreed that Israel should launch a lightning attack across the canal into Egypt. Britain and France would then intervene, supposedly to separate the Israelis and Egyptians, but in reality to help destroy the Egyptian armed forces, especially the air force, and reestablish European control over Suez.

At first all went well with the plan. In 1956 Israel launched a sudden invasion, seizing the Gaza Strip—an Egyptian-administered coastal district adjoining Israel's southern border. The Israelis then defeated the

Aswan, on the east bank of the Nile River, is one of the most important commercial and resort cities in the Nile Valley.

Egyptians in the Sinai Peninsula and advanced toward the canal. Great Britain and France sent an ultimatum to Egypt demanding a cease-fire. They also insisted on temporary British-French occupation of the canal. When Egypt refused, British and French troops seized the Mediterranean end of the canal. Both sides placed ships in the canal and sank them to block it.

Worried that the Soviets would be drawn into the crisis, the United States, under President Eisenhower, decided to intervene. Privately, Eisenhower threatened to cut off all American aid to Britain unless the invasion ended and the Anglo-French forces withdrew. Unable to withstand such a threat, the British agreed and the invasion collapsed.

In a settlement negotiated at the United Nations, Britain and France withdrew their forces. The Israelis gained a vague guarantee to allow Israeli ships in the canal, which Egypt later blockaded. Then they also withdrew. A UN force was sent to patrol the cease-fire line between the Israelis and the Egyptians in the Sinai Desert. As Egypt emerged from the war still in control of the canal, Nasser claimed victory over the European imperialists and Israel. Throughout the world, the Suez Crisis was seen as the final defeat of European imperialism. Nasser himself became the most popular leader in the Arab world. In the aftermath of the Suez Crisis, many Middle Eastern countries began to pursue new courses of political and social development.

Political and Social Change

As the countries of the Middle East became independent, they also confronted more clearly than ever the challenges of modernization. Unlike Africa, where most states had been led to independence by younger, Western-educated leaders, most of the new Middle Eastern states had been granted independence under an older generation of traditional elites. Iraq and Jordan, for example, had become Arab kingdoms under the sons of Sharif Husayn (Husayn ibn 'Ali) of Mecca. Saudi Arabia too was a traditional Arab kingdom ruled by the house of Ibn Saud. Syria and Lebanon were both ruled by wealthy landowning and merchant elites who had prospered under French rule. Only in Egypt did revolution precede real independence, when officers of the army deposed King Farouk and then negotiated Britain's withdrawal.

The Egyptian revolution began as a reaction to the corruption of the monarchy. Under Nasser it also developed a political ideology designed to bind together not only Egypt but all of the Arab world. Although Nasser always made his appeal for support in Islamic terms that would appeal to his listeners, he insisted that modernization along socialist lines was the key to independence:

"Revolution is the way in which the Arab nation can free itself of its shackles, and rid itself of the dark heritage which has burdened it. . . . [It] is the only way to overcome underdevelopment which has been forced on it by suppression and exploitation . . . and to face the challenge awaiting the Arab and other underdeveloped nations: the challenge offered by the astounding scientific discoveries which help to widen the gap between the advanced and backward countries. . . . Freedom today means that of the country and of the citizen. Socialism has become both a means and an end: sufficiency and justice."

Under Nasser the Egyptian government put an end to the practice of absentee landownership, in which wealthy landowners living in the cities made enormous profits from overworked laborers and tenants who actually worked the land. As the government took control of most industry and businesses such as banks and insurance companies, it also proclaimed laws limiting the hours of work, establishing a minimum wage, and creating a whole host of social services. Education was extended even further, and the government tried to improve the status of women.

Similar plans were embraced by members of the Ba'ath Party, which first emerged in Syria. Although at first the Ba'athists had emphasized a kind of Pan-Arab nationalism, by the mid-1950s they had also adopted socialism as a basis for bringing about major reforms in Arab society. The Ba'athists appealed primarily to the new generation of Western-educated intellectuals who had begun to emerge in the Middle East under colonial rule. Ba'athism soon spread to neighboring countries, especially Iraq and Lebanon. In 1958 a Ba'athist-inspired revolution broke out in Iraq, and a Ba'athist government took over in Syria. There also emerged a new generation of leaders who similarly believed in socialism as the best model for further modernization. Socialism, however, whether exercised by the various civilian or military governments that came to power in the 1960s in several Middle Eastern and North African countries, proved to be but the first step toward dictatorship.

Meanwhile, the old ideal of Pan-Arabism also resurfaced to complicate political developments in the Middle East. Nasser in particular began to preach a new brand of Pan-Arabism combined with socialism. In 1958, partly to coordinate efforts against Israel, Nasser convinced Syria to merge with Egypt in what became the United Arab Republic, or UAR. As new Arab leaders began to emerge in Syria and Iraq, however, so too did their own fears of Egyptian domination. In 1961, despite all the talk of Pan-Arabism, Syria broke away from the UAR once again. Perhaps the only point of agreement among all Arab leaders was their ongoing opposition to the state of Israel.

Iran

At the end of World War II, Great Britain and the Soviet Union still occupied Iran. Although American and British pressure eventually forced the withdrawal of Soviet forces from northern Iran, the country remained under heavy British influence. In particular, Britain owned the majority of the Anglo-Iranian Oil Company, which controlled Iran's oil industry. Many Iranian nationalists resented this continuing British domination of their country. At the same time, they believed that political reform along truly democratic, constitutional lines was the key to Iranian development.

In 1951, the popular Iranian nationalist leader Mohammad Mosaddeq (MOHS·ad·dek), became prime minister of Iran. Dr. Mosaddeq had two goals: to firmly establish constitutional government in Iran and to free Iran from foreign interference. Consequently, he tried to limit the power of the shah and to strengthen the power of the *Majlis*, the Iranian parliament. He also decided to establish Iran's sovereignty over the country's primary source of income, the oil industry. Shortly after coming to power, he therefore nationalized the Anglo-Iranian Oil Company. These moves outraged both the British government and the Iranian conservatives who supported a strong monarchy.

The British denounced nationalization as illegal and organized a worldwide boycott of Iranian oil. American officials were alarmed not only by the nationalization but by Mosaddeq's acceptance of political support from Iranian communists. The United States feared that under communist influence, the Soviet Union might gain control of Iran. For this reason, in 1953 the U.S. Central Intelligence Agency helped Mosaddeq's opponents engineer a coup that overthrew his government. The United States then supported the restoration of full power to the young shah of Iran.

Thereafter, the shah worked to establish his power and to impose rapid modernization upon his country. He relied on close ties with the United States and on his army and secret police. By the early 1960s, the shah was firmly in control of Iran.

Turkey

While the Arab Middle East struggled to throw off the last traces of Western imperialism, Turkey, too, faced significant challenges after World War II. Following the war, the secularist and modernist policies of Atatürk continued under his successor Ismet Inönü (i·nuh·NOO). By careful diplomacy, Inönü managed to keep Turkey neutral throughout World War II, only declaring war on Germany and the other Axis Powers once it became clear they were going to lose. Consequently, Turkey avoided the destruction that would certainly have come with war.

After World War II, however, Turkey came under increasing pressure from the Soviet Union, which continued to push south just as imperial Russia had once done. Turkish leaders responded to this threat by allying themselves more closely with the United States and the Western world. In 1952 Turkey joined NATO.

Meanwhile, Inönü also moved away from Atatürk's autocratic rule toward a more democratic government. In 1945 he announced the end of the one-party state and allowed the formation of other political parties. In May 1950, the first free elections brought the opposition party to power under their leader Adnan Menderes. When Menderes began to lose support in the late 1950s, however, he began to impose restrictions on his opposition rather than give up control. He also threatened to undo some of the reforms imposed by Atatürk. Alarmed at these innovations, in 1960 the Turkish army intervened and deposed Menderes, who was later executed. The army soon restored civilian rule but made it clear that future efforts to stray from the path laid down under Atatürk and Inönü might also be met with intervention.

Throughout this political turmoil, Turkey continued to industrialize and to look toward Europe for its model. Education continued to increase, and the Turkish economy generally prospered. On the other hand, many Turks also began to be privately irritated at continuing restrictions on religion. Eventually, some Turks organized themselves in an effort to lift the restrictions on Islam and restore it to a central role in national life.

1. **Define** *colons*, FLN, kibbutz
2. **Identify** David Ben-Gurion, Chaim Weizmann, King Farouk, Gamal Abdel Nasser, Adnan Menderes
3. **Locate and Explain the Significance** Aswan High Dam
4. **Understanding Ideas** How did events in Algeria affect the French in other areas of North Africa and the Middle East?
5. **Summarizing Ideas** Describe what occurred in Palestine in the postwar years.
6. **Determining Cause and Effect** How did past history affect events in Turkey and Iran after World War II?

Section 4

War, Oil, and Revolution in North Africa and the Middle East

Focus Questions

- How did conflicts between Arabs and Israelis shape the history of North Africa and the Middle East?
- How did the presence of oil fields in the Middle East affect political stability in the region?
- What types of new leadership emerged in the Arab world in the 1960s and after?

By 1962 most countries in North Africa and the Middle East had achieved independence. The remaining British protectorates in the Persian Gulf area gained full independence in the early 1970s. The major issues during the final decades of the 1900s concerned the Arab-Israeli confrontation, oil, and political instability within the nations of North Africa and the Middle East.

The Arab-Israeli Confrontation

After the breakup of the union between Egypt and Syria in 1961, Nasser became more cautious about Pan-Arabism. Yet Egypt's president did not want to forfeit his country's leadership role in the Arabic-speaking world. He therefore faced a difficult choice when tension rose along Israel's border with Syria and Jordan in the late 1960s. Nasser could support his Arab neighbors at the risk of war with a militarily strong Israel, or he could hold back at the risk of losing his standing as leader of the Arabic-speaking world. Nasser decided to act.

In May 1967, Nasser demanded the withdrawal of the UN troops that had been policing the border between Egypt and Israel since the end of the Suez crisis in 1956. He also announced a blockade of the Gulf of Aqaba to cut Israel's direct sea route to Africa and Asia. (See map on this page.)

The Six-Day War. Realizing the danger of delay, Israel launched a lightning attack on June 5, 1967. In six days of fighting, Israel captured the Sinai Peninsula and the Gaza Strip from Egypt, seized the Golan Heights from Syria, and took from Jordan the entire west bank of the Jordan River. The so-called West Bank, part of the original Palestine mandate, had remained in Arab hands after the Arab-Israeli war of 1948. Israel also captured the Jordanian section of Jerusalem. Israel then annexed Jerusalem, despite a UN ruling making it an international city.

The Six-Day War, as the brief hostilities came to be called, radically changed Middle Eastern politics. Israel confirmed its military superiority over its neighbors, but peace remained elusive. Many displaced Palestinians lost faith in the Arab governments' ability to recapture what had been Palestine. As a result, they increasingly relied on their own guerrilla organization, the Palestine Liberation Organization (**PLO**), led by Yasir Arafat.

All parties involved on the international level had reason to seek a compromise settlement after 1967. Realizing that they might be drawn into an Arab-Israeli war, the United States and the Soviet Union became interested in arranging a permanent peace settlement in the area. Egypt, Jordan, and Syria wished to regain lost territory. Mutual suspicions and fears, however, doomed many efforts to work out a peace.

Egypt Under Sadat

Nasser died in September 1970 and was succeeded by Anwar Sadat. Under Sadat's leadership, Egypt and Syria secretly planned a war against Israel that began on October 6, 1973. Although the Arabs were successful at first, Israeli troops pushed them back and crossed the Suez Canal to occupy Egyptian land. The Israelis, however, suffered severe losses during their drive into Egypt.

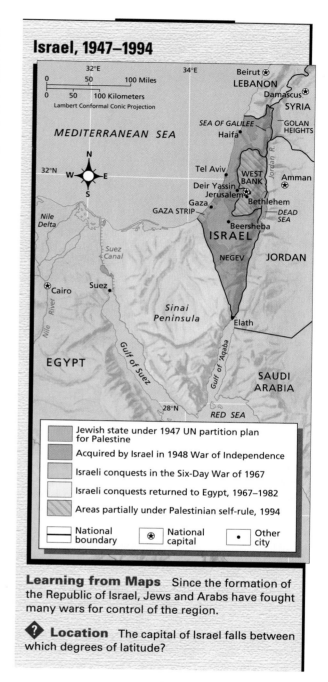

Israel, 1947–1994

Jewish state under 1947 UN partition plan for Palestine

Acquired by Israel in 1948 War of Independence

Israeli conquests in the Six-Day War of 1967

Israeli conquests returned to Egypt, 1967–1982

Areas partially under Palestinian self-rule, 1994

National boundary | National capital | Other city

Learning from Maps Since the formation of the Republic of Israel, Jews and Arabs have fought many wars for control of the region.

Location The capital of Israel falls between which degrees of latitude?

As had been true after the Six-Day War, all sides had reason to seek a compromise settlement. U.S. secretary of state Henry Kissinger began an intensive campaign of **shuttle diplomacy**—moving back and forth from Israel to Egypt and Syria to try to obtain an agreement. He eventually achieved two settlements, one between Israel and Egypt and one between Israel

The Camp David Accords, agreements between Israeli prime minister Menachem Begin and Egyptian president Anwar Sadat, were mediated by American president Jimmy Carter in September 1978 at Camp David, Maryland.

and Syria. Thereafter, the movement toward peace seemed to run out of steam. In November 1977, however, Sadat surprised the world. He went to Israel to speak in person to the Israeli parliament and to Israeli prime minister Menachem Begin.

Sadat's action opened a new dialogue between Egypt and Israel, which the United States openly supported. Many months of delicate negotiations followed, aided by the direct support of President Jimmy Carter. In September 1978, Carter invited the two leaders to Camp David, the presidential retreat in Maryland. After meetings and negotiations there, Sadat and Begin agreed on the framework for a peace settlement. The **Camp David Accords** were followed by a peace treaty that Egypt and Israel signed in March 1979.

Egypt and Israel had achieved a great breakthrough, but many people doubted it would end the Arab-Israeli confrontation. Most Israelis supported the peace with Egypt, but many resisted the idea of a process that might lead to a Palestinian state. The Camp David Accords led to division within the Arab world as well. While Sadat had many supporters, his

opponents claimed that the Egyptian leader had sold out the Palestinians to regain Egyptian territory. In 1981 a group of Egyptian radicals assassinated Sadat, darkening hopes for peace in the Middle East.

Continued Arab-Israeli Conflict

After the Camp David Accords, the PLO and other Palestinian guerrilla organizations stepped up their operations. From camps in neighboring Lebanon, the PLO launched attacks that spread terror throughout northern Israel. Determined to end the PLO threat for good, the Israelis invaded Lebanon in 1982. For two months, they bombed Lebanon's capital, Beirut, where the PLO had its headquarters. Eventually, a settlement was reached whereby the PLO withdrew its forces to Tunisia.

Even though the Israelis finally withdrew from Lebanon in 1985, their invasion had a lasting impact on the region. Rather than destroying the PLO, the invasion had helped strengthen the organization's standing among Palestinians. Moreover, the Israeli intrusion into Lebanon intensified an already bitter civil war being fought there, and many Israelis, including some prominent military commanders, had been opposed to the invasion. This caused a deep split within Israeli society.

Israelis also disagreed about how to handle problems in the occupied territories, the zones Israel had acquired during the Six-Day War. (See map on page 833.) Since the 1970s, Israelis had been moving into these zones, where they were establishing settlements. Palestinians living in these territories started demonstrating against the Israeli presence. In December 1987, the demonstrations turned violent, in an uprising the Palestinians called the *intifada*, an Arabic word meaning "shaking." Day after day, young Palestinians threw rocks and bottles at army patrols and other symbols of Israeli authority. The Israeli army responded with armed military suppression. During the first year alone, the *intifada* claimed the lives of more than 300 Palestinians. Thousands more were wounded, and another 20,000 imprisoned.

Many Israelis supported the harsh measures the authorities used to put down the *intifada*. Others, however, believed that it might be time to withdraw from the occupied zones, exchanging land for a peace settlement with the Palestinians. Unfortunately, events in 1990 seemed to dash any hope for peace.

Under the leadership of Mikhail Gorbachev, the Soviet Union had relaxed restrictions on the emigration of Jews. As a result, Soviet Jews began to move to Israel in huge numbers—200,000 in 1990 alone. Much to the anger of the Palestinians, the Israeli government seemed determined to settle most of these new arrivals in the occupied zones. As a result, violence exploded in the occupied zones once again in October 1990.

The specific incident involved the Temple Mount in Jerusalem, one of Judaism's most holy places. It is also holy to Muslims, who know it as al-Haram ash-Sharif, or "the Noble Holy Place." On October 8, 1990, responding to rumors that their mosques were going to be attacked, hundreds of Palestinians gathered at the Temple Mount. They threw rocks, and Israeli police answered with volleys of rifle fire. At least 20 Palestinians were killed and some 150 were wounded.

New Moves Toward Peace

Despite the continuing *intifada*, not all hope for peace was lost. A growing Israeli peace movement combined with the Israeli general election of 1992 reoriented the situation. Israel's Labor Party won control of the government from the Likud bloc, an alliance of several conservative parties. Yitzhak Rabin (rah·BEEN), a former army chief of staff who had led Israeli forces to their spectacular victory in the Six-Day War, became prime minister. Committed to reaching a settlement with the Palestinians, Rabin authorized secret negotiations with Palestinian leaders.

Israeli and Palestinian representatives met in Oslo, Norway, during 1993. Eventually, the Israeli foreign minister, Shimon Peres, met with PLO Chairman Arafat. Israel agreed to Palestinian autonomy—or self-government—in the West Bank and Gaza Strip, while the PLO officially recognized Israel's right to exist. On September 13, 1993, as a surprised world looked on, Rabin, Peres, and Arafat met in Washington, D.C., to sign a preliminary agreement. The three leaders jointly received the 1994 Nobel Peace Prize for their efforts.

Not everyone was satisfied with the new move toward peace, however. Extremists on both sides opposed aspects of the peace process. As the Israeli army prepared to withdraw from parts of the occupied territories, many Israelis who had settled on the West Bank feared harassment and violence at the hands of the new self-governing Palestinian Authority. In 1994 one radical Israeli settler with an automatic rifle killed 29 Palestinians in the West Bank city of Hebron. At the same time, a radical Palestinian organization known as Hamas, which opposed recognition of Israel and Arafat's leadership, launched a campaign of terrorism within Israel.

By the end of 1995, the peace process had begun to falter yet again. In November an Israeli radical who opposed handing over any territory to Palestinian control assassinated Prime Minister Rabin. Although Rabin's successor, Shimon Peres, remained committed to the settlement with the Palestinians, Israelis grew increasingly skeptical of the peace process as Hamas continued to wage its terror attacks. In 1996 Israeli voters returned the conservative Likud bloc to power. While the new prime minister, Benjamin Netanyahu, pledged his support of the peace process, he stressed that henceforth Israel would move more cautiously.

As the century drew to a close, the Arab-Israeli confrontation remained unsettled and the future uncertain. Although Israel had reached an agreement with neighboring Jordan in 1995, conflict over the border with Syria remained an ominous possibility as of 1998. While implementation of Palestinian self-government in some areas of the West Bank and in the Gaza Strip went forward, personal friction between Israeli and Palestinian leaders combined with sporadic outbreaks of violence continued to put the peace process under enormous strain.

Oil and World Energy Needs

The development of ships, automobiles, and aircraft fueled by petroleum products greatly increased the demand for oil during the early 1900s. As the growing demand threatened to outstrip the production from existing oil fields, a search for new sources of oil began. One area that attracted attention was the Middle East. In 1901 the shah of Persia (present-day Iran) granted a concession, or land-use lease, to a British prospector. Seven years later, the prospector struck oil. Other countries in the region soon granted oil concessions to foreign prospecting companies, mostly from Britain and the United States. Over the next 30 years, these companies discovered major oil fields in Iraq, Saudi Arabia, Kuwait, Bahrain, and elsewhere in the region around the Persian Gulf as well as in Libya in North Africa.

The rulers of these countries, many of whom were absolute monarchs, received a share of the profits from the oil companies' operations. As the oil fields of the Persian Gulf were increasingly developed after World War II, these rulers and many of their citizens became very rich. While critics pointed out that the profits from oil—sometimes called **petrodollars**—

served largely to expand the personal fortunes of local rulers, much of the money went to improve the lives of their citizens. Petrodollars laid the foundation for social welfare systems and giant economic development projects throughout the Persian Gulf. They provided the funds to build roads, schools, and plants to supply precious fresh water to the desert region by desalinating seawater.

With the rising tide of nationalism following World War II, many of the oil-producing countries began to demand that the western oil companies grant them a larger share of the profits. Often the foreign companies were unwilling to grant these demands. In Iran, for example, the Anglo-Iranian Oil Company and the government were unable to reach any kind of agreement. As a result, the Iranian government, as mentioned earlier, nationalized the country's oil industry in 1951. Iran, however, gained little from this action. The Anglo-Iranian Oil Company managed to organize an international boycott of Iranian oil. Because oil was easily bought from other countries, the boycott of Iranian oil sales had little impact on the world market.

Iran's experience showed that, individually, oil-producing countries had little power when negotiating with the oil companies. Together, however, they could bargain from a position of strength. Therefore, in 1960 Iran, Iraq, Kuwait, Saudi Arabia, and the Latin American oil-producing nation of Venezuela created the Organization of Petroleum Exporting Countries (OPEC). Other oil-producing nations joined the organization later.

As the bargaining agent of the oil-producing nations, OPEC worked to set oil production levels and world oil prices. OPEC's power soon became apparent. During the Arab-Israeli War of 1973, the Arab members of OPEC used their oil as an economic weapon. They temporarily cut off shipments of oil to the United States as punishment for supporting Israel. Although this embargo was later eased, not least because the boycott of oil sales to the West harmed the finances of OPEC members, the price of oil rose sharply, from about $3 to more than $12 per barrel.

The discovery and development of new oil fields, especially in Alaska and the North Sea, helped Western nations reduce their dependency on Middle Eastern oil in the years after 1973. The oil fields of the Persian Gulf, however, remain the world's largest. They still constitute a critical source of energy for the industrialized world, and particularly for the rapidly developing economies along Asia's Pacific Rim. Experts predict that as production declines in oil fields outside the Middle East early in the next century, oil produced in the five nations of Iran, Iraq, Kuwait, Saudi Arabia, and the United Arab Emirates will become more important than ever to the world economy. Consequently, the Persian Gulf is likely to remain a principal focus of international attention in the future.

Political Instability

Despite the wealth generated by oil, the Middle East has seen considerable political instability.

Under severe financial strain late in the 1960s, Britain announced plans to withdraw most of its remaining military forces from the Persian Gulf and to grant full independence to Qatar (KAH·tuhr), Bahrain, and the Trucial States (today called the United Arab Emirates). By 1971 each of these former protectorates was fully independent, although British advisers remained influential in their affairs. In neighboring Oman, British troops remained active into the 1970s. They helped successfully put down a communist rebellion in Oman, which is located astride the vital route for the shipment of oil out of the Persian Gulf through the Strait of Hormuz.

As a result of Britain's withdrawal from the Persian Gulf, Iran emerged as the leading power in the region. Western nations, including the United States, looked to the shah of Iran as the main guarantor of the region's security. To many observers in the mid-1970s, the shah's regime appeared militarily strong and politically stable. Discontent was growing within Iran, however.

The Iranian Revolution

Many Iranians continued to oppose Mohammad Reza Shah Pahlavi even after the ouster of Mosaddeq in the 1950s. Some were socialists, while others were Islamic traditionalists eager to rid the country of Western influences. By the late 1970s, social forces at work in Iran had reached an explosive stage.

Throughout the 1960s, the Iranian government had carried out ambitious modernization programs. These included land distribution to the peasants, a campaign against illiteracy, and increased industrialization. As a result, millions had left the countryside for Iran's cities. When an economic slump hit Iran in the 1970s, these uprooted masses rapidly grew anxious. As their prospects for prosperity seemed to vanish, many of these Iranians became ready to support the call for revolution.

Building History Study Skills

READ
WRITE
INTERPRET
CONNECT
THINK

Interpreting Visuals: Reading a Special-Purpose Map

Historians use many different types of special-purpose maps. A special-purpose map relates data to the geographic setting shown on the map.

How to Read a Special-Purpose Map

To read a special-purpose map, follow these steps.
1. Determine the purpose of the map. Is it designed to give you information on troop movements? Resources? Land use?
2. Formulate conclusions about the information presented on the map. For example, if the map shows troop movements, can you learn why the troops took the particular routes they did?

Developing the Skill

Study the map entitled "Oil Deposits in the Middle East and North Africa, 1990," below. The map shows the oil reserves of countries in the region. The purpose of the map, then, is to show which countries in North Africa and the Middle East contain major deposits of oil. The map also shows the oil reserves of North Africa as well as of each of the major producers in the Middle East. It further shows which of the major producers are OPEC members. One conclusion that you can draw from the map is that the Persian Gulf is a vital source of oil.

Practicing the Skill

What other conclusions can you formulate from the information shown on the map of oil deposits in the Middle East and North Africa shown on this page?

To apply this skill, see Applying History Study Skills on page 843.

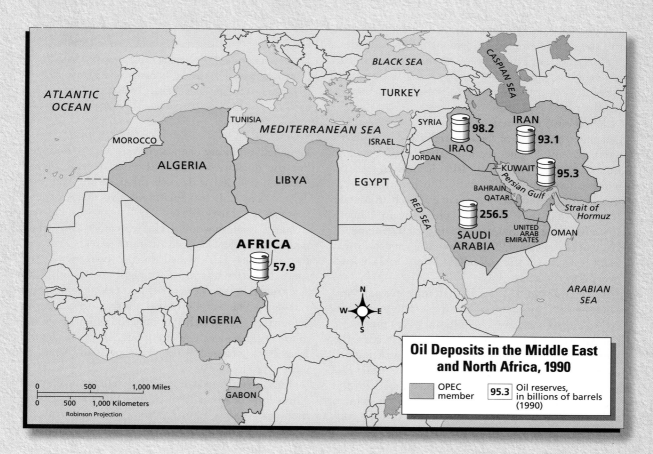

Oil Deposits in the Middle East and North Africa, 1990

OPEC member

95.3 Oil reserves, in billions of barrels (1990)

Compounding the problem, the shah had failed to win loyalty even from those Iranians who had directly benefited from the modernization programs. The shah's government had paid for thousands of young Iranians to go abroad for higher education, but many of these same Iranians feared and detested the shah's rule. They pointed to the atrocities believed to have been committed by the SAVAK, the Iranian secret police, as a symbol of the shah's tyranny. Moreover, the shah tried to keep all control and power in his hands. As a result, not even his own ministers felt strong loyalty to him.

Much of the opposition to the shah found expression in a revived interest in Islam. Conservative Islamic leaders who had long opposed the modernization programs of the shah began to attract wide support in their calls to rid Iran of Western influences. The Ayatollah Ruhollah Khomeini (koh·MAY·nee) soon emerged as the leader of religiously based opposition to the shah. Banished from Iran since 1964, the 76-year-old religious leader had directed a propaganda campaign against the shah from exile in France. By 1978, as the shah's regime entered its final phase, Khomeini's supporters prepared for his return to Iran.

Iran's Islamic republic. In 1978 discontent with the shah's rule erupted in demonstrations and riots throughout Iran. The shah was unable to contain the unrest. Finally, in January 1979, he left the country, appointing a prime minister to preside over Iran in his absence.

Khomeini returned to Iran in February. He demanded abolition of the monarchy and its replacement by an Islamic republic that would govern Iran according to strict Islamic principles. By mid-February Khomeini's revolution had triumphed. Iranians overwhelmingly voted to establish an Islamic republic, and they elected a president in January 1980. Real power, however, remained with Khomeini. His supporters rapidly eliminated other political forces, such as the socialists, who had helped overthrow the shah.

On November 4, 1979, Iranian militants captured the American embassy in Tehran, seizing more than 60 American hostages. The militants were protesting the American decision to let the ailing shah enter the United States for medical treatment. They demanded that the shah be returned to Iran to stand trial. The shah left the United States in December 1979 and died in Egypt in July 1980. Even though the Iranian militants faced worldwide condemnation, they continued to hold the hostages. The United States

On November 4, 1979, Iranian revolutionaries seized the American embassy in Tehran and held more than 50 people hostage until January of 1981.

launched a military operation to rescue the hostages, but the mission was recalled when several aircraft involved collided with each other on the way into Tehran. The militants finally released the American hostages in January 1981.

Iran's situation worsened in September 1980, when neighboring Iraq launched an attack to take control of the waterway that divided the two countries in the south. A bitter war raged for eight years, with both sides suffering heavy casualties but making few territorial gains. The war also posed a serious threat to the stability of the oil-rich Persian Gulf region, worrying many world leaders. Under enormous economic strain from damage caused by the war, Iran finally agreed to a cease-fire in 1988.

Iran's road to recovery proved difficult, even after Khomeini's death in 1989. Although somewhat more moderate leaders took control of the government, many Western nations, including the United States, remained reluctant to do business with the Islamic republic. Iran's continued support of terrorism around the world and calls for Islamic revolution in the Middle East undermined the country's efforts to win international aid.

By the late 1990s, Iran's situation finally seemed to be improving. Foreign oil companies were eagerly seeking deals with Iran, and the gains made by comparatively liberal Iranian leaders in the election of 1997 appeared to hold the promise of improved relations with the United States. However, with traditionalist, anti-Western elements still extremely powerful in the government, Iran's future remained uncertain.

New Leadership in the Arab World

When Anwar Sadat succeeded Nasser, he assumed two roles—leader of Egypt and symbolic leader of the Arab world. After he signed the Camp David Accords, however, most Arabs rejected Sadat's and Egypt's leadership. Thereafter, a struggle over which country would lead the Arab world began. Two major contenders were Syria and Iraq.

Syria. In 1961 Syria seceded from the United Arab Republic and was reestablished as an independent state by a military coup. The government changed hands a number of times in the next few years. This process ended in 1970, when General Hafiz Asad took control. He quickly consolidated his power, ruthlessly putting down any challenge to his authority.

Like other Arab leaders, Asad's foreign policy was driven by the Arab-Israeli conflict. After a devastating defeat at the hands of the Israelis in 1973, however, Asad turned his attention to building his influence in the Arab world. He offered assistance, training, and safe haven to a number of Palestinian guerrilla groups. Yet his great opportunity came in 1975 with the outbreak of civil war in neighboring Lebanon. He first acted as a mediator, trying to bring the warring factions to the peace table. Then, in early 1976, he sent a large peacekeeping force to Lebanon. Nevertheless, many observers felt that Asad was more interested in gaining control of Lebanon than in bringing peace to that nation. That certainly seemed to be the opinion of the Israelis. When they invaded Lebanon in 1982, Syrian positions outside Beirut were among their early targets.

When Israel withdrew from Lebanon in 1985, at least 30,000 Syrian troops remained. In 1990 these troops played a major role in defeating the forces of General Michel Aoun, the last faction opposing the Lebanese government. This gave the Lebanese people real hope for a lasting peace. However, many observers feared that in return for Asad's assistance, the Lebanese authorities might allow him to play a major role in Lebanon's future.

Asad played a leading role in other regional issues. In 1980 he supported Iran in the Iran-Iraq War. In 1990 he condemned Iraq once again for its invasion of Kuwait. In addition, he sent troops to join the coalition forces in the Gulf War against Iraq.

Iraq. In 1968 the radical, nationalist Ba'ath Party seized power in Iraq. A driving force behind the Ba'ath Party was Saddam Hussein. The deputy leader of the government, Saddam was in charge of internal security. Using assassination, execution, imprisonment, and terror tactics he removed threats to the party with brutal efficiency. Saddam continued this approach when he took control of the government in 1979. One of his most ruthless acts was the use of chemical weapons against the Kurds, a minority group in northern Iraq. They had angered Saddam by calling for a degree of self-government.

Saddam began a march to power in the region by laying claim to Iranian territory that had once been part of Iraq—the Shatt al Arab waterway. This resulted in the war between the two countries in 1980. Badly disorganized after the revolution of 1979, the Iranian army was caught by surprise. In the first few months of the war, Iraq made major territorial gains. The Iranians rallied, however, and by 1982 the Iraqis had been pushed back and were on the defensive.

At this point, the Iraqis were faced with the possibility of an internal uprising. About 55 percent of the Iraqi population are Shi'ah Muslims, as are the vast majority of Iranians. Iranian Shi'ah leaders called on the Muslim faithful in Iraq to overthrow their government.

As the war went on, the destruction increased. Both sides shelled, bombed, and fired missiles against each other's major cities. Huge frontal assaults cost the lives of tens of thousands of soldiers. Iraq even resorted to chemical warfare. Eventually, the Iraqi army regained the advantage. The Iranians, devastated by eight years of war, agreed to make peace.

The Iran-Iraq War left Saddam Hussein in a strong position. He began a program of reconstruction and negotiations with neighboring countries. Further, he had built up the country's armed forces. Iraq now had the largest and best-equipped army in the Arab world. However, the country faced terrible economic problems. Iran had targeted Iraq's oil facilities during the war, leaving them in ruins, and Iraq had to pay off huge war debts.

The Gulf War. In mid-1990, Saddam Hussein charged that the small neighboring state of Kuwait was waging economic warfare against Iraq by pumping Iraq's share of oil from a jointly owned oil field. Kuwait's high level of production was driving down the price of oil. Attempts by the Kuwaitis to negotiate a settlement of these and other issues failed, and on August 2, Iraq launched a surprise invasion of Kuwait. Iraq quickly took possession of the smaller country and formally annexed Kuwait on August 8.

Although the leaders of most Arab countries denounced Saddam's actions, the region's poor and dispossessed—especially the Palestinians—looked on him as a hero. Huge demonstrations in support of Saddam spread across North Africa and the Middle East.

World opinion was solidly against the Iraqi invasion. When Iraq seemed poised to invade Saudi Arabia, opinion was backed up by action. Led by the United States, a coalition of about 30 nations launched Operation Desert Shield, sending more than 600,000 troops to defend Saudi Arabia. The United Nations also took action. The General Assembly passed resolutions imposing economic sanctions on Iraq if it did not withdraw from Kuwait. A later resolution set January 15, 1991, as the date for Iraqi withdrawal. After that date, UN members were authorized to use military force to oust Iraq from Kuwait.

The deadline passed with Iraq still occupying Kuwait. The following day, Desert Shield became Desert Storm as coalition forces, led by the United States, launched an air attack. Unable to challenge the coalition for control of the skies, the Iraqis made little response. Their only retaliation was to launch missile attacks against Saudi Arabia. They also made good on an earlier threat to fire missiles against Israel.

The coalition forces kept up an almost constant air barrage against Iraq for nearly 40 days. Then ground forces began to move into Kuwait and southern Iraq. Worn down by weeks of bombing, the Iraqi troops had no heart for a fight. The war ended in 4 days, and Kuwait was liberated.

With his army destroyed and economic sanctions against Iraq remaining in place, Saddam's ambitions seemed checked. Yet he continued to survive, defying international law and opinion throughout the 1990s. In the first days after the war, Shi'ah Muslims in Iraq's south and Kurds in the north attempted to overthrow Saddam's government. Both uprisings failed, leaving Saddam in control. Later UN inspectors arrived in Iraq to ensure Saddam's compliance with UN orders that he dismantle his programs to develop weapons of mass destruction. However, on several occasions the Iraqis deliberately hindered UN inspections, finally expelling the American members of the inspection team. The American inspectors were later allowed to return, but Iraq continued to make UN inspections difficult.

An Uncertain Future

People throughout the world hoped that the end of the Persian Gulf War would create opportunities for a lasting peace in North Africa and the Middle East. U.S. secretary of state James Baker shuttled between Israel and various Arab nations in an effort to get them to agree to a peace conference. However, no major breakthroughs occurred.

The war had left deep divisions between Arab nations. Relations between Saudi Arabia and Kuwait, on one side, and nations such as Jordan that had sided with Iraq on the other, were icy at best. Further, the Saudis and Kuwaitis had been among the PLO's major financial supporters. Because PLO head Yasir Arafat favored Saddam Hussein, however, the Saudis and Kuwaitis reexamined their support of the PLO.

Problems also existed within Saudi Arabia and Kuwait. The ordinary people of these countries had few political rights. After their efforts in the Persian Gulf War, many expected to play a greater role in governing their countries. Islamic radicals in Saudi Arabia, who opposed the country's monarchy and its cooperation with Western nations such as the United States, resorted to terrorism. During the 1990s, they set off bombs in Riyadh (ree·AHD), the Saudi capital, and outside an American military barracks in the city of Dhahran. The attack in Dhahran killed several American personnel.

Terrorism remained a major problem in many parts of the Middle East and North Africa. The use of terror by fanatics on both sides posed an ongoing threat to the peace process between Israel and the Arab world. In Egypt, Islamic radicals repeatedly attacked Egyptian Christians, government officials, and Western tourists. In Algeria, Islamic revolutionaries retaliated against government efforts to suppress their movement by launching attacks on high-ranking officials, security forces, foreigners, and others. The bombing of the World Trade Center in New York City in 1993 highlighted the potential of Middle Eastern terrorism to reach the West.

A major concern of world leaders in the 1990s was the sponsorship of terrorism by various governments in the Middle East and North Africa. The nations of Iran, Iraq, Syria, and Sudan were suspected of supporting terrorist organizations with money, arms, and advice. The government of Libya was linked to several terrorist attacks during the 1980s, including the mid-air destruction of an American airliner over Lockerbie, Scotland, in 1989.

The danger of major war in the Middle East also remained high in the late 1990s. Considerable tensions continued to exist between Israel and Syria. In the Persian Gulf, Saddam Hussein remained entrenched in power and apparently committed to the development of weapons. As of early 1998, his continued interference with UN inspectors in Iraq still threatened to reignite military conflict between Iraq and the United States, Britain, and their Middle Eastern allies.

In addition to these political and military problems, the nations of North Africa and the Middle East confronted a number of other issues. As they experienced modernization, many people sought a greater sense of security by reasserting traditional values. Perhaps the most important movement in this regard was a revival of traditional Islamic values and a rejection of Western culture. This resurgence of Islamic fundamentalism, however, raised other issues. For example, one issue concerned the status of women. During the 1900s and especially after World War II, women in many countries of North Africa and the Middle East won new rights and social freedoms, including education for girls and professional employment. The resurgence of traditional Islam seemed to many to reverse some of the strides that had been made and drew criticism from the West. On the other hand, many women in the region identified with their Islamic heritage and embraced Islamic values and the social restrictions that accompanied these Islamic values.

Serious economic problems also persisted at century's end in much of North Africa and the Middle East. Poverty and the lack of resources, combined with ballooning populations, placed many national economies under great strain. The unequal distribution of wealth between the oil-rich states of the Persian Gulf and poor, heavily populated countries such as Egypt, Sudan, and Yemen created resentments and laid a foundation for conflict. All in all, the nations of North Africa and the Middle East faced an uncertain future.

While many women in the Middle East today wear traditional clothing, others have adopted Western-style clothes.

Section 4 Review

1. **Define** PLO, shuttle diplomacy, Camp David Accords, *intifada*, petrodollars
2. **Identify** Anwar Sadat, Ayatollah Khomeini, Hafiz Asad, Saddam Hussein
3. **Locate and Explain the Significance** Persian Gulf, Beirut, Bahrain, Qatar, United Arab Emirates, Oman, Tehran
4. **Summarizing Ideas** Describe the efforts to attain peace in North Africa and the Middle East after the Arab-Israeli war of October 1973.
5. **Analyzing Ideas** (a) How has OPEC demonstrated its power in world affairs? (b) Has it succeeded in fulfilling its goals? Explain.
6. **Interpreting Ideas** (a) What factors led to the Iranian revolution of 1979? (b) Why did Iranian militants seize American hostages in 1979?
7. **Evaluating Ideas** (a) Why has there been a struggle for the leadership of the Arab world since 1979? (b) Do you think the Gulf War helped or hindered the leadership struggle? Why?

Chapter 30 Review

A.D. 1976
Violence in
Soweto erupts.

A.D. 1979
• Revolution in
Iran occurs.
• Hostage crisis
in Iran begins.

A.D. 1980
Rhodesia is
renamed Zimbabwe.

A.D. 1967

A.D. 1971

A.D. 1975

A.D. 1979

A.D. 1965
Joseph Mobutu takes
full control of the Congo.

A.D. 1967
• Civil war erupts in Nigeria.
• Israel fights Six-Day War
against its Arab neighbors.

A.D. 1975
• Civil war in Angola begins.
• Angola and Mozambique
become independent.

A.D. 1979
Israel and Egypt sign
Camp David Accords.

Chapter Summary

The following list contains the key concepts you have learned about Africa and the Middle East since 1945.

1. Independence came rapidly to the African nations after World War II. Most African countries achieved independence peacefully, but a few resorted to violence.
2. South Africa and Rhodesia resisted any efforts to give the black majority of their populations a real voice in government. The South African government instituted the apartheid system that separated the races.
3. Africa's new nations faced a number of difficulties. There was often hostility among the groups within a country. This led to violence in Nigeria. In Angola the superpowers intervened, as they did in the conflict between Ethiopia and Somalia in the Horn of Africa.
4. Africans also faced economic difficulties, ethnic violence, and environmental challenges.
5. African culture experienced a revival after independence. African writers, musicians, and sculptors allowed westerners to appreciate the achievements of African arts.
6. Many nations in the Middle East also gained independence after 1945. Nations that had gained independence earlier reduced the influence of foreign governments.
7. A continuing problem in the Middle East was the relationship between Israel and its Arab neighbors. Several Arab-Israeli wars were fought between 1948 and 1973. An offer of peace by Egypt led to the signing of a peace treaty in 1979, but the other Arab nations rejected the pact.
8. The nations of the Middle East vary enormously in size, population, and wealth. A number of them gained considerable power as a result of the rise in oil prices in the 1970s.
9. A revolution in Iran resulted in the overthrow of the shah and the establishment of an Islamic republic.
10. In 1991 Iraq occupied and annexed the country of Kuwait. A coalition of about 30 countries opposed Iraq and liberated Kuwait. Saddam Hussein, the leader of Iraq, continued to cause problems for UN forces after his defeat in the Persian Gulf War.
11. The rapid changes of the period after World War II led to upheaval and a revival of Islam. The region faced continuing uncertainties and tension in the 1990s. The use and support of terrorism by certain Middle Eastern and North African governments continues to undermine efforts for peace.

Reviewing Important Terms

On a separate sheet of paper, supply the term that correctly completes each statement.

1. The South African policy based on the principle of racial separation became known as _____, the Afrikaans word for apartness.
2. The movement that promotes the cultural unity of people of African heritage in order to struggle for freedom together is known as _____.
3. Unwise land use patterns have led to _____, or the spread of the desert in Africa.
4. A form of collective farm in Israel is known as a(n) _____.
5. In the 1970s, Secretary of State Henry Kissinger began an intensive campaign of _____ _____, in which he moved back and forth from Israel to Egypt to Syria to try to reach a peace agreement.
6. Profits made from oil are often called _____.

Developing Critical Thinking Skills

1. **Comparing Ideas** (a) How did nationalists after 1945 differ from earlier African leaders? How did each of the following contribute to the rise of nationalism in Africa? (b) Kwame Nkrumah; (c) Jomo Kenyatta; (d) Robert Mugabe
2. **Analyzing Ideas** (a) Which African nations achieved independence with relatively little opposition? (b) Which did not? (c) What reasons might account for these different experiences?
3. **Interpreting Ideas** How is the history of Ghana representative of the postindependence experience of most African nations?
4. **Determining Cause and Effect** What were the causes and results of the Arab-Israeli War of 1948–1949?
5. **Interpreting Ideas** Of the changes that occurred in the Middle East after 1945, which do you think has had the most impact on the rest of the world? Why?

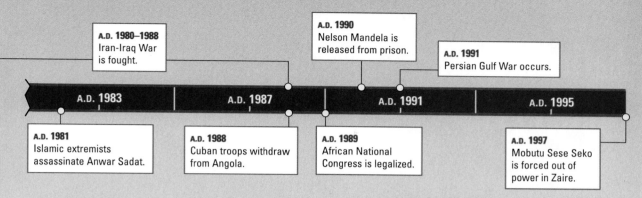

A.D. 1980–1988
Iran-Iraq War is fought.

A.D. 1990
Nelson Mandela is released from prison.

A.D. 1991
Persian Gulf War occurs.

A.D. 1983

A.D. 1987

A.D. 1991

A.D. 1995

A.D. 1981
Islamic extremists assassinate Anwar Sadat.

A.D. 1988
Cuban troops withdraw from Angola.

A.D. 1989
African National Congress is legalized.

A.D. 1997
Mobutu Sese Seko is forced out of power in Zaire.

6. **Classifying Ideas** Name the country that each of the following political and cultural leaders considered their home country; **(a)** Robert Mugabe; **(b)** Kwame Nkrumah; **(c)** Chaim Weizmann; **(d)** Anwar Sadat; **(e)** Jomo Kenyatta; **(f)** Gamal Abdel Nasser; **(g)** Ayatollah Khomeini; **(h)** Hafiz Asad; **(i)** Menachem Begin; **(j)** Saddam Hussein.

Relating Geography to History
Study the map on page 837. **(a)** How do the oil reserves of Africa compare with the oil reserves of the Middle East? **(b)** How might this affect the history and politics of the nations of Africa and the Middle East?

Relating Past to Present
1. In the 1990s, the situation in the Middle East has remained unsettled. Do library research to locate recent articles on events in one of the following nations: Egypt, Israel, Saudi Arabia, Iran, Iraq, Syria, Jordan, or Lebanon. **(a)** How have conditions in this country changed in recent years? **(b)** How have other nations responded to these changing conditions in the Middle East?
2. Find examples of contemporary and historic African art in sources such as *National Geographic* or general histories of Africa. Identify in which time period each piece of art was created. On the basis of evidence in these pictures that you examine, support or challenge the following statement: Modern African art reflects a pride in the cultural achievements of earlier African civilizations.

Applying History Study Skills
Before completing this activity, review Building History Study Skills on page 837.

Study the map entitled "The World: Land Use and Economic Activity" on pages R8–R9 and answer the following questions.
1. In what countries outside the Middle East is drilling for oil a major economic activity?
2. How is most of the land on Madagascar used?

Building Your Portfolio
1. **Preparing an Oral Report** The novels of Chinua Achebe give westerners a glimpse into Nigerian society and

internet connect

Search the Internet through the HRW Web site for information on President Clinton's 1998 trip to Africa. Find and be prepared to discuss what countries he visited, what the purpose of the visit was, and what agreements or changes came about as a result of his trip.

HRW GO TO: go.hrw.com
KEYWORD: SCØ
President Clinton

a changing Africa. Read one of these novels and prepare an oral report on the effects of modernization and the struggle to save or adapt old ways. Possible works include *Man of the People* (Doubleday), *No Longer at Ease* (Doubleday), and *Things Fall Apart* (Doubleday). Place your notes in your portfolio.

2. **Preparing a Panel Discussion** Work with a group of your classmates to find information on the capture of the American embassy in Tehran and the seizure of more than 50 American hostages by Iranian militants on November 4, 1979. Find information that describes the effects of the incident on the Iranians, the hostages, the United States, and the world. Then use the information you have collected to prepare a panel discussion on the effects of the incident. Place the information you collect in your portfolio.

3. **Dramatizing History** In recent decades, the Organization of Petroleum Exporting Countries (OPEC) has been prominent in world affairs. Work with several of your classmates to find out how OPEC conducts its meetings. Then conduct a mock OPEC meeting in which the ministers discuss how to raise the price of oil and how to enforce their decisions. Place a report of the panel meeting in your portfolio.

4. **Conducting a Debate** Prepare a debate on the following topic to present to the class.

    Resolved: The world community of nations should agree never to meet any terrorist demands.

As you and other students prepare your debate, you might find it useful to research some of the terrorist incidents that have taken place in the world in recent years. Place notes from the debate in your portfolio.

CHAPTER 31

Latin America Since 1945

TIME

A.D. 1945–the present

A.D. 1945–the present

3.7 million B.C.   4000 B.C.   A.D. 2100

PLACE

Latin America

Latin America

The Andes Mountains

Significance

Latin America, rich in human and natural resources, persists in working for political, economic, and social progress.

For many years Latin America was overshadowed by the colossus to the north—the United States. The region's governments and economies, particularly of those countries bordering the Caribbean, depended on the United States. However, this situation is fast changing as the 1900s draw to a close. These developing nations have begun to steer their own courses.

Terms to Define

multinational corporations	PRI
monoculture	campesinos
import substitution	Contras
hyperinflation	FMLN
North American Free Trade Agreement	Contadora Principles
	dissidents
demographic transition	Operation Bootstrap
Organization of American States	*desaparecidos*
	Sendero Luminoso
geopolitical region	Medellín cartel

People to Identify

Carlos Salinas de Gortari	Jean-Bertrand Aristide
Daniel Ortega	Eva Perón
José Napoleón Duarte	Fernando Collor
Manuel Noriega	Salvador Allende
Oscar Arias	Patricio Aylwin
Fidel Castro	Alberto Fujimori
Luis Muñoz Marín	

Places to Locate

Mexico	Cuba
Nicaragua	Puerto Rico
El Salvador	Dominican Republic
Panama	Haiti

Chapter Theme Questions

- **Economic Organization** In what ways might economic factors affect the political development of a nation?
- **Social Relations** How might rapid population growth and urbanization affect a society?
- **Politics and Law** What challenges might occur when countries make the transition from authoritarian to democratic forms of government?

The death in 1952 of Eva ("Evita") Perón, first lady of Argentina, sparked an outpouring of national grief. In Evita, the former stage and radio actress, the lower economic classes believed that they had found their champion. Whether she truly had their interests at heart remains a matter for conjecture. The following is a description of the flamboyant Evita as she declined the nomination for vice president in 1951.

❝The woman who mounted the steps and looked out upon the frenzied crowd was a far cry from the fledgling first lady of 1946, or the glamour queen of the Rainbow Tour. The blonde curls and gaudy attire had long since given way to what one scholar has called 'the streamlined, eternally classic style which was to be hers—and uniquely hers at that time—until her death.' Her hair was pulled back severely, accentuating the growing gauntness of her features. Tears flooded her eyes. She raised her arms in response to the delirium, and a look of uncertainty clouded her expression.❞

Like Argentina, other nations of Latin America have witnessed dramatic changes in government during the recent chapters of their history.

Section 1

Facing New Challenges

Focus Questions

- **What economic challenges did Latin America face after World War II?**
- **What challenges has the region faced in terms of population, urbanization, poverty, and the environment?**
- **What social and political forces have emerged in Latin America?**

The countries of Latin America underwent enormous changes after World War II. Once largely rural and agricultural, and with a secondary role in world affairs, Latin America became a focus of world attention. Its growing population, the discovery of its petroleum deposits and other resources, and its rapid industrialization increased Latin America's presence in the world.

Since achieving independence in the early 1800s, most Latin American societies had followed traditional social and economic patterns. After 1945, however, Latin America seemed to be not merely catching up with the industrialized world, but creating its own patterns.

Economic Development

During World War II, Latin America had provided vast quantities of raw materials and food to the Allies. After the war, Latin American nations found economic stability difficult to achieve. There was, however, increased demand for their raw materials and agricultural products.

Most political leaders in Latin America saw internal economic development as the key to resolving the region's problems. Economic development would provide jobs for the increasing population. Industrialization would lessen these countries' dependence on foreign sources for vital manufactured goods and would provide consumer goods for everyone. Throughout the region, the drive for economic development became a major government-driven project. To finance these projects, Latin American nations sought economic aid from foreign governments and took out loans from commercial banks.

Latin American leaders also invited foreign corporations and manufacturers to establish businesses in their countries. They hoped that the foreign corporations' investments and technology would help spur industrialization. Since foreign participation would bring in machinery and capital, it seemed like an inexpensive and rapid way to promote economic development.

Relations between foreign-owned businesses, known as **multinational corporations**, and their host countries developed into a major political issue. Many Latin Americans resented the foreign ownership of important factories. In addition, factory owners often took their profits out of the country instead of reinvesting the funds.

The problem of monoculture. Among the serious economic challenges facing Latin America was the region's reliance on a limited number of crops. The dependence of a region or country on one crop is known as **monoculture**. Monoculture contributed to Latin America's considerable economic instability. Almost every country in the region depended on one or two crops or minerals for the bulk of its export income. For example, Venezuela and Mexico relied on oil; the major cash export of Colombia and many of the Central American countries was coffee. The economic fortunes of countries with one or two cash crops rise and fall with the prices of those products on the world markets. Thus, when world prices of various commodities rose sharply in the 1970s, for instance, only to plunge in the 1980s, Latin American countries were caught on an economic roller coaster.

Patterns of industrialization. In Chapter 26, you read that most Latin American countries followed a policy of economic nationalism during the 1930s. They took action to encourage industry, promote economic self-sufficiency, and reduce dependency on foreign imports. One policy designed to accomplish these goals was known as **import substitution**, or import-substituting industrialization (ISI). Under import substitution, governments chose to replace certain imported manufactured products with goods produced by industries inside the country. Various kinds of favors were granted to encourage manufacturers to produce these items. At the same time, tariffs or quotas would be set to discourage or prevent importation of similar goods, giving the local industries a chance to develop.

Import substitution worked fairly well in the largest countries—Brazil, Mexico, and Argentina—because they had large markets and enough of their own resources to accomplish the task. Starting in the 1950s, these countries produced steel, heavy machinery, automobiles, pharmaceuticals, and many consumer goods. Between 1950 and 1978, the manufacturing sector in Latin America grew at an annual rate of 6.5 percent. Some other Latin American countries, such as Chile, Colombia, and Guatemala, experienced lower, but still significant, rates of development.

By the mid-1980s, all of the easier substitutions of imports had been made. Further growth was obstructed by the fact that the majority of people in many Latin American countries could not afford to purchase consumer products in great volume. The market for the goods, therefore, was sharply limited. In addition, a worldwide recession had begun to affect Latin American economies.

International debt crisis. Adding to Latin America's economic difficulties was the huge burden of foreign debt.

READ
WRITE
INTERPRET
CONNECT
THINK

Making Connections with History: Linking Economics to History

All societies have access to limited amounts of resources that can be used to produce goods and services to satisfy people's wants and needs. Specifically, at any one time, each society has a given amount of labor, capital, and natural resources. In every society, people's wants seem to exceed what can possibly be produced. This condition is called scarcity, and it creates a basic economic problem. Because we cannot have everything we want, we make choices. Much of economics involves the ways and reasons why institutions, people, and societies make the choices that they do.

Opportunity cost, another key economic concept, deals with the economic choices that are made in relation to the sacrifices involved. For example, if you are given a choice of going to a play or to a concert, and you choose the play, the concert becomes your opportunity cost because you sacrificed it when you chose the play.

Economic systems determine the manner in which people decide what to produce, how to produce it, and for whom to produce it. These are the basic economic decisions that every society must make. They are based upon scarcity and opportunity cost. The economic system of a society affects people's relationships with one another, the kind of government they create, and the history of the society.

How to Link Economics to History

To link economics to history, follow these steps.
1. Identify and define the economic concept being discussed. It is either scarcity, opportunity cost, or an economic system.
2. Describe the effects of the economic concept on government or society.

Developing the Skill

Read the following excerpt. How does the description of a hacienda in Latin America help us to understand the development of the society there? "The hacienda as a society may be described by saying that it was—and is—an economic and social system that seeks to achieve self-sufficiency . . . on a local scale. . . . Each unit

Highland farming in Peru

expands until it has within its own borders all that it needs—salt from the sea, *panela* (black, unrefined sugar) from its own cane fields, corn, barley, wheat, coconuts, bananas, apples, and pears. All of this depends upon where the hacienda is located. . . . [I]t can run from the seacoast to the mountain top. . . . Not all haciendas . . . satisfy this ideal completely, but that is the aim of hacienda organization: to buy nothing; to raise and make everything within the limits of its own boundaries. The big house is built from the timbers found on the land. . . . [T]he furniture is made at home. The cloth is woven there from wool shorn off home-grown sheep. The llamas that graze in the hills, the oxen and the horses are raised and broken where they were born. . . . The wooden plow, the wagon, the windmill for the grinding of the corn, or the water mill for the grinding of the cane are all fabricated [made] locally."

The passage describes an economic system. The decisions about what to produce, how to produce it, and for whom to produce it are made by the owner of the hacienda. The goal of the owner is to make and keep this economic unit self-sufficient and self-governing. The problem of scarcity is solved by the planned use of natural resources. The opportunity cost comes in when the owner makes the choice of what is to be produced on the hacienda.

Practicing the Skill

In the free enterprise system of the United States, who answers the three basic economic questions?

To apply this skill, see Applying History Study Skills on page 871.

Foreign debt plagued most of the nations of Latin America. To finance their industrialization and modernization plans, most Latin American governments borrowed enormous sums of money from foreign countries and commercial banks. Between 1970 and 1980, the region's total foreign debt rose by more than 1,000 percent.

Many of Latin America's loans were made in the late 1970s, when interest rates were high. By the early 1980s, with their economies in decline, most Latin American governments had difficulty meeting their loan payments. Many made only token payments. To prevent the debtor nations from completely defaulting on their loans, the lenders agreed to renegotiate repayment schedules. Some nations were also forgiven on a part of their principal—the original amount they had borrowed. Other nations were granted lower interest rates. Still others were allowed a longer time to repay. Even with this help, the Latin American foreign debt still amounted to hundreds of billions of dollars.

This foreign debt greatly contributed to another economic problem—inflation. During the late 1980s, most Latin American countries spent a huge percentage of their revenues on interest payments. At the same time, these countries continued to fund government programs, state-run industries, and bureaucracies to administer them. They did this simply by printing more and more paper money. With so much money in circulation, the value of Latin American currencies plunged, and prices soared. By the 1980s, many Latin American countries were experiencing extremely high rates of inflation, or **hyperinflation**. Several countries had annual inflation rates of over 1,000 percent.

To combat hyperinflation, most Latin American governments raised taxes, cut spending, and eliminated most subsidies to industries. In addition, they drastically reduced the numbers of government workers and strictly controlled the wages of those who remained. In most cases, these measures worked. However, inflation rates remained high compared to those of Western industrial nations. Furthermore, to cut inflation most governments had brought their economies almost to the point of recession. Hardest hit by the burden of these government measures were the people of the working class, who sometimes responded with demonstrations and strikes. It appeared that in the years ahead, Latin America would continue to face significant economic hurdles: limited growth, burdensome foreign debt, high inflation, and widespread unemployment.

Regional economic alliances. In the postwar years, Latin American countries tried new forms of economic relations in an effort to lessen their dependence on industrialized countries and to cooperate in areas of production, tariffs, and trade. The Andean Pact, enacted in 1969, restricted foreign investment and encouraged both lower tariffs and economic cooperation among the Andean nations—Colombia, Ecuador, Peru, Bolivia, and Chile.

Many Latin American countries have strengthened economic links in the 1990s by making agreements with the United States and establishing regional free-trade agreements with one another. For example, the **North American Free Trade Agreement** (NAFTA), which went into effect in 1994, brought together Mexico, Canada, and the United States into one of the largest free-trade zones in the world. Argentina, Brazil, Paraguay, and Uruguay formed a free-trade alliance under the Mercosur Treaty, which took effect in 1995. The Mercosur group subsequently negotiated free-trade agreements with Chile and other Andean nations.

NAFTA, a trade pact signed by leaders of Mexico, Canada, and the United States in 1992, went into effect on January 1, 1994. Standing from left to right are Mexican president Carlos Salinas de Gortari, U.S. president George Bush, and Canadian prime minister Brian Mulroney.

Changes and Challenges

With Latin America's industrialization came many benefits, including economic growth, higher standards of living, and improved health care. However, industrialization created problems, too.

Population growth. In 1950 the population of Latin America totaled about 160 million. This figure had nearly tripled by the mid-1990s, reaching 470 million. Today the region's population continues to grow. The graph on this page shows how the population in selected Latin American countries is expected to grow by the year 2025.

A decline in the death rate—especially the infant mortality rate—spurred this population explosion. Public health measures reduced the number of deaths from disease each year. For example, the spraying of insecticides to kill the mosquitoes that carry malaria and yellow fever, the chlorination of water, and expanded programs of vaccination had a great effect. In addition, improved health care and technology have enabled people to live longer. Since the 1960s, improved socioeconomic conditions have also boosted population growth.

Latin America's population surge was typical of the kind of **demographic transition**—change in the characteristics of a population—that occurs when a nation gradually becomes industrialized. Typically, before industrialization takes place in a country, both birthrates and death rates are high. Industrialization decreases death rates by improving standards of living, including sanitation, nutrition, and medical care. Over time, birthrates also decline; women have fewer babies, knowing that their children will probably survive. During the period of transition, however—when birthrates continue to be high while death rates have declined—a population boom occurs. At present, Latin American countries are at varying points in this period of transition.

The growth of cities. Latin American cities, like cities all over the world, exercise a powerful attraction because they contain a concentration of social services, schools, and popular entertainments. Hospitals, universities, and secondary schools are mostly found in the region's cities. Even more important, however, cities in Latin America grew because large numbers of people migrated from rural areas to the cities in search of work.

Over the past several decades, the populations of Latin America's cities have grown much faster than the general population. Population growth in the cities is often twice that of Latin American nations as

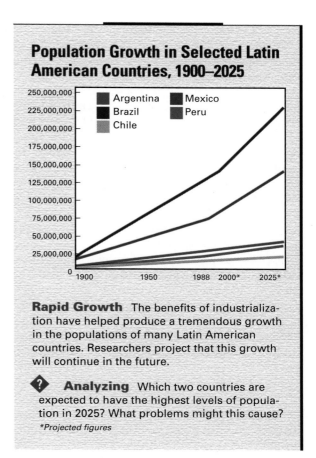

Population Growth in Selected Latin American Countries, 1900–2025

Legend: Argentina, Brazil, Chile, Mexico, Peru

Rapid Growth The benefits of industrialization have helped produce a tremendous growth in the populations of many Latin American countries. Researchers project that this growth will continue in the future.

? Analyzing Which two countries are expected to have the highest levels of population in 2025? What problems might this cause?
Projected figures

a whole. The region's largest cities showed the greatest rate of growth.

City and national governments have had to deal with complex administrative problems. For example, sewer lines, water mains, and electric lines have had to be installed. Large investments have had to be made in road building, public buses, and subway systems. The heavy machinery and other equipment for all of these projects could not be found in most Latin American countries. The need to import these items often created a financial burden.

Many other problems arose in connection with the growth of cities. Most cities faced severe shortages of both housing and jobs. The governments, with so many other new expenses, could not afford to build public housing for the expanding city population. In addition, most of the rural migrants who could find work did not earn enough money to pay for housing. They therefore squatted—took up living space without permission—on whatever empty land they could find, throwing together shacks of scrap metal and other cast-off materials. In recent years many newcomers to Latin American cities have ended up in these shantytown slums, known as *favelas* in Brazil, *barriadas* in Peru, and *colonias* in Mexico.

When large numbers of people live in areas with inadequate sewage systems and no clean running water, a perfect environment is created for the spread of disease. About half the population of Central America lacks safe drinking water, and the situation is similar in other parts of Latin America. In 1991 a cholera outbreak occurred in the slums of Lima, Peru. The outbreak soon became an epidemic and spread to Brazil, Chile, Colombia, and Ecuador. In its first three months, the epidemic killed more than 1,000 people and infected 150,000 others.

Rapidly growing city populations also add to environmental problems. The pollution caused by Mexico City's thousands of factories and 3 million cars is a major hazard to life and health in the city. Half of all infants in Mexico City, for example, have harmful levels of toxins in their blood.

Poverty and frustration. Even though Latin America's economies generally grew during the 1990s, the region's social problems have shown little improvement in recent years. In 1997 almost half of Latin America's people were poor—an increase of 60 million in about 10 years. Rising unemployment made a difficult situation worse. By the mid-1990s, the average unemployment rate for Latin America was almost 8 percent, and five nations had unemployment rates of more than 15 percent. Meanwhile, the gap between Latin America's wealthy people and its poor continued to grow. Social discontent was widespread as people became increasingly frustrated. Many Latin Americans, particularly those in the northern part of the region, migrated to California, Florida, Texas, and other parts of the United States, seeking better-paying jobs and more secure lives.

Environmental problems. Latin America's environment paid a high price for industrialization and the development of natural resources. Millions of acres of land were cleared to make room for buildings, roads, factories, and farms. In Central America alone, more than two thirds of the rain forests have been destroyed. Many plant and animal species have become extinct, and there has been significant soil erosion.

Dangerous pesticides, many of which have been banned in the United States, are still being used in Latin America.

Much of Latin America's rain forest has been destroyed by logging, industrialization, and the development of land for agriculture.

New Political and Social Forces

Events in the last several decades have given rise to new political and social pressures in Latin American society. By the early 1990s, most of the countries of Latin America were moving toward constitutional government.

Women are one emerging political force. The struggle for women's right to vote began in Latin America around World War I. However, not until 1961 did women win the right to vote throughout the region. Their votes increased their influence in government. Even though Latin American women continue to struggle for full equality with men, they have had some political successes. In several of the southern Latin American countries—such as Chile, Uruguay, and Argentina—women were leaders in the struggle against military dictatorships.

Labor also gained political clout in postwar Latin America. As employment in factories increased, labor organizing spread and the union movement grew stronger. Today there are about 40 million union members in Latin America, making up about 20 percent of the workforce. The labor movement has experienced success with strikes and other actions to achieve better conditions.

The Roman Catholic Church represents another emerging political force. In the past, the Catholic Church had supported conservative ideas in Latin American society and politics, which usually translated to church support of those already in power. Historically, however, the church has maintained a concern for the poor and the powerless. Following a meeting of the Catholic bishops of the region in 1968, the church's leaders began to take more liberal stands on the political issues of welfare and human rights.

A theology of liberation emerged, in which many church leaders committed themselves to the struggle for social justice and pledged to change oppressive economic and political systems. Grassroots organizations emerged, often led by priests, and combined religious study with efforts to solve practical social problems.

Although the majority of Latin Americans remained Catholic, Protestantism expanded rapidly in the late 1900s. The emphasis of Protestants on individual spiritual improvement and a close relationship between the clergy and laity differed from Catholicism and appealed to many people.

Political Alliances

During and just after World War II, the nations of the Western Hemisphere entered into several mutual defense pacts. Many political leaders viewed such pacts as necessary steps to contain communism.

Inter-American cooperation went a step further in 1948, when delegates from the nations of the Western Hemisphere met at Bogotá, Colombia, and founded the **Organization of American States** (OAS). The goal of the organization was economic, military, and cultural cooperation among the nations of the Western Hemisphere. The group still exists today and aims to prevent outside states from intervening in the Western Hemisphere and to maintain peace among member nations.

The founding of the OAS represented a continuation of the Good Neighbor Policy, through which the United States sought cooperation with its southern neighbors. This ideal, however, proved difficult to achieve. Although the OAS supported American intervention in the revolution in the Dominican Republic in 1965, the situation soured United States-Latin American relations. Today the OAS has 35 members, including nearly all of the independent countries in the Western Hemisphere.

Section 1 Review

1. **Define** multinational corporations, monoculture, import substitution, hyperinflation, North American Free Trade Agreement, demographic transition, Organization of American States
2. **Interpreting Ideas** How did the drive to industrialize cause economic difficulties in Latin America after World War II?
3. **Analyzing Ideas** What challenges are presented by population growth, the growth of cities, and environmental damage?
4. **Evaluating Ideas (a)** Briefly describe three new political forces that emerged in Latin America in the years after World War II. **(b)** Explain the impact of each on the region.

Section 2

Mexico and Central America

Focus Questions

- **What crises has Mexico faced since World War II?**
- **How did Nicaragua, El Salvador, and Panama move from political instability to the possibility of peace?**
- **What efforts have been made to bring peace to Central America?**

Mexico and Central America are part of what cultural geographers sometimes call Middle America, an area that also includes the Caribbean islands. Geographers also refer to the area as Central America and the Caribbean. (See map on page 854.) This area forms a single **geopolitical region**, one whose communities share similar political and geographic features.

The importance of this region lies in its location at a commercial and military crossroads. The region connects the north-south routes of the hemisphere as well as the routes between the Atlantic and Pacific Oceans via the Panama Canal. Although the largest modern aircraft carriers and supertankers cannot pass through the canal, it is still a major artery for commercial shipping. Such heavy traffic in the waterway results in its continued strategic and commercial importance.

Political and economic turmoil has rocked Central America and the Caribbean in recent decades. As a result, the United States and other nations have focused much attention on this region.

Mexico

Immediately after World War II, Mexico appeared to be one of the most stable countries in Latin America. By 1946, Mexico's Institutional Revolutionary Party, or **PRI**, had a firmly established civilian government. Thereafter, under the policies of a succession of PRI presidents, Mexico made great economic progress, building up its infrastructure and promoting industry. Despite these advances, however, the PRI allowed little opposition. As the party remained entrenched in power, it also became resistant to demands for political reform.

In the late 1960s, student protests racked Mexico, just as they had done in many other nations. This led to numerous confrontations between protesters and police. In 1971 a guerrilla campaign began against the government, further undermining its stability. The government took a hard line, hunting down and capturing or killing the guerrillas. By the mid-1970s, the threat had faded, and Mexico faced very little guerrilla or terrorist activity for some 20 years.

Economic instability. Throughout the three decades following World War II, Mexico experienced economic problems. To remedy these difficulties, the government lowered the value of the currency several times and cut back its spending.

Mexico's economic picture improved greatly with the discovery of huge oil reserves in the 1970s. Mexico's oil earnings soared from $500 million in 1976 to over $13 billion by 1981, and it looked as though the country might finally overcome its economic difficulties. Anticipating these oil revenues, the government borrowed heavily in order to undertake massive development projects.

In the 1980s, however, new problems arose. Corruption in the state-owned oil company, PEMEX, reduced the profits available for government spending. Even more discouragingly, a worldwide slump in oil prices proved devastating for the Mexican economy. Government borrowing during the 1970s had driven up the foreign debt to almost $80 billion. The annual rate of inflation soared; by 1986 it was almost 106 percent. A tremendous earthquake ravaged Mexico City in late 1985, putting additional strain on the nation's economy. The government faced the prospect of rebuilding the shattered capital and providing for the many thousands who were left homeless.

The Mexican economy continued to face challenges through the rest of the decade. By 1988 the annual inflation rate had jumped to 143 percent, and the foreign debt by the end of the decade was approaching $100 billion.

President Carlos Salinas de Gortari, who took office in 1988, attempted to deal with this economic crisis. He loosened controls on the Mexican economy. The government sold some of its business holdings to encourage foreign investors to play a greater role in the economy. Salinas also moved toward establishing free-trade arrangements with Mexico's major trading partners. For example, he pushed hard for approval of the North American Free Trade Agreement (NAFTA), which he hoped would result in heavy investment in Mexico by its northern neighbors.

The earthquake that struck Mexico City in September 1985 killed approximately 9,500 people.

Such investment would further stimulate economic growth and create thousands of new jobs.

Monetary crisis. Despite the government's efforts, however, economic pressures led the next president, Ernesto Zedillo Ponce de León to order the devaluation of the Mexican peso in December 1994. Confidence in the Mexican economy plunged, stifling foreign investment, which had been on the rise. By early 1995, Mexico was caught in a severe monetary and investment crisis. U.S. President Bill Clinton managed to pull together a multibillion-dollar financial aid package, but Mexico's economic woes continued. Inflation rose again, reaching nearly 50 percent, and the country suffered the worst recession in its history. Not until 1996, with the help of government-implemented austerity measures, did the Mexican economy begin to recover.

Emigration problems. New jobs were a constant concern for the Mexican government because of rapid population growth. The economy did not grow nearly as fast as the population, so there were not as many jobs as there were people looking for work. To find employment, tens of thousands of Mexicans slipped illegally into the United States each year. The problem of illegal immigrants troubled United States-Mexican relations.

In 1986 the United States Congress passed the Immigration Reform and Control Act in an attempt to reduce tension between the two countries. The law granted legal status to persons who had entered the United States illegally before January 1, 1982, and had been living in the country continuously since then. The law also required employers to check the residency status of all job applicants, and it established penalties for hiring illegal aliens.

Both the Mexican and U.S. governments hoped that Mexico's economic growth and the creation of new jobs would reduce the number of illegal immigrants crossing the border. However, Mexico's subsequent economic troubles made both unemployment and illegal immigration persistent problems in the 1990s.

Political consequences. The PRI, by now one of the world's longest-ruling parties, had been in power since 1929. However, Mexico's problems in the 1980s and 1990s increased opposition to the PRI. In 1988, for example, the party's candidate for the presidency, Carlos Salinas de Gortari, was—according to many observers—guaranteed election only by resorting to widespread voter fraud. During Salinas's presidency, apparent corruption within the president's own family further rocked confidence in the PRI.

There has been rapid population growth in Mexico since 1915; the number of Mexican immigrants to the United States has also increased drastically. Shown in the photo is a border checkpoint between the United States and Mexico.

Adding to the PRI's problems was an uprising of Maya peasant farmers in the southern state of Chiapas in 1994. After violent clashes between revolutionary guerrillas and Mexican soldiers, the government and the rebels eventually reached an agreement. Additional signs of political unrest were clear, however. These included the assassination later the same year of the PRI presidential candidate.

The PRI's long-standing hold on Mexican politics continued to weaken in 1995 and 1996. For the first time, elections held in 1997 gave control of Mexico's congress to opposition parties rather than to the PRI. Nevertheless, the popularity of President Zedillo, a member of the PRI, was higher than ever, thanks largely to Mexico's improving economy and well-received electoral reforms.

Postwar Conditions in Central America

Following World War II, Central America experienced economic growth. Between 1950 and 1970, cooperation among countries allowed industry to grow and important trade routes, such as highways, to be built. People moved to the cities in great numbers. Between 1970 and 1988, urban populations grew steadily in nearly every country in Central America.

However, only a certain sector of the population benefited from economic growth. The peasants, known as the **campesinos**, did not share in this prosperity. Often the best land in rural areas remained in the hands of the rich. As rents rose, more peasants joined a growing class of landless farm workers.

In addition, earthquakes in Guatemala and Nicaragua in the 1970s, as well as devastating hurricanes that decade and the next, left many already poor citizens homeless. Throughout the 1970s and 1980s, the countries of Central America remained some of the poorest in the world, due in part to inequality in the distribution of wealth.

A lack of sufficient medical help, sanitation facilities, and educational services plagued the countries of Central America. The population increased at a high rate. In the late 1970s and early 1980s, sky-rocketing inflation slowed the economies of the region to a standstill. Faced with almost constant political upheaval, social and economic inequalities, and the threat of natural disasters, thousands of people fled the region. Most entered the United States, often illegally, hoping to find a better life there. Many of those who remained began to demand reforms.

The Nicaraguan Revolution

Following a meeting held by the Catholic bishops of Latin America in 1968, members of the clergy throughout Latin America began to withdraw their support for military dictatorships and other powerful groups. The Latin American Catholic Church began

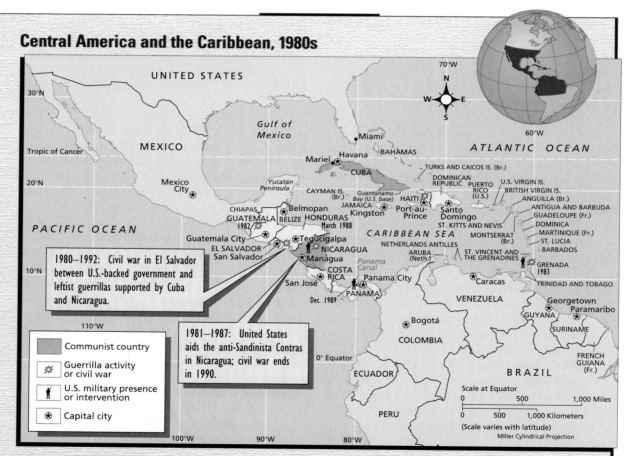

Central America and the Caribbean, 1980s

1980–1992: Civil war in El Salvador between U.S.-backed government and leftist guerrillas supported by Cuba and Nicaragua.

1981–1987: United States aids the anti-Sandinista Contras in Nicaragua; civil war ends in 1990.

Communist country

Guerrilla activity or civil war

U.S. military presence or intervention

Capital city

Scale at Equator
0   500   1,000 Miles
0   500   1,000 Kilometers
(Scale varies with latitude)
Miller Cylindrical Projection

Learning from Maps The countries of Central America and the Caribbean experienced many political upheavals in the 1980s.

? Region In which areas did the United States maintain a military presence in the 1980s?

to believe that it must commit itself to the struggle for social justice, fighting for the oppressed.

In addition, a growing class of educated people joined the ranks of those who opposed corrupt dictators. Both of these factors bolstered the revolutionary movement against the corrupt and oppressive dictator Anastasio Somoza in Nicaragua. Almost the entire population had risen up against his regime by 1979.

A Marxist-inspired revolutionary organization, the Sandinistas, gained control of the anti-Somoza revolution by promising a better life and political pluralism. The Sandinistas took their name from a Nicaraguan nationalist guerrilla leader of the 1920s, Augusto César Sandino. After taking control of Nicaragua, the Sandinistas established a ruling council, or junta, with Daniel Ortega as its head. The junta forged close ties with the Communist governments in Cuba and the Soviet Union. It also began to build a Marxist dictatorship in Nicaragua.

Opposition to the Sandinistas' economic and political policies developed in the early 1980s. In time, the opposition adopted the Sandinistas' approach to political change—armed rebellion. A rebel group called the **Contras** began a guerrilla war to overthrow the Sandinista government. The United States supported the Contras with financial and military aid, while the Sandinista government received support from the Soviet Union and Cuba.

With a civil war raging, survival became the major aim of the Sandinistas. They spent more and more of the national budget on the military, causing severe economic problems. Shortages of manufactured goods were common. As the 1980s wore on, the fighting between government forces and the Contras cost many lives.

El Salvador

The Central American country of El Salvador, located northwest of Nicaragua, was ruled either by wealthy civilians or by military dictatorships from the 1940s to the late 1970s. (See map on opposite page.) Guerrilla groups began to form in the 1970s to fight the inequities imposed by the government. These organizations managed to mobilize people into antigovernment demonstrations.

José Napoleón Duarte of the moderate Christian Democrats led the civilian reform movement and was president through most of the 1980s. During this time, the U.S. government sent military advisers and financial aid to El Salvador to help the government. However, violence marred much of Duarte's administration. The Farabundo Martí National Liberation

Front (**FMLN**), a leftist guerrilla group, undertook a terror campaign of kidnappings, assassinations, and attacks on government buildings. In response, right-wing death squads—many of them backed by the army—hit out at anyone who expressed any kind of support for the FMLN's aims. Their most notorious acts included the 1980 assassination of Oscar Romero, the Catholic archbishop of San Salvador, and the murders of three American nuns and an American volunteer later that year.

In the late 1980s, the government took a turn to the right when the conservative ARENA Party won control of the legislature and the presidency. This spurred the FMLN forces to further violence. In 1989 they attacked a number of large army bases and launched a major offensive against the country's capital, San Salvador, and other urban centers. The message FMLN leaders seemed to be sending was that they could strike anywhere at any time. Right-wing violence increased as well. In November 1989, for example, a death squad murdered six Catholic priests who had expressed anti-ARENA sentiments.

By the end of the decade, the violence had claimed the lives of thousands of Salvadorans. Tired of the killing and the constant turmoil, most people simply wanted peace.

Panama

The country of Panama experienced a political and economic situation similar to that of its Central American neighbors. The only major difference was that the United States controlled the Panama Canal and 10 miles of territory on either side, known as the Canal Zone, that was once part of Panama. American-Panamanian negotiations over control of the canal continued throughout the postwar period. The two nations finally ratified a treaty in 1979. This treaty, which called for the gradual transfer of the canal to Panama by December 31, 1999, caused much controversy in the United States. Many Americans believed that United States security would be in danger when Panama gained control of the canal.

In the late 1980s, relations between Panama and the United States deteriorated. United States officials accused the Panamanian dictator, General Manuel Noriega, of helping South American narcotics dealers send illegal drugs into the United States. President Ronald Reagan attempted to pressure Noriega into resigning. When this failed, Reagan stopped all United States military and economic aid to Panama. Then, in December 1989, after Panamanian forces

Oscar Arias, president of Costa Rica from 1986 until 1990, received the Nobel Peace Prize in 1987 for the plan he proposed and signed with leaders of Guatemala, El Salvador, Honduras, and Nicaragua.

ative economic and political stability—proposed a peace plan for Central America. The plan called for an end to all fighting in the region, a halt to foreign aid to rebels, and economic reforms. The following excerpt from a speech by Arias underscores his belief in the connection between peace and democracy:

66 The democracy in which many American nations live today cannot be consolidated without economic development and social justice. Before any political or economic conditions can be imposed on the democracies of the Americas, there must be a commitment from the Western world to strengthen democracy in all our nations. In the Americas, peace must be democratic, pluralistic, tolerant, and free. While dogmatism [stubborn opinions] and intransigence [stubbornness] persist and there is no dialogue, peace will be impossible. Working together for democracy, freedom, and development is working together for peace. 99

Five Central American countries—Costa Rica, El Salvador, Guatemala, Honduras, and Nicaragua—and the United States endorsed Arias's proposal. For his work, Arias received the Nobel Peace Prize in 1987. Not until the early 1990s, however, did peace seem possible in Central America.

Recent Developments in Central America

As in several other parts of the world, the 1990s brought new hope for peace and democratic change.

Nicaragua. Fighting between the Sandinistas and the Contras finally ended in 1990. In free elections held that year, Violeta Barrios de Chamorro, a candidate who opposed the Sandinistas, was elected president of Nicaragua. Against expectations, the Sandinistas handed over power peacefully. Almost immediately the United States government lifted the trade embargo that it had imposed on Nicaragua in 1985. In addition, the United States and a number of Western European nations provided aid to the new government.

Under Chamorro, the country faced ongoing political instability and severe economic problems, including hyperinflation, massive foreign debt, and 50 percent unemployment. In 1996, Arnoldo Alemán succeeded Chamorro, defeating former Sandinista president Daniel Ortega and many other candidates. Like his predecessor, President Alemán had to deal with Nicaragua's continuing difficulties, including high rates of unemployment and inflation.

killed one American soldier and detained and severely beat another one, U.S. President George Bush sent troops to Panama to restore order and capture Noriega. Noriega was taken to Florida, where he was later convicted and sentenced to 40 years in prison for drug trafficking.

Peace Proposals for Central America

A number of Latin American countries made attempts to find a peaceful settlement to problems in Central America. In 1983, for example, political leaders of Colombia, Mexico, Panama, and Venezuela agreed to the **Contadora Principles**. This document, named for the island where the leaders met, called for a freeze on arms sales and a reduction of foreign military bases and personnel in the area. It also promoted negotiations rather than violence as the only way to settle regional differences.

In 1987, representatives from throughout Central America met in Guatemala City, Guatemala, for a regional peace conference. At this conference Oscar Arias, the president of Costa Rica—a country with rel-

With a series of three lakes and locks—the Gatun, the Pedro Miguel, and the Miraflores—ships can be raised and lowered from one sea level to the next through the Panama Canal.

Section 2 Review

1. **Define** geopolitical region, PRI, campesinos, Contras, FMLN, Contadora Principles
2. **Identify** Carlos Salinas de Gortari, Daniel Ortega, José Napoleón Duarte, Manuel Noriega, Oscar Arias, Violeta Barrios de Chamorro
3. **Locate and Explain the Significance** Mexico, Nicaragua, El Salvador, Panama
4. **Understanding Ideas** Describe the problems faced and the gains made by Mexico since 1945.
5. **Analyzing Ideas** Nicaragua, El Salvador, and Panama moved from political instability to the possibility of peace by the 1990s. Do you agree or disagree with this statement? Why?
6. **Interpreting Ideas** Why do you think some people consider the 1990s a decade of hope for Central America? Do you agree with them? Why or why not?

El Salvador. In El Salvador, President Alfredo Cristiani—who succeeded José Napoleón Duarte in 1989—and FMLN leaders made tentative steps toward peace for their country. By 1992, with the aid of UN mediation, opposing sides had signed a peace treaty. This peace treaty finally brought the costly 12-year civil war to an end. In the first postwar elections, which were held in 1994, Armando Calderón Sol, the ARENA candidate, was elected president of El Salvador. ARENA retained control of the legislature in the 1997 elections, although the FMLN showed considerable strength.

Panama. After the United States intervention in 1989, Panama began the new decade with its first democratically elected government in years. During the early and mid-1990s, the people of Panama seemed determined to hold on to democracy and avoid a return to military dictatorship. However, the country struggled with deep economic and social problems.

With 1999 approaching, preparations were under way for transfer of control of the Panama Canal to Panama. American and Panamanian officials were working to resolve issues concerning future administration of the vital waterway.

Section 3

Nations of the Caribbean

Focus Questions
- How did the revolution in Cuba affect life on the island and its relations with the rest of the world?
- How has the Puerto Rican economy and identity developed since the 1950s?
- What troubles have the Dominican Republic and Haiti experienced?

The islands of the Caribbean Sea, sometimes called the West Indies, stretch from the Bahamas, off the tip of Florida, to the island nations within sight of Venezuela in the south. (See map on page 854.) Of these, Cuba, Puerto Rico, the Dominican Republic, Haiti, and Jamaica are sometimes called the Greater Antilles. The Lesser Antilles are the chain of smaller islands that includes the U.S. Virgin Islands and extends down to Trinidad and Tobago. While some Caribbean islands are independent nations, others remain politically tied to European countries or to the United States.

Revolution in Cuba
In 1959 a revolution in Cuba overthrew Fulgencio Batista, the army officer who had ruled Cuba through

puppet regimes from 1934 to 1944, and then as president beginning in 1952. Led by Fidel Castro, the Cuban Revolution was the greatest political upheaval Latin Americans had experienced since the Mexican Revolution of the early 1900s.

Fidel Castro began his campaign to overthrow the Cuban government in 1953 with an attack on a military barracks in Santiago de Cuba. Jailed for his role in this attack, Castro later went into exile in Mexico, where he trained a group of revolutionaries. He returned to Cuba with a band of men in 1956. For the next three years, Castro, with his brother Raúl and a young Argentine revolutionary named Ernesto ("Ché") Guevara, led guerrilla operations against the Batista government.

Batista answered with brutal, repressive measures. As a result, the Cuban people began to shift their support to the revolutionaries. By 1958 the United States government had reassessed its backing of the Batista regime and suspended arms shipments to his government. Realizing that he faced almost certain defeat, Batista fled, and Fidel Castro's revolutionaries took over the Cuban government.

Cuba under Castro. At first, most Cubans welcomed the revolution. Castro's promises of the reinstatement of civil liberties and agrarian reform were very attractive, as were his pledges to improve education and health care.

Both the lower and middle classes welcomed the change in government. Castro's promise of speedy, open elections seemed to assure a return to democracy.

His statement that he would build a new Cuba, independent of United States influence, was welcomed by many. In a relatively short time, however, the new Cuban government began its swing toward the Soviet bloc. By the end of 1959, Cuba clearly stood on the path to communism.

Castro's now openly communist regime became dictatorial, suppressing the free press. The revolutionaries held public trials of Batista supporters and executed many. The government began to enact a program of Marxist reforms, including land reform and redistribution of income. The government took over the operation of many businesses and agricultural estates owned by Americans.

Castro did enact many of his promised social reforms. His educational reforms concentrated on a literacy campaign. As a result, Cuba's literacy rate has risen to 96 percent, the highest in Latin America. Other social reforms were also enacted. At the same time, however, Castro continued his authoritarian style of rule, maintaining strict censorship on the press and suppressing all dissent.

Although he enjoyed a reasonably high level of support among the poor, Castro lost the backing of many middle- and upper-class Cubans. Businesspeople and landowners were angered by the seizure of their property. Middle-class intellectuals and liberal politicians were shocked by Castro's turn toward authoritarian communism. In time, increasing numbers of Cubans from all classes and walks of life began to flee the island. Many settled in Florida, not far from their homeland.

The population of the West Indies is heterogenous in terms of nationality, language, religion, age, and culture.

Through a guerrilla revolution in 1959, Fidel Castro seized political power in Cuba and pursued a series of Communist reforms.

The Bay of Pigs. In 1960 the Cuban government ordered U.S. owned oil companies on the island to process fuel supplied by the Soviet Union. When the companies refused, Cuba seized their refineries. The United States responded by refusing to import sugar from Cuba. Castro fought back by seizing other U.S. properties in Cuba.

The United States government viewed this situation and the developing relationship between Castro and the Soviets as threats to U.S. national security. The Central Intelligence Agency (CIA) began to funnel money to exiles for the training of anti-Castro troops in Guatemala. In April 1961, a United States-approved rebel landing was made in Cuba. This invasion, which took place on the southern coast at the Bay of Pigs, failed utterly. The expected anti-Castro uprisings did not take place, and the U.S. air support that had been promised was withdrawn. Castro's forces, better armed than the rebels, killed or captured the invasion forces.

The Bay of Pigs invasion was a foreign-policy disaster for the Kennedy administration. Because the rebels had included quite a number of Batista supporters, it appeared to many people that the United States was trying to re-establish a dictatorship in Cuba. Furthermore, the move drove Castro into even closer ties with the Soviet Union.

The Cuban missile crisis. Fearing that the United States would attempt another invasion, Fidel Castro quickly complied with a Soviet request to be allowed to construct nuclear missile sites in Cuba. The resulting crisis (as discussed in Chapter 28) brought the world to the brink of nuclear war in 1962. The agreement reached by the Soviet Union and the United States included a promise that the United States would not invade Cuba.

What If?

The Bay of Pigs
What might have happened if the Bay of Pigs invasion had been successful? Would the Cuban missile crisis have occurred? How might the history of Cuba be different?

Ché Guevara served in various posts under Fidel Castro's leadership. He was later captured and killed while leading a guerrilla attack near Santa Cruz, Bolivia.

Exporting revolution. In the mid-1960s, Castro launched a program to support communist revolutions in other developing nations, particularly in Latin America and Africa. The Cuban government sent arms, troops, and military advisers to Latin American nations such as the Dominican Republic and Nicaragua and to African nations such as Angola and Ethiopia.

Ché Guevara carried out some of the guerrilla activity associated with this effort. A former physician from Argentina, Guevara had become a revolutionary after witnessing the U.S.-sponsored overthrow of President Arbenz of Guatemala in 1954. Guevara personally led a band of guerrillas into the mountains of Bolivia in 1967. Shortly after, he was killed by a troop of U.S.-trained Bolivian rangers.

The United States persuaded the OAS to expel Cuba because of its efforts to export revolution. The American government also called on other nations in the region to join in an economic boycott of Cuba. The island nation thus began a long period of political and economic isolation from its neighbors in the Western Hemisphere.

Economic and social difficulties. This isolation added to Castro's problems in trying to boost the Cuban economy. Industrialization did not proceed as planned, and sugar production declined. As a result, during the 1970s, Cuba became more and more dependent on economic assistance from the Soviet Union.

The failure of Cuba's centrally planned command economy and a lack of consumer goods created social unrest in Cuba. In 1980 this dissatisfaction with the government led many Cubans to seek political asylum in other countries. These people first sought refuge at the Peruvian embassy in Havana. When the Castro government realized how many **dissidents**, or people who disagreed with the government, were among its citizens, it allowed anyone to emigrate, as long as he or she informed the authorities. The total reached 125,000, and most left Cuba from the port of Mariel, in boats provided by Cuban exiles in Miami. However, Castro did more than rid Cuba of dissidents. He also opened the gates of Cuba's prisons and mental hospitals, forcing criminals and mentally ill people onto boats that carried other refugees to the United States.

Throughout the 1980s, Cuba continued its policy of exporting the means for revolution. In addition, it provided support to communist regimes that were already established in African countries such as Angola and Ethiopia. Cuba also maintained its strongly anti-U.S. position in foreign affairs.

In 1994, after Fidel Castro loosened emigration restrictions, thousands of people left Cuba, mainly by boat.

Economically, Cuba remained dependent on the Soviet Union, which in fact subsidized the Cuban economy for many years. However, the Soviet government began to reassess its relations with Cuba after Premier Mikhail Gorbachev's reform programs took effect. (See Chapter 32.) In the late 1980s the Soviets, short of funds themselves, drastically reduced aid to Cuba. Both the Soviet Union and some Eastern European countries also established trade agreements that were less favorable to the Caribbean nation.

Without huge amounts of Soviet aid, and with the continued pressure of the U.S. trade and financial embargo that had been in effect for more than three decades, the Cuban economy came close to collapse in the early 1990s. Nearly every commodity was in short supply, and the government began rationing food and gasoline.

Nevertheless, Castro insisted that the country would continue on the path of communism. By the mid-1990's, however, Castro had allowed some limited private enterprise and had implemented various other economic reforms. The Cuban economy slowly began to show signs of recovery, further benefited by rising tourism and increased foreign investment. In 1997, Cuba also intensified its efforts to improve relations with other Caribbean countries.

Puerto Rico

The United States took control of Puerto Rico in 1898, after the Spanish-American War. The Jones Act, passed by Congress in 1917, established Puerto Rico as a territory of the United States and gave all Puerto Ricans U.S. citizenship. In the early 1930s, however, Puerto Ricans led by Luis Muñoz Marín began to lobby for increased autonomy from the United States. Under pressure from the United Nations, the United States finally permitted Puerto Rico a degree of self-government in 1947. The following year, Muñoz Marín became Puerto Rico's first elected governor.

The forceful Muñoz Marín at first pushed for even greater freedom from the United States. A 1950 act of Congress permitted Puerto Rico to write its own

Although Luis Muñoz Marín (shown with his hands raised) initially advocated Puerto Rico's independence from the United States, he was later elected governor of the U.S. commonwealth and supported social and economic reforms on the island.

constitution, which Puerto Rican voters ratified in 1952. That same year another congressional resolution granted Puerto Rico commonwealth status within the United States.

During the 1940s, Muñoz Marín had drawn up a plan to modernize the Puerto Rican economy. This program, called **Operation Bootstrap**, encouraged outside investment and industrialization of the economy. With the help of the United States government, which gave tax breaks and other special advantages to those who invested in Puerto Rican enterprises, the program made great progress. The Puerto Rican economy thrived over the next two decades. Economic development changed life for Puerto Rico's people. By the 1970s, Puerto Rico—once very poor—had raised its per capita income dramatically.

However, population growth outstripped economic growth, as it did elsewhere in Latin America, and there were not enough jobs for Puerto Rico's growing labor force. As a result, during the 1960s and 1970s, many Puerto Ricans went to the United States in search of work. Today, several million Puerto Ricans live in the United States. Many people believe that this has created two Puerto Rican cultures—a mainland culture strongly influenced by the U.S. way of life and an island culture dominated by the Hispanic heritage.

Puerto Rico's political status has been a constant source of debate on the island and in the United States. However, while public sentiment remains split over the question of commonwealth status versus statehood, only a small but vocal group has called for complete independence from the United States. In 1967, when Puerto Ricans were asked to vote on the matter, 60 percent chose to continue as a commonwealth. In a nonbinding vote taken in 1993, 48.4 percent preferred commonwealth status and 46.2 percent favored statehood, while a small percentage—less than 6 percent—voted for independence. The debate over Puerto Rico's future political status continued into the late 1990s.

Other Caribbean Nations

Cuba was not the only troubled island nation in Latin America in the 1960s. Many countries experienced a shift toward the political left and were disrupted by a series of coups and assassinations.

The Dominican Republic. The Dominican dictator Rafael Trujillo, assassinated in 1961, was succeeded by Juan Bosch, the first president to be democratically elected in the Dominican Republic in more than 30 years. After a coup toppled Bosch in 1963, his

followers, some of whom were Communists, started an uprising to return him to power. Hoping to prevent a communist takeover like the one in Cuba, President Lyndon Johnson of the United States in 1965 sent tens of thousands of marines to support the Dominican Republic's military regime.

After 1965 the Dominican Republic made much political and economic progress. Throughout much of the 1970s and 1980s, the island was stable. Although the economy remained heavily dependent on the export of sugar, efforts to diversify the economy through the development of light industry and tourism met with some success.

In the 1990s, however, the Dominican Republic faced considerable political and economic upheaval. An energy shortage—the nation's utilities were able to meet only 50 percent of demand—disrupted business and industry. Both unemployment and inflation soared.

By the mid-1990s, conditions had improved somewhat. Tourism was up, and inflation—once as high as 100 percent annually—was down to 9.5 percent in 1995. However, the unemployment rate was still about 30 percent, and millions of people lived in poverty. Democratic elections held in 1996 proceeded without incident, but the government faced continuing economic problems and antigovernment unrest.

Haiti. In 1986 the 30-year reign of the Duvalier family ended when "President for Life" Jean-Claude Duvalier was forced into exile. The people of Haiti, the poorest country in the Western Hemisphere, hoped

Armed troops patrol the streets of Port-au-Prince, Haiti, in January 1988.

that they would soon have a democratic government. The military regime that first took control of the government reluctantly allowed an election to be held in 1987. However, this election was canceled because of the violence that erupted among the rival political parties. Another election, held in 1988, brought a civilian government to power, but the military soon seized control again.

The government remained in the hands of the military until 1990, when Jean-Bertrand Aristide, a populist Catholic priest, won, becoming Haiti's first democratically elected president. In September of 1991, however, the military again seized power, forcing Aristide to flee the country. Three years later, mainly through the efforts of the United States, Aristide was able to return to Haiti and once again take office. In 1996 he was succeeded by René Préval—the first time that one elected Haitian civilian had completed his term in office and peacefully passed power to another. Aristide, however, continued to play an important role in Haitian politics, and observers believed that he would again seek the presidency. Meanwhile, Haiti continued to suffer dire economic and social problems, ranging from extreme poverty and widespread illiteracy to rampant crime and corruption.

The Smaller Caribbean Nations

European powers colonized the islands of the West Indies more than two centuries ago. Today, most of these islands have their own governments, and many are independent nations.

In 1958 most of the British islands were joined into a country called the West Indies Federation. The federation was dissolved in 1962, after Jamaica seceded; Jamaica, Trinidad and Tobago, and Barbados soon became independent nations. A number of other small islands have gained their independence relatively recently. For example, Grenada became independent in 1974, Antigua in 1981, and St. Kitts and Nevis in 1983. In response to a request from neighboring Caribbean countries in 1983, President Reagan sent U.S. forces to Grenada to overthrow a communist regime there.

Despite certain physical, historical, and economic similarities, little cohesiveness developed among these Caribbean islands. However, in the mid-1990s, regional groups and associations such as the Caribbean Community and Common Market (Caricom) took on increasing importance as a means of advancing the islands' trade and economic interests.

Section 3 Review

1. **Define** dissidents, Operation Bootstrap
2. **Identify** Fidel Castro, Luis Muñoz Marín, Jean-Bertrand Aristide
3. **Locate and Explain the Significance** Cuba, Puerto Rico, Dominican Republic, Haiti
4. **Analyzing Ideas (a)** Why was Fidel Castro's revolution initially welcomed by many Cubans? **(b)** What caused large numbers of Cubans to lose faith in the revolution?
5. **Contrasting Ideas** How has the experience of Puerto Rico since World War II been different from that of Cuba?
6. **Summarizing Ideas** Describe political developments in the Dominican Republic and Haiti in the past several decades.

Section 4

South America

Focus Questions

- What political and economic problems have the South American countries of Argentina, Brazil, Chile, Peru, and Colombia had in the years since 1945?
- What signs of hope are there for these countries, and what struggles do they continue to face?

Many of the nations of South America experienced turbulent political development in the decades following World War II. Revolutions swept the continent, leaving very few governments and individuals untouched.

Argentina

General Juan Perón rose to power in Argentina in the 1940s, gaining support from lower-class workers and the growing middle class. Elected president by a huge majority in 1946, Perón depended greatly on the advice of his wife, Eva or "Evita," a former film and radio actress. Through the skillful political use of the mass media, Evita built up a huge following, especially among the country's working class. Although Perón held the title of president, his wife was the one loved by the people of Argentina.

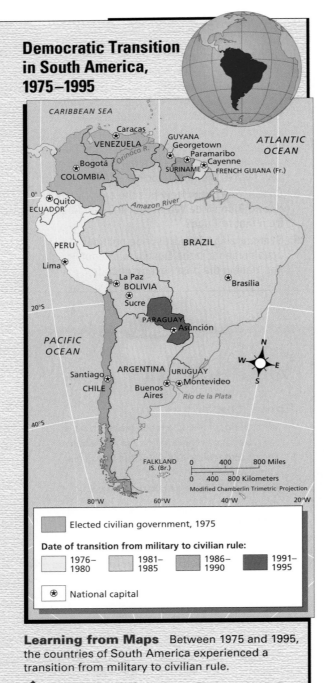

Democratic Transition in South America, 1975–1995

CARIBBEAN SEA

ATLANTIC OCEAN

VENEZUELA — Caracas
Bogotá — COLOMBIA
GUYANA — Georgetown
SURINAME — Paramaribo
Cayenne — FRENCH GUIANA (Fr.)
Quito — ECUADOR
Orinoco R.
Amazon River
PERU
Lima
BRAZIL
La Paz — BOLIVIA
Sucre
Brasília
PARAGUAY — Asunción
PACIFIC OCEAN
ARGENTINA
CHILE — Santiago
URUGUAY — Montevideo
Buenos Aires
Río de la Plata
FALKLAND IS. (Br.)

0   400   800 Miles
0   400   800 Kilometers
Modified Chamberlin Trimetric Projection

80°W   60°W   40°W   20°W
0°
20°S
40°S

| | Elected civilian government, 1975 |

Date of transition from military to civilian rule:

| 1976–1980 | 1981–1985 | 1986–1990 | 1991–1995 |

⊛ National capital

Learning from Maps Between 1975 and 1995, the countries of South America experienced a transition from military to civilian rule.

❓ **Place** Which countries chose to adopt civilian governments between 1976 and 1980?

By promising—and delivering—much to the working class, the Peróns soon had the support of much of the country. Facing little opposition, they

slowly created an authoritarian regime that suppressed political dissent.

During World War II, Argentina had profited from selling beef and grain to the Allies. Although the Perón regime controlled inflation, other attempted reforms did not improve the economy. By the early 1950s, Argentina had many economic troubles.

When Eva Perón died of cancer in 1952, her husband lost his greatest political asset. In death, Evita took on mythical qualities. Juan Perón's popularity, in contrast, plunged. His rule came to an end in 1955, when a military coup forced him into exile.

Over the next 18 years, a succession of military and civilian governments struggled against political and economic instability. A violent terror campaign, begun by leftist guerrillas in the late 1960s, added to the chaos. By 1972 the Argentine people had begun to look back fondly on the Perón years as a time of peace and prosperity. The following year, Perón returned from exile and, in a landslide election victory, again became president. His new wife, Isabel, won election as vice president.

Perón immediately launched an offensive against the left-wing guerrilla groups and made efforts to bring the unruly economy under control. However, he died in 1974, before he could make any progress. His widow succeeded him, becoming the first woman president in the Americas. Incapable of dealing with Argentina's many problems, Isabel was overthrown in 1976 when the military seized control once again.

The dirty war. To put an end to the guerrilla insurrection once and for all, the military regime launched what it called a holy war. Army and police units arrested and imprisoned opposition leaders and anyone else who expressed antigovernment sentiments. Some, perhaps as many as 20,000, were spirited away during the night and never seen again. Most of these ***desaparecidos***—disappeared persons—were tortured before being killed. For this reason, the military's campaign against the guerrillas became known as the "dirty war."

The dirty war and continuing economic problems caused support for the military junta to dwindle. To bolster its popularity, the junta ordered an invasion of the British-held Falkland Islands. Argentina had long laid claim to this territory, which the Argentines called the Malvinas. The junta believed that Britain would not bother to defend these desolate islands, and a quick military victory against a major power would be very popular among Argentines.

The junta's judgment proved disastrously wrong. British prime minister Margaret Thatcher in 1982

Connections: Then and Now

Earlier Battles for the Falklands

On April 2, 1982, a tiny garrison of British Royal Marines was attacked by Argentine soldiers on the Falkland Islands. After two hours of fighting, the marines gave up. The Argentine victory, however, was short-lived. In the brief but bloody war that followed, Britain regained the islands.

The first settlers in the Falklands seem to have been neither Argentine nor British, but French. In 1764 these

Port Howard Settlement, East Falkland Island

French settlers, lured by the prospect of a rich supply of whales and seals—whose oils were in high demand—established a fort on what is now East Falkland. In 1765 the British claimed the islands, establishing Port Egmont on West Falkland. Spain, nervous at having two rivals perched so close to the edge of South America, demanded that both groups of foreigners leave the islands, which it called Las Islas Malvinas. The French left easily after Spain offered them a cash payment. The British were not so easy to dislodge. Spain and Great Britain came to the edge of war in 1770, but Spain backed down and returned Port Egmont to Britain in 1771. By 1774, however, British priorities had changed, and British troops simply withdrew from the

islands, leaving them to the Spanish. They were abandoned by Spain in 1811.

In 1820 the new Argentine nation took possession of the islands, and they once again became a focus of dispute. The new government developed an increasingly strict stance against foreign fishermen, considering them to be intruders and an economic threat. In 1831, ships from the United States were seized off the islands' coast for illegal fishing. The United States attempted to have the islands declared free of government, but by 1833 the British had restored their control of the area. Ever since that time, the Argentines have considered the British action as illegal and imperialist. These disputed claims of ownership set the stage for the Falklands War of 1982.

---

sent an armada of ships and thousands of soldiers to reclaim the territory. The Argentine military was totally mismatched against the well-trained, professional British forces. In a matter of weeks, the British won a decisive victory. This humiliation at the hands of the British greatly angered most Argentines.

A return to democracy. Argentina's defeat in the Falklands led to the downfall of the military government. (See map on opposite page.) Free elections followed in 1983, won by Raúl Alfonsín of the Radical Union Party. Alfonsín had promised to put on trial those military and government officials who had been involved in the dirty war. The promise proved difficult to keep, however. Those who were guilty of crimes probably numbered in the thousands, but only three former presidents and some high-ranking officers went

on trial. This situation, along with continuing economic problems, undermined Alfonsín's popularity. He decided not to run for another term, and in the 1989 elections, Carlos Menem of the Perónist Party became president.

On taking office, Menem faced massive economic problems. Inflation was high. The government had difficulty making its foreign debt payments. Menem also faced difficulties with the armed forces, and the threat of military takeover seemed constant.

Through strict wage and price controls and the privatization of many state monopolies, Menem managed to bring some stability to the economy. To soothe the military, Menem pardoned all but a few of those found guilty of crimes in the dirty war. However, many Argentines resented this action.

Rio de Janeiro stands as a major commercial and financial city with access to Brazil's eastern coast.

In the early 1990s, Argentina's economy continued to improve under the programs of President Menem. Gross national product and annual per capita income both rose sharply, while the rate of inflation declined. Despite a slowdown in the economy, Menem was reelected in 1995. His economic measures helped return Argentina to growth, although the rate of unemployment remained at about 15 percent in 1997.

Brazil

Political unrest and economic chaos characterized Brazil from the postwar period to the early 1990s. Often governments in Brazil were overthrown in an effort to save the economy. Such a situation occurred in the early 1960s, when João Goulart, with the support of a growing labor movement, became president of Brazil. Under Goulart's leadership, inflation worsened and industry declined. Various groups within the society became polarized.

To counter what they viewed as a threat to the economy as well as a political threat from the left, the army overthrew Goulart in 1964. The military government forced wages down by setting a low minimum wage and by pressuring the labor unions. Foreign corporations were also urged to invest in Brazil.

The economy grew so fast that it was widely hailed as the "Brazilian Miracle." People migrated to the cities, where jobs were available. At the same time,

the government suppressed dissent and dissolved political parties. It also went heavily into debt. Brazil emerged from the 1980s with the highest foreign debt among developing countries.

In 1990 a civilian government took office, led by Fernando Collor. Collor's major concern was Brazil's dire economic situation. He attacked inflation, which had risen steadily. To reduce government spending, he drastically cut the government labor force and sold a number of state-owned industries to private concerns. To control private spending, he froze most savings and checking accounts.

Collor's economic program pushed the Brazilian economy into recession. The economy shrank, and inflation jumped. In late 1992 Collor resigned and was succeeded by his vice president Itamar Franco. For most of Franco's 27 months as president, Brazil's problems worsened, with inflation soaring while corruption and crime flourished.

In 1994 Franco's finance minister, Fernando Henrique Cardoso, devised economic reforms which proved so successful that the increasingly popular Cardoso himself went on to become president in 1995. Under Cardoso, Brazil's economy regained some stability. In 1996, inflation fell below 14 percent, and the nation's GDP—the largest in the region by far— grew about 3 percent, in its fourth consecutive year of growth. In 1997, however, volatile financial markets challenged Brazil's ability to maintain the economic progress made in recent years.

Chile

Chile, once the oldest continuing democracy in Latin America, underwent important governmental changes in the 1970s and 1980s. In 1970 an alliance of the Socialist and Communist Parties resulted in the election of Salvador Allende. With Allende as president, a Marxist government had come to power through peaceful means, the first to do so in the Western Hemisphere.

Allende's administration nationalized copper mines and other industries, forced the breakup of many large estates, and implemented an across-the-board wage increase. At the same time, radical supporters seized many farms and factories. Before long the economy was in turmoil. Economic output declined, and food shortages spread. Hard pressed for funds, Allende's treasury printed more money to meet its needs. By 1972 rampant inflation had created hardships for all segments of the population.

As the economy worsened, unrest and disillusionment spread. Meanwhile, the U.S. government supported military leaders who opposed Allende. Finally, in 1973, the army overthrew the government and took power. Allende died in the bloody coup. Once in control, the military swiftly eliminated all forms of opposition.

The new military government executed people who had opposed their coup. Fearing for their lives, thousands of others fled into exile. The military leader, General Augusto Pinochet, dissolved the legislature and outlawed all political parties. He also placed tight controls on the press and cut back many civil liberties.

In addition, he ended all government interference in the economy, allowing it to operate by the forces of supply and demand. This action had a dramatic impact on inflation, which had run wild in the last years of the Allende government. By the end of the 1970s, inflation had fallen to about 30 percent annually, and it ran at about 20 percent a year through most of the 1980s. Such success came at a cost. Unemployment soared. Twenty-one percent of workers had no jobs in the early 1980s. However, Pinochet's economic program, reinforced by a huge inflow of foreign capital, began to work. By the late 1980s, Chile had become one of Latin America's most prosperous countries.

Even so, civil unrest continued to plague the country. Pinochet responded with repressive measures. To strengthen his hold on power, in 1988 Pinochet called for a plebiscite, or special vote, to determine whether he should remain in power. He expected to win, but nearly 55 percent of the electorate said that he should step down. Accepting defeat, Pinochet set free elections for 1989. In that vote, Patricio Aylwin, the candidate of a coalition of parties, was elected president.

Under Aylwin, Chile continued to prosper, the country's economic growth helped by free trade and billions of dollars in foreign investment. Chile's GDP grew by 11 percent in 1992 and 6 percent in 1993, while inflation remained at about 12 percent a year. In December 1993, voters chose Eduardo Frei to succeed Aylwin as president. Chile's stability and economic strength continued into the mid-1990s, even as the government grappled with such problems as widespread poverty and increasing pollution. By 1997, Chile's economy had grown for 14 consecutive years, and Chile had one of the most prosperous economies in Latin America.

To keep its economy growing, the Frei government continued to pursue international trade agreements as a key part of its foreign policy. In 1996, Chile signed free trade agreements with Canada and with the Mercosur group (Argentina, Brazil, Paraguay, and Uruguay). Chile also has agreements with Mexico, Venezuela, Colombia, and other nations.

Peru

In the decades following World War II, Peru's government was run by either military dictators or conservative civilians. Like so many other Latin American nations, Peru faced serious economic problems, including hyperinflation, unemployment, crushing poverty, and mounting foreign debt.

In the 1980s, Peru suffered an economic depression. In addition to its economic crisis, the country faced growing political problems. The greatest challenge to democracy in Peru was the war waged against the government by communist-inspired guerrillas. This war involved two major guerrilla groups.

In the cities, the Tupac Amarú Revolutionary Movement (MRTA) bombed public buildings and utility companies and assassinated police and government officials. Another group, **Sendero Luminoso**, or "Shining Path," carried out a similar terror campaign in the rural highland areas. Shining Path followed a Maoist ideology, believing that the present society had to be destroyed and a new socialist society built on its ruins. Illegal drugs, one of the major problems of the late 1900s, prompted further terrorist activity. Peru is Latin America's leading producer of coca, the plant from which cocaine is obtained. Drug trafficking provided a quick and easy way for the guerrillas to raise funds. The MRTA and Shining Path accepted arms and money in exchange for protecting the profitable cocaine business.

In 1990 a surprise election victory by Alberto Fujimori, son of a Japanese immigrant, set the stage for significant change. The new president took over a country in chaos, with surging hyperinflation (2,800 percent in 1989), huge foreign debt, and a deadly guerrilla war in progress. Austerity measures soon brought inflation down to a manageable level. By the end of 1994, terrorism and violence in Peru had decreased, and the economy was growing. Fujimori easily won re-election in 1995 with 64 percent of the vote, despite criticism of his autocratic approach to government.

By mid-1996, however, slowing economic growth and charges of government corruption had caused Fujimori's popularity to decline. Then, in December 1996, a small group of heavily armed MRTA guerrillas invaded the Japanese embassy in Lima, Peru, taking numerous hostages. The crisis did not end until April 1997, when Fujimori ordered Peruvian soldiers to storm the embassy. All of the guerrillas were killed in the raid, along with one hostage and two soldiers. Popular approval of Fujimori rose again, but not for long.

In subsequent months the president's political position became uncertain. Both Fujimori's power and his popularity appeared to be on the decline. At the same time, Peru's military, which had always played a key role in Fujimori's government, seemed to be taking an ever-increasing share of control. As observers looked ahead to the next election, scheduled for the year 2000, they wondered whether Peru's future would bring democracy or dictatorship.

Colombia

The years immediately following World War II were a time of severe turmoil in Colombia. From 1946 to 1958, both military and civilian dictators came to power amid civil and economic strife. However, by the mid-1960s, Colombia's future appeared brighter. The economy stabilized, and Colombia became known as one of the models of democracy in Latin America.

Unfortunately, the demand for illegal drugs increased in Europe and the United States during the late 1960s and early 1970s. The fertile land of Colombia became a prime region for growing marijuana as well as the coca plant that is used to make narcotics. Huge profits resulting from trade in these illegal products led to an increase in their production. Crime soared, as those who wanted to control this trade jockeyed for power and position. Medellín, once a flourishing industrial city in Colombia, became a headquarters for the **Medellín cartel** that ran the Colombian drug trade.

The Medellín cartel used assassinations and other means of intimidation to gain control of law enforcement agencies. Many officials, especially those at the lower levels of government, were either bribed or threatened by the drug lords until they cooperated with the cartel.

The terror campaigns of many left-wing guerrilla groups added to the violence. The most notorious of these groups, M-19, targeted officials of the justice system for assassination. During the 1980s, actions by M-19 took the lives of hundreds of judges and prosecutors. Right-wing death squads, many connected with the army, added to the death toll by assassinating people who expressed left-wing sympathies. Often dozens of murders would occur in Colombia in one day. Behind all this political violence stood the drug lords, who willingly financed terror groups.

In the late 1980s, the Colombian authorities declared war on the drug cartels. They called on United States law officers and military to assist in this offensive. They also promised to turn over to the United States any drug traffickers they captured. The result was open warfare on the streets of Medellín and Cali, headquarters of the other large drug cartel. The elections of 1990 proved particularly bloody.

Alberto Fujimori, the son of a Japanese immigrant, won the 1990 Peruvian presidential election; he was reelected in 1995.

History Through the Arts

Magic Realism

In the spellbinding fictional worlds of many Latin American writers of the 1900s—such as Gabriel García Márquez, Isabel Allende, and Nélida Piñon—a character may ascend to heaven while clutching bed linens from the clothesline, play the piano without lifting the lid, or be followed everywhere by yellow butterflies. In such a landscape and amidst such characters, real and surreal elements join forces to create the literary style known as magic realism.

Millions of readers around the world have been enchanted in recent decades with the imaginary and marvelous images,

Gabriel García Márquez

settings, and characters that writers of magic realism create. While these elements may seem new and unique, the themes explored are rooted in Latin American everyday town and village life, history, religion, superstition, and myth. As the

Brazilian novelist Nélida Piñon says, "The myths eat with us at our table." Colombian novelist and short-story writer Gabriel García Márquez explains magic realism's lens in this way:

"I have the character Ulises make glass change color every time he touches it. Now, that can't be true. But so much has already been said about love that I had to find a new way of saying that this boy is in love. So I have the colors of the glass change, and I have his mother say, 'Those things happen only because of love.'"

In his best-selling, award-winning novel *One Hundred Years of Solitude*, García Márquez tells the story of Macondo, a small Colombian village. At the same time, he also uses his novel to cry out for his troubled region: where forests are destroyed, political power is abused, and massacres can be covered up and forgotten.

In the early 1990s, Columbian government leaders pledged to continue the fight against the drug cartels. However, corruption funded by drug money was very extensive in this country. Drug trafficking continued into the mid-1990s, as did murder, terrorism, and guerrilla violence.

By 1995 the Cali cartel was thought to control as much as 70 percent of the world trade in cocaine. Moreover, Colombian president Ernesto Samper was himself widely believed to have accepted millions of dollars from the cartel to finance his 1994 election campaign.

The nation struggled with economic difficulties, too. In 1996, inflation in Colombia rose, gross domestic product declined, and unemployment hit an eight-year high. Colombia's political and economic problems continued into 1997. Guerrilla groups, financed by drug money, took more lives, while

President Samper expressed the government's hope for peace talks to end the violence.

Section 4 Review

1. **Define** *desaparecidos*, *Sendero Luminoso*, Medellín cartel
2. **Identify** Eva Perón, Fernando Collor, Salvador Allende, Patricio Aylwin, Alberto Fujimori
3. **Summarizing Ideas** What occurred during the administration of the Peróns in Argentina?
4. **Synthesizing Ideas** What problems are shared by all of the countries discussed in this section?
5. **Understanding Cause and Effect (a)** What caused the growth of the drug trade in Colombia? **(b)** How did this growth affect the government and economy of Colombia?

Chapter 31 Review

| 1962 Cuban missile crisis occurs. | 1965 U.S. Marines are sent to the Dominican Republic. |

A.D. 1945 | **A.D. 1950** | **A.D. 1960** | **A.D. 1965** | **A.D. 1970**

A.D. 1946 Juan Perón is elected president of Argentina.

1952
• Eva Perón dies.
• Puerto Rico becomes a commonwealth of the United States.

1948 OAS is founded.

1961 Bay of Pigs invasion takes place.

1959 Fidel Castro's revolutionaries take control of Cuba.

1967 Ché Guevara dies.

1970 Allende is elected president of Chile.

Chapter Summary

The following list contains the key concepts you have learned about the countries of Latin America from the postwar period to the present.

1. Economic problems faced by nations of Latin America were caused in part by monoculture, import substitution, and large foreign debt. Population growth, rapid urbanization, continued poverty, and environmental problems were major challenges for the region.

2. Women, labor unions, and the Catholic church all emerged as powerful political forces in the Latin American countries.

3. The Organization of American States (OAS) was founded to promote cooperation among the nations of the Western Hemisphere.

4. Revolution in Nicaragua in 1979 brought a Marxist regime to power. A civil war broke out in that country between the government, run by the Sandinistas, and guerrillas called Contras. The United States aided the Contras; Cuba and the Soviet Union aided the Nicaraguan government.

5. The Contadora Principles, along with other Latin American efforts, are bringing hope for peace to Central America.

6. Revolution in Cuba in 1959 brought a communist dictatorship under Fidel Castro to power. Confrontations with the United States occurred with the Bay of Pigs invasion in 1961 and the Cuban missile crisis in 1962. Cuba went through economic difficulties in the early 1990s but has recovered slightly in recent years.

7. Both the Dominican Republic and Haiti overthrew dictators. As the 1990s began, both tentatively established democratic governments.

8. In Argentina, Juan Perón established a dictatorship but was ousted in 1952. In 1976, the military overthrew the government led by his wife, Isabel. After the disastrous Falklands conflict, Argentina returned to civilian government.

9. Political unrest and economic chaos have characterized Brazil in the postwar period. By the 1990s, the country faced massive foreign debt. The economy showed signs of recovery in the late 1900s.

10. Chile's government was a military dictatorship from 1973 to 1988. Chile began to prosper in the 1990s. Both Peru and Colombia faced political unrest through the 1980s. The drug trade has caused problems throughout South America.

Reviewing Important Terms

On a separate sheet of paper, supply the term that correctly completes each statement.
1. A foreign-owned business is called a(n) _____ _____ .
2. _____ _____ is an economic policy in which a country encourages the internal production of goods that the country had been importing.
3. An area whose countries or regions have common geographical and political features is called a(n) _____ _____ .
4. _____ are Central American peasants.
5. The dependence of a country or region on one crop is _____ .
6. People who disagree with the government of a country are called _____ .

Developing Critical Thinking Skills

1. **Understanding Cause and Effect (a)** What were the causes of the population increase in Latin America? **(b)** What were the consequences?
2. **Interpreting Ideas (a)** What benefits did Latin American leaders envision from economic development? **(b)** What efforts did they make to achieve it?
3. **Synthesizing Ideas** How would economic prosperity in Latin America help establish greater political stability?
4. **Understanding Relationships** What were the results of the United States involvement in **(a)** Nicaragua; **(b)** Cuba; **(c)** the Dominican Republic?
5. **Analyzing Ideas** "Demand, not supply, needs to be brought under control." Do you agree that this

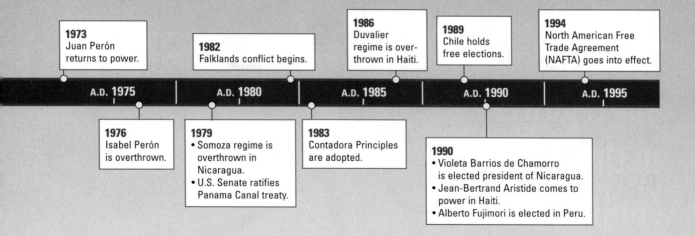

1973
Juan Perón returns to power.

1982
Falklands conflict begins.

1986
Duvalier regime is overthrown in Haiti.

1989
Chile holds free elections.

1994
North American Free Trade Agreement (NAFTA) goes into effect.

A.D. **1975**   A.D. **1980**   A.D. **1985**   A.D. **1990**   A.D. **1995**

1976
Isabel Perón is overthrown.

1979
• Somoza regime is overthrown in Nicaragua.
• U.S. Senate ratifies Panama Canal treaty.

1983
Contadora Principles are adopted.

1990
• Violeta Barrios de Chamorro is elected president of Nicaragua.
• Jean-Bertrand Aristide comes to power in Haiti.
• Alberto Fujimori is elected in Peru.

approach will end the Latin American drug trafficking problem? Explain your answer.
6. **Comparing Ideas (a)** How were the revolutions in Cuba and Nicaragua different? **(b)** How were they similar?

Relating Geography to History
Turn to the map of Central America and the Caribbean on page 854. **(a)** How many of these nations have communist governments? **(b)** How many miles are they from the United States? **(c)** What effect might the presence of communist governments throughout this region have on United States security?

Relating Past to Present
1. Political affairs in many Latin American countries remain unsettled. Choose one Latin American country and do research to find articles on recent developments there. How have changes in Central America affected U.S. foreign policy?
2. Find out how many governments in Latin America today came to power by either a coup or a revolution. Are these governments secure? How many are dictatorships?

Applying History Study Skills
Before completing this activity, review Building History Study Skills on page 847.

Read the following paragraph describing what takes place on a hacienda during a revolution.

"[W]hat we call social revolutions have all occurred in agricultural countries where the mass of the people lived on what they themselves raised from the soil. In such a society, a revolution is a simple thing. First, you cut off the head of the *hacendado,* then you divide the wheat, corn, and barley stored in the barn and the *hacendado*'s cows, horses, sheep, and chickens. Similarly the plows, digging sticks, and other tools are distributed. The land is taken by the peasants and the revolution is over. What really happens is that the stored consumer goods are divided up among the surrounding peasants, and the limited producers' goods, in the form of seed, animals, tools, and the land itself, fall into the hands of those who have used the tools and animals and worked the land."

1. What economic questions are raised by the passage?
2. How is scarcity dealt with after a revolution?
3. What does the passage imply might be some of the causes of the revolution?

⛫ internet**connect**

Search the Internet through the HRW Web site for recent statistics on per capita gross domestic product, major exports, and major imports of these countries: Mexico, Guatemala, El Salvador, Honduras, Belize, Nicaragua, Costa Rica, Panama, Cuba, the Dominican Republic, Haiti, Colombia, Venezuela, Bolivia, Peru, Chile, Brazil, Paraguay, Uruguay, and Argentina. Then assemble the information you have gathered into a chart to display.

HRW
GO TO: go.hrw.com
KEYWORD: SCØ LA Stats

Building Your Portfolio
1. **Presenting an Oral Report** Although the Brazilian economy grew rapidly in the 1960s and 1970s, many Brazilians still lived in poverty. Find out about living conditions in the slums, and present an oral report to the class. Place your notes in your portfolio.
2. **Preparing a Panel Discussion** Work with a group of your classmates to find more information on how the nations of Latin America are dealing with low rates of economic growth, high rates of unemployment and population growth, and burgeoning foreign debts. Then use the information you have collected to prepare a panel discussion detailing possible solutions to these problems. Place your notes or an audiotape of the discussion in your portfolio.

The Superpowers in the Modern Era

TIME

A.D. **1969–the present**

A.D. **1969–the present**

| 3.7 million B.C. | 4000 B.C. | A.D. 2100 |

PLACE

**Africa, Asia, Europe,
the Americas, and Australia**

Europe

Australia

ARCTIC OCEAN

NORTH
AMERICA

EUROPE

ASIA

PACIFIC
OCEAN

AFRICA

Equator

AUSTRALIA

SOUTH
AMERICA

PACIFIC
OCEAN

ATLANTIC
OCEAN

INDIAN
OCEAN

ANTARCTICA

The
Americas

Africa

Asia

The fall of communism in Russia

Significance

The final decades of the 1900s marked a period of transition among the industrialized nations of North America and Europe.

Indeed, the late 1900s were also a period of contrasts. The United States remained a leading power in world affairs, while the Soviet Union as one nation disappeared. As the Soviet Union unraveled, the nations of Western Europe moved toward closer union as the fall of communism reawakened old ethnic divisions in Eastern Europe. At the same time, Canada survived challenges to its unity, notably from separatists in Quebec.

Terms to Define

Vietnamization	Helsinki Accords
Watergate scandal	Maastricht Treaty
stagflation	Brezhnev Doctrine
trade deficit	perestroika
détente	glasnost
Carter Doctrine	Commonwealth of
weapons of mass	Independent States
destruction	ethnic cleansing
Meech Lake Accord	Dayton Accord
Irish Republican Army	Implementation Force
Ostpolitik	

People to Identify

Jimmy Carter	Helmut Kohl
Ronald Reagan	Juan Carlos
Bill Clinton	Mikhail Gorbachev
Margaret Thatcher	Boris Yeltsin
François Mitterrand	Lech Walesa
Jacques Chirac	Vaclav Havel
Helmut Schmidt	Nicolae Ceausescu

Places to Locate

Estonia	Czech Republic
Latvia	Slovakia
Lithuania	Bosnia and
Republic of Georgia	Herzegovina
Caspian Basin	

Chapter Theme Questions

- **War and Diplomacy** How and why might international conflict continue after the end of the Cold War?
- **Economic Organization** How might nations benefit from pursuing free trade and free enterprise?
- **Cross-Cultural Interaction** How might cultural differences within societies in Europe and North America give rise to conflict?

On Christmas Day 1991, Soviet leader Mikhail Gorbachev appeared on television to make an extraordinary announcement. The Soviet Union, he said, would in a few days cease to exist. Less than a week later the world watched with amazement as one of the century's mightiest totalitarian powers officially ceased to exist.

For more than seven decades, the Soviet Union had been a primary force in international politics. Now it had crumbled under the weight of its own economic inefficiency and the spread of democratic ideals. Across the vast stretch of Eurasia, to the borders of the Middle East in the south and to the Pacific in the east, 19 independent republics, with Russia as the largest, eventually emerged in its place.

Challenges remained, however. Would democracy and free enterprise take hold? As the appeal of communism faded, the strength of nationalism resurged—sometimes with bloody consequences. At the dawn of a new millennium, a new set of international relationships took shape.

The Industrial Powers of North America

Focus Questions

- How did the Vietnam War and the Watergate scandal affect political attitudes in the United States in the late 1900s?
- What changes have occurred in the United States's economy since 1970?
- What major changes did American foreign policy undergo in the 1970s, 1980s, and 1990s?
- What major challenges did Canada face in the late 1900s?

During the late 1900s, the United States confronted a number of challenges. Defeat in Vietnam created doubts about America's military power, but the Persian Gulf War appeared to relieve those doubts. The U.S. economy fluctuated through the 1970s, but recovered in the mid-1980s and generally grew through the 1990s. Canada similarly grappled with serious political and economic problems, somewhat reluctantly moving toward closer relations with its neighbor to the south.

U.S. naval vessels like the one in this photo helped evacuate South Vietnamese citizens in 1975.

Ending the Vietnam War

In 1969, Richard M. Nixon became president of the United States. Foremost among the challenges that he faced was the increasingly unpopular and economically burdensome war in Vietnam. Hoping to avoid outright defeat, Nixon sought a way to end American involvement in Vietnam "with honor."

American withdrawal. Nixon first began the process of **Vietnamization**, preparing the South Vietnamese to take over the fighting while gradually withdrawing American forces. By January 1973 the number of American troops in Vietnam had decreased from well over 540,000 (in 1969) to some 24,000.

At the same time, Nixon increased military pressure against the communists in order to compel their leaders to negotiate on American terms. He ordered the invasion of Cambodia in 1970 and subsequently stepped up the bombing of North Vietnam. On January 27, 1973, Communist negotiators finally accepted a comprehensive agreement, known as the Paris Peace Accords, to end the Vietnam War. The accords provided for the withdrawal of all U.S. and allied forces from Vietnam in exchange for the return of all prisoners. Within two months the last major U.S. combat units in Vietnam had returned home, although some troops remained until 1975.

The impact of the Vietnam War. President Nixon managed to extract the United States from Vietnam, but the effects of the war on American society persisted. The war left particularly deep scars on the American national identity. It had inflicted a heavy human toll and placed a substantial burden on the nation's economy. Moreover, with the fall of South Vietnam to the Communists in April 1975, the war seemed an utter failure of U.S. power. As a result, many Americans began to doubt the wisdom of the United States continuing to play a leading role on the world stage.

The Vietnam War bitterly divided the American people. Although Nixon had appealed to what he called a "silent majority" of Americans in 1970 to support the Vietnam War, the antiwar movement that had begun in the mid-1960s continued to gain strength through the Nixon administration. Actions such as the invasion of Cambodia appeared to contradict Nixon's promise to end the war. Demonstrations on college campuses became routine. Some turned violent, and a few turned deadly. At Kent State University in Ohio, four students were killed during a demonstration on May 4, 1970. Ten days later, two students were killed in another protest at Jackson State College in Mississippi. In the end, as the government's estimations of success in Vietnam proved exaggerated, growing numbers of Americans began to question the trustworthiness of their leaders.

Watergate and Its Legacy

A major scandal involving President Nixon added to the disillusionment with government that many Americans experienced after Vietnam. In 1972, burglars were caught breaking into the headquarters of the Democratic National Committee in the Watergate complex in Washington, D.C. In 1972, journalists from the *Washington Post* charged that officials of Nixon's re-election campaign had planned the break-in. An investigation by the Senate followed and found that Nixon's White House staff had used money from an illegal secret fund to conceal the incident's connection to the president. It soon became clear that Nixon himself had known about the cover-up. Facing impeachment by Congress, Nixon chose to

ARCHITECTURE

Maya Ying Lin

Among the 1,421 people who entered the competition to design a memorial to the veterans of the Vietnam War was Maya Ying Lin, a 21-year-old senior at Yale University. Her design for the memorial, shown at right, was simple: two long black granite walls, rising out of the earth and meeting at an angle. Written on these walls would be the names of the more than 58,000 soldiers declared killed or missing in action in Vietnam.

What drew the judges to the work of this young sculptor and architect? Like all great architecture, Lin's design was uniquely suited to its location, the sweeping lawns of the Constitution Gardens on the Mall in Washington, D.C. The design inspired contemplation and reflection; it was dignified and eloquent.

Lin chose a design that entered the earth and came back out again, feeling that such a design suitably symbolized death and remembrance. She also considered the symbolism of a scar—a painful reminder of loss that can heal but never really disappear.

Carved into the walls are the names of the dead and missing. They are arranged chronologically on each wall by the date of death or disappearance. On the east wall, the names begin at the center and travel toward the end. On the west wall, the names begin at the end and travel toward the center. In this way, at the intersection of the walls the first and last deaths meet.

Lin chose black granite rather than white marble for several reasons. Black is, after all, a traditional color of sorrow in the American culture. In a practical sense, the names would be easier to read on black than on white. Also, black granite could be highly polished, allowing it to reflect the Mall and the people who were reading the names. In this way, finally, the dead and those who wished to remember them could once again be brought together.

---

resign his office in August of 1974. He was succeeded by his vice president, Gerald R. Ford.

The **Watergate scandal** shook the faith of many Americans in their political system. People began to sense that politicians generally lacked integrity. President Ford's decision to pardon Nixon did not help to restore public confidence in government. In the minds of many people, as a result of Watergate, Washington politics increasingly became synonymous with dishonesty and corruption. As a result, several post-Watergate candidates for the presidency campaigned as outsiders with no ties to Washington. They vowed to clean up corruption in the political system. In 1976, James Earl ("Jimmy") Carter, a former governor of Georgia, was elected president. Carter proved to be a man of high integrity, but his presidency suffered from some serious problems. Carter upset many people by announcing his belief that the United States had lapsed into a "national malaise." Despite all efforts, the economy remained sluggish. Several reversals in foreign policy also afflicted Carter's presidency. Not least among these was the seizure in 1979 of the American embassy in Iran by Muslim militants, followed by a disastrous rescue attempt and a hostage crisis that Carter was unable to resolve.

In 1980, President Carter lost his bid for re-election to another outsider: Ronald Reagan, a former governor of California. Reagan's abiding optimism in the United States inspired many Americans and helped him to win reelection in 1984. During Reagan's second term, however, scandal once again captured public attention. Members of the National Security Council staff had become involved in illegal transactions involving the sale of arms to Iran in order to win the release of U.S. hostages in Lebanon. Proceeds of the arms sales were diverted and used to support anticommunist rebels—known as Contras—in Nicaragua. Some observers compared the situation to Watergate, dubbing the new scandal "Irangate." President Reagan's public image was tarnished, yet he remained popular.

Although Reagan's vice president, George Bush, a longtime Washington insider, won the presidency in 1988, the appeal of outsiders to American voters remained strong. In 1992, Bill Clinton, the governor of Arkansas, ran as an outsider and defeated President Bush. Accusations of questionable financial dealings and sexual misconduct dogged Clinton even before he took office. In the mid-1990s, an investigation into these accusations turned up evidence of possible crimes. In late 1998, the House of Representatives voted to begin an inquiry into possible grounds for the impeachment of President Clinton.

The U.S. Economy

During the late 1960s, government spending had skyrocketed as President Johnson tried to finance both his Great Society programs and the Vietnam War at the same time. This dramatic increase in government spending, combined with rising energy costs and higher prices for other commodities due to the devaluation of the dollar, led to inflation—a general increase in prices and a decline in the buying power of the dollar. Instability of the U.S. economy became an issue of some concern in the 1970s. It was not until the mid-1980s that the economy began a recovery, and the United States entered a period of general growth and renewed prosperity.

Attempts to stabilize the economy. Attempts to stabilize the U.S. economy in the 1970s proved unsuccessful. President Nixon tried to stimulate the economy by proposing tax changes. His policies, however, had little effect on inflation and actually helped to trigger a recession. The resulting combination of decreased economic activity, high unemployment, and rising prices, known as **stagflation**, remained a problem through the rest of the decade. Presidents Ford and Carter tried to fight stagflation through tight controls on federal spending, tax cuts, and voluntary price and wage freezes, but the economy showed little improvement.

The 1980s saw the return of economic growth. President Reagan took office in 1981, promising to improve the economy. He proposed new reductions in government spending, but it was largely a recession in the early 1980s that finally brought inflation down. To increase economic activity, Reagan called for tax cuts that would encourage spending by consumers and investment by business. This spending in turn would generate economic growth. By the mid-1980s, unemployment had dropped significantly as the economy entered a period of sustained growth. Despite a brief downturn in the early 1990s, the economy would continue its upward trend into the mid-1990s.

Not all was well, however. During the 1980s, the debts of the United States government ballooned. Although Congress had approved Ronald Reagan's proposed tax cuts and increased military expenditures, his proposed reductions in the growth of spending on various government social programs proved harder to implement. As a result, until the late 1980s, the government ran at increasingly larger annual deficits as it spent more than it took in from taxes. To make up the difference, the government borrowed money—much of it from foreign lenders.

As the debt and the interest on it grew, many American leaders became increasingly concerned. In 1985, Congress ordered across-the-board cuts in federal spending if the government failed to meet targeted yearly reductions in the deficit. The debt continued to grow, though at a slower rate. In 1994 the Republicans won majorities in both houses of Congress for the first time since the 1950s. They promised to reform expensive social programs and to press for reductions in the growth of spending to balance the budget. President Clinton, a Democrat, stated his agreement in principle, winning congressional passage of a $500 billion deal in taxes and spending cuts in 1993. The process of balancing the budget, however, proved politically contentious. In the late-1990s, overall growth of the economy made it possible to balance the budget for the first time in almost 30 years. However, the national debt remained a major challenge for the United States.

Changes in the U.S. economy. In many ways the economy lay beyond the control and influence of the government. Changes in the world economy, for example, significantly affected the U.S. economy. During the 1970s and 1980s, the United States began to lose its long-standing lead in heavy industry to other nations. American steel companies, shipbuilders, and automakers found it increasingly difficult to compete with their counterparts in countries like Japan and Germany. As a result, many Americans lost their jobs through the closing of steel mills, ship-yards, and automobile plants in the 1980s.

The decline of American heavy industry contributed to the creation of a **trade deficit**. Beginning in the 1970s, the United States imported more goods than it exported. Still, even as Americans began to buy more from abroad and some U.S. businesses had difficulty selling their products overseas, many U.S. enterprises proved very successful in the world marketplace. Through the 1980s and 1990s, U.S. products dominated such important industries as aerospace engineering and pharmaceuticals. U.S. companies pioneered the revolution in computers and information technology during the 1980s, and these same companies remained the leaders in that field in the 1990s.

In fact, during the 1980s and 1990s, the creation of new jobs outpaced the loss of jobs in heavy industry. Many of the new jobs were in advanced technology and the so-called service industries, such as banking, retail, and restaurants. Economists suggested that this development reflected a transition to a more modern economy, much as heavy industry had replaced agriculture as the basis of the American economy a century earlier. They pointed out that the new economy would demand higher levels of education and more advanced skills than most people had needed in the past. Some worried that while educated people would do well, unskilled and low-skilled workers would fare poorly. Then American society would consist of a small group of extremely wealthy people, a shrinking middle class, and a large class of extremely poor people. On the whole, however, Americans in the mid-1990s enjoyed a comparatively high level of prosperity, and their country still boasted the world's largest economy.

Energy. The cost and availability of energy was one of the determining factors in the performance of the U.S. economy. Fossil fuels such as coal, natural gas, and especially oil were the most important sources of energy for the United States in the late 1900s. The fact that by the 1970s the United States was importing much of its oil, particularly from the Middle East, posed a serious problem. Shortages and price hikes

The accident on March 28, 1979, at the nuclear power station on Three Mile Island led to new health and safety concerns regarding this source of power. Protesters like these called for alternative sources of energy.

stemming from the OPEC oil embargo of 1973 and the Iranian revolution of 1979 added significantly to the instability of the U.S. economy in the years following Vietnam.

Worried about future supplies of oil, Americans began to consider alternative sources of energy. A greater emphasis on the use of coal was one possibility, but many people found the option unattractive because of the pollution created by coal. Some Americans began to demand the development of solar and wind power as clean and renewable sources of energy. President Carter called for research into such alternatives, combined with measures to conserve fossil fuels. The Reagan administration, however, discontinued many of these programs in the early 1980s.

Nuclear power attracted considerable interest as an economical alternative to fossil fuels. Critics worried, however, about the safety of nuclear energy. In 1979, an accident at the Three Mile Island nuclear power plant in Pennsylvania brought widespread attention to these worries. In 1986 the much more serious accident at the Chernobyl nuclear power plant in the Soviet Union further reinforced the growing popular dissatisfaction with nuclear energy.

In the meantime, oil companies had begun to develop previously untapped oil fields, many within the United States. The most notable example was in Alaska. New and significant discoveries of oil continued to be made in such places as the Gulf of Mexico and the Caspian Sea into the 1990s. By the mid-1990s, oil remained the single most important source of energy for the United States and the world.

But even as fears of severe oil depletion in the near future began to diminish, many Americans expressed other concerns about dependence on oil, particularly as fuel for automobiles. One such concern was the pollution caused by heavy oil usage. Other observers noted the strategic danger posed by continued reliance on imported oil. Many of the world's major oil fields lay in politically unstable regions. The Persian Gulf War of 1991 underscored these concerns.

Changes in Foreign Policy

American foreign policy underwent several changes in the late 1900s. In the 1970s, American leaders sought to ease the tensions behind the Cold War through improved relations with the communist world. Responding to continued Soviet expansion, however, the United States increased pressure on the Soviet Union in the 1980s. In the 1990s, U.S. foreign policy confronted a host of new problems that emerged in the wake of the Cold War's end and the collapse of the Soviet Union.

Relations with the Soviet Union. Efforts to improve relations with the Soviet Union began under President Nixon. In 1972, Nixon became the first U.S. president to visit Moscow. During his visit, President Nixon and Soviet leader Leonid Brezhnev signed the Strategic Arms Limitation Treaty, or SALT. This agreement limited each country's production and deployment of certain nuclear weapons. Nixon and Brezhnev also signed several accords related to environmental, health-related, and technological cooperation. The general improvement in Soviet-American relations that followed became known as **détente** (day·TAHNT), a French word meaning an easing of strain.

Presidents Ford and Carter continued the policy of détente throughout much of the 1970s. By the end of the decade, however, renewed tensions between the United States and the Soviet Union began to show. President Carter, insisting that human rights be made a major factor in U.S. foreign policy, began to speak out against Soviet treatment of dissidents—opponents of government policies. He also criticized Soviet and Cuban intervention in Africa, specifically in the Angolan and Ethiopian civil wars.

The most serious break in the relationship came in December 1979, when the Soviet Union invaded Afghanistan. The invasion threatened the security of the oil-rich and economically vital Persian Gulf. In what became known as the **Carter Doctrine**, President Carter declared in his 1980 State of the Union Address that the United States would regard any attempts by outside forces to gain control of the Persian Gulf region as an assault on the vital interests of the United States—an assault that might be answered by military force. He restricted U.S. trade with the Soviet Union and called for an international boycott of the 1980 Olympic Games in Moscow. Carter also called for a delay in ratifying a second Strategic Arms Limitation Treaty—SALT II—that was pending at the time.

By the early 1980s, détente had come to an end. Some Americans believed that the reduction of the U.S. military after Vietnam had served to encourage the aggressive actions of the Soviet Union. On taking office in 1981, President Reagan consequently called for substantially increased defense spending. Congress approved his request, and the United States soon began to build up its conventional forces, modernize its nuclear arsenal, and provide new aid to anticommunist forces that existed overseas.

Looking Beyond Planet Earth

The successful mission of the space shuttle *Discovery* in October 1988 reaffirmed the American commitment to space exploration that had faltered some two years before with the loss of the *Challenger* and its crew of seven. President Ronald Reagan underscored this rekindled commitment when he declared that the United States fully intended to expand human activity beyond Earth into the solar system. In the 1990s, progress toward cooperation with Russia in reaching these goals has been impressive.

The National Aeronautics and Space Administration (NASA) has already begun planning journeys to the farther reaches of the solar system. The first step involved the construction of a space station, a permanently manned outpost in orbit. The space station is designed to serve as a base for scientific observation and experimentation, a refueling station, and a base for launching other satellites or spacecraft.

Earth, as viewed from the space shuttle

The first successful experimental space station was launched by the United States in May 1973. Called *Skylab,* it remained in orbit for nearly a year. During that time, the astronauts made observations of the Sun and conducted experiments on how the body responds to zero-gravity conditions on extended missions. From 1974 to 1982, the Soviet Union also orbited a series of smaller space stations. In 1986 the Soviets launched a new space station called *Mir,* designed to be the core of a permanent manned orbiting facility. Between 1995 and 1998, in a sign of Russian-American cooperation, *Mir* hosted a series of NASA astronauts as crew members.

Both American and Russian scientists also want to explore other parts of the solar system, however. Throughout the 1960s and 1970s, both nations sent out deep-space probes. It was during this period that the Viking landings on Mars; the Voyager fly-bys of Jupiter, Saturn, and Uranus; and the Venera explorations of the surface of Venus were accomplished.

In July 1997 the Mars *Pathfinder* descended to the surface of Mars. Fascinating photographs of the Martian surface were transmitted back to Earth, and a rover vehicle called *Sojourner* moved over the Martian surface.

In the past, historical events and the personalities engaged in them were confined to the surface of Earth. However, the plans of the space programs of both the United States and Russia ensure that a new history will soon unfold in a new geography—that of the planets that lie in the vastness of space far beyond our own world.

Many feared that the United States was now pushing the Soviet Union too hard. The administration, however, maintained the pressure, believing it would ultimately force a more conciliatory policy from the Soviets.

By the mid-1980s, Soviet-American tensions had begun to ease. Recognizing the burden of the Cold War on his country's economy, the new Soviet leader, Mikhail Gorbachev, decided to pursue a friendlier relationship with the United States. In 1985, Reagan and Gorbachev held a summit meeting in Geneva, Switzerland. The two leaders met again in 1986 in Reykjavik (RAY·kyah·veek), Iceland. In 1987, Gorbachev visited Washington, D.C., where he and Reagan signed a new arms agreement eliminating short- and medium-range nuclear weapons.

By the end of the decade, Soviet-American relations had improved significantly. The Soviets began to reduce their military presence around the world, and in 1989 they finally withdrew their forces from Afghanistan. When democratic movements swept communist governments from power in Eastern Europe, the Soviets did not try to stop them. With its satellite states gone, racked by ethnic discord, and still straining under economic inefficiency, the Soviet Union itself faced imminent demise by the early 1990s. In December 1991, the Soviet Union formally ceased to exist. It was replaced by a loose association of many of its former republics, now independent nations.

The "new world order." Numerous threats to world stability, however, persisted after the Cold War ended. Ambitious regional powers represented a major concern of U.S. leaders in the 1990s. In 1990, for example, Iraq invaded Kuwait. In 1991 the United States launched its largest military operation since Vietnam, leading an international coalition in the Persian Gulf that succeeded in expelling Iraq from Kuwait. Iraq's continued efforts to acquire **weapons of mass destruction**—nuclear, chemical, and biological weapons—remained a major concern in the mid-1990s. American officials also worried about the proliferation of such weapons, which might spread from producers like Russia and China to potentially hostile regimes in countries like Iran and North Korea. During the Persian Gulf crisis, President Bush suggested to the United Nations that it was time for all nations to work toward a "new world order" based on peace and mutual cooperation and to defend weaker countries against aggressors. However, some suggested that the international community might defend only those weaker countries that possessed a valuable commodity, like the oil in Kuwait.

Another major concern was the resurgence of militant nationalism and ethnic conflict after the end of the Cold War. The disintegration of Yugoslavia in the early 1990s attracted particular attention. Worried that the ensuing civil war in the province of Bosnia and Herzegovina threatened the stability of Europe, American diplomats mediated a settlement between the Republic of Croatia, Bosnia's Muslim-led government, and Serbian separatists in 1995. To enforce the agreement, President Clinton ordered American troops to Bosnia and Herzegovina, often called Bosnia, as part of a multinational peacekeeping force. Clinton also dispatched American forces to support multinational peacekeeping missions in Somalia and Haiti.

Despite reductions in its military forces after the Cold War ended, the United States seemed to be playing an increased role in world politics in the mid-1990s. In addition to regional conflicts and civil strife, issues such as trade, terrorism, narcotics, and the environment loomed large in American foreign policy. Presidents Bush and Clinton focused on settling the Arab-Israeli dispute. In addition, some observers cautioned that Russia, heir to most of the Soviets' vast nuclear arsenal, still represented a potentially serious threat. China, too, might pose a significant danger, especially as the countries of Asia were growing in importance to the world's economy as the 1900s drew to a close.

Relations with China. American relations with China improved steadily through the 1970s and 1980s. In 1972, President Nixon visited China, beginning a period of diplomacy that culminated in full diplomatic relations with the People's Republic of China starting on January 1, 1979. While many Americans saw opportunities for investment and trade in China's rapidly growing economy, mutual distrust of the Soviet Union provided much of the basis for the improvement of Sino-American relations.

With the end of the Cold War, however, differences between China and the United States began to surface once again. Following China's crackdown on pro-democracy demonstrators in Tiananmen Square in 1989, many Americans expressed misgivings about China's record on human rights. Others worried about China's export of advanced weapons to potentially hostile states like Iran—and about China's own military buildup. By the mid-1990s, the question of how to deal with China—through incentives, such as trading advantages, or through stepped-up economic and military pressure—had become a major issue of debate among American policymakers.

Although the Meech Lake Accord failed to become part of the Canadian constitution, many Québécois continue to favor separation from Canada.

Canada

Canada is the world's second-largest country in terms of geographic area and possesses a vast wealth of raw materials. Although much of its territory—especially in the north—is unsuitable for habitation, Canada is also one of the world's most highly developed countries. In general, Canadians enjoy a relatively high standard of living and a quality of life envied by many people around the world. Nonetheless, Canada confronted difficult political and economic challenges during the late 1900s.

Led by Prime Minister Pierre Trudeau, Canada's Liberal Party controlled the government throughout the 1970s. Trudeau was committed to preserving Canada's federal union, and he emphasized constitutional issues during his years in office. A recession led many Canadians to call for significant economic reform in the early 1980s. In 1984 the Progressive Conservative Party won a general election. To improve the economy, the new government under Prime Minister Brian Mulroney pursued the privatization of various industries, the deregulation of business, and reform of the tax structure. But if economic problems had led to the rise of the Conservative Party in the 1980s, they contributed to its downfall in the 1990s.

A deepening recession in the early 1990s contributed to a major shake-up in Canadian politics. Facing a crisis of confidence, the Conservatives decided to replace Mulroney as their party leader. They chose Kim Campbell to take his place, and she became

Canada's first woman prime minister in mid-1993. Within a few months, however, the Conservatives suffered catastrophic defeat in a general election. The Liberal Party won control of the government for the first time since 1984. In late 1993, Jean Chrétien, who was the leader of the Liberal Party, took office as prime minister.

Chrétien faced many of the same problems that had confronted his predecessors. Many Canadians called for constitutional reform at the federal level. French Canadian separatism and relations with the United States were two of the most important issues.

Separatism. Although the majority of Canadians are of English-speaking descent, people of many cultural backgrounds make Canada their home. American Indians make up one important segment of Canada's population. Many immigrants have come to Canada from South and East Asia as well as from Europe. In one of Canada's 12 provinces, Quebec, French-speaking Canadians form the majority of the population. Approximately 80 percent of Quebec's inhabitants claim French as their first language.

Throughout Canada's history, Quebec's French-speaking population has struggled to preserve its distinctiveness, both in its language and in its French-based traditions. During the 1960s a separatist movement gained strength among the French-speaking population of Quebec. French Canadians sought special recognition for their language and heritage. They also demanded a greater role in both provincial and national government and protections against discrimination. French Canadians gained a notable victory in 1969 with the passage of the Official Languages Act. This act made both French and English official languages of Canada.

Many French Canadians remained unsatisfied, however. The Parti Quebécois favored the complete separation of Quebec from Canada. In 1976 it won control of the provincial government. Four years later, in 1980, it held a referendum on separation, but the people of Quebec voted by a majority of 60 percent to remain a part of Canada. Nonetheless, French Canadian demands for special status for Quebec persisted through the 1980s and into the 1990s.

In 1987, Canadian leaders met at the resort of Meech Lake. There they agreed to accept Quebec as a "distinct society" within Canada. Had Parliament and all of Canada's provincial legislatures ratified the **Meech Lake Accord** by 1990, it would have become part of the Canadian constitution. Many Canadians, however, believed that the accord gave too much power to Quebec. The agreement failed to win the unanimous endorsement necessary for implementation.

The failure of the Meech Lake Accord reinvigorated separatist sentiments. In 1995 the issue of separation for Quebec was once again put to a referendum. Once again the separatists lost—but only by the narrowest margin. Quebec remained part of Canada, but with 49.4 percent of the vote in favor of separation, the issue was far from settled.

Relations with the United States. Most Canadians live within several hundred miles of the border with the United States. This border is the longest undefended international frontier in the world. Indeed, relations between Canada and the United States have become very close during the 1900s. As the century drew to a close, the flow of trade across the Canadian-U.S. border remained the heaviest bilateral trade traffic in the world.

Despite the general friendliness between the two countries, however, Canada and the United States have experienced periodic friction. Disputes over fishing rights in the Atlantic and the Pacific continued to occasionally afflict their relations into the 1990s. By far the greatest strains have resulted from Canada's uneasiness over American involvement in its economy.

Many Canadians were especially unsure about free trade. They voiced particular concern after the announcement of the United States-Canada Free Trade Agreement in 1988. The agreement proposed to eliminate almost all tariff barriers between Canada and the United States. Opponents feared that the agreement would reduce Canada to the status of an economic colony of the United States. The debate over free trade grew even more heated in the early 1990s, when the possibility of adding Mexico to the 1988 agreement was raised just as the Canadian economy went into a major recession. In the end, however, Canada joined with the United States and Mexico in 1992 to sign the North American Free Trade Agreement, or NAFTA. This agreement went into effect on January 1, 1994.

Section 1 Review

1. **Define** Vietnamization, Watergate scandal, stagflation, trade deficit, détente, Carter Doctrine, weapons of mass destruction, Meech Lake Accord

2. **Identify** Jimmy Carter, Ronald Reagan, Bill Clinton

3. **Understanding Ideas** What events caused many Americans to lose confidence in their government after 1970?

4. **Summarizing Ideas** Describe the U.S. economy from 1970 through 1990.

5. **Contrasting Ideas** How did the foreign-policy challenges facing the United States after the end of the Cold War contrast with President Bush's concept of a "new world order"?

6. **Synthesizing Ideas** What have been the main issues in Canadian politics since the 1970s?

Section 2

Europe

Focus Questions

- **How did the British and French governments respond to economic problems in the late 1900s?**
- **What changes have taken place in Germany since 1960?**
- **How have the nations of southern Europe changed politically in the late 1900s?**
- **What strides were made toward greater unity among the nations of Western Europe?**

During the late 1900s, many countries in Western Europe tried to consolidate the economic gains they had made in the early postwar period. Other countries made political advances, turning from dictatorships and military governments toward democracy. Although progress was far from smooth, Western Europe in general made significant strides toward political and economic integration.

Great Britain

By the mid-1960s, Britain's postwar recovery seemed uncertain. By the end of the decade, the country faced severe economic problems and had decided to pull back from major defense commitments overseas. Outdated factories, low productivity, and worker apathy made it difficult for Britain to compete with other industrial nations. The economy came under even greater stress as the government raised taxes and increased borrowing. The 1980s would witness a turnaround for British productivity, but unemployment and inflation would continue.

Margaret Thatcher. In a decisive victory in the general election of 1979, Britain's Conservative Party came to power. The party's leader, Margaret Thatcher, became prime minister—the first woman to hold that office. She argued that the government regulated business and industry too closely and that it taxed the British people too heavily. She planned to start Britain on the road back to prosperity by substantially reducing the government's role in the economy.

Over the next few years, Thatcher began to implement her ideas. She oversaw cuts in social spending, including the complete elimination of some programs. Her opponents charged that Thatcher's real intention was to dismantle the welfare state completely. Thatcher pressed ahead nonetheless, leading successful efforts to reduce taxes and to ease government regulation of business. She also began to privatize Britain's many government-owned industries. Not least, Thatcher managed finally to break the overwhelming influence that Britain's labor unions had exercised over the economy since the 1970s.

Aided by the development of new oil fields in the North Sea, the economy had begun to rebound by the mid-1980s, most notably in southern England. The country's northern areas did not fare as well, however. In this predominantly industrial region, unemployment remained very high. This was partly the result of a general shift in Britain's economy, like that in the United States, from heavy industry to services. Although Thatcher pointed to an overall improvement in the economy, critics charged that her policies favored the wealthy and created an unequal society.

One reason for the harmonious relationship between the United States and Great Britain was the personal friendship between Prime Minister Margaret Thatcher and President Ronald Reagan.

Thatcher brought a tough, no-nonsense approach to Britain's foreign policy as well as to economic affairs. In 1982 she ordered British troops and naval forces to retake the Falklands after Argentina's invasion of the British-held islands in the South Atlantic. The maintenance of strong ties with the United States represented a consistent theme of Thatcher's approach to foreign policy. In 1990 she played an important role in the formation of the international coalition that ultimately forced Iraq to withdraw from Kuwait in 1991.

Changes in leadership. With a downturn in the British economy during the late 1980s, Thatcher began to lose popularity. Even her support within the Conservative Party began to weaken. Her situation became critical following her implementation of the so-called poll tax. This tax, which replaced property taxes as the source of funds for local government, charged all taxpayers the same rate, or percentage, regardless of their income level. The tax proved extremely unpopular with the British people. Many Conservatives began to realize that they would have to reverse the tax if their party was to win the next election. Thatcher, however, continued to support the poll tax as the most fair and efficient way of financing local government.

As Thatcher's popularity continued to fall, her opponents in the Conservative Party challenged her leadership. Convinced by her closest advisers that she could not win the fight for leadership of the party, she stepped down in November 1990. When she left, more than a decade after first taking office, Margaret Thatcher had served longer than any British prime minister in this century.

In her place the Conservatives chose John Major, a leading member of Thatcher's cabinet. Major was generally considered more moderate than Thatcher in many of his views, especially on closer union with Europe, but he shared Thatcher's belief in free-enterprise economics and her support for especially close relations with the United States. Major was a strong supporter of the United States in the Persian Gulf crisis of 1991. During his term of office, Britain's economy began to pick up once again.

After nearly 18 years of Conservative government, however, the British electorate decided on a change, prompted by scandals and incompetence in the government. In 1997 the Labour Party, led by the young moderate Tony Blair, won control of the government for the first time since 1979. Although Labour promised a number of changes, they did not propose to restore the British welfare state to the level it had reached in the 1970s. Many of Thatcher's political and economic ideas had taken hold. A number of challenges faced Blair nonetheless. Among them was the lingering problem of Northern Ireland.

Northern Ireland. After the creation of an independent Republic of Ireland in 1922, Northern Ireland had remained part of Britain. Many people hoped that the old antagonism between Britain and Ireland would finally diminish, but new disagreements soon emerged. Over the years, the Protestant majority in Northern Ireland gained control of the government and dominated the country's economy. The lack of political power and the limited economic opportunities among Northern Ireland's Catholic minority increasingly produced resentment and ultimately erupted in violence.

In the late 1960s, Catholics in Northern Ireland began to demonstrate for an end to discrimination in areas such as employment and housing. At first peaceful, these demonstrations soon turned violent. To keep the peace, in 1969 the British government sent troops to Northern Ireland, and these troops were seen by the Catholics as representatives of a foreign power. This stationing of soldiers in Northern Ireland

A series of bombings and assassinations occurred in Northern Ireland during the 1970s. IRA gunmen are shown here in Londonderry in 1973.

became a permanent policy. Large numbers of British troops remained garrisoned there into the mid-1990s.

Throughout the 1970s, the violence in Northern Ireland escalated as Catholic and Protestant extremists alike took advantage of the situation. Assassinations, car bombings, and attacks on British troops became an almost daily occurrence. The most active extremist group was the **Irish Republican Army (IRA)**. Almost entirely Catholic, the IRA wanted to drive the British out of the north and unite all of Ireland. The IRA took its "war of liberation" far beyond Irish borders, bombing public sites in a number of British cities and attacking British soldiers in other parts of Europe.

In addition to taking strong military measures, the British government tried to end the violence in Northern Ireland through political means. Progress came in the Anglo-Irish Agreement of 1985, which gave the Republic of Ireland a voice in the affairs of Northern Ireland. In time, however, both Catholics and Protestants denounced the agreement. In the early 1990s, generally improving relations between Britain and the Republic of Ireland—combined with growing pressure from Europe and the United States—brought new hope for a settlement in Northern Ireland. In 1993 the British and Irish prime ministers jointly pledged their commitment to the principle of self-determination in Northern Ireland. The IRA declared a cease-fire the following year, but the British insisted that the IRA would have to disarm before talks could begin. The IRA refused and in 1996 renewed its campaign of terror. Peace talks resumed, however, following the Labour Party's victory in the British elections of 1997. A major breakthrough seemed to come with the Good Friday peace accords, signed in 1998. Hopes were high that a lasting peace might soon become a reality.

France

After Charles de Gaulle resigned in 1969, his prime minister, Georges Pompidou, replaced him as president. Although the two men had worked together for many years, they viewed French interests differently. De Gaulle saw France as a major player on the world stage. In contrast, Pompidou believed that France should limit its overseas involvement and focus instead on domestic issues.

Pompidou and Giscard d'Estaing. Pompidou believed that changes in the international situation had made de Gaulle's nationalist approach to foreign affairs impractical. A more realistic strategy, Pompidou argued, would seek close cooperative relations with traditional allies. He therefore worked to strengthen ties with the United States and ended French opposition to British membership in the European Economic Community, or EEC. Within the EEC, Pompidou pursued cooperation rather than French leadership.

Pompidou focused on domestic issues for much of his time in office. He introduced a number of social programs, which he hoped would ease the problems that had given rise to the political upheavals of the late 1960s. He also embarked on an ambitious plan to renovate much of Paris, which was not only France's capital but a major tourist attraction. Pompidou had to curtail many of his plans, however, in the face of an economic crisis that was largely brought on by the OPEC oil embargo and price increases of 1973.

On Pompidou's sudden death in 1974, Valéry Giscard d'Estaing became president. Giscard d'Estaing wanted to improve French standing abroad and encourage social change at home. He continued Pompidou's foreign policy, moving toward fuller cooperation with other countries. On the domestic front, he reduced state controls in the economy. However, high rates of unemployment and inflation undermined Giscard d'Estaing's plans for social change, making his programs virtually impossible to implement.

From Mitterrand to Chirac. Disappointed with Giscard d'Estaing's failure to fulfill his promises of prosperity and social change, in 1981 French voters elected a socialist president, François Mitterrand. Mitterrand faced severe economic problems, including high inflation, growing trade deficits, and rising unem-

ployment. In contrast to Margaret Thatcher in Britain, Mitterrand sought to bolster his country's economy by expanding the government's role. Several industries and banks were nationalized, and taxes were raised for people with high incomes. Mitterrand expanded government programs for the unemployed. In the wake of further economic reversals in the mid-1980s, however, Mitterrand was forced to pursue a more conservative approach to economics.

Under Mitterrand, France once again adopted an assertive foreign policy. French troops were especially active in Africa, frequently operating in support of former French colonies. For example, France assisted Chad in its border war with Libya during the 1980s. France also made major military contributions to multinational peacekeeping operations in Lebanon and Bosnia and participated in the international coalition against Iraq in 1990 and 1991.

Although Mitterrand had moved away from traditional socialist policies by the 1990s, support for his Socialist Party's policies wavered when Mitterrand's popularity waned. In 1993 Mitterrand's party lost significant ground in midterm elections. Economic problems, such as unemployment and recession, persisted. Immigration of Arabs from North Africa into

François Mitterrand, the first socialist president of France, served two terms between 1981 and 1995.

France was an increasing source of substantial social tension. Many people voiced concern about France's ability to balance the economic and political power of a reunified Germany. A deep sense of uncertainty over the future afflicted France in the mid-1990s.

In 1995, French voters elected a new president. They chose Jacques Chirac, mayor of Paris and a member of the conservative Gaullist Party, or RPR. Chirac promised reforms and a fresh approach to France's economic problems. Chirac's government, however, soon encountered difficulties, including disruptive protests by various groups of laborers, farmers, and truckers who feared the loss of jobs and income as France dropped barriers to trade with its European neighbors. Chirac provoked controversy abroad by ordering a new round of nuclear weapons tests in the South Pacific during 1996, though he stopped the testing after international protests. In 1997, Chirac's political future appeared uncertain as his party suffered a setback at the polls.

Germany

By the late 1960s, West Germany had become a major economic power in Western Europe. Even so, the country still faced certain political problems. Access to West Berlin and relations with East Germany, the Soviet Union, and other communist countries posed difficult foreign policy challenges.

Ostpolitik. After his election in 1969, Chancellor Willy Brandt, a member of the liberal Social Democratic Party, tried to meet these challenges. Brandt believed that West Germany had to remain firmly allied with the rest of Western Europe and the United States. At the same time, however, he concluded that tensions between his country and the communist countries of Eastern Europe had to be reduced. Brandt's effort to improve relations between East and West, known as *Ostpolitik* (German for "Eastern Policy") resulted in West German treaties with the Soviet Union and Poland in 1970. *Ostpolitik* eventually led to the mutual recognition of East and West Germany in 1973, and ultimately to the Helsinki Accords in 1975 (see page 889).

In 1974, Helmut Schmidt became chancellor of West Germany after Brandt resigned following the revelation that a member of his staff was an East German spy. Schmidt admired and continued Brandt's *Ostpolitik*. He also pursued closer economic and political cooperation with Western Europe. In the early 1980s, however, recession hit the West German economy. For the first time since the early postwar period,

West Germans faced the prospect of rising unemployment coupled with widespread inflation.

Helmut Kohl. As in both Britain and France, economic troubles led to political change in the early 1980s. In 1982 the Christian Democrats regained control of the government after more than a dozen years out of power. Helmut Kohl, the new chancellor, charged that Schmidt and the Social Democrats had brought on the recession through high levels of government spending. The conservative Kohl promised to return the country to prosperity through policies similar to those of Prime Minister Thatcher in Britain and President Reagan in the United States.

Chancellor Kohl also made changes in West German foreign policy. He strongly reaffirmed West Germany's commitment to the NATO alliance, though he criticized the deployment of American intermediate-range nuclear missiles in West Germany. Kohl worked to improve relations between West Germany and the United States. This relationship remained generally strong into the 1990s, although the reunification of Germany early in the decade created new anxieties among some of Germany's neighbors in Europe.

Reunification. The reunification of Germany was perhaps Kohl's greatest challenge. The process of reunification began almost immediately after the fall of the Berlin Wall in 1989. Talks involving the two Germanies and the four victorious Allies of World War II—Britain, France, the Soviet Union, and the United States—set October 1990 as the date for reunification. Two months later Helmut Kohl, benefiting

Chancellor from 1982 until 1998, Helmut Kohl witnessed the unification of West and East Germany in 1990.

from the goodwill created by this great change, was elected as chancellor of a reunified Germany.

Although initially seen as a hero, Kohl soon began to lose popularity. By the summer of 1991, unemployment was widespread in the former East Germany, and much of the promised investment and reindustrialization was yet to be seen. Germans in the western part of the country also became disillusioned as the enormous costs of reunification became apparent. The reintegration of East Germany became an increasing burden on the German economy through the mid-1990s. Helmut Kohl, however, remained in office until 1998, when he was defeated in September by Gerhard Schroeder and his Social Democratic Party. Schroeder pledged to reduce unemployment and stimulate the economy.

Northern Europe

The smaller but still highly developed nations of northern Europe enjoyed a general period of prosperity during the late 1900s. The small principalities of Monaco and Liechtenstein managed to maintain their sovereignty, while Belgium, Luxembourg, and the Netherlands worked to foster European unity.

Denmark, Iceland, and Norway, members of the NATO alliance, contributed vitally to Western Europe's defense during the Cold War. Despite a sometimes heated dispute with Britain over fishing rights, the island nation of Iceland played a key role in the protection of the Atlantic shipping lanes. So did Norway, which benefited greatly from the discovery and development of North Sea oil in the 1980s.

Although Finland, Sweden, Austria, and Switzerland maintained good relations with the rest of Western Europe, each country remained neutral throughout the Cold War. Recession in the early 1990s, however, offered a strong incentive for these countries to strengthen political and economic ties with Western Europe. Finland, Sweden, and Austria all chose to join the new European Union, while Swiss voters narrowly decided to maintain their country's traditional neutrality. On the domestic front, Sweden implemented free-enterprise reforms, steering away from its socialist policies of the past.

Southern Europe

During the 1970s and 1980s, the nations of southern Europe underwent major political changes. Italy, once one of the more stable European nations, experienced almost constant political turmoil. At the same time, Spain, Portugal, and Greece returned to democratic forms of government.

In August 1961, East Germany sought to restrict travel to and from West Berlin by erecting a wall to separate East Berlin from West Berlin. This photo shows remnants of the Berlin Wall, which came down in 1989.

Italy. The world economic recession of the early 1970s hit Italy especially hard. For much of the decade, unemployment levels soared and inflation was rampant. During the same period, the country's political system experienced a great deal of turmoil. None of the more than 14 political parties could gain a majority in the Italian parliament, so governments had to be formed through coalitions. Since few of these coalitions lasted very long, little could be done to lessen the country's severe political and economic problems. Late in the decade, Italy experienced a wave of terrorism. These acts of terrorism only added to Italy's problems.

Italy's situation improved greatly during the 1980s. By the mid-1980s, the power of the terrorist cells had largely been broken. The economy took off after the introduction of a number of free-enterprise reforms.

By 1994, Italy ranked eighth among all industrialized nations and fourth among the countries of the European Economic Community. Its economy, however, remained burdened by a huge national debt. Moreover, a marked social division existed between Italy's prosperous, industrialized north and the poor, mostly rural south.

In the mid-1990s, however, Italy continued to face serious political instability. Corruption scandals, particularly some that involved organized crime, racked the government. By 1997, the implementation of reforms, begun in 1994 concerning the allotment of seats in parliament, had lent Italy at least some measure of stability.

Spain. During the 1970s, Spain made the transition from dictatorship to democracy. On the death of Spanish dictator Francisco Franco in 1975, Juan Carlos became king. Juan Carlos immediately set about the task of returning Spain to democracy. In 1977, Spain held its first free elections in more than 40 years. In those elections, moderate political parties led by socialists won the majority of the seats in the Cortes, or parliament. Spain's new democracy was not yet secure, however. In 1981 a group of army officers tried to seize control of the government. Although the attempt failed, it demonstrated the fragility of democratic government.

Other challenges to Spain's new democracy included the questions of Basque separatism and of economic development. The Basque people, who possess a distinct language and culture and inhabit a region in Spain's mountainous northwest, have long sought independence from Spain. In 1980, they won self-government within Spain, but some remained unsatisfied. The Basque separatist group, ETA, demanded complete independence and resorted to the use of terrorism throughout the 1980s.

Spain also faced the same economic problems that confronted many other European nations: high levels of unemployment and inflation. One way in which Spanish leaders sought to improve the economy was through trade. In 1986, Spain joined the European Economic Community. Although the issue of Basque separatism lingered and economic problems persisted, in the mid-1990s Spain remained democratic and numbered among the leading economic powers of Western Europe.

Portugal. Like its Spanish neighbor, Portugal also made the transition from dictatorship to democracy in the late 1900s. Ironically, the process began with a military coup. In 1974, army officers led by General Antonio de Spinola ousted the dictator Marcello Caetano. Spinola quickly granted independence to most of Portugal's remaining colonies, including Angola and Mozambique. Spinola then resigned, after calling for elections. Portugal grappled with serious economic and political instability over the next several years. In 1986, Portugal joined the European Economic Community. At the same time, the government introduced a series of free-enterprise reforms. These measures helped spur economic growth and reinforce the stability of Portugal's democracy into the 1990s.

Greece. During the late 1900s, Greece entered a period of political uncertainty. From 1967 to 1974, a repressive military junta ruled Greece. Its interference in the affairs of Cyprus led to its downfall. In 1974, Greek voters chose to make Greece a republic rather than restore the monarchy. In 1981 they elected a socialist government, which implemented various social reforms. Although a more conservative government in the 1990s promised closer cooperation with the West, Greece remained at odds with many Western governments.

European Cooperation

The spirit of cooperation among the nations of Western Europe that had developed in the years after World War II continued to grow during the later part of the 1900s. Formal institutions, such as NATO and the European Economic Community, grew in both strength and membership. The collapse of communism

Living in the Pyrenees Mountains on both sides of the French-Spanish border, the Basque maintain their own culture and government.

in Eastern Europe left the structure and purpose of some of these organizations open to question. At the same time, however, it opened the possibility of an even wider union of European nations.

The Helsinki Accords. In 1975, representatives of 35 nations, including the United States and the Soviet Union, met in Helsinki, Finland, to discuss the topics of security and cooperation in Europe. The meeting resulted in a series of agreements known as the **Helsinki Accords**. These agreements specified ways of improving economic and technological cooperation between East and West, endorsing the use of peaceful means rather than force to settle disputes between nations. The accords also settled a major Cold War issue by recognizing the legitimacy of certain boundaries in Eastern Europe that were established after World War II but were disputed by some countries. Perhaps the most important part of the accords, however, concerned the protection of human rights, including freedom of speech and freedom of worship. The Helsinki Accords called on all nations to respect the basic human rights of their citizens.

Although the Helsinki Accords provided for no real means of enforcement, they proved to be an important symbolic step. By showing little interest in complying with the human rights aspects of the accords, the Soviets and other Communist bloc countries undermined their own credibility in the international community. The accords also formed an important foundation for the democratic movement that ultimately swept across Eastern Europe in the late 1980s. In the 1990s, following the collapse of communism, European nations worked to reaffirm their commitment to the principles set forth in the Helsinki Accords.

NATO. Although the North Atlantic Treaty Organization (NATO) remained the cornerstone of Western European security as the 1900s drew to a close, its policies and future role increasingly came into question. Friction between Greece and Turkey, both members of NATO, led to Greece's withdrawal from the alliance in 1974. Greece eventually rejoined, but its relations with other NATO countries remained strained. The deployment of American nuclear weapons in Europe during the Cold War proved especially controversial. Some member countries refused to allow American nuclear weapons on their soil; others expressed serious reservations. At the same time, the United States demanded that other members agree to take on a larger share of the burden of defending Europe.

NATO's future grew increasingly uncertain following the collapse of the Soviet Union in the early 1990s. With the military threat from the Eastern bloc diminished, NATO seemed to many people to have outlived its usefulness. Others pointed out that threats to European security still existed, and that NATO provided a framework to deal with problems like containing the civil war in the countries of what had been Yugoslavia, or a possible revival of Russian military power. Many countries of Eastern Europe sought to join NATO. Critics argued that any expansion of NATO eastward would require a burdensome commitment from current members and might provoke Russian hostility. In 1997, despite Russian objections, NATO leaders agreed to invite Poland, Hungary, and the Czech Republic to join the alliance.

From EEC to EU. The late 1990s saw the evolution of the European Economic Community (EEC) into the even more closely knit European Union (EU). A general expansion of the EEC preceded this transformation.

After the Maastricht Treaty, the European Economic Community became the European Union, continuing the quest for economic and political cooperation among European countries. The common European currency, euro, is shown.

During the 1970s and 1980s, the EEC grew from 6 members to 12. After lengthy negotiations, Britain finally joined in 1973. Ireland and Denmark also joined in that year. In 1981 Greece became a full member, followed by Spain and Portugal in 1986. In the early 1990s, Austria, Finland, and Sweden joined.

As the EEC grew, it made headway toward setting common practices for its members in taxation, credit, and labor and monetary policies. In 1993 the EEC countries implemented the **Maastricht Treaty**, creating the European Union (EU). Under the terms of the treaty, they dropped trade barriers among themselves, agreed to pursue closer cooperation in defense and foreign relations, and accepted the idea of a common currency.

The implementation of the Maastricht Treaty had not come easily, however, and many problems remained unresolved in the mid-1990s. Several members of the EEC worried that the EU would undermine their sovereignty. British leaders in particular voiced misgivings. In Denmark, voters barely chose to ratify the Maastricht Treaty, but in Norway they rejected membership in the EU. As the century drew to a close, the future of the EU remained unclear. Aligning the economies of Western Europe was proving especially difficult, and the EU remained divided over whether or not to admit Turkey and various Eastern European countries. The nations of Western Europe had nonetheless achieved a real degree of unity in a century marked by two world wars.

Section 2 Review

1. **Define** IRA, *Ostpolitik*, Helsinki Accords, Maastricht Treaty
2. **Identify** Margaret Thatcher, François Mitterrand, Jacques Chirac, Helmut Schmidt, Helmut Kohl, Juan Carlos
3. **Understanding Ideas** How did the leaders of Great Britain and France respond to economic challenges after 1970?
4. **Explaining Ideas** When did Germany reunify, and what challenges followed its reunification?
5. **Summarizing Ideas** What major political changes took place in southern Europe during the late 1900s?
6. **Evaluating Ideas (a)** How have the nations of Western Europe moved toward greater unity? **(b)** What are some potential points of conflict among members of the EU?

The Fall of Communism

Focus Questions

- **How did Mikhail Gorbachev attempt to reform the Soviet Union?**
- **What happened in Russia after the collapse of the Soviet Union?**
- **What major problems faced Russia, the other republics of the former Soviet Union, and the nations of Eastern Europe in the aftermath of communism?**

By the early 1980s, the division of Europe between the communist East and the free West appeared permanent. However, the 1980s and 1990s witnessed the total breakdown of communist rule in Eastern Europe. Although some countries looked forward to a prosperous future, political and economic instability prevailed throughout much of Eastern Europe and the former Soviet Union.

The Soviet Union and Its Successors

At the end of the 1970s, the power of the Soviet Union appeared unshakable to many outside observers. Soviet leaders, however, faced a huge and rapidly growing problem in their country's inefficient economy. The 1980s brought an attempt at fundamental reform, but the Soviet predicament proved overwhelming. After losing its Eastern European satellites to a wave of democratic reform in the late 1980s, the Soviet Union itself finally disintegrated in 1991.

The Brezhnev years. Leonid Brezhnev led the Soviet Union throughout the 1970s. He proved to be a forceful leader. With the invasion of Czechoslovakia in 1968, Brezhnev demonstrated that the Soviet government would tolerate no dissent among its satellite nations in Eastern Europe. He subsequently announced the **Brezhnev Doctrine**, declaring that the Soviet Union would intervene in any satellite nation that seemed to be moving away from communism. As a result, no satellite government attempted reforms on the scale of the Prague Spring during the Brezhnev years. Brezhnev also cracked down on dissent at home. Basic human rights such as the freedoms of speech, worship, and movement were seriously curtailed in the Soviet Union.

While seeking to crush all opposition both domestically and in the Soviet satellites of Eastern Europe,

Brezhnev worked to strengthen his country's position in the balance of world power. Through détente, he tried to stabilize relations with the United States. The Soviet Union's continued military buildup and support for anti-Western forces during the Brezhnev years, however, called into question the sincerity of Soviet commitments to peace. The Soviet invasion of Afghanistan in 1979 proved to be the last straw. Relations with the United States had substantially deteriorated by the time Brezhnev died in 1982.

Gorbachev and reform. Many Soviets experienced a decline in their standard of living during the Brezhnev years, and the Soviet economy remained extremely inefficient. Agricultural failures, an inadequate transportation infrastructure, and outmoded factories all contributed to the dire state of the Soviet economy. Heavy military spending compounded the problem severely. The critical need for reform became increasingly apparent and helped to prompt a struggle for power in the Soviet Union following Brezhnev's death.

At first the old guard—made up of Soviet leaders born before the revolution of 1917—held out. Many of them recognized the need for reform but worried that it might lead to the weakening of the Soviet state. Hoping to improve the economy without endangering the political survival of communism, they named Yuri Andropov, a former head of the secret police, as Brezhnev's successor. Andropov was in poor health, however, and held office only 15 months. His elderly successor, Konstantin Chernenko, lasted little more than a year. On Chernenko's death a younger generation of Communist Party leaders finally gained control of the Soviet government.

In 1985 a rising young star in the Politburo, Mikhail Gorbachev, became the new leader of the Soviet Union. Gorbachev came to office with a background in agricultural and economic affairs. He planned nothing less than a complete overhaul of Soviet political and economic systems. He pledged himself to a course of dramatic reforms known as **perestroika** (per·uh·STROY·kuh), or restructuring, and **glasnost** (GLAZ·nohst), or openness. Gorbachev relaxed government controls on the economy and eased restrictions on dissent, allowing Soviet citizens a greater freedom to speak their minds and to read whatever they liked. Recognizing the burden that military spending put on the Soviet Union, Gorbachev planned to reduce the armed forces and increase their efficiency. He also sought a way to end the bloody, protracted, and increasingly unpopular Soviet occupation of Afghanistan.

Gorbachev's reform-minded attitude won wide acclaim abroad. Relations between the Soviet Union and the United States soon began to improve. Gorbachev met several times with President Reagan, and in 1987 the two men signed agreements to keep fewer nuclear weapons of certain types and to limit the production of others. In 1988, Gorbachev told the United Nations that the Soviet Union would soon begin reducing the number of troops it deployed in Eastern Europe, and in the following year he oversaw the full withdrawal of Soviet forces from Afghanistan.

At home, however, Gorbachev's program of reform ran into problems. Results came slowly and were often ineffective. Liberal supporters complained that Gorbachev was proceeding too cautiously. Despite perestroika, consumer goods remained in short supply, and there were shortages in basic necessities, including bread. In 1990, Gorbachev introduced a program to establish a mixed economy—one combining private ownership with government control—in the Soviet

Mikhail Gorbachev, leader of the Soviet Union from 1985 to 1991, received the Nobel Peace Prize in 1990. He is shown here with his wife, Raisa.

Union, but he soon had to abandon it under pressure from hard-line Communists.

Gorbachev also faced intense criticism from people who worried that he was moving too fast. Many Soviet citizens became discouraged as reforms designed to increase efficiency on the national level seemed only to impose personal hardship. Perestroika represented a drastic change in the way of life to which Soviet citizens were accustomed. No longer did they enjoy guaranteed lifetime employment and secure incomes. As a result, many Soviet citizens questioned the wisdom of Gorbachev's new policies.

The most serious challenge came in the summer of 1991, when some strictly conservative members of the government and military attempted a coup. They arrested Gorbachev, but Boris Yeltsin, the liberal-minded president of Russia, rallied popular opposition to the coup. The coup ultimately failed after Soviet soldiers refused to carry out orders to eliminate the opposition. Gorbachev's popularity never recovered, however. Boris Yeltsin emerged from the crisis as the new champion of reform.

The collapse of the Soviet Union. As Gorbachev's reforms took effect, holding the Soviet Union together became one of the primary challenges facing the Soviet leader. Glasnost helped to fuel tensions among the various nationalities and ethnic groups of the Soviet Union as people began to express opinions that they would previously have kept to themselves. In the late 1980s, ethnic fighting erupted in the predominantly Muslim Soviet republic of Azerbaijan following a territorial dispute with the neighboring and predominantly Christian Soviet republic of Armenia.

After democratic movements swept communist governments in Eastern Europe from power in 1989, some Soviet republics began to demand their own independence. In an attempt to hasten reform, all three Baltic republics—Estonia, Latvia, and Lithuania—legalized non-communist parties, and in 1990 they called for secession from the Soviet Union. Gorbachev responded by deploying troops and threatening the republics with economic boycotts. The attempted crackdown backfired, however, prompting angry demonstrations across the Soviet Union and condemnation from abroad.

The dissolution of the Soviet Union soon became a foregone conclusion. Throughout 1991, one republic after another demanded independence. This trend began to move even faster after the failed coup in August 1991. In December, Gorbachev stepped down as president of the Soviet Union. While an amazed world looked on, the Soviet Union ceased to exist at the end of 1991.

Russia under Yeltsin. Led by President Boris Yeltsin, the Russian Federation—generally referred to simply as Russia—emerged as the largest and most powerful of the newly independent states. During the 1990s, Russia began to make the transition to democracy and an economy based on free enterprise. Many observers believed that the success of that transition depended on the political survival of the reform-minded Yeltsin. Both frequently seemed in doubt in the mid-1990s.

Yeltsin faced numerous challenges. First among them was the state of the economy. During the early 1990s, inflation soared and industrial output plummeted. High unemployment and shortages of food and housing persisted across Russia.

Throughout the 1990s, Yeltsin expressed his personal commitment to liberalization of the Russian economy. Under his leadership, many industries were privatized. Russia increasingly opened its doors to foreign investment. Yeltsin also sought financial assistance from the West, but political disagreements over issues such as Russian arms sales to aggressive states in the Middle East jeopardized such aid.

Economic improvement was slow in coming for Russia. By the late 1990s the Russian economy remained in poor condition. Although a growing class of entrepreneurs enjoyed newfound wealth in Russia, many Russians still suffered severe deprivations as the 1900s drew to a close.

Russia's persistent economic troubles contributed to political uncertainty. Yeltsin faced several political challenges throughout the 1990s. Early on, he encountered strong hostility in the Russian legislature, which still included many Communists. When Yeltsin tried to dissolve the legislature in 1993, defiant members denounced the move as unconstitutional and declared a new government under Alexander Rutskoi. Yeltsin had the army surround the legislature building in Moscow with tanks, but Rutskoi refused to surrender. Hoping to rally public sympathy and turn the army to his side, Rutskoi called on supporters to seize Moscow's television station. Yeltsin then ordered the army to open fire. Rutskoi gave up and was arrested.

Yeltsin's position, however, remained shaky. Ultranationalists and Communists who were opposed to democratic and free-enterprise reform began to win growing support by the mid-1990s. There was also the danger of a coup as the military grew increasingly

In June 1990, Boris Yeltsin became the first popularly elected leader in the history of Russia.

resentful over low pay and poor living conditions. To appease the growing number of critics, Yeltsin began to appoint conservative leaders to key government positions in place of reformers. Amid questions about his health, Yeltsin faced a formidable challenge in the presidential elections of 1996 from Communists led by Gennady Zyuganov. Only by offering a government post with broad powers to a charismatic former general named Alexander Lebed did Yeltsin manage to cement his re-election.

Groups outside the government also wielded considerable influence in the new Russia. The Orthodox church experienced a general revival. It enjoyed a restoration of property and power that had been lost over several decades of communist rule—not always to the liking of democratic reformers. In 1997 the Orthodox church won special status under a new religious law that restricted the activity of non-Orthodox groups such as evangelical Christians in Russia.

A particularly harmful influence on Russian life was the growth of organized crime in the wake of communism's fall. By 1993, observers estimated that between 3,000 and 4,000 crime gangs dealing in drugs, prostitution, and black-market goods operated in Russia.

Although ethnic Russians make up about 80 percent of the population of the Russian Federation, another pressing problem was separatism among various non-Russian minorities. The most serious case involved a small region in southern Russia called Chechnya. A largely Muslim group, the Chechens had long fought their Russian conquerors. Under the Soviet regime, Stalin had deported the Chechens to Central Asia. With the disintegration of the Soviet Union in 1991, Chechnya saw an opportunity to gain freedom and declared its independence.

President Yeltsin, however, soon made it clear that Chechnya—a region with rich oil resources—would not be allowed to break away. In 1994, Yeltsin ordered the Russian army to capture the capital city and put down Chechen resistance. Russia's brutal war on

What If?

Gorbachev
What might have happened if Gorbachev had been more successful in achieving his goals and had not been forced to resign in 1991? Would the history of the Soviet Union and Eastern Europe be any different?

Chechnya brought international criticism, and Russian forces took heavy casualties. Eventually a compromise was reached, keeping Chechnya within the Russian Republic but granting the region almost complete self-government.

Russia and the world. Russia was not the only successor state to the Soviet Union. The dissolution of the Soviet Union created 14 other independent republics. To coordinate economic and defense policies among the newly-created states, Russia engineered the establishment of the **Commonwealth of Independent States (CIS)**. (See map on opposite page.) Eventually, 12 of the republics joined the CIS. In 1992 the members of the CIS agreed to a mutual security treaty, under which they largely entrusted their defense to Russia. In 1997, except for the three Baltic states, the Russian army had troops deployed in all of the former Soviet republics.

Despite the formation of the CIS, however, relations between Russia and the other republics were often strained in the 1990s. In particular, several points of conflict emerged between Russia and the second largest republic, Ukraine. One such conflict involved the division of former Soviet military resources between Russia and Ukraine. Another matter of conflict concerned the status of predominantly Russian-speaking regions in Ukraine, including the Crimea and the economically vital Don River basin.

In the Caucasus region, where Russia remained particularly active, Russian tactics often appeared heavy-handed. In 1992, Russia incited a rebellion in a northeastern region of the Republic of Georgia. The Georgian government had previously been reluctant to join the Russian-dominated CIS. The rebellion forced Georgia to appeal to Russia for assistance, to join the CIS, and to permit the stationing of Russian troops on its soil.

In the mid-1990s, observers began to express concern that Russia was pursuing an aggressive policy in the former Soviet republics surrounding the oil-rich Caspian basin. These concerns gave rise to suggestions that the eight new nations comprising the Caucasus and former Soviet Central Asia were still effectively dominated by Moscow.

Although Yeltsin's government, in critical need of economic aid, generally pursued cooperative relations with the West, a number of differences emerged. Considerable progress was made between Russia and the United States in the area of arms limitation and reduction, but disagreements erupted over issues such as expansion of the NATO alliance into Eastern Europe. Many Western leaders expressed concern over the future of the demoralized but still extensive Russian military—especially about the security of Russia's vast arsenal of nuclear weapons.

Eastern Europe

During the 1970s, although dissent continued, the threat of Soviet intervention under the Brezhnev Doctrine prevented any real liberalization in the nations of Eastern Europe. The reforms implemented by Gorbachev, however, gave new encouragement to democratic forces in the region. In 1989 a tide of democratic reform swept communist governments from power across Eastern Europe. The fall of communism, however, left new and serious problems in its wake.

The growth of dissent. During the 1970s the communist governments of Eastern Europe followed the Soviet lead and imposed repressive measures to end internal dissent. Even so, many people in Eastern Europe continued to voice their opposition to totalitarian rule. Anticommunist writers skirted government censors by issuing *samizdat*, or self-published editions of their work. Following the announcement of the Helsinki Accords in the late 1970s, dissidents in Czechoslovakia called on their government to abide by the human rights articles of the accords. Dissidents throughout Eastern Europe subsequently began to make similar demands.

In Poland, economic troubles during the 1970s fueled the growth of dissent. In 1980 huge price increases spawned a series of labor strikes. Led by an unemployed electrician named Lech Walesa (LEK vah·LEN·suh) and a group of shipyard workers, the strikers demanded political and economic reforms. In response the government agreed to allow labor unions to organize outside of the Communist Party. An independent trade union, known as Solidarity, was then formed. Under Walesa's leadership, Solidarity pressed for further concessions from the Polish government. Fearing Soviet invasion, however, the government refused and imposed martial law. Demonstrations in support of Solidarity continued nonetheless through the 1980s; these demonstrations eventually culminated in the downfall of the communist government following the spread of glasnost and perestroika into Eastern Europe.

Initially, both communist governments and dissidents in Eastern Europe were skeptical of Gorbachev's reforms. Although they faced tremendous economic

The Breakup of the Soviet Sphere

Learning from Maps In 1989, Soviet republics began to demand their independence.

? Region Which former Soviet republics did not become part of the Commonwealth of Independent States?

difficulties of their own, many Eastern European governments, controlled by old-guard communists, were uneasy about restructuring along Soviet lines. In Hungary, however, the government believed that Gorbachev's economic reforms did not go far enough. Reaction among dissidents was also mixed at first. Many expressed outright disbelief, but in the end they overwhelmingly threw their support behind the new policies as the best hope of winning freedom. By 1988 the citizens of Eastern Europe were widely citing glasnost and perestroika as they demanded democratic reform.

The revolutions of 1989. In 1989 the growing pressure on the communist governments of Eastern Europe

reached a critical level as demands for democratic reform swept uncontrollably across the entire region. Poland led the way. In April 1989 the Polish government legalized Solidarity. The result of this action was the election of Poland's first noncommunist prime minister in more than 40 years. In 1990 the Communist Party was dissolved in Poland and replaced by two social democratic parties.

Other nations soon followed Poland's example. In Czechoslovakia, people took to the streets of the capital to demand reform. The government tried to break up the demonstration by force, but the police began to join the demonstrators. Having lost the backing of its security forces, the Czech government quickly gave in to demands for reform. In December, only six weeks after the first demonstrations had begun, the national legislature selected Vaclav Havel, a playwright and former dissident leader, as the country's new president. So smooth was the transition from communism in Czechoslovakia that people dubbed it the "Velvet Revolution."

The transition to a non-communist government proved less peaceful in Romania. Ruled by the ruthless dictator Nicolae Ceausescu (chow·SHES·koo), the people of Romania suffered one of the most repressive regimes in Eastern Europe. Ceausescu tried to crush pro-reform demonstrations with a brutal crackdown by Romania's secret police, but the demonstrators fought back. A brief civil war followed. By the end of the year, pro-democracy forces had captured Ceausescu, whom they executed for treason.

In East Germany the government came under increasing pressure throughout 1989 to open its borders. As communist governments in Czechoslovakia and Hungary loosened restrictions on their own borders with Western countries, many East Germans obtained permission to visit Czechoslovakia and Hungary. Once there, they fled to West Germany. Amid growing protest, the East German government agreed to open East Germany's borders at midnight on November 9, 1989. That night thousands of Berliners from East and West Germany alike assembled on either side of the infamous Berlin Wall—perhaps the most powerful symbol of the Iron Curtain. On the stroke of midnight, they raced to break holes in the wall or to climb over it. More than any other event, the fall of the Berlin Wall came to symbolize the triumph over communist tyranny.

The aftermath of communism. The end of communist rule in Eastern Europe held the promise of greater prosperity but also left many problems in its wake. The new governments of Eastern Europe soon set about the task of implementing democratic reform. Many adopted free-enterprise reforms to boost their economies. In March 1991 the member countries of the Warsaw Pact voted to disband the

The Berlin Wall came down in November of 1989 after dividing East and West Germany for nearly 30 years.

alliance. Some governments hoped for closer cooperation with the West, and in 1997, Poland, Hungary, and the Czech Republic were invited to become members of NATO.

At the same time, serious problems afflicted many countries. Eastern Europe lost its largest trading partner with the fall of the Soviet Union, and inefficient industries and outmoded factories rendered many regional economies uncompetitive with the West. Rising energy costs added to the economic problems of Eastern Europe as the region also lost its cheap supply of fuel with the fall of the Soviet Union. On top of these problems, decades of communist rule had taken an especially heavy toll on the environment. By the late 1990s, Eastern Europe remained among the world's most polluted regions.

Finally, the new freedoms that had been gained in Eastern Europe released old ethnic tensions. In 1992, Czechoslovakia split in two following the rise of a Slovak nationalist party in the eastern portion of the country. The result was the creation of the more prosperous Czech Republic and the poorer country of Slovakia. The breakup of Czechoslovakia came peacefully through the ballot box. Other areas were less fortunate. Massive civil unrest gripped Albania in the mid-1990s. In Yugoslavia, ethnic divisions produced one of the most hostile civil wars in the history of modern times.

Yugoslavia comprised a patchwork of ethnic groups, including Serbs, Croats, Slovenians, Macedonians, and Albanians. Many Yugoslavs shared a mutually comprehensible language; the main distinctions ran along religious lines. The Serbs were predominantly Eastern Orthodox; the Croats and Slovenians were predominantly Roman Catholic. The single largest segment of the population in the central province of Bosnia and Herzegovina, which had once formed part of the Ottoman Empire, adhered to Islam. These divisions erupted in bloody conflict as anticommunist reform took hold in Yugoslavia.

Yugoslavia began to unravel with the fall of communist governments across Eastern Europe. Serbia tried to exert dominance over the other groups, but the effect instead was to encourage Croatian and Slovenian nationalism. In 1991, Croatia and Slovenia declared their independence. As a result, bitter fighting broke out between Serbia and Croatia, ending in a truce that was mediated by the EEC and the United States. A UN peacekeeping force soon arrived to monitor the cease-fire. Though Croatia

Eastern European countries such as Poland, the former East Germany, the Czech Republic, Slovakia, and Hungary became some of the most polluted regions in the world.

paid a high price for its demand for freedom, Slovenia had managed to escape the fighting. Both had secured independence, however. In 1992, Bosnia followed suit and declared its independence.

In Bosnia's case, the greatest problem was the ethnic mix within the province. Muslims formed the single largest group, but they did not represent a majority. Nearly a third of Bosnia's population identified themselves as Serbian, while 17 percent claimed Croatian descent. Led by Radovan Karadzic, many Bosnian Serbs wished to remain part of Serbian-dominated Yugoslavia. Receiving aid from the Yugoslavian government in Belgrade, Bosnian Serb military units engaged in a program of **ethnic cleansing**—a campaign of terror and murder to drive Muslims out of those parts of Bosnia that the Bosnian Serbs claimed for themselves.

The United Nations imposed an arms embargo in an effort to end the fighting. The result harmed the Muslim-controlled Bosnian government's ability to resist the better-armed Serbs. In response to repeated Serb attacks, the UN declared certain areas of Bosnia to be "safe havens" under the protection of UN forces. The UN then began an investigation of Serbian atrocities.

Building History Study Skills

READ
WRITE
INTERPRET
CONNECT
THINK

Thinking About History: Conducting a Debate

A debate is a formal competition between two teams to determine which team has the greater skill in speaking and reasoning. The two sides publicly dispute an issue in a systematic way, appealing to logic and reason rather than to emotion.

How to Conduct a Debate

To conduct a debate, follow these steps.

1. Select the teams. There should be two teams, each composed of two or three members, although the size of the team may vary depending on the debate topic or the format used.

2. State the proposition. A proposition is a thesis statement or conclusion that the teams research and then discuss in the debate. The proposition is often stated as a resolution.

3. Prepare for the debate. Assign members of each team research on the proposition. Team members should organize the information into an orderly and logical outline called a brief. Arrange the points of the brief on index cards that may be used during the debate.

4. Conduct the debate. The debate itself should consist of two parts separated by an intermission. In the first part—the constructive speeches—each team presents its arguments. Members of each team speak alternately, beginning with the affirmative team. Each constructive speech is limited to eight minutes. Intermission follows. After the intermission, each team refutes the arguments of the opposing team in four-minute speeches called rebuttals.

Developing the Skill

Read the following proposition, the constructive speech of the affirmative side, and the rebuttal of the negative side.

Resolved: As a leading power in the Western alliance, the United States should contribute troops to the NATO Implementation Force (IFOR) deployed in Bosnia and Herzegovina to maintain the peace established by the Dayton Accord in 1995.

Affirmative Speech: The Dayton Accord has brought an end to the brutal civil war that gripped Bosnia between 1992 and 1995. The United States played a key role in mediating the agreement and must now play a key role in its implementation.

The dispatch of well-equipped American troops is critical to the effectiveness of the NATO IFOR in Bosnia. With advanced air power on hand, some question the need to send ground forces. Although modern air power offers a powerful means of retaliation, it cannot, however, hold territory.

Finally, the credibility of the United States as a world leader depends on a willingness to share in the danger and popular criticism of missions it expects allied governments to undertake.

Negative Rebuttal: While the United States should certainly use its diplomacy to re-establish peace in Bosnia, the deployment of American troops as part of IFOR is a flawed policy.

American leaders should have learned from the disastrous peacekeeping mission to Somalia in the early 1990s that troops cannot *impose* a lasting peace. Fighting is likely to resume once the troops are withdrawn. Aggressors will simply wait out the presence of peacekeeping forces. The alternative will be a permanent and unpopular stationing of troops in Bosnia.

Finally, throughout the postwar era the United States has carried the largest burden for European defense—not least because the Soviet Union posed a direct threat to the United States as well as to Europe. Bosnia, however, is essentially a European problem. Primary responsibility for its resolution should fall to our European allies.

Practicing the Skill

In a recent issue of your local newspaper or a news magazine, find an article that deals with a controversial issue. Use the article to write a proposition, and from this, develop and conduct a debate.

To apply this skill, see Applying History Study Skills on page 901.

American troops in a Bosnian village

This photo shows children playing at a new playground in a suburb of Dobrinja, Sarajevo. This same area had been totally surrounded by Serb forces for six months as part of their ethnic cleansing campaign.

Serbian aggression continued nonetheless. Continued shelling of Sarajevo, the Bosnian capital, combined with Serbian attacks on UN "safe havens," eventually prompted NATO to carry out extensive air strikes on Serbian targets in 1995.

The Bosnian Serbs agreed to enter peace talks mediated by the United States in Dayton, Ohio. The resulting agreement, known as the **Dayton Accord**, gave the Bosnian Serbs a degree of autonomy in certain areas, at the same time recognizing the overall sovereignty of Bosnia's Muslim-led government. In December 1995, NATO sent a joint military **Implementation Force**, or **IFOR**, to Bosnia to enforce the new peace. IFOR included large numbers of American troops.

At first the peace established in Bosnia by the Dayton Accord seemed to be holding. Its survival, however, seemed to depend on the continued presence of foreign troops. The future of Bosnia, like that of much of Eastern Europe, remained uncertain as the 1900s drew to a close.

Section 3 Review

1. **Define** Brezhnev Doctrine, perestroika, glasnost, CIS, ethnic cleansing, Dayton Accord, IFOR
2. **Identify** Mikhail Gorbachev, Boris Yeltsin, Lech Walesa, Vaclav Havel, Nicolae Ceausescu
3. **Locate and Explain the Significance** Estonia, Latvia, Lithuania, Republic of Georgia, Caspian Basin, Czech Republic, Slovakia, Bosnia and Herzegovina
4. **Understanding Ideas (a)** What kinds of reforms did Gorbachev introduce in the Soviet Union? **(b)** What role did these reforms play in the breakup of the Soviet Union?
5. **Synthesizing Ideas** How did the fall of communism affect the people of the former Soviet Union?
6. **Determining Cause and Effect** How did the fall of communism contribute to the resurgence of ethnic tensions in Eastern Europe?

Chapter 32 Review

A.D. 1974
Valéry Giscard d'Estaing becomes president of France.

A.D. 1975
Helsinki Accords are signed.

A.D. 1977
Free elections are held in Spain.

A.D. 1970   **A.D. 1972**   **A.D. 1974**   **A.D. 1976**   **A.D. 1978**

A.D. 1969
West Germany's *Ostpolitik* begins.

A.D. 1972
Watergate break-in occurs.

A.D. 1973
• OPEC oil embargo occurs.
• American troops are withdrawn from Vietnam.

A.D. 1976
Jimmy Carter is elected president of the United States.

A.D. 1979
• Full diplomatic relations begin between People's Republic of China and the United States.
• Soviet Union invades Afghanistan.
• Margaret Thatcher becomes prime minister of Great Britain.

Chapter Summary

The following list contains the key concepts you have learned about North America and Europe from 1969 to the present.

1. The Vietnam War had a long-lasting impact on the United States.

2. Many Americans lost faith in their government when the Watergate scandal was brought to the attention of the public in 1973.

3. Inflation and unemployment were among the economic problems that plagued the United States throughout the 1970s and into the mid-1980s. After a recovery during President Reagan's administration, the economy generally grew in the 1990s.

4. The nature of the American economy changed significantly during the 1970s and 1980s.

5. Efforts were made during the 1970s to ease tensions between the United States and the Soviet Union. The invasion of Afghanistan by the Soviet Union ended these efforts. However, by the mid-1980s, the two countries once again sought to establish better relations.

6. A separatist movement in Quebec threatened Canadian unity in the 1970s and again in the 1990s.

7. Relations between Canada and the United States have been close despite periodic friction.

8. During the 1970s many Western European nations turned to conservative governments to solve their economic problems.

9. The purpose and policies of NATO came under close scrutiny after the collapse of communism in Eastern Europe in 1989 and 1990.

10. The European Economic Community (EEC) grew in membership during the 1970s and 1980s; in 1993, with the Maastricht Treaty, it became the European Union (EU).

11. During the 1970s the Soviet Union repressed dissent both at home and in its satellite nations. At the same time, it sought to improve its relations with the West.

12. Mikhail Gorbachev introduced a number of reforms in the Soviet Union through the policies of glasnost and perestroika.

13. The nations of Eastern Europe moved from communism to democracy but continued to face economic and political problems.

14. Late in 1991 Gorbachev resigned, and the Soviet Union ceased to exist. Russia, one of the 15 independent nations created from this dissolution, engineered the Commonwealth of Independent States (CIS). Twelve of these nations joined the CIS.

Reviewing Important Terms

On a separate sheet of paper, supply the term that correctly completes each statement.

1. _____ is the name given to the improvement in relations between the United States and the Soviet Union during the 1970s.

2. West German chancellor Willy Brandt's efforts to create better relations between East and West became known as _____ .

3. Mikhail Gorbachev's policy of _____ loosened the reins of censorship and eased the repression of the Brezhnev years.

4. Through _____ , or restructuring, Mikhail Gorbachev planned to overhaul the political and economic systems of the Soviet Union.

5. _____ _____ is the name for a campaign of terror and murder to drive Muslims out of those parts of Bosnia that the Bosnian Serbs claimed for themselves.

Developing Critical Thinking Skills

1. **Analyzing Ideas (a)** What economic problems faced the United States in the 1970s and 1980s? **(b)** What policies did Presidents Ford, Carter, Reagan, Bush, and Clinton use to try to solve these problems?

2. **Comparing Ideas** What similarities and differences are there between the political changes that took place in Great Britain and those that took place in West Germany during the 1970s and 1980s?

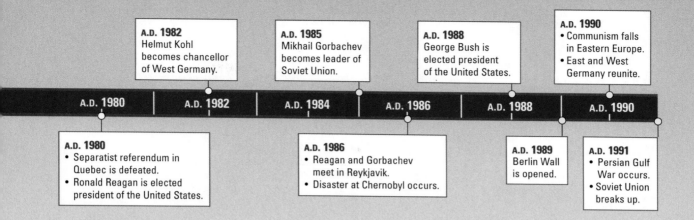

A.D. 1982
Helmut Kohl becomes chancellor of West Germany.

A.D. 1985
Mikhail Gorbachev becomes leader of Soviet Union.

A.D. 1988
George Bush is elected president of the United States.

A.D. 1990
• Communism falls in Eastern Europe.
• East and West Germany reunite.

A.D. 1980   A.D. 1982   A.D. 1984   A.D. 1986   A.D. 1988   A.D. 1990

A.D. 1980
• Separatist referendum in Quebec is defeated.
• Ronald Reagan is elected president of the United States.

A.D. 1986
• Reagan and Gorbachev meet in Reykjavik.
• Disaster at Chernobyl occurs.

A.D. 1989
Berlin Wall is opened.

A.D. 1991
• Persian Gulf War occurs.
• Soviet Union breaks up.

3. **Understanding Ideas** Why were the purpose and policies of NATO reassessed after the fall of communism in Eastern Europe?

4. **Summarizing Ideas** What progress has the EU made toward political unity in Western Europe?

5. **Organizing Ideas** How did glasnost and perestroika change life in the Soviet Union?

6. **Evaluating Ideas** The Nissan plant in Tennessee (below) is an example of Japan's economic expansion. Why did it become increasingly difficult for the United States to compete economically with Japan?

Relating Geography to History

Turn to the map on page 895. **(a)** Which former Soviet republics have not joined the Commonwealth of Independent States? **(b)** Which members of the Commonwealth of Independent States border Europe? **(c)** What benefits and disadvantages do you think are associated with joining the Commonwealth of Independent States?

Relating Past to Present

1. Canada's uneasiness about its relationship with the United States is not new. Using information in this textbook and in encyclopedias, trace the development of this feeling among Canadians, describing when such feelings have surfaced in the past.

2. Many political scientists have noted similarities between the reforms introduced in Czechoslovakia during the Prague Spring and Mikhail Gorbachev's policies of glasnost and perestroika. **(a)** What similarities do you see between the two? **(b)** Explain your answer.

Applying History Study Skills

Before completing this activity, review Building History Study Skills on page 898.

Conduct a debate, using the following steps and proposition or thesis statement.

Resolved: The nations of Western Europe should achieve political as well as economic unity.

1. Select teams.
2. State the proposition.
3. Prepare for the debate.
4. Conduct the debate.

internet**connect**

Search the Internet through the HRW Web site for recent events in one of the countries discussed in this chapter. Find out about major events in that country, and either create a time line of recent events or write a paragraph that could be added to the existing text about that country.

GO TO: go.hrw.com
KEYWORD: SCØ Current Events

Building Your Portfolio

1. **Presenting an Oral Report** Relations between Canadians who speak English and Canadians who speak French have occasionally been tense. Present an oral report on the differences between these two cultural groups. Your report should include a discussion of recent trends toward separatism and away from it. Place your notes and other research materials in your portfolio.

2. **Constructing a Chart** Use resources in the library to gather information on the economies of the nations of Eastern Europe. Note each nation's major industries, leading imports and exports, and chief trading partners. Construct a chart showing your findings. Place the chart in your portfolio.

The World in the Twenty-First Century

TIME

A.D. 1945–the present

A.D. 1945–the present

3.7 million B.C.   4000 B.C.   A.D. 2100

PLACE

The world and beyond

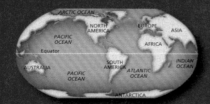

Lunar landing

Significance

The emotional scars of World War II remained, but people rebuilt their lives. Advances in technology and communication unified the world community. Satellites made it possible for millions of television viewers, otherwise separated by distance and ideas, to witness historic events as they occurred. Although it was a U.S. spacecraft that first achieved a manned lunar landing, astronaut Neil Armstrong represented all people on Earth when in 1969 he became the first human being to set foot on the moon.

In the 1970s and 1980s the United States embarked on an ambitious space exploration program. Television coverage of successful launches became almost routine. Then on January 28, 1986, millions of horrified television viewers watched in disbelief as the space shuttle *Challenger* disintegrated into a ball of flame shortly after liftoff.

Terms to Define

Discovery	acid rain
Spacelab	greenhouse effect
miniaturization	abstract
supercomputers	expressionism
laser	pop art
antibiotics	op art
DNA	conceptual art
genetic code	performance art
cloning	

People to Identify

Yuri Gagarin	Lina Wertmuller
Alan Shepard	Steven Spielberg
Neil Armstrong	Arthur Miller
Jackson Pollock	Ralph Ellison
Louise Nevelson	Alice Walker
George Balanchine	Salman Rushdie
Martha Graham	

Place to Locate

Chernobyl

Chapter Theme Questions

- **Technology** How might technological change affect ideas and behavior?
- **Social Relations** What challenges to well-being can people expect in the future?
- **The Arts** What direction did the arts and literature follow after World War II?

Throughout history the lure of the unknown has challenged people's courage, tested their ingenuity, and inspired them to embark on dangerous quests. Many individuals and groups of people have blazed the trail of human progress. Each era of history has provided unique challenges to its people.

We live in a time of rapid change—a time of promise and possibility. Many ideas that existed only in dreams and science fiction 50 years ago have become reality in the 1990s. Children in the 1940s could only imagine what it would be like to travel in space. Today children can watch the massive space shuttle slice through the clouds on its way to dock with an orbiting space station. Robot spaceships have even journeyed to Mars and beyond, gathering information about the universe.

Other frontiers remain on Earth—in science labs where researchers are discovering new treatments and cures for disease; in industry and business, where advancing technology is changing our lives; in the oceans, where scientists and engineers are exploring and tapping mineral resources on the ocean bottoms; and in classrooms, where traditional knowledge and fresh ideas are sparking a new generation to meet today's challenges, explore tomorrow's frontiers, and strive to enhance the quality of human life.

Section 1

Science and Technology

Focus Questions

- **What advances in travel and in space exploration have occurred since 1945?**
- **What impact have miniaturization and computerization had on modern life?**
- **What technological improvements have been made in medical science?**

Dramatic advances in science and technology after World War II affected all the nations of the world. Although industrialized societies felt the effects most directly, inventions, discoveries, and new technological devices also brought changes to developing nations. It is impossible to list all the discoveries and applications of new ideas that affected the way people thought and lived after 1945. However, a look at some spectacular developments illustrates the broad range and sweeping significance of the advances that have taken place in these decades of rapid change.

Faster Travel

Improvements in airplanes transformed travel throughout the world. Advances in air travel were a direct result of World War II. In the United States and Germany, for example, the search for better weapons led to the development of jet airplanes. After the war was over, these designs were adapted for civilian travel.

The first jetliner, the Boeing 707, began passenger service between the United States and Europe in 1958. By the mid-1960s, jetliner travel had become commonplace. The first commercial jumbo jet, the Boeing 747, began service in 1970. At speeds of more than 400 miles per hour, jets like the 747 could allow travel to nearly anywhere in the world in a matter of hours. Supersonic transport is a more recent development in air travel. The Concorde, a sleek airliner developed by the British and the French, travels at speeds of more than 1,000 miles per hour. It slashed travel time from Europe to the United States to three hours, though traveling on it was too expensive for most people. Meanwhile, complex traffic-control systems powered by sophisticated computers helped airports deal with ever-increasing air traffic.

While air travel became the most popular and convenient way to reach distant places, other means of transportation also advanced rapidly. Trains in Japan and Europe sped through the countryside at more than 150 miles per hour. Automobile use increased around the world. From 1950 to 1995, annual world production of motor vehicles jumped from about 10.5 million to nearly 50 million. And in 1994 Europeans welcomed a new link between Great Britain and France with the completion of the Channel Tunnel under the English Channel.

Space Exploration

Although Canada, Japan, and several Western European nations have developed space exploration programs, the United States and the Soviet Union have dominated the space race. The Soviets achieved the earliest successes. As the 1960s progressed, however, the United States stepped up its program.

Early successes. The Space Age began on October 4, 1957, when the Soviet Union launched *Sputnik*, the world's first space satellite, into orbit around Earth. Then in 1961 the Soviets built a rocket with enough power to put a person into orbit around Earth, and Soviet astronaut Yuri Gagarin became the first person to orbit Earth.

The United States had already begun its own ambitious program for space exploration. Now, however, the United States space program expanded rapidly. In 1958 the United States successfully launched an unmanned satellite into space, and in 1961 Alan Shepard became the first American to travel in space. In March 1965 the first Soviet astronaut walked in space, and by August the United States had responded with the 20-minute space walk of Edward White.

Lunar landing. On July 20, 1969, the United States won the intense race to put the first person on the moon. The Apollo XI mission transported three American astronauts—Neil Armstrong, Edwin E. Aldrin, Jr., and Michael Collins—to the moon aboard the spaceship *Columbia*. While Collins stayed behind on the *Columbia* to help coordinate the mission, Armstrong and Aldrin descended to the surface of the moon aboard the lunar module, the *Eagle*. The following excerpt from the transmission between *Eagle* at Tranquility Base on the moon, the orbiting spacecraft *Columbia*, and two control teams—Apollo XI Control and Mission Control—in Houston, Texas, illustrates the triumph of this historic event.

> **"EAGLE:** Houston, Tranquility Base here. The *Eagle* has landed. . . .
> HOUSTON: Roger, Tranquility. Be advised there are lots of smiling faces in this room and all over the world. . . .
> HOUSTON (10:37): Neil, this is Houston. What's your status on hatch opening?
> TRANQUILITY BASE: Everything is go here. . . . We're going to try it. The hatch is coming open. . . .
> ARMSTRONG: Okay, Houston, I'm on the porch. . . .
> HOUSTON: We're getting a picture on the TV. . . .
> ARMSTRONG: I'm at the foot of the ladder. . . . the surface appears to be very, very fine-grained. . . . I'm going to step off the LM [lunar module] now.
> That's one small step for a man, one giant leap for mankind.**"**

Edwin Aldrin joined Neil Armstrong on the moon's surface and for the next two hours the astronauts took photographs, collected lunar soil and rocks, planted a U.S. flag on the moon's surface, and conducted experiments. About 22 hours after the *Eagle* had landed, the astronauts left the moon and returned to the command module. On July 24, 1969, they returned to Earth.

The world watched, listened, and followed the quest for knowledge about space into the 1970s, when the main results of space exploration came from unmanned spacecraft.

Unmanned spacecraft. After a series of manned moon landings from 1969 to 1972, the U.S. space program shifted its emphasis to unmanned spacecraft that explored deep into our solar system. Late in 1973, 21 months after its launch, *Pioneer 10* became the first spacecraft to fly by Jupiter. Then in mid-1976, *Viking 1* and *Viking 2* landed on Mars, the "red planet." For several years they sent information back to Earth that provided a vivid picture of the planet's makeup.

Voyager 1 and *Voyager 2*, launched in 1977, explored the more distant planets of the solar system. Both made flybys of Jupiter and Saturn between 1979 and 1981, sending back spectacular photographs. Then *Voyager 2* continued to the outer reaches of the solar system. It encountered the planet Uranus in 1986 and by 1989 had reached Neptune.

After a break of some years, the United States restarted its unmanned space exploration program in 1989 with the *Magellan* and *Galileo* missions. *Magellan* began orbiting and sending back information from Venus in 1990, mapping nearly the entire surface of the planet. *Galileo* went into orbit around Jupiter in December 1995, transmitting data about the planet and its moons. In 1997 the *Cassini* spacecraft was launched on a mission to Saturn.

One of the most dramatic accomplishments in the mid-1990s was the landing of another U.S. spacecraft on Mars. The *Pathfinder*, which touched down on July 4, 1997, provided scientists with strong evidence that there had once been water on Mars—the key ingredient for creating and sustaining life.

Satellites. The United States, the Soviet Union, and other countries have launched satellites into

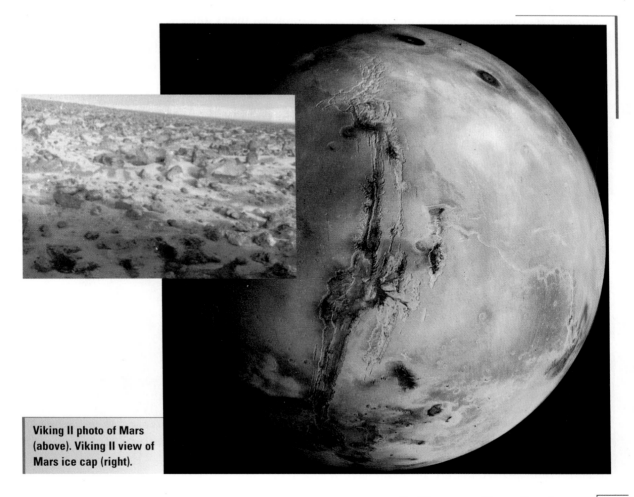

Viking II photo of Mars (above). Viking II view of Mars ice cap (right).

orbit around Earth. These satellites are divided into several types: communications, weather, Earth observation, navigation, and military.

Communications satellites act as relay stations, receiving radio signals from one location and transmitting them to another. Weather satellites help scientists study and forecast the weather. Earth observation satellites locate resources—such as minerals and water—on Earth. They also allow scientists to study the sources and effects of pollution. Navigation satellites allow people operating aircraft, ships, and land vehicles to determine their locations. Military satellites track movements of military equipment and determine where weapons are placed.

New frontiers in space. The 1980s and 1990s brought even greater American and Soviet advances in manned space flight. A new phase of space exploration began in 1981 with the launch of the first U.S. space shuttle, *Columbia*. By 1986 these reusable shuttles, which incorporated elements of both the traditional space capsule and the airplane, had completed two dozen successful missions. Everyone thought that the launch of the *Challenger* on January 28, 1986, would be another routine success. However, 73 seconds after liftoff the shuttle broke apart, disintegrating into a ball

of flame. The *Challenger* and its crew of seven were lost. The disaster halted the United States' manned exploration of space until the successful launch of the shuttle *Discovery* in 1988. That same year, the Soviet Union successfully launched an unmanned space shuttle.

The United States and the Soviet Union also challenged each other in the development of space stations, which are orbiting observation centers. The Soviets led the way with the launch of *Salyut 1* in 1971. Two years later, the United States followed with *Skylab*. These two craft provided an opportunity to do experimental work in geography, engineering, medicine, and many other fields of study. They also allowed scientists to test the effects of long-term space travel on humans. The Soviets launched several more space stations, including *Mir* in 1986, but the United States ended its space station program and focused on the development of the shuttle. *Spacelab*, a joint venture of several European nations, took the place of a permanent space station. This module, carried in the space shuttle's cargo bay, provided the facilities needed to carry out large-scale experiments in space. In 1990, the crew of the shuttle *Discovery* placed into orbit the Hubble Space Telescope, a sophisticated orbiting observatory.

Science experiments were performed in a weightless environment during the Life and Microgravity Mission aboard *Columbia* in 1996. This photograph shows an earlier launch of the reusable shuttle.

Although for many years the United States and the Soviet Union raced against each other in the conquest of space, the end of the Cold War has brought about a greater spirit of cooperation. In 1975, for example, the Soviet *Soyuz* craft docked in orbit with the U.S. *Apollo*. The Soviet cosmonauts and U.S. astronauts then worked together on experiments for two days. In 1995 the United States space shuttle *Atlantis* docked with Russia's space station *Mir*. However, by 1997, *Mir* was experiencing increasing problems, and the station's continued operation was called into question.

Miniaturization

Possibly the most important influence on the design of aircraft and spacecraft is weight. Researchers are always looking for ways to decrease the weight of equipment without making it weaker or less effective. Therefore, inventing ways to make machines, especially electrical equipment, smaller and lighter was a significant consequence of air and space travel. This process is known as **miniaturization**.

The best-known device that resulted from miniaturization is the transistor. This tiny electronic device, invented in 1947, came to replace the much larger vacuum tube. In fact, one transistor could do the work of many vacuum tubes more efficiently. Within 25 years, numerous transistors and other components could be placed on an integrated circuit—a tiny wafer of material, usually silicon.

Miniaturization made possible dozens of new products that affect the activities of people around the world. Portable radios, pocket calculators, digital watches, and automatic cameras were developed as part of this process. Initially, these products were expensive and not widely available. However, costs fell rapidly as technology advanced and the demand for such products increased.

Computerization

The most remarkable product of miniaturization was the modern computer. In the 1600s the French scientist Blaise Pascal invented the first automatic calculator, which worked by means of wheels linked to each other by gears. The idea intrigued scientists and engineers over the next 300 years. In the 1830s Charles Babbage designed a mechanical calculating machine that he called the "analytical engine." His machine is often seen as the forerunner of the modern computer, since it included all of a computer's basic elements: data storage, memory, a system for moving between the memory and storage components, and an input device. Babbage was not, however, able to construct the device he had designed.

ENIAC (Electronic Numerical Integrator and Calculator) was an enormous computer built in 1946. It took up an entire room at the University of Pennsylvania, where it was constructed. The discovery of transistors and later development of integrated circuits made possible much smaller machines capable of storing and rapidly processing information. These computers, which scientists improved year after year, quickly

Computer chips, such as this one, seem astoundingly small considering the extensive amount of information they contain.

made an impact on society. They advanced in both speed and efficiency, while requiring less and less space to store gigantic amounts of information. Integrated circuits opened the door to wider application of computer power. They found their way into machines and appliances of all shapes and sizes, from automobiles to self-focusing cameras to microwave ovens.

By the 1990s computers were performing a multitude of functions and affecting people's lives in dramatic ways. For example, computers make it possible for doctors to diagnose diseases and treat patients more effectively than ever before. CAT (computerized axial tomography) scanners, MRI (magnetic resonance imaging) machines, and other complex devices allow doctors and technicians to view the human body in incredible detail. As a result, many medical problems that once would have required exploratory surgery can now be diagnosed with little risk or discomfort to the patient. Outside the medical field, computers serve to guide spacecraft, operate manufacturing equipment, record airline reservations, print newspapers, construct maps, diagnose automotive problems, and perform a broad range of other functions.

In addition, large and powerful **supercomputers** help provide solutions to complex scientific and engineering problems that not long ago would have been all but impossible to solve. Because supercomputers have more than one processing unit, they can perform billions of computations per second. Supercomputers have revolutionized methods of research, development, and experimentation. For instance, scientists and engineers use supercomputers in the aerospace, petroleum, and automotive industries. They allow engineers to create exact models of what they are studying. Supercomputers are now used widely in weather forecasting, where numerical models are part of the forecasting process.

Today computers increasingly affect people's daily lives. Desktop and lightweight laptop computers are common in offices, homes, schools, and libraries. Businesses use computers to process and store enormous amounts of financial and administrative information—everything from customers' credit-card transactions to employees' retirement benefits. The range of activities controlled or facilitated by computers is growing daily. Meanwhile, computers continue to increase in power and speed while shrinking in size and cost.

Communications

In the decades after World War II, technological advances made radio and then television affordable to more people. Radio and television made it possible to transmit ideas and information more rapidly and widely than ever before.

Computers and the Internet. The advent of computers added a dramatically new dimension to the information revolution. The Internet, a vast global network that connects many computer networks, allows computer users to communicate with one another over telephone lines. Through the Internet, people all over the world can exchange information—words, pictures, and sound—nearly instantaneously. By the mid-1990s, the Internet linked millions of computers all over the globe.

The impact of computer communications is profound. In the comfort of their homes or offices, computer users have worldwide electronic access to stunning amounts of information. In addition, individuals can communicate with one another through e-mail—electronic messages transmitted almost instantaneously. Furthermore, companies can use the Internet to transact business, carry out research, and market their products.

Other innovations. Besides desktop computers, many other important communications innovations came into use over the past several decades. In the 1970s photocopiers established themselves as essential business machines. In the 1980s and 1990s fax machines became affordable and widespread. By the mid-1990s, cellular phones were common. Fiber-optic cables, which use light instead of electricity or radio waves to send signals, offered a faster and better alternative to other types of cables for telecommunications.

The thick layer covering this statue in Venice, Italy, was built up through hundreds of years of rain and air pollution, and was removed by laser cleaning.

Lasers

In 1960 a U.S. scientist built the first laser, although the idea of the laser had been conceived during the 1950s. A **laser** concentrates light and releases it in an intense beam that travels in a straight line. The laser's uses are extraordinarily varied, including applications in medicine, industry, and communications.

Doctors use lasers to repair damaged tissue in the eye and to burn away unhealthy tissue. Lasers help manufacturers cut precisely into hard substances, such as metal or diamonds. Lasers also transmit radio, television, and telephone signals. They can even be used to clean delicate pieces of art. Scientists are continuing to find new uses for this versatile invention.

Medical Science

Not all the advances that followed World War II involved physics or electronics. Biologists and other scientists made significant breakthroughs in their battle against disease.

Antibiotics. In 1928 the British scientist Alexander Fleming discovered a substance he called penicillin, noting that it stopped the growth of many types of bacteria. Thus it could help cure illnesses caused by those bacteria. In the years after Fleming's discovery, other substances were found to have similar effects. Streptomycin, which was discovered in 1944, attacked some bacteria that could resist penicillin. Substances that destroy or limit bacterial growth are called **antibiotics**, and after 1945 these "wonder drugs" transformed the fight against disease. They cured certain illnesses, such as tuberculosis, that previously had had no cure, and they lessened the risk of infection following surgery. Although some bacteria came to resist antibiotics, these medicines became essential in reducing sicknesses and preventing the contamination of food.

Vaccines. Medical researchers also made remarkable progress in preventing disease. Jonas Salk's polio vaccine was released for general use in 1954. In 1960, Albert Sabin produced an oral polio vaccine, which began to be used in 1961. As a consequence, polio has been all but eliminated in developed countries. Similarly, a worldwide campaign against smallpox virtually eliminated the disease by the 1980s. The last known naturally occurring cases of smallpox occurred in 1977.

AIDS. The first cases of AIDS (acquired immunodeficiency syndrome) in the United States were reported in the early 1980s. From the beginning of the epidemic to the middle of 1996, the United Nations

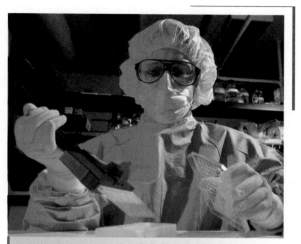

Medical researchers, such as this one, continue studying HIV, the virus that causes AIDS.

UNAIDS program had recorded 30 million cases of HIV/AIDS around the world.

While there is as yet no known cure for the disease and no vaccine to prevent it, researchers have had increasing success in fighting the progress of the disease with combinations of powerful new drugs. Research continues, but until a cure is found or a vaccine developed, efforts to combat the disease rely on education programs that teach people how HIV, the virus that causes AIDS, is spread and how it can be prevented.

Genetic Research and Biotechnology

In 1962 the Nobel Prize for medicine, the most prestigious scientific award in the world, was given to an American, James D. Watson, and two British scientists, Maurice Wilkins and Francis Crick, who had discovered the structure of **DNA** (deoxyribonucleic acid) in 1953. DNA is an essential component of genes—the small units of chromosomes that convey characteristics, such as color of hair and eyes, from parent to child. By understanding DNA, one can understand how a gene is structured—what scientists call the **genetic code**.

By unraveling the genetic code, the DNA experimenters came closer to explaining how different life forms are created. This breakthrough made possible new research into viruses, bacteria, human cells, and diseases such as cancer.

Cloning. The process of manipulating a cell from an animal so as to produce a genetically identical duplicate of that animal is referred to as **cloning**.

The Global Economy

In one day, traders on Wall Street buy and sell a record number of shares as confidence in the market soars. The next day, stock markets in London, Paris, and Tokyo rally. A month later, discouraging economic trends in Japan cause Asian markets to dive sharply. Within minutes, investors across the globe are selling stocks in record numbers. Both scenarios are possible in today's global economy. Modern digital communication allows information to spread almost instantaneously. One result is a global economy in which many economic entities are linked and react to one another's activities. Though the nature of today's global economy is historically unprecedented, economic interdependence has existed for thousands of years.

By the second millennium B.C., the Phoenicians dominated the world trade scene. By about 1100 B.C., Phoenician colonies which bordered the Mediterranean Sea in present-day Spain, northern Africa, and Sicily connected commerce throughout the entire region. Purple-dyed garments were instantly recognizable as the work of Phoenician craftspeople, and the glass, cedar, wine, metalwork, and ivory of Phoenicians could be found in virtually any major trade center located along the Mediterranean Sea.

Unlike the sea routes of the Mediterranean, the Silk Road served as an overland link between east and west.

Established between about 300 B.C. and 200 B.C., the 4,000 mile trade route stretched from China to a point in Southwest Asia. Goods were then transferred to ports located along the Mediterranean, where they eventually found their way to western markets. The Chinese traded their valuable silks for western wools, gold, and silver.

Sea and river routes determined the trade landscape of the Middle Ages. Generally, the northern trade routes dealt in common bulk goods, and southern traders specialized in luxury items from the east, such as spices and silks. These separate European trading contingents occasionally overlapped. At large-scale international fairs in Flanders and Champagne, goods from virtually anyplace in the known world could be bought and sold.

In the 1200's, a group of about 150 north German merchants formed the Hanseatic League. For several hundred years, the trade association dominated economic exchanges in northern Europe. They obtained trading rights in the Baltics, Flanders, England, and Scandinavia. Traders might start with goods from the Baltics, exchange those goods in transactions from Norway to England to Flanders, and return to the Baltics with items that would normally be unavailable in the region. Goods that were traded included everyday staples, such as English wool, Baltic

Left: Medieval Port of Venice

Above: Phoenician trading ship (c. 700 B.C.)
Right: The Steelyard-Depot of the Hanseatic Merchants in London

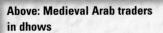

Above: Medieval Arab traders in dhows

grains, Flanders cloth, and Scandinavian fish. The trading partners of the Hanseatic League benefited from guidelines that promoted independence while at the same time encouraging cooperation among the trading partners.

In the southern European trading sphere, Asian spices and luxurious fabrics traveled from the eastern Mediterranean to central and northern European centers, where nobles purchased them. Favorably situated between the Byzantine Empire to the east and European states to the north and west, Venice became a dominant international trade force of the Middle Ages and was a key mover of exotic goods.

In the 1600's and the 1700's, European conquest and colonization on the Indian subcontinent and in the Americas radicalized the character of the global economy. Through special charters, Britain, France, Spain, and the Netherlands gained nearly exclusive trade rights and authority over the inhabitants of certain regions.

However, the growing number of western trade routes had the greatest impact on the global economy. Interests in sugar plantations in the Caribbean—and slave laborers from Africa to work them—soon made trade routes across the Atlantic the most lucrative in the world.

Today, the largest trade organization in the modern Western world is the European Union (EU). The EU boasts 15 member nations that engage in tariff-free trade, bolstering their own economies while enjoying the benefits of trade with other members. In addition to trading with member countries, EU nations also trade with nations across the globe.

In 1992, the North American Free Trade Agreement (NAFTA) eliminated all existing tariffs and trade barriers among Canada, the United States, and Mexico. Such trading partnerships can foster interdependence of nations by creating a larger, unified market of people buying and selling goods and services. However, economic interdependence can create inequities, as well. Opponents of NAFTA have argued that for the

Signing of NAFTA agreement

Meeting of the New European Commission

United States, for instance, the enticement of lower manufacturing costs in Mexico might lead to lost jobs in the United States. Such perceived imbalances must be negotiated in a global economy.

In the past, the international economy was often dominated by one trading power that was virtually unaffected by its trading partners. Today, this scenario is unlikely. Modern nations have forged economic links in which every partner feels the effects of the others' actions. In the early 1990s, for example, when many Asian countries experienced phenomenal economic growth, nations around the globe saw investment opportunities and sank money into the region. In the late 1990's, when markets in Japan, Hong Kong, and other Asian countries suffered serious financial setbacks, the global economy reeled. Markets in North America, Europe, and Latin America experienced losses of varying degrees.

English dignitary of the East India Company being transported by elephant

Genetic Engineering

Since the dawn of humanity, our ancestors have struggled to alter their environment in order to survive. Prehistoric people shaped the natural resources around them into tools, weapons, clothing, and shelter. Through thousands of years of human history, we have learned to effectively control our environment through new developments in food production, housing, travel, and communication. We have learned to control the microscopic environment around us by stopping the spread of infectious diseases, curing infections with antibiotics, and preventing disease with vaccination. Today we are on the edge of being able to control our "internal environment"—the genes that determine our physical heredity—the color of our eyes, our height, and our susceptibility to colon cancer or heart disease.

In the 1980s, scientists began to use genetic engineering to alter genes in plants and animals to produce bigger or better food sources. Today, scientists are involved in perhaps the most dramatic project since the development of the atomic bomb—the Human Genome Project, which is mapping all the genes of the human body. As scientists discover the location and function of individual genes, they have identified genes that cause or contribute to certain diseases: Alzheimer's disease,

Dr. Ian Wilmut and his cloned ewe Dolly

breast cancer, and skin cancer. Scientists are also learning how to use gene therapy—replacing defective genes with normal ones.

This new knowledge and ability has raised some thorny ethical questions: Will insurance companies be able to refuse coverage based on genetic information? Can criminals claim their gene for excessive aggression is responsible for their criminal behavior? Should people be allowed to create "designer babies" by selecting specific characteristics such as hair color, eye color, or musical ability? Bioethicists are still struggling with such questions as our ability to control our genetic structures continues to grow.

In 1997 researchers at the Roslin Institute in Edinburgh, Scotland, successfully cloned a sheep. This was the first mammal ever cloned from a single cell of an adult animal. Some experts believe that within the next decade scientists might have the ability to clone humans.

The Atom

Just as biologists were able to probe inside the cell, physical scientists became more knowledgeable about the smallest of nature's building blocks, the atom. With increasingly powerful instruments, scientists could examine the tiny particles within the atom. They soon learned how to use the energy released when the structure of the atom is altered.

Atomic energy was first used to build more powerful bombs. Later it was used to develop efficient

generators to produce electricity for a growing population. Whenever atomic energy is tapped, dangerous radiation, known as radioactivity, is released. When carefully controlled, radioactivity can have extremely beneficial medical uses—for example, in the treatment of cancer. Extensive uncontrolled exposure to radioactivity, however, can alter genes and kill life forms.

The disastrous explosion at the Chernobyl nuclear power plant in the Soviet Union in 1986 provided a vivid illustration of radiation's dangers. (See Chapter 32.) The explosion spread significant amounts of radioactive material over parts of Europe. Tens of thousands of people living near Chernobyl had to be evacuated. Numerous people subsequently died of radiation-related illnesses. Cancer rates jumped, as did the frequency of birth defects, a trend that doctors anticipated would continue for decades.

The explosion at Chernobyl was the world's worst nuclear accident, and it brought into focus people's doubts about the safety of nuclear energy. Consequently, opposition to nuclear power increased in many countries. Nevertheless, by 1995, there were 437 nuclear power plants in 31 countries. And even though disenchantment with nuclear power had grown, advances in the understanding of the atom continued to offer benefits. For example, researchers in nuclear physics developed new methods for diagnosing and treating disease. Other scientists devised new approaches to preserving food.

Plastics

The first synthetic substances—substances that do not occur in nature—were developed by chemists in laboratories in the 1800s. A few of these substances began to have wide applications. For example, celluloid was used to make movie film, and Bakelite was used for telephones, pot handles, and electrical equipment. It was not until the 1940s, however, that these synthetic substances, called plastics, began to appear in every area of life.

Plastics became an essential part of daily existence. They completely altered the appearance as well as the manufacture of most of the products people use, from toothbrushes to telephones. Synthetic fibers were woven into easy-care fabrics for clothing and upholstery. By the mid-1990s, plastics were being used to make everything from automobiles and household appliances to desktop computers and disposable medical products. Many plastics are made from petroleum products. Therefore, the petroleum industry became increasingly important as the demand for plastics grew.

Technology's Continuing Impact

Since 1945 technological advances have virtually transformed the world. Devices such as telephones, radios, refrigerators, and cameras existed before 1945. However, only after 1945 were they manufactured inexpensively enough for millions of people to buy them. These products are more common in the industrialized nations, but they have also had an enormous impact on life in the developing nations of the world.

What was so remarkable in the period after 1945 was the widespread application of these modern products. New industries, such as television and computer manufacturing, sprang up. Millions of people were employed in new kinds of jobs, and world markets flourished as nations traded the products of the new technological age.

Scientists working for the military also found applications for these advances in technology. Some of their developments were used in battle for the first time during the Persian Gulf War of 1991. Computer guidance systems directed Tomahawk cruise missiles toward targets hundreds of miles away. Computer-operated Patriot missiles intercepted and destroyed Iraqi SCUD missiles. Radar guidance warned the Patriots' computers of the SCUDs' approach.

These "smart" weapons systems and such everyday consumer items as portable computers, video recorders, microwave ovens, and laser printers represent extraordinary advances in the field of technology. Yet, these technological advances are only a hint of technological developments still to come.

Section 1 Review

1. **Define** *Discovery, Spacelab,* miniaturization, supercomputers, laser, antibiotics, DNA, genetic code, cloning
2. **Identify** Yuri Gagarin, Alan Shepard, Neil Armstrong
3. **Locate and Explain the Significance** Chernobyl
4. **Summarizing Ideas** Describe how exploration of space has moved from competition between major powers to cooperation.
5. **Classifying Ideas** List three technological or scientific advances that have taken place since 1945. Explain the importance of each.
6. **Analyzing Ideas** Explain how technology can be both a benefit and a burden.

Section 2

Health and Human Rights

Focus Questions

- How do population pressures affect the well-being of the people of the world today?
- What types of environmental problems are the people of the world trying to solve?
- What are human rights abuses, and how are the nations of the world dealing with them?

The second half of the 1900s was a time of significant political, economic, and social change. In industrialized nations, standards of living generally improved and opportunities multiplied. Change in developing nations was less dramatic, but there, too, most people's lives benefited from technological and scientific advances. Still, progress brought new challenges, and global cooperation became more important than ever as a means of dealing with the world's problems.

Population Pressures

One of the most noteworthy—and startling—developments to occur during the postwar decades was the rapid growth in world population. Between 1930 and 1950, world population increased by about 23 percent. In the next four decades, however, population increased by 112 percent, reaching 5.3 billion people in 1990. And by mid-1997, the world population had soared to 5.8 billion. The U.S. Census Bureau projects it will reach 7.6 billion by 2020 and 9.3 billion by 2050.

This explosive growth resulted from a combination of factors. Medical advances and improvements in health and sanitation practices caused a striking decline in death rates, both in infants and adults.

While better medical care helped keep people alive, scientific research helped feed them. In the 1960s scientists developed seeds that yielded much more rice and wheat than ever before. The use of chemical fertilizers and advances in irrigation methods and farming techniques further improved crop yields. This Green Revolution, as it came to be known, increased food production in many poor countries, helping people to lead longer, healthier lives.

Most of the world's population growth occurred in developing nations, such as those in Asia and Latin America. The most rapidly growing region of all, however, was Africa. As the number of people on Earth continued to multiply, scientists and economists became increasingly concerned with the consequences of overpopulation.

Although populations are increasing in developing countries, increases have been slowing throughout the century in North America and Europe. Many economists are concerned that the rapidly growing populations in developing countries will cancel the economic advances of these areas. Moreover, rapid population growth in some of the world's poorer nations has contributed to political instability and social discontent, particularly when there is a great gap between the rich and the poor.

Human migration. Adding to the challenges of population growth are the effects of large-scale migrations. After World War II, some 400,000 refugees came to the United States. Since the 1960s, the United States has experienced an influx of immigrants from Asia and Latin America. This is a change from the historical immigration pattern of the United States, in which most immigrants came from Europe.

Large-scale migrations occur for many reasons, including war, famine, political changes, a search for fertile soil, and ethnic rivalries. In the Middle East in the early 1990s, as many as 5 million people sought safety in Turkey, Iran, and other countries during the 1991 Persian Gulf War. In Rwanda in the mid-1990s a bloody civil war between the country's two major ethnic groups caused the movement of large numbers of people.

Urban growth. Migration from rural areas to urban areas—a trend known as urbanization—has swelled city populations around the world. Indeed, urban populations in many countries are increasing much more rapidly than rural populations.

Thirty years ago, about 25 percent of the world's population lived in cities of 20,000 or more. By 1980, this figure had increased to about 40 percent. By 2000, that number is estimated to approach 50 percent. Such explosive urban growth has severely challenged the resources of cities.

From Mexico City to Cairo to Calcutta, overcrowding has strained governments' ability to provide adequate health and human services. As cities have expanded, both jobs and housing have become scarce. Some cities have experienced water shortages.

Positive steps. Various efforts are under way to deal with problems related to world population growth. Some governments have promoted programs to limit the birth rate. The Chinese government, for example, undertook a campaign in the 1970s to persuade families to have no more than one child. Still, in many parts of the world, large families continue to be common.

Scientists are working to develop further agricultural methods and technology in order to increase world food production. For example, they are exploring ways to make deserts fertile and to farm the oceans. In addition, using genetic engineering, they are trying to produce food crops that can grow in Earth's driest regions.

While researchers work to produce more food for the world's hungry, the Red Cross, United Nations agencies, and other groups try to help those in need. For example, after the famine and severe economic problems in Nigeria in the 1960s and 1970s and the destruction in Cambodia in the 1970s, relief organizations fed millions of starving people. Governments and organizations are also trying to improve food distribution so that available food reaches victims of famine and malnutrition.

Environmental Concerns

Technological and scientific advances, while improving the quality of life for many people in the world, did not come without cost. As industries grew and as developing countries struggled to build their own industries, industrial waste products polluted Earth's air, water, and land. Moreover, pollution and land development posed a growing danger to animal and plant life. People around the world came to realize that cooperative efforts were essential to clean up, preserve, and protect the environment.

Acid rain. One of the most devastating kinds of pollution is **acid rain**. Acid rain forms when precipitation falls through air polluted by toxins produced by the burning of fossil fuels. Acid rain pollutes water, kills fish, and ravages forests. It can also damage buildings. The destructive effects of acid rain have been felt in North America, Europe, and other parts of the world. In recent years many nations have cooperated to reduce emissions from motor vehicles and factories. Unfortunately, according to studies in 1996, the acidity of waters in Europe had not yet decreased.

Pesticides. Industrialization was not the only cause of pollution. Farming methods of the Green Revolution relied in part on the use of pesticides. Pesticides increase crop production, but they can be dangerous. As biologist Rachel Carson pointed out in her 1962 book *Silent Spring,* pesticides are not selective; they poison all living things with which they come into contact.

When sulfur dioxide and nitrogen oxide are released into the atmosphere, they combine with water vapor to produce sulfuric and nitric acids. This highly acidic precipitation is particularly damaging to aquatic organisms and plant life. Shown in the photo is the Giant Mountains National Park in northeast Bohemia. The park is dying from acid rain.

Waste disposal. Industrialization and population growth increased the amount of waste produced. National and local governments looked for ways to handle both toxic and nontoxic waste. Some governments wanted to export their waste elsewhere, but environmentalists objected that one city or country should not become the waste dump for another. Government and industry leaders in many nations are working to reduce waste products, encourage recycling, and find safe ways to dispose of hazardous wastes.

Endangered species. World population growth and industrialization increases the need for land and other natural resources, leading to the destruction of forests, wetlands, and other areas. Losing these natural habitats threatens the survival of numerous plant and animal species. Rain forests, for example, are being destroyed so quickly that thousands of species are being lost each year. Scientists are concerned about this reduction of biodiversity, the natural variety of plants and animals that naturally occurs in the environment. This loss of biodiversity could have damaging effects on humans as well as the environment.

Ozone depletion. Some scientists warn that pollution is depleting the ozone layer of the stratosphere. Ozone is a gas that shields Earth against the Sun's ultraviolet rays, which can cause skin cancer in humans and damage animal and plant life. Some scientists believe that a leading cause of ozone depletion is the use of chemicals called chlorofluorocarbons (CFCs), used in aerosol sprays, coolants, and the manufacture of electronic parts and plastics. Although scientists did not agree on the cause of ozone depletion, during the 1980s and 1990s many countries began to phase out or ban the use of CFCs.

Global warming. Carbon dioxide and other gases in Earth's atmosphere allow the Sun's rays to warm the planet but do not let the heat radiating from Earth to escape. This **greenhouse effect** helps keep Earth's temperature at levels suitable for life. According to many scientists, the burning of oil, coal, and natural gas has increased the amounts of these gases in the atmosphere, trapping more heat and contributing to a rise in global temperatures. While scientists do not agree on just how great a danger global warming represents, many warn that temperatures may rise by as much as 6°F by 2100. Such an increase could have devastating consequences. For example, if portions of the polar ice caps were to melt, sea levels would rise, and low-lying areas of the world would be flooded.

Global responses. People around the world are making an increasing effort to deal with environmental concerns. Numerous organizations have been established to meet challenges to the environment. For example, Greenpeace, an international organization, has fought against various practices that they believe are dangerous to the environment, such as offshore oil drilling, dumping of radioactive wastes into the oceans, and whaling.

In the past several decades, the United Nations has sponsored international meetings on environmental matters. During this time, several international agreements have addressed such issues as endangered species, the ozone layer, and hazardous wastes. In 1992, delegates from 178 nations attended the United Nations environmental conference, nicknamed the "Earth Summit," in Brazil. Several significant agreements emerged from this conference, including one on the prevention of climate change and one on the preservation of biodiversity.

Human Rights Issues

The horrors of World War II underscored the need to protect human rights around the world. In the preamble to its 1945 charter, the newly formed United Nations (UN) declared:

> **"**We the peoples of the United Nations, determined . . . to reaffirm faith in fundamental human rights, in the dignity and worth of the human person, in the equal rights of men and women and of nations large and small, . . . have resolved to combine our efforts to accomplish these aims.**"**

In 1948, the UN adopted the Universal Declaration of Human Rights, outlining basic human rights to which every person is entitled.

However, while the Declaration and subsequent UN agreements demonstrated the international community's concern for human rights, they were not binding on all nations, and they provided no means of enforcement. Indeed, most countries insisted that any attempt at enforcement would violate their national sovereignty. This opposition to external interference in internal affairs persists as a major obstacle to international human rights protection.

The pursuit of human rights. Even though the United Nations continues to address human rights abuses around the world, such abuses remain all too common. Human rights violations often have political, ethnic, racial, or religious roots. For example, brutal "ethnic cleansing" during the civil war in Bosnia resulted in thousands of deaths. Terrorist violence carried out by extremists in Northern Ireland has killed or injured many innocent people. In many parts

South Africa held its first free presidential election in April 1994. Millions of people waited patiently in line to cast their votes. Nelson Mandela won by a landslide.

of the world, repressive governments have imprisoned, tortured, and executed people who have spoken out against them.

Still, there has been significant progress. For instance, international pressure helped bring an end to apartheid in South Africa, and in 1994 that nation held its first truly democratic election. Political changes in the Soviet Union, both before and after the collapse of the Soviet system, also led to improved human rights.

Besides the United Nations, various other organizations work in pursuit of human rights. For example, Amnesty International, a private organization, investigates and reports on human rights abuses around the world. Numerous regional organizations, such as the Council of Europe, also try to advance the cause of human rights.

In addition to human rights in general, people in many countries have actively supported the rights of specific groups. The women's liberation movement, for example, sought to eliminate barriers to women's equality with men. In the United States, various groups, including the American Association of Retired Persons, work to protect the rights of elderly people.

Differing perspectives. The concept of human rights does not have a single, universal meaning. Different cultures have different perspectives. For example, some people, especially in non-Western countries, place greater emphasis on the interests of the community than on the rights of the individual. Many of these people criticize Western nations for trying to impose their ideals and values on other nations.

Similarly, such concepts as women's rights have different meanings in different societies. In the Islamic world, for instance, women's rights are viewed within the context of the Qur'an, the holy book of Islam. Thus, while the world's many nations may be able to agree on certain basic human rights, all nations must try to understand cultures and values that are different from their own.

Section 3

The Arts and Literature

Focus Questions

- **What trends occurred in painting, sculpture, and architecture after World War II?**
- **What innovations appeared in music, dance, film, and drama since 1945?**
- **How did poetry and novels express the mood of the times?**

In the decades after World War II, the arts and literature reflected the political turbulence and social changes of the times. Artists and writers moved beyond past methods and attitudes, exploring different perspectives and new means of self-expression. Two trends became particularly noticeable after 1945. One trend was the commitment to experimentation, which had been evident since the early 1900s. The other trend was the enormous popular interest in artistic and intellectual developments.

Painting and Sculpture

After 1945 New York City became one of the liveliest centers of new ideas and painting styles. The dominant style of painting became known as **abstract expressionism**. The leading abstract expressionist was an American, Jackson Pollock. Pollock believed that art comes from a person's unconscious mind. A painting is a personal expression, he thought, and should be judged by how authentically it reflects the nature of the artist. Pollock chose to express himself by randomly dripping different colors of paint onto a canvas that was spread out on the floor. Other abstract expressionists used

different techniques. Mark Rothko, a Russian-born American, placed large areas of color next to each other, blurring them together and creating a dazzling effect.

In the 1950s painters moved away from abstract expressionism to experiment in other ways. It was no longer possible to speak of one dominant style. In Great Britain and the United States, a number of artists returned to showing reality—but a special kind of reality. Developing a style called **pop art**, these artists chose as their subjects common objects such as soup cans, comic strips, or road signs. Experimentation also occurred in sculpture. The U.S. sculptor Louise Nevelson, for example, created large wooden sculptures. Many are wall units, like her sculpture *Black Chord*, filled with objects placed within boxed compartments.

New styles of painting arose in the late 1950s and 1960s. One group of artists concentrated on **op art**—a type of art that used optical illusions. These artists rejected reality as the subject of paintings, instead concentrating on the manipulation of brilliant colors and shapes for visual effect. Another type of painting, called hard-edge painting, used geometric areas of bright color with precisely defined contours.

The 1970s and 1980s saw some return to realism in paintings of scenes, objects, and people. Some European and U.S. painters, such as the neo-expressionist German artist Anselm Kiefer, turned away from abstract painting and returned to portraying recognizable objects. Often Kiefer, in particular, dealt with the moral problems posed by Nazism in his painting. Experiments continued, however, and many styles of art seemed acceptable.

The modern age has led artists to incorporate futuristic technology into their work. Today the title "artist" has come to include photographers, filmmakers, ceramists, glassblowers, and many others. The artist's materials range from the traditional canvas, paint, marble, and bronze to materials such as plastic and scrap metal. Modern art forms may be welded, wired, glued, sewn, or lighted. Some artists even construct and paint images from sand, create artistic patterns in plowed fields, or—like the contemporary artist Christo—wrap islands or buildings in fabric. Indeed, the line between sculpture and other art forms is not nearly as clear as it once was.

Another art trend of the modern age is **conceptual art**. Often conceptual art reduces the emphasis on isolated art objects and focuses instead on the arrangement of "environments" composed of both objects and people. Conceptual artists believe that the act of creating the art is more important than the actual art object.

Sydney Opera House

The Sydney Opera House, which dominates the harbor in Sydney, Australia, in appearance resembles a ship with its sails set for the future. Built on a peninsula, the building consists of a series of concrete shells that house a center for the performing arts.

Australia, despite its geographical isolation from Europe, has continued to maintain a strong British heritage. After World War II many European refugees settled in this island continent. They have helped to make the nation's culture more international.

When the Australian government decided to build a center to celebrate the arts, it sponsored a worldwide competition to choose an architect. Joern Utzon, a Dane, was the winner. His building rests on a high platform, and the shells rise more than 200 feet above sea level. Utzon's structure contains four theaters—a concert hall, an opera theater, a drama theater, and a playhouse that was originally designed for chamber music—each acoustically perfect for the type of performance it holds. Opened in 1973, the Sydney Opera House is among the most recognizable buildings in the world and is considered by many to represent a masterpiece of modern architecture.

Another trend that arose in a new form in the 1970s is **performance art**. In performance art, the artist himself or herself becomes a kind of living work of art. The German artist Joseph Beuys, for example, spent a week caged in a New York gallery with a coyote. In another example of performance art, by Nam June Paik, a Buddha contemplates himself on television.

Architecture

The search for new ideas and techniques dominated architecture, as it had since the invention of the skyscraper in the early 1900s. Since 1945 materials have changed frequently. One popular material was reinforced concrete, which was used by French architect Charles-Édouard Jeanneret, known as Le Corbusier, one of the most influential architects of the century. He admired the clean, precise shapes of machinery, and his buildings reflect this preference.

Smoothness and polish also interested architects, who created this smoother look mainly by using huge walls of glass. Le Corbusier himself took this approach when he, along with a committee of other designers, designed the headquarters of the United Nations in New York City.

Architects also experimented with new ways of building houses. Some houses were cast in concrete in standard units and then shipped to the building site. Others made use of new plastic materials.

New shapes appeared in architectural designs. Notable among these unusually shaped buildings is the group of concrete shells that make up the Sydney Opera House in Australia. Another new architectural design is the spiral-shaped form of the Guggenheim Museum in New York City. This was designed by the U.S. architect Frank Lloyd Wright, a leader in the use of unconventional shapes.

The Guggenheim Museum in New York City, designed by Frank Lloyd Wright to display Solomon R. Guggenheim's modern art collection, contains a spiral ramp that encircles the inside of the building for six stories.

Throughout the 1970s and 1980s, architectural designs assumed more contemporary lines. The rapid development of new engineering techniques prompted the construction of domed stadiums such as the Astrodome in Houston, Texas. Designs of the late 1980s emphasized spaciousness and employed innovative features. Some modern homes combined attractive and practical design with solar energy or other devices to save fuel. Many cities had buildings with unique designs, large expanses of glass, or gleaming mirrored tiles.

However, no single design or method of building has dominated architecture in the years since 1945. Experimentation has led to a wide variety in architectural styles, which often are found side by side in city centers. Some observers criticize such mixture of styles, particularly when modern additions are made to historic buildings.

Music and Dance

Experimentation has been equally apparent in the world of music. New uses of instruments, rhythm, harmony, and melody were introduced. Some composers, however, did write traditional types of music. The British composer Benjamin Britten, for example, wrote operas. The later work of Russian composer Dmitry Shostakovich included symphonies built on Baroque structures.

After 1945 new kinds of sound entered the world of serious music. Experimenters found that computers could produce sounds. Innovative composers wrote pieces for synthesizers or for combinations of traditional instruments and synthesizers. Composers also began to write music that gave performers—and even the audience—a major role in determining how a piece would sound. The unorthodox ideas of U.S. composer John Cage, for example, had a profound influence on the music of his time.

The determination to break new ground and to leave the past behind was especially obvious in popular music. During the 1950s, a form of music known as rock 'n' roll emerged in the United States. It had roots in many different places, including African American rhythms and the blues of the rural southern United States. Rock had a heavy, accented beat and a simple, repetitive melody. During the 1960s, the Beatles, a group from Liverpool, England, became one of the most popular and influential rock bands in history. A number of different styles, with such names as folk rock, hard rock, punk rock, and disco, developed. Another form of popular music, country-western, usually consisted of sentimental ballads, and African American musicians developed popular styles such as soul music, rhythm-and-blues, and rap.

In the 1980s and 1990s music videos became increasingly popular, helping to spread popular music and win worldwide fans for many musicians. At the same time, interest grew in the music of other cultures, and artists drew inspiration from the music of Africa, the Caribbean, South America, and other parts of the world.

The world of dance also followed new directions after 1945. Artists who had left Russia after its revolution were especially influential in ballet. The most influential was George Balanchine. Balanchine was founder, artistic director, and chief choreographer/director of the New York City Ballet. In the 1960s and 1970s, young ballet stars such as Rudolf Nureyev, Mikhail Baryshnikov, and Natalia Makarova defected from the Soviet Union to make their careers in the West.

After 1945 the freer and looser forms of modern dance began to influence ballet. As in all the performing arts, the tendency was to leave uniformity behind, to experiment, and to allow more individual expression. Martha Graham, an American, was a very influential teacher of modern dance. Her work expressed powerful emotions.

Building History Study Skills

READ
WRITE
INTERPRET
CONNECT
THINK

Making Connections with History: Linking Architecture to History

Architecture often reflects the values of a culture. The skyscraper is both the triumphant symbol of—and at the same time, an unwelcome intruder into—the city. It shatters scale and steals light, yet it suggests the personality of the city of which it is a part. It has also made the city's character a reflection of its own quality. For example, the Sears Tower in Chicago and the Empire State Building in New York City are the symbols of these metropolitan areas just as the Cathedral of Notre Dame is a symbol of Paris. Linking architecture to history helps historians explain how the environment affects a society, determine the individual's reaction to the environment, and visualize the society's values.

How to Link Architecture to History

To link architecture to history, follow these steps.
1. Establish the historical context of the piece of architecture.
2. Identify the society that built the structure.
3. Identify the major characteristics of the piece of architecture.
4. Describe characteristics of the environment.
5. Relate the environmental characteristics to the historical context.
6. Identify the values expressed by linking the historical context of the piece of architecture and the environmental characteristics.

Developing the Skill

Analyzing the skyscraper's architecture helps you link architecture to modern history. The skyscraper has become the symbol of the U.S. city of the 1900s. It defines life in the metropolis.

Skyscrapers began to rise above 40 stories by 1907. These towering symbols of urbanization housed more than offices—they also included stores and restaurants. Their lobbies became so large that they became gathering places.

One example of the skyscraper is the Woolworth Building in New York City. Completed in 1913, it gracefully extends 792 feet above the ground. Although the building is perceived as a sheer tower, its base consists of a 30-story

The Gateway Arch, St. Louis, Missouri

U-shaped mass. Rising from the center front of the structure is a square tower that culminates in an ornate crown at the top. The vertical lines of the base shoot up into the tower, melding the upper and lower masses together.

The architecture of a particular society also reveals more than cultural values—it reveals information about the economic characteristics of a society. An impressive building is a symbol of a successful corporation. The visual effect of massive buildings suggests corporate glory and represents human ability and technical achievement. In the modern age, skyscrapers have become the cathedrals of commerce.

Practicing the Skill

The Gateway Arch in St. Louis, Missouri, is shown on this page. Research this piece of architecture. Link this piece of architecture to the city where it was built as well as the history of the United States.

To apply this skill, see Applying History Study Skills on page 927.

In recent decades U.S. choreographers such as Alvin Ailey, Jr., Twyla Tharp, Paul Taylor, and Alwin Nikolais have been especially influential in dance.

Film

Traditional subjects—adventures, comedies, and social dramas—dominated most filmmaking after 1945. Spectacular productions, costing millions of dollars, continued to be popular. Other films tried to break free of traditional restrictions.

In the 1940s and 1950s, Italian directors such as Federico Fellini produced shattering and sometimes bizarre commentary on social and political injustice. At the end of the 1950s, a group of young French directors known as the "New Wave" further revolutionized film. These directors, including Louis Malle and Jean-Luc Godard, believed that the director should act as the *auteur,* or author, of a film. That is, a film should be the conception of one person—the director—not a commercial package put together by a movie studio. The "New Wave" directors often rejected traditional filmmaking techniques. They used hand-held cameras and often edited their works in new ways. They believed that the visual style of a film—not necessarily the storyline—was what was most important.

Some of the most interesting but disturbing films made in the 1960s and 1970s came from Japan. Akira Kurosawa and other Japanese directors used violence and a melancholic atmosphere to create startling and frightening new effects. Meanwhile, director Lina Wertmüller was making deeply satirical films concerning Italian politics and society as well as the relations between men and women.

Technical mastery was increasingly evident in American films from the 1970s on. George Lucas's *Star Wars* series, Steven Spielberg's *E.T.—The Extraterrestrial* (1982), and James Cameron's *Titanic* (1997), for example, depended heavily on visual effects. The creative application of advanced computer technology dazzled viewers in *Jurassic Park* (1993), *Toy Story* (1995), and *Twister* (1996).

Computers can be used to generate spectacular effects in movies today. This movie still is from *Jurassic Park*.

Meanwhile, independent moviemakers took film in a new direction. Largely free of ties to the big studios, they made films with strong social commentary. Director Spike Lee, for example, made such provocative movies as *Do the Right Thing* (1989) about the experiences of African Americans in urban America. Despite numerous multimillion-dollar successes, the American filmmaking industry had financial setbacks. Although the explosion of videotapes and VCRs in the homes of the 1980s stimulated interest in films of all kinds and from many countries, some large studios lost huge amounts of money on unsuccessful big-budget movies. The widespread use of cable television in American homes also gave movie theaters increasing competition. In the 1990s economic considerations led many movie studios to become part of large entertainment conglomerates.

Drama

In the theater, too, important new techniques developed. In East Germany the company founded by playwright Bertolt Brecht staged plays with an emphasis on artificiality. Audience members were not to be drawn in but were to be constantly reminded that they were watching a play.

Perhaps the most powerful new vision of the modern age was the biting social commentary of the playwrights of the so-called theater of the absurd. Its leaders were Samuel Beckett and Eugène Ionesco, an Irishman and a Romanian, respectively, who lived in France. Bewilderment and absurdity run throughout Beckett's works, including his most famous play, *Waiting for Godot* (1953).

More realistic but no less biting attacks on modern society were apparent in the works of other playwrights of this period. The most notable of these dramatists were John Osborne, an Englishman, and Arthur Miller, an American. Osborne addressed the bleakness of the lives of the British working class, and Miller's powerful dramas, particularly *Death of a Salesman* (1949), explored human weaknesses and the tensions in families. Another American, Tennessee Williams, explored similar themes concerning the American South.

Social analysis and commentary even entered the boisterous world of U.S. musical theater. Perhaps the most remarkable musical of the post-1945 period was *West Side Story* (1957), based on Shakespeare's *Romeo and Juliet*. Composer and conductor Leonard Bernstein wrote the score, and Jerome Robbins handled choreography for the musical.

During the 1980s and 1990s, many musicals, such as *The Phantom of the Opera* (shown above) and *Les Misérables,* became dramatic successes.

The 1980s and 1990s saw the production of "blockbuster" musicals in theaters all over the world. These musicals involved spectacular stage sets and lavish musical arrangements and often had unusual themes or settings. *The Phantom of the Opera* (1986), by British composer Andrew Lloyd Webber, told of the fascination between a young opera singer and a "ghost" that haunted an opera house located in Paris. A novel written by French author Victor Hugo inspired the hit musical *Les Misérables*. In 1996, *Cats*, based on the work of British poet T.S. Eliot, became the longest-running Broadway show in history.

Poetry and Novels

Many poets and novelists took a stand against the comfortable self-satisfaction they saw in the world around them. For example, society's most prosperous citizens and their values became the target of a group of writers who made up what was called the Beat Generation. These writers, most of them living in San Francisco, Los Angeles, and New York City, began writing in the 1950s. Beat novelist Jack Kerouac and poet Allen Ginsberg attacked the conventions of the American way of life, such as commercialism, materialism, and insensitivity. They thought writing should be completely spontaneous and rejected the traditional forms of the novel and the poem.

Protest was a major theme of the leading writers of the postwar years. Among the most powerful African American writers were Ralph Ellison and James Baldwin. Each explored, with dismay and anger, the life of African Americans in the United States. Nigerian novelist Chinua Achebe examined the effects of colonial rule on his native land. West German novelists Günter Grass and Heinrich Böll explored Hitler's impact on Germany. Boris Pasternak and Alexander Solzhenitsyn wrote of the repressions of the Soviet system. The dissident writers of Eastern Europe, too, wrote about the hardships of life under communism. In fact, these "underground" works were the only source of truth for many Eastern Europeans.

Scientific and technological advances after World War II boosted interest in science fiction, making it one of the most popular forms of literature. Writers such as Ray Bradbury, Robert Heinlein, and Isaac Asimov stimulated the imaginations of millions of readers with tales of space travel, robots, and distant planets.

Naguib Mahfouz became the first Arab writer to be awarded the Nobel Prize for Literature in 1988; his collection of work includes novels, short stories, and plays.

A related theme of literature written during the postwar period was escape from an increasingly hostile and confusing world. Writers such as the American Kurt Vonnegut, Jr., created fantasies about imaginary worlds. The writers of this period used these fantasies to suggest pessimistic and satirical alternatives to what they saw as the dehumanizing attitudes of the times.

Prominent Latin American writers chose a similar approach. Nobel Prize winner Octavio Paz, a Mexican author, used contrasting images of the inevitable loneliness of people and their desire for companionship in surrealistic, dreamlike poems. The Colombian Gabriel García Márquez, also a Nobel Prize winner, wrote haunting, mystical novels and stories about ordinary subjects.

Not all authors and poets wrote of protest or other worlds. Some writers, like American poet Wallace Stevens, explored the interaction of reality and what one can make of that reality in one's own mind. Another American poet, Marianne Moore, used subjects from nature to write about, often as symbols of steadfastness and honesty.

In recent years the voices of minority women have become increasingly powerful in the United States, and their novels and poems have often been best-sellers. Pulitzer Prize winners Alice Walker (*The Color Purple*) and Toni Morrison (*Beloved*) confronted the issues of African American life from the period of slavery through contemporary times. Maya Angelou's poetry explored the black experience in the South. And in her novels Laura Esquivel similarly explored the Hispanic experience of feminism in repressed countries like her native Mexico.

Some writers provoked controversy. For example, in 1988 Western critics acclaimed Anglo-Indian author Salman Rushdie's satirical novel *The Satanic Verses*. Many Muslims, however, called it blasphemous. Some governments banned the book, and violent demonstrations against it occurred in Pakistan and other countries. Then Ayatollah Ruhollah Khomeini of Iran issued a death sentence against Rushdie, forcing the writer into hiding. In 1994 Egyptian author Naguib Mahfouz, the first Arab writer to win the Nobel Prize, was attacked by an assailant who objected to Mahfouz's treatment of Islam in his works.

In the 1990s novelists and poets continued to share their unique insights and personal experiences with readers around the world. Notable writers of this decade included Japanese novelist

Maya Angelou, known for her autobiographical works, read her poem "On the Pulse of Morning" during President Clinton's inauguration ceremony in 1993.

Kenzaburo Oe, American novelist John Updike, and Irish poet Seamus Heaney.

The Audience for the Arts

The excitement of postwar artistic and literary activity generated enormous public appeal, particularly in the United States. After World War II, museums responded to a better-educated society. Of the existing museums in 1988, 75 percent were founded after 1950 and 40 percent since 1970. More Americans paid to go to museums, concerts, operas, ballets, and theaters each year than to attend sporting events.

Around the world, more people are completing the equivalent of a high school education, and more people are attending college. People have more time for leisure activities, particularly in the industrialized nations. Television exposes millions of viewers to films, plays, concerts, and a wide range of other cultural activities. Many people continue to pursue similar entertainment outside the home. Thus education, increased leisure time, and expanding cultural awareness have combined to give the arts and literature greater exposure and support than ever before.

Section 3 Review

1. **Define** abstract expressionism, pop art, op art, conceptual art, performance art
2. **Identify** Jackson Pollock, Louise Nevelson, George Balanchine, Martha Graham, Lina Wërtmuller, Steven Spielberg, Arthur Miller, Ralph Ellison, Alice Walker, Salman Rushdie
3. **Summarizing Ideas** Describe some of the changes in artistic and architectural styles since 1945.
4. **Interpreting Ideas** How did new trends in music and dance reflect some of the same themes as painting and sculpture since 1945?
5. **Analyzing Ideas** Using specific examples, describe how film and theater reflected new techniques and themes.
6. **Interpreting Ideas** Do you agree or disagree with the statement that novels, films, and poetry often give a truer picture of the condition of a country than news reports or other nonfiction? Explain.

Chapter 33 Review

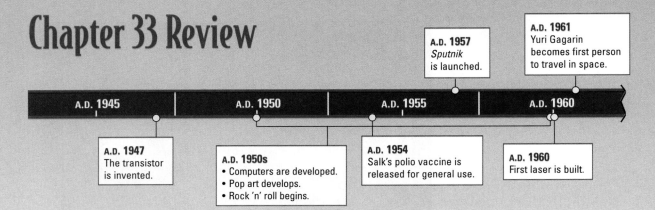

A.D. 1957
Sputnik
is launched.

A.D. 1961
Yuri Gagarin
becomes first person
to travel in space.

A.D. 1945

A.D. 1950

A.D. 1955

A.D. 1960

A.D. 1947
The transistor
is invented.

A.D. 1950s
• Computers are developed.
• Pop art develops.
• Rock 'n' roll begins.

A.D. 1954
Salk's polio vaccine is
released for general use.

A.D. 1960
First laser is built.

Chapter Summary

The following list contains the key concepts you have learned about the modern age.

1. Major technological advances brought about changes in ideas and behavior after 1945. Advances in air travel and space exploration changed the way people thought about their world. Miniaturization, computers, and advances in communication changed the ways people lived and worked. Medical knowledge grew and expanded rapidly. Scientists' growing understanding of the power of the atom had both positive and negative effects.

2. Population grew rapidly in the years after 1945. Most of the world's growth occurred in the developing nations. Rapid population growth can lead to a number of problems. When urban populations increase, for example, city resources are strained.

3. Environmental concerns of recent decades include acid rain, the effects of pesticide use, waste disposal, endangered species, ozone depletion, and global warming. Countries are working together to solve many of these problems.

4. Human rights issues became important in the postwar years. Human rights violations often have political, ethnic, racial, or religious roots. Differing cultural views of human rights sometimes made consensus difficult.

5. The arts and literature continued the experimentation that had marked their development since the early 1900s. New forms of painting, notably abstract expressionism, pop art, and op art, transformed the visual arts. Sculpture and architecture also took new forms.

6. Musicians experimented with new kinds of sounds, both in serious compositions and in popular forms. New styles of creativity were also evident in dance and filmmaking. Drama moved in new directions as traditional plays were transformed by the theater of the absurd.

7. Writers after 1945 expressed many different ideas, including a stand against complacency and various forms of protest. Science and technological advances promoted an interest in science fiction. Other writers focused on an escape from a hostile and confusing world. The voices of minorities, including women, have been heard in greater numbers.

Reviewing Important Terms

On a separate sheet of paper, supply the term that correctly completes each statement.

1. The process of making machines, especially electrical equipment, smaller is called _____ .
2. _____ are medicines used to treat bacterial infections.
3. The style of art dominant after 1945 and demonstrated by Jackson Pollock is called _____ _____ .
4. Paintings of common objects such as soup cans are examples of an art style called _____ _____ .
5. _____ _____ forms when precipitation falls through air polluted by toxins produced by the burning of fossil fuels.
6. The trapping of heat by a layer of gases in the atmosphere is called the _____ _____ .
7. The manipulation of a cell from an animal so as to produce a genetically identical duplicate of the animal is called _____ .

Developing Critical Thinking Skills

1. **Comparing Ideas (a)** How were the early successes of the space exploration programs of the United States and the Soviet Union similar? **(b)** Compare more recent advances in manned space flight and space stations of these two countries.
2. **Debating Ideas (a)** What are some of the benefits and the dangers of atomic power? **(b)** What other technological advances of the 1900s have both positive and negative impacts?
3. **Evaluating Ideas** How might rapid population growth in a developing country slow down other types of growth and development?
4. **Analyzing Ideas** How did changes in the arts during the modern age reflect other changes in society?
5. **Determining Cause and Effect (a)** How did lifestyles in America change after World War II? **(b)** What factors account for these changes?

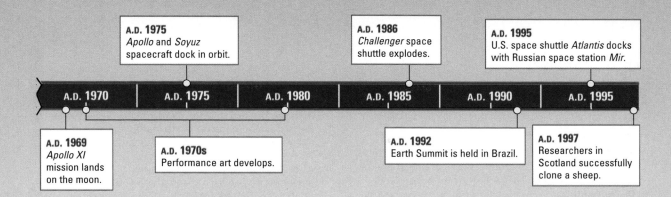

A.D. 1975
Apollo and *Soyuz* spacecraft dock in orbit.

A.D. 1986
Challenger space shuttle explodes.

A.D. 1995
U.S. space shuttle *Atlantis* docks with Russian space station *Mir*.

A.D. 1970 A.D. 1975 A.D. 1980 A.D. 1985 A.D. 1990 A.D. 1995

A.D. 1969
Apollo XI mission lands on the moon.

A.D. 1970s
Performance art develops.

A.D. 1992
Earth Summit is held in Brazil.

A.D. 1997
Researchers in Scotland successfully clone a sheep.

Relating Geography to History

Select a writer, a composer, or an artist from the United States or a foreign country. Write a short biographical essay and describe how that person's environment influenced his or her contribution to the arts.

Relating Past to Present

1. In 1970 Alvin Toffler wrote a book about the effect of rapid change, about people facing the future too soon. Read the passage below from Toffler's *Future Shock* and then answer the questions that follow.

    "The high velocity [rapid rate] of change can be traced to many factors. Population growth, urbanization, the shifting proportions of young and old—all play their part. Yet technological advance is clearly a critical node in that network of causes; indeed, it may be the node that activates the entire net. One powerful strategy in the battle to prevent mass future shock, therefore, involves the conscious regulation of technological advance."

    a. According to Toffler, what factors bring about rapid change?
    b. Which of these factors is most important?
    c. Based on what you learned in this chapter and on your knowledge of current events, do you agree with Toffler? Explain your answer.

2. **(a)** Using a tape recorder, prepare a program of popular music of the 1990s. Then prepare a similar tape for a previous decade. Possible sources of recordings include friends, relatives, and your school or local library. **(b)** What do the tapes reveal about each period? **(c)** How have popular tastes changed? **(d)** What, if any, new instruments are used today? **(e)** How might musical recordings contribute to an understanding of history?

Applying History Study Skills

Before completing this activity, review Building History Study Skills on page 921.

Locate and compare photographs of the medieval cathedral located at Salisbury in England and the Trump Tower building located in New York City. Then answer the following questions.

1. **(a)** What characteristics of Gothic architecture can you find in the photographs? **(b)** How are these characteristics similar? **(c)** How are they different?
2. Which values of medieval society did Gothic architecture tend to reflect?
3. Which values of modern society do skyscraper architecture tend to reflect?
4. Write a brief essay that compares the cathedral to the skyscraper.

 internet**connect**

Search the Internet through the HRW Web site for information about one of the writers or artists mentioned in this chapter or about another contemporary individual working in the arts or literature. Locate an interview or other information about the person. Prepare a short oral report that tells what you learned about the person and his or her art or writings.

HRW GO TO: go.hrw.com
KEYWORD: SC0 Artists

Building Your Portfolio

1. **Writing a Report** The Space Age began in 1957 with the launching of the Soviet satellite *Sputnik 1*. Using reference materials, prepare a report on why the United States has emerged as the world leader in space exploration. Based on your research, what are some reasons for the success of the United States space program? Place the report in your portfolio.

2. **Preparing an Oral Presentation** Technological advances have had an impact not only on developed nations but also on developing nations. Select one area of scientific or technological progress, and present information to the class on how advances in this area have changed life in the developing nations of Asia, Africa, and Latin America. Place your notes and other research materials in your portfolio.

Unit Summary

The following list contains the key concepts you have learned about the challenges that faced the world from 1945 to the present.

1. After World War II, conflicts between Communist and Western nations resulted in the Cold War that threatened world peace.

2. When communist North Korea invaded South Korea in 1950, its troops were repulsed by UN forces, and an armistice was eventually signed.

3. In Southeast Asia, the United States became heavily involved in fighting in Vietnam.

4. Independence came rapidly to the African nations after World War II. Until 1994 the white government of South Africa resisted giving the country's black majority any significant power in government.

5. North Africa and the Middle East experienced several wars after 1945. Arab-Israeli conflicts, civil war in Lebanon, and wars in the Persian Gulf took place during this period.

6. Many countries of Latin America were racked by military upheaval after World War II. However, these developing nations are beginning to work for peace and economic growth as the 1900s come to an end.

7. After Mikhail Gorbachev instituted his policies of glasnost and perestroika, United States–Soviet relations began to improve.

8. The future of NATO grew increasingly uncertain after the collapse of communism in Eastern Europe and the former Soviet Union.

9. After 1945 technological changes transformed communications, the understanding of the universe, the processing of information, the products people used every day, economic activities, medicine, and food production.

Reviewing Concepts

On a separate sheet of paper, supply the term that correctly completes each statement.

1. _____ is a term used to describe the communist nations that supported the Soviet Union.

2. The South African policy based on the principle of racial separation became known as _____, the Afrikaans word for "apartness."

3. _____ is the name given to the improvement in relations between the United States and the Soviet Union during the 1970s.

4. Through _____, or restructuring, Mikhail Gorbachev planned to overhaul the political and economic systems of the Soviet Union.

Applying Critical Thinking Skills

1. **Organizing Ideas** What was the purpose of the alliance systems set up by the Western nations and by the Communist bloc after 1945?

2. **Synthesizing Ideas** How did the work of civil rights leaders such as Dr. Martin Luther King lead to changes in the United States government's policy toward equal rights for all of its citizens?

3. **Comparing Ideas** How did the Korean War and the Vietnam War differ in terms of causes and effects?

4. **Evaluating Ideas** How did each of the following individuals contribute to the rise of nationalism in Africa? **(a)** Kwame Nkrumah; **(b)** Jomo Kenyatta; **(c)** Gamal Abdel Nasser.

5. **Summarizing Ideas** What changes occurred in the nations of the Middle East after 1945?

6. **Analyzing Ideas** How might economic prosperity in Latin America help bring political stability?

7. **Understanding Relationships** What were the results of the United States involvement in each of the following countries: **(a)** Panama, **(b)** Puerto Rico, **(c)** Cuba, **(d)** the Dominican Republic.

8. **Synthesizing Ideas** Should there be a set time period after which war crimes and violations of human rights cannot be punished? Why or why not?

9. **Interpreting Ideas (a)** What are some of the many reasons that people study history? **(b)** How can a knowledge of the past help people understand the present?

Relating Geography to History

Refer to the maps in Chapter 27 and Chapter 28. How did the spread of communism affect the map of Europe after the end of World War II?

Writing About History

Write a report that summarizes three major areas of disagreement between the United States and the Soviet Union between 1945 and 1991. Which was the most threatening to world peace? Why?

Further Readings

Allende, Isabel. *The House of the Spirits*. Bantam, 1986. Uses magic realism to explore the importance of family and political allegiance in Latin America.

Fitzgerald, Frances. *Fire in the Lake: The Vietnamese and the Americans in Vietnam*. Random House, 1989. Describes the Vietnam War.

Yergin, Daniel, and Thane Gustafson. *Russia 2010: And What It Means for the World*. Random House, 1995. Offers a clear and concise assessment of the key problems facing Russia and other former Soviet republics and their possible outcomes.

Date	Politics	Science and Technology	Society and Culture
1945–1955	Formation of UN **28**,* OAS **31**, NATO **28**, Warsaw Pact **28** Filipino **29**, Indian **29**, and Israeli **30** independence Egyptian **30**, Chinese **29**, and Viet Minh **29** revolutions Nuremberg trials **28** Truman Doctrine and Marshall Plan **28** Berlin blockade **28** Korean War **28** *Brown v. Board of Ed.* **28** Suez Crisis **30**	Synthetics and plastics **33** Nuclear power **32** Computer revolution **33** Transistor **33** DNA research **33** Television **33**	Léopold Senghor **30** Le Corbusier **33** Abstract expressionism **33** Mark Rothko **33** Science fiction **33** Britten and Shostakovich **33** Baldwin and Ellison **33** Beat Generation **33** John Cage **33**
1955–1965	United States in Vietnam **29** Martin Luther King Jr. and civil rights **28** OPEC **30** Berlin Wall built **28** Cuban revolution and missile crisis **28, 31**	St. Lawrence Seaway **28** *Sputnik 1* **33** Laser technology **33** Green Revolution **33**	Pop and op art **33** French "New Wave" movies **33** Miller and Williams **33** *West Side Story* **33** Pasternak and Solzhenitsyn **33** The Beatles **33**
1965–1975	Six-Day War **30** Soviet invasion of Czechoslovakia **28** Arab-Israeli War of 1973 **30**, PLO **30** SALT, détente **32** Watergate **32** OPEC embargo **32** Helsinki Accords **32** Pol Pot executes intellectuals **29**	Lunar landing **33** Japanese industrialization **29** Asian economic revolution **29** Jumbo jets **33**	Chinese Cultural Rev. **29** Vonnegut and García Márquez **33** *Samizdat* **32** Objection to Vietnam War **28, 32**
1975–1997	Camp David Accords **30** Solidarity **32** Assassinations of Sadat **30**, Indira and Rajiv Gandhi **29** Perestroika, glasnost **32** Gorbachev and Reagan summit **32** Berlin Wall torn down **32** Persian Gulf War **30** Breakup of Soviet Union **32** NAFTA **31, 32** Transfer of Hong Kong to China **29**	Three Mile Island **32** *Columbia, Challenger* shuttles **33** Chernobyl **32, 33** *Mir* space station **33** AIDS research and education **33** Channel Tunnel **33** Cloning **33**	Protests against apartheid **30** Steven Spielberg and Spike Lee **33** Wole Soyinka **30** Webber's *The Phantom of the Opera* **33** Rushdie's *The Satanic Verses* **33**

*Indicates chapter in which development is discussed

The World Since 1945

CHAPTER 28

Europe and North America in the Postwar Years

The Soviet Union was one of the Allied Powers in World War II, and at the end of the war the Allies had seemed to reach agreements about Germany and Eastern Europe. However, differences dividing the Western democracies and the communist Soviet Union re-emerged. Suspicions between communist and Western nations led to the so-called Cold War, a conflict waged primarily by political and economic means.

Aftermath of the War in Europe

As postwar hostility between the Western democracies and the Soviet Union grew, Allied decisions about Eastern Europe, Germany, and Austria became more and more difficult to reach. For example, it took 10 years to reach an agreement about Austria, and no final agreement was ever reached on Germany. Instead, Germany remained occupied by American, British, French, and Soviet troops. Despite disagreements, however, the United Nations was founded as a body dedicated to preserving peace.

Origins of the Cold War

As the war was ending, Stalin placed governments friendly to Soviet interests in Eastern and Central Europe. Other Soviet actions seemed to indicate a policy of expansionism. In response, early in 1947 President Truman, announcing what came to be called the Truman Doctrine, dedicated the United States to helping countries threatened by communism. With a policy known as containment, the United States would contain, or restrict, the spread of communism.

The United States also instituted the European Recovery Program, often called the Marshall Plan, to help Europe recover from the war. Between 1948 and 1952, the United States spent more than $13 billion with tremendous success. Industrial and agricultural production in Europe rose above prewar levels.

New alliances made clear the extent of the split between East and West. In April 1949 the nations of Western Europe founded the North Atlantic Treaty Organization (NATO), a mutual defense pact. The Soviets and other countries of the European communist bloc responded by founding the Warsaw Pact. The Warsaw Pact greatly outnumbered NATO in terms of ground troops, which reinforced a Western reliance on nuclear deterrents.

Reconstruction, Reform, and Reaction in Europe

In a relatively short time, postwar Western Europe experienced a remarkable economic and political recovery. Eastern Europe also revived, but not nearly as quickly or successfully as the West did.

In 1957 the European Economic Community (EEC)—usually called the Common Market—was founded. It provided for the gradual abolition of tariffs and import quotas among the six member nations.

Stalin's successor, Khrushchev, began a policy of destalinization, loosening some of the government's control on the economy. His economic policies, however, failed to produce desired results.

Immediately after the war, the communist bloc seemed to be a solid group, but dissatisfaction with Soviet domination soon became apparent. In 1956 there was a revolt in Hungary, and in 1968 Czechoslovakia tried to institute reforms. The Soviets crushed the rebels in both countries.

The United States and Canada

At home, the United States aimed to resolve social and political problems and to maintain a flourishing economy. In response to the civil rights movement, in the 1960s Congress passed several acts that promised political equality for African Americans and other minorities. The United States's foreign policy revolved around containment. For example, the United States committed large numbers of troops to help noncommunist South Vietnam defend itself against communist North Vietnam.

After World War II, Canada became a vigorous supporter of the United Nations and an important member of NATO. It loaned billions of dollars to other countries and welcomed thousands of refugees from Europe. Canada also experienced considerable economic development.

CHAPTER 29

Asia Since 1945

The years after World War II saw major political, economic, and social changes in Asia.

South Asia After Empire

In 1947, the British granted independence to India, but violence erupted between Muslims and Hindus when Britain partitioned the subcontinent along religious lines. The governments of India and East and West Pakistan struggled to cope with several problems: rapidly growing populations, poverty, illiteracy, and great cultural and linguistic differences.

By the 1980s, India's economy had made considerable progress, but economic growth had difficulty keeping pace with the ever-growing population. In 1971 civil war between East and West Pakistan resulted in the formation of the new nation of Bangladesh. Frequent natural disasters, economic instability, and a legacy of ill will between the major political parties made Bangladesh's future uncertain. Pakistan, too, faced political instability. India and Pakistan sought to improve relations, but a history of distrust and violence between them made peace an elusive goal.

The Rise of Communist China and Taiwan

By 1949 the Communists took control of the Chinese mainland and forced the Nationalists to flee to Taiwan. In 1966, Mao Zedong launched a Cultural Revolution, a violent attempt at social change that had disastrous effects on the economy. In time, the moderates won control and instituted more liberal economic policies and some political reforms. Calls for more political reforms in 1989, however, were brutally suppressed. Chinese leaders continue to maintain a tight hold on Chinese society.

After World War II China was first closely aligned with the Soviet Union, but Chinese-Soviet relations worsened and China's relations with the United States improved. In 1979 the United States formally recognized the People's Republic of China, but China's refusal to meet international human rights standards continued to cast a shadow over foreign relations in the mid-1990s.

Korea. Korea was divided at the end of World War II. North Korea's attempt to conquer South Korea in 1950 was prevented by the intervention of the United Nations. However, concern grew in the mid-1990s that a famine in North Korea could cause the government to launch new attacks on South Korea. In 1998, the president of South Korea pledged that democratic reforms in his country would go hand-in-hand with economic growth.

Taiwan. Run by a one-party system until the 1990s, Taiwan nevertheless enjoyed economic success under its free enterprise economy. In the 1990s a move toward official independence was viewed in a negative light by the People's Republic of China.

The Japanese Miracle

Japan made rapid economic progress after the war by producing highly advanced technology for a world market. By the end of the 1980s Japan was Asia's leading economic power. Postwar economic developments brought about far-reaching social changes in Japan. In the 1990s, however, Japan became mired in a stubborn recession, and political scandals caused governmental changes.

Ho Chi Minh City

Independence Struggles in Southeast Asia

Southeast Asia consists of 10 countries: the Philippines, Indonesia, Malaysia, Singapore, Brunei, Vietnam, Thailand, Laos, Myanmar (formerly Burma), and Cambodia. Except for Thailand, all of these countries were once colonies. After the war, they gained independence. For some, it was a peaceful transition. In others, violence occurred.

In the Philippines, Fidel Ramos, who became president in 1992, made efforts to strengthen the economy and encourage foreign investment. Indonesia continued to make economic progress in the 1990s, and its political and economic importance in the world grew.

By 1996, Malaysia's economy had become one of the strongest in the Asia-Pacific region, although the country still faced serious problems. Singapore had become the center of economic activity in Southeast Asia, and the country's people enjoyed one of the highest standards of living in Asia. Myanmar had some success in attracting foreign investment, but relations with the United States remained troubled.

Communist North Vietnam and pro-Western South Vietnam were at war more than 20 years. The United States intervened on behalf of South Vietnam. The Communists prevailed and united the country in 1976. The years of war drained the nation's resources, and many people have fled the country since 1976. The Communist government added some elements of free enterprise to the economy, which boomed in the 1990s.

The Communist Khmer Rouge, under the leadership of Pol Pot, captured the government of Cambodia in 1975. Between 1975 and 1977, 1.2 million Cambodians met their deaths by execution or starvation. Thousands fled to Thailand. In 1996, the Khmer Rouge showed signs of weakening, and in 1998 the notorious Pol Pot died of natural causes.

In recent years control of the government of Thailand has shifted back and forth between civilian and military leaders. Between 1985 and 1994 Thailand had one of the world's fastest growing economies. However, by 1997 a severe economic crisis made its future uncertain.

Asian Paths to Prosperity and Security

After independence, most new Asian nations attempted to build democratic societies. However, three factors gave rise to and helped sustain authoritarianism in Asia: (1) ethnic and cultural diversity that sometimes caused violent conflicts; (2) fear about national security; and (3) the desire for economic growth.

In the 1990s, roughly 3 billion people, more than half of the total population of the world, lived in Asia. A significant number of Asia's people lived in poverty and suffered its consequences—malnutrition, illiteracy, and reduced life expectancy.

By the mid-1990s, many parts of Asia had experienced economic expansion. China was an especially dramatic example, and there was no question about the Pacific region's continuing—and increasingly important—role in the world economy.

CHAPTER 30

Africa and the Middle East Since 1945

The African and Middle Eastern nations that became independent in the years after World War II faced problems of economic development, drought, famine, and disease. As the colonial era faded, ethnic and political divisions throughout Africa and the Middle East re-emerged.

Independence for African Nations

The struggle for independence in Africa took many forms. Some colonies followed a constitutional process while others suffered lengthy wars of national liberation. Eventually, even the most reluctant colonial powers had to grant independence. South Africa's experience differed from that of any other African nation. The white minority continued to rule and impose apartheid, a system of complete separation of races that oppressed nonwhites. In 1994, however, Nelson Mandela became president of South Africa, and a new era of multiracial cooperation began.

Africa Since Independence

Having achieved independence, African nations still faced serious problems. Practically all the new nations struggled with economic difficulties. Ethnic tensions also plagued most of them. In addition, drought, disease, and superpower rivalries took their toll. Despite

African National Congress rally

these problems, independence stimulated a revival and development of new cultural expressions. Africans found a new pride in their ancient heritage and its unique contribution to world culture. A mixture of African and outside influences gave an unusual vitality to the arts on the continent.

Nationalism in North Africa and the Middle East

World War II was a turning point for North Africa and the Middle East. During the war, the British had reestablished their control over strategic countries such as Egypt and Iran. Such control angered these countries and fueled the development of nationalism in the region. French North Africans also fought to be free of colonial rule. The establishment of the Jewish nation of Israel angered Palestinian Arabs and neighboring Arab countries. It has been a source of continuing conflict.

War, Oil, and Revolution

By 1962 most countries in North Africa and the Middle East had achieved independence. The remaining British protectorates in the Persian Gulf area gained full independence in the early 1970s. The major issues concerning the nations of the area during the final decades of the 1900s were oil, political instability, and the Arab-Israeli conflict, which continued despite the peace process begun with signing of the Camp David Accords by Egypt and Israel in 1979. Experts predict that after production peaks in oil fields outside the Middle East early in the next century, oil produced in the nations of Iran, Iraq, Kuwait, Saudi Arabia, and the United Arab Emirates will become more important than ever to the world economy. Consequently, the Persian Gulf is likely to remain a principal focus of international attention in the future.

A revolution in Iran and the growing aggression of Iraq drew the world's attention to this strategically important region. The danger of a major war in the Middle East remained high in the final years of the 1900s. In 1991 the Persian Gulf War drew many nations into conflict. In addition to political and military problems, the nations of North Africa and the Middle East confronted social and economic issues.

CHAPTER 31

Latin America Since 1945

Latin America, rich in human and natural resources, stands on the threshold of dynamic change and development, although countries in this region continue to suffer political and economic instability.

Facing New Challenges

A growing population, petroleum deposits and other resources, and rapid industrialization increased Latin America's presence in the world after World War II. With industrialization came many benefits, including higher standards of living, improved health care, and economic growth. However, economic hurdles remained.

Mexico and Central America

By the late 1980s, a huge foreign debt had nearly crippled Mexico's economy. Not until 1996, with the help of government-implemented austerity measures, did the economy begin to recover. The Marxist-inspired Sandinistas took control of the Nicaraguan government in 1979. Opposition to their policies led to a civil war that finally ended in 1990, when free elections were held. In El Salvador, violence from left-wing and right-wing groups claimed thousands of lives in the 1980s. In 1992 opposing sides signed a peace treaty, and the first postwar elections were held. In December 1989, after Panamanian forces killed an American soldier, United States' troops restored order and captured Manuel

Noriega, the country's dictator. Noriega, tried and convicted in Florida of drug trafficking, was sent to prison.

The Nations of the Caribbean

The presence of a communist government led by Fidel Castro in Cuba, a country in close proximity to the United States, alarmed American leaders. Clashes such as the Bay of Pigs invasion and the Cuban missile crisis occurred in 1960 and 1961. Later, an uneasy peace typified relations between the two countries. By the mid-1990s, to boost an economy close to collapse, Castro allowed limited private enterprise.

The people of Haiti overthrew the ruling Duvalier regime in 1986. Jean-Bertrand Aristide, the country's first democratically elected president, was succeeded in 1996—the first time that one elected Haitian civilian had peacefully passed power to another.

South America

In Argentina a succession of military and civilian governments characterized the postwar period. Carlos Menem was elected president in 1989 and again in 1995, and the economy improved. In Brazil political unrest and economic chaos marked the postwar period into the early 1990s. Under Cardoso, who was elected president in 1995, Brazil's economy regained some stability, but in 1997 volatile financial markets challenged the country's ability to maintain economic progress. In Chile, once the oldest continuing democracy in Latin America, a peacefully elected communist regime was overthrown by a military dictatorship, but a civilian government was elected in 1989 and again in 1993. The country enjoyed economic growth. In Peru there were political problems and the government teetered between dictatorship and democracy. In Colombia, growing cocaine traffic threatened to tear the nation apart.

CHAPTER 32

The Superpowers in the Modern Era

The final decades of the 1900s marked a period of transition—the Cold War ended and a "new world order" emerged. Free enterprise and democracy advanced as communism declined. The United States remained a leading power, while the Soviet Union as an entity disappeared.

The Industrial Powers of North America

The Vietnam War left deep scars on America's national identity and placed a substantial burden on the American economy. Also, the Watergate scandal shook the faith of many Americans in their political system and helped to make Washington, D.C., a symbol of corruption. As a result, several post-Watergate presidential candidates campaigned successfully as outsiders to Washington.

High inflation rates and unemployment plagued the nation in the 1970s. Both, however, had been brought under control by the 1980s. Despite a brief downturn in the early 1990s, the economy continued an upward trend into the mid-1990s.

Responding to continued Soviet expansion, the United States increased pressure on the Soviet Union in the 1980s. In the 1990s, American foreign policy confronted a host of new problems, such as the resurgence of militant nationalism and ethnic conflict. These problems emerged in the wake of the Cold War's end and the collapse of the Soviet Union.

Challenges also faced Canada in this period. The nation struggled with a determined French Canadian separatist movement but maintained close, although at times strained, relations with the United States.

Europe

Western Europe in general made significant strides toward political and economic integration, although

The fall of communism in Russia

the reunification of East and West Germany proved an increasing burden on the German economy through the mid-1990s. In the last decades of the century, formal institutions such as NATO and the European Economic Community—which evolved into the European Union in 1993—grew in strength and membership. The collapse of communism in Eastern Europe made possible an even wider union of European nations.

The Fall of Communism

By the early 1980s, the division of Europe between the Communist East and the free West appeared permanent. However, by the 1990s all the former satellites had broken off from the Soviet Union and had thrown out their Communist governments. Finally, the Soviet Union itself broke up into 15 nations. Although some countries looked forward to a prosperous future, political and economic instability prevailed throughout much of Eastern Europe and the former Soviet Union in the wake of communism.

CHAPTER 33

The World in the Twenty-First Century

Vast changes in people's lifestyles and attitudes marked the years following 1945.

Science and Technology

Dramatic advances in science and technology affected all the nations of the world. The United States and the Soviet Union dominated the space race. An important consequence of space exploration was the shift toward smaller and lighter machines. The most remarkable product of miniaturization was the modern computer. Today computers increasingly affect people's lives, and the range of activities controlled or facilitated by them grows daily. The Internet, a vast global network that connects many computer networks, allows computer users around the world to communicate with one another over telephone lines.

Biologists and other scientists made significant breakthroughs in their battle against disease with the development of vaccines, antibiotics, and other powerful new drugs.

Health and Human Rights

The second half of the 1900s was a time of significant political, economic, and social change. In industrialized nations, standards of living generally improved and opportunities continued to multiply. Change in developing nations was less dramatic, but in most areas of the world people's lives benefited from technological and scientific advances. One of the most noteworthy developments during the postwar decades was the rapid growth in world population. Rapid population growth in some of the world's poorer nations has contributed to political instability and social discontent. People around the world are continuously making an effort to deal with environmental concerns brought about by world population growth and industrialization.

The Arts and Literature

In the decades after the war, arts and literature reflected the political turbulence and social changes of the times. Artists and writers moved beyond earlier methods and attitudes, exploring different perspectives and new means of self-expression. Two trends became particularly noticeable after 1945. One was the commitment to experimentation, which had been evident since the early 1900s. The other was the enormous popular interest in artistic and intellectual developments.

Synthesis Review

1. **Understanding Ideas** What was the Cold War and what effect did it have on world events?
2. **Summarizing Ideas** In what ways did Asia change since 1945?
3. **Interpreting Ideas** Why is the Persian Gulf likely to play a part in world affairs in the future?
4. **Determining Cause and Effect** What types of problems have been caused by population growth in Latin America?
5. **Seeing Relationships** What were the results of the breakup of the Soviet Union?
6. **Analyzing Ideas** How did scientific and technological breakthroughs affect ordinary people's lives?
7. **Synthesizing Ideas** How are events in Latin America since 1945 like those in Asia? How are they different?

REFERENCE SECTION

GREENLAND

Baffin Bay

West

Arctic Circle

60°N

BERING SEA

Hudson Bay

BRITISH ISLES

English Channel

R O C K Y

N O R T H

A M E R I C A

ATLANTIC OCEAN

M T S .

Mississippi R.

APPALACHIAN MTS.

SARGASSO SEA

30°N

Strait of Gibraltar

ATLAS

Tropic of Cancer

Gulf of Mexico

Disputed

S

HAWAIIAN ISLANDS

W E S T

I N D I E S

CARIBBEAN SEA

Cape Verde

S A

PACIFIC OCEAN

Central America

0°   Equator

Amazon R.

SOUTH AMERICA

ATLANTIC OCEAN

A

Tropic of Capricorn

N

D

30°S

E
S

ATACAMA DESERT

N

W   E

S

The World: Physical

—— National boundary

0	1000	2000 Miles
0	1000	2000 Kilometers

Miller Projection

Cape Horn

60°S

150°W   120°W   90°W   60°W   30°W

Antarctic Circle

ARCTIC OCEAN

EUROPE

ASIA

AFRICA

URAL MTS.

CARPATHIAN MTS.

Danube R.

ALPS

BLACK SEA

CAUCASUS MTS.

CASPIAN SEA

BALTIC SEA

MEDITERRANEAN SEA

RED SEA

Persian G.

RA

NUBIAN DESERT

Arabian Peninsula

Undefined

ARABIAN SEA

Disputed

HIMALAYAS

Ganges R.

Huang He

GOBI

Chang Jiang

Bay of Bengal

SOUTH CHINA SEA

EAST CHINA SEA

SEA OF OKHOTSK

Tropic of Cancer

PACIFIC OCEAN

Congo R.

INDIAN OCEAN

Strait of Malacca

INDONESIA

Equator

KALAHARI DESERT

MADAGASCAR

AUSTRALIA

Tropic of Capricorn

Cape of Good Hope

Antarctic Circle

ANTARCTICA

30°E   60°E   90°E   120°E   150°E

The World: Political

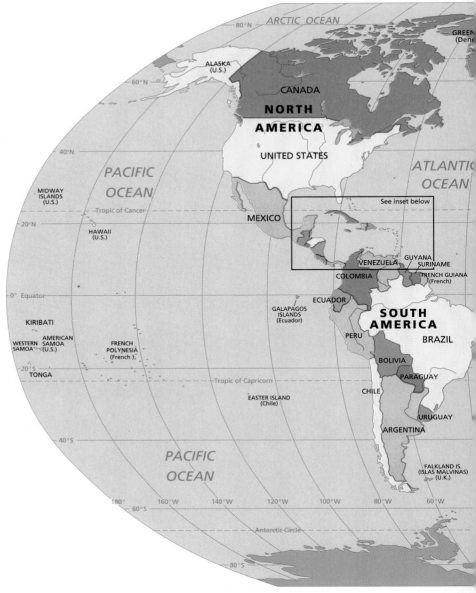

ARCTIC OCEAN

GREEN
(Den

ALASKA
(U.S.)

CANADA

NORTH
AMERICA

UNITED STATES

PACIFIC
OCEAN

ATLANTIC
OCEAN

MIDWAY
ISLANDS
(U.S.)

Tropic of Cancer

MEXICO

See inset below

HAWAII
(U.S.)

VENEZUELA
COLOMBIA

GUYANA
SURINAME
FRENCH GUIANA
(French)

Equator

GALAPAGOS
ISLANDS
(Ecuador)

ECUADOR

SOUTH
AMERICA

PERU

BRAZIL

KIRIBATI

WESTERN
SAMOA

AMERICAN
SAMOA
(U.S.)

FRENCH
POLYNESIA
(French)

BOLIVIA

PARAGUAY

TONGA

CHILE

Tropic of Capricorn

EASTER ISLAND
(Chile)

URUGUAY

ARGENTINA

PACIFIC
OCEAN

FALKLAND IS.
(ISLAS MALVINAS)
(U.K.)

Antarctic Circle

National boundary

Abbreviations

BOS.-HER.	BOSNIA & HERZEGOVINA
DEM. REP. OF THE CONGO	DEMOCRATIC REPUBLIC OF THE CONGO
DEN.	DENMARK
CZECH REP.	CZECH REPUBLIC
FR.	FRANCE
F.Y.R. MACEDONIA	FORMER YUGOSLAV REPUBLIC OF MACEDONIA
GR.	GREECE
LIECH.	LIECHTENSTEIN
NETH.	NETHERLANDS
NOR.	NORWAY
PORT.	PORTUGAL
REP. OF THE CONGO	REPUBLIC OF THE CONGO
SWITZ.	SWITZERLAND
U.A.E.	UNITED ARAB EMIRATES
U.K.	UNITED KINGDOM
U.S.	UNITED STATES

Central America and West Indies

FLORIDA (U.S.)

Gulf of Mexico

BAHAMAS

Tropic of Cancer

CUBA

ATLANTIC OCEAN

HAITI
DOMINICAN
REPUBLIC

VIRGIN ISLANDS
(U.S. and U.K.)

JAMAICA

MEXICO

BELIZE

PUERTO RICO
(U.S.)

ST. KITTS
AND NEVIS

ANTIGUA AND
BARBUDA

GUADELOUPE (Fr.)
DOMINICA

CARIBBEAN SEA

GUATEMALA

HONDURAS

MARTINIQUE (Fr.)

EL SALVADOR

NICARAGUA

ARUBA
(Neth.)

NETHERLANDS
ANTILLES
(Neth.)

ST. LUCIA

ST. VINCENT &
THE GRENADINES

BARBADOS

GRENADA

PACIFIC OCEAN

COSTA RICA

TRINIDAD & TOBAGO

0   200   400 Miles
0   200   400 Kilometers
Mercator Projection

PANAMA

COLOMBIA

VENEZUELA

GUYANA

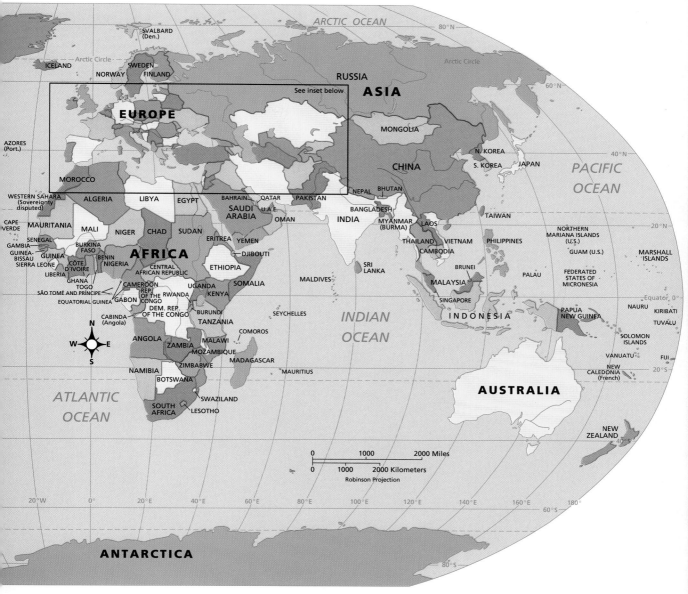

Europe and Central Asia

The World: Elevation

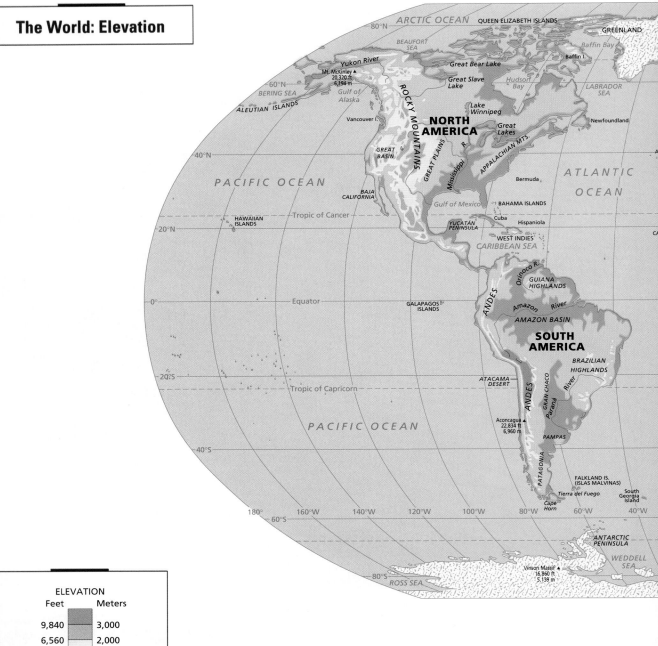

ARCTIC OCEAN QUEEN ELIZABETH ISLANDS

GREENLAND

BEAUFORT SEA

Baffin Bay

80°N

Great Bear Lake

Baffin I.

Mt. McKinley ▲
20,320 ft
6,194 m

Yukon River

Great Slave Lake

Hudson Bay

LABRADOR SEA

60°N
BERING SEA

Gulf of Alaska

ROCKY MOUNTAINS

ALEUTIAN ISLANDS

Vancouver I.

NORTH AMERICA

Lake Winnipeg

Great Lakes

Newfoundland

GREAT BASIN

GREAT PLAINS

Mississippi R.

APPALACHIAN MTS.

40°N

PACIFIC OCEAN

ATLANTIC OCEAN

Bermuda

A2

BAJA CALIFORNIA

Gulf of Mexico

BAHAMA ISLANDS

Tropic of Cancer

HAWAIIAN ISLANDS

YUCATÁN PENINSULA

Cuba

Hispaniola

20°N

WEST INDIES

CAR

CARIBBEAN SEA

Orinoco R.

GUIANA HIGHLANDS

0°

Equator

GALAPAGOS ISLANDS

ANDES

Amazon River

AMAZON BASIN

SOUTH AMERICA

BRAZILIAN HIGHLANDS

20°S

Tropic of Capricorn

ATACAMA DESERT

ANDES

GRAN CHACO

Paraná River

Aconcagua ▲
22,834 ft
6,960 m

PACIFIC OCEAN

PAMPAS

40°S

PATAGONIA

FALKLAND IS.
(ISLAS MALVINAS)

Tierra del Fuego

South Georgia Island

Cape Horn

180°   160°W   140°W   120°W   100°W   80°W   60°W   40°W

60°S

ANTARCTIC PENINSULA

WEDDELL SEA

Vinson Massif ▲
16,860 ft
5,139 m

80°S

ROSS SEA

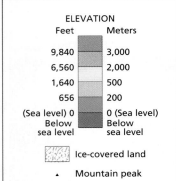

ELEVATION

Feet		Meters
9,840		3,000
6,560		2,000
1,640		500
656		200
(Sea level) 0		0 (Sea level)
Below sea level		Below sea level

░ Ice-covered land

▲ Mountain peak

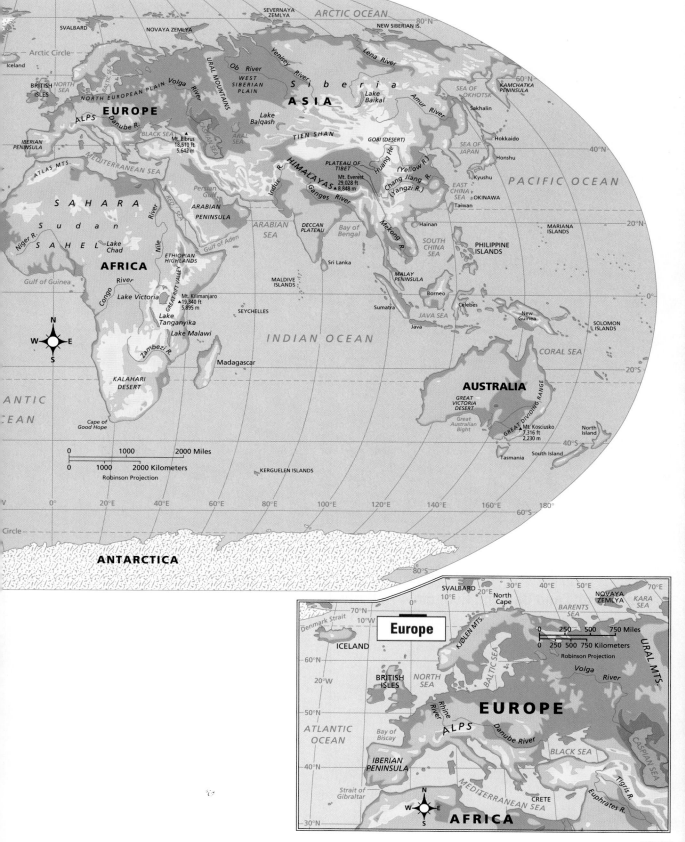

ARCTIC OCEAN

SEVERNAYA
ZEMLYA
NEW SIBERIAN IS.

SVALBARD
NOVAYA ZEMLYA

Arctic Circle
Iceland

BRITISH
ISLES
NORTH
SEA

EUROPE

ALPS
Danube R.

IBERIAN
PENINSULA

ATLAS MTS.

MEDITERRANEAN SEA

URAL MOUNTAINS

Volga River

NORTH EUROPEAN PLAIN

BLACK SEA

Mt. Elbrus
18,510 ft
5,642 m

Ob River

WEST
SIBERIAN
PLAIN

Yenisey River

Lena River

S i b e r i a

ASIA

Lake
Baikal

Amur River

SEA OF
OKHOTSK

KAMCHATKA
PENINSULA

Sakhalin

60°N

40°N

URAL SEA

ARAL
SEA

TIEN SHAN

GOBI (DESERT)

Hokkaido

SEA OF
JAPAN

Honshu

PACIFIC OCEAN

SAHARA

S u d a n

SAHEL

Niger R.

AFRICA

Gulf of Guinea

Congo

River

Lake Victoria

Lake
Chad

Persian
Gulf

RED SEA

Nile

ARABIAN
PENINSULA

Gulf of Aden

ETHIOPIAN
HIGHLANDS

HIMALAYAS

PLATEAU OF
TIBET

Mt. Everest
29,028 ft
8,848 m

Indus R.

Ganges River

ARABIAN
SEA

DECCAN
PLATEAU

Bay of
Bengal

Sri Lanka

MALDIVE
ISLANDS

Huang He

Chang Jiang R.
(Yangzi R.)

(Yellow R.)

EAST
CHINA
SEA

Taiwan

Hainan

SOUTH
CHINA
SEA

Mekong R.

MALAY
PENINSULA

Kyushu

OKINAWA

MARIANA
ISLANDS

20°N

0°

PHILIPPINE
ISLANDS

GREAT RIFT VALLEY

Mt. Kilimanjaro
19,340 ft
5,895 m

Lake
Tanganyika

Lake Malawi

Zambezi R.

SEYCHELLES

INDIAN OCEAN

MADAGASCAR

Sumatra

Borneo

Celebes

JAVA SEA

Java

New
Guinea

SOLOMON
ISLANDS

N
W   E
S

KALAHARI
DESERT

Cape of
Good Hope

20°S

CORAL SEA

AUSTRALIA

GREAT
VICTORIA
DESERT

Great
Australian
Bight

GREAT DIVIDING RANGE

Mt. Kosciusko
7,316 ft
2,230 m

North
Island

0   1000   2000 Miles
0   1000   2000 Kilometers
Robinson Projection

KERGUELEN ISLANDS

Tasmania

South Island

40°S

60°S

ATLANTIC
OCEAN

ANTARCTICA

80°S

Circle

0°   20°E   40°E   60°E   80°E   100°E   120°E   140°E   160°E   180°

ATLANTIC
OCEAN

SVALBARD
30°E
North Cape
10°E   20°E
0°
10°W

70°N

20°W

ICELAND

Denmark Strait

BRITISH
ISLES

60°N

NORTH
SEA

50°N

Bay of
Biscay

IBERIAN
PENINSULA

40°N

Strait of
Gibraltar

N
W   E
S

30°N

KJØLEN MTS.

BARENTS
SEA

40°E   50°E

NOVAYA
ZEMLYA

70°E

KARA
SEA

BALTIC SEA

Rhine
River

ALPS

Danube River

MEDITERRANEAN SEA

EUROPE

Volga   River

BLACK SEA

CRETE

URAL MTS.

CASPIAN SEA

Tigris R.

Euphrates R.

AFRICA

Europe

0   250   500   750 Miles
0   250   500   750 Kilometers
Robinson Projection

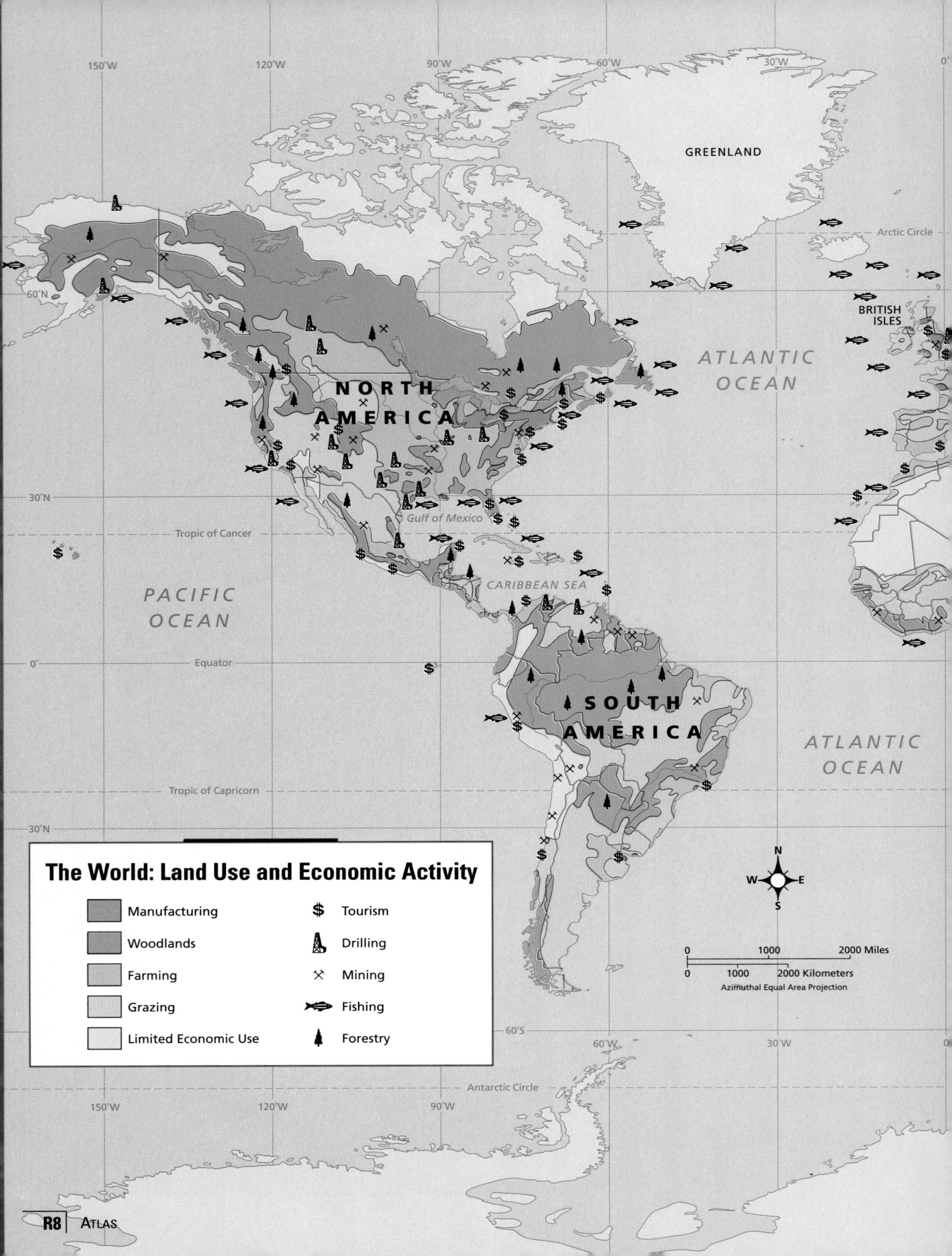

150°W 120°W 90°W 60°W 30°W 0°

GREENLAND

Arctic Circle

60°N

BRITISH
ISLES

NORTH
AMERICA

ATLANTIC
OCEAN

30°N

Tropic of Cancer

Gulf of Mexico

PACIFIC
OCEAN

CARIBBEAN SEA

Equator 0°

SOUTH
AMERICA

ATLANTIC
OCEAN

Tropic of Capricorn

30°N

The World: Land Use and Economic Activity

▨	Manufacturing	$	Tourism
▨	Woodlands	⬧	Drilling
▨	Farming	✕	Mining
▨	Grazing	🐟	Fishing
▨	Limited Economic Use	♠	Forestry

N
W — E
S

0	1000	2000 Miles
0	1000	2000 Kilometers

Azimuthal Equal Area Projection

60°S

60°W 30°W

Antarctic Circle

150°W 120°W 90°W

ARCTIC OCEAN

EUROPE

BALTIC
SEA

BLACK SEA

MEDITERRANEAN SEA

AFRICA

MADAGASCAR

ASIA

INDONESIA

INDIAN
OCEAN

PACIFIC
OCEAN

Tropic of Cancer

Equator

AUSTRALIA

Tropic of Capricorn

NEW
ZEALAND

ANTARCTICA

30°E   60°E   90°E   120°E   150°E

30°E   60°E   90°E   120°E   150°E

Antarctic Circle

ASIA

RUSSIA

ARCTIC OCEAN

North Pole

GREENLAND
(KALAALLIT NUNAAT)
(DENMARK)

ICELAND

EU

Baffin Bay

Bering Strait

BEAUFORT SEA

ALEUTIAN ISLANDS

Yukon River

Anchorage

Gulf of Alaska

Mackenzie R.

Great Bear Lake

Great Slave Lake

Hudson Bay

PACIFIC OCEAN

ROCKY

Peace River

Athabasca River

Saskatchewan River

CANADA

Nelson River

Gulf of St. Lawrence

Vancouver

Calgary

Lake Winnipeg

Québec

St. Lawrence River

Halifax

Seattle

Portland

Missouri River

Montréal

Ottawa

Boston

CASCADE RANGE

COASTAL RANGE

SIERRA NEVADA

M O U N T A I N S

Lake Superior

Minneapolis

Lake Michigan

Lake Huron

Toronto

Lake Ontario

New York

Great Salt Lake

Snake River

Milwaukee

Chicago

Detroit

Lake Erie

Cleveland

Philadelphia

San Francisco

River

Omaha

Pittsburgh

Baltimore

Washington D.C.

Denver

Kansas City

St. Louis

Ohio River

Cincinnati

ATLANTIC OC

Colorado River

UNITED STATES

Mississippi

Memphis

APPALACHIAN MTS.

BERMUDA
(U.K.)

Los Angeles

San Diego

Phoenix

El Paso

Red River

Dallas

Atlanta

Charleston

Savannah

BAJA CALIFORNIA

Rio Grande

San Antonio

Houston

New Orleans

Jacksonville

Tampa

Gulf of Mexico

Miami

Nassau

TURKS AND CAICOS IS. (U.K.)

PUERTO RICO (U.S.)

ST. (N

VIRGIN IS. (U.S.)

Gulf of California

SIERRA MADRE

MEXICO

SIERRA MADRE

Monterrey

Havana

BAHAMAS

CUBA

Santiago de Cuba

DOMINICAN REPUBLIC

HAITI

Port-au-Prince

Santo Domingo

GUADELOUPE MARTI

MONTSE

Guadalajara

Mexico City

Cuernavaca

Veracruz

YUCATÁN PENINSULA

CAYMAN ISLANDS (U.K.)

Kingston

JAMAICA

ST. VINC THE GRE

Oaxaca

BELIZE

Belmopan

CARIBBEAN SEA

CURAÇAO (Neth.)

ARUBA (Neth.)

BONAIRE (Neth.)

TRINIDAD

GUATEMALA

Guatemala

HONDURAS

Tegucigalpa

San Salvador

EL SALVADOR

NICARAGUA

Managua

COSTA RICA

San José

PANAMA

Panama City

SOUTH AMERIC

North America

⊛ National capital

• Other city

— National boundary

Tropic of Cancer

N
W   E
S

0   500   1000 Miles

0   500   1000 Kilometers

Azimuthal Equal Area Projection

CARIBBEAN SEA

Barranquilla

Maracaibo • Caracas

VENEZUELA

Orinoco River

Medellín

Magdalena River

Bogotá

COLOMBIA

Georgetown

GUYANA • Paramaribo

• Cayenne

SURINAME FRENCH
GUIANA
(Fr.)

ATLANTIC
OCEAN

Quito

ECUADOR

Guayaquil

Iquitos

Manaus *River*

Amazon

Equator 0°

10°N

BRAZIL

Fortaleza

ANDES PERU

Lima

Recife

10°S

Lake
Titicaca

La Paz

BOLIVIA

Sucre

Brasília

São Francisco River

Salvador

CHILE

PARAGUAY

River

Paraná River

Belo Horizonte

Rio de Janeiro

São Paulo

20°S

Paraguay

Asunción

ANDES

Uruguay River

Pôrto Alegre

ATLANTIC
OCEAN

30°S

Cordoba

URUGUAY

PACIFIC
OCEAN

Valparaíso • Santiago

Rosario

Buenos Aires

Montevideo

Río de la Plata

ARGENTINA

N

W E

S

40°S

South America

⊛ National capital

• Other city

— National boundary

| 0 | 250 | 500 | 750 | 1000 Miles |

| 0 | 250 | 500 | 750 | 1000 Kilometers |

Azimuthal Equal Area Projection

Stanley

FALKLAND IS.
(ISLAS MALVINAS)
(U.K.)

*TIERRA
DEL
FUEGO*

Cape Horn

90°W 80°W 70°W 60°W 50°W 40°W 30°W 20°W

Europe

⊛ National capital

• Other city

⊢⊣ Canal

— National boundary

ICELAND

Reykjavík

Arctic Circle

FAROE IS.
(Den.)

SHETLAND IS.
(U.K.)

Trondheim

SWEDEN

NORWAY

Bergen

Stavanger

Oslo

Uppsala

Stockholm

Göteborg

Gulf of Bothnia

BALTIC SEA

BORNHOLM
(Den.)

Gdánsk

Vistula R.

NORTHERN
IRELAND
(U.K.)

SCOTLAND

Glasgow

Edinburgh

Belfast

NORTH SEA

DENMARK

Copenhagen

Dublin

UNITED
KINGDOM

Liverpool

Manchester

IRELAND

WALES

ENGLAND

Birmingham

Cardiff

London

Bristol

Thames R.

Dover

Hamburg

Bremen

NETHERLANDS

The Hague

Amsterdam

Rotterdam

Berlin

Oder

POLAND

GERMANY

Elbe R.

English Channel

Calais

Brussels

BELGIUM

Bonn

Leipzig

Prague

Kraków

River

CZECH
REPUBLIC

ATLANTIC OCEAN

Le Havre

Seine River

Paris

LUXEMBOURG

Luxembourg

SLOVAKIA

Loire River

Strasbourg

Rhine R.

Stuttgart

Danube River

FRANCE

Dijon

Munich

LIECHTENSTEIN

Vienna

Bratislava

Budapest

Bay of Biscay

La Rochelle

Geneva

Bern

Vaduz

SWITZERLAND

AUSTRIA

HUNGARY

Bordeaux

Garonne River

Lyon

ALPS

Ljubljana

Trieste

SLOVENIA

Zagreb

Porto

PYRENEES

Milan

Turin

Po River

Venice

CROATIA

Ebro River

ANDORRA

Genoa

BOSNIA-
HERZEGOVINA

PORTUGAL

Madrid

Tagus River

SPAIN

Barcelona

Marseille

Nice

MONACO

SAN
MARINO

APENNINES

Sarajevo

ADRIATIC SEA

MONTENEGRO

Lisbon

Florence

Tiber R.

Valencia

Corsica
(Fr.)

VATICAN
CITY

Rome

ITALY

Tiranë

ALBANIA

Seville

Cadiz

Sardinia
(It.)

BALEARIC ISLANDS
(Sp.)

Naples

TYRRHENIAN SEA

Strait of Gibraltar

GIBRALTAR
(U.K.)

MEDITERRANEAN

Palermo

Sicily

IONIAN SEA

AFRICA

MALTA Valletta

SEA

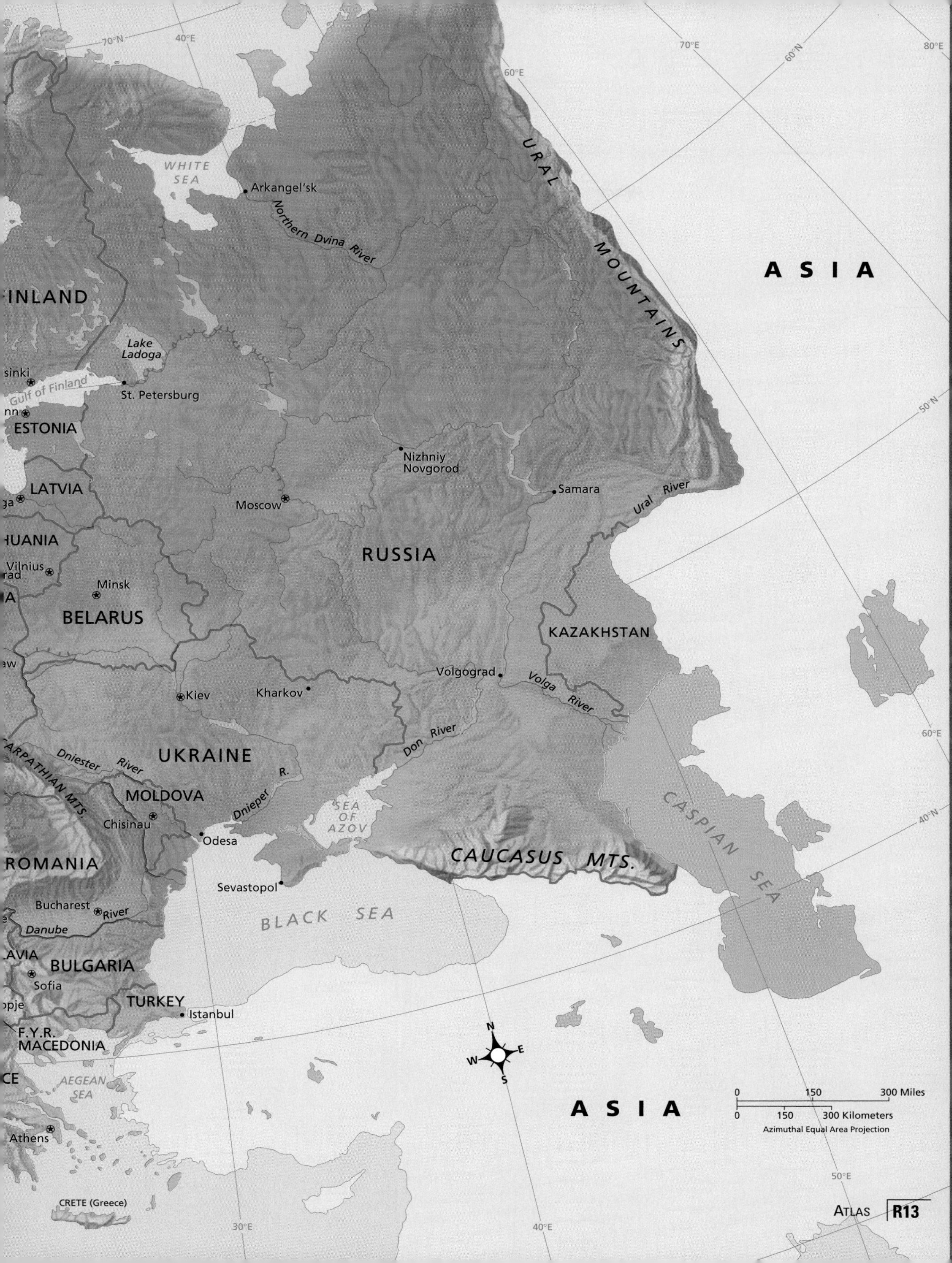

70°N
40°E
70°E
60°N
80°E
60°E
WHITE SEA
Arkangel'sk
Northern Dvina River
URAL MOUNTAINS
ASIA
FINLAND
Lake Ladoga
sinki
Gulf of Finland
St. Petersburg
nn
ESTONIA
50°N
Nizhniy Novgorod
Samara
Ural River
LATVIA
ga
Moscow
HUANIA
RUSSIA
Vilnius
rad
Minsk
A
BELARUS
KAZAKHSTAN
aw
Volgograd
Volga River
Kiev
Kharkov
60°E
Don River
ARPATHIAN MTS.
Dniester River
UKRAINE
R.
MOLDOVA
Dnieper
SEA OF AZOV
CASPIAN SEA
40°N
Chisinau
Odesa
ROMANIA
CAUCASUS MTS.
Sevastopol
Bucharest
River
Danube
BLACK SEA
LAVIA
BULGARIA
Sofia
pje
TURKEY
Istanbul
F.Y.R. MACEDONIA
N
E
W
S
CE
AEGEAN SEA
ASIA
0
150
300 Miles
0
150
300 Kilometers
Azimuthal Equal Area Projection
Athens
50°E
CRETE (Greece)
30°E
40°E

75°N

Arctic Circle

60°N

EUROPE

45°N

BLACK SEA

GEORGIA

Tbilisi

Baku

Ankara

ARMENIA

Yerevan

TURKEY

CAUCASUS

AZERBAIJAN

CASPIAN SEA

KAZAKHSTAN

Astana

Lake Balqash

ARAL SEA

UZBEKISTAN

Bishkek

KYRGYZSTAN

Tashkent

Samarkand

Dushanbe

TAJIKISTAN

TURKMENISTAN

Ashgabat

Ob

River

Irtysh

River

Yekaterinburg (Sverdlovsk)

Chelyabinsk

Omsk

Novosibirsk

URAL MOUNTAINS

Yenisey

River

Nicosia

CYPRUS

Beirut

LEBANON

Damascus

SYRIA

Euphrates R.

Tigris R.

Baghdad

IRAQ

IRAN

Tehran

Kabul

AFGHANISTAN

Islamabad

Disputed

Lahore

HIMALAYAS

Brahmaputra R.

NEPAL

MEDITERRANEAN SEA

Jerusalem

Amman

ISRAEL

JORDAN

Kuwait

KUWAIT

Persian Gulf

PAKISTAN

Indus R.

New Delhi

Kathmandu

Ganges R.

BANGLAD

30°N

SAUDI

Manama

BAHRAIN

QATAR

Doha

Abu Dhabi

OMAN

Muscat

Karachi

INDIA

Dhaka

Tropic of Cancer

RED SEA

Riyadh

UNITED ARAB EMIRATES

ARABIA

OMAN

Calcutta

Jidda

Mecca

Undefined

Mumbai (Bombay)

ARABIAN SEA

Bay of Beng

15°N

Sanaa

YEMEN

Aden

Gulf of Aden

Socotra I. (YEMEN)

LAKSHADWEEP ISLANDS (India)

Chennai (Madras)

ANDAM
ISLA
(In

AFRICA

SRI LANKA

Colombo

N

W   E

S

Male

MALDIVES

0° Equator

INDIAN OCEAN

30°E

0	500	1000 Miles

0	500	1000 Kilometers

Robinson Projection

45°E

60°E

75°E

90°E

105° 120°E 135°E 150°E 165°E 180° 165°W 150°W

ARCTIC OCEAN

75°N

Arctic Circle

R U S S I A

Lena River

60°N

BERING SEA

Lena   River

KAMCHATKA PENINSULA

SEA OF OKHOTSK

Lake Baikal

Amur

River

45°N

M O N G O L I A

• Ulaanbaatar

GOBI

• Harbin

• Vladivostok

KURIL ISLANDS

SEA OF JAPAN

Yalu R.

N. KOREA

Beijing ⊛

⊛ P'yŏngyang

JAPAN

Tianjin•

Seoul ⊛

Tokyo•

C H I N A

Huang He

YELLOW SEA

S. KOREA

Kobe•

• Yokohama

Osaka•

Jiang

• Shanghai

30°N

Chang

• Chongqing

EAST CHINA SEA

PACIFIC OCEAN

RYUKYU IS.
(Japan)

Xi

River

Taipei•

Tropic of Cancer

TAIWAN

• Guangzhou

YANMAR
(URMA)

Mekong

Macao•
(Port.)

• Hong Kong

Hanoi•

LAOS

LUZON STRAIT

15°N

165°E

Yangon
(Rangoon)•

Vientiane•

Luzon

PHILIPPINE SEA

THAILAND

SOUTH CHINA SEA

Bangkok•

CAMBODIA **VIETNAM**

Manila ⊛

PHILIPPINES

Phnom ⊛
Penh

• Ho Chi Minh City

COBAR
LANDS
dia)

BRUNEI

BRUNEI ⊛ Bandar Seri Begawan

M A L A Y S I A

⊛ Kuala Lumpur

⊛ Singapore
SINGAPORE

Sumatra

JAVA SEA

Equator

⊛ Jakarta

I N D O N E S I A

105°E 120°E 135°E 150°E 165°E

Asia

⊛ National capital

• Other city

— National boundary

EUROPE

ASIA

AZORES
(Port.)

MADEIRA IS.
(Port.)

Strait of Gibraltar
Tangier
Casablanca Rabat
Oran
Algiers
Tunis

MEDITERRANEAN SEA
Suez Canal

CANARY IS.
(Sp.)

MOROCCO

TUNISIA
Tripoli

Benghazi
Alexandria
Cairo

WESTERN
SAHARA
(Sovereignty
Disputed)

ALGERIA

LIBYA

EGYPT

Nile

Tropic of Cancer

S   A   H   A   R   A

RED SEA

MAURITANIA

MALI

NIGER

CHAD

Khartoum

Blue Nile
River

ERITREA
Asmara

Nouakchott

Tomboctou

Niger

Lake Chad

SUDAN

DJIBOUTI
Djibouti

Gulf of

Dakar
SENEGAL
Banjul
GAMBIA
Bissau
GUINEA-
BISSAU
Conakry
SIERRA LEONE
Freetown

Bamako

BURKINA
FASO
Ouagadougou

Niamey

River

Kano

N'Djamena

NIGERIA
Abuja

CENTRAL AFRICAN
REPUBLIC

White Nile

Addis Ababa

ETHIOPIA

SOMALIA

GUINEA

BENIN
TOGO

CÔTE
D'IVOIRE GHANA
Yamoussoukro
Monrovia
LIBERIA
Abidjan

Ibadan
Lomé
Accra
Porto-
Novo

Lagos

CAMEROON
Bangui

Mogadishu

Malabo
EQUATORIAL GUINEA
SÃO TOMÉ
AND PRÍNCIPE
São
Tomé

Gulf of Guinea

Yaoundé

Congo   River

Kisangani

UGANDA
Kampala

KENYA

Nairobi

Equa

INDIAN
OCEAN

0° Equator

Libreville
GABON
REP. OF
THE
CONGO
Brazzaville

DEMOCRATIC
REPUBLIC
OF THE
CONGO

Kigali
RWANDA
Bujumbura
BURUNDI

Lake
Victoria

N
W   E
S

CABINDA
(Angola)

Kinshasa

Kananga

Lake
Tanganyika

Mombasa
Pemba I.
Zanzibar I.
Dar es-Salaam

TANZANIA

SEYCHELL

ATLANTIC
OCEAN

Luanda

COMOROS
Moroni

ANGOLA

Lake Malawi

Nampula

MADAGASCA

Prime Meridian

Zambezi
River

ZAMBIA
Lusaka

Lake
Kariba

MALAWI
Lilongwe

Zambezi R.

Harare

MOZAMBIQUE

Mozambique Channel

Antananarivo

20°S

ZIMBABWE

Victoria
Falls

Bulawayo

Beira

REUNIO

NAMIBIA

BOTSWANA

Windhoek
WALVIS BAY
(S. Africa)

Gaborone

Limpopo

R.

Tropic of Capricorn

Johannesburg
Orange
Vaal
R.
Maseru
LESOTHO

Pretoria
Maputo
Mbabane
SWAZILAND

SOUTH
AFRICA

Cape Town

Port Elizabeth

Africa

⊛ National capital

• Other city

⊣⊢ Cataracts of the Nile

─ National boundary

0   500   1000 Miles

0   500   1000 Kilometers
Azimuthal Equal Area Projection

PHILIPPINE SEA

120°E

135°E

150°E

NORTHERN MARIANA IS. (U.S.)

WAKE ISLAND (U.S.)

165°E

180°

HAWAII (U.S.)

165°W

150°W

135°W

15°N

GUAM (U.S.)

Koror
PALAU

CAROLINE ISLANDS

Pohnpei

MARSHALL ISLANDS

Majuro

PACIFIC OCEAN

FEDERATED STATES OF MICRONESIA

Tarawa

Equator 0°

MARQUESAS ISLANDS

ARAFURA SEA

TIMOR SEA

Darwin

Port Moresby

PAPUA NEW GUINEA

SOLOMON ISLANDS

Honiara

NAURU

Yaren District

TUVALU

Funafuti

KIRIBATI

TOKELAU IS. (N.Z.)

WESTERN SAMOA

WALLIS & FUTUNA (Fr.)

Apia

AMERICAN SAMOA (U.S.)

COOK ISLANDS (N.Z.)

SOCIETY IS.

TAHITI

FRENCH POLYNESIA (Fr.)

TUAMOTU ARCH.

15°S

Gulf of Carpentaria

Great Barrier Reef

CORAL SEA

VANUATU

Port-Vila

FIJI

Suva

TONGA

Nuku'alofa

NIUE I. (N.Z.)

Tropic of Capricorn

AUSTRALIA

Alice Springs

NEW CALEDONIA (Fr.)

LOYALTY IS. (Fr.)

Monday Sunday

30°S

Perth

Great Australian Bight

Broken Hill

Adelaide

Brisbane

Port Macquarie

Sydney

Canberra

Geelong

Melbourne

Bass Strait

TASMAN SEA

NORFOLK ISLAND (Aust.)

Auckland

NORTH ISLAND

NEW ZEALAND

International Date Line

INDIAN OCEAN

0   500   1000 Miles
0   500   1000 Kilometers
Mercator Projection

TASMANIA

Hobart

SOUTH ISLAND

Wellington

Christchurch

CHATHAM ISLANDS (N.Z.)

Dunedin

120°E

135°E

150°E

165°E

180°

165°W

150°W

135°W

45°S

Australia, New Zealand, and the South Pacific

⊛   National capital

•   Other city

—   National boundary

PACIFIC OCEAN

160°W

140°W

120°W

100°W

80°W

SOUTH AMERICA

60°W

50°S

60°S

Antarctic Circle

AMUNDSEN SEA

BELLINGSHAUSEN SEA

Ellsworth Land

ANTARCTIC PENINSULA

Antarctica

■   Stations

☐   Ice shelf

Marie Byrd Land

70°S

ROSS SEA

Ross Ice Shelf

McMurdo (U.S.)

Ronne Ice Shelf

WEDDELL SEA

40°W

160°E

Victoria Land

South Pole
Amundsen-Scott (U.S.)

Gen. Belgrano (Argentina)

Halley (U.K.)

Dumont d'Urville (France)

20°W

South Magnetic Pole

40°E

Wilkes Land

Vostok (Russia)

Queen Maud Land

Antarctic Circle

ATLANTIC OCEAN

60°S

500   1000 Miles
500   1000 Kilometers
Azimuthal Equal Area Projection

DAVIS SEA

Syowa (Japan)

20°E

20°E

INDIAN OCEAN

Mawson (Australia)

Enderby Land

100°E

80°E

40°E

0°

ATLAS   **R17**

130°W   50°N   120°W   110°W   100°W

·Seattle
·Olympia   WASHINGTON

Portland·   Columbia   River

COAST RANGES   Salem·
CASCADE RANGE   OREGON   IDAHO   MONTANA
·Helena   NORTH DAKOTA
·Bismarck   Far

·Boise   ·Billings
Snake
River   BLACK HILLS   SOUTH DAKOTA
·Pierre   Sioux F
Missouri R

40°N   WYOMING

R O C K Y

Great Salt Lake   ·Salt Lake City   Cheyenne·   NEBRASKA   Lin

COAST   ·Carson City   NEVADA   UTAH   M O U N T A I N S   ·Denver
SIERRA NEVADA   Sacramento·
·San Francisco   COLORADO   KANS.

CALIFORNIA   Las Vegas·   Colorado   River   ·Santa Fe   Oklaho
RANGES   ·Los Angeles   Colorado   Albuquerque·   OKLAH
ARIZONA   ·Amarillo

PACIFIC OCEAN   NEW MEXICO   ·Lubbock

·San Diego   ·Phoenix

30°N   120°W   ·Tucson   TEXAS

·El Paso   Austin

110°W   Rio Grande   ·San Antonio

Inset — Hawaii:

Kauai   22°N
Niihau   Oahu
Honolulu★   Molokai   HAWAII
160°W   Lanai   Maui
Kahoolawe
PACIFIC OCEAN   Hawaii·
0   75   150 Miles   19°N
0   75   150 Kilometers   155°W

Inset — Alaska:

ARCTIC OCEAN   180°
Arctic Circle
ALASKA
170°E   Yukon River
Fairbanks·
160°W   Mount McKinley
(20,320 ft/   MEXICO
6194 m)
50°N   ·Anchorage   60°N
0   250   500 Miles
0   250   500 Kilometers   BERING SEA
PACIFIC OCEAN   Juneau★   140°W
180°   170°W   ALEUTIAN ISLANDS   Gulf of Alaska
160°W   150°W   140°W

CANADA

90°W   50°N   80°W   70°W

St. Lawrence River

MAINE

MINNESOTA

Lake Superior

Duluth

Augusta ★

VERMONT
Montpelier ★

NEW
HAMPSHIRE

Lake Huron

GREEN MTS.

Concord ★

Minneapolis

St. Paul ★

Mississippi

WISCONSIN

Lake Michigan

MICHIGAN

Lansing ★

Lake Ontario

Rochester •

Albany ★

Boston ★

MASSACHUSETTS

River

Milwaukee •

Madison ★

Detroit •

Buffalo •

NEW
YORK

Hudson River

Hartford ★

Providence ★

RHODE ISLAND

CONNECTICUT

IOWA

Des Moines ★

Chicago •

Gary •

Lake Erie

Cleveland •

PENNSYLVANIA

New York City •

Trenton ★

OHIO

Harrisburg ★

Pittsburgh •

Philadelphia •

NEW
JERSEY

ILLINOIS

INDIANA

Columbus •

MD.

Dover ★

DELAWARE

Springfield ★

Indianapolis ★

Cincinnati •

Ohio River

WEST
VIRGINIA

Washington,
D.C.

Annapolis ★

Kansas
City

St. Louis •

Frankfort ★

Louisville •

Charleston ★

Richmond ★

Chesapeake Bay

Jefferson
City

KENTUCKY

VIRGINIA

Norfolk •

MISSOURI

ATLANTIC
OCEAN

Nashville ★

Raleigh •

70°W

ARKANSAS

TENNESSEE

Tennessee River

NORTH CAROLINA

Charlotte •

APPALACHIAN MTS.

Memphis •

SOUTH

Columbia ★

Wilmington •

Little Rock ★

Birmingham •

Atlanta ★

CAROLINA

Charleston •

Red

Mississippi River

ALABAMA

GEORGIA

MISSISSIPPI

Montgomery ★

Savannah •

Jackson •

River

Mobile •

Jacksonville •

Tallahassee ★

Houston

Baton Rouge •

LOUISIANA

New Orleans •

FLORIDA

Orlando •

Gulf of Mexico

Tampa •

N
W   E
S

Miami •

The United States

⊛   National capital

★   State capital

•   Other city

——   National boundary

——   State boundary

0   250   500 Miles

0   250   500 Kilometers

Albers Equal Area Projection

90°W   80°W

50°N
120°W
110°W
100°W

★ Seattle
Olympia ★
WASHINGTON
CASCADE RANGE
Portland • Columbia River
Salem ★

R O C K Y

Missouri River
Helena ★
MONTANA
• Billings

NORTH DAKOTA
Bismarck ★
Farg

OREGON
IDAHO
• Boise
Snake River

40°N

WYOMING

BLACK HILLS
SOUTH DAKOTA
Pierre ★
Sioux Fal

COAST
SIERRA
Carson City ★
Sacramento ★
San Francisco •
NEVADA

Great Salt Lake
★ Salt Lake City
UTAH

M O U N T A I N S

Cheyenne ★

NEBRASKA

Lincol

RANGES
Death Valley
CALIFORNIA
Las Vegas •

Colorado River

Denver •
COLORADO

KANSAS
To

PACIFIC OCEAN

Grand Canyon

Santa Fe ★
Albuquerque •

Oklahoma City •
OKLAHO

Los Angeles •
ARIZONA
• Phoenix
NEW MEXICO

Amarillo •

Red River

San Diego •

• Lubbock

30°N
120°W
110°W

To understand the relative locations of
Alaska and Hawaii as well as the vast
distances separating them from the rest of
the United States, see the map on page R4.

Gulf of California
• Tucson
★ El Paso

TEXAS

Austin ★

San Antonio ★

Rio Grande

MEXICO

Kauai
Niihau Oahu
Honolulu ★ Molokai HAWAII
160°W Lanai Maui
Kahoolawe
PACIFIC OCEAN
Hawaii
22°N
19°N
155°W
0 75 150 Miles
0 75 150 Kilometers

ARCTIC OCEAN
180°
Arctic Circle
60°N

ALASKA
Yukon River
Fairbanks •
▲ Mount McKinley
(20,320 ft.
6,194 m)

• Anchorage

170°E
0 250 500 Miles
0 250 500 Kilometers
BERING SEA
160°W
150°W
140°W
50°N
180°
170°W
ALEUTIAN ISLANDS
PACIFIC OCEAN
Gulf of Alaska
Juneau ★
60°N
140°W

100°W

CANADA

MINNESOTA
Duluth

Lake Superior

MICHIGAN

Lake Huron

MAINE

★ Augusta

VERMONT
Montpelier ★

NEW HAMPSHIRE
★ Concord

Minneapolis
● ★ St. Paul

WISCONSIN

Madison ★
● Milwaukee

Lansing ★

Lake Ontario
Rochester ●

Albany ★

Boston ●
MASSACHUSETTS
Providence ●

Lake Michigan

IOWA

● Des Moines ★

Chicago ●

Detroit ●

Lake Erie

NEW YORK
● Buffalo

Hartford ★
RHODE ISLAND
CONNECTICUT

Mississippi River

● Gary

Cleveland ●

PENNSYLVANIA

● New York City

ILLINOIS

INDIANA

OHIO
Columbus ★

Harrisburg ★

Pittsburgh ●

NEW JERSEY
Trenton ★
Philadelphia ●

Springfield ★

Indianapolis ★

Cincinnati ●

Baltimore ●

Dover ★
DELAWARE

Kansas City ●

St. Louis ●

Louisville ●

Ohio River

Frankfort ★

WEST VIRGINIA
Charleston ●

Washington D.C. ⊛

Annapolis ★
MARYLAND

Chesapeake Bay

Jefferson City ★

MISSOURI

KENTUCKY

Richmond ★

VIRGINIA

Norfolk ●

ATLANTIC OCEAN

ARKANSAS

★ Nashville

TENNESSEE

Tennessee River

NORTH CAROLINA
★ Raleigh

Charlotte ●

APPALACHIAN MTS.

Little Rock ★

Memphis ●

Wilmington ●

Columbia ●

SOUTH CAROLINA

Birmingham ●

★ Atlanta

Mississippi River

Charleston ●

ALABAMA

GEORGIA

Jackson ★

Montgomery ★

Savannah ●

MISSISSIPPI

Mobile ●

Jacksonville ●

Baton Rouge ★

★ Tallahassee

LOUISIANA

New Orleans ●

Gulf of Mexico

Orlando ●

FLORIDA

Tampa ●

Miami ●

Albers Equal Area Projection

The United States: Elevation

Feet	Meters
9,840	3,000
6,560	2,000
1,640	500
656	200
(Sea level) 0 Below sea level	0 (Sea level) Below sea level

⊛ National capital
★ State capital
● Other city
━━ National boundary
── State boundary

0   250   500 Miles
0   250   500 Kilometers

Gazetteer

Acre (AH-kruh) (33°N 35°E) seaport in present-day Israel; last stronghold of Crusaders in the Holy Land, captured by Muslims in 1291 *m*252, *m*253

Aegean Sea sea between Greece and Turkey *m*102, *m*118

Afghanistan landlocked country between Iran, Pakistan, and the Central Asian republics; invaded by the Soviet Union in 1979 *m*R14-15

Africa world's second largest continent; surrounded by the Atlantic Ocean, the Indian Ocean, and the Mediterranean Sea *m*297, 815, R16

Aix-la-Chapelle (eks-lah-shah-PEL) (50°N 6°E) capital of Charlemagne's empire; today the German city of Aachen (AH-kuhn) *m*227

Aksum ancient kingdom in what is now Ethiopia *m*300

Alexandria (31°N 30°E) historic city in north central Egypt; major commercial center of the Roman Empire; important Christian center around A.D. 100 *m*155

Algeria North African country; gained independence from France in 1962 after a long and bitter war of liberation *m*815, R16

Alps mountain system of south central Europe; crossed by Hannibal and his army in 218 B.C. *m*149, *m*155, R12-13

Alsace-Lorraine region in western France taken by the German Empire in 1871, restored to France in 1918 at the Treaty of Versailles, taken again by Germany in World War II, and returned to France at the end of the war *m*584, *m*644, *m*659

Amazon River major river in South America; second-longest river in the world *m*R11

Andes Mountains great mountain range of South America *m*309, R11

Angola country in Southwest Africa; gained independence from Portugal in 1975 *m*815, R16

Antioch (37°N 37°E) ancient city in Asia Minor, now in ruins; captured by crusaders in the First Crusade *m*252, *m*253

Apennines mountain range that runs the length of the Italian peninsula *m*144, R12-13

Appalachian Mountains mountain system of eastern North America *m*306, R10

Aquitaine historical region of southwest France, much of which was acquired by English kings in 1100s through marriage; won back by the French king Philip II *m*244

Arabian Peninsula peninsula in southwestern Asia bounded by the Red Sea, the Persian Gulf, and the Arabian Sea; today occupied mostly by Saudi Arabia *m*6, *m*134, *m*209

Arctic Ocean ocean north of the Arctic Circle, line of latitude located at 66 1/2° north of the equator *m*R2-3

Argentina second largest country in South America *m*864, R11

Armenia independent country of the Caucasus region of Asia; former Soviet republic *m*895, R14-15

Asia world's largest continent; located between Europe and the Pacific Ocean *m*R2-3, R14–15

Asia Minor peninsula in south western Asia bounded by the Black Sea and the Mediterranean Sea *m*36, 38, 102

Athens (38°N 24°E) capital and largest city in Greece; ancient polis *m*105, *m*118

Atlantic Ocean body of water between the continents of North and South America and the continents of Europe and Africa; about half the size of the Pacific Ocean *m*362-362, *m*370-371, R2-3

Australia only country occupying an entire continent (also called Australia); located between the Indian Ocean and the Pacific Ocean *m*551, R17

Austria country in west central Europe south of Germany, center of former Habsburg Empire *m*659, 717, R12-13

Avignon (44°N 5°E) city in southern France, seat of the Roman Catholic Church in 1300s *m*271

Azerbaijan country west of the Caspian Sea in the Caucasus region of Asia; former Soviet republic *m*895, R14-15

Babylon (32°N 45°E) ancient capital of Babylonia, now ruins near Hilla, Iraq *m*32, *m*33, *m*34

Babylonia ancient country in the lower Euphrates River valley *m*34

Baghdad (33°N 44°E) capital of Iraq; capital of one of the Muslim caliphates; captured and looted by Timur in the early 1400s *m*209

Bahamas independent country consisting of a chain of islands in the Atlantic Ocean southeast of Florida *m*854, R10

Balkan Peninsula peninsula in southeastern Europe bounded by the Adriatic, Ionian, Mediterranean, Aegean, and Black seas *m*102, *m*659

Balkans countries occupying the Balkan Peninsula—Albania, Bulgaria, Greece, Romania, the former Yugoslavia, and northwestern Turkey; ruled by the Ottomans in the 1300s *m*594

Baltic Sea body of water east of the North Sea and Scandinavia *m*383, *m*648, *m*659

Bangladesh South Asian country surrounded by India on north, west, and east; formerly East Pakistan, gained independence in 1971 *m*777, R14-15

Batavia (7°S 107°E) now Jakarta, Indonesia; city on the northwest coast of the island of Java; first colony of the Dutch in Asia *m*362-363, *m*370-371

Beijing (40°N 116°E) historic city in China, became the capital under the Mongol emperors; capital of the People's Republic of China *m*284, *m*454, *m*783

Belgium country between France and Germany in west central Europe *m*644, 649, R12-13

Bengal important region in the northwestern part of the Indian subcontinent; controlled by the British from 1763 to 1947; divided in 1947 into West Bengal, India, and the western section of Pakistan *m*473

Berlin (53°N 13°E) capital of united Germany; former capital of East Germany, divided into four zones after World War II *m*726, *m*858

Bethlehem (32°N 35°E) city in West Bank area administered by Palestine National Authority; birthplace of Jesus *m*166

Black Sea inland sea between Europe and Asia; connected to the Aegean Sea and, thence, the Mediterranean *m*383, *m*644, *m*645

Bolivia landlocked western South American country; conquered by the Spanish in 1538, gained independence in 1825 *m*568, *m*864, R11

Bombay (Mumbai) (19°N 73°E) India's largest city, located on the western coast; important trading post established by the British East India Company in the 1600s *m*362-362, R14-15

Bonn (51°N 7°E) city in western Germany; capital of the former West Germany, replaced by Berlin as the national capital of the reunified country *m*753, *m*761

Bosnia and Herzegovina mountainous former Yugoslav republic located between Serbia and Croatia in eastern Europe; seceded from Yugoslavia in 1992 *m*644, *m*895, R12-13

Bosporus narrow straits in Turkey that link the Black Sea with the Sea of Marmara *m*189

Brazil largest country in South America; gained independence from Portugal in 1822 *m*568, R11

Brest-Litovsk (52°N 22°E) Russian city on the Bug River on the border with Poland; site of treaty between Russia and Germany in 1918 *m*648

Britain island of Great Britain; part of the United Kingdom in northern Europe *m*R12-13

British Isles island group consisting of Great Britain and Ireland *m*R2-3

Buenos Aires (34°S 59°W) capital of Argentina *m*864, R11

Bulgaria country occupying part of the eastern side of the Balkan Peninsula in Eastern Europe *m*594, *m*645, *m*659, *m*761, R12-13

Burma (Myanmar) mainland Southeast Asian country between India, China, and Thailand *m*733, R14-15

Byzantium (41°N 29°E) ancient city at the site of present-day Istanbul, Turkey; later named Constantinople; capital of the Byzantine Empire *m*118

Calcutta (23°N 88°E) giant industrial center and seaport in eastern India; important trading post established by the British East India Company in the 1600s R14

Cambodia country west of southern Vietnam in mainland Southeast Asia; formerly a French colony *m*796, *m*803, R14-15

Canaan historical name for the region in present-day Israel near the east coast of the Mediterranean *m*38

Canada country occupying most of northern North America, created by the British North America Act of 1867 *m*549, R10

Cape of Good Hope point of land at the tip of southern Africa *m*362-363, *m*370-371

Caracas (11°N 67°W) capital of Venezuela *m*568

Caribbean Sea arm of the Atlantic Ocean between North America and South America *m*854, R10

Carthage (37°N 10°E) city on the northeastern coast of present-day Tunisia; powerful Mediterranean empire in the 300s and 400s B.C.; led by Hannibal in battles against Rome during the late 200s B.C. *m*149

Caucasus region, also known as Caucasia, between the Black and Caspian Seas, now the countries of Georgia, Azerbaijan, and Armenia *m*895

Caucasus Mountains mountain range between the Black Sea and the Caspian Sea in the southern part of the former Soviet Union *m*134

Central America narrow southern portion of the North American continent; consists of the countries of Belize, Guatemala, El Salvador, Honduras, Nicaragua, Costa Rica, and Panama R4

Chang-an (Xi'an) (34°N 108°E) city in east central China on the Wei He; capital of several Chinese dynasties; beginning of the Silk Road *m*77, 278

Chang Jiang (Yangzi River) major river in China that flows from the Kunlun Shan across China to the East China Sea *m*10-11, *m*70

Château-Thierry (49°N 3°E) city in northern France; site of important Allied victory late in World War I *m*649

Chechnya region in southern Russia; declared independence in 1991; after Russian invasion in 1994, Chechnya once again became part of Russia, but with almost complete self-government *m*895

Chichén Itzá (chee-CHEN eet-sah) (21°N 89°W) site of extensive ancient Mayan ruins on the Yucatán Peninsula, Mexico *m*309

Chile country in western South America; liberated from Spanish rule in 1818 *m*568, R11

China, People's Republic of communist country in East Asia, established in 1949; world's most populous country *m*783, R15

Colombia country in northern South America *m*864, R11

Concord (42°N 71°W) Massachusetts town, with Lexington, where the first fighting of the Revolutionary War took place *m*421

Congo, Democratic Republic of the, formerly Zaire; country in Central Africa; gained independence from Belgium in 1960 *m*815, R16

Congo River river that forms part of the western boundary of the Democratic Republic of the Congo, flows to the Atlantic Ocean; one of the largest rivers in the world *m*297, *m*607, *m*815, R16

Constantinople (42°N 28°E) ancient city in the European part of Turkey, once the capital of the Byzantine Empire; sacked by crusaders in 1204; seized by Ottoman Turks in 1453; now known as Istanbul *m*170, *m*189, *m*191, *m*470

Córdoba (38°N 5°W) city in southern Spain; capital of one of the Muslim caliphates *m*209, *m*270

Corsica Mediterranean island of France; birthplace of Napoleon *m*R12-13

Costa Rica country in Central America *m*R10

Côte d'Ivoire formerly Ivory Coast, Atlantic coast country of West Africa; gained independence from France in 1960 *m*815, R16

Crete Greek Mediterranean island south of the mainland; home of the ancient Minoan civilization *m*102, 105, 118, 594

Crimea small peninsula of Ukraine that juts southward into the Black Sea *m*594

Croatia Eastern European country and former Yugoslav republic; seceded from Yugoslavia in 1991 *m*895, R12-13

Cuba country and largest island of the Greater Antilles in the Caribbean; under communist rule since 1959 *m*854, R10

Cuzco (14°S 72°W) city southeast of present-day Lima, Peru; ancient capital of the Inca Empire *m*309

Cyprus island in the eastern Mediterranean Sea *m*594

Czechoslovakia Eastern European country formed after World War I; communist-ruled from 1948 to 1989; now divided into the Czech Republic and Slovakia

Dahomey former French colony, now known as Benin, in West Africa R16

Danube River major river in Central Europe that flows into the Black Sea *m*386, *m*388,

Danzig (54°N 18°E) important Polish port city on the Baltic, now known as Gdansk *m*648, *m*659, *m*726

Delhi (29°N 77°E) city north of New Delhi, India; important city in the Mughal Empire; sacked by Persians in 1739, ending the power of the Mughals *m*220

Delphi (38°N 22°E) sacred Greek site *m*118

Denmark one of the Scandinavian countries of northern Europe; occupied by Germany during World War II; one of the original 12 members of NATO *m*761, R12-13

Dien Bien Phu (21°N 102°E) town in northwestern Vietnam where French troops were defeated by Viet Minh troops in 1954, leading to the end of French involvement in Indochina *m*796, *m*803

Dnieper (NEE-puhr) **River** major river in Ukraine that empties into the Black Sea *m*197

Dunkirk (51°N 2°E) French city on the English Channel to which the Allied forces retreated in 1940, leaving France to fall to the Germans *m*726

E

East Berlin (53°N 13°E) the eastern half of Berlin, which was divided at the end of World War II; became the capital of communist East Germany *m*753, *m*761

Eastern Hemisphere the part of the world east of longitude 0° (the prime meridian) and west of longitude 180°

East Germany See German Democratic Republic

East Indies term often used to refer to the Malay Archipelago *m*362-363

East Pakistan See Bangladesh

East Prussia region once part of Prussia, separated in 1919, divided between the Soviet Union and Poland in 1945 *m*385, *m*388

Ecuador country in western South America on the equator *m*864, R11

Edessa (37°N 38°E) city in Asia Minor captured by crusaders in the First Crusade and recaptured by the Muslims in the Second Crusade; today the city of Urfa in southern Turkey; *m*252, *m*253

Egypt country of North Africa east of Libya; gained independence from Great Britain in 1922 *m*815, R16

Elba island off the northwest coast of Italy where Napoleon was exiled in 1814 *m*442

El Salvador small country on the Pacific side of Central America *m*854, R10

England southern part of Great Britain and part of the United Kingdom in northern Europe *m*408, R12

English Channel waterway separating Great Britain from the European continent *m*408, R12-13

Estonia small Baltic country; became territory of the Soviet Union in 1939; gained independence in 1991 *m*659, *m*726, *m*895, R12-13

Ethiopia East African country in the Horn of Africa *m*607, *m*717, *m*815, R16

Euphrates River major river primarily in Iraq in southwestern Asia; Mesopotamian civilization grew up between the Euphrates and Tigris Rivers *m*6, *m*10-11, *m*28

Europe continent between the Ural Mountains and the Atlantic Ocean *m*R2-3, R12-13

Falkland Islands islands in the South Atlantic Ocean belonging to the United Kingdom but claimed by Argentina *m*568, R11

Fertile Crescent wide arc of productive land that runs from the eastern shore of the Mediterranean Sea, through the plains along the Tigris and Euphrates Rivers, to the Persian Gulf *m*28

Finland country of northern Europe between Sweden, Norway, and Russia *m*659, *m*726, R12-13

Florence (44°N 11°E) important art and cultural city on the Arno River in central Italy; historic home of the ruling Medici family *m*326

France country in Western Europe northeast of the Iberian Peninsula *m*659, R12-13

G

Ganges (GAN-jeez) **River** major river in India flowing from the Himalayas southeastward to the Bay of Bengal; center of Indian civilization by the 600s B.C. *m*62, *m*63

Gaul ancient country covering parts of present-day France and Belgium; attacked in the mid-400s by Attila *m*170

Gaza Strip area in southwest Asian, formerly part of the British protectorate of Palestine; occupied by Israel from 1967 to 1994; under Palestinian self-rule in 1994 *m*833

Geneva (46°N 6°E) diplomatic city in southwestern Switzerland; center of Calvinism in the 1500s *m*340

German Democratic Republic former nation in north central Europe; formed in 1949 of Russian zone of Germany; reunified with West Germany in 1990 *m*753, *m*761

Germany country in Western Europe; created in 1871 out of Prussia and surrounding states; member of the Central Powers in World War I; fascist aggressor nation in World War II; divided into East and West Germany after World War II; reunified in 1990 *m*659, *m*726, R12-13

Germany, Federal Republic of former nation in west central Europe; formed in 1949 of American, British, and French zones of Germany; reunified with East Germany in 1990 *m*753, *m*761

Ghana as a British colony, known as Gold Coast; gained independence from Great Britain in 1957, the first sub-Saharan colony to become independent *m*815, R16

Gibraltar (36°N 5°W) small territory of the United Kingdom situated at the entrance to the Mediterranean Sea from the Atlantic Ocean R12-13

Gilbert Islands South Pacific island group that makes up part of the country of Kiribati; controlled by Japan in World War II until the Allies took control in late 1943 *m*733

Gobi vast desert that makes up part of the Mongolian plateau in East Asia *m*70, R14-15

Gold Coast colonial name for Ghana in West Africa *m*607

Granada (37°N 4°W) city in southern Spain; capital of the Moorish kingdom of Granada, captured by Spain in 1492 *m*270

Gran Colombia nation formed in 1819; included the present-day countries of Venezuela, Colombia, Panama, and Ecuador; broke apart in 1830 *m*568

Grand Duchy of Warsaw kingdom created by Napoleon from Prussia's Polish lands; divided among Prussia and Russia at the Congress of Vienna *m*442

Great Britain the largest island of the British Isles composed of Britain, Scotland, and Wales; major island of the United Kingdom *m*408

Greater Antilles the Caribbean islands of Cuba, Puerto Rico, Hispaniola (the countries of the Dominican Republic and Haiti), and Jamaica R10

Great Lakes largest freshwater lake system in the world comprising Lakes Erie, Huron, Ontario, Michigan, and Superior; located in North America R6-7

Great Plains plains region in the middle of the United States between the Interior Plains to the east and the Rocky Mountains to the west R6-7

Great Rift Valley geological fault line in eastern Africa that runs from the Mediterranean Sea to Mozambique *m*297, R6-7

Greece country in southern Europe located at the southern end of the Balkan Peninsula *m*594, R12-13

Grenada Caribbean island country; invaded by the United States in 1983 *m*854, R10

Guadalcanal South Pacific island that is part of the Solomon Islands; controlled by the Japanese during World War II until 1943 when the Allied Forces took control *m*733

Guam (14°N 143°E) South Pacific island and U.S. territory in Micronesia; became U.S. territory in 1898; occupied by the Japanese in World War II *m*733, R17

Guangzhou (GWAHNG-JOH) (23°N 113°E) major Chinese port on the Xi Jiang; formerly known as Canton by English-speakers *m*280, *m*456

Guatemala most populous country in Central America, area of ancient Maya culture *m*854, R10

Guatemala City (15°N 91°W) capital of Guatemala; site of 1987 peace conference of representatives from Central American countries *m*854

Hague, The (52°N 4°E) seat of the government of the Netherlands and location of the International Court of Justice, the UN organization that decides questions of international law *m*761

Haiti country occupying western third of the Caribbean island of Hispaniola; gained independence from France in 1804 *m*565, *m*568, *m*854

Hanoi (21°N 106°E) capital of North Vietnam; capital of Vietnam after unification of North and South Vietnam in 1975 *m*796, *m*803

Harappa (31°N 73°E) ancient city in the Indus River valley, seat of the Harappan civilization *m*10-11, *m*54

Havana (23°N 82°W) capital of Cuba; the U.S. battleship Maine was blown up in the harbor of Havana, leading to the Spanish-American War *m*624, *m*854

Himalayas mountain system in South Asia; site of world's highest mountains *m*62, *m*63, R14-15

Hindu Kush high mountain range that forms the western section of the mountain barrier separating the Indian subcontinent from the rest of Asia *m*62, *m*63

Hiroshima (34°N 132°E) city on Honshu island in Japan; site of first atomic bombing during World War II *m*733

Ho Chi Minh City (11°N 107°E) formerly Saigon, major city in southern Vietnam; capital of the former country of South Vietnam *m*796

Holland See Netherlands

Holy Land Palestine (see m166), referred to in Bible as Holy Land; birthplace of Judaism and Christianity *m*252

Honduras country south of Belize in Central America *m*854, R10

Hong Kong (22°N 115°E) prosperous British colony in southeast China, established in 1842 by the Treaty of Nanjing; transferred to the control of China in 1997 *m*619, *m*733

Huang He (Yellow River) one of the world's longest rivers, located in northern China; site of early civilizations *m*6, *m*10-11, *m*70

Hudson Bay inland sea almost surrounded by Canada; named for Henry Hudson, who explored the area in the early 1600s *m*370-371, *m*549

Hungary country in Eastern Europe between Romania and Austria; settled by the Magyars in the 800s; became independent nation in 1919; came under Soviet influence after World War II; communist rule officially ended in 1990 *m*659, *m*761, *m*895, R12-13

Iberian Peninsula peninsula in southwestern Europe composed of Spain and Portugal m102

India country of South Asia and second-most populous country in the world; under British rule from 1765 until 1947 *m*777, R14-15

Indochina the southeast peninsula of Asia, consisting of Burma, Thailand, Laos, Cambodia, Vietnam, and West Malaysia

Indonesia largest island country in Southeast Asia; composed of 13,660 islands in the Indian and Pacific Oceans *m*796, R14-15

Indus River major river in Pakistan; site of earliest civilizations *m*6, *m*10-11, *m*54

Iran oil-rich country of southwestern Asia north of the Persian Gulf; formerly Persia *m*837, R14-15

Iraq oil-rich country between Iran and Saudi Arabia in southwestern Asia *m*837, R14-15

Ireland country west of Great Britain in the British Isles of northern Europe; unified with the United Kingdom in 1801, after civil war the country was divided into the Irish Free State and Northern Ireland in 1922 *m*R12-13

Islas Malvinas (EES-luhs mahl-VEE-nuhs) Argentina's name for the Falkland Islands *m*568, R11

Israel eastern Mediterranean country of southwestern Asia; made a state by UN partition of Palestine in 1948 *m*833, R14-15

Istanbul (41°N 29°E) largest city and leading seaport in Turkey; see Constantinople *m*726

Italy country consisting of a boot-shaped peninsula stretching southward from Europe into the Mediterranean Sea and the major islands of Sicily and Sardinia *m*761, R12-13

Iwo Jima small island about 650 miles southeast of Tokyo, Japan; captured by the United States in World War II after heavy fighting with the Japanese *m*733

Japan prosperous East Asian country consisting of four large "home" islands and more than 3,000 smaller islands in the western Pacific Ocean *m*465, R14-15

Jerusalem (32°N 35°E) capital of Israel—the ancient kingdom and the modern nation; captured by crusaders in 1099, recaptured by Muslims in 1187 *m*38, *m*166, *m*252, *m*253, *m*833

Jidda (21°N 39°E) port on the Red Sea in western Saudi Arabia; the seaport of Mecca *m*209

Jordan Southwest Asian country stretching east from the Dead Sea and the Jordan River into the Arabian Desert; formerly the British protectorate of Transjordan *m*833, *m*837, R14-15

Kaifeng (35°N 114°E) city in northeast China; capital of the Song Dynasty until 1125 *m*280

Karakorum (kahr-uh-KOHR-uhm) (43°N 103°E) ancient city, now in ruins, in present-day Mongolia; made a capital city by Genghis Khan *m*284

Kashmir mountainous region in the north of the Indian subcontinent; claimed by both India and Pakistan *m*777

Kenya East African country; gained independence from Great Britain in 1963 *m*815

Kiev (50°N 30°E) city on the Dnieper River; served as the capital of Russia from about 882 to 1169; now the capital of Ukraine *m*197, *m*895

Korea peninsula on east coast of Asia divided between the countries of North Korea and South Korea; controlled by China for much of its history *m*790

Kush African kingdom in present-day Sudan, reached the height of its power between 250 B.C. and A.D. 150 *m*300

Kuwait small, oil-rich country on the northwest coast of the Persian Gulf in southwestern Asia; seized in 1990 by Iraq, leading to Persian Gulf War *m*837, R14-15

Kyoto (kee-oht-oh), Japan (35°N 136°E) formerly Heian, the ancient capital of Japan; present-day manufacturing city on the island of Honshu *m*465

Kyyiv See Kiev

Laos landlocked and mountainous country of mainland Southeast Asia; formed as a French protectorate in 1899; became independent in 1975 *m*796, R14-15

Latin America in general, the Spanish- and Portuguese-speaking countries of Middle and South America

Latvia small Baltic country; became a territory of the Soviet Union in 1939; gained independence in 1990 *m*659, *m*726, *m*895, R12-13

Lebanon country lying between Israel and Syria on the Mediterranean coast; gained independence from France in 1943 *m*833, R14-15

Leipzig (51°N 12°E) city in eastern Germany, where Napoleon was defeated by Russian, Prussian, Austrian, and Swedish armies in 1813 *m*442

Leningrad See St. Petersburg

Lesser Antilles chain of small islands beginning at the U.S. Virgin Islands and extending down to Trinidad and Tobago

Lexington (42°N 71°W) Massachusetts town, with Concord, where the fighting in the American Revolutionary War began *m*421

Leyte Gulf (11°N 125°E) gulf in southern Philippines; site of the largest naval engagement in history, in October 1944, between Japan and the Allies *m*733

Liberia country in southern West Africa; founded in 1817 for the resettlement of freed African-American slaves *m*607, R16

Lima (12°S 77°W) capital of Peru *m*568

Lithuania Baltic country made a territory of the Soviet Union in 1939; gained independence in 1990 *m*659, *m*726, *m*895, R12-13

London (52°N 0°W) capital and largest city of the United Kingdom *m*408, *m*726, R12-13

Lydia ancient country in present-day Turkey; the Lydians were the first people in history to use coined money *m*36, *m*38, *m*118

Macao (22°N 113°E) Portuguese territory near Hong Kong; trading station established by the Portuguese in 1557; transferred to China in 1999 *m*456, R14-15

Macedonia name of the powerful empire led by Alexander the Great; fell to Rome in 168 B.C.; also modern-day independent Balkan country; former Yugoslav republic; *m*134, *m*895

Machu Picchu (13°S 73°W) ancient Inca city, now in ruins, high in the Andes Mountains of Peru *m*309

Malacca (muh-LAK-uh) (2°N 102°E) city on the west coast of the Malay Peninsula; historic center of spice trade, captured by Portugal in 1515 *m*362-363, *m*370-371

Malay Peninsula peninsula in southeast Asia consisting of West Malaysia and the southwestern part of Thailand *m*619

Malaysia country in Southeast Asia consisting of most of the Malay Peninsula and part of the island of Borneo *m*796, R14-15

Mali country of West Africa along the Niger River; area where the Mali Empire flourished *m*815, R16

Manchukuo name given by the Japanese to Manchuria, 1932–1945 *m*700, *m*713

Manchuria region of northeastern China bordering the Korean Peninsula; invaded by Japan in 1931 *m*280, *m*456, *m*616, *m*700, *m*713

Marathon plain northeast of Athens and ancient city on that plain; site of legendary battle between Athens and Persia in 490 B.C. *m*118

Mariana Islands South Pacific island chain; site of fighting in World War II between Japan and the Allies *m*733, R17

Marne River river in northeastern France, site of early battle, near Paris, of World War I *m*649

Marshall Islands South Pacific island country; site of fighting in World War II between Japan and the Allies *m*733, R17

Mecca (Makkah) (21°N 40°E) important Islamic city in western Saudi Arabia; birthplace of Muhammad *m*209

Medellín (6°N 76°W) city in northwestern Colombia; once a flourishing industrial center, now headquarters of a drug cartel *m*R11

Medina (Al-Madīnah) (24°N 40°E) important Islamic city in western Saudi Arabia *m*209

Mediterranean Sea sea surrounded by Europe, Asia, and Africa *m*102, R2-3

Meroë capital of the ancient African kingdom of Kush; one of the earliest centers of ironworking in the world *m*300

Mesopotamia ancient name for plains along the Tigris and Euphrates Rivers; area known as the location of one of the world's first civilizations *m*10-11, *m*28

Mexico country in southern North America; site of Aztec and Maya civilizations; won independence from Spain in 1821 *m*568, R10

Mexico City (19°N 99°W) capital of Mexico, once the center of the Aztec Empire *m*568 See Tenochtitlán

Middle America region that includes Mexico, Central America, and the Caribbean islands

Midway Island U.S. island territory in the North Pacific Ocean; site of decisive naval victory for the United States in World War II *m*733

Mississippi River major river in the central United States *m*423, R20-21

Mohenjo-Daro (27°N 68°E) ancient city in the Indus Valley *m*10-11, *m*54

Moluccas (muh-LUKH-uhz) group of islands in eastern Indonesia; see Spice Islands.

Montreal (46°N 74°W) financial and industrial center of Quebec, Canada, founded by French settlers in 1642; second largest French-speaking city in the world *m*549, R10

Morocco nation on the Mediterranean and Atlantic coasts of Africa; gained independence from France in 1956 *m*607, *m*815, R16

Moscow (56°N 38°E) capital of Russia; formerly the capital of the Soviet Union; site of major defeat of Napoleon's army in 1812 *m*197, 687, 726, 895

Mount Olympus (38°N 24°E) mountain (9,570 ft.; 2,917 m) in northeastern Greece, believed to be the home of the Greek gods *m*105, *m*118

Mozambique country in Southeast Africa; gained independence from Portugal in 1975 *m*815, R16

Munich (48°N 12°E) major city and manufacturing center in southern Germany; site of the Munich Conference in 1938 *m*717

Myanmar See Burma

Nagasaki (33°N 130°E) Japanese port city on the island of Kyushu; trading post established by the Dutch in 1600s; site of second atomic bombing in World War II *m*465, *m*733

Nanjing (32°N 119°E) Chinese industrial city on the Chang Jiang; imperial capital during the early Ming dynasty; occupied by the Japanese during World War II *m*733

Naples (41°N 14°E) major seaport in southern Italy *m*577

Nazareth (31°N 35°E) ancient city in present-day Israel; where Jesus grew up *m*166

Netherlands flat, low-lying country in Northwest Europe *m*761, R12-13

Netherlands East Indies former name of Indonesia *m*733

New France former possessions of France from the St. Lawrence River to the Mississippi River in present-day Canada and the United States *m*370-371

New Zealand island nation southeast of Australia *m*551, R17

Nicaragua country in Central America *m*854, R10

Nile River world's longest river; flows into the Mediterranean Sea in Egypt *m*6, *m*10-11

Normandy region of northwestern France; 60-mile stretch of beaches west of Caen, France, where Allied forces landed in 1944, beginning the final stages of World War II in Europe *m*726

North America continent including Canada, the United States, Mexico, Central America, and the Caribbean islands *m*R2–3, R10

Northern Ireland the six northern counties of Ireland that remain part of the United Kingdom; also called Ulster R12–13

North Korea Communist country on the northern part of the Korean Peninsula *m*790, R14-15

North Sea sea between Great Britain, Denmark, and the Scandinavian Peninsula R12-13

North Vietnam Communist nation in Southeast Asia established in 1954; began aiding liberation movement in South Vietnam in 1964; eventually took over South Vietnam in 1975 *m*803

Norway Europe's northernmost nation; one of the Scandinavian countries *m*761, R12-13

Nuremberg (49°N 11°E) city in southern Germany where Nazi war criminals were tried after World War II *m*753

O

Oder River river in Poland forming part of the border with Germany *m*726

Okinawa (26°N 128°E) largest of the Ryukyu Islands; captured by U.S. forces in World War II after heavy losses *m*733

Olympia (38°N 22°E) site of original Olympic Games *m*118

P

Pacific Ocean Earth's largest ocean; located between North and South America and Asia and Australia *m*362-363, *m*370-371, R2-3

Pakistan mainly Muslim country created by the partition of India in 1947 *m*777, R14-15

Palestine region in Southwest Asia at the eastern end of the Mediterranean Sea; now occupied primarily by Israel *m*166, See Holy Land

Panama country in Central America; invaded by the United States in 1989 in order to capture Manuel Noriega, the dictator involved in drug-trafficking *m*854, R10

Panama Canal canal allowing transport between the Pacific Ocean and the Caribbean Sea, located in central Panama; opened in 1914 *m*624

Paraguay landlocked country in central South American *m*864, R11

Pearl Harbor (21°N 158°W) port in the Hawaiian Islands where the U.S. Pacific Fleet was heavily damaged by a Japanese surprise attack in 1941 *m*733

Persian Gulf body of water between Iran and the Arabian Peninsula *m*837, R14-15

Peru country in northwestern South America; area of ancient cultures, including the Inca; much of the country liberated from Spanish rule in 1821 *m*568, R11

Petrograd See St. Petersburg

Philippines country of islands in Southeast Asia lying north of Indonesia and across the South China Sea from mainland Southeast Asia; became territory of the United States in 1898, gained independence in 1946 *m*619, 796, R14-15

Phoenicia (fi-NI-shuh) ancient country on the eastern coast of the Mediterranean Sea famed for its commerce *m*38

Phnom Penh (12°N 105°E) capital of Cambodia *m*796, 803

Poland Eastern Europe's largest and most populous country; invaded by Germany at the beginning of World War II; under communist rule until 1989 *m*726, *m*761, *m*895, R12-13

Portugal country in southern Europe just west of Spain on the Iberian Peninsula R12-13

Prague (50°N 14°E) capital of the former Czechoslovakia, now capital of the Czech Republic; site of demonstrations against Soviet domination of Czechoslovakia in 1968 *m*761

Prussia former German state *m*388, *m*442, *m*446

Puerto Rico island commonwealth of the United States in the Greater Antilles in the Caribbean Sea; became a U.S. possession in 1898 *m*854, R10

Pyrenees mountain range along the border of France and Spain *m*209, R12-13

Q

Qingdao (CHING-DOW) (36°N 121°E) port city in eastern China; German naval base seized by Japan during World War I *m*616,

Quebec mainly French-speaking province in eastern Canada; permanent French settlement established there in 1608 *m*549

R

Red Sea inland sea between the Arabian Peninsula and northeastern Africa *m*209, *m*815,

Rhine River major river in Western Europe that flows through Germany into the North Sea in the Netherlands *m*379, *m*659

Romania country in Eastern Europe between Ukraine and Bulgaria; gained independence from the Ottoman Empire in 1878; under communist rule from mid-1940s to 1989 *m*594, 761, 895, R12-13

Rome (42°N 13°E) capital of Italy; center of the Roman Empire *m*149, *m*155, *m*166, *m*577

Russia giant nation stretching from the center of Europe and the Baltic Sea to the eastern tip of Asia and the coast of the Bering Sea; gained its independence from Mongols in 1480 *m*442, 446, 895, R12-13

S

Sahara immense desert region in northern Africa *m*297, R16

Saigon See Ho Chi Minh City

St. Lawrence River major river linking the Great Lakes with the Gulf of St. Lawrence and the Atlantic Ocean in southeastern Canada; explored by Jacques Cartier in the mid-1530s *m*549

St. Petersburg (60°N 30°E) formerly Leningrad; called Petrograd 1914 to 1924; Russia's second largest city and former capital; located on the Gulf of Finland in northwestern Russia *m*383, *m*648

Samoa group of South Pacific islands divided between American Samoa, which was annexed by the United States in the 1880s, and the independent country of Western Samoa *m*619

São Paulo (24°S 47°W) Brazil's largest city and the heart of South America's largest and wealthiest industrial area; located in southeastern Brazil R11

Sarajevo (44°N 18°E) capital of Bosnia and Herzegovina in Eastern Europe; where Archduke Francis Ferdinand was assassinated, setting off World War I *m*644

Saratoga (43°N 74°W) city in New York state; site of Revolutionary War battle fought in 1777 and won by American colonists *m*421

Sardinia large Italian island in the Mediterranean Sea west of Italy, ruled by Carthage in 200s B.C.; later seized by Rome; the Kingdom of Sardinia, which included parts of mainland Italy, led the drive for Italian unification in the second half of the 1800s *m*577

Saudi Arabia oil-rich country occupying much of the Arabian Peninsula in southwestern Asia *m*837, R14-15

Savoy region that includes parts of southeast France and northwest Italy *m*577

Scandinavia region including Denmark, Norway, Sweden, and sometimes Finland and Iceland

Scotland northern part of the island of Great Britain *m*408

Seoul (SOHL) (38°N 127°E) capital of South Korea *m*790

Serbia republic in Eastern Europe, part of what was Yugoslavia *m*594, *m*644, *m*645, *m*895, R12-13

Siam See Thailand.

Siberia vast region of Russia extending from the Ural Mountains to the Pacific Ocean *m*895

Sicily large Mediterranean island off the southern Italian mainland *m*144, *m*149, *m*726

Silesia region in Central Europe; seized by Prussia from Austria in 1742, divided and given to Poland and Czechoslovakia after World Wars I and II *m*385, 388, 584

Sinai Peninsula peninsula of northeastern Egypt between the Gulf of Suez, Gulf of Aqaba, and Mediterranean Sea *m*38, *m*833

Singapore tiny but prosperous island-country situated at the tip of the Malay Peninsula of Southeast Asia *m*619, *m*733, *m*796, R14-15

Slovenia independent country in Eastern Europe and a former Yugoslav republic; gained independence in 1991 *m*895, R12-13

Solomon Islands South Pacific island chain in Melanesia; controlled by Japan in the early years of World War II *m*733

South Africa country in southern Africa, ruled by the system of apartheid until the 1990s *m*607, 815, R12-13

South America world's fourth largest continent; extends from Colombia to Cape Horn R2-3, R11

South China Sea body of water between Vietnam and the Philippines R14-15

South Korea country occupying the southern half of the Korean Peninsula *m*790, R14-15

South Vietnam former nation in Southeast Asia; fell to North Vietnam in 1975 *m*803

Southern Hemisphere the part of the world south of the equator

Soviet Union former giant northern Eurasian country, the Union of Soviet Socialist Republics (USSR) composed of 15 republics, including Russia *m*687, *m*761

Spain country in southern Europe occupying most of the Iberian Peninsula *m*R12-13

Spanish Netherlands historic region in the southern part of the Netherlands that became Belgium; was part of the Spanish Habsburg Empire until the War of Spanish Succession *m*340

Sparta ancient Greek militaristic city-state *m*118

Spice Islands former name of the Moluccas; once famed producers of spices, captured by Portugal in 1511, then by the Dutch in the early 1600s *m*362-363, *m*370-371

Sri Lanka formerly Ceylon; island country south of India; settled by the Portuguese in the early 1500s *m*362-363, 370-371, R14-15

Stalingrad (49°N 42°E) city on the Volga River in the Soviet Union, now known as Volgograd, Russia; site of a major battle during World War II *m*726

Strait of Magellan narrow waterway running between mainland South America and Tierra del Fuego that connects the Atlantic and Pacific oceans *m*362-363, *m*370-371

Strait of Malacca channel between the Malay Peninsula and the Indonesian island of Sumatra that links the Indian Ocean with the South China Sea *m*619,

Strait of Messina narrow strait separating Sicily from the southern tip of Italy *m*149

Sudan East African country; largest country in Africa; gained independence from Britain in 1956 *m*815,

Sudetenland (soo-DAYT-uhn-land) region in northern Czechoslovakia with large German-speaking population; seized by Germans in 1938, returned to Czechoslovakia in 1945 *m*717

Suez Canal canal linking the Red Sea to the Mediterranean Sea in northeastern Egypt *m*726, *m*815, *m*833

Sumer ancient kingdom in Mesopotamia *m*10-11, 28

Sweden nation in northern Europe; largest of the Scandinavian countries *m*761, R12-13

Syracuse ancient Greek city-state on Sicily *m*149

Syria southwest Asian country between the Mediterranean Sea and Iraq; gained independence from France in 1946 *m*833, *m*837, R14-15

T

Tabriz (38°N 46°E) historic commercial city in northwestern Iran, occupied in 1501 by the Safavids who made it their capital *m*470

Taiwan prosperous, industrialized island country off the southeastern coast of China; Chiang Kaishek and the Chinese Nationalists fled here in 1949 *m*783

Tannenberg (54°N 20°E) city in northern Poland; part of Germany prior to 1945; site of World War I battle *m*648

Tenochtitlán (tay-NAWCH-teht-LAHN) (19°N 99°W) capital of the Aztec Empire on the site of present-day Mexico City, Mexico *m*309, *m*362-363

Thailand country of mainland Southeast Asia between Burma, Laos, and Cambodia *m*796, R14-15

Tiber River river that flows through Rome in central Italy *m*144

Tigris River major river in southwestern Asia, flowing from Turkey through Iraq toward the Persian Gulf, forming, with the Euphrates River, Mesopotamia *m*6, *m*10-11, *m*28

Timbuktu (17°N 3°W) city in Mali and an ancient trading center in West Africa *m*304

Tokyo (36°N 140°E) Japan's national capital and the heart of a giant urban area; formerly known as Edo *m*465, *m*733

Tombouctou See Timbuktu

Tours (47°N 1°E) city on the Loire River in France where Muslim invaders were stopped in 732 *m*209

Transjordan See Jordan

Turkey country of the eastern Mediterranean occupying Anatolia and a corner of southeastern Europe *m*761, R14-15

Tyre (33°N 35°E) known today as Sur, Lebanon; renowned commercial city, once the capital of Phoenicia *m*38

Ukraine independent Eastern European country and the second most populous of the republics of the former Soviet Union; gained independence in 1991 *m*895, R12-13

Union of Soviet Socialist Republics (USSR) See Soviet Union.

United Kingdom country occupying most of the British Isles of northern Europe; Great Britain and Northern Ireland *m*761, R12-13

United States North American country between Canada and Mexico *m*R18-19

Ural (YOOR-uhl) **Mountains** mountain range running north to south through Russia and Kazahkstan; considered the boundary between the European and Asian continents *m*197

Uruguay country on the northern side of the Río de la Plata between Brazil and Argentina in eastern South America *m*568, *m*864, R11

Venezuela country in northern South America; liberated from Spanish rule in 1811 *m*864, R11

Versailles (ver-SY) (49°N 2°E) city west of Paris; royal palace built in the 1700s by Louis XIV; treaty ending World War I signed there *m*379

Vienna (48°N 16°E) capital of Austria; center of the Austrian Empire ruled by the Habsburgs *m*442, *m*446, *m*470, *m*761

Vietnam long, narrow country that occupies the eastern portion of the Indochina Peninsula; former French colony; divided into North and South Vietnam in 1954, then unified in 1975 after North Vietnam's conquest of the south *m*796, *m*803, R14-15

Volga River Europe's longest river; located in west central Russia *m*726

Wake Island (19°N 167°E) U.S. Pacific island territory north of the Marshall Islands; captured by Japan in World War II *m*733

Warsaw (52°N 21°E) capital of Poland; occupied by Germans in World War II, fell to Soviet troops in 1944 *m*726

Western Hemisphere the part of the world west of longitude 0° (the prime meridian) and east of longitude 180°

West Germany See Germany, Federal Republic of

West Indies Caribbean islands lying between North and South America R2-3

West Pakistan western half of Pakistan, a Muslim nation created by the partition of India in 1957; the eastern half, Bangladesh, became independent in 1971 *m*777

Xianyang capital of the Qin dynasty in the 200s B.C.; located just to the northwest of Chang-an (Xi'an) *m*77

Yalu River river forming the border between China and North Korea *m*790

Yangzi River See Chang Jiang.

Yucatán Peninsula peninsula in southeastern Mexico, site of several ancient civilizations *m*309

Yugoslavia Eastern European country formed of six republics after World War I; now composed of Serbia and Montenegro *m*659, *m*761, R12-13

Yukon Territory northern Canadian territory bordering Alaska; organized in 1898 after the Klondike gold rush *m*549

Zimbabwe country in southern Central Africa; formerly British colony of Rhodesia; name changed in 1980, when the country achieved full independence *m*815, R16

Phonetic Respelling Guide

Many of the key terms in the textbook have been respelled to help readers pronounce them. The following Phonetic Respelling Guide has been adapted from several common dictionaries. Using the guide along with the text respellings will allow readers to pronounce difficult terms, including biographical and place names.

Mark	As In	Respelling	Example
a	a̲lphabet	a	*AL·fuh·bet
a	A̲sia	ay	AY·zhuh
ä	ca̲rt, to̲p	ah	KAHRT, TAHP
e	le̲t, te̲n	e	LET, TEN
ē	e̲ven, lea̲f	ee	EE·vuhn, LEEF
i	i̲t, ti̲p, Bri̲ti̲sh	i	IT, TIP, BRIT·ish
ī	si̲te, bu̲y, Ohi̲o	y	SYT, BY, oh·HY·oh
	i̲ris	eye	EYE·ris
k	c̲ard	k	KAHRD
kw	qu̲est	kw	KWEHST
ō	o̲ver, rainbo̲w	oh	oh·vuhr, RAYN·boh
u̇	boo̲k, woo̲d	ooh	BOOHK, WOOHD
o̍	a̲ll, o̲rchid	aw	AWL, AWR·kid
äu̇	ou̲t	ow	OWT
ə	cu̲p, bu̲tte̲r	uh	KUHP, BUHT·uhr
ü	ru̲le, foo̲d	oo	ROOL, FOOD
yü	fe̲w	yoo	FYOO
zh	visi̲on	zh	VIZH·uhn

*A syllable printed in small capital letters receives heavier emphasis than the other syllables in a word.

Glossary

This GLOSSARY contains many of the terms you need to understand as you study world history. After each term there is a brief definition or explanation of the meaning of the term as it is used in world history. The page number in parentheses after each definition refers to the page on which the term is boldfaced in the textbook. A phonetic respelling is provided to help you pronounce many of the terms.

A

abbot: elected head of a monastery **(p. 236)**

absolute monarchy: system of government in which the ruler determines policy without consulting either the people or their representatives **(p. 355)**

abstract expressionism: painting style characterized by form, colors, and shapes rather than recognizable objects **(p. 918)**

acid rain: rain formed from precipitation that falls through air polluted by toxins produced by the burning of fossil fuels. **(p. 915)**

acropolis: hill or mountain in Greece that included a fort as well as temples and other public buildings **(p. 105)**

acupuncture: Chinese medicinal practice that involves insertion of needles into designated parts of the body to enable the life-force energy to move properly **(p. 87)**

adobe: sun-dried brick used to build communal houses **(p. 307)**

aerodynamics: principles governing the movement of air around an object **(p. 517)**

agora: marketplace in Greece that was also a public meeting area where all citizens could gather **(p. 105)**

agriculture: raising crops and livestock for food **(p. 8)**

Allied Powers: World War I alliance of Great Britain, France, Russia, and their partners, later including the United States **(p. 645)**

almanacs: books that predict the weather and the prospects for growing crops, and also contain such things as calendars, maps, and medical advice **(p. 344)**

Analects, The: collection of Confucius's writings that became known as Confucianism **(p. 181)**

anarchists: persons who believe in the abolition of all governments **(p. 562)**

anarchy: absence of any government **(p. 170)**

anthropologists: scientists who study the skeletal remains of early humanlike creatures and people to determine how they looked, how long they lived, and other physical characteristics **(p. 4)**

Anti-Comintern Treaty: agreement between Germany and Japan to work together to oppose Russian communism **(p. 716)**

antibiotics: substances that limit or stop the growth of bacteria **(p. 909)**

antisepsis: process of killing disease-causing germs **(p. 522)**

apartheid: official policy of racial separation followed by the South African government for many years **(p. 820)**

appeasement: policy of attempting to preserve peace by yielding to the demands of the aggressor **(p. 718)**

apprentice: person who undergoes training to become a candidate for membership in a craft guild **(p. 260)**

aqueducts: bridgelike structures that carried water **(p. 158)**

arch: curved structure over an opening **(p. 30)**

archaeologists: scientists who excavate ancient settlements and study artifacts **(p. 4)**

archons: elected rulers in the early government of Athens **(p. 113)**

aristocracies: city-states in ancient Greece governed by nobles; later came to mean a privileged social class **(p. 110)**

armistice: agreement to stop fighting **(p. 655)**

artifacts: human-made material objects, for example, a tool, a weapon, or a coin **(p. 4)**

artisans: skilled craft workers **(p. 13)**

ASEAN: Association of Southeast Asian Nations **(p. 808)**

assimilation: situation in which people of a colony abandon their local culture and adopt all aspects of another culture **(p. 610)**

astrolabe: instrument used to calculate latitude **(p. 356)**

Atlantic Charter: 1941 statement of shared national policies by the United States and Britain **(p. 725)**

atrocities: brutal crimes of war, often committed against defenseless civilians **(p. 651)**

Auschwitz: Nazi extermination camp in Poland **(p. 729)**

authoritarian socialism: economic and political system in which the government owns almost all the means of production and controls economic planning; communism **(p. 511)**

autocracy: form of government in which the ruler holds total power **(p. 78)**

autocrat: a ruler who holds absolute power **(p. 588)**

Awami League: political party dedicated to East Pakistan's independence from West Pakistan **(p. 780)**

Axis Powers: alliance including Germany, Italy, and Japan **(p. 716)**

B

Babylonian Captivity: period of relocation of the papacy to Avignon, France, from 1309 to 1377 **(p. 272)**

balance of power: principle of maintaining equilibrium in international politics **(p. 378)**

Balkan League: alliance between Bulgaria, Serbia, Greece, and Montenegro against the Ottoman Empire **(p. 595)**

Balkan "powder keg": description of the international rivalries and instability focused on the Balkans before World War I **(p. 642)**

barter: exchange of one commodity or service for another **(p. 39)**

barter economy: economic system in which goods and services are exchanged for other goods and services without the use of money **(p. 258)**

Battle of Britain: combat between the German and British air forces in World War II **(p. 723)**

belligerents: warring nations **(p. 643)**

Bessemer process: method of making steel that involves the forcing of air through molten iron to burn off carbon and other impurities **(p. 494)**

Bhagavad Gita: the last 18 chapt s of the Mahabharata, stressing the idea of proper conduct for one's status **(p. 57)**

Bill of Rights: the first 10 amendments to the U.S. Constitution **(p. 422)**

biological sciences: sciences that deal with living organisms **(p. 518)**

blitzkrieg: German word for "lightning war" **(p. 720)**

"bobbies": nickname for London police **(p. 529)**

bourgeoisie: (boorzh'wah'ZEE) city-dwelling middle class, made up of merchants, manufacturers, and professional people such as doctors and lawyers; in Marxist philosophy, owners of property **(p. 424, 510)**

boyars: members of the social class of nobles in Kievan society **(p. 197)**

Brahmins: priests in the Indo-Aryan religion; also, members of the priestly class **(p. 55)**

Brezhnev Doctrine: declaration that the Soviet Union would intervene in any satellite nation that seemed to be moving away from communism **(p. 890)**

broadsides: single printed sheets, distributed by publishers, that might contain a royal decree, news of a crime, or some other event **(p. 344)**

burgesses: merchants and professional people from towns and cities **(p. 397)**

Bushido: samurai code of behavior that stressed bravery, loyalty, and honor **(p. 288)**

business cycle: pattern consisting of alternating periods of prosperity and decline **(p. 503)**

Bundesrat: upper house of the German legislature **(p. 582)**

C

cabinet: leaders of Parliament who acted as advisers to the English monarch **(p. 407)**

caliph: Islamic title meaning "successor to the prophet" **(p. 208)**

caliphates: three divisions of the Muslim Empire **(p. 211)**

calligraphy: artistic form of writing used by the Chinese **(p. 75)**

Camp David Accords: Framework for a peace settlement between Egypt and Israel **(p. 834)**

campesinos: Central American peasants **(p. 854)**

canon law: church code of law (**p. 237**)

capital: wealth earned, saved, or invested in order to produce profits (**p. 259**)

capitalism: economic system in which private individuals rather than the government control the factors of production (**p. 501**)

caravans: groups of people traveling together for safety over long distances (**p. 24**)

cartels: combinations of corporations that control an entire industry (**p. 503**)

Carter Doctrine: declaration that the United States would regard any attempts by outside forces to gain control of the Persian Gulf region as an assault on U.S. interests (**p. 878**)

caste system: form of social organization composed of four classes, which originated in India (**p. 58**)

caudillos: military leaders (**p. 569**)

cavalry: military units of soldiers on horses (**p. 34**)

censors: Roman magistrates who registered citizens according to their wealth, appointed candidates to the Senate, and oversaw the moral conduct of all citizens (**p. 145**)

Central Powers: World War I alliance of Germany, Austria-Hungary, Bulgaria, and the Ottoman Empire (**p. 645**)

Chartists: group in 1830s Great Britain who called for social reforms such as universal male suffrage and payment for members of Parliament (**p. 546**)

checks and balances: system that prevents any one part of a government from becoming too powerful (**p. 145**)

chinampas: raised fields, formed from mud scooped up from the bottom of shallow lakes, used by Aztecs for farming (**p. 310**)

Chinese Eastern Railway: railroad across Manchuria built by Russia (**p. 615**)

chivalry: code of conduct for knights (**p. 233**)

citadel: strong central fortress (**p. 51**)

city-state: form of government that consisted of a town or city and the surrounding land it controlled (**p. 28**)

civil rights: the rights of personal liberty guaranteed by the U.S. Constitution (**p. 768**)

civil service: system that administers the government on a day-to-day basis (**p. 78**)

civilization: highly organized society with complex institutions and attitudes that link a large number of people together (**p. 3**)

cloning: manipulation of a cell from an animal to produce a genetically identical duplicate of that animal (**p. 909**)

coalitions: political groups organized in support of a common cause (**p. 562**)

Cold War: suspicion and hostility between the communist and Western nations, waged primarily by political and economic means rather than with weapons (**p. 751**)

collaborators: persons willing to assist their country's enemies (**p. 721**)

collective bargaining: process of negotiation between union members and management (**p. 509**)

collective farms: land pooled into large farms on which people can work together as a group (**p. 685**)

collegia: (kuh˙LEE˙jee˙uh) workers' trade associations in ancient Rome (**p. 168**)

colons: European settlers in Algeria (**p. 826**)

colonus: Roman tenant farmer who replaced slaves on large estates (**p. 159**)

colony: area in which a foreign nation gained complete control over a given region and its local population (**p. 602**)

comedies: early Greek plays that mocked ideas and people (**p. 132**)

Cominform: Communist Information Bureau, which included all European Communist Parties (**p. 759**)

Comintern: Communist International, organized to spread revolution throughout the world (**p. 687**)

command economy: economic system in which government planners make all economic decisions (**pp. 685, 762**)

commercial capitalism: early phase of capitalism involving merchants who bought, sold, and exchanged goods (**p. 502**)

Commercial Revolution: changes and developments in the European economy from 1400 to 1750, which improved ways of doing business (**p. 357**)

common law: law based on judges' decisions rather than on a code of statutes (**p. 243**)

communism: economic and political system in which the government owns almost all the means of production and controls economic planning; authoritarian socialism (**p. 511**)

compass: instrument used for navigational purposes, which includes a magnetized piece of metal that points to the north (**p. 356**)

conceptual art: art trend based on the idea that the act of creating the art is more important than the actual art itself (**p. 918**)

Concordat: agreement made between Napoleon and the pope by which Napoleon acknowledged Catholicism as the religion of most French citizens, and the church gave up claims to property in France that had been seized and sold during the Revolution (**p. 440**)

condominium: region ruled jointly by two nations (**p. 603**)

conscription: draft adopted in France that made unmarried, able-bodied men from 18 to 45 years of age eligible for military service (**p. 435**)

conservatives: persons who do not want to change existing conditions (**p. 432**)

constitution: document outlining the fundamental laws and principles that govern a nation (**p. 401**)

consulates: diplomatic offices headed by consuls (**p. 468**)

consuls: chief executives in early Rome who ran the government and served as army commanders (**p. 145**)

containment: policy aimed at restricting the spread of communism (**p. 759**)

Contadora Principles: 1983 agreement aimed at reducing armed conflict in Central America (**p. 856**)

contraband: war materials supplied by a neutral to a belligerent nation (**p. 651**)

Contras: rebels seeking to overthrow Nicaragua's Sandinista government (**p. 855**)

corporation: business organization in which individuals buy shares of stock, elect directors to decide policies and hire managers, and receive dividends according to the number of shares they own (**p. 503**)

corporatist state: nation in which the major economic activities, such as agriculture, transportation, manufacturing, and commerce, are organized into syndicates that resemble corporations **(p. 680)**

Counter-Reformation: reform movement in the Catholic Church, beginning in the 1530s, that fostered a more spiritual outlook, clarified church doctrines, and pursued a campaign against Protestantism **(p. 338)**

counterrevolution: activities aimed against, or counter to, a revolution; in France, organized by supporters of the Old Regime **(p. 435)**

coup d'état: (koo day'TAH) seizure of power by force **(p. 439)**

covenant: solemn agreement or promise **(p. 399)**

CPP: Convention People's Party, a pro-independence group in the Gold Coast (Ghana) **(p. 816)**

craft guilds: organizations of skilled workers engaged in one particular craft **(p. 260)**

creoles: white persons who were born in a Spanish or Portuguese colony in Latin America **(p. 563)**

crop rotation: the practice of alternating crops of different kinds to preserve soil fertility **(p. 490)**

Crusades: expeditions to regain the Holy Land for Christians **(p. 252)**

cubism: art style that emphasizes geometric forms, shapes, and design **(p. 668)**

cultural diffusion: spread of culture from one area of the world to another **(p. 13)**

Cultural Revolution: violent attempt at social change in China, begun in 1966 **(p. 785)**

culture: what humans acquire by living together—language, knowledge, skills, art, literature, and life styles **(p. 4)**

cuneiform: (kyooh'NEE'uh'fawrm) Sumerian method of writing using a stylus to make combinations of wedge shapes **(p. 29)**

czar: Russian word for caesar **(p. 200)**

D

daimyo: (DY'mee'oh) samurai leader who gained the loyalty of the lesser samurai **(p. 288)**

Dayton Accord: agreement mediated by the United States that gave Bosnian Serbs a degree of autonomy while recognizing the sovereignty of the Bosnian Muslim-led government **(p. 899)**

democracy: government in which all citizens take part **(p. 111)**

democratic socialism: political system in which the government takes over the means of production peacefully; people retain basic human rights and partial control over economic planning **(p. 511)**

demographic transition: change in the characteristics of a population that gradually occur as a nation becomes industrialized **(p. 849)**

denazification: Allied policy of removing former Nazis from positions of authority in government, industry, and education **(p. 754)**

departments: administrative districts of France **(p. 428)**

depression: lowest point of a business cycle **(p. 504)**

desaparecidos: "disappeared persons" in Argentina's "dirty war" **(p. 867)**

desertification: spread of the desert **(p. 825)**

détente: (day'TAHNT) era of improved Soviet-American relations **(p. 878)**

DEW Line: radar stations along the Arctic Circle **(p. 770)**

dharma: Hindu belief in fulfillment of moral duty so that the soul can progress toward deliverance from punishment in the next life **(p. 58)**

Diamond Sutra: a Buddhist religious text, the world's first printed book **(p. 281)**

Diet: Japan's national legislature **(p.797)**

direct democracy: form of government in which all citizens participate directly in making decisions, rather than making them through elected representatives **(p. 115)**

Discovery: U.S. space shuttle **(p. 906)**

dissidents: persons who are dissatisfied with the government **(p. 860)**

divine right of kings: belief that God ordained certain individuals to govern **(p. 377)**

division of labor: characteristic of civilizations in which different people perform different jobs **(p. 9, 502)**

DNA: deoxyribonucleic acid, the small units of chromosomes that convey characteristics from parent to child **(p. 909)**

domestication: to tame animals, such as the dog **(p. 8)**

domestic system: method of production in which work is done in homes rather than in a shop or factory **(p. 259, 491)**

domino theory: belief that if one nation in a region fell to communism, other nations in the region would also fall to communism **(p. 802)**

dower: groom's marriage gift to his bride **(p. 212)**

dowry: money or goods a woman brings to a marriage **(p. 188)**

dramas: plays containing action or dialogue and usually involving conflict and emotion **(p. 131)**

Duma: Russian parliament formed in 1905 **(p. 591)**

dynamo: electric generator **(p. 516)**

dynasty: family of rulers whose right to rule is hereditary **(p. 20)**

E

Easter Rising: Irish nationalist revolt in 1916 **(p. 677)**

economic boom: sudden increase in prosperity **(p. 671)**

economic nationalism: policy that a nation uses to try to improve its economic well-being by establishing protective tariffs and similar restrictions on the import and export of goods **(p. 671)**

economic sanctions: refusal to trade with an offending nation **(p. 661)**

Emancipation Edict: 1861 proclamation that freed all Russian serfs **(p. 588)**

emigrations: movements of people to other lands **(p. 528)**

émigrés: nobles who fled France during the Revolution **(p. 428)**

empire: form of government that unites different territories and peoples under one ruler **(p. 21)**

enclosure movement: practice of fencing or enclosing common lands into individual holdings **(p. 490)**

enlightened despotism: system of government in which absolute monarchs ruled according to the principles of the Enlightenment **(p. 418)**

Enlightenment: period in the 1700s when philosophers believed that they could apply the scientific method and use reason to explain human nature logically **(p. 415)**

ephors: one of five rulers or overseers elected by the assembly in Sparta **(p. 112)**

epics: long poems describing heroes and great events **(p. 57)**

equites: class of Roman business and land-owning people who had wealth and political power **(p. 150)**

ethical monotheism: Hebrew form of monotheism, or belief in one god, that emphasizes proper conduct **(p. 45)**

ethnic cleansing: a campaign of terror and murder to drive out certain ethnic groups from a country or region **(p. 897)**

evolution: the belief that organisms develop through change over time **(p. 519)**

excommunication: official edict that bars a person from church membership and from taking part in any church ceremonies **(p. 193)**

executive branch: branch of government that enforces the laws **(p. 422)**

export: good or service that is sold to another country or region **(p. 110)**

extraterritoriality: exemption of foreigners from the laws of the nation in which they live or do business **(p. 460)**

F

factors of production: basic resources necessary for industrialization, such as land, capital, and labor **(p. 490)**

factory system: production of goods in a factory through the use of machines and a large number of workers **(p. 491)**

fascism: governmental doctrine that relies on dictatorial rule and a totalitarian regime, in which the state maintains rigid control of the people through force and censorship **(p. 679)**

Falange: Spanish fascist party **(p. 714)**

Fashoda crisis: military confrontation between Great Britain and France in the Sudan in 1898 **(p. 605)**

favorable balance of trade: situation that exists when a country sells more goods than it buys from a foreign country **(p. 358)**

federal system of government: system of government in which power is divided between a central, or federal, government, and individual states **(p. 422)**

feudalism: political system of local government based on the granting of land in return for loyalty, military assistance, and other services **(p. 230)**

"Final Solution": Hitler's program to annihilate the entire Jewish population of Europe **(p. 729)**

Five Classics, The: the most important works of Chinese literature **(p. 86)**

fief: grant of land given by a feudal lord to a vassal **(p. 230)**

FLN: Algerian National Liberation Front, known by its French initials **(p. 827)**

FMLN: Farabundo Martí National Liberation Front, a leftist guerilla group in El Salvador **(p. 855)**

Fourteen Points: President Woodrow Wilson's plan for a just world based on the Allies' aims to end World War I **(p. 654)**

"Four Tigers": South Korea, Taiwan, Singapore, and Hong Kong; noted for their strong economic growth **(p. 809)**

free enterprise: economic system based on supply, demand, and competition, where laws and regulations are thought to interfere with the working of the system **(p. 506)**

free trade: practice based on the belief that government should not restrict or interfere with international trade **(p. 460)**

frescoes: paintings done on a wet plaster wall **(p. 103)**

functionalism: form of architecture based on the principle that a building should be designed for its specific use rather than according to any predetermined style **(p. 669)**

G

galleys: long ships used for European coastal trade **(p. 356)**

general strike: refusal by laborers in various industries to work until demands are met **(p. 675)**

genetic code: the structure of a gene **(p. 909)**

genetics: study of the ways in which inborn characteristics of plants and animals are inherited by their descendants **(p. 520)**

Geneva Accords: agreement signed in 1954 that called for French withdrawal from Vietnam and division of the country into two zones **(p. 801)**

gentry: class of English population who owned land and had social position but held no title **(p. 397)**

geocentric theory: theory that Earth is at the center of the universe **(p. 346)**

geopolitical region: area in which neighboring countries share similar political and geographic features **(p. 851)**

German-Soviet nonaggression pact: 1939 agreement dividing eastern Europe into spheres of influence **(p. 719)**

glaciers: large, slowly moving masses of snow and ice **(p. 5)**

glasnost: (GLAZ'nohst) Soviet policy of openness under which government controls on the economy were relaxed and restrictions on dissent were eased **(p. 891)**

Good Neighbor Policy: policy of the United States during the 1930s stressing cooperation among American nations **(p. 706)**

Great Depression: worldwide depression beginning in 1929 **(p. 672)**

Great Leap Forward: Chinese government's second Five-Year Plan, begun in 1958 **(p. 785)**

Great Schism: division of the Catholic Church into two hostile groups from 1378 to 1417 **(p. 273)**

Great Society: President Lyndon Johnson's program of social reform **(p. 768)**

Greek fire: flammable liquid used as a weapon by the Byzantine navy **(p. 190)**

greenhouse effect: warming of the earth's surface caused by an excess of carbon dioxide and other gases in the earth's atmosphere; the gases let the sun's rays warm the earth but do not let the heat escape **(p. 916)**

guerrilla warfare: military technique relying on swift raids by small bands of soldiers **(p. 373)**

Guomindang: Chinese nationalist party, founded by Sun Yixian, which grew out of reform movement after Boxer Rebellion **(p. 697)**

habeas corpus: legal right protecting individuals from arbitrary arrest and imprisonment **(p. 405)**

Hagia Sophia: magnificent church in Constantinople, begun in A.D. 532 **(p. 193)**

haciendas: (hah·see·EN·duh) large, self-sufficient farming estates **(p. 563)**

heliocentric theory: theory that the sun is at the center of the universe **(p. 347)**

Hellenistic culture: culture founded on Greek ideas and features from other cultures of the Mediterranean region **(p. 125)**

helots: (HEL·uht) social group in Sparta consisting of slaves; made up of peoples conquered by the Spartans **(p. 111)**

Helsinki Accords: a series of agreements that, among other things, specified ways of improving economic and technological cooperation between East and West, endorsed the use of peaceful means to settle disputes between nations, and protected human rights **(p. 889)**

heresy: opinion that conflicts with church doctrine **(p. 193)**

hieroglyphics: (hy·ruh·GLI·fiks) method of Egyptian writing that used pictures or symbols to indicate words or sounds **(p. 19)**

hijrah: (hi·JY·ruh) migration of Muhammad and his followers to Al-Madinah in 622, marking the first year in the Muslim calendar **(p. 206)**

history: record of events since people first developed writing, about 5,000 years ago **(p. 3)**

Holocaust: systematic elimination of European Jews by the Nazis **(p. 729)**

home rule: self-government **(p. 547)**

hominids: human beings and earlier human-like creatures **(p. 4)**

hoplite: member of a group of heavily armed Greek infantry soldiers who typically fought in phalanx formation **(p. 110)**

hubris: (HYOO·bruhs) excessive pride in oneself or one's accomplishments, often seen in heroes in Greek drama **(p. 132)**

humanists: people who specialize in the humanities, the study of grammar, rhetoric, history, and poetry **(p. 326)**

hyperinflation: extremely high inflation **(p. 848)**

Ice Age: time when Earth had extremely cold weather **(p. 5)**

icons: small religious pictures set up in a church or home, or carried on a journey as aids to worship **(p. 191)**

iconoclastic controversy: argument between the supporters and the opponents of icons **(p. 191)**

iconoclasts: Byzantines who opposed the use of icons in worship **(p. 191)**

IFOR: Implementation Force, NATO joint military force sent to Bosnia to enforce the Dayton Accord **(p. 899)**

imams: spiritual leaders who, according to some Shi'ah Muslims, should be direct descendants of Muhammad **(p. 210)**

imperialism: ambition of a powerful nation to dominate the political, economic, and cultural affairs of another nation or region **(p. 599)**

import: good or service that is bought from another country or region **(p. 110)**

import substitution: economic policy in which governments choose to replace certain imported manufactured products with goods produced by industries inside the country **(p. 846)**

impressionists: French painters who attempted to give vivid impressions of people and places as they might appear at a particular moment in a particular light **(p. 538)**

indemnity: compensation paid to a nation for damages inflicted on it, as in war **(pp. 148, 447)**

indulgences: pardons from punishment for sin **(p. 333)**

industrial capitalism: type of capitalism occurring during the Industrial Revolution when capitalists were involved in producing and manufacturing goods themselves, often using mechanized and industrialized methods of production **(p. 502)**

Industrial Revolution: term for changes beginning in the 1700s, when power-driven machines began to do much of the work that people had done before **(p. 489)**

infantry: group of soldiers trained and equipped to fight on foot **(p. 133)**

inflation: rise in prices caused by a decrease in the value of the medium of exchange **(pp. 168, 345)**

Inquisition: institution of the Roman Catholic Church that sought to eliminate heresy by seeking out and punishing heretics **(p. 239)**

intendants: regional administrators of a French province **(p. 376)**

interchangeable parts: parts that can go equally well in other components **(p. 502)**

interdict: church's punishment of an entire region, involving closing churches and withholding sacraments **(p. 238)**

international style: style of architecture that was functional, plain, and severe, using uninterrupted expanses of steel and glass **(p. 669)**

intifada: Palestinian uprising against Israeli presence in the late 1980s and early 1990s **(p. 834)**

Irish Republican Army (IRA): Northern Irish extremist group **(p. 884)**

irrigation: method of transporting water for crops based on the use of ditches and canals **(p. 10)**

island hopping: American strategy in the Pacific campaign in World War II, calling for only certain Japanese islands to be captured while the rest were bypassed **(p. 732)**

isolationists: persons who believe that their own country should not become involved in relations with other nations, especially alliances **(p. 724)**

Jabal Tariq: the "Mountain of Tariq," known in Europe as Gibraltar **(p. 210)**

jihad: (ji-HAHD) struggle to defend the faith **(p. 208)**

Johnson Act: 1934 law that prohibited loans to countries that owed war debts to the United States **(p. 674)**

joint-stock company: business organization that raised money by selling investors stock, or shares, in the company **(p. 358)**

journeyman: skilled artisan who worked for a master for daily wages **(p. 260)**

judicial branch: branch of government that interprets and applies the laws **(p. 422)**

jungle: thick growth of plants found in a tropical rain forest **(p. 296)**

junks: large Chinese ships **(p. 454)**

kaiser: title of the German emperor **(p. 582)**

kami: gods or nature spirits believed by the Japanese to live in natural objects such as sand, waterfalls, and trees **(p. 287)**

karma: Hindu belief that the present condition of a person's life reflects what that person did during a previous life **(p. 58)**

Kellogg-Briand Pact: 1928 international agreement that made war "illegal" **(p. 712)**

kibbutz: collective farm in Israel **(p. 828)**

kingdom: term for monarchy, a form of government headed by a king or queen **(p. 20)**

Kulturkampf: Bismarck's anti-Catholic "culture struggle" **(p. 585)**

laissez-faire: (le'say-FAR) belief that government should not interfere with the operations of business **(p. 506)**

laser: device that concentrates light and releases it in an intense beam that travels in a straight line **(p. 909)**

latifundia: large Roman estates **(p. 150)**

latitude: distance north or south of the equator **(p. 356)**

League of Nations: world organization formed after World War I to maintain peace **(p. 657)**

legion: most important military unit of the Roman army, consisting of 4,500 to 6,000 soldiers **(p. 146)**

legislative branch: branch of government that makes the laws **(p. 422)**

legitimacy: principle involving restoring former ruling families to their thrones **(p. 445)**

Lend-Lease Act: 1941 legislation allowing the United States to supply war materials to Great Britain on credit **(p. 724)**

liberalism: political movement extending the principles of the American and French Revolutions, stressing individual rights and the rule of law rather than the rule of a monarch **(p. 448)**

limited constitutional monarchy: government led by a monarch whose powers were limited by a constitution, and who was required to consult Parliament **(p. 408)**

linguists: scholars who study language **(p. 296)**

Locarno Pact: a number of treaties signed in 1925 guaranteeing existing Franco-German boundaries and negotiating other outstanding issues **(p. 675)**

loess: (LES) extraordinarily fertile yellow soil **(p. 71)**

Long March: 6,000-mile journey by Chinese Communists to escape Nationalist troops in 1934–1935 **(p. 700)**

Long Parliament: English Parliament elected in 1640, which reconvened periodically for 20 years **(p. 400)**

Loyalists: American colonists who opposed independence from Great Britain **(p. 419)**

Luftwaffe: the German air force in World War II **(p. 723)**

Lytton Commission: investigating commission sent by the League of Nations to Manchuria during Japanese invasion **(p. 712)**

Maastricht Treaty: treaty that created the European Union **(p. 890)**

MacArthur Constitution: U.S.-imposed constitution adopted by Japan in 1947 **(p. 794)**

Maginot Line: French fortifications along the borders of Germany and Luxembourg **(p. 675)**

Magna Carta: English document intended to protect the liberties of nobles **(p. 241)**

Maine: U.S. battleship that exploded in Havana harbor in 1898, contributing to the Spanish-American War **(p. 621)**

Mahabharata: epic poem based on themes from the Upanishads **(p. 57)**

mandate: area, usually a former colony, to be administered by the government of another nation **(p. 661)**

Mandate of Heaven: right to rule claimed to have been granted to ancient Chinese rulers by the gods **(p. 76)**

manor: economic unit of the early Middle Ages; a large estate that included a manor house, pastures, fields, and a village **(p. 232)**

market economy: an economy in which land, labor, and capital are controlled by individuals **(pp. 259, 762)**

market speculations: risky investments in the stock market in the hope of quick, high profits **(p. 672)**

martyrs: persons put to death because they refuse to renounce certain beliefs **(p. 166)**

mass production: system of manufacturing large numbers of identical items **(p. 502)**

matrilineal: describes a society in which people trace their ancestors or inherit property through their mothers rather than through their fathers **(p. 299)**

Mau Mau: Kikuyu organization that waged a guerilla battle against the British presence in Kenya in the 1950s **(p. 817)**

maya: according to Hinduism, the illusory world of the senses **(p. 58)**

mechanization: use of automatic machinery to increase production **(p. 491)**

Medellín cartel: powerful Colombian criminal organization **(p. 868)**

medieval: term that describes the period A.D. 500 to 1500 in western European history; also known as the Middle Ages **(p. 225)**

Meech Lake Accord: failed accord that would have recognized Quebec as a "distinct society" within Canada **(p. 882)**

Mein Kampf: book written by Adolf Hitler in the 1920s expressing the spirit of the Nazi movement **(p. 681)**

mercantilism: economic theory stating that there is a fixed amount of wealth in the world and that in order to receive a larger share, one country has to take some wealth away from another country (**p. 358**)

merchant guild: organization of merchants (**p. 260**)

mestizos: persons of American Indian and European descent (**p. 564**)

metics: person living in Athens who was not an Athenian citizen, who could work and who paid taxes but was not allowed to own land or take part in government (**p. 112**)

metropolitan: chief bishop of the Kievan church (**p. 198**)

Middle Ages: period in western European history between the collapse of the Roman Empire and the Renaissance (**p. 225**)

Middle Passage: second stage of the triangular trade system, which involved the shipping of slaves across the Atlantic Ocean to the Americas (**p. 366**)

militarism: glorification of armed strength (**p. 640**)

millets: communities of religious minorities within the Ottoman Empire (**p. 215**)

miniaturization: process of making electronic equipment smaller and lighter (**p. 907**)

mixed economy: economy characterized by the private ownership of some industries and government ownership of others (**p. 778**)

mobilized: organized a nation's army and other resources for combat (**p. 640**)

moderates: persons who have no extreme views, who may side with either conservatives or radicals depending on the issues at hand (**p. 432**)

monarchy: term for kingdom, a form of government headed by a king or queen (**p. 20**)

monasticism: way of life in monasteries and convents in which Christians withdraw from the world to lead a life of prayer, fasting, and self-denial (**p. 236**)

money economy: economic system based on the use of money rather than on barter (**p. 39**)

monism: Hindu belief that God and human beings are one (**p. 58**)

monoculture: region or country's dependence on one crop (**p. 846**)

monopoly: complete control of the production or sale of a good or service by a single firm (**p. 503**)

monotheism: belief in one God (**p. 22**)

Monroe Doctrine: 1823 statement that the United States would oppose any attempt by European nations to interfere in the Western Hemisphere (**p. 568**)

monsoons: seasonal wind named for the direction in which it blows or the season in which it occurs (**p. 50**)

mosaics: pictures or designs formed from inlaid pieces of stone, glass, or enamel (**p. 193**)

mosques: Muslim places of worship (**p. 208**)

MPLA: Marxist Popular Movement for the Liberation of Angola (**p. 823**)

mulattoes: persons of African and European ancestry (**p. 564**)

multinational corporations: foreign-owned businesses in a host country (**p. 846**)

mummification: preservation process that involved treating a corpse with various chemicals (**p. 27**)

Munich Conference: meeting called by Hitler in 1938 to discuss Czech problem, which led to the annexation of the Sudetenland by Germany (**p. 718**)

Muslim League: political group formed by Indian Muslims in 1906 to protect their interests (**p. 613**)

myths: traditional stories about the deeds and misdeeds of gods, goddesses, and heroes, sometimes explaining the origins of a particular group of people (**p. 108**)

N

NAACP: National Association for the Advancement of Colored People (**p. 768**)

nationalism: love of one's country rather than love of one's native region (**p. 441**)

nationalized: put industry under government control or ownership (**p. 676**)

naturalists: persons who emphasizes scientific observation of life in his or her writing, refusing to avoid the ugly or the sordid (**p. 538**)

negritude: "blackness" (**p. 825**)

Neolithic Revolution: shift from food gathering to food production in prehistoric times (**p. 8**)

Neutrality Acts: laws passed between 1935 and 1937 aimed at keeping the United States neutral in future wars (**p. 724**)

"New Order": Adolf Hitler's plan for organizing Europe into a single political and economic system ruled by Germany (**p. 727**)

95 theses: Martin Luther's protests against indulgences, which he posted on the church door at Wittenberg (**p. 334**)

nirvana: a perfect peace, part of Buddhist belief, which releases the soul from the endless cycle of reincarnation (**p. 60**)

nomads: wanderer who travels from place to place in search of food (**p. 8**)

nonalignment: a nation's policy of refusing to ally with either the United States or the Soviet Union (**p. 778**)

North American Free Trade Agreement: (NAFTA) agreement bringing Mexico, Canada, and the United States into one large free-trade zone (**p. 848**)

Northwest Ordinance: law passed by the U.S. Congress in 1787 to provide government for the Northwest Territory (**p. 552**)

Nuremberg Trials: postwar trials of Nazi leaders (**p. 754**)

O

oasis: place in the desert where water allows plant and animal life (**p. 18**)

on margin: practice of buying stocks using only the value of the stock or its expected profit as security (**p. 672**)

Operation Bootstrap: plan to modernize Puerto Rico's economy begun in the 1940s (**p. 862**)

op art: type of art that uses optical illusions and manipulates brilliant colors and shapes for visual effect (**p. 918**)

Open Door Policy: right of all foreign nations to trade equally in China (**p. 697**)

Operation Overlord: codename for the Allied invasion of northwest France **(p. 732)**

oracles: religious sanctuaries where Greek gods were believed to speak about the future through priests and priestesses **(p. 108)**

oracle bones: bones used by Chinese priests, who wrote questions on the shoulder bones of cattle or the bottom of tortoise shells and then interpreted answers to the questions from cracks that developed when the bones were heated **(p. 75)**

oral traditions: passing of poems, songs, and stories by word of mouth from one generation to another **(p. 296)**

orators: public speakers **(p. 133)**

Organization of American States: (OAS) organization formed to promote economic, military and cultural cooperation among nations of the Western hemisphere **(p. 851)**

Ostpolitik: term used to describe German chancellor Willy Brandt's effort to improve relations between East and West **(p. 886)**

Pan-Africanism: movement that promotes the cultural unity of people of African heritage in their struggle together for freedom **(p. 814)**

Pan-Slavism: nationalist movement that pressed for the political and cultural unity of all Slavs under Russian leadership **(pp. 588, 642)**

papyrus: writing material made by the ancient Egyptians out of plant stems; plural papyri **(p. 19)**

Paris Peace Accords: 1973 cease-Fire agreement calling for withdrawal of U.S. troops from South Vietnam **(p. 803)**

Paris Peace Conference: meeting of victorious nations to write terms for the peace following World War I **(p. 655)**

partnership: business owned and controlled by two or more people **(p. 503)**

passive resistance: a form of civil disobedience; peaceful refusal of citizens to cooperate with their government in order to win concessions from it **(p. 694)**

pasteurization: process of heating liquids to kill bacteria and prevent fermentation **(p. 522)**

paterfamilias: (pah·tuhr·fuh·MI·lee·uhs) father of a Roman family who had absolute authority **(p. 147)**

paternalism: system of governing colonies in much the same way that parents guide their children **(p. 610)**

patriarchs: bishops of the five administrative centers for the church in the last years of the Roman Empire **(pp. 167, 191)**

patricians: powerful aristocratic class that controlled Roman government and society **(p. 145)**

patriotism: feeling of loyalty to a country **(p. 267)**

Patriots: American colonists who favored independence from Great Britain **(p. 419)**

Pax Romana: period of Roman peace from the beginning of Augustus's reign in 27 B.C. until the death of Marcus Aurelius in A.D. 180 **(p. 157)**

pedagogue: in ancient Greece, a male slave who taught a young boy **(p. 116)**

peninsulares: Europeans living in colonial Spanish America **(p. 563)**

People's Will: Russian terrorist group in the late 1800s **(p. 589)**

perestroika: (per·uh·STROY·kuh) Soviet restructuring policy designed to overhaul the Soviet political and economic systems **(p. 891)**

performance art: art form in which the artist becomes a living work of art **(p. 919)**

perspective: art technique that involves making distant objects smaller than those in the foreground and arranging them to create the illusion of depth on a flat canvas **(p. 329)**

petrodollars: profits from oil **(p. 835)**

phalanx: (FAY·langks) military formation composed of rows of soldiers standing shoulder to shoulder and equipped with long spears **(p. 133)**

pharaoh: Egyptian ruler's title **(p. 20)**

philology: history of literature and language **(p. 457)**

philosophes: (fee·luh·ZAWF) thinker or philosopher of the Enlightenment **(p. 416)**

philosopher: literally "lover of wisdom;" one who studies philosophy **(p. 128)**

philosophy: study of the most fundamental questions of reality and human existence **(p. 128)**

"phony war": early phase of World War II marked by little activity in western Europe **(p. 721)**

physical sciences: sciences concerned with the properties of energy and inanimate, or nonliving, matter **(p. 518)**

Platt Amendment: provision of the Cuban constitution giving the United States the right to intervene in Cuba **(p. 622)**

plebeians: citizens of Rome not of the aristocratic class **(p. 145)**

plebiscite: (PLEB·uh·syt) procedure used to submit the constitution of a new government to the people for a vote **(p. 439)**

PLO: Palestine Liberation Organization **(p. 833)**

pogroms: (POH·gruhmz) government-sponsored riots resulting in the massacre of Jews in Russia **(p. 590)**

polis: Greek word for city-state, originally meant a fort **(p. 105)**

Politburo: the Political Bureau of the Communist Party; the small committee that held most of the power in the Soviet Union **(p. 686)**

polygyny: marriage of a man to more than one wife **(p. 64)**

polytheism: belief in the existence of many gods **(p. 22)**

pop art: style used by artists who painted common objects such as soup cans, pictures from comic books, or road signs **(p. 918)**

pope: title assumed by the patriarch of Rome and head of the Christian church; from the Latin word meaning "father" **(p. 167)**

Popular Front: left-wing coalition government of France in the late 1930s **(p. 675)**

popular government: idea that people can and should rule themselves and not be ruled by others **(p. 111)**

popular sovereignty: governmental principle based on just laws and on a government created by and subject to the will of the people **(p. 417)**

Portsmouth, Treaty of: agreement, mediated by Theodore Roosevelt, which ended the Russo-Japanese War **(p. 702)**

praetors: (PREET´uhrz) military commanders and overseers of the legal system in ancient Rome **(p. 145)**

Prague, Treaty of: agreement that ended the Seven Weeks' War between Prussia and Austria **(p. 581)**

Pravda Russkaia: law code in Kievan Russia **(p. 197)**

predestination: belief that at the beginning of time God decided who would be saved **(p. 337)**

prehistory: period of time before people kept written records **(p. 3)**

PRI: Mexico's Institutional Revolutionary Party **(p. 852)**

prime minister: the head of government in Great Britain **(p. 408)**

primogeniture: (pry´moh´JE´nuh´choohr) system under which only the eldest son could inherit his father's property **(p. 230)**

Prohibition: law forbidding the manufacture, sale, and transportation of alcoholic beverages **(p. 671)**

proletariat: (proh´luh´TAYR´ee´uht) name given by Marx to the working class **(p. 510)**

propaganda: ideas, facts, or rumors spread deliberately to further one's cause or to damage an opposing cause **(p. 648)**

protectorate: colony in which the native ruler keeps his title, but officials of the foreign power actually control the region **(p. 603)**

psychiatry: study and treatment of mental illness **(p. 527)**

psychoanalysis: process of revealing and analyzing the unconscious **(p. 527)**

purge: act of forcing people to leave an organization or an area **(p. 686)**

Q

quantum: the Latin word for "how much" **(p. 524)**

quantum theory: Max Planck's theory concerning matter and energy that describes it as being divided into particular units, or "packages" **(p. 524)**

queue: single braid that characterized hair style for Chinese men during the Qing dynasty **(p. 455)**

quipu: (KEE´poo) kind of knotted string used by the Inca to assist the memory **(p. 311)**

Qur'an: holy book of Islam **(p. 206)**

R

rabbis: Jewish scholars knowledgeable about the scriptures and about commentaries on religious law **(p. 164)**

radicals: persons who want to institute far-reaching changes **(p. 432)**

radioactivity: process in which atoms of certain elements constantly disintegrate and release energy **(p. 523)**

radiocarbon dating: technique that allows the age of organic matter to be identified by measuring the rate of decay of radiocarbon atoms **(p. 4)**

raja: prince who ruled an Indo-Aryan city-state **(p. 55)**

Ramayana: epic poem based on themes from the Upanishads **(p. 57)**

rationalism: belief that truth can be arrived at solely by reason, or logical thinking **(p. 416)**

reaction: period of time during which those in authority desire a return to the orderly conditions of an earlier era **(p. 447)**

reactionaries: extremists who not only oppose change, but generally would like to return to the way things were before certain changes occurred **(p. 447)**

realism: a method of dealing with the realities of everyday life and expressing a keen observation of social settings, characteristic of literature and art in the mid-1800s **(p. 536)**

recessions: periods of temporary business slowdown and increased unemployment **(p. 768)**

Reformation: religious revolution that split the Christian church in western Europe and created a number of new churches **(p. 333)**

regionalism: portrayal of everyday life in particular locales **(p. 538)**

Reichstag: the lower house of the German legislature **(p. 582)**

reincarnation: Hindu belief in the transmigration, or rebirth, of the soul **(p. 58)**

Renaissance: movement following the Middle Ages that centered on revival of interest in the classical learning of Greece and Rome; French word meaning "rebirth" **(p. 325)**

reparations: payment for war damages **(p. 657)**

representative democracies: forms of government in which citizens elect representatives to run the government for them **(p. 115)**

republic: form of government in which voters elect officials to run the state **(p. 145)**

revolution: radical attempt to change the structure of a country's government and society **(p. 394)**

rhetoric: study of oratory, or public speaking **(p. 116)**

risorgimento: Italian word for "resurgence"; used as a name for the Italian nationalist movement of the 1800s **(p. 574)**

Roaring Twenties: nickname for the 1920s because of the booming economy and fast pace of life during that era **(p. 671)**

romanticism: trend followed by many writers of the early 1800s whose work appealed to sentiment and imagination and dealt with the romance of life **(p. 534)**

Rome-Berlin Axis: alliance formed in 1936 between Germany and Italy **(p. 684)**

Roosevelt Corollary: extension of the Monroe Doctrine stating that the United States would guarantee that Latin American nations would meet their international obligations **(p. 623)**

Russification: program to force non-Russian people to adopt the Russian language, Orthodox religion, and Russian customs **(p. 588)**

S

sacraments: special ceremonies at which participants receive the direct favor, or grace, of God to help them ward off the consequences of sin **(p. 235)**

salons: gatherings of the social, political, and cultural elite in France during the Enlightenment **(p. 416)**

samurai: Japanese warriors devoted to protecting their lords and clans **(p. 288)**

Sanskrit: Indo-Aryan language that is the classical language of India **(p. 54)**

San Stefano, Treaty of: 1878 agreement in which the Ottoman Empire granted independence to Romania, Serbia, and Montenegro **(p. 593)**

savannas: vast areas of relatively dry grassland **(p. 296)**

scholasticism: attempt of medieval philosophers to reconcile Christian faith and reason **(p. 264)**

scientific method: method of inquiry that includes carefully conducted experiments and mathematical calculations to verify the results of the experiments **(p. 346)**

Scientific Revolution: transformation in thinking that occurred during the 1500s and 1600s caused by scientific observation, experimentation, and the questioning of traditional opinions **(p. 346)**

scorched-earth policy: tactic of burning or destroying crops and anything else that might be of value to an invader **(p. 443)**

scribes: clerks who read or wrote for those who could not do so themselves **(p. 26)**

sea dogs: adventurous group of English sea captains who lived in the late 1500s **(p. 409)**

secede: to withdraw from a union **(p. 554)**

sects: religious societies of a few people, usually with a preacher as their leader **(p. 335)**

sectionalism: rivalry among the various sections of a country **(p. 554)**

Sendero Luminoso: guerilla group in Peru **(p. 867)**

sepoys: (SEE´poyz) local troops in India trained and led by British officers **(p. 474)**

seppuku: (se´POO´koo) form of ceremonial suicide in feudal Japan **(p. 288)**

serfs: persons bound to the land, who could not leave without permission **(p. 232)**

Shimonoseki, Treaty of: 1895 treaty forcing China to recognize the complete independence of Korea **(p. 614)**

Shinto: religion of Japan involving prayers and rituals to appease nature spirits **(p. 287)**

shires: governmental districts in early England **(p. 240)**

shogun: chief military and governmental officer in feudal Japan **(p. 288)**

shuttle diplomacy: process in which a negotiator travels back and forth between countries for the purpose of helping them to reach an agreement **(p. 833)**

silt: fertile soil carried as sediment in river water **(pp. 18, 71)**

simony: (SY´moh´nee) purchase of a church position, common during early medieval times **(p. 239)**

social Darwinism: the application of Charles Darwin's theory of natural selection to society, leading to the conclusion that those who have acquired wealth and social standing have done so because of their superior abilities **(p. 526)**

Social Democratic Labor Party: Russian socialist party formed in 1898 **(p. 590)**

Social Democratic Party: German socialist party formed in 1869 **(p. 586)**

socialism: political and economic system in which the government owns the means of production **(pp. 509–510)**

social sciences: branches of knowledge that scientifically studiy people as members of society, covering such areas as economics, political institutions, history, and relations among people **(p. 525)**

sole proprietorship: business owned and controlled by one person **(p. 503)**

Social Security Act: 1935 law providing for unemployment and old-age benefits for Americans **(p. 673)**

"soft underbelly of the Axis": Winston Churchill's description of Italy and the Balkans during World War II **(p. 731)**

Spacelab: module designed to carry out large-scale experiments in space, joint venture of several European nations **(p. 906)**

special theory of relativity: Einstein's theory that no particle of matter can move faster than the speed of light and that motion can be measured only relative to a particular observer **(p. 524)**

sphere of influence: region in which one nation has special, sometimes exclusive, economic and political privileges that are recognized by other nations **(p. 603)**

St. Lawrence Seaway: 2,300-mile waterway linking the Great Lakes with the Atlantic Ocean **(p. 770)**

stagflation: combination of decreased economic activity and rising prices **(p. 876)**

standard of living: measure of the quality of life of a people or a country **(p. 345)**

Statute of Westminster: 1931 act of Britain's Parliament that recognized Canada, Australia, New Zealand, and South Africa as independent **(p. 694)**

steppe: vast, grassy, largely treeless plain in southeastern Europe and southern Central Asia **(p. 196)**

strike: bargaining method involving the refusal of workers to work until their demands have been met **(p. 508)**

stupa: hemispherical or dome-shaped shrine that held objects associated with the Buddha **(p. 64)**

subsidies: government grants of money **(p. 359)**

suburbs: residential areas on the outskirts of a city **(p. 529)**

suffrage: voting rights **(p. 546)**

suffragettes: women who fought for voting rights for all women **(p. 548)**

sultan: Turkish ruler **(p. 215)**

supercomputers: large and powerful computers **(p. 908)**

surrealism: art movement that attempts to merge conscious and unconscious ideas to portray and interpret life in a dreamlike way **(p. 666)**

suttee: Indian ritual in which a widow commits suicide after the death of her husband **(pp. 64, 216)**

taiga: (TY´gah) forest zone in northern region of Kievan Russia **(p. 198)**

tariffs: import taxes on foreign goods **(p. 358)**

tax farming: selling the right to collect taxes to private individuals called tax farmers **(p. 375)**

Tennessee Valley Authority: U.S. government agency that built dams and provided other services in the valley of the Tennessee River starting in the 1930s **(p. 673)**

tepees: cone-shaped tents made of buffalo hide **(p. 307)**

terracing: creating small, flat plots of land by building low walls around the hillsides and filling the space behind them with soil **(p. 115)**

terrorism: bombings, kidnappings, and other acts of violence by political groups or governments, sometimes against innocent people, to force governments to grant their demands **(p. 589)**

Tet Offensive: North Vietnamese and Viet Cong offensive in early 1968 **(p. 802)**

The Tale of Genji: the world's first novel, written around A.D. 1000 by the Lady Murasaki Shikibu **(p. 288)**

theocracy: government ruled by the clergy claiming God's authority **(p. 337)**

Third Reich: Adolf Hitler's name for his regime **(p. 684)**

"third Rome": Russian Orthodox interpretation of their leading role in bringing spiritual light to the world **(p. 201)**

tithe: church tax collected from Christians in early times that represented one tenth of their income; later became a gift to a church representing one tenth of a person's income **(pp. 238, 424)**

Toleration Act: 1689 act of British Parliament granting some religious freedoms to non-Anglican Protestants **(p. 407)**

Tordesillas, Treaty of: 1494 agreement between Spain and Portugal dividing all newly discovered lands **(p. 364)**

totalitarian regimes: highly centralized governments that do not allow opposition and maintain total control **(p. 665)**

total war: strategy that involves targeting an enemy's military and civilian resources **(p. 556)**

trade deficit: situation in which a country imports more than it exports **(p. 877)**

tragedies: form of Greek drama that shows the major character struggling against fate **(p. 132)**

triangular trade: system of trade involving three stages, one of which was the transatlantic slave trade **(p. 366)**

tribunes: officials elected by Rome's popular assemblies **(p. 145)**

Triple Alliance: 1881 alliance between Germany, Austria-Hungary, and Italy **(p. 641)**

Triple Entente: 1907 alliance between France, Russia, and Great Britain **(p. 642)**

tropical rain forests: forested regions receiving more than 100 inches of annual rainfall **(p. 296)**

troubadours: traveling singers who entertained people during the Middle Ages **(p. 262)**

tyrants: in ancient Greece, someone who seized power by force but who ruled with the people's support; later came to refer to rulers who exercise brutal and oppressive power **(p. 110)**

U-boats: German submaries used in World War I **(p. 648)**

ultimatum: demand in which one party threatens harmful action to another party if the other party rejects its proposals **(p. 642)**

Union of Soviet Socialist Republics: name given to Russia in 1922 **(p. 685)**

unions: associations of workers that plan actions and coordinate demands for workers **(p. 509)**

UNITA: National Union for the Total Independence of Angola; U.S.-backed group in Angolan civil war **(p. 823)**

Upanishads: philosophical explanations of the Vedic religion **(p. 57)**

usury: (YOO-zhuh˙ree) policy of charging interest on loans **(p. 259)**

utilitarianism: belief that the principle of utility, or usefulness, was the standard by which to measure a society and its laws **(p. 506)**

utopian socialists: persons who believe that people can live at peace with each other if they live in small cooperative settlements, owning all of the means of production in common and sharing the products **(p. 510)**

vassal: person granted land from a lord in return for services **(p. 230)**

Vedas: the great literature of the Indo-Aryan religion **(p. 54)**

V-E Day: May 8, 1945, the day of victory in Europe in World War II **(p. 734)**

vernacular languages: everyday speech that varies from place to place **(p. 262)**

Versailles, Treaty of: treaty between Germany and the Allied Powers at the end of World War I **(p. 657)**

veto: to refuse to approve a measure **(p. 145)**

veto power: power to defeat a measure with a single vote **(p. 755)**

viceroys: representatives of the Spanish monarch in Spain's colonial empire **(p. 368)**

Vietnamization: the process of preparing the South Vietnamese to take over the fighting of the Vietnam War to allow for the withdrawing of American troops **(p. 874)**

V-J Day: September 2, 1945, the day of victory in the Pacific during World War II **(p. 736)**

war of attrition: slow wearing-down manner of warfare in which each side tries to outlast the other **(p. 651)**

Waste Land, The: 1922 poem by T.S. Eliot **(p. 667)**

Watergate scandal: the break-in at the Democratic National Committee headquarters in 1972 that led to President Nixon's resignation **(p. 874)**

weapons of mass destruction: nuclear, chemical, and biological weapons of great power **(p. 880)**

welfare state: state in which the government undertakes primary responsibility for the social welfare of its citizens **(p. 763)**

Western civilization: civilization that evolved in Europe and later spread to the Americas **(p. 101)**

"White Man's Burden": attitude that Europeans had toward people in non-Western nations **(p. 601)**

World Court: the Permanent Court of International Justice, located at The Hague in the Netherlands **(p. 660)**

yoga: Hindu religious practice of physical and mental discipline that harmonizes the body with the soul **(p. 59)**

Young Italy movement: society of Italian nationalists formed in 1831 **(p. 574)**

Zen: a sect of Buddhism that developed around A.D. 700 **(p. 280)**

ziggurats: Sumerian temples built in layers, each one smaller than the one below it **(p. 30)**

Zionism: nationalist movement to build a homeland for Jews in Palestine **(p. 692)**

Zollverein: customs union of German states begun in 1834 **(p. 578)**

For permission to reprint copyrighted material, grateful acknowledgment is made to the following sources:

American Heritage Magazine, a division of Forbes, Inc.: From pp. 160-161 from "The Gold of Sofala" and excerpts from pages 179 and 184 from *The Horizon History of Africa*, edited by Alvin M. Josephy, Jr. Copyright © 1971 by American Heritage Publishing Co. Inc. From p. 606 from *The American Heritage Picture Book of World War II* by C. L. Sulzberger. Copyright © 1966 by American Heritage Publishing Co., Inc.

Asian Humanities Press, a division of Jain Publishing Co., Inc.: From "The Yoga of Meditation (Dhyana Yoga): Part 6, Lines 10-14 from *The Bhagavad Gita: A Scripture for the Future*, translated by Sachindra K. Majumdar. Copyright © 1991 by Sachindra Kumar Majumdar.

Anthony Bonner: From "Cercamon" from *Songs of the Troubadours*, edited and translated by Anthony Bonner. Copyright © 1972 by Schocken Books Inc.

Cambridge University Press: From "The Ten Commandments" from *The New English Bible*. Copyright © 1961, 1970 by the Delegates of the Oxford University Press and the Syndics of the Cambridge University Press. From "A June Morning" from *Life on the English Manor: A Study of Peasant Conditions,1150-1400* by H. S. Bennett. Published by Cambridge University Press, 1937. From *The Stages of Economic Growth* by W. W. Rostow. Copyright © 1960 by Cambridge University Press.

Frank Cass & Co. Ltd.: From "Conclusion: Value of of British Rule" (retitled "A Justification of British Colonialism in Africa") from *The Dual Mandate in Tropical Africa* by Lord Lugard. First published in 1922.

Lionel Casson: From "The way things were at the first Olympics" by Lionel Casson from *Smithsonian*, vol. 15, no. 3, June 1984, pp. 64-73. Copyright © 1984 by Lionel Casson.

Leon E. Clark: From "A Closed Society: 1600-1853" from *Through Japanese Eyes* by Richard H. Minear, edited by Leon E. Clark. Copyright © 1974, 1981 by Leon E. Clark and Richard H. Minear.

Armand Colin: From "Peasantry and Working-Class Leadership" from *The Political Thought of Mao Tse-tung* by Stuart R. Schram. Copyright © 1963 by Frederick A. Praeger, Inc.

Columbia University Press: From "Supreme Happiness" from *Chuang Tzu: Basic Writings*, translated by Burton Watson. Copyright © 1964 by Columbia University Press.

Coronado Press Inc., a division of Pro Print Incorporated: From "Funeral Oration of Pericles" from *The Speeches of Thucydides* by H. F. Harding. Copyright © 1973 by H. F. Harding.

Dembner Books, a division of Red Dembner Enterprises Corporation: From "About Kings" from *Isaac Asimov's Book of Facts*. Copyright © 1979 by Red Dembner Enterprises Corp.

J. M. Dent & Sons, Ltd.: From "Letter to an English Friend" by Giuseppe Mazzini from *Giuseppe Mazzini: Selected Writings*, translated by Alice de Rosen Jervis.

Doubleday, a division of Bantam Doubleday Dell Publishing Group, Inc.: From *An Introduction to Haiku* by Harold G. Henderson. Copyright © 1958 by Harold G. Henderson.

Dutton, a division of Penguin Putnam Inc.: From *Lost City of the Incas* by Hiram Bingham. Copyright 1948 by Hiram Bingham; copyright renewed © 1976 by Alfred Bingham.

Harcourt Brace & Company: From *Elizabeth and Essex: A Tragic History* by Lytton Strachey. Copyright 1928 by Lytton Strachey; copyright renewed © 1956 by James Strachey.

The John Hopkins University Press: From "Book VIII" from *The Metamorphoses of Ovid*, translated by David R. Slavitt. Copyright © 1994 by The John Hopkins University Press.

Jean Kistler Kendall, Executrix of the Estates of Elizabeth Bothwell Kistler and Jean Bothwell: From *The Story of India* by Jean Bothwell. Copyright 1952 by Harcourt Brace & Company.

Alfred A. Knopf, Inc.: From "Castro and Social Change" and from "The Hacienda" from *Ten Keys to Latin America* by Frank Tannenbaum. Copyright © 1960, 1962 by Frank Tannenbaum.

Judy Barrett Litoff: From "Germany, 12 October 1944" from *Miss You: The World War II Letters of Barbara Wooddall Taylor and Charles E. Taylor* by Judy Barrett Litoff, David C. Smith, Barbara Wooddall Tayor, and Charles E. Taylor. Copyright © 1990 by Taylor Thomas Lawson.

John Murray (Publishers) Ltd.: From "Reproach" by Muhammad Iqbal from *Poems from Iqbal*, translated by V. G. Kiernan. Copyright © 1955 by John Murray (Publishers) Ltd.

National Geographic Society: From "Florence Rises from the Flood" by Joseph Judge from *National Geographic*, July 1967. Copyright © 1967 by National Geographic Society. From "Viking Trail East" by R. P. Jordan from *National Geographic*, March 1985. Copyright © 1985 by National Geographic Society. From "The Search for Our Ancestors" by Kenneth F. Weaver from *National Geographic*, November 1985. Copyright © 1985 by National Geographic Society.

National Geographic Society: From "La Navidad, 1462: Searching for Columbus's Lost Colony" by Kathleen A. Deagan from *National Geographic*, November 1987. Copyright © 1987 by National Geographic Society.

Jawaharlal Nehru Memorial Fund: From "A Tryst with Destiny" from *Jawaharlal Nehru: An Anthology*, edited by Sarvepalli Gopal. Copyright © 1980 by Indira Gandhi.

W. W. Norton & Company, Inc.: From "The Sources of the Cold War" from *On Every Front: The Making of the Cold War* by Thomas G. Paterson. Copyright © 1979 by W. W. Norton & Company, Inc.

Penguin Books Ltd.: From "Prologue" from *The Canterbury Tales* by Geoffrey Chaucer, translated by Nevill Coghill (Penguin Classics, Fourth Revised Edition 1977). Copyright © 1951, 1958, 1960, 1975, 1977 by Nevill Coghill. From *The Song of Roland*, translated by Dorthy L. Sayers (Penguin Classics, 1937). Copyright © 1957 by Executors of Dorothy L. Sayers. From *Procopius: The Secret History*, translated by G. A. Williamson (Penguin Classics, 1966). Copyright © 1966 by G. A. Williamson.

Playboy Magazine: "Interview with Gabriel Garcia Marquez" from *Playboy*, February 1982. Copyright © 1982 by Playboy.

Prometheus Books, Amherst, NY: From "Letter to Menoeceus" from *The Essential Epicurus*, translated by Eugene O'Connor. Copyright © 1993 by Eugene O'Connor. All rights reserved.

Random House, Inc.: "Knowing Oneself" from *The Wisdom of China and India* by Lao-Tzu, edited by Lin Yutang. Copyright © 1942 and renewed © 1970 by Random House, Inc.

Marian Reiner: From *More Cricket Songs*, Japanese haiku translated by Harry Behn. Copyright © 1971 by Harry Behn.

Simon & Schuster: From "They that Turn the Cheek" from *I Found No Peace: The Journal of a Foreign Correspondent* by Webb Miller. Copyright © 1936, 1963 by Webb Miller. From "Garibaldi's Conquest of the Kingdom of Naplea" from *Prologue: A Documentary History of Europe 1846-1960*, edited by M. Christine Walsh. Copyright © 1968 by Cassell Australia Ltd. Originally published by Cassell Australia Ltd.

Time-Life Books Inc.: From *Great Ages of Man: Imperial Rome* by Moses Hadas and the Editors of Time-Life Books. Copyright © 1965 by Time-Life Books Inc.

Charles E. Tuttle Co., Inc.: From *The Code of the Samurai*, translated by A. L. Sadler. Copyright © 1941 by The Japan Foundation.

The University of Chicago Press: From *Feudal Society* by Marc Bloch, translated by L. A. Manyon. Copyright © 1961 by The University of Chicago Press.

University of Pennsylvania Press, Philadelphia: From *History Begins at Sumer* by Samuel Noah Kramer. Copyright © 1981 by the University of Pennsylvania Press.

University Press PLC: From "Constitutional Basis" from *The People's Republic* by Obafemi Awolowo. Copyright © 1968 by Obafemi Awolowo.

Viking Penguin, a division of Penguin Putnam Inc.: From "The Body Social: Paris During the Hundred Years War" by John of Salsbury, translated by J. Dickinson from *The Portable Medieval Reader*, edited by James Bruce Ross and Mary Martin McLaughlin. English translation copyright 1927 by Appleton Croft on.

Vintage Books, a division of Random House, Inc.: From *The Odyssey of Homer* by Homer, translated by Robert Fitzgerald. Copyright © 1961, 1963 by Robert Fitzgerald; copyright renewed © 1989 by Benedict R. C. Fitzgerald.

SOURCES CITED

From "Men Walk on Moon" from *New York Times*, July 21, 1969. Published by The New York Times Company, New York, NY, 1969.

Speech by Winston Churchill March 5, 1946, from *A Treasury of the World's Great Speeches*. Published by Simon & Schuster, New York, NY 1954.

"Table 2: Selected Soviet Economic Growth Rates 1928-1965" from *Economic Development in the Soviet Union* by Stanley H. Cohn. Published by D. C. Heath and Company, Lexington, MA., 1970.

From "A Relativistic World" from *Modern Times: The World from the Twenties to the Nineties, Revised Edition* by Paul Johnson. Published by HarperCollins Publishers, Inc., New York, NY, 1991.

From "Eastern Asia and Oceania: Mohenjo-Daro, Pakistan" from *The Atlas of Past Worlds: A Comparative Chronology of Human History 2000 BC-AD 1500* by John Manley. Published by Cassell Publishers Limited, London, England, 1993.

From "The First Radio Signal across the Atlantic, 12 December 1901" by Guglielmo Marconi from *Scrapbook 1900-1941* by Leslie Bailey. Published by Frederick Muller, 1957.

Figures for Chart on Election Results, 1932, 1933 from *The Anchor Atlas of World History, Vol. II: From the French Revolution to the American Bicentennial*, translated by Ernest A. Menze with maps designed by Harald and Ruth Bukor. Published by Anchor Books, Anchor Press/Doubleday, Garden City, NY, 1978.

From "The Civil Service" from *China: An Introduction* by Lucian W. Pye. Published by Little, Brown and Company, Boston, MA, 1972.

From *All Quiet on the Western Front* by Erich Maria Remarque, translated by A. W. Wheen. Published by Little, Brown and Company, Boston, MA, 1929.

From *The Guns of August* by Barbara Tuchman. Published by Macmillan Publishing Company, a division of Simon & Schuster, New York, NY, 1962.

PHOTO CREDITS

Positions are shown in abbreviated form as follows: *t*-top, *b*-bottom, *c*-center, *l*-left, *r*-right, *i*-inset, *bckgd*-background.

i (bkgd), Michael Holford; ii-iii Bibliotheque Nationale, Paris, France/Bridgeman Art Library, London/New York; iii (c), K. Scholz/H. Armstrong Roberts; vii (b), Scala/Art Resource; vii (t), K. Scholz/H. Armstrong Roberts, Inc.; viii (t), SCALA/Art Resource; viii (b), David Ball/The Stock Market; ix, Blaine Harrington/The Stock Market; x (t), Werner H. Muller/Peter Arnold; x (b), Steve Vidler/Nawrocki Stock Photo; xi (b), Kunsthistorisches Museum, Vienna; xi (t), Bury Art Gallery and Museum, Lancashire, UK/Bridgeman Art Library, London/New York; xii (t), ChinaStock; xii (b), Museum of the North American Indian, New York/Bridgeman Art Library, London/New York; xiii (t), Scala/Art Resource; xiii (b), Musee de Grenoble, France/Peter Will/Bridgeman Art Library, London/New York; xiv, Christie's Images, London, UK/Bridgeman Art Library, London/New York; xv (b), Corbis-Bettmann; xv (t), Corbis-Bettmann; xvi, AKG London; xvii (t), Photri; xvii (b), Photoworld/FPG ; xviii (b), UPI/Corbis-Bettmann; xviii (t), Franklin D. Roosevelt Library; xix (b), Hulton Getty/Gamma-Liaison; xix (t), Magnus Bartlet/Woodfin Camp & Associates; xx (b), Velasco-Afrapix/Gamma-Liaison; xx (t), Robert Frerck/Woodfin Camp & Associates; xxi (t), Orlando Sentinel/Sygma Photos; xxi (b), Itar-Tass/Sovfoto; xxvi (tr), Stock Market; xxvi (bl), Peter Van Steen; xxx, John Reader/Science Photo Library/Photo Researchers, Inc.; 1 (t), Marilyn Kazmers/Peter Arnold; 1 (c), Brian Brake/Photo Researchers; 1 (bl), Museum of Anatolian Civilizations, Ankara, Turkey; 2-3, Scala/Art Resource; 4, Jonathan Blair/Woodfin Camp & Associates; 7, Erich Lessing/Art Resource; 8 G. Tortoll/Sheridan Ancient Art & Architecture Collection; 16-17, Adam G. Sylvester/Photo Researchers; 19, John Launois-Rapho/Black Star; 20, Michael Holford; 23, K. Scholz/H. Armstrong Roberts, Inc.; 24, ZEFA/H.Armstrong Roberts, Inc.; 25 (b), Erich Lessing/Art Resource; 25 (t), Erich Lessing/Art Resource; 26, Carlos Sanuvo/Bruce Coleman, Inc.; 29, Erich Lessing/Art Resource; 30, Georg Gerster/Photo Researchers; 31, British Museum, London/Bridgeman Art Library/SuperStock; 37, SEF/Art Resource; 40 (l), Cotton Coulson/Woodfin Camp & Associates; 40 (r), Jim Amos/Photo Researchers; 41 (bl), Courtesy of the New York State Museum; 41 (tl), Robert B. Pickering/Nawrocki; 41 (tr), John Wilson/Nawrocki; 41 (bc), Nawrocki; 41 (br), Nawrocki; 42, Jewish Museum/Art Resource; 44, Photri; 45, Henry Friedman; 48-49, AKG London; 51, J. Hiebeler/Leo de Wys; 52 (tl), SCALA/Art Resource; 52 (c), Jehangir Gazdar/Woodfin Camp & Associates; 52 (tr), SCALA/Art Resource; 52 (bl), SCALA/Art Resource; 52 (br), SCALA/Art Resource; 55, SCALA/Art Resource; 56, Richard Nowitz/The Stock Market; 59, Michael Holford; 65 (r), Culver Pictures; 68-69, David Ball/The Stock Market; 71, He Jianfu/ChinaStock; 74 (tr), Courtesy of the Freer Gallery of Art , Smithsonian Institution, Washington, D.C.; 75 (br), Ronald Sheridan Ancient Art & Architecture Collection; 78 (r), SuperStock; 80, P. Belzeaux/Photo Researchers; 81, Bibliotheque Nationale, Paris/Bridgeman Art Library, London/New York; 82 , G. Neri/Woodfin Camp & Associates; 83, Giraudon/Art Resource; 84, J. Alex Langley/Uniphoto; 85 (t), Joe Viesti/Viesti Associates; 85 (c), ChinaStock; 85 (b), Corbis-Bettmann; 87, Sylvain Grandadam/Tony Stone Images; 93, Adam G. Sylvester/Photo Researchers; 95, AKG London; 96, David Ball/The Stock Market; 98, David Smith Collection, Columbia University; 99 (t), Scala/Art Resource; 99 (b), AKG London; 100-101, David Pollack/The Stock Market; 103, Nimatallah/Art Resource; 104 (br), Nimatallah/Art Resource; 104 (bl), Dan J. McCoy/Rainbow; 104 (t), Ronald Sheridan/Ancient Art & Architecture Collection; 107, Musee du Bardo, Tunis/Bridgeman Art Library, London/New York; 108, AKG London; 109 (t), Michael Holford; 109 (c), James Ranoklev/Tony Stone Images; 109 (b), Peter Van Steen; 111, William Hubbell/Woodfin Camp & Associates; 113, SCALA/Art Resource; 116, Scala/Art Resource; 117 (t), British Museum, London/Bridgeman Art Library, London/New York; 117 (b), Giraudon/Art Resource; 121, J. Paul Kennedy/The Stock Market; 124-125, AKG London; 126, Nimatallah/Art Resource; 127, Scala/Art Resource; 130, Scala/Art Resource; 131, Robert Frerck/Odyssey Productions; 132, Ronald Sheridan/Ancient Art & Architecture Collection; 135 (l), Fitzwilliam Museum, University of Cambridge/Bridgeman Art Library, London/New York; 135 (c), Louvre, Paris, France/Bridgeman Art Library, London/New York; 135 (r), The Greek Ministry of Culture & Sciences, Prof Manolis Andronikos/Art Resource; 136 (t), Scala/Art Resource; 136 (b), Nimatallah/Art Resource; 137 (l), Rare Books Division, The New York Public Library, Astor, Lenox and Tilden Foundations; 139, Erich Lessing/Art Resource; 142-143, Blaine Harrington/The Stock Market; 146, The British Museum; 147, Louvre, Paris, France/Bridgeman Art Library, London/New York; 152, The British Museum; 153, Robert Emmett Bright/Photo Researchers; 154 (bl), Mary Evans Picture Library/Photo Researchers; 156, Casa di Lucrezio Frontone, Pompeii/Bridgeman Art Library, London/New York; 158, Robert Frerck/Odyssey Productions; 160, Erich Lessing/Art Resource; 161 (t), Blaine Harrington/The Stock Market; 161 (b), Fridmar Damm/Leo de Wys, Inc.; 162, AKG London; 164, Scala/Art Resource; 168 (t), Erich Lessing/Art Resource; 172 (br), Scala/Art Resource; 173 (tl), Everett C. Johnson/Tony Stone Images; 173 (tr), Randy Wells/The Stock Market; 173 (b), Michael Holford; 178, David Pollack/The Stock Market; 181, AKG London; 182, Blaine Harrington/The Stock Market; 184, Werner Forman/Art Resource; 185 (t), Houses of Parliament, Westminster, London, UK/Bridgeman Art Library, London/New York; 185 (cl), British Library, London, UK/Bridgeman Art Library, London/New York; 185 (b), Thomas Rampy/The Image Bank; 185 (c), Bibliotheque Royale Albert I er, Bruxelles; 185 (cr), Peter Willi/Musee des Beaux-Arts, Rouen/Brigeman Art Library, London/New York; 186-187, Robert Emmett Bright/Photo Researchers; 190, Victoria & Albert Museum, London/Bridgeman Art Library, London/New York; 191, Florence, Museo Del Bargello; SCALA/Art Resource; 192 (t), AKG London; 192 (b), AKG London; 194, Michael Holford; 195 (t), Milton & Joan Mann/Cameramann International; 195 (b), Ulf Sjostedt/FPG International; 195 (c), K. Scholz/H. Armstrong Roberts, Inc.; 198, Art Resource, NY; 200, Steve Vidler/Nawrocki Stock Photo; 201, Werner H. Muller/Peter Arnold, Inc.; 204-205, Steve Vidler/Nawrocki; 207, Free Library of Philadelphia/Scala/Art Resource; 210, Roland & Sabrina Michaud/Woodfin Camp & Associates; 211 (r), Index/Bridgeman Art Library, London/New York; 211 (l), Masjid-i-Jami (Great Mosque) Cordoba, Spain/Bridgeman Art Library, London/New York; 212, Roland & Sabrina Michaud/Woodfin Camp & Associates; 213 (l), Stever Dunwell/The Image Bank; 213 (r), Ciaro, Bib. National; Giraudon/Art Resource; 214, The Metropolitan Museum of Art, Bequest of Joseph V. McMullan 1973. (1974.149.18). Photograph ©1998 The Metropolitan Museum of Art; 217, AKG London; 218 (r), AKG London; 218 (l), Steve Vidler/Nawrocki Stock Photo; 219 (bl), Michel Gotin; 219 (br), Rafael Macia/Photo Researchers; 219 (t), E. Simanor/Explorer/Photo Researchers; 221, Thomas Rampy/The Image Bank; 224, Erich Lessing/Art Resource; 227, Kunsthistorisches Museum, Vienna, Austria/The Bridgeman Art Library, London/New York; 231, Bettmann; 232, Chantilly, Musee Conde/Giraudon/Art Resource; 234, AKG London; 236, Scala/Art Resource; 237, British Library, London/Bridgeman Art Library, London/New York; 238, Giraudon/Art Resource; 240, The British Library; 242, Victoria & Albert Museum, London/Art Resource; 243, Bettmann; 245, Kunsthistorisches Museum, Vienna; 246, AKG London; 250-251, Michael Holford; 254, Ancient Art & Architecture Collection; 256, Ancient Art & Architecture Collection; 257 (t), Culver Pictures; 257 (b), Peter Van Steen; 258, Bibliotheque Nationale, Paris, France/Bridgeman Art Library, London/New York; 260, Museo Correr, Venice/Bridgeman Art Library, London/New York; 263, Art Resource; 264, Bury Art Gallery and Museum, Lancashire, UK/Bridgeman Art Library, London/New York; 265, Susan McCartney/Photo Researchers; 266 (l), Steve Vidler/Leo Dy Wys, Inc.; 266 (r), Ancient Art & Architecture Collection, Ltd.; 272, Giraudon/Art Resource; 276-277, Private Collection/Christie's Images/Bridgeman Art Library, London/New York; 279, AKG London; 283, Private Collection/Bridgeman Art Library, London/New York; 285 (t), Bibliotheque Nationale, Paris/Bridgeman Art Library, London/New York; 285 (b), Bibliotheque Nationale, Paris/Bridgeman Art Library, London/New York; 286, ChinaStock; 289, Boston Museum of Fine Arts/Corbis-Bettmann; 294-295, Wolfgang Kaehler; 298 (t), Boltin Picture Library; 298 (bl), Sam Emerson/Sygma; 298 (br), Robert Weaver/Gamma-Liaison; 300 (t), Mike Yamashita/Woodfin Camp & Associates; 300 (b), Mike Yamashita/Woodfin Camp & Associates; 302, Smithsonian Institution, Museum of African Art, Aldo Tutino/Art Resource; 303, Boltin Picture Library; 307 (t), Corbis-Bettmann; 307 (b), Museum of the North American Indian, New York, USA/Bridgeman Art Library, London/New York; 308, Laurence Parent; 310, Michael Fogden/Bruce Coleman, Inc.; 311 (l), Boltin Picture Library; 311 (r), Bettmann; 317, Steve Vidler/Nawrocki Stock Photo; 318, Erich Lessing/Art Resource; 319, Michael Holford ; 320, Private Collection/Christie's Images/Bridgeman Art Library, London/New York; 322 (t), Victoria & Albert Museum, London/Art Resource; 322 (c), Cappella Sistina Vaticano/Scala/Art Resource; 322 (b), The Pierpoint Morgan Library/Art Resource; 323 (tl), AKG London; 323 (tr), American Philosophical Society ; 323 (c), AKG London; 323 (b), Library of Congress; 324-325, AKG London; 327 (t), Scala/Art Resource; 327 (b), G. Neri/Woodfin Camp & Associates; 328, Musee Des Beaux-Arts De Lille, Jardin Du Muss/Giraudon/Art Resource; 329, Erich Lessing/Art Resource; 330 Scala/Art Resource; 331, Scala/Art Resource; 332, Scala/Art Resource; 334, Scala/Art Resource; 335, Giraudon/Art Resource; 337, British Museum; 338, Giraudon/Art Resource; 339, Erich Lessing/ Art Resource; 342, Erich Lessing/Art Resource; 343 (t), Erich Lessing/Art Resource; 343 (b), SuperStock; 344, Erich Lessing/Art Resource; 347, Erich Lessing/Art Resource; 348, Scala/Art Resource; 349 (r), Scala/Art Resource; 349 (l), Royal Society, London, UK/Bridgeman Art Library, London/New York; 350, Erich Lessing/Art Resource; 351, Giraudon/Art Resource; 353, Scala/Art Resource; 354-355, Louvre, Paris/Reunion des Musees Nationaux/Bridgeman Art Library, London/New York; 356, Reunion des Musees Nationaux/Bridgeman Art Library; 357, Florence, Museum of Science; Scala/Art Resource; 358, Giraudon/Art Resource, NY; 359, Herzog Anton Ulrich-Museum; 361, AKG London; 364, Courtesy of Nettie Lee Benson Latin American Collection, University of Texas at Austin; HRW photo; 365, Royal Geographical Society, London/Bridgeman Art Library, London/New York; 367, Culver Pictures; 368, Corbis-Bettmann; 372, Giraudon/Art Resource; 373, The Metropolitan Museum of Art, Marquand Collection, Gift of Henry G. Marquand, 1889. (89.15.21) Photograph ©1993 The Metropolitan Museum of Art; 375, AKG London; 377, Musee de Grenoble, France/Peter Will/Bridgeman Art Library, London/New York; 380, J. Messerschmidt/Stock Market; 382, Corbis-Bettmann; 383, Collection of Countess Bobrinskoy/Michael Holford; 384, Erich Lessing/Art Resource; 387, Kunsthistorisches Museum, Vienna, Austria/Bridgeman Art Library, London/New York; 392-393, AKG London; 394, AKG London; 396 (l), Michael Holford; 396 (tr), Richard Turpin/Arcaid; 396 (tr), Richard Turpin/Arcaid; 398, Picture Library/American Bible Society; 399, Louvre, Paris/Reunion des Musees Nationaux/Bridgeman Art Library, London/New York;

401, Corbis-Bettmann; 403, Dreweatt Neate Fine Art Auctioneers, Newbury/Bridgeman Art Library, London/New York; 404, Private Collection/Bridgeman Art Library, London/New York; 405, AKG London; 409, Kunsthistorisches Museum, Vienna/Bridgeman Art Library, London/New York; 410, Michael Holford; 411, Culver Pictures; 414-415, AKG London; 417, Erich Lessing/Art Resource; 419, Culver Pictures; 420, Culver Pictures; 424, Erich Lessing/Art Resource; 426, Giraudon/Art Resource; 427 (t), Historical Society of Pennsylvania/Bridgeman Art Library, London/New York; 427 (bl), Pablo Bartholomew/Gamma Liason ; 427 (br), Cesar Vera/Leo De Wys ; 429, AKG London; 430 (t), New York Historical Society, USA/Bridgeman Art Library, London/New York; 430 (b), Architect of the Capitol; 431 (t), Giraudon/Art Resource; 431 (c), AKG London; 431 (b), Giraudon/Art Resource; 433, AKG London; 435, P. Boulat/Cosmos/Woodfin Camp; 436, P. Boulat/Cosmos/Woodfin Camp & Associates; 437, Musees Royaux Des Beaux-Arts De Belgique, Bruxelles; 438, Scala/Art Resource; 441, Giraudon/Art Resource; 445, AKG London; 448, Culver Pictures; 452-453, Steve Vidler/Nawrocki; 457, Victoria & Albert Museum, London, UK/Bridgeman Art Library, London/New York; 458, SEF/Art Resource; 459, Royal Geographical Society, London/Bridgeman Art Library, London/New York; 460, The Metropolitan Museum of Art, Purchase, The Lucille and Robert H. Gries Charity Fund, 1970 (1970.220.1). Photograph ©1998 The Metropolitan Museum of Art.; 461, National Maritime Museum, London/Bridgeman Art Library, London/New York; 462, Corbis-Bettmann; 464, Palubniak Studios; 466, Art Resource; 467, Palubniak Studios; 468 (r), Christie's Images, London, UK/Bridgeman Art Library, London/New York; 468 (l), Private Collection/Bridgeman Art Library, London/New York; 469, Ronald Sheridan/Ancient Art & Architecture; 471, Ronald Sheridan/Ancient Art & Architecture; 473, Brown Brothers; 475, Hulton Getty/Liaison Agency; 480, AKG London; 483, AKG London; 484, AKG London; 486 (b), Ann Ronan Picture Library/Art Resource; 486 (cr), Scottish National Portrait Gallery, Edinburgh, Scotland/Bridgeman Art Library, London/New York; 486 (cl), HRW Photo; 487 (t), Library of Congress; 487 (b), The Smithsonian Institution; 487 (cl), Snark/Art Resource; 487 (cr), Metropolitan Museum of Art, New York, USA/Bridgeman Art Library, London/New York; 488-489, Peter Van Steen; 491, Ann Ronan Picture Library/Art Resource; 492 (b), Christie's Images/Bridgeman Art Library, London/New York; 492 (t), Trades Union Congress, London, UK/Bridgeman Art Library, London/New York; 493 (t), Brown Brothers; 493 (b), Brown Brothers; 495, Brown Brothers; 496, Palubniak Studios; 499, Private Collection/Bridgeman Art Library, London/New York; 501, Snark/Art Resource; 502, Ford Archives, Henry Ford Museum; 507, Hulton Getty/Liaison Agency; 508, Corbis-Bettmann; 511, AKG London; 514-515, Guildhall Library, Corporation of London, UK/Bridgeman Art Library, London/New York; 516, Art Resource, NY; 517, Corbis-Bettmann; 518, Topham/The Image Works; 519, Brown Brothers; 520, Erich Lessing/Art Resource; 521 (t), Culver Pictures; 521 (b), NASA; 521 (c), The Museum of Modern Art/Film Stills Archives; 522, Gernsheim Collection, Harry Ransom Humanities Research Center, The University of Texas at Austin; 524, AKG London; 526, Egyptian Expedition/The Metropolitan Museum of Art; 527, Giraudon/Art Resource; 529, Culver Pictures; 531, Culver Pictures; 532, Winslow Homer, American, 1836-1910, Croquet Scene, oil on canvas, 1866, 15 7/8 x 26 1/16in, Friends of American Art Collection, 1942.35, photograph ©1998, The Art Institute of Chicago, All Rights Reserved.; 533, Scala/Art Resource; 535, Giraudon/Art Resource; 536, Stock Montage/SuperStock; 537, Erich Lessing/Art Resource; 538, Giraudon/Art Resource; 539, The Metropolitan Museum of Art, H.O. Havemeyer Collection, Bequest of Mrs. H.O. Havemeyer, 1929. (29.100.370). Photograph ©1981 The Metropolitan Museum of Art; 542-543, National Museum of American Art/Smithsonian Institute, Washington DC/Art Resource; 545 (t), HBJ Photo; 545 (b), HBJ Photo; 546 (t), Topham/The Image Works; 546 (b), AKG London; 548, Culver Pictures/Superstock; 550, Culver Pictures; 551, Royal Geographical Society, London, UK/Bridgeman Art Library, London/New York; 556, Seneca Falls Historical Society; 559, Musee d'Orsay, Paris, France/Reunion des Musees Nationaux/Bridgeman Art Library, London/New York; 560, Private Collection/Bridgeman Art Library, London/New York; 561, Giraudon/Art Resource; 563, Giraudon/Art Resource; 566 (b), Topham/The Image Works; 566, Corbis-Bettmann; 567, Topham/The Image Works; 572-573, Scala/Art Resource; 575, SEF/Art Resource; 576, Scala/Art Resource; 579, Culver Pictures; 580, AKG London; 582, AKG London; 583, Giraudon/Art Resource; 585, AKG London; 587, Culver Pictures; 589, Walters Art Gallery, Baltimore, Courtesy of Robert Forbes Collection; 590, SEF/Art Resource; 595, AKG London; 598-599, AKG London; 601, Brown Brothers; 602, Culver Pictures; 604, Culver Pictures; 609, Milton & Joan Mann/Cameramann International; 610, Culver Pictures; 611, HRW Photo; 613, HRW photo; 615, Private Collection/The Bridgeman Art Library; 617, The Metropolitan Museum of Art, The Helena Woolworth McCaan Collection, Winfield Foundation Gift, 1958. (58.52); 621, Brown Brothers; 622, Library of Congress; 623, Library of Congress; 625, Brown Brothers; 630, Christie's Images/Bridgeman Art Library, London/New York; 631, Guildhall Library, Corporation of London, UK/Bridgeman Art Library, London/New York; 633, Scala/Art Resource; 635, AKG London; 636 (t), HRW Photo; 636 (b), Brown Brothers; 636 (c), Brown Brothers; 637 (t), Gamma Liaison; 637 (bl), Johnson Family Photo, LBJ Library Collection; 637 (br), Brown Brothers; 637 (cl), Brown Brothers; 637 (cr), Topham Picturepoint/Image Works; 638-639, Stapleton Collection/Bridgeman Art Library, London/New York; 641, HRW photo by Sam Dudgeon; 643, UPI/Corbis-Bettmann; 646 (t), Corbis-Bettmann; 646 (bl), Bibliotheque Nationale, Paris, France/Bridgeman Art Library, London/New York; 646 (br), The British Library; 647 (tl), UPI/Bettmann Newsphotos; 647 (tr), SIPA-Press; 647 (bl), George Hall/Tony Stone Images; 647 (br), PHOTRI; 650 (t), Topham/The Image Works; 650 (c), Dreweatt Neate Fine Art Auctioneers, Newbbury/Bridgeman Art Library, London/New York; 650 (b), Topham/The Image Works; 652, Brown Brothers; 653, Novosti/Bridgeman Art Library, London/New York; 655, Culver Pictures; 656, Scottish National Gallery of Modern Art, Edinburgh, UK/Bridgeman Art Library, London/New York; 658, R.B. Flemming/The Trustees of the Imperial War Museum, London; 661, Corbis-Bettmann; 664-665, Topham/The Image Works; 667, The Museum of Modern Art/Film Stills Archive; 669, Topham/The Image Works; 670, Ezra Stoller/Esto; 670, Ezra Stoller/Esto; 673, Bettmann; 674, Photoworld/FPG; 676, Brown Brothers; 677, Topham/The Image Works; 680, AP/Wide World Photos; 681, UPI/Corbis-Bettmann; 682, Corbis-Bettmann; 684, UPI/Corbis-Bettmann; 686, Corbis-Bettmann; 690-691, Schalwijk/Art Resource; 693, UPI/Corbis-Bettmann; 695, UPI/Corbis-Bettmann; 698, Corbis-Bettmann; 699, Camera Press, London; 700, Collection of J.A.F./Paris/Magnum Photos; 702, AKG London; 703, Culver Pictures; 705, Schalkwijk/Art Resource; 707, AP/World Wide Photos; 710-711, Topham/The Image Works; 714, David Seymour/Magnum Photos; 715, Giraudon/Art Resource/Artist Rights Society; 718, AP/World Wide Photos; 719, Franklin D. Roosevelt Library; 721, UPI/Corbis-Bettmann; 723, U.S. Postal Stamp; 724, Imperial War Museum/Archive Photos; 728, Topham/The Image Works; 730, Franklin D. Roosevelt Library; 734, Nicolas Reynard/Gamma-Liaison; 736, UPI/Corbis-Bettmann; 737, UPI/Wide World Photos; 742, Stapleton Collection/Bridgeman Art Library; 744, Topham/The Image Works; 746, Schalwijk/Art Resource; 747, Topham/The Image Works; 748 (tl), Photoassist/Woodfin Camp & Associates; 748 (tr), Dan Budnik/Woodfin Camp & Associates; 748 (bl), Woodfin Camp & Associates; 748 (br), Topham Picturepoint/The Image Works; 748 (c), J. C. Francolon/Gamma-Liaison; 749 (t), Express Newspapers/Archive Photos; 749 (b), I. Kostin/Leh/Nov/Woodfin Camp & Associates; 749 (cl), Topham Picturepoint/ The Image Works; 749 (cr), Ed Carlin/Archive Photos; 750-751, Diana Walker/Gamma-Liaison; 754, FPG International; 756, UPI/Corbis-Bettmann; 758, AP/Wide World Photos; 760 (b), Hulton Getty/Gamma-Liaison; 760 (t), Hulton Getty/Gamma-Liaison; 763, AKG London; 765, E. Streichan/SuperStock; 766, UPI/Corbis-Bettmann; 769, UPI/Bettmann Newsphotos; 771, Archive Photos; 774-775, Andrew Holbrooke/The Stock Market; 778, Baldev/Sygma; 779, Tibor Bognar/The Stock Market; 781, Alfred/SIPA Press; 782, China Stock; 784, Wu Yinxian/China Stock; 786, Harvey Lloyd/The Stock Market; 787, Stuart Franklin/Magnum Photos; 789, D. Groshong/Sygma; 791, AKG; 792, P. Durand/Sygma Photos; 793, Robin Moyer/Gamma-Liaison; 795, Catherine Karnow/Woodfin Camp & Associates; 797, Reuters/Corbis-Bettmann; 799, HRW photo by Sam Dudgeon; 800, David Stoecklein/The Stock Market; 802, Archive Photos; 804, Magnus Bartlet/Woodfin Camp & Associates; 807, Noel Figaro/Gamma-Liaison; 808, Frank Wing/Stock Boston; 812-813, Velasco-Afrapix/Gamma-Liaison; 816, John Moss/Black Star; 818, Robinson/Black Star; 821, Raymond Preston/Sipa Press; 823, Betty Press/Woodfin Camp; 825, Gideon Mendel/Magnum Photos; 827, AKG/AP; 829, Art Resource; 830, Antonio Ribeiro/Gamma-Liaison; 834, Wally McNamee/Woodfin Camp & Associates; 838, Reza/Sipa Press; 841, Robert Azzi/Woodfin Camp & Associates; 844-845, Robert Frerck/Woodfin Camp & Associates; 847, Robert Frerck/Odyssey Productions; 848, Reuters/Gerald Schuman/Archive Photos; 850, Antonio Ribeiro/Gamma-Liaison; 852, T. Campion/Sygma; 853, A. Ramey/Woodfin Camp & Associates; 856, Bleibtreu/Sygma ; 857, Robert Frerck/Woodfin Camp & Associates; 858, Lynn Hughes/Gamma-Liaison; 859, Issi Kato/Oshihara/Sipa Press; 860 (t), AKG London; 860 (b), Olivier Rebbot/Woodfin Camp & Associates; 861, AP/Wide World Photo; 862, P. Chauvel/Sygma Photos; 865, Adam Woolfitt/Woodfin Camp & Associates; 866, David Pollack/The Stock Market; 868, AP/Wide World Photos; 869, Ulf Andersen/Gamma-Liaison; 872-873, Itar-Tass/Sovfoto; 874, Nik Wheeler/SIPA; 875, Wally McNamee/Woodfin Camp; 877, Martin Benjamin/The Image Works; 879, NASA; 881, Steve Liss/Time Magazine; 883, Gamma Liason; 884, Leif Skoogfoors/Woodfin Camp; 885, Bernard Bisson/Sygma; 886, Attal/REA/SABA; 887, G. Pietro Agostini /Contrasto/SABA; 888, Christiana Dittmann/Rainbow; 889, Christian Vioujard/Gamma Liason; 891, Gamma Liason; 893, Peter Blakely/SABA; 896, B. Annebicque/Sygma; 897, Jerry Bergman/Gamma-Liaison; 898, Filip Horuat/SABA; 899, M. L. Corvetto/The Image Works; 901, William Strode/Woodfin Camp & Associates; 902, NASA; 905 (l), NASA; 905 (r), NASA; 906, Orlando Sentinel/Sygma ; 907, Courtesy of Advanced Micro Devices; 908, Marvin Newman(c)1990/Reprinted with permission of Discover Magazine; 909, Eric Sander/Gamma Liason; 910 (cl), Culver Pictures; 910 (t), Culver Pictures; 910 (cr), Culver Pictures; 911 (b), Victoria & Albert Museum/Michael Holford; 911 (t), Jeffrey Markowitz/SYGMA; 911 (c), SYGMA; 913, Gamma Liason; 915, C.T.K./Gamma Liason; 917, South Light/Gamma-Liason; 919, Harvey Lloyd/The Stock Market; 920, Steve Elmore/The Stock Market; 921, Steve Vidler/Nawrocki; 922, Gamma Liason; 923, Clive Barda/Woodfin Camp & Associates; 924, Jean-Claude Aunos/Gamma Liason; 925, Wally McNamee/SYGMA; 931, Andrew Holbrooke/The Stock Market; 933, Velasco-Afrapix/Gamma-Liaison; 934, Itar-Tass/Sovfoto; 936, Victoria & Albert Museum, London/Art Resource; R1, K. Scholz/ H. Armstrong Roberts; R1 (bkgd), Michael Holford